Economics and the Interpretation and Application of U.S. and E.U. Antitrust Law

Richard S. Markovits

Economics and the Interpretation and Application of U.S. and E.U. Antitrust Law

Volume II Economics-Based Legal Analyses of Mergers, Vertical Practices, and Joint Ventures

Springer

Richard S. Markovits
School of Law
The University of Texas
Austin
USA

ISBN 978-3-642-24312-7 ISBN 978-3-642-24313-4 (eBook)
DOI 10.1007/978-3-642-24313-4
Springer Heidelberg New York Dordrecht London

Library of Congress Control Number: 2014939296

Printed on acid-free paper

Springer is part of Springer Science+Business Media (www.springer.com)

To Robert Leslie Markovits, my brother,
for his intelligence, sense of humor, generosity,
and courage—for always doing the best that
he can.

Foreword to Volume II

This two-volume study of *Economics and the Interpretation and Application of U.S. and E.U. Antitrust Law* has two parts. Part I (which is presented in Chapters 1–9 and appears entirely in Volume I) focuses on Basic Concepts and Approaches. Part II (which is presented in Chapters 10–15 and is divided between Volumes I and II) focuses on Applications. Oligopolistic conduct and predatory conduct are examined in Volume I (respectively in Chapters 10 and 11). Horizontal mergers, conglomerate mergers, vertical mergers and the pricing techniques, contract-of-sale provisions, and sales/consignment policies that are surrogates for vertical integration, and joint ventures and other types of functionally-analogous collaborative arrangements are examined in Volume II (respectively in Chapters 12, 13, 14, and 15). Volume II also contains a lengthy Conclusion, which (1) reviews the most important economic and legal concepts the study uses, its critique of market-oriented approaches to the analysis of antitrust-law issues, and the basic features of the non-market-oriented approaches to such issues it proposes; (2) compares post-1950 U.S. antitrust law as written with pre-EMCR and post-EMCR E.C./E.U. competition law as written; and (3) analyzes the extent to which errors in interpretation and application made respectively by U.S. and E.C./E.U. government antitrust authorities have increased or decreased the divergence between U.S. and E.C./E.U. antitrust law as applied. Detailed summaries of each of Volume II's chapters and of the Conclusion to the study that Volume II contains appear in Volume I in its Introduction to Part II: Applications, starting with the last paragraph of page 326 and continuing through the end of page 342.

This two-volume Law Study is written as a continuous work—*i.e.*, I have not included in Chapters 12–15 definitions of concepts those chapters use that are articulated in Volume I or summaries of analyses that those chapters rely on that are executed in Volume I. Still, much of Volume II should be fully comprehensible to readers who have not read Volume I. Thus, Chapter 13's critique of the toe-hold-merger doctrine and most of its critique of limit-pricing theory, Chapter 14's economic analyses of the functions of vertical integration and its various surrogates, and Chapter 15's economic analyses of joint ventures and the restraints that joint-venture agreements impose on the joint venture and/or its parents can be understood without reading Volume I. Moreover, although some of Part II's legal analyses are critically affected by specific features of Part I's conclusions about the legally-correct way to interpret respectively (1) the (specific-anticompetitive-intent) test of illegality, which I claim is promulgated by the Sherman Act, the object-branch of Article 101's test of illegality, and the exclusionary-abuse branch of Article 102's test of illegality and (2) the (lessening-competition) test of *prima facie* illegality, which I claim is promulgated by the Clayton Act, the effect-branch of Article 101's test of illegality, and the EMCR, many of its legal analyses do not turn on any non-obvious elements of the operationalizations of these tests that I believe are correct as a matter of law.

Nevertheless, I think it would be helpful for me to supply at this juncture definitions of some of the key concepts developed in Volume I and a summary of some related conclusions reached in Volume I on which Volume II relies. Volume I argues that antitrust law is concerned not only with price competition but also with "quality-or-variety-increasing-investment (QV-investment)" competition—the process through which product rivals compete away their potential profits by introducing additional, sometimes-superior product variants, opening up additional, sometimes-superior distributive outlets, or adding to their capacity or inventory (which enables them to offer buyers faster average speed of supply throughout a fluctuating-demand cycle). Volume I also develops a QV-investment-focused conceptual system, which it uses to analyze the determinants of equilibrium QV investment in any area of product-space, the impact of business conduct on the intensity of QV-investment competition in a relevant area of product-space, the conditions under which potential competition will be effective, the soundness of limit-price theory, when and why firms that face an effective potential competitor will find it most profitable to respond to the threat of entry by making a limit QV investment to deter entry, and the economically and legally correct definition of the concept of a predatory QV investment. That conceptual system distinguishes three QV-investment equilibria, which differ according to the relationship between the equilibrium QV-investment level in an area of product-space and the entry-preventing QV-investment level in that area of product-space, four barriers to entry and four counterpart barriers to QV-investment expansion that may be faced by an established firm (each of which refers to a specified subset of the factors that can cause the certainty-equivalent post-investment supernormal rate-of-return for a new QV investment [QV-investment incentives and disincentives aside—see below] to be lower than the pre-investment supernormal rate-of-return generated by the most-supernormally-profitable QV investments in the relevant area of product-space), the monopolistic QV-investment incentives or disincentives an established firm faces in relation to its making an additional QV investment in an area of product-space in which it is already operating (which reflect the impact that the new QV investment will have on the profit-yields of the investor's pre-existing projects by taking sales from them, by inducing rivals to make non-retaliatory responses, and/or by deterring rivals from making QV investments in the relevant area of product-space that would reduce the profit-yields of the investor's pre-existing projects in the above two ways more or less than its contemplated QV investment would do), and the natural oligopolistic QV-investment disincentives an established firm faces to make a QV investment when that investment's overall profitability will be reduced not only by monopolistic QV-investment disincentives but also by its inducing a rival to make an additional QV investment in the relevant area of product-space that would not otherwise be made.

Volume I also develops a conceptual system for describing the supra-competitiveness of prices, determining whether actual prices manifest horizontal price-fixing ("contrived oligopolistic pricing") or predatory pricing, and analyzing the impact of business conduct on the intensity of price competition. Although the details of this system vary according to whether the sellers in the relevant area of product-space set prices on an "individualized," customer-by-customer basis or establish a set of terms that apply "across-the-board" to all potential buyers, five concepts play an important role in the system's account of the gap between a seller's price and (conventional) marginal costs in all pricing contexts: (1) the seller's highest non-oligopolistic price (HNOP), the highest price the seller would find profitable to charge if its rivals know that it cannot react to their responses; (2) the seller's natural oligopolistic margin (NOM), the price-increase the seller obtains because its rivals know that, if they beat its initial offer, the buyer will give the seller an opportunity to rebid and the seller will find it inherently profitable to beat their offers; (3) the seller's contrived oligopolistic margin, the price-increase the seller obtains (or tries to obtain) by informing its rivals that it will react to their responses to its offer in inherently-unprofitable ways that will make it unprofitable for them to beat its offer—*viz.*, by retaliating against their beating its offer in one or more inherently-unprofitable ways to inflict harm on them and/or reciprocating to their foregoing the opportunity to make profits by beating its offer by allowing them to make additional profits by supplying other buyers by passing up the inherently-profitable opportunity to beat their contrived oligopolistic prices to those other buyers; (4) the seller's basic competitive advantage (BCA) in relation to a particular buyer (the sum of the number of dollars [monetary units] by which the buyer prefers the seller's product over the product of the buyer's second-placed supplier [the best-placed seller's buyer preference advantage or BPA] and the number of dollars by which the conventional marginal [or incremental] cost the best-placed seller must incur to supply the buyer in question are lower than their counterpart for that buyer's second-placed supplier [the best-placed seller's marginal cost advantage or MCA]); and (5) the contextual marginal costs (CMC) a best-placed individualized pricer's closest competitor must incur to match the best-placed seller's HNOP-containing offer (costs that arise primarily because the price that the second-placed supplier must include in its bid to match the best-placed supplier's HNOP-containing offer is discriminatory) or those costs' across-the-board-pricing counterpart (the number or dollars by which the price that an across-the-board pricer would find most profitable to charge if no-one engaged in oligopolistic pricing is increased by the fact that its rivals' BCAs would make it profitable for them to charge supra-marginal-cost prices even if no one practiced oligopolistic pricing).

Volume I also explains why definitions of both classical economic markets and (allegedly-functional) antitrust markets are inevitably arbitrary, not just at their peripheries but comprehensively, indicates that for this reason this study usually substitutes the acronym ARDEPPS (for arbitrarily-defined portion of product-space) for the conventional term "market," critiques a large number of protocols for market definition proposed by economists and government antitrust authorities, and explains why market-oriented approaches to analyzing the antitrust legality of business conduct can never be cost-effective (because market definitions achieve the remarkable double of increasing cost while decreasing accuracy in that data on the non-market-aggregated parameters that are used to define markets have more predictive power than data on any market-aggregated parameter could have).

Finally, I think it would be helpful for me to articulate the operationalizations of the two tests of illegality that Volume I argues are promulgated by both some provisions of U.S. antitrust legislation and some provisions of the E.C./E.U. treaty (or the EMCR). In my judgment, correctly interpreted as a matter of law, the specific-anticompetitive-intent test declares covered conduct illegal if its perpetrator's or perpetrators' *ex ante* perception that the conduct would be profitable was critically affected by the perpetrator's or perpetrators' belief that it would or might increase its or their future profits by reducing the absolute attractiveness of the best offers against which it or they would have to compete in one or more ways that would render the conduct profitable though economically inefficient if the profits the conduct would yield would not otherwise diverge from the conduct's impact on economic efficiency. In my judgment, correctly interpreted as a matter of law, the lessening-competition test declares covered conduct *prima facie* illegal if the conduct inflicts a net equivalent-monetary loss on the potential customers of the perpetrator(s) and the potential customers of the perpetrator's or perpetrators' product-rivals "combined" by reducing the absolute attractiveness of the best offers they respectively receive from any inferior supplier.

I hope that the preceding material will enable those readers of Volume II who have not read Volume I to fully comprehend Volume II. Readers of Volume II who are experiencing difficulties that they think can be traced to their not having read Volume I can always refer to the relevant sections of that volume, which the chapter-by-chapter summaries in pages 1–5 of Volume I should help them identify.

Introduction to This Study

This Study's Coverage and Distinctive Features

This study analyzes the non-monopolizing private functions, possible monopolizing or abusive character, and competitive impact of the various types of business conduct that antitrust laws cover. More specifically, it addresses these issues as they apply to

1. the so-called "abuse" of monopoly power,
2. the various types of oligopolistic conduct in which firms can engage,
3. the various types of predatory conduct in which firms can engage and some types of business conduct that have been incorrectly characterized as predatory,
4. horizontal mergers and acquisitions,
5. conglomerate mergers and acquisitions,
6. various contractual and sales/consignment-policy surrogates for vertical integration—price discrimination of different sorts, tie-ins, reciprocity, systems rivalry, bundling, resale price maintenance, vertical territorial restraints and customer-allocation clauses, long-term full-requirements contracts, single-brand and non-single-brand exclusive dealing, and sales (consignment) policies of supplying only those independent distributors (using only those independent consignees) whose pricing, promotion, and other choices the supplier deems appropriate,
7. vertical mergers and acquisitions, and
8. horizontal, conglomerate, and vertical joint ventures (including R&D joint ventures and patent pools).

In addition to developing its own economic analyses of these types of business conduct and explaining how U.S. and E.U. antitrust "agencies" and courts should analyze their legality, it criticizes the standard economic analysis of many of these types of conduct, the conclusions that economists and legal scholars have reached about the way in which courts should analyze their legality, and the ways in which U.S. and E.U. antitrust agencies and courts have actually handled such conduct.

There is nothing unusual about the set of business practices this study investigates or the broad issues it addresses. However, the study's approach to these issues is in several respects unique. This Introduction provides preliminary accounts of the study's five major distinguishing features. The separate Introductions to the study's two parts and the Table of Contents contain respectively chapter-by-chapter and section-by-section summaries and outlines of the study's coverage.

This study's first major distinguishing feature is its explicit definition of various key antitrust-economics concepts. The study provides a basis for its definitions by delineating the criteria one should use to evaluate definitions of the kinds of concepts in question—*viz.*, (1) the extent to which the definition conforms with professional and, when relevant, popular usage and intuitive understanding and (2) the extent to which the definition creates a concept that can play a useful role in a valuable analysis. It then articulates operational definitions of such concepts as "the impact of a choice on economic efficiency," "the impact of a choice on the intensity of competition," "monopolization," "oligopolistic conduct," and "predatory conduct" and applies the criteria it has delineated to justify the definitions it proposes.

This feature of this study rectifies a deficiency in the literature: economists and lawyers that use economics to execute antitrust-law analyses (1) have never discussed the criteria one should use to evaluate definitions of these sorts of concepts, (2) have never articulated explicit definitions of "oligopolistic conduct" and "predatory conduct" and have articulated various underspecified, inconsistent, and I believe inappropriate or "incorrect" operationalizations of "the impact of a choice on the intensity of competition" and "the impact of a choice on economic efficiency," and (3) have never tried to justify the definitions of these concepts they have implicitly or explicitly adopted.

Even at this juncture, an example may be useful. This study defines a choice to be a "primary oligopolistic choice" if and only if the chooser's *ex ante* perception that it would be profitable was critically affected by its perception that its rivals would or might realize that it could react to their responses to the choice in question. The study further refines this concept to distinguish between primary oligopolistic choices to initiate a "contrived" oligopolistic interaction and primary oligopolistic choices to initiate a "natural" oligopolistic interaction. On this study's definition, an oligopolistic interaction is "contrived" if its initiator induced the responder to believe that the initiator would react to its response in a way that would render unprofitable for the responder a non-cooperative response the responder would otherwise have found profitable by promising to reciprocate to the responder's otherwise-unprofitable cooperation (*i.e.*, to react to a cooperative response in an inherently-unprofitable[873] way that would benefit the cooperative responder) and/or

[873] In my vocabulary, a business believes that a choice it is contemplating making is "inherently profitable" if its perception that the choice will be profitable does not depend on any tendency it believes the choice may have to reduce the absolute attractiveness of the offers against which the business will have to compete in the future in some way that would tend to make the choice more profitable than economically efficient in an otherwise-Pareto-perfect economy—most commonly, by driving a rival out or inducing a rival to compete less hard against it. By way of contrast, in my vocabulary, a business choice is said to be "strategic" if the business' *ex ante* perception that the

by threatening to retaliate[874] against a responder that made a non-cooperative response (*i.e.*, to react to a non-cooperative response in an inherently-unprofitable way that would impose losses on the non-cooperative responder). By way of contrast, on this study's definition, an oligopolistic interaction is "natural" if its initiator did not have to rely on any such anticompetitive promise and/or threat to induce the responder to conclude that the initiator would react to the responder's cooperative and non-cooperative responses in ways that would render unprofitable for the responder non-cooperative responses the responder would otherwise find profitable—more positively, if the initiator could rely on the responder's realization that it would be both possible and inherently profitable for the initiator to react to a non-cooperative response in a way that would render unprofitable for the responder a non-cooperative response the responder would otherwise find profitable (for example, on the responder's realization that the relevant buyer would give the initiator the opportunity to rebid and that the initiator would find it inherently profitable to beat any non-cooperative response-offer the responder would otherwise find profitable to make to the buyer in question).

As we shall see, although some "oligopolistic pricing" models focus on conduct that is oligopolistic in my sense, other so-called "oligopolistic pricing" models focus on conduct that is not oligopolistic in my sense—specifically, focus on conduct that is influenced by the actor's realization that the pay-off to its choice will be affected by the response it elicits from one or more particular, identifiable rivals. As we shall also see, economists and lawyers have also not distinguished contrived and natural oligopolistic interactions. This study explains why both (1) the distinction between the three-stage interaction I denominate "oligopolistic" and the two-stage interaction economists consider to be oligopolistic and (2) the distinction between oligopolistic interactions that are contrived and natural in my sense are legally critical.

The study's second major distinguishing feature is its recognition that the economy generates a wide variety of categories of economic inefficiency whose magnitudes business conduct and antitrust policies can affect and that the impact of business conduct on the magnitudes of only some of these categories of economic

choice would be profitable is critically affected by the business' belief that the choice will or may reduce the absolute attractiveness of the offers against which it will have to compete in the future in some way that would tend to make the choice more profitable than allocatively efficient in an otherwise-Pareto-perfect economy. For an explanation of the point of the qualification articulated at the end of the preceding sentence, see Chaps. 3 and 4 *infra*.

[874] In my usage, a business' response to a rival's choice is said to be retaliatory if it is a strategic response that is designed to increase the retaliator's future profits by deterring rivals that it does not drive out from competing as hard against the retaliator in the future as they would otherwise have done. This usage distinguishes "retaliatory responses" not only from non-strategic responses but also from "predatory" strategic responses—*i.e.*, responses made by actors that would not have found them profitable *ex ante* but for their belief that they would or might increase their profits in the long run by driving a rival out or deterring a rival from entering when this effect would make the choice in question profitable through economically inefficient in an otherwise-Pareto-perfect economy.

inefficiency are relevant to the conduct's legality under either U.S. antitrust law or E.C./E.U. competition law. Thus, the study explains why the impact that business conduct has on the amount of misallocation the relevant economy generates (1) by producing the goods it does produce in economically-inefficient proportions, (2) by allocating too many resources from the perspective of economic efficiency to the creation of quality and variety in some areas of product-space relative to the amount of resources it allocates to creating quality and variety in other areas of product-space, (3) by allocating too many resources from the perspective of economic efficiency to research designed to discover more-economically-efficient production processes to use to produce goods in some areas of product-space relative to the amount of resources it allocates to research designed to discover more-economically-efficient production processes to produce goods in other areas of product-space, and (4) by allocating resources among unit-output-increasing, quality-or-variety-creating, and production-process-research-executing uses in economically-inefficient proportions are irrelevant to its legality under both U.S. antitrust law and E.C./E.U. competition law while any tendency business conduct has to increase economic efficiency (5) by increasing the proficiency with which its perpetrator or perpetrators produce their products using known technologies, distribute their products, and finance their operations, (6) by increasing the intrinsic economic efficiency of the product and production-process research-projects they undertake, (7) by increasing the proficiency with which they execute the research projects they undertake, and (8) by increasing the economic efficiency of the portfolio of research projects a group of businesses execute by enabling them to avoid executing a set of projects that is less-economically-efficient than an alternative set of the same magnitude could be because the projects they executed were economically-inefficiently duplicative is relevant to its legality under U.S. antitrust law and E.C./E.U. competition law.

The study's third major distinguishing feature is the conceptual system it uses to analyze the impact of conduct on the intensity of price competition. Conventional analyses (1) focus on the total difference between price and marginal cost and (2) do not analyze separately the determinants of the intensity of price competition in individualized-pricing contexts (in which sellers set separate prices to each of their potential customers) and in across-the-board-pricing contexts (in which sellers set a single per-unit price that applies to all buyers). This study distinguishes a number of components of the gap between price (P) and marginal cost (MC) and focuses separately on individualized-pricing and across-the-board-pricing contexts. Chapter 2 delineates in detail all the components of the difference between a seller's actual price and marginal cost that are useful to distinguish, including various components of the gap between a seller's actual price and the price it would find most profitable to charge if no-one made any relevant error and its rivals assumed that it could not react to their responses to its price (the firm's NEHNOP or no-error highest-non-oligopolistic price) and various components of the gap between a firm's NEHNOP and its conventional marginal cost. I argue that one should distinguish the components in question because only by doing so can one understand the relationships between or among the components in question, accurately predict the impact of various types of conduct such as horizontal mergers on the prices the merger partners and their independent rivals charge, or accurately assess whether the price a given seller is charging is "oligopolistic" or "predatory." The study focuses separately on individualized-pricing and across-the-board-pricing contexts because some of the components of the P–MC gap of a seller that is setting individualized prices that are useful to distinguish have no exact across-the-board-pricing counterpart, because the determinants of the magnitudes of some of the components of the gap between an individualized-pricing seller's P–MC gap are different from the determinants of the magnitudes of the counterpart components of an across-the-board-pricing seller's P–MC gap, and because one therefore cannot accurately predict the impact of given conduct on the P–MC gap of its perpetrator(s) and its (their) rivals or accurately assess whether a given seller's price is oligopolistic or predatory without paying attention to this distinction between individualized and across-the-board pricing.

The study's fourth major distinguishing feature is (1) the fact that it analyzes the impact of business choices and government policies on quality-or-variety-increasing-investment (QV-investment) competition separately from their impact on price competition and (2) the conceptual system it uses to analyze the impact of business choices or government decisions on QV-investment competition. In my vocabulary, the expression "QV-investment competition" refers to the process in which firms compete away their supernormal profits by making quality-or-variety-increasing (QV) investments in a given area of product-space—*i.e.*, by introducing additional or superior product variants, by opening up additional or superior distributive outlets, or by adding to their capacity or inventory to increase the average speed with which they can supply their customers throughout a fluctuating-demand cycle.

Obviously, economists recognize that firms engage in QV-investment competition as well as price competition. However, because they think that (1) the same factors have the same impact on the intensities of price and QV-investment competition, (2) increases of the same magnitude in price and QV-investment competition (*i.e.*, of equal net equivalent-dollar value to relevant buyers) have the same positive impact on economic efficiency, and (3) increases of the same magnitude in price and QV-investment competition have the same impact on the distribution of income and/or its desirability, they see no need to analyze the impact of any business choice or government decision on the intensity of QV-investment competition—*i.e.*, they believe that one can learn everything one needs to know about the competitive impact, economic efficiency, distributive desirability, and overall desirability of any business choice or government decision by analyzing its impact on price competition. I disagree with this conclusion because I reject all of its predicates. In particular, I believe that

1. as Chap. 2 makes clear, the determinants of the impact of a business choice or government decision on the intensity of price competition are different from the determinants of such a choice's impact on the intensity of QV-investment competition and a given choice can increase price competition while decreasing QV-investment competition and *vice versa*;

2. for reasons that The Welfare Economics of Antitrust Policy and U.S. and E.U. Antitrust Law explains in great detail, although increases in price competition almost always increase economic efficiency in our actual, highly-Pareto-imperfect economy, increases in QV-investment competition usually decrease economic efficiency on balance in our actual economy; and
3. because increases in price competition usually benefit the poor more than do comparable increases in QV-investment competition, both the distributive impact of and the distributive desirability from a wide variety of normative perspectives of increases in the two types of competition are almost certainly quite different.

This study, therefore, analyzes the impact of the business choices and government decisions it examines on QV-investment competition as well as on price competition, and its policy companion analyzes separately the economic efficiency/overall desirability of any tendency that relevant business choices and government decisions have on QV-investment competition and price competition. For this purpose, I have developed another unique conceptual scheme. This scheme defines eleven determinants of the intensity of QV-investment competition in any arbitrarily-designated area of product-space (ARDEPPS)[875]: four barriers to entry, four barriers to expansion, the monopolistic QV-investment incentive a potential QV investor that is already operating in the relevant area of product-space may face, the monopolistic QV-investment disincentive such a potential QV investor may face, and the natural oligopolistic QV-investment disincentives that two or more such potential QV investors may face. Chapter 2 carefully defines all of these concepts.

I have already indicated that this conceptual system is unique. Admittedly, economists do talk about "barriers to entry." However, they do not define such barriers in the way I have done—indeed, do not define them clearly or consistently and do not use them to analyze QV-investment competition (use them instead to predict whether established firms will engage in "limit pricing"—*i.e.*, will charge lower prices than they would otherwise charge to deter new entry). Moreover, to my knowledge, economists have never discussed either the barriers to expansion established firms face or any of the QV-investment incentives and disincentives I identify.

The study's fifth major distinguishing feature is its rejection of market-oriented approaches to the measurement of monopoly and oligopoly power, the analysis of the monopolizing character of any type of business conduct, or the prediction of the competitive impact of any type of business conduct. None of the analyses this study executes uses such an approach—*i.e.*, bases predictions or post-dictions on any kind of market-aggregated data (for example, on market-share figures, four-firm or

[875] The text refers to an arbitrarily-designated portion of product-space rather than a market because, for reasons that the text of this Introduction outlines below and Chap. 6 explains in detail, regardless of the plausible criterion one uses to evaluate any set of market definitions, market definitions are inherently arbitrary not just at their periphery but at their core.

eight-firm seller-concentration ratios, post-merger Hirschman-Herfendahl Indices [HHIs—the sum of the squares of the market shares of all firms placed inside an allegedly-relevant market], or merger-induced increases in HHIs). Admittedly, the study's definitions of barriers to entry and expansion and its analyses of the impact of business choices and government decisions on the intensity of QV-investment competition do make reference to arbitrarily-designated areas of product-space (ARDEPPSes). However, my use of these concepts is not inconsistent with my claim that the study consistently rejects market-oriented approaches. At no point do I propose doing anything that requires the oxymoronic non-arbitrary definition of an ARDEPPS—*i.e.*, my use of the concept of an ARDEPPS is always purely heuristic.

As Chap. 6 explains, I reject market-oriented approaches to any of the issues with which this study and/or its policy sequel are concerned for two partially-overlapping reasons. First, I reject market-oriented approaches to any type of antitrust-economics analysis because, regardless of whether one evaluates sets of market definitions (approaches to market definition) by the extent to which they (the market definitions they yield) (1) satisfy professional (and perhaps popular) assumptions about the competitiveness of products placed within the same market and the difference between the competitiveness of products placed in the same market and the competitiveness of products placed in different markets or (2) play a useful role in a valuable analytic protocol,[876] market definitions (the choice among alternative approaches to market definition) are arbitrary not just at their periphery but at their core. Second, I reject market-oriented approaches to antitrust-economics analyses because, even if (contrary to my conclusion) some set of market definitions could be shown to be superior to all its alternatives, market-oriented approaches would not be cost-effective. In my judgment, regardless of the question at issue, market-oriented approaches always achieve the remarkable double of increasing cost while decreasing accuracy because (1) market definitions are costly and (2) the non-market-aggregated data one uses to define relevant markets have more predictive power than the market-aggregated figures (on market shares, market-concentration ratios, and HHIs) that market-oriented approaches use market definitions to generate.

Five final introductory points. First, I want to admit at the outset that the question to ask about conceptual systems and analytic approaches is not whether they are "right" or "wrong" but whether they are useful—whether (1) the conceptual systems call attention to important issues that could not be articulated without them (or, at least, without paying attention to the distinctions they draw) and (2) whether the conceptual systems and theoretical approaches enable the analyst to resolve more accurately or cost-effectively both the novel issues the conceptual systems enable the analyst to identify and important issues that have been or can be

[876] Note that the criteria in question are exemplars of the two criteria by which I think one should evaluate any conceptual definition of the type to which the concept of a market belongs: respectively, (1) is the definition consistent with professional and, when relevant, popular usage and intuitive understanding and (2) will the definition create a concept that can perform a valuable role in a useful analysis.

articulated without making reference to any of the conceptual innovations under scrutiny. Second, I want to assure readers that all the innovative concepts and approaches just outlined will be described and discussed in far more detail in the chapters that follow. Third, and relatedly, I want to point out that readers will not be able to assess the value of the distinguishing conceptual and analytic features of this study until they have seen them in use (until they have read the study). The proof of this pudding is in the eating. Fourth, a vocabulary point: throughout this text, I refer to the *categories* of resource allocation and resource misallocation I distinguish (while referring to *types* of Pareto imperfections and resource-uses) to remind readers that the categories in question are usually counterfactual (though analytically useful—*i.e.*, are in one sense artificial as opposed to natural).

And fifth, because the two volumes in which this study is being printed have been given different ISBN numbers, the first page of Vol. 2 must begin with page-number 1. To differentiate the page-numbers in the two volumes, upright page-numbers are used in Vol. 1, and italicized page numbers are used in Vol. 2. The Index incorporates this font-practice—*i.e.* in the Index, upright page-reference numbers refer to page-numbers in Vol. 1, and italicized page-reference numbers refer to pages in Vol. 2.

Contents

Chapter 12
Horizontal Mergers and Acquisitions

A merger or acquisition (hereinafter a merger) is horizontal to the extent that the merger partners are well-placed to compete for the patronage of the same buyers in relation to given purchasing decisions. This chapter analyzes the determinants of the economic effects of horizontal mergers that are relevant to their legality under U.S. and E.C./E.U. antitrust law and states and criticizes both the approaches that U.S. and E.C./E.U. authorities have taken to the analysis of the antitrust legality of such mergers and various conclusions they have reached about the legal relevance of various facts.

The chapter has five sections. Section 1 lists the various Sherman-Act-licit and Sherman-Act-illicit ways in which horizontal mergers can increase their participants' profits. Section 2 focuses on the ways in which horizontal mergers can increase and decrease competition in the Clayton Act sense of those expressions. More specifically, Section 2A delineates the ways in which and the determinants of the extent to which horizontal mergers that generate no efficiencies that can benefit Clayton-Act-relevant buyers will tend to impose equivalent-dollar losses on such buyers by reducing the absolute attractiveness of the best offer they respectively receive from any inferior supplier. Section 2B delineates the ways in which and the determinants of the extent to which any static or dynamic efficiencies a horizontal merger generates will benefit Clayton-Act-relevant buyers and explains why, in exceptional circumstances, such efficiencies may impose an equivalent-dollar loss on such buyers. Section 3 analyzes the legality of horizontal mergers under U.S. antitrust law and E.C./E.U. competition law, correctly interpreted and applied. Section 4 delineates the approaches that U.S. courts and the U.S. DOJ and FTC (the "Agencies") have taken to analyzing the legality of horizontal mergers. Section 4A delineates and criticizes the U.S. courts' traditional market-oriented approach to horizontal-merger analysis, which focuses primarily on the merger partners' market shares and the traditional seller-concentration ratio of the relevant market(s). Section 4B delineates the other facts that U.S. courts traditionally considered when analyzing the legality of horizontal mergers and criticizes their assessment of the economic and legal relevance of these facts. Section 4C (1) delineates and criticizes the approach to horizontal-merger analysis that the DOJ and FTC

R.S. Markovits, *Economics and the Interpretation and Application of U.S. and E.U. Antitrust Law*, DOI 10.1007/978-3-642-24313-4_1,

indicated their intention to take in the 1992 Horizontal Merger Guidelines and the 1997 Revision of those Guidelines and (2) two other approaches that do not conform to the Guidelines' approach—the merger-simulation approach and an approach that generates predictions by drawing inferences from natural events—that the DOJ and FTC have actually used in recent years. Section 4D delineates and criticizes the Horizontal Merger Guidelines that the DOJ and FTC promulgated on August 19, 2010, just as the manuscript for this study was headed for copy-editing. Section D focuses on the differences between and commonalities shared by the 2010 Guidelines and their 1992/1997 precursor and argues that although the 2010 Guidelines are more in line with the approach I am recommending than even the 1992/1997 Guidelines were, they continue to make some errors whose importance I have been stressing and, more puzzlingly, persist in insisting that the Agencies are continuing to follow a market-oriented (post-merger-HHI/merger-induced change-in-HHI) approach when they clearly are not doing so in anything but name. Section 5 describes and assesses the economic and legal correctness of the EC's positions and the E.C./E.U.-court case-law on horizontal mergers.

1. The Ways That Horizontal Mergers Can Generate Sherman-Act-Licit and Sherman-Act-Illicit Profits

Horizontal mergers can yield their participants profits or gains in at least seven Sherman-Act-licit ways:

(1) by creating a merged firm that can increase the proficiency with which it makes use of the MPs' QV investments by taking fuller advantage than its antecedents could of real economies of scale in purchasing, production, advertising, distribution, and/or financing and/or by combining assets that are complementary for non-scale reasons: if such static efficiencies lower fixed costs, the associated profit-increase equals the efficiencies, but if they lower MC, the associated profit-increase depends on the original competitive-position distribution of the perpetrator(s)—*e.g.*, if the perpetrator(s) set individualized prices and I ignore CMC-related and OM-related effects, the profit-increase equals (the units of output they were originally best-placed to sell *times* the MC-reduction) *plus* (the units of output the MC-reduction made them best-placed to sell *times* [the difference between the MC-reduction and their original BCD on the relevant sales]);

(2) by creating a firm that faces lower (Π_D + R) barriers to expansion than did either merger partner (MP) by combining firms whose assets are complementary for non-scale reasons (*e.g.*, by combining a firm with excess managerial capacity in production with a firm with excess managerial capacity in distribution, by combining a firm with QV-investment ideas and the personnel to execute them proficiently but no ability to finance them with a firm that has substantial retained earnings but no investment-ideas, or by combining a start-up with a potentially-profitable product with another firm that has the financial wherewithal and promotional and other distributive skills to market it)—the associated profits equal the dynamic efficiencies in question if a perpetrator

would have made the relevant QV investment in any case or the amount by which the QV investment the dynamic efficiencies induced the perpetrator(s) to make increased their overall profits;
(3) by enabling an owner or owner/manager of a small firm that wants to retire to liquidate his or her assets and escape the burden of management;
(4) by enabling a firm that has a tax loss that it cannot fully use itself to offset future profits because the loss exceeds its predicted taxable income during the period in which such losses can be carried forward (*i.e.*, can be used to offset taxable income) to make profits by "selling" itself and its losses to another firm that will have enough taxable income during the relevant period to make fuller use of the tax loss in question;
(5) by helping the MPs and perhaps their remaining rivals (*R*s)—where the *R* is italicized to differentiate the *R* that stands for a rival of one or more firms (say, the MPs) from the unitalicized R that stands for the risk barrier to entry or expansion—to overcome the "public-good-type" problem that prevents them from spending as much money on campaign contributions and participation in legislative, administrative, and adjudicative decisionmaking processes as would be in their collective interest;
(6) by creating a merged firm that can obtain more NOMs than could its antecedents because the merger generates static efficiencies that give the merged firm higher OCAs—see point (1) in this list—and because the merged firm is better-placed than its antecedents to initiate a series of premature price announcements and/or to take advantage of economies of scale in changing initially-announced prices; and
(7) by creating an across-the-board-pricing merged firm that is better-placed than its across-the-board-pricing antecedents were to initiate or organize a series of price-announcements that are sequenced in the order that would raise the height of the across-the-board-HNOP array of the merged firm and its *R*s.

However, as Section 2A will explain in more detail, horizontal mergers can also benefit their participants in at least five Sherman-Act-illicit ways:

(1) by increasing their OCAs and derivatively their NOMs and possibly their COMs by freeing the MPs from each other's price competition;
(2) by freeing the MPs from each other's QV-investment competition—*i.e.*, by putting the merged company in a position not to make a QV investment that one of the MPs would have made pre merger in circumstances in which the expansion would have reduced the non-expanding MP's supernormal profits by more than it increased the expanding MP's supernormal profits (*i.e.*, in circumstances in which the merged firm would face critical *M* disincentives when the relevant MP or MPs would not have faced critical *M* disincentives);
(3) possibly, but probably not, for various reasons Section 2 will also delineate, by enabling the merged company to obtain more COMs than the MPs would have obtained;
(4) by creating a merged company that can retaliate more cost-effectively against a potential competitor that executed a new entry and/or an established rival that executed a QV-investment expansion because the merged company can better

coordinate the MPs' retaliatory price-cuts, because the merged company does not face the risk that one or both MPs will misinterpret the other MP's retaliation against an *R* to be an aggressive price-move against it, and because the merged company can take advantage of any increase in its reputation for retaliating when selling a larger set of products (often) in a larger set of markets and hence will earn more profits than its antecedents would have earned combined by erecting retaliation barriers to entry or expansion that are critically higher than the retaliation barriers the relevant potential entrant or expander would otherwise have faced; and

(5) by creating a merged company that, for the same reasons, earns more profits by engaging in predation that is designed to drive its target(s) out than its antecedents would have done.

2. Possible Clayton-Act-Relevant Impacts of Horizontal Mergers and These Impacts' Magnitudes' Determinants

A. The Ways That a Horizontal Merger That Yields No Static Marginal (Hereinafter Marginal-Cost) Efficiencies Can Generate Clayton-Act-Relevant Effects and These Effects' Magnitudes' Determinants

Horizontal mergers that generate no static marginal-cost efficiencies can injure Clayton-Act-relevant buyers in the following general Clayton-Act-relevant ways: by increasing the HNOPs, NOMs, and COMs of the MPs, by increasing the HNOPs, NOMs, and COMs of the MPs' *R*s, and by reducing the intensity of QV investment competition in the relevant area of product-space (1) by creating a merged company that faces higher (Π_D + R) barriers, higher L barriers, and/or higher *M* or *O* disincentives than its antecedents faced, (2) by raising the L barriers facing the merged firm's actual and potential *R*s, and (3) by causing a relevant actual *R* of the merged firm to face *M* or *O* disincentives.

(1) The Ways in Which a Horizontal Merger That Yields No Static Marginal-Cost Efficiencies Would Increase Prices If It Did Not Raise the Equilibrium QV-Investment Level in the ARDEPPS in Which It Took Place

(A) The Impact of a Horizontal Merger That Yields No Static Marginal-Cost Efficiencies on the Competitiveness of Prices at the ARDEPPS' Pre-Merger Equilibrium QV-Investment Level When the Merged Firm and Its *R*s Charge Individualized Prices

I will now list the determinants of the impact that a horizontal merger that generates no static marginal-cost efficiencies will have on the merged firm's OCAs (HNOPs), NOMs, and COMs relative to those of its antecedents (the MPs) and the determinants of such a merger's impact on the merged firm's *R*s' OCAs (HNOPs), NOMs, and COMs when the merged firm and its *R*s charge individualized prices. (The text that follows ignores the possibility that the relevant merger might produce these effects by creating a merged company that engages in more predation than its antecedents would have done.) This section provides little explanation. More detailed explanations can be found in Chaps. 2 and 10.

The magnitude of the equivalent-dollar loss that a horizontal merger between individualized pricers that generates no static marginal-cost efficiencies will inflict on the MPs' customers by raising the merged firm's OCAs and HNOPs (QV-investment consequences aside) above those of the MPs by reducing the absolute attractiveness of the best offer each of these buyers receive from any inferior supplier (by reducing the absolute attractiveness of the best offer against which the merged firm must compete below the absolute attractiveness of the best offer against which the individual MPs would have to compete) is

(1) directly related to the absolute number of times that the MPs are respectively uniquely-best-placed and uniquely-second-place (or are uniquely-equal-best-placed);
(2) directly related to the average amount by which the second-placed MP (each MP) was better-placed pre merger than the third-placed supplier of the buyers in question when pre merger the MPs were uniquely-second-placed and uniquely-best-placed (uniquely-equal-best-placed); and
(3) inversely related to the amount by which the merger reduces the average OCD of the *R*s that are second-placed post-merger (when in individual cases the *R* that was better-placed than any other *R* to obtain the patronage of the relevant buyers pre merger may not be the *R* that is second-placed post-merger) by reducing the average CMC the relevant *R*s must incur to match the merged firm's HNOP-containing offers to the buyers the merged firm is best-placed to supply below the average CMC the pre merger third-placed suppliers would have had to incur to do so by making the prices in the relevant post-merger matching offers less discriminatory than the prices in the relevant pre-merger-matching offers.[877]

[877] Some explanation is required. I will start by assuming that the *R* that was third-placed from supply any buyer the MPs were respectively best-placed and second-placed (or were uniquely-equal-best-placed) to supply pre merger will be second-placed to supply that buyer post-merger. Pre-merger, that *R* would have had to incur CMC to match the best-placed (equal-best-placed) MP's (MPs') HNOP-containing offer because the price the *R* would have had to charge the MP's (MPs') customer to match that offer would be lower than the price the *R* was charging its own customers—*viz.*, would equal its marginal costs *minus* the amount by which it was worse-placed than the best-placed MP (MPs) to supply the buyer in question while its price to its own customers would equal its marginal costs *plus* the OCAs it enjoyed in its relations with them *plus* the NOM + COM it obtained from them. If I ignore the fact that (for reasons that will be discussed below) the merger may increase the prices the relevant *R* is charging its own customers, the post-merger prices that the *R* will have to charge the merged firm's customers to match the merged firm's HNOP-containing offers will be higher and therefore less discriminatory and CMC-generating—*viz.*, will equal (rather than be lower than) the *R*'s marginal cost (since, post-merger, the *R* is second-placed). Admittedly, this reduction in the *R*'s relevant CMC will be lower to the extent that

The magnitude of the equivalent-dollar loss that such a merger inflicts on the MPs' customers by creating a merged firm that can obtain NOMs when the MPs could not (*i.e.*, by naturally deterring Rs that would have prevented an MP from obtaining an NOM from undercutting the merged firm's NOM-containing price) is directly related to

(1) the amount by which the merger increased the merged firm's OCAs above the best-placed MP's (MPs') OCAs and

---

the merger increases the *R*'s prices to its own customers, which it may do in three ways. First, the MPs' merger will increase the relevant *R*s' prices to their own customers by increasing their OCAs in their relations with buyers one or both of the MPs were second-placed to supply pre merger by causing the average CMC the merged firm would have to incur to match the *R*s' pre-merger HNOP-containing offers to exceed the CMC the second-placed MP(s) would have had to incur to do so pre merger by enabling the merged firm to obtain higher prices from its customers than the MPs would have obtained from/charged the same buyers pre merger (by increasing the merged firm's OCAs, NOMs, and COMs above the MPs')—*i.e.*, by making the merged firm's relevant-matching-offer price more discriminatory than its antecedents' relevant-matching-offer prices would have been. Second, and derivatively, any associated increase in the *R*s' OCAs will tend to increase the frequency with which they can obtain NOMs from the buyers in question. And third, for reasons that will be enumerated below, the merger will also increase the *R*s' COMs. (I should perhaps add that, to the extent that the *R*s whose prices to their own customers the merger increased are second-placed to obtain buyers the merged firm is best-placed to supply post-merger, any associated increase in the *R*s' relevant CMC will increase the merged firm's OCAs not only directly but also indirectly by increasing the CMC the merged firm has to incur to match the post-merger HNOP-containing offer of an *R* to a buyer the merged firm was or would otherwise have been second-placed to supply, thereby raising the *R*'s OCA and prices to its own customers, thereby raising the CMC the *R* would have to incur to match relevant offers the merged firm might make to its own customers, and so on and so forth.) I now need to explain the first sentence of this note—*i.e.*, why the *R* that was third-placed to obtain the patronage of an MP's customer pre merger may not be the *R* that is second-placed to obtain the patronage of that buyer post-merger. We have just seen that a horizontal merger can cause the CMC that a given *R*—*viz.*, the *R* that was third-placed to obtain a relevant buyer's patronage pre-merger—will have to incur to match the merged firm's HNOP-containing offer post-merger to differ from the CMC that that *R* had to incur to match the MP's (MPs') HNOP-containing offers pre-merger. The impact of a horizontal merger on the CMC in question may differ from *R* to R—*e.g.*, such a merger could reduce the CMC that an *R* that was fourth-placed or worse-than-fourth-placed pre merger had to incur to match the relevant HNOP-containing offers by more than it reduced the CMC that an *R* that was third-placed pre merger would have to incur to make such matching offers or could increase the CMC that an *R* that was second-placed pre merger to match the relevant HNOP-containing offers by more than it increased the CMC that an *R* that was worse-than-second-placed to match the relevant HNOP-containing offers. When either of these possibilities eventuates, an *R* that was fourth-placed or worse-than-fourth-placed to supply a buyer one or both MPs were best-placed to supply pre merger may be second-placed to supply that buyer post-merger. In such cases, the associated reduction in the amount by which the merged firm's OCA exceeds the best-placed MP's OCA will equal the reduction in the relevant CMC the post-merger second-placed *R* had to incur to match the relevant HNOP-containing offers *minus* the amount by which that firm was worse-placed pre merger than the *R* that was better-placed pre merger than any other *R* to obtain the relevant buyer's patronage. A final admission: neither the text to which this note is attached nor this note lists the determinants of the size of this effect. Those determinants are listed later in the text in paragraphs that focus on the possible effect of a horizontal merger on the OCAs, NOMs, and COMs of the MPs' *R*s.

(2) the frequency with which pre merger the strategic and mechanical cost the best-placed MP would have had to incur to change its initially-announced price exceeded its OCA by a small amount—*i.e.*, more precisely, is directly related to the frequency with which the merged firm's higher OCAs exceed the bargaining, legal, goodwill, buyer-expectation-related, and mechanical cost it must incur to change its initially-announced price when a best-placed MP's lower OCAs were lower than those costs.

Both the courts and the antitrust-enforcement agencies have been concerned about the possibility that horizontal mergers might increase price-fixing, but their analyses has focused primarily on the possibility that such a merger might eliminate a "maverick," defined implicitly to be a firm that for one or more unspecified reasons would not cooperate in a price-fixing conspiracy. My analysis of contrived oligopolistic pricing has far more specific implications. I will discuss them in detail.

The magnitude of the equivalent-dollar loss that a horizontal merger that generates no relevant efficiencies will inflict on the MPs' customers by increasing the COMs the merged firm obtains from them above the COMs the MPs would have obtained from them is directly related to (1) the frequency with which, pre-merger, contrived oligopolistic pricing was either profitable or unprofitable by a smaller amount than the amount by which the merger made such contrivance more profitable for the merged firm than it would have been for its antecedents and (2) the amount by which contrived oligopolistic pricing was more profitable for the merged firm than for its antecedents and relatedly the average amount by which the most profitable COMs for the merged firm to attempt to contrive exceeded the average COMs it was most profitable for its antecedents to attempt to contrive.

I will start by delineating and discussing the determinants of the first item in the preceding two-item list. Before doing so, however, I should admit that the need for information on these factors would be substantially reduced if it could be shown that the MPs and the merged firm's *R*s had successfully practiced contrived oligopolistic pricing prior to the relevant merger's proposal or execution, though even then information on the determinants of the profitability of such pricing would be useful to the extent that it would enable the relevant decisionmaker to assess whether conditions in the ARDEPPS had changed between the time that the relevant actors had engaged in such pricing and the time of the merger proposal in ways that would make such pricing unprofitable at the later date absent the merger. In any event, at any point in time, the frequency with which contrived oligopolistic pricing will be profitable for an individualized-pricing MP (or only slightly unprofitable for it) is

(1) inversely related to the number of rivals that were either second-placed or close-to-second-placed to obtain the patronage of the MPs' customers,
(2) directly related to the strength of the MPs' reputations for estimating their costs and OCAs accurately (a strong reputation for accuracy will increase their ability to communicate their contrived oligopolistic intentions cheaply simply by charging an oligopolistic price),
(3) directly related to the strength of the MPs' reputations for making and carrying out contrived oligopolistic threats and promises (a strong reputation for

contrivance will increase the profitability of such behavior both by reducing the cost of making the necessary communications [by enabling them to communicate simply by charging an oligopolistic price] and by increasing the credibility of the MP's anticompetitive threats and promises [by reducing the probability of undercutting]),

(4) directly related to the stability through time of the MPs' repeat-sales, sales-to-other-suppliers'-customers, and sales-to-new-buyers' percentages (which is positively correlated with the number of buyers in each of the three categories) and to the ability of the MPs to identify and measure the causes of fluctuations in these percentages other than the undercutting conduct of rivals and inversely related to the likely differences between relevant future and past conditions that are difficult to measure (the greater the MPs' ability to detect undercutting from such circumstantial sales-record evidence),

(5) directly related to the MPs' ability to identify their undercutter—inversely related to the number of rivals that would find undercutting the MP's contrived oligopolistic price profitable if the MP would not react strategically to any response to the MP's contrived oligopolistic price and directly related to their ability to identify their closest rivals for particular individual customers and their ability to identify the new suppliers of their old customers, of the former customers of their rivals, and/or of any new buyers in the market by inspecting deliveries, inventories, or goods sold,

(6) directly related to the amount of benefits the MPs can provide their potential undercutters (Us) by promising not to undercut the contrived oligopolistic prices of any cooperating rival and then foregoing the inherently-profitable opportunity to undercut the contrived oligopolistic prices the Us charged (relative to the profits the relevant undercutters could realize by undercutting the MPs, absent the MPs' strategic responses)—*i.e.*, directly related to the frequency with which and the amount by which the MPs were their potential Us' closest competitors (or were their potential Us' closest competitors among those rivals whose cooperation the Us had not secured),

(7) directly related to the ratio pre merger of the harm each MP could inflict on an undercutting *R* by engaging in individualized-price retaliation to the loss the MP must incur to do so for the amount of harm the MP had to inflict on that *R* to make the *R* regret undercutting sufficiently to deter the *R* and its counterparts from undercutting the MPs in the future—*inter alia*, and roughly speaking, directly related to the frequency with which the MPs were second-placed or close-to-second-placed to obtain each potential U's customers relative to the frequency with which that potential U was able to steal the relevant MP's customers and directly related to the size of each relevant U's OCAs in the U's relations with the buyers the MPs will find most cost-effective to steal in retaliation,

(8) inversely related to each MP's OCAs in the relevant "market"—*i.e.*, inversely related to the safe profits each MP had to put at risk to contrive an OM, and

(9) directly related to the company-wide sales of each MP to buyers from which it might contrive OMs—*i.e.*, to the extent to which pre merger each MP could

take advantage of company-wide economies of scale in building and maintaining a reputation for making contrived oligopolistic offers and carrying out contrived oligopolistic threats and promises.

Somewhat relatedly, the amount by which contrived oligopolistic pricing will be more profitable for the merged firm than for the MPs (*i.e.*, both the difference between the frequency with which the merged firm and the MPs will contrive OMs and the difference in the average COMs they contrive) is

(1) directly related to the frequency with which the elimination of MP2 as a potential undercutter of MP1 (and *vice versa*) reduces the number of potential Us because pre merger MP2 belonged to a group of second-placed or close-to-second-placed suppliers relative to the frequency with which the elimination of MP2 as a potential undercutter of MP1 (and *vice versa*) increased the number of MP1's potential undercutters because pre merger MP2 was MP1's closest competitor by a considerable margin and more than one *R* was or was close to being the third-placed supplier of the buyer in question,
(2) directly related to the contribution the merger makes to the MPs' ability to estimate their costs and OCAs (by enabling the MPs to share information about their product-*R*s' costs or the relative attractiveness of their own products versus those of their product-*R*s to particular buyers),
(3) directly related to the extent to which the merged firm has a stronger reputation for making contrived oligopolistic offers and carrying out its threats and promises than one or both of its antecedents (because it inherits the reputation of the tougher MP or because it creates a merged firm with a greater stake in deterring undercutting by enabling the whole company to profit from the reputational effects of any act of retaliation or reciprocation the merged company commits),
(4) directly related to the extent to which the merged company's ability to infer undercutting from circumstantial evidence exceeds its antecedents' because the merger enables the company to pool its antecedents' repeat-sales, sales-to-other-suppliers'-customers, and new-buyer-sales records (an effect that will probably increase with the sales of the MPs and the extent to which they have common product-*R*s, ["probably" because increases in MP sales cut in both directions since the value of any given amount of additional sales-record information will be inversely related to the original amount of such information available to the seller in question]),
(5) directly related to the extent to which the merged company's ability to identify its undercutter from sales-record circumstantial evidence exceeds its antecedents' because it has access to the relevant sales-records and rival-competitive-position information of both MPs (directly related to the sales of the MPs, the extent to which they have common product-*R*s, and the complementarity of the rival-competitive-position information in their possession),
(6) directly related to the amount by which the merger increases each MP's ability to reciprocate (directly related to the extent to which one MP had excess reciprocatory power pre merger and directly related to the frequency with

which the MPs were a rival's closest two rivals not to be co-opted pre merger and, in those instances in which they were the relevant rival's two closest non-co-opted rivals, directly related to the amount by which the worse-placed MP was better-placed than the next-placed supplier of the relevant rival's customer not to be co-opted),

(7) directly related to the extent to which the merger reduced the harm-inflicted to loss-incurred ratio for MP-retaliation by enabling the MPs to pool their power (by combining MPs with different marginal harm-inflicted to loss-incurred ratios for the last act of retaliation that would have been necessary for each had they remained separate in relation to a given potential U), and

(8) inversely related to the amount by which the merger increased the MPs' OCAs (at least if, as I suspect, increases in a seller's OCAs reduce the average COMs it will find most profitable to attempt to contrive by increasing the safe profits it must put at risk to do so by more than they raise those COMs by increasing the credibility of its related anti-competitive threats and promises by increasing the amount of profits it can protect by carrying them out).

The magnitude of the equivalent-dollar loss that such a merger inflicts on the MPs' product-*R*s' customers by increasing the MPs' product-*R*s' OCAs in their relations with buyers that an MP would have been second-placed to supply post-merger by raising the CMC that the merged firm would have to incur to charge the *R*'s customers the prices that would make the merged firm's offer to these buyers match the *R*'s HNOP-containing offer to them above the CMC that the second-placed MP would have had to incur to do so post-merger by increasing the prices the merged company charged its own customers above the prices the MPs charged their customers pre merger is

(1) directly related to the frequency with which one of the MPs was some *R*'s closest competitor for the patronage of a buyer that that *R* was best-placed to supply,

(2) directly related to the amount by which the MPs' merger will increase the prices the merged firm charges its customers above the prices the best-placed MP charged those buyers by causing the OCAs the merged firm enjoyed in its relations with those buyers and the NOMs and COMs it obtained from them to exceed the OCAs, NOMs, and COMs the MPs would have enjoyed and obtained post-merger, and

(3) directly related to the extent to which the CMC the merged firm will have to incur to match the *R*'s HNOP-containing offer exceed the CMC the relevant MP would have had to incur to do so post-merger (*i.e.*, after the date of the merger had the merger not been executed) because the merged firm's relevant matching-offer prices are more discriminatory than the MPs' relevant post-merger matching-offer prices would have been and/or because the merger made it more likely that the merged company would be prosecuted/sued and convicted/found liable on any set of evidentiary facts than would have been the case for the MPs post-merger—*i.e.*, directly related to (A) the frequency with which the merged firm exaggerated its costs in negotiations with buyers, (B) the proclivity of buyers to place a negative value on the profits they give sellers that

have discriminated against them, (C) the proclivity of buyers to assume that sellers that have reduced their initial prices to some buyers or in one time-period will repeat that conduct in relations with other buyers or in future time-periods and the ability of buyers to delay their purchases in anticipation of such price-reductions, (D) the extent to which the State or potential private plaintiffs are more likely to prosecute or sue recently-merged firms, (E) the extent to which triers-of-fact are more likely to find against recently-merged firms on a given set of evidentiary facts, (F) the extent to which the probability that a price discriminator will be prosecuted/sued and convicted/found liable for price discrimination increase with the discriminatoriness of its pricing, and (G) the extent to which the criminal penalties, fines, and damage-awards a defendant found guilty or liable for price discrimination must pay will increase with the discriminatoriness of its discrimination, and (H) the magnitude of the prescribed penalties, civil fines, and civil-damage-awards.

The magnitude of the equivalent-dollar loss that a horizontal merger between MPs that set individualized prices that generates no static marginal-cost efficiencies will impose on the merged firm's *R*s' customers by enabling those *R*s to obtain OMs naturally is directly related to the frequency with which the increases in those *R*s' OCAs that such a merger generates makes those OCAs higher than the various costs the relevant *R* must incur to change an initially-announced price when pre merger its lower OCA was lower than those costs—*i.e.*, is directly related to the amount by which the merger in question raises the *R*s' OCAs and the frequency with which an *R* whose OCA the merger increased could not obtain an OM naturally pre merger because its pre merger OCA was a small amount below the costs it had to incur to change its initially-announced price.

Finally, the magnitude of the equivalent-dollar loss that such a horizontal merger will impose on the customers of the merged firm's *R*s by increasing the COMs those *R*s contrive is

(1) inversely related to the amount by which the merger increases the *R*s' OCAs and NOMs (*i.e.*, increase the safe profits the *R*s must put at risk to engage in contrivance),
(2) directly related to the frequency with which both MPs were potential Us of a given product-*R* pre merger (directly related to the frequency with which pre merger such an *R* would have had to communicate with both MPs separately and would have had to consider the possibility that either MP might be their actual U and the greater the associated communication and identification costs),
(3) directly related to the amount by which the MPs' merger raises the amount of benefits an *R* can give the merged firm by reciprocating to the merged firm's decision not to undercut the *R* above the sum of the benefits the *R* could provide the two independent MPs in this way—the greater the frequency with which the two MPs were best-placed and second-placed when the *R* was third-placed and the greater the frequency with which the MPs were best-placed and third-placed when the *R* was second-placed and the greater the amount by which in this latter

case the third-placed MP was better-placed than the fourth-placed supplier of the buyer in question,
(4) directly related to the frequency with which the merger enables a given *R* to take advantage of any excess reciprocatory power it enjoyed vis-à-vis one MP because the *R* did not have sufficient reciprocatory power in relation to the other MP to secure its cooperation solely through reciprocation, and
(5) directly related to the amount by which the merger raises the harm-inflicted to loss-incurred ratio for the *R*'s inflicting a relevant amount of harm on the merged firm by retaliating against the merged firm's undercutting below its counterpart for the MPs by increasing the merged firm's OCAs, NOMs, and COMs above the MPs'.

Any effect a horizontal merger has on the HNOPs, NOMs, and COMs of MP *R*s that were best-placed to supply one or more customers one or both MPs were uniquely-second-placed to supply will have further ripple effects that will inflict equivalent-dollar losses on Clayton-Act-relevant buyers. Thus, for the same reason that any increase the merger generated in the merged firm's prices relative to those of the MPs would cause MP rivals some of whose customers one or both MPs were uniquely-second-placed to supply to raise their prices to their own customers, the increase in the prices these MP rivals were charging their customers would cause those rivals of the relevant MP rivals (both the MP/merged firm and other firms) one or more of whose customers the MP rivals in question were respectively uniquely-second-placed to supply to raise their prices (by increasing their OCAs and NOMs) and so on and so forth until the cycling is stopped by the competitive position of unaffected, worse-placed potential suppliers of the buyers in question.

(B) The Impact of a Horizontal Merger That Yields No Static Marginal-Cost Efficiencies on the Competitiveness of Prices at the ARDEPPS' Pre-Merger Equilibrium QV-Investment Level When the Merged Firm and Its *R*s Set Across-the-Board Prices

In the general case in which the marginal costs of the merger partners and their rivals vary over the relevant range of outputs, a complete analysis of the impact of a horizontal merger between firms that set across-the-board prices would have on the HNOPs of both the merged firm (relative to the HNOPs of the MPs) and its product-*R*s would proceed in the following way:

(1) identify the order in which the MPs and the merged firm's *R*s announced their prices pre merger (or, when necessary and more trickily, the order in which they would have announced their prices post-merger had they not engaged in oligopolistic pricing);
(2) determine each such firm's buyer-to-buyer pre merger BPA or BPD position in relation to each buyer one of them supplied pre merger or was close to supplying pre merger for each buyer one of the firms either supplied or was close to supplying post-merger and each such firm's marginal costs at, above,

and below its pre merger output; (to estimate the BPA/BPD and MC positions that each MP would have occupied in the post-merger period had the merger not been consummated);

(3) calculate the price that each such firm would have found most profitable to charge pre-merger and after the date of the merger had no merger been executed had it assumed that it could not react to its rivals' responses to its price, that its rivals understood this fact, and that its respective rivals would respond to its price and any other price announced before the rival in question announced its price on the assumption that the rival in question could not react to rival responses to that rival's price and that all other rivals understood this fact;
(4) identify the order in which the merged firm and its rivals would announce their prices post-merger if they did not engage in oligopolistic pricing;
(5) determine each such firm's post-merger buyer-by-buyer BPA or BPD position relative to its independent rivals in relation to each buyer one of them supplied pre merger or was close to supplying pre-merger (primarily by estimating each firm's pre-merger BPA/BPD array) and each such firm's likely post-merger MC curve (by estimating each's pre-merger MC curve);
(6) calculate the prices that each such firm would find most profitable to charge post-merger on the assumptions delineated in (3) above; and
(7) compare the pre merger across-the-board-pricing HNOP array generated by Steps (1)–(3) of this protocol with the post-merger across-the-board-pricing HNOP array generated by Steps (4)–(6) of this protocol.

In the special case in which the relevant firms' MC curves are horizontal over the relevant ranges of outputs (a condition that I think will often be satisfied), the protocol will be somewhat different: Step (2) of the protocol's analysis of the pre merger buyer-by-buyer across-the-board-pricing BCA and BCD positions of the merger partners and the other suppliers of all relevant buyers, and Step (5)'s analysis of the predicted post-merger buyer-by-buyer across-the-positions of board-pricing can focus exclusively on the BPA/BPD positions of the merged firm and the other suppliers of all relevant buyers.

Since it probably will not prove cost-effective to use even a crudely-executed version of this protocol to analyze the impact of the kind of horizontal merger with which we are now concerned on the relevant ARDEPPS' across-the-board-pricing HNOP array, I will restrict myself here to a few observations:

(1) such a merger will tend to increase the prices in an across-the-board-pricing ARDEPPS' HNOP array more when it creates a merged company that is in a better position than its antecedents were to alter the sequence in which it and its product-*R*s announce their prices in a way that raises the prices in the ARDEPPS' HNOP array;
(2) not surprisingly, the amount by which such a horizontal merger would increase the merged firm's HNOPs above the MPs' HNOPs even if it did not alter the HNOPs of the merged firm's *R*s will increase with (A) the frequency with which the MPs were either respectively uniquely-best-placed and uniquely-second-placed to obtain the patronage of given buyers (in BCA/BCD terms) or

uniquely-equal-best-placed to obtain the patronage of given buyers and (B) the average size of the advantage the second-placed MP (the two MPs) had over the third-placed supplier of the buyer in question in those cases in which the MPs were either uniquely-best-placed and uniquely-second-placed or uniquely-equal-best-placed;

(3) controlling for the factors delineated in item (2) in this list, the amount by which such a horizontal merger will increase the HNOPs of the merged firm's *R*s will increase with the frequency with which and the amount by which an MP was that seller's closest competitor, the closest competitor of that seller's closest competitor, or the closest competitor of the closest competitor of the sellers in question; and

(4) controlling for the factors delineated in item (2) in this list, the amount by which such a horizontal merger increases the HNOPs of the merged firm above those of the MPs will increase with the amount by which it increases the HNOPs of those of the MPs' *R*s that were its closest competitors for a significant percentage of its customers' patronage and so on and so forth.

To the extent that a horizontal merger that generates no static marginal-cost efficiencies raises the across-the-board HNOPs of the merged firm and its *R*s at the ARDEPPS' pre merger QV-investment level, it will tend on that account to increase the probability that they can obtain OMs naturally because, by increasing the amount by which their HNOPs exceed their marginal costs, the merger will increase the likelihood that the non-strategic profits the relevant firms will be able to earn by reducing an initially-announced price that has been undermined will exceed the various costs they will have to incur to change their initially-announced price. I should add, however, that any related tendency of such a horizontal merger to increase the merged firm's NOMs above the MPs' NOMs will be counteracted to the extent that the probability that the merged firm will be prosecuted/sued and convicted/found liable for reducing its initially-announced prices non-strategically is higher than the probability that the MPs would be prosecuted/sued and convicted/found liable for doing so (even though such conduct does not violate U.S. antitrust law: it does in my opinion violate E.C.I.E.U. competition law).

A horizontal merger that is executed in an ARDEPPS in which prices are set across-the-board and that generates no static marginal-cost efficiencies will affect the COMs that the merged firm and its *R*s attempt to contrive in many ways. I will focus first on the ways in which such a merger will affect the merged firm's practice of contrived oligopolistic pricing and then on the ways in which it will affect the merged firm's *R*s' practice of contrived oligopolistic pricing.

So far as the merged firm is concerned, such a merger will

(1) decrease the OMs it attempts to contrive (relative to the OMs the MPs would have attempted to contrive) by increasing the amount of safe profits it must put at risk to do so (by increasing the merged firm's [HNOP + NOM − MC] figure),
(2) increase the OMs it attempts to contrive by creating a larger firm that can take advantage of company-wide economies of scale in building and maintaining a reputation for contrivance,

(3) increase (decrease) the OMs it attempts to contrive if the merged firm inherits the reputation for contrivance of the MP with the stronger (weaker) reputation for contrivance,
(4) increase (decrease) the OMs it attempts to contrive if it inherits the reputation (ability) of the MP that was more (less) able to estimate its HNOP and NOM accurately,
(5) increase (decrease) the OMs it attempts to contrive if it decreases (increases) the number of rivals that would find it inherently profitable to undermine prices that contain given, relevant COMs,
(6) increase the OMs it attempts to contrive by increasing its rivals' (HNOP + NOM − MC) figures, thereby making them more vulnerable to retaliation and less likely to undermine the merged firm's contrived oligopolistic price on that account, and
(7) increase the OMs it attempts to contrive by increasing its ability to coordinate the retaliatory pricing of both MPs' products and perhaps by increasing as well its ability to induce other firms whose prices the undercutter undermined to retaliate against the underminer and to coordinate its own retaliation with these other firms (or less ambitiously, by increasing the ability of the merged firm to prevent such other firms from misperceiving its retaliation to be aggressive price-cutting and instigating an all-out price-war).

I cannot say whether, all things considered, across all relevant cases, horizontal mergers that yield no static marginal-cost efficiencies will increase or decrease the OMs that merged firms attempt to contrive.

So far as the merged firm's *R*s are concerned, a horizontal merger that is executed in an area of product-space in which prices are set across-the-board and that generates no static marginal-cost efficiencies will

(1) decrease the OM each *R* attempts to contrive by increasing the amount of safe profits it individually must put at risk to do so by increasing its (HNOP + NOM − MC) figure (but will do so far less than it will reduce the OMs the merged firm attempts to contrive in this way because it will increase the individual Rs' [HNOP + NOM − MC] figures far less than it increases the merged firm's [HNOP + NOM − MC] figure),
(2) increase the OM any *R* attempts to contrive to the extent that both MPs were potential underminers by enabling each *R* to substitute one communication to the merged firm for separate communications to each MP,
(3) increase the OM each *R* attempts to contrive to the extent that both MPs were potential underminers by increasing the merged firm's (HNOP + NOM − MC) figures above those of the MPs, thereby making the merged firm more vulnerable to retaliation than were the MPs and unlikely on that account to undermine any *R*'s contrived oligopolistic prices than were the MPs,
(4) increase the OM each *R* attempts to contrive by enabling it to reciprocate more to the merged firm's cooperation than it could to the MPs' by freeing each MP from the other's competition (by rendering the *R* second-placed to the merged

firm when it would have been third-placed behind either two uniquely-equal-best-placed MPs or one uniquely-best-placed MP and one uniquely-second-placed MP and by enabling the *R* to increase the benefits it can confer on the merged firm above those it could have conferred on an MP in cases in which one MP was best-placed, the *R* was second-placed, and the other MP was uniquely-third-placed),

(5) increase the OM each *R* attempts to contrive to the extent that the MPs were potential underminers by spreading the merged firm's defenses—*i.e.*, by making the merged firm more vulnerable to retaliation and less inclined to undermine a rival's contrived oligopolistic price on that account by permitting the *R* to reduce the loss it must incur to inflict given relevant amounts of harm on the merged firm by retaliating against it below the loss the *R* would have had to incur to inflict the same total amount of harm on the two MPs by retaliating more against the merged firm's MP1 division and less against the merged firm's MP2 division (or *vice versa*) when the marginal harm-inflicted to loss-incurred ratio for additional retaliation against the MP1 division beyond the amount that would have been executed against the independent MP1 was greater than its counterpart for the last act of retaliation that would have been executed against the independent MP2, and

(6) increase the OM each *R* attempts to contrive by enabling it to piggyback on the enhanced ability of the merged firm to retaliate against underminers, to induce other rivals to join in such retaliation, and to increase the cost-effectiveness of all retaliators' retaliation (unless the merger reduces the amount of contrived oligopolistic pricing that the merged firm practices sufficiently below the amount its antecedents practiced for this effect to outweigh its predecessor).

All things considered, my suspicion is that, across all cases, horizontal mergers that generate no static marginal-cost efficiencies will tend to increase the amount of COMs the across-the-board-pricing *R*s of across-the-board-pricing merged firms attempt to and actually do obtain.

(2) The Impact That a Horizontal Meger That Yields No Dynamic Efficiencies Will Have on the Intensity of QV-Investment Competition

The preceding analyses all assumed that the horizontal merger in question would not affect the equilibrium QV-investment level in the ARDEPPS in which it takes place. This assumption is obviously unrealistic. *Ceteris paribus*, any increase that a horizontal merger generates in the prices that are charged at the relevant ARDEPPS' pre merger equilibrium QV-investment level will tend to cause additional QV investments to be introduced into the relevant area of product-space (by raising the $H\Pi_E$, $I\Pi_E$, and $H\Pi_N$ curves in the ARDEPPS in question). Such induced QV investments will benefit the customers of the merged firm and the customers of its *R*s both directly by increasing the quality and variety of goods available to them and indirectly by decreasing the prices of the products that were produced in the

ARDEPPS pre merger and will on both these accounts reduce the net equivalent-dollar loss the relevant horizontal merger imposes on Clayton-Act-relevant buyers. Obviously, however, to the extent that a price-increasing horizontal merger that generates no dynamic efficiencies reduces the intensity of QV-investment competition in the ARDEPPS in which it is executed, it will generate a smaller increase in that ARDEPPS' equilibrium QV-investment level than it otherwise would have done and therefore will impose a larger net equivalent-dollar loss on the combination of the customers of the merged firm and the customers of its *R*s than it otherwise would have done.

A horizontal merger that generates no dynamic efficiencies can reduce QV-investment competition in the ARDEPPS in which it is executed either (1) by deterring the merged firm from making a QV investment that one of the MPs would have made pre merger when no other established firm or potential entrant would otherwise have introduced an additional QV investment into the relevant area of product-space (because all other established firms faced barriers to expansion and/or monopolistic QV-investment disincentives that were critically higher than those that confronted the relevant MP and because all potential competitors faced barriers to entry that exceeded the sum of the barriers to expansion and *M* or *O* QV-investment disincentives facing the relevant MP) or (2) by deterring one or more actual or potential *R*s of the merged firm from adding a QV investment to the relevant area of product-space when the deterred QV investment would not be replaced by a QV investment made by someone else. I will first explain the various reasons why a horizontal merger that generates no dynamic efficiencies may deter the merged firm from making a QV investment that would increase the ARDEPPS' equilibrium QV-investment level, then explain why such a merger may deter an actual or potential rival of the merged firm from making a QV investment that would increase the ARDEPPS' equilibrium QV-investment level, and finally explain why, perversely, in a few situations such a merger may induce the merged firm or one of its actual rivals to make a QV investment that would increase the relevant ARDEPPS' equilibrium QV-investment level.

A horizontal merger that generates no dynamic efficiencies can reduce QV-investment competition in the ARDEPPS in which it is executed by deterring the merged firm from making a QV investment one of its antecedents would have made in five ways:

(1) by causing the merged firm to face higher (Π_D + R) barriers than the relevant MP faced pre merger by making it profitable for the merged firm to devote to consolidation resources the MP would have used to execute a QV-investment expansion;
(2) by raising the L barriers the merged firm faces above the L barriers the relevant MP would have faced had no merger been executed by decreasing the cost that potential retaliators would have to incur to inflict relevant amounts of harm on an expanding merged firm below the costs they would have had to incur to inflict these amounts of harm on an expanding MP by raising the merged firm's (OCA + NOMs) in individualized-pricing contexts and its (HNOP + NOM − MC) in across-the-board-pricing contexts above their counterparts for the relevant MP and creating

a merged firm whose defenses are more spread than were those of the relevant MP (a merged firm against which rivals can retaliate by lowering prices to or affecting the profits yielded by sales to the customers of both MPs rather than solely the customers of the MP that would have expanded) when these effects (as I expect they usually will) exceed any tendency the merger has to reduce the L barriers facing the merged firm below those that would have faced the relevant MP (A) by creating a merged company that has inherited the reputation of the tougher MP for not being deterrable, (B) by creating a merged company that would in any event be thought to be less deterrable than the relevant MP would have been deemed to be because the merged company can take better advantage of company-wide economies of scale in establishing and maintaining a reputation for not being deterrable, and (C) by eliminating the possibility that the MP that would not have expanded pre merger but might have retaliated against the other MP's expansion pre merger will retaliate against the merged company's expansion;

(3) by causing the merged firm to face higher monopolistic QV-investment disincentives than the relevant MP would have faced by making the profits the expansion will yield the merged firm depend not only on the amount by which it will reduce the profit-yields of the pre existing (and possible future) projects of the MP that would have expanded but also on the amount by which it will reduce the profit-yields of the projects of the MP that would not have expanded pre-merger: admittedly, this difference in the *M* disincentives faced by the merged firm and the *M* disincentive the relevant MP faced will be lower to the extent that the merged firm can increase the profits an expansion yields by introducing a QV investment that is less competitive with the projects of the MP that would not have expanded than the QV investment of the MP that would have expanded would have been (to the extent that the resulting profit-loss reduction exceeds the amount by which the conventional profit-yield of the less-competitive project falls below the conventional profit-yield of the project the MP would have executed);

(4) by creating a merged firm that faces higher natural oligopolistic QV-investment disincentives *O* than a relevant MP would have faced because the profits yielded by any QV-investment expansion the merged firm executes depend, *inter alia*, on the amount by which any rival QV investment that expansion induces lowers the profits yielded by the other projects of both MPs whereas the profits yielded by any QV-investment expansion the relevant MP might have executed depend, *inter alia*, on the amount by which any rival QV investment that expansion induces lowers the profits yielded by only its other projects; and

(5) by converting (A) a situation in which both MPs, both MPs and one or more of their established rivals, or one MP and one or more of their established rivals would have added to the relevant ARDEPPS' QV-investment level because (i) the ARDEPPS' pre existing QV-investment level equaled or exceeded its entry-preventing QV-investment level, (ii) the barriers to expansion facing both MPs and one or more of their established *R*s were not in themselves preclusive, and (iii) the MPs and *R*s in question did not cause each other to face natural oligopolistic QV-investment disincentives because, *inter alia*, three or more of

them would not have faced preclusive barriers to expansion into (B) a situation in which the merged firm and one or more of its established rivals face (preclusive) *O* disincentives by reducing by one the number of independent established firms not facing preclusive barriers to expansion.

I should add that, in some cases, a horizontal merger will also reduce QV-investment competition in the area of product-space in which it is executed by creating a merged firm that finds it profitable to withdraw one or more of the MPs' QV investments in circumstances in which such a choice will not lead a rival to make a QV investment (or an equally-large amount of QV investments). The merged firm will find such consolidation or rationalization profitable when the profits the use of the removed QV investment generated for that MP were lower than the amount by which the relevant QV investment reduced the profit-yields of the projects of the other MP or, more to the point, the other projects of the merged firm and the merged firm knows that the withdrawn QV investment will not be replaced by a rival QV investment (or possibly by an equally-competitive rival QV investment).

A horizontal merger that generates no dynamic efficiencies can reduce QV-investment competition in the ARDEPPS in which it is executed by deterring an established rival or potential competitor of the merged firm from making a QV investment that rival would have made had no merger been executed in two ways:

(1) by critically raising the retaliation barrier to expansion or entry that rival faces (A) by creating a merged firm that can better coordinate the retaliation that its antecedents and perhaps the retaliation its remaining rivals and its antecedents direct at an expanding established firm or new entrant, *inter alia*, by reducing the risk that defensive retaliation will lead to a price-war because one or more non-underminers mistake a retaliator's retaliation for non-retaliatory price-cuts aimed at them (and perhaps others); (B) by increasing the harm-inflicted to loss-incurred ratio for retaliation against a relevant expander for both the merged firm and other potential retaliators by raising the expander's (OCA + NOM) figures in individualized-pricing contexts and its (HNOP − NOM − MC) figure in an across-the-board-pricing context; and (C) by creating a merged firm that will find maintaining and building a reputation for retaliating against rival QV investments (and other rival competitive moves) more profitable than its individual antecedents would have done because the merged firm can take advantage of company-wide economies of scale in building and maintaining such a reputation when, as I suspect will usually be the case, those effects are stronger than the countervailing tendency of such a merger to reduce the retaliation barriers to QV investing the merged firm's rivals face by increasing the law-related costs the merged firm will face if it retaliates above those the relevant MP would have faced if it retaliated; and (D) by increasing the harm-inflicted to loss-incurred ratio for the investing *R*'s retaliating against the merged firm's retaliation above its counterpart for the investing *R*'s retaliating against the relevant MP's retaliation by raising the merged firm's (OCA + NOM)s or (HNOP + NOM − MC) figure (s) above the MPs' and by creating a merged firm whose defenses are more spread than those of its individual antecedents and

(2) by causing an established rival that would not otherwise have faced *M* disincentives to expansion (indeed, that might otherwise have had a monopolistic QV-investment incentive to expand) because it knew that, if it did not expand, an MP would have expanded instead to face critical *M* disincentives (not to have critical *M* incentives) by creating a merged company that would not expand despite the fact that one of its antecedents would have done so after the date of the merger or by causing two or more established rivals that would not otherwise have faced *O* disincentives to do so by substituting for an MP that would not have been deterred from expanding by the (Π_D + R + S + L) barriers it faces a merged firm that faces one or more barriers of these kinds that are critically higher.

I turn now to the various ways in which a horizontal merger that generates no static or dynamic efficiencies can increase QV-investment competition in the ARDEPPS in which it is executed. First, some horizontal mergers that generate no static or dynamic efficiencies will increase QV-investment competition by reducing the retaliation barrier to expansion faced by the merged company and/or one or more of its rivals.[878] Such a horizontal merger can create a merged company that faces lower L barriers than a relevant MP would have faced if the merged company's stake in avoiding a reputation of being deterrable and for other reasons the merged company's ability to retaliate cost-effectively against those that have retaliated against it exceed the relevant stakes and abilities of its antecedents, though I suspect that these effects will rarely outweigh the tendency of such mergers to increase the

[878] I should note that, in a few cases, such reductions in L barriers might reduce QV-investment competition. In particular this result will obtain when the following conditions are fulfilled:

(1) the pre merger L barriers would have rendered any additional QV investment unprofitable for the relevant MP or merged-firm *R*;

(2) the monopolistic QV-investment disincentive that another firm faced as a result would not have been critical—*i.e.*, the other firm in question would have made a QV investment pre-merger;

(3) the merger-generated reduction in L would make it profitable for the merged firm or merged-firm *R* whose L barrier was reduced to execute a QV investment if its doing so would not induce another firm to make a QV investment that that other firm would not otherwise make;

(4) the merger-generated reduction in L would not make it profitable for the merged firm or merged-firm R whose L barrier was reduced to make a QV investment if its doing so would induce another firm to make a QV investment that that other firm would not otherwise make but will make it profitable for the established firm in question to make a QV investment once the other firm has made one (since, then, the former firm's investment will not induce the latter firm to make such an investment); and

(5) the other firm that would have made a QV investment pre merger despite the fact that it faced a monopolistic QV-investment disincentive will not make a QV investment post-merger if the established firm whose L barrier the merger reduced does not do so because the profits its QV investment would yield if it did not induce another firm to make a QV investment are lower than the loss another firm's QV investment would impose on it and, as indicated in (4), post-merger, the established firm's QV investment would induce the other firm whose L barrier the merger reduced to make a QV investment.

In brief, when these conditions are fulfilled, the reduction in L barriers the merger generated will reduce QV-investment competition because it will cause relevant potential investors to face critical natural oligopolistic QV-investment disincentives when otherwise the relevant potential investor would have had a non-critical monopolistic QV-investment disincentive.

retaliation barriers faced by the merged firm above those the MPs would have faced by increasing the merged firm's OCAs, NOMs, and COMs above those of its antecedents and by creating a merged firm that a retaliator can attack by cutting prices to both MPs' customers. Such a horizontal merger can reduce the L barriers faced by an *R* of the merged firm below those it would have faced by creating a merged firm that (1) faces retaliation-related law-related costs that are higher than the retaliation-related law-related costs its antecedents would have faced and (2) had higher OCAs, NOMs, and COMs and defenses that are more-widely spread, which will increase the harm-inflicted to loss-incurred ratio the *R* would face in relation to its retaliation against the merged firm's retaliation against the *R*'s investing. However, once more, I suspect that these effects will rarely outweigh the tendency of such a merger to increase the L barriers the MPs' *R*s face by creating a merged company that has a higher stake in building and maintaining a reputation for retaliating, that can retaliate through the products of both MPs, and that is more able than are the individual MPs to induce other *R*s to participate in retaliation against a target *R* that has made a QV investment. Second, horizontal mergers that generate no static marginal-cost efficiencies or dynamic efficiencies can also increase QV-investment competition by substituting for two MPs that would have faced critical natural oligopolistic QV-investment disincentives (that their respective abilities to expand imposed on each other) a merged firm that faced a non-critical monopolistic QV-investment incentive (that created a merged firm that could make one QV investment when, collectively, the two MPs "together" would have been able to make either no QV investment or two QV investments and also created a firm that could increase the profitability of its expansions by choosing to execute a QV investment that was less damaging to its pre existing projects' profit-yields than the QV investment either MP would have been to the profit-yields of the two MPs' pre existing projects). Horizontal mergers that generate no static or dynamic efficiencies but do create a merged company that faces higher ($\Pi_D + R$) barriers than its antecedents faced can also increase QV-investment competition by converting a situation in which one or both MPs and a merged-firm *R* originally caused each other to face critical natural oligopolistic QV-investment disincentives into one in which the merged-firm *R* faces non-critical monopolistic QV-investment disincentives by raising the ($\Pi_D + R + L$) barriers the merged firm faces sufficiently to deter it from making a QV investment if the rival makes one (or, indeed, even if the rival does not). I hasten to add that I doubt the practical importance of these last two possibilities: given the fact that the conditions for their realization are evanescent (and the related fact that the increase in competition with which they will be associated will be small), the substantial cost of establishing their factual predicates will almost always be prohibitive.

B. The Determinants of the Magnitude of the Equivalent-Dollar Gains That Any Static and Dynamic Efficiencies a Horizontal Merger Generates Will Confer on the Customers of the Merged Firm and the Customers of the Merged Firm's Rivals

Virtually all the procompetitive effects horizontal mergers can have derive from the organizational economic efficiencies they are capable of generating. Previously, I distinguished two types of such efficiencies that a merger can generate. In my vocabulary, a merger is said to generate *static* organizational economic efficiencies to the extent that the merged firm can operate the MPs' QV-investment projects more proficiently than the MPs did—*e.g.*, to the extent that the merged firm produces a relevant quantity of an MP's product more cheaply than the MP did. And, in my vocabulary, a merger is said to generate *dynamic* efficiencies to the extent that the merged firm faces lower (Π_D + R) barriers to expansion than the MP that was better-placed to expand did.[879]

Purely-static efficiencies will not benefit the customers of the MPs' rivals or the customers of the MPs if the efficiencies are fixed-cost or non-marginal-or-incremental-cost variable-cost efficiencies. However, any tendency of a horizontal merger to reduce the marginal or incremental cost of the merged firm below that of an MP will usually confer a net equivalent-dollar gain on Clayton-Act-relevant buyers.

Assume that the horizontal merger in question reduces the merged firm's marginal costs below its antecedents' marginal costs. The determinants of the impact of any static marginal-cost efficiencies a horizontal merger generates on Clayton-Act-relevant buyers will be somewhat different when the merged firm, the MPs, and their *R*s set individualized prices from their counterparts when across-the-board-pricing is practiced in the relevant ARDEPPS. I will focus first on individualized-pricing contexts and then on across-the-board-pricing contexts.

The individualized-pricing-context analysis will initially assume that (1) the static marginal-cost efficiencies that horizontal mergers generate will not affect the CMC that the merged firm and its *R*s must incur to compete for the patronage of buyers they are not best-placed to supply (*i.e.*, to match the HNOP-containing offers that these buyers receive from their respective best-placed suppliers), (2) the static marginal-cost efficiencies that horizontal mergers generate will not cause any merged-firm *R*s to exit, and (3) both of the MPs and, more to the point, the merged firm face marginal-cost curves that are horizontal between the MPs' pre merger outputs and the outputs of the MPs' products that the merged firm would sell. All of these assumptions will be relaxed at the end of the discussion.

---

[879] Mergers can generate dynamic efficiencies either by generating static efficiencies that carry over to expansions or by generating specifically-dynamic efficiencies—*e.g.*, by combining one MP that has a clever idea for a profitable QV investment with another MP that can finance the project with retained earnings and has the ability to recognize the profitability of the venture when outside financiers would be less perspicuous.

I will also initially make a fourth assumption that, though unrealistic, is expositionally attractive. This fourth assumption is that the variations in price on which the analysis focuses will not affect the number of units of the relevant product that any buyer purchases—more specifically, that each buyer will buy one unit of the product in question, regardless of the prices that are being charged for the relevant products. (The exposition that follows will ignore the fact that, if the number of units purchased exceeds one, the analysis should focus on incremental [variable] costs rather than on marginal costs.) This fourth assumption is convenient because it allows me to focus on sets of buyers rather than on the sales that various sellers are best-placed or worse-than-best-placed to make. I will also drop this fourth assumption when discusing the way in which the impact that any static marginal-cost efficiencies a horizontal merger generates will have on Clayton-Act-relevant buyers will be affected by any tendency of the merged firm's marginal-cost curves to rise to the right of the MPs' pre merger outputs of their products. I hasten to add, however, that this assumption that the relevant variations in prices will not affect the quantity of any good a relevant buyer purchases does not critically affect any important conclusion I reach.

As previously indicated, this fourth assumption enables me to analyze the effect of the static marginal-cost efficiencies a horizontal merger generates on Clayton-Act-relevant buyers in individualized-pricing contexts by analyzing separately their effect on each of five sets of buyers, distinguished by the combination of how well-placed the most-advantageously-placed (highest-ranking) MP was to obtain their patronage pre merger and how well-placed the merged company is to supply them post-merger. The first set contains buyers for which both MPs were much-worse-than-second-placed pre merger and the merged company is also much-worse-than-second-placed post-merger (though the merged firm's competitive disadvantage is lower than that of the better-placed MP—equals that MP's OCD *minus* the marginal-cost reduction the merger enabled the merged firm to achieve). CMC-related and exit possibilities aside, the static marginal-cost efficiencies the relevant horizontal merger generated will have no effect on the prices these buyers must pay—*i.e.*, will have no impact on their best-placed supplier's OCA and hence HNOP, no effect on the OM that firm can obtain naturally from them, and no effect on the OM it can contrive from them (unless the relevant best-placed supplier was able to co-opt all of those inferior suppliers that were better-placed than the merged firm to supply the buyers in question).

The second set of buyers contains those buyers that both MPs were considerably worse-than-second-placed to supply pre merger but the merged firm was either equal-second-placed or close-to-second-placed to supply. CMC-related and exit possibilities aside, the static marginal-cost efficiencies that the relevant horizontal merger generated will also not affect the prices these buyers must pay by altering their respective best-placed suppliers' HNOP (since they will not affect their OCAs), will therefore also not affect the NOMs these buyers must pay, but may reduce the COMs they must pay by increasing the number of rivals whose cooperation their best-placed supplier must secure to obtain a COM it would otherwise have tried to obtain—by creating a merged firm about which their best-placed supplier must be concerned when the MPs would not have been able to profit by undercutting its contrived oligopolistic price if that response elicited no reaction.

The third set of buyers contains those buyers that the MPs were either worse-than-second-placed to supply or second-placed to supply and the merged firm was not only better-placed to supply than was either MP but uniquely-second-placed to supply. CMC-related and exit possibilities aside, the static marginal-cost efficiencies the horizontal merger generated will benefit each such buyer by lowering its best-placed supplier's HNOP by the difference between the marginal-cost reduction the merger generated for the product that was second-placed post-merger and any amount by which the MP that produced that product was worse-than-second-placed pre-merger. Concomitantly, the static marginal-cost efficiencies the merger generated would reduce the probability that these buyers would have to pay NOMs (the probability that their respective best-placed suppliers could obtain NOMs). Finally, the static marginal-cost efficiencies in question would have an uncertain effect on the COMs the buyers in question would have to pay—would tend to increase those COMs by reducing the safe profits the buyers' respective best-placed suppliers would have to put at risk to contrive an OM, would have an uncertain effect on those COMs by changing the number of rivals that were second-placed or close-to-second-placed to obtain the relevant buyers' patronage (whose cooperation the best-placed supplier would have to secure to obtain a COM, to which it would have to communicate its contrived oligopolistic intentions, and that it would have to consider when trying to identify its actual undercutter) since the efficiencies could either increase or decrease that number, and for analogous reasons would also have an uncertain effect on such determinants of the profitability of contrived oligopolistic pricing as the ability of the best-placed supplier to reciprocate to its rivals' cooperation and the cost it would have to incur to inflict relevant amounts of harm on its undercutters through retaliation.

The fourth set of buyers contains those buyers that neither MP was best-placed to supply pre merger but the merged firm was either best-placed to supply or equal-best-placed to supply post-merger. CMC-related and exit possibilities aside, the static-marginal-cost efficiencies the relevant horizontal merger generated would improve the most attractive offers those buyers would receive if their best-placed suppliers did not engage in oligopolistic pricing by their pre merger best-placed supplier's OCA (which the merger would at least wipe out).[880] If the merged firm's post-merger average OCA in its relations with these buyers is higher than the average OCA the other suppliers that were best-placed to supply them pre merger enjoyed in their relations with them pre-merger, the associated gain to the buyers in question will tend to be reduced by the related tendency of the efficiencies to increase the NOMs they pay. However, if the merged firm's post-merger average

[880] The buyers in question would not benefit directly from any positive difference between the marginal-cost reduction the merger generated and the amount by which the MP that produced the product that became best-placed post-merger was worse-than-best-placed pre merger (the pre merger OCD of the MP in question): any such difference would yield a profit for the merged company.

OCA in its relations with these buyers is lower than the average OCA the suppliers that were best-placed to supply them pre merger enjoyed pre merger in their relations with them, the associated gain to the buyers in question will tend to be increased by the related tendency of the static efficiencies the merger generates to reduce the NOMs these buyers pay. Across all cases in this category, if CMC-related and exit possibilities are ignored, I see no reason to believe that the static marginal-cost efficiencies that horizontal mergers generate will either increase or decrease the NOMs that the buyers in question pay: the impact of the efficiencies on these NOMs will depend on whether the merged firm's post-merger OCAs are larger or smaller than the OCAs the *R* that was best-placed pre merger enjoyed pre-merger and on whether the costs the merged firm had to incur to change its initial price post-merger were higher or lower than the costs the *R* in question had to incur pre merger to change its initial price. If the static marginal-cost efficiencies the relevant merger generates had no effects on CMC and led to no exits, I would also be unable to predict the effect that they would have on the COMs these buyers pay across all cases: *ceteris paribus*, the sign of this effect will depend on whether the efficiencies caused the merged firm's post-merger average OCA in its relations with these buyers to be larger or smaller than the average OCA the other firms that were best-placed to supply them pre merger enjoyed in their relations with them at that time, on whether and the extent to which the merged firm was more able than the *R* that would otherwise have been their best-placed supplier to detect undercutting from sales records, on whether and the extent to which the merged firm would be more able than the relevant *R* to reciprocate to cooperators, on whether and the extent to which the retaliation-related harm-inflicted to loss-incurred ratio would be higher for the merged firm than for that *R*, *etc*.

On balance, if the static marginal-cost efficiencies a horizontal merger generates have no relevant CMC consequences and lead to no exits and the horizontal mergers that generate static marginal-cost efficiencies all involve MPs and merged firms whose marginal-cost curves are horizontal between the MPs' outputs and the merged firm's outputs, I would have no doubt that the static marginal-cost efficiencies in question would confer a net equivalent-dollar gain on all of the first four sets of buyers I have just distinguished. Unfortunately, I suspect that, even on the above assumptions, such efficiencies will, if anything, tend to inflict a net equivalent-dollar loss on the fifth set of buyers I want to distinguish—buyers that one MP was uniquely-best-placed to supply pre merger or both MPs were uniquely-best-placed to supply pre-merger. Admittedly, CMC-related and exit possibilities aside, the static marginal-cost efficiencies a horizontal merger generates will have no impact on this set of buyers by changing their best-placed supplier's HNOPs because the efficiencies in question will not make the merged firm's HNOP differ from the best-placed MP's HNOP. However, any static marginal-cost efficiencies a horizontal merger generates will tend to impose equivalent-dollar losses on these buyers by increasing the NOMs they must pay by increasing the merged firm's OCAs above its best-placed antecedent's OCAs. My uncertainty about whether horizontal mergers that generate static marginal-cost efficiencies will inflict a net equivalent-dollar loss on this fifth group of buyers reflects the fact that they could decrease the COMs these buyers must pay. The impact of such efficiencies on these COMs is unclear because, although they may tend to increase the COMs the merged firm attempts to receive by enabling it to reciprocate more to cooperators than the MPs could (by making it second-placed more often than the MPs were) and by increasing its harm-inflicted to loss-incurred ratio for retaliation against undercutters (in the same way), they will also tend to decrease the COMs the merged firm tries to obtain by increasing the safe profits it must put at risk to do so (by increasing its [OCA + NOM]s). Nevertheless, all things considered, I suspect that, even if CMC-related and exit possibilities are ignored, any static marginal-cost efficiencies a horizontal merger generates will, if anything, tend to inflict a net equivalent-dollar loss on this fifth set of buyers.

I now turn to the CMC-related, exit, and non-horizontal marginal-cost curve possibilities I have so far ignored. First, how will the CMC consequences of any static marginal-cost efficiencies a horizontal merger generates affect Clayton-Act-relevant buyers if the relevant marginal-cost curves are horizontal over the relevant ranges? To the extent that such efficiencies reduce the prices that a merged-firm *R* charges buyers it was best-placed to supply pre merger and is best-placed to supply post-merger by lowering its HNOP (by reducing the OCD of the merged firm in relation to the buyers in question below the pre merger OCD of its better-placed antecedent, derivatively by eliminating the relevant *R*'s ability to obtain OMs naturally from the buyers in question, and/or by eliminating or reducing the OMs it contrives from them), the efficiencies may also benefit buyers these *R*s were second-placed or close-to-second-placed to supply pre merger (regardless of whether these buyers' best-placed supplier was the merged firm or another *R*) by reducing the CMC the *R*s in question will have to incur to match the HNOP-containing offers of these latter buyers' best-placed suppliers in circumstances in which this CMC reduction makes a relevant *R* second-placed that was not originally second-placed or reduces the OCD of a relevant *R* that was originally second-placed—*i.e.*, by reducing the HNOPs of these buyers' best-placed suppliers in this way and possibly derivatively their ability to obtain OMs naturally.[881] I hasten to add that this effect will be reduced by the tendency of the relevant static marginal-cost efficiencies to increase the CMC the merged firm must incur to match the relevant *R*s' HNOP-containing offers (by increasing the prices—the NOMs and possibly the

[881] The text ignores one type of NOM-related efficiency a horizontal merger can generate—*viz.*, the ability of a horizontal merger to reduce the cost the merged firm must incur to change its initially-announced prices below the costs its antecedents would have had to incur to do so by creating a company that can take more advantage of economies of scale in changing advertising, prices posted on shelves or affixed to products, or prices entered into computers. Any such efficiencies will clearly make it more possible for the merged company than for its antecedents to obtain OMs naturally. Obviously, to the extent that such efficiencies do increase the merged firm's NOMs above the MPs', they will inflict equivalent-dollar losses on the customers of the MPs on this account. Derivatively, to the extent that such efficiencies increase the merged firm's NOMs above the MPs', they will also tend to inflict equivalent-dollar losses on the customers of the *R*s that the MPs were originally second-placed to supply by raising the CMC the merged company would have to incur to match the pre-merger HNOP-containing offers of these buyers' best-placed suppliers above the CMC the MPs had to incur to do so pre-merger.

COMs—the merged firm obtains from its own customers above those the MP charged them) at the same time that they reduce the conventional marginal costs the merged firm must incur to supply the relevant buyers.

Second, why may the static marginal-cost efficiencies a horizontal merger generates induce one or more of the merged firm's *R*s to exit, and, if the efficiencies do induce such an exit, how will they affect Clayton-Act-relevant buyers on this account? To the extent that the static marginal-cost efficiencies a horizontal merger generates reduces the OCAs of the remaining rivals (*R*s) of the MPs and merged firm, to the extent that derivatively they prevent those *R*s from obtaining OMs naturally, and to the extent that they reduce the COMs those *R*s obtain, they will obviously tend to induce the relevant *R*s to exit—in particular, will induce those *R*s to exit whose related losses exceed the supernormal profits they would otherwise have realized by operating or renewing their QV investments. Moreover, to the extent that the QV investment of any such *R* that exits is not replaced or is replaced by a QV investment that puts less competitive pressure on the other projects in the relevant area of product-space than the withdrawn QV investment did, the static marginal-cost efficiencies that induced the exit will inflict an equivalent-dollar loss not only on the buyers of the withdrawn product or outlet that obtained buyer surplus by purchasing it but also on buyers of other products whose prices the withdrawn product reduced by more than they were reduced by any QV investment whose creation was induced by the withdrawal of the exited QV investment. Of course, any equivalent-dollar loss these two sets of buyers sustained will be somewhat offset by any gains that buyers of other products obtain because the induced QV investment put more pressure on their suppliers than the withdrawn QV investment did. (The exit and withdrawal of a QV investment will also affect relevant buyers to the extent that the buyer surplus the customers of the withdrawn QV investment realized by patronizing its owner differs from the buyer surplus the customers of the "replacement" QV investment realize by purchasing the good it creates.) All things considered, I have no doubt that, in the vast majority of instances, any exits induced by the static marginal-cost efficiencies a horizontal merger yields will inflict net equivalent-dollar losses on Clayton-Act-relevant buyers.[882]

Third, how will any tendency of the merged firm's marginal-cost curves to rise to the right of the MPs' pre merger outputs affect the impact that any static marginal-cost efficiencies the horizontal merger generates will have on Clayton-Act-relevant buyers? Unfortunately, the analysis of this issue is complicated. I will analyze it initially on the assumption that, at the time that the merged firm makes any individualized bid from either a best-placed position or a position of competitive inferiority, it knows how many of its other bids have been and will be accepted—in particular, it knows that all the bids it makes from a best-placed position will be accepted and that none of the bids it makes from a position of competitive inferiority

[882] Of course, if the Clayton Act is interpreted to contain an organizational-allocative-efficiency defense, the losses that a merger imposed on Clayton-Act-relevant buyers in this way will never critically affect its Clayton Act legality.

will be accepted. (Admittedly, if it were not for the ability of unaccepted bids to yield keeping-in-touch advantages, the second part of the preceding assumption would be inconsistent with my general assumption that all relevant sellers are sovereign maximizers.) This assumption will be relaxed at the end of the analysis.

The analysis that follows will also be based on a second assumption, which differs from the assumption just described in two ways: it is realistic, and it complicates the relevant analysis. In particular, the analysis that follows takes account of the reality that variations in the prices that a given seller charges a given buyer for a particular good or service may affect the number of units of that good that the buyer purchases from the seller in question if it patronizes that seller—*i.e.*, will take account of the fact that particular potential purchasers of any good from a particular supplier will often place different values on the successive units of that good they may choose to purchase and will sometimes vary their unit purchases with the terms they are offered. This assumption makes the exposition somewhat more awkward. Once one recognizes that a seller that is best-placed to sell one or more units of its product to a given buyer may be second-placed to sell other additional units to that buyer and worse-than-second-placed to sell some units of its product to that buyer, it is no longer useful to focus separately on four categories of buyers distinguished by the competitive positions that the MPs and the merged firm respectively had and have in relation to them—*viz.*, (1) buyers that an MP was and the merged firm is best-placed to supply, (2) buyers that no MP was best-placed to supply but the merged firm is best-placed to supply, (3) buyers that the highest-ranked or higher-ranked MP was second-placed or worse-than-second-placed to supply and the merged firm is second-placed to supply and better-placed to supply than was the pre-merger second-placed supplier of the buyer in question, and (4) buyers that no MP was best-placed or second-placed to supply and the merged firm is also not uniquely-second-placed to supply but is better-placed to supply than any MP was and is sufficiently-well-placed to supply to reduce the best-placed supplier's weighted-average-expected COMs and/or to raise the probability that the merged firm will beat the best-placed supplier's contrived oligopolistic price when no MP would have done so. Instead, it becomes necessary to focus on analogous categories of unit sales (analogous in that they are also defined by the competitive positions of the MPs and the merged firm)—*viz.*, (1) unit sales that an MP and the merged firm were best-placed to make, (2) unit sales that no MP was best-placed to make but the merged firm is best-placed to make, (3) unit sales that no MP was either best-placed or second-placed to make but the merged firm is second-placed to make—*i.e.*, is better-placed to make than was the firm that was second-placed to make them pre-merger, and (4) unit sales that the merged firm is worse-than-second-placed to make but is more of a hindrance to the best-placed supplier's charging and obtaining COMs than the MPs would have been. I will now analyze the impact of the rising-MC-curves fact on the equivalent-dollar gain that the static marginal-cost efficiencies a horizontal merger generates confers on buyers in relation to their purchases of the units of output placed respectively in each of the four unit-sales categories just delineated.

Because the rising-MC-curves fact on which we are focusing has no bearing on the shape of the merged firm's MC curve over the range of output that an MP would have been and the merged firm is best-placed to supply, the rising-MC-curves fact would have no impact on the terms the buyers involved in the sales of these units received (and therefore on the relevant impact that any static marginal-cost efficiencies that the horizontal merger generates have on the buyers that purchased the units that an MP would have been and the merged firm is best-placed to supply) if it did not affect the merged firm's rivals' CMC in relation to these sales or the merged firm's rivals'/ potential rivals' exit/entrance decisions. In fact, however, the rising-MC-curves fact will tend to increase the CMC that the merged firm's rivals (*R*s) will have to incur to match the merged firm's HNOP-containing offers on these units by reducing the amount by which the merger's static marginal-cost efficiencies decrease the *R*s' BCAs, NOMs, and probably COMs on the sales they are best-placed to make by reducing the frequency with which the MP that was better-placed than the other MP to make the sales the *R* was best-placed to make (1) was second-placed to make the relevant sales, (2) was worse-than-second-placed to make those sales by an amount that was smaller than the amount by which the merger reduced the merged firm's marginal costs below those of the relevant MP, and (3) was worse-than-second-placed to make those sales by an amount that exceeded the amount by which the merger reduced the merged firm's marginal costs by a sufficiently-small sum for the improvement in the merged firm's competitive position relative to that of the better-placed MP to deter the *R* from attempting to obtain a COM, to induce the *R* to lower the COM it attempted to obtain, or to induce the merged firm to beat the *R*'s contrived oligopolistic price when the better-placed MP would not have done so. Moreover, for the same reasons that the rising-MC-cost-curves fact will tend to increase the CMC that the merged firm's *R*s will have to incur to match any relevant offer the merged firm might make in relation to units it is best-placed to sell, that fact will tend both (1) to reduce the likelihood that the static marginal-cost efficiencies a horizontal merger generates will lead one or more of the merged firm's *R*s to exit (will deter one or more of the merged firm's rival potential QV investors from investing in the relevant area of product-space) and (2) to reduce the total magnitude of the exits that result (of the rival QV investments that are deterred). Since the tendency of the rising-marginal-cost-curves fact to increase the merged firm's rivals' CMC (actually to reduce the amount by which a merger's static marginal-cost efficiencies increase the merged firm's *R*s' relevant CMC) will tend to cause the merged firm to obtain higher prices for the units it is best-placed to sell (by increasing its OCAs and on that account its ability to secure NOMs [though the effect on its COMs is uncertain]) while the tendency of the rising-MC-curves fact to reduce the extent to which any static marginal-cost efficiencies a horizontal merger generates will induce the merged firm's *R*s to exit or deter them from making rival QV investments will tend to cause the merged firm to charge lower prices for the units an MP would have been best-placed to sell and the merged firm is best-placed to sell (by reducing its OCAs, NOMs, and COMs), *a priori* analysis cannot reveal the direction in which the rising-MC-curves fact will affect the equivalent-dollar effect that the static marginal-cost efficiencies that a horizontal merger generates have on the gains that buyers obtain from purchasing from the merged firm product-units with which an MP would have been best-placed to supply them and the merged firm is best-placed to supply them. I have no informed guess about the relative magnitudes across all cases of the CMC-related and exit/QV-investment-related effects of the rising-MC-curves fact on the impact that horizontal-merger-generated static marginal-cost efficiencies will have on the buyers of the units that an MP would have been best-placed to supply and the merged firm is best-placed to supply by purchasing those units. I will therefore assume that the rising-MC-curves fact will have no net impact on the effect of the efficiencies in question on the indicated buyers.

The second and third sets of unit-sale-oriented competitive-position-defined situations that is useful to distinguish contains those in which no MP was best-placed (though one or both MPs could have been second-placed) to make the unit sale (sales) in question but the merged firm is best-placed to make the relevant unit sale(s) or second-placed to do so and at a smaller disadvantage than the firm that was second-placed to make the relevant unit sale(s) pre-merger. If the merger in question had no effect on relevant merged-firm *R* CMCs or merged-firm *R* exit/QV-investment incentives, the static marginal-cost efficiencies a horizontal merger generates would benefit the buyers of the units that neither MP was best-placed to supply but the merged firm was second-placed or best-placed to supply per unit by (1) the difference between the marginal-cost reduction in question and any amount by which the higher-or-highest-ranked MP was worse-than-second-placed up to the amount by which the pre merger second-placed supplier of the unit in question was worse-than-best-placed to supply it *minus* (2)(A) any NOM(s) and COM(s) the merged firm would obtain on the sale(s) in question when it was best-placed *minus* (B) the NOM(s) and COM(s) that the pre merger best-placed supplier of the unit(s) in question would have obtained on the relevant sale(s) had the merger not been executed. The rising-MC-curves fact (which, by definition, applies to the MC curves of both the merged firm and the MPs) will reduce the equivalent-dollar benefits that the static marginal-cost efficiencies a horizontal merger generates confer on buyers of product-units in relation to which the competitive-position condition on which this paragraph focuses is fulfilled by reducing (1) the number of product-units for which this condition is fulfilled (by reducing the number of units on which the better-placed MP was either second-placed or worse-than-second placed by less than the marginal-cost reduction generated) and (I suspect) (2) the average amount by which the marginal-cost reduction in question makes the merged firm better-placed to sell units that it is second-placed or best-placed to supply but no MP was best-placed to supply (by increasing the average amount by which the better-placed MP was worse-than-second-placed when it was not second-placed [or, of course, best-placed]). This conclusion ignores the CMC-related and *R*-exit/QV investment consequences of the rising-MC-curves fact. The rising-MC-curves fact will increase the equivalent-dollar gains that the static marginal-cost efficiency a horizontal merger generates for the buyers involved in the sales on which this paragraph focuses by influencing relevant CMCs. In particular, when a merged-firm *R* is best-placed to supply the unit in question post-merger, the CMC consequences of the rising-MC-curve fact will increase the gains to the relevant buyers by lowering in three ways the CMC the merged firm would have to incur to match any offer the relevant *R* might make and thereby decreasing the relevant *R*'s NEHNOP when the merged firm was its closest competitor for the sale in question: (1) by lowering the merged firm's average NEHNOP for those sales it is best-placed to make by reducing (I suspect in virtually all cases) the average OCA the firm enjoys on the additional product-units the merger-generated efficiencies make the merged firm best-placed to sell and reducing both the quantity of such sales and the percentage of all the sales the merged firm is best-placed to make that these additional sales constitute, (2) by reducing the number of offers that the merged firm's matching offer to the relevant *R*'s customer would render discriminatory by reducing the number of sales the merged firm is best-placed to make, and (3) by reducing the number of sales the merged firm's matching offer to the *R*'s customers would put in jeopardy by putting the lie to the merged firm's cost-claims to its own customers or giving its own customers the impression that it could be bargained down (by reducing the number of sales the merged firm is best-placed to make). When the merged firm is best-placed to supply the unit in question post-merger, the CMC consequences of the rising-MC-curve fact will decrease the gains to the relevant buyers by increasing the CMC that the merged-firm *R* that was best-placed to supply the relevant units pre merger but is second-placed to do so post-merger must incur to match any offer the merged firm makes post-merger both (1) by increasing the average OCA the *R* enjoys post-merger on sales it is best-placed to make and hence its average NEHNOP on those sales by reducing the amount by which the merged firm is better-placed to supply the units in question than was the pre merger second-placed supplier of those units and (2) by increasing the volume of sales the *R* is best-placed to make post-merger by decreasing the volume of sales that the merger-generated marginal-cost reductions renders the merged firm best-placed to make (and hence the number of offers the *R*'s post-merger matching offers to the merged firm's customers will render discriminatory, the number of cost-claim lies to its own customers *R*'s matching offers to the merged firm's customers will reveal, and the number of sales in relation to which *R* will have to bargain harder or make concessions because its lower price to the merged firm's customers leaves the impression that it can be bargained down). Since the rising-MC-curves fact will benefit buyers of units in this category that a merged-firm *R* remains best-placed to supply and harm buyers of units in this category that the merged firm becomes best-placed to supply, *a priori* analysis cannot reveal the sign of the equivalent-dollar impact that the rising-MC-curves fact will have via its CMC consequences on the gains that buyers obtain by purchasing product-units in this competitive-position category. The rising-MC-curves fact can also affect the impact that the static marginal-cost efficiencies that horizontal mergers generate will have on buyers of product-units in the competitive-position category on which we are now focusing by affecting those efficiencies' impact on the exit decisions of merged-firm established *R*s and the QV-investment incentives of potential investors in the merged firm's area of product-space. In particular, by reducing the likelihood that the marginal-cost reductions in question will induce one or more *R*s to exit or critically reducing the relevant investment incentives of any otherwise-effective potential investor in the merged firm's area of product-space as well as the total magnitude of the exits that are induced and the new investments whose execution is rendered *ex ante* unprofitable, the rising-MC-curves fact will increase the equivalent-dollar gains that the efficiencies in question confer on the buyers that purchase units that no MP was best-placed to supply but the merged firm is either best-placed to supply or second-placed to supply and better-placed to supply than was their pre merger second-placed supplier.

It is conceivable that in some cases this exit/QV-investment-related effect of the rising-MC-curves fact would exceed its "more direct" tendency to reduce the equivalent-dollar gains that a horizontal merger's static marginal-cost efficiencies confer on Clayton-Act-relevant buyers by reducing the amount of sales in these second and third categories and the average amount by which the efficiencies in question benefit the purchaser of the units in this category. But I would be astounded if this occurred very often and am certain that, across all cases, the rising-MC-curves fact will reduce the equivalent-dollar gains that a horizontal merger's static marginal-cost efficiencies confer on Clayton-Act-relevant buyers that purchase units in these categories.

The fourth unit-sale-oriented competitive-position-defined category that is useful to distinguish contains those unit sales (1) that no MP was best-placed or second-placed to make and (2) that the merged firm is also not best-placed or second-placed to make but is better-placed to make than any MP was pre merger and is well-enough-placed to make for its substitution for the relevant MP to deter the best-placed supplier of the unit in question from attempting to obtain a COM, to reduce the COM the best-placed supplier attempts to contrive, and/or to cause the merged firm to beat the best-placed supplier's contrived oligopolistic offer when no MP would have done so. The impact of the rising-MC-curves fact on the number of sales for which these conditions obtain depends on the distribution of competitive positions the MPs and merged firm would have but for the relevant rise in the merged firm's MC curve: if the rise in the relevant MC curve over the relevant range prevented the merger-generated static marginal-cost efficiencies from rendering the merged firm second-placed in many instances in which no MP was second-placed, it might actually increase the number of sales made in situations in which this third set of unit-sales-oriented competitive-position conditions is fulfilled. However, in any situation in which the rising-MC-curve fact had this effect, it will reduce the equivalent-dollar benefits that the horizontal-merger-generated static marginal-cost efficiencies confer on the buyers involved in categories-two-through-four unit-sales categories combined in that (1) the amount by which the rising-MC-curve fact will reduce the offer-improvements from the relevant buyers' perspective that those efficiencies will generate when (2)(A) the merged firm is second-placed when no MP was second-placed, (B) the merged firm is second-placed and an MP was second-placed, or (C) the merged firm is best-placed and no MP was either best-placed or second-placed *will exceed* (3) any amount by which the rising-MC-curve fact can increase the offer-improvements from the relevant buyers' perspectives that those efficiencies will generate when both the merged firm and the MPs are worse-than-second-placed. Admittedly, (1) since in this situation an R of the merged firm is always best-placed to make the sale in question, the CMC consequences of the rising-MC-curve fact will increase the gains the relevant buyers secure by purchasing the units in question for the same reasons that they will have this effect in the second and third unit-output-oriented competitive-position-defined situations just analyzed, and (2) the rising-MC-curve fact will also benefit the buyers of the category-four units by reducing static-marginal-cost-efficiency-induced exits and reducing the extent to which the efficiencies in question critically reduce the QV-investment incentives of otherwise-effective merged-firm-*R* potential QV investors. Nevertheless, I am confident that, on the assumption that sellers will always make the sales they are best-placed to make and will never make any sale they are not best-placed to make, the rising-MC-curve fact will reduce the net combined equivalent-dollar benefits that any static marginal-cost efficiencies a horizontal merger generates will confer on the buyers that purchase the units that belong in the second and third categories I distinguished.

All things considered, then, on the assumption to which the preceding sentence referred, the rising-MC-curve fact will reduce the net equivalent-dollar benefits that the static marginal-cost efficiencies a horizontal merger generates will confer on Clayton-Act-relevant buyers in individualized-pricing contexts, though I suspect that the impact of the rising-MC-curve fact on Clayton-Act-relevant buyers would be smaller in such situations than most experts would predict if induced to address this issue. Nor do I think that the preceding conclusion about the impact of the rising-MC-curve fact on the equivalent-dollar impact of the static marginal-cost efficiencies that a horizontal merger generates on Clayton-Act-relevant buyers will have to be significantly altered to take account of the reality that some product-units will be sold by individualized pricers that are not best-placed to sell them.

I turn now to the impact that any static marginal-cost efficiencies that are generated by a horizontal merger in an area of product-space in which across-the-board-pricing is practiced will have on Clayton-Act-relevant buyers. In across-the-board-pricing contexts as in individualized-pricing contexts, such static marginal-cost efficiencies can affect Clayton-Act-relevant buyers by changing their suppliers' HNOPs, NOMS, and COMs.

When the merged firm and its *R*s are setting across-the-board prices, the HNOPs that the merger's static marginal-cost efficiencies can alter will be across-the-board HNOPs. If perfect data could be costlessly collected and perfect analyses could be costlessly executed, one would predict the impact of the static marginal-cost efficiencies a horizontal merger generates on the HNOPs of the merged firm and its rivals by using the seven-step protocol previously delineated to determine the impact the merger would have on the merged firm's and its *R*s' HNOPs if it would generate no static marginal-cost efficiencies (*i.e.*, if the merger would not change the relevant firms' BCA/BCD distributions and conceivably the order in which they announce their prices by generating static marginal-cost efficiencies) and then revising Steps (4) and (5) and derivatively Steps (6) and (7) of that protocol to take account of the possibility that the static marginal-cost efficiencies might change the order in which the merged firms and its *R*s would announce their prices if they do not engage in oligopolistic pricing (say, by increasing the prominence—*i.e.*, the sales of—the merged firm and hence its ability to induce its rivals to announce their prices in the order that is in their collective interest) and would change the BCA/BCD distributions of the merged firm and many, if not all, of its *R*s. I suspect, however, that frequently it may not prove cost-effective to use even a crude variant of this protocol to predict the impact of any static marginal-cost efficiencies a horizontal merger generates on the HNOPs of the merged firm and its *R*s. For this reason, it may be useful for me to indicate some of the parameters that I suspect will determine the impact of such efficiencies on the HNOPs of across-the-board-pricing firms.

Roughly speaking, the amount by which the static marginal-cost efficiencies a horizontal-merger generates will decrease an across-the-board-pricing merged firm's HNOP will be directly related to (1) the magnitude of the static marginal-cost efficiencies in question, (2) the ratio of the number of buyers whose patronage the MPs were close to securing pre merger to the number of buyers they supplied pre-merger, and (3) the difference between the MPs' pre merger HNOPs and MCs. The second of these relationships reflects the following reality: the higher the ratio in question, the greater the ratio of the additional profits a price-reduction will enable the merged firm to obtain on new sales (because the greater the amount of new sales the price-reduction will enable it to secure) relative to the profits the price-reduction will cause the merged firm to lose on sales it would have made at the MPs' prices—*i.e.*, *ceteris paribus*, the more profitable the price-reduction in question. The third of the above relationships reflects the following reality: controlling for the additional sales a price-reduction of any size will enable the merged firm to make, the greater the gap between the MPs' pre merger HNOPs and MCs, the greater the amount of profits the price-reduction will yield by generating new sales. Obviously, the amount by which the static marginal-cost efficiencies a horizontal merger generates will decrease the HNOPs of the merged firm's *R*s will be directly related to the amount by which they lower the HNOPs of the merged firm and the percentage of its *R*s' customers whose patronage the merged firm was close to securing pre-merger. I hasten to add that the preceding analysis is crude, *inter alia*, because it does not take account of the determinants of the non-strategic response of the merged firm's *R*s to the various price-reductions it could make.

Any static marginal-cost efficiencies a horizontal merger generates will also tend to increase the probability that an across-the-board-pricing merged firm will be able to obtain OMs naturally by increasing the inherent profitability of its reacting to undermining responses to any supra-HNOP price it charges initially by reducing its originally-announced price sufficiently to make those responses unprofitable by increasing its (HNOP–MC) figure and the number of buyers it supplies. Relatedly, I suspect that the static marginal-cost efficiencies a horizontal merger generates will tend to decrease the probability that the merged firm's *R*s will be able to obtain OMs naturally by reducing their respective (HNOP − MC) figures and the number of buyers they respectively supply—*i.e.*, by reducing on these accounts the probability that they will find it inherently profitable to react to an undermining set of responses to their initially-announced price by reducing those initially-announced prices sufficiently to make those responses unprofitable.

The static marginal-cost efficiencies a horizontal merger generates are also likely to have significantly-different impacts on the OMs that the merged firm contrives on the one hand and those that the merged firm's *R*s contrive on the other. I suspect that such efficiencies will tend to reduce the COMs that across-the-board-pricing merged firms attempt to obtain below the COMs their antecedents would have attempted to secure: I reach this conclusion because (1) such efficiencies will tend to reduce the merged firm's COMs by increasing the safe profits it must put at risk to attempt to contrive OMs, (2) such efficiencies will tend to increase the merged firm's COMs by increasing the number of buyers the merged firm supplies (the number of buyers in relations with which it could take advantage of a maintained or enhanced reputation for contrivance), (3) such efficiencies will have an uncertain effect on the costs the merged firm will have to incur to inflict a given, relevant amount of harm on an underminer (since it will have an uncertain effect on the ratio of buyers the merged firm would be close to securing at the most profitable non-retaliatory price it could charge to the number of buyers it would supply at that price), and (4) the first of the three preceding effects this list delineates will almost always be bigger than the second of these effects. By way of contrast, I suspect that the static marginal-cost efficiencies a horizontal merger generates will tend to increase the OMs the merged firm's *R*s attempt to contrive: I reach this conclusion because (1) such efficiencies tend to increase the OMs the *R*s will attempt to contrive by decreasing the amount of safe profits they must put at risk to do so, (2) will decrease the OMs the *R*s will attempt to contrive by reducing the number of buyers they supply in relation to which they could take advantage of a reputation for contrivance, (3) (I suspect) will tend to increase the OMs the individual *R*s will attempt to contrive more by decreasing the cost it will have to incur to inflict a given, relevant amount of harm on the merged firm through retaliation should the merged firm choose to undermine its contrived oligopolistic price (by increasing the merged firm's [HNOP + NOM − MC] figure) by more than they reduce the OMs the individual *R*s will attempt to contrive by reducing the cost each will have to incur to inflict a given, relevant amount of harm on the merged firm's other *R*s if they should undermine the contrived oligopolistic price of the *R* in question by decreasing these other *R*s' (HNOP + NOM − MC) figures, and (4) the effect that item (1) in this list delineates is almost certainly bigger than the effect that item (2) in this list delineates.

Now that I have analyzed the ways in which any static marginal-cost efficiencies a horizontal merger generates may affect Clayton-Act-relevant buyers at the relevant ARDEPPS' pre merger equilibrium QV-investment level, I will analyze the ways in which any dynamic efficiencies a horizontal merger generates will affect Clayton-Act-relevant buyers by increasing (or, in rare instances, decreasing) QV-investment competition in the ARDEPPS in which the merger is executed—*i.e.*, by increasing (or, rarely, decreasing) the extent to which the overall loss the merger would otherwise impose on such buyers is reduced by its tendency to increase equilibrium QV-investment in the ARDEPPS in question. In the vocabulary Chap. 2 defined, a horizontal merger will generate dynamic efficiencies to the extent that it reduces the (Π_D + R) barriers the merged firm faces below the (Π_D + R) barriers the individual MPs faced. In some cases, the dynamic efficiencies a horizontal merger generates will have no effect on equilibrium QV investment in the relevant area of product-space. Unfortunately, because (1) the relevant merger will often make it profitable for the merged firm (and one or more of its actual and potential *R*s) to execute additional QV investments in the relevant ARDEPPS even if it does not generate any dynamic efficiencies (by increasing prices at the ARDEPPS' pre merger QV-investment level) and (2) the (Π_D + R) barriers a firm faces will tend to increase as it makes successive QV-investment expansions, the conditions under which the dynamic efficiencies a horizontal merger generates will have no effect on its ARDEPPS' equilibrium QV-investment level are complicated to articulate: basically, such efficiencies will have no such effect even if they carry over to the next expansion the merged firm could execute once its ARDEPPS' QV investment reached the level it would have in equilibrium if the merger generated no dynamic efficiencies if, under those conditions at that ARDEPPS QV-investment level, the merged firm would be sufficiently worse-placed to expand than the ARDEPPS' best-placed potential expander or entrant for the dynamic efficiencies the merger generated not to make it better-placed to invest in that ARDEPPS than any other potential investor (or, more precisely, not to make it sufficiently better-placed to invest than any other potential investor for it to find an investment profitable when no-one would otherwise have found it profitable to raise the ARDEPPS' QV-investment level). Of course, in some cases, the dynamic efficiencies a horizontal merger generates will increase equilibrium QV investment in the ARDEPPS in which it is executed—*i.e.*, will critically increase the profitability of the merged firm's making a relevant QV-investment expansion when no-one else would otherwise have added to the ARDEPPS' QV-investment total. In some such cases, the relevant dynamic efficiencies will cause the merged firm to make a QV investment that raises total QV investment in the ARDEPPS in question to a level it would not otherwise have attained. In other such cases, the relevant dynamic efficiencies will raise the relevant ARDEPPS' equilibrium QV-investment level by inducing an *R* of the merged firm to make a QV investment that will raise total QV investment in the relevant ARDEPPS to a level it would not otherwise have obtained by eliminating or critically reducing a critical monopolistic QV-investment disincentive it would otherwise have faced. Obviously, the probability that one or the other of these two procompetitive sequences of conduct will result will be directly related to the magnitude of the dynamic efficiencies the relevant horizontal merger generates and the extent to which the merged firm can realize them not just on its first post-merger expansion but on the post-merger expansion it would have to be willing to execute for them to raise its ARDEPPS' equilibrium QV-investment level and will be inversely related to the extent to which, in their absence, the merged firm would have been worse-placed to raise its ARDEPPS' QV investment above the level that would have been its equilibrium level in their absence than the other potential investor that would otherwise have been best-placed to increase the ARDEPPS' total QV investment above the level that would have been its equilibrium level in their absence. Finally, in a few cases, the dynamic efficiencies a horizontal merger generates will reduce equilibrium QV investment in the ARDEPPS in which it is executed by converting a situation in which an *R* would have invested because the monopolistic QV-investment disincentives it would have faced would not have been critical into a situation in which neither that *R* nor the merged firm will invest because they cause each other to face (critical) natural oligopolistic QV-investment disincentives. Once more, however, I doubt the practical relevance of this last, perverse possibility: the conditions for it to occur will be fulfilled too rarely and will be too difficult to investigate and the effects of such disincentives will be too evanescent for an effort to consider this possibility to be warranted.

* * *

I have now reviewed all the ways in which a horizontal merger can harm and benefit Clayton-Act-relevant buyers by decreasing seller competition and discussed the various factors that determine whether an individual horizontal merger will affect Clayton-Act-relevant buyers in each of the ways in question and the magnitudes of any such effects that do result. If perfect data on all these parameters could be costlessly collected and perfect analyses of the implications of these facts for the net equivalent-dollar impact of any horizontal merger on Clayton-Act-relevant buyers could be costlessly executed, the optimal way to analyze the impact of a horizontal merger on Clayton-Act-relevant buyers would be to collect perfect data on the parameters whose relevance the preceding discussions established and perfectly analyze their implications for the horizontal merger's impact on Clayton-Act-relevant buyers. Of course, I realize that data and analysis are inevitably costly and that at least data is virtually always imperfect. Still, I am confident that some more or less refined version of the protocols that would be ideal if perfect data could be costlessly collected and perfect analyses could be costlessly executed will prove to be optimal for courts and antitrust-enforcement agencies to use to assess the legally-relevant effects of horizontal mergers. I am also confident that pre-merger-notification programs of the sort that Sect. 4 will describe should require firms that are proposing a horizontal merger or acquisition to supply the antitrust-enforcement agencies with data on the parameters whose relevance this section has identified—*inter alia*, with data on the frequency with which and the amount by which the MPs were each other's closest competitors for particular buyers' patronage, the type and magnitude of the static and dynamic efficiencies their merger/acquisition would generate, the frequency with which an MP was second-placed to obtain the patronage of a buyer an *R* was best-placed to supply pre-merger, the frequency with which an MP was close-to-second-placed to obtain the patronage of such a buyer and the amount by which it was worse-than-second-placed when it was close-to-second-placed, whether an MP was or was close to being the relevant ARDEPPS' best-placed potential investor, and the various parameters that are relevant to the transaction's likely impact on COMs.

So far, this section has focused solely on the ways in which horizontal mergers can inflict net equivalent-dollar losses on Clayton-Act-relevant buyers by reducing seller competition. I want to close by discussing briefly the argument that horizontal mergers between firms that compete against each other as *buyers* will violate the

Clayton Act by inflicting net equivalent-dollar losses on Clayton-Act-relevant customers of the merging firms. The consensus among economists[883] is that horizontal mergers that yield the merged firm monopsony power or create a merged firm that has more monopsony power than the individual MPs would have had will inflict an equivalent-dollar loss on Clayton-Act-relevant buyers by *increasing* the MCs and hence prices of the merged firm above the prospective MCs and hence prices of the MPs. It is true that, if a monopsonist engages in non-discriminatory, single-pricing buying—*i.e.*, if it offers all its potential suppliers the same single per-unit price and purchases as much of their products as they are willing to supply it at that price—and the relevant suppliers are price-takers (some of which can obtain economic rents, given that the relevant supply curve is upward-sloping), the marginal cost of any *n*th unit of input to the monopsonist will be higher than the marginal cost its non-monopsonist counterparts would have had to incur to buy that *n*th unit of input by paying the price that would elicit its supply since the non-discriminating, single-price-offering monopsonist (which [this argument implicitly assumes] by definition faces an upward-sloping supply curve) would have to pay a higher price for the $(n - 1)$ units it could otherwise have purchased at a lower price to purchase the *n*th unit whose supply it can only elicit at a higher price while the non-monopsonists (which individually face horizontal supply curves) would not. It is also true that any such increase in the marginal cost to the monopsonist of purchasing the last unit or units of the inputs it uses to produce its product or service will increase its marginal costs of supply and hence the price it charges. However, for two reasons, this result does not imply that real-world non-monopsonists will have to pay more for the last unit of input than their monopsonistic counterparts would have paid (and will therefore face higher marginal costs of production at their non-monopsonistic counterparts' unit-output level and will hence produce fewer units of output and charge higher prices than their non-monopsonistic counterparts would have done): (1) real-world monopsonists will not usually find if profitable to engage in non-discriminatory, single-pricing buying—will usually engage in substantial amounts of inter-supplier price discrimination and will come much closer to practicing perfect price discrimination in their dealings with individual suppliers—and (2) real-world monopsonists will often face suppliers that are not price-takers—that have some degree of monopoly and oligopoly power and make significant pricing-choices. Even if the suppliers of real-world monopsonists are just price-takers (and the monopsonist faces an upward-sloping supply curve), the marginal cost to the monopsonist of the last unit of the relevant input its non-monopsonistic counterparts would buy will be the same as the cost to them of that unit of input if the monopsonist engages in (presumably-usually-conventionally-discriminatory) perfect price discrimination in its dealings with its individual suppliers. And if the monopsonist's suppliers are not simply price-takers (and the

[883] This consensus was generated by an article and subsequent book by Roger Blair and Jeffrey Harrison. See Roger D. Blair and Jeffrey L. Harrison, *Antitrust Policy and Monopsony*, 76 CORNELL L. REV. 297 (1991) and ROGER BLAIR AND JEFFREY HARRISON, MONOPSONY (Princeton Univ. Press, 1993).

monopsonist does not face an upward-sloping supply curve determined by the marginal costs of its suppliers), the monopsonist (*i.e.*, a buyer with bargaining power) may well be able to buy the last unit of input its non-monopsonist counterparts purchased (and one or more additional units as well) at a lower marginal (purchase) cost than its non-monopsonist counterparts would have to incur to do so because the monopsonist will be able to secure price-concessions that its non-monopsonist counterparts could not. To the extent that this is the case, the monopsonist will face lower (total) marginal costs of producing its product than its non-monopsonist counterparts would, and a merger that increased its participants' monopsony power will benefit Clayton-Act-relevant buyers on this account regardless of whether the monopsonist and its product rivals practice across-the-board pricing or individualized pricing. When the monopsonist sets individualized prices, the analysis is identical to the analysis of the procompetitive effect of the static marginal efficiencies a horizontal merger can generate: the merger-induced increase in monopsony power will benefit Clayton-Act-relevant buyers to the extent that one or both MPs was (1) second-placed pre-merger, (2) worse-than-second-placed by less than the associated reduction in the merged firm's marginal costs, or (3) worse-than-second-placed by an amount that exceeds the associated reduction in the merged firm's marginal costs by sufficiently little for the improvement in the merged firm's competitive position to reduce the COMs the relevant buyer's best-placed supplier obtained. Since I grant that monopsonists that face price-taking suppliers will sometimes (actually usually) not find it possible or profitable to practice perfectly-discriminatory perfect price discrimination as buyers and that monopsonists whose monopsonistic power was created or enhanced by a horizontal merger will sometimes face price-taking suppliers, I admit that the sign of the net equivalent-dollar impact on Clayton-Act-relevant buyers of any tendency that a horizontal merger has to increase its participants' monopsony power will vary from case to case. However, far from agreeing with the current consensus among economists that any such tendency will always cause Clayton-Act-relevant buyers to suffer an equivalent-dollar loss, I am confident that, across all cases, horizontal-merger generated increases in monopsony power will confer equivalent-dollar gains on Clayton-Act-relevant buyers even if the possibility to which the next section refers is empirically significant. That possibility is that merger-generated increases in the monopsony power that the merged firm possesses relative to the monopsony power that the MPs would possess may result in the merged firm's inducing its suppliers to drive out or discipline the merged firm's product rivals by refusing to supply them. For two reasons, I do not think that this possibility critically affects the probable impact of any tendency of a horizontal merger to increase its participants' monopsony power: (1) I think that such mergers will lead to such behavior only rarely, and (2) I believe that, even when such a merger does, its doing so will usually not critically affect the net equivalent-dollar impact on Clayton-Act-relevant buyers of the merger's tendency to increase the merged firm's monopsony power. In part, these conclusions reflect my assumption that the antitrust authorities will be able to deter such post-merger conduct or take action that enables affected buyers to obtain compensation from the perpetrators of any induced illegal refusals to deal. In any event, it is not clear that the tendency of a horizontal merger to induce its participants and/or anyone else to engage in this type of illegal conduct (which I think is detectable and provable) is relevant to the merger's Clayton Act legality.

3. The Legality of Horizontal Mergers Under U.S. Antitrust Law and E.C./E.U. Competition Law, Correctly Interpreted and Applied

A. The Legality of Horizontal Mergers Under U.S. Antitrust Law, Properly Interpreted and Applied

(1) The Legality of Horizontal Mergers Under the Sherman Act, Correctly Interpreted and Applied

Correctly interpreted, the Sherman Act prohibits a horizontal merger if, but only if, its participants' *ex ante* perception that it would be profitable was critically increased by their belief that it would or might reduce the absolute attractiveness of the offers against which they (as the merged firm) would have to compete in ways that would critically *inflate* the profitability of their merger in an otherwise-Pareto-perfect economy—*e.g.*, by freeing them from each other's price and/or QV-investment competition, by increasing the profits they can realize by engaging in contrived oligopolistic pricing, by increasing the cost-effectiveness of their efforts to deter remaining rivals from undercutting or undermining a relevant contrived oligopolistic price they might charge, by increasing the profits they can realize by raising the retaliation barriers faced by actual and potential rivals that would otherwise have made an additional QV investment, and/or by enabling them to profit by engaging in predation to drive a rival out. With one possible qualification, this test of illegality implies that, even if the State or a private plaintiff can establish the requisite probability that the participants in a horizontal merger perceived *ex ante* that it would increase their profits in one or more of the preceding ways (usually by demonstrating that it will or did increase their profits in one or more of these ways but sometimes by introducing documentary evidence or oral testimony about the MPs' *ex ante* beliefs), the horizontal merger will not violate the Sherman Act if this perception did not critically affect their conclusion that the merger would be profitable—*i.e.*, if they perceived *ex ante* that their merger would be rendered at least normally profitable by the profits it would yield them (1) by generating static and/or dynamic efficiencies (even if these efficiencies did not enable them to profit by engaging in contrivance or predation or by inducing a rival to exit without their practicing predation), (2) by enabling the owner of one MP to liquidate his or her assets and escape managerial responsibilities, (3) by enabling an MP to sell tax losses it could not fully utilize itself, (4) by enabling the MPs to overcome to a greater extent the public-good problem that militates against their and their *R*s' spending as much money on campaign contributions and government-decision-making-process participation as is in their collective interest, (5) by increasing their NOMs, and (6) by increasing their ability to get themselves and their *R*s to announce their across-the-board prices in a sequence that is more in their collective interest. The qualification is that, if the Sherman Act is properly interpreted to be a fence law, horizontal mergers that are predicted to be requisitely likely to increase contrived oligopolistic or predatory conduct will violate the Sherman Act on that account even if they were not perpetrated with specific anticompetitive intent.

The analysis that follows assumes that it would be incorrect as a matter of law to interpret the Sherman Act to be a fence law. In my judgment, Sherman Act horizontal-merger trials should be structured in the following way. The government should be required to make out a *prima facie* case against the defendant by establishing the requisite probability that their merger would generate more than a *de minimis* decrease in the absolute attractiveness of the offers against which the merged firm would or did have to compete relative to the absolute attractiveness of the offers against which the MPs would have had to compete in one or more of the ways just listed (*e.g.*, when the merger takes place in an individualized-pricing context, by establishing that the MPs were sufficiently often either best-placed and second-placed or uniquely-equal-best-placed to obtain a given buyer's patronage and sufficiently better-placed than the third-placed supplier of the buyer in question for the merger to produce on that account a sufficient decrease in the absolute attractiveness of the offers against which the merged firm would have to compete). If the government has put on enough such evidence to survive a motion for summary judgment and the defendant(s) have failed to undermine that evidence sufficiently to win a directed verdict on that account, the defendants should be given the opportunity to exonerate themselves by establishing that their *ex ante* perception that their merger would be profitable was not critically affected by any such effects they perceived *ex ante* their merger would or might have—*i.e.*, by putting on evidence that establishes the requisite probability that they believed *ex ante* that their merger was rendered profitable by the profits it would yield them in one or more of the six Sherman-Act-licit ways listed in the preceding paragraph or in one or more of those ways and one or more other licit ways I failed to include in that list. When the merger cases are adjudicated after the merger has been executed, defendants will, I suspect, usually be best able to establish that they did not have specific anticompetitive intent by demonstrating that their merger actually did increase their profits sufficiently in licit ways to be profitable on that account. However, when the mergers are being evaluated *ex ante* or when the MPs mistakenly believed *ex ante* that their merger would be profitable for licit reasons, they may want to introduce documentary evidence and/or testimony about their *ex ante* perceptions about the prospects of their merger's yielding them profits in Sherman-Act-licit ways. I should add that, in my judgment (1) the State or private plaintiff should have to bear not just the burden of persuasion on the facts they must prove to establish their *prima facie* case but the burden of paying the cost of producing the evidence that relates to those facts (though the defendants may be required to produce some relevant evidence—*e.g.*, about how competitive they were with each other) and (2) the defendants should bear both the burden of persuasion on the facts they would need to establish to exonerate themselves once a *prima facie* case had been made against them and the burden of producing the associated evidence. To be honest, I am not sure how the cost of producing the relevant evidence should be allocated. Economic efficiency would probably be served by allocating to the defendants the cost of producing the evidence on which they would bear the burden of production (though this allocation might be economically inefficient if it led the State or private plaintiffs to bring economically-inefficient suits against horizontal-merger participants). However, it does seem unfair to me to make innocent defendants pay all the costs of defending themselves.

I want to address one final issue whose resolution could critically affect the conclusion one reaches about the Sherman Act legality of a horizontal merger—the "compared to what" issue, which has historically been most important in horizontal-merger cases when one of the MPs was alleged to be a "failing company." I will use a numerical illustration to make the relevant point. Assume first that the MPs will have to incur $1,000,000 in legal and other costs to consummate a merger and that the normal rate-of-return for the MPs in question on this $1,000,000 investment is 10 %—that normal profits on the merger will be $100,000. Assume second that, relative to the situation that would prevail if the MPs engaged in no merger, the merger they executed (proposed to execute) would yield them $150,000 in Sherman-Act-licit profits and $200,000 in profits by reducing the absolute attractiveness of the offers against which the merged company would have to compete—*i.e.*, a total of $350,000 in profits. Now, assume third that the MP that initiated the merger in question could have executed an equally-risky merger that would also have cost it and its alternative merger partner $1,000,000 to consummate whose normal profits would also be $100,000 and that would have yielded it $170,000 in profits in Sherman-Act-licit ways but only $100,000 in profits by reducing the absolute attractiveness of the offers against which this alternative merged firm would have to compete below the absolute attractiveness of the offers against which the initiating MP and its alternative MP had to compete—*i.e.*, a total of $270,000 in profits ($80,000 less than the profits the merger it executed/proposed did/would generate for its participants). In my view, the merger that the defendants executed or proposed would not violate the Sherman Act because its participants' *ex ante* perception that it would be more profitable than *executing no merger at all (doing nothing)* was not critically increased by its reducing the absolute attractiveness of the offers against which the merged company would have to compete below the absolute attractiveness of the offers against which the executed/proposed merger's individual participants had to compete even though the initiator's *ex ante* perception that the executed/proposed merger would be more profitable than *an alternative merger it could have executed* was critically increased by its belief that the executed/proposed merger would reduce the absolute attractiveness of the offers against which the merged firm that merger would create would have to compete below the absolute attractiveness of the offers against which its participants would have had to compete by more than some alternative merger the initiator could have executed would have reduced the absolute attractiveness of the offers against which the alternative merged firm the alternative merger would have created below the absolute attractiveness of the offers against which the initiator and its alternative merger partner would have had to compete. For Sherman Act purposes (and for Clayton Act purposes), the relevant baseline for comparison is the defendants' do-nothing option, not the member of the set of options that were more profitable than doing nothing that would have been most-procompetitive or least-anticompetitive for it to choose or the most-procompetitive or least-anticompetitive member of that set of options that it would have been able to identify had it made a "reasonable" effort (whatever that means) to identify such an option.

(2) The Legality of Horizontal Mergers Under the Clayton Act, Correctly Interpreted and Applied

Correctly interpreted, the Clayton Act prohibits an executed/proposed horizontal merger if, and only if, the merger partners' decision to participate in the merger rather than do nothing created a reasonable probability that it would inflict a net equivalent-dollar loss on the combination of the customers of the MPs and the customers of the merged firm's *R*s by reducing the absolute attractiveness of the best offer they respectively received from any inferior supplier unless (if I am right that the Clayton Act should be read to recognize an organizational-economic-efficiency defense) the defendants can establish the requisite probability that their merger would not have imposed a net equivalent-dollar loss on these buyers had it not led one or more of the merged firm's *R*s to exit by generating static marginal-allocative-cost efficiencies that would critically reduce the profits these *R*s could earn even if they did not lead the merged firm to engage in predation.

I want to make eight points about the test of illegality I believe the Clayton Act is properly read to promulgate. First, although the Clayton Act's text—in particular, its use of the expression "*may be* substantially to lessen competition" (emphasis added)—seems to imply that it prohibits mergers that create *some risk* of a significant reduction in competition, legislative history indicates that the drafters and ratifiers intended the Act to prohibit only those mergers that created a "*reasonable probability*" that competition would be reduced significantly,[884] and I believe (as some courts have assumed) that the Act should be read to prohibit only those mergers that are more likely than not to reduce competition significantly. Second, as I indicated both in Chap. 4 and when discussing the Sherman Act's test of illegality in this chapter, I believe that the baseline for analyzing the competitive impact of a horizontal merger (or any other type of conduct) under the Clayton Act is the conditions that would prevail if the defendants did nothing relevant, not the conditions that would prevail if they made the most-procompetitive choice of the relevant kind they could make that would still be

[884] The statute condemns horizontal mergers whose effect *may be* substantially to lessen competition (emphasis added). Although this is not much of an advance in operationality, it was understood that "[t]he use of these words means that the bill, if enacted, would not apply to the mere possibility but only to the reasonable probability of the pr[o]scribed effect...." See S. Rep. No. 1775 at 6, U.S. Code Cong. & Admin News 4293, 4298 (1950).

more profitable than doing nothing or the most-procompetitive choice that would be more profitable than doing nothing they could identify if they made "reasonable" efforts to identify such options. Third, as I also indicated in Chap. 4, my claim that, correctly interpreted, the Clayton Act would be deemed to permit defendants to exonerate themselves by establishing an organizational-economic-efficiency defense is highly contestable because the text of the statute makes no reference to such a defense. Fourth, the legality of an executed horizontal merger under the Clayton Act depends on its actual consequences, not on its participants' *ex ante* beliefs about those consequences—indeed, not even on the predictions that a well-informed, highly-skilled, objective expert would have made about the Clayton-Act-relevant consequences of the merger before it was executed. Fifth, a horizontal merger that did not inflict a net equivalent-dollar loss on Clayton-Act-relevant buyers by reducing the absolute attractiveness of the best offers they respectively received from any inferior supplier from the date of its execution until the end of time cannot properly be proven to violate the Clayton Act by demonstrating that it will inflict a net equivalent-dollar loss on such buyers in this way during a period that begins on some date after the date of the merger's execution and lasts until the end of time, regardless of whether a federal court had previously found the merger lawful under the Clayton Act. Sixth, any tendency of a horizontal merger to inflict a net equivalent-dollar loss (confer a net equivalent-dollar gain) on Clayton-Act-relevant buyers by increasing (decreasing) the net NOMs they pay is uncontestably relevant to the merger's legality under the Clayton Act. Seventh, the relevance to a horizontal merger's Clayton Act legality of any tendency it has to inflict a net equivalent-dollar loss on Clayton-Act-relevant buyers by increasing the COMs their suppliers obtain from them is contestable. The conclusion that any such tendency a horizontal merger has should be deemed irrelevant to its Clayton Act legality is favored by the argument that (1) the State/private plaintiff can prevent the additional contrivance to which the merger might otherwise lead by standing ready to prosecute/sue contrivers, (2) the victims of contrivance can prevent contrivers from profiting from their illicit behavior and themselves from being harmed by the contrivers' contrivance by suing contrivers post-merger, and (3) firms do not always take advantage of their opportunities to earn profits by engaging in contrived oligopolistic pricing. The conclusion that any such tendency a horizontal merger has should be counted against its Clayton Act legality is favored by the difficulty and cost of proving that contrived oligopolistic pricing has been practiced (which Chap. 10 established). My own judgment is that any tendency a horizontal merger has to increase the likely incidence of contrived oligopolistic pricing should be counted against its Clayton Act legality. Eighth, for the same reason, the relevance to a horizontal merger's Clayton Act legality of any tendency it has to reduce QV-investment competition in the ARDEPPS in which it takes place by increasing the retaliation barriers to QV investment the merged firm's actual and potential *R*s face and/or the merged firm faces is also contestable. Once more, I am persuaded by the counterpart argument for counting any such tendency a horizontal merger has against its Clayton Act legality.

So far, this discussion of the legality of horizontal mergers under U.S. antitrust law, properly interpreted and applied, has focused exclusively on mergers that might violate U.S. antitrust law by reducing the competition firms face as sellers. I turn now to the legality under U.S. antitrust law, properly interpreted and applied, of horizontal mergers that increase their participants' monopsony power.

In my judgment, such mergers violate the Clayton Act if, but only if, the increase in monopsony power they generate inflicts a net equivalent-dollar loss on Clayton-Act-relevant buyers by reducing the absolute attractiveness of the best offer they respectively receive from an inferior supplier. As I indicated at the end of Sect. 2 of this chapter, although I admit that this result will obtain in some cases—*viz.*, when the merged company does not practice inter-buyer and perfect price discrimination perfectly, the relevant suppliers are price-takers and the associated increase in the marginal cost of inputs to the merged company inflicts on equivalent-dollar loss on buyers by increasing the prices the merged company charges buyers an MP was either best-placed or second-placed to supply pre-merger, I believe that, in most cases, horizontal mergers that increase their participants' monopsony power will confer an equivalent-dollar gain on Clayton-Act-relevant buyers by reducing the marginal cost the merged firm must incur to purchase relevant units of inputs. Moreover, although I acknowledge that horizontal mergers that increase their participants' monopsony power may impose an equivalent-dollar loss on Clayton-Act-relevant buyers by creating a merged firm that induces its suppliers to boycott the merged firm's product rivals, I doubt that this result occurs often, suspect that even when it does occur, it will often not cause the merger to inflict a net equivalent-dollar loss on relevant buyers, and am inclined to conclude that, given the feasibility of detecting and proving such post-merger illegal refusals to deal, the possibility that mergers may lead to such conduct by increasing the merged firm's monopsony power should not count against *the merger's* legality.

I also do not think that the fact that a horizontal merger will increase its participants' monopsony power will count against its legality under the Sherman Act if that statute is properly interpreted and applied. This conclusion is obviously correct when the prospect of the merger's benefitting the MPs in this way did not critically affect their *ex ante* belief that it was profitable. However, with one exception, I also think that this conclusion is correct when this prospect did critically affect the MPs' *ex ante* belief in the merger's profitability: even then, I do not think one could say that the merger in question would restrain trade or that it constituted an act of monopolization or an attempt to monopolize. I acknowledge that an exception is in order: if the MPs' *ex ante* belief in the merger's profitability was critically affected by their belief that it would enable them to increase their profits by using the monopsony power it gave them to induce suppliers to refuse to deal with the merged firm's product rivals (a possibility that I consider to be remote at best), the merger's perceived tendency to increase its participants' monopsony power would render it illegal under the Sherman Act, properly interpreted and applied.

B. The Legality of Horizontal Concentrations Under E.C./E.U. Competition Law, Correctly Interpreted and Applied

In 1989, on the (to my mind, mistaken) assumption that the 1957 Treaty and its various sequels did not cover mergers, the Council of Ministers promulgated the EC Merger Control Regulation (Regulation 4064/89). Article 2 of that regulation articulated its test of illegality:

> A concentration which creates or strengthens a dominant position as a result of which effective competition would be significantly impeded in the common market or in a substantial part of it shall be declared incompatible with the common market.[885]

From the perspective of the goal of maintaining competition, this Regulation was still inadequate in that it did not prohibit competition-reducing concentrations between or among firms that did not have a dominant position either pre merger or post-merger. In 2004, the Council of Ministers tried to remedy this deficiency of its 1989 Regulation by promulgating a new regulation[886] whose text seems to me initially to correct but then to repeat the 1989 Regulation's "error." According to Article 2(3) of Regulation 139/2004:

> A concentration which would significantly impede effective competition, in the common market or a substantial part of it, in particular as a result of creating or strengthening a dominant position, shall be declared incompatible with the common market.[887]

At least in U.S. English, the clause that begins with the words "in particular" defeats the purpose of the new regulation, which its text would otherwise have achieved. (If the words "for example" had been used instead of the words "in particular," the inclusion of the clause in question would not have made the regulation's text inconsistent with its drafters' and ratifiers' intention.) Although U.S. courts often "interpret" texts that are inconsistent with their drafters' and ratifiers' established intentions in a way that is inconsistent with the text but consistent with those intentions, I believe that European courts are much less prone to do this. (As I indicated in Chap. 4, this difference may reflect the fact that it is more difficult to correct poor drafting through new legislation in the U.S.' congressional system than in any of Europe's or the E.U.'s parliamentary systems.)

---

[885] Council Regulation 4064/89 on the Control of Concentrations Between Undertakings, Article 11 of the 1989 Regulation OJ L395/1 (1989) delineated the criteria that should be used to determine whether an otherwise-prohibited concentration would "significantly impede[]" effective competition. Those criteria focused on the total revenue of the MPs in the E.C. and its distribution in the E.C.'s member states. These criteria ignore the fact that mergers may decrease competition not only by increasing the prices the merged firm charges above those charged by the MPs but also by increasing the prices the merged firm's *R*s charge. They also ignore the fact that the total revenue of the MPs in the E.C./E.U. is not a good indicator of the extent of the equivalent-dollar loss their horizontal merger will impose on their own E.C./E.U. customers.

[886] Council Regulation 139/2004 on the Control of Concentrations Between Undertakings (EMCR) at Article 2, OJ L 24/1 (2004).

[887] *Id.* at Article 2(3).

In any event, the Council of Ministers proceeded to take care of this problem by promulgating Recital 25:

> The notion of 'significant impediment to effective competition' in Article 2(2) and (3) should be interpreted as extending, beyond the concept of dominance only to the anticompetitive effects of a concentration resulting from the non-coordinated behavior of undertakings which would not have a dominant position on the market concerned.[888]

I should add that, although by itself, this sentence would imply that concentrations that do not create or enhance a dominant position would violate the EMCR only if they imposed a requisitely-large equivalent-dollar loss on relevant consumers by increasing the HNOPs and NOMs of their suppliers—*i.e.*, would not prohibit concentrations whose critical effect on relevant consumers was critically affected by their tendency to increase COMs and retaliation barriers to expansion and entry, this implication of the sentence in question would seem to be contradicted by an earlier sentence in the Recital that implicitly assumes that the effects of a merger on contrivance is relevant to its legality:

> [U]nder certain circumstances, concentrations involving the elimination of important competitive restraints that the merger parties had exerted upon each other, as well as on a reduction in the competitive pressure on the remaining competitors, may even in the absence of a likelihood of coordination between members of the oligopoly, result in a significant impediment to effective competition.[889]

Although this statement recognizes the legal significance of the impact that a concentration will have on relevant buyers by increasing contrivance only implicitly (and ignores the effects the merger will have on the merged firm by reducing the competitive pressure it faces from remaining rivals), it does seem to me to justify an interpreter's concluding that the 2004 EMCR does make contrivance-related effects relevant to the legality of a concentration.

Recital 26 adds nothing of practical importance but may have been promulgated as a sop to supporters of the 1989 EMCR's test of illegality, under which a concentration was deemed illegal only if it "create[d] or strengthen[ed] a dominant position":

> A significant impediment to effective competition generally results from the creation or strengthening of a dominant position. ...[A] concentration with a Community dimension which would significantly impede effective competition, in the common market or in a substantial part thereof, in particular as a result of the creation or strengthening of a dominant position, is to be declared incompatible with the common market.[890]

(The first quoted sentence's use of the word "generally"—instead of the word "definitionally"—probably reflects the fact that the EC and the E.C./E.U. courts operationally determine whether a firm has a dominant position and, if it does, the strength of its dominant position by its market share—an operationalization that, for reasons that Chap. 6 and 8 explained, I would reject.)

---

[888] *Id.* at Recital 25.

[889] *Id.*

[890] *Id.* at Recital 26.

Recital 29 clarifies the relevance of any efficiencies a concentration generates to its legality under the EMCR:

> In order to determine the impact of any concentration on competition in the common market, it is appropriate to take account of any substantiated and likely efficiencies put forward by the undertakings concerned. It is possible that the efficiencies brought about by the concentration counteract the effects on competition, and in particular the potential harm to consumers, that it might otherwise have and that, as a consequence the concentration would not significantly impede competition in the common market or in a substantial part of it, in particular as a result of the creation or strengthening of a dominant position.[891]

If one ignores the language beginning with "in particular" at the end of this statement, it represents a useful clarification of the legal relevance of any efficiencies a concentration generates as well as establishing that, unlike the Article numbered 101 in the Lisbon Treaty, the EMCR does not require firms to give relevant consumers a "fair share" of the gains those efficiencies (or the defendants' conduct) generates for the defendants and relevant buyers combined.

All things considered, with two possible exceptions, the new EMCR as clarified by Recitals 25, 26, and 29 seems to me to promulgate the same test of illegality as the U.S. Clayton Act. The first possible exception relates to the fact that, unlike the Clayton Act, the EMCR does not contain any language that implies that mergers that do not inflict a net equivalent-dollar loss on all Clayton-Act-relevant buyers combined but do impose such a loss on the buyers in one or more individual markets are illegal on the latter account. In my judgment, the EMCR is superior to the Clayton Act in this respect. I characterize this as a possible exception because I do not think that the relevant Clayton Act language should, as a matter of law, be interpreted literally—*i.e.*, because I think that, correctly interpreted, the Clayton Act would not be deemed to prohibit mergers that harm the buyers in one or more markets but do not impose a net equivalent-dollar loss on all Clayton-Act-relevant buyers combined. The second possible exception relates to the organization-allocative-efficiency defense that I think it is legally correct to read into the Clayton Act. Neither the EMCR nor the Clayton Act contains language promulgating an organizational-economic-efficiency defense to exonerate defendants whose mergers would not have inflicted a net equivalent-dollar loss on relevant buyers had it not generated static marginal-cost efficiencies that led one or more of the merged firm's *R*s to exit by reducing their total OCAs (and/or perhaps had it not generated dynamic efficiencies that induced the merged firm to make an expansion that prevented an actual or potential *R* from creating a QV investment that would have been more procompetitive). I list this as a possible exception because the E.C./E.U.'s general industrial policy does not favor reading such a defence into the EMCR to the same extent that the general industrial policy of the U.S. favors reading such a defense into the Clayton Act. Thus, one of the elements of the efficiency defence that Article 101(3) creates is that defendants prove that relevant buyers obtain a "fair share" of the equivalent-dollar gains that the efficient conduct

[891] *Id.* at Recital 29.

in question confers on them and the relevant buyers combined. Article 102 prohibits exploitative abuses as well as exclusionary abuses, and European and E.C./E.U. IP law are less favorable to discoverers than is U.S. IP law. For this reason, although I do believe that the Clayton Act should be interpreted to promulgate an organizational-economic-efficiency defense—*i.e.*, a special type of efficiency defense in cases in which the relevant conduct does inflict a net equivalent-dollar loss on Clayton-Act-relevant buyers, I doubt that the EMCR should be interpreted to do so.

I turn finally to the legality under E.C./E.U. competition law, properly interpreted and applied, of any tendency of a horizontal merger to increase its participants' monopsony power. Two legal issues are salient in this context: (1) does the impact of a merger on "effectiveness of competition" depend on its impact on Clayton-Act-relevant buyers or on its impact on the market shares of individually-or-collectively-dominant firms and on whether any firm has a high enough market share to qualify as a dominant firm and (2) if the trier-of-fact concludes that a horizontal merger has a tendency to enable the merged firm to induce its suppliers to boycott one or more of its product rivals by increasing its monopsony power (conduct that would constitute an independent violation of now-Article 101 and of now-Article 102 if the merged firm was either individually dominant or belonged to a set of collectively-dominant rivals), does that fact favor the conclusion that the merger violates the EMCR (or now-Article 101 or now-Article 102 if those Articles are deemed to cover horizontal mergers)?

The first issue is important because horizontal mergers that raise the cost to the merged firm of purchasing the input-unit that would have been the marginal input-unit for the MPs by increasing the merged firm's monopsony power will simultaneously inflict an equivalent-dollar loss on relevant buyers and reduce the merged firm's market share (by raising its marginal cost of production and decreasing the sales it makes—*i.e.*, the number of buyers it is best-placed to supply) while horizontal mergers that lower the cost to the merged firm of purchasing the unit of input that would have been the marginal input-unit for the MPs by increasing the merged firm's monopsony power will simultaneously confer an equivalent-dollar gain on relevant buyers and increase the merged firm's market share (make it more individually dominant if it was already individually dominant, possibly make it individually dominant when it was not so pre-merger, make the dominant group more collectively dominant if some of the additional sales the merged firm made are taken from suppliers that were not part of the dominant group, or make a group of firms that were not collectively dominant pre merger collectively dominant post-merger in the above circumstances—at least if, contrary to my conclusions about the way that "market power" should be measured, dominance is measured by market share). I believe that Recital 29 on efficiencies removes any doubt that under the EMCR the effectiveness of competition is measured by relevant-buyer equivalent-dollar welfare rather than by seller market share. If that is true and if I am correct in believing that any increases in monopsony power a horizontal merger generates will usually, if not virtually always, confer a net equivalent-dollar gain on relevant buyers—at least if it does not lead the merged firm to induce its suppliers to boycott the merged firm's rivals, then (with that possible exception) any tendency of a horizontal merger to increase its participants' monopsony power will favor its legality under the EMCR.

I also believe that—given the detectability and provability of any illegal refusals to deal to which a merger-generated increase-in-merged-firm monopsony power leads, the possibility that a merger might induce such illegal conduct by increasing the merged firm's monopsony power should not count against *the merger's* legality under the EMCR. I might add that I suspect that mergers that increase their participants' monopsony power will rarely lead to such illegal boycotts and believe that, even when they do, all tolled, the merger's tendency to increase monopsony power will usually confer an equivalent-dollar gain on relevant buyers.

4. The U.S.. Courts' Traditional Market Share/Market-Concentration Approach to Horizontal Mergers and the Various DOJ/FTC Approaches to Horizontal Mergers

Both the content and the structure of this section are strongly influenced by two facts. First, although I believe that, correctly interpreted, the Sherman and Clayton Acts promulgate significantly-different basic tests of illegality, both the U.S. courts and the U.S. antitrust-enforcement agencies have assumed that—in relation to mergers—they do not. Most horizontal-merger cases have been and continue to be brought under Section 7 of the Clayton Act rather than under Section 1 of the Sherman Act because it has always been assumed that the probability that has to be established that a merger violated or would violate the Clayton Act test of illegality to win a Clayton Act case against merger-participants is lower than the probability that has to be established that a merger violated or would violate the Sherman Act test of illegality to win a civil Sherman Act case against merger-participants (though this issue has never been litigated and contemporary Clayton Act practice does not support the existence of such a difference).

Second, for over 30 years, U.S. horizontal-merger "regulation" has been largely administrative as opposed to judicial. In fact, since 1976, the U.S. Supreme Court has not heard a single horizontal-merger case, and very few such cases have reached the lower federal courts. The application of U.S. horizontal-merger law has been left almost entirely to the Department of Justice (DOJ) and the Federal Trade Commission (FTC). This feature of horizontal-merger-law administration can be traced almost exclusively to the U.S. Congress' passage in 1976 of the Hart-Scott-Rodino Act,[892] which established a system of pre merger notification.

Hart-Scott-Rodino requires firms that are proposing to engage in a merger or acquisition to file a detailed "Notification and Report Form" if the dollar value of their assets or annual sales exceed specified amounts (which are adjusted periodically). The DOJ or FTC (the two "agencies" have come to specialize in different industries) have 30 days (15 days for cash-tender offers) either to approve

[892] 15 U.S.C. Section 15a (1976).

the proposed merger/acquisition or to make a "second request" for additional information, which they have actually done in about 5 % of the cases. After considering the additional information the merger/acquisition participants have submitted and possibly additional information it had collected in previous investigations, the DOJ or FTC can (1) approve the merger or acquisition as originally proposed, (2) negotiate structural alterations (divestitures) and/or (conceivably) conduct commitments from the participants[893] and approve the transaction as altered and/or with the behavioral constraints to which the participants agreed, or (3) seek a preliminary injunction of the merger/acquisition from the courts. The U.S. courts generally grant such injunctions if the relevant "agency" "has raised questions going to the merits so serious, substantial, difficult and doubtful as to make them fair ground for thorough investigation, study, deliberation, and determination by the... [agency] in the first place and alternately by the Court of Appeals."[894]

For at least four reasons, firms that have proposed a merger or acquisition usually abandon their plans once the DOJ or FTC has decided to oppose their proposal and almost never choose to litigate their case once a preliminary injunction has been issued against them: (1) the cost of litigation is often prohibitive; (2) it will sometimes be difficult or impossible to maintain merger-financing until the court case is decided; (3) MPs that want to combine assets that are complementary for non-scale reasons will find it prohibitively costly to maintain the availability of their respective complementary assets (say, distribution managers and production managers or good ideas and financing) for the period of a protracted litigation; and (4) MPs have good reason to suspect that the U.S. courts will tend to view their proposed merger or acquisition less favorably than the antitrust-enforcement agencies viewed it. Hence, agency decisions to oppose a proposed merger or acquisition rarely lead to litigation.

Nor is litigation likely to occur when the relevant agency decides not to challenge a proposed merger or acquisition or to approve a proposal that has been altered through negotiation. Clayton-Act-relevant buyers will usually have standing to challenge a horizontal merger (competitors usually will not), but they will usually be deterred not only by the collective-action problem they face but also by their lack of access to the information the government has collected, their inability to conduct discovery before the merger has been executed, the reluctance of courts to break up companies that have been meaningfully combined, and the difficulty of proving damages with the certainty the law requires.

The fact that contemporary U.S. horizontal-merger law in action is agency law rather than court law has affected the content and structure of this section in two ways. First, the fact that the U.S. Supreme Court has not heard a horizontal-merger case since 1976 and the related fact that it has not had the occasion to reconsider a

---

[893] Quite properly to my mind, the agencies strongly prefer structural alterations to conduct commitments. See United States Department of Justice and Federal Trade Commission, Commentary on the Horizontal Merger Guidelines (hereinafter 2006 Commentary) (2006).

[894] See Federal Trade Commission v. H.J. Heinz Co., 246 F.3d 708, 714–15 (D.C. Cir. 2001).

number of holdings it made in canonical decisions that are inconsistent with (much more anti-merger than) current agency practice (law in action) and that, I suspect, it would no longer follow have led me not to include a detailed discussion of these canonical U.S. cases. However, because the general market-oriented (market-share/market-concentration) approach to horizontal-merger analysis that U.S. courts historically took has, in important respects, been taken over by both (1) the U.S. agencies' Horizontal Merger Guidelines and (2) the EC and E.C./E.U. courts, I have decided to include in Sect. 4A(1) a detailed critique of that approach (which, I hope, will also reveal the usefulness of the conceptual systems that Chap. 2 developed and the theoretical analyses that Chap. 10 and Sect. 2 of this chapter developed). (Section 4B will discuss some more specific elements of the canonical "case"-law that the agencies have developed.)

Second, the fact that the contemporary living law of horizontal mergers in the U.S. is made by its antitrust-enforcement agencies (as well as the fact that the EC and E.C./E.U. courts have been substantially influenced by the 1992 U.S. Horizontal Merger Guidelines) has led me to include a lengthy discussion of the 1992 Guidelines and the other methods the DOJ and FTC use to assess the competitive impact of horizontal mergers.

A. The U.S. Courts' Traditional MP-Market-Share/Seller-Concentration-Ratio Approach to Horizontal-Merger Analysis, Some Elements of That Approach That the Agencies Have Respectively Rejected and Taken Over, and a Brief Account of Some More Contemporary U.S. Lower-Court Horizontal-Merger Opinions

(1) The U.S. Courts' Traditional MP-Market-Share/Seller-Concentration-Ratio Approach to Horizontal Merger Analysis: A Statement and Critique

The U.S. courts' traditional approach to horizontal-merger competitive-impact analysis was a market-share/market-concentration-oriented approach that assumed that any such merger will be more likely to reduce competition the higher the sum of the MPs' market shares, the smaller the disparity between the MPs' market shares, and the higher the total market share of the leading four or eight firms in the markets in which both MPs were placed. Although at different times analysts that used the traditional approach took other factors (such as trends in concentration or height of the barriers to entry) into consideration,[895] the traditional approach essentially consisted of rules that established a set of combinations of weighted pre-merger

---

[895] For an exhaustive compilation, see BETTY BOCK, MERGERS AND MARKETS (National Indus. Conf. Bd. Stud. in Bus. Econ. No. 100, 1968).

MP-market-shares and pre merger traditional-concentration figures that would render a horizontal merger illegal. Although the courts never explicitly stated this fact, the weighted MP-market-share figure was calculated by assigning a greater weight to the lower MP-market-share—in particular, by weighting that share three to four times more heavily.[896] The weighted MP-market-share figure that would render a merger illegal was inversely related to the relevant market's traditional concentration. The judges and DOJ and FTC officials that used this traditional approach were never very forthcoming about the way in which they defined the relevant market(s). The discussion that follows will assume that markets have been defined in an unidentified though supposedly-identifiable functionally-ideal way.

In part because U.S. courts have not distinguished between the Sherman Act and Clayton Act tests of illegality in horizontal-merger cases, in part because the effects of horizontal mergers on relevant buyers that disfavor the merger's legality under the Clayton Act tend to be associated with merger-partner benefits that are Sherman-Act-illicit and the effects of horizontal mergers on relevant buyers that favor the merger's legality under the Clayton Act tend to be associated with merger-partner benefits that are Sherman-Act-licit, and in part because most horizontal-merger cases are brought under the Clayton Act, this section will focus on how accurately the U.S. courts' traditional approach to horizontal-merger analysis will predict such mergers' Clayton Act legality. More specifically, Subsection 4(A)(1) analyzes the extent to which the various sets of non-market-aggregated determinants of the competitive impact of a horizontal merger (determinants that Sect. 2 of this chapter delineated) can be accurately predicted from the MPs' market shares or from a combination of data on the MPs' market shares and the relevant market's four-firm or eight-firm concentration ratio, assuming that the market in question has been defined in a functionally-ideal way, and Sect. 4(A)(2) analyzes the extent to which the competitive impact of the efficiencies that a horizontal merger will generate can be predicted from market-share and market-concentration data.

---

[896] This practice of weighting the smaller market share more heavily is consistent with the traditional assumptions that the firms established inside a market are equally competitive with each other and that all firms have the same ratio of best-placed to second-placed positions. Assume, for example, that all sellers (whose market shares do not exceed 50 %) are second-placed the same number of times they are best-placed, that each firm in a market is second-placed to obtain the same percentage of the customers that each other market-insider is best-placed to supply, and that all second-placed firms always enjoy the same advantage over the third-placed supplier of the buyers they are second-placed to supply. Assume in addition that the market in question has 100 buyers. In this case, a merger between two firms with 20 % market shares will combine established firms that are each other's closest competitors by the standard amount for 20 %(20) + 20 %(20) = 8 buyers while a merger between firms with 30 % and 10 % market shares (the same total market share of 40 %) will combine established firms that are each other's closest competitors by the standard amount for 30 %(10 %) + 10 %(30 %) = 6 buyers. The practice of giving more weight to the market share of the smaller MP—*i.e.*, of counting in favor of a merger any disparity in the market shares of the MPs, given the sum of their market shares—is consistent with this outcome. As we shall see, perhaps for the same reason, the 1992 Guidelines also assume that, *ceteris paribus*, a horizontal merger is less likely to be anticompetitive the greater the disparity in the MPs' market shares. See the text of Subsection 4A(1)(A)(i)(a) of this chapter.

(A) The Accuracy of Any Approach That Attempts to Predict the Competitive Impact of a Horizontal Merger That Generates No Relevant Efficiencies From MP-Market-Share and Traditional-Seller-Concentration-Ratio Data

(i) The Accuracy with Which the Traditional MP-Market-Share/Seller-Concentration-Ratio Approach Can Predict the Impact of a Horizontal Merger That Generates No Relevant Efficiencies and Does Not Change the Equilibrium QV-Investment Level of the Market in Which It Takes Place Will Have on the Prices That the Merged Firm Will Charge Relative to Those That the MPs Would Have Charged and on the Prices That the Merged Firm's Rs Will Charge

(a) MP Market Shares, Traditional Market-Concentration Ratios, and the Effect of Such a Horizontal Merger on the OCAs and HNOPs of the Merged Firm and Its *R*s How accurately will MP-market-share and traditional seller-concentration-ratio data predict the impact of a horizontal merger on the OCAs of the MPs and the merged firm's *R*s if the efficiencies it generated and (partially relatedly) its impact on QV investment could be ignored. I will focus first on the impact of a horizontal merger on the MPs' OCAs and then on its impact on the *R*s' OCAs. In each case, I will focus first on individualized-pricing contexts and then consider some of the additional factors that will affect the MPs' and *R*s' HNOPs in across-the-board-pricing contexts.

In individualized-pricing contexts, a merger's impact on the HNOPs of the MPs (and their *R*s) depends solely on its impact on the OCAs of the merged firm relative to those of the MPs (and on the OCAs of the merged firm's *R*s). The first determinant of the impact of such a horizontal merger on the OCAs of the merged firm relative to those of the MPs in an individualized-pricing context is the frequency with which the MPs were each other's closest competitors. Obviously, if (1) every product in a given market were the closest competitor of each of its insider-rivals for the same percentage of each such rival's customers, (2) every firm's best-placed-to-second-placed-to-an-insider ratio were the same, and (3) the above ratios were the same in all markets, (A) one could predict the frequency with which if not the amount by which the MPs were each other's closest competitors from their market shares, (B) that frequency would be directly related to the MPs' average market shares, and (C) that frequency would also be inversely related to the difference between the MPs' market shares, controlling for their total or average market share. For example, if one assumes that the relevant market consists of a given number of sellers with a one-to-one best-placed-to-second-placed ratio (which would be the only assumption compatible with equal ratios if the closest competitor of any firm in a given market for a particular buyer's patronage were always another insider) and (for simplicity) 1,000 buyers of equal size, (i) a merger between two MPs with 10 % market shares would combine sellers that were each other's closest competitors a total of 20 times—*i.e.*, would combine sellers each of which was the other's closest competitor for 10 buyers (10 % of the 100 [which is 10 % of 1,000] buyers the other was best-placed to serve); (ii) a merger between two MPs with 20 % market shares would combine sellers that were each other's closest competitors a total of 80 times—*i.e.*, would combine sellers each of which was the other's closest competitor for 40 (which is 20 % of 200) buyers; and (iii) a merger between one firm with a 15 % market share and another with a 5 % market share would combine sellers that were each other's closest competitors a total of 15 times (15 %[5 %]1,000 + 5 %[15 %]1,000 = 7.5 + 7.5 = 15). However, in practice, the effects of these tendencies are likely to be overwhelmed by the effects of those facts that make the above assumptions (1), (2), and (3) inaccurate. Thus, in practice, I expect that variations in different MPs' best-placed-to-second-placed ratios or in the ratio of the percent of each other's customers they are best-placed to obtain to the percent of all other insiders' customers that given MPs are best-placed to obtain—*i.e.*, in the extent to which the different pairs of MPs are more competitive (or less competitive) with each other than they are with their average other insider-*R*s—will have at least as much to do with the absolute frequency with which a given pair of MPs are each other's closest competitors as will the size of their market shares. Thus, one will not be able to predict accurately the frequency with which the MPs are each other's closest competitors from data on their market shares. Nor is there any reason to believe that one will be able to predict this determinant more accurately by combining MP-market-share data with traditional seller-concentration-ratio data.

The second set of determinants of the effect of a horizontal merger on the MPs' OCAs is the average amount by which the second-placed MP was better-placed than the third-placed supplier of a buyer that the MPs were respectively uniquely-best-placed and uniquely-second-placed to supply and the average amount by which both MPs were better-placed than the third-placed supplier of a buyer that the MPs were uniquely-equal-best-placed to supply. A very similar argument to the one developed in the preceding paragraph can be used to demonstrate that the sum of the MPs' market shares, the disparity in their market shares, and the traditional concentration of the market are not accurate predictors of the amount by which (1) the second-placed MP is better-placed than the third-placed supplier of those buyers the MPs are respectively uniquely-best-placed and uniquely-second-placed to serve and (2) both MPs are better-placed than the third-placed supplier of buyers the two MPs are uniquely-equal-best-placed to supply. In this case, the argument that the MPs' average market share is a good predictor of the amount by which the MPs are each other's closest competitors when they are each other's closest competitors would probably be based on the following three possible relationships: (1) the larger the MPs' combined market shares, the smaller the number of non-MP insider-products; (2) the smaller the number of non-MP insiders, the smaller the number of products that will be close-to-second-placed; and (3) the smaller the number of close-to-second-placed products, the larger the gap between the second-placed MP and the third-placed supplier of the buyers the MPs were respectively uniquely-best-placed and uniquely-second-placed (or uniquely-equal-best-placed) to serve. Although this argument is not completely unfounded, each of the relationships on which it is based is too weak for the MPs' market shares to be good predictors of the amount by which they are each other's closest competitors when they are respectively uniquely-best-placed and uniquely-second-placed (uniquely-equal-best-placed) to supply a given buyer. Thus, in the real world, the relationships between non-MP market shares (or non-MP contributions to the relevant market's HHI) and the number of non-MP insiders is very weak: even if one constrains the analysis by controlling for the non-MP contribution to the relevant market's traditional concentration ratio, any number of independent firms could be operating in the market in question. Similarly, in the real world, the relationship between the number of non-MP insiders and the number of such products that were close to being second-placed to serve those customers the MPs were respectively uniquely-best-placed and uniquely-second-placed (or uniquely-equal-best-placed) to serve is also likely to be very weak across markets. In general, I suspect that the percentages of the non-MPs that are close-to-second-placed when the MPs are respectively uniquely-best-placed and uniquely-second-placed (or uniquely-equal-best-placed) and the average gap between the second-placed MP (the MPs) and the third-placed supplier of the buyer in question will be respectively lower and higher in markets whose products are heterogeneous than in markets whose products are homogeneous. The preceding argument implies not only that one will not be able to predict accurately the average amount by which the MPs will be each other's closest competitors when they are each other's closest competitors for the patronage of a buyer one MP is or both MPs are best-placed to supply from data on their market shares but also that such predictions will not be rendered significantly more accurate by combining such MP-market-share data with traditional seller-concentration-ratio data.

The third set of determinants that is relevant to the impact of the merger on the MPs' OCAs contains those that affect the extent to which the merger will raise the MPs' OCAs by raising their *R*s' OCAs by raising the contextual marginal costs the MPs will have to incur to match what would otherwise be the *R*s' HNOP-containing offers to the *R*s' customers—

(1) the frequency with which one MP was the closest competitor of some *R* that either was the closest competitor of the merged firm post-merger or would be were it not for the effect of the merger on the *R*'s relevant contextual marginal costs (CMC),
(2) the amount by which the merger increased the CMC that the merged firm would have to incur to match the *R*'s pre merger HNOP-containing offer to its customers above the CMC that the relevant MP would have had to incur to do so

    (A) by increasing the prices that the merged firm charged its customers above the prices the relevant MP charged its own customers and hence the discriminatory character of any relevant matching-offers that the merged firm might make and
    (B) (i) by increasing the probability that the antitrust authorities or the MPs' competitors would sue the merged firm post-merger for undercutting rivals above the probability that they would sue the relevant MP pre merger for doing so, (ii) by increasing the probability that triers-of-fact would find the merged firm liable for doing so above the probability that triers-of-fact would find against the relevant MP (controlling for the [other] evidence of contrivance that has been introduced), and (iii) by increasing the penalties

and damages that would be imposed on or assessed against the merged firm if found liable relative to those that would be imposed on the relevant MP (once more, controlling for the [other] evidence),

(3) the amount by which any such increase in the merged firm's relevant CMC relative to the relevant MP's would enable the *R*s to raise their prices to their own customers—an amount whose upper limit is the advantage the MPs originally had when second-placed to that *R* over the third-placed supplier of the *R*-customers in question, and
(4) the various factors that affect the amount by which any related increase in the relevant *R*s' prices to their own customers would raise the CMC they had to incur to match the merged firm's HNOP-containing offers to its customers post-merger relative to those they had to incur to match the relevant MP's HNOP-containing offers pre-merger.

I have already argued that the MPs' market shares are very poor predictors of the frequency with which they would be second-placed *inter alia* to a best-placed *R* and *a fortiori* to an *R* that was second-placed to them. I have also already argued that the MPs' market shares are a poor indicator of the amount by which their merger will increase the prices they charge their own customers by increasing their OCAs by freeing them from each other's competition. The text that follows will show that the MPs' market shares and the relevant market's traditional concentration are equally-poor predictors of the amount by which their merger will induce them to increase the prices they charge their own customers by increasing their NOMs and COMs (both by changing their OCAs and in other ways). The MPs' market shares and the traditional concentration of their market also have little bearing on the extent of the MPs' advantages over the independent third-placed supplier of those of the *R*'s customers that the MPs are second-place to supply. Hence, although there may be a positive correlation between the MPs' market shares and their market's traditional concentration on the one hand and the likelihood that they will be sued and convicted or held liable if they take an *R*'s customers post-merger, I doubt that this relationship significantly increases the accuracy of any approach that attempts to predict the *R*-CMC-related tendency of a horizontal merger to increase the MPs' prices from market-aggregated data, especially if one considers the possible offsetting tendency of increases in the MPs' market shares and their market's traditional concentration to decrease the probability that at least smaller *R*s will be sued and convicted for undercutting the MPs' prices.

Everything considered, then, any approach that uses MP-market-share data and traditional seller-concentration-ratio data to predict the amount by which a horizontal merger would increase the OCAs of an individualized-pricing merged firm above the OCAs the MPs would have had (and hence on the amount by which it will increase the merged firm's HNOPs above the HNOPs the MPs would have had) if the merger did not generate any efficiencies or alter QV investment in any other way will be extremely inaccurate.

The same conclusion is justified when the merged firm and its *R*s charge across-the-board prices. For reasons that Chap. 2 explained, the analysis of the amount by which a horizontal merger will increase an across-the-board-pricing merged firm's HNOPs above the HNOPs the MPs would have had differs from individualized-pricing counterpart in two respects: (1) rather than considering CMC consequences, the across-the-board-pricing analysis must consider the effect the merger has on the BCA/BCD distributions not only of the merged firm relative to those of its antecedents but also on the BCA/BCD distributions of the merged firm's *R*s and of the *R*s of the merged firm's *R*s, *etc*., and (2) relatedly, the across-the-board-pricing analysis must also consider the impact of the merger on the order in which the prices of the products in the relevant ARDEPPS are announced. Although the preceding demonstration that the MPs' market shares and the ARDEPPS' concentration have little bearing on the impact of their merger on the merged firm's customer-by-customer OCAs applies *mutatis mutandis* to the impact their merger will have on the BCA/BCD distribution of all relevant firms, the preceding analysis cannot be extended so straightforwardly to cover the relevance of the MPs' market shares and the relevant ARDEPPS' traditional concentration to the impact their horizontal merger will have on the HNOPs of the merged firm (and its *R*s) by changing the order in which the prices of the products produced by the MPs and the merged firm's *R*s are announced. Horizontal mergers can alter the sequence of these price-announcements so as to increase the HNOP array of the merged firm and its *R*s in two ways:

(1) by eliminating as an independent decisionmaker an MP that announced its price later in the relevant price-announcement sequence than was in its and its merger partner's joint interest (both when the former MP's timing choice was in its interest [roughly speaking] because the MP in question was "second-placed" in BCA/BCD terms much more often than it was "best-placed" in those terms and when the MP in question's price-announcement-timing choice was against its own interest) and
(2) by creating a merged firm that, unlike the MPs, had the status, knowledge, and skill to lead its rivals and itself to announce their prices in a sequence that was more in its individual and their collective interest.

I do not think that the extent to which a horizontal merger increases the relevant ARDEPPS' across-the-board-HNOP array in the first of the above two ways is positively correlated with the MPs' market shares. It would be only if the ratio of (the dollar volume of sales in relation to which a firm has a BCA) to (the dollar volume of sales in relation to which the firm's BCA position is second or close to second) were inversely related to its market share, and I suspect that, if anything, across all cases this ratio is strongly positively correlated with firm market shares—that firms with high market shares tend to have BCAs far more often than they are second-placed or close-to-second-placed in BCA terms while firms with low market shares tend to be second-placed or close-to-second-placed far more often than they are best-placed in BCA terms. (This contestable suspicion is based on an assumption that in developed countries firms with small market shares tend to produce generics rather than highly-differentiated product variants that appeal strongly to the few buyers that purchase them.) I also see no reason to believe that the extent to which a horizontal merger will increase the HNOP array in the across-the-board-pricing ARDEPPS in which it will take place will be correlated in any way with the concentration of the ARDEPPS in question. Admittedly, there may be some reason to believe that the larger the smaller MP, the more likely a horizontal merger will be to create a merged firm that is critically more able to improve the timing of the merged firm's and its rivals' price announcements from their collective perspective if the merged firm is the largest firm in the relevant ARDEPPS. However, this relationship provides support for at most a weak positive correlation between the MPs' market shares and the extent to which their merger will increase across-the-board HNOPs in the second way delineated above and for no correlation between the relevant ARDEPPS' concentration and the extent to which a horizontal merger in it will increase across-the-board HNOPs in this way.

I turn now to the correlation between the MPs' market shares and their ARDEPPS' concentration on the one hand and the amount by which their no-relevant-efficiency-generating horizontal merger will increase the HNOPs of the merged firm's *R*s on the other. The earlier discussion of the circumstances in which and amount by which in individualized-pricing contexts such a merger will increase the *R*s' HNOPs by increasing the CMC the merged firm will have to incur to match the *R*s' pre merger HNOP-containing offers implies that the amount by which such a merger will increase the *R*s' HNOPs cannot be inferred from the MPs' market shares or the relevant market's concentration. And the earlier discussions of the extent to which one can predict the impact of such a merger on (1) the merged firm's OCA distribution and (2) the ability of the ARDEPPS' firms to announce their prices in the sequence that is in their collective interest imply that the amount by which such a merger will increase across-the-board-pricing *R*s' HNOPs in these ways can also not be predicted accurately from the MPs' market shares or the relevant market's concentration.

(b) MP Market Shares, Traditional Seller-Concentration Ratios, and the Effect of Such a Horizontal Merger on the NOMs of the Merged Firm and Its *R*s It will also not be possible to derive from MP-market-share data and "relevant"-market-concentration data accurate predictions of the extent to which a horizontal merger that generates no relevant efficiencies will increase the NOMs of the merged firm and its *R*s. As we have seen, such mergers can affect the frequency with which the MPs and their *R*s can obtain NOMs only by changing their OCAs, by critically affecting their ability to make a series of premature price announcements that would lower the cost to them of reducing their initially-announced prices, or by lowering in some other way the mechanical, bargaining, buyer-expectation-related, or legal costs they have to incur to reduce their initially-announced prices. I will now address each of these three possibilities. First, we have just seen that one cannot accurately predict the impact of a horizontal merger on the OCAs of the MPs and their *R*s from the MPs' market shares and the ARDEPPS' concentration. Second, the preceding explanation of why one cannot accurately predict the likelihood that a horizontal merger will enable the established firms in the relevant ARDEPPS to time their mature price announcements in their collective interest from data on the MPs' market shares and the ARDEPPS concentration implies that one also cannot predict from such data the likelihood that such a merger will enable the members of the ARDEPPS to make premature price announcements that permit them to obtain OMs naturally. Third and finally, such a horizontal merger seems unlikely to increase the ability of the merged firm or its *R*s to obtain NOMs by lowering the cost it or they must incur to reduce an initially-announced price in reaction to an undercutting or undermining response by one or more rivals—indeed, the MPs' market shares and the market's concentration seem likely to be positively related to the legal cost that a recently-merged firm should expect it will incur if it reacts to a rival's undercutting or undermining response to its initial price by making a perfectly-legal, non-strategic price-reduction (will be positively related to the probability that the firm in question will be prosecuted/sued and convicted/found liable for reacting in this way and will also be positively related to the penalty/damages that are likely to be assessed against it if it is convicted/found liable).

(c) MP Market Shares, Traditional Seller-Concentration Ratios, and the Effect of Such a Horizontal Merger on the COMs of the Merged Firm and Its *R*s This subsection will execute four related but separate analyses of the accuracy with which one can predict the impact that a horizontal merger will have on the COMs paid by Clayton-Act-relevant buyers from the MPs' market shares and the relevant ARDEPPS' traditional seller-concentration ratio:

(i) an analysis that focuses on the relationship between the COMs that the merged firm will try to obtain relative to the COMs that the MPs would have tried to obtain and assumes that the MPs, the merged firm, and the merged firm's *R*s all charge individualized prices;
(ii) an analysis that focuses on relationship between the the COMs the merged firm's *R*s will try to obtain and assumes that all relevant firms charge individualized prices;
(iii) an analysis that focuses on the relationship between the COMs that the merged firm will try to obtain and the COMs the MPs would have tried to obtain but assumes that the firms in question all set across-the-board prices; and
(iv) an analysis that focuses on the COMs that the merged firm's *R*s will try to obtain but assumes that all relevant firms charge across-the-board prices.

As we saw, it is useful to distinguish two sets of determinants of each of these impacts:

(1) the determinants of whether contrived oligopolistic pricing was profitable for the firm or firms in question pre-merger—*i.e.*, (A) the determinants (i) of the percentage of an individualized pricer's customers in relation to which it was profitable pre merger for the individualized-pricing firm in question to attempt to contrive an OM and (ii) of whether it was profitable pre merger for an across-the-board pricer to attempt to contrive OMs and (B) the determinants of the amount by which contrived oligopolistic pricing was unprofitable for an

individualized pricer or across-the-board pricer when it was unprofitable for the firm in question and
(2) the determinants of the amount by which the relevant merger increased the profitability of contrived oligopolistic pricing for the firm in question.

All four of the analyses this subsection executes will focus separately on these two sets of factors.

(i) MP Market Shares, the Market's Traditional Seller-Concentration Ratio, and the Amount by Which Such a Merger Will Raise the Merged Firm's COMs Above the MPs' When Prices Are Individualized

How accurately can one predict the amount by which a horizontal merger that generates no relevant efficiencies will raise the COMs that an individualized-pricing merged firm will try to obtain relative to those that the MPs would have tried to obtain from accurate data on the MPs' market shares and the relevant ARDEPPS' traditional seller concentration? First, how accurately can one predict the pre merger profitability of contrived oligopolistic pricing for individualized-pricing MPs from accurate data on their market shares and their market's traditional seller concentration? The answer is: not accurately at all. Thus, since the MPs' market shares and their market's traditional seller-concentration ratio are inaccurate predictors of the MPs' average OCA + NOM in relation to those buyers they were best-placed to supply pre-merger, data on MP pre merger market shares and pre merger market concentration will not accurately predict the extent to which the MPs will be deterred from engaging in contrived oligopolistic pricing by the safe profits they must put at risk to do so. Similarly, since the average number of rivals that were either second-placed or close-to-second-placed to obtain the patronage of the MPs' customers pre merger will not be highly correlated with either the MPs' pre merger market shares or their market's pre merger traditional concentration (given that the latter will not reflect the number of small firms in the competitive fringe that were in such positions), MP-market-share and traditional seller-concentration data will be poor predictors of the communication costs the MPs had to incur to contrive OMs pre merger or the cost to them of identifying their undercutters pre-merger. Such data will also be poor predictors of the MPs' pre merger reputations (1) for estimating their costs and OCAs accurately and (2) for making and carrying out oligopolistic threats and promises. MP-market-share and traditional seller-concentration-ratio data are also poor predictors as well of the MPs' respective pre merger abilities to detect undercutting from circumstantial sales-record evidence: such market-aggregated data is not at all correlated with the stability of the determinants of the MPs' relevant sales-percentages through time or the ability of the MPs to identify and measure the determinants of their relevant sales-percentages other than rival-undercutting and (because the ratio of buyers to sellers varies tremendously from market to market) are at most only weakly positively correlated with the number of old buyers each MP was best-placed to supply pre-merger, the number of old buyers each MP's *R*s were best-placed to supply pre merger (the number of customers they would expect to obtain from their *R*s as a result of spontaneous defections), and the number of new buyers that usually entered the market each season pre merger (the number of new buyers they would expect to obtain as customers if no-one engaged in undercutting). MP-market-share and traditional seller-concentration-ratio data are also poor indicators of the MPs' respective pre merger knowledge of the identities of their customers' second-placed or close-to-second-placed suppliers, of the inclinations of various rivals to engage in undercutting, or of the MPs' ability to identify the actual suppliers of the various buyers in the market by inspecting deliveries, inventories, or goods sold. And again, MP-market-share and traditional seller-concentration-ratio data are poor indicators of the extent to which pre merger each MP could make it profitable for its potential undercutters (Us) to forego inherently-profitable opportunities to undercut that MP's contrived oligopolistic prices by foregoing any similar opportunities the Us gave that MP—*i.e.*, are poor indicators of the frequency with which and amount by which pre-merger each MP was the second-placed supplier of a buyer the *R* was best-placed to supply (or was better-placed than any inferior supplier of such a buyer than any other firm the U could not co-opt or the amount by which the MP was better-placed than the third-placed supplier of those buyers the *R* was best-placed to supply and the MP was second-placed to supply). Similarly, MP-market-share and traditional seller-concentration-ratio data are not strongly correlated with the factors that determine the cost to each MP pre merger of inflicting any given amount of harm on an undercutting U by engaging in individualized-price retaliation—the frequency with which each MP was the U's closest competitor or was close to being the U's closest competitor and the size of the U's (OCA + NOM)s in those cases in which the MP was or was close to being the U's closest competitor. Finally, since the MPs' shares of the markets to which they are both assigned do not indicate the absolute volume of sales each is best-placed to make across all the "markets" in which each operates (indeed, does not even indicate the *absolute* volume of sales each makes in the market to which both have been assigned), MP-market-share data is a poor predictor of the extent to which each MP could take advantage of company-wide-reputation-related economies of scale when practicing contrived oligopolistic pricing. Everything considered, then, MP-market-share and traditional seller-concentration-ratio data will be poor predictors of the pre merger profitability of contrived oligopolistic pricing for individualized-pricing MPs in the market in which both were deemed to be operating.

Second, how accurately can one predict the amount by which a horizontal merger that generates no relevant efficiencies will raise the profits the merged firm can realize by engaging in contrived oligopolistic pricing in the market in which both MPs have been deemed to be operating above the profits the MPs could have realized from data on the MPs' pre merger shares of that market and that market's traditionally-measured seller concentration? Once more, the answer is: not at all accurately. Thus, since MP-market-share and traditional seller-concentration-ratio data are inaccurate predictors of the amount by which a merger increases the merged firm's average (OCA + NOM) above each of the MPs' average (OCA + NOM), data on these parameters will have little bearing on the extent to which the merger reduces the profitability of contrived oligopolistic pricing for the merged firm below the profitability of such contrivance for the MPs by increasing the average amount of safe profits the merged firm must put at risk to engage in such contrivance above the average amount of safe profits the MPs had to put at risk to do so. The MPs' market shares and the relevant market's traditional concentration will also not accurately predict the amount by which their merger will raise the profits the merged firm can obtain by engaging in contrived oligopolistic pricing above the profits the MPs could realize by doing so by reducing the number of rivals that would find it inherently profitable to undercut the contrived oligopolistic prices that the merged firm might charge below the average number of rivals that would find it inherently profitable to undercut the MPs' contrived oligopolistic prices—*i.e.*, by reducing the number of rivals to which the merged firm must communicate its contrived oligopolistic intentions, must co-opt, and must sort through to identify its actual undercutter below the average number of rivals the MPs would have to deal with to practice contrived oligopolistic pricing successfully. This conclusion reflects the fact that MP-market-share data and relevant-market traditional-concentration data have no bearing on the relative frequencies with which the MPs' merger (1) will reduce the number of potential undercutters the merged firm must deal with to contrive an oligopolistic price below the number a best-placed MP had to deal with to contrive an oligopolistic price because pre merger the other MP belonged to a larger set of second-placed or close-to-second-placed suppliers and (2) will increase the number of potential undercutters the merged firm must deal with to contrive an oligopolistic price above the number a best-placed MP had to deal with to do so because pre merger either (A) the MPs were uniquely-equal-best-placed to supply a buyer that had two or more third-placed and close-to-third-placed suppliers all of which were much-worse-than-best-placed or (B) the MPs were respectively uniquely-best-placed and uniquely-second-placed to supply a buyer that had two or more third-placed and close-to-third-placed suppliers all of which were much-worse-placed to supply them than was the second-placed MP. MP-market-share and traditional seller-concentration-ratio data will also be poor predictors of the extent to which the merger will increase the profitability of contrivance to the merged firm above its profitability to the MPs by reducing the communication costs the merged firm must incur to practice contrivance below the communication costs the MPs had to incur to do so by creating a merged firm that can communicate its contrived oligopolistic intentions more cheaply simply by setting an oligopolistic price because the merged firm has a stronger reputation for estimating its HNOPs and NOMs accurately and/or for practicing contrived oligopolistic pricing than the average MP had (since MP-market-share data is not highly correlated with the extent to which the merged firm's relevant abilities or reputations will be greater than its antecedents'). Although the MPs' market shares will be directly related to the extent to which the merger will create a merged firm that is more able than its antecedents to infer undercutting from circumstantial evidence relating to its sales (since the larger the MPs' market shares, the greater their sales and hence the greater the advantage the merged firm can obtain by pooling MP sales-information), the fact that the number of buyers placed in a given market varies widely from market to market, the fact that the stability through time of the relevant sales-percentages of the average seller in a given market varies widely from market to market, and the fact that the ability of the average seller in a given market to identify and measure the magnitude in any relevant time-period of the determinants of its relevant sales-percentages other than rival undercutting varies widely from market to market all imply that market-share data will be a poor predictor of the absolute amount by which a merger will raise the profitability of contrived oligopolistic pricing for the merged firm relative to its profitability for the MPs in this way. MP-market-share and traditional-market concentration data also provide little information about the amount by which the cost to the merged firm of identifying its undercutter is lower than the cost to the MPs of doing so (1) because (as has already been stated) such data indicate little about the difference between the number of potential undercutters the merged firm faces and the average MP faced but also (2) because it has little bearing on the extent to which each MP has information about remaining rivals that will help the other identify its potential undercutters. MP-market-share and traditional seller-concentration-ratio data are certainly not good predictors of the difference between the merged company's ability to reward cooperators through reciprocation and the average MP's ability to do so—a difference that depends on the frequency with which the MPs were respectively second-placed and third-placed to obtain a cooperating *R*'s customer's patronage (or were the *R*'s closest competitors whose cooperation the *R* had not yet secured) and the amount by which the third-placed MP was better-placed than the fourth-placed supplier of the buyers in question. Nor are such market-aggregated data good predictors of whether or the extent to which pre merger one MP had excess reciprocatory power in relation to some *R* (could give more benefits to that *R* by reciprocating than were necessary to secure that *R*'s cooperation) that the other MP could use post-merger. MP-market-share and traditional seller-concentration-ratio data can also not accurately predict the likelihood that or the extent to which the competitive relationships between the two MPs and one or more *R*s were complementarily asymmetric—*i.e.*, caused the harm-inflicted to loss-incurred ratio for the last necessary act of retaliation by one MP against a relevant *R* to be lower than its counterpart for the other MP's last necessary act of price-retaliation against that *R* (can also not accurately predict the likelihood that or the extent to which the merger would increase the profitability of contrived oligopolistic pricing to the merged company above its profitability for the MPs by enabling the merged firm to engage in retaliatory-power pooling [to retaliate against an *R* by making more price-cuts on one MP's product[s] and fewer on the other MP's product[s] than the two MPs would have made as independents]). MP-market-share data and traditional seller-concentration-ratio data can also not accurately predict the extent to which the merger will increase the profitability of contrived oligopolistic pricing to the merged firm relative to its profitability to the MPs by creating a merged firm that can take better advantage of company-wide economies of scale in building, maintaining, and using a reputation for contrivance both because the total sales of different (antitrust) markets vary enormously and because such ARDEPPS-data ignore the volume of sales the MPs have in other

ARDEPPSes. In addition, MP-market-share data and traditional seller-concentration-ratio data cannot accurately predict the impact such a horizontal merger will have on the COMs the merged firm will attempt to obtain relative to the COMs its antecedents would attempt to contrive by creating a company whose management had different attitudes toward violating the law than did the weighted-average management of its antecedents. Admittedly, in a legal system in which the legality of horizontal mergers depends on the MPs' market shares and the relevant ARDEPPS' traditional-market-concentration, increases in these parameters may tend to decrease the COMs the merged firm attempts to contrive by raising the likelihood that contrivance will lead to prosecution and conviction or private suits and civil liability, by raising the probability (controlling for the other evidence) that the merged firm will be found guilty or liable, and by raising (controlling for the other evidence) the magnitude of the penalties/damage-awards that will be imposed on/assessed against it. However, even if this bootstrapping is taken into account, it seems clear that the MP-market-share and relevant-market traditional-concentration data on which U.S. courts claim to base their decisions in horizontal-merger cases can accurately predict neither the pre merger profitability of contrived oligopolistic pricing to the MPs nor the extent to which the merger increases the profitability of such pricing for the merged firm relative to its profitability for the MPs. Such data cannot accurately predict the effect that horizontal mergers that generate no relevant efficiencies would have on the merged firm's COMs relative to the MPs' COMs.

(ii) MP Market Shares, the Market's Traditional Seller-Concentration Ratios, and the Amount by Which Such a Horizontal Merger in an Individualized-Pricing Market Will Increase the COMs of the Merged Firm's Rs

How accurately can one predict from accurate MP-market-share and accurate relevant-market traditional-concentration-ratio data the impact that a horizontal merger that generates no relevant efficiencies and takes place in a market in which individualized prices are charged will have on the COMs that the merged firm's *R*s attempt to contrive? Not surprisingly, the answer is: even less accurately than one can predict the impact of such a merger on the COMs that the merged firm will attempt to obtain relative to those that the MPs would attempt to obtain. Thus, MP-market-share and relevant-market traditional-concentration-ratio data will be even a worse predictor of the pre merger profitability of contrived oligopolistic pricing to the merged firm's *R*s and to the impact of the merger on the profitability of such pricing to those *R*s than there were the counterpart figures for the merged firm.

To save space, I will be brief. First, MP-market-share data will, if anything, be a worse predictor of the following determinants of the impact of a horizontal merger on an individualized-pricing *R*'s COMs than on the counterpart determinants of the impact of such a merger on the merged firm's COMs relative to the MPs' COMs: (1) the merged firm's *R*s' average pre merger individualized (HNOP + NOM − MC) figure and the impact of the merger on that figure, (2) the *R*s' pre-merger and post-merger reputations for assessing their HNOPs and NOMs accurately and for practicing contrived oligopolistic pricing and the impact of the merger on those reputations, (3) the pre merger ability of the competitive *R*s to take advantage of company-wide economies of scale in building and maintaining a reputation for contrivance and practicing contrived oligopolistic pricing and the impact of the merger on those reputations, and (4) the dispreference of the managers of the various *R*s pre-merger for breaking the law by engaging in price-fixing and the impact of the merger on those attitudes. Second, MP-market-share data will be a poor predictor of a number of other determinants of the impact of a merger on the *R*s' individualized COMs. Thus, since the MPs' market shares are a poor predictor of the frequency with which they were both second-placed or close-to-second-placed to obtain the patronage of an *R*'s customer, MP-market-share data will not be a good predictor of the amount by which the MPs' merger will increase the profitability of contrived oligopolistic pricing to the MPs' *R*s by reducing by one the number of possible undercutters to which the *R* must communicate its contrived oligopolistic intentions and by reducing by one the number of possible undercutters whose behavior the *R* may have to investigate if its contrived oligopolistic price is undercut—*i.e.*, by reducing the *R*'s relevant communication and undercutter-identification costs. Similarly, since the MPs' market shares and the relevant market's traditional concentration are poor predictors of the effect of the merger on the OCAs, NOMs, and COMs of the merged firm relative to those of the MPs, market-aggregated data of these kinds are not good indicators of the amount by which the MPs' merger will increase the profitability of contrived oligopolistic pricing to their *R*s by increasing the amount of harm the *R*s can inflict on the MPs by stealing any given number of customers from them or, more importantly, by incurring any amount of losses to do so. Moreover, since the MPs' market shares and the relevant market's traditional concentration ratio are poor predictors of the average difference between the harm-inflicted to loss-incurred ratios for the merged firm's *R*s' last necessary act of retaliation against MP1 and MP2, data on these parameters will provide little insight into the extent to which a horizontal merger will increase the COMs the merged firm's *R*s will find profitable to attempt to contrive by creating a merged firm whose defenses are more spread than those of its antecedents. And again, since the MPs' market shares and the relevant market's traditional concentration ratio will be poor indicators of the frequency with which the MPs are best-placed and second-placed when an *R* is third-placed, in such cases the amount by which (pre-merger) the *R* is better placed than the fourth-placed supplier of the buyer in question, the frequency with which they are best-placed and third-placed when the *R* is second-placed, and in this latter case the amount by which the third-placed MP is better-placed than the fourth-placed supplier of the buyer in question, such market-aggregated data will be poor predictors of the extent to which the MPs' merger will increase the profitability of contrivance to an *R* by increasing the latter's ability to reciprocate to the MPs' cooperation. In addition, since such market-aggregated data are poor indicators of the frequency with which an *R* has excess reciprocatory power in relation to one MP and insufficient reciprocatory power in relation to the other, such data will not be good predictors of the extent to which a horizontal merger will increase the profitability of contrived oligopolistic pricing to the MPs' *R*s by enabling them to take advantage of any excess reciprocatory power they enjoy in relation to one MP. All things considered, then, it is clear that, if anything, MP-market-share and relevant-market traditional-concentration-ratio data will be even poorer predictors of the impact of a horizontal merger that generates no relevant efficiencies on the COMs that the merged firm's *R*s attempt to obtain than on the COMs the merged firm attempts to obtain relative to those the MPs attempted to obtain.

(iii) MP Market Shares, the Market's Traditional Seller-Concentration Ratio, and the Amount by Which Such a Horizontal Merger Will Raise the COMs of an Across-the-Board-Pricing Merged Firm Above the COMs the MPs Would Have Obtained

Assume a horizontal merger that yields no static efficiencies and does not change the equilibrium level of QV investment in the market in which it takes place. How accurately will one be able to predict the amount by which such a merger will raise the COMs the merged firm will obtain above the COMs the MPs would obtain when the MPs, the merged firm, and their *R*s set across-the-board prices from the MPs' shares of the market in question and that market's traditionally-defined seller-concentration? Once more, the answer is: not accurately at all.

First, MP-market-share data and traditional concentration ratios will have no more bearing on the amount of safe profits the MPs would have to put at risk to attempt to secure a COM or on the amount by which the merger would increase that figure when the firms in question set across-the-board prices than when they set individualized prices. Roughly speaking, when the firms in question practice across-the-board pricing, the safe profits in question depend (1) on the MPs' average BCAs, their closest *R*s' average BCAs, and their closest *R*s' closest *R*s' average BCAs and (2) on the order in which the MPs, the MPs' closest *R*s', and the MPs' closest *R*s' closest *R*s make their mature price announcements. I see no reason to believe that the MP-market-share figures or the traditional seller-concentration ratio of the relevant market will have any more bearing on either the pre merger magnitude of these figures or the impact of the merger on them than they do on the average pre merger OCAs of individualized-pricing MPs and the amount by which the merger raises the average OCA of an individualized-pricing merged firm above the average OCA of its antecedents.

Second, regardless of the relative extents to which the relevant firms' reputations for contrivance are based on their or their antecedents' past conduct or on an assessment of the profitability of their engaging in such conduct, MP-market-share data and traditional seller-concentration ratios have no more bearing on the MPs' reputations for contrivance or on the extent to which the merged firm's reputation for contrivance is stronger than the average reputation for contrivance of the MPs when the sellers in question practice across-the-board pricing than when they charge individualized prices. Thus, regardless of whether the sellers in question are setting across-the-board or individualized prices, such data is a poor predictor of the relevant actors' past conduct, of the extent to which the MPs could take advantage of company-wide economies of scale in building and maintaining a reputation for contrivance, and of the impact of the merger on the ability of the merged firm relative to that of its antecedents to take advantage of such company-wide economies of scale.

Third, MP-market-share data and traditional seller-concentration ratios are poor predictors of the dispreferences of the managers of the MPs and the dispreferences of the managers of their *R*s pre merger for breaking the law by engaging in price-fixing as well as of the impact of the merger on the relevant attitudes of the managers of the merged company relative to the attitudes of the MPs' managers and the relevant attitudes of the managers of the relevant merged-firm *R*s, regardless of whether the companies in question set across-the-board or individualized prices.

Fourth, MP-market-share data and traditional seller-concentration ratios are also as poor predictors of (1)(A) the pre merger abilities of across-the-board-pricing individual MPs and their fellow undermined *R*s to retaliate cost-effectively against their underminers and (B) the impact of the MPs' merger on this ability as they are of (2)(A) the pre merger abilities of individualized-pricing MPs and their fellow undercut *R*s to retaliate cost-effectively against a rival that has undercut their contrived oligopolistic prices and (B) the impact of the merger on the ability of individualized-pricing merged firms relative to that of the MPs and the ability of the merged firm's individualized-pricing undercut *R*s to retaliate cost-effectively against such an undercutter. Primarily, such market-aggregated data will predict these facts poorly in across-the-board-pricing markets because (1) the impact of the underminer's undermining cannot be assumed to be spread among all established firms proportionate to their sales and (2) the MPs' market shares will therefore have little bearing on the extent to which their merger will create a merged firm that bears a higher share of the relevant seller-loss than either MP did. This reality is salient because, as we saw in Chap. 10, one factor that will affect the ability of the rival-victims of across-the-board undermining prices to retaliate effectively against the underminer is the "concentratedness" of the victim group: when the victim group is not concentrated, its members may not be able to overcome the public-good-type problem that can prevent them from engaging in the amount of retaliation that is in their joint interest and may also find it difficult to coordinate their retaliatory moves to make them as cost-effective as possible on the positive side and to avoid misperceptions that could lead to more general price-wars on the negative side. MP-market-share data and traditional seller-concentration ratios will also be poor predictors of the ability of the MPs and their *R*s to retaliate cost-effectively against underminers and the impact of the MPs' merger on the ability of victims of undermining to retaliate cost-effectively against the underminer because these parameters are also insensitive to the extent to which the undermined firms can devise retaliatory responses whose effects are concentrated on the actual underminer.

I am therefore confident that MP-market-share data and traditional seller-concentration ratios are poor predictors of the amount by which a horizontal merger in an across-the-board-pricing market that generates no static efficiencies and does not change the relevant market's equilibrium QV-investment level will raise the merged firm's COMs above the MPs' COMs.

(iv) MP Market Shares, the Market's Traditional Seller-Concentration Ratio, and the Effect of Such a Merger on the COMs of the Merged Firm's Rs When Both the Merged Firm and Its Rs Set Across-the-Board Prices

When a merger that yields no static efficiencies and generates no change in the relevant market's equilibrium QV-investment level takes place in a market in which prices are set across-the-board, MP-market-share data and the relevant market's seller-concentration ratio will, if anything, be a worse predictor of the merger's impact on the *R*s' COMs than of its impact on the merged firm's COMs relative to those of the MPs. In across-the-board-pricing situations, such a merger's impact on the COMs that the merged firm's *R*s attempt to contrive will reflect its impact both on the COMs the *R*s attempt to contrive by responding cooperatively to the merged firm's attempt to initiate a contrived-oligopolistic-pricing sequence relative to the MPs' pre merger attempts to initiate such a sequence and on the COMs the *R*s attempt to contrive by attempting to initiate such a sequence themselves. I will now address each of these possibilities in turn.

For the merger to increase the merged firm's *R*s' responsive COMs, it must (1) increase the COMs the merged firm will attempt to contrive relative to those the MPs would attempt to contrive without reducing the extent to which the *R*s respond cooperatively to the merged firm's contrivance-initiatives sufficiently to prevent this outcome, (2) increase the extent to which the *R*s will respond cooperatively to any attempts the merged firm will make to initiate a successful contrived-oligopolistic-pricing sequence without reducing the merged firm's attempts to initiate such sequences sufficiently to prevent this outcome, or (3) increase both the attempts the merged firm will make to initiate a successful contrived-oligopolistic-pricing sequence and the extent to which the *R*s will respond cooperatively to the merged firm's relevant initiatives. The preceding analysis explained why the MPs' market shares and the relevant market's traditional concentration ratio are not accurate predictors of (1) the impact such a merger will have on the COMs the merged firm will attempt to obtain relative to those the MPs would attempt to contrive by initiating contrived-oligopolistic-pricing sequences and (2) the impact such a merger will have on the probability that the *R*s will respond cooperatively to any such attempt the merged firm will make relative to the probability that the *R*s would respond cooperatively to any such attempt the MPs would make by affecting the relative probabilities that the merged firm and the MPs (perhaps together with non-undermining *R*s) would retaliate effectively against any undermining response that one or more *R*s made respectively to the merged firm's and the MPs' attempts to contrive OMs. There is also no reason to believe that the MPs' markets shares or the relevant ARDEPPS' traditional seller-concentration ratio will be a good predictor of the other determinants of the *R*s' cooperative-response rates that such a horizontal merger might affect—*e.g.*, the *R*s' (HNOP + NOM − MC) figures (which determine their vulnerability to retaliation). All things considered, then, the MPs' market shares and the relevant market's traditional concentration ratio are clearly poor predictors of the impact that a horizontal merger in an across-the-board-pricing market that generates no relevant efficiencies and does not change the relevant market's equilibrium QV-investment level will have on the OMs the merged firm's *R*s will attempt to contrive by responding cooperatively to the merged firm's or the MPs' contrived-oligopolistic-pricing initiatives.

Accurate data on these parameters will be no better predictors of the impact that such a merger will have on the OMs the merged firm's *R*s will try to contrive by initiating contrived-oligopolistic-pricing sequences themselves. Thus, the MPs' market shares and the relevant market's concentration ratio are poor predictors of (1) the impact that such a merger will have on the merged firm's (OCA + NOM − MC) figures relative to their MP counterparts (figures whose relationship to the merged firm's willingness to cooperate with an *R*'s contrived-oligopolistic-pricing initiative is, in any event, unclear since increases in this sum increase the vulnerability of the merged firm both to the initiator's retaliation and to the undermining responses of other *R*s) or (2) the impact that the merger will have on the cost-effectiveness of a particular *R*'s retaliation against the merged firm relative to the cost-effectiveness of the *R*'s retaliation against the MPs (by spreading the merged firm's defenses relative to those of the individual MPs).

Everything considered, then, the MPs' markets shares and the relevant market's traditional concentration ratio are poor predictors of both the COMs the merged firm's *R*s will try to obtain by initiating a contrived-oligopolistic-pricing sequence and the COMs they will try to obtain by responding cooperatively to the merged firm's (versus the MPs') attempts to initiate a successful contrived oligopolistic-pricing sequence.

* * *

I have now explained why, regardless of whether the relevant mergers take place in individualized-pricing or across-the-board-pricing markets, MP-market-share data and relevant-market traditional seller-concentration-ratio data will be poor predictors of the impact that a merger that generates no relevant efficiencies and does not change the relevant market's equilibrium QV-investment level will have on the prices charged both by the merged firm relative to those charged by the MPs and by the merged firm's *R*s.

(ii) MP Market Shares, Traditional Seller-Concentration Ratios, and the Effect of a Horizontal Merger That Generates No Relevant Efficiencies on QV-Investment Competition in the Market(s) in Which Both MPs Are Deemed to Be Operating

MP-market-share and traditional seller-concentration-ratio data are also poor indicators of the factors that influence the impact of a horizontal merger that generates no relevant efficiencies on QV-investment competition. Thus, such data will inaccurately predict

(1) whether and the extent to which the merger will create a company that faces higher (Π_D + R) barriers than its antecedents did because it finds it profitable to devote to consolidation resources they would have used to execute QV-investment expansions,
(2) the difference between (A) the amount by which the merger will increase the L barriers the merged company faces above those its antecedents faced by raising the merged company's OCA and NOMs, by spreading its defenses, and by creating a new company that suffers from the weak reputation of its weaker predecessor and (B) the amount by which the merger will reduce the merged firm's L barriers below those of its weighted-average antecedent by creating a new company that inherits the tough reputation of its tougher antecedent and can take advantage of company-wide economies of scale in building and maintaining a reputation of being undeterrable by retaliation, and
(3) the amount by which the merger will increase the L barriers the MPs' *R*s face by facilitating the MPs' coordination of retaliation, by creating a new company that inherits the reputation for retaliating of its tougher antecedent, and by creating a new company that can take advantage of company-wide economies of scale in building and maintaining a reputation for retaliating.

MP-market-share and traditional seller-concentration-ratio data are also poor predictors of whether absent the-merger one MP was or both MPs would be close to being the established firm that was best-placed to make an additional QV investment in the relevant ARDEPPS as well as of whether absent the merger the equilibrium QV-investment level (as opposed to the actual QV-investment level) would be above, at, or below the entry-preventing QV-investment level—whether, controlling for the relevant $(M + O)$s, any changes the merger would generate in the (Π_D + R + L) barriers the merged firm would face relative to those the MPs faced would affect its QV-investment decision and thereby equilibrium QV-investment in the relevant area of product-space. Similarly, MP-market-share and traditional seller-concentration-ratio data are also poor indicators of whether the merger would change the L barriers the merged firm's *R*s face and of whether any change the merger generated in the L barriers facing the merged firm's *R*s would affect equilibrium QV investment in the relevant area of product-space if one ignored monopolistic QV-investment incentives and disincentives or oligopolistic QV-investment disincentives. Finally, MP-market-share and traditional seller-concentration-ratio data are also poor indicators of the following sets of $(M + O)$-related factors:

(1) whether absent the merger one MP would face monopolistic QV-investment disincentives, whether those disincentives would be critical, whether the merger would increase those incentives by causing the merged company to be concerned with the impact of its expansion on the profit-yields of both its antecedents' pre existing projects or decrease those disincentives by enabling the merged company to make a different QV investment from the one that the better-placed potential-expander MP would have made, whether any tendency the merger might otherwise have to increase QV-investment competition by

reducing the L barrier the merged company faced would be offset by the fact that the merged company would face monopolistic QV-investment disincentives;

(2) whether absent the merger one or both MPs would have monopolistic QV-investment incentives, whether these incentives would be critical, whether the merger would eliminate those incentives because the two MPs would be the only firms not deterred from expanding by the expansion or entry barriers they would face pre merger or because the merger would critically increase the L barriers that would be faced by an established *R* or potential competitor that would otherwise not be deterred by the barriers it would face; and

(3) whether absent the merger one or both MPs would face natural oligopolistic QV-investment disincentives, whether the merger would induce the merged firm to make one to two QV investments that *O*s would have deterred one or both of its antecedents from making because absent the merger these two MPs would be the only firms that were giving each other *O*s and post-merger the merged company would have the option of making one QV-investment expansion rather than two QV-investment expansions and of choosing to make one or two QV investments that were less damaging to the profit-yields of the two MPs' other projects than the investments that would have been made by the independent MPs would have been, because the merger would induce the merged firm to make one or two QV investments that *O*s would have deterred it or anyone else from making because absent the merger one MP and an established rival would be the only two firms not deterred by barriers from expanding in circumstances in which they confronted each other with *O*s and the merger would raise the L barriers the *R* confronted sufficiently to make the total barriers it would face preclusive, whether the merger would induce an *R* to make a QV investment that neither it nor either MP nor anyone else would have made absent the merger because (A) absent the merger, everyone but the *R* in question and one or both MPs would face preclusive barriers pre-merger, (B) the relevant *R* and one or both MPs would confront each other with *O*s, and (C) the merger would eliminate those *O*s by raising the $(\Pi_D + R + L)$ barriers facing the merged company sufficiently above the counterpart sum for its relevant antecedents to make the sum of the barriers the merged firm would face prohibitively high.

* * *

I have now demonstrated that, individually, MP-market-share and traditional seller-concentration-ratio data are poor predictors of each determinant of the competitive impact of a horizontal merger that generates no relevant efficiencies. Admittedly, this demonstration leaves open the possibility that one might be able to predict this impact accurately from such data because the errors one would make if one tried to predict this impact exclusively from one of these parameters would perfectly or close-to-perfectly offset the errors one would make if one tried to predict this impact exclusively from the other of these two parameters. However, there is absolutely no reason to believe that this is the case. Therefore, I conclude that one cannot accurately predict the competitive impact of a horizontal merger that generates no relevant efficiencies through an approach that focuses exclusively on MP-market-share and tradition-seller-concentration-ratio data—*i.e.*, through the approach that the U.S. courts traditionally claimed they were taking to this issue.

(B) The Accuracy of Any Approach That Attempts to Predict from MP-Market-Share and Traditional-Seller-Concentration-Ratio Data the Extent to Which a Horizontal Merger Increases Competition by Generating Static and Dynamic Efficiencies

Obviously, the traditionally-measured concentration ratio of any market in which both MPs are placed has no bearing on the size of the static and dynamic efficiencies their merger generates. Admittedly, the absolute size of the MPs' operations may have some bearing on whether their merger will generate efficiencies by creating a merged firm that can take better advantage of economies of scale than the MPs did. However, the fact that minimum efficient absolute scale varies widely from market to market and the fact that the total sales made in markets vary widely from market to market imply that absolute-economies-of-scale considerations will yield at most an extremely-weak negative correlation between the MPs' market shares and the amount of minimum-efficient-scale-related efficiencies their merger generates. *Ceteris paribus*, then, to the extent that the amount by which the efficiencies that a horizontal merger generates increases competition is directly related to the magnitude of the efficiencies in question, one will not be able to predict such a merger's efficiency-related procompetitive impact from such market-aggregated data. I suspect that this argument and conclusion surprises no-one. However, judges, antitrust-enforcement officials, and antitrust analysts may be surprised by how poorly such market-aggregated data predicts the procompetitive effects of horizontal mergers in combination with accurate data on the efficiencies the relevant merger generates. This section begins by analyzing the accuracy of any approach that attempts to predict from MP-market-share and traditional seller-concentration-ratio data the extent to which the known static efficiencies of a horizontal merger will tend to increase price competition and then proceeds to investigate the accuracy with which such an approach can predict the impact on QV-investment competition of a horizontal merger's dynamic efficiencies.

(i) The Accuracy of Any Approach That Attempts to Predict From MP-Market-Share and Traditional Seller-Concentration-Ratio Data the Net Equivalent-Dollar Impact of a Horizontal Merger's (Marginal) Static Efficiencies on Clayton-Act-Relevant Buyers

The rest of this section will assume that the static efficiencies in question are marginal in the sense that they improve the competitive position of the MPs by changing the attractiveness of their products to particular buyers and/or the marginal costs they have to incur to supply different buyers in ways that increase their OCAs when they were originally best-placed and decrease their OCDs (overall competitive disadvantages) when they were originally worse-than-best-placed. For simplicity, I will assume henceforth that all static marginal efficiencies involve exclusively reductions in variable and marginal costs. Only static marginal efficiencies will affect Clayton-Act-relevant buyers directly—*i.e.*, static efficiencies that relate to the fixed costs or only the intra-marginal variable costs of the MPs will affect such buyers only indirectly, if at all, by carrying over to any expansions the MPs might make and hence affecting the intensity of QV-investment competition. The question for investigation is: How accurately can one predict the net equivalent-dollar gain that the static marginal efficiencies of given size that a horizontal merger generates will confer on Clayton-Act-relevant buyers from data on the merger partners' market shares and the relevant market's seller concentration? For simplicity, the analyses that follows will ignore the impact that the static marginal efficiencies a horizontal merger generates may have on Clayton-Act-relevant buyers by raising the CMC that sellers that would otherwise have been uniquely-second-placed to supply a rival's customers would have to incur to match the offer that would otherwise have been that rival's HNOP-containing offer to the buyers in question.

(a) Individualized-Pricing Contexts To simplify this analysis still further, I will assume (1) that the static marginal efficiency in question is a reduction in the seller's marginal costs, (2) that, prior to the merger, all Clayton-Act-relevant buyers would purchase only one unit of any relevant good produced by a relevant seller, and (3) that the merger will not change that fact (despite any impact it may have on the prices charged for the relevant good). On those assumptions, the static marginal efficiencies a horizontal merger generates

(1) will inflict a net equivalent-monetary loss on each buyer that either one MP was uniquely-best-placed to supply or both MPs were uniquely-equal-best-placed to supply because the efficiencies will not alter such a buyer's best-placed supplier's HNOP, will tend to enable that supplier to obtain an NOM (by increasing its HNOP − OMC gap), and will be highly unlikely to lower the COM the relevant buyer pays when purchasing the product in question by as much as they increase the total NOM it pays when purchasing that product (though the efficiencies may tend to decrease the COMs in question),
(2) will confer a net equivalent-monetary gain on each buyer that one MP was uniquely-second-placed to supply or that both MPs were uniquely-equal-second-placed to supply equal to the lower of the marginal-cost reduction in question and the amount by which the uniquely-second-placed MP or both uniquely-equal-second-placed MPs were worse-than-best-placed if they do not affect the relevant buyers' suppliers' (NOMs + COMs) (the impact of the efficiencies on the relevant [NOM + COM]s will depend on whether in these cases, they increase or decrease the [possibly-changing] best-placed supplier's OCAs),

(3) will confer a net equivalent-monetary gain on each buyer that no MP was second-placed to supply but the merged firm would be second-placed or third-placed to supply equal to (A) the lower of (i) the difference between the marginal-cost reduction in question and the amount by which the relevant MP(s) were worse-than-second-placed and (ii) the amount by which the original second-placed supplier(s) of the buyers in question were worse-than-best-placed *plus* (*minus*) (B) the amount by which the efficiencies increased (decreased) the NOMs the relevant buyer had to pay (where it would decrease the NOMs unless the merged firm was the buyer's best-placed supplier and the merged firm's OCAs were as high or higher than the OCA of the non-MP that was best-placed to supply the buyer pre-merger) *plus* (*minus*) the positive (negative) difference the efficiencies made in the COM the buyer had to pay (I wrote "gain" at the beginning of this item because I am confident that the above sum will virtually always be positive), and
(4) will confer a net equivalent-monetary gain on each buyer that the merged firm and both MPs were worse-than-second-placed to supply because the efficiencies caused the merged firm to reduce the COMs the relevant buyers had to pay by more than the MPs reduced those COMs by making the amount by which the merged firm was worse-than-second-placed smaller than the amount by which the MPs were worse-than-second-placed.

At the crudest level, these conclusions imply that the net equivalent-monetary gain that the static marginal efficiencies that a horizontal merger generates will confer on Clayton-Act-relevant buyers will be higher the higher the ratio of the number of buyers in categories (2)–(4) to the number in category (1), the higher the ratio of the number of buyers in category (2) to the numbers in categories (3) and (4), and the higher the ratio of the number of buyers in category (3) to the number in category (4). At a somewhat-more-refined level, the preceding conclusions imply that the net equivalent-monetary gain that the static marginal efficiencies a horizontal merger generates will confer on Clayton-Act-relevant buyers will be inversely related to the amount by which the MPs were worse-than-second-placed to supply buyers in category (2) and directly related to the amount by which the supplier that was second-placed to supply those buyers pre merger was worse-than-best-placed to do so.

What do these conclusions imply for the accuracy with which one can predict from market-aggregated data the magnitude of the equivalent-monetary gains that the given-size static marginal efficiencies a horizontal merger generates will confer on Clayton-Act-relevant buyers? I want to make four points or sets of points.

First, although (A) given the number of buyers in the defined market, the number of buyers in category (1) and the ratio of that number to the number of buyers in categories (2), (3), and (4) combined will increase with the MPs' market shares and (B) given the fact that the number of buyers in different markets will almost inevitably vary substantially, there will be virtually no cross-market correlation between the MPs' market shares and the number of buyers in category (1) or the ratio of that number to the sum of the buyers in categories (2), (3), and (4).

Second, since the relevant efficiencies will inflict equivalent-monetary losses on category (1) buyers, any correlation that exists between MP market shares and the gain that is of interest will be negative, not positive on this account.

Third, since the only reason for believing that there is a correlation between the frequency with which a firm is best-placed and the frequency with which it is second-placed or sufficiently close-to-second-placed for the efficiency to make it a potential undercutter is that the higher the percentage of customers a firm is best-placed to supply the lower the percentage of customers for which it could be worse-than-best-placed to supply, there is virtually no correlation either within a given market or, *a fortiori*, across markets between the MPs' market shares and the ratios of the number of customers in category (1) to the number of categories (2), (3), and (4) respectively. Moreover, there is absolutely no correlation between the MPs' market shares and the ratio of the number of buyers in category (2) to the number in category (3), the ratio of the number of buyers in category (2) to the number in category (4), or the ratio of the number of buyers in category (3) to the number in category (4). Nor is there any reason to believe that there is any correlation between the MPs' market shares and the amount by which an MP is worse-than-second-placed to supply a buyer in category (2) or the size of the OCA of the best-placed supplier of a buyer in category (2).

Fourth, it should be obvious that data on the seller concentration of the market in which a horizontal merger takes place will have even less bearing than MP-market-share data on any determinant or the magnitude of the equivalent-monetary gains that the given static marginal efficiencies a horizontal merger generates will confer on Clayton-Act-relevant buyers.

(b) Across-the-Board-Pricing Contexts Basically, the same arguments and conclusions apply in across-the-board-pricing contexts as in individualized-pricing contexts.

(ii) The Accuracy of Any Approach That Attempts to Predict the Impact of the Dynamic Efficiencies of Given Magnitudes That a Horizontal Merger Generates on QV-Investment Competition from MP-Market-Share and Traditional Seller-Concentration-Ratio Data

MP-market-share and traditional seller-concentration-ratio data are also poor predictors of the "situational" factors that determine the effect of dynamic efficiencies of a given magnitude on QV-investment competition. Thus, such market-aggregated data are poor indicators of

(1) whether absent the merger one or both MPs would be as well-placed as any established rival to expand their "market's" QV investment,
(2) whether, if they would not be, the amount by which they would be worse-placed to expand than the best-placed established potential expander would be smaller than the amount by which their merger would reduce the barriers to expansion they faced,

(3) whether if after the merger the merged company would be as well-placed as any other established firm to expand the total amount of QV investment in the relevant market, one or more potential competitors would be as well-placed as the merged firm would be to make a QV investment in the relevant market,
(4) the size of the monopolistic QV-investment disincentives the merged firm would face post-merger if it were the only firm that would not face prohibitive barriers post-merger (a factor that would be directly related to the MPs' market shares though I suspect the correlation would be relatively weak, given the "fact" that the extent to which any new QV investment is differentially competitive with the other QV investments in its market varies substantially across markets),
(5) whether and the extent to which any expansion the merger's relevant efficiencies would induce the merged company to make would increase competition more or less in comparison with the *status quo ante* than competition would have been increased by the QV investment that would have been introduced by another established company or by a potential competitor had the merged company not expanded (when post-merger not only the merged company but also one or more other firms would find it profitable to add one QV investment to the market), and
(6) whether, perversely, the efficiencies in question will reduce QV-investment competition by creating a situation in which the merged company and an established rival face natural oligopolistic QV-investment disincentives that deter the rival from making a QV investment it would otherwise have made as well as the merged company from adding to the market's QV-investment stock.

Once more, there is no reason to believe that the errors that the traditional market-oriented approach will implicitly make when predicting the preceding individual determinants of the effects of any dynamic efficiencies a horizontal merger generates on QV-investment competition will tend to be offsetting. Hence, the preceding analysis justifies the conclusion that, even in conjunction with accurate data on the dynamic efficiencies a merger generates, MP-market-share and traditional seller-concentration-ratio data cannot yield accurate predictions of the effect the dynamic efficiencies a horizontal merger generates will have on QV-investment competition. It therefore follows that the traditional market-oriented approach to predicting the impact that a horizontal merger's dynamic efficiencies would have on QV-investment competition will be highly inaccurate.

* * *

We have now seen that one cannot accurately predict either the direct effect on price competition or the effect on QV-investment competition of the static marginal and dynamic efficiencies a horizontal merger generates by combining data on the nature and magnitudes of those efficiencies with data on the MPs' market shares and their market's traditional seller-concentration ratio. There is absolutely no reason to believe that the errors that this approach makes when predicting the magnitude of the equivalent-monetary gains that the static marginal and dynamic efficiencies a horizontal merger will generate will confer on Clayton-Act-relevant buyers will tend to be offsetting. Hence, the preceding arguments demonstrate that one cannot accurately predict the overall competitive impact of the efficiencies a horizontal merger generates in the traditional market-oriented way even if one assumes that one knows the magnitudes of the efficiencies in question.

* * *

Previously, we saw that the traditional market-oriented approach also predicts only very inaccurately the competitive impact that a horizontal merger would have if it generated no economic efficiencies. There is absolutely no reason to believe that the errors that the traditional market-oriented approach makes on this non-efficiency-related issue will tend to offset the errors this approach makes when used to predict the competitive impact of the economic efficiencies that a horizontal merger generates. It therefore follows that the traditional market-oriented approach to horizontal merger competitive-impact prediction will be highly inaccurate even if the relevant markets are defined in a functionally-ideal way.

(2) Twelve Other Elements of the U.S. Courts' Traditional Approach to Analyzing the Legality of Horizontal Mergers

(A) Four Additional Elements That the Contemporary DOJ and FTC Have Taken Over

The first element of the U.S. courts' traditional approach to horizontal-merger analysis that the DOJ and FTC have taken over is the courts' (intermittent) use of buyer-oriented market definitions. Chapter 6 argued that, although an appropriate non-market-oriented approach to competitive-impact analysis is superior to any market-oriented approach that could be devised, market-oriented analyses that incorporate buyer-oriented market definitions (that define individual markets to contain those sellers that are well-placed to obtain buyers with similar dollar preferences) are superior to analyses that incorporate traditional seller-oriented market definitions. Section 4 of Chap. 7 pointed out that, in several important decisions (which were strongly criticized at the time on this account by economists and legal scholars) U.S. courts adopted buyer-oriented market definitions. Thus, in *Philadelphia National Bank*,[897] the Supreme Court stated that (1) the area of effective competition is the area "to which the purchaser can practicably turn for supplies"[898] and (2) this area may be different for different groups of buyers. In other cases, the Court shifted from seller-oriented to buyer-oriented market definitions by focusing on "submarkets," which were defined in a buyer-oriented way to contain suppliers and products that are

[897] United States v. Philadelphia National Bank, 374 U.S. 321 (1963).

[898] The quotation, from Tampa Electric Co. v. National Coal Co., 365 U.S. 320, 327 (1961), is quoted by the *Philadelphia National Bank* Court at 374 U.S. 321, 359 (1963).

well-placed to obtain the patronage of a particular subset of buyers.[899] The shift to buyer-oriented market definitions was also manifest by the Court's recognition in *Rome Cable*[900] and *Continental Can*[901] that competitive-impact predictions would be more accurate if firms and products were placed in a series of "markets" whose membership varied with the preferences (and sometimes supply-cost positions) of different groups of buyers. Thus, since some buyers of containers had a strong preference for bottles, some had a strong preference for cans, and some were indifferent between these two types of containers, the Supreme Court in *Continental Can* held that there were three separate markets—one occupied by bottle producers, one by can producers, and one by bottle producers and can producers. I am not claiming that in these cases the Court arrived at the best set of buyer-oriented market definitions one could devise. I do not know whether the *Rome Cable* Court's decision to define a submarket that contained both insulated and uninsulated aluminum conductor made good sense within the market-oriented paradigm (whether there were buyers whose preference for insulated over non-insulated aluminum conductor just equaled or approximated the extra cost of the insulation), and I am confident that the *Continental Can* Court's decision to exclude plastic containers from any of the markets in which the merger partners (a can producer and a glass producer) were found to be operating was cost-ineffective. Still, even though partial and imperfect, this shift by the U.S. courts to buyer-oriented market definitions is clearly a move in the right direction.

I am therefore pleased that the contemporary DOJ and FTC have shifted to a considerable extent from seller-oriented to buyer-oriented market definitions. Their shift to buyer-oriented market definitions is manifest in Section 1.22 of the 1992 Horizontal Merger Guidelines, headed "Product Market Definition in the Presence of Price Discrimination," which states (in essence) that "the Agency"—the name the Guidelines assign to the DOJ and FTC—will consider defining a separate product market for each group of buyers charged a given price. The "Agency's" shift to buyer-oriented market definitions is also manifest in their analyses of individual merger proposals. Thus, in 1995, in *Interstate Bakeries-Continental*,[902] the DOJ defined the seller-side of the markets on which it focused to contain those sellers that were well-placed to supply supermarkets in particular geographic locations; in 1994 and 1996, respectively in *Thrifty-Payless*[903] and *Rite*

---

[899] The term "submarket" was first used by the Supreme Court in Brown Shoe Co. v. United States, 370 U.S. 294, 325 (1962).

[900] United States v. Aluminum Company of American (Rome Cable), 377 U.S. 271, 274–76 (1964).

[901] United States v. Continental Can Co., 378 U.S.441 (1964).

[902] See 2006 Commentary at 8. See also United States v. Interstate Bakeries Corp. and Continental Baking Co., (N.D. Ill., filed July 20, 1995), 60 Fed. Reg. 40, 195 (August 7, 1995), 1996–1 Trade Cas. (CCH) ¶ 71,271, materials available at http://www.usdoj.gov/atr/cases/inters0.htm.

[903] See 2006 Commentary at 13. See also Thrifty Drug Stores (TCH Corp.) and PayLess Drug Stores (1994), 59 Fed. Reg. 15,736 (Apr. 4, 1994), materials available at http://www.ftc.gov/os/closings/staffclosing.htm.

Aid-Revco,[904] the FTC recognized that the sellers that were well-placed to supply third-party payers such as health plans and pharmacy-benefit managers should be placed in a separate market from those that were well-placed to supply so-called "cash customers," who pay out-of-pocket for prescription drugs; in 2000, in *Dairy Farmers-SODIAAL*,[905] the DOJ defined a market to contain only those sellers that supplied branded butter because a significant group of buyers had a sufficient preference for such butter over private-label butter, margarine, and other substitutes for the sellers in question to be better-placed to obtain these buyers' patronage than suppliers of any of the other products just listed; in 2003, in *Quest Diagnostics-Unilab*,[906] the FTC placed in a separate market those suppliers that were well-placed to supply clinical-laboratory-testing services to physician groups in Northern California; and again in 2003, in *Nestle-Dreyer's*,[907] the FTC placed in a separate market those sellers that were well-placed to supply buyers whose dollar preferences for super-premium ice cream were sufficiently strong for suppliers of such ice cream to be generically better-placed to obtain these buyers' patronage than were suppliers of premium or economy ice cream. I hasten to admit that the Agency may not have fully understood the point of adopting buyer-oriented market definitions. The DOJ and FTC sometimes appear to believe that it makes sense to adopt buyer-oriented markets only if the relevant sellers discriminated among or would find it profitable to discriminate among the separate groups of buyers in question[908] when, in fact, this belief is false: if different groups of sellers are well-placed to obtain the patronage of different sets of buyers not because of inter-buyer-group differences in the dollar values the buyers place on the products of the members of the different sets of sellers in question but because of inter-seller-group differences in the costs that the sellers in question would have to incur to supply any relevant set of buyers, it will make analytic sense to adopt buyer-oriented market definitions even if no seller can increase its profits by obtaining different prices from the members of different sets of buyers. Still, even if the DOJ and FTC have not fully understood the rationale for the shift to buyer-oriented market definitions, their making this shift is a step forward.

The second element of the U.S. courts' traditional handling of horizontal-merger cases that the Agency has taken over that merits attention is also desirable. U.S. courts have consistently insisted that the MP-market-share and seller-concentration

[904] See 2006 Commentary at 13. See also Rite Aid Corp. and Revco D.S., Inc. (1996), materials available at http://www.ftc.gov/opa/1996/04/riterevc.htm.

[905] See 2006 Commentary at 9. See also United States v. Dairy Farmers of American (E.D. Pa., filed March 31, 2000), 65 Fed. Reg. 44,820 (July 19, 2000), 2001–1 Trade Cas. (CCH) ¶ 73,136, materials available at http://www.usdoj.gov/atr/cases/indx4450.htm.

[906] See 2006 Commentary at 33–34. See also Quest Diagnostics, Inc. and Unilab Corp. (2003), 69 Fed. Reg. 9,082 (Feb. 27, 2003), materials available at http://www.ftc.gov/opa/2000/03/wsl.htm.

[907] See 2006 Commentary at 28–29. See also Nestle Holdings, Inc.; Dreyer's Grand Ice Creamings Holdings, Inc.; and Dreyer's Grand Ice Cream, Inc. (2003), 68 Fed. Reg., 39,464 (July 2, 2003), materials available at http://www.ftc.gov/opa/1999/11/pcc2.htm.

[908] See 1992 Horizontal Merger Guidelines at Section 1.22.

figures that are relevant under the traditional approach include not just the figures at the time the merger is proposed or is being assessed but also the figures that would appear likely to be accurate in the future even if the merger were not executed. In most cases that referred to this second set of figures, the court believed and was concerned that the relevant market would become more concentrated over time (in the court's words, that there was a "trend toward concentration")[909] but in some cases, the court's point was that either because one of the MPs was a failing company[910] or because, though not currently failing, a relevant MP faced other obstacles (such as its ownership of a fixed stock of coal of the type it had the technical skill to mine in circumstances in which it was unlikely to be able to discover or buy more coal deposits of the relevant type)[911] the court believed that the merger under investigation was less likely to reduce competition because one MP's market share would decline over time if it did not merge. The DOJ and FTC have fully accepted this element of the courts' approach. It is manifest in the 1992 Guidelines' treatment of failing firms (Sect. 5.1), in the 1992 Guidelines' more general provision on "Changing Market Conditions" (Section 1.521), and in paragraph 2 of Sect. 5.2 of the 2010, Guidelines.

The third and fourth elements of the courts' handling of horizontal-merger cases that the DOJ and FTC have accepted are features of the failing-company defense that the Supreme Court first articulated in *International Shoe Co. v. Federal Trade Commission.*[912] The third, which reappears in a number of conglomerate-merger cases in which one of the MPs is a potential competitor of the other and in some geographic-diversification conglomerate-merger cases, is that, in addition to demonstrating that its "resources [are] so depleted and the prospect of rehabilitation is so remote that it faced the grave probability of business failure," a defendant that wishes to establish a failing-company defense must demonstrate that it had tried to identify but failed to identify a merger partner with which it could execute a merger that would be both profitable for it and more procompetitive than the proposed/executed merger.[913] In my judgment, this requirement changes the baseline for competitive-impact analysis in a way that is incorrect as a matter of law. As I will discuss in some detail in Chap. 13, U.S. courts have also deviated from the law's do-nothing baseline when analyzing conglomerate mergers between potential competitors (by focusing on whether the merger in question deterred the MPs from making separate QV investments that would have increased competition by more than it was increased by the merged firm's choices) and when analyzing some geographic-diversification mergers (by focusing on whether an outside firm that wishes to enter a new geographic market by merger could execute a more procompetitive merger with another firm in the market in question that would be

[909] United States v. Von's Grocery Co., 384 U.S. 270, 277 (1966).

[910] Citizen Publishing Co. v. United States, 394 U.S. 131 (1969).

[911] United States v. General Dynamics Corp., 415 U.S. 486 (1974).

[912] 280 U.S. 291 (1930).

[913] *Id.* at 302.

more profitable than not merging at all or had made a reasonable effort to identify such an alternative merger). (I should add that U.S. courts have also deviated from the standard, do-nothing "baseline" when analyzing some joint-venture cases by focusing on whether the joint venture made more QV investments or more-competition-increasing QV investments than its parents would have executed on their own had they not participated in the joint venture.) (I admit that a parallel move seems to me to be legally justifiable if the relevant question is not the Clayton Act competitive-impact question but the Sherman Act specific-anticompetitive-intent question; however, in such cases, the move cannot be said to involve a shift in the baseline for competitive-impact calculation since no competitive impact is being assessed.) Regrettably, the failing-firm defense that the DOJ and FTC recognize seems to have accepted the competitive-impact-baseline-shift that is built into the U.S. courts' failing-company-defense doctrine. Thus, Section 5.2 of the 1992 Horizontal Merger Guidelines states that, to establish a failing-firm defense, a defendant must demonstrate *inter alia*, that

> it has made unsuccessful good-faith efforts to elicit reasonable alternative offers of acquisition of the assets of the failing firm that would both keep its tangible and intangible assets in the relevant market and pose a less severe danger to competition than does the proposed merger....

The 2010 Horizontal Merger Guidelines make what I take to be the same error. Thus, its Section 11 states that a failing-company defense will not be available to a company "whose assets would otherwise exit the market" unless, *inter alia*, "it has made unsuccessful good-faith efforts to elicit reasonable alternative offers that would keep its tangible and intangible assets in the relevant market and pose a less severe danger to competition than does the proposed merger" and that a failing-company defense will not be available to a company that is proposing to sell a failing division in a transaction that would cause the division's assets to "exit the relevant market in the near future" unless, *inter alia*, "the owner of the failing division has made good-faith efforts to elicit reasonable alternative offers that would keep its tangible and intangible assets in the relevant market and pose a less severe danger to competition than does the proposed acquisition."

The preceding quotations from the 1992 and 2010 Horizontal Merger Guidelines also reveal a fourth element of the U.S. courts' traditional handling of horizontal mergers that the DOJ and FTC have taken over, at least in the context of horizontal mergers that involve failing companies. In particular, the failing-company-defense sections of both these Guidelines imply that the Agencies will reject a failing-company defense if the proposed merger would lessen competition in the failing company's market even if it would not lessen competition overall because it would increase competition in the other market in which the merged firm would utilize the failing company's assets by at least as much as it would lessen competition in the market in which the failing company is operating. As I have previously indicated, although textual argument favors the conclusion that the Clayton Act prohibits all mergers that lessen competition in any market, I think that this conclusion (which is disfavored by consequentialist-prudential—*i.e.*, policy—argument) is incorrect as a matter of U.S. law. I hasten to add that I do not know whether the DOJ and FTC take this position more generally—*i.e.*, believe that covered conduct that does not lessen competition overall is lawful under the Clayton Act even if it does lessen competition in one or more markets.

(B) Five Additional Elements That the Contemporary DOJ and FTC Have Rejected

In Chap. 7, I argued that, in the past, the U.S. courts not only failed to articulate an operational protocol for defining markets but in practice "cooked" the market definitions they used to secure the anti-defendant conclusion they preferred—*i.e.*, to yield MP-market-share and traditional-market-concentration-ratio figures that, under the market-share/market-concentration-based test of illegality they had enunciated, led to the conclusion that the merger under consideration violated the Sherman Act. This is the practice that underlies Justice Stewart's claim in dissent in *Von's Grocery* that "[t]he sole consistency that I can find in litigation under § 7. . .[is that] the governmental always wins. . ..."[914] As we saw in Sect. 2 of Chap. 7, although many scholars have accepted the claim of the DOJ and FTC that the 1992 Guidelines effectively prevent the "Agencies" from cooking their concrete-market-definition conclusions, both the 1992 Guidelines' lengthy statement of the formal definition of antitrust markets that the DOJ and FTC will use and those Guidelines' detailed account of the protocol for market definition they incorrectly insist will identify the concrete definition(s) that best fit their formal definition are sufficiently vague and inconsistent to allow the Agencies to cook their market-definition conclusions. (The 2010 Guidelines are not different in this respect. Thus, in my judgment, the 2010 Guidelines' statement in the penultimate paragraph of Section 4 that "[t]he Agencies [will] implement . . .[their] principles of market definition flexibly" constitutes an admission that they intend to cook their market definitions. In my judgment, the same is true for the statements in Sections 5.1 and 5.2 of the 2010 Guidelines that, when firms that would not be placed in a relevant market if the Agencies' normal market-definition principles were used have an impact on competitive outcomes in that market, the Agencies will include such firms in the market in question and assign them the market shares that result in the Agencies' market-oriented approach's yielding correct conclusions.) In my judgment, however, at least prior to 2010, the DOJ and FTC did not cook their market definitions. As Sect. 4B of this chapter will point out, when confronted with a situation in which their honest use of their definition and protocol yields a market definition that was associated with post-merger HHI figures and merger-induced change-in-HHI figures to which the 1992 Guidelines assigned a competitive-impact and legal significance that the Agency considered to be unwarranted, the Agency responded not by changing its market definition but by choosing not to follow the Guidelines' "General Standards"—either to override them without justifying doing so with a "qualifying-

[914] See Vons's Grocery v. United States, 384 U.S. 270, 301 (Stewart, J. dissenting) (1966).

factor" analysis or to override them and justify doing so by citing special conditions whose presence makes the General Standards non-determinative.[915]

The second element of the U.S. courts' handling of horizontal-merger cases that the DOJ and FTC have rejected is the use of data on cross-elasticities of demand to define markets. Section 4 of Chap. 7 explained both that in *United States v. E.I. du Pont de Nemours & Co.*[916] the Supreme Court claimed that "cross-elasticity of demand" figures should be used to define markets and that this claim was mistaken. Although the DOJ and FTC do sometimes make some use of calculations of cross-elasticities of demand their use of estimates of cross-elasticities of demand is far more limited and careful than the use of such data that the U.S. courts say they think is appropriate—*i.e.*, the FTC and DOJ do not commit the so-called *Cellophane* fallacy. More specifically, the DOJ and FTC use calculations of cross-elasticities of demand to predict the competitive impact of mergers between firms independently placed in the same market, not to define the markets in which firms are placed. I hasten to add that my claim that U.S. courts traditionally used cross-elasticity-of-demand figures to define markets is contestable: although the *Cellophane* Court said that one should use cross-elasticity-of-demand estimates to generate market definitions, it did not do so in practice in that case, and, although U.S. courts subsequently often made reference to the importance of cross-elasticity-of-demand figures for market definition, the courts that did so also did not really use estimates of cross-elasticities of demand to define markets.

The third element of the U.S. courts' traditional handling of horizontal-merger cases that the contemporary DOJ and FTC reject is the set of market-share/market-concentration-oriented tests of illegality the courts' legal conclusions implicitly promulgated. For example, neither the 1992 Horizontal Merger Guidelines nor *a fortiori* the DOJ/FTC's more lenient actual practice, nor the 2010 Guidelines would deem illegal (1) the horizontal merger declared illegal in *Brown Shoe*,[917] a merger that created a firm with 5 % of an admittedly-ill-defined market, (2) the type of merger deemed presumptively illegal in *Philadelphia National Bank*,[918] a merger that would create a firm with a 30 % market share and raise the combined share of the market's two biggest firms from 44 % to 59 %, or (3) the type of merger deemed presumptively illegal in *Von's Grocery*,[919] a merger that created a firm with a 7.5 % market share (of an ill-defined market) and increased the market share of the two largest firms by 1.4 % (in a market that, admittedly, had exhibited a trend toward concentration).

The fourth element of the U.S. courts' traditional handling of horizontal mergers that the DOJ and FTC reject relates to the general legal relevance of any efficiencies

[915] See Subsection 4B(1) of this chapter for a detailed discussion of the Guidelines' "General Standards" and "Qualifying Factors."

[916] 351 U.S. 377 (1956).

[917] Brown Shoe v. United States, 370 U.S. 294 (1962).

[918] United States v. Philadelphia Natural Bank, 374 U.S. 321 (1963).

[919] United States v. Von's Grocery, 384 U.S. 270 (1966).

such mergers may generate. Traditionally, U.S courts have been somewhat ambivalent about the legal significance of efficiencies. On the one hand, U.S. courts have consistently stated that the attainment of monopoly power through "skill, foresight, and industry" is not prohibited by the antitrust laws and that the U.S. antitrust laws aim at "the protection of competition, not competitors." In the other direction, at least in the 1960s, the Supreme Court stated on more than one occasion that the Celler-Kefauver Act (which amended Section 7 of the Clayton Act) was designed to prevent concentration even when efficiency had to be sacrificed to do so[920]: indeed, this view played a critical role in the Court's conclusions that the mergers involved in *Brown Shoe*[921] and *Von's Grocery*[922] (which it seems to have believed put Ma and Pa shoe-stores and grocery stores at greater risk) violated the Clayton Act. Indeed, even if the *Brown Shoe* Court's statement that any efficiencies a merger generates disfavor its legality[923] did not accurately portray the Court's position during the relevant period, the Court's statement in another case of that era (*Clorox*) that "[p]ossible economies cannot be used as a defense to illegality" in Section 7 merger cases[924] clearly does express a position to which the Supreme Court of that period subscribed. The DOJ and FTC have no such ambivalence toward the efficiencies that horizontal mergers can generate. Section 4 of the 1992 Guidelines, the improved Section 4 that the Agency introduced in the 1997 Revision of the 1992 Guidelines, and the counterpart section (Sect. 10) in the 2010 Guidelines make it clear that the Agency believes that the efficiencies a merger generates favor its Clayton Act legality by reducing the probability that the merger will inflict a net equivalent-dollar loss on Clayton-Act-relevant buyers.[925]

The U.S. courts' traditional approach to horizontal mergers may not contain the fifth and last element I want to discuss under this heading: the practice of counting in favor of the legality of a horizontal merger between marginal or small firms the efficiencies the merger will generate on the ground that those efficiencies will help such firms survive or increase the competitive pressure the firms in question can put on their larger rivals while counting against the legality of horizontal mergers

[920] This proposition is certainly contestable and probably false.

[921] Brown Shoe v. United States, 370 U.S. 294 (1962).

[922] Von's Grocery v. United States, 384 U.S. 270 (1966).

[923] See Brown Shoe v. United States, 370 U.S. 294, 344 (1962): "...[w]e cannot fail to recognize Congress' desire to promote competition through the protection of viable, small locally owned businesses. Congress appreciated that occasional higher costs and prices might result from the maintenance of fragmented industries and markets. It resolved these competing considerations in favor of decentralization. We must give effect to that decision."

[924] Federal Trade Commission v. Procter & Gamble Co. (Clorox), 386 U.S. 568, 580 (1967).

[925] Neither the 1992 Guidelines' section on efficiency nor the 1997 Revision's revision of that section nor the counterpart section in the 2010 Guidelines directly addresses the scenario to which the organizational-allocative-efficiency defense that I believe can properly be read into the Clayton Act relates—*viz*., the case in which the efficiencies a horizontal merger generates cause it to inflict a net equivalent-dollar loss on Clayton-Act-relevant buyers when it would not otherwise have done so by leading one or more established rivals of the merged firm to exit or deterring one or more actual or potential rivals of the merged firm from making a QV investment.

involving a non-marginal or large firm the efficiencies its merger will generate on the ground that those efficiencies will tend to drive the well-established firm's marginal competitors out. As I indicated in Chap. 4, the Supreme Court took this pari-mutuel approach in at least one vertical-practice case.[926] However, although I suspect that the U.S. courts were influenced by a disposition to use horizontal-merger law to handicap economic competition, I cannot point to any specific case in which they explicitly did so. Nevertheless, it is worth pointing out that the contemporary DOJ and FTC have shown no inclination to engage in such handicapping.

(C) Three Additional Elements of the U.S. Courts' Traditional Handling of Horizontal-Merger Cases That Either Can Play No Role in DOJ/FTC Decisionmaking or Have Been Neither Taken Over nor Rejected by the DOJ or FTC

The first element of the U.S. courts' traditional handling of horizontal-merger cases that I want to consider under this heading may actually be a deviant holding in a vertical-merger case that, if part of the merger-case tradition, would have important implications for horizontal-merger cases. In its 1957 decision in *du Pont-General Motors*,[927] the Supreme Court held that, even if *over its lifetime* the (vertical) acquisition by du Pont of a 23 % stock interest in General Motors did not reduce competition in the Clayton Act sense, du Pont's continued ownership of these shares would violate the Clayton Act test of illegality[928] if *from the date of the time of the suit* (some 30 years after the actual acquisition) *forward* it would impose a net equivalent-dollar loss on Clayton-Act-relevant buyers. Although I would be shocked if the contemporary DOJ or FTC followed this decision, because they have focused on proposed rather than past mergers, they have never addressed the issue. (Of course, the DOJ and FTC are not prohibited from attacking consummated mergers.)

The second element of the U.S. courts' traditional handling of horizontal-merger cases I want to address under the current heading is their conclusion that a (horizontal) merger violates the Clayton Act even if it does not impose a net equivalent-dollar loss on Clayton-Act-relevant buyers (indeed, even if it confers a net equivalent-dollar gain on them) if it reduces competition in the Clayton Act sense in one or more individual markets.[929] As I argued in Chap. 4, although textual

[926] White Motor Co. v. United States, 372 U.S. 253 (1963).

[927] United States v. E.I. du Pont de Nemours & Co., 353 U.S. 586 (1957).

[928] Because the case was brought in 1949, a year before the Clayton Act was amended *inter alia* to cover vertical mergers, it could not be brought under Section 7 of the Clayton Act. However, in its 1957 decision, the Supreme Court applied the "policy" of the Clayton Act as amended, and the case is now treated as if it were a Section 7 vertical-merger case.

[929] See United States v. Philadelphia Bank, 374 U.S. 321, 370–71 (1963).

argument does favor this conclusion, it is so inconsistent with the objectives of the statute that I consider it to be wrong as a matter of law (because disfavored by legislative history and prudential arguments). As I indicated previously, the 1992 and 2010 Horizontal Merger Guidelines' sections on failing-company defenses implicitly adopt this conclusion. However, the DOJ and the FTC have never explicitly addressed this issue, and their general policy-orientation strongly favors the conclusion that they would not subscribe to this position if they were given the opportunity to address it forthrightly.

The third and final element of the U.S. courts' handling of horizontal-merger cases that belongs in this category is the courts' adoption of limit-price theory (which it sometimes calls "wings theory"). Limit-price theory most often plays a role in U.S. case-law when the conduct under scrutiny is (1) a conglomerate merger that "eliminates" a potential competitor or (2) a joint venture that involves two or more parents that were potential entrants into the joint venture's market. The U.S. courts' acceptance of limit-price theory is also manifest in their assertions that horizontal mergers are less likely to reduce competition if barriers to entry into the relevant area of product-space are low since that claim probably reflects the courts' implicit mistaken premise that, in such circumstances, the merged firm (and its *R*s) will not take advantage of any opportunity the merger would otherwise give them to make additional profits by raising their prices—will, instead, keep their prices down (charge lower prices than would otherwise be profitable) to prevent entry. To my knowledge, neither the contemporary DOJ nor the contemporary FTC has ever addressed the defensibility of limit-price theory. However, the conclusion that the contemporary DOJ and FTC reject limit-price theory is favored by two features of the 1992 Horizontal Merger Guidelines, the 1997 Revision of the Guidelines, and the 2010 Horizontal Merger Guidelines—*viz*., (1) the fact that none of these states that the impact that a horizontal merger will have on the prices charged *at the relevant market's pre merger QV-investment level* will be affected by the height of the barriers to entry into the market in question or, more explicitly, by whether limit pricing would be effective and profitable for its established firms and (2) the fact that the 1992 Guidelines' section on entry (Section 3) focuses on the Agencies' belief that entry will prevent the merged firm and its *R*s from maintaining any price-increases the merger would enable them to make.[930] However, in the absence of more information, I am classifying the U.S. courts' traditional acceptance of

[930] Although the 1992 Guidelines err in assuming that when entry is not blockaded it will prevent a horizontal merger that would otherwise inflict a net equivalent-dollar loss on Clayton-Act-relevant buyers from doing so, that mistake does not imply that the DOJ and FTC believe that when potential competition is effective it will affect outcomes by inducing the established firms to limit price. I should note that the 2010 Horizontal Merger Guidelines do not assume that the presence of effective potential competitors will always prevent a horizontal merger that would otherwise have reduced competition in the Clayton Act sense from doing so. Thus, paragraph 2 of Section 9.1 states: "Even if the prospect of entry does not deter the competitive effects of concern, post-merger entry may counteract them."

limit-price theory as an element of their approach whose acceptance by the DOJ and FTC is open to question.

The preceding account of the U.S. courts' traditional approach to analyzing the legality of horizontal mergers—though detailed—focused only on cases in which the relevant issue was the merger's impact on the competition that the merged firm (relative to the MPs) and the merged firm's *R*s would face as sellers. A far smaller number of cases focused on the legality of horizontal mergers that are predicted to increase the monopsony power of their participants. Relying in part on a Supreme Court case that ruled illegal a buying cartel in a regional sugar-beet market despite the absence of any proof that it would raise the price of refined sugar,[931] at least one old lower-court case[932] condemned a horizontal merger on the ground that it would increase its participants' monopsony power over an input in the absence of any evidence that the exercise of such power would increase final-product prices. As I indicated in Sect. 2, I believe that these decisions are wrong as a matter of economics, and derivatively, as a matter of law.

(3) Six Horizontal-Merger-Related Issues or Related Sets of Issues on Which More-Contemporary U.S. Courts Have Taken Positions

As previously indicated, no horizontal-merger case has reached the Supreme Court since the passage of the Hart-Scott-Rodino Act in 1976. In fact, since that time, relatively-few horizontal-merger cases have been decided by the lower federal courts. This subsection will concentrate on the modern case-law's handling of six issues or sets of issues: the conditions under which the DOJ or FTC can obtain a preliminary injunction against a horizontal merger, two entry-related issues, two efficiency-related issues, the relevance of the fact that relevant buyers are sophisticated for the competitive impact of a horizontal merger, the legal relevance of submarkets, and the legal relevance of the Horizontal Merger Guidelines.

I start with the lower courts' position on the showing that the DOJ or FTC must make to obtain a preliminary injunction against a horizontal merger. According to the U.S. lower courts, two issues are relevant to whether the FTC or DOJ should be granted a preliminary injunction to block a horizontal merger: (1) the likelihood that the FTC or DOJ will prevail on the merits and (2) the balance of the relevant "equities." In general, the lower courts seem to me to have accepted the operationalization of these considerations adopted by a U.S. District Court in *Federal Trade Commission v. Staples, Inc.*[933] According to the *Staples* court, although a demonstration that the relevant Agency has a "'fair and tenable' chance of ultimate success on the merits" will not satisfy the first criterion, the Agencies can satisfy

[931] Mandeville Island Farms v. American Crystal Sugar, 334 U.S. 219 (1948).

[932] United States v. Pennzoil, 252 F. Supp. 962 (D. Pa. 1965). The input market involved in *Pennzoil* was the Pennsylvania market for crude oil, and the final-good market involved in the case was the worldwide market for refined oil.

[933] 970 F. Supp. 1066 (D.D.C. 1997).

this first criterion without "prov[ing] to a certainty that the merger will have an anticompetitive effect" by establishing "a 'reasonable probability' that the transaction will substantially impair competition...."[934] I have enquoted the word "equities" in my statement of the second criterion because the considerations that the courts have in mind are not really "equitable"—*viz.*, are (1) the reduction in competition a failure to grant a preliminary injunction will generate if (A) the merger would impose a net equivalent-dollar loss on Clayton-Act-relevant buyers in a Clayton-Act-relevant way but (B) post-merger, the deciding court will be unwilling to break up the merged firm because doing so will only make things worse from the relevant perspective (the "unscrambling the eggs" difficulty) and (2) the reduction in competition the grant of a preliminary injunction will generate if the merger would confer a net equivalent-dollar gain on Clayton-Act-relevant buyers at a minimum by delaying the execution of the merger and frequently by preventing the merger because the MPs will find it unprofitable to maintain their abilities to participate in the merger until the date on which they would be allowed to consummate it.[935] Chapter 4 discusses the first of these issues. The courts' discussion of the "equitable" issue seems peculiar in that it ignores the "general deterrence" and "general 'inducement'" effects respectively of decisions to grant and decisions not to grant the injunctions in question.

In relatively-recent times, U.S. lower courts have also taken positions on two entry-related issues: (1) the circumstances in which entry will be effective—in this context, in which the possibility of entry will reduce (perhaps critically) the equivalent-dollar loss that a horizontal merger that would otherwise generate such a loss will impose on Clayton-Act-relevant buyers—and (2) the likelihood that entry that is effective will prevent a horizontal merger that would otherwise impose a net equivalent-dollar loss on Clayton-Act-relevant buyers from doing so. In my judgment, the relevant opinions' claims about the circumstances in which entry will be effective are deficient in four respects:

(1) they ignore the fact that the benefits they correctly assume entry will confer on Clayton-Act-relevant buyers will also be conferred on such buyers by established-firm QV-investment expansions;
(2) they never define what they mean by the height of the barriers to entry into a particular market—*inter alia*, by low and high barriers to entry;
(3) they mistakenly assume that the fact that a potential entrant (the best-placed potential entrant) faces low barriers implies that it will be effective and the fact that a potential entrant (the best-placed potential entrant) faces high barriers to entry implies that it will be ineffective when—at least when the concept is defined in any of the ways in which I and other contemporary economists define it—no such connection is present: on my definition, for example, a firm that faces high barriers to entry will be effective if the barriers it faces are lower than the barriers faced by any other potential entrant and the sum of the barriers and

[934] *Id.* at 1072.
[935] *Id.* at 1093.

disincentives that would face any potential expander if entry were barred at what in its absence would be the market's equilibrium QV-investment level; and

(4) some of them mistakenly assume that the fact that entry has not taken place for a considerable period of time implies that barriers to entry are high and potential competition is ineffective[936] when in reality the absence of entry could manifest instead (A) the facts that QV-investment opportunities arise discontinuously and are very product/location specific and established firms always learn of them sooner than outsiders and/or (B) the fact that the established firms always chose to deter new entry by expanding themselves—*i.e.*, by making limit QV investments.

In my judgment, the modern lower-court case-law also exaggerates the likelihood that the entry a horizontal merger will induce if barriers to entry are low will prevent it from imposing a net equivalent-dollar loss on Clayton-Act-relevant buyers.[937] Even if the courts were right in assuming that the amount of actual entry a horizontal merger would induce (or the effectiveness of entry) was inversely correlated to the height of the barriers to entry into the relevant market, entry would only reduce the loss that a merger that would otherwise impose a net equivalent-dollar loss on Clayton-Act-relevant buyers imposes on such buyers.

The third set of issues that more-modern lower-court case-law has addressed is efficiency-related. I have already indicated that the Supreme Court case-law of the 1960s declared that the efficiencies a horizontal merger generated either counted against its Clayton Act legality or were irrelevant to its Clayton Act legality. However, by 1980, the lower courts were splitting over the availability of an efficiency defense.[938] Indeed, as the Court of Appeals recognized in 2001 in *Federal Trade Commission v. H.J. Heinz Co.*, since that time "the trend among lower courts is to recognize the defense."[939] By way of contrast, my impression is that the courts are being niggardly both in "measuring" the efficiencies a merger has generated and

---

[936] See, *e.g.*, Federal Trade Commission v. H.J. Heinz Co., 246 F.3d 708, 717 and n.13 (D.C. Cir. 2001).

[937] See, *e.g.*, United States v. Country Lake Foods, 754 F. Supp. 669 (D. Minn. 1990); United States v. Baker Hughes, Inc. 908 F.2d 981 (D.C. Cir. 1990); and United States v. Waste Management, Inc., 743 F.2d 976 (2d Cir. 1984). I should add that the first two of these courts may have been encouraged to adopt this position by a Supreme Court dicta in a predatory-pricing case. In Cargill v. Montfort of Colorado, Inc., 479 U.S. 104 (1986), the Supreme Court said that a competitor could not challenge a merger on the ground that it would facilitate predatory pricing if some of the market's potential competitors faced low barriers to entry.

[938] Compare, *e.g.*, RSR Corp. v. Federal Trade Commission, 602 F.2d 1317, 1325 (9th Cir. 1979) (stating that the argument for an efficiency defense has been rejected repeatedly) with Federal Trade Commission v. Universal Health, 938 F.2d 1206, 1222 (recognizing the defense).

[939] 246 F.3d 708, 720 (D.C. Cir. 2001), citing not only Universal Health but also Federal Trade Commission v. Tenet Health Care Corp. 816 F.3d 1045, 1054 (8th Cir. 1999); Federal Trade Commission v. Cardinal Health, Inc., 12 F.2d 34, 61 (D.D.C. 1998); Federal Trade Commission v. Staples, Inc. 970 F. Supp. 1066, 1088–89 (197); and ABA Antitrust Section, *Mergers and Acquisitions: Understanding the Antitrust Issues* 152 (2000).

in assessing whether those efficiencies are "merger-specific"—*i.e.*, whether the MPs would have created the efficiencies on their own had they not engaged in the merger. The *Heinz* opinion itself manifests these tendencies. The Heinz/Beech-Nut merger at issue in that case would have generated efficiencies by combining a Heinz company that had a new plant that it was operating at 40 % of capacity to produce its lower-quality baby food with a Beech-Nut company that was producing in an antiquated plant constructed in 1907 better-quality baby food that could compete on the merits with Gerber's products. Producing Beech-Nut's products in Heinz' plant would have reduced their "variable conversion cost" of production by 43 %. The *Heinz* court articulated three objections to the defendant's claimed efficiency defense. First, it pointed out that variable conversion costs constituted only part of Beech-Nut's total variable manufacturing costs and that the claimed efficiencies constituted only 22.3 % of the company's total variable manufacturing cost. Second, it argued that the efficiencies in question should be expressed as a percentage not just of Beech-Nut's total variable manufacturing costs but as a percentage of both costs. I must say that I do not grasp the point of either of these two objections. The relevant question is whether the efficiencies in question will generate sufficient benefits for Clayton-Act-relevant buyers to make it sufficiently unlikely that the proposed merger will inflict a (sufficiently-large?) net equivalent-dollar loss on these buyers for the merger to be illegal. The answer to that question does not depend in any way on whether the relevant cost-savings are expressed as an amount per unit of Beech-Nut's product, as a percentage of Beech-Nut's total variable conversion cost, as a percentage of Beech-Nut's total variable manufacturing cost, or as a percentage of Beech-Nut's and Heinz' total variable manufacturing costs. I should add that the court's interest in this last percentage is particularly bewildering, given that the merged company will undoubtedly produce more units of Beech-Nut products and fewer of Heinz' products than the MPs would absent the merger. The *Heinz* court's third objection to the defendant's efficiency-defense argument was that the alleged efficiencies might not have been merger-specific: in its words, "neither the District Court nor the...[MPs] addressed the question whether Heinz could obtain the benefit of better recipes by investing more money in product development and promotion"—in particular, whether Heinz could achieve this benefit in this way by spending "an amount less than the amount Heinz would spend to acquire Beech-Nut."[940] Even if this argument's implicit rejection of the U.S. antitrust law's do-nothing benchmark for competitive-impact analysis were legally justifiable, it seems to ignore the facts that (1) acting on its own, Heinz would have to improve not only its product but its reputation for quality and (2) the latter objective might be both difficult and time-costly to achieve.

One more-contemporary U.S. court has argued (in an opinion by Justice Thomas when he was a Court of Appeals judge) that horizontal mergers that would otherwise reduce competition and therefore violate the Clayton Act may not do so if the

[940] Federal Trade Commission v. H.J. Heinz Co., 246 F.3d 708, 722 (2001).

relevant buyers are sophisticated.[941] Then-Judge Thomas did not fully explain the basis of this claim. However, although I cannot see how a buyer's sophistication will help it combat the tendency of a merger to increase the price it must pay by raising its best-placed supplier's HNOP and NOM, in some circumstances, such a buyer may be able to combat the tendency of a merger to increase the COM it must pay by insisting on its potential suppliers' using a bidding system that makes it more difficult for them to police a price-fixing arrangement.

As I indicated in Sect. 4 of Chap. 7, starting at least with *Brown Shoe* in 1962, the United States Supreme Court and various lower courts used the concept of a submarket to analyze the competitive impact of a horizontal merger—*i.e.*, proceeded on the assumption that a horizontal merger could violate the Clayton Act by reducing competition in a submarket even if the MP-market-share and seller-concentration-ratio figures for the larger market within which the submarket was located would, under the Court's "rules," imply that the merger was lawful. In Chap. 7, I also explained that, although many economists and legal scholars of the period condemned such submarket analysis, I thought it justifiable (within the confines of a market-oriented analysis). However, over the years, lower U.S. courts stopped using the concept of a submarket. I am glad to report that two more recent cases have engaged in submarket analysis.

In 1997, in *Federal Trade Commission v. Staples, Inc.*, a District Court not only recognized the "possibility...that the sale of consumable office supplies by office superstores may qualify as a submarket within a larger market of retailers of office supplies in general"[942] but found that it did,[943] basing its conclusion on the various criteria *Brown Shoe* had proposed using for this purpose—most relevantly, whether the prices of products placed in the submarket are "affected primarily" by prices of other products placed in that submarket, whether firms thought in terms of the submarket when considering entry decision, whether (in the case of retail stores) the stores placed in the submarket were physically different from retailers of the same products placed outside the submarket, and whether the industry and public recognized the submarket as a "separate economic entity."[944] More recently still, in *Federal Trade Commission v. Whole Foods Market, Inc.*, the Court of Appeals for the D.C. Circuit in effect found that "premium natural and organic supermarkets" constituted the seller-side of a submarket within the larger market in which all types of supermarkets belong.[945]

In addition, in several cases, more-contemporary U.S. lower courts have taken positions on whether the DOJ/FTC Horizontal Merger Guidelines are a source of law and, assuming that they are not, the extent to which they can inform the judgment of U.S. courts. The *Staples* court expressed the lower-court consensus on these issues:

---

[941] See United States v. Baker Hughes, Inc. 908 F.2d 981, 986 and 992 (D.C. Cir. 1990).

[942] 970 F. Supp. 1066, 1075 (D.D.C. 1997).

[943] *Id.* at 1080.

[944] *Id.* at 1075.

[945] Case 07–5276 at 18 (July 29, 2008).

> The *Merger Guidelines*, of course, are not binding on the Court, but, as this Circuit has stated, they do provide "a useful illustration of the application of the HHI. . . ."[946]

Finally, at least two more-contemporary U.S. lower courts have taken a position on the economic effects of monopsony and the legal significance of any tendency of a horizontal merger to increase its participants' monopsony power. In the Court of Appeals decision in *Khan v. State Oil Co.*,[947] Judge Posner stated that "monopoly and monopsony are symmetrical distortions of competition from an economic standpoint," meaning that they both inflict equivalent-dollar losses on ultimate buyers, and in *United States v. Rice Growers Association*,[948] a District Court condemned a horizontal merger that it found would give its participants monopsony power in the California paddy-rice market even though there was no reason to believe that it would raise the price of milled rice in any "geographic market."

B. The Approaches That the U.S. Antitrust-Enforcement Agencies (the DOJ and FTC) Have Taken to Horizontal-Merger Analysis

I have already explained the primary reason why, since the passage of the Hart-Scott-Rodino Act, the DOJ and FTC (the Agencies) have been the most important antitrust-law decisionmakers in the central government:

(1) firms that want to participate in mergers or acquisitions above a relatively-modest size must obtain the approval of the DOJ or FTC (or a court that overturns a negative Agency decision) before doing so;
(2) decisions by the Agencies to oppose a proposed merger almost always result in the MPs' abandoning their merger plans; and
(3) private plaintiffs rarely challenge any horizontal merger the Agencies choose not to oppose.[949]

In fact, the Agencies' various positions also play an increasingly-important role in merger litigation: the Merger Guidelines have figured importantly in dozens of cases since 1984.

In practice, both the DOJ and the FTC now take two different approaches or sets of approaches to horizontal-merger analysis: (1) the part of the approach delineated in the 1992 Horizontal Merger Guidelines as revised in 1997 that the 2010 Horizontal Merger Guidelines appear to accept and (2) any of a number of non-Guidelines-based approaches including merger simulations of various sorts and the investigation

---

[946] Federal Trade Commission v. Staples, 970 F. Supp. 1066, 1082 (D.D.C. 1997).

[947] 93 F.3d 1358, 1361 (7th Cir. 1996), *vacated on other grounds*, 522 U.S. 3 (1997).

[948] 1986–2 Trade Cas. (CCH) ¶ 67, 288 (E.D. Cal. 1986).

[949] The DOJ and FTC challenge only a small percentage of the mergers they consider under Hart-Scott-Rodino. Indeed, they make a "second request" for information in only about 5 % of the cases.

of the implications of various sorts of natural experiments that bear on the likely competitive impact of the merger the Agencies are scrutinizing. After devoting a great deal of attention to the 1992 Horizontal Merger Guidelines' approach to horizontal-merger analysis (in part because the E.C./E.U. has taken a similar approach), this subsection will discuss the various non-Guidelines-based approaches the Agencies now take to horizontal-merger competitive-impact prediction and the 2010 Horizontal Merger Guidelines' approach to horizontal-merger analysis.

(1) The DOJ/FTC 1992 Horizontal Merger Guidelines' Approach to Horizontal-Merger Analysis

Section 2 of Chap. 7 delineated and criticized the 1992 Guidelines' approaches to market definition. This subsection focuses on the rest of the Guidelines' approach to competitive-impact prediction. That approach always begins by predicting the proposed merger's impact on the HHI(s) of the market(s) in which the MPs have both been placed and the magnitude of those markets' post-merger HHIs (where HHI is a measure of the concentration of the seller-side of a market that equates that concentration with the sum of the squares of the market shares of all firms placed in the market in question). In fact, as I will describe in more detail below, the 1992 Guidelines (1) establish "safe harbors" for mergers that are associated either with specified post-merger HHI figures alone or with specified combinations of post-merger HHI figures and merger-generated increase-in-HHI figures and (2) state that the DOJ and FTC have adopted a difficult-to-rebut presumption that mergers associated with other specified combinations of post-merger HHI figures and merger-generated increase-in-HHI figures reduce competition and are therefore unlawful. However, the 1992 Guidelines also state that the Agencies' evaluation of mergers that do not fall into either of these two categories will be influenced by a number of non-HHI-oriented considerations: so-called qualifying factors related to product heterogeneity, which the Agencies believe reduce the predictive power of post-merger-HHI and merger-generated increase-in-HHI figures; attributes of the condition of entry; the efficiencies the merger should be predicted to generate; and the fact that one of the companies involved in the merger under scrutiny is a "failing company." Indeed, although any suggestion of this kind is inconsistent with the provisions in the 1992 Guidelines' General Standards section that assert that the Agencies will irrebuttably presume that mergers associated with specified post-merger-HHI and merger-generated increase-in-HHI figures are illegal, the later sections of the Guidelines that focus on these non-HHI-oriented factors seem to claim that one or more of them may lead the DOJ or FTC to declare any horizontal merger lawful, regardless of the post-merger-HHI and merger-generated increase-in-HHI figures with which it is associated.

This subsection will (A) describe the 1992 Guidelines' HHI-oriented classifications of mergers and criticize the Guidelines' irrebuttable presumptions of legality and illegality on the admittedly-contestable assumptions that they really are irrebuttable, (B) describe and evaluate the 1992 Guidelines' account of the various ways in which a horizontal merger can affect the intensity of price competition in the area of product-space in which it is executed, the 1992 Guidelines' discussion of the various "qualifying factors" that make the HHI-oriented figures on which the General Standards focus less reliable predictors of a horizontal merger's impact on such price competition, and the 1992 Guidelines' approach to taking these qualifying factors into consideration, (C) describe and criticize the 1992 Guidelines' position on the relevance of "entry conditions" for the competitive impact of a horizontal merger, (D) describe and criticize the 1992 Guidelines and the 1997 Guidelines-revision's treatment of the economic significance and legal relevance of the efficiencies a horizontal merger can generate, (E) describe and criticize the failing-company defense the 1992 Guidelines recognize, and (F) describe and criticize the 1992 Guidelines' positions on the likely economic effects and legal significance of any tendency a horizontal merger has to increase the monopsony power of its participants and (G) delineate and comment on the relationship between the 2010 Guidelines' positions on all these issues and their 1992 counterparts'.

Before proceeding, however, I want to describe a practice reality that some might think make the 1992 Guidelines unimportant and explain why I think the detailed analysis of the 1992 Guidelines this subsection provides is warranted despite this practice reality. I fully recognize that, in practice, from 1992 until 2010, the DOJ and FTC's treatment of horizontal mergers was far more lenient than the 1992 Guidelines indicate it would be. According to data the DOJ and FTC have themselves released in a praiseworthy, self-conscious attempt to increase transparency, the 1992 Guidelines' implications to the contrary notwithstanding,

(1) the Agencies virtually never challenge non-oil-market mergers in markets whose post-merger HHI is below 2,000 (though they often challenge oil-market mergers in markets whose post-merger HHIs are between 1,800 and 2,000 and frequently challenge non-oil-market mergers in markets whose post-merger HHIs are between 2,000 and 3,000 where "often" and "frequently" are used absolutely, not relatively: the figures the Agencies released do not indicate the number of mergers in the relevant category that they did not challenge)[950];
(2) the probability that the FTC will challenge a merger that leaves the relevant market with four significant sellers is below 40 % when the market's post-merger HHI is under 4,000, the probability that the FTC will challenge a merger that leaves the market with three significant sellers is below 50 % when the market's post-merger HHI is below 4,000, and the probability that the FTC will

[950] See FTC–DOJ, Merger Challenge Data, Fiscal Years 1999–2003, Tables 3–10 (200_). See also Federal Trade Commission, Horizontal Merger Enforcement Data: Fiscal Years 1996–2005, Table 3.1 (2007), indicating that, of the 37 horizontal mergers it investigated between 1996 and 2005 inclusive in which the post-merger HHI was between 1800 and 2000 and the merger-generated increase in HHI was between 100 and 300, it challenged only 18.

challenge a merger that leaves the relevant market with only two significant sellers rises to 50 % only when the market's HHI is over 3,000[951];

(3) between 1996 and 2003, the average post-merger HHI of the markets involved in mergers that the FTC did not challenge after making a second request varied from 3,055 to 3,271, and the average change in HHI the mergers in question generated varied from 703 to 825 while the counterpart average figures for the mergers that the FTC did challenge varied respectively from 5,220 to 5,833 and 1,774 to 1,903[952]; and

(4) "mergers that increase HHI by 100 to a level between 1000–1800 are rarely subjects of enforcement and those that produce an HHI over 1800 are not, in fact, 'presumed'... likely to create or enhance market power or facilitate its exercise."[953]

I can understand why a reader might wonder why the facts that the Agencies did not make use of the 1992 Guidelines' presumptions in the 1992–2010 period and, as subsection (3) will indicate, explicitly stated in their 2010 Guidelines that (roughly speaking) they were committed to continuing their 1992-Guideline-inconsistent enforcement practices have not deterred me from including the detailed consideration of the 1992 Guidelines that follows. In part, the answer is that (as I indicated earlier) the 1992 Guidelines (including their General Standards) do influence U.S. courts, continue to have some impact on the U.S. DOJ and FTC, and (as I will explain in Sect. 5 of this chapter) have had a substantial impact on the E.C./E.U.'s treatment of horizontal mergers, but primarily it is that (1) my analysis of the 1992 Guidelines focuses not so much on their HHI-oriented presumptions but on the economic and legal assumptions that underlie the 1992 Guidelines' sections on Qualifying Factors, Entry, Merger-Generated Efficiencies, and Failing Companies and (2) many of those assumptions are wrong, influentially and highly deleterious (though they are also made by a large number of respected Industrial Organization economist, legal academics, and lawyers who specialize in antitrust and are conversant with economics). (I hasten to add that the discussion that follows will also point out various ways in which the 1992 Guidelines manifest real progress by rejecting various incorrect assumptions and conclusions that many economists and lawyers previously made—*i.e.*, that the 1992 Guidelines' approach is half-way between the traditional market-oriented approach to horizontal-merger

---

[951] See Malcolm Coate and Shawn Ulrick, *Transparency at the Federal Trade Commission: The Horizontal Merger Review Process 1996–2003*, 73 ANTITRUST L.J. 531, 557 (2006).

[952] *Id.* at 543. The same data reveals that the probability of enforcement is best predicted by the relevant market's post-merger HHI when the FTC is most concerned with the merger's increasing "coordinated behavior" and is best predicted by the number of significant sellers in the market post-merger when the FTC is concerned with the possible unilateral effects of the merger. See Malcolm Coate, *Empirical Analysis of Merger Enforcement Under the 1992 Merger Guidelines*, 27 REV. IND. ORG. 279 (2005).

[953] See EINER ELHAUGE AND DAMIEN GERADIN, GLOBAL ANTITRUST: LAW AND ECONOMICS 899–900 (Foundation Press, 2007), quoting Section 1.51(c) of the 1992 Horizontal Merger Guidelines. I should add that the three preceding items in the above list were also adapted from a paragraph in the ELHAUGE AND GERADIN book at 900.

competitive-impact analysis and the essentially-non-market-oriented approach to this task Sect. 2 of this chapter proposed.)

(A) The 1992 Guidelines' HHI-Oriented "General Standards"

The first paragraph of the 1992 Guidelines' version of the non-market-definition part of the DOJ and FTC's approach to horizontal-merger analysis explicitly states their view that

> [a] merger is unlikely to create or enhance market power or to facilitate its exercise unless it significantly increases concentration and results in a concentrated market, properly defined and measured. Mergers that either do not significantly increase concentration or do not result in a concentrated market ordinarily require no further analysis.[954]

Given this introduction, it should not be surprising that the 1992 Guidelines' "General Standards," which articulate the basic presumptions that the DOJ and FTC use when deciding whether to challenge a horizontal merger, focus exclusively on the post-merger concentration of the market(s) in which both MPs have been placed and the increases in the concentration of those markets that the horizontal merger under investigation generated. As I have already stated, the 1992 Guidelines adopt the HHI operationalization of the seller-side of any market—*i.e.*, define the concentration of the seller-side of any market to equal the sum of the squares of the market shares of the firms placed within the market. The 1992 Guidelines also claim that this operationalization of seller concentration implies that a horizontal merger between two firms with market shares of x and y will increase the relevant market's HHI by $2xy$.[955] Although this claim would be correct if the merger of two firms with market shares of x and y would create a merged firm with a market share of $(x + y)$ and not affect any non-MP market share, for at least four reasons this premise of this Guidelines' claim will usually be inaccurate. Thus, if, as is usually the case, a firm's market share is calculated by the percentage of market sales it makes:

(1) even if the merger does not make the merged firm best-placed to obtain the patronage of buyers neither MP was best-placed to supply pre merger by generating static marginal efficiencies, does not induce the merged firm to make a QV investment it would not otherwise have made by generating dynamic efficiencies or causing it to face *M* disincentives that are lower than the *O* disincentives its antecedents faced, and does not cause the merged firm to withdraw one of the MPs' QV investments by increasing the *M* disincentives it faced above the *M* disincentives the relevant MP faced, it will increase the merged firm's dollar sales and hence (*ceteris paribus*) market share above the sum of the MPs' dollar sales and market shares (A) by freeing the MPs from each other's competition, (B) by producing CMC-related increases in its CCAs and HNOPs (when individualized pricing is practiced in the relevant market) or increase-in-rival-price-generated and sequence-of-rival-price-announcement-related increases in the merged firm's HNOPs (when across-the-board pricing

[954] See 1992 Horizontal Merger Guidelines at Section 1.0.

[955] See *id.* at Section 1.51 at note 18.

is practiced in the relevant market), (C) by generating related increases in the merged firm's NOMs, and (D) by increasing the COMs the merged firm contrives (though in many cases it may reduce these COMs);

(2) in many cases, *ceteris paribus*, a horizontal merger will increase the merged firm's market share above the sum of the MPs' market shares (A) by generating static marginal-cost efficiencies that make it best-placed to supply buyers neither MP was best-placed to supply pre merger (or, when the marginal efficiency in question reflected the merger's enabling the merged firm to produce a product that was more attractive to consumers, by enabling it to obtain a higher price from buyers an MP was already best-placed to supply than the MP could have obtained) and/or (B) by inducing the merged firm to make a QV investment neither MP would have made though the merger may also reduce the merged firm's market share by inducing it to withdraw a QV investment that the relevant MP would not have withdrawn;

(3) in some cases, a horizontal merger will tend to decrease the merged firm's dollar sales and market share above the sum of the MPs' market shares by increasing the prices the merged firm's *R*s obtain from their customers by increasing the CMC the merged firm would have to obtain to supply their customers at relevant prices, derivatively the NOMs they secure, and possibly the COMs they obtain as well; and

(4) in many cases, a horizontal merger will alter the market shares of one or more rivals of the merged firm (A) by generating efficiencies that make the merged firm best-placed to supply buyers a merged-firm rival was best-placed to supply pre merger or that reduce the OCA of a merged-firm rival (and possibly prevent it from obtaining an NOM on that account), (B) by increasing the profitability of contrived oligopolistic pricing for the merged firm's rivals by making the merged firm more vulnerable to retaliation than the MPs were (by increasing the merged firm's [OCA + NOM]s above the MPs' and creating a merged firm whose defenses are more spread than the MPs'), and (C) by increasing the CMC the merged firm must incur to match a rival's pre merger HNOP to a buyer the rival was best-placed to supply and an MP would have been uniquely-second-placed to supply.

The failure of the 1992 Guidelines to recognize the various reasons why a merger between firms with market shares of x and y may not yield a merged firm with a market share of $(x + y)$ and may change the market shares of the merged firm's rivals is primarily important because it suggests that the 1992 Guidelines' authors (and their successors) are unaware of or tend to forget or ignore many of the ways in which horizontal mergers can affect competition.

It is also important to note that the 1992 Guidelines' assumption that a merger between MPs with market shares of x and y will yield a merged firm with a market share of $(x + y)$ implies that the amount by which horizontal mergers raise the HHI of any market in which they take place will increase with both the sum of the market shares of the MPs and the disparity between their market shares. Indeed, I am confident that this conclusion would not be affected by the substitution of a more accurate assessment of the relationship between the merged firm's market share and the sum of the MPs' market shares. I want to point out that (1) this latter fact implies that the 1992 Guidelines place more weight on the market share of the merger partner with the lower market share than on the market share of the merger partner with the higher market share, given the sum of their market shares, and (2) in so doing, the 1992 Guidelines are repeating the practice of the traditional market-oriented approach, which implicitly placed three to four times the weight on the larger MP's market share relative to the smaller MP's market share when predicting the impact that a merger would have on competition in the relevant area of product-space.

I will now (1) delineate the various presumptions that the 1992 General Standards establish and (2) analyze whether these presumptions seem to reflect appropriately-accurate conclusions about the absolute and relative likelihood that the horizontal mergers to which they apply would or would not decrease competition (whether the virtually-irrebuttable presumptions they establish are accurate and whether the more-or-less-rebuttable presumptions they establish provide accurate starting points for analysis).

(i) The Three Types of HHI-Based Presumptions That the 1992 Guidelines Establish

The first set of presumptions that the 1992 Guidelines establish are virtually-irrebuttable or totally-irrebuttable presumptions that the mergers to which they apply are lawful because they "are unlikely to have adverse competitive effects...." This type of presumption applies to three categories of horizontal mergers: (1) those that leave their market's HHI below 1,000, (2) those that generate an increase of fewer[956] than 100 points in the HHI of a market whose post-merger HHI is between 1,000 and 1,800,[957] and (3) those that produce an increase in the HHI of fewer than 50 points in a market whose post-merger HHI is above 1,800.[958] Although the 1992 Guidelines' initial articulation of this set of presumptions leaves the impression that they are rebuttable in that the 1992 Guidelines state that cases in these categories "*ordinarily* require no further analysis"[959] (emphasis added), subsequent statements in the 1992 Guidelines imply that these presumptions of legality are in fact irrebuttable. Thus, the 1992 Guidelines' discussion of the relevance of evidence suggesting that the merging firms' products are more likely to be best-placed and second-placed to obtain the patronage of given buyers than their "market shares would alone suggest"[960] states that such evidence will be taken into consideration

[956] The 1992 Guidelines incorrectly use the word "less": if a number can be placed on the referent, "fewer" should be used, not "less."

[957] *Id.* at Section 1.51, subsection "a)."

[958] *Id.* at Section 1.51, subsection "c)."

[959] *Id.*

[960] *Id.* at Section 2.211, paragraph two, sentence one.

only if the relevant "market concentration data fall outside the *safeharbor* regions of Sect. 1.5"[961] (emphasis added).

The second type of presumption that the 1992 Guidelines establish is a rebuttable presumption of illegality. Thus, the 1992 Guidelines state:

> Where the post-merger HHI exceeds 1800, it will be presumed that mergers producing an increase in the HHI of more than 100 points are likely to create or enhance market power or facilitate its exercise. The presumption may be overcome by a showing that [certain] factors [*viz.*, the non-HHI-oriented factors on which the succeeding parts of this subsection will focus]. . .make it unlikely that the merger will create or enhance market power or facilitate its exercise, in light of market concentration and market shares.[962]

Note that this presumption is strong in the sense that it can be overcome only by showing that the merger is "*unlikely*" to be anticompetitive (though perhaps this part of the 1992 Guidelines' text does no more than reflect the fact that the Clayton Act text condemns mergers whose effect "*may be* substantially to lessen competition" [emphasis added]).[963]

The third set of presumptions that the 1992 Guidelines establish could in fact be said to be no presumptions at all since they seem to imply no more than that the DOJ and FTC will take seriously the possibility that the mergers to which they apply may lessen competition. Perhaps this set of presumptions might best be described as anti-presumptions in that the 1992 Guidelines seem to be indicating that in the cases to which they apply the DOJ and FTC will not rely on their and the 1992 Guidelines' normal assumption that most horizontal mergers are "procompetitive or competitively neutral."[964] In any event, the 1992 Guidelines indicate that two categories of horizontal mergers "potentially raise significant competitive concerns depending on the factors. . ."[965] on which the next parts of this subsection will focus: (1) "[m]ergers producing an increase in the HHI of more than 100 points in moderately concentrated markets postmerger"[966]—*i.e.*, in markets with post-merger HHIs between 1,000 and 1,800— and (2) "[m]ergers producing an increase in the HHI of more than 50 points [but fewer than 100] in highly concentrated markets postmerger"[967]—*i.e.*, in markets with post-merger HHIs over 1,800.

---

[961] *Id.* at Section 2.211, paragraph one in the sentence after the sentence that closes with note 22. See also *id.* at Section 2.211, paragraph 3.

[962] *Id.* at Section 1.51, subsection "c)." I assume that the reference to facilitating the exercise of market power refers to the illegal exercise of market power—*e.g.*, by taking advantage of the opportunity to profit by engaging in contrived oligopolistic pricing. As Chapter 4 explained, U.S. antitrust law does not proscribe a firm's taking advantage of its lawful monopoly power (exploiting a given demand-curve marginal-cost-curve combination) or committing an act that facilitates its taking advantage of its lawful monopoly power.

[963] See Clayton Act at Section 7.

[964] See the 1992 Guidelines, paragraph two, sentence two.

[965] See *id.* at Section 1.1, subsections "b)" and "c)."

[966] See *id.* at Section 1.51, subsection "b)."

[967] See *id.* at Section 1.51, subsection "c)."

(ii) The Accuracy of the 1992 Guidelines' Three Market-Aggregated-Data-Based Presumptions

This section analyzes (1) whether horizontal mergers that do not raise their market's HHI above 1,000 are extremely unlikely to lessen competition, (2) whether horizontal mergers that produce an HHI increase of more than 100 points in a market whose post-merger HHI is at least 1,800 are extremely likely to lessen competition, and least troublingly (3) whether the competitive impact of mergers that produce an HHI-increase of more than 100 points in a market whose post-merger HHI is between 1,000 and 1,800 or that produce an HHI-increase of more than 50 points in a market whose post-merger HHI is over 1,800 deserve to be carefully scrutinized.

Before proceeding to a detailed analysis of the above questions, three preliminary points that apply to the analysis of each should be made. First, the analyses that follow assume (contrary to fact) that the 1992 Guidelines' market-definition protocol will always place into at least one shared market the participants in any horizontal merger that will reduce competition by injuring on balance the customers of the MPs and the customers of the MPs' product-rivals by reducing the absolute attractiveness of the best offer these buyers respectively receive from any inferior supplier.

Second, the fact that the MPs belong to the smallest hypothetical-combinant set whose combination would enable its members to profit by increasing their prices by 5 % if no non-combinants would respond to the combinants' price-increases does not guarantee either (1) that the actual merger will enable its participants to profit by raising their prices by 5 % or (2) that the actual merger would lead its participants to raise their prices by 5 % even if it made such price-increases profitable in the sense of more profitable than no price-increases or lower price-increases. Thus, the actual merger may not make it profitable for the MPs to raise their prices by 5 % or at all despite the fact that the hypothetical combinants would find a 5 % price-increase profitable in the above sense (1) because some of the members of the hypothetical-combinant group may be non-MPs that will not follow the MPs' price-increases and (2) because some firms that are not part of the hypothetical-combinant group may respond to any 5 % price-increase the group attempts by cutting their prices. Moreover, if the 5 % price-increase that the hypothetical combination would make profitable consisted entirely of increased contrived OMs, the MPs might not raise their prices even if it would be profitable for them to do so because they valued obeying the law.[968]

---

[968] Indeed, as I indicated in Section 3 of this chapter, even if one knew that the merged firm would take advantage of any opportunity it had to profit by raising its COMs above those the MPs would charge and that the merger would also induce the merged firm's *R*s to secure more COMs, one *might* argue that any tendency of the merger to increase prices on this account should not be counted against the merger's legality since the effect in question would result from an independent illegal act. The word "might" is emphasized in the preceding sentence because, given the difficulty of proving contrived oligopolistic pricing, the only effective way to deter it is often to prevent the development of conditions that make the practice profitable. I admit, however, that my position on this "fence law" issue is highly contestable.

Third, even if the market definition reflected the fact that each hypothetical combinant would find a price-increase of 5 % profitable (*i.e.*, more profitable than no price-increase or any lower or higher price-increase) given that no non-combinant would change its price in response, the horizontal merger might in reality make it profitable for the merged firm to raise its prices by more than 5 % above the prices the MPs would charge absent the merger because in reality the merged firm's actual remaining rivals might increase their prices in response to the increase in the merged firm's prices.

I will now develop an example that calls into question the claim of the 1992 Guidelines' General Standards that horizontal mergers in markets whose post-merger HHIs are below 1,000 are sufficiently unlikely to be anticompetitive for it to be appropriate for the DOJ and FTC to presume (virtually or totally irrebuttably) that such mergers will not lessen competition and therefore are not illegal. Assume that the horizontal merger in question takes place between two firms that are operating in an individualized-pricing "market" that, absent the merger, would conventionally be said to contain 23 sellers—in particular, in a conventional market that would contain seller *R25* (whose market share is 25 %), seller *R10* (whose market share is 10 %), sellers *R8A* and *R8B* (whose market shares are 8 %), sellers *R5A-C* (whose market shares are 5 %), sellers *R3A-F* (whose market shares are 3 %), sellers *R2A-E* (whose market shares are 2 %), and sellers *R1A-F* (whose market shares are 1 %). Assume that the relevant market were defined to include all these firms and that the relevant merger would be between *R5A* (MP1) and *R3A* (MP2)—*i.e.*, would increase the number of sellers with 8 % market shares to three while decreasing the number of sellers with 5 % market shares to two and the number with 3 % market shares to five. The 1992 Guidelines would irrebuttably presume that this merger would not lessen competition since it would produce only a 30-point rise (since $[5 + 3]^2 - [5^2 + 3^2] = 64 - 34 = 30$) in the HHI of a market whose post-merger HHI was between 1,000 and 1,800—in particular, was ($1{,}038 = 25^2 + 10^2 + 3[8]^2 + 2[5^2] + 5[3^2] + 5[2^2] + 6[1^2] = 625 + 100 + 192 + 50 + 45 + 20 + 6$).

However, the 1992 Guidelines' protocol might not result in all the above products' being placed in the market in which MP1 and MP2 were placed. To explain why this might be the case, it will be necessary to demonstrate that a hypothetical combination involving the MPs and a subset of the sellers that would be placed in the above conventional market could enable the combinants to profit by raising their prices by 5 % if no-one else responded to their price-changes. Since a fully-worked-out example would be very elaborate, I will articulate one set of circumstances in which the combination of MP1 with MP2 and a subset of the remaining firms in the above conventional market would make it profitable for the MP1 division of the merged firm to raise its prices by 5 % and then simply explain why the combination of the same subset of the conventional market's products could enable the merged firm to raise its prices by 5 % to the customers of all the hypothetical combinants.

Assume that (1) MP2 (otherwise known as *R3A*) was MP1's closest competitor for the patronage of 20 % of the buyers that MP1 (otherwise known as *R5A*) was best-placed to supply, (2) *R8A* was MP1's closest competitor for another 8 % of MP1's customers, (3) *R5B* and *R5C* were second-placed to obtain 6 % of MP1's customers, (4) *R3B–D* each were second-placed to obtain the patronage of 5 % of MP1's customers, (5) *R2A–F* each were second-placed to supply 4 % of MP1's customers, (6) *R1A–C* each were second-placed to supply 3 % of MP1's customers, (7) each of the firms that was second-placed to supply some of MP1's customers had an average advantage over the third-placed supplier of those buyers equal to 3 % of MP1's average pre merger price to them, and (8) the combination of MP1 with the other firms just listed would raise the merged firm's HNOP to the buyers that MP1 was best-placed to supply and one of these other hypothetical combinants was second-placed to supply by an amount equal to 6 % of MP1's pre merger price to these buyers because on the average the non-combinant that was better-placed than any other non-combinant to supply the buyers in question was worse-than-second-placed to supply these buyers by an amount equal to 3 % of MP1's average pre merger price to those buyers (because the hypothetical combination also often included the third-placed or third-placed and fourth-placed, *etc*., suppliers of the buyers in question).

On these facts, the combination of the two MPs, *R8B*, *R5B–C*, *R3B–D*, *R2A–F*, and *R1A–C* would enable the MP1 division of the merged firm to raise its prices to (88 % = 20 % + 8 % + 2[6 %] + 3[5 %] + 6[4 %] + 3[3 %]) of MP1's customers—*i.e*., would enable the merged firm to raise its average price to all of MP1's customers by (88 %)(6 %) = 5.28 % even if it did not enable it to obtain oligopolistic margins naturally from any of the buyers in question or to secure additional COMs from them.

I should note that these facts are not at all unrealistic. If the market shares of the firms in the conventional market are highly correlated with the extent to which their products are differentiated, *R25* and *R10* may not be placed in *R5A*'s and *R3A*'s market by the 1992 Guidelines' protocol because they are rarely these MPs' closest competitors even though they would conventionally be placed in the same market as *R5A* and *R3A* because the latter are the former's closest competitor a significant number of times or because *R5A* and *R3A* are highly competitive with *R8A* and *R8B*, which are in turn highly competitive with *R25* and *R10*.

Unfortunately, there is no reason to believe that the market that the 1992 Guidelines would construct by adding firms to MP1 will be the same as the market it would construct by adding firms to MP2 even if MP1 and MP2 are put into each other's markets. Moreover, there is also no reason to believe that the competitive positions of any two firms will be symmetric in the sense that the percentage of firm X's customers that MP1 is second-placed to supply will be the same as the percentage of MP1's customers that X is second-placed to supply or that MP1's advantage over the third-placed supplier of those of X's customers MP1 is second-placed to supply will equal X's advantage over the third-placed supplier of those of MP1's customers that X is second-placed to supply. And again, there is no reason to believe that competitive positions are "transitive"—that the facts that MP1 is "highly competitive" in my sense with *R5B* and that *R5B* is highly competitive in my sense with *R3A* imply that MP1 is highly competitive with *R3A*. For these and other reasons, the fact that a given combination would enable the merged firm to profit by raising its prices to MP1's customers 5 % above the prices that MP1 would charge them if no non-combinant would alter its price in response does not guarantee that the combination in question would create a merged firm that could profit by raising its prices to all of the combinant's customers 5 % above the prices the best-placed individual combinant would charge them. However, in many cases, the 1992 Guidelines' market-definition criterion would be satisfied by the smallest combination that would enable the merged firm to profit from raising its prices to all of the combinants' customers 5 % above the prices they would charge them. I will simply assume that this relationship obtains in the case just described.

On this assumption, the market in which the 1992 Guidelines would place MP1 (*R5A*) and MP2 (*R3A*) would contain as well *R8A*, *R5B–C*, *R3B–D*, *R2A–F*, and *R1A–C*—firms that collectively had (5 % + 3 % + 8 % + 2[5 %] + 3[3 %] + 6 [2 %] + 3[1 %] = 50 %) of the conventionally-defined market. Since the 1992 Guidelines' protocol excluded firms from MP1's and MP2's market that had 50 % of the conventional market's sales, the shares of the members of the merged firm's 1992-Guidelines-defined market are twice the shares that those firms would have of the conventional market I originally assumed would be the relevant market. Post-merger, then, the market into which the 1992 Guidelines' protocol would place the MPs would contain two firms with 16 % market shares (one of which is the merged firm), two firms with 10 % market shares, three firms with 6 % market shares, six firms with 4 % market shares, and three firms with 2 % market shares. The post-merger HHI of the MPs' market would therefore equal ($928 = 2[16^2] + 2[10^2] + 3[6^2] + 6[4^2] + 3[2^2]$). This result implies that under the 1992 Guidelines the merger between *R5A* and *R3A* would be irrebuttably presumed not to be anticompetitive (to be lawful). Even though the merger would be found to have increased the MPs' market's HHI by over 100 points (since their shares of the 1992-Guidelines-defined market are 10 % and 6 %), their merger will increase their contribution to this market's HHI by 120 points from $[10^2 + 6^2 = 136]$ to $[16^2 = 256]$, it would not be scrutinized because the post-merger HHI of the market in which it would be found to have taken place was under 1,000.

Clearly, however, the horizontal merger just described would lessen competition substantially. It would raise the merged firm's MP1 division's HNOP to 20 % of MP1's customers above the HNOP MP1 would be able to charge those buyers by an average of 3 % of MP1's average price to these buyers by freeing MP1 from MP2's competition. As we have seen, this immediate increase in the merged firm's prices to MP1's customers might lead to further increases in the merged firm's OCAs and HNOPs by raising the CMC that the merged firm must incur to bid for and supply various remaining rivals' customers, hence the prices these *R*s charge their customers, and hence the CMC these *R*s must incur to bid for and supply the merged firm's customers. Moreover, as we have seen, any increase in the merged firm's OCAs that the merger generates either directly by freeing MP1 from MP2's competition or indirectly by raising an *R*'s CMC will tend to increase the frequency with which the merged firm can obtain OMs naturally. And, of course, although I have not specified the facts that are relevant to the importance of this possibility, the

MP1–MP2 merger could increase the OMs that the merged firm contrives in all the ways that Subsections 4A(1)(A)(i) and (iii) of this chapter listed—*i.e.*, the fact that the relevant market's post-merger HHI is under 1,000 is perfectly compatible with the merger's increasing the COMs the merged firm will obtain from MP1's customers above those MP1 would obtain from them.

Obviously, the MP1–MP2 merger will affect not only the prices MP1's customers are charged (and, derivatively, the prices charged to some of the customers of the merged firm's *R*s that MP1 was second-placed to supply) but also the prices charged to MP2's customers in all the ways it affected the prices charged MP1's customers. Moreover, since the fact that the relevant market's post-merger HHI is under 1,000 is also perfectly compatible with various *R*s' finding it profitable to contrive OMs post-merger, the MP1-MP2 merger may also increase some *R*s' COMs for the various reasons that Sect. 4A (1) (A) (ii) and (iv) of this chapter delineated.

The fact that the "relevant market's" post-merger HHI is under 1,000 is also compatible with the MP1–MP2 merger's reducing QV-investment competition since, for example, it is compatible with either of the following two sets of facts:

(1) (A) absent the merger, one MP or both MPs would be the only firm(s) willing to add to QV investment in the relevant area of product-space,
(B) the merger would critically raise the (Π_D + R) barriers the merged firm faces above those faced by its antecedents by making it profitable for the merged firm to devote to company-consolidation resources its antecedents would have used to create and operate an additional QV investment,
(C) the merger would critically raise the retaliation barriers the merged firm faces above those that confronted its antecedents, and/or
(D) the merger would critically raise the *M* disincentives the merged firm faces above the *M* disincentives the relevant MP or MPs faced and/or

(2) (A) one or more established or potential *R*s of the merged firm are the only firms willing to add a QV investment to the relevant area of product-space pre-merger, and
(B) the merger would critically raise the retaliation barriers the *R*(s) in question faced.

The safeharbor provision of Section 1.51a of the 1992 Guidelines indicates that, when its conditions are fulfilled, the DOJ and FTC will not investigate either the possibility that an MP1–MP2 merger will reduce competition by freeing them from each other's competition or the possibility that it will reduce competition in the other ways just listed—*i.e.*, that the DOJ and FTC will simply presume that these effects will not result or will not be "substantial." There is absolutely no justification for this presumption. The assumption that underlies the safeharbor provision of Section 1.51a—that the percentage of the mergers to which it applies that will lessen competition is extremely low—is almost certainly highly inaccurate.

Similar examples could be used to illustrate my reasons for doubting the accuracy of the competitive-impact predictions that underlie the 1992 Guidelines' two other "safeharbor" provisions: Section 1.51(b)'s placement of horizontal mergers that add fewer than 100 points to the HHI of a market whose post-merger HHI is between 1,000 and 1,800 into a safeharbor, and Section 1.51(c)'s placement of horizontal mergers that generate an increase of fewer than 50 points in the HHI of a market whose post-merger HHI is over 1,800 into a safeharbor. However, considerations of both space and reader patience lead me to leave those examples to your imagination.

Still, I do want to develop an example to illustrate my reasons for believing that—as the 1992 Guidelines appear to acknowledge—it will sometimes be possible to overcome their other strong presumption: Section 1.51(c)'s presumption that mergers that generate an increase of more than 100 points in an HHI that is over 1,800 post-merger lessen competition. For this purpose, I will take a case in which the 1992-Guidelines-defined market will be the same as the conventionally-defined market—a case involving the merger of producers F20 and F5A, which respectively have shares of 20 % and 5 % of an across-the-board-pricing market that also contains one firm (F30) with a 30 % market share, one firm (F15) with a 15 % market share, two firms (F10A–B) with 10 % market shares, and two other firms (F5B–C) with 5 % market shares. The 1992 Guidelines indicate that the DOJ and FTC will rebuttably presume this merger to lessen competition because it will increase the HHI of a 1992-Guidelines-defined market whose post-merger HHI is over 1,800 by more than 100 points—in particular, because it will increase by $(25^2 - [20^2 + 5^2] = 200)$ points the HHI of a market whose post-merger HHI is $(30^2 + 25^2 + 15^2 + 2[10^2] + 2[5^2] = 2{,}000)$.

To see why this merger might not reduce competition, assume the following facts: (1) F30 is second-placed to obtain 50 % of F20's customers, (2) F15 is second-placed to obtain 25 % of F20's customers, (3) F10A is second-placed to obtain 15 % of F20's customers, (4) F10B is second-placed to obtain 10 % of F20's customers, and (5) F5A–C are never second-placed to obtain any of F20's customers. This pattern could reflect the combination of (1) the fact that F20 and the four larger firms just listed produce highly-differentiated goods while F5A–C produce undifferentiated products and (2) the fact that F20's customers prefer differentiated goods (*e.g.*, because they value being seen to be purchasing and using higher-priced goods or because they assume that price and quality are highly correlated and value quality highly). Assume in addition that because many of F30's customers do not have this preference or belief (6)(A) F5A–C are each second-placed to supply 20 % of F30's customers (that are more willing to trade off differentiation for a lower price) and (B) F20, F15, F10A, and F10B are each second-placed to supply 10 % of F30's customers—all of which have a buyer preference for F30's product-variant that is smallest vis-à-vis the product of the respective rival in question. Finally, assume (7) that F5A–C are each second-placed to supply each other's customers 40 % of the time—a fact that could reflect their customers' not valuing product-differentiation very highly.

In such a situation, the Guidelines' market-definition protocol might place F5A into F20's market even though F5A was never F20's closest competitor because (1) F30 was F20's closest competitor often enough for its inclusion in the hypothetical combination to be essential to F20's finding a 5 % price-increase profitable and (2) F5A was sufficiently often (A) F30's closest competitor and (B) the closest competitor of firms that were important close competitors of F30 (F5B and F5C) for its inclusion in F20's market to be essential to F30's finding a 5 % price-increase profitable.

Of course, this simply demonstrates that in the case described a merger that would trigger Section 1.51c's rebuttable presumption of illegality would not induce one of the MPs to raise its prices by increasing its HNOPs by freeing it from the other MP's competition or relatedly by increasing its NOMs or its and its rivals' OCAs by raising each other's relevant CMCs. Nothing in the stated "facts" precludes the merger in question's increasing (1) F20's COMs, (2) increasing F5A's (the other merger partner's) HNOPs, NOMs, and COMs, or (3) raising various remaining *R*s' COMs. On the other hand, nothing guarantees that these various possible negative effects on price competition will take place. Nor does anything guarantee that the merger in question will decrease QV-investment competition if it does not generate any relevant efficiencies or that any efficiencies the merger generates (many of which may be hard to prove) will not increase competition more than the merger would have decreased competition in their absence.

Admittedly, I have given you no more than one, very partial example. However, I hope it suffices to suggest why I believe the general prediction that underlies Section 1.51c's rebuttable presumption of illegality is highly inaccurate.

As already noted, the final set of presumptions that the 1992 Guidelines' General Standards establish are really no presumptions at all. The relevant provisions simply indicate that horizontal mergers that are not covered by the 1992 General Standards' safeharbor provisions or rebuttable-presumption-of-illegality provisions are sufficiently likely to decrease competition for this possibility to deserve consideration but sufficiently likely not to do so for any presumption of illegality to be unwarranted. I consider these basically-non-predictive predictions to be highly accurate. In fact, I believe they are warranted for all horizontal mergers, not just for those for which the 1992 Guidelines make them.

In short, in my judgment, the predictions on which the real presumptions the 1992 Guidelines establish are based are extremely inaccurate. In part, the inaccuracy of the competitive-impact predictions that the 1992 Guidelines base on market-aggregated (HHI-oriented) data reflects the fact that, contrary to the 1992 Guidelines' authors' apparent beliefs,

(1) a firm's share of a 1992-Guidelines-defined market will not normally be a good predictor of the percentage of the market's sales it is second-placed to make,[969]

[969] The 1992 Guidelines acknowledge that a product's market share may not be "reflective of...its relative appeal as a second choice, and hence as a competitive constraint to the first choice." See the 1992 Guidelines at Section 2.211. However, their authors clearly assume that normally one will be able to predict accurately the frequency with which a product is second-placed from its market share.

(2) all firms in a 1992-Guidelines-defined market will not be equally competitive or even nearly-equally-competitive with each other,[970] and
(3) pairs of firms in a 1992-Guidelines-defined market will often not be symmetrically competitive with each other.[971]

However, even if the 1992 Guidelines' implicit assumptions on these issues were far more accurate than I believe, the competitive-impact predictions that the 1992 Guidelines' General Standards reflect would be highly inaccurate.

The conclusion that the HHI-based competitive-impact predictions of the 1992 Guidelines are highly inaccurate should not be surprising to anyone who has read Chap. 6 or Sect. 2 of this chapter. There is no reason to believe that the difference between the market definitions that the 1992 Guidelines generate and the functionally-ideal market definitions Sect. 2 of this chapter assumed traditional analyses employed will make the 1992 Guidelines' General Standards' predictions more accurate than the traditional approach's. Indeed, as Sect. 2 of Chap. 7 showed, the Guidelines' formal market definition and market-definition protocol are far from ideal. There is also no reason to believe that the 1992 Guidelines' HHI-measure of market concentration is sufficiently superior to the traditional four-firm or eight-firm concentration ratio to make the 1992 General Standards' predictions significantly more accurate than the traditional approach's. In fact, absolutely no empirical evidence supports the claim that the HHI measure of concentration is superior, and the theoretical argument for its superiority is far from convincing. Admittedly, (1) unlike traditional concentration measures the HHI does give some weight to the market shares of smaller sellers (that are often described as belonging to the competitive fringe), and (2) such small sellers often make a far greater contribution to the competitiveness of prices than analysts that think that the competitive importance of a seller is proportionate to its market-share would think (because small sellers are frequently second-placed or close-to-second-placed far more often than they are best-placed and are particularly likely in part on that account to undercut contrived oligopolistic prices). However, the HHI also gives inadequate weight to small market shares. Moreover, the imperfection that the HHI measure removes or reduces by giving some weight to the shares of the smallest firms in a market is likely to be small and randomly related to the other imperfections in its measure of market concentration (if that concept is supposed to predict the competitive impact of a horizontal merger). Hence, even if the HHIs' giving some weight to small market shares would make it superior to the traditional measure of concentration if no other imperfections afflicted either its or the traditional measure of concentration, there is no reason to believe that the HHI measure of concentration will be superior to the

[970] The 1992 Guidelines acknowledge that "different products in the market may vary in the degree of their substitutability for one another" and that "individual sellers compete more directly with those rivals selling closer substitutes." *Id.* at Section 2.211, paragraph one. However, their authors clearly underestimate the frequency and extent to which this is the case.

[971] In part, the 1992 Guidelines' failure to recognize the possibility that its market-definition protocol might place MP2 in MP1's market but not place MP1 in MP2's market reflects their authors' failure to appreciate the existence or importance of competitive asymmetries.

traditional measure, given the other imperfections in both measures that yield *ceteris paribus* distortions in their operationalization of the concept of market concentration. Finally, there is no reason to believe that the 1992 Guidelines' HHI "rules" are closer to being ideal HHI rules than the courts' traditional-market-concentration-oriented rules are to being ideal rules of this kind. Both sets of rules seem to have been picked out of a hat. Neither has any theoretical or empirical basis.

(B) The 1992 Guidelines' Analysis of the "Qualifying Factors" Other Than the Condition of Entry, Efficiencies, and the Failing-Company Status of a Merger Partner That Can Reduce the Relevance of the HHI-Related Determinants of a Horizontal Merger's Competitive Impact on Which Their General Standards Focus

The 1992 Horizontal Merger Guidelines, the 1997 Revision of those Guidelines, and the 2006 Commentary all acknowledge that in some circumstances one will not be able to predict the competitive impact of a horizontal merger from its impact on the defined market's HHI and the post-merger HHI of the defined market—that so-called Qualifying Factors (factors other than the merger-induced increase-in-HHI and the post-merger HHI) will have to be taken into account to predict a horizontal merger's impact on competition acceptably accurately. Indeed, all these Government publications' discussions of Qualifying Factors leave the impression that all such factors (including those this subsection ignores) must be taken into account even when the merger-induced increase-in-HHI and post-merger HHI figures for the merger in question would place it into a General Standards' "irrebuttably presumed to be lawful" category.

(i) The 1992 Guidelines' Analysis of the Qualifying Factors Other than the Condition of Entry, Efficiencies, and the Failing-Company Status of a Merger Partner That Can Affect a Merger's Impact on Price Competition in the Defined Market, Given Its Array of QV Investments

According to the 1992 Guidelines, horizontal mergers can reduce price competition both by promoting "coordinated interaction"[972] and by generating "unilateral effects"[973]—in my terminology, respectively by increasing COMs and HNOPs. Surprisingly, the 1992 Guidelines' recognition of these "unilateral effects" represents real progress. Although in one sense economists obviously know better, they have persisted in ignoring the fact that sellers that are not pure monopolists may enjoy OCAs in their dealings with particular buyers[974] and that horizontal mergers (or other business practices) that do not create pure monopolies may

---

[972] See 1992 Guidelines, Section 2.1.

[973] See *id.* at Section 2.2.

[974] For example, as Chapters 10 and 11 revealed, many of the tests for "oligopolistic pricing" and "predatory pricing" that economists and economist-lawyers have proposed assume that the sellers in question have no OCAs.

increase OCAs and HNOPs in ways that have legal significance (should be deemed to reduce competition).[975] The general reaction of economists to the 1984 Guidelines' market-definition protocol (which, basically, the 1992 Guidelines took over) manifested this pattern: in general, economists praised the 1984 Guidelines' market-definition protocol because, in their view, it made a breakthrough in defining markets in terms of a "minimum collusive group."[976]

However, I should point out that, to my mind, the progress that the 1992 Guidelines make in this respect is reduced by the fact that they discuss the possible unilateral effects of horizontal mergers only after discussing the possible impact of a merger on "coordinated interaction." I reach this conclusion for three reasons. First, this organization ignores the fact that a horizontal merger's impact on COMs will be significantly affected by its impact on OCAs. Second, this organization ignores the fact that even if the relevant horizontal mergers' impact on COMs were as big as their impact on OCAs, the legal significance of their impact on COMs might be smaller because, as I indicated both in Chap. 4 and in Sect. 2 of this chapter, it might not be appropriate to count against a horizontal merger any tendency it may have to induce its participants and/or their product-rivals to engage in subsequent illegal behavior. And third, in part for the above two reasons, this organization leaves the impression that the relevant horizontal mergers' direct "unilateral effects" are empirically less important than their effects on "coordinated interaction": I believe the opposite to be the case. In any event, for all these reasons, I will first discuss the 1992 Guidelines' treatment of the factors that affect a horizontal merger's impact on unilateral action (OCAs and HNOPs) and then discuss their treatment of the factors that affect a horizontal merger's impact on coordinated interaction (COMs).

(a) The 1992 Guidelines' Analysis of the Qualifying Factors This Subsection Covers That Can Affect the Unilateral Impact of a Horizontal Merger on Prices

The 1992 Guidelines do recognize that

(1) horizontal mergers can reduce competition unilaterally by increasing the MPs' OCAs by freeing them from each other's competition when they were uniquely-equal-best-placed to supply a given buyer or respectively best-placed and second-placed to supply a given buyer,[977]

---

[975] As Chapter 4 explained, a horizontal merger (or any other business practices) that increases a best-placed seller's OCAs directly by generating efficiencies should not be considered to be anticompetitive on that account. As Chapter 4 argued as well, in my judgment, a horizontal merger whose efficiencies increase the MPs' OCAs not only directly but also indirectly by worsening the competitive-position distribution of one or more of the merged firm's *R*s sufficiently to induce the *R*(s) to exit should also not be held to violate either the Sherman Act or the Clayton Act on this account.

[976] See, *e.g.*, Ian Ayres, *A Private Revolution: Markovits on Markets*, 64 CHI.-KENT L. REV. 861, 864 (1988).

[977] See 1992 Guidelines Section 2.21 and Guidelines' note 21, which is attached to Section 2.21.

(2) the amount by which a horizontal merger will increase the price an individual buyer will have to pay on this account in an individualized-pricing situation equals the advantage the two MPs had over the third-placed supplier of a given buyer that they were uniquely-equal-best-placed to supply or the advantage that the second-placed MP had over the third-placed supplier of a buyer that the MPs were best-placed and second-placed to supply,[978]

(3) the frequency with which this result occurs depends on the frequency with which the MPs are each other's closest competitors for the patronage of a given buyer that no-one else is best-placed to supply,[979] and

(4) one cannot predict the frequency with which this result will obtain from MP-market-share data since "different products in the market may vary in the degree of their substitutability for another."[980]

However, the 1992 Guidelines' discussion of these issues is sometimes misleading and scattered. Thus, in referring to "close substitutes" rather than close competitors, they leave the impression that all that counts in this context is the relevant products' buyer preference advantages—though this impression is somewhat offset by the fact that the 1992 Guidelines must be assuming that the relevant "substitutability" is not "pure" but is at current prices, which presumably reflect the cost of supplying the relevant products. Nevertheless, it is unfortunate that the 1992 Guidelines mention the relevance of cost-differences only in a footnote that deals with situations in which there are no buyer preference advantages.[981] It is also unfortunate that the 1992 Guidelines' only reference to the second proposition listed above is in that footnote.

Moreover, not only is the 1992 Guidelines' articulation of the factors that determine the extent to which horizontal mergers reduce price competition by increasing the MPs' OCAs by freeing them from each other's competition not so clear as it might be, the 1992 Guidelines also qualify their conclusions on this issue incorrectly by stating that horizontal mergers will decrease competition on this account only if and to the extent that repositioning of the non-parties' product-lines to replace the localized competition lost through the merger is unlikely.[982] Although such repositioning will clearly reduce the extent to which a horizontal merger will increase the MPs' OCAs by freeing them from each other's competition and lessen the profits the merger yields them on this account, such repositioning will not reduce to anything like the same extent or perhaps at all the amount by which a horizontal merger reduces Clayton Act competition by injuring the relevant

[978] See *id.* Section 2.21, paragraph two, sentence three. See also *id.* at last sentence of the Guidelines' note 21, which is attached to Section 2.21.

[979] See *id.* at Section 2.21, last sentence. I assume that this sentence's reference to "price rise" really refers to the frequency with which a price-rise will take place on this account and hence to the average price-rise the MPs' customers experience on this account.

[980] See *id.* at Section 2.21, first paragraph, second sentence.

[981] See 1992 Guidelines' note 21.

[982] See *id.* at Section 2.212.

buyers in the relevant way on this account: presumably, any equivalent-dollar gain that the repositioning confers on the buyers that would otherwise have been harmed by the merger's increasing the MPs' OCAs by freeing them from each other's competition will be more or less offset by the equivalent-dollar loss the repositioning imposes on the buyers whose patronage the product that was eliminated by the repositioning was best-placed, second-placed, or perhaps (if contrivance is a possibility) close-to-second-placed to obtain.[983]

In addition, both the 1992 Guidelines and the 2006 DOJ/FTC Commentary on the Horizontal Merger Guidelines suggest that the DOJ and FTC will use a peculiarly-circuitous protocol to determine how often two MPs were respectively best-placed and second-placed to obtain a given buyer's patronage or uniquely-equal-best-placed to obtain a given buyers' patronage:

(1) calculate the "diversion ratio" from one MP to another—"the proportion of the decrease in the quantity of. . .the purchases [of one MP's product] resulting from a small increase in its price that is accounted for by the increase in quantity purchased for the other [MP's] product" and
(2) analyze the implications of that ratio for the unilateral effects of the merger in question taking into account the fact that "[a] merger may produce significant unilateral effects even though a large majority of the substitution away from each merging product goes to non-merging products"—indeed, "even though a non-merging product is the 'closest' substitute for every merging product in the sense that the largest diversion ratio for every product of the merged firm is to a non-merging firm's product."[984]

My point is that the second of these two points, which is clearly correct, implies that one should not collect data on diversion *ratios* at all: although the absolute number of sales that MP1 will lose to MP2 if MP1 raises its prices (*the diversion amount*) is relevant to the merger's unilateral effects, *the diversion ratio* is not. Why should the Agencies predict a merger's unilateral effects by calculating diversion ratios, analyzing in the circumstances in question the connection between the MP1 to MP2 and MP2 to MP1 diversion ratios and the MP1 to MP2 and MP2 to MP1 diversion amounts, and then base their predictions on those diversion amounts? Why not calculate the diversion amounts directly and proceed from there? I have chosen to make this point not only because it is important in itself but also because the 1992 Guidelines contain other analogous "errors"—most importantly in their statement that, when making competitive-impact predictions, one should always use HHI-oriented figures as a "starting point" even when extant conditions require such predictions to be adjusted when, in fact, it would be far more cost-effective to

---

[983] For a discussion of other instances in which analysts have failed to distinguish between the effects of something on a seller's profits and its competitive impact, see Richard S. Markovits, *Monopolistic Competition, Second Best, and* THE ANTITRUST PARADOX: *A Review Article*, 77 MICH. L. REV. 567, 635–39 (1979).

[984] See 2006 Commentary at 27–28.

ignore the HHI-related data altogether and generate predictions directly from the non-HHI-related facts that make predictions based solely on HHI-related facts inaccurate. The next subsection will explain this point in more detail.

The 1992 Guidelines' discussion of the non-HHI factors that may yield unilateral effects is also deficient in that it ignores in individualized-pricing situations the ways in which horizontal mergers that increase the MPs' OCAs when they were best-placed and second-placed or uniquely-equal-best-placed pre merger (or, for that matter, that increases the MPs' prices by raising their NOMs and COMs) may increase some *R*s' OCAs by raising the MPs' CMCs. Indeed, as we saw, any such increase in the *R*s' OCAs will in turn raise the MPs' OCAs by causing the *R*s to raise their prices to the customers they are best-placed to supply and thereby raising the CMCs the *R*s will have to incur to charge given lower prices to the MPs' customers. The 1992 Guidelines also ignore the across-the-board counterpart to this CMC possibility—the tendency of any OCA-increase-related increase in the MPs' across-the-board HNOPs and prices to increase the across-the-board HNOPs of their *R*s and thereby produce a cycle of feedbacks to the HNOPs of the MPs and their *R*s—as well as the possibility that a horizontal merger in an across-the-board-pricing market may increase the HNOPs of the merged firm and its *R*s by enabling them to change the sequence in which they announce their prices.

The 1992 Guidelines' discussion of the non-contrivance-related determinants of the prices charged in any area of product-space given the amount of QV investment it contains also ignores the fact that firms can obtain oligopolistic margins naturally—*i.e.*, ignores all the determinants of the ability of the merged firm and its *R*s to obtain NOMs and all the determinants of the size of the OMs they can obtain naturally. (I admit that NOM effects may not be correctly characterized as unilateral even if they also cannot be properly said to manifest changes in coordinated conduct.)

Of course, virtually all these omissions make the 1992 Guidelines' account of the various ways in which horizontal mergers can generate pricing effects without affecting the extent of "oligopolistic cooperation" in the sense of contrivance partial. Not surprisingly, the 1992 Guidelines do not consider the possibility that horizontal mergers may yield unilateral effects by changing the value of any of those determinants of the magnitude of a firm's (HNOP + NOM) figure their discussions of such determinants ignores.

The "unilateral effects" section of the 1992 Guidelines also ignores the tendency of any static marginal efficiencies that the merger under investigation generates to reduce the number and average size of the OCAs of the MPs' *R*s[985] and thereby to set up a cycle of CMC-related reductions in the MPs' and *R*s' OCAs, HNOPs, and prices. This omission would be inconsequential if the 1992 Guidelines' section on

[985] As I indicated in Chapter 4 and Section 2 of this chapter, the tendency of any such efficiencies to increase the MPs' OCAs in their relations with customers one of them was best-placed to supply pre merger or to make an MP best-placed when it was not pre merger (to give it an OCA when it generally was at a disadvantage) is legally irrelevant.

efficiencies took up this issue, but the efficiency section makes no mention of this possibility—indeed, as we shall see, does not specify any of the ways in which any merger-generated efficiency may increase competition.

Finally, I want to report and make nine comments on the purportedly-more-concrete positions the 1992 Guidelines take on the probable unilateral effects of horizontal mergers. In the confirming words of Section 2 of the 2006 DOJ/FTC Commentary on the Horizontal Merger Guidelines:

> Section 2.21 [of the 1992 Horizontal Merger Guidelines] provides that significant unilateral effects are likely with differentiated products when the combined market share of the merging firms exceeds 35 % and other market characteristics indicate that market share is a reasonable proxy for the relevant appeal of the merging products as second choices as well as first choices. Section 2.2.2 provides that significant unilateral effects are likely with undifferentiated products when the combined market share of the merging firms exceeds 35 % and other market characteristics indicate that non-merging firms would not expand output sufficiently to frustrate an effort to reduce total market output.

Here are my comments. First, although I agree that mergers between rival producers of differentiated products with combined market shares of more than 35 % will have significant unilateral effects in markets in which prices are set on an individualized basis if (1) the firms' market shares indicate the percentage of buyers they are second-placed to supply (as well as the percentage of buyers they are best-placed to supply), (2) they are second-placed to supply the same percentage of the customers of all firms placed in the market in question, and (3) the average advantage each MP has over the third-placed suppliers of the other MP's customers when the former MP is second-places is substantial, this conclusion may not be justified if the second and/or third of the three conditions just listed (which the 1992 Guidelines do not articulate) are not satisfied since, in such situations, a merger between two firms in the same 1992-Guidelines-defined market (if one defines that market to satisfy the Guidelines' formal definition as opposed to using the Guideline's protocol to define it) that have a combined market share over 35 % will not have significant unilateral effects if (1) the sum of the MPs' market shares is far higher than the percentage of the buyers in the relevant market they are second-placed to supply, (2) the percentage of the MPs' customers that each is second-placed to supply is far lower than the percentage of all of their respective rivals' customers each is second placed to supply, and/or (3) the average advantage each MP has over the third-placed supplier of the other MP's customers when the former MP is second-placed is very small.

Second, on my understanding of "substantial," when all three of the above conditions are completely satisfied and in many situations in which one or more of them are only partially satisfied, it would be correct to say that mergers between rival, individualized-pricing producers of differentiated products whose combined market share is far lower than 35 % will generate *substantial* negative unilateral effects (if they do not generate significant positive unilateral effects by yielding static marginal efficiencies and neither of the MPs is a failing company).

Third, although I admit that condition (2) in the list my first comment delineated is not so important in across-the-board-pricing contexts (since the feedback effects generated by changes in across-the-board prices are more substantial than the CMC-related feedback effects that occur in individualized-pricing contexts), conditions (1) and (3) in the list in question are equally important in across-the-board as in individualized-pricing contexts.

Fourth, in my judgment, many mergers between across-the-board-pricing producers of differentiated products whose combined market shares does not exceed 35 % will generate substantial negative unilateral effects if the mergers do not yield counteracting static marginal efficiencies or involve a failing company.

Fifth, a point on which the next subsection will focus: given the importance of conditions (1), (2), and (3) and the reality that they are often far from fully satisfied in markets in which differentiated products are produced, it will not be cost-effective to predict the unilateral effects of a horizontal merger by defining markets, calculating the MPs' market shares, basing an initial prediction of the relevant unilateral effects on the MPs' combined market shares, investigating the extent to which conditions (1), (2), and (3) are satisfied, and adjusting one's initial prediction to reflect the extent to which they are not satisfied. In individualized-pricing contexts, the cost-effective approach is to collect the facts to which conditions (1), (2), and (3) relate—how often the MPs are best-placed and second-placed or uniquely-equal-best-placed to supply a relevant buyer and, in those situations in which the MPs do occupy such positions, what is the OCA of the second-placed MP or the uniquely-equal-best-placed MPs over the third-placed supplier of the buyer in question—and to base one's predictions of the merger's unilateral effects directly on those facts. And in across-the-board-pricing contexts, the cost-effective approach is to collect not only the facts one should collect to predict the unilateral effects that a horizontal merger in an individualized-pricing market will have but also the facts that relate to the possible impact of the merger on the sequence in which relevant sellers announce their prices and to base one's prediction of the merger's unilateral effects directly on these two sets of facts.

Sixth, although I agree that the merger of rival producers of undifferentiated products whose combined market shares exceed 35 % will probably yield substantial unilateral effects if (1) remaining rivals could not expand their outputs sufficiently to prevent the merged firm from raising prices by reducing output and (2) one or both MPs could expand their outputs substantially pre-merger, such a merger will not generate substantial unilateral effects if the second of these two conditions (which the 1992 Guidelines do not articulate) is not satisfied.

Seventh, on my understanding of "substantial" in this context, if the above two conditions are fulfilled, mergers of producers of undifferentiated products whose combined market share is far lower than 35 % will generate *substantial* negative unilateral effects if they do not yield significantly-offsetting static marginal efficiencies or involve a failing company.

Eighth, given the importance of the two conditions delineated in the sixth point and the fact that they are often far from fully satisfied, it will not be cost-effective to predict the unilateral effects of mergers in markets in which undifferentiated products are produced by defining the relevant market, calculating the MPs' market shares, basing an initial estimate on the MPs' combined market shares, investigating the extent to which the two conditions in question are satisfied, and adjusting one's initial prediction of the merger's unilateral effects to reflect the extent to which those conditions are not satisfied: the cost-effective way to proceed is to calculate the sales of the MPs and the extent to which the two conditions are satisfied and generate a prediction from those figures directly.

Ninth and finally, in light of the fifth and eighth comments I have just made, I take some solace from the DOJ and FTC's statement in the first sentence of the last paragraph of Section 1 of their 2006 Commentary on the [1992] Horizontal Merger Guidelines that "market concentration may be unimportant under a unilateral effects theory of competitive harm." I just wish they would extend this statement to include MP-market-share data and, as I will recommend in the next subsection, abandon their market-oriented (HHI-oriented) approach to horizontal-merger competitive-impact prediction altogether.

In short, although the 1992 Guidelines' discussion of the non-market-aggregated market factors that affect the "unilateral effects" of the relevant horizontal mergers represents real progress, it is far from perfect. However, for a balanced assessment, some historical perspective is required. Starting in the late 1960s, I tried without success to get the DOJ and FTC or anyone else to recognize and think about the unilateral effects of horizontal mergers. From that perspective, the 1992 Guidelines' and 2006 Commentary's treatments of these effects represent an important step forward.

(b) The 1992 Guidelines' Analysis of the Qualifying Factors This Subsection Considers That Can Affect the Impact of a Horizontal Merger on Coordinated Conduct

I turn now to the 1992 Guidelines' discussion of the non-HHI factors that affect the COMs a market's constituent firms obtain and the impact that a horizontal merger between two of its constituent firms will have on those COMs. The first point I want to make in this connection is partly expositional but does have some substantive implications as well: with one exception (the possibility that a horizontal merger may increase the profitability of contrivance by eliminating a "maverick-firm"[986]), the Guidelines focus exclusively on the factors that affect the determinants of the profitability of contrived oligopolistic pricing—*i.e.*, never focus explicitly on how a horizontal merger can affect those factors. Clearly, the appropriate approach would have been to discuss both (1) the factors that determine the pre merger profitability of contrived oligopolistic pricing for the MPs and their *R*s and (2) the factors that affect the impact of a horizontal merger on the determinants of the profitability of such pricing for the MPs and their *R*s. However, having made this basic objection, I will now focus on the points that the 1992 Guidelines, the DOJ/FTC 1997 Revision of the

[986] See 1992 Guidelines, Section 2.12, fifth (last) paragraph.

1992 Horizontal Merger Guidelines, and the DOJ/FTC 2006 Commentary on the revised Horizontal Merger Guidelines make about the contrived-oligopolistic-pricing-related issues they do address.

I will begin by discussing their overview of the general determinants of the profitability of "coordinated interaction" and then discuss their analysis of the more specific determinants of the profitability of such pricing. According to the 1992 Guidelines, the probability that a group of sellers will find it profitable to engage in coordinated interaction will depend on their ability to establish the "terms of coordination," the presence of firms that can realize substantial immediate returns by undercutting and/or can protect themselves against immediate retaliation, and the "ability [of the possible contrivers] to detect and punish deviations that would undermine the coordinated interaction."[987] Section 2.1 of the DOJ/FTC 1997 Revision of the 1992 Horizontal Merger Guidelines elaborates on those Guidelines' account of these determinants in a number of ways—*inter alia*, by stating that

(1) the extent of coordinated interaction will be affected by "[t]he availability of key information concerning market conditions, transactions and individual competitors; the extent of firm and product heterogeneity; pricing or market practices typically employed by firms in the market; the characteristics of buyers and sellers; and the characteristics of typical transactions";
(2) "[i]t is likely that market conditions are conducive to coordinated interaction when the firms in the market have previously engaged in express collusion and when the salient conditions in the market have not changed appreciably since the most recent such incident. Previous express collusion in another geographic market will have the same weight when the salient characteristics of that other market at the time of collusion are comparable to those in the relevant market. . ..";
(3) "reaching terms of coordination may be facilitated by product or firm homogeneity and. . .by standardization of pricing or product variables on which firms could compete";
(4) "[k]ey information about rival firms and the market may also facilitate reaching terms of coordination";
(5) "if key information about specific transactions or individual price or output levels is available routinely to competitors, it may be difficult for a firm to deviate secretly";
(6) "[i]f orders for the product are frequent, regular and small relative to the total output of a firm in the market, it may be difficult for the firm to deviate in a substantial way without the knowledge of rivals and without the opportunity of rivals to react";
(7) "[i]f demand or cost fluctuations are relatively infrequent and small, deviations may be relatively easy to deter";

[987] See *id.* at Section 2.1, paragraphs 1 and 2.

(8) "[w]here large buyers likely would engage in long-term contracting so that the sales covered by such contracts can be large relative to the total output of a firm in the market, firms may have an incentive to deviate"; and
(9) "a firm is more likely to be a maverick the greater is its excess or divertible capacity in relation to its sales or total capacity, and the lower are its direct and opportunity costs of expanding sales in the relevant market."

Section 2 of the U.S. DOJ/FTC 2006 Commentary on the 1992 Horizontal Merger Guidelines makes only one relevant additional point, which reiterates the Agencies' belief in the usefulness of market-aggregated figures. The additional point is that "the Agencies not only assess whether the market conditions for viable coordination are present, but also ascertain specifically whether and how the merger would affect market conditions to make successful coordination after the merger significantly more likely." The reiteration is that "[t]he number of rival firms remaining after a merger, their market shares, and market concentration are relevant factors in determining the effect of a merger on the likelihood of coordinated interaction."

Four points need to be made about these statements. First, they focus on contrived oligopolistic pricing by groups, presumably operating in across-the-board-pricing situations—*i.e.*, they ignore contrivance by an individualized pricer. Second, and relatedly, they assume that contrivance always involves agreements—*i.e.*, they ignore the possibility that one or more sellers may be able to obtain COMs exclusively by threatening retaliation. This second point is related to the first because, in across-the-board-pricing situations, the seller that is charging contrived oligopolistic prices to its own customers automatically charges them to its rivals' customers as well—*i.e.*, automatically reciprocates to its rivals' collaboration. Only in individualized-pricing contexts is the distinction between retaliatory and reciprocatory price-moves and hence the distinction between contrivance through agreement and contrivance exclusively through threat viable. Third, and again relatedly for the same reason, the 1992 Guidelines' general description assumes that responses to non-cooperation will always involve retaliation as opposed to the withdrawal of reciprocation. Fourth and finally, the statements fail to distinguish two components of the ability of a firm to "detect. . .deviations": its ability to determine that it has been undercut (undermined) and its ability to identify its undercutter (underminer).

I will now analyze the various non-HHI factors that determine the profitability of contrivance (and the impact of a horizontal merger on that profitability) by affecting the cost and efficaciousness of the necessary communications, the number of firms that need to be deterred, the ability of the potential contrivers to determine whether they have been undercut (undermined), the ability of the potential contrivers to identify their undercutter (underminer), and the cost to a potential contriver of deterring deviations by punishing undercutters (underminers) and/or rewarding collaborators. (The discussion that follows will omit "underminer" and its cognates.)

The DOJ/FTC's discussions of the costs of the necessary communication focus exclusively on the problems that can arise because of product heterogeneity or firm heterogeneity (for example, firm differences that relate to their degree of vertical integration or whether they produce complements to the relevant product). I suspect that it will be more difficult to arrange a price-fixing agreement when cost and quality vary from product to product—*e.g.*, when some products represent low cost-quality combinations and others, high cost-quality combinations. However, the DOJ/FTC's claim that this problem relates to product and firm heterogeneity is imprecise. Although this difficulty cannot arise if products are homogeneous (from the buyers' perspective), its importance is not highly correlated with product heterogeneity since a set of strongly-differentiated products may all have the same cost and quality. I should add that, to the extent that the 1992 Guidelines, their 1997 Revision, and the 2006 Commentary give the impression that product heterogeneity disfavors the profitability of contrived oligopolistic pricing on balance, their argument does not justify this conclusion. As we have seen, product heterogeneity affects the profitability of contrived oligopolistic pricing in a number of ways other than by complicating the required agreement, and its net effect on the profitability of such pricing clearly varies from situation to situation and defies generalization. Thus,

(1) to the extent that the products in a heterogeneous-product market (including geographic as well as material or image heterogeneity) are not equally competitive with each other (or that such heterogeneity and such inequalities are positively correlated), heterogeneity will tend to increase the profitability of contrived oligopolistic pricing by reducing the percentage of the "market's" products and producers for which undercutting would be inherently profitable and hence

   (A) the number and cost of the necessary communications,
   (B) the cost of identifying the undercutter (by decreasing the number of suspects), and
   (C) in across-the-board-pricing contexts, the probability that retaliation will be rendered ineffective by the "public good" character of abstentions from undercutting from the perspective of the group of potential undercutters;

(2) to the extent that product heterogeneity and inequalities of competition between various in-market product-pairs are positively correlated, product heterogeneity will increase the profitability of across-the-board contrivance

   (A) by increasing the ability of an undercut group to coordinate their retaliation by reducing the number of members of the relevant group and
   (B) by increasing the benefits that individualized-pricing contrivers can convey to their collaborators by reciprocating to their cooperation (by increasing the frequency with which and amount by which they are their collaborators' closest competitors);

(3) to the extent that product heterogeneity is positively correlated with the potential contriver's OCAs, it will reduce the profitability of contrivance by increasing the safe profits that contrivance puts at risk and increasing the probability that the seller in question will be able to obtain OMs naturally, though these

effects will be somewhat offset by the tendency of high OCAs to increase the profitability of contrivance by increasing the credibility of the potential contriver's threats and promises by increasing the profits it must protect against undercutting (if the high OCAs do not reduce the profits it puts at risk by contriving as a result of their tendency to reduce the frequency with which it attempts to contrive an OM); and

(4) to the extent that product heterogeneity is positively correlated with the potential undercutters' OCAs, it will increase the profitability of contrivance by increasing the harm that an undercut contriver can inflict on its undercutter by price-retaliation at any given cost to itself.

The Agencies correctly point out that it will be easier for potential contrivers to reach agreement on the "terms of coordination" when product-unit size is standardized and when all firms use the same type of pricing (make only per-unit charges, charge only lump-sum fees, or mix these two types of charges). The DOJ and FTC do not explain this point, but I do not think it requires explanation.

By way of contrast, it is regrettable that the DOJ and FTC fail to explain their claim that differences in the extent to which the relevant producers are vertically integrated or produce goods that are complementary to the products in question will make it more difficult to establish terms of coordination. In particular, this failure is regrettable because I think both of these claims are exaggerated. Admittedly, when potential contrivers produce intermediate products, the fact that one or more but not all of them are vertically integrated will make it necessary for them to control the downstream prices of the integrated firms as well as the price of the intermediate product that they all produce. But I really do not believe that the necessity of exercising such control will cause significant additional problems, and, in any case, any problem that does arise on this account will not be exacerbated by differences in the extent to which the "market's" firms or the relevant firms are vertically integrated. I also do not believe that significant problems will arise because some but not all of the potential contrivers produce complements to the goods whose prices they want to "fix." Admittedly, sellers may have valid reasons to want to control the quality of the complements their customers use together with their product[988] and to coordinate the pricing of complementary goods.[989] However, sellers that do not themselves produce the relevant complement(s) are virtually as likely to want on those accounts to use tie-ins involving complements as are sellers that do produce the complements themselves. I therefore do not think that differences in the extent to which the potential contrivers produce complements will complicate the process of coordination, though the need of the potential conspirators to control the quality and prices of the complements their customers use may make it more difficult for them to agree on terms of coordination.

---

[988] See Chapter 14 *infra* and Richard S. Markovits, *Tie-ins, Reciprocity, and the Leverage Theory (the Non-Leverage Functions of Tying Agreements)*, 76 YALE L. J. 1397, 1459–61 (1967).

[989] See *id.* at 1434–42 and Chapter 14 *infra*.

The DOJ/FTC discussion of the factors that determine the cost of the communications necessary to practice contrived oligopolistic pricing is also deficient in that it ignores the possibility that in some cases the necessary communications may be made simply by charging an oligopolistic price. Correlatively, the DOJ and FTC ignore the factors that affect the ability of firms to communicate in this way and the factors that affect a horizontal merger's impact on the ability of the merged firm relative to that of the MPs to use this cheap method of communication—*viz.*, whether the merger will create a company with a better reputation for estimating its HNOPs and NOMs accurately and a stronger reputation for practicing contrived oligopolistic pricing.

In short, the 1992 Guidelines, 1997 Guidelines Revision, and 2006 Commentary mis-specify some of the factors that are relevant to the cost of the communications that are essential to contrived oligopolistic pricing, fail to justify the impression they leave of the on-balance effect of one of the factors they discuss (product heterogeneity) on the profitability of contrivance, exaggerate the importance of some relevant factors that they do discuss, and ignore other factors that are relevant in this context.

The second general determinant of the profitability of contrived oligopolistic pricing that the 1992 Guidelines, the 1997 Revision, and the 2006 Commentary all discuss is the presence of "maverick-firms—firms that have a greater economic incentive to deviate from the terms of coordination than do most of their rivals."[990] The DOJ and FTC are correct in stressing the importance of this factor. They are also correct in pointing out that the disruptive character of a firm is likely to increase with "its excess or divertable capacity in relation to its sales or its total capacity,"[991] though the "in relation to" part of the factor in question is relevant only in across-the-board-pricing contexts. However, the 1992 Guidelines fail to indicate how the Agencies will determine whether a merger partner is a maverick—whether they will base their conclusions solely on the firm's historic conduct or whether they will also take into consideration whether the firm's competitive-position array makes it profitable for the firm to be non-cooperative. Concomitantly, the Guidelines make no effort to determine the attributes of a firm's competitive-position array that will make it profitable for it to be a maverick—*e.g.*, to undercut or undermine its rivals' contrived oligopolistic prices. My analysis implies that such maverick conduct will be more profitable for a firm the higher its ratio of (second-placed and close-to-second-placed competitive positions) to (best-placed competitive positions) and the lower its average (OCA + NOM) sum when it is best-placed in individualized-pricing contexts or its average (HNOP + NOM − MC) sum in its relations with those buyers it is best-placed to supply in across-the-board-pricing contexts. I suspect that on both these accounts maverick behavior will tend to be more profitable for small sellers that

[990] See the 1992 Guidelines, Section 2.12, last paragraph.

[991] *Id.* at Section 2.12, paragraph 2.

produce relatively-undifferentiated products as members of the so-called "competition fringe."

The third determinant of the profitability of contrived oligopolistic pricing that the 1992 Guidelines, 1997 Revision, and 2006 Commentary discuss is the ability of possible undercutters to protect themselves against short-run price-retaliation in the market in which it has been undercutting its rivals by making sales equal to their capacity at the cut price. As the DOJ and FTC point out, this ability will be greater if the market contains one or more large buyers whose needs could occupy the capacity of an individual seller. However, even though an undercutter will be able to protect itself against short-run price-retaliation against its operations in the market in question by entering into a sufficiently-substantial and long-term supply-contract with such a buyer, one should not exaggerate the extent of the protection it will thereby secure: if the undercutter is operating in other geographic or product markets, those victims of its undercutting that are operating in these other markets as well will be able to retaliate against it there, and, even if it is not, the victims of an undercutter will often have long memories—will retaliate against it in the market in which it engaged in undercutting by cutting their prices later on to buyers it would like to supply after the expiration of the contract that protected the undercutter at first.

As I have already indicated, the 1992 Guidelines do not explicitly distinguish the fourth general determinant of the profitability of contrived oligopolistic pricing—the ability of the potential contriver to determine whether it has been undercut (lost a sale to a competitive inferior)—from the fifth—the ability of a potential contriver to identify its undercutter. Nevertheless, a number of the more specific factors they discuss are relevant to a seller's ability to detect the fact that it has lost a sale as a result of undercutting rather than through a spontaneous change in the relevant buyer's taste (or an acceptable change in the location of a rival in the relevant area of product-space). Thus, information about specific transactions or about the price and output levels of particular sellers may help a contriver determine whether it has been undercut by an aggressive rival (particularly in individualized-pricing contexts, in which such information may not be public).[992] Similarly, sellers will be more able to determine that they have been undercut the more "frequently, regular and small" "orders. . .[are] relative to the total output of a firm in a market,"[993] at least to the extent that these factors correlate positively and strongly with the number of buyers in the market or the number of truly-separate purchase-decisions buyers make. As we have seen, such information is relevant because, through the law of large numbers, it affects how certain individual sellers will be about the percentage of sales to their former customers they will retain, the percentage of their rivals' former sales to their rivals' customers they will secure,

[992] For a discussion of inter-seller information-exchanges that can provide sellers with information that would not otherwise be available to them because it is not public and the various judicial opinions that have analyzed their legality, see Chap. 10 *supra*.

[993] See the 1992 Guidelines, Section 2.12, paragraph 2 and Chap. 4.

and the percentage of new buyers whose patronage they will obtain if no-one engages in undercutting—*i.e.*, to their ability to infer undercutting from circumstantial evidence relating to these percentages. And again, sellers will be more able to determine that they have been undercut from such circumstantial evidence if "demand or cost fluctuations are relatively infrequent and small,"[994] at least to the extent that these factors are correlated with the extent of difficult-to-detect changes in circumstances that leave a seller uncertain about the three percentages in question that would result if no-one engages in undercutting. I should say, however, that although the 1992 Guidelines do refer to these factors, I doubt that their authors realized their connection to the ability of firms to determine that they have lost a sale to an inferior (that has been undercutting them). In part, my skepticism relates to the fact that the factors the 1992 Guidelines, the 1997 Revision, and the 2006 Commentary specify are not really the factors that are relevant in these contexts and, in part, it reflects the fact that the DOJ and FTC state that these factors are relevant to the ability of sellers to distinguish undercutting-based price fluctuations from price fluctuations that have other causes or to the general ability of sellers to deter deviations.[995]

The DOJ and FTC's treatment of the factors that affect a contriver's ability to identify its undercutter is equally deficient. They do point out the obvious fact that information on specific sellers' prices and outputs will facilitate such identification.[996] However, they ignore the importance of inter-product-pair competitiveness-differences that reduce the percentage of firms in the market that would find undercutting inherently profitable (that are either second-placed or worse-than-second-placed by a smaller margin than the COM being sought). They also ignore the relevance of evidence about (1) the percentage of a contriver's customers that particular rivals are second-placed or close-to-second-placed to obtain and (2) circumstantial evidence relating to the expected and actual percentages of the contriver's customers that each particular rival was well-placed to steal, the percentages of each particular rival's customers that the contriver was well-placed to obtain, and the percentage of new buyers that the contriver and each particular rival were well-placed to secure.

The 1992 Guidelines, 1997 Revision, and 2006 Commentary also suggest that their authors understood only one of the two ways in which the final factor that they mention is relevant to the profitability of contrived oligopolistic pricing. Thus, although these publications point out that the fact that contrived oligopolistic pricing was practiced in the relevant market in the past is good evidence of its being profitable post-merger,[997] they do not indicate that a particular seller's past contrivance is likely to increase the profitability of its engaging in contrivance in the future both by making its anticompetitive threats and offers more

---

[994] *Id.*

[995] *Id.* at paragraph 3.

[996] *Id.* at paragraph 2.

[997] *Id.* at Section 2.1, paragraph 4.

credible and by increasing the likelihood that it will be able to communicate its contrived oligopolistic intentions cheaply simply by charging an oligopolistic price (though, admittedly, these effects will be offset to the extent that the Agencies or private plaintiffs are more likely to sue contrivers that have contrived in the past, judges and juries are more likely to convict such firms, and/or judges and juries are likely to impose harsher penalties on them or require them to pay higher damage-awards).

The 1992 Guidelines', 1997 Revision's, and 2006 Commentary's discussion of the factors that affect the profitability of contrived oligopolistic pricing is also deficient in that it totally ignores the determinants of (1) the amount of benefits that an individualized-pricing contriver can confer on its cooperative potential undercutters by reciprocating to their cooperation, (2) the harm-inflicted to loss-incurred ratio for different amounts of harm that an individualized pricer can inflict on its undercutters by cutting its individualized prices to their customers, (3) the ability of a group of across-the-board contrivers to maximize the cost-effectiveness of their price-retaliation against an undercutter that has hurt them all, (4) the extent to which a group of potential undercutters can avoid undercutting that (because of the retaliation or abandonment of contrivance it will generate) would be against their joint interest, and (5) the ability of contrivers to retaliate by targeting advertising on their undercutters' customers, cutting prices in outlets that are closest to their undercutters' outlets, and/or locating new QV investments closer to their undercutters' operations.

A final point before concluding this section. As I indicated earlier, the 1992 Guidelines and their 1997 Revision both correctly state that evidence that the MPs and their *R*s have engaged in contrived oligopolistic pricing in the past favors the conclusion that such pricing is profitable for them in the present as well (though as the Guidelines recognize, one must take account of changes in relevant conditions before reaching any final conclusion on this issue). However, the 1992 Guidelines and their 1997 Revision both seem to assume that, whenever contrived oligopolistic pricing is profitable pre merger in the market in which a proposed horizontal merger would take place, the consummation of that merger would increase the profitability of such contrivance and presumably the amount of OMs the MPs and their *R*s contrive. For reasons that Sect. 2 of this chapter delineated, this latter conclusion is highly contestable: although, on balance, there may be reason to believe that horizontal mergers will tend to increase the profitability of contrived oligopolistic pricing to the merged firm's *R*s, I suspect that, if anything, such mergers will tend to reduce the profitability of contrived oligopolistic pricing to the merged firm relative to its profitability to the MPs.

In short, the DOJ and FTC's discussion of "coordinated interaction" hardly focuses at all on the ways in which horizontal mergers may increase the profitability of contrived oligopolistic pricing, mis-specifies several determinants of the profitability of such pricing, misanalyzes the relevance of some of the factors it indicates do affect the profitability of such pricing, gives a misleading impression of the overall effect of some factors on the profitability of contrived oligopolistic pricing, and totally ignores some general and a substantial number of specific determinants of the profitability of contrived oligopolistic pricing.

(ii) The 1992 Guidelines' Conclusions About the Cost-Effective Way to Take Account of the Non-HHI Qualifying Factors Other Than Conditions of Entry, Efficiencies, and the Failing-Company Status of a Merger Partner That They Admit Reduce the Relevance of the HHI-Related Factors on Which the General Standards Focus to the Impact of the Merger on Price Competition

The 1992 Horizontal Merger Guidelines, their 1997 Revision, and the 2006 Commentary claim that the most-cost-effective way for the DOJ and FTC to take account of the Qualifying Factors that reduce the relevance of the HHI figures on which the General Standards focus (as well as of entry, efficiencies, and [business] failure) when analyzing the competitive impact and hence legality of horizontal mergers that fall outside their safeharbor provisions is to use the HHI figure as "a starting point" and then "assess the other [non-HHI-oriented] market factors that pertain to competitive effects as well as entry, efficiency and failure"[998] to see how their initial prediction should be adjusted. I think that this proposal is fundamentally misguided: in those cases in which qualifying factors must be considered (all or virtually all cases in my judgment), the Qualifying-Factor analysis should be *substituted for*, not *combined with*, the General Standards' HHI-oriented analysis.

The preceding conclusion is extremely important, not only in itself but also because its justification reveals why, even if antitrust markets could be defined non-arbitrarily, no antitrust-market-oriented approach to horizontal-merger competitive-impact prediction could be cost-effective. For this reason, I want to articulate at some length two justifications for my conclusion that the fact that qualifying factors must be taken into account when their magnitudes deviate from their "normal" values actually implies that not only in such uses but in all cases an exclusively-non-market-oriented qualifying-factor-based approach to predicting the competitive impact of horizontal mergers will be cost-effective.

The first justification is in one sense negative: it focuses on what the Agencies or anyone else would have to demonstrate to justify the conclusion that the most-cost-effective way to analyze the competitive impact of a horizontal merger is to combine an (initial) HHI-oriented approach with a qualifying-factor-oriented initial-conclusion-adjustment analysis—*i.e.*, it focuses on the reality that no such demonstration has ever been provided. To prove that some variant of the Agencies' "combination" protocol could be cost-effective, either the Agencies or someone else must

(1) (A) identify the non-market-aggregated parameters that the Agencies acknowledge will require their market-aggregated-parameter-based competitive-impact predictions to be adjusted if those parameters' magnitudes deviate from their "normal" values and (B) identify the normal magnitudes of the non-market-aggregated parameters in question,

[998] *Id.* at Section 2.0.

(2) state and provide a theoretical and/or empirical justification for the conclusion that would be warranted about the net competitive impact that all horizontal mergers associated with each possible combination of post-merger-HHI and merger-induced increase-in-HHI figures would have if the relevant non-market-aggregated parameters had their normal magnitudes, and
(3) state and provide a theoretical and/or empirical justification for the conclusions that are warranted about the ways in which the competitive impact of all horizontal mergers associated with each particular combination of post-merger-HHI and merger-induced increase-in-HHI figures will vary with all possible sets of deviations in the magnitudes of the various relevant non-market-aggregated parameters from their normal magnitudes.

Clearly no-one has executed any of these analyses.

The second justification for my conclusion is in one sense more positive: it explains at least some of the reasons for doubting that anyone could make the factual demonstrations necessary to establish the cost-effectiveness of the Agencies' combination-protocol. The first reason is that there is no theoretical or empirical basis for the belief that each pair of HHI-related figures has a normal implication for the likely competitive impact of a horizontal merger. Indeed, there is every theoretical reason to believe the contrary. Thus, a given pre-merger HHI figure can be generated by an infinite number of market-share distributions, a given merger-generated increase-in-HHI figure can also be generated by an infinite set of MP-market-share combinations, and a given market-share distribution can be associated with wildly-different distributions of OCAs, wildly-different distributions of NOMs, and wildly-different distributions of COMs.

The second positive reason for rejecting the preceding argument for the cost-effectiveness of the Agencies' combination-protocol is the incorrectness of its premise that, when the Qualifying Factors must be taken into account, the HHI figures on which the General Standards focus continue to have some predictive power. Assume, for example, that MP1 has a 20 % market share and that the 1992 Guidelines assume that this implies that MP1 will be second-placed to supply 20 % of MP2's customers. The non-market-aggregated factors will not be factors that indicate that, although the HHI-relevant-data continues to be relevant, in this case MP1's market share will "overstate" by 25 % the percentage of MP2's customers MP1 is second-placed to supply. Instead, the non-market-aggregated factors will be market-research or buyer-behavior-based data that reveal that the HHI-related data is not relevant at all—that indicate directly that MP1 is MP2's closest competitor for only 15 % of the buyers MP2 is best-placed to supply.

Or assume that of the ten firms the 1992 Guidelines place within a given individualized-pricing market only four would be in a position to undercut or undermine MP1's contrived oligopolistic price, not all ten as the 1992 Guidelines normally assume. This fact would be relevant to the profitability of contrived oligopolistic pricing because it affects the cost of the necessary communications and the cost of identifying any undercutter. In this case as well, the relevant competitive-position data will not indicate that the HHI-related data is less relevant than it normally would be and that any conclusions derived from it must be adjusted to take the non-HHI-related data into account. Instead, the non-HHI-related data will reveal that the HHI-related data is irrelevant—*i.e.*, will directly inform the analyst that only four rivals would find it inherently profitable to undercut the MP's contrived oligopolistic price.

In these situations, it would be highly-cost-ineffective to proceed by *combining* HHI-related data and non-HHI-related data—in particular, by collecting HHI-related data, making an initial prediction based on that data, collecting the non-HHI-related data, making a correct prediction based on the latter data, and then adjusting the conclusion initially derived from the HHI-related data to make it coincide with the correct conclusion derived from the non-HHI-related data by *adjusting* market-aggregated data to take account of certain non-market-aggregated factors. The analysis that is based on non-HHI-related data should be *substituted for* not *combined with* the analysis based on HHI-related data. The collection of the HHI-related data and the derivation of predictions from it consume resources and achieve absolutely nothing.

This criticism is not "merely linguistic" in the pejorative sense of being a language quibble. Throughout, the 1992 Guidelines fail to recognize that, at least in a world in which, as they acknowledge, Qualifying Factors are important, HHI-related data is useless.

* * *

I should not conclude this critique of the 1992 Guidelines' use of market-concentration data without addressing one excuse that a leading economist at the Division has offered for this approach. Although the economist in question—Gregory Werden—does believe that "a structural merger policy—one built on market delineation and market shares—finds support in economic theory and empirical research, and, in industries with relatively-undifferentiated products, a structural [*i.e.*, market-oriented] approach to mergers is probably the best we can do given our current state of knowledge,"[999] he also maintains that "[t]he [1992] Guidelines' use of market delineation as the first step of a largely structural analysis was compelled by case law precedent"[1000]: "Failing to delineate a market most likely would have resulted in the dismissal of any cases filed in court, so the

---

[999] See *Werden Delineation* at 523, citing George A. Hay and Gregory Werden, *Horizontal Mergers: Law, Policy, and Economics*, 83 AM. ECON. REV. (PAPERS & PROC.) 117 (1993).

[1000] See *Werden, Delineation* at 521 text and n. 13. According to Werden at *Werden Delineation* at 521 n. 13:

In *Brown Shoe Co. v. United States*, 370 U.S. 294, 335 (1962), the Supreme Court held that "the proper definition of the market is a 'necessary predicate' to an examination of competition that may be affected by the horizontal aspects of [a] merger." The market delineation-market share approach was further solidified in *United States v. Philadelphia National Bank*, 374 U.S. 321, 355–69 (1963), and *United States Marine Bancorporation*, 418 U.S. 602, 618 (1974), and it continues to be followed by the lower courts.

Department of Justice may have had little choice but to delineate markets and assign market shares."[1001]

I do not find this excuse compelling. Even if the DOJ has to make arguments before the courts that begin by defining markets and focus on market-aggregated seller-concentration data, it does not have to use such an approach when deciding whether to challenge particular mergers or joint ventures. The Guidelines state that "[t]hey describe the analytical framework and specific standards normally used by the Agency in analyzing mergers."[1002] They are said to state the Agency's policy.[1003] Even if, contrary to practice, prosecutorial offices in the United States were morally and legally obligated to take the approach to making prosecutorial decisions that are most consistent with the text of the statute or ordinance they are enforcing or will best achieve the goals that led to the passage of the legislation or ordinance in question, nothing suggests that prosecutors are bound by incorrect judicial operationalizations of legislation or ordinances. If market-oriented approaches are not cost-effective ways of enforcing the American antitrust laws, the DOJ and FTC are not obligated to and ought not to use them in their internal decisionmaking processes. The case-law therefore does not excuse the 1992 Guidelines' adoption of a market-oriented approach even if it would obligate the Justice Department to use such an approach before the courts.

Moreover, I do not think that the case-law makes it desirable for the DOJ and FTC to use market-oriented approaches before the courts. Although, as the cases Werden cites imply, the courts have assumed that antitrust analysis should be based on market-oriented approaches, that judicial position primarily reflects the way in which the government has argued antitrust cases. Indeed, even if the courts would react negatively to the Justice Department's refusal to use a market-oriented approach—even if the Department's substituting good arguments for bad arguments would cause it to lose some cases, the Department might do more good than harm in the long run by proceeding in this way (might change the judges' minds in the longer run or might persuade the legislature to pass clarifying legislation that would induce the courts to respond appropriately to good and bad arguments).

I should add that I doubt that the DOJ and FTC's focus on seller-concentration figures does, in fact, reflect the relevant officials' belief that they are constrained to do so by the case-law. The argument that the relevant officials felt obligated or compelled by the courts to use a market-oriented approach to horizontal-merger analysis is undercut by the fact that the 1992 Guidelines rejected case-law conclusions in relation to many other issues such as the correct way to define markets, the MP-market-share/market-concentration figures that render a merger illegal or presumptively illegal, the persuasiveness of "limit price," "perceived potential entrant," or "waiting in the wings" theory, and the legal significance of the efficiencies a horizontal merger may generate.

[1001] *Id.* at 522.

[1002] See the 1992 Guidelines, Section 0., paragraph 1, sentence 2.

[1003] *Id.*, Section O., paragraph 1, sentence 3.

(C) The 1992 Guidelines' Analysis of the Factors That Relate to Entry and QV-Investment Expansions by the Merged Firm's Established Rivals

I will begin by summarizing the 1992 Guidelines' positions on the possible relevance of entry and QV-investment expansions by the merged firm's established *R*s and then comment on the correctness of these 1992 Guidelines' positions.[1004] The 1992 Guidelines and the 1997 Revision state that in markets where entry or expansions by one or more of the merged firm's established *R*s pass their "tests of timeliness, likelihood, and sufficiency," "a merger raises no antitrust concern and ordinarily requires no further analysis."[1005] According to the 1992 Guidelines (and the 1997 Revision), an entry or expansion is "timely" if (1) less than two years will elapse between "initial planning" and "significant market impact" or (2) when the product in question is a durable good, enough consumers would respond to any merger-generated price-increase by delaying their purchases if one or more of the MPs' potential or actual competitors made a significant commitment to executing a relevant expansion or entry that would take more than two years to complete for the prospective entry or expansion to deter or counteract the feared tendency of the merger to lessen competition.[1006] Again, according to the 1992 Guidelines (and the 1997 Revision), an entry (or expansion) alternative is "likely" if it would be profitable.[1007] And finally, according to the 1992 Guidelines (and the 1997 Revision), entry (or expansion) would be sufficient if it would eliminate the increases in the prices of the merged firm (relative to those of the MPs) that the merger would generate either *before* the entry or *but for* the prospective entry. Thus, the 1992 Guidelines point out that when the concern is the tendency of the merger to increase the merged firm's OCAs and prices by freeing the MPs from each other's competition, an entry will not be "sufficient" unless it involves "a product so close to the products of the merging firms" that it renders unprofitable the price-increase that would otherwise have resulted.[1008]

I have two positive comments and seven criticisms to make about the 1992 Guidelines' and 1997 Revision's positions on entry. First, the positive comments. The 1992 Guidelines' and the 1997 Revision's acknowledgment that the negative effects of a horizontal merger on price competition can be counteracted by any

---

[1004] Although the heading and text of the relevant section of the 1992 Guidelines (Section 3) refer to entry, the 1992 Guidelines' note 24 makes it clear that QV-investment expansions by the MPs' established *R*s have the same consequences and must be analyzed in the same way as entry. The 1992 Guidelines classify a supply-response as an entry (a committed entry) or expansion if it "requires expenditure of significant sunk costs of entry and exit." See *id.* at Section 3.0, paragraph 3.

[1005] *Id.* at Section 3.0, paragraph 2.

[1006] *Id.* at Section 3.2.

[1007] The 1992 Guidelines' articulation of this point is more complex but no more informative. Thus, although the Guidelines do state that "an entry ultimately is likely if it would be profitable at pre merger prices, and if such prices could be secured by the entrant," the very next sentence admits that a new entrant may not be able to secure pre merger prices post-merger. See *id.* at Section 3.3. *Id.* at Section 3.2.

[1008] *Id.* at Section 3.4.

tendency the associated price-increases have to induce the merged firm's established rivals to make additional QV investments in the relevant area of product-space (to expand) as well as by any tendency they have on this account to induce new entry represents real progress. Although economists clearly in one sense know better, many standard economic analyses implicitly assume that established firms cannot create additional QV investments in their area of product-space. The 1992 Guidelines and 1997 Revision explicitly reject this view. Although it is regrettable that they do not address the possible differences in the position of potential entrants and potential expanders (the differences in the barriers they face and the monopolistic QV-investment incentives and monopolistic and oligopolistic QV-investment disincentives that potential expanders but not potential entrants can face), they do prepare the way for such discussions, which will probably take place if future Guidelines move the treatment of the expansion-possibility from a footnote to the text.

In addition, the 1992 Guidelines and 1997 Revision make a tremendous contribution by (implicitly) rejecting limit-price theory[1009] (sometimes called "wings" theory by the Supreme Court[1010])—the theory that effective potential competition affects competition by inducing the relevant market's established firms to lower their prices to deter entry. The 1992 Guidelines and 1997 Revision do not explicitly discuss this hypothesis. However, they clearly do assume that potential entry or expansions will make a difference not by inducing entry-deterring limit pricing to be practiced but by causing actual entry or expansions to be executed that will make a difference. This has been my position for 40 years.[1011] In particular, I have argued that (1) limit pricing would only rarely be able to deter entry, (2) even if limit pricing could deter entry, it would only rarely be more profitable than allowing entry to occur, and (3) even if limit pricing could deter entry and would be more profitable than allowing entry to occur, it would only rarely be more profitable than many other moves established sellers could make to deter entry—most importantly, making additional QV-investments (what I call "limit investments") themselves. In fact, both these theoretical arguments and my perusal of the relevant "empirical" literature led me to conclude that limit pricing is a theory in search of a phenomenon. Moreover, I argued that, rather than being praiseworthy, limit pricing would actually be illegal—is a form of predatory pricing. Until now, economists have rejected all these conclusions—have insisted that the problems with "limit price" theory could

[1009] For a discussion of the history of the development of limit-price theory and citations to much of the relevant literature, see Richard S. Markovits, *Potential Competition, Limit Price Theory, and the Legality of Horizontal and Conglomerate Mergers under the American Antitrust Laws* (hereinafter *Markovits Limit Pricing*), 1975 WIS. L. REV. 658, 659–64 (1975). See also Chapter 13 *infra* and Section 2 of this chapter *supra*.

[1010] See, *e.g.*, United States v. Penn-Olin Chem. Co., 378 U.S. 158 (1964). See also United States v. Falstaff Brewing Corp., 410 U.S. 526 (1973) and Federal Trade Commission v. Proctor & Gamble Co. (Clorox), 386 U.S. 568 (1967).

[1011] See RICHARD S. MARKOVITS, POTENTIAL COMPETITION, PRICING, AND INVESTMENT (DOCTORAL DISSERTATION SUCCESSFULLY SUBMITTED TO THE LONDON SCHOOL OF ECONOMICS, 1966) and *Markovits Limit Pricing*.

be solved by making limit-pricing models stochastic and/or dynamic.[1012] In fact, these standard moves of traditional science do nothing to remedy the central deficiencies of "limit pricing" theory. The 1992 Guidelines and 1997 Revision deserve high praise for rejecting this theory, even if they do so only implicitly.

Unfortunately, the 1992 Guidelines' and 1997 Revision's treatment of entry and expansion is still deficient in seven respects. First, they leave the impression that the presence of a potential competitor or potential expander will counteract the tendency of a horizontal merger to lessen competition only if that potential entrant or expander enters. In fact, in many situations, a potential competitor or expander will affect results by inducing someone else that would not otherwise have made a QV investment to make such an investment to deter the entry or expansion in question.

Second, although the 1992 Guidelines are correct in focusing in this context on entries (and expansions) that are induced by the merger,[1013] some of the factors they list as being relevant to whether the merger will induce entry are inconsistent with that focus. In particular, their discussion of "growth or decline" in market demand is inappropriate in this context. The relevant issues are whether the merger (1) will deter the creation of one or more QV investments by increasing the $(\Pi_D + R)$ barriers to expansion or *M* or *O* disincentives faced by the merged firm above those faced by the MPs or by increasing the L barriers or *O* disincentives faced by an established or potential *R* of the merged firm or (2) will induce the creation of one or more QV investments by reducing the $(\Pi_D + R)$ barriers and/or $(M + O)$ disincentives faced by the merged firm below those faced by the MPs, not whether increases in market demand would lead additional QV investments to be introduced into the market in question independent of the merger or, indeed, whether the merger would lead to the introduction of additional QV investments into the relevant market by raising the prices that are charged at its pre merger QV-investment level. Admittedly, one might argue the point if the claims were that (1) a growth in market demand that would not itself make an entry or expansion profitable might do so in conjunction with any price-increase to which the horizontal merger in question would otherwise lead and (2) a decline in market demand that would in itself lead to a QV investment's being withdrawn might not do so because of the tendency of the horizontal merger in question to decrease price competition directly. Clearly, however, if the 1992 Guidelines and 1997 Revision are making either or both of the above two points, they should make them explicitly.

Third, the 1992 Guidelines' and 1997 Revision's analyses of the factors that influence the profitability of entry (or expansion) is impoverished. They do refer to what I call the scale barrier to entry and do mention other considerations that contribute to barriers that I denominate profit-rate-differential and risk barriers to entry, but much more needs to be said about these issues. Moreover, as I have

[1012] See, *e.g.*, Darius W. Gaskins, *Dynamic Limit Pricing: Optimal Pricing Under Threat of Entry*, 3 J. ECON. THEORY 306 (1971).

[1013] See the 1992 Guidelines, Section 3.3 at note 27.

already indicated, they say nothing about the difference between the relevant barriers to expansion and the counterpart barriers to entry nor do they mention the QV-investment disincentives and incentives a potential expander may face. Finally, because standard economics does not provide an appropriate conceptual system for this type of analysis and because the 1992 Guidelines' and the 1997 Revision's authors have not developed one on their own, the 1992 Guidelines and 1997 Revision do not analyze the connection between (1) the profitability of entry or expansions and (2) the relative size of the entry-preventing QV-investment level and the entry-barred expansion-preventing QV-investment level.

Fourth, the 1992 Guidelines and 1997 Revision ignore the various ways other than by decreasing the intensity of price competition in which a horizontal merger can affect the profitability of entry and expansion. As Sect. 2 of this chapter pointed out, horizontal mergers that do not generate any relevant efficiencies can affect the profitability of entry by changing the retaliation barrier to entry, can affect the profitability of expansion by a rival of the merged firm by changing the retaliation barrier to expansion as well as by changing the monopolistic QV-investment incentives or disincentives and the oligopolistic QV-investment disincentives a relevant *R* faces, and can affect the profitability of expansion by the merged firm not only in the above ways but also by raising the ($\Pi_D + R$) barriers the merged firm faces above their counterparts for the antecedent that was best-placed to expand. Moreover, as Sect. 2 of this chapter also pointed out, the efficiencies that horizontal mergers generate can also affect the ($\Pi_D + R$) barriers and correlatively the QV-investment incentives and disincentives the merged firm faces and by so doing the QV-investment incentives and disincentives one or more of its *R*s face. The 1992 Guidelines' and 1997 Revision's failure to deal with these efficiency-related possibilities in its section on entry would not be a problem if they examined them in their section that is concerned with efficiencies, but they do not do so there either.

Fifth, the 1992 Guidelines and 1997 Revision make a clear error in assuming that entry cannot convert a horizontal merger that would otherwise lessen competition into one that does not unless it takes place in the part of the market in question in which the merger would otherwise have caused prices to rise—*e.g.*, in the part of the market in which the MPs' products were located if their merger enabled them to increase their prices by raising their OCAs directly by freeing them from each other's competition.[1014] Admittedly, in such a case, entry would be unlikely to stop or reduce the harm that the MPs' merger would otherwise continue to inflict on those of their customers that they were respectively best-placed and second-placed to supply or both "uniquely-equal-best-placed" to supply pre merger unless it took place in that local area of product-space. Nor would entry in some other part of the relevant area of product-space be likely to stop the MPs from profiting on this account. But these conclusions do not imply that an entry that the merger induced to

[1014] *Id.* at Section 3.4.

be made elsewhere in the market in question could not reduce the amount by which it decreases competition by as much as an entry in the directly-affected area would do. In the Clayton Act context, the competitive impact of a horizontal merger is defined in terms of (*i.e.*, the legality of a horizontal merger under the Clayton Act depends on) its equivalent-dollar impact on the customers of the MPs and the customers of the merged firm's product-*R*s combined. Since an entry elsewhere would presumably improve the position of the other customers of the MPs and of customers of the merged firm's *R*s by as much as an entry in the directly-affected area would benefit the buyers it helped, the "sufficiency" of any entry the merger induces does not depend at all on where in the market it takes place. As I stated in Chap. 4, read literally, the Clayton Act does seem to prohibit any horizontal merger that reduces competition in one or more markets even if that merger does not reduce competition across all the markets it affects, and the Supreme Court has stated in dicta[1015] (mistakenly, I believe) that the Act does prohibit mergers that reduce competition in any market, regardless of whether they reduce competition on balance. But nothing in the Act or in any Supreme Court opinion implies that it prohibits mergers that injure any buyer or significant group of buyers in a market if it does not impose an equivalent-dollar loss on all buyers in that market on balance (by reducing the attractiveness of the best offer they respectively receive from any inferior supplier). I hasten to repeat that my belief that the Supreme Court dicta described above is mistaken reflects my conclusion that in the U.S. legal culture courts are authorized to interpret a civil statute non-literally when a literal interpretation would produce results that are contrary to the policy goals of the legislature that passed it.[1016]

Sixth, in my judgment, the 1992 Guidelines and 1997 Revision manifest an unrealistic view of the ability of the entries and/or expansions that a horizontal merger may induce because of its tendency to reduce price competition to prevent that merger from harming the relevant buyers in the post-entry or post-expansion period and indeed, in some cases (*e.g.*, when the good in question is a durable good and consumers can delay their purchases) from doing so in the pre-entry or pre-expansion period as well. Even if one considers (as the 1992 Guidelines and 1997 Revision do not) the equivalent-dollar gains that any merger-induced entries and/or expansions confer on the relevant buyers by increasing the quality or variety of the products available to them, the quality or variety of the distributive outlets at which they can shop, and the average speed with which they get supplied, mergers that lead to increases in QV investment by reducing price competition will still harm the buyers in question. The authors of the 1992 Guidelines and 1997 Revision seem to think that the investments that a horizontal merger may induce by decreasing price competition may be able to bring prices back down to or below their pre merger level. I doubt that the QV investments that

---

[1015] United States v. Philadelphia National Bank, 374 U.S. 321 (1963).

[1016] The same conclusion would apply to criminal statutes when the non-literal interpretation would favor the defendants.

a horizontal merger induces by reducing price competition will have this effect very often, in part because if they would the merger would probably not be made in the first place. To see why, note that if the QV investments that a horizontal merger induces have this effect on market prices, the horizontal merger will reduce the profits the market's established firms realize in the post-induced-investment period on their pre merger QV investments below the profits they realized on those investments pre merger unless it generates sufficient static efficiencies to overcome the facts that (1) prices in the later period are equal or below their pre merger counterparts and (2) more alternatives are available to buyers in the later period. Hence, for the MPs to find their merger profitable in the face of its tendency to induce the execution of new QV investments that would lower prices to or below their pre merger level, the sum of (1) the profits the merger generates for the MPs because of the static efficiencies it yielded, (2) the profits it enables them to realize before the induced QV investment becomes operative because it reduces competition in various ways, and (3) the profits the merger enables the MPs to realize on any additional QV investments it causes them to make (either by increasing their absolute ability to expand or by opening up an investment opportunity by raising prices) must exceed (4) the loss it imposes on them by reducing the profit-yields of their pre existing projects in the whole post-induced-investment period by lowering prices and reducing unit sales (increasing the options available to buyers). I doubt that this condition will be satisfied very often. In any event, I think that the 1992 Guidelines and 1997 Revision are far too sanguine about the likelihood that entry (or expansion) will be "sufficient" in the sense in which they define that term.

Seventh and finally, the 1992 Guidelines and 1997 Revision take an unacceptable position on the relevant-consumer losses that can be ignored as being "not substantial" or *de minimis*. Basically, they state that if the DOJ or FTC concludes that a horizontal merger will not harm the relevant consumers in the period that begins two years after its execution (or, worse yet, two years after the merger-induced entry or expansion is "initially plann[ed]"), it will allow the merger (conclude that the losses the merger imposes or the relevant consumers in the intervening period are *de minimis*). I do not find that position acceptable.

My overall assessment of the 1992 Guidelines' and 1997 Revision's treatment of "entry alternatives" is therefore quite similar to its counterpart for their discussions of the non-HHI-related qualifying factors that are relevant to a horizontal merger's impact on unilateral price-increases and coordinated price-interactions. Real progress has been made, but many errors and omissions still need to be corrected.

(D) The 1992 Guidelines' Analysis of the Economic Effects and Legal Relevance of the Efficiencies That a Horizontal Merger May Generate

The 1992 Guidelines represent an improvement on the previous position of the Executive Branch on the legal relevance of any efficiencies a horizontal merger may generate.[1017] Thus, they improve on the 1984 Guidelines' position[1018] on such efficiencies in two respects: (1) they make it clear that efficiencies are relevant only to the extent that they benefit the "combination" of the customers of the MPs and the customers of the MPs' product-*R*s,[1019] and (2) they explicitly state that the benefits that a horizontal merger's efficiencies confer on the relevant consumers will make an otherwise-unlawful merger legal only if they exceed the relevant losses the merger would otherwise impose on the buyers in question.[1020] (I should add that, although these two positions of the 1992 Guidelines are correct as a matter of law if the question is the legality of a horizontal merger under the Clayton Act, they are not correct as a matter of law when the question at issue is the legality of a horizontal merger under the Sherman Act: for the latter purpose, the crucial issue is not the effect of the economic efficiencies on the merger's net equivalent-dollar impact on Clayton-Act-relevant buyers but the effect of the economic efficiencies on the profits of the merger partners—more specifically, on whether the perpetrators' *ex ante* belief that the merger would yield them profits by generating economic efficiencies would have critically affected their conclusion that its licit effects would render it at least normally profitable [had they addressed this issue].)

I want to make five points about the 1992 Guidelines' and 1997 Revision's treatment of efficiencies. The first is the least important: although the 1992 Guidelines identify the competitive benefits that a merger's efficiencies can generate with their tendency to "result in lower prices to consumers,"[1021] the 1997 Revision recognizes that efficiencies can also benefit consumers by leading to the introduction of "new or improved products." As we have seen, the efficiencies a horizontal merger generates can benefit the customers of the MPs as well as the customers of the merged firm's product-*R*s by increasing the quality and variety of the product-and-service options available to them. Second, although the 1992 Guidelines' treatment of efficiencies fails to distinguish among static fixed-cost efficiencies that do not carry over to QV-investment expansions, static variable-cost non-marginal-cost efficiencies that do not carry over to QV-investment expansions, static marginal-cost efficiencies that do not carry over to QV-investment expansions, dynamic efficiencies (including static efficiencies of all kinds that do carry over to QV-investment expansions), and efficiencies that relate to the cost a seller has to incur to change its initially-announced price, the 1997 Revision does, at least, contain a separate reference to the possible special effects of any marginal-cost reductions a merger enables the merged firm to achieve. Third, the 1992 Guidelines contain no analysis whatsoever of the factors that influence the impact that the above

---

[1017] See the 1992 Guidelines, Section 4.

[1018] As indicated in Subsection 4A of this chapter, they also represent an improvement on the 1960s U.S. courts' position that such efficiencies either count against the legality of the merger in question (at least if the MPs were larger firms) or are legally irrelevant.

[1019] See the 1992 Guidelines, Section 4, paragraph 1.

[1020] See *id.* at Section 4, paragraph 2.

[1021] See the 1992 Guidelines at Section 4, paragraph 1.

kinds of efficiencies may have on price competition and QV-investment competition, and the 1997 Revision's discussion of this topic is limited to the statements that (1) "merger-generated efficiencies may enhance competition by permitting two ineffective (*e.g.*, high cost) competitors to become an effective (*e.g.*, lower cost) competitor," (2) "[i]n a coordinated interaction context, marginal cost reductions may make coordination less likely or effective by enhancing the incentive of a maverick to lower price or by creating a new maverick-firm," (3) "[i]n a unilateral effects context, marginal costs reductions may reduce the merged firm's incentives to elevate prices," and (4) "[e]fficiencies also may result in benefits in the form of new or improved products." To see why I find this treatment unsatisfactory, compare these statements with Sect. 2's analysis of the various determinants of the competitive impact of any static marginal or dynamic efficiencies a horizontal merger generates. Fourth, the 1992 Guidelines and 1997 Revision fail to discuss their assumption that a merger's efficiencies will not count in its favor if the efficiencies are not "merger-specific"—*i.e.*, "if equivalent or comparable savings can reasonably be achieved by the parties through other means."[1022] At a minimum, this assumption is highly contestable. In general, the American antitrust laws have been interpreted to establish a "what would happen if the defendant did nothing" baseline—to instruct the courts to analyze the competitive impact of any conduct the laws cover on the assumption that the alternative to a defendant's doing what it did was its doing nothing. The 1992 Guidelines' and 1997 Revision's position on what counts as a merger-generated efficiency radically changes the baseline for competitive-impact analysis—in effect, imposes a duty on any company that wants to increase their organizational economic efficiency to do so in the way that would increase competition the most relative to what would happen if it did nothing rather than simply to avoid organizational-efficiency-enhancing moves that would decrease competition in comparison with the do-nothing position. Even if I would approve of a legislature's adopting this baseline-shift, I do not think it appropriate for Executive-Branch officials or courts to make it. I will return to this issue in the next section. Fifth and finally, the 1992 Guidelines almost certainly implicitly reject the organizational-economic-efficiency defense that I think it is correct as a matter of law to read into the Clayton Act. I say "almost certainly" because, although the Guidelines state that efficiencies can form the basis of a defense only if they result in the relevant merger's not imposing an equivalent-dollar loss on Clayton-Act-relevant buyers, Sect. 4 also includes the statement that "[e]fficiencies *almost never* justify a merger to monopoly or near-monopoly (emphasis added)," which almost certainly should be read to reflect the Agencies' view that (regardless of the efficiencies they generate) such mergers will almost always inflict a significant equivalent-dollar loss on Clayton-Act-relevant buyers but might also be read (not by me) to reflect the Agencies' conclusion that an organizational-economic efficiency defense should be read into the Clayton Act.

[1022] *Id.* at Section 4, paragraph 2.

My bottom-line assessment of the 1992 Guidelines' treatment of the efficiencies that a horizontal merger may generate will sound familiar. Once more, real progress has been made. Once more, many additional advances still have to be achieved.

* * *

It seems to me that this is an appropriate juncture to note a deficiency of the 1992 Guidelines that appears in its treatment of each of the subject-matters whose 1992-Guidelines discussion this section has previously addressed—*viz.*, the failure of the 1992 Guidelines to recognize or respond to the facts that a firm can obtain natural as well as contrived oligopolistic margins, can face natural oligopolistic QV-investment disincentives instead of monopolistic QV-investment disincentives or incentives, and can also face natural oligopolistic disincentives to execute accident-and/or-pollution-loss-reducing PPR projects or to inform the public of the dangerousness of using its product (even when its product is safer than its rivals' products). A complete analysis of the determinants of the competitive impact of a horizontal merger would have to take account *inter alia* of the determinants of its impact on the NOMs of the merged firm relative to those of the merger partners and on the NOMs of the merged firm's rivals, the determinants of the impact of any changes in relevant firms' NOMs on their COMs, and the determinants of the impact of a horizontal merger on the *O* disincentives faced by the merged firm and by its rivals.

(E) The 1992 Guidelines' Analysis of the Legal Significance of the Fact That One of the MPs Is a Failing Company or a Failing Division of a Non-Failing Company

According to the 1992 Guidelines[1023] and the 1997 Revision, the DOJ and FTC will allow any horizontal merger or acquisition for which the following four conditions are fulfilled on the ground that if these conditions are fulfilled the merger or acquisition in question would not be "likely to create or enhance market power or facilitate its exercise":

(1) "the allegedly failing firm [or division] would be unable to meet its financial obligations in the near future";
(2) it would not be able "to reorganize successfully under Chap. 11 of the Bankruptcy Act";
(3) "it has made unsuccessful good-faith efforts to elicit reasonable alternative offers of acquisition of...[its] assets...that would both keep its tangible and intangible assets in the relevant market and pose a less severe danger to competition than does the proposed merger" (where the concept of a "reasonable offer" is unclear but may be equatable with "an offer that exceeds the liquidation value of the firm's tangible assets" and the legal conclusion is that the failing firm would be legally obligated to accept such an "alternative

[1023] *Id.* at Section 5.1.

reasonable offer" even if it were less favorable to the firm than the proposed merger if its acceptance would create a more competitive market than the acceptance of the proposed merger-offer would); and

(4) "absent the acquisition, the assets of the failing firm [or division] would exit the relevant market."

I want to make three points about the DOJ/FTC Guidelines' failing-company position. The first relates to the fourth point in the preceding list. That point seems to manifest an assumption that a proposed merger with a market outsider that would result in the failing company's tangible assets being used in a market other than the market in which the failing company is operating will violate the Clayton Act even if such a use of the failing company's assets would increase competition in the market in which they would be used by as much or more than competition would be lessened in the market in which the failing company is operating by the withdrawal of the failing company's tangible assets from that market. Although this legal conclusion is consistent with the interpretation of the Clayton Act that asserts that it prohibits any merger that lessens competition in any market even if the merger does not lessen competition overall, I consider that interpretation to be incorrect as a matter of U.S. law, even though it is favored by a literal reading of the Clayton Act's text.

The second point is that if the goal of the 1992 Guidelines or, more to the point, of the Clayton Act is to increase competition in the market in which the failing company is operating, its failing-company rules may well be counterproductive. In particular, these rules will tend to decrease competition in the markets in question in two ways: (1) by requiring failing companies (A) to search not just for a buyer to which they can sell themselves profitability but for the buyer to which they can sell themselves profitably in a transaction that would be more procompetitive than any other they could make and (B) by requiring them to accept a less attractive offer than the best offer they receive, the rules of the 1992 Guidelines and 1997 Revisions may deter failing companies from searching for and locating buyers that would keep their assets in the market (from participating in mergers that would increase competition relative to what it would be if they did nothing to find merger partners or acquirers), and (2) by increasing the loss that the failure of a failing company imposes on its owners in both the above ways, the DOJ/FTC failing-company rules may reduce competition by deterring managers of established companies from leaving their jobs to set up companies of their own (companies that may well fail). Of course, in some cases, the 1992 Guidelines' failing-company rules might well increase competition on balance despite their two tendencies to reduce competition—*i.e.*, might increase competition more by causing the failing company's assets to be sold to an in-market buyer or potential entrant whose use of them will increase competition more than it would be increased by the more profitable in-market sale the 1992 Guidelines' rules prohibit. However, the assumption that the 1992 Guidelines' failing-company rules will increase competition on balance is clearly contestable.

Like the first point I made about the 1992 Guidelines' and 1997 Revision's position on failing companies, the third point is legal. Even if the 1992 Guidelines' failing-company rules would increase competition on balance, I doubt that the DOJ and FTC are authorized to adopt them. My reason for doubting the legitimacy of the 1992 Guidelines' failing-company rules is the same reason that led me to doubt the legitimacy of one part of the 1992 Guidelines' efficiency-rules: the fact that they change the baseline for competitive-impact analysis. Thus, in requiring the failing company to make good-faith efforts to elicit the offer whose acceptance would increase competition in the failing company's market to the greatest extent possible and then to forego more profitable offers whose acceptance would increase competition less in the relevant market in favor of less profitable offers whose acceptance would increase competition more in the relevant market, the 1992 Guidelines implicitly reject the normal do-nothing baseline for competitive-impact analysis—*viz.*, what would have happened had the defendant done nothing—in favor of a much more activist baseline—*viz.*, what would have happened had the defendant made a good-faith effort (whatever that is) to identify and make the choice of the relevant kind that would increase competition as much as possible in its market. Even if I were convinced that this shift in baseline would increase competition in the failing company's market or overall, I would not think that the DOJ and FTC are authorized to make it. I admit that both the "Agencies" and some courts have made this baseline-shift in a few other areas of antitrust law—*e.g.*, (1) in requiring firms that wish to enter a market through merger or acquisition to merge with a small rather than a large seller in the market in question (to make a so-called toe-hold merger),[1024] (2) when assessing the competitive impact of a conglomerate merger that eliminates a potential competitor by comparing the situation it created with the situation that would have been created had the outsider entered independently (taking into consideration the probability that such an independent entry would have been effectuated),[1025] and (3) when assessing the competitive impact of a joint venture by comparing the situation it created with the situation that would have been created had one or both parents of the joint venturer entered independently (taking into consideration the probability that such independent entries would have been effectuated).[1026] However, the opinions and enforcement-practices that adopt this baseline-shift are deviant, and the weight they should be given is diminished by

[1024] See, *e.g.*, Bendix Corp., 77 F.T.C. 731 (1970), vacated on procedural grounds, 450 F.2d 534 (6th Cir. 1971), consent order, 84 F.T.C. 1291 (1974) and United States v. Falstaff Brewing Corp., 410 U.S. 526 (1973). For a critique of the premise that the toe-hold-merger doctrine will increase competition, see Chapter 13 *infra*.

[1025] See, *e.g.*, Federal Commission v. Proctor & Gamble Co. (Clorox), 386 U.S. 568 (1967). For an analysis of the determinants of the competitive impact of conglomerate mergers involving a potential competitor, see Chapter 13 *infra*.

[1026] See, *e.g.*, United States v. Penn-Olin Chem. Co., 378 U.S. 158 (1964) and United States v. Pan American World Airways, 193 F. Supp. 18 (S.D.N.Y. 1961), rev'd on other grounds, 371 U.S. 296 (1963). For an analysis of the determinants of the competitive impact of joint ventures, see Chapter 15 *infra*.

the failure of the defendants' lawyers in the cases in question to point out that the approach the courts adopted radically changed the baseline for competitive-impact analysis. In any event, I have real doubts about the legitimacy of the 1992 Guidelines' requirement that a failing company that wants to accept an offer for its assets whose acceptance would not decrease competition in comparison with what would happen if it made no sale at all make a good-faith effort to secure and accept an alternative offer that would increase competition in its market by more than competition would be increased by its acceptance of the offer it wished to accept.

(F) The 1992 Guidelines' Positions on the Economic Effects and Legal Relevance of Any Tendency a Horizontal Merger Has to Increase Its Participants' Monopsony Power

The 1992 Guidelines and the 1997 Revised Guidelines both state that "[t]he exercise of market power by buyers ('monopsony power') has adverse effects comparable to those associated with the exercise of market powers by sellers" in that both will "depress output" and "[t]hat in order to assess potential monopsony concerns [*i.e.*, the possibility that a horizontal merger will inflict an equivalent-dollar loss on Clayton-Act-relevant buyers by increasing its participants' monopsony power], the Agency will apply an analytic framework analogous to the framework of these Guidelines. . . ."[1027] I have already explained (in Sect. 2 of this chapter[1028]) why I reject the Agencies' conclusion that across all cases the exercise of buyer power by the producers that engage in horizontal mergers will tend to increase the prices that final consumers pay (to "depress output")—*viz.*, because although this conclusion would be warranted if the relevant producers were traditional pure monopsonists that faced an upward-sloping supply curve and did not practice price discrimination when buying the good in question, in most cases in which horizontal mergers increase the buying power of the MPs the merged firms will be operating as a buyer in a bilateral-monopoly situation so that any tendency of the merger to increase its buying power relative to the buying power of the separate MPs will reduce rather than increase the cost it has to incur to purchase the marginal (and many intra-marginal) units of the product in relation to which it has buying power relative to the price the MPs had to incur to purchase those units.

* * *

I want to conclude this subsection by reviewing the 8 most important things the 1992 Guidelines get right and the 19 most important things the 1992 Guidelines continue to get wrong. The 1992 Guidelines make real progress by getting 8 things right:

[1027] See 1992 Guidelines at Section 0.1.

[1028] See, more specifically, the text accompanying footnote 762.

(1) they recognize the importance of distinguishing between what I call across-the-board-pricing contexts and individualized-pricing contexts (which they refer to as price-discrimination situations);
(2) they recognize that, even when conditions are not likely to change, market-aggregated data will not always adequately describe the competitiveness of a situation or provide an acceptably-accurate basis for predicting the competitive impact of a horizontal merger;
(3) they recognize the importance of what I call OCAs and the possible effects of horizontal mergers on OCAs (on what they call unilateral price-moves);
(4) they recognize the importance of data on the competitive positions of sellers in their relations with particular buyers both for the analysis of the competitiveness of a market pre merger and for the analysis of a horizontal merger's impact on OCAs and COMs;
(5) they correctly if somewhat inarticulately analyze the determinants of the extent to which a horizontal merger will increase the MPs' OCAs directly by freeing the MPs from each other's competition;
(6) they reject limit-price theory (if only implicitly);
(7) they recognize that horizontal mergers can induce QV-investment expansions by established firms as well as entries by potential competitors and that any such expansions that a horizontal merger induces will have very similar effects on its net competitive impact as any new entry it induces; and
(8) they recognize that the efficiencies that horizontal mergers may generate can increase competition, that the legal relevance of such efficiencies to the Clayton Act legality of the mergers that generate them derives from their net equivalent-dollar impact on Clayton-Act-relevant buyers (their competitive impact), and that any tendency a horizontal merger has to increase competition by generating efficiencies will make it legal only if the efficiency-generated equivalent-dollar gains they confer on Clayton-Act-relevant buyers (the increase in competition they generate) exceed or equal (or are nearly as large as) the net equivalent-dollar loss the merger would have imposed on Clayton-Act-relevant buyers (decrease in competition the merger would generate) if it did not generate the relevant efficiencies.

However, the 1992 Guidelines continue to be deficient in 19 respects:

(1) they continue to insist that markets can be defined non-arbitrarily and usefully;
(2) the protocol they delineate for market definitions is poorly drafted, incorrectly assumes that the products it will place in a given market will be each other's successive next-best substitutes, and is based on a peculiar assumption that the price of any product placed outside a given market will not be affected by price-changes that take place within that market;
(3) they fail to recognize that the arguments that led them in certain cases to supplement HHI-related data with non-HHI-related data actually destroy the case for using HHI-related data at all—justify the conclusion that data on the relevant non-HHI-related factors should be substituted for rather than combined with HHI-related data;

(4) in individualized-pricing contexts, they ignore contextual marginal costs and hence the CMC-related ways in which horizontal mergers can affect price competition;
(5) they ignore NOMs and hence the various ways in which horizontal mergers can affect price competition by affecting NOMs;
(6) they present an impoverished analysis of the determinants of the profitability of contrived oligopolistic pricing that ignores, *inter alia*,

(A) the ability of contrivers to reduce the cost of communication by communicating their intentions simply by charging an oligopolistic price,
(B) the relevance and determinants of the number of firms to which a contriver must communicate its intentions (which is also the number of its potential undercutters),
(C) the ability of contrivers to use circumstantial sales-evidence records to detect the fact that they have been undercut and identify their undercutter,
(D) the ability of individualized-pricing contrivers to secure cooperation by promising to reciprocate to rival cooperation,
(E) the determinants of the harm-inflicted to loss-incurred ratio for price-retaliation that inflicts various amounts of harm on undercutters,
(F) the determinants of the ability of across-the-board-pricing contrivers to collaborate in ways that increase the cost-effectiveness of their price-retaliation,
(G) the determinants of the ability of a victim of undercutting to increase the cost-effectiveness of its retaliation by making non-pricing retaliatory moves (*e.g.*, by targeting its undercutter's customers in its advertisements or by locating new products or outlets near its undercutter's operations),
(H) some of the determinants of the likelihood that an individual firm will find undercutting profitable—*i.e.*, will be a maverick,
(I) the determinants of the ability of a group of potential undercutters in an across-the-board-pricing context to eschew undercutting when doing so is in their joint interest,
(J) the relevance of a firm's reputation for contrivance both for its ability to communicate its contrived oligopolistic intentions cheaply and for the credibility of its anticompetitive threats and promises,
(K) the relevance of the amount of profits across all its operations a potential contriver can make by contriving or can protect by deterring undercutting for the credibility of its contrivance-related anticompetitive threats and promises, and
(L) the tendency of increases in a potential contriver's OCAs to reduce the profitability of its contriving by increasing the safe profits it must put at risk to contrive an OM;

(7) they fail to analyze at all the ways in which a horizontal merger can affect the profitability of contrived oligopolistic pricing both for the merged firm relative to the MPs and for the merged firm's *R*s;

(8) they give a misleading impression that contrivance will be less profitable on balance when products are heterogeneous in the market in question;
(9) they mis-state the conditions under which potential competition will be effective in a given area of product-space;
(10) they fail to recognize that the presence of potential entrants and potential expanders may counteract the tendency of a horizontal merger to inflict equivalent-dollar losses on Clayton-Act-relevant buyers not only by reducing the extent to which the merger raises prices but also by increasing the extent to which it increases the quality and variety of the options available to the relevant buyers;
(11) they fail to recognize that potential entrants and expanders can increase competition not only by investing themselves but also by inducing the MPs to make (limit) QV investments to deter their established and potential competitors from making QV investments;
(12) they fail to recognize that, to offset the tendency of a horizontal merger to impose a net equivalent-dollar loss on Clayton-Act-relevant buyers, any entry, merged-firm-established-rival expansion, or merged-firm limit investment the relevant horizontal merger induces need not take place in the "sub-market" in which the reduction in price competition will occur;
(13) they fail to recognize that any QV-investment relocations a horizontal merger generates will be likely to inflict equivalent-dollar losses on buyers that the investment that was relocated was well-placed to supply that are as big as the equivalent-dollar gains the investment that was substituted for the original investment confers on the buyers it is well-placed to supply (buyers the merged firm is well-placed to supply);
(14) they imply that the fact that potential competition will be effective post-merger in the market in which a horizontal merger will take place guarantees or at least creates the possibility that a merger that would otherwise have imposed a net equivalent-dollar loss on Clayton-Act-relevant buyers will not do so;
(15) they fail to to give a coherent account of QV-investment competition and to analyze the determinants of the impact a horizontal merger may have on QV-investment competition;
(16) they fail to analyze the determinants of the ways in which the various kinds of efficiencies that a horizontal merger does generate will affect OCAs, NOMs, COMs and the intensity of QV-investment competition in the "market" in which it takes place (indeed and relatedly, they fail to distinguish the various kinds of economic efficiencies that a horizontal merger can generate that one should distinguish because they affect competition in different ways and their impact is determined by different factors);
(17) they fail to accept the organizational-economic-efficiency defense that I think should, as a matter of law, be read into the Clayton Act;
(18) their sections on efficiencies and failing companies shift the baseline for competitive-impact analysis in a way that may be counterproductive but is, I believe, in any case incorrect as a matter of law; and

(19) their section on failing companies at least leaves the impression that a failing-company merger that would lessen competition in the market in which the failing company is operating would violate the Clayton Act even if it would not lessen competition overall because it would result in the reallocation of the failing company's tangible assets to a different market in which they would increase competition by at least as much as the amount by which their withdrawal from the failing company's market would lessen competition in the latter market.

Much progress has been made. Far more work needs to be done.

(2) Merger Simulations and Inferences from Natural Events

Merger simulation is a technique for predicting the competitive impact of a merger that "seeks to fit a structural model to historical industry data (back-casting) and then use that model to predict price levels after the merger (forecasting)."[1029] In the words of the DOJ and FTC, merger simulation "'calibrates' a model to match quantitative aspects (*e.g.*, demand elasticities) of the industry in which the merger occurs and uses the calibrated model to predict the outcome of the competitive process after the merger."[1030] Over the past 15 years, the DOJ and FTC (as well as economists not at the Agencies) have increasingly used merger simulations to predict the competitive impact of horizontal mergers. The use of this technique has been stimulated by three developments: (1) increases in the availability of point-of-sale scanner data on the prices of rival goods and the quantities of those goods that were sold at different price-arrays as well as data on various types of promotional expenditures that were made on the goods in question; (2) decreases in the cost of computer time; and (3) improvements in econometric theory.

The DOJ and FTC also recognize that, in appropriate circumstances, it may be possible to predict the competitive impact of a proposed merger (1) from information about the effect of past mergers executed either in the market in question or in other geographic markets in which the same products are sold, (2) from information about the differences in the prices charged in other geographic markets in which the same product was sold that had, respectively, the number of relevant sellers that the market in which the proposed merger would take place had pre merger and the number it would have post-merger, and (3) from information about the way in which firms had reacted to relevant past entries and expansions—*i.e.*, by inference from natural events or natural situational analogs.

The Agencies claim that their use of these approaches to horizontal-merger competitive-impact prediction is consistent with the 1992 Horizontal Merger

[1029] Carl Shapiro and Joseph Farrell, Antitrust Evaluation of Horizontal Mergers: An Economic Alternative to Market Definition (unpublished manuscript posted at the Scholarship Repository, University of California—http://repositories cdlib.org/Berkeley_econ221/spring2009/5)25 (2008)).

[1030] See 2006 Commentary at Section 2.

Guidelines—that these techniques do no more than implement the approach articulated by the 1992 Guidelines' Qualifying Factor section. In fact, however, this claim cannot bear scrutiny: both merger simulations and natural-event/natural-analogous-situation inference-protocols are inconsistent with the Guidelines in that they do not use an HHI-figure-based prediction as a starting point and generate a final prediction by adjusting that starting prediction to take account of the Qualifying Factors that are present in the situation in question.

I will now discuss briefly some of the difficulties that must be overcome to generate accurate predictions from merger simulations or information about natural events or natural situational analogs. I start with the merger-simulation approach,[1031] which the DOJ and FTC have used in several cases—*e.g.*, in *Interstate-Bakeries-Continental* (1995) where the DOJ used scanner data to estimate cross-elasticities of demand and the elasticity of demand for two classes of products, in *Maybelline-Cosmair* (2006) where the DOJ used point-of-sale scanner data to estimate demand elasticities, in *Vail Resorts-Ralston Resorts* (1997) where the DOJ used a buyer (skier) survey to estimate price-effects, and in *General Mills-Pillsbury* (2001) where the FTC used scanner data to estimate cross-price elasticities of demand to determine which products should be placed in the relevant market.

The first set of problems that merger-simulation approaches to horizontal-merger competitive-impact prediction must overcome are data problems.[1032] Merger simulations can obtain data from a wide variety of sources: POS (point-of-sale) scanner data on buyers' actual purchases; seller reports of promotional activities and expenditures; and Agency-commissioned or business-commissioned[1033] survey research into the value that buyers place on various product and supplier attributes and the way in which buyers responded to price-differences, promotional campaigns, and changes in their circumstances.[1034] Problems arise with each of these types of data.

Although the DOJ and FTC or a private plaintiff could collect scanner data themselves, I will assume that, in practice, they will have to rely on the data of this sort that others have already collected. In the United States, "[t]he two leading providers of scanner data are A.C. Nielsen (Nielsen) and Information Resources Incorporated (IR). Both firms. . .[cover] a number of channels of [retail] distribution

---

[1031] The following discussion of merger-simulation problems borrows heavily from Daniel Hosken, Daniel O'Brien, David Scheffman, and Michael Vita, Demand System Estimation and Its Application to Horizontal Merger Analysis (2002) (hereinafter Hosken et al.)—unpublished manuscript forthcoming in THE USE OF ECONOMETRICS IN ANTITRUST (John D. Harkrider, ed.) (American Bar Assoc. Section on Antitrust) (forthcoming).

[1032] I hasten to admit that all the data problems I am about to discuss also afflict the protocols I think should be used to predict the competitive impact of horizontal mergers.

[1033] Businesses commission such research both to determine the prices that would be most profitable to charge for a given product and to assess the profitability of introducing a new product (of entering, expanding, or repositioning themselves by introducing a new product).

[1034] See 2006 Commentary at 1.

(supermarkets, drug stores, mass-merchandisers and convenience stores) for various geographic regions throughout the U.S. . . .[T]he scanner data provides data on total revenue and total units sold. . .[of specified product brands and package sizes]. . . .IRI and Nielsen also collect [data on] three general [variants of advertising in circulars]. . ., [on] in-store promotional displays [of different kinds],. . .[and on product-discount] coupons. . .." Although Nielsen and IRI typically sell only aggregated data to their clients—"aggregates of total sales in dollars and units" by brand and package size either at "the level of chain within a specific geographic area" or "over all chains and stores within a geographical area for a given channel" of distribution, I assume that the DOJ/FTC or a private plaintiff would have access to the raw data.[1035] If they do not, various aggregation problems will arise: for example, (1) if the available data aggregates information across different distribution channels (convenience stores, supermarkets, mass-merchandisers), the data will not reveal differences in the elasticities of demand (or OCA/OCD distribution) of the buyers that patronize these different types of distributors,[1036] (2) if the available data aggregates information across retailers in a given channel-of-distribution category that supply different buyer populations (characterized, for example, by economic class, race, or ethnicity), it will not reveal inter-buyer-population differences in elasticities of demand (or OCA/OCD distributions),[1037] and (3) if the data is reported at the brand level (Pepsi) as opposed to the more specific product-size/product-package level (21/12 oz. and bottle/can), it will not reveal inter-product differences in the elasticities of demand (or OCA/OCD distributions).[1038] Indeed, even if the DOJ/FTC or a private plaintiff does have access to the raw data, that data will be deficient in at least two important ways (even when it covers the firms engaged in the merger and their product *R*s):

(1) the IRI and Nielsen price data does not reflect the discount the buyer received because it used a conventional coupon or "club" or "loyalty card," and
(2) the IRI and Nielsen data is collected and recorded in weekly intervals and shelf prices often vary during the recording weeks (*e.g.*, because promotion periods do not correspond to collection periods).[1039]

The second set of scanner-data problems might be called "absence of data" problems. If the DOJ/FTC or private plaintiff in question cannot generate the scanner data itself in a timely fashion or at non-prohibitive cost, it will have to rely on IRI, Nielsen, or some other firm's scanner data, and these companies will often not have such data on the relevant MPs and the merged company's *R*s. Sometimes, the problem will be that the companies in question will not have

[1035] Hosken *et al.* at 2–3.

[1036] *Id.* at 6.

[1037] Additional problems will arise when the retailers in the relevant category charge different prices for the same specific product. See *id.* at 8–12.

[1038] *Id.* at 6.

[1039] *Id.* at 6–7.

covered retailing in the relevant geographic "markets," and sometimes it will be that the merger is between wholesalers or manufacturers, types of firms for which these companies do not collect point-of-sale price data (because their sales are not recorded on "scanners") or promotion data. Admittedly, in some retailer-merger cases, the DOJ/FTC or a private plaintiff may be able to draw useful inferences from scanner data on retail sales in geographic markets in which the MPs do not operate, and in some wholesaler-merger or manufacturer-merger cases, they may be able to draw useful inferences from scanner data on retail sales of the products involved, but both these moves are problematic. It will not be easy to establish the relationship between the competitiveness of various possibly-relevant pairs of products in the markets for which data is available and the competitiveness of the MPs or of each MP and its various other rivals, and it is extremely difficult to infer accurately-derived demand curves and demand-curve elasticities and cross-elasticities (the facts that pertain to wholesalers or manufacturers) from estimates of retailer demand curves and demand-curve elasticities and cross-elasticities.[1040] Even when data is available on the prices manufacturers and wholesalers charge their direct customers, its use will often be complicated by the fact that the sellers in question are charging the relevant buyers positive lump-sum (franchise) fees as well as per-unit prices, paying the relevant buyers to engage in certain promotional activities, obligating them to engage in activities of these kinds without payment, and agreeing to engage in certain promotional activities themselves. (I should say that many, if not all, of the same problems will afflict the execution of the protocol I recommend, whose object is to estimate wholesaler or manufacturer OCA/OCD distributions rather than demand elasticities or cross-elasticities of demand.)

Of course, as I have already indicated, the DOJ/FTC can also make use of consumer-research surveys that the Agencies execute themselves, that independent consumer-research companies have completed, or that businesses have executed or commissioned to improve their pricing, product-positioning, and/or entry/expansion decisions. However, relevant data of this kind may not be available, and even when it is, there may be some ground to believe that (1) even if the surveyed consumers are providing as reliable information as they can and the sample of consumers surveyed is not biased, their reports of their dollar preferences and responses to past situations will be less reliable than inferences drawn from their actual choices, (2) in a few instances, the responses of consumers with stakes in pending or future litigation may be influenced (whether consciously or not) by those stakes, and (3) more significantly, the samples of consumers studied by and the questions posed by businesses that are proposing or expect to propose mergers to whose legality the consumer-responses would be relevant may be biased on this account.

The second set of problems that merger-simulation approaches to horizontal-merger competitive-impact predictions must overcome are econometric. Even when the analysis is not attempting to estimate a derived demand curve from data on retail sales and terms of sale, hard choices must be made about the functional

[1040] *Id.* at 22–29.

form of the equation one is trying to estimate.[1041] The number of difficult and contestable choices that will have to be made to estimate the elasticity of the derived demand curves that wholesalers and manufacturers face from retail-price data is far greater.[1042]

Finally, to produce accurate elasticity estimates through merger simulations, analysts will often have to resolve correctly various tricky endogeneity issues. Although econometricians have developed various methods for isolating demand relationships when changes in prices reflect a combination of a change in the demand curve and a change in the supply curve, many of these methods require amounts of data on so-called cost-shifters that available scanner data is not likely to provide.[1043]

I have already admitted that the approach to horizontal-merger competitive-impact prediction I recommend will have most of the same data problems that afflict the merger-simulation approach. However, my approach—which is in one sense more complicated in that it distinguishes HNOP effects, NOM effects, and COM effects whereas merger simulations look at price effects that reflect all three of the effects I distinguish—is less econometrically demanding.

I have even less to say about the natural-event-inference approach to horizontal-merger competitive-impact prediction. The FTC used this approach in *Staples* (as we have seen), the DOJ used this approach in 1997 in *Cargill-Akzo Nobel* (to demonstrate that the winning bids in formal sealed-bid auctions to supply government agencies in the eastern portion of Lake Erie with rock salt for de-icing purposes were significantly lower when there were four bids rather than three), and the DOJ and FTC both noted the usefulness of natural-experiment inferences in Section 2 of their 2006 Commentary on the Horizontal Merger Guidelines. The major problems with the natural-experiment-inference approach to horizontal-merger competitive-impact prediction is (1) the fact that, in many (probably most) cases, no relevant natural experiments will be available and (2) the fact that, even when a natural experiment from which something can be learned is available, the analyst must carefully identify and analyze the significance of relevant differences between (A) the situation in which the natural experiment took place and the situation in which the merger under investigation or related entry would be executed, (B) the merger that is being proposed or entry/expansion that it might deter and the merger or entry/expansion that constitutes the natural experiment, and (C) the firms that the proposed merger would involve. This second difficulty is perfectly analogous to the difficulty one would have to overcome to use the inter-temporal or inter-regional comparison method I propose using to investigate the oligopolistic or predatory character of prices (a proposal that involves the same kind of natural-experiment inference that can be used to predict the competitive impact of a horizontal merger).

[1041] *Id.* at 12–27.

[1042] *Id.* at 21–29.

[1043] *Id.* at 17–18.

(3) The August 19, 2010 DOJ/FTC Horizontal Merger Guidelines[1044]

This section summarizes the 2010 DOJ/FTC Horizontal Merger Guidelines, explains how they differ from their 1997-revised 1992 Guidelines' counterparts, and evaluates the differences.

(A) The 2010 Guidelines' HHI-Oriented "General Standards"

(i) The Relationship Between the 1992 and 2010 Guidelines' Positions on Market Definition and "General Standards" Presumptions

I will begin by making five points about the relationship between the 2010 Guidelines' discussion of relevant-antitrust-market definition and the 1992 Guidelines' treatment of this issue. First, with one important exception, the 2010 Guidelines accept (or, at least, as an initial matter, claim to accept) the 1992 Guidelines' abstract definition of a relevant antitrust market.[1045] Second, the 2010 Guidelines change the 1992 Guidelines' abstract definition of a relevant antitrust market by specifying that the SSNIP that plays a critical role in identifying the hypothetical monopolist or combinants that constitute the seller-side of the defined market refers not to the prices of all in-market products (of all products in the hypothetical combination) but to "at least one product in the market, including at least one product sold by one of the merging firms."[1046] (I should note that this change leaves incompletely specified the set of products to which the SSNIP analysis applies. I should also note that the 2010 Guidelines make no attempt to justify this change and that I have no idea whether it is a change for the better.) Third, the 2010 Guidelines' discussions of "target customers" and "price-discrimination markets"[1047] as well as their discussion of geographic markets based on the location of customers[1048] strengthen the message of the 1992 Guidelines that the Agencies will sometimes use buyer-oriented market definitions rather than seller-oriented market definitions. Fourth, the 2010 Guidelines almost certainly should be read to reject the 1992 Guidelines' "add to each merger-partner product its closest and then successively-next-closest substitute (read: rival product)" protocol for identifying the hypothetical monopolist (set of hypothetical combinants) the Guidelines claim constitute the seller-side of each relevant antitrust market.

[1044] United States Department of Justice and the Federal Trade Commission, Horizontal Merger Guidelines (hereinafter 2010 Horizontal Merger Guidelines) (August 19, 2010)

[1045] *Id.* at Section 4.1.1 ¶¶ 1–2.

[1046] *Id.* at Section 4.1.1 ¶ 4.

[1047] *Id.* at Section 4.1.4.

[1048] *Id.* at Section 4.2.2.

Thus, the 2010 Guidelines do not refer to this protocol, and, when discussing the hypothetical-monopolist test, they state: "When applying the hypothetical monopolist test to define a market around a product offered by one of the merging firms, if the market includes a second product, the Agencies will normally include a third product *if that third product is a closer substitute for the first product than is the second product* (emphasis added)."[1049] (I should note that this sentence's implication that in some cases the Agencies will decide that the first product that its abstract market definition implies should be added to a merger-partner product will not be the merger-partner product's closest substitute [rival] is a step in the right direction: when the profitability to the hypothetical combination of raising the price of the merger-partner product's closest-rival product at the same time that it raises the price of the merger-partner product is reduced more by the ability of producers of products that are competitive with the merger-partner product's closest-rival product to profit by undercutting or undermining the latter's increased price than the profitability to the hypothetical combination of raising the price of some less-close rival of the merger-partner product at the same time that it raised the price of the merger-partner product could be reduced by the ability of the less-close rival's rivals to profit by undercutting or undermining its increase price, the first product to add to the merger-partner product may not be its closest competitor. On the other hand, for related reasons, I doubt the sentence's claim that, when the first product that should be added to the merger-partner product is not its closest rival, the second product that should be included in the hypothetical combination should normally be more competitive with the merger-partner product than the first product that was included in the hypothetical combination.) Fifth, unlike the 1992 Guidelines, the 2010 Guidelines contain a large number of statements that imply that their authors do not really believe in the cost-effectiveness of market-oriented approaches to predicting the competitive impact of horizontal mergers—*i.e.*, in the soundness of their definition of relevant antitrust markets or in the accuracy of any predictions that are generated from derived HHI-oriented figures (even in standard cases).[1050]

[1049] *Id.* at Section 4.1.1 ¶ 4.

[1050] Thus, at Section 4.1.1 ¶ 5, the 2010 Guidelines state that the Agencies will "*usually*" (emphasis added) employ the hypothetical-monopolist test for market definition; at Section 4.1.2, they indicate that the Agencies will sometimes operationalize the SSNIP (which usually refers to a price-increase of 5%) to refer to "a price increase that is larger or smaller than 5%"; at Section 4.1.1 ¶5, they state that the Agencies will "usually" *(i.e.*, not always) define the relevant antitrust market to be the smallest market that satisfies the hypothetical-monopolist test; respectively at Sections 5.2 ¶5 and 5.2 ¶6, the 2010 Guidelines state that the Agencies will base their attribution of a market share to a particular firm not on its share of existing sales made in the defined market but on its "capacity or reserves" or its sales to "a broader group of customers" if doing so will generate HHI figures that better reflect the firm's contribution to competition (that yield competitive-impact predictions that are more accurate); at Sections 5.1 ¶1 and 5.2 ¶1, the Guidelines state that the Agencies will place a firm in the Guidelines' defined relevant market and attribute to the firm a market share that increases the accuracy of the Guidelines' HHI-oriented competitive-impact predictions despite the fact that the Guidelines' hypothetical-monopolist test would not result in the firm's being placed in the market in question; at ¶8 of Section 5.3 (the last

I turn now to the 2010 Guidelines General Standards. I will start with two short and one long quotation from the 2010 Guidelines. The first short quotation is: "unconcentrated markets are unlikely to be vulnerable to coordinated conduct."[1051]

The long quotation is:

> Based on their experience, the Agencies generally classify markets into three types:
> - Unconcentrated Markets: HHI below 1500
> - Moderately Concentrated Markets: HHI between 1500 and 2500
> - Highly Concentrated Markets: HHI above 2500
>
> The Agencies employ the following general standards for the relevant markets they have defined:
> - *Small Change in Concentration*: Mergers involving an increase in the HHI of less than 100 points are unlikely to have adverse competitive effects and ordinarily require no further analysis.
> - *Unconcentrated Markets*: Mergers resulting in unconcentrated markets are unlikely to have adverse competitive effects and ordinarily require no further analysis.
> - *Moderately Concentrated Markets*: Mergers resulting in moderately concentrated markets that involve an increase in the HHI of more than 100 points potentially raise significant competitive concerns and often warrant scrutiny.
> - *Highly Concentrated Markets*: Mergers resulting in highly concentrated markets that involve an increase in the HHI of between 100 points and 200 points potentially raise significant competitive concerns and often warrant scrutiny. Mergers resulting in highly concentrated markets that involve an increase in the HHI of more than 200 points will be presumed to be likely to enhance market power. The presumption may be rebutted by persuasive evidence showing that the merger is unlikely to enhance market power.[1052]

---

paragraph of that section), the Guidelines state that "[t]he purpose of... [its HHI-oriented] thresholds is not to provide a rigid screen to separate competitively benign mergers from anticompetitive ones"; the 2010 Guidelines' general standards, articulated in Section 5.3 ¶7 and quoted in the text that follows, manifest this reality by using such language as "*ordinarily* (emphasis added) require no further analysis," "often warrant scrutiny," "will be presumed to be likely to enhance market power," and "[t]he presumption may be rebutted by persuasive evidence"; at Section 4.1.1 ¶5, the Guidelines refer to "the overarching principle that the purpose of defining the market and measuring market shares is to illuminate the evaluation of competitive effects"; at Section 1 ¶4, the Guidelines state that "[t]hese Guidelines should be read with the awareness that merger analysis does not consist of uniform application of a single methodology"; at Section 2.1.2 ¶1, the Guidelines indicate that the Agencies will sometimes base their competitive-impact predictions (at least in part) on "natural experiments"—a methodology that in practice has usually not been market-oriented; in Section 6.1 the Guidelines state that the Agencies will sometimes "construct economic models" or rely on "merger simulation methods," both of which need not rely on market definition; and in Section 4 ¶4, the Guidelines state that "[w]here analysis suggests alternative and reasonably plausible candidate markets, and where the resulting market shares lead to very different inferences regarding competitive effects, it is particularly valuable to examine more direct forms of evidence concerning those effects."

[1051] *Id.* at Section 7.1 ¶ 1.

[1052] *Id.* at Section 5.3 ¶¶ 6–7.

The second short quotation is: "The increase in the HHI [that will be generated by a horizontal merger] is equal to twice the product of the market share of the merging firms"[1053] This claim is then illustrated by a numerical example: "For example, the merger of firms with shares of five percent and ten percent of the market would increase the HHI by 100 ([by] $5 \times 10 \times 2 = 100$)."[1054]

I want to make four points about these quotations. First, all reflect the Agencies' assumption that data on merger-partner market shares and the concentration of the seller-side of any relevant market bear strongly on the competitive impact of a horizontal merger.

Second, the third quotation reveals that, like the authors of the 1992 Guidelines, the authors of the 2010 Guidelines are not aware of many of the ways that horizontal mergers can affect competition and are also not aware of many of the determinants of the magnitudes of various effects on competition that horizontal mergers can generate whose causes the authors do understand.

Third, the long quotation indicates that the Agencies will no longer make use of any HHI-oriented irrebuttable presumptions—*i.e.*, that they reject not only the HHI-oriented irrebuttable presumptions of the 1992 Guidelines but all such irrebuttable presumptions. Hurray!

Fourth, the long quotation also implies that, even when various factual conditions cause the Agencies to believe that competitive-impact predictions based on HHI-oriented figures will be inaccurate, the Agencies will proceed by calculating the HHI figures on which they normally rely and then adjusting the competitive-impact prediction they generate from these figures to reflect the facts that they think require a conclusion-adjustment. I have already explained why this decision-protocol (which the 1992 Guidelines also state the Agencies will use in relevant cases) is indefensible. The appropriate way to analyze cases in which such adjustment-requiring facts are present is not to *combine* an adjustment-analysis with a standard HHI-oriented analysis but to *substitute* for the HHI-oriented analysis a non-market-oriented analysis that focuses on the adjustment-requiring qualifying-factor facts and various other facts as well. Don't get it wrong and then make it right: get it right in the first place.

(ii) The Accuracy of the 2010 Guidelines' "General Standards" Presumptions

Counterparts to the examples I used to explain why I believe that the 1992 Guidelines' HHI-figure-oriented presumptions are highly inaccurate would be equally effective at undermining the 2010 Guidelines' HHI-figure-oriented

[1053] *Id.* at ¶ 5.

[1054] *Id.* at note 10.

presumptions. Given the nature of my critique of market-oriented approaches to the analysis of the competitive impact of horizontal mergers, it should not be surprising that I have no idea about which set of presumptions is more inaccurate.

(B) The 2010 Guidelines' Analysis of the So-Called "Qualifying Factors" Other Than the Condition of Entry, Efficiencies, and a Merger/Acquisition Target's Failing Company/Division Status

(i) The 2010 Guidelines' Analysis of the Qualifying Factors Other Than the Condition of Entry, Efficiencies, and the Failing-Company Status of a Merger/Acquisition Partner/Target That Can Affect a Merger's Impact on Price Competition in the Defined Market, Given Its Array of QV Investments

(a) The 2010 Guidelines' Analysis of the Qualifying Factors Other Than Those Listed Above That Can Affect the Unilateral Impact of a Horizontal Merger on Prices

The 2010 Guidelines discuss various non-HHI determinants of the unilateral impact of a horizontal merger on prices other than the condition of entry, efficiencies, and the failing-company status of a merger partner or acquired division. I will limit myself here to three sets of positive observations on and three related sets of criticisms of the 2010 Guidelines' analyses of these parameters.

My first and most important positive observation is that, like the 1992 Guidelines, the 2010 Guidelines recognize that the unilateral impact of a horizontal merger is significantly affected by how closely competitive and how uniquely-closely-competitive the merger partners are and that one will sometimes (probably often) not be able to predict these facts from the merger partners' market shares and the relevant market's seller concentration. More specifically, the 2010 Guidelines state that, when products are differentiated, "[the] extent of direct competition between the products sold by the merging parties is central to the evaluation of unilateral price effects,"[1055] that "[i]n differentiated product industries, some products can be very close substitutes [the Guidelines should say: 'can be very close competitors'] and compete strongly against each other, while other products are more distant substitutes and compete less strongly,"[1056] and that "[a]nticompetitive unilateral effects...are likely in proportion to the frequency or probability with which, prior to the merger, one of the merging sellers had been the

[1055] *Id.* at Section 6.1 ¶ 3.

[1056] *Id.* at Section 6.1 ¶ 1.

runner-up when the other won the business" and "[t]hese effects are likely to be greater, the greater the advantage the runner-up merging firm has over other suppliers in meeting customers' needs."[1057] The fact that the 2010 Guidelines devote a subsection[1058] to situations in which the competitive position of sellers is significantly affected by their and/or the relevant buyers' geographic locations implies that their authors recognize that virtually all sales are of "products" that are differentiated (if "differentiation" is broadly defined).

My second positive observation is that the 2010 Guidelines correctly state that, in some circumstances, a horizontal merger between producers of a homogeneous product may generate unilateral price-increases by creating a merged firm that finds it profitable to reduce its output when neither merger partner would have found it profitable to do so. I should add that the 2010 Guidelines also specify what the Agencies take to be the determinants of the likelihood of this outcome's obtaining: a unilateral output suppression strategy is more likely to be profitable when (1) the merged firm's market share is relatively high; (2) the share of the merged firm's output already committed for sale at prices unaffected by the output suppression is relatively low; (3) the margin on the suppressed output is relatively low; (4) the supply response of rivals is relatively small; and (5) the market elasticity of demand is relative low.[1059]

My third positive observation is that the 2010 Guidelines correctly note the possibility that a horizontal merger can also generate unilateral price-increases by creating a merged firm that engages in predation when neither merger partner would have done so.[1060]

I have three sets of corresponding criticisms. I will begin with two criticisms that relate to the first set of positive observations. It is important to recognize that, like the 1992 Guidelines, the 2010 Guidelines do not pay attention to the way in which a horizontal merger can generate unilateral price-increases by affecting CMCs in individualized-pricing contexts and their counterparts in across-the-board-pricing contexts. Thus, the 2010 Guidelines ignore the fact that a horizontal merger between two firms that practice individualized pricing can raise above its relevant-merger-partner counterpart the contextual marginal costs that the merged firm would have to incur to charge a rival's customer the price that would have enabled the merger partner that would have been that buyer's second-placed supplier to match what would have been the HNOP-containing offer of the merged-firm rival that was that buyer's best-placed supplier, derivatively the contextual marginal costs that the rival in question will have to incur when it is second-placed to match the HNOP-containing offers the best-placed suppliers of the buyers the merged-firm

[1057] *Id.* at Section 6.2 ¶ 3. Although Section 6.2's heading indicates that it is concerned with bargaining and auctions, there is every reason to assume that the enquoted propositions apply more generally.

[1058] *Id.* at Section 4.2.

[1059] *Id.* at Section 6.3 ¶ 2.

[1060] *Id.* at Section 6.3 ¶ 4.

rival in question would otherwise have been second-placed to supply, and so on and so forth. Similarly, the 2010 Guidelines ignore the fact that any initial impact a horizontal merger between two firms that charge across-the-board prices has on the merged firm's prices relative to those that the merger partners would have charged will have indirect unilateral effects on the prices the merged firm's closest rivals charge and thereby on the prices that those firms' closest rivals will charge and so on and so forth, and that these indirect effects will in turn affect the merged firm's prices and derivatively the prices of all other firms in the relevant area of product-space and so on and so forth. Obviously, because the 2010 Guidelines ignore these possibilities altogether, they also do not address the determinants of the effects in question. Like the 1992 Guidelines, the 2010 Guidelines also ignore the fact that a horizontal merger can generate unilateral increases in across-the-board prices by creating a merged firm that can induce the relevant sellers to lock themselves into prices in the order that will maximize their HNOP arrays or by eliminating a firm that was a maverick in relation to its "timing of price announcement" and related "locking in" choices.

The second set of criticisms relates to the 2010 Guidelines' listing of the determinants of the profitability to a producer of a homogeneous product of suppressing its output. The Guidelines articulate one of these determinants poorly (refer to "the share of the merged firm's output already committed for sale at prices unaffected by the output suppression" as opposed to referencing "the extent to which the merged firm can reduce its output") and refer to certain relative figures when the relevant factors are absolute figures.

My third set of criticisms relates to the 2010 Guidelines' brief statement that "exclusionary unilateral effects can arise."[1061] This criticism is that it would have been useful for the Agencies to have made at least the following three additional points about this possibility:

(1) horizontal mergers can increase prices or prevent price-decreases not only by creating a merged firm that will drive extant firms out to a greater extent than the merger partners would have done but also by creating a merged firm that will deter rival entries and QV-investment expansions by erecting retaliation barriers to entry and expansion to a greater extent than the merger partners would have done;
(2) horizontal mergers can also increase prices or prevent price-decreases by creating a merged firm that is more likely to be a target of predation than the merger partners would have been or against which rivals are more likely to erect retaliation barriers to expansion because the merged firm's defenses are more spread out than the merger partners' would have been (though such outcomes are made less likely by the fact that the merged firm is larger than either MP and is on that account more able to withstand predatory attacks and

[1061] *Id.* at Section 6 ¶ 2.

more likely to find it profitable to build or preserve a reputation for not succumbing to predation or retaliation);

(3) it is not clear that it is legally correct for the Agencies to take account of any tendency of a horizontal merger to increase the extent to which the merged firm or its rivals will engage in post-merger (illegal) exclusionary conduct when assessing the legality of the merger in question.

(b) The 2010 Guidelines Analysis of the (Non-Excluded) Qualifying Factors That Can Affect the Impact of a Horizontal Merger on Coordinated Conduct (Contrived Oligopolistic Pricing)

The 2010 Guidelines' discussion of the determinants of the profitability of what they call coordinated conduct and of the ways in which horizontal mergers can affect the profitability of such contrivance is not much better than the 1992 Guidelines' treatment of these issues. The relevant sections of the 2010 Guidelines[1062] contain many statements on these issues that are clearly correct though entirely obvious. Thus, paragraph 1 of Section 7.2 correctly states that evidence establishing that firms in a given market had previously engaged in express collusion in that market or (more contestably) had unsuccessfully attempted to engage in such collusion in that market would favor the conclusion that "market conditions are conducive to coordinated interaction" "unless competitive conditions in the market have since changed significantly." Paragraph 1 of Section 7.2 also correctly points out that evidence of "[p]revious collusion or attempted collusion in another product market" also supports the conclusion that conditions in the market involved in the merger under review favor contrivance "if the salient characteristics of that other market at the time of collusion are closely comparable to those in the relevant market." (I must add, however, that I would be more encouraged by these correct statements if the 2010 Guidelines as a whole led me to conclude that the Agencies had a good understanding of the determinants of the profitability of contrivance.) In the same vein, paragraph 2 of Section 7.2 observes correctly if obviously that contrivance will be more likely if "the terms offered to customers are relatively transparent." Slightly less obviously and equally correctly, paragraph 3 of Section 7.2 states that contrivance will be more likely "if sales are small and frequent," and paragraph 7 of Section 7.2 states that contrivance will be less likely if sellers can enter into "large and long-term contracts." Paragraph 6 of Section 7.2 adds the unremarkable observation that "coordinated interaction . . . [is] more likely the more the participants stand to gain from successful coordination."

The 2010 Guidelines expand on the 1992 Guidelines' statements about the significance of the fact that one of the merger partners is a maverick. In particular, Section 2.1.5 points out that firms can be mavericks not only by disrupting

[1062] *Id.* at Sections 7, 7.1, and 7.2.

coordinated pricing but also by making QV investments that raise the equilibrium QV-investment level in the relevant area of product-space (which the Guidelines state is more likely if the alleged maverick has "a new technology or business model"). However, like the 1992 Guidelines, the 2010 Guidelines do not state whether the Agencies will base their conclusions about the maverick status of a merger partner in relation to pricing on its past conduct or on an assessment of the profitability of non-cooperative pricing to the firm, does not analyze the evidence that would be relevant to the latter inquiry, and leaves the impression that a merger that eliminates a merger partner that would have been able to introduce a QV-investment project that was more profitable than any existing project might create a merged firm that would choose not to execute that project (an outcome that I regard as extraordinarily unlikely).

In addition, Sections 7.1 and 7.2 of the 2010 Guidelines contain various assertions that are either dubious or wrong. Thus, paragraph 1 of Section 7.1 states that "unconcentrated markets are unlikely to be vulnerable to coordinated conduct." Paragraph 2 of Section 7.2 contains the contestable claim that "[p]rice transparency can be greater [I interpret this to mean: will tend to be greater] for relatively homogeneous products." And paragraph 3 of Section 7.2 states that contrived oligopolistic prices are more likely to be undermined "if there are few significant competitors" and "if products are relatively homogeneous."

Unfortunately in my judgment, like the 1992 Guidelines' treatment of coordinated pricing, the 2010 Guidelines' discussion of contrived oligopolistic pricing suffers more from sins of omission than from sins of commission. The 2010 Guidelines' comments on "coordinated conduct" do not advert to the vast majority of the determinants of the profitability of contrived oligopolistic pricing whose salience Chapter 10 establishes, and Section 7.1 of the 2010 Guidelines does not discuss the ways in which horizontal mergers can affect the magnitudes of any of the parameters that determine the profitability of contrived oligopolistic pricing—not only of those parameters the 2010 Guidelines ignore but even of those parameters that their Section 7.2 identifies. (That is why I expressed doubts about whether the Agencies would do a good job of determining whether competitive conditions in a merger-involved market in which the merger partners and/or their rivals had previously practiced contrivance had changed or whether competitive conditions in another market in which the merger partners and/or their rivals had previously practiced contrivance were similar to those in a relevant merger-involved market.) (I hasten to add that I also think that, if the Agencies recognized the relevance of various determinants of the profitability of contrived oligopolistic pricing that the 2010 Guidelines ignore, they would change their minds about both the definability of markets and the connection between a market's seller concentration and its vulnerability to what they call coordinated conduct.)

* * *

At this juncture of my discussion of the 1992 Horizontal Merger Guidelines, I pointed out that those Guidelines paid no attention whatsoever to natural oligopolistic pricing, natural oligopolistic QV-investment disincentives, or the natural oligopolistic disincentives that can deter a firm from executing PPR projects designed to discover less-accident-and/or-pollution-loss-prone production processes or from informing buyers of the dangers of using the products it and its rivals produce (even if its product is safer than its rivals' products). The 2010 Guidelines make a small step toward remedying this deficiency. Although they do not explicitly define the concept of natural oligopolistic interactions, do not analyze the determinants of such conduct's feasibility or the ability of firms to make choices that will render such conduct feasible, and do not recognize that—unlike contrived oligopolistic conduct—natural oligopolistic conduct does not violate the Sherman Act, they do contain the statement "coordinated interaction includes conduct not otherwise condemned by the antitrust laws,"[1063] which seems to advert to natural oligopolistic conduct (though the reference is somewhat compromised by the Guidelines' failure to define "coordinated conduct" and the statement's failure to explain that, for both economic and legal reasons, it is important to distinguish natural and contrived oligopolistic conduct).

(C) The 2010 Guidelines' Analyses of Factors That Relate to Entry, to the Ability of the Merged Firm Relative to That of the Merger Partners to Make Additional QV Investments, and to the QV-investment Decisions of the Merged Firm's Established Rivals

The 2010 Guidelines' analyses of these issues are somewhat better than the 1992 Guidelines'. Thus, the 2010 Guidelines recognize that (1) horizontal mergers can increase equilibrium QV investment in a relevant area of product-space by reducing what I denominate the (Π_D + R) barriers to expansion faced by the merged firm below their counterparts for the merger partners,[1064] (2) horizontal mergers can reduce equilibrium QV investment in a relevant area of product-space either by deterring the creation of a new QV investment or by inducing the exit of an existing QV investment by creating a merged firm that faces what I would call critically-higher monopolistic QV investment disincentives than those that would face a relevant merger partner,[1065] (3) a horizontal merger that increases equilibrium QV investment in a relevant area of product-space can confer an equivalent-dollar gain on Clayton-Act-relevant buyers on that account even if it does not reduce

[1063] *Id.* at Section 7 ¶ 2.

[1064] *Id.* at Section 6.4 ¶ 3 and Section 10 ¶ 10.

[1065] *Id.* at Section 6.4 ¶ 2 and ¶ 4.

prices by increasing the quality and variety of the products they can buy[1066] and a merger that leads to the elimination of a product will inflict a net equivalent-dollar loss on Clayton-Act-relevant buyers even if it does not lead to any price-increases by reducing the quality of variety of the products on offer,[1067] and (4) a horizontal merger can also benefit Clayton-Act-relevant buyers by creating a merged firm that finds it profitable to change the product-space location of its products in a way that makes them more differentiated from each other than the merger partners' products would have been.[1068]

However, it is also true that the 2010 Guidelines' treatment of QV-investment competition shares many of the deficiencies of the 1992 Guidelines' approach to such competition: (1) ignores the fact that the intensity of QV-investment competition depends not only on the effectiveness of potential competition and the ability of the merger partners/merged firm to expand but also on the ability of the merged firm's established rivals to make profitable QV-investment expansions and concomitantly that the impact of a horizontal merger on QV-investment competition depends on its impact on all three of these factors (it is telling that the heading of Section 9 of the 2010 Guidelines is simply "Entry"), (2) does not develop a comprehensive account of what I call barriers to entry, barriers to expansion, monopolistic QV-investment incentives and disincentives, and natural oligopolistic QV-investment disincentives, (3) does not distinguish the entry-preventing and entry-barred expansion-preventing QV-investment levels in any area of product-space, relatedly (4) does not distinguish the three kinds of QV-investment equilibria that can be established in any area of product-space, relatedly (5) does not contain any analysis of the different ways in which the various barriers to entry, barriers to expansion, and QV-investment incentives and disincentives interact to determine equilibrium QV investment in each of the three types of equilibrium situations it is useful to distinguish in this context, therefore (6) fails to identify many of the ways in which a horizontal merger can affect QV-investment competition in "relevant markets" by changing barriers to entry, barriers to expansion, or QV-investment expansion-related monopolistic QV-investment incentives and disincentives or natural oligopolistic QV-investment disincentives or the conditions under which any of the impacts that a horizontal merger can have on these intermediate determinants of the intensity of QV-investment competition will actually affect equilibrium QV investment in the relevant area of product-space, and (7) in Section 9 (its section on entry), makes explicit reference to the effect of entry (or effective potential competition) only on price—*i.e.*, ignores their impact on quality and/or variety.

[1066] *Id.* at Section 10 ¶ 1.

[1067] *Id.* at Section 6.4 ¶ 5.

[1068] *Id.* at Section 6.4 ¶ 4.

(D) The 2010 Guidelines' Analyses of the Economic Effects and Legal Relevance of the Efficiencies That a Horizontal Merger Can Generate

The 2010 Guidelines preserve all the improvements in the Agencies' 1992 Guidelines' positions on the relevance of efficiencies and, equally importantly, in the 1997 Revision of those Guidelines' positions on the relevance of efficiencies. Thus, like the 1997 Revision of the 1992 Guidelines, the 2010 Guidelines state that the efficiencies a horizontal merger generates will be relevant to the legality of the merger under the Clayton Act only if they critically affect the net equivalent-dollar impact of the merger on Clayton-Act-relevant buyers.[1069] In fact, as I have already indicated, in one respect, the 2010 Guidelines improve on the 1997-Revised 1992 Guidelines by recognizing that any QV-investment-increasing dynamic efficiencies a horizontal merger generates will benefit Clayton-Act-relevant buyers not only indirectly by generating unilateral price-decreases but also directly by increasing quality and variety.[1070]

However, the 2010 Guidelines' section on efficiencies does not make any significant other improvements in the 1997-Revised 1992 Guidelines. Thus, the 2010 Guidelines

(1) still fail to analyze the determinants of the equivalent-dollar gains that any static efficiencies a horizontal merger generates will confer on Clayton-Act-relevant buyers;
(2) still fail to analyze the determinants of the equivalent-dollar gains that any dynamic efficiencies a horizontal merger generates will confer on Clayton-Act-relevant buyers (or, less seriously, do not recognize that in a few cases such efficiencies can harm Clayton-Act-relevant buyers by creating a situation in which relevant established firms face natural oligopolistic QV-investment disincentives);
(3) (A) still fail to address the possibility that the efficiencies a horizontal merger generates may harm Clayton-Act-relevant buyers by causing one or more merger-firm rivals to exit by improving the competitive-position array of the merged firm relative to those of the merger partners and concomitantly worsening the competitive-position arrays of the exiting merged-firm rivals and (B) still imply that the Agencies would not accept the organizational-economic-efficiency defense I think the Clayton Act should as a matter of law be read to promulgate to cover situations in which horizontal mergers that would not otherwise have inflicted a net equivalent-dollar loss on Clayton-Act-relevant buyers do so in the way just described; and

[1069] *Id.* at Section 10 ¶ 6.

[1070] *Id.* at Section 10 ¶ 1.

(4) still ignore the possibility that their position that only those efficiencies that are "merger-specific"[1071] can count in favor of a horizontal merger's legality may be incorrect as a matter of law in that it departs from the U.S. antitrust laws' normal do-nothing baseline for competitive-impact calculation.

(E) The 2010 Guidelines' Analysis of the Legal Significance of the Fact That One of the MPs Is a Failing Company or a Failing Division of a Non-failing Company

The 2010 Guidelines' section on mergers and acquisitions that involve failing companies and on acquisitions of failing divisions of non-failing companies (Section 11) is essentially the same as the 1992 Guidelines' section on such transactions. My comments on the 1992 Guidelines' section therefore apply equally to Section 11 of the 2010 Guidelines.

(F) The 2010 Guidelines' Positions on the Economic Effects and Legal Relevance of any Tendency a Horizontal Merger Has to Increase Its Participants' Monopsony (Buying) Power

I do not think that the 2010 Guidelines change the Agencies' position on the economic effects or legal relevance of any tendency of a horizontal merger to increase the buying power of the merged firm relative to that of the merger partners. Section 12 of the 2010 Guidelines (Mergers of Competing Buyers) does say that a horizontal merger that enables the merged company to take advantage of real-economies-of-scale buying-efficiencies will tend to increase competition on that account but does not advert to the issue of whether a merger that increases buyer (bargaining) power will tend to increase or decrease the marginal cost to the buyer of purchasing units of the good in question and hence will tend to increase or decrease downstream prices. The 2010 Guidelines imply that the fact that a merger between the only two buyers in an agricultural-product market (whose seller-side is presumably competitive) will increase the merged firm's power as a buyer relative to that of each MP and will thereby cause "a transfer of wealth from farmers" and an inefficient reduction in supply will disfavor the merger's legality even if the merger does not "lead to any increase in the price charged by the merged firm for its output."[1072] Although this hypothetical does not raise the issue of how the increase in the merged firm's buying power would affect the merger's legality if it caused the

[1071] *Id.* at Section 10 ¶ 2.

[1072] *Id.* at Section 12 Example 24.

merged firm to charge buyers lower prices than they would have been charged by the merger partners, I suspect that, even in such a case, the Agencies would continue to conclude that the fact that the merger would increase the merged firm's buying power would disfavor its legality. Admittedly, the Guidelines' Overview Section does contain the statement that "[t]he Agencies presume, absent convincing evidence to the contrary, that adverse effects on direct customers also cause adverse effects on final consumers,"[1073] but I doubt that one should read this statement to imply that—in increase-in-buyer-bargaining-power cases—the Agencies will employ a test of illegality in which covered conduct's equivalent-dollar impact on final consumers plays a critical role. Certainly, such a reading is disfavored by the following statement in the same section of the 2010 Guidelines: "Enhancement of market power by buyers, sometimes called 'monopsony power,' has adverse effects comparable to enhancement of market power by sellers."[1074] As I have already indicated, although this conclusion (which focuses on the impact of monopsony power) on ultimate consumers, would be correct if the buyer involved was not involved in a bilateral-monopoly situation, (1) it most likely is wrong when the buyer faces a supplier with economic power, and (2) I suspect that most of the relevant buyers do face such suppliers. I should add that both of the preceding critiques of this Guidelines position assume that the Guidelines are designed to implement the Clayton Act. As I have also already indicated, the significance of the fact that a merger increases a relevant buyer's monopsony power for its legality under the Sherman Act is contestable. In one direction, the conclusion that any tendency of a merger to create a merged firm that has more bargaining power than the MPs would have had counts against its legality under the Sherman Act (1) is favored by textual argument and (2) would be favored by the argument that the Sherman Act was passed in part to instantiate the moral position that conduct motivated by specific anticompetitive intent is immoral if that position applied not only when the actor is a seller but also when the actor is a buyer even if the buyer's exercise of the relevant additional power benefits final consumers. In the other direction, the claim that any such tendency of a merger to produce this effect counts for its legality under the Sherman Act when ultimate consumers are benefitted is favored by the argument that the Sherman Act was passed at least in part to yield direct benefits to ultimate consumers when that can be done without compromising the incentives of defendants to create competitive advantages in ways that would be economically efficient in an otherwise-Pareto-perfect economy and derivatively would be beneficial to final consumers.

* * *

I will close with a factual observation and an evaluative comment. The factual observation is that the 2010 Guidelines provide far more detail than the 1992

[1073] *Id.* at Section 1 ¶ 7.

[1074] *Id.* at Section 1 ¶ 8.

Guidelines did about the kinds of evidence on which the Agencies intend to base their competitive-impact predictions and the sources from which they intend to secure this evidence[1075] as well as about the various methodologies they expect to use to generate relevant predictions. The evaluative comment is that the Agencies should "own up" to the reality that they are no longer using any market-oriented approach to predict the competitive impact of horizontal mergers. "Fessing up" would serve the Agencies' avowed goal in promulgating the Guidelines[1076]—"assist[ing] the business community and antitrust practitioners by increasing the transparency of the analytical process of the Agencies' enforcement decisions"—and would also, I suspect, accelerate the development of superior, practical non-market-oriented approaches to predicting the competitive impact of horizontal mergers.

5. Contemporary EC Positions and the E.C./E.U. Case-Law on Horizontal Concentrations

A. Contemporary EC Positions on Horizontal Concentrations

E.C./E.U. competition law requires actual or potential participants in mergers or acquisitions to notify the EC not more than one week after entering into a relevant agreement, announcing a public bid for another firm, or acquiring a controlling interest in another undertaking.[1077] Although Articles 11–13 of the EMCR give the EC authority to secure any information the undertakings have that bears on the legality of their actual or proposed conduct, the parties usually provide the required information by phone or e-mail shortly after notifying the Commission. Like U.S. law, E.C./E.U. law provides a possible two-stage review. At Stage I, the EC makes a preliminary review of the request for approval. If, at this stage, it decides that the merger or acquisition in question is not "incompatible with the Common Market," the EC must declare it compatible (perhaps conditional on the parties' fulfilling certain commitments). If the EC has serious doubts about the legality of the merger or acquisition in question, it must proceed to Stage II, in which it investigates the

[1075] See, *e.g.*, *id.* at Section 2.1 (types of evidence relevant to adverse competitive effects); Section 2.2 (sources of evidence); Section 4.1.3 (evidence that relates to implementing the hypothetical-monopolist test—see text below); Section 4.2.1 ¶ 4 (evidence that relates to customer-reactions to price-increases); Section 6.1 ¶¶ 3 and 5 (evidence and methods that relate to direct price competition between MPs); Section 9.1 ¶ 5 (evidence that relates to the timeliness, likelihood and sufficiency of entry); and Section 10 ¶¶ 3–4 (evidence that relates to merger-specific efficiencies).

[1076] *Id.* at Section 1 ¶ 3.

[1077] EMCR Article 4.

merger more carefully. Also, like the U.S. DOJ and FTC, the EC must conduct its investigations under severe time-constraints:

> The time frame for decisions under both stage I and stage II investigations was lengthened in 2004: the old limits of one month and four months respectively proved too tight. Article 10(1) now provides that decisions at stage I shall be taken within 25 days of receiving complete notification, which is increased to 35 working days if, under article 9, a Member State makes a request that the matter be referred to it or if, after negotiation, the parties offer commitments.... Article 10(2) now requires the Commission to make a decision...[at stage II] within 90 days of initiating proceedings for stage II, or the concentration will be deemed to have been approved.... The period is increased to 105 working days when the parties offer commitments 55 days or more after proceedings were initiated. A further 15 working days is possible...but usually only [at the initiative of] the Commission with the consent of the parties.[1078]

I will now delineate and comment on the EC's various positions on the ways in which horizontal mergers can affect relevant buyers and the factors that will influence the existence and magnitude of each such possible effect. More specifically, I will discuss in this order (1) the EC's general position on the relevance of MP-market-shares and market-concentration figures or post-merger HHI figures and merger-generated change-in-HHI figures to a horizontal merger's impact on non-coordinated and coordinated price and QV-investment conduct,[1079] (2) its positions on the determinants of the impact of a horizontal merger on legally-relevant non-coordinated conduct,[1080] (3) its position on the determinants of the extent of coordinated conduct and the impact of a horizontal merger on coordinated conduct,[1081] (4) its discussion of the legal relevance of entry,[1082] (5) its discussion of the impact of the efficiencies a horizontal merger can generate and the legal relevance of such efficiencies under the EMCR,[1083] (6) its discussion of the legal relevance under the EMCR of the fact that one of the undertakings participating in the merger or acquisition under scrutiny is a failing company,[1084] and (7) its positions on the legal relevance of any tendency of a horizontal merger to create or strengthen buyer power in upstream markets[1085] and the legal relevance of any counteracting buyer power possessed by the customers of the merged firm and their *R*s.[1086] I should say at the outset that although the EC Horizontal Merger Guidelines are clearly modeled on their U.S. counterparts, they do deviate from them in a number of significant ways.

[1078] VALENTINE KORAH, AN INTRODUCTORY GUIDE TO EC COMPETITION LAW AND PRACTICE 298–99 (Hart Publishing Co., 9th ed., 2007) (hereinafter KORAH).

[1079] EC Guidelines on the Assessment of Horizontal Mergers at Section III, OJ C 31/5 (2004).

[1080] *Id.* at Section IV.

[1081] *Id.*

[1082] *Id.* at Section VI.

[1083] *Id.* at Section VII.

[1084] *Id.* at Section VIII.

[1085] *Id.* at Section V.

[1086] *Id.* The text that follows will not repeat this or the preceding seven citations.

(1) The EC Guidelines' General Position on the Relevance of MP-Market-Share/Market-Concentration and Post-Merger-HHI/Merger-Generated Change-in-HHI Figures for the Competitive Impact of Horizontal Concentrations

As Sect. 5 of Chap. 7 stated, the EC 1997 Relevant-Market Notice adopts the same SSNIP abstract definition of a relevant antitrust market that the U.S. 1992 Guidelines adopt (and the U.S. 2010 Guidelines continue to use with one important change). The Notice also adopts the same "add closest substitute and successive-next-closest substitutes" protocol for identifying the products that its abstract definition asserts belong in a relevant antitrust market and includes in another provision a reference to the relevance for market definition of all potentially-includable products' prices that reveals that the EC understands that its protocol should refer to closest rival-product and successive next-closest rival products.

The EC Guidelines resemble the U.S. Guidelines as well in asserting that both MP-market-share/market-concentration figures and post-merger-HHI/merger-generated change-in-HHI figures are determinants of the net equivalent-monetary impact of a horizontal merger on relevant buyers. Like their U.S. counterparts, they claim that data on these parameters is a useful starting point for analysis (though they use different language—"initial indication"—to express this position). The EC Guidelines also resemble their U.S. counterparts in providing post-merger-HHI/merger-induced change-in-HHI-figure-oriented guidelines to the enforcement authority's likely reaction to proposed mergers. The EC Guidelines resemble their U.S. counterparts as well in recognizing that, in some circumstances, current market shares will not be good indicators of the future shares the relevant firms would have absent the merger. The EC Guidelines differ from the 1992 U.S. DOJ/FTC Guidelines and resemble the U.S. 2010 Guidelines in that the EC HHI/ΔHHI-based guidelines establish no safe harbors (promulgate no HHI/ΔHHI-based irrebuttable presumptions of legality), establish no HHI/ΔHHI-based irrebuttable presumptions of illegality, and establish no HHI/ΔHHI-based rebuttable presumptions of illegality: in the EC's words, the post-merger HHI and ΔHHI figures are only "initial indicators," "do not give rise to a presumption of either the existence or the absence of. . .concerns. . . ." The EC HHI/ΔHHI-based guidelines and the actual practice of the DOJ and FTC prior to 2010 also resemble their 2010 U.S. Guidelines more than they do the 1992 U.S. Guidelines in terms of their leniency: (1) state that mergers that yield a post-merger HHI below 1,000 normally will not require extensive analysis, and (2) state that mergers that yield a post-merger HHI between 1,000 and 2,000 and a ΔHHI below 250 are unlikely to cause concern.

The EC's general comments on the usefulness of market-aggregated data differ from their U.S. counterparts in two other ways. First, for understandable legal reasons, the EC's general comments include a discussion of the relationship between a firm's market share and its possession of a dominant position or the strength of its dominant position. The EC states that the fact that a firm's market share exceeds 50 % *may* itself evidence its occupancy of a dominant position and that mergers that yield a merged firm with a market share between 40 % and 50 % and in some cases that yield a merged firm with a market share below 40 % may create a firm with a dominant position or strengthen the dominance of an already-dominant firm. For reasons that Sect. 3 of Chap. 8 delineated, I do not think that market share is much connected to dominance. The EC Guidelines recognize that the connection is undermined by inter-market differences in the number and "strength" (whatever that means) of the allegedly-dominant firm's rivals and capacity-constraints faced by rivals that produce close substitutes of the merged firm's products (which are relevant because they affect the merged firm's MCAs over those rivals for the patronage of the buyers the allegedly-dominant firm is best-placed to supply [though the EC Guidelines do not explain this relationship]).

The EC Guidelines also list, without explaining the relevance of, six factors that the Commission recognizes may reduce the predictive power of post-merger-HHI and ΔHHI figures:

(1) the fact that the merger involves a potential entrant or a recent entrant with a small market share (which [to my mind] is relevant to the extent that the new entrant's share would be likely to grow in the future);
(2) the fact that one or more merging parties are important innovators in ways not reflected in their market shares (which [to my mind] may be relevant because it suggests that the innovators' market shares would grow in the future or because mergers that involve one or more innovative MPs may be more or less likely to create a merged firm that faced lower (Π_D + R) barriers than those that faced either MP, more likely to increase QV-investment competition by substituting a merged firm that faced lower *M* disincentives for an MP that faced higher *O* disincentives, more likely to reduce QV-investment competition by substituting a merged firm that faced higher *M* disincentives for an MP that faced lower *M* disincentives, and more likely to reduce QV-investment competition by substituting for a situation in which an *R* faced non-critical *M* disincentives a situation in which that *R* and the merged firm face *O* disincentives);
(3) the fact that "there are significant cross-shareholdings among participants" (which [to my mind] suggests both that pre merger the market is really more concentrated than market-share data suggests but which also may suggest that the merger will increase concentration less than the market-share data would suggest if the MPs had shares in each other pre-merger);
(4) the fact that "one of the maverick-firms is a maverick-firm with a high likelihood of disrupting coordinated conduct" (which [to my mind] increases the probability that the merger will raise COMs and reduce QV-investment competition);
(5) the existence of "indications of past or ongoing coordination, or facilitating practices" (which [to my mind] increases the likelihood that the merger will increase COMs and generate QV-investment restrictions by increasing L barriers to entry or expansion); and
(6) the fact that "one of the merging partners has a pre merger market share of 50 % or more" (which strikes me as much less relevant than I suspect the EC believes it is).

(2) The EC Guidelines' Position on the Determinants of the Non-Coordinated-Conduct Effects of a Horizontal Concentration

The EC Guidelines' discussion of non-coordinated effects has both the strengths and the weaknesses of the U.S. DOJ/FTC's discussion of unilateral effects: The most important shared strengths are (1) the EC's and DOJ/FTC's recognition that the non-coordinated-conduct impact of a merger will be substantially determined by the frequency with which the merger partners are best-placed and second-placed (or, though the Guidelines do not mention this possibility, are both uniquely-equal-best-placed) to supply the same customers and the amount by which when they do occupy such positions the second-placed MP (or both MPs in the uniquely-equal-best-placed case) are better-placed than the buyer's third-placed supplier, (2) the EC's and DOJ/FTC's realization that one can use "customer preference surveys" and analyses of "purchasing patterns" to estimate these figures, and (3) the EC's and DOJ/FTC's realization that one can also derive estimates of the likely impact of a merger on prices (though the fact that they reference this possibility in a section on non-coordinated effects is unfortunate) by analyzing historical bids (*i.e.*, comparing the outcomes of bidding records in which both MPs bid and one in which only one MP bid, presumably controlling for relevant factors that might account for the difference in participation). The most important shared deficiencies of the EC's and DOJ/FTC's discussion of non-coordinated effects are (1) their failure to focus on natural oligopolistic pricing (either in this section or in the section on coordinated interactions), (2) their failure to note the possible relevance of the distinction between individualized-pricing and across-the-board-pricing contexts and their related failure to focus on the CMC-related possibilities and the possibility that a horizontal merger might increase across-the-board HNOPs by altering the sequence in which firms announced their prices, (3) their claim that the frequency with which the MPs are first-placed and second-placed (or uniquely-equal-best-placed) to obtain the patronage of the same buyer depends on "the degree of substitutability" of their products (*i.e.*, their failure to recognize that MCAs as well as BPAs are relevant in this context), and (4) their belief that a firm's market share is "normally" an important determinant of its OCA ("market power" in their words) and that the merger's impact on a firm's market share is "normally" an important determinant of its impact on the firm's OCAs. The EC Guidelines attempt to justify this last claim with the incorrect argument that "[t]he larger the increase in the sales base on which to enjoy higher margins after a price increase, the more likely it is that the merged firms will find such a price increase profitable despite the accompanying reduction in output"—an argument that is wrong both because it ignores the fact that the relevant reduction in output will also tend to increase with the merged firm's sales and because it incorrectly assumes that, across all markets, sales and market shares are highly and strongly positively correlated.

The EC Guidelines also leave the unfortunate impression that the Commission believes that two factors that actually relate to the size of the second-placed MP's advantage over the third-placed supplier of buyers the MPs are best-placed and second-placed to supply are, in fact, independent determinants of the impact of the merger on non-coordinated conduct: (1) "switching costs"—the extent to which buyers will have difficulty switching to other suppliers, which may tend to be high when the buyer "used dual sourcing from the two merging firms"—and (2) the ability of "competitors of the merging parties. . .to increase their supply substantially if prices increase"—whether "rival firms have enough capacity and [would] find it profitable to expand output sufficiently" in response to a merged-firm price-increase to make that price-increase unprofitable for the merged firm.

The EC Guidelines' section on "non-coordinated effects" also contains a peculiar paragraph headed "*Merged entity able to hinder expansion by competitors*," which discusses not only the extent to which the merged entity will hinder rival expansions or entry by refusing to supply production inputs or distribution services to expanders or entrants and refusing to sell to them the right to use information protected by patents (behavior that might violate what is now Article 102 if the merged entity is a dominant firm or part of a set of collectively-dominant rivals)—a possibility that fits the heading—but also the extent to which expansions and entries will be deterred by the merged firm's products' positive brand-recognition and the greater financial strength of the merged entity (whose relevance is unexplained, though it might be relevant to the likelihood that the merged firm would retaliate against an entry or expansion or try to drive the new QV investment out).

On the positive side, this section of the EC Guidelines recognizes that a horizontal merger can either increase or decrease QV-investment competition, though the Guidelines do not explain how and when horizontal mergers can generate these effects.

(3) The EC Guidelines' Position on the Determinants of the Coordinated-Conduct Effects of Horizontal Concentration

The EC Guidelines' discussion of coordinated effects begins with a reference to the possibility that firms may be "able to coordinate their behavior. . .without entering into an agreement or resorting to a concerted practice within the meaning of Article 18 of the Treaty." Although this passage could be addressing natural oligopolistic pricing, it seems far more likely to manifest the Commission's failure to understand that firms can enter into contrived-oligopolistic-pricing agreements without linguistic communications—a failure shared by economists in general and the U.S. authorities as well, which shows up in the relevant experts' confusing discussions of the nature and legality of tacit collusion.

The EC Guidelines proceed to state that for coordination to be achieved, firms must (1) agree on the terms of coordination, (2) monitor behavior to determine "whether the terms of coordination are adhered to," (3) "establish a "credible deterrent mechanism," and (4) prevent current competitors that are not participants in the fix, potential entrants, and customers from undermining it. It would seem to me that the third item in this list would cover the part of the fourth item that refers to established non-participants and potential entrants, and I do not understand how buyers can undermine coordinated behavior other than by informing the authorities or suing the participants themselves.

The first three items in this list are also found in a counterpart list in the U.S. Guidelines. Like its U.S. counterpart, this list ignores various non-behavioral determinants of the profitability of "coordination" that may be affected by horizontal mergers—*e.g.*, the OCAs of the merged firm and its rivals (the amount of safe profits these firms must put at risk to contrive an oligopolistic margin) and the amount of company-wide sales on which a firm can take advantage of a reputation for contrivance or refusing to be deterred from undercutting contrived oligopolistic prices or making other competitive moves.

The EC Guidelines then discuss the factors that affect the ability of potential contrivers to do the first three things the initial list correctly states they must do to successfully coordinate their behavior. Those more specific discussions also share the strengths and weaknesses of their counterparts in the DOJ/FTC Guidelines, including the latter's failure to focus separately on the determinants of the pre merger profitability of coordination and the determinants of the merger's impact on the profitability of coordination.

Like the U.S. Guidelines, the EC Guidelines recognize that it will be easier for firms to reach agreement on the "terms of coordination" (1) the more homogeneous their products, (2) the more homogeneous the firms in terms of their cost structures, market shares, capacity levels, and degrees of vertical integration (which the EC presumably thinks are relevant because it believes these affect the firms' respective HNOPs), (3) the less likely it is that demand and supply conditions will vary through time (presumably in ways that affect the HNOPs of the participants differently), (4) the simpler the pricing-techniques the firms in question employ, (5) the greater the public availability of data on parameters to which prices can be keyed, and (6) the greater cross-shareholders between or among firms (which presumably facilitate communication). This list is fine so far as it goes, but it ignores the possibility that price-fixing can be engaged in by an individual firm (in an individualized-pricing context), that, in some circumstances, coordination can be achieved non-linguistically simply by announcing a contrived oligopolistic price, and that the cost of linguistic communications depends in part on the number of rivals to which such communications must be made, the attention that the antitrust authorities are paying to the relevant parties' conduct, and (even in the E.C./E.U.) the attitudes that potential triers-of-fact have toward the likely guilt of the potential coordinators in question. Relatedly, it ignores the factors that determine the importance of these possibilities and the magnitude of these costs in individual cases, many of which can be affected by horizontal mergers—*e.g.*, the reputation of a firm both for contrivance and for estimating its (HNOP + NOM) correctly.

Like its U.S. DOJ/FTC's counterparts', the EC Guidelines' treatment of "monitoring deviations" also has strengths and weaknesses. The EC correctly points out (1) that monitoring will be easier the more public the relevant prices and transactions and the fewer the number of possible undercutters/underminers, (2) that it may be more difficult for a firm to determine whether it has lost sales because of undercutting or changes in buyer preferences in an "unstable environment," and (3) that the inclusion of meeting-competition or most-favored-customer clauses in contracts of sale facilitate monitoring by inducing buyers to report the prices they have received from other suppliers. However, the EC Guidelines (1) fail to distinguish clearly the task of determining whether one has been undercut by a firm operating from an inferior position from the task of identifying one's undercutter, (2) fail to delineate many of the factors that determine whether a firm can infer undercutting from circumstantial evidence about its repeat sales, sales to former customers of rivals, and new buyers—*e.g.*, the number of buyers in the relevant market, the stability through time of each firm's sales to the three sets of buyers just distinguished, the extent to which sellers have or can obtain reliable data on the non-undercutting-by-competitive-inferior causes of fluctuations in the percentages of sales they make to such buyers, (3) fail to recognize the importance of sellers' having information about the identities of those rivals in the market in question that are well-placed to obtain the seller's customers, (4) fail to recognize the importent of the ability of sellers to identify their former customers' new suppliers by monitoring the deliveries those customers receive, inspecting those customers' input or final-product inventories, and/or examining those customers' final products (when the seller's product is an input), (5) fail to recognize the importance of the factors that determine whether buyers will report to their best-placed suppliers superior offers they receive from one or more inferior suppliers in the hope of securing an even better deal from their best-placed supplier (whether the buyers are repeat buyers in the relevant market and, if not, whether the fact that they "told on" and did not patronize the inferior suppliers that made them a superior offer will become known in the other areas of product-space in which they operate and thereby deter the inferior suppliers they have there from undercutting their best-placed suppliers' contrived oligopolistic offers), and (6) fail to recognize the importance of buyers' adopting a practice of switching suppliers even when it is against their short-run interest to do so to make it more difficult for their best-placed supplier to infer undercutting from their switching suppliers.

The EC Guidelines' discussion of "deterrent mechanisms" is superior to the DOJ/FTC's discussion of these mechanisms in two important respects: it recognizes that (1) "retaliation need not necessarily take place in the same market as the deviation" and that (2) "retaliation may take many forms, including cancellation of joint ventures or other forms of cooperation or selling of shares in jointly owned companies." However, the EC discussion (1) ignores the fact that, in individualized-pricing contexts, "deviation" can be deterred by promises of reciprocation as well as or instead of by threats of retaliation, relatedly (2) fails to discuss the determinants of a firm's ability to reciprocate to a cooperator and the related determinants of the impact that a horizontal merger will have on that ability, (3) fails to discuss the determinants of the loss an individualized-pricing firm that has been undercut will have to incur to inflict various amounts of harm on an undercutter through individualized price-retaliation and of the related determinants of the impact of a horizontal merger on the relevant harm-inflicted to loss-incurred ratios, (4) ignores the deterrent effect of a firm's reputation for contrivance and the determinants of a merger's impact on the reputation of the merged firm for contrivance relative to that of the MPs, (5) fails to discuss the determinants of the profitability to an individual across-the-board pricer of retaliating against an undercutter and of the ability of a group of across-the-board pricers that have been undercut to make the retaliatory moves that are in their collective interest and the determinants of the impact of a horizontal merger on this ability—*e.g.*, fails to note that the uniformity of market shares it believes will facilitate agreement on the terms of cooperation will militate against effective joint across-the-board retaliation (will make the "public good" problem that potential across-the-board retaliators face more severe), and (6) ignores the determinants of the ability of a group of potential across-the-board-pricing underminers to abstain from undermining behavior that is not in their collective interest and the related determinants of the impact of a horizontal merger on this ability.

In short, although the EC Guidelines' discussion of "coordinated effects"—*i.e.*, effects on coordinated behavior—gets a lot right and little wrong, it fails to consider a large number of factors that affect the impact of horizontal merger on such conduct.

(4) The EC Guidelines' Treatment of the Possible Effect of Entry on the Competitive Impact of a Horizontal Concentration

The EC Guidelines borrow the U.S DOJ/FTC Guidelines' focus on the "likelihood, timeliness, and sufficiency" of entry and, like the U.S. Guidelines, claim that "likely, timely, and sufficient...[entry will] deter or defeat any anticompetitive effects of...[a horizontal merger]." Indeed, the EC appears to believe that not just actual entry but even the threat of entry will constrain the merged firm: "When entry barriers are low, the merging parties are more likely to be constrained by entry"—*i.e.*, appears to accept the limit-pricing hypothesis. As already indicated, I think that (1) the effectiveness of potential competition depends not on the height of the barriers to entry but on whether the barriers to entry facing the best-placed potential entrant are higher or lower than the sum of the barriers to expansion and monopolistic or natural oligopolistic QV-investment disincentives that would confront the firm that would be the ARDEPPS' best-placed potential expander at the entry-barred expansion-preventing QV investment level, (2) that the prospect of entry will rarely if ever cause a merged firm not to take advantage of the opportunity its merger gave it to raise its prices (*i.e.*, that the prospect of entry will rarely if ever cause a merger that would otherwise cause prices to be raised not to do so because it induces the merged firm and its *R*s to limit price), (3) effective potential competition will affect outcomes by leading either to entry or to one or more established firms' making QV investments (limit investments) to deter entry, and (4) although actual entry will reduce the equivalent-dollar loss Clayton-Act-relevant buyers suffer from a horizontal merger that would otherwise inflict such a loss on them, it will not eliminate that loss.

The EC guidelines do a better job than their U.S. counterparts of describing the various barriers to entry a potential competitor faces—in effect, make reference to the scale barrier, the risk barrier (thought they define it implicitly in terms of the risk costs incumbents face on "most profitable" QV-investment projects), and Π_D barriers (which they recognize can be generated by the ownership of essential facilities, natural resources, IP rights, superior technological skill, brand preferences, and consumer loyalty). However, the EC Guidelines' entry section (1) does not refer to the retaliation barrier to entry (though its reference to the possibility that the merged firm might deter expansions by small established firms by refusing to deal with them in its section on non-coordinated effects might be interpreted as a reference to retaliation), (2) does not refer to the possibility of expansion by established *R*s of the merged firm (though, as I have just indicated, a paragraph in the Guidelines' non-coordinated-effects section does so), relatedly (3) does not therefore refer to the fact that the effectiveness of potential entry depends, *inter alia*, on the ability of established firms to expand (or the related fact that the effectiveness of potential expansion depends on the ability of potential competitors to enter), and relatedly (4) in essence asserts incorrectly that the effectiveness of potential competition depends on the height of the barriers to entry facing the market's best-placed potential competitor(s).

(5) The EC Guidelines' Treatment of the Legal Relevance of Any Efficiencies a Horizontal Concentration Generates

Like the U.S. DOJ/FTC Horizontal Merger Guidelines, the EC Guidelines state that, for the efficiencies a horizontal merger generates to be legally relevant, they must "benefit consumers, be merger-specific and be verifiable" and for efficiencies to critically affect the legality of a merger they must cause relevant "consumer[s]. . . not [to] be worse off as a result of the merger." The EC Guidelines improve on the 1997 Revision of the U.S. Guidelines' implicit recognition that static marginal efficiencies may have a competitive impact that other sorts of static efficiencies do not (itself an improvement on the 1992 Guidelines) by stating that reductions in variable and marginal costs are more likely to benefit relevant buyers than reductions in fixed costs. The EC Guidelines also improve on the U.S. Guidelines by stating that "the incentive on the part of the merged entity to pass efficiency gains on to consumers is often related to the existence of competitive pressure from the remaining firms in the market," though they do not move from that general point to a consideration of the competitive-position determinants of the relevant pass-on rates and err by stating that the relevant competitive pressure can come not only from established *R*s but also from "potential entry"—*i.e.*, by accepting limit-price theory in this context as well. Like the 1997 Revision of the 1992 U.S. Guidelines, the EC Guidelines recognize that dynamic efficiencies can benefit relevant consumers by leading to the introduction of additional or improved products (even if they do not cause prices to drop). Like the 1997 Revision of the 1992 U.S. Guidelines, the EC Guidelines also claim that efficiencies "may. . .lead to a lower risk of coordinated effects in the relevant market" by "increas[ing] the merged entity's incentive to increase production and reduce prices...." I believe that this claim mischaracterizes the tendency of the static marginal efficiencies a horizontal merger generates to reduce some HNOPs in individualized-pricing contexts and all across-the-board HNOPs as a tendency to reduce COMs: the static marginal efficiencies a horizontal merger generates will reduce the merged firm's incentives to practice contrived oligopolistic pricing relative to those of the MPs by increasing the safe profits it must put at risk to do so, but they will also affect the profitability of contrivance for the merged firm and its *R*s in a host of other ways that Sect. 2 of this chapter indicated that both the EC Guidelines and their U.S. counterparts ignore. For reasons that Sect. 2 explained, the net impact that the static marginal efficiencies a horizontal merger generates will have on contrived oligopolistic pricing in the market in which the merger will be executed is difficult to predict. The EC Guidelines contain one other statement that the U.S. Guidelines contain—a pronouncement that "it is highly unlikely that a merger leading to a market position approaching that of a monopoly, or leading to a similar level of market power, can be declared compatible with the common market on the ground that efficiency gains would be sufficient to counteract its potential anticompetitive effects." I agree though I am surprised that the two Guidelines' authors thought this issue sufficiently important to warrant the inclusion of this sentence.

Finally, two comparative legal points. When discussing the U.S. Guidelines' position on efficiencies, I stated that I believed that both (1) their requirement that the merger's efficiencies be merger-specific to be legally relevant and (2) their implicit rejection of the organizational-economic-efficiency defense that I think should be read into the Clayton Act are wrong as a matter of law—in the former instance because the position alters the U.S. law's do-nothing baseline for competitive-impact analysis and, in the latter instance, because the position is incompatible with a general element of U.S. industrial policy, the practice of encouraging firms to increase their efficiency even when their doing so results in their possessing and exercising monopoly power. The EC Guidelines take the same positions as their U.S. counterparts on the two issues in question. I want to conclude by emphasizing that, even if my contestable conclusions about the individual answers to these issues that are correct as a matter of U.S. law are right, the same answers may not be correct as a matter of EC law, which may not have adopted the relevant do-nothing baseline and may not be as generally supportive of efficiency-enhancing conduct as U.S. industrial policy has been.

(6) The EC Guidelines' Treatment of the Legal Relevance of the Fact That One of the MPs Involved in a Horizontal Concentration Is a Failing Firm

The EC Guidelines' position on failing-firm defenses is identical to the U.S. DOJ/FTC's position. The two purely-economic criticisms I had of the U.S. DOJ/FTC failing-company-defense position therefore apply fully to the EC failing-company-defense position:

(1) the requirement that "in the absence of a merger, the assets of the failing firm would inevitably exit the market"[1087] will reduce competition in those cases in which the proposed merger with an established firm in the relevant area of product-space would benefit relevant buyers more than would any available merger with a market-outsider (perhaps because the merger with the inside firm was more economically efficient than any available merger with an outside firm would be), and
(2) both the above requirement and the requirement that the failing firm show that it could not have executed a more procompetitive merger with another incumbent that would also have been more profitable than not merging at all may reduce competition by deterring failing firms from searching for buyers and by deterring managers of established companies from starting their own new companies or shifting to new companies.

The legal criticism I made of the U.S. DOJ/FTC's failing-company-defense position may not be applicable to the identical EC position: if EC competition law did not adopt the do-nothing baseline for competitive-impact prediction that I believe U.S. law adopted, the EC's requirement that the failing firm establish that "no less anticompetitive alternative purchase" was available to it and that "in the absence of a merger,. . .[its] assets would inevitably exit the market" would be less problematic as a matter of EC law than the U.S. Guidelines' counterpart requirements are as a matter of U.S. law.

(7) The EC Guidelines' Treatment of Buyer Power

The first horizontal-merger-related buyer-power issue is the likely economic impact and legal relevance of any tendency of a horizontal merger to increase the merged firm's buyer power relative to the MPs'. The EC Guidelines correctly state that, if the merged entity is "likely to use its [enhanced] buyer power vis-à-vis its suppliers to foreclose its rivals," any tendency of a merger to increase the merged firm's market power will tend, on this account, to inflict an equivalent-monetary loss on relevant buyers. However, I suspect that the EC greatly exaggerates the likelihood of this possibility. I hasten to add that several items in the clause (a)–(e) list in Article 101(1) and in the clause (a)–(d) list in Article 102 do support the EC's legal conclusion that any tendency of a horizontal merger to impose a net equivalent-euro loss on relevant ultimate consumers by creating a merged firm that has more buying power than the MPs would have had disfavor its legality—*i.e.*, that what are now Articles 101 and 102 are correctly interpreted to be fence laws. I think that the same conclusion applies to the EMCR. But it is also important to emphasize that the EC recognizes that not all mergers that would create a merged firm that would have

[1087] EC Guidelines on the Assessment of Horizontal Mergers at ¶ 90, OJ C3115 (2004).

more buying power than the MPs would have had harm ultimate consumers on that account. Thus, the EC Guidelines correctly state that any "increase[] [in the] buying power [of the merged firm] may be beneficial for competition...[because] a proportion of...[the associated input] cost reductions...[is] likely to be passed on to consumers in the form of lower prices."[1088] For reasons that I explained in Sect. 4B, I think that the EC has this right (whereas the DOJ/FTC and most contemporary U.S. economists wrongly conclude that any increase in the merged firm's buyer power will lead it to increase prices and decrease output by raising its marginal costs).

The second horizontal-merger-related buyer-power issue is the economic effect and legal relevance of any buyer power the customers of the merged firm and its *R*s possess. Although I agree with the EC (and U.S. DOJ/FTC) that any buyer power these firms' customers possess (partly as a result of their ability to threaten to integrate forward and supply themselves) will reduce the extent to which a horizontal merger will enable the merged firm and its *R*s to raise their prices, I reject any suggestion (the Guidelines are unclear) that such prices will prevent a significant number of mergers that would otherwise have resulted in relevant buyers' paying significantly-higher prices from doing so.

B. A Brief Account of the E.C./E.U. Court Case-Law on Horizontal Concentrations

Very few horizontal-merger cases have been decided since the 2004 revision of the 1989 European Merger Control Regulation became effective on May 1, 2004 and the issuance of the EC's Guidelines on the Assessment of Horizontal Mergers in the same year. Hence, the brevity of this subsection. The horizontal-merger case-law discussions of E.C./E.U. competition-law experts tend to focus on a few pre-1989 EMCR cases and a number of post-1989 but pre-2004 cases on either side of the turn of the millennium.

Prior to 1989, the EC and apparently the E.C./E.U. courts believed that the Treaty prohibited only mergers that involved an MP that was already a dominant firm and that created a merged company that had a stronger dominant position than the dominant MP. Although in 1973 in *Continental Can*,[1089] the EC prohibited a merger that in its view satisfied these requirements, it took no other formal actions against proposed or actual mergers (though it did act informally to block or modify a few large mergers between 1973 and 1989[1090]). The EC and the E.C./E.U. courts did not believe that the Treaty (in particular, what is now Article 101) prohibited

---

[1088] *Id.* at Section IV.

[1089] E.U.R. 215 (6/72) (1973).

[1090] See KORAH at 389–90.

mergers that reduced competition without creating a dominant firm or making a set of rivals collectively dominant.[1091]

A number of pre-2004, turn-of-the-century cases focused on the legality under the 1989 EMCR of horizontal mergers that might decrease competition by making the merged firm and some subset of its *R*s collectively dominant. I should state at the outset that, in these cases, the EC and the E.C./E.U. courts were not as clear as they might have been about how such collective dominance would be manifest: unilateral effects were rarely mentioned and references about "tacit collusion" on price or capacity were mixed with expressions of concern that the merger might enable firms to increase their prices (above their HNOPs in my terminology) "without having to enter into an agreement or resort to a concerted practice within the meaning of Article 101. . . ." Although the words themselves could be referring to the possibility that the merger would enable the merged firm and some of its *R*s to practice oligopolistic pricing naturally, the fact that, like their U.S. counterparts, the EC and the E.C./E.U. courts do not recognize the existence of this phenomenon implies that the statement actually reveals those authorities' failure to realize that collusion that is tacit in the sense of not involving verbal communication can still involve the creation of an agreement (that would violate now-Article 101) and/or the communication of a threat (which, regrettably, would not violate now-Article 101 and would also not violate now-Article 102 if the threatener[s] was [were] not individually dominant or member[s] of a set of collectively-dominant rivals).

The collective-dominance cases began in 1992 when the EC decided in *Nestlé/ Perrier*[1092] that the 1989 EMCR applied to cases involving firms with a collectively-dominant position (a conclusion made contestable by the fact that, unlike now-Article 102 of the Treaty, the 1989 EMCR did not refer to the dominant position on the part of one *or more* undertakings—*i.e.*, did not include the italicized words). In 1998 in *Kali & Salz* (also called *France v. Commission* in its appellate iteration),[1093] the ECJ confirmed that a merger might violate the 1989 EMCR by creating a firm or cross-ownership arrangement that made a set of rivals collectively dominant. In *Gencor/Lornho*,[1094] the EC condemned on the ground that it would create a situation of collective dominance a merger (as opposed to a stock acquisition) that would create a merged firm with a 30–35 % share of the world market for platinum and other metals usually found in the same ore when that market (1) was also occupied by another firm with a similar market share, (2) had high barriers to entry and other characteristics conducive to contrivance, and (3) contained a 10 %

[1091] Admittedly, in 1987 in BAT, the ECJ stated that the provision of the 1957 Treaty that is now Article 101 of the 2009 Treaty of Lisbon might prohibit the acquisition of a minority shareholding in a competitor if the acquisition restricted competition. According to KORAH at 390, this surprising judgment created sufficient uncertainty to induce the business community to conclude that a Community-level merger-control system was needed.

[1092] OJ L356 (1992).

[1093] Kali und Salz/MdK/Treuhand (IV/M. 308) OJ L186/38 (1994), on appeal France v. Commission (C68/94 & 30/95) (1998), ECR I-1453 (1998), 4 CMLR 829.

[1094] Gencor/Lornho (IV/M. 619) OJ L11/30 (1999), 4CMLR 1076 (1997).

seller whose stocks the EC believed were nearly exhausted (so that the merged firm and its other large rival's shares would increase to 40 % each in the near future). On appeal, the CFI upheld the EC's decision, stating that "...particularly in the case of a duopoly, a large market share is, in the absence of evidence to the contrary...a strong indication of the existence of a collective dominant position."[1095] In 2000, in *Airtours/First Choice*,[1096] the EC found that a merger that reduced the number of large firms in a market (in this case, the British market for package tours—airline seats and hotel accommodations) from four to three (as opposed to from three to two) violated the EMCR by creating a situation of collective dominance. On appeal,[1097] the CFI confirmed the legal validity of the Commission's merger-to-collective-dominance position but required the Commission to provide convincing evidence not based solely on the market shares of the MPs and concentration of the market that the proposed merger would, in fact, create a condition of collective dominance: "it is incumbent on...[the Commission] to produce convincing evidence" that the proposed merger "will create a situation of collective dominance"—evidence about "market transparency" (the ability of firms to detect each other's pricing and capacity-creation/production decisions), about the ability of firms to retaliate effectively against undercutters, and about the inability of non-participating incumbents and potential entrants to undermine any coordinated conduct or of consumers to protect themselves by shifting to other suppliers or bargaining. The CFI decision in this case is notable not just or even primarily because of the positions just articulated or the court's finding in the case at issue that the EC had not met its burden but for (1) the fact that the opinion made no reference to the possible (probable?) unilateral effects of the merger in question and (2) the doubtfulness of several of the objections the court had to the Commission's evidence on the issues the court deemed critical.

I have no doubt that British buyers have preferences among package-tour suppliers that reflect such matters as their experience with different suppliers, the suppliers' general reputation, and the suppliers' expertise and connections in relation to particular trip-destinations in which the buyer is interested and that, despite the fact that the industry contained three fairly-large tour operators and

---

[1095] Gencor Ltd. v. Commission, ECR-II 753 (1999), 4 CMLR 971 (1999).

[1096] Airtours/First Choice (2000/276) EC, (IV/M 1524) OJ L9311 (2000), 5 CMLR 494 (2000).

[1097] See Airtours v. Commission, Case T342-99, ECR II-2585 (2002). The greater reluctance of the courts to prohibit mergers may also be manifest in two later cases: Tetra Laval BV v. Commission, case T-5/02, ECR II-4381 (the CFI decision) and Commission v. Tetra Laval, Case C 12–03, ECR I-1113 (2005) (the ECJ decision); and Independent Music Publishers and Labels Association v. Commission, Case T-464-04 (2006). However, the significance of these decisions is undercut by the high likelihood that, in the cases in question, the courts were right and the Commission, wrong—in the former case, because the leverage theory the EC used to predict the competitive consequences of an essentially-conglomerate merger is erroneous (though an alternative theory of cross-market contrivance may have been applicable) and in the latter case, because one cannot infer contrivance from parallel price movements (or even from consciously-parallel price decisionmaking).

hundreds of small tour operators as well as four large tour operators, there were buyers for which Airtours and First Choice were respectively first-placed and second-placed (or uniquely-equal-best-placed)—buyers whose third-placed suppliers were significantly worse-placed than the second-placed (or both) MPs. Perhaps the CFI and EC did not mention this reality and its implications for the competitive impact of the proposed merger because the case was handled as a collective-dominance case and collective dominance is defined to relate solely to the ability of firms to coordinate their behavior but, if so, this explanation would provide no more than an excuse (as opposed to a justification).

Several of the CFI's objections to the Commission's assessment of the likely impact of the proposed merger on COMs also seem misguided. It is true that volatility of market shares will disfavor contrivance (whether arranged through verbal communication or tacitly [as the court assumes]) to the extent that sellers cannot detect the causes of changes in their market shares other than rival undercutting (because in such situations volatility will make it more difficult for sellers to detect the causes of changes in their market shares other than rival undercutting (because in such situations volatility will make it more difficult for sellers to detect undercutting from circumstantial sales-evidence records) but, the CFI position to the contrary notwithstanding, this reality does not imply that market-share volatility caused by sellers' acquiring each other makes it more difficult for firms to engage in contrivance. Similarly, the CFI's assumptions to the contrary notwithstanding, there is no obvious negative correlation between the rate of growth of market demand and the profitability of contrived oligopolistic pricing (unless the growth in demand is associated with an increase in HNOP – MC differences as it may well not be). And again, the CFI's assumptions to the contrary notwithstanding, the fact that small tour operators may face Π_D barriers to expansion and that foreign tour operators may face Π_D barriers to entry does suggest that any such expansions and entries that merger-induced increases in COMs elicit will be less damaging to the contrivers than they would otherwise have been, and, as I have argued before, although such expansions and entry will reduce the equivalent-dollar loss a merger inflicts on relevant buyers by increasing COMs at the market's pre merger QV-investment levels, they will not in any case eliminate that loss.

European commentators cite *Airtours* for its confirmation of the EC's position that horizontal mergers can violate the EMCR by creating a collective-dominance situation and for its insistence that high market-share and high market-concentration figures do not shift the burden of proof to defendants—that the Commission still bears the burden of proving through non-structural evidence that the proposed merger is likely to enable the MPs and their *R*s to obtain COMs (or higher COMs). Although I agree that *Airtours* is important for these reasons, I think the court's failure to consider unilateral effects and its reluctance to find coordinated-conduct effects (manifest in the errors it makes when analyzing the likelihood that such effects will result) are, if anything, more important.

To an American, the most striking feature of the E.C./E.U.-court case-law on horizontal mergers is the absence of discussion of unilateral effects (though I admit that the pre-1992 U.S. Horizontal Merger Guidelines also did not discuss unilateral effects). This gap in the E.C./E.U. case-law has a simple explanation, which just shifts the focus of surprise one stage further back in the "regulatory" process: the EC has executed only a few, partial investigations of the non-coordinated-conduct effects of horizontal mergers. The Commission did raise this issue in one case in which it chose not to pursue it[1098] and has based one decision in a five-to-four merger case on the ground that the proposed merger "would give rise to non-coordinated effects"[1099] but seems otherwise to have been discouraged from addressing this issue by objections that have been made to various econometric approaches to pursuing it.[1100]

The post-1989 E.C./E.U.-court case-law also contains a case that focuses on the failing-company defense and the relevance of the buyer-power consideration. Thus, in *Kali-Salz/MDK/Treuhand*,[1101] the ECJ formulated a version of the failing-company defense that is more strict than the version that appears in the EC Guideline or the U.S. DOJ/FTC Horizontal Merger Guidelines in that it requires the defendant to demonstrate that "the acquiring undertaking would gain the market share of the acquired undertaking if it were forced out of the market," which it will virtually never be able to do if it is not the only seller other than the failing company in the market in question.

The last case I will discuss is *Enso/Stora*.[1102] In that case, in 1999, the EC concluded that a merger that would reduce the number of sellers from four to three (one large and two smaller sellers) in a market that had one large buyer and two small buyers would not injure the relevant buyers because the buyers' countervailing power was sufficiently great "to remove the possibility of the parties' exercising market power" despite the Commission's recognition that the two small buyers were much less able to protect themselves than the one larger buyer. May I express my doubts?

* * *

In 1979, I was invited to give a lecture—a "Distinguished Guest Lecture," I believe it was called—by the Antitrust Division of the United States Department of Justice. I chose to lecture on the deficiencies of the traditional market-oriented (MP-market-share/market-concentration-oriented) approach to horizontal-merger competitive-impact analysis that the U.S. courts, DOJ, and FTC were all using at that time and on what I took to be the correct way to predict the competitive impact

[1098] Oracle/PeopleSoft, M3216, OJ L218/6, 4 CMLR IS93 at ¶¶ 197–204 (1994).

[1099] T-Mobile/Tele-ring, M 3916, IP/06/535.

[1100] See Oracle/PeopleSoft, M3216, OJ L218/6 at paras 197–204 (2004) and Volvo/Scania OJ L 143/74, 5 CMCR 11 (2001).

[1101] Kali und Salz/Mdk/Treuhand (IV/M.308) OJ L186/38 (1994), on appeal France v. Commission (C68/94 & 30/95) (1998), ECR I-1453 (1998, 4CMLR829.

[1102] (M. 2243) OJ L254/9 (1999), 4 CMLR 372 (2000) (summary only).

of a horizontal merger. The lecture (and the article on which it was based[1103]) made the following positive points, which should be familiar to readers of this chapter:

(1) analyses of the competitive impact of horizontal mergers must consider their impact not only on price competition but also on QV-investment competition (which the U.S. courts and antitrust-enforcement agencies had so far ignored);
(2) analyses of the competitive impact of horizontal mergers on price competition must focus separately on individualized-pricing situations (where something called contextual marginal costs played an important role) and across-the-board-pricing situations (where the outcome was influenced both by the fact that sellers charged the same price to their own customers and to the customers of their rivals and by the order in which sellers announced their prices);
(3) horizontal mergers affect the prices that are charged in the area(s) of product-space in which they are executed not only by affecting the extent to which price-fixing is practiced in them (in modern terms, by affecting the extent of coordinated pricing behavior) but also by affecting what I called the highest non-oligopolistic prices the sellers in question could charge and the oligopolistic margins they could obtain naturally (whereas the courts and the Agencies at the time completely ignored what they now call unilateral-conduct effects and natural oligopolistic pricing [which they still totally ignore]);
(4) the impact of a horizontal merger that generates no relevant efficiencies on the HNOPs of the merged firm depends substantially on (A) the frequency with which the MPs were respectively best-placed and second-placed to obtain the patronage of the same buyer (or were uniquely-equal-best-placed to obtain a given buyer's patronage) and the amount by which, when they were, the second-placed MP was better-placed to obtain the relevant buyer's patronage than was the buyer's third-placed supplier, (B) the extent to which horizontal mergers that raise the merged firm's OCAs above the MPs' will tend on that account to enable the merged firm to obtain NOMs from buyers from which the MPs could not have done so, (C) the impact of a horizontal merger on the contrived oligopolistic margins the merged firm obtains relative to those the MPs obtained and on the COMs the merged firm's *R*s obtain (which depend on its impact on the amount of safe profits the merged firm must put at risk relative to those the MPs had to put at risk to attempt to contrive an OM and on the safe profits the *R*s must put at risk to attempt to contrive an OM, its tendency to increase the OMs the merged firm attempts to contrive by enabling it to take advantage to a greater extent than the MPs could of company-wide economies of scale in practicing contrivance, its impact on the cost to the merged firm relative to the cost to the MPs of communicating its [their] contrived oligopolistic intentions, its impact on the ability of the merged firm relative to the ability of the MPs and on the ability of the merged

[1103] Richard S. Markovits, *Predicting the Competitive Impact of Horizontal Mergers in a Monopolistically Competitive World: A Non-Market-Oriented Proposal and Critique of the Market Definition-Market Share-Market Concentration Approach*, 56 TEX. L. REV. 587 (1978).

firm's *R*s to infer undercutting from sale records, its impact on the ability of the merged firm relative to the MPs and on the abilities of the merged firm's *R*s to identify their undercutter once they conclude that they have been undercut by a firm operating from an inferior competitive position, [in individualized-pricing contexts] its impact on the ability of the merged firm relative to the ability of the MPs to elicit cooperation by promising reciprocation, its impact on the loss that the merged firm must incur to inflict given relevant amounts of harm on its undercutters through price retaliation relative to the loss the MPs had to incur to do so, its impact on the counterpart costs of contrivance to the *R*s, and its effect on the host of factors that determine these impacts), and (D) the extent to which the merger's initial impact on the merged firm's prices to its own customers cause the HNOPs and NOMs of the merged firm's *R*s to rise and the extent to which any such initial rises in these *R*s' prices to their own customers increase the merged firm's HNOPs and NOMs and so on and so forth;

(5) in individual cases, the impact that a horizontal merger has on QV-investment competition can depend not only (A) on whether it raises the profits the merged firm can earn by expanding above the profits either MP could earn by doing so or lowers the profits the merged firm can earn by expanding below the profits either MP could earn by doing so and (B) on whether it decreases the profits the relevant market's best-placed potential competitor can earn by entering but also on (C) whether it increases or decreases the profits the merged firm's established rivals can earn by expanding (where the courts, which ignored the possibility that established rivals of the merged firm might expand, paid no attention to this third possible impact);

(6) horizontal mergers can affect the incentives of the merged firm and its established and potential rivals to expand not only (A) by raising the prices charged in the relevant area(s) of product-space at its (their) pre merger QV-investment level(s) but also (B) by raising the (Π_D + R) barriers the merged firm faces above those the MP that was best-placed to expand would face or lowering the (Π_D + R) barriers the merged firm faces below those that that MP would face; (C) by increasing or decreasing the retaliation barriers the merged firm faces above those the relevant MP would face and/or by increasing the retaliation barriers to QV investing facing the merged firm's established and potential competitors; (D) by creating a merged firm that faces higher monopolistic QV-investment incentives than did either MP; (E) by substituting a situation in which the merged firm faces monopolistic QV-investment disincentives for one in which the MPs caused each other to face higher natural oligopolistic QV-investment disincentives or one or both MPs and a rival caused each other to face higher natural oligopolistic QV-investment disincentives; or possibly (F) by substituting a situation in which the merged firm and one of its *R*s face critical natural oligopolistic QV-investment disincentives post-merger for one in which pre merger the relevant *R* faced critically-lower monopolistic QV-investment disincentives (whereas the courts and antitrust-enforcement agencies had no conceptual structure for analyzing

the impact of horizontal mergers on QV-investment competition, did not define clearly or consistently the various barriers to entry and expansion that merit consideration, and completely ignored the phenomena I call monopolistic QV-investment incentives and disincentives and natural oligopolistic QV-investment incentives);

(7) the static marginal efficiencies a horizontal merger generates will almost always confer equivalent-dollar gains on Clayton-Act-relevant buyers and the extent of those gains will depend not only on the size of the efficiencies in question but also on the frequencies with which an MP was best-placed, second-placed, worse-than-second-placed by a smaller amount than the amount by which the efficiencies improved the merged firm's position relative to the MPs' positions, and worse-than-second-placed by an amount that exceeded the efficiency in question by a sufficiently-small amount for the efficiencies to reduce the COMs the relevant buyers' unchanged best-placed suppliers obtain from them;

(8) except for a few perverse cases (in which the reductions in competition would clearly be ephemeral), the dynamic efficiencies a horizontal merger generates will also confer equivalent-dollar gains on Clayton-Act-relevant buyers by increasing the quality and variety of the products from which they can choose and, derivatively, by reducing the prices they are charged;

(9) in all but a few cases—see Point (10), the net equivalent-dollar impact a horizontal merger will have on the customers of the MPs and the customers of the merged firm's rivals by altering the absolute attractiveness of the best offer they respectively receive from any inferior supplier will depend on the relative sizes of the equivalent-dollar gains that the efficiencies the merger generates confer on them and the equivalent-dollar loss the merger would, in the absence of these efficiencies, inflict on them; and

(10) in a few cases, the static and dynamic efficiencies a horizontal merger generates will inflict an equivalent-dollar loss on Clayton-Act-relevant buyers by improving the position of the merged firm relative to that of the MPs sufficiently to make it profitable for an established *R* to exit or unprofitable for an established *R* to expand or a potential competitor to enter.

The U.S. DOJ and FTC (and their EC counterparts) have, from my perspective, vastly improved their approach to horizontal-merger competitive-impact analysis since 1979. They have accepted Point (2), Point (3), much of Point (4), much of Point (5), much of Points (7) and (8), and all of Point (9) in the preceding list. I do not know the extent to which my lecture and scholarship contributed to this improvement (though two economists that were present at the 1979 lecture have recently told me that I did have a significant impact). But the important point is that progress has been made. I hope that this study will contribute to further improvements.

Chapter 13
Conglomerate Mergers and Acquisitions

This chapter focuses on the legally-relevant economic effects and legality of conglomerate mergers and acquisitions (hereinafter conglomerate mergers) under U.S. antitrust law and E.C./E.U. competition law. Conglomerate mergers are mergers that are neither horizontal nor vertical—*i.e.*, are mergers between MPs that (1) are not equal-best-placed, respectively best-placed and second-placed, or respectively best-placed and well-enough-placed to affect the oligopolistic margins that a best-placed MP would find *ex ante* profitable to attempt to contrive and (2) are not in a supplier-supplied relationship to each other. Three types of conglomerate mergers can be distinguished:

(1) product-diversification conglomerate mergers (between MPs whose products would not be well-placed to obtain the patronage of any common buyer even if geographic location were not an issue);
(2) geographic-diversification conglomerate mergers (between MPs that produce products that would be rivalrous if they produced them in the same geographic area but, for reasons of geography, are not well-placed to supply any common buyer despite this fact); and
(3) conglomerate mergers that eliminate an effective potential competitor, which may or may not yield product or geographic diversification but whose defining characteristic is that they eliminate an effective potential competitor (a potential entrant that will enter if the established firms do not engage in otherwise-unprofitable conduct to prevent its doing so [or perhaps that was misperceived by the relevant established firm to be sufficiently likely to enter if nothing were done to prevent this outcome]).

R.S. Markovits, *Economics and the Interpretation and Application of U.S. and E.U. Antitrust Law*, DOI 10.1007/978-3-642-24313-4_2,

1. The Sherman and Clayton Act Tests for the Illegality of Conglomerate Mergers

The Sherman Act's "specific anticompetitive intent" test of illegality applies to conglomerate mergers just as it does to the other types of conduct the Act covers, and the Clayton Act's "organizational-economic-efficiency-defense-qualified competitive-impact test" is defined in the same way when the Clayton Act legality of conglomerate mergers is at issue as when the Clayton Act legality of all other Clayton-Act-covered types of conduct is at issue. It is important to emphasize that the Clayton Act test for the illegality of conglomerate mergers incorporates the same "defendant-do-nothing" baseline for competitive-impact measurement as does the Clayton Act test for the illegality of all the other types of conduct the statute covers: the Clayton Act does not obligate firms that propose to execute a conglomerate merger to execute the most-procompetitive conglomerate merger they would find more profitable than doing nothing—just prohibits such parties from executing any conglomerate merger that would reduce the intensity of competition below the level it would have if they did nothing. As we shall see, this feature of the Clayton Act test of illegality renders lawful under the Clayton Act

(1) any geographic-diversification conglomerate merger whose substitution for no attempt to enter into the acquired or merged-with firm's territory would not reduce competition in that area of product-space when the prohibition of the proposed merger would have made it profitable for the firm seeking geographic diversification to execute an alternative, more procompetitive geographic-diversification conglomerate merger in the same market or to execute a more procompetitive independent entry into that market,
(2) any product-diversification conglomerate merger whose substitution for no attempt to diversify into the acquired or merged-with firm's product market would not reduce competition in that market when the prohibition of the proposed merger would have made it profitable for the firm seeking to enter the acquired/merged-with firm's product market to execute an alternative, more procompetitive product-diversification conglomerate merger in the same product market or to execute a more procompetitive independent entry into that market, and
(3) any conglomerate merger that would eliminate a particular effective potential competitor whose substitution for no attempt to prevent the merged-with firm's entry would not decrease competition when the prohibition of the proposed merger would have led the non-potential-competitor MP to execute a more procompetitive merger with a firm that was not an effective potential competitor or with a different effective potential competitor.

2. The Sherman-Act-Licit and Sherman-Act-Illicit Ways in Which Conglomerate Mergers That Do Not Eliminate an Effective Potential Competitor Can Increase Their Participants' Profits and the Appropriate Structure of Trials About the Legality of Such Conglomerate Mergers Under the Sherman Act

A. The Sherman-Act-Licit Ways in Which Conglomerate Mergers That Do Not Eliminate an Effective Potential Competitor Can Increase Their Participants' Profits

The Sherman Act regards as illicit any tendency of a choice to increase the chooser's profits by reducing the absolute attractiveness of the offers against which it must compete in some way that would critically inflate the profitability of the choice in an otherwise-Pareto-perfect economy but regards as licit any tendency of a choice to increase the chooser's profits in any other way. Conglomerate mergers of all sorts can increase their participants' profits in all the Sherman-Act-licit ways that horizontal mergers can do so—in particular,

(1) by generating static and/or dynamic purchasing, production, distribution, marketing, R&D, and finance economic efficiencies;
(2) (in my judgment, though this is not the view of the U.S. antitrust-enforcement authorities or the U.S. courts) by increasing the merged firm's bargaining power as a buyer above the sum of the MPs' pre-merger bargaining powers as buyers when this effect benefits ultimate consumers;
(3) by creating a merged firm that must incur lower mechanical costs to change its initially-announced prices (which may increase the merged firm's profits both directly when the MPs obtained NOMs pre-merger and indirectly by enabling the merged firm to obtain OMs naturally from buyers from which the MPs could otherwise not have done so);
(4) by enabling the merged firm to obtain NOMs the MPs could not have secured by creating a merged firm that would be able to orchestrate a series of natural-oligopolistic-pricing-enabling premature price-announcements that the MPs and their *R*s would not have made;
(5) in across-the-board-pricing contexts, by creating a merged firm that can orchestrate a sequence of mature price-announcements (by itself and its rivals) that will increase the HNOP array for it and its rivals;
(6) by enabling the owners of one MP to profit by selling tax losses that the MP in question could not use to the other MP, which could use them; and
(7) by enabling the owner of one of the MPs to obtain an equivalent-dollar gain by liquidating his or her holding in the MP company (for money or for more liquid shares in the merged company) and perhaps by enabling the owner in question to turn over his or her managerial responsibilities to the merged company.

B. The Sherman-Act-Illicit Ways in Which Conglomerate Mergers That Do Not Eliminate an Effective Potential Competitor Can Increase Their Participants' Profits

Conglomerate mergers that do not eliminate an effective potential competitor can increase their participants' profits in all the Sherman-Act-illicit ways that horizontal mergers can do so except by freeing the merger partners from the price (or, more generally, the non-QV-investment) competition they waged against each other pre-merger. Thus, conglomerate mergers can yield their participants' Sherman-Act-illicit profits by increasing the profits the merged firm obtains by securing through contrivance the cooperation of remaining rivals, by erecting retaliation barriers against other rivals' expansions or entries, and by engaging in predation above the sum of the profits the MPs would have obtained over the same time-period in these ways. And conglomerate mergers between an established firm and an effective potential competitor can yield Sherman-Act-illicit profits by reducing the QV-investment competition the established firm faces.

To facilitate my explanation of these contrivance, retaliation-barrier, and predation claims, I will assume (1) that the conglomerate merger in question is being proposed by firms MP1 and MP2, (2) that the firm the merger would create would have an MP1 division and an MP2 division, and (3) that contrived oligopolistic pricing, the creation of retaliation barriers to entry or expansion, and predation were not so unprofitable for each MP pre-merger for any tendency of the merger to increase the profitability of such conduct to leave such conduct still unprofitable for the merged firm post-merger. I focus first on how such a merger can increase the profits that the merged firm can make by engaging in contrived oligopolistic pricing above the profits that MP1 and MP2 could have made by engaging in such pricing. First, even if the MPs do not have a common conglomerate rival—*i.e.*, even if the economy does not contain a conglomerate firm that is requisitely-well-placed to obtain the patronage of at least one buyer each MP is best-placed to supply, their conglomerate merger could increase the profits the merged firm could realize by engaging in contrived oligopolistic pricing in at least the following five ways:

(1) by enabling the division of the merged firm whose MP-antecedent had a weaker reputation for contrived oligopolistic pricing to take advantage of the other MP's stronger reputation for such contrivance when the merged company will inherit the reputation of the MP with the stronger reputation for contriving;
(2) by enabling the merged company to take advantage of economies of scale in estimating its HNOPs and NOMs accurately or one division of the merged company to take advantage of the other division's expertise in making such estimates;
(3) when one MP has personnel that are more skilled at contrivance than are the personnel of the other MP or has developed better contrived-oligopolistic-pricing-related data-collection protocols and delivery/inventory-inspection regimes by enabling the division of the merged company whose MP-antecedent had less-relevantly-skilled personnel and less-cost-effective protocols and regimes to use the other MP's personnel and regimes or obtain training from the other division;

(4) in individualized-pricing contexts in which pricing is secret and it is therefore more difficult for an undercut firm both to determine whether it has been undercut by a rival that is worse-placed to obtain the patronage of the buyer in question and to identify its undercutter, by enabling the merged company to take advantage of economies of scale in collecting sales-data, observing deliveries, and inspecting inventories; and
(5) by enabling the merged company to take advantage of company-wide economies of scale (related to the number of customers that the company is best-placed to supply and hence from which it could secure a COM) in building and maintaining a reputation for carrying out contrived-oligopolistic-pricing-related threats and promises.

Second, when the MPs do have a common conglomerate rival, their conglomerate merger may increase the profits the merged firm can realize from contrived oligopolistic pricing in at least the following five additional ways:

(1) by reducing the mechanical and legal costs the merged firm would have to incur to communicate its contrived oligopolistic intentions to such *R*s below those the MPs would have to incur to do so by enabling the merged firm to use one communication to each such *R* to convey its intention to practice contrived oligopolistic pricing on the products of both MPs that that *R* was well-placed to steal (instead of the separate communications the MPs would have to make to communicate their respective intentions) and by enabling the merged firm to communicate its contrived oligopolistic intentions simply by charging a contrived oligopolistic price (when the merged firm has a stronger reputation for contrivance and for estimating its [HNOP + NOM]s accurately than one or both of the MPs had);
(2) in individualized-pricing contexts in which pricing is secret, by increasing the ability of the merged firm to infer from circumstantial sales-evidence whether it has been undercut by an *R* that was worse-placed to secure a relevant buyer's patronage above the ability of the MPs to do so by enabling the merged firm to pool the sales-data of the MPs that relate to customers the relevant *R*s are well-placed to supply;
(3) in individualized-pricing contexts in which pricing is secret, by increasing the ability of the merged firm to identify the rival that has undercut it from a position of inferiority by enabling it to pool the information the MPs have about their common *R*s' relevant competitive positions and dispositions to undercut;
(4) by enabling the merged company to take advantage of any excess reciprocatory power one MP had in its relations with such a common *R*; and
(5) by enabling the merged company to "pool the MPs' retaliation power"—*i.e.*, to reduce the loss it must incur to inflict some relevant amount of harm on any such common *R* that undercut it from a position of inferiority by facilitating its engaging in more retaliation (more retaliatory price-cuts, more retaliatory advertising, and conceivably more creations of retaliatory QV investments) through one MP division and less through the other MP division than the separate MPs would have practiced on their own when the harm-inflicted to

loss-incurred ratio for the additional retaliation by the former division is higher than the harm-inflicted to loss-incurred ratio for the foregone retaliation of the latter division.

I hasten to add that conglomerate mergers that (do or) do not eliminate an effective potential competitor may also tend to reduce the profits that the merged firm can make by engaging in contrived oligopolistic pricing in at least two ways:

(1) by increasing the amount of safe profits the merged firm must put at risk to attempt to contrive an OM (A) by yielding static marginal efficiencies that increase its OCAs directly, (B) in across-the-board-pricing situations, by creating a merged firm that can orchestrate an HNOP-array-raising change in the sequence in which it and its rivals announce their prices, (C) by increasing the NOMs the merged firm can obtain by enabling it to take advantage of economies of scale in changing initially-announced prices and enabling it to orchestrate a series of natural-oligopolistic-pricing-facilitating premature price-announcements, and (D) by increasing the prices its customer-by-customer best-placed rivals charge its customers (in individualized-pricing situations by raising the relevant CMC it and they must incur and, in across-the-board-pricing contexts, by raising the prices it would charge its own customers in the above ways even if its pricing would not affect its rivals' prices and thereby raising the prices its rivals charge their customers and hence its customers as well) and
(2) by increasing (A) the inclination of antitrust authorities and potential private plaintiffs to pay attention to the merged firm's conduct and prosecute/sue it if it engages in contrivance, (B) the likelihood that on any given evidence a trier-of-fact will find the merged firm guilty of contrived oligopolistic conduct, and (C) the sentences, fines, or damage-awards that will be imposed on or assessed against the merged firm or its managers if it is convicted/found liable.

I also hasten to repeat a point I made in the preceding three chapters: the fact that a particular type of conduct (in this case, contrived oligopolistic pricing) is more profitable for an actor (in this case, for the merged firm relative to the MPs) does not guarantee that the actor will engage in the conduct in question (in this case, contrived oligopolistic pricing): the firm's managers' preference for obeying (desirable) laws may lead them to reject such profit opportunities.

With two exceptions, the preceding ways in which a conglomerate merger that does not eliminate an effective potential competitor can increase the profits the merged firm can realize by engaging in contrived oligopolistic pricing applies *mutatis mutandis* when the issue is the possible tendency of such a conglomerate merger to increase the profits the merged firm can make by erecting retaliation barriers to the entry of an effective potential competitor and/or the QV-investment expansion of an established firm that is an effective potential expander. Thus, conglomerate mergers that do not eliminate an effective potential competitor can also increase the profits the merged firm can make by erecting retaliation barriers above those that the independent MPs could realize by doing so by creating a merged firm that inherits the reputation for retaliating against new investors of the MP with the stronger such reputation, by creating a merged firm that can take advantage of company-wide economies of scale in building such a reputation, and (when the MPs face common conglomerate *R*s) by enabling the merged firm to communicate its barrier-erection-relevant intentions in relation to the markets in which both MPs operate in one rather than two communicative acts, to take advantage of any excess reciprocatory power one MP had in its relations with a potential rival investor or co-barrier-erector,[1104] and to pool the MPs' retaliatory power in relation to any such investor or co-barrier-erector, *etc*. The two exceptions are:

(1) since the identity/identities of the potential entrant and/or potential expander in question is/are usually known and cannot in any event be inferred from circumstantial sales-evidence, the parts of the contrived-oligopolistic-pricing analysis that relate to the possibility that any such conglomerate merger that was executed in an individualized-pricing context would tend to facilitate the merged firm's (A) determination of whether it has been undercut by a rival that occupied an inferior competitive position and (B) identification of its undercutter have no counterpart in the "erection of retaliation barriers to entry or expansion" analysis, and
(2) any tendency a conglomerate merger that does not eliminate an effective potential competitor has to increase the amount by which the merged firm's actual price exceeds its overall marginal costs above the amount by which the MPs' actual prices exceeded their overall marginal costs will tend to *increase* the profits the merged firm can make by erecting retaliation barriers to expansion or entry by increasing the amount of profits a new rival QV investment will take away from it whereas, as we saw, the same tendency of a conglomerate merger will tend to *decrease* the profits the merged firm can make by practicing contrived oligopolistic pricing by increasing the safe profits its attempts to engage in such contrivance put at risk.

With the same two exceptions, the analysis of the ways in which a conglomerate merger that does not eliminate an effective potential competitor can increase the profits the merged firm can make by engaging in contrived oligopolistic pricing will apply *mutatis mutandis* when the issue is the possible tendency of such conglomerate mergers to increase the profits the merged firm can realize by driving an established rival out of business (or inducing an established rival to sell out to it at a distressed price after threatening to drive it out).[1105]

[1104] The text assumes that, in some cases, the merged firm and the MPs might find it profitable to deter an entry or rival QV-investment expansion *inter alia* by rewarding the potential investor for not investing by allowing it to make COM-containing deals the barrier-erector would otherwise have found profitable to prevent.

[1105] The tendency of a conglomerate merger to enable the merged firm to take advantage of any excess reciprocatory power an MP has in relation to a particular rival could increase its ability to induce a target rival to exit or sell out to the extent that it will increase the merged firm's ability relative to the MPs' to secure this outcome by promising to increase the profits the target's other QV investments yield by allowing the target to secure COMs when selling the products those investments created when neither MP would otherwise have done so. Admittedly, unless the effort to secure the exit of a rival involved a threat to engage in inherently-unprofitable conduct to inflict a loss on the target, it would be inappropriate to label it "predatory." However, the conduct in question would still violate the Sherman Act.

3. The Various Ways in Which Conglomerate Mergers That Do Not Eliminate an Effective Potential Competitor Can Decrease and Increase Competition in the Clayton Act Sense and the Appropriate Structure of Trials About the Legality of Such Conglomerate Mergers Under the Clayton Act

A. The Various Ways in Which Conglomerate Mergers That Do Not Eliminate an Effective Potential Competitor Can Decrease Competition in the Clayton Act Sense of That Expression

I will first examine the various ways in which such conglomerate mergers that do not generate any purchasing, production, distribution, or finance economic efficiencies can impose a net equivalent-dollar loss on Clayton-Act-relevant buyers by reducing the absolute attractiveness of the best offer they respectively receive from any inferior supplier and then examine the two (unusual) sets of circumstances in which, perversely, the purchasing, production, distribution, or finance economic efficiencies that such a conglomerate merger can generate can impose a net equivalent-dollar loss in this way on Clayton-Act-relevant buyers.

First, in across-the-board-pricing contexts, to the extent that the merged firm is able to orchestrate an HNOP-array-raising sequence of price-announcements that would not otherwise have been made in the order in question, the merger will inflict an equivalent-dollar loss on the customers of the merged firm and its *R*s on this account. Second, to the extent that the cost to the merged firm of changing its initial prices is lower than the cost to the MPs of doing so (because the merged firm can take advantage of economies of scale in making such changes), a conglomerate merger that does not eliminate a potential competitor will tend to inflict an equivalent-dollar loss on the Clayton-Act-relevant customers of the merged firm by increasing the NOMs they pay—in particular, will do so to the extent that the cost-reduction critically affects the ability of the merged firm to secure OMs naturally. Third, to the extent that the merger in question creates a firm that can orchestrate a series of premature price-announcements that would not otherwise have been made and that permit both the merged firm and its rivals to secure OMs naturally, it will inflict an equivalent-dollar loss on the customers of both the merged firm and the customers of its rivals on this account. Fourth, to the extent that the merged firm chooses to take advantage of the merger-generated increase in its opportunity (see Sect. 2A(2)) to profit by contriving OMs, erecting retaliation barriers to new entry or established-rival expansions, or engaging in predation, the merger will tend to inflict equivalent-dollar losses on both the merged firm's customers and the customers of its rivals on those accounts as well. Fifth, to the extent that the merged firm faces one or more conglomerate *R*s that compete against both the MP1 and MP2 division of the merged firm, the merger will inflict an equivalent-dollar loss on the customers of such conglomerate *R*s by increasing the COMs those *R*s obtain from them if the *R*s in question choose to take advantage of the tendency of the merger to increase the profits they can make by contriving OMs (1) by reducing the cost to them of communicating their contrivance intentions to the merged firm relative to the cost they had to incur to do so separately to each MP, (2) by enabling the *R*s to take advantage of any excess reciprocatory power they had in relation to one MP, (3) by spreading the merged firm's defenses—*i.e.*, by reducing the loss the *R*s have to incur to inflict some relevant amount of harm on the merged firm below the loss they had to incur to inflict the same total amount of harm in appropriate proportions on the two MPs separately by enabling the *R*s to inflict the requisite total amount of harm on the merged firm by inflicting more harm on the MP1 division of the merged firm than they had to inflict on MP1 pre-merger and less harm on the MP2 division of the merged firm than they had to inflict on MP2 pre-merger (or *vice versa*) when the harm-inflicted to loss-incurred ratio for the additional harm inflicted on the MP1 division was higher than its counterpart for the foregone retaliation on the MP2 division, and (4) by increasing the harm-inflicted to loss-incurred ratio for retaliating against the merged firm by stealing one of the merged firm's customers below its counterpart for retaliating against the relevant MP by stealing the same customer from the MP pre-merger by increasing the NOM and COM components of the merged firm's price to that buyer above their counterparts for the relevant MP. Sixth, to the extent that such a merger increases the prices the merged firm and its *R*s charge their own respective customers in one or more of the preceding five ways, it will increase the prices the *R*s and the merged firm secure from their customers indirectly: in individualized-pricing contexts, because the higher prices the merged firm charges its own customers (the Rs charge their own customers) will increase the CMC it (they) have to incur to match any offer the *R*s (the merged firm) charge their (its) customers, and, in across-the-board-pricing contexts, because the fact that the merged firm (*R*s) will be charging the *R*s' (merged firm's) customers the same price it is (they are) charging its (their) own customers means that the merged firm (the *R*s) can piggyback ride on the higher prices the *R*s (the merged firm) is charging, and so on and so forth. Seventh, conglomerate mergers that generate static marginal efficiencies that (1) would increase the merged firm's BCAs above the BCAs a best-placed MP enjoys in its relations with buyers it is best-placed to supply and/or (2) would give the merged firm a BCA in relation to a buyer that no MP is best-placed to supply that exceeds the BCA that the *R* that is best-placed to supply that buyer pre-merger enjoys in its relations with the buyer in question may inflict an equivalent-dollar loss on the relevant buyers by increasing the NOMs they pay (by more than any amount by which the static marginal efficiencies reduce the COMs they must pay by increasing the amount of safe profits the merged firm must put at risk to attempt to contrive an OM [though this effect may be outweighed by the possible tendency of the efficiencies in question to increase the merged firm's ability to reciprocate to competing rivals and to retaliate cost-effectively against undercutters]). Eighth, conglomerate mergers that do not eliminate an effective potential competitor can also inflict an equivalent-dollar loss on the customers of the merged firm and its *R*s by deterring the merged firm from making a QV-investment expansion that no-one else will replace either at all or with a project that is as beneficial to Clayton-Act-relevant buyers by critically raising (1) the (Π_D + R) barriers the merged firm would face above those that face an effective-potential-expander MP pre-merger (by making it profitable for the merged firm to allocate to consolidation resources the MP would have devoted to expanding) and/or (2) the retaliation barriers the merged firm would face above the L barriers the relevant MP faces by enabling the merged firm to obtain higher prices from the MPs' customers and by spreading the merged firm's defenses—*i.e.*, by enabling a conglomerate *R* that competes against both MP1 and MP2 to retaliate against the merged firm's execution of an expansion that one of the MPs would otherwise have executed on its own by retaliating against both divisions of the merged firm (and conceivably, by enabling individual *R*s that compete against either MP1 or MP2 but not against both to make more cost-effective "cross-market" joint-retaliation arrangements). Ninth, perversely, rarely, and I suspect practically irrelevantly, a conglomerate merger that does not eliminate an effective potential competitor can also inflict an equivalent-dollar loss on Clayton-Act-relevant buyers by generating dynamic efficiencies that convert a situation in which an *R* of the MPs would otherwise execute a QV-investment expansion even though it would face a monopolistic QV-investment disincentive to make the investment in question into a situation in which the merged firm and that *R* would confront each other with critical natural oligopolistic QV-investment disincentives. Tenth, finally, perversely, rarely, but I suspect occasionally possibly relevantly, such a conglomerate merger can inflict an equivalent-dollar loss on Clayton-Act-relevant buyers if the static efficiencies it generates leads enough of these *R*s to exit (by improving the merged firm's competitive-position arrays and concomitantly making the MPs' *R*s' competitive-position arrays worse) to produce this effect.

Now that I have explained the various ways in which a conglomerate merger that does not eliminate an effective potential competitor can inflict equivalent-dollar losses on Clayton-Act-relevant buyers, I want to repeat two points I made in the horizontal-merger context about the Clayton Act relevance of some of these possibilities. First, if as I argued in Chap. 4 it is correct as a matter of law to read an organizational-economic-efficiency defense into the Clayton Act, a conglomerate merger that would not inflict a net equivalent-dollar loss on Clayton-Act-relevant buyers if it did not lead one or more *R*s of the merged firm to exit by worsening their competitive-position arrays by improving the merged firm's competitive-position array by generating organizational efficiencies that are allocative as well as private will not violate the Clayton Act (though the burden of proving the elements of this defense will fall on the defendants). Second, if contrary to my own conclusion it is incorrect as a matter of law to hold against a conglomerate merger any tendency it has to inflict an equivalent-dollar loss on Clayton-Act-relevant buyers by inducing the merged firm and/or its *R*s to engage in illegal oligopolistic or predatory conduct post-merger, these possible effects of such mergers will be irrelevant to their legality under the Clayton Act. (As I indicated in Chap. 12, I do not think it legally incorrect to consider the tendency of mergers to induce subsequent illegal conduct that is difficult to detect, prove, and deter when assessing their Clayton Act legality, though, of course, I agree that defendants must be given the opportunity to rebut any claim that they will take advantage of any opportunity their merger will give them to make additional profits by committing illegal acts that will harm Clayton-Act-relevant buyers by putting on evidence of their past conduct or current intentions and/or evidence that suggests that it will be easy for the authorities or a potential private plaintiff to detect and prove any such illegal conduct the merged firm might engage in.)

Conglomerate mergers that do not eliminate an effective potential competitor can generate both static and dynamic efficiencies. Thus, since the production of goods that are non-rivalrous can "consume" identical inputs that share certain production steps, conglomerate mergers can enable their participants to take advantage of purchasing and production economies of scale; since given distributors often resell non-rivalrous products and the separate resellers of non-rivalrous products often are located conveniently near to each other, conglomerate mergers can enable their participants to take advantage of distribution economies of scale; since readers and viewers of given media often are interested in purchasing various non-rivalrous products, conglomerate mergers can enable their participants to take advantage of promotional economies of scale; since there are some economies of scale and scope in both product R&D and production-process R&D, conglomerate mergers can enable their participants to execute both these types of research more proficiently; and since it is possible to finance more than one non-rivalrous operation at one time and one can sometimes reduce risk costs by developing an appropriate portfolio of QV-investment projects, conglomerate mergers can also enable their participants to take advantage of finance economies of scale and to reduce risk costs by creating a risk-cost-reducing portfolio of projects. Conglomerate mergers can also generate allocative efficiencies for non-scale (or scope) reasons by enabling their participants to combine assets that are complementary for non-scale non-risk-related reasons—*e.g.*, by combining one firm with excess production-management personnel and insufficient distribution-management personnel with another firm with a production-management-personnel shortage and a distribution-management-personnel glut.

Although, as Sect. 3A stated, both the static and the dynamic efficiencies that a conglomerate merger generates can in some circumstances inflict an equivalent-dollar loss on Clayton-Act-relevant buyers, I am confident that in the overwhelming majority of situations such efficiencies will confer an equivalent-dollar gain on such buyers. The analysis of the impact of such efficiencies on such buyers in the normal case in which they benefit them is the same as the counterpart analysis of the impact of the efficiencies that a horizontal merger can generate.

I start with the static efficiencies. To save space and simplify the exposition, I will assume that

(1) the MPs, the merged firm, and their *R*s all set individualized prices,
(2) the static efficiencies in question are marginal-cost reductions,
(3) each relevant buyer will buy one unit of the relevant product regardless of whether the merger is executed,
(4) the magnitude of the static efficiency in question equals the marginal-cost reduction that the relevant conglomerate merger will generate, and
(5) unless otherwise specified, the static efficiencies in question will not cause any rival of the merged firm to exit or affect the NOMs or COMs any relevant buyer pays for any other reason.

On these assumptions, the equivalent-dollar impact of the static efficiencies a conglomerate merger generates on any given buyer will depend not only on the magnitude of the relevant static efficiencies but on the competitive position of the better-placed MP in relation to that buyer:

(1) when the better-placed MP is best-placed in relation to a buyer, the static efficiency will not directly affect that buyer (though it may inflict a loss on the buyer by enabling the merged firm to obtain an OM naturally or confer a benefit on the buyer by deterring the merged firm from attempting to contrive an OM);
(2) when the better-placed MP is second-placed pre-merger, the static efficiency will benefit the buyer in question: the equivalent-dollar gain will equal the smaller of the static efficiency and the original OCD of the better-placed MP;
(3) when the better-placed MP is worse-than-second-placed by an amount that is smaller than the static efficiency, the static efficiency will benefit the relevant buyer: the equivalent-dollar gain will equal the smaller of the original best-placed supplier's OCA and the positive difference between the static efficiency and the amount by which the better-placed MP is worse-than-second-placed; and
(4) when the better-placed MP is worse-than-second-placed by an amount that exceeds the static efficiency that is generated, there will be no effect on the buyer in question unless the improvement in the position of the merged firm reduces the OMs the buyer's best-placed supplier attempts to contrive by making it inherently profitable for the merged firm to beat a contrived oligopolistic offer that the relevant best-placed firm would otherwise have made.

I turn now to the dynamic efficiencies that a conglomerate merger can generate for one or more of the reasons that such mergers can generate static efficiencies. In the normal case, any such reductions in the (Π_D + R) barriers to expansion the merged firm faces will—if anything—confer an equivalent-dollar gain on Clayton-Act-relevant buyers. In particular, to the extent that such efficiencies would make it profitable for the merged firm to make a QV investment if no rival made a limit QV investment to deter it from doing so when it would not be profitable for any MP to expand and would otherwise also not be profitable for any potential competitor or other established firm to add to total QV investment in the relevant area of product-space, the dynamic efficiencies would benefit relevant buyers either by inducing the merged firm to make such an investment or by inducing an *R* to make a limit QV investment to deter the merged firm from doing so.

B. The Appropriate Structure of Trials About the Clayton Act Legality of Conglomerate Mergers That Do Not Eliminate an Effective Potential Competitor

We have just seen that, like horizontal mergers, a conglomerate merger that does not eliminate an effective potential competitor will tend to decrease competition in the Clayton Act sense if they generate no static or dynamic efficiencies but will not decrease such competition on balance if (1) it generates static and/or dynamic efficiencies and (2) those efficiencies confer sufficient equivalent-dollar gains on Clayton-Act-relevant buyers to fully offset the net equivalent-dollar loss the merger would impose on the relevant buyers if it did not generate any such efficiencies. I suspect that conglomerate mergers that do not eliminate an effective potential competitor are less likely to violate the Clayton Act than are horizontal mergers: any tendency of conglomerate mergers to yield buyers lower efficiency-related equivalent-dollar gains than horizontal mergers yield is likely to be outweighed by the fact that, unlike horizontal mergers, conglomerate mergers that do not eliminate an effective potential competitor do not inflict equivalent-dollar losses on Clayton-Act-relevant buyers by freeing the MPs from each other's non-QV-investment competition. However, I do not think that this difference affects the appropriate structure of trials about the Clayton Act legality of such conglomerate mergers.

In my judgment, the appropriate structure for trials about the Clayton Act legality of conglomerate mergers that do not eliminate an effective potential competitor is the same as the appropriate structure for trials about the legality of such mergers under the Sherman Act. First, the government should be required to establish a *prima facie* case against the legality of a proposed merger of the relevant type by providing evidence that (1) one of the MPs had orchestrated premature price-announcements in the areas of product-space in which it operated and that natural oligopolistic pricing was not currently being practiced in the other MP's "markets," (2) one of the MPs had orchestrated an HNOP-array-increasing sequence of mature price-announcements in across-the-board-pricing markets in which it operated and that the other MP operated in an across-the-board-pricing "market" in which the sequencing of mature price-announcements was suboptimal from the sellers' perspective, (3) one MP had a stronger reputation for contrivance and/or predation than the other and that the merged company was likely to inherit that MP's reputation, and/or the fact that the merged firm would be best-placed or second-placed to supply more buyers than either MP would have been would critically increase the profitability to the merged firm of building and maintaining a reputation for engaging in strategic conduct (4) the merged firm would face conglomerate rivals that competed against both MPs, and/or (5) the MPs and their *R*s had engaged in contrived oligopolistic pricing in the past. (If the merger in question has already been consummated, the government can establish its *prima facie* case not only by introducing a requisite amount of evidence on these matters but also by putting on evidence about post-merger contrivance and predation, post-merger increases in prices, and post-merger rejections of expansion and entry plans.) Second, once the government has made out its *prima facie* case, the defendants should be permitted to defeat the government's case by rebutting the government's evidence, explaining that any post-merger rival exits (and related price-increases and/or QV-investment decreases) that the government had documented resulted from the organizational allocative efficiencies the merger generated, and/or establishing the requisite probability that the merger would (or did) benefit Clayton-Act-relevant buyers sufficiently by generating static and dynamic efficiencies to leave them no worse-off in equivalent-dollar terms. Third, the government should be permitted to rebut the defendants' evidence, and fourth and finally, the defendants should be permitted to rebut the government's rebuttal evidence.

4. The U.S. Case-Law and DOJ/FTC Positions on the Economic Consequences and Antitrust Legality of Conglomerate Mergers That Do Not Eliminate an Effective Potential Competitor

A. Conglomerate Mergers That Do Not Eliminate an Effective Potential Competitor, Will Not Induce the Merged Firm to Engage in Additional Reciprocity or Execute Additional Tie-Ins, and Do Not Enable One MP to Achieve Sought-After Geographic Diversification

I have argued that conglomerate mergers in this category can reduce competition (1) by increasing the COMs the merged firm will obtain relative to the COMs the MPs would have secured and by increasing the COMs the merged firm's rivals obtain, (2) by increasing the amount of predatory conduct in which the merged firm will engage above the amount in which the MPs would have engaged, (3) by increasing the retaliation barriers the merged firm will erect against its established rivals' and potential competitors' making QV investments above the L barriers the MPs would have erected, (4) by increasing the retaliation barrier to expansion the merged firm will face above the L barriers the MPs would have faced, and (5) by increasing the $(\Pi_D + R)$ barriers to expansion the merged firm will face above those the MPs would have faced. Neither the U.S. courts nor the U.S. antitrust-enforcement agencies have ever adverted to any of the last three of these possibilities. In the late 1960s, both the FTC[1106] and the Justice Department[1107] believed that conglomerate mergers could facilitate and encourage price-fixing (though they were unable to explain how such mergers would do so). However, the courts were not always so willing to accept this contention. Admittedly, in *Procter & Gamble (Clorox)*,[1108] the Supreme Court accepted the proposition that, in the Court's words, "the substitution of the powerful acquiring firm [Procter & Gamble] for the smaller, but already dominant, firm [Clorox]. . .may substantially reduce [competition]. . .by dissuading the smaller firms from aggressively competing...." However, it is not clear whether the desired "aggressive competition" was a refusal to cooperate with contrivance or the execution of more positive competitive moves. And, in at least one case, the courts did not seem to grasp the contrived-oligopolistic-pricing argument even when it was presented to them—in particular, interpreted a government contention that "the most important anticompetitive effect of the trend toward conglomeration by merger is 'conglomerate interdependence and forbearance'" to be a social and political argument for preventing the concentration of society's resources across the economy as a whole rather than as an argument for preventing decreases in competition.[1109] By way of contrast, not only the DOJ but also the courts in the 1960s did seem to believe that conglomerate mergers could lead to predation. Once more, however, the Agencies' and courts' understanding of how conglomerate mergers could increase the profitability of predation was limited—*viz.*, focused on the possibility that a conglomerate merger could create a merged firm that engaged in predation in which neither MP would have engaged on its own because the merged firm could have a larger pool of capital to use to finance a predation campaign[1110] and ignored the possibility that the conglomerate merger could also encourage predation by creating a merged company that had a stronger related reputation for engaging in such conduct than did either or both MPs, by creating a merged company that could pool the MPs' retaliatory and reciprocatory power (particularly when the MPs faced common conglomerate rivals), by creating a merged company that was best-placed and second-placed more often than either MP was and could on that account profit more by building and maintaining a reputation for engaging in strategic conduct, and by generating static efficiencies that increased the cost-effectiveness of the merged company's predatory moves.

[1106] See FTC Staff, An Economic Report on Corporate Mergers at 458–71 (1969), reprinted in Antitrust and Monopoly Subcommittee, Senate Judiciary Committee, 91st Cong., 1st Sess., Hearings on Economic Concentration, pt. 8-A (1969).

[1107] See the Justice Department argument in United States v. International Tel. and Tel. Corp., 324 F. Supp. 19 (D. Conn., 1970).

[1108] Federal Trade Commission v. Procter & Gamble Co. (Clorox), 386 U.S. 568, 578 (1967).

[1109] United States v. International Tel. and Tel. Corp., 324 F. Supp. 19, 53 (D. Conn. 1970).

[1110] United States v. Aluminum Co. of Am. (Cupples), 233 F. Supp. 718 (E.D. Mo. 1964), aff'd per curiam, 382 U.S. 12 (1965), and 233 F. Supp. 718 (E.D. Mo. 1964), aff'd per curiam, 382 U.S. 12 (1965) and Reynolds Metal Co. v. FTC, 309 F.2d 223 (D.C. Cir. 1962).

B. Conglomerate Mergers That Do Not Eliminate an Effective Potential Competitor and Do Not Enable One MP to Achieve Sought-After Geographic Diversification but Do Create a Merged Firm That Will Enter Into More Tying and Reciprocity Agreements Than the MPs Would Have Done

Conventionally, tie-ins are defined to be agreements in which a seller either (1) conditions its willingness to supply one product on stated terms on the buyer's agreeing to purchase one or more other products on stated terms or (2) agrees to supply a buyer with a package of products for a stated total price. In fact, tie-ins can also be arranged by a buyer that either (1) conditions its agreement to buy one product on stated terms on the seller's agreement to supply it with another product on stated terms or (2) agrees to purchase a package of products from a given seller for a stated total price. Conventionally, reciprocity agreements are defined to be agreements in which a buyer conditions its agreement to purchase a product from a given seller on stated terms on that seller's agreeing to purchase a product from the buyer on stated terms. Once more, however, in some situations it will be more accurate to say that reciprocity involves a seller's conditioning its agreement to supply a buyer with a product on stated terms on the buyer's agreeing to supply the seller with another product on stated terms. As Chap. 14 explains, for close to 100 years, U.S. courts and antitrust-enforcement agencies assumed that the exclusive or inevitable function of tie-ins is to enable a seller that has market power in the sale of one of the goods the tie-in involves (the so-called tying product) to use that power to lever itself into a position of market power in the sale of the second (so-called tied) product. Since reciprocity agreements perform the same functions as tying agreements, one should expect that those that subscribe to this leverage theory of tie-ins would also believe that the exclusive or inevitable function of reciprocity is to enable an actor that has market power when *buying* one good to use that power to lever itself into a position of market power when *selling* the other good. One would also expect decisionmakers that believe in the leverage theory of tie-ins and reciprocity to conclude that any tendency of a conglomerate merger to increase the extent to which the merged firm employs tie-ins and practices reciprocity (because enforcement of the alleged prohibition of such agreements was imperfect) should count against its legality. It is therefore not surprising that, at a time at which U.S. officials believed in the leverage theory of tie-ins and reciprocity (1965), the U.S. Supreme Court in *Consolidated Foods* held that an acquisition that is conventionally deemed to be conglomerate but might better be classified as vertical violated the Clayton Act because (1) the acquiring firm purchased a large share of the final products (processed foods of various types) for whose production the acquired firm's products (dehydrated onion and garlic) was an input and (2) the merger put the merged firm in a position to condition its purchase of those final products on their producers' purchasing the acquired firm's products.[1111] However, although this case

[1111] See Federal Trade Commission v. Consolidated Foods Corp., 380 U.S. 592 (1965).

has never been overruled, I am confident that the DOJ and FTC will no longer attack conglomerate mergers on the ground that they will lead the merged firm to employ more tie-ins and reciprocity agreements than the MPs would have done and suspect that the Supreme Court would either overrule or work its way around *Consolidated Foods* if it were presented with a case to which that precedent applied.

I base those conclusions on the following "facts" that Chap. 14 discusses in more detail:

(1) neither the leverage theory of tie-ins and reciprocity nor the legal conclusions it would warrant can bear scrutiny:

   (A) there is a generation gap in the leverage theory—although in a wide variety of circumstances and in a wide variety of ways tie-ins and reciprocity agreements can increase their employer's profits, they cannot "generate leverage" in the sense of that expression that is relevant to Sherman Act and Clayton Act legal analysis;
   (B) most of the functions of tie-ins and reciprocity are Sherman-Act-licit, and most tying and reciprocity agreements perform only Sherman-Act-licit functions;
   (C) many of the minority of such agreements that perform the illegitimate function of concealing the existence or extent of independently-illegal behavior conceal tax and contract frauds and price-regulation violations rather than antitrust violations;
   (D) the fact that a tie-in or reciprocity agreement has been used to conceal an independent antitrust violation is irrelevant to the illegal status of the underlying violation (though in some instances it may make the perpetrator's conduct a violation of the Clayton Act as well as the Sherman Act when it otherwise would have been only a Sherman Act violation);
   (E) if the Clayton Act is correctly interpreted to make the legality of a firm's use of tying and reciprocity agreements depend on the consequence of a rule allowing it and its rivals to use such agreements, the use of tie-ins and reciprocity agreements to perform Sherman-Act-licit functions will rarely inflict a net equivalent-dollar loss on Clayton-Act-relevant buyers by reducing the absolute attractiveness of the best offer they respectively receive from any inferior supplier and, in some of the few instances in which the general availability of such agreements does impose such a loss on such buyers in this way, the perpetrators will be able to make out an organizational-economic-efficiency defense for their conduct;

(2) in conversations with me, economists at the DOJ have made it clear that they recognize the truth of all or virtually all of the preceding claims;
(3) the DOJ's 1984 Vertical Merger Guidelines come close to abandoning the foreclosure theory of vertical mergers, which is related to the leverage

theory of tie-ins and reciprocity; since 1984, the DOJ has not challenged a single vertical merger; and between 1996 and 2003, the FTC issued second requests (for additional information) in response to only 12 vertical-merger proposals[1112];

(4) despite the fact that *Consolidated Foods* had not been reversed, the DOJ's 1984 Conglomerate Merger Guidelines made no reference to the possibility that a conglomerate merger might be rendered illegal by its tendency to cause the merged firm to engage in more reciprocity or enter into more tying agreements than the MPs would have done;

(5) in 1993, without explanation, the DOJ rescinded its 1985 Vertical Restraints Guidelines, which while acknowledging the fact that tie-ins can perform some legitimate functions state incorrectly that (even when the tying seller does not have dominant power in the tying-product market) tie-ins that require the buyer to enter into a full-requirements contract on the tied product can endanger competition in the tied-product market;

(6) in recent years, the DOJ has virtually stopped bringing suits against firms for

   (A) employing tie-ins or engaging in reciprocal dealing or
   (B) for including vertical territorial restraints, customer-allocation clauses, or resale-price-maintenance terms in their contracts with their distributors—a fact that is relevant because the argument for the illegality of such practices has many of the same deficiencies as the leverage theory of tie-ins and reciprocity;

(7) more specifically, in 2000, the DOJ decided not to challenge a proposed merger between GE and Honeywell that the EC believed would reduce competition by putting the merged company into a position to engage in reciprocity by refusing to buy airplanes that did not include Honeywell equipment[1113];

(8) although the Supreme Court has not yet disavowed the leverage theory of tie-ins—indeed, has relied on it in some recent cases, in other cases the Court has upheld the legality of tie-ins in circumstances in which the leverage theory implies they should be deemed illegal simply by refusing to acknowledge that the business conduct in question involved the use of the tie-ins[1114]; and

(9) the Supreme Court has recently held that the legality of (A) vertical territorial restraints and customer-allocation clauses[1115] and (B) the vertical fixing of

---

[1112] See FTC, Horizontal Merger Investigation Data: Fiscal Years 1996–2003 at Table 1 (2004).

[1113] For an official explanation that admittedly focuses more on the facts of the case than on the deficiencies of the leverage theory of reciprocity, see William J. Kolasky, Deputy Assistant Attorney General, U.S. DOJ, *Conglomerate Mergers and Range Effects: It's a Long Way From Chicago to Brussels* (2001).

[1114] See Broadcast Music, Inc. v. Columbia Broadcasting System, Inc., 441 U.S. 1 (1979).

[1115] See Continental T.V., Inc. v. GTE Sylvania, Inc. 433 U.S. 36 (1997).

maximum and minimum resale prices[1116] should be determined on a case-by-case basis through the application of a Rule of Reason analysis.

I should add, however, that (for reasons that Sect. 7 of this chapter and Subsect. 3B(2) of Chap. 14 will explain) although the EC and the E.C./E.U. courts have come to a better understanding of the functions and consequences of tie-ins and reciprocity, it is still uncertain whether they would count any tendency of a conglomerate merger to create a merged firm that would participate in more tying and reciprocity agreements than the MPs would have done against the legality of the merger in question.

C. Conglomerate Mergers That Do Not Eliminate an Effective Potential Competitor and Do Not Create a Merged Firm That Will Enter Into More Tying and Reciprocity Agreements Than the MPs Would Have Done but Will Enable One MP to Achieve Sought-After Geographic Diversification: The "Toe-Hold Merger" Doctrine

Since 1970, both the U.S. antitrust-enforcement agencies and the U.S. courts have been developing and applying a special, somewhat-unclearly-specified, so-called "toe-hold merger" doctrine to prevent firms K that are seeking to achieve geographic diversification from achieving this goal by merging with or acquiring another established firm E that sells a product that is intrinsically rivalrous with the K-firm's product in a different geographic market when, in their view, the merger or acquisition in question would violate the Clayton Act. According to the version of this doctrine that I think one should read the U.S. courts and antitrust-enforcement agencies to have developed,[1117] in order for such a merger to pass Clayton Act scrutiny, the firm K must demonstrate both (1) that it would not enter E's market independently if it were prohibited from entering it through merger or acquisition and (2) that either (A) the E it merged with or acquired was a relatively-small firm (E_S)—*i.e.*, was small relative to the other firms in its market—or (B) if the K was proposing to merge with or acquire a relatively-large E-firm (E_L), it had made

[1116] State Oil Co. v. Khan, 522 U.S. 3 (1997) reached this conclusion about the vertical fixing of maximum resale prices, and Leegin Creative Leather Products v. PSKS, Inc., 555 U.S. 877 (2007) reached this conclusion about the vertical fixing of minimum resale prices.

[1117] I find this reading of the doctrine appropriate because it brings it into line with the failing-company doctrine that the U.S. courts announced in Citizen Pub. Co. v. United States, 394 U.S. 131 (1969)—*i.e.*, at about the same time that the FTC first relied on the "toe-hold merger" doctrine in Bendix Corp. 77 F.T.C. 731 (1976), vacated on procedural grounds, 450 F.2d 534 (6th Cir. 1971), consent order, 84 F.T.C. 1291 (1974)—and that the DOJ and FTC adopted in their 1992 Horizontal Merger Guidelines, the 1997 Revision of those Guidelines, and the 2010 Horizontal Merger Guidelines.

reasonable efforts to identify a relatively-small firm in that market whose "acquisition" would be more profitable than not entering that market through merger or acquisition at all and failed to identify an E_S that would satisfy this criterion.[1118] I have described the "toe-hold merger" doctrine as a "special" doctrine because it implies *inter alia* that (1) K–E_S or K–E_L geographic-diversification conglomerate mergers that would not decrease the intensity of competition in the E-firm's market below the level it would have if the K-firm did nothing to enter the E-firm's market or would increase the intensity of competition in the E-firm's market above what it would be if the K-firm did nothing to enter that market will violate the Clayton Act if the prohibition of the merger in question would lead the K-firm to enter the E-firm's market independently and (2) K–E_L geographic-diversification conglomerate mergers that would not decrease the intensity of competition in the E-firm's market below the level it would have if the K-firm did nothing to enter the E-firm's market or would increase the intensity of competition in the E-firm's market above what it would be if the K-firm did nothing to enter that market will violate the Clayton Act if the prohibition of the K-firm's executing a merger with a relatively-large firm E_L in the E-firm's market would make it profitable for the K-firm to execute a merger with a relatively-small firm E_S in the E-firm's market. (I should add that, although the "toe-hold merger" doctrine has been applied only in geographic-diversification conglomerate-merger cases [and the text that follows will assume that it applies only to such mergers], if valid it would be equally applicable to product-diversification conglomerate-merger cases.)

I should admit at the outset that the positive-law status of the "toe-hold merger" doctrine is somewhat uncertain. As already noted, a version of it was first used by the FTC in 1970 in a case in which the Commission found a geographic-diversification conglomerate acquisition of a relative-large E-firm (an E_L) in a concentrated market unlawful on the ground that the K-firm would have entered the firm's market by acquiring an E_S firm had it not merged with the E_L firm in question.[1119] Since that time, the FTC has accepted the doctrine in cases that hold geographic-diversification conglomerate mergers lawful on the ground that the E-firm was an E_S firm or unlawful on the ground that the E-firm was an E_L firm,[1120] and the DOJ implicitly accepted the doctrine in its 1984 Conglomerate Merger Guidelines.[1121] Moreover, several Court of Appeals opinions have

---

[1118] The alternative versions of the "toe-hold merger" doctrine that the U.S. courts and antitrust-enforcement agencies may have in mind would respectively (1) establish an irrebuttable presumption that K–E_L geographic-diversification conglomerate mergers violate the Clayton Act or (2) empower the government to establish the illegality of a K–E_L geographic-diversification conglomerate merger by demonstrating that the K-firm would have found either independent entry or some K–E_L merger more profitable than not diversifying into the E market at all.

[1119] See Bendix Corp., 77 F.T.C. 731 (1970).

[1120] See, *e.g.*, SKF Indus., 1979 Trade Reg. Rep. ¶21595 at 21724 (FTC) and Budd Co., 86 F.T.C. 518, 582–83 (1975).

[1121] See United States Justice Department 1984 Conglomerate Merger Guidelines, 2 Trade Reg. Rep. ¶¶ 14490–4495 (1984).

expressed sympathy for the doctrine,[1122] and a number of lower-court opinions have implicitly relied on it.[1123] The positive-law status of the "toe-hold merger" doctrine is uncertain despite all this because the Supreme Court has never ruled on the doctrine—indeed, has in *Falstaff Brewing* expressly reserved the question of its correctness.[1124]

However, given the empirical importance of geographic-diversification conglomerate mergers, the doctrine is potentially sufficiently significant to merit detailed consideration. In my judgment, all variants of the "toe-hold merger" doctrine are unjustified and/or incorrect for two economic reasons (which relate primarily to its "privileging" $K\text{–}E_S$ mergers over $K\text{–}E_L$ mergers) and one legal reason (which relates equally to its "privileging" independent entry over merging and its "privileging" $K\text{–}E_S$ mergers over $K\text{–}E_L$ mergers). I will now discuss these three objections to the doctrine in turn.

(1) The Doctrine's Economic Assumption That the Less-Profitable $K\text{–}E_S$ Merger That a Firm Seeking Geographic Diversification Will Find More Profitable Than No Merger Will Be More Procompetitive Than the More-Profitable $K\text{–}E_L$ Merger the Firm Would Prefer So That, if the Doctrine Always Leads K-Firms to Substitute the Less-Profitable $K\text{–}E_S$ Merger for the More-Profitable $K\text{–}E_L$ Mergers, It Will Increase Competition on That Account

The first economic reason that the "toe-hold merger" doctrine is wrong relates to its premise that—if the doctrine succeeds in inducing K-firms to substitute less-profitable $K\text{–}E_S$ mergers for the more-profitable $K\text{–}E_L$ mergers they would have preferred to execute—it will always or at least across all cases tend to increase competition on that account. This premise is based on two, more-basic assumptions both of which I think are clearly unjustified and probably incorrect:

(1) from the perspective of the goal of increasing competition or preventing decreases in competition, there is a bias in favor of Ks' finding $K\text{–}E_L$ mergers more profitable than $K\text{–}E_S$ mergers—*i.e.*, if $P\pi$ stands for the private profits yielded by any merger, $\uparrow C$ stands for the increase in competition the relevant merger generates, and the parentheticals $(K\text{–}E_L)$ and $(K\text{–}E_S)$ indicate the type of merger in question, the relevant bias will be present to the extent that $P\pi(K\text{–}E_L)\text{–}P\pi(K\text{–}E_S) > \uparrow C(K\text{–}E_L)\text{–}\uparrow C(K\text{–}E_S)$, and
(2) this bias must be sufficiently large relative to the $P\pi$ difference in question for the $K\text{–}E_L$ mergers that would be executed in the absence of a "toe-hold merger" doctrine (because they were the most-profitable conglomerate mergers the

[1122] See Bendix Corp., 450 F.2d 534, 541–42 (6th Cir. 1971) and Kennecott Copper Corp. v. FTC, 467 F.2d 67, 79 (10th Cir. 1972), cert. denied, 416 U.S. 909 (1974).

[1123] See, *e.g.*, Washington Mt. Sav. Bank v. Federal Dep. Ins. Corp., 347 F. Supp. 790, 798–800 (W.D. Wash. 1972), aff'd, 482 F.2d 459 (9th Cir. 1973) and United States v. Phillips Petro. Co., 367 F. Supp. 1226, 1258 (C.D. Cal. 1973), aff'd mem. 418 U.S. 906 (1974).

[1124] See United States v. Falstaff Brewing Corp., 410 U.S. 526, 537 (1973).

parties identified) to be less procompetitive on balance than the K–E_S mergers we are currently assuming would be substituted for them if the "toe-hold merger" doctrine were applied.

Mathematically, the profit bias just defined (hereinafter "πB") will be critical wherever ↑C(K–E_S)>↑C(K–E_L) despite the fact that Pπ(K–E_L)>Pπ(K–E_S), which will occur whenever the bias—(Pπ[K–E_L]–Pπ[K–E_S])–(↑C[K–E_L]–↑C[K–E_S])—exceeds the amount by which the K–E_L merger was more profitable than the K–E_S merger: Pπ(K–E_L)–Pπ(K–E_S). The amount by which the K–E_L merger whose profitability was actually biased (from the perspective of the goal of increasing competition) would have increased competition by less than the K–E_S merger we are assuming would be substituted for it if the "toe-hold merger" doctrine were applied would be the bias just defined *minus* (Pπ[K–E_L]–Pπ[K–E_S]). And if we let (1) "#" stand for the number of cases in which the K–E_L merger would be more profitable than the K–E_S merger, (2) "%(*πB)" stand for the percentage of the relevant K–E_L mergers for which there was a critical profit-bias in favor of the K–E_L merger from the perspective of the goal of increasing competition, (3) "(1–%[*πB])" stand for the percentage of such mergers for which there was no such critical profit-bias, (4) "ave(↑C[K–E_L]–↑C[K–E_S])$_{N*\pi B}$" stand for the average amount by which the K–E_L mergers were more procompetitive than the K–E_S mergers that we are now assuming the "toe-hold merger" doctrine would cause to be substituted for them in those cases in which there was "no critical profit-bias"—N*πB, and (5) "ave(πB–[Pπ(K–E_L)–Pπ(K–E_S)$_{*\pi B}$])" stand for the average amount by which the K–E_L mergers would be less procompetitive than the K–E_S mergers we are now assuming the "toe-hold merger" doctrine would cause to be substituted for them in those cases in which there was a critical profit bias—*πB, the K–E_S mergers we are now assuming the "toe-hold merger" doctrine will cause to be substituted for all the more-profitable K–E_L mergers that would be executed by their potential participants in its absence only if

$$\#(1\text{–}\%[^*\pi B])(\text{ave}[\uparrow C(K\text{–}E_L)\text{–}\uparrow C(K\text{–}E_S)]_{N^*\pi B}])<$$
$$\#(\%[^*\pi B])(\text{ave}[\pi B\text{–}(P\pi[K\text{–}E_L]\text{–}P\pi[K\text{–}E_S])_{^*\pi B}]),$$

where the first expression indicates the total reduction in competition that the "toe-hold merger" doctrine will generate by causing less procompetitive K–E_S mergers to be substituted for more procompetitive K–E_L mergers and the second expression indicates the total increase in competition the doctrine will generate by causing more procompetitive K–E_S mergers to be substituted for less procompetitive K–E_L mergers.

To see whether the first of the above two conditions is fulfilled, one must list the various ways in which a conglomerate merger can increase the profits of its participants or the pre-merger stockholders of one of its participants and then examine whether the size of the established merger partner (whether the merger involves an E_L or an E_S) will affect the relationship between the contribution the merger makes to the relevant profits and the intensity of competition (in the relevant sense) in each of these ways. A conglomerate merger can increase the profits of the merging companies or the welfare of the pre-merger owners of its initiator in the following ways:

(1) by enabling an initiator's pre-merger stockholders to take advantage of investor misperceptions of the likely impact of such mergers on the MPs' profits[1125];
(2) by yielding tax advantages—*e.g.*, when one MP can take advantage of tax losses of the other MP that the other MP cannot use;
(3) by enabling the pre-merger owner of an E (probably an E_S) whose stock is not publicly traded to retire without damaging its company and to exchange its interest for assets (cash or stock in the K company) that are more liquid;
(4) by enabling the acquiring firm to profit by purchasing the acquired firm at a bargain-basement price by threatening to enter particularly close to it in product-space and/or to make it the target of predatory or retaliatory moves post-entry;
(5) by generating static efficiencies and dynamic efficiencies (including static efficiencies that carry over to QV-investment expansions);
(6) when the MPs and the merged company set across-the-board prices, by creating a merged company that can enable its rivals and itself to lock themselves into prices in a sequence that maximizes its and their HNOP array;
(7) by increasing the profits that the merged firm can realize through natural oligopolistic pricing above the profits that K and E realized in this way pre-merger by generating static marginal efficiencies that increase the merged firm's BCAs above the MPs' BCAs, by creating a company that can initiate a series of facilitating premature price-announcements, and by creating a merged company that can take advantage of economies of scale in changing its initially-announced prices;
(8) by enabling the merged company to earn more profits through contrivance than K and E would have earned after the date of the merger in this way;
(9) by enabling the merged firm to earn more profits through predation or threatening predation than K and E would have earned after the date of the merger in these ways.

I will now discuss whether a bias in favor of K–E_L mergers relative to K–E_S mergers from the perspective of the goal of increasing competition is likely to be operative in relation to these respective possible sources of conglomerate-merger profits. I will first discuss the bias issue as it relates to profit-sources for which the analysis is not difficult and then discuss it in relation to profit-sources for which the analysis is more complex.

From the perspective of the goal of increasing competition, the facts that investor misperceptions and tax considerations can make conglomerate mergers

[1125] Admittedly, although there is some evidence that this consideration played an important role in the 1960s and 1970s, I doubt its significance today—*i.e.*, I think that investors have learned to be more skeptical about claims that mergers are inevitably advantageous to their participants.

profitable create a bias in favor of firms' engaging in conglomerate mergers (as opposed to doing nothing) since no increase in competition will be associated with the profits that investor errors and tax considerations can yield. Indeed, these purely-private advantages may actually cause conglomerate mergers to be executed that decrease competition because they are profitable despite the fact that they reduce the organizational economic efficiency of their participants. However, these factors will be likely to bias a merger-partner-size choice from the perspective of the goal of increasing competition only to the extent that there are transaction-cost economies of scale in executing mergers: otherwise, the K-firm could achieve the same gains by executing more conglomerate mergers with (E_S)s rather than fewer with (E_L)s. Indeed, to the extent that (E_L)s are less likely to have tax losses of which they cannot take advantage, the tax consideration might be associated with a bias in favor of K–E_S mergers from the perspective of the goal of increasing competition.

Some conglomerate mergers are initiated by the owner of a closely-held corporation who wants to retire and convert his property into more liquid assets that will be of more use to him during his retirement and can be more fruitfully passed on to his beneficiaries. Since these mergers tend to maintain the competitive position of their E_S-participants (which would otherwise have declined as the company's single-person or small-team management grew older and less able or willing to function), the associated private gain may not be associated with any bias in favor of their profitability in comparison with their not merging at all. However, since many of the E_S-firms in question were founded by middle-level or high-level managers of larger concerns that decided to strike out on their own—in essence, to divest themselves from well-established firms—and since decisions by K_S-firms to merge with such (E_S)s rather than with (E_L)s will tend to increase competition by encouraging managers of well-established firms to set out on their own by increasing the ability of such owners of E_S-firms to sell out when they want to do so and the attractiveness of the terms on which they can effectuate their company's sale, this possibility may be associated with a bias against K–E_S and in favor of K–E_L mergers from the perspective of the goal of increasing competition.

The ability of a firm to profit by inducing a non-rival to accept a bargain-basement buy-out or merger offer by threatening to make an otherwise-unprofitable location-decision and/or to make retaliatory or predatory moves after locating also obviously creates a bias in favor of conglomerate mergers from the perspective of the goal of increasing competition. Once more, however, unless there are transaction-cost economies of scale in executing such mergers, this possibility will create no bias in favor of K–E_L mergers over K–E_S mergers. Indeed, to the extent that the (E_L)s of this world are less intimidatable than the (E_S)s, this possibility may be associated with a bias in favor of K–E_S mergers relative to K–E_L mergers.

The same conclusions apply in relation to the ability of conglomerate mergers to increase their participants' profits by facilitating their contrived oligopolistic pricing, predation, or retaliation against rival QV investors. However, two additional points do need to be made in this context. First, the bias (from the perspective of competition) toward firms' engaging in conglomerate mergers that will yield contrived-oligopolistic-pricing, predation, and retaliation-barrier advantages to the MPs will be increased by the tendency of such mergers to increase the OMs that the MPs' conglomerate rivals can obtain (*e.g.*, by increasing the MPs' OCAs and natural OMs, creating a merged firm whose defenses are spread, *etc.*) as well as the L barriers that the merged firm faces. Second, those oligopolistic and predatory realities will be less likely to create a bias in favor of K–E_L mergers relative to K–E_S mergers (indeed, may tend to create the opposite bias) because (E_L)s may have less need of the information and retaliatory and reciprocatory abilities of K_S than do (E_S)s, though this consideration will be offset to the extent that contrived oligopolistic pricing is less likely to have been so unprofitable for an E_L (than for an E_S) pre-merger for the practice still to be unprofitable for the "E division" of the merged concern post-merger and by the fact that the E_L firm will have more buyers in relation to which it will be able to obtain gains by engaging in these types of conduct.

Conglomerate mergers can increase the NOMs of the merger partners not only by generating static efficiencies that increase their OCAs but also by enabling the K and E firms to take advantage of economies of scale in changing their initially-announced prices (say, of changing their advertising or instructing their distributors of a price-change or altering their posted prices or computer entries) and/or by substituting for E a K-firm whose reputation increases its ability to organize a facilitating series of premature price-announcements. Once more, however, although those possibilities create a bias in favor of conglomerate mergers, a bias which in some cases reflects the fact that the mergers in question will increase the NOMs not only of the MPs but also of their *R*s, it is not so clear that it creates a bias in favor of K–E_L mergers relative to K–E_S mergers. This conclusion partially reflects the fact that (E_L)s may be more likely than (E_S)s to have been able to obtain OMs naturally pre-merger, though the fact that the E_L has more sales than the E_S favors the conclusion that this NOM-possibility creates a bias in favor K–E_L mergers over K–E_S mergers because the E_L firm has more sales on which it can obtain NOMs.

All things considered, I do not think that the various possibilities so far canvassed suggest the existence of a strong bias in favor of K–E_L conglomerate mergers over K–E_S conglomerate mergers from the perspective of the goal of increasing competition. Unfortunately, it will be far more complicated to analyze whether any such bias is created by the two remaining sources of conglomerate-merger profits—static efficiencies and dynamic efficiencies (including static efficiencies that carry over to QV-investment expansions). I will analyze these issues despite this fact not only because they critically affect the competitive impact of the "toe-hold merger" doctrine but also because the extant analyses of these issues are completely inadequate[1126] (in large part because the relevant analysts were not accustomed to thinking in non-market-oriented terms).

[1126] Thus, in addition to assuming incorrectly either (1) that the effect of any event or act on the intensity of competition in the Clayton Act sense is monotonically related to its impact on economic efficiency and/or (2) that the Clayton Act promulgates an economic-efficiency as

I focus first on static efficiencies that will not carry over to any new QV investments the MPs execute. If the efficiencies relate to the fixed costs of the merged concern, they will increase the merged company's profits by an amount equal to the efficiency in question but will have no effect on Clayton-Act-relevant buyers (assuming that they do not critically affect K's or E's survival) since they will not affect K's or E's competitive position vis-à-vis any buyer. If the efficiencies are "marginal"—*i.e.*, entail a simple reduction in the marginal costs of the merged concern or an improvement in its competitive position in relation to particular buyers that reflects an increase in the attractiveness of its product to those buyers not fully offset by any related increase in its marginal costs, a decrease in the attractiveness of its product to some buyers that is smaller than the associated decrease in its marginal costs, or an increase in the attractiveness of its product to some buyers that is not accompanied by an increase in its marginal costs, four cases will have to be distinguished. For simplicity, I will assume that in each case prices are being set on an individualized basis.

First, to the extent that the static marginal efficiencies affect the merged company's position in relation to buyers that one MP would have been best-placed to supply after the date of the merger and the merged company was best-placed to supply after the merger, the efficiencies will increase the merged company's profits by the amount of the marginal efficiency in question (since it will increase the relevant OCA by that amount) *plus* any NOM that the increase in the relevant OCA enables the merged concern to realize *minus* any loss the efficiency imposes on the merged concern by reducing the profits it can realize by practicing contrived oligopolistic pricing (by increasing the amount of safe profits it must put at risk to do so) and/or by reducing the profits the merged concern realizes by undercutting its rivals' oligopolistic prices (by increasing the merged company's vulnerability to retaliation). By way of contrast, to the extent that the efficiencies relate to buyers K or E would have been best-placed to supply after the date of the merger and KE was best-placed to supply post-merger, they will impose an equivalent-dollar loss on Clayton-Act-relevant buyers by the amount of additional NOMs they enable KE to obtain *minus* the amount by which they reduce KE's COMs *plus* the amount by which they increase the KE's *R*s' HNOPS (by increasing KE's prices to its own

---

opposed to a competitive-impact test of illegality, Bork's analysis of the "toe-hold merger" doctrine assumes that the contribution that a conglomerate merger's efficiencies make to the MPs' profits is monotonically related to their contribution to both the intensity of competition and economic efficiency. See ROBERT H. BORK, THE ANTITRUST PARADOX: A POLICY AT WAR WITH ITSELF 260–62 (Basic Studies, 1978). I critiqued Bork's analysis of the competitive impact of the "toe-hold merger" doctrine in Richard S. Markovits, *Monopolistic Competition, Second Best, and* THE ANTITRUST PARADOX: *A Review Article*, 77 MICH. L. REV. 567, 635–39 (1979). As I pointed out in Chap. 12, the 1992 Horizontal Merger Guidelines, their 1997 revision, and the 2010 Guidelines also fail to analyze the factors that determine the competitive impact of any efficiencies a horizontal merger may generate (though, unlike their 1984 predecessor, they do recognize that the legal relevance of a merger's efficiencies relates to their competitive impact as opposed to their contribution to economic efficiency and do identify this competitive impact with the effect of the efficiencies on the welfare of the customers of the MPs and their product-*R*s).

customers and hence the CMCs KE will have to incur to charge any given lower price to an *R*'s customers relative to the CMCs the relevant merger partner would have had to incur to do so) *plus* the amount by which they increase the *R*s' NOMs by increasing their OCAs on the preceding account *plus* the amount by which they increase the *R*s' COMs by reducing KE's willingness to undercut the *R*s' contrived oligopolistic prices by increasing KE's vulnerability to retaliation (by raising KE's [OCA + NOM + COM]s and spreading its defenses when the relevant *R* operates in both K's and E's markets) and its rivals' ability to reciprocate to KE's collaboration: note that the preceding analysis assumes that any efficiency-related increase in KE's OCAs will not improve the terms the merged concern offers its customers—that, for example, the merged firm will not pass on any reduction in its marginal costs the merger generates.

Second, to the extent that the static marginal efficiencies that a conglomerate merger generates affect KE's position in relation to buyers either K or E would have been second-placed to supply after the date of the merger and that KE was second-placed to supply post-merger, they will not increase KE's profits at all but will increase competition by the size of the efficiency in question (which will reduce the OCA of the *R* that is the best-placed supplier of the relevant buyer) *plus* any NOM the efficiencies preclude the relevant best-placed *R* from securing (by reducing its OCA) *plus or minus* any amount by which it reduces or increases the *R*'s COM, by increasing or reducing the number of firms in a position to profit by beating any given contrived oligopolistic offer it makes.

Third, to the extent that the static marginal efficiencies that a conglomerate merger generates affects KE's position in relation to buyers that K or E would have been third-placed to supply to nth-placed after the date of the merger and KE was second-placed to supply after the merger, they will not increase KE's profits at all but will confer an equivalent-dollar gain on the buyers in question equal to the positive difference between the efficiency and the amount by which the relevant K or E would have been worse-than-second-placed after the date of the merger *plus* any associated reduction the efficiency generates in the relevant *R*'s NOMs and COMs.

Fourth, to the extent that the static marginal efficiencies that a conglomerate merger generates affect KE's position in relation to buyers that K or E would have been worse-than-best-placed to supply after the date of the merger and KE is best-placed to supply post-merger, the efficiencies will increase the merged company's profits by the OCAs they enable KE to enjoy post-merger (the difference between the sum of the static marginal efficiencies that the merger enabled KE to secure in its relations with the buyers in question and the sum of the OCDs under which the K or E whose products became best-placed post-merger would have operated after the date of the merger in its relations with the buyers in question) *plus* any NOMs KE secured from the relevant buyers *plus* any COMs it secured from them *minus* any reductions in the COMs it secured from others caused by any related increase in its vulnerability to retaliation *minus* any reduction in the profits it realized by undercutting others' contrived oligopolistic prices attributable to the efficiency-related increase in its vulnerability to retaliation. By way of contrast, to the extent that the efficiencies in question make KE best-placed, it will benefit the relevant buyers by the OCAs of their no-merger best-placed suppliers *plus* any decrease or *minus* any increase in the sum of the NOMs and COMs the buyers that the efficiencies made KE best-placed to supply had to pay *minus* any amount by which the efficiencies raised the COMs other buyers paid by reducing KE's willingness to undercut its rivals from a position of inferiority by increasing its vulnerability to retaliation (as well as its rivals' ability to reciprocate to its cooperation).

This analysis suggests that the relative number of cases in these four categories will substantially affect whether, from the perspective of the goal of increasing competition in the Clayton Act sense, there is a static-marginal-efficiency-related bias in favor of (1) firms' engaging in conglomerate mergers as opposed to doing nothing to enter and (2) K–E_L mergers relative to K–E_S mergers. I will focus on this second issue and address it in a crude way. Roughly speaking, there will be a static-marginal-efficiency-related bias in favor of K–E_L conglomerate mergers over K–E_S conglomerate mergers if the ratio of the number of customers for which larger established firms are best-placed to the number for which they are second-placed or close-to-second-place is greater than its counterpart for small established firms—*e.g.*, if (E_L)s tend to be best-placed more often than they are second-placed or close-to-second-placed while (E_S)s tend to be best-placed less often than they are second-placed or close-to-second-placed. I have no hard data and no real basis for guessing about whether this condition is fulfilled. To the extent that (E_L)s tend to produce highly-differentiated products that consumers either strongly prefer or prefer by far less than their extra cost while (E_S)s tend to produce undifferentiated products, (E_L)s will tend to be best-placed far more often than they are second-placed or close-to-second-placed while (E_S)s will tend to be second-placed or close-to-second-placed far more often than they are best-placed. However, although this description clearly fits some (E_L)s and some (E_S)s, some (E_S)s produce highly-differentiated products that a small number of devotees adore, and some (E_L)s produce generics or old reliables that are not strongly differentiated. I simply do not trust my hunch about which of these situations is typical. I therefore do not know whether there is a static-marginal-efficiency-related bias in favor of K–E_L conglomerate mergers over K–E_S conglomerate mergers from the perspective of the goal of increasing competition.

The final source of conglomerate-merger profits that might create a bias in favor of K–E_L mergers over K–E_S mergers from the perspective of competition are the dynamic efficiencies such a merger may generate. Unfortunately, the relationship between the private-profit-yield and competitive impact of such efficiencies is at least as complicated to analyze as its counterpart for static marginal efficiencies that do not carry over to expansions. I will initially assume that in any given situation the relevant K–E_L and K–E_S mergers will generate the same amount and types of dynamic efficiencies and that the relevant E_L and E_S firms' QV-investment-expansion-related positions are the same. On those assumptions, six categories of situations must be distinguished.

In the first, the dynamic efficiencies that I am now assuming that either the relevant K–E_L or the relevant K–E_S merger would generate would not affect equilibrium QV investment in the relevant area of product-space even though the merged firm will make a QV investment that takes advantage of them because the relevant K or E merger partner would have expanded anyway. In this case, the efficiencies will increase the profitability of the merger by an amount equal to the number of buyers the efficiencies cause KE's new investment to be best-placed to supply and the average difference between the OCD under which the new QV investment would have otherwise operated in those instances and the size of the per-unit efficiency in question (if each buyer is assumed to buy one unit) *plus* the number of buyers (if any) that the efficiencies cause KE's new investment to be best-placed to supply and obtain (by raising KE's OCAs on its new investment) *plus* the related amount by which the efficiencies raise KE's NOMs above the NOMs the relevant MP would have obtained *minus* the amount by which they reduce the OMs KE contrives (by increasing the safe profits KE would have to put at risk to practice contrived oligopolistic pricing on its new product) *minus* the amount by which they reduce the profits KE realizes by undercutting its rivals' contrived oligopolistic prices (by increasing KE's vulnerability to retaliation and its rivals' ability to reciprocate to KE's collaboration) *plus* or *minus* any increase or decrease in the damage KE's new QV investment does to the profit-yield of its pre-existing QV investments in the relevant ARDEPPS. If the dynamic efficiencies are fixed-cost efficiencies and do not affect the product the merged company introduces, they will have no effect on competition—*i.e.*, on the welfare of the customers of K, E, and their product-*R*s. However, if the dynamic efficiencies are marginal efficiencies (as I will hereinafter assume), they will increase competition by the amount by which they reduce the *R*s' OCAs (which will depend not only on the size of the efficiencies but on the amount by which they increase the frequency with which the [perhaps changed] product the merged firm introduces is second-placed and reduce the amount by which it is worse-than-best-placed when it is second-placed)[1127] *plus* the related amount by which they reduce the *R*s' NOMs (by reducing their OCAs) *minus* the amount by which they increase the KE's NOMs (by increasing its OCAs) *plus* the net amount by which they reduce or *minus* the net amount by which they increase the sum of the COMs of KE and its product-*R*s (through producing a variety of effects that I will not review here). These conclusions suggest that, in the case now under investigation, the sign of the bias that dynamic efficiencies create in the profitability of the conglomerate merger that generate them from the perspective of the goal of increasing competition will depend substantially on the ratio of the number of times the new product is best-placed to the number of times it is second-placed. Relatedly, they suggest that there will be a dynamic-efficiency-related bias in favor of K–E_L mergers over K–E_S mergers if the preceding ratio is sufficiently higher for (E_L)s than for (E_S)s to overcome any bias against K–E_L mergers in favor

[1127] If the relevant efficiencies do not change the product the merged firm introduces, this impact will depend not only on the size of the marginal dynamic efficiencies in question but also on the frequency with which after the date of the merger the relevant MP would have been either second-placed or worse-than-second-placed by less than the improvement in its position yielded by the efficiencies in question.

of K–E_S mergers created by the greater *M* disincentive the K–E_L firm will have to expand relative to the *M* likely to confront the K–E_S firm.

In the second situation that needs to be distinguished, the dynamic marginal efficiencies that I am now assuming that either the relevant K–E_L or the relevant K–E_S merger would generate would not affect equilibrium QV investment in the relevant ARDEPPS either because, despite them, expansion would still be unprofitable for the merged firm or because a rival of the merged firm that would have made the additional QV investment anyway makes the investment in question (because, despite the efficiencies, expansion would still be more profitable for this rival than for KE). In this case, the dynamic efficiencies will have no impact either on the profits the merger yields its participants or on Clayton-Act-relevant buyers, and no dynamic-efficiency-related bias will affect the choice of whether to engage in the merger rather than not doing anything at all or whether to execute a K–E_L merger rather than a K–E_S merger.

In the third relevant situation, the relevant dynamic efficiencies have no effect on equilibrium QV investment but do cause the merged firm to make an investment that deters an *R* from making an alternative, equally-large QV investment (by making expansion more profitable for KE than for an *R* or by making expansion profitable for a K-firm that can commit itself to making a new QV investment more quickly than can the relevant *R*). In this case, the relevant dynamic efficiencies will increase the profitability of the merger by the sum of the nominal supernormal profits yielded by the QV investment they enable KE to make *plus* the amount by which the substitution of the KE's QV investment for the rival QV investment it deters reduced the damage the additional QV investment did to the profit-yields of the relevant K's or E's pre-existing projects in the relevant area of product-space (a monopolistic-QV-investment-incentive-related amount that will probably tend to be larger for [E_L]s than for [E_S]s.) Unfortunately, in this case, it is complicated to predict the competitive impact of the dynamic efficiencies a conglomerate merger generates. The efficiency-induced substitution of the KE expansion for the *R* expansion will affect competition in three ways:

(1) by altering the sum of the pre-expansion OCAs of the sellers that lose their best-placed position to the new investor,
(2) by altering the amount by which the new investment reduces the OCAs of other sellers whose patronage the new product is second-placed to secure, and
(3) by altering the NOMs and COMs of both the new investor and its rivals as well as the OCAs of the new investor's rivals by changing the new investor's CMCs.

I will assume that the fact that the KE makes the new QV investment implies that its QV investment is more profitable than the QV investment it deters (and not that KE was able to commit itself to investing before the relevant *R* could do so) and that the greater profitability of the KE's QV investment reflects the fact that the product it creates is best-placed more often than the product that would have been created by the QV investment that was deterred (rather than the fact that KE enjoyed higher OCAs when dealing with the buyers in relation to which its new product was best-placed than the deterred *R* would have enjoyed when dealing with the buyers in relation to which its deterred QV investment's product would have been best-placed and/or the fact that KE had higher monopolistic QV-investment incentives to make its QV than the deterred *R* had to make its QV investment). To the extent that these assumptions are justified (and I do believe that to some extent they are), the dynamic efficiencies a conglomerate merger generates will increase competition in the Clayton Act sense by substituting a QV investment that totally removes more OCAs than would have been removed by the QV investment it deters. However, although I do suspect that dynamic efficiencies will increase competition in the preceding way, I am far less certain that they will increase competition by reducing the OCAs of sellers that were best-placed prior to the QV-investment expansion and remain best-placed post-expansion though by a smaller margin (since the product created by the new QV investment is second-placed post-expansion). Once more, my doubts reflect my suspicion that there is little correlation between the frequency and amount by which a product is best-placed and the frequency and amount by which it is second-placed (as opposed to worse-than-second-placed). To the extent that there is a negative correlation between these components of a product's competitive-position array (and I would not be at all surprised to discover that there were), the dynamic efficiencies a conglomerate merger generated would tend to decrease competition on this account. Finally, to the extent that the dynamic efficiencies in question raise the average OCA the (changing) new investor enjoys when dealing for the patronage of the buyers in relation to which the new product is best-placed, they may decrease competition in various ways—by enabling KE to realize more NOMs than the relevant *R* would have done, by raising KE's CMCs and hence its various non-deterred and deterred *R*s' HNOPs by more than the deterred QV investment would have raised the deterred *R*'s CMCs and hence the HNOPs of the sellers that were best-placed to supply buyers the deterred *R* was originally second-placed to supply, and perhaps by increasing COMs by increasing KE's vulnerability to retaliation by more than the deterred *R*'s QV investment would have increased its vulnerability to retaliation and by substituting an expansion by KE for a new entry. On balance, I suspect that in this case the dynamic efficiencies a conglomerate merger generates will cause it to confer an equivalent-dollar gain on Clayton-Act-relevant buyers, though the size of the gain to the relevant buyers will have little connection to the contribution the efficiencies made to the merged company's profits.

Unfortunately, in this case, I cannot even speculate in a worthwhile way as to whether, from the perspective of the goal of increasing competition, there is a bias in favor of the conglomerate merger in question. Moreover, although, *ceteris paribus*, monopolistic-QV-investment-incentive considerations will create a bias in favor of K–E_L mergers over K–E_S mergers from the above perspective, this consideration seems likely to be dwarfed by other factors.

In the fourth situation that should be distinguished, the dynamic efficiencies that I am assuming that either the relevant K–E_L or the relevant K–E_S conglomerate merger would generate would increase equilibrium QV investment by making it profitable for KE to introduce an additional QV investment into the ARDEPPS when no-one else would otherwise have done so. In this case, these efficiencies will increase the merged firm's profits by the difference between the nominal supernormal profits the investment in question will yield and the amount by which its execution will reduce the profit-yield of KE's pre-existing projects. By way of contrast, in this case, the relevant efficiencies will confer an equivalent-dollar gain on Clayton-Act-relevant buyers equal to the OCAs enjoyed pre-expansion by the sellers that were best-placed to supply the buyers the new product became best-placed to supply *plus* the amount by which the new product reduced the OCAs of sellers that continued to be best-placed post-expansion (because the new product was second-placed to supply the relevant buyers) *plus* any related reduction in the relevant *R*s' NOMs *minus* any increase in the COMs the new QV investment enabled KE's *R*s to obtain by increasing their ability to reciprocate to KE's collaboration and/or to retaliate against its undercutting.

Once more, in this case, I am unable to put a sign on the dynamic-efficiency-related bias in the profitability of the relevant conglomerate mergers. Once more as well, although a bias in favor of K–E_L over the K–E_S mergers from the perspective of the goal of increasing competition will be produced by *M* considerations, this bias is likely to be sufficiently small relative to and uncorrelated with the bias in this choice created by all the other biasing factors combined to make me reluctant to reach any conclusions on this basis.

In the fifth relevant type of situation, the dynamic efficiencies that I am assuming that either the relevant K–E_L or the relevant K–E_S conglomerate merger would generate would raise equilibrium QV investment in the relevant ARDEPPS by inducing a rival of the merged firm to make a QV investment when neither it nor anyone else would otherwise have added a QV investment to the ARDEPPS. The efficiencies in question could produce this effect by eliminating or reducing the monopolistic QV-investment disincentive the R faced or giving it a monopolistic QV-investment incentive when it previously faced a disincentive by making it profitable for KE to expand when neither the relevant E nor any other rival of the R in question would otherwise have found a QV investment profitable. In this case, the relevant efficiencies will decrease the profits of the MPs by the amount by which the QV investment they induce R to execute reduces the profit-yield of the investment(s) KE owns in *R*'s ARDEPPS. By way of contrast, in this case, the dynamic efficiencies in question will confer an equivalent-dollar gain on Clayton-Act-relevant buyers by producing the same types of equivalent-dollar impacts on the relevant buyers that the induced KE expansion did in the preceding case.

Hence, in this type of situation, the relevant efficiencies will clearly create a bias against the MPs' merging as opposed to doing nothing from the perspective of the goal of increasing competition. However, since the QV investment the relevant efficiencies will induce R to make will presumably reduce an E_L's pre-existing projects' profit-yields by a larger absolute amount than the sum by which it would reduce an E_S's pre-existing projects' profit-yields (in that E_L has more such projects than E_S), there will tend to be a dynamic-efficiency-related bias against E_L mergers and in favor of E_S mergers in this type of case.

The sixth and final situation worth distinguishing presents a perverse case. In it, the dynamic efficiencies that I am assuming that either the K–E_L or the K–E_S conglomerate merger would generate would cause one or more QV investments not to be added to the relevant ARDEPPS that would otherwise have been made by converting a situation in which a given *R* originally faced non-preclusive monopolistic QV-investment disincentives into one in which the *R* and KE would face preclusive natural oligopolistic QV-investment disincentives (by critically raising the nominal profitability to KE of expanding). In this type of situation, the efficiencies in question will increase the profitability of the merger to KE by an amount equal to the loss the deterred rival QV investment(s) would otherwise have imposed on KE but will decrease competition by preventing the relevant buyers from obtaining the net benefits the deterred QV investment(s) would have conferred on them (as explained when discussing dynamic efficiencies that increase equilibrium QV investment in the ARDEPPS in question). In this type of situation, the dynamic efficiencies that the relevant conglomerate merger would generate will clearly create a bias in favor of the merger from the perspective of the goal of increasing competition. Moreover, since an E_L would tend to gain more from the relevant QV investment's or QV investments' being deterred than would an E_S, the dynamic efficiencies in question will also create a bias in favor of K–E_L mergers over K–E_S mergers in this type of case.

Across all the relevant types of situations, if the relevant K–E_L and K–E_S mergers would generate the same amount and type of dynamic efficiencies and the QV-investment-expansion-related positions of the relevant E_L and E_S firms and of their rivals were the same, the fact that geographic-diversification conglomerate mergers can generate dynamic efficiencies probably would create a small *ceteris paribus* bias in favor of K–E_L mergers over K–E_S mergers if the only distortion in the private profitability of that choice related to the effect of new QV investments in the ARDEPPS on the profit-yields of the MPs' pre-existing projects. Clearly, however, any final assessment of the likely bias in merger-partner selection from the perspective of the goal of preventing the lessening of competition or of increasing competition that is associated with the fact that geographic-diversification conglomerate mergers can generate dynamic efficiencies will also have to take account of any systematic differences in the quantity and types of the dynamic efficiencies that would be generated respectively by relevant K–E_L and K–E_S mergers and any systematic differences in the QV-investment-expansion positions of the relevant (E_L)s and (E_S)s and of their rivals whose salience the preceding analyses reveal. Because there are some limits to even my willingness to try my readers' patience, I will comment no further on these issues.

Having reviewed all the ways in which a conglomerate merger can either increase its participants' profits or the welfare of the owners of one of its participants, it should now be possible to assess whether, from the perspective of the goal of increasing competition, there is a net bias in favor of K–E_L mergers relative to K–E_S mergers. As we have seen, although some factors do create such a bias, others (such as tax considerations and the desire of owners of small businesses to preserve the value of their businesses in the face of their prospective retirement or to exchange their holdings for liquid assets that put them in a position to retire and to benefit their beneficiaries) create the opposite bias. More importantly, the individual biases to which I have been able to give a sign seem likely to be small and uncorrelated with the net sum of the other biases whose size and magnitude I cannot even usefully guesstimate. Surely, even if this complicated analysis does suggest that on balance there is a bias in favor of K–E_L mergers relative to K–E_S mergers from the perspective of the goal of increasing competition, there is absolutely no reason to believe that this bias is likely to be sufficiently large relative to the relevant profit-difference to justify the conclusion that a "toe-hold merger" doctrine whose only relevant effect was to cause K–E_S mergers to be substituted for K–E_L mergers to be procompetitive on balance. The contrary assumption of the developers and proponents of the "toe-hold merger" doctrine is clearly unjustified and probably incorrect. Perhaps the most important implications of the preceding analysis of the relevant profit-bias claim are that those who make this claim have no idea about the proper way to assess it and that the conceptual structures Chap. 2 developed can play a useful role in its assessment.

(2) The Doctrine's Economic Assumption That—If It Will Increase Competition in Those Cases in Which It Will Lead K-firms to Substitute K–E_S Mergers for K–E_L Mergers—It Will Increase Competition

The second economic objection to the claim that the part of the "toe-hold merger" doctrine that privileges K–E_S mergers over K–E_L mergers will increase competition is that, even if, *ceteris paribus*, the doctrine would increase competition by inducing K-firms to substitute K–E_S mergers for K–E_L mergers, it might not increase competition all things considered because, in at least some cases, the doctrine will cause K-firms that would otherwise have executed K–E_L mergers that would have increased competition relative to the defendant-do-nothing baseline to do nothing—*i.e.*, not to enter the firm's market at all rather than to execute an (assumed to be) procompetitive merger with E_S. If K-firms know *ab initio* that they will not be allowed to execute K–E_L mergers that they would find most profitable unless they can show that they made unsuccessful "reasonable efforts" to identify an E_S-firm whose acquisition would be more profitable than not entering the firm's market at all, the cost of making the relevant search (which includes not only the cost of identifying acquisition targets or merger partners but also the cost of negotiating the terms of the acquisition or merger [which in the case of the merger might include the cost of revealing to the relevant E proprietary information about the K's customer lists, costs, trade secrets, and expected merger-generated efficiencies]) might be prohibitively high. Although, admittedly, the probability that the "toe-hold merger" doctrine will produce this outcome depends in part on how the requirement that K-firms that want to merge with an E_L establish that they made "reasonable efforts to identify a suitable E_S firm and failed to do so" is interpreted and applied, I suspect that the prospect of having to engage in such a search and having to forego a more profitable E_L merger if a "suitable" E_S partner is identified may render the search for an E acquisition-target or merger-partner *ex ante* unprofitable for at least some (I suspect, many) Ks that would otherwise attempt to achieve geographic diversification by executing conglomerate mergers or acquisitions. Obviously, to the extent that this is the case, the substitution of the part of the "toe-hold merger" doctrine that privileges K–E_S mergers over K–E_L mergers might not increase competition even if all the substitutions of K–E_S for K–E_L mergers it induces do increase competition. I must admit, however, that the argument that the toe-hold-merger doctrine will increase competition if the K–E_S mergers it causes to be substituted for K–E_L mergers are more procompetitive than the K–E_L mergers will be strengthened to the extent that—by increasing the market value of E_S firms—the doctrine increases the extent to which managers of well-established firms leave their positions to set up their own new companies.

(3) The Doctrine's Legal Assumption That, If It Will Increase Competition, It Is Correct as a Matter of Law

The DOJ, FTC, and those U.S. courts that have promulgated, applied, or commented positively on the "toe-hold merger" doctrine have all assumed that—if its application would increase competition—the doctrine would be correct as a matter of law. I disagree. The doctrine assumes that the Clayton Act forbids a firm from achieving geographic diversification (1) by merging with or acquiring an established firm of any relative size in the target area even when the merger or acquisition in question would not decrease the intensity of competition in the target market below the level it would have if the K-firm did nothing to enter the market in question or if the K-firm could execute an independent entry into that market that would be more profitable than not diversifying into the territory in question at all on the usually-accurate assumption that the independent entry would be more procompetitive than the merger or acquisition and (2) by merging with a relatively-large established firm (E_L) in the target area rather than with a relatively-small established firm (E_S) in the target area even when its merger with or acquisition of the E_L firm would not reduce or would increase the intensity of competition in the target area relative to what it would be if the K-firm did not enter the target market unless the K-firm can show that it had made a reasonable effort to identify an E_S whose acquisition would be more profitable than not entering the target market at all and had failed to do so (on the dubious assumption that K–E_S mergers that would be more profitable for the K-firm than not entering the firm's market at all would be more procompetitive than the K–E_L merger the K-firm would find more profitable to execute). Both these branches of the "toe-hold merger" doctrine therefore assume that the Clayton Act imposes a duty on any firm that wants to achieve geographic diversification not just to avoid doing so in a way that would decrease competition but in some respects to do so in a way that would increase competition. (I say "in some respects" because the doctrine does not require firms that would find one independent entry into a new geographic market more profitable than not entering that market at all to choose the number or the set of independent-entry projects that were more profitable than not entering at all that was most procompetitive.) In my view, because the "toe-hold merger" doctrine imposes (1) a duty to increase competition when choosing between (A) geographic-diversification mergers and geographic-diversification entries and (B) geographic-diversification mergers or acquisition partners as opposed to (2) a duty not to decrease competition by choosing to engage in geographic diversification through merger or acquisition instead of not achieving such diversification at all, the doctrine is wrong as a matter of Clayton Act law in that it rejects the Clayton Act's "defendant-do-nothing" baseline for competitive-impact measurement.

* * *

To my knowledge, no U.S. case about the legality of a conglomerate merger that does not eliminate an effective potential competitor has ever argued (1) that the static efficiencies such a merger generates will reduce competition by causing one or more of the merged firm's established competitors to exit by worsening its array or their arrays of OCAs or by deterring a rival entry or expansion by worsening the potential investor's array of prospective OCAs or (2) that the dynamic efficiencies such a merger generates will reduce competition by inducing a merged-firm expansion that deterred a more procompetitive entry or by substituting a situation in which the merged firm and an established rival faced critical natural oligopolistic QV-investment disincentives for one in which the rival faced non-critical monopolistic QV-investment disincentives. Nor, to my knowledge, has any U.S. case on such conglomerate mergers ever had to respond to a situation in which one of the MPs or the acquired firm was a failing company. However, although as Sect. 6C(1) will indicate some 1960s opinions on the legality of conglomerate mergers that would eliminate an effective potential competitor did express the then-popular view that the efficiencies yielded by any type of merger count against its legality, I am confident that contemporary courts would take the opposite position on this issue not only in potential-competition conglomerate-merger cases but also in cases about the legality of conglomerate mergers that do not eliminate an effective potential competitor. I also see no reason to believe that contemporary courts would not follow the *Citizen Publishing Co.*/1992 and 2010 Horizontal Merger Guidelines failing-company doctrine in conglomerate-merger cases, regardless of whether the merger eliminated an effective potential competitor.

5. The Conditions Under Which Competition Will Be Effective and the Economic Effects of the Fact That a Conglomerate Merger Has Eliminated or Would Eliminate an Effective Potential Competitor

A. The Conditions Under Which Potential Competition Will Be Effective and the Competitive Impact of Effective Potential Competition

(1) The Conditions Under Which Potential Competition Will Be Effective

If (as I will do in this section) one ignores the possibility that an ARDEPPS' established firms may incorrectly believe that an entry will be executed if they do nothing to prevent it, potential competition will be effective in a given ARDEPPS if one or more entries would be executed at the level of ARDEPPS QV investment that would be the equilibrium QV-investment level in that ARDEPPS if entry were barred—*i.e.*, if the entry-preventing QV-investment level were higher than the entry-barred, expansion-preventing QV-investment level. In the QV-investment-competition-related terminology that Chap. 2 developed, the preceding (obvious) claim implies that potential competition will be effective in a given ARDEPPS if the sum of the barriers to entry facing the firm that would be the ARDEPPS' best-placed potential competitor at the ARDEPPS' entry-barred, expansion-preventing QV-investment level were lower than the sum of the barriers to expansion and monopolistic or natural oligopolistic QV-investment disincentives that would (I will assume) just deter the established firm that would be the ARDEPPS' best-placed potential expander at the entry-barred, expansion-preventing QV-investment level from executing a QV-investment expansion. As we shall see, it is important to note that, on this account, the effectiveness of potential competition in a given ARDEPPS depends not exclusively on the height of the barriers to entry facing its best-placed potential competitor (at a particular ARDEPPS QV-investment level) but on the magnitude of those barriers *relative to* the magnitude of the counterpart barriers and possible additional disincentives facing the established firm that would be the ARDEPPS' best-placed potential expander at the relevant QV-investment level if entry were barred.

So far, this discussion of the conditions under which potential competition will be effective has been static in the sense that it has made no reference to the reality that conditions in virtually all ARDEPPSes change through time—in particular, that most ARDEPPS' $H\Pi_E$ curves vary through time as technological developments and changes in the prices of relevant inputs alter the cost of producing the ARDEPPS' products and changes in population size, population wealth, and consumer preferences alter the demand curves for the ARDEPPS' products. *Ceteris paribus*, the faster an ARDEPPS' "$H\Pi_E$" curve (the quotation marks are necessary because I am ignoring related changes in the monopolisticness of the ARDEPPS' pricing) moves to the right through time (because of cost reductions and/or demand increases), the more likely potential competition will be effective at at least some point in time because the barriers to expansion that an ARDEPPS' individual established firms will face on their first, second,...*n*th expansion will increase *inter alia* with the rate at which they are expanding through time and, *ceteris paribus*, the rate at which they will have to expand through time to deter new entry will increase with the rate at which the ARDEPPS' "$H\Pi_E$" curve is moving to the right through time.

(2) The Competitive Impact of Effective Potential Competition (and Hence of Conglomerate Mergers That Eliminate an Effective Potential Competitor)

I believe that in the overwhelming majority of situations effective potential competition will affect competitive outcomes either (1) by becoming kinetic (*i.e.*, by leading to entry) and thereby benefitting Clayton-Act-relevant buyers both directly by providing them with more quality or variety and indirectly by causing prices to drop in the relevant area of product-space or (2) by inducing one or more established firms to make limit investments (QV investments they would not otherwise have made to deter entry) and thereby benefitting Clayton-Act-relevant buyers in the same two ways. As Sect. 5(B)(2) discusses, this conclusion is at odds with the conclusion to which many economists seem to continue to subscribe—*viz.*, the conclusion of limit-price theory that in a broad range of circumstances effective potential competition will affect competitive outcomes by inducing the relevant ARDEPPS' established firms to charge lower prices than they would otherwise have charged to deter entry (to limit price to limit entry). In my judgment, the presence of an effective potential competitor will induce an established firm to lower its prices to deter the potential competitor's entry in only four, empirically-unimportant situations:

(1) a relatively inefficient producer in a little-explored area of product-space that cannot increase the proficiency of its current project, make a new, more-efficient QV investment in the relevant niche, or sell to a potential investor that would be able to operate more proficiently its knowledge of the existence of a profitable investment opportunity may keep its prices down to conceal the profit-potential of the relevant area of product-space to deter the entry of more-efficient firms whose (non-predatory) operation would reduce its profits even more than they were reduced by its low pricing and might even lead to its exit;
(2) a producer in a little-explored area of product-space may keep its prices down in the short run if it believes that if it prevents the "outside" firms that could profit by entering its niche from identifying this opportunity in the short run they will alter their entry positions by using their entry-relevant resources and capital in other ways;
(3) a producer in a little-explored area of product-space may keep its prices down if it fears that any revelation of the profit-potential of its niche will lead to more

QV investments being made in that area of product-space than can be sustained in equilibrium; and

(4) a seller that faces a strong buyer that is threatening to integrate backward into the seller's field of production may offer the buyer a price-reduction to deter the buyer from entering (though I would hesitate to characterize such price-reductions as "limit pricing" because they are not designed to deter entry in any of the ways in which it is claimed limit pricing would do so).

Obviously, the preceding analysis yields the conclusion that, in the vast majority of cases, the fact that a conglomerate merger eliminates an effective potential competitor implies that it (1) will yield the merger partners Sherman-Act-illicit profits either by freeing them from the competition with which the new entry it prevents on this account would have confronted them or by obviating their making a limit investment that would have been unprofitable had it not deterred the relevant new entry and (2) will impose either a larger equivalent-dollar loss on Clayton-Act-relevant rivals by deterring a new entry or a somewhat-smaller equivalent-dollar loss on Clayton-Act-relevant buyers by deterring one or more established firms' making a limit QV investment (smaller because a limit investment by an established firm will tend to be less procompetitive than a new entry). The preceding analysis also yields the conclusion that, in a few cases, the fact that a conglomerate merger eliminates an effective potential competitor implies that it (1) will yield the merger partners Sherman-Act-illicit profits by obviating the relevant established firms' lowering their prices (though the illicitness of these profits may be contestable when the foregone price-reduction would have been executed because the incumbent feared that investors would otherwise bring total QV investment in the ARDEPPS to a supra-equilibrium level) and (2) will impose an equivalent-dollar loss on Clayton-Act-relevant buyers by obviating the incumbents' making price-reductions to deter entry.

B. A Statement and Critique of Limit-Price Theory: The Conditions Under Which the Theory Alleges Potential Competition Is Effective, How Limit Pricing Allegedly Deters Entry, Its Alleged Effectiveness, and Its Profitability Relative to Allowing Entry If Bribing or Buying the Potential Entrant Is Impossible

(1) The Conditions Under Which, According to at Least Some Limit-Price Theorists, Potential Competition or a Particular Potential Competitor Will Be Effective

I have not done a systematic empirical study of the extent to which contemporary Industrial Organization economists support limit-price theory, but my impression is that most Industrial Organization graduate students are still taught limit-price theory not as an historical curiosity but as a correct analysis of the impact of effective potential competition. I also do not know the proportion of those IO economists who subscribe to limit-price theory who agree with the position its major developer—Joe Bain—took on the conditions under which potential competition would be effective. However, both Bain and his signature work on limit pricing[1128] appear to me to be sufficiently-highly-regarded today to justify my recounting and criticizing his position on the conditions under which potential competition will be effective. According to Bain, a market's best-placed potential competitor(s) will be effective whenever the barriers to entry they face are either low (in which case the established firms will not limit price and the potential competitor will enter) or moderate to substantial (in which case the established firms will not limit price and entry will be deterred) but not when the barriers to entry they face are high since in high-barrier-to-entry situations entry will be "blockaded" in that the highest profitable price the established firms could manage to set if they were not concerned about entry will be lower than the limit price (the price that will deter entry).[1129] I should state at the outset that Bain does not define the concept of a barrier to entry in the same way that I do.[1130] However, the relevant

[1128] BAIN BARRIERS.

[1129] *Id.* at 34–41.

[1130] For Bain, barriers to entry are factors that raise the potential entrants' post-entry average total costs above technological minimum average total cost (where the product is defined without reference to any images that advertising could link to it and without reference to the speed with which it will be supplied at different stages of a fluctuating-demand cycle). More specifically, Bain distinguishes three types of barriers to entry: (1) absolute cost barriers to entry, which reflect the fact that the potential entrant would have to pay more to use a patented or secret production process than its established firm "owner" had to pay to discover it or buy it, would have to pay more for raw materials or other types of inputs than the established firms have to pay for them, or can make less-profitable labor and management "purchases" than the established firms made; (2) product-differentiation barriers to entry, which equal the additional cost per unit the potential entrant would have to incur to overcome the product-differentiation-related advantage of the established firms; and (3) scale barriers to entry, which he defines to equal the amount by which entry would cause the established firm's average total costs to exceed technological minimum average total cost by reducing its output further below the average-total-cost-minimizing level (and simultaneously cause the new entrant's costs to be higher by causing its sales to be lower than they would be if its entry did not raise QV investment in the ARDEPPS in question). (Bain should also have included in his scale barrier to entry category the amount by which the established firms' pre-entry average total costs exceeded technological minimum average total cost because even pre-entry their sales were lower than their average-total-cost-minimizing outputs.) Bain argued that the limit price depended as well on what he called the "percentage effect" of entry—the amount by which entry would reduce prevailing prices in the market in question. According to Bain, the limit price equaled (actually, was infinitesimally below) minimum average total cost *plus* the three barriers to entry *plus* the percentage effect of entry. In Bain's view, limit pricing would deter entry because if the established firms charged that price (P_L) the potential entrant would realize that the price it could obtain post-entry—P_L *minus* the percentage effect of entry—would be lower than its post-entry average total costs—minimum average total cost *plus* the three barriers to entry. This arithmetic argument would be incorrect even if Bain altered the definition of his scale barrier to entry to include the amount by which the established firms' pre-entry average total costs exceeded technological minimum average total cost because even pre-entry they could not take full

definitional difference is not relevant to the point I am making. I should also say that even if one believed that limit pricing would deter entry, would be more profitable than any other means of deterring entry, and would be more profitable than allowing entry to occur (see below) there would be no reason to believe that entry will be blockaded so that potential competition will be ineffective when barriers to entry are high. Admittedly, on Bain's account of the limit price, the height of the limit price (P_L) in any market—more precisely the difference between P_L and minimum average total cost in that market—will increase with the barriers to entry into that market. However, on Bain's account of the various barriers to entry, the height of the conventional-profit-maximizing price in any market will also increase with the height of its various barriers to entry: product differentiation tends to be associated with higher OCAs and NOMs, and absolute cost differences and high economies of scale relative to the extent of the market tend to be associated with higher OCAs and NOMs as well (given the degree of product differentiation) by being linked to what would conventionally be denominated higher seller-concentration ratios. Hence, even if I accepted Bain's "theory" of limit pricing (which I do not—see below), there would be no reason to believe that the limit price in a market (P_L) will be especially likely to be higher than the profit-maximizing price in that market when P_L is high relative to average total cost (ATC) or marginal cost (MC)—*i.e.*, there would be no reason to conclude that there was a positive relationship between the height of the barriers to entry into a given market and the likelihood that entry into it would be blockaded.

The preceding analysis focused on Bain's position about whether *any potential entrant* into a particular market would be effective. Some economists have also expressed to me their agreement with a position that the U.S. DOJ took in its 1984 Conglomerate Merger Guidelines on a different "potential-competitor-effectiveness" issue—*viz.*, whether *a particular potential competitor* is effective. Although I have no idea whether the economists at the DOJ were responsible for this position, the

advantage of the available technological economies of scale. In particular, Bain's arithmetic argument for the efficacy of limit pricing would be wrong even if it were improved in this way because it is based on the highly-unrealistic assumption that what he denominates the percentage effect of entry will not be affected by whether the established firms were limit pricing pre-entry. Assume that, if the established firms were charging the highest conventionally-profitable prices they could charge pre-entry, the entry would cause them to reduce their prices by X cents (by reducing their OCAs, NOMs, and COMs and perhaps by causing them to retaliate). If, alternatively, pre-entry, the established firms were charging prices that did not take advantage of their OCAs, their ability to secure NOMs, and their ability to profit by charging contrived oligopolistic prices, post-entry they would almost certainly reduce their prices by less than X cents—*e.g.*, having failed to deter entry by deceiving the potential competitor into underestimating the highest price they could charge, the established firms would give up attempting to do so and would charge the most-conventionally-profitable price they could charge post-entry (a price that might even be higher than the limit price though it would presumably be lower than the most-conventionally-profitable price they could have charged pre-merger).

1984 Guidelines state that—unless there is strong evidence that a particular potential competitor will enter—the Department will assume that only the best-placed, second-placed, and third-placed potential entrant into a given market are effective potential competitors. I disagree with this position. In many situations, no potential competitor is effective because the entry-barred, expansion-preventing QV-investment level is higher than the entry-preventing QV-investment level; in many situations, only one or two potential competitors are effective because (1) the $H\Pi_E$ curve for the relevant ARDEPPS is not rising quickly and either (2) (A) the entry-barred, expansion-preventing QV-investment level is only one or two QV investments below the entry-preventing QV-investment level and/or (B) the barriers to entry facing the second-placed potential competitor are much higher than those facing the best-placed potential competitor and/or the barriers to entry facing the third-placed potential competitor are much higher than those facing the second-placed potential competitor; and in many situations, more than three potential competitors are effective because (1) the entry-barred, expansion-preventing QV-investment level is now or will become more than three QV investments below the entry-preventing QV-investment level (given the rate at which the relevant ARDEPPS' $H\Pi_E$ curve is rising through time) and (2) the barriers facing the fourth-placed, fifth-placed, *etc.*, potential entrants are not significantly higher than those facing the best-placed potential competitor. I am also not sure why the fact that a particular potential entrant that was part of a group of four or more equally-well-placed potential entrants was clearly going to enter should make one conclude that it was effective: its prospective entry would not increase the effectiveness of potential competition if its entry would deter the entry of another equally-well-placed potential entrant unless the fact that its plans were well-advanced meant that, if it were not eliminated, it would enter more quickly than the firm its entry deterred would have done.

I want to close this subsection by commenting on one relevant evidentiary point that several economists have made to me and that various courts have also accepted—*viz.*, the claim that the fact that no entry has taken place into a given ARDEPPS for a considerable period of time implies that potential competition is not effective in that ARDEPPS. In my judgment, this claim is wrong because it ignores the fact that potential competition can be effective even if it never becomes kinetic by inducing one or more of an ARDEPPS' established firms to make a limit investment to deter the effective potential competitor from entering.

(2) The Alleged Competitive Impact of Effective Potential Competition, How Limit Pricing Allegedly Deters Entry, Its Alleged Effectiveness, and Its Alleged Profitability Relative to Allowing Entry If Bribing or Buying the Potential Entrant Is Impossible

A considerable number of economists in both the U.S. and Europe continue to believe that in a broad range of circumstances effective potential competition will affect competitive outcomes not by leading to entry or inducing incumbents to make limit investments but by inducing incumbents to charge lower prices than they would otherwise have found profitable to charge to deter entry. Bain claimed that the established firms in a market would respond to potential competition by engaging in limit pricing whenever the best-placed potential entrant faced moderate to substantial barriers to entry (because he believed that potential competitors that faced moderate to substantial barriers to entry would always be effective and that limit pricing—which he assumed would always be effective—would be more profitable than conventional profit-maximization when the potential competitor that had to be deterred faced moderate to substantial as opposed to low barriers to entry).[1131] Some limit-price-theory supporters appear to believe that limit pricing will always be profitable for established firms confronted by an effective potential competitor, while others seem to think that limit pricing will sometimes be profitable for such incumbents and sometimes not be profitable for them but that the profitability of the practice does not depend solely on the height of the barriers to entry the best-placed, effective potential competitor faces.[1132] However, all limit-price theorists believe that limit pricing will always deter entry, will sometimes be more profitable than allowing entry to occur, and when it is more profitable than allowing entry to occur will be the most profitable way for established firms to deter entry. I will now explain why I reject all three of these claims.

[1131] I should also point out that Bain's explanation of the efficacy of limit pricing would not imply that limit pricing will tend to be more profitable than conventional profit-maximization when barriers to entry are moderate to substantial and less profitable than conventional profit-maximization when barriers to entry are low even if it did imply that the limit-price rate-of-return (Π_L) in a given market would increase with the barriers to entry into that market. More particularly, Bain's limit-price "theory" would not imply this result because there are good reasons to believe that the conventional-profit-maximizing rate-of-return in a given market will also increase with "the height of its barriers to entry" on Bain's definition. Thus, to the extent that Bain's absolute cost barriers to entry are positively correlated with what I call Π_D barriers to entry and expansion and Bain's scale barriers to entry are highly correlated with what I call the scale barrier to entry and expansion, the profit-maximizing rate-of-return in a given market would also be positively correlated with the height of its barriers to entry in Bain's sense of this concept. Hence, if I let Π_L stand for the limit-pricing rate-of-return (which on Bain's assumption that limit pricing will always deter entry will be constant through time) and Π_M stand for the conventional-profit-maximizing rate-of-return—which will equal the weighted-average of the before-entry conventional-profit-maximizing rate-of-return (Π_M^B) and the after-entry conventional-profit-maximizing rate-of-return (Π_M^A), more specifically which will equal $(c\Pi_M^B + d\Pi_M^A)/(c + d)$ where "c" is the length of the before-entry period and "d" is the length of the after-entry period—the strong, positive correlation between Π_L and Π_M implies that there is no reason to believe that (Π_L) will be higher than $(c\Pi_M^B + d\Pi_M^A)/(c + d)$ when barriers to entry are moderate to substantial and lower than $(c\Pi_M^B + d\Pi_M^A)/(c + d)$ when barriers to entry are low.

[1132] These scholars have not provided an account of the determinants of the profitability of limit pricing for established firms that confront an effective potential competitor.

With one partial exception,[1133] limit-price theorists all assume that limit pricing will always deter entry. As I have already noted, because Bain assumed that the fact that a market's established firms were practicing limit pricing pre-entry would not affect the impact that entry would have on their prices, he believed that one could establish the inevitable efficacy of limit pricing arithmetically (at least if one assumed that the relevant potential entrants were sovereign maximizers). However, in a world in which the fact that an ARDEPPS' established firms were charging limit prices pre-entry will affect the post-entry price-change that is most profitable for them, Bain's type of arithmetic proof of limit pricing's efficacy will no longer work. To be fair, limit-price theorists have offered four non-arithmetic explanations for the supposed efficacy of limit pricing, and I can think of at least two others that deserve some attention. However, even if one takes account of the possibility that individual acts of limit pricing could tend to deter entry in more than one way, such pricing will clearly be far less effective at deterring entry than the limit-price theorists suppose.

Bain offered the first explanation of the supposed ability of limit pricing to deter entry—that limit pricing would deceive potential investors into underestimating the price the ARDEPPS' established firms could have charged pre-entry and hence would charge post-entry[1134] (in my terms but not his, into underestimating the height of the ARDEPPS' $H\Pi_E$ curve—*inter alia*, the OCAs, NOMs, and COMs the established firms enjoyed or could have obtained pre-entry). I think that the current literature exaggerates the extent to which limit pricing can function in this way. Although limit pricing might totally deceive some potential competitors, there are several reasons for doubting that such deception would often take place. Thus, since the best-placed potential entrants into many ARDEPPSes are already-established firms in closely-allied fields, they will often know too much about the shape of the ARDEPPS' demand curve and the intensity of its price competition to be fooled by limit pricing. Indeed, even if the potential entrants do not discover the ruse themselves, the character of the ARDEPPS' prevailing price might very well be revealed to them (for a price—perhaps a superior job-offer) by a knowledgeable employee of an established firm in the ARDEPPS in question. The existence of interlocking directorates, the mobility of top-level management, and the huge sums that are currently spent on intercompany spying also support the conclusion that such deception could not succeed for long.

A second possibility, which Bain and others have ignored, is related to the first: even if limit pricing does not deter entry or expansions by deceiving the potential investors in question into underestimating the height of the relevant ARDEPPS'

[1133] The exception is Darius Gaskins, who assumes that limit pricing will always reduce the probability that entry will occur. See Darius Gaskins, *Dynamic Limit Pricing: Optimal Limit Pricing Under Threat of Entry*, 3 J. ECON. THEORY 306 (1971).

[1134] See Joe S. Bain, *A Note on Pricing in Monopoly and Oligopoly*, 39 AM. ECON. REV. 448, 453 (1949).

$H\Pi_E$ curve, it may deter risk-averse potential investors from making a QV investment by increasing their uncertainty about the height of the $H\Pi_E$ curve at the ARDEPPS' pre-entry QV-investment level (by increasing the risk barrier to entry or expansion). However, the fact that the relevant potential investors will almost always be well-established firms in the ARDEPPS in question or in closely-allied ARDEPPSes reduces the ability of limit pricing to function in this way as well by reducing both its ability to create such uncertainty and the relevant investors' risk-averseness.

Milgrom and Roberts proposed a third possible basis for the supposed deterrent effect of limit pricing—*viz.*, that limit pricing would deter entry by deceiving potential competitors into underestimating the established firms' costs.[1135] For two reasons, I doubt that limit pricing would have much of an impact on entry for this reason. First, I think that artificially-low prices would be more likely to deceive potential investors into underestimating the established firms' OCAs and attainable NOMs and COMs than to induce them to underestimate the established firms' MCs. Second, since potential investors' post-entry profits will be directly determined by their rivals' post-entry prices rather than by their rivals' post-entry costs, their entry decision will be affected by their rival-cost underestimates only to the extent that (1) they lead them to underestimate the prices that the established firms would find conventionally-most-profitable post-entry, (2) they lead them to overestimate the probability that the established firms will respond to entry by engaging in a fight to the finish by making the potential investors underestimate their own chances of survival in such a battle, and (3) they induce them to spend resources to determine why their predicted costs are so much higher than their rivals' apparent costs—how they could improve their planned production and distribution techniques. Once more, the fact that the relevant potential investors will usually be well-established firms in the same or allied ARDEPPSes reduces both the likelihood that limit pricing will induce them to underestimate the established firms' costs and the extent to which any such induced underestimates would deter them from investing.[1136]

Bain also suggested a fourth way that limit pricing might deter entry—*viz.*, by communicating a threat that the established firms would retaliate against any new entrant. Although limit pricing could deter entry in this way, the force of this argument is vitiated by two considerations (even if we ignore the fact that limit

[1135] Paul Milgrom and John Roberts, *Limit Pricing and Entry Under Incomplete Information: An Equilibrium Analysis*, 50 ECONOMETRICA 443 (1982).

[1136] Milgrom and Roberts' article induced a response that argued that an established firm whose potential competitors were uncertain of their own likely costs might be able to deter entry by charging prices above its inherently-most-profitable price. I regard the suggestion that such behavior would tend to deter entry by inducing the relevant potential competitors to overestimate their costs as essentially silly since the relevant pricing would also tend to make them overestimate their prospective rivals' post-entry prices. See Joseph Harrington, *Limit Pricing When the Potential Entrant Is Uncertain of Its Cost Function*, 54 ECONOMETRICA 429 (1986).

pricing is an extremely-expensive way of communicating such a threat). First, limit pricing cannot simultaneously (1) communicate a threat and (2) deceive a potential investor into underestimating the price the established firms could succeed in obtaining pre-entry and post-entry or the costs the established firms had to incur to produce and distribute their products. Second, the efficacy of this kind of threat will obviously be lower when the relevant potential investors are already-established firms that have the financial wherewithal to withstand retaliation and a stake in avoiding a reputation of being deterrable.

I can think of a fifth way in which limit pricing could deter entry or expansions that is related to this threat-possibility. Limit pricing could deter such investments by increasing the credibility of the established firms' threat of retaliation by reducing the law-related costs the sellers in question will have to incur to carry out the threats in question. Thus, to the extent that established firms that are limit pricing can retaliate against a new entrant simply by maintaining their original limit price—*i.e.*, without responding to entry by reducing their prices, the practice of limit pricing will reduce the probability that their retaliation will lead to their being tried and/or convicted under the antitrust laws (and concomitantly the certainty-equivalent cost to them of retaliating). Obviously, the lower the cost of retaliation, the more believable any related threats, and the less attractive actual entry, other things' being equal.

Sixth and finally, some limit-price theorists have argued that limit pricing will deter entry by protecting the goodwill of the established firms. According to this group of theorists, limit pricing will protect the established firms' goodwill and thereby deny the potential entrant the opportunity "to establish the essential connection in the market, which is the condition *sine qua non* of the efficient and continuing manufacturer."[1137] More specifically, they argue that "the general situation. . .is that so long as its price is right, an established firm will have a more or less clearly defined market, and would be protected from the efforts of would-be competing businesses to cut into the market."[1138] "But in the event that the price is *not* right—then experience suggests not only that new competition will appear but at least as often as not the new competitor will succeed,"[1139] for "the resentment of the buyers the price now revealed to have been not warranted by costs provides a reservoir of ill-will which, properly exploited, will ensure the new entrant access to the market."[1140] In short, these limit-price theorists (1) implicitly

---

[1137] ROY HARROD, ECONOMIC ESSAYS 125 (Macmillan, 1952).

Harry R. Edwards, *Price Formation in Manufacturing Industry and Excess Capacity*, 7 OX. ECON. PAPERS 94, 96 (1955).

[1138] P.W.S. ANDREWS, MANUFACTURING BUSINESS 148 (Macmillan, 1949).

[1139] Harry R. Edwards, *Price Formation in Manufacturing Industry and Excess Capacity*, 7 OX. ECON. PAPERS 94, 96 (1955).

[1140] *Id.* at 97.

define a seller's goodwill in terms of the satisfaction customers obtain from providing the seller with income, (2) argue that goodwill will be positive if buyers believe that their supplier has given them "fair" terms but will become negative if buyers discover that the seller has been charging more than a "reasonable" markup over costs, (3) assume that buyers will always draw the latter inference if a new entrant offers them more attractive terms, and therefore (4) conclude that limit pricing will deter new entry by precluding new entrants from turning goodwill into bad. I find this goodwill argument almost totally unpersuasive, at least in the more generalized industrial context in which it has been made. Thus, although village butchers might very well possess the kind of goodwill on which the theory focuses, I doubt that many consumers place a positive value on the profits their purchases generate for major industrial concerns. Indeed, even if such goodwill were more pervasive than I believe, I would not be persuaded by this hypothesis, for (1) it is not at all clear to me why shoppers who are offered more attractive terms by a newcomer would not attribute this fact to the newcomer's lower costs or promotional pricing rather than to their previous supplier's "excessive" margins, and (2) large new entrants that want to undermine their established rival's goodwill might be able to do so in the face of limit pricing simply by sustaining short-run losses in order to establish a market position.

In sum, I do not think that limit pricing would deter entry nearly so effectively as the limit-pricing theorists have assumed. I will now explain why I think that the limit-price theorists exaggerate the frequency with which—if limit pricing would always deter entry—it would be more profitable than allowing entry to occur. I have already indicated that in three sets of circumstances sellers may find a practice that could properly be labeled limit pricing not only an effective deterrent to entry but a method of deterring entry that is more profitable than allowing entry to occur or deterring entry in any other way. These three cases aside, however, I do not think that limit pricing would be more profitable than allowing entry to occur even if it would effectively deter entry. Even if the number of best-placed potential competitors the established firms faced was sufficiently large to create a situation in which the potential competitor that would make the last entry that would be executed absent limit pricing or established-firm expansions would face the same barriers to entry that confronted the first potential competitor to enter the ARDEPPS in question during the analysis-period, limit pricing that was effective would not be more profitable than allowing entry to occur unless it would reduce the relevant potential competitors' certainty-equivalent expected rates-of-return by more than it reduced the limit pricers' rates-of-return. If limit pricing that reduced the supernormal rate-of-return the established firms realized on each of their QV-investment projects by X%—*i.e.*, from (Y + X)% to Y%—deterred all entry by reducing their best-placed potential competitors' certainty-equivalent expected rates-of-return by X%, it would have no effect on the established firms' long-run rates-of-return even if the potential competitor that was best-placed to make the last entry that would be made absent limit pricing or established-firm expansion would face the same barriers as the potential competitor that would otherwise have made the first entry. And if an X% limit-pricing-induced reduction in the established firms' rates-of-return deterred all entry by reducing all potential competitors' certainty-equivalent expected rates-of-return by X%, it would reduce the established firms' long-run rates-of-return if the last entry that would otherwise have been made would have been introduced by someone that faced higher barriers than those that confronted the first entrant in the analysis-period (because at least one of the potential competitors that would have to enter to establish equilibrium QV investment would face higher barriers to entry than the [original] best-placed potential competitor faced). Hence, outside the three exceptional cases described previously, limit pricing would not be more profitable than allowing entry to occur unless its practice would reduce the potential competitors' expected certainty-equivalent rate-of-return by more than it reduces the limit pricers' actual rates-of-return.

I doubt that this condition will ever be fulfilled. Clearly, if limit pricing works by deceiving the potential competitors into underestimating the height of the relevant ARDEPPS' $H\Pi_E$ curve, this condition is unlikely to be fulfilled. The most favorable assumption one could make on this issue from the perspective of those who claim that limit pricing would be more profitable than allowing entry to occur is undoubtedly that such deception will reduce the potential competitors' estimates of the height of the relevant $H\Pi_E$ curve by the same amount that it reduces its practitioners' rates-of-return. Nor do things look brighter for the profitability of limit pricing if we shift to the other ways in which it could deter entry. Thus, limit pricing seems unlikely to increase the risk barrier to entry by creating uncertainty about the height of the $H\Pi_E$ curve by as much as it would reduce the incumbent's short-run rate-of-return—much less to increase the relevant short-run rate-of-return sufficiently to compensate for the effects of any tendency of the relevant barriers to entry faced by the last entrant in the analysis-period to exceed those facing the first. Similarly, although limit pricing that communicates a threat or makes the threat more credible will raise the potential competitors' retaliation barrier to entry, I doubt that the practice will increase this barrier as much as it reduces the established firms' rates-of-return. Indeed, I suspect that the profit-difference in question will virtually always exceed the profits the threat will enable the limit pricer to realize in other ways—*i.e.*, by practicing predation in other contexts, by contriving oligopolistic prices, and by undercutting or undermining its rivals' contrived oligopolistic prices. This conclusion is crucial because, as already mentioned, these threat-effects are alternatives to the deception-effect first considered—*i.e.*, will not be present for any potential competitor that limit pricing deceives into underestimating the height of the relevant ARDEPPS' $H\Pi_E$ curve. Moreover, as I have already indicated, although the goodwill argument can be combined with any of the above possibilities, I doubt its empirical importance. Nor do I find it conceivable that limit pricing will decrease the relevant potential entrant's expected supernormal rate-of-return by more than it will reduce the limit pricers' rates-of-return by performing any combination of the above functions that it could simultaneously perform.

In short, in my judgment, unless one is dealing with (1) a relatively inefficient producer in a business niche whose profit-potential is seriously underestimated, (2) a seller that fears that more accurate information about the profit-potential of its ARDEPPS will lead to a frenzy of QV-investment activity that will raise ARDEPPS QV investment above its equilibrium level, or (3) a seller that believes that, if its limit pricing deters an entry or expansion in the short run, it will raise the barriers faced by the best-placed potential entrant or expander in its ARDEPPS (and hence its limit price) because the potential competitor or expander that was originally best-placed to add a QV investment to the relevant ARDEPPS will become worse-placed to do so over time, perhaps because it will use elsewhere the financial, managerial, and/or non-managerial labor resources it would have used to execute its entry into or QV-investment expansion in the relevant ARDEPPS in the short run, limit pricing would virtually never be more profitable than allowing entry to occur even if it were effective. (Recall: I do not think that the practice in which a seller reduces its price to a buyer to deter the latter from integrating backwards should be called "limit pricing.")

I turn now to the possibility that, even if limit pricing would be both effective and more profitable than allowing entry, it would not be more profitable than other entry-deterring strategies. In practice, I expect that limit pricing will almost never be as profitable as other means of deterring entry. Thus, even if limit pricing could successfully communicate a threat, sellers would probably prefer to communicate threats verbally or by reducing their prices for a short time in response to specific rumors that entry was being contemplated. Similarly, even if limit pricing could increase goodwill, sellers would probably find it more attractive to accomplish this result by providing superior service. Indeed, despite the risk of prosecution, established firms would probably find buying off or buying up a potential competitor preferable to limit pricing. Most important, however, I suspect that sellers will almost always find it more profitable to deter entry by making one or more QV investments themselves—*i.e.*, by making what I call limit investments, QV investments that would not be profitable but for their tendency to reduce the amount of QV investments others make in the ARDEPPS in question. Since many types of limit investments (for example, an investment in a new product variant or in capacity) are not really rescindable in the way in which limit-pricing price-cuts can be reversed, they clearly will tend to deter entry by reducing the potential entrant's prospective OCAs and increasing its costs by reducing its sales and hence its ability to take advantage of economies of scale in production and distribution. Since any potential entrant that is deterred by limit investments would have expected to realize at least a normal rate-of-return on its investment had the limit investment not been executed, an established firm will find it profitable to make a limit investment of $X that will deter someone else's QV investment of $X unless the difference between the barriers to expansion it faced and the barriers to entry facing the potential competitor whose entry its expansion would deter exceed the sum of (1) the supernormal profit-rate the deterred potential competitor would otherwise have realized on its entry and (2) the amount by which the limit investment's actual rate-of-return was increased by the fact that its execution would reduce (in comparison with the *status quo ante*) the nominal profits the limit investor's pre-existing projects would generate in the future by less than those profits would otherwise have been reduced by the new entry (or rival expansion) it deterred. Unless one is dealing with an ARDEPPS in which demand is growing or costs are falling extremely rapidly, established firms will virtually always find limit investments that deter the same amount of QV investment that they create privately profitable.

In short, (1) limit pricing will be a far-less-effective deterrent of entry or expansion than the limit-pricing theorists claim; (2) except in three very special cases, limit pricing would almost certainly not be more profitable than allowing entry to occur even if it were as effective as its "supporters" assert; and (3) even if limit pricing were as effective as limit-price theorists claim and would be more profitable than allowing entry to occur, it would almost certainly not be so profitable as various alternative moves the relevant established firms could make to deter entry or expansion.[1141] Although these conclusions would be surprising if there were a substantial body of direct evidence that established firms threatened with entry did engage in limit pricing or if limit-price theorists had confirmed their theory through some other type of valid empirical procedure, no such direct evidence or sound empirical test exists. To my knowledge, no-one (no limit-price theorist and no-one else) has ever described a case in which an established firm practiced limit pricing: the historical stories that have been provided are all accounts of limit investing. Limit-price "theory" is a "theory" in search of a phenomenon. And the supposed empirical tests of limit-price theory—which claim to be testing the theory by demonstrating that, controlling for seller concentration, rates-of-return increase with barriers to entry[1142]—are no tests of the theory at all since the relevant relationship would obtain (assuming away the problematic character of any related market definitions and the somewhat related dubiousness of the relevance of seller concentration) regardless of whether the sellers in question limit priced or charged conventional-profit-maximizing prices.

[1141] Rather than confronting the deficiencies of limit-price theory, academic economists have tried to rescue it by building stochastic limit-pricing models (which claim that limit pricing reduces the probability of entry). See Darius Gaskins, *Dynamic Limit Pricing: Optimal Limit Pricing Under Threat of Entry*, 3 J. ECON. THEORY 306 (1971).

[1142] See BAIN BARRIERS at 182–204.

6. The Reasons Why It May Be More Profitable to Prevent Entry by Merging With the Potential Competitor Than by Bribing It Not to Enter and/or Threatening to Retaliate Against Its Entry, the Relevance of the Fact That a Conglomerate Merger Eliminates an Effective Potential Competitor to Its Legality Under the Sherman and Clayton Acts, Correctly Interpreted, and the U.S. Courts' and the Antitrust-Enforcement Agencies' Positions on This Legal Issue

A. The Reasons Why It May Be More Profitable to Prevent Entry by Merging With the Potential Competitor Than by Bribing It Not to Enter and/or Threatening to Retaliate Against Its Entry

Why might it be more profitable to eliminate an effective potential competitor by merging with it than by deterring its investment by paying it a bribe or threatening it with retaliation or allowing the entry to take place? The merger will be more profitable than deterring the new entry by paying the potential competitor a bribe (not accompanied by a threat of retaliation) if the following sum is positive:

(1) the gains the merger will confer on the merger partners by generating efficiencies, by creating a merged firm whose buying power exceeds the sum of the MPs' buying power, by creating a merged firm that can earn more profits through contrivance and predation, and in the other ways that conglomerate mergers can yield profits than the MPs could have done *minus*
(2) the loss the merger generates by creating a merged firm that is less efficient in specific ways than the MPs were and generating risk costs that are unrelated to the possibility that the potential competitor may accept the bribe and enter anyway *minus*
(3) the certainty-equivalent cost the briber incurs because the potential competitor may accept the bribe and enter anyway *minus*
(4) any positive difference between the mechanical transaction cost of the merger and the mechanical transactions cost of the bribe *minus*
(5) any positive difference between the law-related cost of the merger and the law-related cost of the bribe.

The merger will be more profitable than deterring the new entry by threatening the potential competitor with retaliation and, if necessary, carrying out that threat if the following sum is positive:

(1) the gains the merger will confer on the merger partners in the ways listed in item (1) of the immediately-preceding list *plus*
(2) the gains that the threats and associated acts of retaliation will confer on the incumbent if they succeed in deterring the new entry by strengthening its reputation for engaging in successful strategic conduct *minus*

(3) the loss the merger generated by creating a merged firm that is less efficient in specific ways than the MPs were and by generating risk costs that are unrelated to the possibility that the threats and acts of retaliation may fail to deter the new entry *minus*
(4) the certainty-equivalent cost the incumbent incurs because its threats and acts of retaliation may not deter the new entry (which includes the cost it incurs because the episode weakens its reputation for engaging in successful strategic conduct) *minus*
(5) any positive difference between the mechanical transaction cost of the merger and the mechanical transaction cost of the threats *minus*
(6) the cost to the incumbent of any retaliation it must engage in (which includes both mechanical costs and the loss it would have to incur to retaliate even if the retaliation were mechanically transaction-costless) *minus*
(7) any positive difference between the law-related cost of the merger and the law-related cost of the threat of retaliation and any associated acts of retaliation (a difference that might be negative).

The merger will be more profitable for the incumbent than allowing entry to occur if the following sum is positive:

(1) the difference between the amount by which the potential competitor's entry would reduce the merger-partner incumbent's profits and the supernormal profits the new entrant would realize on its new entry *plus*
(2) the gains the merger would confer on the merger partners by generating efficiencies, by creating a merged firm whose buying power exceeds the sum of the MPs' buying power, and by creating a merged firm that profits more from contrivance and predation than the MPs would have done *minus*
(3) the loss the merger generates by creating a merged firm that is less efficient in specific ways than the MPs were and by generating risk costs *minus*
(4) any supernormal profits the potential competitor would earn on the merger (the potential competitor might actually realize a loss on the merger if the incumbent threatened it with retaliation if it did not agree to the merger) *minus*
(5) the transaction cost of the merger *minus*
(6) the law-related cost of the merger.

Admittedly, it will often by more profitable to use a combination of anticompetitve offers (bribes) and threats of retaliation to deter the entry of a uniquely-effective potential competitor than to merge with or acquire it. Still, there clearly will be many situations in which the most profitable way to deter such a potential competitor's entry will be to merge with it or acquire it.

B. The Relevance of the Fact That a Conglomerate Merger Eliminates an Effective Potential Competitor to Its Legality Under the Sherman and Clayton Acts, Correctly Interpreted

Three points are salient. First, although the profits that a conglomerate merger yields its participants by eliminating an effective potential competitor of one or both of the MPs in question (in the latter case, when each MP was a potential competitor of the other [in different markets]) are Sherman-Act-illicit, the fact that a conglomerate yields Sherman-Act-illicit profits in this way will not cause it to violate the Sherman Act unless the MPs' *ex ante* perception that their merger was *ex ante* profitable was critically affected by their belief that it would or might yield them profits by eliminating one or both as a potential competitor of the other. This condition for "criticality" will not be satisfied if (1) the MPs believed *ex ante* that their merger would yield sufficient profits legitimately (*e.g.*, by generating static and/or dynamic efficiencies, tax advantages, or benefits to an MP-owner who wanted to increase the liquidity of his assets and/or escape his managerial responsibilities) to be *ex ante* profitable on that account or (2) if the MPs believed *ex ante* that although their merger would not generate sufficient Sherman-Act-licit profits to be *ex ante* profitable on that account the Sherman-Act-licit profits it would yield and the Sherman-Act-illicit profits it would yield by enabling them to increase their COMs, to increase the retaliation barriers to QV investing they erected against their rivals, and to practice predation more profitably—even if it did not eliminate an effective potential competitor—would render it *ex ante* profitable.

Second, although the fact that a conglomerate merger eliminates an effective potential competitor of one or both MPs counts against its Clayton Act legality since the elimination of such a competitor will tend to inflict an equivalent-dollar loss on Clayton-Act-relevant buyers by reducing the absolute attractiveness of the best offer they respectively receive from any inferior supplier, it will not critically affect the Clayton Act legality of the merger in question unless it causes a merger that would not otherwise have inflicted a net equivalent-dollar loss on Clayton-Act-relevant buyers to do so. This criticality-condition is salient because even conglomerate mergers that eliminate an effective potential competitor can generate sufficient static and dynamic efficiencies for it not to inflict a net equivalent-dollar loss on Clayton-Act-relevant buyers.

Third, the "defendant-do-nothing" baseline for measuring the competitive impact and hence legality of conduct covered by the Clayton Act can also critically affect the Clayton Act legality of conglomerate mergers that eliminate one or more potential competitors. Thus, this feature of the Clayton Act approach to measuring a business choice's competitive impact implies that an effective-potential-competitor-eliminating conglomerate merger whose substitution for no conglomerate merger at all would not impose a net equivalent-dollar loss on Clayton-Act-relevant buyers by reducing the absolute attractiveness of the best offer they respectively received from any inferior supplier would not violate the Clayton Act even if the prohibition of the proposed or consummated merger in question would have conferred an equivalent-dollar gain on Clayton-Act-relevant buyers by inducing the "acquiring" firm to execute a more procompetitive conglomerate merger with a different potential competitor (a more procompetitive merger that would have yielded more static and dynamic efficiencies but would have deterred an entry that would have been less competitive with the "acquiring" firm's projects than the entry that was/would have been deterred by its consummated/proposed merger) or with a firm that was not one of its potential competitors.

C. The U.S. Courts' and the DOJ/FTC's Position on the Legal Relevance of the Fact That a Conglomerate Merger Eliminates an Effective Potential Competitor and on the Economic-Efficiency Issues and Failing-Company Issues That Have Arisen or Could Arise in Such Potential-Competition Conglomerate-Merger Cases

(1) The U.S. Courts' Positions

U.S. courts seem to have fully accepted the limit-price theorists' central claims that limit pricing will always deter entry, that limit pricing will be more profitable than allowing entry to occur in a broad range of circumstance, and that limit pricing will be the most profitable way for established firms to deter entry. In a series of cases in the 1960s and early 1970s, U.S. courts endorsed limit-price theory, which they denominated "wings theory" (the reference was to firms' waiting just offstage in the theatrical "wings") or "edge" theory (where the misleading reference is to firms' waiting at the edge of a market, misleading because an ARDEPPS' best-place potential competitor may not currently be operating at its edge).[1143] Lower U.S.

[1143] The first case in which the Supreme Court used the expression "potential competition"—United States v. El Paso Natural Gas Co., 376 U.S. 651 (1964)—actually involved a misuse of the expression to cover an actual rival that had already unsuccessfully bid against the acquiring firm. The Supreme Court used the expression correctly in FTC v. Procter & Gamble Co. (Clorox), which involved a merger between (1) a manufacturer of household products including laundry detergent but not bleach that was allegedly the best-placed potential entrant into the bleach market and (2) the leading manufacturer of bleach. The notion of potential competition also played a significant role in United States. v. Falstaff Brewing Co., 410 U.S. 526 (1973)—the geographic-diversification conglomerate-merger case discussed in Sect. 4C. Perhaps most importantly, limit-price theory (in fact, an even more dubious misperceived-potential-competitor variant of limit-price theory) played a critical role in the joint-venture case United States v. Penn-Olin Chemical Co., 378 U.S. 158 (1964). In that case, the Court found a joint venture to violate Section 7 of the Clayton Act (which actually does not apply to joint ventures) on the ground that, if it did not take place, one of the parents would have entered the market the joint venture would have entered (which, apparently, one parent would have done) while the other parent's continuing presence as a potential competitor—indeed, as a potential competitor that the market's established firms would have incorrectly believed would enter if they did nothing to prevent its entry—would have induced the established firms to limit price to keep it out. (The Court implicitly

courts have never given any indication that they are aware of the deficiencies of limit-price "theory"—*i.e.*, continue to appear to subscribe to it. However, post-1973, U.S. courts have been less willing to conclude that particular potential entrants were in fact effective[1144] and have left the impression that they would recognize a potential competitor to be effective only if convincing evidence were introduced establishing that the potential competitor in question intended to act on well-developed independent-entry plans if it could not gain entrance to the target ARDEPPS through merger or acquisition.[1145] I hasten to add, however, that post-1980, the government has sometimes won conglomerate-merger cases in lower courts on the ground that the merger in question would eliminate an effective potential competitor.[1146]

U.S. courts have never addressed the general issue of when potential competition will be effective or when limit pricing will be practiced. Nor have they ever focused on Bain's contentions (1) that potential competition will not be effective when barriers to entry are high[1147] or (2) that limit pricing will be practiced if but only if the best-placed potential competitor faces moderate to substantial barriers to entry. Relatedly, U.S. courts have not recognized that this latter claim—which, as I noted, is inconsistent with Bain's claims about the efficacy and profitability of limit pricing—implies that horizontal mergers that would raise the conventional-profit-maximizing prices of the MPs and their *R*s will not reduce competition on that account if the barriers facing the best-placed potential competitor for the market in question are moderate to substantial since the incumbents in question will practice limit pricing in such situations and (on Bain's account) the merger will not alter the limit price. U.S. courts have also not noticed that limit pricing would almost certainly be illegal if it were ever practiced. As described by the proponents of limit-price theory, limit pricing involves one or more sellers' setting lower-than-conventionally-profitable prices to increase their profits in the long run by reducing the absolute attractiveness of the best offers against which they will have

---

assumed—probably correctly—that, if the joint venture had gone forward, the parents' stake in it would have made it unprofitable for them to enter its market independently even if the joint-venture agreement did not prohibit them from doing so.)

[1144] See, *e.g.*, United States v. Marine Bancorporation, 418 U.S. 602 (1974), where the cause of skepticism was state and federal regulations against branching in the banking industry, and Tenneco, Inc. v. FTC, 689 F.2d 346 (2d Cir. 1982), where the cause of skepticism was high barriers to entry.

[1145] HOVENKAMP at 300.

[1146] See, *e.g.*, Yamaha Motor Co. v. FTC, 657 F.2d 971 (9th Cir. 1981).

[1147] Indeed, even those U.S. courts that recognize the possibility that a potential competitor that would face high barriers to entry for an independent entry might be able to reduce the barriers it faced by executing a toe-hold conglomerate merger do not seem to recognize that the effectiveness of a best-placed potential competitor depends not on the absolute height of the barriers to entry it faces but on the relationship between the height of the barriers to entry it faces and the sum of the barriers to expansion and QV-investment disincentives that would face the ARDEPPS' best-placed potential expander at its entry-barred expansion-preventing QV-investment level. See Tenneco, Inc. v. FTC, 689 F.2d 346 (2d Cir. 1982).

to compete by deterring the entry of a potential competitor. As I indicated in Chap. 11, such pricing would appear to be a textbook example of predatory pricing, which is prohibited by the Sherman Act. Admittedly, one might contest this claim by pointing out that, unlike predatory price-cuts, which the predator can reverse after its target has exited, limit-pricing price-cuts cannot be profitably reversed post-deterrence or, at least, could not be profitably reversed if the effective potential competitor did not increase the (Π_D + R) barriers it faced by allocating to some other project the resources it was originally going to use to enter the market in question. I am not persuaded by this counterargument (1) partially because in practice best-placed potential competitors will tend to allocate to other projects the resources they were planning to devote to entry but (2) primarily for the formalist reason that the asserted fact does not alter the reality that limit pricing satisfies all of the Sherman Act's formal requirements for illegality.

One 1962 Supreme Court potential-competition conglomerate-merger opinion—*Procter & Gamble*[1148]—did address the legal relevance of the "efficiencies" that the merger in question reputedly would generate and concluded that those efficiencies counted against the merger's legality. However, I am confident that contemporary U.S. courts would reach the opposite conclusion about any real efficiencies that a potential-competition-eliminating conglomerate merger would generate. This element of the *P&G* opinion primarily reflected the now-outdated judicial view of the 1960s that the efficiencies that any type of conduct generated would tend to reduce competition by inducing the actor's established competitors to exit (by worsening their array of competitive positions) and by deterring potential entrants to and potential expanders in the actor's market from making a QV investment (by worsening such potential investments' prospective arrays of competitive positions). It also reflected the *P&G* Court's view that some of the "efficiencies" in question would be purely private (would reflect the fact that the merged firm would have more bargaining power than Clorox) and that the other efficiencies the merger would generate would stem from P&G's ability to profit more than Clorox from engaging in misleading advertising (about the superiority of the Clorox product). (I should add that the latter fact would be irrelevant to the economic-efficiency impact of the efficiencies in question if the relevant private gain reflected the fact that the merged company could place the same quantity of advertising at lower private and allocative cost but would be relevant to the associated economic-efficiency gain to the extent that it reflected the fact that the profits in question reflected P&G's finding it profitable to place more such advertisements than Clorox did.)

Finally, to my knowledge, no U.S. court has ever addressed the legal significance of the fact that a potential-competitor-eliminating conglomerate merger involved a failing company. The absence of opinions on this point partly reflects the fact that a failing company cannot be an effective potential competitor of its acquirer, but some

[1148] FTC v. Procter & Gamble Co. (Clorox), 386 U.S. 568 (1967).

cases in this category must involve a conglomerate merger in which the acquiring firm is a potential entrant into a failing company's market. I am confident that U.S. courts will handle the failing-company issue in such cases in the way that *Citizen Publishing Co.* and the 1992 and 2010 U.S. Horizontal Merger Guidelines recommend. My critique of this approach applies *mutatis mutandis* in the current context.

(2) The DOJ's and FTC's Positions

Six points are salient. First, in a substantial number of cases, including those cited in the preceding six footnotes, the DOJ or FTC argued that the fact that a conglomerate merger (or joint venture) would or did eliminate an effective potential competitor rendered it illegal under U.S. antitrust law. Second, in its 1997 review of Bell Atlantic Corporation's proposed acquisition of Nynex Corporation, the government was concerned that Philadelphia-based Bell Atlantic would enter the New York market independently if it were not allowed to merge with Nynex. Third, between 1996 and 2003, the FTC issued second requests in 12 potential-competition conglomerate-merger cases asking for information about the possibility that the mergers in question might reduce competition by eliminating an effective potential competitor. Fourth, the Agencies' arguments in several pre-1992 potential-competition conglomerate-merger cases accepted limit-price theory, and the DOJ's 1984 Conglomerate Merger Guidelines assumed that limit-price theory was correct as a matter of economics. Fifth, as I stated in Chap. 12, both the 1992 and the 2010 Horizontal Merger Guidelines seem to me to reject limit-price theory, and, to my knowledge, the Agencies have not made a limit-price-theory argument since the 1992 Guidelines' publication. Sixth, the 1984 Conglomerate Merger Guidelines make a number of other potential-competition-related assumptions and claims that the DOJ and FTC have never disavowed that are both wrong and undermine the Agencies' positions on a broader range of business conduct:

(1) assume that potential competition will not be able to induce established firms to lower their prices unless the relevant ARDEPPS' seller concentration is conducive to monopolization and collusion—an assumption that ignores the fact that firms that could not be considered to be monopolists can find it profitable to charge supra-competitive prices even if they do not engage in predation or contrivance (because they can possess OCAs and obtain NOMs without engaging in predation);
(2) assume that firms will be able to profit by engaging in predation or contrived oligopolistic pricing only if the ARDEPPS' concentration is high or its leading firm's market share is high;
(3) assume that an individual potential competitor is unlikely to be effective if three or more other firms are better-placed or equally-well-placed to enter or if other firms that are worse-placed to enter will enter unless the evidence that the firm

in question will enter is "particularly strong"—assumptions that respectively ignore (A) the fact that more than three firms can be effective potential competitors (when actual QV investment is more than three QV investments below current or future equilibrium QV investment) and (B) the fact that a firm's willingness to enter if it is not "eliminated" through merger or acquisition does not guarantee that it was effective; and

(4) assume that an individual potential competitor will not be effective if another potential competitor would be willing to replace any QV investment the firm did not make (an assumption that will be wrong if the eliminated potential competitor would have executed its entry sooner than its entry would be replaced by the entry of a fellow potential competitor).

7. The Legality of Conglomerate Mergers Under E.C./E.U. Competition Law, Both as Correctly and as Actually Interpreted and Applied

A. The Legality of Conglomerate Mergers Under E.C./E.U. Competition Law as Correctly Interpreted and Applied

The various provisions of E.C./E.U. competition law that apply to horizontal mergers apply in precisely the same ways to conglomerate mergers. In particular, the EMCR and its Clayton-Act-type lessening-competition test are fully applicable to conglomerate mergers; now-Article 102 and both its Sherman-Act-type exclusionary-abuse test and its unique exploitative-abuse test apply to conglomerate mergers at least one of whose participants is individually or collectively dominant; and now-Article 101 and both its "*object* of preventing, restricting, or distorting competition" test and its "*effect* of preventing, restricting, or distorting competition" test apply to all conglomerate mergers if my interpretation of now-Article 101(1) is correct and to those conglomerate mergers that are requisitely likely to create a merged company that will engage in more contrived oligopolistic or predatory conduct than its participants would otherwise have done if, contrary to my view, it would be legally correct to read the "clause (a)–(e)" list in now-Article 101(1) to be comprehensive.

As I indicated in Chap. 4, although I am certain that—properly interpreted—the Clayton Act would be read to prescribe a do-nothing baseline for competitive-impact measurement, I am not certain whether it would be correct as a matter of the E.C./E.U. competition law to interpret now-Article 101(1) and the EMCR to prescribe the use of that baseline.

B. The Legality of Conglomerate Mergers Under E.C./E.U. Competition Law as Actually Interpreted and Applied

(1) The EC's and the E.C./E.U. Courts' Positions on the Ways in Which Conglomerate Mergers Can Lessen Competition and the Kinds of Procompetitive Economic Efficiencies That Conglomerate Mergers Can Generate

The discussion that follows takes into consideration the way in which, prior to 2008, the EC addressed and resolved cases about mergers and acquisitions it classified as conglomerate (see below), the CFI's and ECJ's review of those EC decisions on appeal, the relevant portions of the 2008 EC Guidelines on the Assessment of Non-Horizontal Mergers Under the Council Regulation on the Control of Concentrations Between Undertakings (hereinafter 2008 EC Non-Horizontal Merger Guidelines)[1149]—which the EC promulgated at least in substantial part to reconcile its position to the courts', and the post-2008 EC conglomerate-merger decisions.

Prior to 2008, the CFI and ECJ both agreed (1) that conglomerate mergers were far less likely than horizontal concentrations to impede effective competition significantly and (2) that mergers they classified as conglomerate could reduce competition in four different ways. I will initially list and then comment on the four ways in which the EC and the E.C./E.U. courts claimed and continue to believe that conglomerate mergers can lessen competition.

First, both the EC and the E.C./E.U. courts assert that mergers they classify as conglomerate because, at the time of the merger's proposed execution, its participants were not both well-placed to obtain the patronage of any individual buyer and were not in a vertical relationship with each other will reduce competition if foreseeable changes in buyer preferences and/or production and distribution marginal costs would cause both to be well-placed to secure the patronage of one or more individual buyers—*i.e.*, if for this reason the merger would reduce competition by eliminating future competition between the participants.[1150] Although I agree with this conclusion, such mergers should be classified as horizontal mergers and would be so classified in the U.S.

Second, both the EC and the E.C./E.U. courts believed prior to 2008 and continue to believe that conglomerate mergers and acquisitions will tend to lessen competition to the extent that the business entity they create will be more able to use

[1149] OJ C 265/07 (2008). The relevant portions are Section II—Overview (points 10–22), Section III—Market Share and Concentration Levels (points 23–27), and Section V—Conglomerate Mergers (points 91–121).

[1150] See, *e.g.*, Tetra Laval/Sidel, M2416, OJ L43/13 (2004) and Commission v. Tetra Laval, C13/03, ECRI-1113 (2005). I am glad to say that no mention of this possibility is made in the 2008 EC Non-Horizontal Merger Guidelines.

tying agreements or engage in additional bundling to foreclose competition.[1151] Somewhat more specifically, both prior to 2008 and now the EC and the E.C./E.U. courts believe that, if the conglomerate merger creates an entity that has "a significant degree of market power, which does not necessarily amount to dominance in one of the markets concerned,"[1152] any additional tie-ins and bundling that the conglomerate merger causes their participants to use may enable the conglomerate both to "gain. . .market power in the tied goods market" and to "protect. . .[its] market power in the tying goods market."[1153] I consider this claim to be almost totally unwarranted for reasons that Chap. 14's critique of the related leverage theory of tie-ins and reciprocity explains.

As I will argue then, the leverage theory is based on the clearly-false premise that a firm that enjoys competitive advantages when selling one product to a particular buyer (regardless of whether it is a dominant firm or the product in question is a "leading brand" or a "must stock item") can somehow increase the profitability of inducing relevant buyers to make concessions to it by accepting disadvantageous terms of sale on other products or by accepting other disadvantageous obligations (say, not to deal with the seller's rivals) by conditioning its sale of the first product to the buyer in question on the buyer's accepting these other unfavorable terms of sale or other obligations—a premise that in essence assumes that the relevant sellers can have their cake and eat it too (can extract these concessions without making concession on the first product, on which they enjoy competitive advantages). As we shall see, tie-ins and bundling can perform many functions for their employers, will often increase economic efficiency, and will not generate the kind of leverage with which this theory is concerned even when the benefits they yield are purely private. Moreover, even if I grant that a few tie-ins (*viz*., a few tie-ins that impose a long-term full-requirements obligation on the other party whose imposition is not inherently profitable) might be exclusionary, the probability that a given tie-in of the relevant type will fall into this category has little to do with the tying seller's market power in or its share of the so-called tying-product market. This conclusion reflects the following facts: (1) the crucial question is whether the tie-ins in question leave "un-locked-up" enough suppliers or distributors to enable others to operate proficiently, (2) even if all suppliers and all distributors were fungible, the answer to this question would depend not on the percentage of them that are locked-up but on the quantity not locked-up relative to the quantity of inputs or distributorship-services the potentially-excluded firm requires, and (3) not all input suppliers or distributors are fungible, so that the actual answer depends on the relative quantities of available, appropriate (best-placed or well-placed) inputs and distributorship-services. Moreover, the preceding discussion implicitly assumed that potentially-excluded competitors would be restricted to purchasing inputs or distributive services from

---

[1151] See, *e.g*., General Electric v. Commission, Case T-210/01, ECR II-000 ¶¶ 327, 362–63, 405 (2005); GE/Amersham, Case COMP/M. 3304, points 35 and 37 (2004); and GE/Smiths Aerospace, Case COMP/M. 4561, points 116–26 (2007), OJ C 133/02 (2007).

[1152] This position was reiterated by the EC in its 2008 Horizontal Merger Guidelines at point 99.

[1153] This position was reiterated by the EC at *id*. at point 108.

extant independents. In reality, even if such a firm were prevented from using suitable extant independents, it might be able to overcome this problem by entering on its own, participating in a joint-venture entry, or inducing an independent entry (by providing information, direct monetary subsidies, and/or long-term full-requirements purchase or supply guarantees to independent entrants). Although the EC and the E.C./E.U. courts recognize the relevance of truly-independent entry and the possibility that a firm that would otherwise be foreclosed might be able to facilitate an entry by an independent firm, they do not devote appropriate attention to the possibilities that a firm that would otherwise be injured by foreclosure could reduce or eliminate the loss in question by entering itself or as a parent of a joint venture. Admittedly, the 2008 EC Non-Horizontal Merger Guidelines do mention other "counterstrategies" such as changing production processes to reduce dependence on a foreclosed input or deciding "to price more aggressively to maintain market share."[1154] However, I suspect that the first of these options will rarely be available and the second will rarely be efficacious. One final law-related point is relevant in this context. If the additional tie-ins and bundling that a conglomerate merger would cause its participants to use not only would have the *effect* of reducing competition but would have reducing competition as their *critical object* (*i.e.*, would be exclusionary), that fact would reduce to the persuasiveness of the tie-ins/bundling arguments against the legality of conglomerate mergers in that the illegality of the feared merger-induced conduct (1) should call into question the assumption that the merger will create a merged firm that will engage in the conduct and (2) raises the possibility that the legally-appropriate response to the risk that a conglomerate merger will lead the resulting company to use additional exclusionary tie-ins is to bring cases against it if it does rather than to prohibit the merger.

So far, I have been critical of this tie-in/bundling leverage-argument against conglomerate mergers. I should admit that the EC's and the E.C./E.U. courts' discussions of this possibility gets some things right. In particular, the EC and the E.C./E.U. courts are correct in arguing that, for the tie-ins to foreclose there must be a "large common pool of customers for the products concerned,"[1155] the products will usually have to be bought simultaneously by the same customers,[1156] and the arrangements must be "lasting."[1157] The EC's and the E.C./E.U. courts' claim that for tie-ins to foreclose they must cover "a sufficiently large fraction of market output" to "significantly impede effective competition,"[1158] *inter alia*, by precluding extant firms or potential competitors from taking advantage of economies of

---

[1154] *Id.* at point 103.

[1155] This position was reiterated by the EC at *id.* at point 100.

[1156] This position was reiterated by the EC at *id.* at point 98, citing GE/Amersham, point 35 Case COMP./M. 3304 (2004).

[1157] This position was reiterated by the EC at EC 2008 Non-Horizontal Merger Guidelines at point 102.

[1158] This position was reiterated by the EC at *id.* at point 113.

scale or network effects[1159] is less persuasive, given the non-fungibility of all input suppliers on the one hand and all resellers on the other.

Third, both prior to and after 2008, the EC and the E.C./E.U. courts claimed that conglomerate mergers and acquisitions can lessen competition by generating what they seem to regard to be two other, "exclusionary" "portfolio effects"—*i.e.*, will enable the resulting company to gain advantages by threatening to withdraw supplies of both participants' products from buyers who want to purchase both participants' products (particularly when at least one of the products in question is a "leading brand") and will enable the resulting company to take advantage of economies of scale and scope whose realization will cause rivals to exit and/or reduce competition by raising barriers to entry.[1160] It might have been appropriate for me to enquote the word "third" with which this paragraph began because the first of these "portfolio effects" fears is really just the negative counterpart of the tie-in/bundling concern—*i.e.*, the concern that a seller can obtain leverage by refusing to supply two or more products to a given buyer is the negative counterpart of the concern that a seller can obtain leverage by requiring buyers to purchase two or more products from it. Chapter 14's critique of the leverage theory of tie-ins applies *mutatis mutandis* to this portfolio concern. I should add that, although neither the EC nor the E.C./E.U. courts have explained why the economies of scale and scope that a conglomerate merger or acquisition can generate can reduce competition by inducing one or more rivals to exit or deterring rival QV investments, such economies can reduce competition both in these ways by worsening an established firm's competitive-position array and by critically raising the barriers to QV investment facing one or more otherwise-effective potential QV investors by worsening their prospective competitive-position arrays. However, not only have the EC and the E.C./E.U. courts failed to delineate the conditions under which either such outcome would eventuate, their assumption that any tendency of a conglomerate merger or acquisition to generate such effects counts against its legality is inconsistent with their general insistence that E.C./E.U. competition law does not prohibit even dominant firms from competing on the merits. (I have not said that this assumption is inconsistent with the EC's and E.C./E.U. courts' assertion that the economic efficiencies a conglomerate merger or acquisition yields favor its legality because that assertion may reflect an implicit premise that the efficiencies in question will benefit relevant buyers.)

Fourth, the EC and the E.C./E.U. courts are also concerned that conglomerate mergers can increase competition-lessening coordination (contrivance in my terms) in the areas of product-space in which their participants operate (1) by reducing the number of effective competitors[1161] (presumably by leading to additional,

---

[1159] This position was reiterated by the EC at *id.* at point 101.

[1160] See, *e.g.*, Commission v. Tetra Laval, C-13/03, ECR I-1113 (2005) and Tetra Laval v. Commission, Case T-502, ECR II-4381, ¶¶ 150–55 (2002). See also General Electric v. Commission, Case T210/01, ECR II-5575, 65–76 (2005).

[1161] 2008 EC Non-Horizontal Merger Guidelines at point 120.

exclusionary tie-ins and bundling, by generating analogous portfolio effects, and by yielding economies of scale and scope)—*i.e.*, the number of rivals a contriver must induce to comply with its wishes, (2) by rendering some rivals whose compliance is required "more vulnerable,"[1162] and (3) by increasing the extent to which contrivance can take place across markets.[1163] The concern that conglomerate mergers will increase contrivance by reducing the number of firms in the relevant areas of product-space piggybacks on the exclusionary-leverage/portfolio-effect claims but would be relevant if those were justified and the legally-appropriate response to the behavior in question were not to attack it when it occurs—in particular, would be relevant on the above assumptions because any such secondary effects that should be considered might critically influence the net equivalent-dollar impact of a merger that generated some economic efficiencies that benefitted relevant consumers. However, if I am right that conglomerate mergers will rarely if ever reduce the number of sellers in a relevant area of product-space, the concern that conglomerate mergers will increase contrivance by reducing the number of relevant competitors is unwarranted. I also disagree with the EC's and E.C./E.U. courts' claim that conglomerate mergers will tend to increase contrivance by making some sellers "more vulnerable" in a way that affects their willingness to oppose contrivance, though I doubt that the EC and the E.C./E.U. courts understand when and why this will occur—*viz.*, that the merger may make the merged firm less willing to undercut its rivals from a position of inferiority than the MPs were both by increasing the merged firm's (OCA + NOM)s by generating static marginal efficiencies and by spreading the merged firm's defenses when it faces conglomerate rivals that operate in both MPs' ARDEPPSes. As the preceding sentence indicates, I also agree with the Guidelines' claim that conglomerate mergers can facilitate cross-market contrivance.

Having listed and discussed the various ways in which the EC and the E.C./E.U. courts believe conglomerate mergers may lessen competition, I should point out various ways in which conglomerate mergers can lessen competition that the EC and the E.C./E.U. courts have ignored and the specific reasons why conglomerate mergers can facilitate cross-market contrivance—*viz.*, by

(1) creating a merged firm that engages in more single-market price contrivance and QV-investment contrivance (generates more L barriers) than its antecedents would have done by increasing the profits it can realize by doing so because the firm the merger creates inherits the reputation for contrivance of the merger participant that has a stronger reputation for contrivance, because the merged firm will tend to have more retained and current earnings to invest in contrivance, because there are company-wide economies of scale in contrivance (in building a reputation for contrivance), and because in some circumstances

[1162] *Id.*

[1163] *Id.* at point 121.

(see below), the conglomerate merger will increase the profitability of contrivance in other ways,

(2) reducing QV-investment competition by creating a firm that is less willing to expand than one or both antecedents were by increasing the (Π_D + R) barriers the resulting firm faces by leading it to devote to consolidation resources that the antecedents would have devoted to executing a QV investment and by increasing the L barriers the resulting firm faces above those the antecedents faced by increasing the resulting firm's average OCAs (by generating static marginal efficiencies), NOMs, and COMs above those of its antecedents and spreading the resulting firm's defenses when the resulting firm faces a conglomerate *R* that was a rival of both antecedents,

(3) reducing price and QV-investment competition by creating a firm that engages in more predation than the participants would have practiced in all the ways that the merger in question could increase the amount of contrivance the merged firm practiced above the combined amount its participants would have, perhaps[1164]

(4) reducing QV-investment competition directly and price competition indirectly by eliminating an effective potential competitor, and

(5) when the merged company faces one or more conglomerate rivals that operate in one or more of the markets in which each merger participant operated, by creating a merged firm that engages in more price and QV-investment contrivance than its antecedents would have done by enabling the merged firm to make one anticompetitive communication when each of its antecedents would have had to make one, by enabling the merged firm to take advantage of any excess reciprocatory power that one of its participants had in its relations with a conglomerate rival in relation to which the other participant did not have sufficient reciprocatory power to secure collaboration on that basis alone, by enabling the merged firm to reduce the loss it had to incur to inflict any given amount of harm on such a conglomerate rival through retaliation by enabling it to execute more retaliation through one of the participant's products and less through the other's than the participants would have found necessary and optimal as separate entities, and relatedly and conceivably (but doubtfully) by making it profitable for the merged firm when it would not have been for the merger participants to retaliate against non-cooperators by inducing buyers/

[1164] I say "perhaps" because the evidence for the claim is weak since (1) it consists solely of the fact that (at least to my knowledge) neither the EC nor any E.C./E.U. court has even considered the possibility that a conglomerate merger that eliminated or would eliminate a potential competitor might reduce competition because the potential competitor in question was effective (would have entered had the market's established firms done nothing to prevent it from doing so) and (2) that "fact" may reflect nothing more than their never having been presented with such a case. The fact that in a series of cases the EC considered the possibility that likely entry from potential competitors might prevent a merger it would otherwise have concluded would decrease competition from doing so is beside the point. See, *e.g.*, Mercedes-Benz/Kässbohrer, Case IV/M. 477, OJ L211/1 (1995); Gubain/Wacker Chemie/NUM, Case IV/M. 744, J L247/1 (1996); Aerospatiale-Alenialde Havilland, Case IV/M. 53, OJ L334/42 (1991); and Boeing-McDonnell-Douglas, Case IV/M. 877, OJL 336/16 (1997).

suppliers of both participants' products to boycott a non-cooperator by threatening the buyers/suppliers with retaliation.

The EC and the E.C./E.U. courts recognize that conglomerate mergers that would tend to impose an equivalent-monetary loss on relevant buyers by lessening competition might not do so if they generate economic efficiencies.[1165] Three economic-efficiency-related points are relevant at this juncture. First, although, as previously indicated, the EC and the E.C./E.U. courts do recognize that the economies of scale and scope that conglomerate mergers and acquisitions generate may lessen competition, they agree that the economic efficiencies that such transactions generate will normally benefit relevant consumers. Second, the EC and the E.C./E.U. courts have no more idea of the factors that determine whether and by how much the economic efficiencies that conglomerate mergers/acquisitions generate will benefit relevant consumers than they (or their U.S. counterparts) have of the counterpart factors for horizontal mergers. Third, although the 2008 EC Guidelines do explain how conglomerate mergers can generate various "economies of scope"[1166] and do allude to the possibility that conglomerate mergers involving producers of complementary products may facilitate the coordination of their pricing to prevent privately-unprofitable and perhaps-presumptively-economically-inefficient substitutions among them,[1167] their discussion of the latter possibility ignores the ability of firms to prevent such substitutions by using tie-ins, reciprocity agreements, and endproduct-royalty schemes (see Chap. 14), and their more general comment about the relationship between the economic efficiencies that can be generated respectively by conglomerate and vertical mergers/acquisitions[1168] does not instill confidence about the EC's understanding of the economic efficiencies that vertical but not conglomerate mergers and acquisitions can generate.

(2) The Probability That the EC Must Establish That a Conglomerate Merger Will Reduce Competition to Be Justified in Declaring It Illegal on That Account and Various Kinds of Evidence That the EC Must Consider When Calculating the Probability in Question: Two Issues on Which the EC and the E.C./E.U. Courts Originally Disagreed

The preceding discussion focused on abstract theoretical issues on which the EC and the E.C./E.U. courts seem largely to have agreed. However, my impression is that, although the EC and the E.C./E.U. courts agreed that "conglomerate mergers

[1165] 2008 EC Non-Horizontal Merger Guidelines at points 13, 92, and 115.

[1166] *Id.* at point 118.

[1167] *Id.* at point 117.

[1168] *Id.* at point 116.

in the majority of circumstances will not lead to any competition problems"[1169] and agreed as well about the ways in which conglomerate mergers and acquisitions can lessen competition and the general conditions under which they pose a risk to competition, the E.C./E.U. courts believed that one factor that could influence the competitive impact of conglomerate mergers was more important than the EC recognized and also believed that stronger evidence of possible reductions in competition must be supplied to warrant the prohibition of a conglomerate merger than the EC thought was necessary.

The factor that the CFI and ECJ found more important than the EC did was the possibility that the competition-reducing conduct in which the EC and the E.C./E.U. courts feared conglomerate mergers might induce the resulting entity to engage would be illegal under E.C./E.U. law or the laws of its member states. In particular, the ECJ has required the EC to devote considerable attention to the possibility that E.C./E.U. and member-nation prohibitions of leveraging and exclusionary conduct may deter the firm created by a conglomerate merger from engaging in such conduct (though, unlike the CFI, the ECJ did not require the EC to execute an exhaustive analysis of the applicable laws and actual enforcement-practices).[1170] On other matters of required proof, the CFI and ECJ have (1) stated that the EC should take account of whether the merged company's management has made statements indicating their intention to engage in relevant leveraging or exclusionary conduct post-merger (which I suspect they will rarely do once such evidence is utilized),[1171] (2) noted that evidence on an MP's use of reciprocity or tie-ins involving one set of products in one time-period has only limited bearing on the probability that the firm would engage in such conduct on other paired products in a different time-period,[1172] (3) called into question the EC's reliance on studies by one or more academic economists of the possible effects of a conglomerate merger it was considering when other economists challenged those studies' conclusions by questioning their empirical premises,[1173] and (4) stated that "where the Commission takes the view that a [conglomerate] merger should be prohibited because it will create or strengthen a dominant position within a foreseeable period, it is incumbent on it to produce convincing evidence thereof."[1174]

The EC is bound by the ECJ's judgments. It is therefore not surprising that both the relevant portions of the 2008 EC Non-Horizontal Merger Guidelines (in particular, point 46, which addresses the relevance for the legality of a conglomerate merger of the fact that the competition-decreasing conduct that the EC would otherwise find conglomerate mergers might generate was illegal under E.C./E.U.

[1169] *Id.* at point 92.

[1170] See Commission v. Tetra Laval, Case C-13/03, ¶ 89 (2005) and Tetra Laval BV v. Commission, Case T-5/03, ECR II-4381 (2002).

[1171] See General Electric v. Commission, Case T210/01, ECR II-5575 (2005).

[1172] *Id.*

[1173] *Id.*

[1174] Tetra Laval v. Commission, Case T-5/02, ¶¶ 150–55, ECR (2002) II-4381 (2002).

or member-country national laws) and the EC's more-recent decisions appear to conform to the ECJ's substantive, "burden of proof," and evidentiary conclusions.[1175]

* * *

The conglomerate-merger analyses of academic economists, antitrust-enforcement agencies, and courts are disappointing. All of these actors have ignored the ways in which conglomerate mergers can reduce competition by increasing contrived oligopolistic pricing, (Π_D + R) barriers, and predation. Many economists and the courts continue to subscribe to a limit-price theory whose premises are unrealistic, whose specific conclusions do not follow from its premises, and that cannot be tested in the way that they have attempted to test it.[1176] The EC and E.C./E.U. courts continue to subscribe to a leverage theory and a theory of exclusion that, as Chap. 14 will show, cannot bear scrutiny. And at least the lower U.S. courts seem to be committed to a "toe-hold merger" doctrine that is incorrect both as a matter of economics and independently as a matter of law. Given the current empirical importance of conglomerate mergers and the fact that they are likely to become even more common if horizontal-merger regulation is tightened, these deficiencies of the applicable economic and legal analyses are likely to have significant social consequences.

[1175] See Peder Christensen, Kyriakos Founotoukakos, and Dan Sjöblom, *Mergers* in THE EC LAW OF COMPETITION 421 at 505 (Jonathan Faull and Ali Nikpay, eds.) (Oxford Univ. Press, 2d ed., 2007), citing GE/Amersham, Case COMP/M. 3304.

[1176] See Sect. 2B of Chap. 10 and Sect. 4 of Chap. 12.

Chapter 14
Vertical Mergers and the Pricing-Techniques, Contract-of-Sale Provisions, and Sales/ Consignment Policies That Are Surrogates for Vertical Integration

Business integration is said to be vertical when the integrators are in a supplier-supplied relationship to each other. Vertical integration can be initiated or carried out by producers, distributors, or buyers. However, for expositional reasons, this chapter will assume that the vertical-integration initiator is a final-goods producer. Such a firm can vertically integrate either backward or forward—backward into the production of inputs and forward into distribution and/or final-good consumption. Firms can execute vertical integration through merger, acquisition, or internal growth. As we shall see, firms can also achieve some of the benefits that vertical integration can generate by using complicated pricing-techniques, contract-of-sale provisions, and sales and consignment policies all of which I call "surrogates for vertical integration."

Vertical mergers (and acquisitions) can perform many of the Sherman-Act-licit functions that horizontal and conglomerate mergers can perform—*e.g.*, can enable one participant to take advantage of the other's tax losses when the other could not do so, can enable one participant to liquidate his or her assets and escape managerial responsibilities, can enable both participants to take advantage of economies of scale in financing, and can enable one (both) participant(s) to take better advantage of its (their) managerial capacity. However, vertical mergers and acquisitions and vertical integration through internal growth can also perform two Sherman-Act-licit functions that horizontal and conglomerate mergers cannot perform: (1) can enable their participants to take advantage of continuous-flow economies and (2) can enable a producer to use hierarchical controls to reduce the losses it sustains because its independent customers' purchasing decisions have spillover effects (*viz.*, affect the amount of seller surplus it obtains by selling its product to them) and because its individual independent distributors' resale-pricing decisions, demand-increasing-expenditure decisions, and complement-choices have spillover effects (deprive it of transaction surplus both directly by reducing the seller surplus it obtains on its sales to the individual independent distributor in question and indirectly by reducing the seller surplus it obtains on its sales to other distributors or final consumers of its product). (The surrogates for vertical integration to which

R.S. Markovits, *Economics and the Interpretation and Application of U.S. and E.U. Antitrust Law*, DOI 10.1007/978-3-642-24313-4_3,

I previously referred function by enabling their employer to reduce or internalize such spillover effects or by prohibiting independent distributors or final consumers from making the choices that would generate them.)

It is important to note that, even when vertical integration would benefit a producer in one or more of the ways just described, a non-integrated producer might not find it profitable to integrate forward into distribution and consumption for one or more of the following four reasons that have nothing to do with any legal prohibitions:

(1) the vertical integration may itself be transaction-costly;
(2) if the vertical integration is to be achieved through internal growth, it may increase QV investment in the area of product-space in which the integrating investment is located;
(3) spillover effects aside, the vertically-integrated concern may not be as proficient at performing the relevant production, distribution, and/or consumption tasks as independent actors would be; and
(4) the hierarchical controls that the vertically-integrated concern would have to use to induce its employees and managers to make the decisions that would maximize the organization's profits may be transaction-costly and less-than-perfectly effective.

It is also important to note that, even when the various surrogates for vertical integration I have listed would benefit their employer in the manner described (or would do so if they succeeded in altering the relevant distributors' or final consumers' behavior), they might be rendered unprofitable (law-related costs aside) by the transaction cost of devising and implementing them and by the losses the relevant distributors and consumers impose on their employer by violating the obligations the associated contractual provisions impose on them or by failing to accept the recommendations the associated sales or consignment policies convey to them.

Chapter 14 has five sections. Section 1 describes the spillover effects that the choices of a product's independent final consumers and individual distributors can generate. Section 2 delineates the economic functions and examines the probable competitive impact of the various practices I call "surrogates for vertical integration" and comments on some contrary positions on these issues taken by economists. Section 3 analyzes the legality of these surrogates for vertical integration under U.S. and E.C./E.U. antitrust law, properly interpreted and applied, and discusses the U.S. and E.C./E.U. case-law and antitrust-enforcement-agency positions on these practices. Section 4 delineates the Sherman-Act-licit and Sherman-Act-illicit economic functions of vertical mergers and acquisitions, examines the probable competitive impact of such transactions, and comments on some contrary positions on these issues taken by some economists. Section 5 analyzes the legality of vertical mergers and acquisitions under U.S. and E.U. antitrust law, properly interpreted and applied, and discusses the U.S. and E.C./E.U. case-law and the U.S. and E.C./E.U. antitrust-enforcement-agency positions on the legality of such transactions.

1. The Spillover Effects That Perfectly-Coordinated Vertical Integration Will Prevent and That Surrogates for Vertical Integration Are Designed to Combat

This section is executed from the perspective of a final-product producer and focuses on the spillover effects that can be generated by four types of decisions that the distributors and final consumers of the final-product producer's product make. The first such set of spillover-effect-generating decisions are the purchasing decisions of the producer's customers (be they final consumers or distributors). Non-integrated final-good producers will make lower profits than a fully-vertically-integrated firm would make if the integration generated none of the four "costs" that I previously indicated vertical integration can generate because the non-integrated producer's independent buyers will not take account of the seller surplus their decision not to purchase units of the producer's product prevents the producer from obtaining—*i.e.*, of the negative spillover generated by their decision not to purchase additional units of the good in question. For this reason, if the producer charges a buyer a per-unit price for its product that exceeds the producer's marginal cost at its transaction-surplus-maximizing output (the output at which the demand curve it faces cuts its marginal cost curve from above), the buyer will not purchase some units of the good in question that the fully-vertically-integrated firm would find profitable to supply to its own distribution or consumption "division." When the producer faces a downward-sloping demand curve, conventional "profit-maximizing" pricing—the setting of the most-profitable per-unit price the producer could charge—fails to prevent this spillover effect and hence yields profits that fall below those the perfectly-coordinated, fully-and-costlessly-vertically-integrated firm would realize not only by the buyer surplus such pricing enables the buyer in question to realize but also by the transaction surplus such pricing destroys by causing the buyer to purchase fewer units of the good in question than the fully-vertically-integrated producer would find profitable to supply to itself. (I hasten to add that—if the analysis were focused on the non-integrated buyer—the sub-optimal outcome would be attributed to the positive spillover that would be generated by any decision of the producer to lower its per-unit price from the conventional profit-maximizing level toward or to its transaction-surplus-maximizing level.)

The second set of spillover-effect-generating decisions that is relevant at this juncture contains the resale-pricing decisions of a non-integrated producer's independent distributors. I will begin this discussion by pointing out that, for the profits of an integrated producer-distributor to be maximized, two conditions must be satisfied: (1) each final consumer it is best-placed to supply must pay the highest price for the organization's product that that buyer would be willing to pay, and (2) each such buyer must purchase that product from the distributive outlet that is best-placed to supply it (*ceteris paribus*, the outlet for which distributor-delivery or buyer-pick-up costs are lowest). If the per-unit price an independent producer charges its independent distributors for its product is lower than the price that equals the highest price a relevant buyer would be willing to pay for the product *minus* the non-cost-of-goods-sold marginal costs that the distributors would have to incur to supply the buyer in question, the individual independent distributors may find it profitable to offer the relevant buyer prices that are lower than the highest price that buyer would be willing to pay for the product in question despite the fact that, by engaging in such intra-brand competition, they will reduce the sum of the profits the producer and all its independent distributors realize both by reducing the difference between the total revenue the sale of the product generates and the variable cost of producing the goods sold and by increasing total distribution costs (by increasing bidding costs and other sorts of distribution costs when the successful distributor is not the lowest-cost distributor for the buyer in question). Individual independent distributors will often find it profitable to behave in this way despite the fact that such intra-brand competition reduces the profits of the producer and all its distributors combined because such individual-independent-distributor conduct generates negative spillovers both for the other independent distributor that was best-placed to supply the buyer in question and for the producer (given that, the lump-sum [franchise] fees the producer's independent distributors will be willing to pay the producer for the right to purchase its product at a given price will be reduced by such intra-brand competition). I should add that this problem is salient because, for various reasons that will be discussed below, most producers would otherwise find it most profitable to charge their independent distributors sufficiently-low per-unit prices for their product to create this problem (and to remove the buyer surplus such an arrangement would yield the distributors by charging them a lump-sum fee for the right to purchase the producer's product at the low per-unit price in question).

Spillover effects can also deter independent distributors from making another type of pricing decision that would be in the joint interest of the producer and all the producer's distributors combined—*viz.*, decisions to charge promotional prices (which are lower than the prices that would maximize the seller's current profits) to increase future sales. To the extent that the future sales such promotional pricing would generate would be made by another distributor of the good in question, the non-internalization of this positive spillover may critically reduce the profitability of such pricing to individual independent distributors.

This discussion of promotional pricing provides a segueway to the analysis of the third type of decision that the non-internalization of spillover effects can critically affect—decisions by independent distributors to make demand-increasing expenditures on or resource allocations to out-of-store advertising, in-store shelf-space or other sorts of displays, in-store sales-efforts (including the giving of pre-sales advice), door-to-door salesmanship, and in-store post-sales warrantee services. To the extent that the demand-increasing expenditures or resource allocations that an individual independent distributor makes generate positive spillovers by increasing the profits that other distributors of the product in question make by increasing their sales and/or by increasing the profits that the producer makes because it profits from the additional sales the expenditures yield both the distributor that made them and other distributers of the product in question (because its per-unit prices to these distributors exceed its marginal costs and/or because any increase in the operating profits its independent distributors make increase the lump-sum fees it can collect from them in the future), the non-internalization of these positive spillovers may deter the individual independent distributors from making demand-increasing expenditures and resource allocations that would be profitable for a fully-integrated firm. In the other direction, to the extent that such demand-increasing expenditures or resource allocations generate negative spillovers by reducing the sales of other distributors of the product in question, the non-internalization of these spillovers may render it profitable for individual independent distributors to make expenditures or resource allocations of those kinds that a perfectly-coordinated fully-vertically-integrated firm would not make—that would reduce the profits of the "organization" taken as a whole (that would disserve the producer's interests).

The fourth and final type of decision that spillover effects may make profitable for a buyer despite the fact that the decision reduces the sum of the buyer's and producer's profits relates to the complements that the buyer combines with the producer's product—for example, with the producer's durable machine or franchise idea. Buyers of durable products or restaurant franchises may find it profitable to use or sell lower-quality complements than is in their and the producer's joint interest because the tendency of their doing so to reduce the sales the producer makes through other distributors or franchisees to other buyers or in the future to the buyer that is using the inferior complement is a spillover effect (which is not internalized to the relevant complement-chooser).

I will illustrate this possibility first when the basic good is a durable machine and then when it is a restaurant franchise. Assume that one or more final consumers of a durable machine want to combine it with lower-quality complements (believe [correctly or incorrectly] that the associated cost-savings are greater than the cost to them of the machine's performing less well than it would with higher-quality complements). If these buyers' use of lower-quality complements reduce the demand for the producer's machine because others who observe its performance when the inferior complement is used attribute its poor performance to the machine rather than to the buyers' complement-choice, because the buyers who use the inferior complements tell others of the machine's poor performance and do not attribute that reality to their complement-choice, or because the buyers who use the inferior complements do not themselves appreciate the fact that its poor performance is attributable to their complement-choice and therefore do not buy the machine again, the buyers' complement-choice will produce a negative spillover whose non-internalization may make a complement-choice that is in the buyer's actual or perceived interest against the producer's interest. An analogous spillover may generate a profit-loss for the producer when the immediate buyer of the producer's product is an independent distributor of the producer's machine and that distributor's use or sale of inferior complements costs the producer profits (1) by reducing the demand curve faced by other independent distributors of its product or by in-house distributors of its product and/or (2) by reducing the sales of the inferior-complement-supplying-or-using distributor in circumstances in which the product producer would have made profits by supplying the distributor in question with the extra units of the product the distributor would otherwise have bought and resold.

I turn now to the restaurant-franchise example. In this case, the basic good is the franchise idea and the complements are foodstuffs, physical environment, cleaning services, and waitperson services. Assume that (1) the "complement-choosing" franchisee has both repeat local customers who prefer to pay lower prices for lower-quality complements and non-repeat transient customers who prefer to pay higher prices for higher-quality complements, (2) it is impracticable for a distributor to offer different-quality complements (ketchup, salad bars, cleanliness, physical environment, waitperson services) to different buyers, (3) the transients cannot evaluate the quality of the complements a given franchisee will supply without incurring a significant cost to visit its outlet (so that the transient's restaurant choice will be guided by the chain's reputation or the transient's experience with individual franchises), and (4) the complement-quality choice that is most profitable for the individual distributor in question is lower than the complement-quality choice that would maximize the organization's profits because the relevant individual distributor's choice of low-quality complements would yield negative spillovers by reducing the purchases transients make at other outlets. In this case as well, the non-internalization of the relevant spillover will induce the local independent distributor to make complement-choices that reduce the sum of its, the other franchisees', and the franchisor's profits.

2. The Functions of the Various Surrogates for Vertical Integration

A. Single-Product Pricing-Techniques

(1) Single-Product Non-Discriminatory Single Pricing

In practice, firms that are not vertically integrated forward into consumption will not place a $1 value on each dollar of buyer surplus its customers obtain by engaging in transactions with it. Indeed, such firms' legal obligations to their shareholders require them to ignore the buyer-surplus consequences of their decisions (except to the extent that such buyer surplus creates goodwill from which the firms in question can subsequently profit). These realities account for the fact that, if a non-integrated firm is constrained to engage in single-product single pricing (to sell each of its products separately and to set a uniform ["single"] per-unit price for each product it sells), the single per-unit price it will choose to charge (the conventional profit-maximizing price of all elementary-economics textbooks) will be higher than the transaction-surplus-maximizing (hereinafter TSM) price—*i.e.*, will equal the height of the demand curve it faces for the product in question at the output at which its single-pricing marginal revenue curve cuts its marginal cost curve from above rather than the height of the relevant demand curve at the higher output at which that demand curve cuts its marginal cost curve from above.

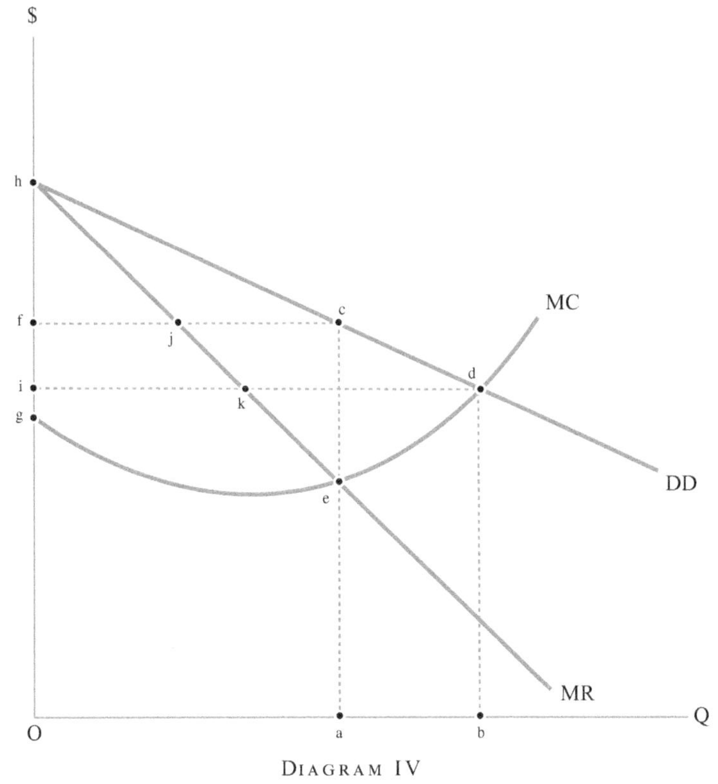

Diagram IV Diagram to Illustrate the Advantages and Disadvantages of Various Pricing-Techniques

Diagram IV illustrates this reality. In Diagram IV, the demand curve (DD) is assumed to be linear solely to facilitate the construction of the single-pricing marginal revenue curve (MR)—the marginal revenue curve the firm would face if it charged no lump-sum fee and secured additional sales simply by reducing its per-unit price. In particular, DD is constructed to be linear in Diagram IV solely because, when DD is linear, the single-pricing MR will bisect the horizontal line between the vertical axis and the DD curve at every height. Thus, in Diagram IV, fj = jc and ik = kd. In Diagram IV, MC represents the marginal cost curve facing the seller in question. In Diagram IV, the TSM price is db—the price that equals the height of the DD curve at the output (Ob) at which the DD curve cuts the MC curve from above (at point d). In Diagram IV, the single-pricing profit-maximizing price is ca—the price that equals the height of the DD curve at the output (Oa) at which the single-pricing marginal revenue curve cuts the MC curve from above (at point e). Diagram IV can also be used to illustrate the fact that the spillover effects that the non-integrated firm's pricing generates will lower the profits it realizes by single-pricing its products (area fceg in Diagram IV) below the profits that a completely-integrated firm would realize by producing and consuming the product in question (area hdeg in Diagram IV). In particular, the profits the non-integrated firm will realize by single-pricing its product will fall below the profits the integrated firm would realize by producing and consuming the product in question by the sum of the buyer surplus the single-pricing would allow to escape (area hcf in Diagram IV) and the amount of transaction surplus the seller's supra-marginal-cost pricing would destroy (area cde in Diagram IV) by reducing its sales from the TSM quantity Ob to the smaller quantity Oa.

(2) Single-Product Discriminatory Per-Unit Pricing—Conventional Price Discrimination

In many situations, incompletely-integrated sellers will be able to increase the profits they realize (reduce the "cost" to them of their being incompletely integrated) by engaging in conventional per-unit-pricing price discrimination—*i.e.*, by charging different buyers different per-unit prices. The simplest variant of such discrimination involves the seller's establishing two per-unit prices—*i.e.*, separating its potential customers into two groups and charging one of these groups' members a different per-unit price from the per-unit price it is charging the members of the other group. However, sellers can also engage in more-refined versions of conventional price discrimination in which three or more groups of buyers are distinguished and each group is charged a different price. Indeed, at the extreme, a conventional price discriminator could charge each of its customers a different per-unit price (though, by definition, the price charged each such buyer would not vary from unit to unit). For conventional price discrimination to yield its practitioner additional profits, two conditions must be fulfilled:

(1) the profit-maximizing per-unit price for two or more of its customers must be different, and
(2) the costs it must incur to practice some variant of conventional price discrimination must not exceed the profits that variant would otherwise yield it by increasing the profits it makes both from those buyers that it charges a price that exceeds its non-discriminatory, profit-maximizing single-pricing per-unit price and from those buyers that it charges a price that is lower than that non-discriminatory price.

The relevant costs include the consumer-research cost it will have to incur to identify the subgroups of buyers to which it can profitably charge different per-unit prices and to identify the separate conventional profit-maximizing price for each such subgroup of buyers, the additional mechanical costs it will have to incur to charge different buyers different prices as opposed to setting a uniform price and allowing all buyers to make purchases at that price, the cost it will have to incur to prevent arbitrage—*i.e.*, to prevent buyers to which it is charging a lower price from reselling the product to buyers from which it is trying to obtain a higher price (which will depend, *inter alia*, on the ability of the firm to alter its product so as to render the variant it sells to some buyers at a lower price unsuitable for use by the buyers to which it is trying to sell another variant at a higher price, the ability of buyers that have been charged the lower price to identify higher-valuing buyers, the ability of buyers that are being charged the higher price to identify buyers that have been charged a lower price, the perishability of the product, the cost of transporting the product [its bulkiness, weight, and fragility and the proximity of the possible arbitrage participants], the losses it will suffer when such arbitrage takes place, the costs it will incur in bilateral-monopoly situations if the lower price puts the lie to the cost-claims it made or would otherwise make to buyers from which it is trying to extract a higher price, the costs it will incur if its discrimination against some buyers reduces the goodwill it enjoys in its relations with them, and the law-related costs of practicing conventional price discrimination in a jurisdiction in which such pricing is or is thought to be at least sometimes illegal).

(3) Perfect Price Discrimination (Which May or May Not Discriminate Between or Among Buyers)

Regardless of whether it is practicing inter-buyer price discrimination, a firm that is not integrated forward into consumption may also be able to realize more profits than single-product per-unit pricing would yield it by engaging in "perfect price discrimination"—*i.e.*, by making each of its individual customers pay the presumably-different prices each could break even by paying for the successive units of the firm's product the buyer in question purchases. Diagram IV can be used to illustrate the three superficially-different but ultimately-coincident forms in which perfect price discrimination can be practiced. In its first variant, perfect price discrimination involves no lump-sum fee and a per-unit price for each successive unit that equals the buyer's usually-varying demand price for the units in question. If, for this purpose, I interpret the DD curve in Diagram IV to be the demand curve of an individual buyer and assume for simplicity that the seller's substitution of perfect price discrimination for single pricing will not alter the dollar value that the relevant buyer places on any relevant unit of the seller's product (in essence, by changing the buyer's real wealth), the seller who used this variant of perfect price discrimination would charge the buyer in question hO for the first unit it bought and progressively-lower prices equal to the varying heights of the DD curve for the second through Obth unit it bought, including a price of ca for the Oath unit it bought and a price of db for the Obth unit it bought. In its second variant, perfect price discrimination involves no per-unit price but a lump-sum fee—in particular, the seller that uses this variant of perfect price discrimination offers the buyer the right to purchase the output of the product in question that is transaction-surplus-maximizing for it to purchase for a lump-sum fee equal to the total value of the output in question to the buyer. In Diagram IV, this offer would be an offer to sell Ob units of the product in question for a lump-sum fee equal to area hdbO. In its third variant, perfect price discrimination involves both a per-unit price and a lump-sum fee—in particular, the seller that uses this variant of perfect price discrimination offers to sell the buyer the right to purchase any quantity of the product in question up to the quantity that is transaction-surplus-maximizing for the buyer to purchase for a per-unit price equal to the relevant TSM marginal cost for a lump-sum fee equal to the buyer surplus the buyer would otherwise realize on the deal in question. In Diagram IV, this offer would be to sell to the buyer for a lump-sum fee equal to area hdi the right to purchase as much of the product in question as it wanted up to Ob units for a per-unit price of db. If perfect price discrimination could be practiced without generating any mechanical transaction or other costs, it would not just increase its incompletely-integrated practitioner's profits but totally eliminate the difference between those profits and the profits that would be realized by an equally-proficient firm that was completely integrated forward into consumption.

The preceding analysis assumed that the relevant seller would have to incur no transaction costs to implement any of the three forms of perfect price discrimination just delineated. This assumption is obviously unrealistic:

(1) to practice any of the variants of perfect price discrimination, a seller must incur the cost of calculating the TSM output and the value the buyer places on each successive unit of that output or on the whole TSM output;
(2) to practice any of the variants of perfect price discrimination, the seller must incur the transaction cost of negotiating, drafting, and signing the associated contract (which, for transaction-cost reasons, will cover a substantial period of time);
(3) to practice the first variant of perfect price discrimination, the seller will have to incur the extra cost of calculating not only the value to the buyer of each unit of the good it is transaction-surplus-increasing for the buyer to purchase but also the cost of determining the number of units of the product in question the relevant buyer has already purchased during the contract period (which is a determinant of the value the buyer places on the next unit of the product in question) when setting the price the buyer must pay for an additional unit of the relevant product (which will include the cost of the associated checkout-counter delays); and
(4) to practice any of the variants of perfect price discrimination, the seller will also have to incur the cost of preventing or allowing buyer arbitrage (cross-selling), including *inter alia* the cost of determining whether the buyer has purchased more than its TSM volume of the good in question (with the intention of cross-selling it to the seller's other potential customers) (since under perfect price discrimination the higher of any per-unit price the buyer must pay for a unit and any opportunity cost it must incur to not use a unit it purchased in its own business will be lower than the sum of the per-unit price and average lump-sum fee the relevant seller is offering its other potential customers).

The preceding analysis also assumed that, to practice perfect price discrimination, a seller will have to incur no direct or indirect risk costs and no seller-error or buyer-error costs. These assumptions are unrealistic as well.

I will start by explaining why and when perfect price discrimination may increase the risk-related costs its practitioners will bear. I have used the expression "risk-related costs" rather than "risk costs" because, if the buyer takes some account of the risk costs the transaction imposes on it, the seller will be somewhat concerned about the risk costs its transaction with the buyer imposes on the buyer because those risk costs will reduce the lump-sum fee the buyer will be willing to pay the seller for any quantity of the seller's product or for the right to purchase at a specified per-unit price (or for the varying per-unit prices in a specified per-unit-price schedule) a specified quantity, as many units as it wants, or as many units as it wants up to some specified maximum number of units of the seller's product. More specifically, if, as I will be assuming, the buyer is a sovereign maximizer in relation to its risk costs, the seller will be equally concerned with the risk costs its pricing imposes on the buyer as with the risk costs its pricing causes it to bear directly because the lump-sum fee that the buyer will be willing to pay the seller for any quantity of the seller's product or for the right to purchase for a specified per-unit price (or for the varying prices in a specified per-unit-price schedule) a specified quantity, as many units as it wants, or as many units as it wants up to some specified maximum number of units of the seller's product will decrease by $1 for each dollar in risk costs any such arrangement imposes on the buyer, and a shift from conventional day-by-day single pricing to a longer-term perfect-price-discrimination arrangement will be risk-costly to the seller to the extent that it increases the sum of the risk costs that the buyer and seller respectively directly bear. To see how the shift from single pricing to perfect price discrimination will affect this sum, I will first analyze the way in which it will shift risk between the buyer and the seller and then analyze the determinants of the impact of the risk-shift in question on the sum of the buyer's and seller's risk costs.

The sellers and buyers involved in perfect price discrimination face transaction-generated risk costs because (1) for reasons related to the transaction cost of negotiating, drafting, and signing perfect-price-discrimination contracts, it will be profitable for the seller to write such contracts to cover the purchases the buyer makes over a significant period of time and (2) the seller and buyer are uncertain about the buyer's demand curve for the relevant product for that time-period (and perhaps about the relevant MC curve as well). The DD curve in Diagram IV is really a weighted-average-expected demand curve rather than (as I have so far been assuming) an actual demand curve.

The effect that a shift from conventional single per-unit pricing to perfect price discrimination will have on the demand-related risk borne by the buyer and seller respectively (and relatedly on the sum of the buyer's and seller's transaction-generated risk costs) will be substantially affected by the variant of perfect price discrimination the contract implements. If the perfect-price-discrimination contract simply sets out a schedule of the per-unit prices the buyer will have to pay for successive units of the relevant product over the time-period it covers but does not obligate the buyer to purchase the weighted-average-expected TSM quantity or any other quantity of the product for prices indicated in the schedule, the shift from single pricing to this contract will not significantly affect the risk borne by the seller and buyer: if the buyer's demand for the product turns out to be lower than expected, the seller will still be worse off under the perfect-price-discrimination contract in question than the seller expected to be on the weighted average, and the buyer will not suffer any transaction-related loss (unless the buyer had some bargaining power that enabled it to strike a bargain that was expected to give it some surplus, its actual demand did not allow it to obtain as much surplus by buying the seller's product at the agreed-upon price schedule, and for some reason renegotiation was not practicable). However, if the perfect-price-discrimination contract (1) sets out a schedule of per-unit prices and does obligate the buyer to purchase its weighted-average-expected TSM quantity or some other minimum quantity of the product in question for the specified prices (the least likely possibility), (2) requires the buyer to pay a lump-sum fee for its weighted-average-expected TSM purchase-quantity of the good in question equal to the weighted-average-expected value of the units in question to it *minus* the risk costs it would have to bear under this arrangement *minus* any buyer surplus its bargaining power enabled it to obtain, or, most likely, (3) requires the buyer to pay a lump-sum fee for the right to purchase up to its weighted-average-expected TSM purchase-quantity of the good in question for a per-unit price equal to the producer's weighted-average-expected marginal cost for the last unit in question—in particular, requires the buyer to pay a lump-sum fee equal to the difference between the weighted-average-expected value of those units to the buyer *minus* the total per-unit payments it would have to make for its weighted-average-executed unit purchases *minus* the risk costs it would have to bear under this arrangement *minus* any buyer surplus its bargaining power enabled it to secure, all the risk created by the parties' imperfect information about the buyer's demand for the product in question will be borne by the buyer (at least if I assume that the lump-sum fee will be paid and that the buyer will make any contractually-required per-unit payments in a timely fashion)—*i.e.*, the shift from day-to-day conventional single pricing to longer-term perfect price discrimination will shift both the beneficial risk that the buyer's demand will turn out to be higher than expected on the weighted average and the harmful risk that the buyer's demand will turn out be lower than expected or the weighted average from the seller to the buyer. Put crudely, this reality reflects the fact that under each of these three variants of perfect price discrimination a large part of the buyer's payments to the seller do not vary with the value the buyer turns out to place on successive units of the seller's product.

I suspect that for two reasons this shift in risk will normally increase the sum of the risk costs generated by the seller's selling its good to the buyer: (1) in most cases, the seller will tend to be larger than the buyer—to have larger capital reserves that enable it to withstand worse-than-expected outcomes—and (2) in those cases in which the buyers are distributors of the seller's final good or final-good producers that use the intermediate product or raw material the seller produces, perfect-price-discrimination contracts of these sorts will increase the risk to the buyers by more than they reduce the risk to the seller because the buyers must be concerned not only with variations in final-consumer demand for the seller's product (when the seller is a final-good producer and the buyers are distributors) or with variations in final-consumer demand for the final good it produces (when the seller is a producer of an intermediate product or raw material and the buyers are final-goods producers) but also with their share of the sales of the seller's final product or of the type of product the buyer produces whereas the seller need not be concerned in this context with the *relative* sales of its own distributors or of the final-goods producers to which it sells its intermediate products or raw materials.

Sellers may also have to incur buyer-error-related (buyer-pessimism-generated) and seller-error-generated (seller-pessimism-generated) costs to practice perfect price discrimination. I will address each of these possibilities in turn. If the perfect-price-discrimination contract covers purchases the buyer will make over a substantial period of time and, at the time of contracting, the buyer underestimates the dollar value it will place on the units it will buy under the contract at the time that it will purchase those units, the seller will suffer a loss on this account if it practices perfect price discrimination since this pricing-technique makes the payments the seller can induce the buyer to render depend on the value the buyer predicts at the time of contract it will place on the units it will purchase under that contract at the later time at which it actually purchases those units. (Of course, if at the time at which the buyer enters into the perfect-price-discrimination contract the buyer overestimates the value it will place on the units it will purchase under that contract at the later date on which it will make those purchases, perfect price discrimination will tend to be more profitable than single pricing on that account.) Similarly, if at the time of perfect-price-discrimination-contract formation the seller underestimates the dollar value the buyer places on successive units of the seller's product at that time and will place on those units at the time of purchase, the shift from single pricing to perfect price discrimination will cost that seller money on this account because this seller error will cause the seller to charge the buyer lower per-unit prices and/or lump-sum fees than the buyer would have been willing to pay both at the time of the formation of the perfect-price-discrimination contract and at the later date on which the buyer will purchase units of the seller's product, and the fact that the perfect-price-discrimination contract covers a substantial period of time will preclude the seller from taking advantage of any better information it obtains in the interim. Although the associated loss may be particularly high when the contract allows the buyer to purchase as many units as it wishes at a specified per-unit price and the seller's estimate of its weighted-average-expected TSM sales to the buyer is too low, the possibility that the seller might be making this type of error can also make perfect price discrimination less profitable for the seller when the error relates to the value the buyer places on its TSM purchases rather than on the number of units it is TSM for the buyer to purchase.

I want to consider one additional type of cost a seller may have to incur to practice perfect price discrimination. I am considering this category of cost last because its existence is contestable. If the perfect-price-discrimination arrangement deprives a distributor of any profits it would otherwise make on the sales it obtains because it has advertised the producer's product and/or devoted useful shelf-space or other sorts of display-space to it, the producer's perfect price discrimination will impose losses on it equal to the profits it would otherwise have obtained because the distributor would otherwise have made the advertising, shelf-space, and other-sort-of-display-space decisions that were in its and the producer's joint interest. The existence or at least the non-*de-minimis* magnitude of this type of cost is questionable for two reasons: (1) the producer could avoid this loss by arranging its lump-sum-fee and/or per-unit-price schedule to make all such jointly-profitable distributor decisions infinitesimally profitable for the distributor and (2) as Subsect. 2B will explain, producers will also be able to avoid these losses in other ways. For these reasons, I will ignore this type of cost of perfect price discrimination in the rest of my discussion of the profitability of such pricing, though I do think it will be transaction-costly for a producer to avoid them.

In short, the choice by a seller to substitute perfect price discrimination for pure per-unit pricing in its dealings with an individual buyer will increase the seller's profits whenever the sum of the buyer surplus that that choice would prevent from escaping if the relevant buyer did not have the buying power it would need to have to be able to retain some such surplus and the transaction surplus it would keep from being destroyed (if perfect price discrimination could be practiced perfectly accurately at no cost) exceeds the sum of the "costs" the seller would have to incur to engage in the relevant perfect price discrimination.

(4) A Mixed Pricing-Technique That Combines a Lump-Sum Fee with a Supra-TSM-Marginal-Cost Per-Unit Price

In some circumstances an incompletely-integrated firm that is restricted to pricing its individual products separately will find it most profitable to combine (1) a positive lump-sum fee that is lower than the lump-sum fee it would charge in the variant of perfect price discrimination in which the buyer is charged a lump-sum fee for the right to purchase any quantity it wants of the product in question up to its TSM quantity for that buyer at a price equal to the product's TSM marginal cost and (2) a supra-marginal-cost per-unit price—*i.e.*, to substitute for pure supra-marginal-cost (single) per-unit pricing not perfect price discrimination (which could be denominated "pure-lump-sum pricing") but a pricing-technique that mixes some amount of supra-marginal-cost per-unit pricing with some amount of lump-sum pricing. I will first describe the costs and benefits for a seller of substituting this mixed technique for pure-lump-sum pricing (perfect price discrimination) and then discuss in more detail the determinants of the magnitude of the costs.

The shift from pure-lump-sum pricing to a mixed technique in which a lower lump-sum fee is combined with a supra-marginal-cost per-unit price will generate two types of "costs." The first such "cost" is the transaction surplus the supra-marginal-cost per-unit pricing the mixed technique entails will destroy: every dollar of transactions surplus that is destroyed reduces by $1 the maximum amount of profits the incompletely-integrated firm can earn by selling the product in question below the amount of profits that the ideally-and-completely-integrated firm would realize by producing and consuming it.

The second type of "cost" that a shift from pure-lump-sum-pricing to a mixed technique that includes a supra-marginal-cost per-unit price will generate relates to the demand-increasing expenditures or resource allocations that the seller's customers can make both in relation to the seller's product when they are its distributors and in relation to their own product when the seller produces an intermediate product or raw material and the "buyer" is a final-good producer. In both these situations, the seller's supra-marginal-cost per-unit price may destroy transaction surplus and reduce the seller's own profits by rendering it unprofitable for the seller's customer to make demand-increasing expenditures that would be in the customer's and the seller's joint interest by creating a situation in which some of the benefits the customer's expenditures would generated for the customer and seller combined by increasing the customer's sales would go to the seller. Although these costs are important, as we shall see, sellers can take steps to reduce the losses they incur on this account.

The benefits of substituting the mixed technique for pure-lump-sum pricing all relate to the risk-cost cost, buyer-pessimism-generated cost, seller-pessimism-generated cost, and arbitrage-related cost of pure-lump-sum pricing. I will start with the risk costs that the relevant seller and buyers bear because they are not perfectly informed about the individual buyers' demand curves for the seller's product. As we saw, the shift from pure supra-marginal-cost per-unit pricing to perfect price discrimination will—by shifting risk from the seller to the buyer—increase the sum of the risk costs that the seller and buyer bear because they do not have perfect information about the buyer's demand for the product whenever the buyer is more risk-averse than the seller and whenever the shift increases the sum of the individual buyer's risks more than it decreases the seller's (in that, unlike the seller, who must be concerned only with the overall sales of its final product or the overall sales of the products its intermediate product is used to produce, each of the seller's individual customers must be concerned not only with these overall-sales figures but also with its individual share of the relevant final product's sales). Since the shift from perfect price discrimination (pure-lump-sum pricing) to the mixed technique will shift risk back from the buyers (whose total payments it makes more dependent on their actual demands) to the seller, it will reduce these costs whenever the shift from pure supra-marginal-cost per-unit pricing to pure-lump-sum pricing would increase them.

The shift from pure-lump-sum pricing to a mixed technique that involves a lower lump-sum fee and a higher per-unit price will also reduce the amount of "costs" the seller's departure from pure supra-marginal-cost per-unit pricing causes it to bear because, at the time at which it would have to enter into the perfect-price-discrimination contract, the buyer would underestimate its demand for the seller's product. If the perfect-price-discrimination contract entitles the buyer to purchase as many units of the seller's product as it wants to purchase at a stipulated per-unit price or as many units up to a specified maximum number at that per-unit price, to the extent that the buyer's pessimism is manifest in its underestimating the quantity of the seller's good it will want to purchase at the contract price during the period of time the contract covers, the buyer's error will result in its underestimating the amount the contract's supra-marginal-cost per-unit price will cost it at the same time that it underestimates the value to it of the right to purchase the seller's product at that price during the period covered by the contract. The buyer will therefore agree to a supra-marginal-cost per-unit price that will cost it more (and benefit the seller more) than the highest lump-sum fee it would be willing to pay.

The shift from pure-lump-sum pricing to a mixed technique that combines a lower lump-sum fee with a per-unit price that is higher than the product's TSM marginal cost will also tend to reduce the losses the producer will sustain when it underestimates the quantity of its product the relevant buyer will purchase at various relevant prices, at least if the variant of perfect price discrimination the seller would practice would involve its charging a lump-sum fee to the buyer for the right to purchase as much as it wants of the producer's product at that product's seller-estimated TSM marginal cost or as much as it wants up to some specified maximum that exceeds the quantity the seller believes the buyer will purchase. The shift from pure-lump-sum pricing to the mixed pricing scheme will provide the seller with some protection against its underestimating the buyer's quantity demand for the seller's product because it will enable the seller to make some profits on the purchases the buyer makes that the seller did not anticipate whereas it would make no such profits on these extra sales under a pure-lump-sum pricing arrangement in which the per-unit price equaled the seller's marginal cost if the marginal cost was horizontal over the relevant range.

The shift from pure-lump-sum pricing to the mixed technique on which I am currently focusing will also tend to reduce the costs the relevant seller must incur to prevent or allow arbitrage. Because the price the buyer will have to pay for its marginal and various relevant intra-marginal units of the seller's product will be higher if the seller substitutes the mixed technique with its supra-marginal-cost per-unit price for pure-lump-sum pricing, in which the seller agrees to supply the buyer with up to the relevant TSM quantity of the seller's product at a per-unit price equal to its TSM marginal cost, the shift from pure-lump-sum pricing to the mixed technique will raise the cost to the buyer of the marginal units and some of the intra-marginal units the buyer would purchase under pure-lump-sum pricing above the value those units would yield the buyer if it used them in its own business (which would be the arbitrage-relevant consideration if the maximum number of units the contract entitled the buyer to purchase does not exceed the number of units the buyer would find profitable to purchase if it could not engage in arbitrage) and, in so doing, will reduce the buyer's incentive to engage in arbitrage and hence the cost the seller will have to incur to prevent or allow arbitrage.

Obviously, the preceding paragraphs imply that a seller will find it profitable to shift from pure-lump-sum pricing to the mixed pricing-technique now under consideration whenever the amount of transaction surplus that will be destroyed by the combination of a reduction in the lump-sum fee and a perfectly-offsetting (from the buyer's perspective) increase in the per-unit price is smaller than the amount by which the shift reduces the sum of the demand-ignorance-related risk costs, buyer-pessimism-related and seller-pessimism-related costs, and buyer-arbitrage-related costs the seller must incur. Equally obviously, there will be some situations in which it will be profitable for an incompletely-vertically-integrated seller to shift from pure supra-marginal-cost per-unit (single) pricing to the mixed pricing-technique when it would not be profitable for it to shift from pure supra-marginal-cost per-unit pricing to pure-lump-sum pricing (to perfect price discrimination).

I now want to discuss the factors that determine the amount of transaction surplus a seller will have to destroy—the (TS–)—to execute a shift from pure-lump-sum pricing to a variant of the mixed pricing-technique that removes a given amount of buyer surplus through supra-TSM-marginal-cost per-unit pricing—for a price-increase that yields a given (BS–)—and reduces the lump-sum fee by an amount that leaves the buyer unaffected on balance. For convenience, I will assume at the outset (usually counterfactually) that the relevant sellers and buyers are perfectly informed about the relevant demand and marginal-cost curves so that the shift from perfect price discrimination to the mixed technique will not affect the risk costs they bear or the losses or gains the relevant sellers or buyers experience because of their own or their transaction-partner's non-sovereignty. This assumption, which will eventually be relaxed, implies that the compensating reduction in the seller's lump-sum fee will equal the amount of buyer surplus its supra-TSM-marginal-cost per-unit pricing removes from the buyers. I should point out at the outset that the factors that influence this (TS–)/(BS–) ratio for any (BS–) will also influence the (SS+)/(BS–) ratio for any such price-increase that eliminates a given amount of buyer surplus—that yields a given (BS–)—where (SS+) stands for the associated increase in seller surplus. This conclusion reflects the fact that (SS+) = (BS–)–(TS–). On the above assumption, three factors will determine the (TS–)/(BS–) and (SS+)/(BS–) ratios for any per-unit-price-increase above TSM marginal cost: the (average) absolute slope of the relevant demand curve over the relevant range of output, the TSM output, and the (average) slope of the MC curve over the relevant range. Diagram IIA–C are designed to illustrate respectively the relevance of each of these factors.

Diagram VA illustrates the relevance of the average absolute slope of the buyer's demand curve for the seller's product. For this purpose, Diagram VA has been constructed to contain three demand curves with different slopes: DD_3 (a kinky oligopoly demand curve) whose absolute slope is infinite (which is vertical) over the relevant range; DD_2, whose absolute slope is lower; and DD_1, whose absolute slope is lowest. DD_2 and DD_1 are constructed to be linear solely to ease the exposition. To enable Diagram VA to reveal the relevance of the absolute slope of the demand curve, it is also constructed on the assumption that the TSM output will be the same (AF) in each of the three demand-curve situations and that the slope of the MC curve over the relevant range will be the same in the three demand-curve situations. To secure the latter control, Diagram VA assumes that the same horizontal MC curve will be present in the three demand-curve situations depicted. To secure the former control, Diagram VA is constructed so that each pair of DD and MC curves intersect at the same output (AF) at the same point (F). Diagram VA reveals that, *ceteris paribus*, the amount of transaction surplus that a seller will have to destroy to remove

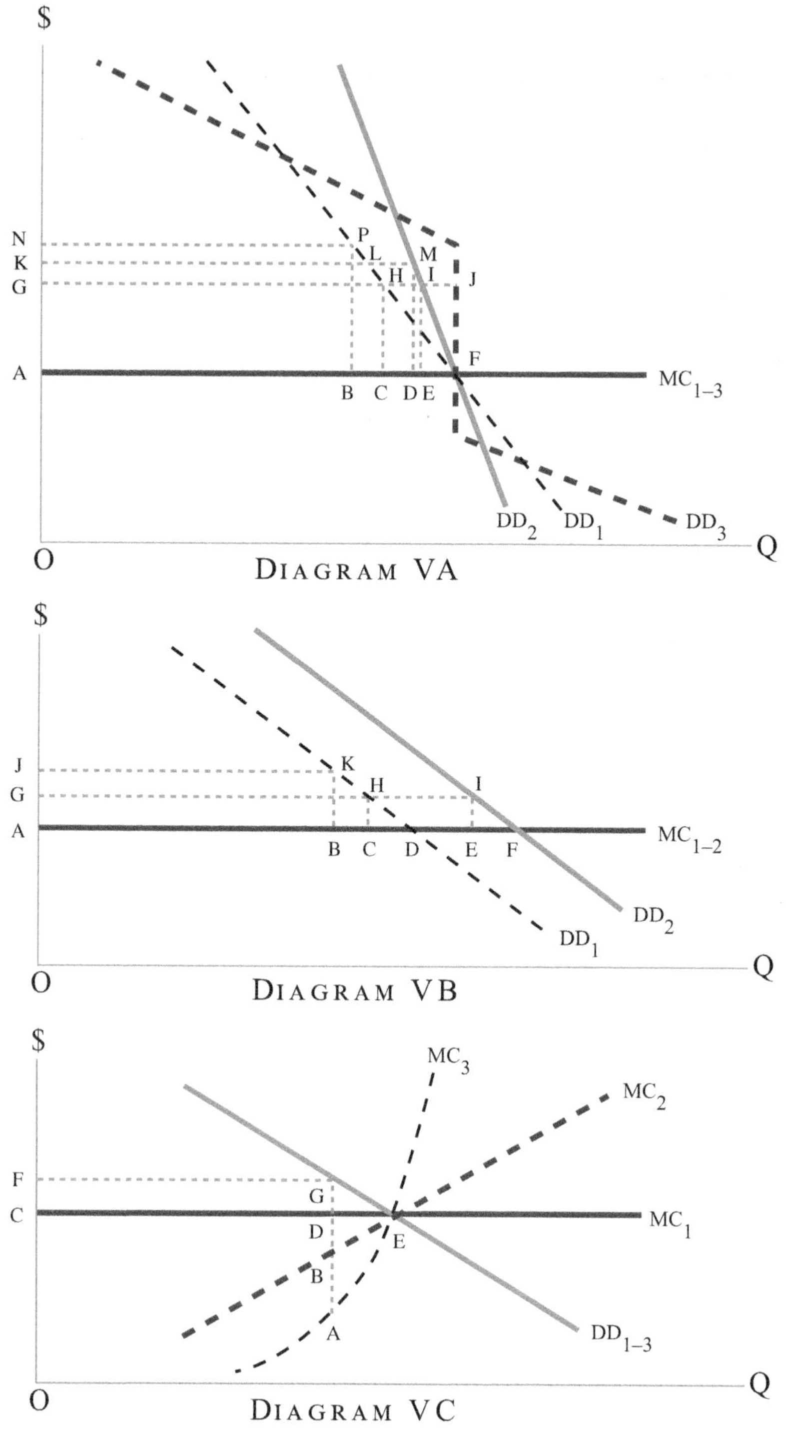

Diagram V The Determinants of (SS+/BS–) for Any Given (BS–) Generated by the Supra-TSM–MC Pricing of a Specified Product

a given amount of buyer surplus through supra-TSM-marginal-cost pricing is inversely related to the slope of the DD curve over the relevant range of outputs. To facilitate the relevant analysis, Diagram VA is constructed so that the amount of buyers surplus (BS) that the seller that faces DD_3 and MC_3 will remove by raising its price JF above its TSM marginal cost (AO)—area GJFA—equals both the amount of buyer surplus that the seller that faces DD_2 and MC_2 will remove by raising its price MD > JF above its TSM marginal cost (AO)—area KMFA—and the amount of buyer surplus that the seller that faces DD_1 and MC_1 will remove by raising its price PB > MD > JF above its TSM marginal cost (AO)—area NPFA. However, the relevant seller's specified price-increases will not destroy the same amounts of transaction surplus (TS) or, concomitantly, yield it the same amounts of seller surplus (SS) (if one ignores the associated reduction in their lump-sum fees). Specifically, the JF price-increase of the seller that faces DD_1 and MC_1 will destroy no transaction surplus (since the relevant DD curve is vertical over the relevant rage—since the absolute slope of its DD curve over the relevant range is infinite) and will yield it SS equal to area GJFA (which equals the BS it will remove from the relevant buyers); the MD price-increase of the seller that faces DD_2 and MC_2 will destroy TS equal to area MFD and will therefore yield the seller in question a gain in seller surplus (SS+)—area KMDA—that is smaller than both the (SS+) the first seller obtained by executing an equivalent (from the buyers' perspectives) price-increase and the (BS–) for the buyers in question—area KMFA, which falls below that amount by the associated (TS–), area MFD; and the PB price-increase of the seller that faces DD_1 and MC_1 will destroy TS equal to area PFB > area MFD and will therefore yield the seller in question an (SS+)—area NPBA—that is smaller than the (SS+)s for both the DD_2/MC_2 seller and the DD_1/MC_1 seller and the (BS–) for the customers of the DD_3/MC_3 seller. Thus, Diagram VA illustrates two concomitant relationships: controlling for the slope of the relevant MC curves over the relevant ranges and the TSM outputs of the relevant products, (1) the (TS–)/(BS–) ratio for a per-unit-price-increase above TSM marginal cost that yields a given (BS–) will be inversely related to the absolute value of the slope of the relevant demand curve over the relevant range, and (2) the (SS+)/(BS–) ratio for such a per-unit-price-increase will be directly related to that absolute value. These relationships reflect two facts: (1) *ceteris paribus*, the size of the price-increase a seller must make to eliminate a given amount of buyer surplus will be inversely related to the slope of the relevant buyer's demand curve for its product, and (2) *ceteris paribus*, the amount of TS that a given price-increase above TSM marginal cost will destroy will be inversely related to the slope of the relevant demand curve.

Diagram VB illustrates the relevance of the TSM output of the product in question. For this purpose, Diagram VB has been constructed to represent two situations in which the TSM output of the product in question is different. In the situation in which the seller in question faces DD_1 and MC_1, the TSM output is AD, and in the situation in which the seller in question faces DD_2 and MC_2, the TSM output is AF > AD (where in each situation the TSM output is determined by the intersection of the DD and MC curves that define it). Diagram VB is also constructed to control for the two other determinants of the (TS–)/(BS–) and

(SS+/BS–) ratios for any given (BS–) caused by a per-unit-price-increase above TSM marginal cost: the absolute slope of the relevant DD curve over the relevant range and the slope of the relevant MC curve over the relevant range. Thus, the fact that the DD_1 and DD_2 are constructed to be both linear and parallel in Diagram VB assures that the slopes of these demand curves are the same over the relevant ranges, and the fact that MC_1 and MC_2 are constructed to be linear and identical in Diagram VB assures that the slopes of these marginal cost curves are the same over the relevant range: MC_1 and MC_2 are constructed to be horizontal purely for visual and expositional reasons. Diagram VB is also constructed so that the amount of buyer surplus that will be removed by a per-unit-price-increase of GA above TSM marginal cost AO (*i.e.*, from AO to GO) if the relevant seller faces DD_2 and MC_2 (*i.e.*, by a price-increase from AO to GO)—area GIFA—equals the amount of buyer surplus that will be removed by a per-unit-price-increase of JA above TSM marginal cost AO if the relevant seller faces DD_1 and MC_1—area JKDA. Diagram VB reveals that, controlling for the slopes of the relevant demand curves and the slopes of the relevant marginal cost curves, (1) the amount of transaction surplus a seller will have to destroy to remove a given amount of buyer surplus by raising the relevant per-unit price above TSM marginal cost will be inversely related to the relevant product's TSM output and hence (2) the amount of seller surplus a seller can obtain by doing so will be positively related to the relevant product's TSM output. Thus, in Diagram VB, the (TS–) for the GA price-increase above TSM marginal cost AO that will yield a (BS–) of area GIFA when the seller faces DD_2 and the relevant TSM output is AF—area IFE—is smaller than the (TS–) of area KDB for the JA price-increase above the TSM marginal cost of AO that will yield the same (BS–) of area GKDA = area GIFA. Concomitantly, Diagram VB reveals that the (SS+) for the GA price-increase above the TSM marginal cost by the seller that faces DD_2—area GIEA—will exceed the (SS+) for the JA price-increase above TSM marginal cost by the seller that faces DD_1—area JKBA; indeed area GIEA will exceed area JKBA by (area KDB–area IFE)—*i.e.*, by the difference between the (BS–)s for the two price-increase by the two sellers in question. Thus, Diagram VB illustrates the fact that, *ceteris paribus*, the (TS–) for a price-increase above TSM marginal cost that yields a given (BS–) will be inversely related to the relevant product's TSM output and that, *ceteris paribus*, the (SS+) for a price-increase above TSM marginal cost that yields a given (BS–) will be directly related to the relevant product's TSM output. These relationships reflect the fact that, controlling for the slopes of both the relevant DD curves and the relevant MC curves over the relevant range, the price-increase that will have to be made above the TSM marginal cost to remove a given amount of buyer surplus will be inversely related to the product's TSM output.

Diagram VC illustrates the relevance of the slope of the MC curve over the relevant range of outputs (between outputs CE and CD). For this purpose, Diagram VC is constructed to contain three MC curves that have different slopes over the relevant range of outputs: MC_1 has a zero slope to the left of the TSM output with which it is associated (CE); MC_2 has a positive slope over the relevant output-range that is lower than the slope of MC_3 over the relevant output-range; and MC_3 has a higher (average) positive slope than does MC_2 over the relevant range of outputs. To enable it to serve its purpose, Diagram VC is also constructed to control for the two other determinants of the (TS–)/(BS–) and (SS+/BS–) ratios on which I am focusing—the slope of the relevant demand curves and the TSM outputs of the product(s) in question. Thus, in all three situations depicted in Diagram VC, the slopes of the relevant portions of the relevant DD curves are the same: this result is achieved by assuming that all three DD curves are not only identical but linear. Similarly, in all three situations depicted in Diagram VC, the TSM outputs are the same (CE): this result is achieved by constructing the three MC curves so that the DD curve (which is the same in all three situations depicted) cuts each from above at the same output (at output CE and point E). Because the demand curve and the TSM output are the same in all three situations depicted by Diagram VC, the price-increase above TSM marginal cost that will remove any given amount of buyer surplus will be the same in the three situations in question. Thus, in all three situations depicted in Diagram VC, a price-increase of FC above TSM marginal cost CO will remove buyer surplus equal to area FGEC. However, the amount of transaction surplus destroyed by that price-increase will not be the same in the three situations. When the slope of the relevant MC curve is zero (as it is for MC_1), the (TS–) will be area GED; when the slope is the lower positive slope of MC_2, the (TS–) will be the larger amount represented by area GEB—*i.e.*, will include not only the area GED in buyer surplus that would be generated by the production and consumption of the DE units of the relevant product whose production and consumption the FC price-increase prevents but also the seller surplus (area DEB) that would have been generated by the sale of the units in question; and when the slope of the relevant MC curve is the higher slope of MC_3, the (TS–) will be the still larger area GEA, which will include not only the area GED in buyer surplus the prevented transactions would have generated but the area DEA in seller surplus those transactions would have generated. Thus, Diagram VC illustrates the fact that, controlling for inter-situational differences in the slopes of the relevant demand curves over the relevant range of outputs and inter-situational differences in the associated TSM outputs, the amount of transaction surplus that a seller will have to destroy to remove a given amount of buyer surplus by raising its per-unit price above its TSM marginal cost will increase with the positive slope of the relevant MC curve over the relevant range of outputs. Concomitantly, Diagram VC illustrates the fact that, *ceteris paribus*, for any per-unit-price-increase-generated (BS–), the (SS+/BS–) ratio will be inversely related to the positive slope of the relevant MC curve over the relevant output-range: that the (SS+/BS–) ratio when the slope of the relevant MC curve is zero as is the slope of curve MC_1—(area FGDC)/(area FGEC)—is higher than the (SS+/BS–) ratio when the slope of the relevant MC curve is positive but relatively low as is the slope of MC_2—([area FGDC–area DEB]/area FGEC)—which is in turn higher than the (SS+/BS–) ratio when the slope of the relevant MC curve is positive and relatively high as is the slope of MC_3—([area FGDC–area DEA]/area FGEC). Both this last relationship and the (TS–) relationship that underlies it reflect the fact that, *ceteris paribus*, the steeper the relevant MC curve, the higher the amount of transaction surplus that will be destroyed by a price-increase above TSM marginal cost that produces a given reduction in output and a given (BS–).

To analyze the (non-strategic) pricing-technique that will be most profitable for a seller that is constrained to price its individual products separately, it is necessary to extend the preceding analysis in an important way and then to take account of the following additional possible effects of a shift from pure-lump-sum pricing to the mixed strategy on which we are currently focusing: its possible impact on the sum of buyer and seller risk cost, its impact on the loss the seller incurs because of buyer or seller pessimism, its impact on the costs the seller must incur to prevent or allow arbitrage, its impact on the losses the producer incurs because its pricing induces a distributor to make advertising, shelf-space, and other-sorts-of-display-space decisions that are not in the distributor's and producer's joint interests, and its impact on the research and contracting costs the relevant seller has to incur to determine the terms that are privately optimal and to explain and negotiate out this more complicated arrangement with the relevant buyer.

I start with the extension of the preceding analysis that must be worked out to determine the (TS–)-related cost a seller will have to incur to obtain the various additional risk-cost-related, buyer-and-seller-pessimism-related, and arbitrage-related benefits that successive *marginal* increases in its per-unit price progressively further above the seller's TSM marginal cost will confer on it. For expositional reasons, the preceding analysis focused on the determinants of the (TS–)-related cost to a seller of increasing its per-unit price *incrementally*, not marginally, above its TSM marginal cost—in particular, sufficiently above its TSM marginal cost to remove a specified, substantial amount of buyer surplus. Clearly, if the relevant research and contracting costs could be ignored, the profit-maximizing seller would focus not on the cost and benefits of one or more discrete, lumpy (*i.e.*, incremental) price-increases but on the costs and benefits of successive, infinitesimally-small price-increases—*i.e.*, would maximize its profits by continuing to increase its price by infinitesimally-small amounts until the (TS–)-related cost of the last marginal price-increase to the seller (which will tend to rise from marginal price-increase to marginal price-increase) just equals the risk-cost/seller-and-buyer-pessimism/arbitrage-related increases in seller surplus the last price-increase confers on it (which, I suspect, will tend to fall from marginal price-increase to marginal price-increase).

If I let (Δ[TS–])/(Δ[BS–]) stand for the ratio of the change in (TS–) to the change in (BS–) that will be generated by a last, marginal (Δ) per-unit-price-increase, that ratio will be (1) inversely related to the absolute slope of the demand curve between the pre-last, marginal-per-unit-price-increase price and the post-last-per-unit-price-increase price, (2) inversely related to the output of the product in question at the pre-last, marginal-per-unit-price-increase price, (3) directly related to the positive slope of the relevant MC curve between the pre-last, marginal-per-unit-price-increase price and the post-last, marginal-per-unit-price-increase price, and (4) directly related to the gap between the pre-last, marginal-per-unit-price-increase price and the pre-last, marginal-per-unit-price-increase marginal cost. If I take into account the transaction-surplus losses that increases in the seller's per-unit price above its TSM marginal cost will generate by deterring its distributors from making demand-increasing expenditures and resource allocations that would be in their and the seller's joint interest as well as the transaction surplus that such increases in the seller's per-unit price will destroy directly by causing relevant buyers to purchase fewer units of its product than would be transaction-surplus-maximizing, given its and its distributors' demand-increasing-expenditure/resource-allocation choices, the relevant (Δ[TS–])/(Δ[BS+]) ratio for successive marginal per-unit-price-increases will reflect the demand-increasing-expenditure (Δ[TS–])/(Δ[BS+]) ratio as well (which in practice will depend, *inter alia*, on the seller's ability to reduce the latter losses profitably by adopting policies I will discuss below).

Once the seller has calculated the (Δ[TS–])/(Δ[BS–]) ratio for successive, marginal per-unit-price-increases—which would be symbolized in calculus as the (d[TS–])/(d[BS–]) figure since assuming the price-changes in question are infinitesimally small (where the "d"s indicate that one is taking a derivative), it must compare these costs with the (risk-cost/buyer-and-seller-pessimism/arbitrage/distributor-advertising-and-shelf-space-related [ΔSS+]/[ΔBS–]) figures for the successive per-unit-price-increases it could make to identify the per-unit-price-increase above TSM marginal cost that would be profit-maximizing if the associated research and contract-negotiation costs could be ignored. As we saw, each per-unit-price-increase will benefit the seller (1) if it is less risk-averse than the buyer and faces less risk on the transaction than does its individual buyers (because the combination of the per-unit-price-increase and the lump-sum-fee decrease will shift risk from the buyer to the seller), (2) if *ex ante* the seller and/or the buyer might underestimate the value to the buyer of the right to purchase the product in question at the seller's TSM marginal cost and the higher per-unit price that the mixed technique would charge because it and/or the buyer underestimate the quantity of the good the buyer will purchase at those prices (because the combination of the per-unit-price-increase and the lump-sum-fee decrease will reduce the seller's dependence on both its and its customer's estimating accurately their quantity demand for its product at the relevant price), and (3) to the extent that the buyer could profit by reselling to other potential customers of the seller some of the units the buyer purchased from the seller (because the per-unit-price-increase to the buyer would increase either the opportunity cost to the buyer in question of reselling one or more of the units it purchased from the seller—the value the buyer would place on the marginal and successive intra-marginal units of the product in question it purchased from the seller if its option under the contract were to purchase at the stated per-unit price no more than the number of units it would purchase for its own use at that price by reducing the number of units it will purchase and hence increasing the value to it of using those last units in its own business or the out-of-pocket cost to the buyer in question of purchasing units for resale if its option under the contract were to purchase as many units as it wanted at the stated per-unit price and in so doing would tend to render unprofitable arbitrage that would otherwise have been profitable).

Of course, in practice, sellers will often have to incur additional research and contracting costs to shift from pure-lump-sum pricing to the mixed pricing-technique now under consideration. Although any seller who has decided to shift from a pricing-technique that involves no lump-sum fee will have to incur additional research costs to calculate the lump-sum fee and various mechanical transaction costs, to draft a written contract (as opposed to selling goods without such a contract at a per-unit price off the shelf), and to explain to the buyer and negotiate out the pure-lump-sum-pricing arrangement, the shift from pure-lump-sum pricing to the mixed pricing-technique will require additional research costs to be incurred even if the seller does not strive to find the combination of lump-sum fee and supra-TSM-marginal-cost per-unit price that would be most profitable, transaction costs aside, and will probably require the seller to incur additional costs to draft and negotiate out the more-refined contract as well. Particularly if, contrary to the assumption I have been implicitly making, the relevant buyer has sufficient buyer power to be able to secure for itself some of the joint gains the mixed pricing-technique would yield once the seller had incurred the fixed cost of doing the associated research, the seller may find the mixed strategy less profitable than pure-lump-sum pricing on these research-cost and contracting-cost accounts. However, I suspect that in a great many situations sellers that are contemplating engaging in inter-business transactions (say, with distributors) will find some more-or-less-refined version of the mixed pricing-technique I have just described most profitable *ex ante* even if they are constrained to sell each of their products separately. And, as we shall see below when discussing the various possible functions of tying and reciprocal-trading agreements, when sellers are not so constrained, they may find it profitable to use a mixed pricing-technique that covers either the terms on which relevant buyers can purchase two or more goods or the terms on which a relevant customer can purchase one good and the seller in question can purchase another good from that customer when such a pricing-technique would not be profitable if the seller had to sell each of its products separately. Of course, as we shall see as well, in many situations in which tie-ins and reciprocity will not *critically* increase the profitability of the mixed pricing-technique, they will increase the profitability of the technique when it would have been profitable if used in relation to the sale of just one good.

B. Producer Subsidies for Distributor Decisions to Make Demand-Increasing Expenditures or Resource Allocations, Contractual Provisions That Obligate Distributors to Make a Specified Quantity of Specified Demand-Increasing Expenditures, and Sales and Consignment Policies That Communicate to Independent Distributors That Their Franchises Will Not Be Renewed If They Do Not Make a Specified Quantity of Such Specified Expenditures

(1) Increasing the Profits a Seller Can Earn by Charging a Supra-TSM-Marginal-Cost Per-Unit Price by Preventing Such Pricing from Imposing a Loss on the Seller by Deterring the Reseller from Making Demand-Increasing Expenditures That Would Be in the Reseller's and Producer's Joint Interest

Assume that the producer would otherwise find it most profitable to charge its distributors a supra-marginal-cost per-unit price for its product. As we saw, in this situation, the producer's supra-marginal-cost per-unit pricing will tend to destroy transaction surplus by deterring the producer's independent distributors from making demand-increasing expenditures that would be in their and its joint interest by causing some of the profits those expenditures yield it and the distributor combined to go to the producer—*i.e.*, by creating a situation in which distributor choices to make such expenditures generate a positive spillover. In many such situations, the producer will not be able to eliminate the loss it sustains because its supra-marginal-cost pricing deflates its distributor's incentives to make demand-increasing expenditures by making those expenditures itself (and raising its franchise fees to internalize the additional surplus its expenditures would otherwise enable its distributors to obtain) because often the local distributor will be in possession of impacted information about the effectiveness of various sales-pitches to its customers, about the effectiveness of different sorts of out-of-store ads, and about the cost and effectiveness for it of different advertising venues. In some such situations, the producer will be able to reduce the loss it sustains because its supra-marginal-cost per-unit pricing would otherwise deter its independent distributors from making demand-increasing expenditures and resource allocations that would be in its and their joint interest by agreeing to pay the percentage of the cost of such expenditures that equals the percentage that the profits they will yield the producer constitutes of the profits they will yield the distributor and the producer combined. In essence, such a subsidy would internalize to the distributor the positive spillover effect of its decision to make a demand-increasing expenditure. However, in other cases, the prospect of distributor fraud may make this response unprofitable—*i.e.*, such a policy may seem too likely to be undermined by the distributor's exaggerating its relevant expenditures and perhaps concealing its fraud by getting newspapers, radio stations, and TV stations to increase the prices they charge them for the ads the producer is subsidizing and decrease the prices they are charging them for other ads. When this is the case, the producer may still be able to reduce the associated losses (1) by contractually obligating the distributor or consignee to place a specified amount of ads, to give it a specified quantity and quality of shelf-space, to provide it with a specified quantity and quality of other sorts of in-store displays, and to provide buyers with a specified quantity and quality of pre-sale advice and post-sales service and/or (2) by communicating to its independent distributors or consignees either verbally or through its conduct its intention to cancel the franchises/contracts of distributors/consignees that do not follow its demand-increasing-expenditure recommendation.

(2) Predation/Contrivance

Although it is inconvenient to have to admit this possibility, a producer may choose to subsidize reseller/consignee demand-increasing expenditures when the producer would not have found some or all of the subsidy in question profitable *ex ante* but for its belief that the induced demand-increasing expenditure would reduce the absolute attractiveness of the offers against which the producer would have to compete by driving an extant rival out or eliciting more cooperation with its future contrivance efforts by penalizing an extant rival that did not cooperate with the producer's past efforts at contrivance by reducing the actual demand curve such rivals face or deterring a rival expansion or entry by reducing the prospective demand curve the rival in question faces/would face. I hasten to add that I believe that few if any demand-increasing-expenditure subsidies are predatory or illegally retaliatory, in part because such subsidies will rarely if ever be the most profitable method of predation or retaliation available to producers that can profit from and are willing to engage in predation or contrivance.

C. Tie-Ins and Reciprocity Agreements

Although a firm can enter into a tying agreement because of the position it occupies or the conditions it faces either as a seller or as a buyer, I will for convenience adopt the conventional assumption that tie-ins are initiated by a firm because of its positions as a seller. On this assumption, a tie-in is either (1) an agreement between a seller and buyer in which the seller agrees to supply the buyer and the buyer agrees to purchase from the seller a specified product (the so-called "tying product") on specified terms on condition that the seller supply the buyer and the buyer purchase from the seller a specified quantity or the buyer's full requirements of a second specified product (the so-called "tied product") on specified terms or (2) an agreement in which the seller agrees to sell a buyer and the buyer agrees to purchase from the seller specified quantities of two or more products for a total (package) price. Similarly, although a firm can enter into a reciprocity agreement because of the position it occupies or the conditions it faces either as a seller or as a buyer, I will for convenience adopt the conventional assumption that reciprocity is initiated by a firm because of its position as a buyer. On this assumption, a reciprocity agreement is either (1) an agreement between two firms in which one firm agrees to purchase from the other a specified quantity, the second firm's total output, or the first firm's full requirements of a specified good on specified terms on condition that the second firm agree to purchase from the first firm a specified quantity, the second firm's full requirements, or the first firm's total output of a second product on specified terms or (2) an agreement in which two firms agree to exchange specified quantities of two or more goods for a monetary transfer payment from one to the other (or perhaps on a pure barter basis).

This subsection analyzes the various functions that (1) tie-ins and (2) reciprocal-trading agreements can perform. As we shall see, several of these functions could be characterized as increasing the profitability of one or more of the pricing-techniques Subsect. 2A investigated. However, with one exception, the initial explanation of these functions will not characterize them in this way, though the relevant connections will always be made at the end of the discussion of each of the functions in question.

(1) Tie-Ins

The discussions that follow will assume that all tie-ins are arranged between a seller X and a buyer Y and that the agreements in question tie the sale of product A to the sale of product B.

(A) Increasing the Cost-Effectiveness of a Seller's Complement-Quality Control

As I indicated in Sect. 1 of this chapter, left to themselves, some of a seller X's customers Y may choose to combine the seller's product A with complements B whose use reduces the seller's profits. A Y may make such a choice either because (1) the B that is most profitable for Y to combine with A is not the B whose use by Y will maximize X's profits or (2) because the Y has made a mistake from its own perspective—has chosen to use a complement when doing so reduces its own profits as well as X's. As we also saw, this problem can arise both when A is a durable material product and when A is a franchise idea. Obviously, in both these types of situations, X will benefit if it can prevent Y from combining A with jointly-unprofitable Bs and will find it profitable to do so if it can achieve this result at non-prohibitive cost. In some circumstances, the most profitable way for X to control the quality of the complements B that Y combines with X's product A will be to impose or enforce a contractual obligation on Y to use complements B of suitable quality. However, in many situations, this straightforward approach may not be practicable: it may be expensive to determine and/or articulate the relevant complement-attributes and costly or impossible to enforce the relevant obligation—*e.g.*, to assess the quality of the B Y is using by inspecting its inventory or examining its final product. For these reasons, X may find it profitable to use a tie-in to control the complements B that buyers of its product A use with it—*i.e.*, to contractually obligate buyers of A to purchase from X or someone else X designates either their full requirements of B or the amount of B they will use together with the quantity of A they purchase. When (1) X can infer the amount of B Y will use together with A from Y's purchases of A and either (2)(A) it would be prohibitively expensive for Y to take delivery of suitable B from X or a supplier that X designates and resell that B and substitute lower-quality, lower-price complements for it or (B) it would be cheap for X to alter the B it supplies Y or arrange for the designated supplier of B to Y to alter the B it supplies Y to make it readily identifiable in Y's inventory or final product (*e.g.*, if B is a button, to notch the button in a particular, hard-to-replicate way), either of these types of tie-ins may be the most-cost-effective way for X to control the quality of the complements Y uses. Indeed, in the circumstances described, this control-method may be foolproof and virtually costless. I should add that if the tie-ins that are performing this function are not designed to perform other functions as well (see below), the price that will be charged for B under the contracts in question will be its normal market price.

I want to point out a possible wrinkle on this complement-quality-control function whose empirical significance is doubtful. It is conceivable that a seller would use a complement-quality-controlling tie-in that would not otherwise be profitable because the improvement in its competitive-position array that its employment of such tie-ins would yield would cause an extant rival to exit or deter a potential investor in its area of product-space from expanding or entering by yielding a concomitant deterioration respectively in such actual and potential rivals' actual and prospective competitive-position arrays. Tie-ins whose perpetrator-perceived *ex ante* profitability was critically increased by the perpetrator's perception that they would or might have any such effect are predatory and do violate the Sherman Act. However, given the low cost and efficacy (*i.e.*, the independent profitability of this functional type of tie-in), I suspect that few if any complement-quality-controlling tie-ins are predatory.

This wrinkle has counterparts for ingredient-quality-controlling reciprocity agreements and for RPM and non-single-brand exclusive dealerships that function by enabling the producer to induce its resellers to make more demand-increasing expenditures, to secure better warranty service for its customers, to prevent its individual resellers from reducing the actual and/or perceived dollar value of its product to some prospective buyers by charging a lower price for its product than would on this account be in the reseller's and its joint interest, and to prevent its resellers from offering a different (usually lower) price/quality combination than the combination the producer (franchisor) wants to be able to assure potential buyers they will receive from any franchisee. However, to save space and because I doubt both the legal significance and empirical importance of this possibility, I will not discuss it again when delineating the functions or analyzing the legality of these other categories of surrogates for vertical integration.

(B) Reducing the Costs the Seller Must Incur to Prevent or Allow Arbitrage

As we have seen, buyers Y that are charged discriminatorily-low per-unit prices by a seller X that is practicing conventional price discrimination and buyers Y that are charged lump-sum fees or varying per-unit prices by a seller that is engaging in perfect price discrimination or using the mixed pricing-technique discussed in Subsect. 2A(4) of this chapter may find it profitable to resell the A they are purchasing from X to other potential customers of X. If (1) X knows the quantity of some complement B to its product A that any buyer of A will combine with the quantity of A it purchased if it used that A in its own business and (2) it will be costly for Y to take delivery of that quantity of B and resell it to someone else if it engages in arbitrage on some of the A it buys from X, an X that is discriminating in Y's favor on A, is charging Y a lump-sum fee for the right to purchase A on specified per-unit terms, or is charging Y a varying per-unit price for A may be able to reduce the associated cost it must incur to prevent or allow Y's arbitrage by using a tie-in that obligates Y to purchase from X or someone else X designates the B Y would purchase anyway if it used all the A it purchased from X in its own business. Indeed, this type of tie-in will be a virtually costless way of reducing Y's incentive to engage in arbitrage on A by the cost it will have to incur to resell the B the tie-in requires it to buy when it purchases the A it would otherwise resell. Once more, if such arbitrage-deterring tie-ins are not designed to perform any other functions (or any other functions other than complement-quality control), the price of B in the contract in question will be its normal market price.

(C) Concealing, Reducing the Apparent Extent of, and/or Changing the Apparent Locus of a Seller's Price Discrimination, Predatory or Illegally-Retaliatory Pricing, Maximum-or-Minimum-Price-Regulation Violations, and Tax or Contract Frauds

For a variety of reasons, a seller may find it profitable to conceal the price it is charging a particular buyer for a particular good A:

(1) the price to the buyer in question may be discriminatorily-low, and the seller may want to prevent other buyers from discovering it because it will put the lie to the cost-claims it has made to them, make them believe for other reasons that they can obtain a price-reduction, and/or cost it goodwill by revealing that it has discriminated against them;
(2) the price may be discriminatorily-low or high, predatory, or retaliatory against a rival that has undercut the seller's contrived oligopolistic price to another buyer or the price may be incorrectly perceived to fall into one of these categories, and the seller may be concerned that its detection will create antitrust problems;
(3) the price may violate a maximum-price regulation or a minimum-price regulation, and the seller may wish to avoid the penalties it would have to pay if its price-regulation violation were detected;

(4) the seller may wish to shift the apparent locus of its profits because the profits the seller earns by selling some goods may be taxed at a higher rate than the rate at which the profits the seller makes by selling other goods are taxed; and
(5) the seller may wish to shift the apparent locus of its revenues or profits because the royalties it must pay on the dollar sales it makes of or the profits it makes on the sales of one product may be higher than the royalties it must pay on its dollar sales of or the profits it makes by selling other products.

In some situations, a seller X of product A may be able to increase its profits by using a tie-in to conceal or change the apparent extent or locus of its price discrimination, predatory pricing, contrived oligopolistic pricing, or maximum-or-minimum-price-regulation violations. Assume, for example, that the buyer Y that is interested in purchasing product A from seller X is also interested in buying some other product B from X—in particular, that Y is interested in purchasing one unit of both A and B from X. Assume in addition that X's normal price for A is $12 and normal price for B is $7 but that Y is willing to pay X $13 for A and $6 for B and X wants to charge Y those prices for these products—*i.e.*, that X wants to discriminate against Y on A and in favor of Y on B. In such a situation, X may be able to conceal its price discrimination by using a package-pricing tie-in in which Y is sold one unit of A and one unit of B for a combined price of $19 or by conditioning its agreement to supply Y with one unit of A at a price of $12 on Y's agreeing to purchase a unit of B for $7. Obviously, tie-ins will be able to perform the same concealing function (1) when X wants to violate a maximum-price regulation when selling A to Y and a minimum-price regulation when selling B to Y, (2) when X wants to price discriminate against Y on A and violate a minimum-price regulation when selling B to Y, and (3) when X wants to price discriminate in favor of Y on A and violate a maximum-price regulation when selling B to Y. Even if the relevant numbers do not make it possible for a tie-in to conceal all of the seller's discrimination and/or price-regulation violations, tie-ins may enable the seller to reduce the apparent extent of its discrimination and/or price-regulation violation. Thus, in a situation in which X wants to (1) discriminate against Y by $2 on product A by charging Y $14 for A when it charges other buyers $12 for A and (2) to discriminate in favor of Y by $1 on product B by charging Y $7 for B when it charges other buyers $8 for B, X will be able to reduce the apparent extent of its price discrimination by charging Y $21 for A and B combined or by offering to supply Y with a unit of B for $13 on condition that Y agree to purchase a unit of A for $8 ($1 more than Y would be willing to pay for B in a separate transaction). Indeed, even if tie-ins cannot enable X to conceal the extent of its violations (for example, because X wants to discriminate against Y on A but charge Y the normal price for B), X may be able to reduce the cost of its pricing conduct by shifting the locus of its apparent "deviance." Assume that X wants to violate a regulation that sets a minimum price of $8 for B by charging $7 for B to a Y that would not be willing to pay more than $7 for B but would purchase A from X for its normal price of $12. If the legal cost of violating the minimum-price regulation on B is higher than the legal and bargaining-related cost of (apparent) price discrimination on A, X may be able to increase its profits by entering into a tie-in in which it agrees to supply Y with one unit of A for $11 ($1 below the normal price for A) on condition that Y purchase one unit of B for the lawful price of $8. The legal cost to a seller of violating (or appearing to violate) anti-price-discrimination laws by engaging in discrimination on different products or of violating maximum-price or minimum-price regulations that apply to different products will differ to the extent that the penalties imposed for violating the anti-price-discrimination law are different from the penalties for violating the maximum-price or minimum-price regulation, the penalties for violating the different maximum-price or minimum-price regulations in question differ, the authorities that enforce one of the regulations are more assiduous than the authorities that enforce the other, the authorities pay more attention to price discrimination in some areas of product-space than in others, or the legally-entitled victims of price discrimination in one area of product-space (or of one maximum-price or minimum-price regulation) are more likely to sue than the legally-entitled victims of price discrimination in another area of product-space (or of another maximum-price or minimum-price regulation) regardless of whether they are legally entitled to recovery.

Mutatis mutandis, the same argument will apply when the conduct that X wants to conceal is not price discrimination in favor of a particular buyer or a minimum-price-regulation violation but predatory pricing or retaliatory pricing that is designed to punish a rival that has undercut or undermined the retaliator's contrived oligopolistic price to one or more other buyers.

Tie-ins can also yield a seller profits by enabling it to practice tax or contract fraud more cost-effectively. Assume, for example, that X is a seller of forest land and timber and that, under the relevant jurisdiction's tax laws, the profits that X makes by selling its land are taxed at a higher rate (*e.g.*, are taxed as normal income) than the profits X makes by selling its timber (which are taxed as capital gains). If X can locate a buyer Y that is willing to purchase both its land and its timber, X can perpetrate a tax fraud by agreeing to sell Y the land for less than its market price on condition that Y agree to purchase the timber for more than its market price. Or assume that X is a producer and distributor of motion-picture films A and B and that the percentage of the revenues that X obtains by distributing film A to which the writers, directors, and actors who worked on film A are contractually entitled is higher than the percentage of the revenues that X obtains by distributing film B to which the writers, directors, and actors who worked on film B are contractually entitled. Assume as well that exhibitor Y is interested in exhibiting both film A and film B. In this situation, a tie-in under which Y is charged less than Y would be willing to pay for the right to exhibit film A on condition that Y agrees to pay more for the right to exhibit film B than it would otherwise be willing to pay may enable X to profit by committing a contract fraud—*i.e.*, by reducing the total royalties it pays to the writers, directors, and actors who have worked on X's films.

I should point out that, although tie-ins that function by perpetrating tax and contact frauds or by concealing maximum-or-minimum price-regulation violations are illegal, they do not violate the antitrust laws. Indeed, even those tie-ins that function by concealing the existence, extent, or location of the seller's antitrust violations do not affect the antitrust legality of the concealed behavior, though they will change the antitrust liability of any buyer that knowingly collaborates with the seller (at least if it knowingly accepts compensation for doing so). (Tie-ins that function by concealing a contrived oligopolistic pricer's retaliating against an undercutter/underminer or a predators predatory pricing do violate U.S. antitrust law—in particular, the Sherman Act—in that they are part of a broader set of conduct whose other components would violate U.S. antitrust law even if no tie-in were involved. For the same reason, such tie-ins would also always violate the exclusionary-abuse branch and sometimes violate the exploitative-abuse branch of now-Article 102 of the E.C./E.U. competition law if the seller in question were either individually dominant or a member of a collectively-dominant set of rivals. However, I do not think tie-ins that conceal individual-firm predation or contrivance executed exclusively through threats of retaliation will violate E.C./E.U. competition law when the perpetrator is not a dominant firm or a member of a set of collectively-dominant rivals. This last conclusion reflects the fact that single-firm predation and contrivance that is pursued solely by the making and carrying out of retaliatory threats do not violate now-Article 101(1): if such tie-ins do not violate now-Article 101(1), tie-ins that are designed to conceal them cannot violate now-Article 101(1).)

(D) Reducing the Market-Research, Personnel-Training, and Checkout-Counter-Delay Costs of Conventional Price Discrimination

In order to practice conventional price discrimination, a seller will normally have to incur market-research costs to determine the price each of its potential customers or various subsets of its potential customers would be willing to pay either for its product or for the right to purchase its product at a specified per-unit price, additional costs to train its point-of-sale personnel to identify particular buyers—*i.e.*, the price that particular buyers would be willing to pay, and additional delay-costs at the checkout counter to charge different buyers different prices. However, if the seller knows that, although individual buyers place different prices on each of the products it could supply them, they place the same value on some package of the products it could supply them, the seller will be able to practice price discrimination on each individual product in the package without doing market research into the price each buyer would be willing to pay for each product in the package, without training its point-of-sale personnel to determine the dollar value that its individual potential customers place on each of the products in question, and without slowing down the processing of buyers through the checkout counter by offering to sell all buyers the relevant package of products for the same package-price. Indeed, this type of package-pricing tie-in will be costless if the dollar value that each relevant buyer places on each member of the relevant package exceeds the marginal cost the seller must incur to supply that buyer with the product in question. (For reasons that were discussed previously, in appropriate circumstances, such a tie-in will also benefit the seller by concealing the fact that it is engaging in price discrimination and by helping the seller prevent buyers in whose favor it is discriminating from engaging in arbitrage.)

Of course, in practice, relevant buyers will rarely place the same value on any relevant package of goods. However, so long as the values that individual buyers place on some package of goods with which the seller could supply them are more homogeneous than are the values they place on the individual products in the package, the package-pricing tie-in may reduce the amount of market research the seller must do to practice price discrimination with any degree of precision. In some cases, a seller in this position may decide to discriminate in its pricing of the relevant package of goods—*i.e.*, (1) to incur additional costs to train point-of-sale personnel to determine which buyers place higher-than-average and lower-than-average values on the package of goods or, more ambitiously, to determine the exact value that each buyer places on the relevant package of goods, (2) to incur the additional cost of paying cashiers to take the time to determine the price that individual buyers are willing to pay for the package and to charge separate prices to each buyer, and (3) to accept the losses associated with the checkout-corner delays the discrimination entails. And in some cases, such a seller may decide that the market-research, personnel-training, and checkout-counter-delay costs of engaging in discrimination on the package of goods are greater than the benefits that such discrimination would confer on it (1) by enabling it not to supply a good to a buyer to which its value is lower than the marginal cost the seller must incur to supply it, (2) by preventing it from losing profits by charging some buyers a price for the package that exceeds the price they are willing to pay for it, and (3) by preventing it from losing profits by charging some buyers less for the package of goods than they would be willing to pay for it. Still, regardless of whether the seller in question engages in price discrimination when selling the relevant package of goods, when the above information-condition is fulfilled, the seller will be able to increase the profits it can make by engaging in *de facto* discrimination when pricing the individual products in the package.

An example may be useful. Assume that the relevant seller X manufactures dishwasher powder and that it realizes that some buyers (say, those that have higher incomes and wealth) are willing to pay a higher price for its product while other buyers (say, those that are poorer) are willing to pay a lower price for its product. Assume in addition that it will be costly for the seller to engage in price discrimination when selling its product separately—*i.e.*, to train its personnel to identify high-valuing and low-valuing buyers, to take the time to charge different buyers different prices, to put the buyers in whose favor it is discriminating in a position to profit by reselling their purchases to the seller's high-valuing potential customers, and to charge the prices in question openly—for the reasons we discussed in Subsect. 2C(1)(C). Assume next that X can also supply buyers with a coupon that would entitle them to purchase inexpensive, low-quality dishes for less than their market price. Assume in addition that X knows that this coupon is worth nothing to its wealthy potential customers, who do not want low-quality dishes at any price, but is positively valued by its poor potential customers, who do value the opportunity to buy even low-quality dishes cheaply. Assume finally but not essentially that the value of the package of goods consisting of the dishwasher powder and the dish-purchasing coupon is the same to both those of its potential customers that place a higher-than-average value on its dishwasher powder and to those of its potential customers that place a lower-than-average value on its dishwasher powder. On these assumptions, the seller in question will be able to practice *de facto* price discrimination on its dishwasher powder by offering to supply all buyers with a package of goods consisting of the dishwasher powder and the dish coupon for the same price without doing market research to identify which potential customer places what value on each of the two products, without training its sales personnel to identify the valuation-class of different buyers, and without slowing down the processing of buyers through the checkout counter by charging different buyers different prices for each good in question. (As we saw earlier, such a tie-in will also benefit the seller by concealing the fact that it is engaging in price discrimination on the individual products in the package. Moreover, if the relevant seller can bury the coupon in the center of the box, such package-pricing tie-ins may benefit X as well by enabling it to discriminate in poor people's favor without providing them with as much of an incentive as straightforward discrimination would give them to resell the dishwasher powder they bought to the high-valuing potential buyers of X's dishwasher powder and without making it profitable for the wealthier buyers to resell the coupon to the poorer buyers.)

(E) Increasing the Profits That a Seller Can Realize by Using the Mixed Pricing-Technique Sect. 2A(4) Explained to Price the Sale of a Durable Machine, Franchise, or Product or Production-Process Idea or Patent by Reducing the Transaction Cost of Determining the Frequency with Which the Buyer Used the Machine or Idea and/or the Cost of Allowing the Buyer to Commit Contract Fraud by Underreporting the Frequency with Which It Used the Relevant Machine or Idea or the Sales or Profits It Made by Using the Relevant Machine or Idea—*i.e.*, Increasing the Profitability of "Meter Pricing"

If one redescribes the outright sale of a machine, the sale of the exclusive right to operate an outlet with a specified franchiser name in a specified territory, the outright sale of a product or production-process idea or patent, or the sale of the right to use an idea for a lump-sum fee as the sale of the right to use the machine, franchise idea, or product or production-process idea or patent for a per-unit price (zero) equal to the marginal cost to the seller of the buyer's using the machine, franchise, or idea in question, the fact that such an arrangement is a variant of pure-lump-sum pricing should become apparent. Relatedly, this redescription of such outright sales should make it apparent that each of the following four arrangements is a variant of the mixed pricing-technique that Sect. 2A(4) discussed: (1) an arrangement in which the seller of a durable machine lowers its lump-sum fee below the fee it could have obtained for the machine in an outright sale, attaches a meter to its machine, and requires its customer to pay not only its reduced lump-sum fee but also a per-use price (a meter rate) for using the machine, (2) an arrangement in which the seller of a durable machine lowers its lump-sum fee below the fee it could have obtained in an outright sale but requires its customer to pay not only the reduced lump-sum fee but a percentage of the sales it makes of the product it uses the machine to produce or a percentage of the profits it otherwise would have made on those sales (an endproduct royalty), (3) an arrangement in which a franchisor lowers its lump-sum franchise fee below the fee it could have obtained in a pure-lump-sum-fee franchise agreement but requires the franchisee to pay not only its reduced franchise fee but also a percentage of the sales it makes or the profits it would otherwise have made on those sales, and (4) an arrangement in which a seller of the right to use another type of product idea or a production-process idea or a seller of the idea itself reduces the lump-sum fee it charges for the right to use the idea in question or for the idea or patent that relates to it below the lump-sum fee it could have obtained for it in a simple sale but requires the buyer to pay not only the reduced lump-sum fee but also (A) a percentage of the sales it makes by producing the product in question, (B) a percentage of the profits it would otherwise have made on those sales, (C) a per-unit price each time it uses the relevant production process to produce a unit of the product in question, (D) a percentage of the sales it makes of that product, or (E) a percentage of the profits it otherwise would have made on that product. Thus, the shift from pure-lump-sum pricing to each of these types of arrangements will increase the seller's profits if the benefits it provides the seller by reducing the sum of the seller's and buyer's risk costs, by helping the seller overcome the buyer's and/or its own underestimation of the buyer's quantity demand for using the seller's product at various relevant per-unit prices, and by reducing the cost to the seller of preventing or allowing buyer arbitrage (*e.g.*, the buyer's using the machine not only to produce its own product but also to produce the product of other potential customers of the seller) exceeds the costs they impose on the seller by destroying transaction surplus by reducing the frequency with which the buyer uses the machine, franchise idea, or other-product or production-process idea and by deterring the buyer from making as high demand-increasing expenditures on the product or idea in question as would be in its and the seller's joint interest, by increasing the cost of drafting and negotiating the relevant sales or franchise agreement, and by generating other types of transaction costs such as the cost of buying, installing, maintaining and repairing, and reading the meter, the cost to the seller of preventing or allowing meter-tampering, the cost to the buyer of submitting sales and profit records, the cost to the seller of verifying those records, and the cost to the seller of preventing the buyer from or allowing the buyer to commit accounting fraud.

In some situations, sellers may be able to increase the profitability of using this mixed pricing-technique to price durable machines, franchise ideas, or product or production-process ideas by substituting appropriate full-requirements tie-ins for meters and meter-rates or endproduct royalties. Under this variant of the mixed pricing-strategy, the seller would reduce the lump-sum fee it charged for its durable machine, franchise idea, or other product or production-process idea A but require the buyer to purchase its full requirements of some complement B it uses together with the machine, franchise idea, or other idea in question for more than that product's normal market price. If I assume for simplicity that the buyer uses one unit of B each time it uses the machine A, uses the franchise idea A to make a sale, produces a unit of the good A the idea identified, or uses once the production process A the idea identified, the difference between the contract price of B and its normal market price will be the meter rate (the difference between the seller's per-use price for the machine or idea and the marginal cost to the seller of its machine's or idea's being used [zero]). More specifically, the full-requirements tie-in will be more profitable to the extent that the cost of policing the full-requirements contract (which can often be reduced by altering the B the buyer is obligated to purchase to make it more easily identifiable) is lower than both (1) the sum of the cost of buying, installing, maintaining, and repairing meters, of reading meters, and of preventing or not preventing meter-tampering and (2) the sum of the cost to the buyer of submitting sales and profit reports, the cost to the seller of verifying those reports, and the cost to the seller of preventing or allowing buyer accounting fraud.

I want to close this discussion by making two additional points. In some circumstances, tie-ins that perform the function just described may also enable the seller to control the quality of the complements the buyer combines with its machine or idea and/or enable the seller to commit tax or contract fraud. Second, because courts have sometimes declared meter-pricing tie-ins illegal on the ground that they effectuate conventional price discrimination (which the courts incorrectly believe is illegal in the circumstances in question), it is important to note that both the mixed pricing-technique and the type of tie-in that increases its profitability may be profitable when neither produces conventional price discrimination—*e.g.*, when the seller supplies only one buyer. Although the mixed technique and this type of tie-in may be used more often by sellers that find price discrimination profitable—*i.e.*, by sellers that have customers that will use their machines or ideas to different extents (since under those conditions the sellers may be more likely to underestimate the relevant quantity demands of one or more buyers), the profitability of the mixed pricing-technique and the type of tie-in on which we are currently focusing does not in general depend on their producing discriminatory outcomes.

(F) Increasing the Cost-Effectiveness of a Seller's Supra-TSM-Marginal-Cost Per-Unit Pricing by Shifting Its Locus from the Seller's Product A to Another Product B When (SS+)/(BS–) for the Relevant Segment of the Full-Requirements Demand Curve for B Is Higher Than |(SS–(BS+)| for the Relevant Segment of the Demand Curve for A and/or the Relevant Supra-MC Pricing of A Destroys More Transaction Surplus by Reducing Reseller Demand-Increasing Expenditures Than the Relevant Supra-MC Pricing of B Destroys in This Way

(i) Increasing the Profits That a Producer X of a Final Product A Can Realize by Using the Mixed Pricing-Technique Sect. 2A(4) Explained to Price Any Type of Product A by Shifting the Locus of the Associated Supra-TSM-Marginal-Cost Per-Unit Pricing from the Seller's (Tying) Product A to a (Tied) Product B That the Tie-In Obligates the Buyer to Purchase Exclusively from the Seller When the Benefits the Tie-In Confers on the Seller Because the Foregone Supra-Marginal-Cost Pricing on A Would Have Destroyed More Transaction Surplus Than the Associated Per-Unit-Price Increase on B Destroys (1) by Reducing the Quantity of Those Products That Are Sold Even If Y Is Not a Retailer of A or the Supra-TSM-Marginal-Cost Pricing of A Does Not Deter Its Distributor from Making Demand-Increasing Expenditures That Would Be in Y's and X's Joint Equivalent-Dollar Interest and (2) by Deterring Y from Making Demand-Increasing Expenditures That Are in Y's and X's Joint Equivalent-Dollar Interest Exceed the Costs the Tie-In Imposes on the Seller X (3) by Raising the Sum of X's and Y's Risk Costs, (4) by Reducing the Protection X's Supra-TSM-Marginal-Cost Per-Unit Pricing Gives X Against Its and/or Y's Underestimating Y's Quantity Demand for the Tying Product at Relevant Prices, (5) by Eliminating the Protection That X's Supra-TSM-Marginal-Cost Per-Unit Pricing of A Would Have Given It Against Y's Practicing Arbitrage on A, (6) by Creating the Risk That Y Will Not Fulfill Its Contractual Obligation to Purchase Its Full Requirements of B from X, and (7) by Increasing the Costs X Must Incur to Draft the Relevant Contract and to Explain It to Y as Well as the Cost to Y of Evaluating the Seller's Offer (Which Will Affect the Buyer Surplus That X Must Allow Y to Retain If It Is to Retain Y's Patronage in the Long Run)

Sorry about that. The alternative was a heading that was either uninformative or inaccurate. The heading also frees me from having to repeat its substance in the text. I will restrict myself to providing examples of the type of tie-in in question, illustrating the first point in the heading's list diagrammatically, explaining why the benefit delineated in the second point is likely to be generated, explaining why and when the costs delineated in the third and fourth points will be lower than one might anticipate, reviewing how the seller may be able to reduce the costs delineated in the fifth and sixth points in the list, and pointing out that tie-ins of this sort will usually make it profitable for the seller that uses them to increase the amount of buyer surplus it removes through supra-TSM-marginal-cost per-unit pricing.

The functional type of tie-in on which this subsection focuses is sometimes referred to as "full-line forcing" tie-ins. The name is misleading in two respects. First, it implies incorrectly that sellers that use this type of tie-in always "force" the buyer to accept the arrangement against the buyer's will. This claim is incorrect because it ignores the facts that (1) this type of tie-in will usually not inflict an equivalent-dollar loss on the buyer (will do so only if perfect price discrimination would not have been profitable for the seller and the mixed pricing-technique would also not have been profitable for the seller if the seller could not have used such a tie-in to increase its profitability), (2) this type of tie-in will sometimes benefit the buyer by enabling it to profit from its or the seller's underestimating its quantity demand for the tying product at relevant prices or, if the buyer has some bargaining power, by enabling it to obtain a share of the transaction-surplus gains the tie-in generates and, most fundamentally, (3) even when this type of tie-in leaves the buyer worse-off than it would have been had the seller been prevented from using it, the tie-in deal will not leave the buyer worse-off than it would have been had it not bought the tying good from the seller at all—*i.e.*, the tying seller will not have had to secure the buyer's agreement by threatening to retaliate against the buyer's rejection of the deal in question (by overbearing the buyer's will). Second, the name is misleading because it implies that the products whose sale is tied will always be part of what would conventionally be called a product-line. Although, as will be explained below, this type of tie-in is more likely to be profitable when variations in the demand curves for the tying and tied products through time are positively correlated and when sellers or buyers that underestimate the buyer's quantity demand for the tying product at relevant prices will also underestimate the buyer's quantity demand for the tied product at relevant prices (conditions that will be more likely to be fulfilled when A and B are part of a given product-line), this reality does not imply that the tying and tied products must be part of a conventional product-line. Indeed, for tie-ins to perform "the function" this type of tie-in performs, the tying seller need not even produce the tied product itself or sell the tied product under the tying product's brand name.

I will provide two concrete examples of this type of tie-in. In the first, the tying product—product A—is a differentiated men's suit sold by a clothing producer X to a retailer Y that owns the only high-quality-men's-clothing store in the relevant geographic area of product-space and the tied product B "is" a set of relatively-undifferentiated dress shirts or neckties that the clothing producer may not even produce itself and that final consumer Z can purchase not only from the haberdasher Y but also from one or two other department stores in the area in question. In the second, the tying product A is a highly-differentiated lawnmower that is sold by its producer X to the only retailer Y of such equipment in the relevant geographic area and the tied product B "is" a set of rakes, hoes, hoses and other sorts of undifferentiated gardening products that may or may not be produced by X and are sold not only by Y but by one or two general stores in the relevant area. In the former situation, the relevant tie-in would be one in which the clothing producer X reduces the per-unit price it charges the retailer Y for its suits on condition that Y agree to purchase from it as well as Y's full requirements of standardized dress shirts and neckties for more than their normal market price. In the latter situation, the relevant tie-in would be one in which the lawnmower-producer X reduces the per-unit price it charges the retailer Y for its lawnmowers on condition that Y agree to purchase from it as well as Y's full requirements of standardized rakes, hoes, and hoses for more than their normal market prices. If one ignores for simplicity any tendency of the tie-in to increase the risk costs Y bears, assumes that Y cannot bargain to secure any of the transaction-surplus gains the tie-in will generate, disregards any tendency the tie-in may have to alter the amount of demand-increasing expenditures (expenditures that will increase the demand for A) Y makes, and ignores the tendency of the tie-in to increase the amount of buyer surplus that it is profitable for X to remove through supra-TSM-marginal-cost per-unit pricing, the amount of buyer surplus that Y will obtain from the price-reduction on A that the tie-in entails will equal the amount of buyer surplus that the price-reduction on B the tie-in entails will remove from Y (if one measures Y's buyer surplus on B on the counterfactual assumption that, even in the absence of the tie-in, X would be the only supplier of B that Y can patronize).

Before proceeding to the illustrative diagram, I want to explain the relevance of some features I have built into the preceding examples to make it more likely that the tie-ins they describe will increase the profits the seller that uses them can realize by employing the mixed pricing-technique Sect. 2A(4) analyzed. In particular, the preceding examples assumed that

(1) the relevant products A are highly differentiated and that their retailers Y are the only retailers of them in the relevant area to make it likely that the demand curve that Y faces when selling A to its final consumers is downward-sloping and continuous,
(2) the relevant products B are standardized and that their retailers Y resell them in competition with one or two other rivals to create the possibility that Y may face a kinky oligopoly demand curve when reselling B—*i.e.*, may be operating in a situation in which any reduction it makes in its price for B below the product's prevailing retail price will be matched by its rivals while any increase it makes in its price for B above B's prevailing market price will not induce its rivals to change their prices so that the slope of the demand curve Y faces when selling B to its final consumers below B's prevailing market price is much steeper than the slope of the demand curve Y faces when selling B to its final consumers above B's prevailing market price, and
(3) buyers that purchase any product A will be likely to purchase some of product B as well to use together with the A to increase the probability that variations in the demand curves for A and B through time will tend to be positively correlated with each other and that any X or Y that underestimates Y's quantity demand for A at relevant prices will be likely to underestimate Y's quantity demand for B at relevant prices.

Although all three of these assumptions favor the profitability of this type of tie-in, the first two are not essential to such tie-ins' profitability—are adopted primarily to make it easier to illustrate the relevant part of the argument diagrammatically.

Diagram VI is constructed to illustrate the explanations of the first point made in the heading of Sect. 2C(1)(F)(i). (At this juncture, the symbols in Diagram VI that are enclosed by brackets should be ignored: they will be relevant when Diagram VI

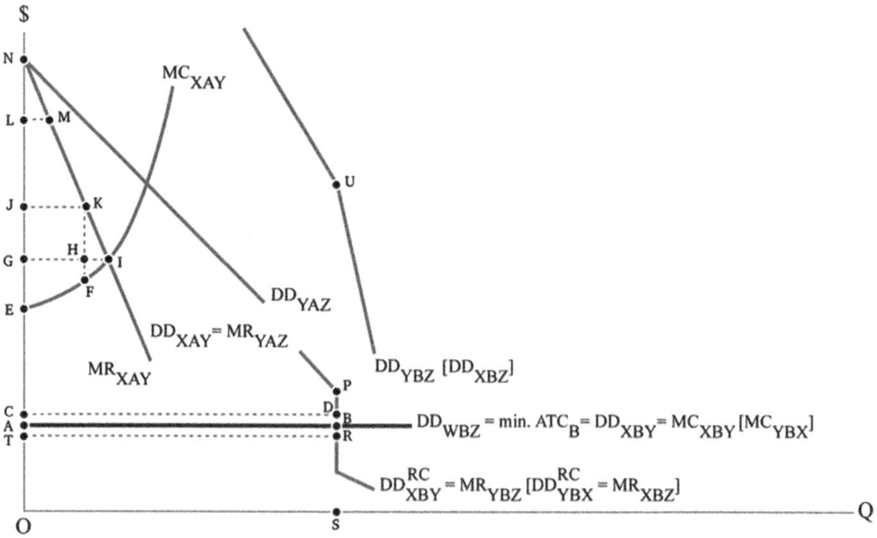

Diagram VI

Diagram VI A Diagram That Illustrates the Relevance of Some of the Determinants of the Profitability of a Full-Requirements Tie-In (Total-Output Reciprocity Agreement) That Functions *Inter Alia* by Enabling Its Perpetrator to Reduce the (TS–) Associated With the (BS–) for a Relevant Amount of Supra–TSM–MC (Supra–TSM–MC or Sub–TSM–MC) Pricing

is used to illustrate when and how reciprocal-trading agreements can perform the same set of functions that this section argues tie-ins can perform.) In the diagram and the text that follows, DD stands for "demand curve"; $DD^{RC}_{\_\,\_\,\_}$ stands for the demand curve the seller indicated by the first subscript in the set of three subscripts in the $DD^{RC}_{\_\,\_\,\_}$ expression in question would face when selling the product indicated by the middle subscript in this set of three subscripts to the buyer indicated by the last of the three subscripts if the indicated buyer had contracted to purchase its full requirements of the indicated product from the indicated seller (RC stands for requirements contract); MR stands for the marginal revenue curve the indicated seller would face when selling the indicated product to the indicated buyer if the seller engaged in single pricing when selling the indicated product to the buyer in question; MC stands for marginal cost curve the indicated seller would face to supply the indicated product to the indicated buyer; min. ATC stands for the minimum average total cost at which the product could be supplied by any possible supplier to the indicated buyer; X (sometimes W) stands for the relevant producer; Y (sometimes V) stands for the relevant retailer; Z stands for the relevant final consumer; A stands for the differentiated, so-called "tying product"; and B stands for the standardized, so-called "tied product"—the product the buyer has agreed to purchase exclusively from the seller. Thus, in Diagram VI, DD_{XAY} stands for the demand curve that producer X faces when selling product A to retailer Y; DD_{XBY} stands for the demand curve X faces when selling product B to Y in circumstances in which Y has not committed itself to purchasing its full requirements of B from X; DD^{RC}_{XBY} stands for the demand curve that X would face when selling B to Y if Y had committed itself to purchasing its full requirements of B from X; DD_{YAZ} stands for the demand curve retailer Y faces when selling A to final consumer Z; DD_{YBZ} indicates the demand curve Y faces when reselling B to Z; DD_{WBV} indicates the demand curve that any producer W of B would face when selling B to any retailer V of B if, as I will assume for simplicity, B is produced under conditions of perfect competition and the marginal cost of supplying each of its retailers is the same; MR_{XAY} indicates the marginal revenue curve that X would face when selling A to Y if it did so by setting a single per-unit price and allowing Y to purchase as much A as Y desired at that price; MR_{YAZ} indicates the marginal revenue curve Y will face when reselling A to final consumers Z if it engages in such single pricing on the product; MR_{YBZ} indicates the marginal revenue curve Y would face when selling B to Z if it engaged in single pricing on B; min. ATC_B, which is constructed on the assumption that B is produced under conditions of perfect competition and that the average total cost of supplying each of its retailers is the same, is a horizontal line equal to the minimum height of the average total cost curve for B; MC_{XAY} indicates the marginal cost that X will have to incur to supply Y with successive units of A; and MC_{XBY} indicates the marginal cost that X will have to incur to supply Y with successive units of B.

Diagram VI does not contain any MC_{YAZ} or MC_{YBZ} curve. However, for simplicity, the analysis that follows will assume that MC_{YAZ} is horizontal at the per-unit price that Y must pay X for A and that MC_{YBZ} is horizontal at the per-unit price that Y must pay X for B. This obviously-unrealistic assumption that the only (marginal) cost Y must incur to supply Z with A or B is the "cost of the good sold" is made solely to reduce by two the number of curves in the diagram. More specifically, this assumption simplifies the diagram by enabling me to assume that DD_{XAY} coincides with MR_{YAZ} and that DD^{RC}_{XBY} coincides with MR_{YBZ}. If the only cost that Y must incur to supply A or B to Z is the cost it has to incur to purchase the relevant unit of A or B from X, the relevant DD_{X_Y} curve will coincide with the relevant MR_{Y_Z} curve because the value to Y of successive units of A or B will equal the marginal revenue Y can obtain by selling those units to Z. If Y has to incur non-cost-of-goods-sold marginal costs to distribute A or B to Z, the value of successive units of A or B to Y will be lower than the marginal revenue their resale would yield Y by the amount of the relevant non-cost-of-goods-sold marginal costs, and DD_{XAY} and DD^{RC}_{XBY} will respectively be below MR_{XAY} and MR_{XBY} by the non-cost-of-goods-sold marginal costs Y must incur to distribute A and B to Y respectively. I repeat: the assumption that Y must incur no non-cost-of-goods-sold marginal costs to distribute A or B to Z is made solely to simplify the diagram and my exposition. It has no effect on any significant conclusion I generate.

I have already indicated that Diagram VI assumes that product B is produced in a perfectly-competitive market. This assumption is manifest in Diagram VI's construction of both DD_{WBV} and MC_{XBY} to be horizontal over the relevant range at the minimum average total cost of B. (MC_{XBY} will equal min. ATC_B on this perfect-competition assumption regardless of whether X produces B itself or buys it from someone else.) Like the "no non-cost-of-goods-sold retail-distribution-cost assumption," this assumption is made solely to simplify the diagram and my exposition and affects no significant conclusion the analysis generates.

In Diagram VI, DD_{YAZ} is constructed to be not only continuous and downward-sloping but linear. I have made this assumption solely to facilitate the construction of MR_{YAZ} (to enable me to create the correct relationship between MR_{YAZ} and DD_{YAZ}).

Finally, in Diagram VI, DD_{YBZ} is constructed to be discontinuous at point U—*i.e.*, to be a kinky oligopoly demand curve, the kind of curve that members of tight oligopolies would face if, at the prevailing market price (US in Diagram VI), each seller realized that if it raised its price its rivals would not raise theirs but if it lowered its price its rivals would cut their prices as well. This kinky-oligopoly-demand-curve assumption strongly favors the profitability of the tie-in that the diagram is being used to analyze because (1) when a demand curve is kinked at a particular price, the (single-pricing) marginal revenue curve with which it is associated will be vertical (have a gap—between points P and R in Diagram VI) at the output in question (output OS in Diagram VI) since the relevant seller will obtain a lot more revenue by reducing its price down to the prevailing price that its rivals are (more or less) charging than it will obtain by lowering its price below the prevailing level (since *ex hypothesis* its rivals will not reduce their prices in response to the seller's reducing its price to the prevailing level but will reduce their prices if the seller reduces its price below the prevailing level) and (2) when the demand curve for a product (here, $DD^{RC}_{XBY} = MR_{YBZ}$) is vertical over some relevant range (PR or, more relevantly, DB in Diagram VI), the relevant seller can raise its price within that range without destroying transaction surplus by deterring buyers from making a purchase that would be in their and its joint interest. However, the kinky-oligopoly DD_{YBZ} assumption of Diagram VI is not essential to my argument (is made solely to increase the visual usefulness of the diagram): for point (1) in the heading's list to be justified, all that is necessary is that the (SS–)/(BS+) ratio (along DD_{XAY}) for the per-unit-price-reduction the tie-in effectuates on A be lower than the (SS+)/(BS–) ratio (along DD^{RC}_{XBY}) for the per-unit-price-increase the tie-in effectuates on B where the (BS+) for the relevant price-reduction on A equals the (BS–) for the relevant price-increase on B, and, for this condition to be fulfilled, it is not necessary for DD^{RC}_{XBY} to be a kinky oligopoly demand curve—*i.e.*, for DD^{RC}_{XBY} to be vertical over the relevant range, for (SS+)/(BS–) over the relevant section of DD^{RC}_{XBY} to have a value of one.

Diagram VI is designed to illustrate the first-listed consequence of seller X's decision to replace (1) what I assume would have been its most-profitable single-product pricing-technique—a mixed pricing-technique in which X charges Y a lump-sum fee equal to area LMKJ for the right to purchase as much A as Y wants to purchase up to the TSM quantity GI for a supra-TSM-marginal-cost per-unit price of JO (where area NML equals the amount of risk costs this arrangement imposes on Y or the sum of those risk costs and any buyer surplus Y's bargaining power allows Y to secure) for (2) a tie-in in which X charges Y a lump-sum fee equal to area LMKJ for the right to purchase as much A as Y wants to purchase up to the TSM quantity GI at the TSM-marginal-cost per-unit price of GO $<$ JO on condition that Y agree to purchase its full requirements of some other product B from X as well for CA more than B's normal market (competitive) price of AO where, by construction, area JKIG (the amount of buyer surplus the price-reduction on A enables Y to obtain on its purchases of that product from X) equals area CDBA (the cost to Y of having to pay CO rather than AO for each unit of B Y purchases from X). Diagram VI's assumption that, *ceteris paribus*, the price-cut X makes on A will benefit Y by the same amount that, *ceteris paribus*, X's price-increase on B will harm Y assumes for convenience that the tie-in will not change the risk costs Y bears as a result of its transaction with X. This assumption will eventually be relaxed.

Diagram VI is designed to illustrate why, although *ceteris paribus* Y will be indifferent to the tie-in just described and the deal that X would have found most profitable to offer Y on A if X were constrained to sell A separately, X will find the tie-in more profitable than the most-profitable deal I am assuming it could arrange if required to sell A separately—*viz.*, because, *ceteris paribus*, the transaction surplus the tie-in would preserve by lowering the per-unit price of A would exceed the transaction surplus it would destroy by raising the per-unit price of B. I will begin by explaining the relationship between DD^{RC}_{XBY} and DD_{XBY} in Diagram VI. Y's agreement to buy its full requirements of B from X is an agreement, in effect, to treat X as if X were a pure monopolistic supplier of B when deciding how many units of B to purchase from X at the price of B set in the tie-in (whereas Diagram VI is assuming that X either does not produce B at all or produces it as a member of a perfectly-competitive industry). Y's decision to treat X as if it were a pure monopolist of B when X charges Y the price for B stipulated in the tying agreement changes the demand curve X faces when selling B to Y. DD_{XBY} is horizontal at B's normal market price (which I am assuming for convenience equals its perfectly-competitive price—min. ATC_B) because, if Y has not committed itself to buying B exclusively from X, Y will have the option of buying B from someone else at a price equal to min. ATC_B—*i.e.*, because under these circumstances the value of successive units of X's B to Y equals the cost Y would have to incur to purchase the unit of B in question from someone else. DD^{RC}_{XBY} exceeds DD_{XBY} to the left of quantity AB in Diagram VI because Y's agreement to buy its B exclusively from X precludes it from purchasing B from someone else so that the value to Y of the successive units of B it would purchase from X equals not their replacement cost but the (net) additional revenue Y could obtain by reselling those successive units of B to Z (which, on our assumption that the only variable cost to Y of selling B to Z is the cost Y must incur to purchase the relevant unit of B from X, equals MR_{YBZ}).

That is why DD^{RC}_{XBY} diverges from DD_{XBY} in Diagram VI—more specifically, why DD^{RC}_{XBY} is higher than DD_{XBY} between output zero and output AB in Diagram VI. In any event, under the full-requirements tie-in, X's sales of B to Y at any per-unit price for B will be indicated by DD^{RC}_{XBY}, not DD_{XBY}. Obviously, Y's agreement to enter into a full-requirements contract on B with X is costly to Y—more specifically, on the assumptions of Diagram VI, Y's agreement to buy its full requirements of B from X despite the fact that B's price under the contract (CO) exceeds B's normal market price of AO will cost Y a number of dollars equal to area CDBA if we ignore any related risk-cost costs, buyer-or-seller-error-related costs, and buyer-demand-increasing-expenditure costs and assume that Y will fulfill its obligation to purchase B exclusively from X. To induce Y to bind itself to buy B only from X despite the fact that X will be charging Y a per-unit price for B that is CA above its normal market price, X must offer Y a reward that at least equals area CDBA. The tie-in provides Y with that reward by committing X to supplying Y with all the A that Y wants up to the quantity GI at a per-unit price of GO and a lump-sum fee of LMKJ—*i.e.*, by committing X to allowing Y to obtain (additional) buyer surplus on A equal to area JKIG = area CDBA. *Ceteris paribus*, then, Y will be indifferent between the deal that X would offer Y on A if constrained to sell A separately—a lump-sum fee of LMKJ and a per-unit price of JO—and the tie-in I am assuming X would substitute for that deal—an arrangement in which X would agree to supply Y with A at the lower per-unit price GO in exchange for the same lump-sum fee LMKJ and Y's agreement to purchase its full requirements of B from X for a per-unit price of CO—a price CA above B's normal market price.

However, *ceteris paribus*, X will not be indifferent to substituting this tie-in for the most profitable (mixed) pricing-technique it could use if it had to sell A separately. In particular, *ceteris paribus*, X will prefer the tie-in to its most-profitable single-product mixed-pricing-technique arrangement because, on Diagram VI's assumptions, the shift to the tie-in will save KIF in transaction surplus and concomitantly, *ceteris paribus*, will increase SS by KIF (on our assumption that it will not affect BS). Thus, on Diagram VI's assumption, the most-profitable pricing-technique X could use to sell A separately would destroy transaction surplus equal to area KIF by reducing Y's quantity purchases of A from the TSM quantity GI to the lower quantity of GH = JK by requiring Y to pay X a per-unit price of JO, JG above A's TSM marginal cost, whereas, on Diagram VI's assumptions, the tie-in will destroy no transaction surplus on either A or B because (1) under it, the per-unit price of A equals A's TSM marginal cost and (2) DD^{RC}_{XBY} is vertical over the relevant price-interval. Since TS ≡ SS + BS, any such (TS) saving will yield an equal SS increase if BS stays constant. Thus, on Diagram VI's assumptions, the seller surplus that the tie-in's price-reduction on A costs X—area JKHG (the profits X will not make under the tie-in by selling Y the first GH units of A Y will buy that X would have made under the deal the tie-in would replace) *minus* area HIF (the seller surplus that X will realize under the tie-in on the additional HI in sales of A the tie-in will enable X to make to Y—will be smaller than the seller surplus the tie-in will enable X to realize by supplying B to Y—area CDBA = area

JKIG). More precisely, if one recalls that, by construction, area CDBA equals area JKIG, the net (SS+) the tie-in generates—the difference between the (SS+) on B (area JKIG) and the (SS–) on A (area JKHG–area HIF) equals ([area JKIG–area JKGH] + area HIF) = area KIH + area HIF = area KIF, which equals the quantity of transaction surplus that the tie-in prevents from being destroyed on product A by preventing its sales from being reduced below the TSM level GI *minus* the quantity of transaction surplus the tie-in causes to be destroyed on B by reducing its sales below the TSM level AB (which is zero on Diagram VI's assumptions).

I turn now to the other benefit that the functional type of tie-in on which we are now focusing can yield the seller X that uses it—reducing the loss that X's supra-TSM-marginal-cost per-unit pricing imposes on X by deterring its retailer-customer Y from making demand-increasing expenditures and resource allocations that would have been in Y's and X's joint interest. I have indicated that this functional type of tie-in will usually involve a differentiated tying product whose per-unit price it reduces and a standardized good whose per-unit price it increases. If the extent to which Y can increase the sum of its and X's profits by making expenditures related to the sale of a product that will increase the demand for the product increases with the extent to which the good in question is differentiated—a contestable relationship that I suspect does exist, the functional type of tie-in under consideration will tend to increase X's profits by reducing the losses X sustains because the retailer Y spends less to increase the demand for A than would be in its and X's joint interest (by reducing the extent to which that product's per-unit price to Y exceeds its marginal cost to X) by more than it increases the losses X sustains because Y spends less to increase the demand for the tied product B than would be in its and X's joint interest (by increasing the amount by which the per-unit price X charges Y for B exceeds the marginal cost to X of supplying Y with B).

Of course, X could obtain the two benefits just discussed without using the functional type of tie-in this subsection is considering "simply" by practicing perfect price discrimination (pure-lump-sum pricing). Indeed, the pure-lump-sum pricing-technique would have certain advantages over this kind of tie-in—*viz.*, (1) would not require X to incur either the cost of preventing Y from violating its contractual obligation to purchase its full requirements of B from X for more than B's normal market price or to absorb the losses that Y's violations of this obligation would impose on X and (2) would not require X to incur the extra contract-drafting, contract-explaining, and contract-negotiating costs the tie-in would entail because the tying agreement is more complicated than the pure-lump-sum-pricing agreement. To be more profitable than pure-lump-sum pricing, "full-line-forcing" tie-ins must do a better job than pure-lump-sum pricing does at (1) reducing the sum of the risk costs that X and Y bear and (2) reducing the certainty-equivalent losses X should anticipate sustaining because it and/or Y underestimate Y's quantity demand for A at various relevant prices. If I compare the tie-in with the most-profitable variant of mixed pricing X could use if it were constrained to sell A separately, the relevant point would be that, to be profitable, (1) the sum of (A) the amount by which the shift from single-product mixed pricing to the tie-in increases buyer and seller risk costs and the losses the seller sustains because it and/or the buyer underestimate the buyer's quantity demand for product A at relevant prices—items (3) and (4) in the heading's list, (B) the additional arbitrage-on-A-related costs the shift to the tie-in will impose on X by reducing the cost Y must incur to purchase successive units of A, (C) the additional contract-drafting/explaining/negotiating costs X will have to incur if it shifts from single-product mixed pricing to the tie-in, and (D) the costs that X will have to incur to enforce Y's obligation to purchase B from X or to allow B to violate its contractual obligation to purchase B from X *must be lower than* the (2) the sum of (A) the transaction surplus the tie-in saves by lowering X's price on A to X's TSM marginal cost (by raising A's unit sales to the TSM level) *minus* the transaction surplus the tie-in destroys by raising the price Y pays for B above the normal market price for B (by lowering Y's unit purchases of B below its TSM level) and (B) the additional transaction surplus the tie-in generates by giving Y a greater incentive to make expenditures or resource allocations to increase the demand it faces on A *minus* the transaction surplus the tie-in destroys by reducing Y's incentive to make expenditures or resource allocations to increase the demand it faces on B. As I indicated earlier, if X can find a product B to tie to product A such that (1) variations in Y's demand for B through time are highly positively correlated with variations in Y's demand for A through time and (2) the amount by which X and Y underestimate Y's full-requirements quantity demand for B at its tie-in price is highly positively correlated with the amount by which X and Y respectively underestimate Y's quantity demand for A at its tie-in price, the shift from single-product mixed pricing on A to the tie-in will produce a much smaller increase in the sum of X's and Y's relevant-transaction-related risk costs and a much smaller increase in the losses X should anticipate sustaining because it and/or Y underestimate Y's quantity demand for A at relevant prices.

Some explanation is required. My analysis of the risk-cost issue will assume that the impact of the relevant transaction on Y's total risk costs equals the risk costs that the transaction would impose on Y if it were the only source of risk to Y but that the risk cost the relevant transaction imposes on X equals the transaction's impact on the total risk costs X bears on its sales of A to all of A's retailers (Y1. . .N). For this reason, I will now use the notation Y^* to refer to the particular Y involved in a given transaction. Before proceeding, I should point out that in the current context DD_{XAY} represents not the actual demand curve X will face when selling A to Y (*i.e.*, Y^*) but X's weighted-average estimate at the time of contracting of the quantities of A Y (*i.e.*, Y^*) will buy at various prices during the period covered by the contract.

The risk costs that the single-product mixed-pricing arrangement will impose on Y^* are generated by the possibility that the value of the right to purchase A at the per-unit price JO that Y^* will be charged under this scheme will turn out to be lower or higher than the lump-sum fee Y^* is required to pay. The risk costs that the single-product mixed-pricing arrangement will impose on X are generated by the possibilities that (1) in practice Y^* will buy less or more A at the per-unit price JO than the JK units of A X predicts on the weighted average Y^* will buy at per-unit price JO to the extent that that per-unit price exceeds the average marginal cost X would have to incur to supply Y^* with the units Y^* unexpectedly does not or does purchase and (2) the possibility that MC_{XAY} will turn out to be higher or lower than X believes it will be at the time of contract. (For simplicity, I will ignore this second source of risk to X.) Under the tie-in, (1) the risk to X will shift from being the risk that Y will buy fewer units of A (the harmful risk) or more units of A (the beneficial risk) than X anticipated on the weighted average to the risk that Y will buy (respectively) fewer units of B (the harmful risk) or more units of B (the beneficial risk) than X anticipated on the weighted average, and (2) the risk to Y will shift from being that Y will buy fewer units of A (the harmful risk) than Y anticipated on the weighted average or more units of A (the beneficial risk) than Y anticipated on the weighted average to the risk that Y will buy more units of B (the harmful risk) than Y anticipated on the weighted average or fewer units of B (the beneficial risk) than Y anticipate on the weighted average. If the sign and percentage by which Y^*'s actual quantity demand for A over the contract period at various relevant prices deviates from Y^*'s weighted-average-expected quantity demand for A are the same as the sign and percentage by which Y^*'s actual quantity demand for B over the contract period at various relevant prices deviates from Y^*'s weighted-average-expected quantity demand for B over the contract period at relevant prices, X's shift from single-product mixed pricing on A to the tie-in will not affect the risk and risk costs that either Y or X bears. More specifically if the preceding condition is fulfilled, the tie-in will give Y^* the same protection against the contingency that its quantity demand for A at its contact price will turn out to be lower than Y^* expected it to be on the weighted average at the time of contracting that the single-product mixed-pricing-technique that would be more profitable for X than any other single-product pricing-technique would have given Y^* because, if that contingency arises, the total extra payments Y^* will make to X under the tie-in for the B that Y^* purchases will be lower than the total extra payments Y^* was expected on the weighted average at the time of contracting to make to X for the B that Y^* purchases (because Y^*'s purchases of B will be lower than expected). Concomitantly, if the preceding condition is fulfilled, the tie-in will leave unchanged the risk and risk costs X faces in relation to the contingencies that Y^*'s purchases of A will be various percentages higher or lower than was expected on the weighted average at the time of contracting because (for example) any time that the tie-in-related price-reduction on A costs X a given unanticipated sum on the profits X would have made on A because Y^*'s purchases of A were any percent higher than was anticipated on the weighted average at the time of contract the tie-in related price-increase on B will confer on X the same amount of unanticipated profits on B because Y^*'s purchases of B will be the same percentage higher than they were anticipated on the weighted average to be at the time of contract. Of course, to the extent that Y^*'s demands for A and B are not linked as perfectly as the condition articulates, the shift from the most-profitable single-product mixed-pricing arrangement to the type of tie-in on which this subsection is focusing could impose costs on X by raising the sum of X's and Y^*'s risk costs. I should add, however, that in some circumstances departures from the "linkages" whose consequences have just been analyzed might result in the tie-in's reducing the sum of the risk costs that X and Y (and hence in the end X) bear.

Under some conditions, the shift from the most-profitable single-product mixed-pricing arrangement X could execute with Y^* on A to the type of tie-in on which we are now focusing will also not impose "costs" on X by reducing the protection that X's shift from pure-lump-sum pricing to some arrangement that involves some supra-TSM-marginal-cost per-unit pricing gives X against its own or Y^*'s underestimating Y^*'s quantity demand for A at the per-unit price Y^* has contracted to pay X for A. In particular, the shift from the most-profitable mixed-pricing arrangement on A to the tie-in involving A and B on which we are focusing will not reduce the protection X's supra-TSM-marginal-cost per-unit pricing affords X against its or Y^*'s making this kind of *ex ante* error if (1) any time that X underestimates Y^*'s quantity demand for A at A's per-unit contract price, X underestimates by the same percentage Y^*'s quantity demand for B under the full-requirements provision of the tie-in at B's per-unit tie-in-contract price and (2) any time that Y^* underestimates Y^*'s quantity demand for A at A's per-unit contract price, Y underestimates by the same percentage Y^*'s quantity demand for B under the full-requirements provision of the tie-in at B's per-unit tie-in-contract price. Thus, if this condition is fulfilled, B's supra-market-price tie-in price will provide X with the same protection against its charging Y too low a lump-sum fee because X underestimated Y^*'s quantity demand for A by assuring that when X makes this error X will underestimate by the same percentage both Y^*'s quantity demand for B and the profits that the tie-in's supra-market-price price of B will bring X—*i.e.*, by assuring that, if X's lump-sum fee would be $\$\alpha$ too low if X's estimate of Y^*'s quantity demand for B were accurate, the tie-in's supra-market-price price on B will cost Y^* $\$\alpha$ more than X anticipated—roughly speaking, will yield X $\$\alpha$ more profits than X anticipated. Similarly, if this condition is fulfilled, B's supra-market-price tie-in price will provide X with the same protection against Y^*'s underestimating its quantity demand for A as would be provided by the supra-TSM-marginal-cost per-unit price X would charge Y^* for A under the most-profitable single-product mixed-pricing arrangement on A. In particular, under these conditions, the tie-in's supra-market-price price on B will provide X with this protection because any time that Y^* underestimates by $\$\beta$ the lump-sum fee Y^* can pay X for the right to purchase A at the per-unit price the most-profitable single-product mixed-pricing arrangement would set for A, Y^* will underestimate by $\$\beta$ the extra amount the tie-in's supra-market-price on B will cost Y^*. Once more, of course, to the extent that the error-linkage condition in question is not satisfied, the shift from the most-profitable single-product mixed-pricing arrangement on A to the tie-in question may increase the losses X sustains because X and/or Y^* underestimate Y^*'s quantity demand for A at its per-unit price under the most-profitable single-product mixed-pricing arrangement.

As I have already indicated, the shift from the most-profitable single-product mixed-pricing arrangement X could make when selling A to Y^* to the type of "full-line forcing" tie-in under consideration will always tend to impose costs on X by providing Y^* with an incentive to violate its contractual obligation to purchase its full requirements of B from X for a supra-market-price per-unit price and by making it necessary for X to think through, draft, explain, and negotiate a tie-in that is more complicated than the most-profitable single-product mixed-pricing arrangement. However, I have no doubt that in many situations, this type of tie-in will be more profitable than the most-profitable single-product mixed-pricing arrangement X could make (or than perfect price discrimination) even if, as I have been assuming so far, B is not a complement of A and the tie-in does not also increase X's profits by reducing the cost X must incur to control the quality of the complements of B Y^* combines with A or the loss X incurs because Y^* uses Bs whose use is against X's interest.

Perhaps it would be useful to complete this discussion by summarizing its implications for the determinants of the profitability to a seller X of shifting from the most-profitable single-product mixed-pricing arrangement it could make on its product A to the most-profitable tie-in it could execute that would require its customer Y^* not only to pay it a lump-sum fee and a (lower) per-unit price but also to agree to purchase from X its full requirements of some product B for more than B's normal market price. The preceding analysis implies that the profitability of such a shift will be

(1) directly related to the ratio of the TSM sales for X to make of B to Y^* to the TSM sales for X to make of A to Y^*,
(2) directly related to the ratio of the average absolute slope of $DD^{RC}_{XBY^*}$ between B's normal market price and its most-profitable per-unit price under the tie-in to the average absolute slope of DD_{XAY^*} between A's most-profitable per-unit price under the most-profitable single-product mixed-pricing arrangement X could make with Y^* and the per-unit price of B under the most-profitable full-requirements tie-in X could execute with Y^*,
(3) directly related to the ratio of the average slope of MC_{XAY^*} between the A prices in question and the average slope of MC_{XBY^*} between the B prices just delineated,
(4) directly related to the extent to which distributor demand-increasing expenditures related to A are "more important" than distributor demand-increasing expenditures on B (which may be directly related to the extent to which A is more differentiated than B) and inversely related to the ability of X to reduce related losses by subsidizing Y^*'s advertising budget or identifying the retailer-decisions of this kind that would be in the retailer's and its joint interest and either making those decisions itself or contractually obligating its retailers to do so,
(5) directly related to the certainty with which X and Y^* can estimate DD_{XAY^*} *ex ante*, inversely related to the extent to which X is less risk-averse than Y^* and X's transaction-risk in its dealings with any Y^* is lower than the Y^*'s transaction-risk, directly related to the extent to which any difference between the actual DD_{XAY^*} and the best weighted-average estimate of DD_{XAY^*} that could be made *ex ante* resembles the difference between the actual $DD^{RC}_{XBY^*}$ and the best weighted-average estimate that could be made *ex ante* of that curve, directly related to the extent to which any error X makes when estimating at the time of contracting Y^*'s quantity demand for A at relevant prices resembles the error X would make at that time when estimating Y^*'s quantity demand for B under the tie-in at relevant prices, and directly related to the extent to which

any error Y^* makes at the time of contracting when estimating its quantity demand for A at relevant prices resembles the error it would make at that time when estimating its quantity demand of B at relevant prices under the full-requirements tie-in,

(6) inversely related to the frequency with which the shift to the tie-in critically increases the profitability to Y^* of practicing arbitrage on A and directly related to X's ability to prevent Y^* from practicing such arbitrage cost-effectively,

(7) directly related to X's ability to prevent Y^* from violating its contractual obligation to purchase its full requirements of B from X for more than its normal market price,

(8) inversely related to the extra cost of researching, drafting, explaining, and negotiating the tie-in relative to the single-product mixed-pricing arrangement, and

(9) when B is a complement of A, directly related to X's need to control the quality of the Bs Y^* combines with A and inversely related to X's ability to control Y^*'s complement-choices in some other way.

(ii) Increasing the Profits That a Producer X of an Input A Against Which Substitution Is Possible Can Realize by Engaging in Supra-TSM-Marginal-Cost Per-Unit Pricing

Assume that Y is a producer of final-good D and that Y produces this product either (1) exclusively with inputs A and B, which can be substituted against each other, or (2) with inputs A and B, which can be substituted against each other, and input C, against which substitution is not possible—*i.e.*, assume in the latter case that the quantity of C that Y must use to produce any quantity of D cannot be varied but that the quantities of A and B that Y must use to product that quantity of D can be varied. Assume in addition that X is a producer of input A and that DD_{XAY} is downward-sloping. Assume finally that, if X were constrained to sell A to Y independently (*i.e.*, not to use a tie-in or reciprocity agreement) and not to use an endproduct-royalty scheme to sell A to Y, X would find it most profitable to charge Y a supra-marginal-cost price for A.

In the situation described, X's supra-marginal-cost pricing of A to Y would reduce X's sales of A to Y in two ways and concomitantly would reduce in the same two ways the profits X would realize by selling A to Y below the profits its production of A would enable it to earn if it were vertically-integrated forward into the production of D and the vertically-integrated X would be as privately proficient at producing A and D as the independent X and Y were: (1) by increasing MC_{YDZ} and thereby decreasing Y's profit-maximizing output of D and concomitantly the quantity of A that Y would buy from X even if A's higher price did not induce Y to substitute B for A (did not induce Y to produce the lower quantity of D it would produce with more units of B and fewer units of A than Y [or an ideally-vertically-integrated firm] would use for this purpose if the per-unit price of A to Y equaled its marginal cost to X) and (2) by inducing Y to substitute B for A (to produce its lower output of D with more units of B and fewer units of A than

Y [or an ideally-vertically-integrated firm] would find profitable to use for this purpose if A's price to Y equaled rather than exceeded its marginal cost to X).

Before proceeding, it might be useful for me to explain why, if inputs A and B can be substituted for each other in a production process used to produce D, any increase in the price of A will tend to induce the producer of D to substitute B for A. The key point is that, to minimize its cost of production, a producer that can use A and B in variable proportions to produce any quantity of D will have to vary the quantities of A and B it uses until the amount of extra D it produces with the last penny it spends on A equals the amount of extra D it produces with the last penny it spends on B. Thus, if Y is not a monopsonist of A and B so that MK_{AY} (the cost [kost] to Y of buying a marginal unit of A) equals P_{AY} (the per-unit price of A to Y) and $MK_{BY} = P_{BY}$ and if we let $MPP_{A/D}$ stand for the marginal physical product of A in terms of D and $MPP_{B/D}$ stand for the marginal physical product of B in terms of D, Y will minimize the cost it must incur to produce any quantity of D by varying its purchases of A and B until $MPP_{A/Y}/P_{AY} = MPP_{B/Y}/P_{BY}$. When the P_{AY} increases, $MPP_{A/Y}/P_{AY}$ (which equaled $MPP_{B/Y}/P_{BY}$ at the pre-price-increase prices of A and B) will fall below $MPP_{B/Y}/P_{BY}$ at the post-price-increase P_{AY} at the pre-price-increase A–B input-mix. To restore the relevant equality, Y will have to decrease its purchases of A (which will increase $MPP_{A/Y}$) and increase its purchases of B (which will decrease $MPP_{B/Y}$).

If Y produces D with inputs A and B, which can be substituted against each other, and input C against which no substitution is possible, X will be able to reduce the amount of transaction surplus it will destroy by removing a given amount of buyer surplus from Y by charging Y supra-marginal-cost prices by shifting from a pricing-technique in which it charges Y a supra-marginal-cost price for A alone to either of two tie-ins: (1) a tie-in in which X agrees to supply Y will all the A that Y wants to buy to produce D itself at a per-unit price equal to MC_{XAY} on condition that Y agree to purchase its full requirements of C from X at a per-unit price sufficiently above its normal market price for the loss Y sustains by doing so to equal the gains the shift to the tie-in confers on Y by reducing the per-unit price Y must pay for A below the per-unit price X would find most profitable to charge Y for A if X were constrained to sell A independently to Y and forbidden to charge Y either a lump-sum fee or a varying per-unit price for A or (2) a tie-in in which X agrees to supply Y with all the A that Y wants to buy to use to produce D itself at a lower but still supra-TSM-marginal-cost per-unit price than X would charge Y in a separate transaction on A on condition that Y agree to purchase from X its full requirements of B for a per-unit price that is the same proportion above the normal market price of B that A's price in the tie-in is above the marginal cost to X of supplying A to Y under the tie-in.

Neither of the above tie-ins will prevent X's supra-marginal-cost pricing to Y from destroying transaction surplus by increasing MC_{YDZ} and hence reducing Y's profit-maximizing output of D and concomitantly its purchases of A, but both will prevent X's supra-marginal-cost pricing to Y from destroying transaction surplus by inducing Y to produce the lower unit output of D it will produce with more units of B and fewer units of A than it would have used to produce that lower output if $P_{AY} = MC_{XAY}$ and

P_{BY} equaled its normal market price. The tie-in involving A and C will prevent X's supra-marginal-cost pricing to Y from engendering transaction-surplus-destroying substitutions because neither A nor any other input can be substituted against C. And the tie-in involving A and B will prevent X's supra-marginal-cost pricing to Y from inducing Y to make any transaction-surplus-destroying input-substitutions because this tie-in will not cause MK_{BY}/MK_{AY} to differ from MC_{AX}/MK_{BX} at Y's actual output of D.

Of course, for these types of tie-ins to be profitable, the gains they would confer on X by preventing transaction-cost-destroying substitutions against A (if Y fulfilled its obligation to purchase its full requirements of C or B from X at their tie-in per-unit prices) must exceed (1) the costs X sustains to prevent Y from violating this duty *plus* (2) any losses X sustains because it does not fully prevent Y's cheating *plus* (3) the extra cost of figuring out, drafting, explaining, and negotiating the tie-in *minus* (4) any benefits the tie-in confers on X by helping X control the quality of the complements Y combines with X's A.

Diagram VII is designed to illustrate the way in which a seller X of an input A against which substitution is possible can increase its profits by substituting for supra-TSM-marginal-cost per-unit pricing on A the A–B or A–C tie-in under discussion because that tie-in will reduce the (TS–) associated with a given (BS–) generated by supra-marginal-cost pricing by preventing that pricing from inducing the buyer from substituting B against A when producing its final product D. Diagram VII contains a DD_{YDZ} curve, a MR_{YDZ} curve, and four marginal cost curves—MC_1, MC_2, MC_3, and MC_4. (It also contains a $P^{RA}_{YDX} = MK^{RA}_{DX}$ curve, which will be used in the analysis of the ability of a seller of an input against which substitution is possible to employ reciprocity agreements to enable it to obtain the benefits of non-marginal-cost per-unit pricing without inducing its customer to make jointly-unprofitable substitutions against its input and two other bracketed curve labels—DD_{XDZ} and MR_{XDZ}—which will be used for the same purpose.)

To simplify the exposition, Diagram VII is constructed on the assumption that D is produced under constant returns to scale (*e.g.*, that one can double Y's output of D by doubling the amount of each of the inputs it uses to produce D). This assumption is useful because it implies both that (1) Y produces each unit of D that it does produce with the same combination of inputs—the combination that is cost-minimizing for Y, given the prices of A, B, and C—and (2) the various MC curves are horizontal. The various MC curves stand for two different kinds of marginal costs: first, and conventionally, the marginal costs Y must incur to produce each unit of D under a specific set of input-price assumptions and second, the sum of the "outside" payments Y and X must make to other parties (*e.g.*, to the producers of B and C if, as I will assume, X does not produce those inputs itself and to the factor suppliers whom X employs to produce A) to pay for the A, B and C that Y employs under stated input-price conditions to produce each unit of D. Thus, this "outside marginal cost curve" does not include the internal payments Y makes to X. More particularly, MC_4 presents the conventional marginal costs Y would have to incur to produce D without A; MC_1 indicates the conventional marginal cost at

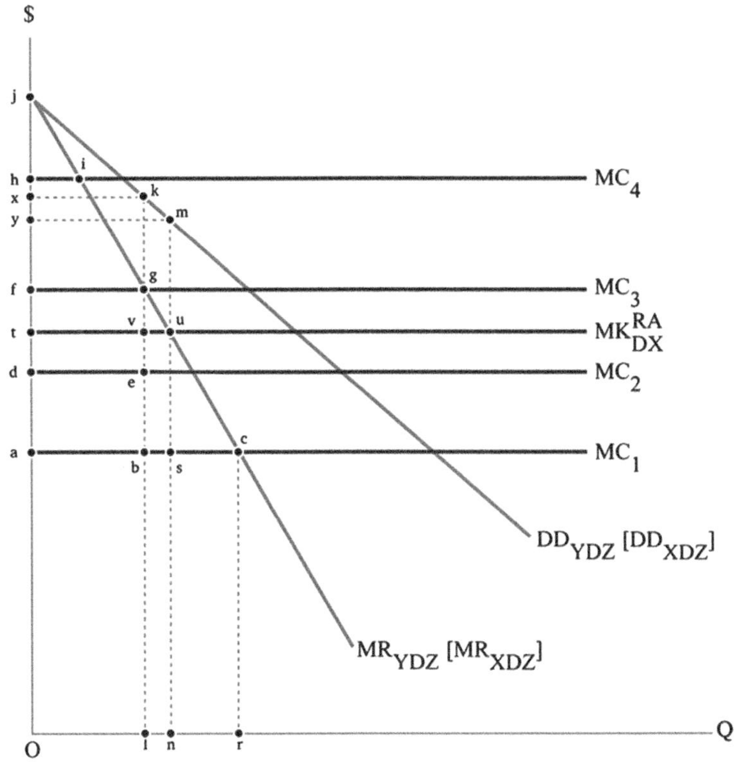

DIAGRAM VII

Diagram VII A Diagram That Illustrates the Ability of Both (1) an Input Tie-In That Shifts the Locus of Some/All of the Supra–TSM–MC Pricing of an Input Against Which Substitution Is Possible to a Complementary Input Against Which Substitution Is Possible/Is Not Possible and (2) an Input/Related-Final-Good Reciprocity Agreement That Exchanges Sub–TSM–MC Pricing of a Final Good for Supra–TSM–MC Pricing of a Related Input Against Which Substitution Is Possible to Increase Its Perpetrators' Profits by Preventing Non–TSM–MC Per-Unit Pricing From Destroying Transaction Surplus by Inducing Input-Substitutions

which Y could produce D if it could purchase A at its TSM marginal cost to X (which is not shown on Diagram VII) as well as the outside marginal costs Y and X would incur under these conditions—*i.e.*, the cost to X of supplying Y with the A that Y uses to produce one unit of D *plus* the cost to Y of the other inputs Y would combine with this TSM-priced A to produce a unit of D; MC_3 equals the conventional marginal cost Y would have to incur to produce one unit of D if X set the price of A at the supra-marginal-cost level that X would find profit-maximizing if X had to price A independently; and MC_2 equals the outside marginal costs Y and X would incur if X priced A in this way—*i.e.*, the cost to X of supplying Y with the A that Y would use to produce each unit of D if X priced A independently *plus* the cost to Y of the B and C that Y would combine with the A in question for this purpose. It is important to note that MC_2 exceeds MC_1 in Diagram VII. This construction reflects the fact that A's supra-marginal-cost price would induce Y to produce each unit of D with fewer units of A and more of B than Y would have employed had A's per-unit price equaled its TSM marginal cost. To see the significance for X of MC_2's exceeding MC_1, note that, since we are assuming that X will realize all the profits that it and Y make on their transaction, any effect that reduces these profits (by reducing the gap between X and Y's outside marginal costs and Y's total revenue) will concomitantly reduce X's returns by the same amount.

Having explained the various referents of our four MC curves, I can analyze how tie-ins might increase X's profits in such a situation. I will begin by analyzing the various ways in which X could price A by itself. MC_4 and MC_1 imply that, if one ignores Y's possible bargaining power, X could charge Y a sum equal to area hica *minus* the associated risk costs Y would have to bear for the right to purchase A at its TSM marginal cost to X (unshown in Diagram VII)—where area hica equals the difference between the profits Y would expect to make by producing D if Y could purchase A at such a per-unit price without paying a lump-sum fee (area jca) and the profits Y would expect to realize by producing D without A (area jih). However, I will assume that X will be able to profit by rejecting such pure-lump-sum pricing for a mixed-pricing approach that involves X's charging Y a lower lump-sum fee and a supra-TSM-marginal-cost per-unit price for A because the shift from the former to the latter arrangement would reduce the sum of X's and Y's risk costs, protect X against its and Y's possible underestimate of Y's quantity demand for A, and reduce the costs X will have to incur to prevent or allow Y from engaging in arbitrage on A. Thus, X might find that its optimal independent pricing arrangement on A would be to reduce its lump-sum fee to area higf *minus* Y's associated risk costs and raise A's per-unit price sufficiently above its TSM marginal cost to increase the marginal cost Y has to incur to produce D from MC_1 to MC_3. Of course, X could not expect to realize (SS+) equal to the (BS–) such a unit-price-increase would destroy (area fgca), for such an increase would simultaneously destroy some TS. In particular, such a price-increase would destroy (1) area gcb in transaction surplus by inducing Y to reduce its output of D from ac to ab and (2) area deba in transaction surplus by inducing Y to substitute B for A and thereby raising X and Y's outside marginal costs from MC_1 to MC_2 (because this behavior increased Y's payments for the necessary B by more than it reduced X's "payments" for the necessary A). Thus, (SS+)/(BS–) for the increase in A's per-unit price would be only (area fged)/(area fgca) in the situation described. As I have suggested, tie-ins can improve this result by preventing Y from substituting B for A—*i.e.*, by reducing the outside payments X and Y make when Y produces D. Thus, X can eliminate area fgca in BS without raising its and Y's outside marginal cost curve above MC_1 by inducing Y to substitute B for A if X reduces the price of A to its TSM marginal cost on condition that Y purchase its full requirements of C for sufficiently more than its normal market price to reduce Y's buyer surplus by the same amount that X's foregone supra-marginal-cost pricing on A would have done (which would also have increased the marginal cost of D to Y to MC_3). As we have seen, X can produce the same result by agreeing to reduce the price of A toward, though not to, its TSM marginal cost on condition that Y agree to purchase its full requirements of B through X for a price that is the same percentage above B's normal market price that A's price under the tie-in is above to its marginal cost to X. In practice, when an input like C is available, X's choice between tying B or C will depend on (1) the extra costs X will have to incur to prevent or allow arbitrage on A under the C as opposed to the B tie-in and (2) the relative costs X must incur to prevent Y from cheating on its agreement to purchase its full requirements of B or C respectively—*e.g.*, on X's relative ability to alter the B and C it supplies to facilitate their identification.

In any case, it should now be clear that in appropriate circumstances producers of substitutable inputs may be able to increase the profitability of their supra-marginal-cost per-unit pricing of those inputs by tying the sale of these inputs to their partial substitutes or to related inputs against which substitution is not possible. In fact, sellers that can employ tie-ins in this way probably will find it profitable to reduce their lump-sum fees and increase the amount of BS they remove with their supra-marginal-cost per-unit prices.

Of course, X could increase the profitability of its supra-TSM-marginal-cost per-unit pricing in other ways. For example, X could also remove area fgca in BS without inducing Y to make any TS-destroying substitutions of B for A by conditioning its sale of A to Y at its TSM marginal cost on Y's agreeing to pay X an endproduct royalty of fa on each unit of D that Y sold. Such an endproduct-royalty scheme will be preferable to a tie-in whenever it is easier for X to determine whether Y has accurately reported its sales of D than to enforce a full-requirements contract on B or C. In practice, tie-ins will tend to be cheaper to enforce than endproduct-royalty schemes when X cannot estimate Y's production or unit sales of D from Y's purchases of A, when X cannot easily determine the price for which Y sells D, and when X can reduce the loss it sustains because of Y's ability to violate its obligation to purchase its full requirements of B or C from X by altering the B and C it supplies Y to facilitate their identification.

(G) Increasing the Profits That a Seller Can Realize by Predatorily Deterring Tied-Product-Market Entry

Sections 9A(1)(B) and 9A(1)(C) of Chap. 11 established three conclusions that are relevant in the current context. First, those sections explained various reasons why the activity of producing and supplying one or more complements of a particular product (or conceivably a non-complement) to that product's customers could reduce the (Π_D + R) barriers to entry that would confront the complement supplier in relation to its entering into the basic-product business. More specifically, Sect. 9A(1)(B) pointed out that producing a complement to a basic product and supplying it or attempting to sell it to a customer of the basic product could reduce the (Π_D + R) barriers the complement-producer faced in relation to its entry into basic-product production and sale by enabling the independent complement-producer

(1) to make profits by producing the complement that it could then use to finance its entry into the basic-product business,
(2) to discover things about the basic product or its production that would enable it to be a more-cost-effective producer of a variant of the basic product,
(3) to learn the names and addresses of the basic product's buyers,
(4) to discover facts about those buyers' needs or responsiveness to certain types of sales-pitches that would improve respectively its prospective "objective" competitive position in relation to those buyers or its ability to make sales to them, or
(5) to obtain the trust of the relevant buyers or induce them to place a positive value on giving it sales or profits.

(Items (2) and (3) in this list would not be relevant when the second good was a non-complement of the first, and item (4) would be less relevant in that case.)

The preceding analyses of this section imply that sellers of complements to a product may also find it more profitable to operate in the basic-product business than they would if they did not produce the complement because in a variety of situations for a variety of reasons it may be more profitable to tie the sale of the basic product to the sale of a complement and there may be some advantage to producing the relevant complement oneself rather than buying it from a third party. (This last possibility may also be less likely to be salient when the second good is not a complement of the first.)

Second, Sect. 9A(1)(B) of Chap. 11 also explained that a firm might be able to deter a potential entrant into the basic-product business from reducing the barriers it faced in relation to entering that business by entering the complement business by producing a basic product that physically incorporated the complement, by changing the basic product in some way that affected the attributes that complements must have to be suitable or even compatible, by making such changes and not informing independent complement-producers of their existence or character, or by contractually prohibiting buyers of the basic product from purchasing complements from specific independent complement-producers or categories of possible independent complement-producers that were likely to or seemed more likely to enter the basic-product business. In addition, Chap. 11 pointed out the possibility that is relevant in the current context—*viz.*, that basic-product producers might also be able to deter potential basic-product rivals from entering into the complement business by requiring buyers of the basic product to purchase their full requirements of relevant complements from it or a designated third party.

Third, Sect. 9A(1)(B) of Chap. 11 explained that although in many if not most cases the profitability of those basic-product-producer decisions that have the effect of deterring others from producing complements will not be critically affected by any tendency they may have to deter the latter firms from entering the basic-product market (because such decisions usually generate profits in a number of perfectly-legitimate ways), in the rare instances in which the relevant basic-product producer believed *ex ante* that its choice's profitability was critically affected by its tendency to deter entry into the basic-product business, its choice would be predatory and Sherman-Act-violative unless it could be justified by claiming that the basic-product producer was entitled to make such choices to preserve its incentive to create the basic product or to protect its customer list or relevant information about its product or the production process through which its product could be most-cost-effectively produced.

I have included this discussion here not just because basic-product-producers might use full-requirements tie-ins to engage in predation, a possibility whose empirical importance I doubt, but because there is a substantial economics literature written by deservedly-highly-respected scholars that focuses on this possibility.[1177]

The reason that I think that this possibility is empirically unimportant is that, in my judgment, in virtually all situations in which basic-product producers can use tie-ins to achieve this result, either

(1) it will be more-cost-effective to use some other means such as predatory price-cuts on the complement to deter the potential basic-product-business entrant from entering the complement-production-and-distribution business or
(2) the reason why the tie-in will be a more-cost-effective method to deter the potential entrant into the basic-product business from entering the complement business (*viz.*, either because [A] a full-requirements tie-in in which the tied complement's per-unit price is higher than it would be if the complement were priced independently and predatorily and the basic product's per-unit price is lower than it would be in an independent sale will prevent the seller's pricing from destroying transaction surplus by inducing the buyer to combine the complement and basic product in proportions that are not in their joint interest—*i.e.*, to make jointly-unprofitable substitutions of the complement for the basic product, regardless of whether the two products are inputs—or because [B] the full-requirements tie-in will enable the seller better to control the quality of the complement the buyer combines with the seller's basic product) will usually result in the tie-in's being profitable on that account or those accounts alone—*i.e.*, because in the vast majority of situations in which the tie-in is the more profitable way to prevent a basic-product-business potential entrant from improving its position as a basic-product-business potential entrant by operating in the complement-production-and-distribution business,

[1177] See, *e.g.*, Dennis W. Carlton and Michael Waldman, *The Strategic Use of Tying to Preserve and Create Market Power in Evolving Industries*, 33 RAND. J. OF ECON. 194 (2002); Jay Pil Choi and Christodoulos Stefanadis, *Tying, Investment, and the Dynamic Leverage Theory*, 32 RAND J. OF ECON. 52 (2001); Michael D. Whinston, *Tying, Foreclosure, and Exclusion*, 80 AM. ECON. REV. 837 (1990); Joseph Farrell and Garth Saloner, *Installed Base and Compatibility: Innovation, Product Preannouncements, and Predation*, 76 AM. ECON. REV. 940 (1986); and Janusz A. Ordover, Alan O. Sykes, and Robert D. Willig, *Nonprice Anticompetitive Behavior by Dominant Firms Toward the Producers of Complementary Products*, in ANTITRUST AND REGULATION: ESSAYS IN MEMORY OF JOHN J. MCGOWAN 115 (Franklin M. Fisher, ed.) (MIT Press, 1985). This literature fails to mention some of the ways in which I argued a firm's operating in the complement-production-and-distribution business will lower the barriers to its entering the basic-product production-and-distribution business, but it does point out (as I did not) that efforts to deter complement-business entry may be particularly successful in the presence of certain complement-related network effects.

the tie-in will not be predatory because its *ex ante* seller-perceived profitability will not depend on the seller's *ex ante* belief that it will or might deter basic-product-business entry.

Admittedly, however, the preceding discussion leaves open the possibility that full-requirements tie-ins of this type might be illegal under Section 3 of the Clayton Act or Articles 101 or 102 of the 2009 Treaty of Lisbon because they lessen competition if the Sherman-Act-licit functions they perform do not provide a basis for an applicable efficiency defense.

I want to close by making three points about the legal significance of the fact that sellers may use tie-ins to execute this type of predation. First, the fact that a particular tie-in has been used to execute predation of this kind does not affect its legality under the type of specific-anticompetitive-intent test I claim the U.S. Sherman Act promulgates: the predation in question would violate that test regardless of whether tie-ins were involved. Second, the fact that some tie-ins fall into this functional category would not justify a conclusion that tie-ins should be deemed *per se* illegal (because both the percentage of tie-ins that violate the antitrust laws for this and other [concealing] reasons and the cost of determining that particular tie-ins are performing lawful functions are too low for such a conclusion to be justified). Third, the fact that some predation is executed through the use of tie-ins (if true) would have some legal significance if the legal regime in question does cover contracts (including tie-ins) but not non-contractual single-firm predation or non-contractual predation by firms that are neither individually dominant nor part of a set of collectively-dominant rivals (see E.C./E.U. competition law) or if the legal regime in question has a statute that prohibits at least some predatory tie-ins but not predation effectuated in other ways and that statute has different penalties/remedies and/or private-suit provisions from those included in its other (say, anticompetitive-intent) statutes that prohibit predation (see the U.S. Clayton Act and its relation to the U.S. Sherman Act).

(2) Reciprocity Agreements

Reciprocal-trading agreements (reciprocity) are agreements (is the practice) in which the seller (buyer) of one good conditions its agreement to supply (purchase) that good on its trading partner's agreeing to supply it (to purchase from it) a second good. Although the literature normally assumes that reciprocity is instigated by firms operating in their capacities as buyers, as we shall see and as the preceding sentence indicates, reciprocity can also emanate from its instigator's position as a seller. Like tying agreements, reciprocity agreements can include quantity terms that specify the number of units of one or both parties' product(s) that that party (each party) will provide the other, that require one party or both parties to purchase its or their full requirements of the product(s) in question from the other party, that specify the relationship between the quantity of the good A that one party X purchases from the other party Y and the quantity of the good B that Y must supply

X, or that require one or both parties to supply the other with its or their total output of the product it obligates it or them to supply the other party. Reciprocal-trading agreements can specify separate prices for the products they involve, can specify the difference between the prices of the products they involve, or can create a pure barter arrangement.

Reciprocal-trading agreements can perform "the same" functions that tie-ins can perform where the expression "the same" is enquoted because in some instances it would be more accurate to say that the relevant function that a reciprocity agreement can perform is *analogous to* one of the functions that tie-ins can perform. However, as we shall see, the probability that the conditions that would have to be satisfied for reciprocity to be able to perform some of the functions the practice can perform will be satisfied may be significantly lower than the probability that the conditions that will have to be fulfilled for tie-ins to be able to perform identical or analogous functions will be fulfilled.

(A) Reducing the Costs That a Firm Y Must Incur to Prevent Its Supplier X of Product D from Using Inferior Ingredients (Inputs) A to Produce the D Y Will Purchase from X

Obviously, buyers (Y) will be interested in preventing their suppliers (X) from using inputs (*e.g.*, ingredients) A of lower-than-expected or contracted-for quality to produce the products the buyers are purchasing from them. In some situations, a buyer will find it most profitable to deter such conduct by specifying the quality of the relevant inputs in its contract of purchase and inspecting either the inputs as they are used or the final products. However, in many instances, this approach will be problematic: it may be difficult to specify the attributes that make an input satisfactory, to assess the quality of the inputs being used, or to assess the quality of the product that has been supplied at or shortly after the date of delivery (*e.g.*, when low-quality inputs affect durability or future performance). For these reasons, a buyer Y will sometimes find it more profitable to prevent its supplier X from using inferior inputs A to produce the good D that X will supply it by requiring X to purchase from Y its full requirements of a suitable variant of A at its normal market price (or at least to purchase from Y its full requirements of a suitable variant of A for use to produce the D it will supply to Y). For reciprocity to perform this function, Y need not produce the A in question itself: it can purchase it for delivery to X from a third party in whose product-quality Y has confidence. (Y will have an incentive to require X to purchase its full requirements of A [as contrasted with all the A X will use to produce D for Y] from Y or a trusted third party to the extent that Y would find it difficult to alter the A it supplied X or arranged to have a third party supply X in a way that would make it readily identifiable and feared that X might use the A Y supplied X or arranged to have supplied to X to produce products for other buyers and substitute lower-quality inputs when producing D for Y.) The associated reciprocity agreement (in which Y conditions its obligation to purchase D from X on X's purchasing from Y or a designated third party the A X will use to make the D X supplies Y or perhaps all the A X buys) will be more profitable (1) the greater the ability of Y to produce suitable A itself at the same cost that independents could produce it or to determine the quality of the A Y purchases from a third party to supply X, (2) the greater the ability of Y or the third party from which Y buys the A it will supply X to render the A it supplies X readily identifiable, (3) the greater the cost to X of reselling the A it is supplied by Y and substituting cheaper inputs for that A, (4) the smaller the ability of X to profit by cheating Y by substituting lower-quality inputs for the A with which Y supplies X when producing D for X and using X's higher-quality A to supply others, and (5) the smaller the loss to X of using the higher-quality A Y requires X to use in all its production activities when X imposes such an obligation on X. I suspect that, in many situations, a buyer Y will find a reciprocity agreement in which it agrees to purchase a specified quantity or its full requirements of some product D from a producer X (or X's total output of D) on condition that X agree to purchase a relevant specified quantity or its full requirements of A from Y at its normal market price the most-cost-effective and profitable response to X's possible incentive to use inferior inputs to produce the D X will supply Y despite the fact that the substitution in question is against X's and Y's joint interest.

(B) Reducing the Cost That a Seller X of an Input A Must Incur to Prevent Its Customer Y—a Producer of D—from Engaging in Arbitrage on A

As we have seen, conventional price discrimination, perfect price discrimination, and mixed lump-sum/supra-TSM-marginal-cost-per-unit pricing strategies all create a risk that the buyers to which the relevant prices are being charged will resell at a lower price some of the units they purchase to buyers the relevant seller could otherwise profitably supply at a higher price. When the relevant product is an input A that the relevant buyer Y uses to produce a final product D, the seller X may be able to reduce the sum of the costs it must incur to prevent Y from engaging in arbitrage on X's product (input A) and the losses it sustains because Y does engage in arbitrage on A by entering into a reciprocity agreement in which X agrees to supply Y with Y's full requirements of A on specified price terms on condition that Y agrees (1) not to engage in arbitrage on A and (2) to supply X at the price Y would otherwise be able to obtain for D either with the quantity of D Y would produce with the A X supplied if Y used all that A in its own business or, if X found it difficult to predict the latter quantity, with Y's total output of D. If X can predict the amount of D Y would produce if Y used all the A Y purchased from X to produce D, such a reciprocity agreement will enable X to prevent Y from engaging in arbitrage on A (by facilitating X's discovery of Y's engaging in such arbitrage to the extent that it would be difficult for X to verify Y's production or sales reports). I suspect that, in many situations, the cost to X of using reciprocity for this purpose—the difference between X's proficiency at distributing D and the proficiency of the distributor that Y would otherwise have chosen to market D or the sum of (1) the difference between the cost X would have to incur to pick a third-party distributor of Y's D and the cost Y would have had to incur to pick such a distributor (zero if Y would otherwise have distributed D itself) and (2) the difference between that third party's proficiency at distributing D and the proficiency of the distributor Y would have chosen to distribute D (which may have been Y)—will be lower than the sum of the costs X would have to incur to verify Y's production and sales reports and the losses X would sustain because its efforts to prevent Y's arbitrage by checking Y's sales would be less successful at preventing arbitrage than the relevant reciprocity agreement would be.

(C) Concealing, Reducing the Apparent Extent of, and/or Changing the Apparent Locus of a Seller's Price Discrimination, Predatory or Illegally-Retaliatory Pricing, Maximum-or-Minimum-Price-Regulation Violations, and/or Tax or Contract Frauds

Section 2C(1)(C) explained when and how tie-ins can perform the functions delineated in the immediately-preceding heading. In some circumstances, reciprocal trading agreements can also perform the functions in question. For example, if two firms that purchase goods from each other want to discriminate in each other's favor by the same amount on their respective products, to charge each other predatorily-low prices that may not be discriminatory but are each equally below their respective lowest-legitimate price, or to violate in each other's favor by the same amount minimum-price regulations that apply to their respective products, they can practice such discrimination, retaliation, or predation or commit such price-regulation violations without charging openly discriminatory, retaliatory, predatory, or regulatorily-prohibited prices by agreeing to sell each other the products in question at their normal prices. Thus, if X wishes to sell Y one unit of A for 2 cents less than its normal, lowest-legitimate, or regulated-minimum price of 20 cents (because Y would not buy X's A for more than 18 cents) while Y wishes to sell X one unit of B for 2 cents less than its normal, lowest-legitimate, or regulated-minimum price of 8 cents (because X would not be willing to pay more than 6 cents for B in an independent sale), they can produce the same result without openly discriminating, openly charging a retaliatory or predatory price, or openly violating the relevant price regulations by entering into a contract in which X agrees to buy a unit of B from Y for its normal, lowest-legitimate, or regulated-minimum price of 8 cents on condition that Y agrees to purchase from X a unit of A for its normal, lowest-legitimate, or regulated-minimum price of 20 cents—*i.e.*, by entering into a contract in which X continues to receive 12 cents net plus B in exchange for A. Clearly, this analysis also applies when each of two sellers wants to violate a maximum-price regulation when supplying the other or discriminate against the other by the same amounts on the products they are supplying each other. Indeed, even when the offsets are not perfect, firms may find it advantageous to use appropriate reciprocity agreements to reduce the apparent extent or to shift the apparent locus of their violations or suspect behavior.

In a very similar way, reciprocity also may enable sellers to conceal their tax and contract fraud by shifting the locus of their apparent profits to goods on which they must pay lower tax-rates or royalty-rates. Thus, if (1) X manufactures A (which it sells to Y) but also resells B (which it buys from Y) and (2) X must pay a percentage royalty on the profits it makes on (or dollar sales it makes of) A but none on the profits it realizes on or sales it makes of B, X may be able to increase its returns by agreeing to sell A to Y for less than it otherwise would charge on condition that Y offer X a similar price-cut on B.

(D) Reducing the Market-Research, Personnel-Training, and Checkout-Counter-Delay Costs of Conventional Price Discrimination

Section 2C(1)(D) explains when and how tie-ins can perform the functions delineated in the immediately-preceding heading. In theory, reciprocity can perform these functions as well. For reciprocity to be able to yield profits by performing these functions, (1) the same firm X that is in a position to discriminate as a seller of A to Y1...N must also be in a position to discriminate when buying B from Y1...N, (2) those Ys that place a higher-than-average value on A must have a higher-than-average supply cost on B, (3) diseconomies of scale or capacity constraints affecting the Ys must make it profitable for X to purchase B from both high-cost and low-cost suppliers, and (4) X must realize that its high-demand (low-demand) buyers of A are high-cost (low-cost) suppliers of B without being able to place any given Y in the high or low category (short of incurring significant expenses). It is just conceivable that these conditions might be fulfilled—*e.g.*, when A is an input whose value tends to rise with managerial or labor-force inadequacies that will also cause the relevant firm to have higher-than-average costs when producing B. I would be very surprised, however, if any significant number of reciprocity agreements could be accounted for in these terms. Although the relevant correlation between demand and supply prices also might be caused by differences in the technologies that various Ys use, X probably would be sufficiently aware of differences it its customers' technologies to obviate its using reciprocity agreements to reduce the relevant costs of discrimination in such circumstances.

(E) Increasing the Profitability of Meter Pricing

Section 2C(1)(E) reviewed why a seller of a durable machine, the franchisor of one or more distributive franchises, or the seller of some other type of product or production-process idea might find it profitable to substitute for the outright sale of the machine, franchise, or right to use the idea for a lump-sum fee a pricing arrangement in which the buyer paid a combination of (1) a lower lump-sum fee than the buyer would have been willing to pay if that were the only payment it had to make and (2) a per-use charge for using the machine or franchise, product, or production-process idea by selling units of the good and/or service it involved.

Section 2C(1)(E) also explained many of the forms that the latter type of mixed lump-sum fee *plus* supra-marginal-cost per-unit-price pricing-technique could take—*viz.*, that the seller could execute this technique (1) by examining the buyer's books to determine how often it used the machine or idea or how many sales it made through the franchise and basing the total per-use charge on the use-figures obtained, (2) by attaching a meter to the machine and charging a meter rate, or (3) by requiring the buyer to pay it an endproduct royalty on each unit of the final product it used the seller's machine to produce or a royalty on the sales or profits it made through the franchise the seller granted it or by using the other sort of idea the seller permitted it to use. Finally, Sect. 2C(1)(E) explained why in some circumstances sellers will find it most profitable to use tie-ins to execute meter pricing—in particular, a tie-in under which the buyer would be required to purchase from the seller for more than its normal market price a product the buyer used each time it made use of the seller's machine, franchise idea, or other product or production-process idea.

In some circumstances, sellers may also find it profitable to use reciprocity agreements to execute a meter-pricing strategy for a durable machine, franchise idea, product or production-process idea, or loan of capital. Under this arrangement, the seller X would reduce its lump-sum fee in exchange for the buyer Y's agreeing to supply X with the buyer's total output of the good it used the product idea, machine, or capital to produce for some per-unit price below the per-unit price for which Y could have sold the good in question (D). If X's product were a machine and Y used that machine once to produce each unit of its product D, the meter rate would equal the difference between the price the reciprocity agreement would obligate Y to charge X for D and the price for which Y would otherwise sell D. Although the substitution of this arrangement for the pure-lump-sum pricing of the machine, franchise idea, product idea, production-process idea, or capital in question will reduce the joint gains of the seller and buyer in question by making it profitable for the original buyer Y to reduce the output of the final product D it uses the machine (idea or capital) to produce below the level that would be in its and the original seller's joint interest (just as a meter fee will destroy transaction surplus by raising the buyer's marginal costs and thereby making it profitable for the buyer to reduce its output below the level that would be in its and its supplier's joint interest), the related losses may be lower than the benefits the shift from pure-lump-sum pricing to this type of reciprocity agreement will confer on X by reducing the costs X incurs (1) because even if X's and Y's weighted-average-expected estimate of the frequency with which the buyer will use the machine, franchise idea, product idea, production-process idea, or capital in question are accurate, they are not certain about that frequency, (2) because X and/or Y may underestimate the frequency with which Y will use the machine or the sales it will make of the product it uses the product idea or capital to produce, and (3) because Y may engage in arbitrage by using X's machine to produce the product of one or more other firms. Moreover, in some situations, X may find it more profitable to use this type of reciprocity agreement rather than a tie-in or endproduct-royalty scheme to execute a meter-pricing arrangement. In some cases in which X's product is a durable machine, no suitable complementary input may be available, meters may be impractical (think of riveting machines), or the cost of preventing tampering and/or reading the meter may be prohibitive. And when the agreement requires Y to supply X with its total output of D, it may be cheaper for X to determine whether Y has broken its promise to supply X with Y's full output of D than to determine whether Y has broken its endproduct-royalty promise by misreporting its unit output or sales or has violated its tie-in promise to purchase its full requirements of the tied product B from X.

(F) Increasing the Cost-Effectiveness of a Firm's Non-MC Per-Unit Price-Charging and Price-Paying by Increasing the Per-Unit Price It Pays and Decreasing the Per-Unit Price It Charges a Trading Partner to Decrease the Amount of Transaction Surplus Its Non-MC Per-Unit Pricing Destroys Both Directly and by Distorting Its and/or Its Trading Partner's Demand-Increasing-Expenditure Incentives From Their Joint Perspective

Sections 2C(1)(F)(i) and (ii) explained when and how tie-ins can increase their employers' profits in the way the immediately-preceding heading indicates respectively (1) when the seller's tying product A is a final good and the tied product B is another final good and (2) when the seller's product A is an input against which substitution is possible and the tied product is either another input B that can be substituted against A that is used by the buyer Y to produce its final product D or another input C against which substitutions is not possible that is, once more, used by the buyer Y to produce its final product D. Sections 2C(2)(F)(i) and (ii) will explain when and how reciprocity agreements can perform this "function" respectively when A is a final good and when A is an input against which substitution is possible that the buyer Y uses to produce a final product D.

(i) When A Is a Final Product

This section explains the circumstances in which and the reasons why a seller X of a final product A will be able to use a reciprocity agreement to increase its profits in the above way—a reciprocity agreement in which X agrees to lower the per-unit price Y must pay for X's final product A below the per-unit price X would find most profitable to charge Y for A if constrained to price A independently in exchange for Y's agreeing to supply X with its full requirements (for its own use—typically for distribution) of some other product B (which Y need not even produce itself) for less than B's normal market price.

Diagram VI can be used to illustrate the relevant analysis. For this purpose, three of its curves (the curves in the right portion of the diagram that relate to product B) must be redefined (and hence relabeled) and one additional line (the dashed line TR) must be defined and explained.

Thus, since in the reciprocity analysis X sells A to Y on specified terms on condition that Y supply X with X's full requirements of B on specified terms—

i.e., since in the reciprocity analysis X is the buyer rather than the seller of B and Y is the supplier rather than the buyer of B, (1) the curve that includes point U that was DD_{YBZ} in the tie-in analysis is DD_{XBZ} in the reciprocity analysis, (2) the curve that includes points A and B that was MC_{XBY} in the tie-in analysis is MC_{YBX} in the reciprocity analysis, and (3) the curve that was $DD^{RC}_{XBY} = MR_{YBZ}$ (where the equality reflected a simplifying assumption that there were no non-cost-of-goods-sold costs of distributing B) in the tie-in analysis is $DD^{RC}_{YBX} = MR_{XBZ}$ (where the equality reflects the same simplifying assumption) in the reciprocity analysis. The relevant definition-changes are indicated in Diagram VI in brackets to the right of the labels defining the curves in question in the way in which they were defined in the tie-in analysis. I should point out that both DD_{XBZ} and $DD^{RC}_{YBX} = MR_{XBZ}$ are defined on the assumption that X will buy B only to retail it itself—will not engage in arbitrage by reselling B to others for retail distribution. (The assumption that B is a final good that X will retail and not an input that X will use to produce some other product is made for expositional reasons.)

The additional line in Diagram VI to which the reciprocity analysis will make reference (line TR) is the counterpart to line CD in the tie-in analysis. In the tie-in analysis, DB was constructed to equal the amount by which the price Y would be required to pay X for product B by the relevant full-requirements tie-in would have to exceed B's normal market price for the (BS–) generated by that price-increase (area DCBA) to equal the (BS+) generated by the associated decrease in A's price under the tie-in from JO to GO (area JKIG). For the purpose of the reciprocity analysis, BR is constructed to equal the amount by which the per-unit price that Y was charging X for X's full requirements of B under the reciprocity agreement would have to fall below the normal market per-unit price for B for the (SS–) generated by that price-cut for Y to equal the (BS+) generated for Y by the associated decrease in A's price under the reciprocity agreement from OJ to OG. (Since DD^{RC}_{XBY} in the tie-in analysis is vertical between points D and B and DD^{RC}_{YBX} in the reciprocity analysis is vertical between points B and R, DB = BR in Diagram VI.)

This section makes two claims. First, it argues that, in appropriate circumstances, X will be able to increase the profits it can make by selling A to Y by shifting from the most-profitable pricing-technique X could use to supply A independently to Y (charging Y a lump-sum fee of LMKJ for the right to purchase its full requirements of A for a per-unit price of JO [where area NML equals the sum of the risk costs Y would bear under this arrangement and any buyer surplus Y is able to extract on the deal]) to a reciprocity agreement in which X agrees to supply Y with Y's full requirements of A at the lower per-unit price of GO on condition that Y agree to supply X with X's full requirements of B for distribution itself (or for resale to other specified distributors for their distribution) for a per-unit price of RS (BR below B's normal price) and to pay X a lump-sum fee equal to LMKJ *minus* any additional risk costs Y must bear under the reciprocity agreement or *plus* any risk-cost savings the reciprocity agreement enables Y to experience where, by construction, the (SS–) Y's supply-obligation imposes on Y (area ABRT) equals the (BS+) the price-cut on

A confers on Y (area JKIG). Second, it argues that, in some circumstances, the reciprocity agreement just described will be more profitable for X than any full-requirements tie-in it could employ for the same purposes.

For the reciprocity agreement to be more profitable than the most-profitable pricing arrangement X could make on A if X were required to price A independently, (1) the amount of transaction surplus that the associated per-unit price-decrease on A generates by increasing Y's purchases of A must exceed the amount of transaction surplus the associated per-unit price-decrease on B destroys by inducing X to purchase more B than is in X's and Y's joint interest and (2) the net transaction-surplus savings the reciprocity agreement generates in the above way must exceed the amount by which the shift from the most-profitable pricing scheme that X could use if constrained to price A independently to the reciprocity agreement reduces X's profits by increasing the sum of the risk costs X and Y bear because they are not certain about Y's quantity demand for A at various relevant prices, by increasing the losses X sustains because of its own and Y's underestimation of Y's quantity demand for A at various relevant prices, by increasing the arbitrage-prevention costs and actual-arbitrage-generated losses X incurs because Y has an incentive to engage in arbitrage on A, by increasing the cost to X of the incentives the reciprocity agreement gives X to engage in arbitrage on B (to purchase B not to retail it itself but to sell it to others who will sell it at retail)—an incentive that will be costly to X because X will have to reduce its lump-sum fee to compensate Y for the certainty-equivalent costs the possibility of X's engaging in such arbitrage imposes on Y, and by imposing costs or losses on X by necessitating Y's supplying X with B (an extra step in the distribution process when Y does not produce B itself) and X's reselling B when X is less proficient at doing so than the retailer that would otherwise have distributed that product would have been.

I have no doubt that in a considerable number of situations X will be able to find a product B with which Y could supply it that X could resell for which the (BS+)/(SS–) ratio along DD^{RC}_{YBX} for a relevant unit-price price-cut on B below B's prevailing market price will be higher than the (BS+)/(SS–) ratio along DD_{XAY} for a relevant unit-price price-cut on A below the per-unit price X would find most profitable to charge Y for A if constrained to sell A to Y independently (where the [SS–] in the first ratio [which is experienced by Y] equals the [BS+] in the second ratio [which will also be experienced by Y] because I am assuming for simplicity that any change the shift to reciprocity generates in the risk costs Y bears is offset by an equal change in the lump-sum fee Y must pay X and that the shift to reciprocity does not induce X to change the amount of non-marginal-cost pricing it practices in relation to Y). In Diagram VI, the combination of (1) the construction of DD_{XBZ} to be kinked at price US (the assumption that X would resell B in a tight oligopoly) and the related construction of DD^{RC}_{YBX} to be vertical between points B and R (to be discontinuous over the relevant range at output OS) and (2) the construction of DD_{YAZ} and MR_{YAZ} to be continuously downward-sloping over the relevant range guarantees that the first condition will be satisfied by guaranteeing that the (BS+)/(SS–) ratio for the price-cut on B will equal 1 (that the price-cut on B will not destroy any transaction surplus by causing X to increase the number of units of B it purchases) while the (BS+)/(SS–) ratio for the price-cut on A will be greater than 1 (that the price-cut will increase transaction surplus [by area KIF] by inducing Y to increase the number of units of A it purchases). More importantly, as I indicated when discussing the ability of tie-ins to increase their employer's profits in this way, the satisfaction of this first condition does not depend on the DD_{XBZ}'s being a kinky oligopoly demand curve: this condition will be satisfied when

(1) the TSM output of B exceeds the TSM output of A, the slope of DD^{RC}_{YBX} is higher than the slope of DD_{XAY} over their relevant ranges, and the absolute slope of MC_{YBX} is lower than the absolute slope of MC_{XAY} over their relevant ranges,
(2) one or two of these relationships obtains when there is no relevant difference between the members of the other parameter-pairs, or
(3) the actual combination of differences between these pairs of parameters produces this effect even when the sign of one or two of the differences in question does not favor this condition's satisfaction.

I will concretize the preceding analysis by developing an example that is related to the one I used to illustrate the tie-in analysis. Assume that X is a producer of highly-valued (designer) suits (product A) that distributes its product both from its own retail outlets in some towns and through independent distributors Y, that some of the Ys in question are the only haberdashers in the towns in which they operate that sell designer suits, that the retail outlets that X (and Y) operate sell not only suits but also good-quality but more-standardized shirts and ties (products B), and that in some of the towns in which X operates not only it but also the town's high-quality department store sells such shirts and ties. In such a case, DD_{XAY} might be continuously downward-sloping (as in Diagram VI) while DD_{XBZ} was kinked at the prevailing market price for B (and DD^{RC}_{YBX} was, derivatively, vertical at the output at which DD_{XBZ} was kinked). In such a case, X might be able to increase its profits by reducing the amount of transaction surplus that a relevant amount of non-marginal-cost pricing destroys directly by altering unit-purchase decisions by substituting for the best pricing-deal it could arrange when selling A independently a reciprocity agreement in which X reduced the per-unit price of its suits (product A) to Y from JO to GO in exchange for Y's agreeing to supply X with X's full requirements in one or more specified outlets of shirts and ties (product B). At least, such an arrangement would be more profitable for X than the independent pricing of A if the transaction-surplus savings in question exceeded the losses the relevant shift would impose on X for other reasons.

I will now examine the factors that will determine the extent of the losses that the relevant shift from the independent pricing of A to reciprocity will impose on X. First, the shift in question will impose costs on X by increasing the sum of the risk costs that X and Y bear because they are not certain about the number of units of A Y will want to purchase during the relevant time-period to the extent that Y is more risk-averse than X, the reciprocity arrangement increases Y's Y-quantity-demand-for-A-related risk more than it reduces X's Y-quantity-demand-for-A-related risk because each buyer Y must be concerned not only with the amount of A final consumers Z1...N purchase but also with its share of those sales whereas X is not concerned with the relative shares that its individual independent distributors Y1...N have of the group's sales of its product, and relevant temporal variations in DD_{XAY} are less-than-perfectly-positively correlated with temporal variations in DD^{RC}_{YBX}. This third factor is relevant because, if these two demand curves are perfectly positively correlated, the reciprocity agreement will give Y the same protection against its quantity demand for A's being lower than Y expected on the weighted average as the higher per-unit price for A (and reduced lump-sum fee) would have given in that when Y's quantity demand for A is any percentage γ lower than expected (so that Y will obtain γ percent lower gains, lump-sum fee aside, than Y expected from purchasing A at the contractual price) X's full-requirements quantity demand for B will be the same percentage lower than expected (so that the duty the reciprocity agreement imposes on Y to supply B to X for less than its market price will cost Y γ percent less than Y expected).

Second, the amount by which the shift in question increases the loss X will expect to incur on the weighted average because X underestimates Y's weighted-average-expected quantity demand for A (and hence accepts a lower lump-sum fee from Y than Y would have been willing to pay) will also be inversely related to the positive correlation between DD_{XAY} and DD^{RC}_{YBX}. Thus, if these two demand curves vary through time in the same direction by the same percentage, the reciprocity agreement will give X the same protection against its being pessimistic about Y's quantity demand for A because each time that X underestimates Y's weighted-average-expected quantity demand for A by γ percent and hence would require Y to pay a lump-sum fee that was (roughly speaking) γ percent too low, X will underestimate its own quantity demand for B under a full-requirements contract by γ percent and hence will impose an obligation on Y to supply X's requirements of B at a cut price that will cost Y γ percent more than X thinks it will cost Y.

Third, for perfectly-analogous reasons, the amount by which the shift in question increases the loss X will sustain because Y underestimates its weighted-average-expected quantity demand for A will also be inversely related to the extent to which Y will underestimate X's weighted-average-expected quantity demand for B to the same extent it will underestimate its own weighted-average-expected quantity demand for A: if these underestimates are identical, the shift to the reciprocity agreement will not increase the losses X suffers on account of Y's pessimism because any time that Y underestimates its quantity demand for A by ε percent (and hence the lump-sum fee it can pay X and break even by ε percent) Y will underestimate X's quantity demand for B by ε percent and hence the cost to it of its supply obligation by ε percent—*i.e.*, will be willing to accept reciprocity-agreement terms relating to B that are in fact ε percent more costly to Y than the lump-sum-fee term Y would have been willing to accept in an independent transaction on A.

Before proceeding to discuss the other reasons why a shift from the most-profitable independent pricing arrangement on A to the reciprocity agreement on which we are focusing might disserve X's interests, I should point out that, in the sort of situation described by the concrete example in which A is designer suits and B is good-quality shirts and ties, DD_{XAY} will often vary through time with DD^{RC}_{YBX} and underestimates by X or Y of Y's quantity demand for A will often be highly positively correlated with underestimates respectively by X or Y of X's quantity demand for B—*i.e.*, the shift in question is likely to reduce X's profits only slightly by increasing the sum of X's and Y's risk costs and the loss that X sustains because X and/or Y underestimates Y's quantity demand for A. Thus, in this sort of situation, the temporal variations in Y's quantity demand for A are likely to be very similar to the temporal variations in X's quantity demand for B because X's quantity demand for B is likely to be highly positively correlated with X's retail sales of A (through its own outlets or the outlets of a specified third party) and X's retail sales of A through its own outlets or the outlets of a specified third party are likely to be highly positively correlated with Y's quantity demand for A—*i.e.*, X's retail sales of A are likely to be highly positively correlated with Y's retail sales of A since both will vary in the same way with macroeconomic conditions and the relative success of X's product-line.

Fourth, although the shift from the most-profitable pricing-technique X could use to sell A to Y independently to the reciprocity agreement on which we are focusing will always tend to cost X money by increasing Y's incentive to engage in arbitrage on A and giving X an incentive to purchase B for resale outside the scope of its "normal" business, the extent of these losses will depend on such things as (1) the size of the lump-sum fee X is charging, (2) the cost to Y of finding non-final-consumer buyers of A, (3) the cost to Y of transporting A to any such non-final-consumer buyers (*inter alia*, A's size, weight, fragility, and perishability), (4) the cost to X of proving that Y has violated their contract by engaging in arbitrage on A, (5) the price-cut the reciprocity agreement requires Y to give X on B, (6) the cost to X of finding a non-final-consumer buyer of B, (7) the cost to X of transporting B to any such non-final-consumer buyer, and (8) the cost to Y of proving that X has violated their agreement by engaging in arbitrage on B.

Fifth, the net effect that the relevant shift to reciprocity has on X by giving Y more-jointly-optimal incentives to make demand-increasing expenditures to increase its sales of A and giving X incentives to make demand-increasing expenditures related to the sale of B that are against its and Y's joint interest depends *inter alia* on (1) the amount by which the associated decrease in A's price to Y would increase X's and Y's joint profits by inducing Y to make additional demand-increasing expenditures if X could not otherwise induce Y to make such jointly-profitable expenditures or substitute expenditures of its own for Y's, (2) the amount by which the associated decrease in B's price would decrease X's and Y's joint profits by inducing X to make expenditures that would increase DD_{XBZ} if Y could not prevent X from doing so, (3) the ability of X to provide Y with jointly-optimal incentives to make expenditures of these kinds when it sells A independently to Y by sharing Y's advertising budget, (4) the ability of X to put Y under and enforce a contractual obligation to make all such expenditures that are in X's and Y's joint interest, (5) the proficiency with which X can substitute its own expenditures for any jointly-optimal expenditures Y does not make, and (6) the ability of Y to put X under and enforce contractual obligations not to make B-demand-increasing expenditures that are not in X's and Y's joint interest. I should point out that, to the extent that the efficaciousness of demand-increasing expenditures increases with the differentiation of the product in question, the fact that product A is more differentiated than product B in the typical reciprocity-situation of this kind favors the conclusion that the functional type of shifts to reciprocity on which we are now focusing will tend to increase X's profits on balance on this demand-increasing-expenditure account—*i.e.*, the demand-increasing-expenditure-related transaction-surplus gain such shifts will yield on products A will exceed the demand-increasing-expenditure-related transaction-surplus losses they will generate on products B.

To be honest, I do not have enough information about the magnitudes in various situations of the determinants of the profitability to sellers of the shift from the independent pricing of some product A to the type of reciprocity agreement on which we have just been focusing to make any reliable prediction of the frequency with which some reciprocity agreements involving final products A and B will be more profitable on this account for the seller involved than the most-profitable pricing-technique the seller could use to sell A independently. However, my guess is that this type of reciprocity agreement will often be more profitable for sellers than the independent pricing of A.

Of course, for reciprocity of this type to be profitable, it must also be more profitable than the tie-ins that X could use to similar effect since in most such situations Y, like X, will distribute B as well as A. In fact, for three reasons, reciprocity agreements may be more profitable than tie-ins in this type of situation:

(1) even if X's outlets have the same demand for B as Y's, MC_B is constant over the relevant range, and DD_{XBY} has the same slope above and below the TSM price, the reciprocity agreement (which increases sales) will have to destroy less transaction surplus than the tie-in (which decreases sales) to provide X with a given expected non-lump-sum gain;
(2) X may find it more difficult to determine whether Y is cheating on its tie-in obligation to purchase its full requirements of B than to prove to Y that it (X) has not engaged in arbitrage on its reciprocity purchases of B; and
(3) X may find it easier to assure Y that it is not overpromoting B under the reciprocity agreement than to prevent Y under the tie-in from underpromoting B.

In short, I suspect that there are many situations in which the type of reciprocity agreement on which we are now focusing would be more profitable than both the independent pricing of A and the most suitable tie-in the relevant seller could employ. I should admit, however, that I do not have the data necessary to substantiate this claim.

(ii) When A Is an Input Against Which Substitution Is Possible

Section 2C(1)(F)(ii) explained why a producer X of input A against which substitution is possible may find it profitable to substitute for the independent pricing of A tie-ins involving A and either another input B that can be substituted against A or another input C against which substitution is not possible—*viz.*, because tie-ins in which the P/MC ratio for A is equated with the P/(normal market price) ratio for B or tie-ins in which the price of A is reduced to its TSM marginal cost but the buyer Y is obligated to purchase its full requirements of C from the seller X as well for more than its normal market price will increase X's profits by enabling X to use supra-marginal-cost per-unit pricing to reduce (1) the sum of its and Y's risk costs related to their uncertainty about Y's quantity demand for A and (2) the costs X bears because of the possibility that it and/or Y may underestimate the quantity of A that Y should be expected on the weighted average to purchase without inducing Y to make jointly-unprofitable substitutions of input B for the seller's input A. As Sect. 2C(1)(F)(ii) pointed out, in some circumstances, the seller X of an input A against which substitution is possible when it is used to produce product D may also be able to make more profits than it could realize by pricing A independently by conditioning its sale of A to Y, the producer of D, at A's TSM marginal cost on Y's agreeing to pay X a per-unit endproduct royalty on each unit of D Y sold that would eliminate all the (unnecessary) buyer surplus Y would otherwise have obtained on the transaction in question. Indeed, to the extent that it will be more cost-effective for X to determine whether Y has accurately reported its sales of D than to enforce the full-requirements obligation on B and/or C that a tie-in would impose on Y, the endproduct-royalty arrangement would be more profitable than the tie-in even if both were perfectly legal.

In terms of Diagram VII, an endproduct-royalty scheme in which Y was obligated to pay X a royalty of fa for each unit of D Y sold would replicate the tie-ins previously discussed in two respects. First, since under the endproduct-royalty scheme A would be priced at its TSM marginal cost, the endproduct-royalty scheme would raise MC_{YDZ} from MC_1 to MC_3 (if we count the royalty as a marginal cost of D to Y) without raising above MC_1 the sum of (1) the cost X incurred to supply Y with the A Y used to produce each unit of D and (2) the cost that the initial purchaser of B and C (here Y) incurred to purchase the B and C Y used to produce each unit of D it produced. (For simplicity, I continue to assume that D is produced under conditions of constant returns to scale.) Second, since DD_{YDZ} will vary through time with DD_{XAY} and since X and Y will respectively be likely to underestimate Z's accurately-estimated weighted-average-expected quantity demand for D by the same percentages as they respectively underestimate Y's accurately-estimated weighted-average-expected quantity demand for A, an endproduct-royalty scheme that eliminates a given amount of BS by requiring Y to pay X a royalty of fa for each unit of D Y sells will be equally adept at reducing the cost to X of the risk costs X and Y bear because of their uncertainty about Y's quantity demand for A and the weighted-average cost X expects to bear because of the possibility that X and/or Y might underestimate the amount of A Y should be expected on the weighted average to buy as would a shift from pure-lump-sum pricing on A to a mixed lump-sum supra-TSM-marginal-cost per-unit price system on A that removes that amount of BS by raising the per-unit price for A or a tie-in that removes that amount of BS by raising the per-unit price that Y must pay for B and/or C.

The point of this section is that, in some circumstances, a seller X of an input A against which substitution is possible when it is used to produce D may find it even more profitable to use a reciprocity agreement than to use a tie-in or endproduct-royalty scheme to enable itself to obtain the risk-cost-related and seller-or-buyer quantity-demand-pessimism-related benefits of non-marginal-cost per-unit pricing without inducing the buyer Y to make jointly-unprofitable substitutions against A in part because, in many circumstances, the relevant reciprocity agreement will destroy less of the surplus that the relevant transactions generate for X and Y combined by reducing Y's output of D below the level that would be in X's and Y's joint interest.

The reciprocity agreement in question would substitute for (1) the obligation the tie-in would impose on Y to purchase its full requirements of B and/or C for a price (prices) above their normal market price(s) or (2) the obligation the endproduct-royalty scheme would impose on Y to pay X a given sum (fa in Diagram VII) for each unit of D Y sells (3) an obligation on Y to supply X with Y's full output of D for "a lower per-unit price than Y would otherwise charge for D." I have enquoted the preceding expression because, as the following analysis (which makes use of Diagram VII) reveals, the substitution of the reciprocity agreement that will be described below for the tie-ins that Sect. 2C(1)(F)(ii) discussed or the endproduct-royalty scheme discussed earlier in this section would change Y's output of D and hence in one sense the price that Y would otherwise have charged for D.

I will now use Diagram VII to illustrate the determination of the price that X could require Y to charge X for D under a reciprocity agreement that would otherwise give Y the same amount of (unnecessary) BS that the tie-ins and endproduct-royalty schemes previously analyzed would give Y if they did not respectively require Y to purchase its full requirements of B and/or C for more than their normal market prices and did not require Y to pay X endproduct royalties on Y's sales of D without making the deal unprofitable for Y and (2) the analysis of why and when the relevant reciprocity agreement may be more profitable for X than the tie-in or endproduct-royalty schemes previously considered. DD_{YDZ}, MR_{YDZ}, and the four MC curves in Diagram VII have the same definition in the current reciprocity analysis as they did in the preceding section's tie-in analysis. Since under the reciprocity agreement X will be selling D to its final consumers Z, in the reciprocity analysis DD_{XDZ} and MR_{XDZ} (indicated in brackets in Diagram VII) will replace the DD_{YDZ} and MR_{YDZ} curves on which the tie-in analysis focused. In Diagram VII, DD_{XDZ} and MR_{XDZ} are assumed to coincide with DD_{YDZ} and MR_{YDZ} respectively—X is assumed to be as attractive a distributor of D as Y would have been.

The assumptions that underlie the definitions of the curves in Diagram VII imply that, since Y could earn profits equal to area jih without using input A, if (1) X chose to agree to supply Y with all the A that Y used in its own operations for a price equal to A's TSM marginal cost to X (so that $MC_{YDZ} = MC_1$) in exchange for Y's paying X a lump-sum fee equal to area higf *minus* the risk costs this arrangement would impose on Y and any buyer surplus Y's bargaining power enabled it to extract and if

(2) I assume for simplicity that the price-cut the relevant reciprocity agreement obligated Y to give X on D affected neither Y's risk costs nor the amount of buyer surplus Y's bargaining power enabled it to extract, the price for which the reciprocity agreement could require Y to supply D to X (without making it profitable for Y to reject the offer) would have to give Y operating profits equal to area jgf in Diagram VII (the certainty-equivalent profits Y could have earned by producing D without A *plus* the lump-sum fee the agreement required Y to pay X *plus* the risk costs Y would bear under the agreement over and above the risk costs Y would bear if it did not use A *plus* the buyer surplus Y's bargaining power enabled it to extract from the deal). By construction, the price for D that would enable Y to earn profits equal to area jgf on the facts assumed in Diagram VII is un—*i.e.*, by construction, area tusa in Diagram VII (the operating profits Y would realize by supplying D to X at a per-unit price of un—see below) equals area jgf. To see why Y would make operating profits equal to area tusa by supplying X's full requirements of D at a per-unit price of un, note that, if we continue our simplifying assumption that the only cost of distributing any product is the cost of the good sold to the distributor so that $MK_{DX}^{RA} = MC_{XDZ}$,

(1) if the price to X of D under the reciprocity agreement is un, X will find it most profitable to buy and sell tu units of D (since MR_{XDZ} will cut MC_{XDZ} from above at point u [output tu] if $MC_{XDZ} = MK_{DX}^{RA} = un$);
(2) Y will obtain revenue equal to area tunO by selling tu units of D to X at a per-unit price of un;
(3) MC_{YDX} under the reciprocity agreement will be MC_1;
(4) the total variable cost to Y of supplying X with tu units of D under the reciprocity agreement will be area asnO; and
(5) the operating profits that Y will realize by selling (tu units of) D to X under the reciprocity agreement will equal area tunO *minus* area asnO—*i.e.*, will equal area tusa.

I will now explain why this type of reciprocity agreement might be more profitable than either the two types of tie-ins or the endproduct-royalty scheme previously described:

(1) because DD_{XDZ} (or DD_{YDZ}) will vary in the same way through time as DD_{XAY}, the reciprocity agreement will have the same effect on the sum of the risk costs that X bears because it and Y are uncertain about Y's quantity demand for A that the input tie-ins or endproduct-royalty schemes would have;
(2) because X and/or Y will underestimate X's quantity demand for D when and to the same extent that they underestimate Y's quantity demand for A, the reciprocity agreement will give X the same protection against X's and/or Y's underestimating the quantity of A Y should be expected to buy on the weighted average that either the input tie-ins or the endproduct-royalty scheme previously discussed will give X;
(3) because, to the extent that X can determine the amount of D Y has produced from the amount of A Y purchased (given the fact that Y can combine that A with B

and/or C purchased at their normal market prices) and/or to the extent that X can require Y to alter the D it produces in a way that makes its D easily identifiable and that Y can do so without incurring any significant cost or altering the quality of the D in question, a reciprocity agreement that obligates Y to alter its D in this way will often reduce the cost to X of the incentives X gives Y to cheat on their agreement (whatever form it should take)—by engaging in arbitrage on A, by buying from someone else some of the B and/or C a tie-in agreement requires Y to purchase from X at more than its or their market price(s), by misreporting its unit or dollar sales of D under an agreement that requires Y to make endproduct-royalty payments to X, or by not supplying X with all the D it produces;

(4) because, like the tie-ins and endproduct-royalty schemes previously analyzed, the reciprocity agreement described will give Y no incentive to make jointly-unprofitable substitutions against X's input A;

(5) because, to the extent that the reciprocity agreement stipulates a price that Y must charge X for the D it obligates Y to supply to X (un in Diagram IV) that is lower than the marginal cost Y would have to incur to produce D under either of the two the tie-in schemes or the endproduct-royalty scheme previously described (MC_3 in Diagram VII) and to the extent that X could distribute D either itself or through a third party as proficiently as it could be distributed if Y distributed it itself or through a third party, the reciprocity agreement will be more profitable for X than either of the two tie-in schemes or the endproduct-royalty scheme previously analyzed in that it will reduce the joint gain to X and Y less by inducing Y to reduce its output of D below that product's jointly-profitable output (Or = ac) for a firm perfectly-vertically-integrated from input production to final-good production (but not to final-good consumption) than would either of the two tie-ins or the endproduct-royalty scheme previously discussed—*i.e.*, will result in the output's being tu = as rather than fg = ab and will therefore preserve (area gusb = area vusb–area fgvt) in possible joint gains to X and Y that the tie-ins or endproduct-royalty scheme would have destroyed (while simultaneously reducing the price of D from kl to mn and increasing the ultimate consumer Z's buyer surplus by xkmy); and

(6) because, to the extent that the marginal cost of D to its actual distributor under the reciprocity agreement is lower than its marginal cost or kost to that distributor under either of the two tie-in schemes or the endproduct-royalty scheme (when one counts any royalty payment Y must make under the royalty scheme to be part of the marginal cost of D to Y), the shift to the reciprocity agreement will increase X's profits by inducing D's distributor to make additional demand-increasing expenditures related to D that are in X's and Y's joint interest.

The preceding analysis assumed that the amount of surplus X would choose to remove from Y (risk-cost effects aside) under the reciprocity agreement by requiring Y to supply it with D for a price lower than Y would otherwise charge for D would equal the amount of surplus X would choose to remove from Y under the A-B tie-in by requiring Y to purchase Y's full requirements of B for more than its normal market price and all the A Y needs for a price that exceeds A's TSM marginal cost, under the A-C tie-in by requiring Y to purchase its full requirements of C from X for more than its normal market price, or under the endproduct-royalty scheme by requiring Y to pay it endproduct royalties. In fact, to the extent that the reciprocity arrangement would increase the profitability of non-marginal-cost per-unit pricing for X, one would expect that X would choose to remove more surplus from Y under the reciprocity agreement by requiring Y to supply it with D for a lower price than Y would otherwise charge for that product (while lowering the lump-sum fee X charged Y) than it would chose to remove from Y through price-increases on B and/or C under the tie-in or through endproduct royalties under the endproduct-royalty scheme.

D. Resale Price Maintenance and Non-Single-Brand Exclusive Dealerships (Vertical Territorial Restraints and Vertical Customer-Allocation Clauses)

(1) Resale Price Maintenance

Resale price maintenance (RPM) is the practice in which a seller higher in a chain of production and distribution requires a distributive customer lower in the chain to resell the product the latter firm buys from the former firm for a stipulated price or for a price that is not below a stipulated minimum price or above a stipulated maximum price. A seller higher in a distribution-chain can try to control the actual, minimum, or maximum prices that resellers charge for its product in a variety of different ways—*e.g.*, by including an RPM clause in its contract of sale, by verbally informing its distributors that it will continue to supply them only if they adhere to the resale-price "recommendation" it gives them and discontinuing its supply of buyers that do not follow its "recommendation," or by making recommendations and discontinuing distributors who do not follow them without forewarning the distributors of its intention to do so or verbally explaining the discontinuance *ex post*. Since such maximum-resale-price controls perform different functions from their minimum-price-control counterparts, their functions will be analyzed separately.

Although RPM can be practiced by producers in relation to wholesalers and by wholesalers in relation to retailers as well as by producers in relation to retailers, the text that follows will always focus on the use of the practice by a producer in its relation with its retailers. Admittedly, RPM between producers or wholesalers on the one hand and retailers on the other can perform some functions that RPM between producers and wholesalers cannot perform. However, the functional difference between RPM involving either producers and retailers or wholesalers and retailers on the one hand and RPM between producers and wholesalers on the other would be significant only if it would critically affect the legal (or policy) case for making RPM between some types of actors *per se* legal or illegal. Since we shall see that it will not, the simplifying locution I will employ will save space without affecting any significant conclusion.

(A) RPM That Is Not Designed to Prevent a Distributor from Charging More Than a Stipulated Maximum Resale Price

(i) Increasing the Profits a Producer Can Realize by Charging Lump-Sum Fees or by Engaging in Conventional Per-Unit-Price Price Discrimination by Preventing Such Pricing from Inducing Resellers to Engage in "Intra-Brand Price Competition" That Would Reduce Producer Profits by Enabling Ultimate Consumers to Pay Less for the Good Than They Would Be Willing to Pay, by Increasing the Total Pricing/Salesmanship Costs of the Producer's Resellers, and/or by Allocating Sales to Worse-Than-Best-Placed Resellers

As we have seen, in many situations, a producer that uses independent retailers to distribute its product may find it profitable to shift from pure, non-discriminatory per-unit (single) pricing to a pricing system in which it charges those retailers some lump-sum fee and a lower per-unit price than it would otherwise have found most profitable to charge them. One drawback of such pricing is the incentive it gives its individual distributors to compete against each other and in so doing to drive the price that buyers pay for the producer's product below the price they would have been willing to pay for its product. Such intra-brand competition is "costly" to the producer because, by driving down the operating profits its independent distributors earn by reselling its product (by reducing the prices they obtain on any sales they make, by increasing the non-cost-of-goods-sold distribution costs they incur per sale by increasing the number of distributors of the product that attempt to obtain each sale, and [possibly] by causing some sales to be made by distributors that were not best-placed to make them), it drives down the lump-sum fees the distributors are willing to pay the producer for the right to purchase its product at a low per-unit price.

As we have also seen, in some circumstances, a producer may also find it profitable to engage in conventional per-unit-price price discrimination. Although our initial treatment of this possibility implicitly assumed that the relevant buyers were final consumers, there is no reason why those buyers might not be (1) retailers some of which were best-placed to supply final consumers that were willing on average to pay a higher price and some of which were best-placed to supply final consumers that were willing to pay a lower price (that would still more than cover the production and distribution cost of supplying them) or (2) wholesalers that differed according to the value that their retailer customers placed on the product in question. One drawback of charging discriminatory per-unit prices to retailers or wholesalers is the incentive the lower per-unit price charged the "favored" retailers (wholesalers) might give them to compete for the patronage of the final consumers (retailers) that the non-favored retailers (wholesalers) were best-placed to supply, thereby driving down the prices the high-valuing final consumers (retailers) had to pay and hence the quantity of the producer's product the non-favored buyers purchase and perhaps their willingness to distribute the producer's product.

Resale price maintenance can prevent intra-brand competition that can drive down the joint profits of the producer and its distributors and hence the profits of the producer alone (1) by driving down the price that resale buyers pay for the producer's product below the price they would be willing to pay for it, (2) by raising distribution costs by inducing more than one distributor of the producer's product to attempt to obtain the patronage of given resale buyers, and (3) by allocating sales to distributors that are not the best-placed distributor of the producer's product to make them. To accomplish this goal in the normal situation in which the reseller charges only per-unit prices, the RPM clause or "recommendation" must set the resale per-unit price that can be charged any resale buyer at the highest price that that resale buyer would be willing to pay for the producer's product. Because, *ceteris paribus*, buyers will tend to prefer the retailer that is geographically best-placed to supply them, this policy will not only prevent the price paid from being driven down but will also make it likely (1) that the distributor that is best-placed to supply any particular buyer (the one that can make most profits by supplying that buyer) will be the only distributor of the producer's product to attempt to obtain the buyer's patronage and (2) that the distributor that is best-placed to supply any buyer will make the sale to it. In the typical case in which the reseller sets a single per-unit price, the RPM clause in question should set a per-unit actual or minimum price that will apply to the price the reseller charges any buyer.

(ii) Increasing the Profits a Producer Can Realize by Charging Lump-Sum Fees or by Engaging in Conventional Per-Unit-Price Price Discrimination by Preventing Such Pricing from Leading to "Intra-Brand Price Competition" That Would Deter Independent Retailers From Making the Demand-Increasing Expenditures (on Media Advertising, Display-Space, Pre-Sales Advice, and Other Sorts of Salesmanship) That Would Be in the Producer's and Resellers' Joint Interest

As we saw, when a producer's per-unit price to an independent retailer exceeds the producer's marginal costs, it may not be profitable for the reseller to make demand-increasing expenditures that would be in its and the producer's joint interest because some of the benefits those expenditures generate by yielding additional sales (*viz.*, the product of the number of additional units sold and the difference between the producer's price to the retailer and the producer's marginal cost) will be realized by the producer. As we also saw, a producer may be able to prevent the losses it would otherwise experience on this account (without sacrificing the advantages of supra-marginal-cost per-unit pricing) by agreeing to pay the percentage of the retailer's demand-increasing expenditures that the producer's profits from any resulting sales constitute of the sum of the producer's and retailer's profits on those sales (gross of the demand-increasing expenditure in question).

This section focuses on the tendency of inter-retailer as opposed to retailer-producer spillovers to deter a producer's retailers from making demand-increasing expenditures that would be in their and the producer's joint interest. To the extent that one or more retailers of a producer's good believe that some of the sales that its media advertising, in-store product-displays, pre-sale advice (*e.g.*, about the hi-fi components that work well together or the type of truck fleet that would be most-cost-effective for a particular buyer), or general sales-efforts will go to another retail distributor of the producer's product, it may not find it profitable to make a demand-increasing expenditure of one or more of these kinds despite the fact that the expenditure in question would be in the joint interest of the producer and all its retailers. And to the extent that the estimate of one or more retailers of a producer's product of the percentage of the sales its demand-increasing expenditures will generate that will go to someone else is increased by the operation of (1) discount houses that offer lower prices but make few such expenditures or even (2) other more-regular retailers that might beat the prices of the retailer that is considering making such expenditures, an RPM policy that prevents any rival of any retailer that makes such expenditures from beating its price by requiring all retailers to charge the same price or prohibiting all retailers from charging less than some stipulated minimum price will reduce the loss that prospective intra-brand price competition imposes on the producer by deterring its individual retailers from making demand-increasing expenditures that would be in the joint interest of all retailers and the producer and hence in the producer's interest. Although RPM will not be able to eliminate the reduction in the incentives that individual retailers have to place media advertisements when other retailers of the producer's product operate in the geographic market the relevant media cover or supply the non-geographically-defined classes of buyers the media in question reach (vertical territorial restraints and vertical customer-allocation clauses will be needed to prevent these types of spillovers), RPM will do a good job of preventing the spillovers that can render unprofitable for the individual retailer display-space, pre-sales-advice, and in-store-salesmanship efforts that are in the joint interest of the producer and all its retailers since buyers that have no price reason to patronize another retailer will (I suspect) usually or almost always buy the producer's product from the retailer in whose store it saw the product displayed or from which it received pre-sales advise or some other type of sales-pitch.

(iii) Preventing the "Intra-Brand" Competition That Would Make It Profitable for an Individual Reseller to Make a Demand-Increasing Expenditure That Would Be Against Its and the Producer's Joint Interest Because It Would Reduce the Sales and Profits of Another Reseller of the Producer's Product

When an individual reseller's demand-increasing expenditure would enable it to take a sale away from another reseller of the producer's product or would cost another reseller of the producer's product a sale to a prospective customer that or who would otherwise have patronized it by annoying that buyer (as a visit from a second door-to-door salesman of a particular product or a telephone call from a second telemarketer of a particular product might), the individual reseller might find such an expenditure profitable despite the fact that it would reduce the sum of its and the producer's profits by reducing the operating profits of other resellers of the producer's product. RPM may be able to reduce the loss that individual resellers impose on producers by making demand-increasing expenditures that will reduce the sales and operating profits of other resellers of its product by reducing the probability that the demand-increasing expenditure will take a sale away from another reseller of the manufacturer's product by reducing the probability that buyers will purchase the producer's product from an inferior-placed reseller.

(iv) Increasing the Profits That a Producer Can Realize by Providing Buyers With an Effective Product-Warranty

For two reasons, producers may find it profitable to offer their customers product-warranties: (1) the producer may be less risk-averse than one or more of its customers and (2) the ability of the producer to predict the percentage of its products that will malfunction may be greater than the ability of its customers to predict the percentage of all the products they individually purchase that will malfunction and the cost the producer must incur to put its malfunctioning products right or replace them may be lower than the cost its customers must incur to put their malfunctioning purchases right or to absorb the loss that the purchased goods' continuing non-performance or poor performance generates. A seller that, for one or both of these reasons, might be able to profit by offering product-warranties can provide warranty-repairs by doing them itself, by paying its distributors a remunerative price to provide the services in question, or by requiring its distributors to provide such services without any (or full) compensation. Each of these methods has its drawbacks:

(1) the producer may be less well-placed than its retailers to supply the warranty-repairs if in the relevant geographic area the number of such repairs to be made is too low to enable the producer to take full advantage of the available economies of scale whereas the retailers can take better or full advantage of such economies of scale by repairing malfunctioning exemplars they sold of all the brands they sell, by combining their warranty-repair business with their non-warranty-repair business, and by combining their warranty-repair business with their efforts to fix up and resell used products they obtain as trade-ins;
(2) the option of paying retailers enough for warranty-repair services to make it profitable for them to provide such services may be rendered less attractive by the difficulty of determining whether retailers are doing unnecessary work to collect the payments or reporting that they have done repair-work that was neither required nor provided; and
(3) the option of contractually obligating retailers to provide warranty-repair services without compensation may be rendered less attractive by the incentives

the retailers will have to save money by providing repair services whose quality is lower than would be in the joint interest of the producer and all its retailers, particularly when the buyer whose product the retailer services under warranty may not make its next purchase of the product in question from the dealer that serviced it well (*e.g.*, because the buyer moves to a different geographic market).

Although RPM cannot counteract the tendency of buyer mobility (*i.e.*, of the fact that some buyers will change their geographic location before making their next purchase of the producer's product) to give individual retailers that are obligated to provide warranty services for free an incentive to supply inferior warranty services that are against the joint interest of the producer and all retailers taken as a group, it can increase the incentives of individual independent retailers to provide warranty-repair services that are in the joint interest of the producer and all distributors of its product by reducing the probability that a buyer that receives good warranty-repair services from one retailer will make future purchases of the producer's product from other retailers in the same geographic area by guaranteeing that buyers will have no price incentive to give their business to another retailer in the same area.

(v) Preventing Individual Retailers from Charging Lower Prices That Would Increase the Individual Retailer's Profits but Would Reduce the Sum of Its and the Producer's Profits by Reducing the Actual or Perceived Dollar Value of the Producer's Product to Prospective Buyers Who or That Would Purchase the Producer's Product from Another Reseller

For at least three reasons, the value that a given buyer places on a product may increase with its price:

(1) the buyer may assume that the physical quality of the product is directly related to its price;
(2) the buyer may value paying a high price in itself—may want to demonstrate his or its wealth or its financial soundness by engaging in conspicuous consumption; or
(3) a product's price may affect one or more non-wealth attributes of its buyers, and some potential buyers may value the product more when its price is high because the buyer wants others to believe that he has the non-wealth attributes of the majority of people who will purchase it when its price is high as opposed to the non-wealth attributes of the majority of people who would purchase it if its price were lower.

For any or all of these reasons, a decision by an individual retailer to sell a producer's product for a low price that is more profitable for it to charge may be against the joint interest of the producer and all its retailers because it reduces the prices that other buyers that might patronize other retailers would be willing to pay for the product. An effective RPM program can increase a producer's profits by preventing its individual retailers from charging a low price that would "damage" the producer by reducing its product's buyer-perceived or actual dollar value to some potential final consumers that would purchase the producer's (or franchisor's) product from another retailer.

(vi) Preventing One or More of a (Restaurant) Franchisor's Individual Franchisees Whose Local Customers Prefer a Lower Quality/Price Combination Than Is Preferred by Transient Potential Buyers Who Might Patronize Other Franchisees as Well From Supplying That Lower Quality/Price Combination When (1) It Is Impracticable for a Franchisee to Offer Both the Higher and the Lower Quality/Price Combination and/or the Supply of the Lower-Quality Combination Reduces the Value of the Higher-Quality Combination to Its Potential Buyers and (2) It Would Be Costly for Transients to Determine the Quality of the Product/Service an Individual Franchisee Supplies Ex Ante Because, to Do So, the Transient Buyer Would Have to Enter the Franchisee's Premises and Perhaps Interact with Its Employees and/or Consume Its Product

Franchisors of various types of retail establishments (most importantly: restaurants, bakeries, ice-cream parlors, coffee houses) will often find it profitable to assure potential customers that their different franchisees will supply a uniform quality of product and service. This reality partly reflects the cost to transient potential customers who might want to patronize more than one franchisee of stopping to check the physical environment and quality of the food and service a particular franchisee offers, particularly when buyers will not be able to determine the quality of the service on offer until they have received it or the quality of the food being supplied until they have consumed it. When a franchisee has local patrons who prefer a lower quality/price combination than transient potential buyers prefer, it may be profitable for the franchisee to supply the lower quality/price combination its local customers prefer despite the fact that doing so is against its and the franchisor's joint interest because the losses the franchisor experiences when the individual franchisee's choice to supply a lower quality/price combination deters transients from patronizing other franchisees are external to the low-quality-supplying franchisee.

This potential problem would not arise if it would be costless and fully effective for the individual franchisee with local patrons who prefer the lower quality/price combination to simultaneously offer a lower and higher quality/price combination. However, in some cases, this response may not be costless and/or fully effective: (1) it may be costly because complicated to supply both higher-quality and lower-quality meat patties, to have some fryers use higher-quality and some use lower-quality frying oil, and/or to have some customers get higher-quality wait-person services and others get lower-quality wait-person services; (2) the franchisee may not be able to supply both high-quality and low-quality products, service, and/or physical environments without sacrificing economies of scale; and (3) it may not be practicable to wall off buyers with preferences for high quality from the low-quality part of the business when the high-quality preferrers do not like to smell the low-quality cooking oil or meat, to see the low-quality physical environment, or (I regret to admit) to see or interact with the customers that prefer the low quality/price combination.

As I argued when discussing tie-ins that are designed to control the quality of the complements that a seller's customers use together with the seller's product, sellers in this position may be able to prevent individual franchisees from offering a lower quality/price combination than is in the franchisor's interest by contractually obligating them to use architectural layouts and furniture and fittings, ingredients, and personnel of stipulated high quality or by requiring them to purchase their full requirements of these "complements" from the franchisor. However, these responses are neither costless nor foolproof. In some situations, therefore, the franchisor may find it profitable to reduce or eliminate the incentive of individual franchisees to supply lower-quality complements than the franchisor wants them to supply by forbidding them to charge a lower price for any lower-quality product/service they supply—*i.e.*, by engaging in minimum-price-setting RPM.

(vii) (vii) Preventing a Retailer From Charging a Lower Price That Is Against Its and the Producer's Joint Interest

RPM can increase a producer's profits by preventing best-placed distributors from undercharging their customers or preventing intra-brand price competition that lowers the prices buyers pay and/or allocates sales to worse-than-best-placed distributors.

(viii) Encouraging Resellers to Inform the Producer or Each Other of Sales-Pitches or Product-Demonstrations That Are Effective or Ineffective or of Functions That the Product Can Perform for Particular Classes of Buyers

It obviously will be in the interest of a producer to obtain information from its resellers about sales techniques that are effective or ineffective (profitable or unprofitable) or (relatedly) about uses to which the product can be put that its producer had not previously recognized. An individual reseller will hesitate to convey such information to the producer or to other resellers if it believes that other resellers will subsequently use that information in resale competition with it. One way to eliminate this disincentive to information-provision is to give each reseller a perpetual exclusive right to make sales in its territory or to a certain class of buyers. However, since this approach has certain drawbacks (*e.g.*, makes it difficult for the producer to drop the reseller if it becomes relatively ineffective), the producer may find it profitable on this account to use RPM to assure each of its resellers that no other reseller will be able to offer buyers that the information-provider is really best-placed to supply a price-reason to buy through them—*i.e.*, to reduce the likelihood that the information provided will be used in intra-brand competition against its provider.

(ix) Facilitating a Producer Price-Fix

Rival producers can use RPM to facilitate their execution of a price-fix by reducing the profits each can make by cheating by giving their retailers secret price-cuts. RPM will produce this effect by precluding the retailers in question and hence the producer from increasing the profits the price-cut enables them to earn by increasing their sales by passing part or all of the price-cuts on to final consumers. It is important to note, however, that RPM cannot completely eliminate the incentive of price-fixing producers to cut their prices secretly: even if the RPM does prevent the producer's existing retailers from responding to producer price-cuts by increasing their and the producer's sales and profits by cutting their resale prices, it cannot prevent them from responding to produce price-cuts by increasing their and the producer's sales and profits by making demand-increasing expenditures, and it cannot prevent producer price-cutting from raising producer sales and profits by increasing the number of retailers that distribute the producer's product.

(x) Facilitating a Retailer Price-Fix

Retailers might require their suppliers to include resale-price-maintenance provisions in their contracts of supply to enable the retailers to contractually obligate their suppliers to enforce the retailers' price-fix by (1) contractually obligating the resellers to charge a particular price (the fixed price) or not to charge any price below a minimum price (the fixed price) and (2) backing up that "requirement" by ceasing to supply retailers that charge a lower price and/or suing violators of a minimum-price-setting RPM clause for breach of contract (in jurisdictions in which RPM is not prohibited by antitrust law or considered to be *contra bones mores*). Indeed, the first U.S. case to condemn resale price maintenance involved an attempt by resellers (the members of various national associations of wholesale and retail druggists) to fix the price of proprietary drugs by inducing their drug-manufacturer suppliers to impose and enforce a resale price-fix.[1178] The RPM that was involved in a 1930's incident in which (1) druggists responded to a decision by the manufacturer of Pepsodent toothpaste to drop RPM "by relegating Pepsodent to second class distribution or not distributing it at all," (2)

[1178] See Dr. Miles Medical Co. v. John D. Park & Sons Co., 220 U.S. 373 (1911).

the druggists' trade association campaigned for a *de facto* boycott, and (3) the manufacturer reinstated RPM[1179] may also have been designed to facilitate a reseller price-fix. I realize that the geographic retail distribution market may be smaller than the geographic manufacturing market. Nevertheless, I suspect that only a tiny number of and an extremely-low percentage of the RPM arrangements one either encounters today or would encounter if RPM were declared *per se* lawful or subjected to a Rule-of-Reason legal analysis would manifest a reseller price-fix: (1) the Pepsodent story is ambiguous (could manifest full-service drugstores' trying to keep discount houses out rather than a drug-store price-fix); (2) manufacturers will still almost always be more likely than their retailers to find price-fixing profitable and any trend in the other direction generated by the replacement of "mom and pop" retail operations by chains is probably more than offset by an increase in the number of buyers who commute to work and a general increase in shopping mobility (attributable, *inter alia*, to the rise in two-car families)—*i.e.*, by the related increase in the geographic distance separating the retailers that are well-placed to supply individual buyers; and (3) for RPM to help resellers enforce their own price-fix, the resellers must secure the cooperation of manufacturers that own a vast majority of the manufacturing capacity and must prevent new entry and QV-investment expansions by potential and actual non-cooperators (results that will be both difficult and expensive to achieve).

(B) RPM That Is Designed to Prevent a Distributor From Charging More Than a Specified *Maximum* Resale Price

(i) Reducing the Amount of Transaction Surplus That the Producer's Supra-TSM-Marginal-Cost Per-Unit Price Destroys by Inducing the Reseller to Charge a Resale Price for the Product That Is Higher Than the Per-Unit Resale Price That Is in Its and the Producer's Joint Interest

As we saw, one disadvantage of supra-TSM-marginal-cost per-unit pricing is its tendency to destroy transaction surplus by inducing the buyer to purchase fewer units of the product in question than would be in its and the seller's joint interest. When the buyer in question is a reseller, this outcome reflects the fact that it will charge buyers further down the distribution-chain (say, final consumers) a higher per-unit price for the product in question than would be in its and the producer's joint interest because the per-unit price it finds most profitable to charge will equal the height of the demand curve it faces at the lower output at which the marginal revenue curve it faces cuts from above its marginal cost curve (a horizontal line whose height equals the per-unit price it is paying the producer for the relevant product, if we continue our simplifying assumption that the only

[1179] See HERBERT HOVENKAMP, FEDERAL ANTITRUST POLICY 451 (hereinafter HOVENKAMP HORNBOOK) (3rd ed.) (Thomson West, 2005) for a discussion of this sequence of events.

distribution cost is the cost to the distributor of the good distributed) rather than the lower height of that demand curve at the higher output at which the marginal revenue curve it faces cuts from above the marginal cost curve the producer faces, which will be lower at the relevant output than the marginal cost curve the reseller faces since *ex hypothesis* the producer's price to the reseller is higher than the producer's marginal cost. One way that a producer can combat this tendency of its supra-TSM-marginal-cost per-unit pricing to induce its reseller to charge a resale price that exceeds the resale price that would be in their joint interest is to control the maximum price for which the reseller can resell the producer's product. I have no doubt that some maximum-price RPM is designed to increase the producer's profits in this way.

(ii) Deterring a Reseller From Charging a Higher Price That Would Reduce the Producer's Profits by Reducing the Demand Curve for the Producer's Product That Other Resellers Face by Precluding a Sale by the High-Pricing Reseller to a Buyer Whose Consumption of the Product Would Lead That Buyer to Purchase It Again From a Different Reseller or Would Induce Someone Else to Whom the Relevant Buyer Would Recommend It or Who Would Observe the Relevant Buyer's Consuming It to Buy It From a Different Reseller

A producer (whose price to its reseller equals the producer's marginal costs) will not have to take any steps to induce a sovereign, maximizing reseller to charge a lower price than would otherwise have been the most profitable price for the reseller to charge when that lower price would serve a promotional function—*i.e.*, would increase the producer's future sales—if the additional sales in question would be made by the reseller charging the lower price. However, even if the producer's price to a reseller equals its marginal costs, the producer will have to take steps to induce the reseller to charge lower, promotional prices that are in the producer's and all resellers' joint interest when some of the sales that result will be made by other resellers. In such a situation, a producer can induce a reseller to charge a lower, promotional price that would not otherwise be in the reseller's interest by contractually obligating the reseller to charge that lower price, by informing the reseller that it will discontinue their relationship if the reseller does not charge the jointly-optimal, lower, promotional price and making good on that threat, or by recommending that resellers charge the lower price and discontinuing its supply of those who do not follow its recommendation without verbally threatening to do so *ex ante* or explaining its decision *ex post*—*i.e.*, by practicing RPM.

(iii) Preventing the Product's Individual Resellers From Charging a Higher Price That Would Maximize the Individual Reseller's Profits but Would Reduce the Reseller's and Producer's Joint Profits Because It Would Reduce the Demand Curve for the Producer's Product That Other Resellers Face by Reducing the Dollar Value of That Product to Potential Customers of Other Resellers Who Do Not Want to Be Perceived to Have Bought a High-Priced Good or Do Not Want to Be Perceived to Have the Non-Wealth Attributes of Those Buyers Who Would Be Willing to Pay the Higher Price

This function is the counterpart of the fourth function of minimum-price-setting RPM discussed above. For two reasons, I suspect that the number of maximum-price-setting RPM arrangements that perform this function is smaller than the number of minimum-price-setting RPM arrangements that perform the counterpart function:

(1) reseller decisions to charge high prices will not induce buyers to underestimate the material quality of the producer's product, and
(2) (regrettably) in our cultures, buyers are less likely to disvalue in itself others' perceiving them to have paid a higher price for a product than others' perceiving them to have paid a lower price for a product, and buyers are less likely to disvalue than to positively value others' perceiving them to have the non-wealth attributes of buyers who are willing to pay a higher as opposed to a lower price for a product.

(iv) Preventing One or More of a Franchisor's Individual Franchisees From Choosing a Price That Will Maximize the Individual Reseller's Profits but Will Reduce the Franchisor's Profits by Reducing the Demand Curve Faced by Other Franchisees When It Is in the Organization's Interest to Guarantee a Nationwide or Regional Price/Quality Combination Because Transient Buyers Are More Price-Sensitive Than Some Franchisees' Local Buyers and It Is Critically Costly for Buyers to Determine Price Ex Ante

RPM is most likely to perform this function for fast-food franchisors some of whose outlets are on or near interstate highways or in tourist sites. Franchisors may find it profitable to use maximum-price-setting RPM for this purpose not just when some franchisees' local customers are willing to pay higher prices than transients are willing to pay for the same fare but also when local-customer dollar-valuations make it profitable for the local franchisee to offer a higher price/quality (food/service/physical environment) package than the franchise-organization normally offers in circumstances in which it is not practicable to offer both the higher price/quality combination and the standard lower price/quality combination or in cases in which the availability of the higher-quality option makes the standard option objectively less attractive to some transient buyers, who dislike seeing other people get better products and services or do not like "interacting" with—*i.e.*, being in the same environment as—wealthier people. In these sorts of situations, individual franchisees may find it profitable to offer a higher quality/price combination that reduces the franchisor's profits by deterring transients who prefer a lower quality/price combination from patronizing other franchises of the franchisor.

Although the franchisor may find it most profitable to prevent its franchisees from offering such a high quality/price combination by forbidding them from doing so contractually or requiring them to purchase their full requirements of foodstuffs, staff, and buildings, furniture, and fittings from it, in some situations, the franchisor will find it profitable instead or as well to remove or reduce its individual franchisees' incentive to supply higher quality by precluding them from raising their prices when they do so—*i.e.*, by employing maximum-price-setting RPM. (I say "*reduce* the individual franchisee's incentive" because even if the franchisee cannot raise its prices when it increases the quality of the good/service package it offers, its supply of a higher-quality package may increase its profits by increasing its quantity-sales to buyers who prefer the higher-quality package.)

(v) Preventing One or More Distributors from Charging a Price That Would Maximize the Distributor's Profits but Would Be Higher Than the Price That Would Maximize the Producer's Profits Because It Would Reduce the Demand for a Related Product That the Producer but Not the Distributor Sells

The paradigm example of this possibility involves a publisher of a newspaper, magazine, or possibly a television program that contains advertising that the publisher sells and a distributor that sells the written publication or visual product in question but does not receive any compensation for the advertising it contains. In this case, the price that maximizes the distributor's profits may be higher than the price that maximizes the "producer's" profits or the sum of the producer's and distributor's profits because the distributor's returns are not affected by its higher price's tendency to reduce the producer's advertising-sales profits by reducing the number of its readers or viewers or possibly by changing one or more of their relevant attributes (*e.g.*, their income and wealth). The one maximum-resale-price case I know in which the agreement seems likely to be performing this function (among others) is a canonical U.S. case that involves a newspaper publisher and distributor—*Albrecht v. Herald.*[1180] However, maximum-price resale-price-fixes may also be rendered profitable by their ability to perform this function when the producer produces both (1) a basic product and (2) replacement parts and/or repair-and-maintenance services (which it sells for more than their marginal or average variable costs) and the distributor resells only the basic product. Unfortunately, I know of no case whose facts fit this description.

(vi) Enabling a Producer to Make More Reliable Statements in Its Advertisements About the Actual (or at Least the Maximum) Resale Price That Buyers Will Have to Pay for Its Product

In some situations, producers may be advertising their product in the hope of inducing potential buyers to further investigate the desirability of purchasing it by going to a store in which it can be physically examined and obtaining further information from

[1180] 390 U.S. 145 (1968).

sales personnel or by checking it out on some website on which further information is provided. In order to decide whether it makes sense to incur such search costs, potential buyers will want to know the actual price or at least the maximum price of the product in question. Although the producer will be able to satisfy this need of its prospective customers partially by indicating its recommended price in its advertisement even if it does not control the actual price its resellers charge for its product, from the prospective buyer's and hence producer's perspective, it will often be more valuable for the producer to indicate the actual or maximum price the buyer will have to pay for the product if it goes to a store to purchase it. From the producer's perspective, a reseller's choice to charge a higher price than the buyer expected (say, than the producer's advertisement indicates it recommended) will be costly not only in that it may cost the producer an immediate sale but also in that it may cost the producer future sales by militating against its persuading the buyer in question and other buyers to whom that buyer tells his story from incurring the cost of investigating the attributes and value to them of the producer's product by providing them with information about its product's resale price. I have no doubt that some maximum-price RPM is designed to enable the producer to prevent these outcomes by preventing resellers from charging a higher price for its product than the maximum or actual price for which the producer's advertisement indicates its product can be purchased. I have not argued that minimum-price-setting RPM can perform an analogous function because I doubt that buyers will be discouraged from investigating the value of a producer's product to them by discovering that the actual price they will have to pay for some good is lower than the producer's recommended price (though I admit that, in rare cases—*viz.*, when the relevant buyers' valuation of a product is directly related to its price, this claim may be wrong).

(vii) Preventing Individual Resellers From Charging Higher Prices That Are Against Their as Well as the Producer's Interest

Just as a reseller's non-sovereignty and/or non-maximization can cause it to charge a resale price that is below its (and the producer's) profit-maximizing resale price, a reseller's non-maximization and/or non-sovereignty can cause it to charge a resale price that is above its (and the producer's) profit-maximizing resale price. In some cases, a producer may find it profitable to prevent this outcome by establishing a maximum resale price that a particular reseller, a specified category of resellers, or any reseller of its product can charge (though, of course, there may be enforcement difficulties and the producer must also be concerned with the possibility that the relevant reseller's or resellers' estimates of the profit-maximizing resale price is correct).

(viii) Facilitating the Price-Fixing of the Resellers by Setting a Purported Maximum Resale Price That Is Actually the Minimum Fixed Price or Facilitating Price-Fixing by the Producer and Its Product Rivals by Setting the Purported Maximum Price Its Product's Resellers Will Charge for It When the Set Price Is Actually the Minimum Price They Will Charge

Since the purported maximum-price-setting RPM on which we are now focusing will not entitle the producer to discontinue supplying or to sue resellers that charge a lower price than the price the purported maximum-price-setting RPM sets, fake-maximum-price RPM will be less effective at facilitating retailer or producer price-fixing than real minimum-price-setting RPM would be. Although I doubt that any significant amount of (purported) maximum-price-setting RPM functions in this way, I include this possibility not only for completeness but also because it precludes me from concluding that no purportedly-maximum-price-setting RPM manifests anticompetitive intent.

(2) Exclusive Dealerships in the Non-Single-Brand Sense

The expression "vertical territorial restrains" (VTRs) refers to contractual arrangements that limit the territory within which a reseller is authorized to sell the producer's product and non-contractual arrangements in which the producer (1) "recommends" that the reseller operate only in a specified territory, states that it will discontinue its relationship with the reseller if the latter does not follow the recommendation in question, and proceeds to carry out that threat by cutting off non-conformers or (2) makes such a recommendation without issuing any such threat verbally and cuts off non-conforming resellers without explanation. When the set of VTR arrangements a producer creates gives one or more or all of its resellers the exclusive right to distribute the producer's product in the reseller's assigned territory, the dealer is said to have been given an exclusive dealership (ED), which may or may not be exclusive in the second, "single-brand" sense of prohibiting the dealer from distributing rival products of the producer's covered product(s). (The text that follows will assume that the EDs on which this section focuses are not exclusive in this single-brand sense.)

Vertical customer-allocation clauses (arrangements) are clauses that restrict (arrangements designed to restrict) the buyers to which or whom the reseller is authorized to resell the producer's product either by name or by category. When the set of vertical customer-allocation clauses or policies a producer employs gives one or more or all of its resellers the exclusive right to distribute the producer's product to the named individual buyers or categories of buyers, the arrangement is also said to have given the reseller(s) in question an exclusive dealership.

This section analyzes the functions of non-single-brand exclusive dealerships created through either vertical territorial restraints or vertical customer-allocation clauses or their non-contractual variants. The section begins by explaining eight functions that such EDs can perform better than RPM arrangements at least in some circumstances and then proceeds to list three functions that, for obvious reasons, such EDs will either not be able to perform at all or not be able to perform in circumstances in which RPM could perform them. A subsequent section focuses on the functions of single-brand exclusive dealerships.

(A) Eight Functions That (Non-Single-Brand) EDs Can Perform Better Than Minimum-Price-Setting RPM at Least in Some Circumstances

(i) Preventing Intra-Brand Reseller Competition from Reducing the Producer's Profits (A) by Driving Down the Price That Next-Level Buyers Pay for the Producer's Product, (B) by Increasing the Sales Cost Per-Unit Sold That Its Distributors Incur, (C) by Causing Sales to Be Made by Worse-Than-Best-Placed Resellers, and (D) by Making It Profitable for an Individual Retailer to Charge a Lower Price That Reduces the Sum of Its and the Producer's Profits by Reducing the Actual or Perceived Value of the Producer's Product to Prospective Buyers Who or That Either Do or Would Otherwise Purchase the Producer's Product From One or More Resellers

As we saw, at least in theory, RPM can prevent these losses by requiring resellers to charge any buyer the highest price the buyer would be willing to pay for the producer's product, precluding a worse-than-best-placed reseller from giving any relevant buyer a price reason to give such a reseller its patronage, and prohibiting resellers from charging lower prices that would reduce the dollar value that some buyers place on the producer's product. In practice, of course, RPM will be a less-than-perfect response to this problem to the extent that the producer is less able than the reseller to determine the highest price that various buyers would be willing to pay for the producer's product and to the extent that worse-than-best-placed resellers can circumvent the RPM pricing-restriction. EDs will be a more-cost-effective response than RPM to the possibilities listed in the heading for two reasons: (1) the ED will decentralize the price-setting task to the reseller and (2) the ED arrangement will do a better job of precluding intra-brand competition if the exclusive territories can be drawn to reduce the frequency with which any non-best-placed reseller is able to profit by beating the offer of the best-placed reseller that contains the highest price the buyer in question would be willing to pay for the producer's product.

(ii) Preventing Individual Resellers from Being Deterred from Making Demand-Increasing Expenditures That Would Increase the Sum of Their and the Producer's Profits by the Prospect That Their Expenditure Would or Might Increase the Sales and Profits of Another Reseller

As we saw, minimum-price-setting RPM will reduce the losses the producer sustains on this account by reducing the probability that a buyer who or that is induced to buy the producer's product by one reseller's media advertising, in-store display, pre-sale advice, or in-store or door-to-door salesmanship of some other type will purchase the good from another reseller by precluding any other reseller from giving the buyer a price-reason to patronize it. EDs will be even more effective at preventing this outcome than RPM since the EDs will forbid the non-spender for competing in the spender's territory or for the spender's assigned customers (though there may be some spillovers if the relevant buyer is a transient that lives or is located in a different territory from the territory in which the relevant spender is located).

(iii) Preventing Individual Resellers From Making Demand-Increasing Expenditures That Are Against the Joint Interest of the Producer and Reseller Because They Take Sales From Other Resellers of the Product

When an individual reseller's demand-increasing expenditure would enable it to take a sale away from another reseller of the producer's product or would cost another reseller of the producer's product a sale by causing the prospective customer to purchase a different product by annoying that buyer, the individual reseller might find such an expenditure profitable despite the fact that it would reduce the sum of its and the producer's profits by reducing the operating profits of other resellers. As we saw, RPM may be able to reduce the loss that individual resellers impose on producers by making demand-increasing expenditures that will reduce the sales and operating profits of other resellers of its product by reducing the probability that the demand-increasing expenditure will take a sale away from another reseller of the manufacturer's product by reducing the probability that buyers will purchase the producer's product from an inferior-placed reseller. However, EDs will be even more effective than RPM at preventing individual resellers from making demand-increasing expenditures that are against their and the producer's joint interest for this reason because EDs will prevent any reseller from taking a sale from another reseller (if we ignore the possibility that a reseller might supply a transient who would otherwise patronize the reseller that is located in its home territory).

(iv) Preventing Individual Resellers from Making Demand-Increasing-Expenditure Decisions That Are Against Their Own Immediate Interest Because They Make Mistakes When Estimating the Impact of Intra-Brand Competition on the Profits Such Decisions Will Yield Them

Three points are relevant in this connection. First, EDs will prevent all such errors if the ED restrictions are perfectly effective because they will eliminate the intra-brand competition whose impact individual resellers may misestimate. Second, even if perfectly enforced, RPM will be less effective at preventing these errors because under even a perfectly-enforced arrangement a reseller of the producer's product that is not as well-placed to obtain the patronage of a buyer as is another reseller of the producer's product may find it *ex ante* profitable to try to obtain that buyer's patronage. Third, a non-economic-efficiency-related second-best-type point: the demand-increasing-expenditure errors that EDs may prevent a producer's individual resellers from making may have promoted the producer's interest. Thus, if the reseller-error the ED would prevent would have caused the individual reseller in question to make a demand-increasing expenditure that would reduce its profits in circumstances in which the error-induced expenditure would increase the sum of the reseller's and producer's profits by increasing another reseller's sales, the ED would disserve the producer's interest by preventing the reseller's error. And again, if the reseller-error the ED would prevent would have caused the individual reseller in question not to make a demand-increasing expenditure that would have increased its profits in circumstances in which the expenditure would have decreased the sum of the reseller's and producer's profits because it would have decreased the sales of another reseller of the producer's product, the ED would also disserve the producer's interest by preventing the reseller's error.

(v) Increasing the Profits the Producer Can Realize by Providing Buyers With Product-Warranties by Increasing Its Ability to Secure Appropriate Warranty Services From Resellers Without Paying Them Separately to Do the Work

As we saw, in some situations, if a producer could rely on its independent resellers to provide appropriate warranty-repair services without being paid for doing so, it would be profitable for it to offer such warranties to its customers and to secure the associated warranty-repair services in this way. As we also saw, (1) resellers that are contractually obligated to supply such warranty-repair services without being directly (adequately) compensated for doing so may have an incentive to provide cheaper, lower-quality services of this kind than would be in the producer's interest, (2) the profitability to the reseller of providing such low-quality warranty-repair services will be inversely related to the likelihood that any buyer that is induced by its providing high-quality warranty-repair services to purchase one or more units of the producer's product in the future will not do so from the reseller that provided the appropriate service, and (3) although RPM cannot prevent buyers that change their geographic location from transferring their patronage to the reseller in their new area even if their decision to purchase the producer's product again was critically affected by the high-quality warranty-repair service they received from the reseller that originally supplied them, it can increase the probability that a buyer that has not moved and was induced by its original reseller-supplier's warranty-repair services to be a repeat buyer of the producer's product will make its future purchases from its original supplier since RPM will prevent any other seller of the producer's product from giving such a buyer a price reason to take its business elsewhere. Clearly, however, giving the buyer's original reseller-supplier an ED will increase the probability that a repeat buyer that has not moved will make its next purchase of the producer's product from the dealer that supplied it with good warranty-repair services by more than an RPM arrangement will, particularly if the dealer's territory is large enough to make it unprofitable for anyone else to beat the offer it would make to a given buyer if that buyer could not purchase the producer's product from anyone else. Indeed, as the size of the exclusive territory the dealer is given increases, the amount by which the original supplier's incentive to supply appropriate warranty-repair services will be reduced by the possibility that the buyer will move out-of-territory will decline.

(vi) Reducing the Probability That an Individual Reseller Will Be Deterred From Communicating Information About Effective Sales-Pitches, Other Demand-Increasing Expenditures, or Valuable Product-Uses to the Producer or to Other Resellers by the Prospect That the Information in Question Will or Might Be Used by Rival Resellers of the Producer's Product in Competition Against Them

As we saw, RPM will reduce the likelihood that any such information that a reseller provides will be used against it by a same-brand reseller by reducing the ability of rival suppliers of the same product to steal buyers the information-provider is best-placed to supply by precluding such rivals from giving the buyers in question a price-reason to give them their patronage. Obviously, however, a properly-defined ED will provide such an information-provider with even more protection of this kind by prohibiting rival resellers of the producer's product from competing for the patronage of the buyers the information-provider is best-placed to supply and possibly by making it unprofitable for them to do so, sanctions aside.

(vii) Facilitating Price-Fixing by the Producer and Its Rivals

If each member of a group of rival producers creates a series of single-brand EDs and if the group's members assign to their respective reseller-groups sets of territories or buyers that do not overlap (*i.e.*, that give each such reseller-group a different, non-overlapping set of territories or customers), the producer group will have used a series of EDs that are simultaneously single-brand and territorial EDs to create a market division that will facilitate their practice of price-fixing. Indeed, such an ED-generated market division will obviously facilitate price-fixing far more than the producer-group's use of minimum-price-setting RPM would do.

(viii) Facilitating Price-Fixing by the Resellers

In the rare instances in which resellers are able to engage in price-fixing when their producer-suppliers are not, the resellers may be able to induce their suppliers to organize a reseller market division that will facilitate their price-fixing by inducing all producers that supply any retailer to impose the same functional or customer restriction on that retailer and varying the restrictions among retailers so that (1) only one retailer is permitted to operate in any territory or to bid for the patronage of any given buyer but (2) taken as a group, the retailers are authorized to operate in all territories in which they might make a profitable sale and to bid for the patronage of all buyers they could profitably supply. I grant that such a producer-created reseller market division would contribute more to the resellers' ability to fix prices than would any RPM arrangement the resellers might induce producers to put in place. However, I doubt the empirical importance of this possibility for the same reason that I doubt the empirical importance of its RPM counterpart.

I want to emphasize my belief that few if any EDs or RPM arrangements are created to or actually do facilitate producer or retailer price-fixing. I have included these possible functions of RPM and vertical-territorial-restraint-created and vertical-customer-allocation-clause-created EDs both for the sake of completeness and because the possibility that these practices may perform these functions preclude me from concluding that RPM, vertical territorial restraints, and vertical customer-allocation clauses never manifest anticompetitive intent.

(B) Three Functions That EDs Will Not Be Able to Perform Either at All or as Well as RPM Can Perform Them in the Relevant Circumstances

The first of these functions is preventing an individual retailer from charging lower prices that would increase its individual profits but would reduce the sum of its and the producer's profits by reducing the actual or perceived dollar value of the producer's product to prospective buyers who or that would have purchased the producer's product from one or more other resellers when the lower price would have been profitable for the individual reseller not because of the intra-brand competition it faced but because of either the inter-brand competition it faced or the relevant buyer's interest in purchasing an entirely-different product. The second of these functions is preventing a reseller from offering a lower quality/price combination that was in its interest because local buyers preferred it but was against its and the franchisor's joint interest because

(1) transient buyers preferred a higher quality/price combination;
(2) it was not practicable for the reseller to offer both a lower quality/price combination to the locals who prefer it and a higher quality/price combination to the transients;
(3) the transients have to incur significant "costs" to determine the quality of the product an individual franchisee was supplying; and
(4) as a result of (3), the supply of a lower-quality product by an individual franchisee will impose losses on the franchisor by deterring transients from patronizing other franchisees.

The third of these functions is preventing errors that resellers make when determining the price that would be most profitable for them to charge or the demand-increasing expenditures it would be profitable for them to make when those errors do not reflect their misestimating the impact of intra-brand competition.

E. Single-Brand Exclusive Dealerships

(1) Preventing the Reseller From Promoting Rival Products or Reducing Rival-Product Prices When Its Doing So Will Decrease the Sum of the Reseller's and Relevant Producer's Profits

As we have seen, when a producer charges a reseller a per-unit price for its product that exceeds the marginal cost the producer must incur to supply the relevant reseller with the product in question, it will (1) make it individually profitable for that reseller to set a resale per-unit price that exceeds the per-unit price that would maximize the sum of the reseller's and producer's profits and (2) more relevantly here, make it individually unprofitable for that reseller to make demand-increasing expenditures on media advertising, in-store displays, pre-sales advice, and other forms of salesmanship that would maximize the sum of its and the producer's profits—in both cases because the producer's supra-marginal-cost per-unit price to the reseller reduces the reseller's profits from any additional sales the price-reduction or demand-increasing expenditure would generate below the sum of the profits that it and the producer would realize on any such additional sales. For perfectly-analogous reasons, when a producer charges a reseller a per-unit price for its product that exceeds the marginal cost that the producer must incur to supply the reseller with that product, it will on that account make it profitable for the reseller to increase its sales of products of the producer's rivals that it also distributes at the "cost" of reducing its sales of the producer's product(s) by charging lower prices for the rivals' products than would maximize the sum of the reseller's and relevant producer's profits and by incurring more expenses to increase the demand for such rival products than would maximize the sum of the profits of the reseller and producer in question. In this case, the behavior in question reflects the fact that, given the producer's supra-marginal-cost price to the reseller, the profits the reseller would have made on the sales of the producer's product it foregoes when it lowers the price of a rival product or makes an expenditure that will increase the demand curve it faces when reselling the rival product when one or more of the additional sales will be made to buyers that would otherwise have purchased the product of the other supplier of the reseller in question do not include the profits the producer in question would have realized on the sacrificed sales of its product. One function of single-brand exclusive dealerships is to enable the producer that creates them to avoid the losses it would otherwise sustain on this account if it used multiple-brand distributors: the losses each such distributors' jointly-unprofitable prices and demand-increasing expenditures would impose on the producer, the cost to it of foregoing some or all of the supra-marginal-cost per-unit pricing that is one of the causes of those losses, and/or the cost of its taking other steps to prevent its supra-marginal-cost per-unit pricing from generating losses of these kinds.

(2) Enabling a Producer to Prevent Independent Resellers of Its Product(s) From Using Training and Information With Which It Provides Them to Sell Rival Products

At least for the life of the single-brand distributorship agreement and in the longer run if combined with an agreement-not-to-compete contractual clause, a producer may be able to prevent its independent distributor from using the training and information it provides about store layouts, personnel structures, media advertising, in-store displays, product-uses, pre-sales-advice-giving, and other forms of salesmanship (as well as any capital it supplies) to sell rival products. Single-brand restrictions in distributorship agreements can prevent the losses the producer would otherwise sustain if its dealers used such information against it or if it took other "costly" steps to prevent this outcome such as not providing as much or any training or information to its independent dealers or vertically integrating forward into distribution itself.

(3) In Combination With an Appropriately-Coordinated Set of Territorial or Customer Restraints on the Relevant Producer-Rivals' Individual Distributors, Enabling the Producers to Divide Up Markets Territorially

As we just saw, in combination with an arrangement in which the members of a set of product-producer rivals divide up territories or customers among themselves, single-brand exclusive dealerships can enable the producers in question to divide up those markets.

(4) Predation—Locking Up Enough Distributors to Induce the Exit of an Established Rival, to Prevent the Expansion of an Established Rival, and/or to Prevent the Entry of a Potential Competitor When the Producer Would Not Have Perceived the Single-Brand Distributorships in Question to Be Profitable *Ex Ante* but for Its Perception That They Would or Might Have Such an Effect

As Chap. 11 indicated, in some situations an individual established firm or two or more incumbents acting concertedly may find it profitable to engage in this variant of predation. If I assume that the producers that create them are not making a mistake, single-brand distributorships cannot be predatory unless the joint economies of distributing more than one brand through the same outlet are sufficiently high for the single-brand arrangement to be inherently unprofitable. For a series of single-brand-distributorship arrangements to succeed in driving out an established producer or in preventing an established rival from expanding or a potential competitor from entering,

(1) the number of distributorships that would otherwise be well-placed to distribute the products of the incumbent or potential investor in question that are not locked up must be too low to support that incumbent or potential investor;
(2) it must be prohibitively disadvantageous for the incumbent that the perpetrators are trying to drive out to invest in distribution or for the potential investor in a relevant production business whose investment the perpetrator or perpetrators are trying to deter to invest on both levels because the firms in question would face Π_D, R, and S barriers at the distribution level; and
(3) it must be prohibitively costly or impossible for the relevant product-investor to identify an independent potential distribution-investor that was sufficiently better-placed than it was to perform that function to make a separate-entry or joint-venture scenario practicable.

For a series of single-brand-distributorship arrangements that drive out an incumbent, deter an incumbent's expansion, and/or deter a new entry to increase the perpetrator's or perpetrators' profits on that account, there must be no firm (other than one or more of the perpetrators) that can replace the exited or deterred investment with one that would be equally competitive with those of the perpetrator(s). I suspect that only a small percentage of single-brand distributorships are predatory. However, as I indicated in Chap. 11, if such predation would otherwise be feasible and profitable, the fact that the distributors in question taken as a group would lose from the exit of an incumbent or the deterrence of a QV investment in the production business would rarely render the predation unprofitable because the distributors would be likely to be tyrannized by their small decisions: if each individual distributor makes a relatively-small percentage of the sales that a relevant incumbent or potential investor would have to make to break even, each would correctly perceive that the perpetrator or perpetrators in question would lock up enough distributors to achieve its or their predatory objective regardless of what the individual distributor in question did, and each would therefore find it profitable to lock itself in for a trivial payment.

F. Slotting Arrangements and Other Sorts of Trade-Promotion Arrangements

Slotting arrangements are contracts in which a producer pays a reseller up front to provide it with a specified quantity and quality of shelf-space (where shelf-space at eye-level, at the end of an aisle, or near the cash register is more highly valued [because more productive of sales] than shelf-space in other locations). Slotting arrangements are common in grocery retailing, drug retailing, book retailing, and record retailing and are increasingly made by producers of perfumes and cosmetics to secure ground-floor counter-space and by mutual funds to secure inclusion in brokers' lists of recommended financial products. Economists and courts sometimes distinguish between slotting arrangements and trade-promotion arrangements, which are arrangements in which producers induce resellers to supply them with more and/or higher-quality shelf-space or floor-space by giving them discounts on the product to be promoted in this way.

The analysis of the relative attractiveness of slotting contracts (contracts in which a producer makes a fixed payment [*i.e.*, pays a lump-sum fee to a reseller for providing in-store promotions of the producer's product[s]]) and trade promotions (contracts in which some or all of the payments to the reseller come in the form of per-unit-price discounts) to a buyer of reseller promotional-services is similar to the analysis previously executed of the relative profitability to a seller of some good or service of pure-lump-sum pricing, single pricing, and mixed lump-sum *plus* supra-TSM-marginal-cost per-unit pricing that Sect. 2A of this chapter executed. By shifting risk from the seller of the promotional services (the reseller of the good) to the buyer of the promotional services (the producer of the good), a shift from a per-unit product-discount (trade-promotion) arrangement to a lump-sum fee (slotting) arrangement (1) will lower the sum of reseller and product-producer risk costs to the extent that the product-producer is less risk-averse than the reseller or has a portfolio of risks that causes the shift to the slotting arrangement to impose less additional risk on the product-producer than it removes from the reseller, (2) will lower the loss the producer suffers because of reseller pessimism to the extent that the reseller would underestimate the number of units of the producer's product it would resell if it supplies the producer with the contracted-for product-promotion (so that the per-unit product-price discount the product-producer would have to offer the reseller would be higher than it should be and on that account would sum to a higher total discount than the lump-sum fee that would be acceptable to the reseller), (3) will lower the loss the product-producer sustains because it underestimates the number of units of its product the reseller will resell if it supplies the producer with the contracted-for promotional services (so that the producer would offer the reseller a higher sum of per-unit discounts than would have been necessary to secure its agreement), (4) will lower the loss the producer suffers because of the incentive the per-unit-price discount would give the reseller to engage in arbitrage (to resell the product to other potential distributors of the producer's product from which it would otherwise be able to obtain a lump-sum [franchise] fee), and (5) will lower the loss the producer sustains because the per-unit-price discount makes it profitable for the reseller to resell the good to final consumers in competition with other resellers of the same product that might be getting a similar per-unit-price discount for providing promotional services for a lower price than those final consumers would be willing to pay for the product if it were distributed by only one reseller.

(1) Enabling a Producer to Prevent Its Supra-Marginal-Cost Per-Unit Pricing From Inducing Its Reseller to Provide It with Less or Lower-Quality Shelf-Space Than Would Be in the Reseller's and Producer's Joint Interest

So far, my discussion of reseller demand-increasing expenditures has ignored the decisions that resellers must make about the quantity and quality of shelf-space and floor-space to allocate to a producer's product(s). The preceding analyses of other reseller demand-increasing-expenditure decisions apply *mutatis mutandis* to such decisions as well: (1) to the extent that the producer is charging the relevant reseller a per-unit price for the producer's product that exceeds the marginal cost the producer must incur to supply the reseller with that product, the producer's use of that pricing-technique will tend to make it unprofitable for the reseller to give the producer as much or as high-quality shelf-space as would be in the reseller's and producer's joint interest because some of the profits that would be generated by the sales that the higher quantity or quality of shelf-space would yield would be realized by the producer and (2) to the extent that some of the sales that the reseller's allocation of additional or higher-quality shelf-space to the producer's product would be taken from another reseller of the producer's product, the reseller may find it profitable to provide the producer with more or better shelf-space and floor-space than would be in the reseller's and producer's joint interest. Producer decisions to pay resellers to provide them with a stipulated quantity and quality of shelf-space (like producer decisions to pay part of the media-advertising costs its resellers incur to market the producer's product) can enable the producer to prevent its charging of supra-marginal-cost per-unit prices from causing the reseller to provide it with less and/or lower-quality shelf-space than would be in their joint interest.

If the reseller were better-placed than the producer to determine the quantity and quality of shelf-space and floor-space whose assignment to the producer would be in their joint interest and if the producer could estimate the opportunity cost to the reseller of assigning it more or better shelf-space and floor-space cheaply and accurately, it would be more profitable for the producer (1) to obligate itself contractually to pay the reseller the percentage of the opportunity cost to the reseller of giving the producer shelf-space and floor-space above some stipulated quantity and quality that equals the percentage that the profits the producer would realize on any resulting sales would constitute of the sum of the profits that it and the reseller would realize on those sales than (2) to pay the reseller a specified sum for giving it a specified quantity and quality of shelf-space and floor-space. I assume that the fact that most slotting arrangements appear to take the "payment for a specified quantity and quality of shelf-space" form implies that one or both of the above two conditions are not satisfied.

(2) Predation

Not all slotting or related trade-promotion arrangements are *ex ante* inherently profitable for their participants: in some instances, the opportunity cost to the reseller of assigning additional or superior shelf-space to the producer's product(s) are sufficiently high to make the arrangement jointly unprofitable if any strategic gains the practice yields the producer are not taken into account. If the producer enters into a slotting contract that it realizes *ex ante* is inherently unprofitable because it believes that the contract in question will be rendered profitable by its tendency to drive an incumbent rival out, to prevent an incumbent rival from making a rival QV investment, and/or to deter a new entry, the slotting arrangement will be predatory. The conditions under which an individual firm's or a group of rivals' slotting/trade-promotion arrangements will produce such an outcome and be predatory are the same as the conditions under which an individual firm's or group of rivals' single-brand exclusive dealerships will be predatory.

I hasten to add that, because virtually all slotting/trade-promotion arrangement contracts have a short duration, it is virtually inconceivable that any significant percentage of extant arrangements of this kind are in fact predatory. That conclusion will obtain even if the slotting arrangement or other type of trade-promotion arrangement is "exclusive" (*i.e.*, prohibits the reseller from giving shelf or floor-space to any rival of the product-producer involved). The conclusion also does not depend on whether the percentage of space contracted for exceeds the percentage of sales in the relevant market that the relevant product made pre-arrangement. The preceding two sentences are included because it appears that U.S. courts think that the factors on which those sentences focus are somehow relevant to the legality of slotting arrangements or other types of trade-promotion arrangements.

G. Long-Term Full-Requirements Contracts

A long-term full-requirements contract is an agreement in which a buyer agrees to purchase its full requirements of some product during the covered period from a particular seller or producer.

(1) Sherman-Act-Licit Functions

As we saw in Chap. 11, long-term full-requirements contracts can perform many legitimate business functions. More specifically, even when such contracts are not part of a tying or reciprocal-trading agreement, they can increase their participants' profits by reducing their contracting costs, encouraging them to adapt their operations in each others' interests, minimizing the sum of their conventional risk costs, and relatedly putting them in a better position to make long-term investments by providing them respectively with an assured source of "sales" and an assured source of supply. Moreover, when incorporated into an appropriate tying or reciprocity agreement, long-term full-requirements contract-clauses can enable their employer to reduce the cost it must incur to control the quality of the complements its customer combines with its product or the quality of the inputs its supplier uses to produce the goods it purchases from the supplier (*i.e.*, the quality of the goods with which its supplier supplies it), to reduce the cost it must incur to implement a meter-pricing scheme (which will reduce the losses it sustains because of its own pessimism about the buyer's quantity demand for its product, the buyer's pessimism about that quantity demand, the risk costs it and its customer incur, and its customer's practice of arbitrage), or to reduce the amount of transaction surplus (buyer *plus* seller surplus) it must destroy to remove a given amount of its customer's buyer surplus through non-marginal-cost per-unit pricing.

(2) Predation

Although I suspect that the vast majority of long-term full-requirements contracts are not predatory (and that only a few such agreements do reduce the absolute attractiveness of the offers against which their employer has to compete), I have no doubt that the defendant-perceived *ex ante* profitability of some long-term requirements contracts is critically affected by the defendant's belief that they will or may deter an entry or expansion or drive an established project out. The use of long-term requirements contracts by an individual firm or a group of rivals will produce this result in the same circumstances in which its or their use of single-brand EDs or slotting arrangements will do so.

3. The Legality of the Various Surrogates for Vertical Integration Under U.S. and E.C./E.U. Antitrust Law Both as Properly Interpreted and Applied and as Actually Applied

A. U.S. Antitrust Law Both as Properly Interpreted and Applied and as Actually Applied

(1) U.S. Antitrust Law as Correctly Interpreted and Applied

(A) The Sherman Act as Correctly Interpreted and Applied

The Sherman Act covers all the surrogates for vertical integration whose possible functions Sect. 2 explored. This subsection analyzes in turn the legality of each of these surrogates for vertical integration under a correctly-interpreted-and-applied Sherman Act.

Single-product non-discriminatory single pricing and single-product discriminatory per-unit pricing (conventional price discrimination) violate the Sherman Act only if (1) they are predatory, illegally retaliatory (as retaliation by a contrived oligopolistic pricer against an undercutter or underminer would be but legitimate, defensive retaliation against a contriver's retaliation or a predator's predation would not be), or illegally "reciprocatory" (as a contrived oligopolistic pricer's failure to undercut or undermine a cooperating rival's price would be) or (2) one or more of the prices charged are primary or secondary contrived oligopolistic prices. The preceding statement implies that uniform single prices, prices that discriminate in favor of a particular buyer, and prices that discriminate against a particular buyer can all violate the Sherman Act since the first two categories in question can be predatory and all three can be contrived oligopolistic. However, in my judgment, the overwhelming majority of prices in all these categories do not violate the Sherman Act—manifest the pricer's attempt to take legitimate advantage of a given demand/marginal-cost-curve combination or to increase its profits legitimately by engaging in promotional, learning-by-doing, or keeping-in-touch pricing or defensive retaliation.

Perfect price discrimination violates the Sherman Act only when the cost of its execution would be prohibitive but for its tendency to drive a rival out or deter a rival expansion or entry by preventing the rival in question from making profitable sales to the discriminator's customer. I doubt that any significant percentage of the small number of incidents of perfect price discrimination violates the Sherman Act for this reason and am virtually certain that it would rarely if ever be possible to establish the illegality of any perfect price discrimination that was Sherman-Act-violative.

A seller's decision to use a mixed pricing-technique that combines a lump-sum fee with a supra-TSM-marginal-cost per-unit price could also conceivably violate the Sherman Act if the rejected alternative involved a higher per-unit price and the seller would not have found the mixed pricing-technique profitable *ex ante* but for its belief that it would drive a rival out or deter a rival QV-investment's execution by reducing the profits the relevant rival could make by supplying the seller's customer. Once more, however, I suspect that the use of mixed pricing-techniques is rarely predatory and that it is extremely unlikely that the State or a private plaintiff will be able to establish the predatory character of any of the few exemplars of this variant of predatory pricing that might exist.

Section 2B explained the various Sherman-Act-licit functions that can be performed by producer subsidies of distributor demand-increasing expenditures, contractual provisions obligating distributors to make a specified quantity of more-or-less-specified expenditures of this kind, or sales policies of dropping distributors that do not make the demand-increasing expenditures that the producer wants them to make. Section 2B also acknowledged that in some instances a producer's conclusion that a decision to pay such subsidies, to negotiate such contractual arrangements, or to employ such sales policies was *ex ante* profitable might be influenced by its belief that the relevant distributor sales-efforts would increase the future demand curve the producer would face by driving a rival out or punishing a rival that did not cooperate with the producer's contrivance efforts by reducing the profits the rival could make by supplying the buyers that the distributor's induced efforts influenced or by deterring a rival QV-investment expansion or entry by reducing the profits the investor would anticipate making by supplying the buyers in question by making the product of the seller that induced its distributors to make additional demand-increasing expenditures more attractive to the relevant buyers. Once more, however, I suspect that only a tiny percentage of such seller decisions is predatory or illegally retaliatory and that the State or a private plaintiff will rarely if ever be able to establish the predatory or illegally-retaliatory character of those exemplars of such conduct that do violate the Sherman Act.

Section 2C explained the various functions that tie-ins and reciprocity agreements can perform for the sellers or buyers that create them. I believe that, with two exceptions that cover only a very small percentage of such agreements, tie-ins and reciprocity do not violate the Sherman Act because the overwhelming majority of such contracts perform only Sherman-Act-licit functions.

The first exception is tie-ins and reciprocity that function by concealing the existence, apparent extent of, and/or actual locus of the seller's predatory or illegally-retaliatory conduct, which would independently violate the Sherman Act. Although the fact that the conduct that the tie-in or reciprocity agreement concealed was independently Sherman-Act-violative reduces the significance of the conclusion that the tie-in that was used to conceal it also violates the Sherman Act, it does not render that conclusion legally irrelevant: if the trading partner of the firm that is using a tie-in or reciprocity agreement to conceal its antitrust violation is aware of the function of the agreement in question, its participation in such an arrangement will also be Sherman-Act-violative, at least when the trading partner obtains some of the benefits the tie-in or reciprocity agreement yields the firm whose conduct it is concealing.

The second exception relates to the same predation/contrivance-related-retaliation possibilities I acknowledged when discussing producer choices that are designed in the first instance to induce a distributor to make relevant demand-increasing expenditures. Consider a tie-in that functions in the first instance by increasing the cost-effectiveness of a seller's attempt to control the quality of the complements a buyer combines with or sells together with the seller's product or a reciprocity agreement that functions in the first instance by increasing the cost-effectiveness of a buyer's efforts to control the quality of the ingredients its supplier uses to produce a product the buyer purchases. If a firm that employs such tie-ins or reciprocity agreements would not, for transaction-cost reasons, have found them *ex ante* profitable but for its belief that such contracts would or might increase the demand curve it would face in the future by driving a rival out by reducing the profits the rival could make by supplying relevant buyers, by inducing its future rivals to cooperate more with its future contrivance efforts by punishing a rival that did not cooperate with its past contrivance efforts by reducing the profits the latter firm can make by supplying relevant buyers, or by deterring a rival QV investment by reducing the profits the potential investor can expect to realize by supplying certain buyers in each case by improving the performance of the tying seller's/reciprocal trader's product, the contracts in question would be Sherman-Act-violative. The same conclusion will be warranted on analogous facts for tie-ins and reciprocity agreements that increase the amount of price discrimination in which the relevant sellers engage when that price discrimination reduces the demand curve its actual and prospective rivals face (as it well may not) or for so-called "full-line forcing" tie-ins when they injure the "forcer's" actual and potential rivals by inducing the "forcer's" distributors to make more demand-increasing expenditures. I hasten to add, however, that (1) I do not think that a significant number of tie-ins or reciprocity agreements fall within this second exception (in part because I doubt that such contracts will often be the most-cost-effective means for practicing predation or engaging in illegal retaliation) and (2) I doubt the ability of the State or a private plaintiff to establish the predatory or illegally-retaliatory character of the small number of such agreements that are predatory or illegally retaliatory.

Section 2D explained the various functions that resale price maintenance, vertical territorial restraints, and vertical customer-allocation clauses can perform. As it demonstrated, the vast majority of these functions are Sherman-Act-licit. For this reason, with three exceptions, RPM, VTRs, and vertical customer-allocation clauses do not violate the Sherman Act.

The first exceptions are (1) RPM agreements used by a series of producers that are participating in a price-fix to facilitate their price-fix by prohibiting their respective resellers from passing on any price-fix-violating price-concessions the producers in question give them and (2) complementary VTRs and vertical customer-allocation clauses used by multiple participants in a price-fix to divide up territories, classes of buyers, or named buyers among themselves. The second are RPM agreements instigated by multiple resellers that are participants in a price-fix to create contractual obligations that put their suppliers in a position to enforce the resellers' price-fix by suing resellers that resell any supplier's product for less than the horizontally-fixed but nominally-vertical resale minimum price. The third is RPM, VTR, or vertical customer-allocation clauses that perform one or more Sherman-Act-licit functions whose employer would not, for transaction-cost reasons, find them *ex ante* profitable but for its belief that—by improving the attractiveness of its product to relevant buyers by inducing resellers to make additional demand-increasing expenditures, provide better warranty services, and/or supply better product complements or by deterring resellers from charging lower prices that lower the perceived or actual value of the product to some potential buyers—it would reduce the absolute attractiveness of the offers against which the producer would have to compete in the future by driving a rival out by reducing the profits it can make by supplying some buyers, by deterring future undercutting of the seller's contrived offers by preventing current undercutters by punishing an undercutter by reducing the profits it can make by supplying some buyers, and/or by deterring rival QV investments by reducing the profits the potential investors would be able to realize by supplying some buyers.

However, I believe that none of these exceptions is empirically significant. The ability of such clauses to facilitate producer price-fixing is too patent for them to be a cost-effective way of organizing a cartel once law-related costs are taken into account; price-fixing is rarely practiced by resellers; and the arguments I have made against the likely empirical importance of the third exception when discussing its counterpart for other types of surrogates for vertical integration apply equally forcefully *mutatis mutandis* in the current context.

I should perhaps add one further point that relates to RPM, VTRs, and vertical customer-allocation clauses that are designed to prevent intra-brand competition that would drive down the price that buyers must pay for the producer's product (and perhaps that are designed to prevent a producer's resellers from spending more on promotion or door-to-door salesmanship than is in the joint interest of the producer and all resellers). Analysts that assume that the Sherman Act (or, more generally, the U.S. antitrust laws) promulgate a buyer-equivalent-dollar-welfare test of illegality almost always conclude that RPMs, VTRs, and vertical customer-allocation clauses that perform these functions violate the Sherman Act. On my account of the Sherman Act's test of illegality, this legal conclusion is wrong—indeed, would be wrong even if the prohibition of the relevant contractual clauses would confer an equivalent-dollar gain on their employer's customers. As I argued in Chap. 4, correctly interpreted, the Sherman Act would not be read to promulgate such a net-equivalent-dollar relevant-buyer-welfare test of illegality. For example, the Sherman Act does not prohibit a seller from raising its single per-unit price despite the fact that the price-increase will inflict an equivalent-dollar loss on its customers, does not prohibit a seller from practicing price discrimination without having specific anticompetitive intent even when its doing so inflicts a net equivalent-dollar loss on its customers, and does not prohibit a firm that makes the following choice without specific anticompetitive intent from shifting from single exclusively-per-unit pricing to perfect price discrimination or a mixed pricing-technique in which it charges a combination of a lump-sum fee and some supra-TSM-marginal-cost per-unit price even in the usual case in which this shift inflicts an equivalent-dollar loss on the buyer concerned.

These facts are salient because from no defensible normative perspective I can imagine will it be sensible to make the legality of a firm's taking better advantage of a given demand/marginal-cost-curve combination or effectuating a privately-advantageous change in the demand/marginal-cost curve combination it faces (whose advantageousness to the firm is not critically affected by the relevant decision's reducing the absolute attractiveness of the best offer[s] against which the firm will have to compete) depend on whether the firm secures those advantages by inducing its own employees and managers to make the relevant choices or by inducing one or more independent contractors it hires to make the relevant choices. If it is desirable to allow a firm to instruct its employees not to underbid each other when competing for the patronage of any buyer, it must be desirable to allow that firm to prohibit its independent contractors from competing against each other in this way as well. I should add that in many situations attempts to benefit a firm's customers by precluding it from prohibiting its independent distributors from undercutting the prices they respectively charge the buyer for the producer's product will backfire in that it will induce the firm either to increase the per-unit price it charges its independent distributors for its product (while presumably reducing the lump-sum [franchise] fee it charges them) or to integrate forward into distribution itself.

Section 2E discussed the Sherman-Act-licit functions of single-brand exclusive dealerships, the possible Sherman-Act-illicit horizontal market-division function such dealerships can perform in combination with an appropriate set of non-single-brand exclusive-dealership arrangements by the individual members of a set of product rivals, and the Sherman-Act-illicit predatory function that such dealerships can perform by locking up enough distributors to prevent an established-rival investment from breaking even (to induce exit) or render a potential rival investment prospectively unprofitable. A seller's creation of one or more single-brand exclusive dealerships that is either contrived oligopolistic or predatory clearly is Sherman-Act-violative. In relation to the predation possibility, I should add that a seller's use of single-brand exclusive dealerships to prevent its dealers from making choices that reduce its profits by increasing its rivals' sales or to prevent its dealers from using the training or information with which it provides them to sell rival products will be predatory if, for transaction-cost reasons, the seller would not have found the arrangement in question *ex ante* profitable but for its belief that it would reduce the absolute attractiveness of the offers against which it would have to compete in the future by driving a rival out, deterring a possible additional QV investment, or making the rival's product less absolutely attractive to relevant buyers (though in the training-and-information-provision case one might contest the characterization of the conduct as predatory or at least the conclusion that it was Sherman-Act-violative by arguing that the single-brand exclusive dealership would be economically efficient in an otherwise-Pareto-perfect economy insofar as it critically affected the profitability of the producer's providing its independent distributor with valuable training and information). I suspect that the vast majority of single-brand exclusive dealerships are Sherman-Act-licit—in fact, are both legitimately profitable and do not lock in distributors whose independence would be critical to an established rival's exit decision or a prospective investor's investment decision (when a decision to exit or not to invest would reduce the competition the relevant seller faced).

Section 2F discussed the Sherman-Act-licit and predatory functions of slotting arrangements. Since such arrangements are functionally identical to the other moves a seller can make to induce its independent distributors to make demand-increasing expenditures on its behalf (discussed in Sect. 2B), the preceding analysis of the legality of those moves under the Sherman Act applies *mutatis mutandis* to slotting arrangements.

Section 2G discussed both the Sherman-Act-licit and predatory functions of long-term full-requirements contracts. As it showed, long-term full requirements will be predatory in the same circumstances in which single-firm exclusive dealerships are predatory. Thus, long-term full requirements will be predatory both when they perform no legitimate functions and are used exclusively to drive an extant rival out or deter a rival QV investment and when they perform legitimate functions when, for transaction-cost reasons, the seller that arranges them would not have found them *ex ante* profitable but for its belief that they would or might reduce the absolute attractiveness of the best offer(s) against which it would have to compete in the future by driving a rival out by depriving that rival of the profits it would otherwise have made by supplying the buyer(s) the agreement(s) locks (lock) up and/or by deterring a potential QV investor from making a rival QV investment by creating a situation in which that firm will realize that it will not make the profits it would otherwise have anticipated making by supplying the buyer(s) the agreement(s) in question locks (lock) up.

* * *

I recognize that a wide variety of contractual or other surrogates for vertical integration will sometimes violate the Sherman Act. However, for the reasons just delineated, I am certain that the vast majority of exemplars of all these categories of surrogates do not violate the Sherman Act and suspect that it rarely will be possible for the State or private plaintiff to establish the illegality under the Sherman Act of most of the small number of surrogates for vertical integration that do violate the Act.

(B) The Clayton Act as Correctly Interpreted and Applied

The Clayton Act covers only some of the surrogates for vertical integration. In particular, Section 2 of the Clayton Act (the Robinson-Patman Act) covers "price discrimination" by sellers in the sale (a category that excludes leases) of "commodities" (a category that excludes, for example, services) of "like grade and quality" on appropriately-similar dates[1181] by the same seller to different buyers[1182] where "price discrimination" is enquoted because the statute defines the expression in a way that diverges from what I take to be the more functional definition of economists to include the charging of prices that are different even when the differences are cost-justified as part of a regime that recognizes a cost-justification as well as a "meeting competition in good faith" defense. The Robinson-Patman Act—more specifically, Section 2(f) of the Clayton Act—also makes it illegal for a buyer "knowingly to induce or receive a [prohibited] discrimination in price" when its doing so injures one or more of its rivals, a provision that manifests the enacting Congress' distributive concern that large chains were obtaining price-concessions not justified by costs that were unfairly disadvantaging and endangering the survival of small resellers. The fact that Sect. 2 covers "price discrimination" by sellers in the sense in which it defines that practice implies that it also covers tie-ins and reciprocity agreements that increase the extent to which their employers practice price discrimination. Section 2 of the Clayton Act covers slotting arrangements when they involve charging different distributors different prices. (However, although any such price-differences would not be "cost-justified" in Clayton Act terms, I doubt that many covered slotting arrangements violate the Clayton Act's standard lessening-competition test of *prima facie* illegality and the perpetrators of those slotting arrangements that do should be able to establish an organizational-economic-efficiency defense for their conduct.) Section 3 of the Clayton Act covers all arrangements that fix a price or discount or rebate of a commodity or lease (as opposed to a service or intellectual property) "on the condition, agreement, or understanding that the lessee or purchaser. . .shall not deal in the goods, wares, machinery, supplies, or other commodities of a competitor or competitors of the lessor or seller. . .." Section 3 therefore covers all single-product full-requirements contracts that involve a commodity and all single-brand exclusive dealerships that involve one or more commodities. It also covers all full-requirements tie-ins in which both products are commodities and the tying seller is a producer or real distributor of the tied product and all full-requirements reciprocity agreements in which both products are commodities and the buyer of one of the commodities is a meaningful producer or distributor of the second commodity (to which the full-requirements term relates). Both Sections 2 and 3 of the statute prohibit the conduct they cover "where [its] effect. . .may be substantially to lessen competition or tend to create a monopoly in any line of commerce. . .."

For both aesthetic and policy reasons, I wish that the preceding sentence stated everything that needs to be said about the tests of illegality that the Clayton Act prescribes for the various surrogates for vertical integration. Unfortunately,

---

[1181] The requirement of contemporaneousness is implicit, though, as will be explained, its operationalization is not straightforward.

[1182] This requirement is definitional. However, as will be explained, its operationalization is not always straightforward.

however, it does not. Although the Clayton Act's "general" "lessening-competition" test of illegality does apply to all the surrogates for vertical integration it covers as well as to vertical mergers and acquisitions, it appears that, legally correctly interpreted, the 1936 Robinson-Patman Act amendment to Section 2 of the 1914 Clayton Act also condemns "price discrimination" in its sense that is not requisitely likely to lessen competition in the Clayton Act sense if it is requisitely likely to injure a disfavored reseller-buyer by worsening its competitive position vis-à-vis one or more favored reseller-buyers. The added words in question are: "or to injure, destroy, or prevent competition with any person who either grants or knowingly receives the benefits [of price discrimination in the Clayton Act sense] or with customers of either of them." I acknowledge that the added text just quoted is confusingly drafted and that its instruction that "price discrimination" be condemned whenever doing so would prevent a disfavored buyer from being injured in the stated way even when the injury to such a competitor is not associated with an injury to competition is inconsistent with the rest of U.S. antitrust law. However, that does seem to be the import of the language of the added text. Moreover, this reading of the text is supported by (1) the fact that the Congress that passed the Robinson-Patman Act was acting in substantial part out of a concern that small resellers (*e.g.*, "mom and pop" grocers) were being driven out as a result of the price-concessions that large chains were able to obtain as well as by (2) the fact that the statute provides some reason to believe that the preceding Congressional concern would not have been eliminated by proof that the price "concessions" the large chains were able to obtain were "cost-justified" in the sense in which economists would define that adjective: the fact that the statute defines "price discrimination" in price-difference terms, places the burden of proof on the "cost-justification" issue on the "discriminator," and provides a list of legitimating cost-differences that might be interpreted to exclude some cost-differences whose existence economists would count against a claim that price discrimination in their sense had been practiced from the set of cost-differences that can justify price-differences in Clayton Act cases (see below).

The deservedly-highly-respected U.S.-antitrust-law expert Herbert Hovenkamp has attempted to refute the argument that the text that the Robinson-Patman Act adds to Section 2 of the 1914 Clayton Act supplements the original Act's "lessening-competition" test with the limited "injury to a competitor" test delineated above by pointing out that the added language covers "price discrimination" "that injures competition."[1183] I would like to be but am not persuaded: the words "injure competition" in the added language refer to the competition that the disfavored buyer can give the favored buyer(s) when competing for resale customers, not to competition in the "competitive-outcome" Clayton Act sense.

I will now analyze the legality of price discrimination under both the general Clayton Act "lessening-competition" test and the "injury to a rival of a favored buyer" test that the Robinson-Patman Act added to the Clayton Act's general test of

[1183] HOVENKAMP HORNBOOK 581.

illegality. In my judgment, the overwhelming majority of price-discrimination exemplars do not violate the Clayton Act's "lessen competition" test of illegality. Admittedly, price discrimination that violates the Sherman Act because it is predatory or illicitly retaliatory will also violate the Clayton Act if it is requisitely likely to achieve its anticompetitive purpose. And price discrimination that does not violate the Sherman Act because its discriminator-perceived (and usually actual) profitability is guaranteed by its ability to help the discriminator take advantage of (1) the fact that its OCAs vary among the buyers it is best-placed to supply and/or (2) the fact that the discriminator is in a position to steal a customer it is not best-placed to supply because the buyer's best-placed supplier overestimated its (*i.e.*, that rival's) NEHNOP, believed incorrectly that it (the rival) could obtain an OM naturally, or was attempting to contrive an oligopolistic margin will nevertheless violate the Clayton Act in the rare instances in which the price discrimination in question (1) is requisitely likely to impose a net equivalent-dollar loss on buyers of the discriminator's product and buyers of the discriminator's rivals' products by reducing the absolute attractiveness of the offers these buyers receive from their inferior suppliers and (2) does not increase the discriminator's organizational economic efficiency. Some explanation of this last possibility is required. In some situations, price discrimination that does not violate the Sherman Act will produce the above relevant so-called "primary-line" loss because—although its profitability to the discriminator is not critically affected by its having this impact—it will drive a rival of the discriminator out by reducing the profits the rival can make (in circumstances in which the exiting firm will not be immediately replaced by an equally-effective competitor) or will deter a rival primary-line QV-investment expansion or entry by reducing the profits that a prospective rival investor should anticipate making in that, in comparison with the relevant firm's non-discriminatory price, the discriminator's discriminatorily-low price reduces the relevant rival's actual or prospective profits by more than the discriminator's discriminatorily-high price-increases the relevant rival's actual or prospective profits. I hasten to add that Sherman-Act-licit price discrimination will not *tend to* produce such effects—indeed, will not even tend to reduce the profits of the discriminator's extant rivals or the prospective profits of potential investors in the discriminator's "market." In general, Sherman-Act-licit price discrimination will be as likely to increase as to decrease the actual profits of the discriminator's extant rivals or the prospective profits of potential investors in the discriminator's area of product-space. However, although it would simplify matters if this were not the case, there will be situations in which a firm's Sherman-Act-licit price discrimination will inflict a loss on its actual and prospective competitors, and there will (I suspect) be situations in which this loss critically affects their decisions to continue to operate or invest (in circumstances in which the exiting or non-investing rival either will not be replaced or will be replaced by a less-competition-enhancing firm). I should say, though, that in my judgment, Sherman-Act-licit price discrimination will rarely lessen primary-line competition and that, even when it is requisitely likely to do so, it will rarely if ever be practicable for the State or a private plaintiff to establish that fact.

Sherman-Act-licit price discrimination can also violate the Clayton Act by lessening so-called secondary-line competition (competition in the "market" in which the discriminator's customers operate). The standard account of this possibility focuses on situations in which the discriminator's favored and disfavored customers compete against each other and the discrimination reduces competition by causing the disfavored customer to exit. I doubt the empirical importance or legal significance of this possibility. In my judgment, firms will rarely if ever find it profitable to engage in price discrimination that will generate this effect (*inter alia*, because it will strengthen the bargaining power of its surviving customer[s]) and will find it profitable to practice price discrimination that generates this effect only when the elimination of the disfavored customer(s) increases the organizational economic efficiency of secondary-line operations (in which case a plausible variant of the organizational-economic-efficiency defense may be available to the discriminator). However, I acknowledge that in some cases in which the discriminator is not discriminating between or among secondary-line competitors but is charging a lower price to one customer than it charges other buyers that are not rivals of the favored customer, the price-concession could lessen competition in the favored customer's "market" by improving its competitive-position array and concomitantly worsening (1) the competitive-position array of its extant rivals, causing one or more of them to exit, and/or (2) the prospective competitive-position arrays of one or more prospective investors in the favored buyer's market, deterring one or more of them from investing even when the profitability of the lower price to the discriminator is not critically affected by its having any such effect. Once more, though, I doubt that this result obtains in a significant number of cases and suspect that, even in the few instances in which the result is sufficiently likely to obtain to render the discrimination illegal under the Clayton Act, the State or a private plaintiff will not be able to establish the relevant facts either at all or at a non-prohibitive cost.

It is also conceivable that a firm's Sherman-Act-licit discrimination in favor of a buyer that itself produces an intermediate good will lessen competition in the so-called tertiary market in which the customer of the discriminator's favored buyer operates by making it inherently profitable for the customer of the discriminator's customer to pass on to its customers some of the "price reduction" the discriminator's price-reduction to its customer caused that firm to pass on to its customer in circumstances in which the final price-reduction in the series of related price-reductions—though inherently profitable—drives a tertiary-line incumbent out or decreases QV-investment competition in the tertiary line by deterring an incumbent expansion or new entry. Once more, however, I doubt both the empirical importance of this possibility and the ability of the State or a private plaintiff to make out such a case at non-prohibitive cost.

As I indicated previously, although I regret this fact, all things considered, the text that the Robinson-Patman Act added to the 1914 Clayton Act warrants the conclusion that, regardless of whether Clayton Act "price discrimination" is requisitely likely to lessen competition or violates the Sherman Act's test of illegality, "price discrimination" in the Clayton Act sense violates the Clayton

Act if it injures a disfavored buyer by depriving it of the profits it would otherwise have been able to realize by competing with favored buyers. However, I suspect that few buyers will be entitled to recovery for this reason because sellers will rarely find it profitable to engage in price discrimination that causes disfavored resellers to lose sales and profits to favored rivals.

Some explanation is required. On the one hand, sellers will normally not find it profitable to practice non-cost-justified Clayton Act discrimination that causes a disfavored buyer to lose sales to a favored buyer because (1) buyers that would make (additional) sales but for the producer's non-cost-justified discrimination against them must be (in the absence of such discrimination) privately-better-placed to make those sales (or use the seller's product) than is the favored "buyer" and (2) producers will find it inherently most profitable to have their product distributed or used by the buyer that would be privately-best-placed to distribute or use it if the producer did not practice price discrimination against the potential buyer in question and in favor of that firm's rival. That is why I suspect that sellers will rarely engage in non-cost-justified Clayton Act price discrimination that injures the disfavored buyer by worsening its competitive position relative to that of favored buyers. On the other hand, sellers may on rare occasions as opposed to never practice price discrimination that injures the disfavored buyer in this way for two reasons. First, in some situations, the disfavored buyer that would have made sales had it not been disfavored will have done so from a position of private competitive inferiority (by waging intra-brand competition that is against its and the seller's joint interest). I think that this situation will arise at most rarely rather than more frequently because sellers that confront such a possibility will normally respond to it in ways other than by practicing price discrimination against the prospective intra-brand competitor—*viz.*, (1) by lowering their lump-sum fees and raising their per-unit prices to all buyers, (2) by engaging in minimum-price-setting RPM or incorporating vertical territorial restraints or vertical customer-allocation clauses into their contracts of sale (when the living law permits them to do so), (3) by threatening to discontinue and/or actually discontinuing the supply of buyers that wage such intra-brand competition, or (4) by engaging in forward vertical integration. (I should add that the Robinson-Patman Act provision in question is inconsistent with the [generally-acknowledged] legality of the relevant vertical integration and sales policy [at least when the latter is not accompanied by threats of supply-terminations or explanations of actual supply-terminations]). Second, in other situations, a seller will find it profitable to practice price discrimination that injures a disfavored buyer that would otherwise have been privately-best-placed to make certain sales by rendering it privately-worse-placed than a favored buyer to do so to prevent the disfavored buyer from entering the upstream, product-production business. I think that this situation will arise rarely rather than more frequently. I should also add—as I indicated previously—that in many situations producers will be legally entitled to prevent buyers from integrating backward into the producer's business in this way (most likely, when the producer's action is designed to protect its intellectual-property rights in its product-design or the production process it uses to produce its product and/or its right to keep its customer list to itself but also, more than conceivably, more generally).

Of course, the preceding conclusions are perfectly consistent with some buyers being legally entitled to recover under the "injury to competitor" test of illegality that the Robinson-Patman Act adds to the Clayton Act's "lessening-competition" test. Under a legal regime in which maximum-price-setting RPM, vertical territorial restraints, and vertical-customer-allocation clauses may well be found illegal, if producers do not find vertical integration forward or relevant sales policies or relevant changes in lump-sum fees possible or profitable at least in the short or medium run, they may find it profitable to prevent intra-brand competition by discriminating against privately-worse-than-best-placed suppliers when their doing so will cause those suppliers to lose sales and profits to favored rivals if the producers believe that they will not be sued for doing so (because the disfavored buyers may not realize that they have been discriminated against or do not want to alienate the producer or because the court may erroneously exonerate the producer).

I turn now to the legality of full-requirements tie-ins, full-requirements contracts more generally, and single-brand-exclusive-distributorship arrangements (which effectuate a variant of a full-requirements contract), all of which are covered by Section 3 of the Clayton Act. As we saw, full-requirements tie-ins can perform a wide variety of Sherman-Act-licit functions—reducing the cost a producer must incur to control the quality of the complements its reseller combines with or sells with the producer's product, reducing the cost the seller must incur to prevent arbitrage, reducing the cost of implementing a meter-pricing arrangement, and increasing the profitability of supra-marginal-cost per-unit pricing in non-metering contexts both when the so-called tying product is a final good and when it is an input against which substitution is possible.

Two questions need to be addressed at this juncture.

(1) can Sherman-Act-licit full-requirements tie-ins that perform one or more of these functions "lessen competition" in the Clayton Act sense of that expression, and
(2) if they can, will the tying seller be able to establish an organizational-economic-efficiency defense for its use of them?

I will address these questions first on the conventional assumption that the relevant unit of analysis is the impact of an individual seller's use of full-requirements tie-ins and then, after explaining why this traditional focus may be inapposite, on the assumption that the relevant unit of analysis is the impact of a decision to allow all members of a relevant set of rivals to use full-requirements tie-ins of the relevant type.

Before proceeding, three background points. First, although as we shall see, U.S. courts have been primarily concerned with the alleged tendency of full-requirements tie-ins—indeed, of all tie-ins—or related sales policies to reduce competition in the so-called tied-product market, the more likely though still unlikely outcome is that an individual seller's tie-ins/related sales policies (or the use of tie-ins by a set of rivals) will reduce competition in the so-called tying-product market. *Inter alia*, this conclusion is favored by the related facts that (1) tying sellers often do not produce the tied product their tie-ins involve—a fact that manifests the reality that the tying seller need not produce the tied product itself for full-requirements tie-ins or related sales policies to perform the various functions they can perform—and (2) a tying seller that does not produce the tied product itself will place a negative value on any tendency its use of tie-ins has to reduce tied-product competition (since it is a buyer of the tied product).

Second, it is important to focus on the "Compared to what?" question. Many analyses of the impact of tie-ins/related sales policies (and such other surrogates for vertical integration as RPM, non-single-brand exclusive dealerships [created by an appropriate series of vertical-territorial restraints and vertical customer-allocation clauses], and non-tie-in full-requirements contracts [including those created by single-brand exclusive dealerships]) assume that the seller that employs such arrangements would respond to their effective prohibition by ceasing to employ them and leaving unchanged all other features of its organizational arrangements, all other clauses in its contracts of sale, and all other elements of its sales policies. This assumption is clearly unjustified.

A seller that finds it profitable to use full-requirements tie-ins or a full-requirements sales policy to control the quality of the complements that one or more of its resellers use or sell together with its product may well respond to an effective legal prohibition of its doing so (1) by contractually obligating its resellers to use complements of specified attributes or complements specified by brand and model and incurring the cost of enforcing its legal right that they fulfill this contractual commitment (the cost of inspecting its customers' inventories and analyzing their products and the cost of suing buyers that violate this contractual obligation or of obtaining redress from them by negotiating a settlement in the shadow of the law), (2) by changing its product to render its extant independently-produced complements incompatible with it and perhaps keeping the nature of the changes in question secret, or (3) by vertically integrating forward into distribution (or final-product production when the potentially-tying product is an input). A seller that finds it profitable to use full-requirements tie-ins to prevent arbitrage may well respond to an effective legal prohibition of its doing so (1) by changing its pricing-technique to make arbitrage less profitable (by reducing its lump-sum fees and raising its per-unit prices or by reducing the magnitude of any differences in the per-unit prices it charges different buyers), (2) by altering the product it supplies those buyers to which it wants to charge per-unit prices that are lower than the average lump-sum fee *plus* per-unit price it is attempting to obtain from other buyers to make the product it supplies the former buyers less attractive to or unsuitable for the latter buyers (by incurring [A] the cost of altering its product to make it cheaper to detect prohibited cross-selling by inspecting non-customers' inventories and/or final products, [B] the cost of spying on its customers and the non-customers with which they may engage in arbitrage, and [C] the cost of suing customers that engage in cross-selling or of obtaining redress from them by negotiating a settlement in the shadow of the law), (3) by including a no-arbitrage clause in its contracts of sale to relevant buyers and enforcing its rights under that clause, or (4) by vertically integrating forward into distribution. A seller that finds it profitable to use full-requirements tie-ins or related sales policies to implement a meter-pricing scheme when selling a durable machine or franchise may well respond to an effective legal prohibition of its doing so (1) by changing its machine to render extant independent complements incompatible with it and perhaps keeping the nature of the changes secret so that it can charge higher per-unit prices for its complements (which it may or may not produce itself) than the standard market price for similar complements, (2) by installing, inspecting, and reading an actual meter, (3) by using a percentage-of-sales-royalty (endproduct-royalty) scheme, or (4) by vertically integrating forward into the machine-using business or the franchisee business. A seller of a final good that finds it profitable to use a full-requirements tie-in to increase the profitability of its non-meter-pricing supra-marginal-cost per-unit pricing that is prohibited from doing so may find it profitable to respond (1) by reducing the extent to which it engages in supra-marginal-cost per-unit pricing, (2) by using demand-increasing-expenditure subsidies or slotting contracts to decrease the extent to which its supra-marginal-cost per-unit pricing of the so-called tying product reduces its profits by deterring its individual resellers from making demand-increasing expenditures that are in their individual and its joint interest, or (3) by vertically integrating forward into the resale business. And finally a seller of an input against which substitution is possible that finds it profitable to use full-requirement tie-ins to increase the profitability of its supra-marginal-cost per-unit pricing that is legally prohibited from doing so may find it profitable to respond (1) by shifting to an endproduct-royalty scheme on the final product or (2) by vertically integrating forward into final-product production. These realities are relevant because they affect (1) whether, in an individual case in which or the likelihood that across all relevant cases in which an individual seller uses tie-ins or sales policies that perform some function or set of functions, the tie-in(s) or sales policies in question will inflict a net equivalent-dollar loss on Clayton-Act-relevant buyers by reducing the absolute attractiveness of the best offer they respectively receive from any inferior supplier, (2) whether a rule allowing all members of a set of rivals to use any particular functional type of tie-in or related sales policy will inflict a net equivalent-dollar loss on Clayton-Act-relevant buyers by reducing the absolute attractiveness of the best offer they respectively receive from any inferior supplier, and (3) the ability of a defendant in a tie-in or related-sales-policy case to make out an organizational-economic-efficiency defense.

Third, a point that relates to the organizational-economic-efficiency defense that I think correct as a matter of law to read into the Clayton Act. In my judgment, for the purpose of applying this defense, it is correct as a matter of law to assess the economic efficiency of the various surrogates for vertical integration that firms can use on an otherwise-Pareto-perfect assumption that implies that, unless the surrogate has an effect that destroys the following equalities, the private cost and benefits of such surrogates will equal their respective allocative counterparts. This assumption is the counterpart to the assumption that, when assessing the legality under the

Sherman Act of conduct that reduces the absolute attractiveness of the best offers against which its perpetrator will have to compete, one should determine whether this consequence of the conduct will render it profitable though economically inefficient on an otherwise-Pareto-perfect assumption.

I begin by analyzing the legality of tie-ins and reciprocity agreements under the Clayton Act on the contestable assumption that the relevant unit for legal analysis is an individual seller's use of such agreements. When if ever will an individual seller's use of tie-ins and reciprocity (1) be covered by the Clayton Act, (2) be requisitely likely to inflict a net equivalent-dollar loss on the combination of the employing seller's customers and the customers of its product rivals by reducing the absolute attractiveness of the best offers they respectively receive from any inferior supplier to violate the Clayton Act's test of *prima facie* illegality, and (3) in those situations in which an individual seller's use of such agreements will be requisitely likely to have such an impact on Clayton-Act-relevant buyers, not increase the perpetrator's organizational economic efficiency in a way that would render its conduct lawful under the Clayton Act?

As I indicated earlier, the Clayton Act does not cover all tie-ins and reciprocity agreements. More specifically, Section 2 of the Clayton Act does not cover tie-ins or reciprocity agreements that do not increase the amount of price discrimination in the Clayton Act sense that the perpetrator practices and/or that increase the amount of such price discrimination practiced in relation to the sale of something that the Clayton Act does not classify as a commodity, and Section 3 does not cover tie-ins or reciprocity agreements that do not contain full-requirements clauses, does not cover tie-ins or reciprocity agreements that do contain full-requirements clauses if the party that is not subjected to the full-requirements obligation does not produce or really distribute the commodity that the other party is under a full-requirements obligation to purchase, and does not cover tie-ins or reciprocity agreements that do contain full-requirements clauses and are not excluded from coverage for the second reason just delineated if one or both of the "goods" involved in the agreement are not commodities in the Clayton Act sense—*e.g.*, are services or intellectual property. I will now analyze the Clayton Act legality of each functional type of tie-in and reciprocity agreement.

I start with tie-ins that increase the proficiency with which a seller can control the quality of the complements its customers combine with or resell with its product. Because such tie-ins always obligate the buyer they involve to purchase its full requirements of the "tied" product (the complement) from the seller, they will be covered by Section 3 of the Clayton Act whenever the two goods they involve are commodities in the Clayton Act sense that the tying seller produces itself or meaningfully distributes. To the extent that a seller's use of such tie-ins improves its competitive-position array by enabling it to increase the actual or buyer-perceived value of its product to at least some buyers by more than the use of such agreements increases the marginal cost the seller must incur to supply the buyers in question, the seller's use of such agreements for this purpose could inflict a net equivalent-dollar loss on Clayton-Act-relevant buyers by reducing the absolute attractiveness of the best offer they respectively received from any inferior supplier in two possible ways:

(1) by inducing one or more extant rivals of the tying seller to exit by reducing the profits it or they can earn by continuing to operate their businesses by making the tying seller best-placed when that rival would otherwise have been best-placed or by reducing that rival's OCA in relation to one or more buyers it remained best-placed to supply by improving the tying seller's competitive position in relation to the relevant buyer(s) in circumstances in which the associated loss to Clayton-Act-relevant buyers would not be eliminated by any related new entries or established-firm expansions and
(2) by deterring a rival potential investor in the tying seller's area of product-space from making a QV investment in that area of product-space by reducing the number of buyers its project would be best-placed to supply and/or the competitive advantage it would enjoy in relation to some buyers it would be best-placed to supply by improving the tying seller's competitive positions in relation to those buyers in circumstances in which the potential associated loss to Clayton-Act-relevant buyers would not be eliminated by the substitution of some other QV investment for the deterred QV investment.

However, if my claim that the Clayton Act should be interpreted to recognize an organizational-economic-efficiency defense is correct, an individual seller's use of tie-ins to control the quality of the complements combined with its product should not be deemed to violate the Clayton Act even if it would be requisitely likely to inflict a net equivalent-dollar loss on Clayton-Act-relevant buyers by driving one or more rivals of the defendant out or deterring one or more potential investors in its area of product-space from making a QV investment in it if the tie-in would not have yielded this outcome had it not increased its perpetrator's organizational economic efficiency. For tie-ins to increase the tying seller's organizational economic efficiency by increasing the proficiency with which it controlled the complements its customers used together with its product, the relevant agreements must reduce the private cost to their perpetrator of exercising any given amount of control on the quality of the relevant complements their customers use, increase the extent to which the perpetrator controls the quality of the relevant product at any given cost, simultaneously reduce private cost and increase quality control, increase the dollar value of the extra quality-control achieved by more than it increased private cost, or create a quality-control cost-saving that exceeded the dollar value of any associated reduction in quality-control. Since on the antitrust laws' otherwise-Pareto-perfect assumption, any associated change in the private cost of quality-control will equal its allocative counterpart and any related change in the private value of the quality-control achieved will equal its allocative counterpart, any exemplar of this functional type of tie-in would be profitable even if it would not reduce the absolute attractiveness of the offers against which its perpetrator will have to compete will have increased its perpetrator's organizational economic efficiency and (on my legal assumption) will not violate the Clayton Act even in what I take to be the rare instances in which it is requisitely likely to inflict a net equivalent-dollar loss on

Clayton-Act-relevant buyers in a Clayton-Act-relevant way if it would not have done so had it not increased the perpetrator's organizational economic efficiency (even if the appropriate focus for the applicable legal analysis were the impact of the individual seller's use of such tie-ins as opposed to the impact of a rule allowing the relevant seller and all its rivals to use such tie-ins).

As we saw, reciprocity agreements can also perform a quality-control function. In particular, a buyer of a final product may find it profitable to control the quality of the product it is purchasing by requiring its supplier to purchase from it or through it the supplier's full requirements of an ingredient or other input used to produce the final product in question. If the "goods" involved are commodities and the buyer of the final product produces or really distributes the ingredient/input in question itself, this arrangement will be covered by Section 3 of the Clayton Act. The analysis of the legality of an individual firm's using such ingredient/input-quality-control reciprocity agreements is exactly parallel to the analysis of the legality of an individual firm's use of complement-quality-controlling tie-ins. (Recall: I think that the appropriate focus for the analyses of the *prima facie* Clayton Act legality of tie-ins and reciprocity is the impact not of an individual firm's use of such agreements but of a rule allowing all members of a set of product-rivals to use such agreements.)

I turn now to non-predatory tie-ins or reciprocity agreements that function by preventing arbitrage. When a tie-in or reciprocity agreement that prevents arbitrage involves a "good" that is a commodity and increases the extent to which its user practices price discrimination in the Clayton Act sense, it will be covered by Section 2 of the Clayton Act. Because tie-ins that prevent arbitrage may neither formally nor in practice prohibit the buyer from purchasing some of the tied good from someone other than the seller (may just require the buyer to purchase from the seller the amount of the tied good it would use in its own business if it used in its own business all the tying good it purchased from the seller), tie-ins in this functional category may not be covered by Section 3 even if they involve commodities and the seller does produce or meaningfully distribute the tied product. Because reciprocity agreements that enable a firm in its capacity as a seller to prevent arbitrage do no prohibit the firm that buys the seller's good from using or dealing in commodities that are rivalrous with "the seller's" products (prohibit "the buyer" from selling its output to anyone other than "the seller"), they are not covered by Section 3 of the Clayton Act.

In any event, an individual firm's use of arbitrage-preventing tie-ins will violate the lessening-competition test of *prima facie* illegality of Section 2 (when it increases the extent to which the firm engages in price discrimination) and the lessening-competition test of *prima facie* illegality of Section 3 when it increases the extent to which the firm includes full-requirements clauses in its contracts of sale if (1) the extra discrimination or full-requirements contracts in question reduce the profits that one or more actual rivals can earn or prospective rival QV investors could earn on their new investments (which need not be the case), (2) the profit-loss or prospective-profit-reduction in question critically affects the relevant rival's decision to stay in business or make the relevant QV investment, and (3) the induced exit or decision not to invest inflicts a net equivalent-dollar loss on Clayton-Act-relevant buyers that exceeds any net equivalent-dollar gains the tie-in would otherwise have conferred on them. I suspect that in the vast majority of cases in which sellers are using non-predatory tie-ins to prevent arbitrage, one or more of these conditions will not be satisfied—*i.e.*, the use of one or more such agreements by a given seller will not inflict a net equivalent-dollar loss on Clayton-Act-relevant buyers in a Clayton-Act-relevant way.

Arbitrage-preventing reciprocity agreements are covered by the Clayton Act only when they increase the extent to which their employer practices price discrimination—*i.e.*, only by Section 2. The portion of the tie-in analysis that relates to this possibility applies fully to discrimination-increasing arbitrage-preventing reciprocity.

Unfortunately, it is not easy to generalize about whether a seller whose arbitrage-preventing tie-in or reciprocity agreement would otherwise violate the Clayton Act will be able to make out an organizational-economic-efficiency defense. Equally unfortunately, some of the points that are relevant will be far more comprehensible to readers who are conversant with the kind of economic-efficiency analysis that will be developed in and dominate the discussion of THE WELFARE ECONOMICS OF ANTITRUST POLICY AND U.S. AND E.U. ANTITRUST LAW.

Three points would be relevant in this connection if the tying seller/reciprocal trader would not respond to a prohibition of its using tie-ins and reciprocal-trading agreements to prevent arbitrage by vertically integrating forward. First, if the agreements in question reduce the private cost their employer incurs to prevent arbitrage (and, on the relevant otherwise-Pareto-perfect assumption, the allocative cost it generates when preventing arbitrage) but do not affect the amount of either conventional price discrimination or lump-sum pricing the perpetrator practices, they will increase economic efficiency on that account in a way that entitles their perpetrator to establish an organizational-economic-efficiency defense. (Of course, if the agreements increase the private costs their employer incurs to prevent arbitrage [as they might if they increase the extent to which their employer prevented arbitrage], given the incentives to cross-selling its pricing would otherwise have generated for its customers, this consideration will count against the seller's ability to establish an organizational-economic-efficiency defense.)

Second, if the agreements in question do not affect the amount of conventional price discrimination or lump-sum pricing in which their employer engages (by reducing the cost it must incur to prevent or allow the arbitrage that such pricing gives its customers an incentive to practice) but do reduce (increase) the amount of arbitrage that their employer's customers practice, they will tend on that account to reduce (increase) economic efficiency on the relevant otherwise-Pareto-perfect assumption because on that assumption the fact that the relevant cross-selling is jointly profitable for its participants implies that it is economically efficient.

Third, to the extent that, for the reason stated in the preceding sentence, the agreements in question increase the amount of conventional price discrimination or pure or mixed lump-sum pricing their employer practices, their use will tend to decrease economic efficiency because both such pricing-techniques are economically inefficient (not only on an otherwise-Pareto-perfect assumption but also on realistic assumptions). Thus, conventional price discrimination tends to be misallocative both because it is allocatively as well as privately transaction-costly and because it causes misallocation by allocating some units of the good in question to buyers that are charged the lower price despite the fact that the dollar value that these buyers place on those units is lower than the dollar value placed on those units by potential buyers that are charged the higher price and value the units in question above the lower price that is charged for them but below the higher price they would be charged for them. Admittedly, lump-sum pricing will sometimes be economically efficient since some of the private benefits it yields its participants are allocative as well as private (*e.g.*, the benefits such pricing can yield [1] by reducing the sum of the seller's and buyer's risk costs and, relatedly, the amount of resources the seller and buyer allocate to estimating the buyer's demand for the seller' product, [2] the benefits such pricing can yield [at least on the otherwise-Pareto-perfect assumption] by making it profitable for a reselling buyer to make the demand-increasing expenditures that are in its and the seller's joint interest, and [3] the economic-efficiency gains the use of this pricing-technique would generate in an otherwise-Pareto-perfect world by rendering profitable the QV investments that created the products and services to whose sale it was applied [by enabling the sellers to profit by eliminating buyer surplus that in an otherwise-Pareto-perfect economy would sometimes render economically-efficient QV investments unprofitable (in our actual, highly-Pareto-imperfect world, I suspect that such buyer surplus will, if anything, almost always increase economic efficiency by rendering unprofitable economically-inefficient QV investments that would otherwise have been rendered profitable by the other Pareto imperfections in the system [most importantly, imperfections in seller price competition])]). However, for three reasons, I suspect that across all situations in which it is employed lump-sum pricing will decrease economic efficiency:

(1) lump-sum pricing will tend to be more privately and allocatively transaction-costly than pricing-techniques that do not involve the charging of any lump-sum fee (in part because lump-sum-pricing arrangements always involve the negotiation and drafting of written contracts);
(2) some of the private benefits of the variant of lump-sum pricing that is almost always employed (a variant that combines the lump-sum fee with a supra-TSM-marginal-cost per-unit price)—most importantly, the benefits such pricing yields the seller by reducing the losses it suffers because of its or its customer's pessimism about the customer's quantity demand for the seller's product during the period covered by the contract—have no allocative counterpart (at least if the seller would not respond to the prohibition of its using such a mixed pricing-technique by doing additional research into the buyer's demand for the product in question); and
(3) as I just indicated, in the real world, the tendency of lump-sum pricing to increase the profits a QV investor can realize on its QV investment will tend to generate economic inefficiency by increasing the extent to which, from the perspective of economic efficiency, the economy devotes too many resources to

the creation of QV investments relative to the amount that it devotes to production-process research and the production of units of extant products.

On our current assumption that the seller in question would not respond to a prohibition of its using tie-ins and/or reciprocity agreements to prevent arbitrage by vertically integrating forward, the preceding points imply that the likelihood that such a seller's use of arbitrage-preventing tie-ins and reciprocity will have increased its organizational economic efficiency (that the seller would be justified in asserting an organizational-economic-efficiency defense for such conduct) will be (1) directly related to the amount by which its use of these agreements for this purpose reduced the transactions costs its attempts to prevent arbitrage generated and (2) inversely related to the extent to which its use of such agreements for this purpose decreases arbitrage and increases its use of price discrimination and lump-sum pricing. In my judgment, (1) the signs and magnitudes of the three effects of such tie-ins and reciprocity agreements that are relevant to whether their perpetrator would be justified in asserting an organizational-economic-efficiency defense will vary from agreement to agreement, (2) it seems most likely that employers of such agreements will frequently be justified in asserting an organizational-economic-efficiency defense but will also frequently not be justified in doing so, and (3) there is no ground for believing that employers of this functional category of tie-ins and reciprocity agreements will be either more than 50 % likely or less than 50 % likely to be justified in asserting such a defense. The only generalization I can therefore offer about this defense in this sort of case is that (1) one will have to analyze on a case-by-case basis whether the tie-ins and reciprocity agreements they involve can be Clayton-Act-justified in this way and (2) the factual complexity of the relevant analysis will in practice make it difficult for defendants to carry the associated burden of persuasion.

The third functional category of tie-ins and reciprocity agreements whose legality under the Clayton Act I will analyze is concealing tie-ins and reciprocity agreements. Such agreements will be covered by the Clayton Act (*viz.*, by Section 2) only when they increase the extent to which their perpetrator practices price discrimination, and even then their legality under the Clayton Act will be completely determined by the legality under the Clayton Act of the price discrimination they make it profitable for their employer to practice, whose determinants were analyzed in the preceding discussion of price discrimination.

The fourth functional type of tie-ins and reciprocity agreements are package-pricing arrangements that are designed to increase the profitability of price discrimination by reducing the market-research cost sellers must incur to discriminate, the cost that sellers must incur to train checkout-counter personnel to determine the different dollar value that various buyers place on the seller's product, the checkout-counter transaction cost of making the relevant determinations and charging the varying prices, the cost the sellers must incur to prevent or allow arbitrage, and/or the law-related, bargaining, and goodwill cost to the sellers of practicing price discrimination (and/or the cost of concealing the discrimination or its extent or locus). Such agreements are covered by Section 2 of the Clayton Act when they increase the extent to which their employer practices price discrimination on a commodity. The preceding discussion of the conditions under which the resulting discrimination will impose a net equivalent-dollar loss on Clayton-Act-relevant buyers in a Clayton-Act-relevant way applies here as well. It is very unlikely that non-predatory price discrimination will violate the Clayton Act. However, even if the discriminator could make out an organizational-economic-efficiency defense for its use of tie-ins or reciprocity agreements to increase the profitability of the rare instances of discrimination that would violate the Clayton Act's test of *prima facie* illegality (in that such agreements reduced the transaction cost of the discrimination), that fact would not render the discrimination itself lawful under the Clayton Act.

The fifth functional category of tie-ins and reciprocity agreements that the Clayton Act covers are agreements that increase the private proficiency with which their perpetrator can practice meter pricing on a durable product, patented product, idea, patented production process, or possibly franchise if franchises are considered to be Clayton Act commodities. Since all meter-pricing tie-ins impose full-requirements obligations on the buyers they involve, all such tie-ins that involve commodities in the Clayton Act sense are covered by Section 3 of the Clayton Act if the tying seller produces or meaningfully distributes the tied good, regardless of whether they generate price discrimination. Meter-pricing tie-ins that increase price discrimination are also covered by Section 2 of the Clayton Act, regardless of whether the tying seller produces or meaningfully distributes the tied good. (I assume, perhaps contestably, that the preceding claim is correct both when the discrimination is *ex ante* discrimination and when it is *ex post* discrimination.) Meter-pricing reciprocity agreements that involve commodities are covered by the Clayton Act in the same or in analogous circumstances as those in which meter-pricing tie-ins are covered by the Clayton Act—*i.e.*, are covered by Section 2 when they increase the extent to which their employer practices price discrimination and are covered by Section 3 if the reciprocal trader really does distribute (or use in its own final-product-production business) its trading-partner's product. An individual seller's use of a meter-pricing tie-in or reciprocity agreement will benefit Clayton-Act-relevant buyers by improving the absolute attractiveness of the best offer they respectively receive from any inferior supplier if it enables a seller that would otherwise have exited to survive when its exit would have reduced competition in the Clayton Act sense or induces its prospective employer to make a QV investment that that firm would otherwise have found unprofitable when the QV investment in question would increase competition in the relevant sense. Given that sellers use this sort of agreement to increase the profits they can realize by supplying a buyer they are in any event best-placed to supply, it is exceedingly unlikely that a seller's use of such agreements will impose a net equivalent-dollar loss on Clayton-Act-relevant buyers in a Clayton-Act-relevant way by driving an extant rival out or deterring a rival QV investments. The only conceivable exception would be a case in which this sort of agreement would make it profitable for its perpetrator to use meter pricing when the pure-lump-sum prices it would otherwise have charged for a Clayton Act commodity would have deterred some buyers it was best-placed to supply from purchasing its product and thereby would have benefitted one or more of the seller's extant rivals or potential investors in its area of product-space by enabling them to make sales to the seller's customers in circumstances in which the associated profits induced them to stay in business or make a QV investment when their survival or investment would have increased competition in the Clayton Act sense. It seems obvious to me that such an outcome is exceedingly unlikely. Unfortunately, it is unclear how often, in cases in which such a result is requisitely likely to obtain, the agreement's perpetrator would be justified in asserting an organizational-economic-efficiency defense. The relevant analysis is similar to its counterpart for arbitrage-preventing tie-ins and reciprocity agreements:

(1) if the meter-pricing tie-in or reciprocity agreement reduces the private (and, on the law's otherwise-Pareto-perfect assumption, the allocative) transaction cost of effectuating a meter-pricing scheme without changing the amount of meter pricing the seller in question practices, the agreement will increase its perpetrator's organizational economic efficiency, and the perpetrator will be justified in asserting an organizational-economic-efficiency defense;
(2) if the meter-pricing tie-in or reciprocity agreement increases the private (and, on the law's otherwise-Pareto-perfect assumption, the allocative) transaction cost of effectuating a meter-pricing scheme but is employed nevertheless because it requisitely reduces the amount of cheating in which the buyer engages (say, by tampering with meters or underreporting final-product sales), this fact will count against the agreement's economic efficiency and the perpetrator's organizational-economic-efficiency defense;
(3) if the meter-pricing tie-in or reciprocity agreement increases the extent to which the perpetrator practices meter pricing, this fact will strengthen the perpetrator's organizational-economic-efficiency-defense agreement if meter pricing is economically efficient and weaken it if such pricing is economically inefficient: although the conclusion that meter pricing is economically efficient is favored by the tendency of such pricing to reduce the sum of buyer and seller risk costs and by the fact that on the law's otherwise-Pareto-perfect assumption (though not on realistic assumptions) it will tend to increase economic efficiency by making economically-efficient QV investments profitable, it is disfavored by the "reality" that (more honestly, my belief that) meter pricing is almost always more transaction-costly than outright sales (even if one takes account of the tendency of such pricing to reduce the research costs the seller and buyer generate to estimate the buyer's demand for the seller's product) and by the fact that the benefits that meter pricing confers on the seller by helping it overcome its own and the buyer's pessimism about the buyer's demand for the seller's product are purely private; and
(4) the relevant impacts of meter-pricing tie-ins and reciprocity and of meter pricing itself seem likely to differ from case to case in ways that are collectively critical too often for any general conclusion about their organizational-economic-efficiency defensibility to be warranted.

The sixth functional category of tie-ins encompasses

(1) tie-ins that increase the profits that a seller X of a final product A can realize by charging supra-TSM-marginal-cost per-unit prices by shifting the locus of its supra-TSM-marginal-cost per-unit pricing to a tied product B that the relevant buyer agrees to purchase exclusively from the sellers in question where the (SS+)/(BS–) ratio over the relevant range of DD^{RC}_{XBY} exceeds the (SS+/BS–) ratio over the relevant range of DD_{XAY} for reasons related to the difference between the TSM output of A and the TSM output of B under the full-requirements contract, the difference between the slopes of DD_{XAY} and DD^{RC}_{XBY} over their relevant ranges, and the difference between the slopes of MC_{XAY} and MC_{XBY} over their relevant ranges and
(2) tie-ins that increase the profits that a producer of an input against which substitution is possible realizes by enabling it to obtain the benefits of charging supra-TSM-marginal-cost per-unit prices without inflicting losses on itself by inducing the buyer to substitute against that input by shifting the locus of its supra-TSM-marginal-cost per-unit pricing by reducing its price on its own input A and obligating the buyer to purchase its full requirements of the substitutable input B for a price that is the same percentage above B's normal market price as A's price in the tie-in agreement is above MC_{XAY} or by reducing the price of its own input A in the tie-in to A's TSM marginal cost and obligating the buyer to purchase its full requirements of another input C against which substitution is not possible for a price sufficiently above its normal market price to cancel out the buyer's gain on A. Because such a tie-in always impose a full-requirements obligation on the buyer it involves, it will be covered by Section 3 of the Clayton Act if the goods it involves are commodities and the seller produces or meaningfully distributes the tied product.

When if ever will such a tie-in violate Section 3's test of *prima facie* illegality? I should note at the outset that such tie-ins are covered by the Clayton Act because they always imposes a full-requirements obligation on the buyer they involve. Of course, the fact that such tie-ins are covered by the Clayton Act does not imply that they are prohibited by the Clayton Act. Many such tie-ins are lawful under the Clayton Act because they do not harm the relevant buyers. To the contrary, such tie-ins will confer an equivalent-dollar gain on Clayton-Act-relevant buyers in a Clayton-Act-relevant way in two sets of circumstances; (1) when they critically increase the profitability of the seller's continuing to sell the extant product in question/creating the product in question in circumstances in which its continued supply of that product/its execution of the relevant QV investment would confer a Clayton-Act-relevant net equivalent-dollar gain on Clayton-Act-relevant buyers and (2) when the relevant buyer's bargaining power enabled it to secure a share of the joint gain the tie-in generated for it and the seller. On the other hand, such tie-ins could also inflict an equivalent-dollar loss on Clayton-Act-relevant buyers in a Clayton-Act-relevant way if such tie-ins reduced the sales that the tying seller's extant rivals made to buyers of the tying product A or the sales that potential investors in the area of product-space in which A is located would expect to make to buyers of A not only by reducing the per-unit price of A but also (when A is a final good rather than an input) by encouraging A's distributors to make additional expenditures that increase the demand for A in circumstances in which (1) this reduction in the profits that the extant/prospective rivals of A's producer realize/will expect to realize will cause the extant rival to exit/the prospective investor not to invest and (2) the rival's decision to exit/decision not to invest will impose a net equivalent-dollar loss on Clayton-Act-relevant buyers by reducing the absolute attractiveness of the best offer they respectively receive from any inferior supplier. However, I think it extremely unlikely that an individual seller's use of this type of tie-in will generate such a Clayton-Act-relevant decrease in competition.

Once more, it is neither easy to assess nor clear whether a seller whose use of this functional type of tie-in is requisitely likely to yield a Clayton-Act-relevant decrease in competition will be justified in asserting an organizational-economic-efficiency defense. I will start by making five points that relate to the organizational-economic-efficiency defensibility of such tie-ins.

First, the fact that the substitution of final-product "full-line-forcing" tie-ins and input-substitution-preventing tie-ins for single-product contracts will tend to increase allocative (as well as private) transaction costs because the tie-ins are more transaction-costly to devise and negotiate than a one-product contract would be, because the tie-ins will cause the seller to use resources to prevent the buyer from cheating on its related full-requirements obligation on B (in the input case, on B and/or C), and because the tie-ins will tend to cause the seller to use additional resources to prevent the buyer from engaging in arbitrage on A (by giving the buyer additional incentives to engage in arbitrage on A by reducing A's per-unit price) militates against the organizational-economic-efficiency defensibility of the tie-ins because it implies that the tie-ins on this account will reduce the seller's organizational economic efficiency. Second, for the same reason, the fact that the substitution of the tie-ins for one-product sales of A will tend to reduce the amount by which the seller's supra-TSM-marginal-cost per-unit pricing reduces the sum of the seller's and buyers' risk costs also militates against such tie-ins' organizational-economic-efficiency-based Clayton Act defensibility. Third, on what I take to be the law's otherwise-Pareto-perfect assumption, the fact that such tie-ins reduce the amount of transaction surplus the seller destroys by removing a given amount of buyer surplus through supra-TSM-marginal-cost per-unit pricing favors their organizational-economic-efficiency-based Clayton Act defensibility because it implies that the tie-ins will increase the seller's organizational economic efficiency on this account. (I should add that, although I do not think that this effect of final-product "full-line forcing" tie-ins favors their economic efficiency in our actual, highly-Pareto-imperfect world, I suspect that it does favor the economic efficiency of input-substitution-preventing tie-ins in the real world. The explanation for these last two conclusions, which are legally irrelevant for reasons that Chap. 5 indicated, will be provided in THE WELFARE ECONOMICS OF ANTITRUST POLICY AND U.S. AND E.U. ANTITRUST LAW.) Fourth, on what I take to be the law's otherwise-Pareto-perfect assumption (though, I suspect, not on more realistic assumptions), the fact that the amount by which final-product "full-line-forcing" tie-ins increase the seller's profits by inducing resellers of A to make additional jointly-profitable expenditures that increase the demand for A *exceeds* the amount by which such tie-ins reduce the seller's profits by deterring resellers of B from making jointly-profitable expenditures that would increase the demand for B will also favor the agreement's economic efficiency and hence organizational-economic-efficiency defensibility by implying that the tie-ins will increase the seller's organizational allocative efficiency on this account. Fifth, if it could be shown that any such tie-in would render the creation of product A profitable when its creation would not otherwise be profitable despite the fact that it would be economically efficient if the economy were otherwise-Pareto-perfect, that fact would also favor the organizational-economic-efficiency defensibility of the tie-in under the Clayton Act. Sixth, for reasons that Chap. 5 explained, the facts that (for reasons that THE WELFARE ECONOMICS OF ANTITRUST POLICY AND U.S. AND E.U. ANTITRUST LAW will explain) any decrease in price competition such a tie-in generates will decrease economic efficiency and any decrease in QV-investment competition such a tie-in generates will increase economic efficiency are irrelevant to the organizational-economic-efficiency defensibility of any such tie-in that decreases one or both types of competition under the Clayton Act. On the otherwise-Pareto-perfect assumption on which antitrust-law analysis proceeds, tie-ins of these sorts that are profitable will always qualify for an organizational-economic-efficiency defense because that assumption rules out the existence of buyer surplus whose reduction by the tie-in would call this conclusion into question. In a world in which the existence of buyer surplus is taken into account, tie-ins that make it profitable for a firm to shift from single pricing (as opposed to the mixed single-product pricing-technique I assumed the tie-in replaced) to the multi-product mixed pricing-technique the tie-in implemented might not increase the relevant seller's organizational economic efficiency—*i.e.*, might not be defensible on the ground that they decreased competition because they increased the perpetrator's organizational economic efficiency. The messiness of this analysis is one more (admittedly-relatively-unimportant) reason to be glad that these types of tie-ins are extremely unlikely to reduce competition.

In short, if the relevant unit for analysis were an individual seller's decision to use tie-ins, only very few tie-ins would violate the Clayton Act, properly interpreted and applied. Moreover, it seems extremely doubtful that the State or a private plaintiff will be able to establish the Clayton Act illegality of even the rare tie-in that does violate the Act.

We have seen that reciprocity agreements can also perform the functions that "full-line forcing" tie-ins can perform. Section 3 of the Clayton Act will cover this functional category of reciprocity agreements if both goods they involve are commodities and the initiating reciprocal trader really distributes the good (itself produces the input to which the full-requirements supply-obligation attaches). The analysis of the legality of any reciprocity agreement covered by Section 3 under that section is the same as its tie-in counterpart.

The seventh and final functional category of tie-ins and reciprocity agreements are predatory tie-ins and reciprocity agreements. Predatory tie-ins and reciprocity agreements that are covered by Section 2 or Section 3 of the Clayton Act will violate these provisions if they seem requisitely likely to be successful or have been successful.

I turn now to an individual firm's decision to use single-brand exclusive dealerships. As we saw, such exclusive dealerships enable the producer to avoid losses it would otherwise sustain because (1) its supra-marginal-cost per-unit prices to its independent-distributors would or do make it profitable for them to make additional sales of rival products by lowering the prices of rival products or making expenditures that increase the demand for such products when such distributor choices are against the joint interest of the producer and distributor or (2) its independent distributors would or do use the training and information the producer provides them to sell the products of one of more of the relevant producer's rivals when it is not in the joint interest of the producer and distributors for them to do so. Single-brand exclusive dealerships clearly are covered by Section 3 of the Clayton Act when the good(s) sold is (are) Section 3 commodities. An individual firm's single-brand exclusive dealership may confer a net equivalent-dollar gain on Clayton-Act relevant buyers (1) by making it profitable for the producer in question to provide training and information to its independent distributors that improve their performance in ways that benefit their customers or (2) by deterring the producer from vertically integrating forward into distribution when, in various relevant respects that matter to consumers, it would be a less proficient distributor than the independent single-brand exclusive dealers would be. However, an individual firm's use of single-brand exclusive dealerships could inflict a net equivalent-dollar loss on Clayton-Act-relevant buyers in a Clayton-Act-relevant way by driving out an established rival of the firm that substituted such dealerships for non-single-brand independent distributors and/or by deterring the entry of other producers of the commodity in question by critically reducing the profits the existing QV investment generated or the deterred QV investment would generate (even if the producer decision to prohibit its independent distributors from selling rival products was not predatory). However, I suspect that at most a low percentage of single-brand exclusive-dealership arrangements will inflict a net equivalent-dollar loss on Clayton-Act-relevant buyers in this way. In any event, an individual firm whose single-brand exclusive dealership(s) would or did lessen competition in the above way might be able to establish an organizational economic efficiency defense for its conduct by establishing that its single-brand exclusive dealership(s) resulted in its providing additional training and information to its independent distributors rather than to vertically integrate forward into distribution when its use of independent distributors was more economically efficient.

Section 3 of the Clayton Act also covers single-product contracts that contain short-term or long-term full-requirements provisions. Three points need to be made about such provisions' legality under the Clayton Act. First, those single-product full-requirements provisions that are not only predatory but requisitely likely to secure their predatory objective violate the Clayton Act (as well as the Sherman

Act). Second, single-product long-term full-requirements provisions that are not predatory because the seller that includes them in its contracts of sale did not believe *ex ante* that their profitability depended on their reducing the absolute attractiveness of the best offers against which it will have to compete may still be requisitely likely to inflict a net equivalent-dollar loss on Clayton-Act-relevant buyers by reducing the absolute attractiveness of the best offer those buyers respectively receive from any inferior supplier because the provisions in question reduce the amount of sales that an extant seller-participant in the relevant area of product-space might make that are not locked up below the amount that the seller in question must make to survive or that a potential investor in that area of product-space might make that are not locked up below the amount that it must make for its prospective investment to at least break even in circumstances in which the induced decision to exit or not invest will cause the full-requirements provision in question to inflict a net equivalent-dollar loss on Clayton-Act-relevant buyers. Third, if I am correct in concluding that it is legally correct to read into the Clayton Act an organizational-economic-efficiency defense in which the economic efficiency of the conduct in question is to be analyzed on otherwise-Pareto-perfect assumptions, no non-predatory full-requirements provision in a single-product contract will violate the Clayton Act because all such provisions will be Clayton Act defensible for organizational-economic-efficiency reasons.

So far, I have been assuming that the relevant analysand for the Clayton Act Section 2 or 3 legal analysis of non-predatory tie-ins, reciprocity, single-brand exclusive dealerships, and single-product full-requirements contracts is the decision of an individual seller to use such a contractual surrogate for vertical integration. In fact, as I have explained, in cases in which no organizational-economic-efficiency defense could be established for the defendant's conduct either because the conduct did not increase its organization's economic efficiency or because [contrary to my view] it is incorrect as a matter of law to read such a defense into the Clayton Act, that conclusion would be incorrect as a matter of law because it would result in courts' violating the U.S. antitrust laws' level-playing-field assumption by implying that it would be correct as a matter of law for them (1) to find illegal a well-established firm's using a surrogate for vertical integration that would improve its competitive-position array if in doing so it decreased Clayton Act competition by driving a marginal rival out or deterring a rival QV investment while (2) finding lawful a marginal established firm's or (prospectively) a potential competitor's or smaller potential expander's using the exact same surrogate for vertical integration to improve its competitive-position array when such a firm's doing so would increase Clayton Act competition by helping it survive or critically reducing the barriers to QV investment it faced. In my judgment, the correct analysand for Clayton Act Section 2 and Section 3 analysis is "a rule permitting all members of a relevant set of rivals to use the contractual surrogate for vertical integration in question." Such an analysand-shift is legally-salient because a rule permitting all members of a set of rivals to use a particular surrogate for vertical integration will be far less likely to reduce competition in the Clayton Act sense than would an individual seller's use of the surrogate in question. Indeed, I think that a rule permitting all such firms to use any such surrogate for vertical integration will rarely if ever reduce Clayton Act competition: (1) such surrogates are likely to be more profitable for marginal competitors and potential entrants than for well-established firms (since marginal and potential competitors are more likely than well-established firms to need to protect their products' reputations, less able than are well-established firms to obtain information about buyer demand or to prevent arbitrage in other ways short of vertical integration, more dependent on their independent distributors' sound performance, more needful of the assured supply or assured sales that full-requirements contracts can secure, and less able than are well-established firms to execute forward vertical integration), (2) even when such surrogates for vertical integration are more profitable for well-established firms than for marginal and potential competitors, their availability will usually not critically affect the survival of a marginal established firm that will not be replaced by an equally-effective competitor or critically raise the barriers to entry faced by an otherwise-effective potential entrant, and (3) even when the general availability of some surrogate for vertical integration will reduce competition in the Clayton Act sense, the well-established firms for which it is more profitable will often be able to establish an organizational-economic-efficiency defense for their using it.

(2) The U.S. Antitrust Law as Actually Applied

(A) Single-Product Pricing-Techniques

(i) Techniques That Do Not Involve Conventional Price Discrimination

U.S. courts and antitrust-enforcement agencies have always understood that—except when single pricing, perfect price discrimination, and the mixed pricing-technique in which a lump-sum fee is combined with a supra-TSM-marginal-cost per-unit price are employed predatorily[1184]—such techniques do not violate the U.S. antitrust laws, regardless of whether the single prices charged are high (relative to any cost figure) or the mixed technique allows the buyer in question to obtain any surplus and despite the fact that, by definition, perfect price discrimination will not allow the buyer to obtain any surplus. I know of no instance in which a U.S. antitrust-enforcement agency or a U.S. federal court has claimed or concluded that an exemplar of any of these techniques that is not predatory violates U.S. antitrust law.

[1184] Because perfect price discrimination and the mixed pricing-technique to which the text refers are used by sellers in relation to buyers they are best-placed to supply, the claim that such pricing-techniques can be used predatorily may be surprising. In fact, exemplars of both pricing-techniques will be predatory if (1) for pricing-cost reasons, their practitioner did not find them inherently profitable *ex ante* but (2) their practitioner did find them profitable *ex ante*, all things considered, because it believed that their substitution for their most-inherently-profitable alternative would reduce the absolute attractiveness of the offers against which it would have to compete in the future by driving a rival out and/or deterring a rival QV investment by reducing the demand curve that the target rival(s) faced or would face by increasing the discriminator's unit sales and/or decreasing the relevant buyer's buyer surplus (and hence wealth and demand for the target's product).

(ii) Conventional Price Discrimination

Conventional price discrimination that is predatory always violates Sections 1 and 2 of the Sherman Act. However, because the Sherman Act illegality of discriminatorily-low, predatory prices does not at all depend on their being discriminatory (*i.e.*, on the fact that the predator charged other buyers higher prices when the price-difference was not cost-justified), this section focuses exclusively on the way in which the U.S. courts and U.S. antitrust-enforcement agencies have dealt with price discrimination under the Clayton Act (or its 1936 Robinson-Patman Act amendment).

The original 1914 statute prohibited any seller operating in interstate commerce "to discriminate in price between different purchasers of commodities of like grade and quality [when making sales in interstate commerce at requisitely-proximate times]. . . where the effect of such discrimination may be to lessen competition or tend to create a monopoly in any line of commerce" except if the defendant can demonstrate that the relevant differences in price make only "due allowance for differences in the cost of manufacturer, sale, or delivery" or that the lower price "was made in good faith to meet an equally low price of a competitor." The 1936 amendment (the Robinson-Patman Act) adds text that prohibits "price discrimination" whose effect is "to injure, destroy, or prevent competition with any person who either grants or knowingly receives. . .[its] benefits, or with customers of either of them."

I will focus first and primarily on the way in which U.S. courts have interpreted and applied both Section 2 of the 1914 statute and the 1936 Robinson-Patman Act amendment to that statute. Thirteen issues will be addressed in the text for the most part in the order in which they are raised by the immediately-preceding paragraph's account of Section 2 of the Clayton Act.

The first issue relates to the "separateness" in the Clayton Act context of separately-incorporated companies. A parent and a wholly-owned subsidiary that charged different prices for the same product are not separate sellers—*i.e.*, are a single seller—for Robinson-Patman Act purposes.[1185] Of course, this conclusion does not resolve in general the extent to which the ownership of two companies must overlap for them to be considered a single seller in Robinson-Patman Act cases.

Second, U.S. courts have held that, to be covered by the Robinson-Patman Act, a seller must be "engaged in" interstate commerce as opposed to merely affecting interstate commerce and that at least one of the sales in question (see below) must be made in interstate commerce.[1186]

[1185] Caribe BMW v. Bayerische Motoren Weke Aktiengesellschaft, 19 F.3d 745 (1st Cir. 1994). Both this cite and most of the others in this section are taken from HOVENKAMP HORNBOOK 578–82.

[1186] See, *e.g.*, Gulf Oil Corp. v. Copp Paving Co., 419 U.S. 186, 200–201 & n. 17 (1974) on remand 618 F.2d 91 (9th Cir. 1980). This second requirement has led to further litigation in situations in which a manufacturer in one state has supplied an agent in another state that has in turn sold the good in question at discriminatory prices in the second state. The consensus appears to be that the sale in the second state would be deemed to be in interstate commerce if but only if the manufacturer knew the identity of the buyers in the second state to which the goods would be sold

Third, U.S. courts have always understood Section 2 to cover a given seller's charging different prices to different buyers (and/or offering different associated services [credit terms, delivery service, etc.] to different buyers that were charged the same price)—*i.e.*, not to cover a seller's charging different buyers the same price despite the fact that the marginal or incremental cost of its supplying them was different. This Clayton Act definition of price discrimination is different from (and, to my mind, creates a concept that is less useful than) the economic definition of price discrimination, according to which prices are discriminatory if and only if the difference between them does not equal the difference in the relevant costs the seller in question would have to incur to supply the buyers concerned.[1187]

Fourth, the U.S. courts have concluded that, to be covered by the Robinson-Patman Act, the relevant transactions must involve sales not leases,[1188] consignments,[1189] or quotations/offers.[1190]

Fifth, U.S. courts have held that, to be covered by Section 2 of the Clayton Act, sales must be consummated on reasonably-proximate dates.[1191]

Sixth, U.S. courts have consistently held that the word "commodities" implies that Section 2 does not cover the pricing of services or intellectual property.[1192]

Seventh, U.S. courts have found that two commodities will not satisfy the "like grade and quality" requirement if they differ physically in ways that buyers not

---

at the time it shipped the goods to the second state. See, *e.g.*, Taggart v. Rutledge, 657 F. Supp. 1420, 1438-40 (D. Mont. 1987), affirmed mem., 852 F.2d 1290 (9th Cir. 1988).

[1187] The Robinson-Patman Act also covers so-called "indirect price discrimination"—the practice in which a seller offers different (1) credit terms, (2) delivery, stocking, storage, and/or advertising services, (3) brokerage allowances, (4) return privileges, *etc.* to different buyers and the value of all such preferential terms to favored buyers exceed any positive difference between the price that the favored and disfavored buyers are charged. In practice, the courts appear to be much more willing to accept evidence that the value to favored buyers of such preferential non-price terms equals the extra amount that they are charged (and to find for this reason that no "indirect discrimination" had been practiced) than to find cost-justification evidence adequate to establish this defense (see below).

[1188] See, *e.g.*, Export Liquor Sales, Inc. v. Ammex Warehouse Co., 426 F.2d 251, 252 (6th Cir. 1970), cert. denied, 400 U.S. 1000 (1971).

[1189] Seaboard Supply Co. v. Congoleum Corp., 770 F.2d 367, 373 (3d Cir. 1985).

[1190] See Reeder-Simco GMC, Inc. v. Volvo GM Heavy Truck Corp. 374 F.3d 701, 708–90 (8th Cir. 2004); S&W Constr. & Materials Co. v. Draro Banc Materials Co., 813 F. Supp. 1214, 1223 (S.D. Miss. 1992), affirmed, 1 F.3d 1288 (5th Cir. 1993); and Terry's Floor Fashions, Inc. v. Burlington Indus., 713 F.2d 604, 615 (4th Cir. 1985).

[1191] See Reeder-Simco GMC, Inc. v. Volvo GM Heavy Truck Corp., 374 F.3d 701, n. 25 at 710–11 (8th Cir. 2004) (sales within 4 months requisitely contemporaneous) and Xeta, Inc. v. Atex, Inc., 85 F.2d 1280 (Fed. Cir. 1988).

[1192] See, *e.g.*, Innomed Laboratories, LLC v. Alza Corp., 368 F.3d 148 (2d Cir. 2004) (intellectual property); Advo, Inc. v. Philadelphia Newspapers, Inc. 51 F.3d 1191, 1995 (3d Cir. 1995) (dictum: print advertising); and Berlyn, Inc. v. The Gazette Newspapers, Inc., 157 F. Supp. 2d 609 (D. Md. 2001) (newspaper advertising); Ball Memorial Hospital v. Mutual Hospital Ins., 784 F.2d 1325, 1340 (7th Cir. 1986), rehearing denied 788 F.2d 1223 (7th Cir. 1986) (medical services); and Alliance Shippers, Inc. v. Southern Pacif. Trans. Co., 675 F. Supp. 105, 1006 (D.C. Cal. 1986), affirmed 858 F.2d 567 (9th Cir. 1988) (freight shipping).

only recognize but value. By way of contrast, U.S. courts have found that, if two products are physically identical or similar, the fact that packaging or advertising has caused (a significant number of) buyers to value them differently (by giving the products different images, by inducing potential buyers to have different associations with them, or by causing potential buyers to misperceive their physical attributes) is irrelevant to their being of "like grade and quality."[1193]

Eighth, as the Supreme Court pointed out in *Brooke Group*, although "Section 2 of the Sherman Act. . .condemn[s] predatory pricing [only] when it poses a dangerous probability of actual monopolization. . ., . . .the Robinson-Patman Act requires only that there be a reasonable possibility of substantial injury to competition. . .."[1194]

The ninth aspect of the actual U.S. case-law on price discrimination that I want to discuss relates to the distinction between the Clayton Act's general "lessening-competition" test of illegality and the additional "injuring a buyer by preventing it from making sales and profits by disfavoring it and favoring one or more of its rivals" test of illegality that the 1936 Robinson-Patman Act amendment to the Clayton Act promulgated in relation to Clayton Act discrimination. I want to make three points about the case-law on this distinction in Clayton Act price-discrimination cases. First, although in primary-line cases, U.S. courts have always taken the position that Clayton Act discrimination can violate the Clayton Act only if it is requisitely likely to substantially lessen competition in the Clayton Act sense,[1195] in practice, for many years, the U.S. Supreme Court has at least substantially and possibly totally eliminated the importance of the distinction between injuring competition and injuring a seller by worsening its competitive position by adopting a presumption that price discrimination that injures a disfavored buyer by worsening its competitive position in relations with one or more downstream potential customers (whose patronage it might otherwise have obtained) relative to that of favored buyers will decrease secondary-line competition on that account. Thus, in 1948, in *FTC v. Morton Sale Co.*, the Supreme Court stated that the FTC's finding "that the competitive opportunities of certain merchants were injured when they had to pay respondent substantially more for their goods than their competitors had to pay" was "adequate" to establish the required probability (*viz.*, the "reasonable possibility") that primary-line competition would be decreased.[1196] And in 1990, the Supreme Court reaffirmed its support of this *Morton Salt* presumption, rejecting the argument of both the FTC and the U.S. government in *amicus* briefs

---

[1193] See FTC v. Borden Co., 383 U.S. 637 (1966). See also Texas, Inc. v. Hasbrouck, 496 U.S. 543, 556 n. 14 (1990), indicating in dicta that chemically-identical branded and non-branded gasoline were products of "like grade and quality" under the Robinson-Patman Act.

[1194] See Brooke Group Ltd. (Liggett) v. Brown & Williamson Tobacco Corp., 509 U.S. 209, 225 (1993), citing Spectrum Sports, Inc. v. McQuillan, 506 U.S. 447, 459 (1993) for the relevant element of the Sherman Act test and Falls City Industries, Inc. v. Vanco Beverages, Inc., 460 U.S. 428, 434 (1983) for the relevant element of the Robinson-Patman Act test.

[1195] See, *e.g.*, Brooke Group Ltd. (Liggett) v. Brown & Williamson Tobacco Corp., 509 U.S. 209 (1993).

[1196] 334 U.S. 37, (1948).

that the presumption should not be adopted in cases in which the favored buyer was a wholesaler and the disfavored buyer was a retailer.[1197] In my judgment, this *Morton Salt* presumption is unwarranted. Second, in secondary-line (and presumably tertiary-line) cases, the Supreme Court not only subscribes to the view that the Section 2 Clayton Act test of illegality is "injury to competition" but does not adopt any presumption that discrimination that injures a secondary-line seller will on that account lessen secondary-line competition. These Supreme Court positions are manifest, for example, in the *Brooke Group* quotation through which I made the eighth point in this list. Third, many circuit courts have implicitly rejected the Supreme Court's position on secondary-line (and presumably tertiary-line) cases—in particular, have argued that, in such cases, the Robinson-Patman Act prohibits covered "price discrimination" not only when it injures competition but also when it injures a seller (a competitor of the favored buyers) by worsening its competitive position when trying to obtain the patronage of one or more downstream buyers.[1198] More specifically, the circuits argue that, although the language that the Robinson-Patman Act took from the 1914 Clayton Act promulgates a "lessening-competition" test of illegality, the language it added to the relevant part of the 1914 Act—"or to injure, destroy, or prevent competition with any person who either grants or knowingly receives the benefits [of discrimination] or with customers of either of them"—supplements the 1914 "injury to competition" test with an "injury to a seller by worsening its competitive position" test. Indeed, according to the Ninth Circuit, the Robinson-Patman Act amendment to the Clayton Act "shifts the focus of the statute from protecting competition to protecting individual disfavored buyers from the loss of business to favored buyers."[1199] As I stated in Sect. 3A(1)(B) of this chapter, I think (1) that the Robinson-Patman Act does add the above "injury to competitor" test to the standard Clayton Act "injury to competition" test in "price-discrimination" cases and (2) that in a legal regime in which courts are declaring maximum-price-setting RPM, vertical territorial restraints, and vertical-customer-allocation clauses illegal—the legal regime that prevailed in the U.S. when many of the relevant price-discrimination cases were brought—a few buyers may be entitled to recovery under this additional test.

The tenth Clayton Act price-discrimination issue the courts have addressed is the meaning of a sale "in interstate commerce." The courts have always concluded that this text implies that, for sales to be covered by the Robinson-Patman Act, one of the relevant sales must involve a seller and buyer located in different states.[1200]

[1197] Texaco v. Hasbrouck, 496 U.S. 543 (1990).

[1198] See, *e.g.*, George Haug Co. v. Rolls Royce Motor Cars, Inc., 148 F.3d 136 (2d Cir. 1998); Chroma-Lighting v. GTE Products Corp., 111 F.3d 653, 655 (9th Cir. 1997), cert. denied, 522 U.S. 943 (1947); and J.F. Feeser, Inc. v. Serre-A-Portion, Inc., 909 F.2d 1524, 1533 (3d Cir. 1990), cert. denied, 499 U.S. 921 (1991).

[1199] See, *e.g.*, Chroma-Lighting v. GTE Products Corp., 111 F.3d 653, 655 (9th Cir. 1997), cert. denied, 522 U.S. 943 (1997).

[1200] Gulf Oil Corp. v. Copp Paving Co., 419 U.S. 186, 200–01 & n. 17 (1974), on remand, 618 F.2d 91 (9th Cir. 1980).

In so doing, the courts have rejected two (or three) possible alternatives: (1) that, to be covered by the Robinson-Patman Act, both the high-priced sale and the low-priced sale must involve a buyer and seller in different states and (2) that, to be covered by the Robinson-Patman Act, the high-priced sale and/or the low-priced sale must "affect interstate commerce" in any of the non-demanding ways that U.S. constitutional-law cases deem sufficient to satisfy the Constitutional "affecting interstate commerce" requirement. U.S. courts have also addressed more specific questions about whether or how the "flow of commerce" between producers, distributors, and final consumers should be divided up when deciding whether a sale involves a seller and buyer in different states (whether "a sale has crossed a state line" in legalese). Assume that a producer in one state sells goods to a distributor in another state that proceeds to resell these goods to final consumers in the second state at different prices. The consensus appears to be that (1) if the producer was aware that the distributor intended to resell the goods shipped to it to *particular customers* at different prices at the time the producer made the sale to the distributor, the sales would be considered to be in interstate commerce but (2) if the producer did not know the identity of the buyers to whom its distributor would resell the goods that it supplied to the distributor, the discriminatory sales would not be deemed to be in interstate commerce—*i.e.*, the flow of commerce would be divided into two segments, a non-discriminatory sale in interstate commerce involving the producer and the distributor and discriminatory sales involving the distributors and its customers that were not in interstate commerce.[1201] In my judgment, one can reasonably disagree about whether it would be desirable to hold producers liable for any illegal discrimination their independent distributors practice with and/or without the producer's knowledge. I am uncertain about how I think courts should resolve this issue. On the one hand, my belief that this kind of issue should be decided by legislatures rather than courts inclines me to conclude that courts should absolve the manufacturer in all cases in which it did not require, advise, or actively facilitate its distributor's illegal discrimination. On the other hand, the facts that this conclusion would provide producers with an artificial disincentive to integrate forward into distribution and that antitrust courts are supposed to take account of any tendency of their decisions to distort the organizational-arrangement incentives of the law's potential addressees incline me to conclude that courts should hold producers liable for any illegal price discrimination their independent distributor practice.

The eleventh and twelfth Clayton Action Section 2 issues U.S. courts have addressed relate to the defenses the Robinson-Patman Act recognizes—respectively the "cost-justification defense" and "the meeting competition in good faith" defense.

[1201] See Taggart v. Rutledge, 657 F. Supp. 1402, 1438–40 (D. Mont. 1987), affirmed mem. 852 F.2d 1290 (9th Cir. 1988); Indiana Grocery v. Super Valu Stores, 647 F. Supp. 254 (S.D. Ind. 1986); Zoslaw v. MCA Dist. Corp., 693 F.2d 870, 880 (9th Cir. 182), cert. denied 460 U.S. 1058 (1983); Walker Oil Co. v. Hudson Oil Co. of Missouri, 414 F.2d 588 (5th Cir. 1969), cert. denied, 396 U.S. 1042 (1970); and Cliff Food Stores, Inc. v. Kroger, Inc. 417 F.2d 203 (5th Cir. 1969). Contra: Rio Vista Oil, Ltd. v. Southland Corp., 667 F. Supp. 575, 762–64 (D. Utah 1987).

Courts have had to decide three important questions that relate to the cost-justification defense.

The first is: "What type of costs are relevant to the defense?" The statute refers to "differences in the cost of manufacture, sale, or delivery." I would have thought that "differences in the cost of manufacture" would include cost-differences that might arise later in any period of time that includes dates that are sufficiently contemporaneous for relevant price-differences to be covered by the Robinson-Patman Act that reflect the fact that later in the time-period production is along either a lower segment of the relevant marginal-cost curve (because over some interval workers become more proficient as the number of hours they work in some time-period increases) or a higher segment of the relevant marginal-cost curve because full capacity has been exceeded (say, given the need to repair and maintain machines after they have been used a certain number of times or given the fact that worker-proficiency decreases and/or the value to workers of marginal and extra-marginal units of leisure increases after they have worked a certain number of hours in the relevant time-period). I would also have thought that "differences in sales costs" would include savings that producers achieve when a sale reduces the advertising, other-promotional, or sales-effort costs they must incur. Moreover, although the following category of cost-difference does not fit neatly into the "manufacturing-cost" difference, the "sale-cost" difference, or the "delivery-cost" difference category, I would also have thought that the difference between the amount by which a large sale and a small sale early in a relevant time-period would enable the relevant seller to reduce the risk costs it bore would also be "price-discrimination-justifying" under the statute. Although I do not know of any opinion that explicitly addresses any of these issues, my impression is that U.S. courts would be at best reluctant to consider any of these types of cost-differences to be "price-discrimination"-justifying.

I have already articulated the second salient cost-justification-defense-related issue: "To establish a cost-justification defense, must a 'price discriminator' establish the requisite probability that the differences in its prices were *proportional to* or *equal to* differences in types of costs that are 'price-discrimination justifying'?" As I have already indicated, Hovenkamp claims that the courts have concluded that "differential prices...[will] not be condemned if the differences...[are] *in direct proportion to* (emphasis added) the differences in marginal costs of serving two customers."[1202] As I have also stated previously, I think that Robinson-Patman Act defendants can justify their discrimination only if they satisfy the more-demanding requirement of showing that their price-differences *are equal to* differences in relevant costs.

The third salient cost-justification-defense-related issue is: "With what degree of certainty must a defendant in a 'price-discrimination' suit establish that the difference in the prices it charged was cost-justified to succeed in making out a cost-justification defense?" Although the U.S. courts have never articulated this question in this way, in practice they have required a very high degree of certainty—a high

[1202] HOVENKAMP HORNBOOK 586.

probability that the price-difference was cost-justified. As Hovenkamp explains, "[t]he Supreme Court has rejected expensive, detailed cost studies because they did not divide purchasers into sufficiently homogeneous groups or did not account for every aspect of cost difference,"[1203] and, although cost studies have been accepted in some cases,[1204] the net effect of the cases on this issue "has been to force many sellers to engage in true economic discrimination by charging the same price to different groups of buyers, even though the cost of serving them differ."[1205]

The twelfth Clayton Act Section 2 issue U.S. courts have addressed relates to the statute's "meeting competition in good faith defense." In a 1945 decision that the Supreme Court has never expressed any doubt about (*A.E. Staley*), the Court held that to make out this defense a defendant must establish that it had first-hand knowledge of an offer from an actual competitor that would beat the seller's normal offer (the actual language referred to a "lower price" of an actual competitor, but I assume the Court would accept my more general formulation).[1206] Although I understand the difficulty of determining whether a defendant that could not establish that it had such first-hand knowledge had made the discriminatorily-attractive offer in good faith to meet what it perceived to be an offer by a rival, I do not think that courts are authorized to substitute operational decision-rules that deviate from statutory meaning for such pragmatic reasons. I therefore think that the holding of *A.E. Staley* is legally incorrect.

The thirteenth and final issue I want to address in the text[1207] relates to the provision of the Robinson-Patman Act that makes it illegal for a buyer "knowingly to induce or receive a discrimination in price which is prohibited. . .." The issue is whether a buyer can violate the statute by inducing a seller to grant it a discount in circumstances in which the seller's doing so does not violate the Act because the seller granted the discount in good faith to meet what it believed was an otherwise-superior offer by a rival. A conclusion that a large buyer would not violate the Act by eliciting discriminatorily-favorable offers from two or more suppliers that had

[1203] *Id.*, citing United States v. Borden Co., 370 U.S. 460 (1962) and one more recent circuit-court case, Allied Accessories & Auto Parts Co., v. General Motors Corp., 825 F.2d 971 (6th Cir. 1987), appeal after remand, 901 F.3d 1322 (6th Cir. 1990).

[1204] Coastal Fuels of Puerto Rico, Inc. v. Caribbean Petroleum Corp., 990 F.2d 25 (1st Cir. 1993); OKI Distributing, Inc. v. Amana Refrigeration, Inc. 850 F. Supp. 637, 648 (S.D. Ohio 1994); FTC v. Standard Motor Products, Inc. 371 F.2d 613 (2d Cir. 1967); and Motor v. National Dairy Prods. Corp., 414 F.2d 403 (3rd Cir. 1969), cert. denied, 396 U.S. 1006 (1970).

[1205] HOVENKAMP HORNBOOK 587.

[1206] FTC v. A.E. Staley Mfg. Co., 324 U.S. 746 (1945).

[1207] I do want to note one further Clayton Act Section 2 conclusion that the U.S. Supreme reached and one related assumption it seems to have made in the case in question. The conclusion is that Clayton Act Section 2 applies to sales that favor state and local governments as buyers if these government buyers proceed to resell the commodity in competition with disfavored buyers. The assumption that the Court made without explicitly addressing the issue is that sales to a state-government or local-government instrumentality for internal consumption are not covered by the Act. See Jefferson County Pharmaceutical Ass'n, Inc. v. Abbott Laboratories, 460 U.S. 150 (1983), rehearing denied, 460 U.S. 1105 (1983), on remand 709 F.2d 8 (5th Cir. 1983).

first-hand knowledge of the offers it had elicited from one or more of each of these supplier's rivals (satisfying *Staley*) or a *fortiori* by convincing one or more suppliers to offer it discriminatorily-favorable terms by persuading each that, contrary to fact, it had received an equally-attractive offer from an alternative supplier (if the "meeting competition in good faith" defense is applied in the way in which I think as a matter of law it should be applied) would be inconsistent with Congress' intention to prevent large buyers from obtaining non-cost-justified discriminatorily-favorable terms. However, in 1979, the Supreme Court held that the Robinson-Patman Act does not prohibit buyers from obtaining discriminatorily-favorable terms from sellers that could make out a "good faith meeting competition" defense even if the discrimination would otherwise violate the Act.[1208]

I turn now to the Robinson-Patman Act enforcement-decisions of the U.S. antitrust authorities. Fortunately, I can be brief. The U.S. Department of Justice (the Antitrust Division) has not brought a Robinson-Patman Act case since 1977, and the Federal Trade Commission has also concluded that price discrimination rarely if ever poses a problem that requires Commission action.[1209] Basically, these enforcement conclusions are consistent with (indeed, have been generated by) the relevant legal and policy conclusions of economists.

(B) Producer-Paid Subsidies to Distributors for Making Demand-Increasing Expenditures, Contract Provisions That Obligate Distributors to Make Such Expenditures, and Sales Policies of Cutting Off Distributors Who Fail to Make the Amount and Types of Such Expenditures the Producer Wants Them to Make

All such conduct is covered by Section 2 of the Sherman Act, contractual arrangements that obligate resellers to make such expenditures are covered by Section 1 of the Sherman Act, and payments of this kind that are actually discriminatory are covered by Section 2 of the Clayton Act. I know of no case-law on such reseller *expenditures*, though as we shall see in Sect. 3A(2)(F) of this chapter, there is a significant amount of case-law on the functionally-identical practice in which a producer pays a reseller to provide it with a specified quantity and quality of shelf-space and floor-space (*i.e.*, on slotting contracts and other related types of trade-promotion arrangements). It may be worth pointing out, however, that the U.S. courts' historic hostility to at least some types of advertising[1210] might incline them to find these sorts of behavior illegal even though I suspect that such conduct virtually never is predatory.

[1208] Great Atlantic & Pacific Tea Co. v. FTC (A&P), 440 U.S. 69 (1979).

[1209] See U.S. Department of Justice, Report on the Robinson-Patman Act (1977) and H.C. Hansen, *Robinson-Patman Law: A Review and Analysis*, 51 FORDHAM L. REV. 1113, 1123 (1988).

[1210] See note 643 *supra*.

(C) Tie-Ins and Reciprocity

(i) Tie-Ins

I start with six points about the U.S. courts' handling of tie-in cases. First, U.S. courts have always maintained that some tie-ins are *per se* illegal under the Sherman Act and/or the Clayton Act and that the legality of those tie-ins that are not *per se* illegal under either statute must still be analyzed through a Rule-of-Reason approach.

Second, in a unanimous opinion in 1953, the Supreme Court stated that the conditions under which a tie-in is *per se* illegal under the Clayton Act are different from the conditions under which a tie-in is *per se* illegal under the Sherman Act. In particular, according to this opinion (*Times-Picayune*), "[w]hen the seller enjoys a monopolistic position in the market for the 'tying product,' *or* if a substantial volume of commerce in the tied product is restrained, a tying arrangement violates. . .§3 of the Clayton Act because from either factor the requisite potential lessening of competition is inferred while a tying arrangement is banned by §1 of the Sherman Act whenever *both* conditions are met" because "it is unreasonable *per se*, [for even a lawful monopolist] to foreclose competitors from any substantial market."[1211] I hasten to add that the requirement that the tied product's sales represent a not insubstantial amount of commerce is reminiscent of the "quantitative-substantiality" test that U.S. courts at one time used to assess the legality of single-brand exclusive dealerships and long-term full-requirements contracts. As we saw in Sect. 9 of Chap. 11, U.S. courts subsequently rejected this "quantitative-substantiality" test for anticompetitive "exclusion" with a "qualitative-substantiality" (share of market locked up) test that has more bearing on the likelihood that the arrangement in question either was predatory or would tend to reduce competition in the Clayton Act sense by leading an established rival to exit or deterring an actual or potential rival QV investment.[1212] One final thought: I am far from convinced that in tie-in cases U.S. courts ever followed much less would now follow the *Times-Picayune* distinction between the conditions for Clayton Act and Sherman Act *per se* illegality.

[1211] See Times-Picayune Publishing Co. v. United States (hereinafter *Times-Picayune*), 345 U.S. 594, 609 (1953). Obviously, the difference in these operational decision-rules for *per se* illegality under the Clayton and Sherman Acts does not track the difference in the tests of illegality that I think it legally incorrect to interpret these statutes to promulgate.

[1212] The quantitative-substantiality test was promulgated by Standard Oil Co. v. United States (Standard Stations), 337 U.S. 293 (1949). Tampa Electric C. v. Nashville Coal Co., 365 U.S. 320 (1961) replaced the quantitative-substantiality test with a qualitative-substantiality test, which focused on the percentage of sales locked in. In a concurring opinion in Jefferson Parish Hosp. Dist. No. 2 v. Hyde (hereinafter *Jefferson Parish*), 466 U.S. 2, 32 (1984) (O'Connor, J., joined by Burger, C.J., Powell, J., and Rehnquist, J., concurring), four justices of the Supreme Court stated that tie-ins should not be found to be *per se* illegal unless they cover a substantial *share* of tied-product sales.

Third, the applicable sections of the Clayton Act, unlike the Sherman Act, do not cover tie-ins that involve services (and, I assume, by extension, intellectual property). In the case of Section 2 of the Clayton Act, this conclusion reflects the fact that its text refers to "commodities." In the case of Section 3, it reflects the fact that the text refers to "other commodities." [1213]

Fourth, for an arrangement that ties together the sale of two items (commodities or goods) that are given separate names to constitute a tie-in for U.S. antitrust purpose, the two items must be separate products rather than components of a single product. Unfortunately, and not surprisingly (once one gives even a small amount of thought to the issue), U.S. courts have found it difficult to articulate a test to determine whether two items to which different names can be given (left shoes and right shoes, tires and the rest of a new automobile, aluminum ingot and the manufacturing process that converts it into an aluminum tube, anesthesiological services and the other services that are part of a surgical procedure) should be deemed two products or one product for the purpose of analyzing the legality of their "tied" sale under U.S. antitrust law. One oft-used test focuses on whether the allegedly-tying product (say, new automobiles without tires or left shoes) is ever sold independent of the allegedly-tied product (say, tires or right shoes).[1214] A second, somewhat-overlapping test focuses on whether joint economies of production or distribution can be achieved by requiring all buyers to purchase both products (or making it prohibitively expensive in practice for a buyer to purchase one product without the other) (advertising in a morning newspaper and in an afternoon newspaper when making the advertising pages in the two papers identical permits the same type-set to be used for both).[1215] In effect, this test for product-separateness allows efficiency-justifications for tie-ins to critically affect legal outcomes in a backdoor way—*i.e.*, enables U.S. courts to reach correct legal conclusions without admitting (as at one stage they were unwilling to do) that tie-ins can generate efficiencies (can perform functions other than suppressing competition [see below]). A third test that U.S. courts have sometimes used to determine whether two products should be deemed separate for the purpose of determining whether some business conduct involves the use of a tie-in that violates the U.S. antitrust laws focuses on whether buyers (or sometimes sellers and buyers) consider the products to be separate (say, bill them separately or purchase them separately). In fact, courts that correctly intuit that an alleged tie-in is not in fact illegal sometimes misapply this test for separateness to exonerate the defendant.[1216]

[1213] The Government's fear that advertising-space might not be deemed to be a "commodity" for Clayton Act purposes appears to have led it to bring the *Times-Picayune* case under the Sherman Act instead of under the Clayton Act. See *Times-Picayune* at 609 and at n. 27 at 609–10.

[1214] See, *e.g.*, *Jefferson Parish* at 11–12.

[1215] See *Times-Picayune* at 609.

[1216] See, *e.g.*, the *Times-Picayune* Court's argument that advertisers could properly be found not to regard advertising-space in the relevant morning newspaper to be a different product from advertising-space in the relevant afternoon newspaper (to consider the two advertising-spaces to be the "'selfsame' product") because they thought that the customers reached by the two kinds of

Fifth, according to U.S. courts, "the tendency of the arrangement [*i.e.*, tie-ins] to accomplishment of monopoly seems obvious"[1217]: in their view, tie-ins enable a seller that has market power on the tying product to use that power to lever itself into a position of market power when selling the full product. The problem is that there is a generation gap in this leverage "theory." If the seller that has market power (competitive advantages, presumably) when selling the tying product to a given buyer has fully exploited that power by charging the buyer in question lump-sum fees for the right to purchase that good at specified per-unit prices and/or supra-marginal-cost per-unit prices for one or more units of that good that prevent the buyer from obtaining any buyer surplus when purchasing that good, the tie-in will not enable it to use its market power on the tying good to improve its ability to sell the tied good to the buyer in question because it will already have exhausted that power: one cannot have one's cake and eat it, too. Of course, as Sect. 2C(1) of this chapter explained, in many circumstances, for a variety of reasons, a seller will be able to profit by conditioning the sale of one good on which it enjoys a competitive advantage when dealing for the patronage of a particular buyer on the buyer's agreeing to purchase from the seller in question a second good on which the seller may or may not enjoy such a competitive advantage (indeed, that it may not even produce itself). However, none of the functions that tie-ins can perform is captured by the simplistic and indefensible leverage theory to which U.S. courts subscribed and continue to subscribe to some extent.

U.S. courts have attempted to buttress their leverage theory of tie-ins by using the language of compulsion, coercion, or forcing. Thus, as early as 1922, the Supreme Court claimed that the system of "'tying' restrictions" involved in the case in question "compels the use" of the tied products.[1218] U.S. courts continue to claim that the fact that buyers that participate in tie-ins accept terms on the tied product to which they would not have been willing to agree in an independent

---

advertising-space were "fungible." *Id.* at 613. Obviously, even if the relevant two sets of newspaper readers were fungible from the advertisers' perspective, the two advertising venues could be separate products: the fact that buyers would find two products equally desirable, all things considered, does not imply that they are the same product: even if buyers would be indifferent between a Mercedes and a BMW (at the same price), the two cars would be different products.

The suggestion that the *Times-Picayune* Court misapplied this third test for separateness is suggested by another quite-remarkably-misleading claim its opinion made that relates to the question whether the morning newspaper (the Times-Picayune) had sufficient market power to render its tie of advertising-space in it with advertising-space in the company's afternoon newspaper "coercing" and therefore illegal—*viz.*, the claim (relevant to this market-power issue because the Court mistakenly believed that a firm's market power was significantly and strongly correlated with its market share) that the Times-Picayune had about a 40% share of general and classified morning and afternoon advertising linage in New Orleans during the relevant years (a market share the Court deemed too low to justify the conclusion that the Times-Picayune paper had sufficient market power to render its tie-in coercive or legally problematic). This market-share claim is misleading because it ignores the fact that the tie-in under scrutiny guarantees that the highest market share that the Times-Picayune paper could have of the defined market was 50%.

[1217] International Salt v. United States, 332 U.S. 392, 396 (1947).

[1218] United Shoe Machinery v. United States, 258 U.S. 451, 458 (1922).

transaction demonstrates that the seller used the tie-in to *compel*, *coerce*, or *force* the buyer to accept the tied-product terms when the more accurate description would be that the seller used the tie-in to *compensate* the buyer for accepting the tied-product terms in question.

In any event, U.S. courts originally maintained that the only function that tie-ins perform is to enable sellers to use their monopoly power over the tying product to secure a second monopoly on the tied product. In the words of the Supreme Court in 1956, "tying agreements serve hardly any purpose beyond the suppression of competition...."[1219] U.S. courts backed up this position by dismissing the claim that tie-ins performed particular legitimate functions (such as controlling the quality of a complement—say, salt—used together with a basic product—say, a salt-packing machine) by arguing that that function could be performed equally-legitimately-profitably through other conduct (such as specifying the attributes of the salt that machine lessors or buyers must use, inspecting the salt the customer used, and using the law or the threat of legal action to enforce their contractual rights[1220]), that would not suppress competition. It is therefore not surprising that for many years U.S. courts tended to find illegal the tie-ins whose legality they were called upon to assess.[1221]

[1219] Northern Pacific Railway Co. v. United States, 356 U.S. 1, 6 (1958), quoting Standard Oil Co. v. United States (Standard Stations), 337 U.S. 293, 305–06 (1949).

[1220] International Salt v. United States, 332 U.S. 392, 397–98 (1947). Perhaps the text does an injustice to the Court: its point may have been that International Salt had not proven (indeed, had not submitted any evidence to establish) the tie-in's greater proficiency at complement-quality control. My defense is that, for the reasons I explained in Section 2C(1)(A) of this chapter, the greater proficiency of the tie-in seems to be obvious.

[1221] See, *e.g.*, Henry v. Dick Co., 224 U.S.1 (1912) (mimeograph machine and complements to the machine); Motion Picture Patents Co. v. Universal Film Manufacturing Co., 243 U.S. 502 (1917) (motion-picture projectors and films); United Shoe Machinery v. United States, 258 U.S. 451 (1922) (leases of one shoe-manufacturing machine and other inputs used to manufacture shoes); Carbice Corp. v. American Patent Development Corp., 283 U.S. 27 (1931) (box for transporting ice cream and dry ice used as a complement to the box); International Business Machines Corp. v. United States, 298 U.S. 31 (1936) (leases of tabulating/other related machines and tabulating cards); Morton Salt Co. v. G.S. Suppiger Co., 314 U.S. 488 (1942) (license to use salt-dispensing machine and salt); International Salt Co. v. United States, 332 U.S. 392 (1947) (leases of either a machine to dissolve rock salt into a brine or to inject salt into canned products during the canning process and the salt or salt tablets that are complements of the machine); United States v. Paramount Pictures, Inc., 334 U.S. 131 (1948) (block booking of copyrighted films into movie theatres); Northern Pacific Railway Co. v. United States, 356 U.S. 1 (1958) (sale of land and "preferential routing clauses" that [with some exceptions] required buyers to ship all commodities produced or manufactured on the land via the land-seller's railroad [if the railroad matched competing carriers' prices and, in some cases, services]); and United States v. Loew's, 371 U.S. 38 (1962) (block booking of copyrighted feature motion pictures for television exhibition). But see FTC v. Sinclair Refining Co., 261 U.S. 463 (1923), finding lawful tie-ins of leases of underground gasoline-storage tanks with pumps with the lessor's gasoline, apparently on the ground that the lessor did not have market power over gasoline and that the lessees retained the right to distribute rival brands of gas and Times-Picayune Publishing Co. v. United States, 345 U.S. 549 (1953) (advertising-space in a morning newspaper and advertising-space in an afternoon newspaper).

Admittedly, U.S. courts now recognize that tie-ins can perform a number of legitimate functions. Thus, already in 1960, a District Court recognized that a tie-in (involving the various components of a community antenna system for towns remote from any TV transmission station) could be legitimized by its proficiency at controlling the quality of the components of the system that buyers used.[1222] In 1984, the Supreme Court recognized that package-pricing tie-ins can perform legitimate functions (though it failed to explain them, confining itself to the comment that "[b]uyers often find package sales attractive"[1223]). Indeed, by 2006, in *Illinois Tool Works*, the Court pointed out that "[o]ver the years,. . .this Court's strong disapproval of tying arrangements has substantially diminished. . . .[O]ur early opinions consistently assumed that '[t]ying arrangements serve hardly any purpose beyond the suppression of competition.' *Standard Stations*. . . .[T]he assumption that 'tying arrangements secure hardly any purpose beyond the suppression of competition". . .[was] rejected in *Fortner II*, has not been endorsed in any opinion since [and] [i]nstead. . .was again rejected just seven years later in *Jefferson Parish*."[1224]

Nevertheless, the Supreme Court has still not rejected the leverage theory or the concern that tie-ins employed by sellers that have market power in the tying-product market may violate the Sherman or Clayton Act. The *Illinois Tool Works* Court explained the Court's current position in the following way: "Rather than relying on assumptions, in its more recent opinions the Court has required a showing of market power in the tying product."[1225] I assume that the "assumptions" on which the current Court believes its predecessors incorrectly relied include the assumption that tie-ins inevitably suppress competition and the somewhat-less-extreme assumption that any tie-in that involves a buyer's accepting terms on a tied product the buyer would not have accepted in an independent transaction must have been arranged by a seller that possessed a quantity of market power over the tying product that guarantees that the tie-in will suppress competition. As I have already indicated, like the Court, I reject both these assumptions. But I do not agree with the *Illinois Tool Works* Court's assumption that tie-ins that are employed by a seller that can be shown in some other way to have substantial marker power over the tying product either should be found illegal on that basis alone or can be presumed on that account to have a significant tendency to suppress competition (though this tendency may be outweighed by various efficiencies the Court recognizes even such tie-ins can generate).

[1222] United States v. Jerrold Electronics Corp., 187 F. Supp. 545 (E.D. Pa. 1960), aff'd per curiam, 365 U.S. 567 (1961).

[1223] See Jefferson Parish at 12.

[1224] Illinois Tool Works, Inc. v. Independent Ink, Inc., 547 U.S. 28, 36 (2006). The citation for Fortner II—not given in the opinion—is United States Steel Corp. v. Fortner Enterprises (II), 429 U.S. 10 (1977).

[1225] Illinois Tool Works, Inc. v. Independent Ink, Inc., 547 U.S. 28, 35 (2006).

The sixth and final tie-in-related issue that U.S. courts have addressed that merits discussion is: "How does one determine whether a tying seller has the amount of market power over the tying product to render its tie-in either *per se* illegal or prone on that account to suppress competition?" I should state at the outset that U.S. courts have never tried to offer an explicit definition of the concept of market power that they are using in tie-in cases. At various times, U.S. courts based their conclusion that a tying firm had market power over the tying good on any one of a number of different facts. Thus, at one point, U.S. courts asserted that one could infer the requisite market power from the fact that the tying product was patented (or copyrighted),[1226] but the Supreme Court now recognizes that any such inference is unwarranted: "the vast majority of academic literature recognizes that a patent does not necessarily confer market power."[1227] Other cases assumed that one could infer the tying seller's market power in the tying-product market from the fact that the tying product was "unique," even if not patented or copyrighted.[1228] Unfortunately, uniqueness of physical attributes is no more a guarantee of market power in the sense of competitive advantages than is patents or copyrights; buyers can place the same value on two or more products that have different sets of attributes, and any buyer preference advantages with which uniqueness is associated may be perfectly offset by marginal-cost disadvantages. In practice, the most important type of evidence that U.S. courts have used to determine whether a tying seller had market power in the tying-product market is the seller's share of that market's sales. This fact should not be surprising, given the U.S. courts' (and antitrust-enforcement agencies') Section 2 Sherman Act practice of assessing a firm's pre-conduct and post-conduct market power by (respectively) its pre-conduct and post-conduct market share.[1229] Unfortunately, for reasons that were explored in some detail in Chap. 7, even if (contrary to the conclusion of Chap. 6) markets could be defined non-arbitrarily, a firm's market share is a poor indicator of its market power over price, its market power over QV investment, and its market power over price and QV investment combined (regardless of the defensible way in which these two variants of market power are combined to produce a concept of total market power). Nevertheless, it is worth pointing out that (1) in 1953 in *Times-Picayune*,[1230] after calculating the relevant market share in a misleading way, the Supreme Court found that a share of the tying-product market that hovered around 40 % was not sufficient to warrant the

---

[1226] See, *e.g.*, International Salt v. United States, 332 U.S. 392, 395–96 (1947).

[1227] Illinois Tool Works, Inc. v. Independent Ink, Inc. 547 U.S. 28, 44 (2006). Prior to *Illinois Tool Works*, the Courts of Appeals disagreed about the related issue of whether one could presume market power from the existence of a copyright. Compare, for example, Digidyne Corp. v. Data General Corp. 734 F.2d 336 (9th Cir. 1984), cert. denied, 473 U.S. 908 (1985) (recognizing the presumption for a copyright) with Grappone v. Subaru of New England, 858 F.2d 792 (1st Cir. 1988) (rejecting the presumption).

[1228] See United States Steel Corp. v. Fortner Enterprises (II), 429 U.S. 610, 619 (1977), citing as an example of a case in which the unique product was not patented or copyrighted, Northern Pacific Railway Co. v. United States, 356 U.S. 1 (1958) (land).

[1229] See Section 3 of Chapter 8.

[1230] Times-Picayune at 612.

conclusion that the tying seller had sufficient market power over the tying product for its tie-in to be *per se* illegal or even legally problematic and (2) in 1984 in *Jefferson Parish*,[1231] the Supreme Court indicated that a 30 % share of the tying-product market did not suffice to establish the tying seller's requisite market power.

I have already pointed out that U.S. courts that fear that their market-power-oriented leverage-theory-based tie-in doctrine may imply that tie-ins that are in fact lawful violate U.S. antitrust laws have sometimes prevented themselves from making such a mistake by finding that the allegedly-different products involved in the alleged tie-in are in fact not separate and by calculating market shares in a misleading way. I want now to point out that U.S. courts that confront this dilemma also have prevented themselves from reaching an incorrect legal conclusion by refusing to take note of the fact that the conduct whose antitrust legality they have been asked to scrutinize is a tie-in. Thus, in *Broadcast Music*, the Supreme Court upheld a blanket-license arrangement in which a distributor of the right to play certain copyrighted music required "buyers" (*i.e.*, licensees) to purchase the right to play all the music that the distributor was authorized to license people to play—an arrangement the Court realized was rendered economically efficient by its ability to reduce both sales costs and monitoring costs (since payments depended on the frequency with which particular songs were played)—in an opinion that did not mention the fact that the blanket licenses in question were package-pricing tie-ins (which doctrine probably implied were illegal, given the share of the market the license grantor supplied and the volume of tied-product sales involved).[1232] Lower federal courts are also now ruling for defendants in types of tie-in cases that were previously resolved in plaintiff's favor.[1233]

The contemporary Antitrust Division and the FTC also seem to be convinced that the vast majority of tie-ins are lawful. For some time now, virtually all tie-in litigation has been initiated by private plaintiffs seeking damages.

As the preceding accounts imply, contemporary U.S. courts are far less likely to find that a tie-in has violated the Sherman Act or the Clayton Act than their predecessors were. Although the courts have not formally abandoned the leverage theory or stated that they are now no more concerned with long-term full-requirements tie-ins than they are with single-brand exclusive dealing or long-term single-product requirements contracts, it is not clear that future U.S. courts will often find that tie-ins violate the U.S. antitrust laws.

[1231] Jefferson Parish at 7.

[1232] See Broadcast Music, Inc. v. Columbia Broadcasting System, Inc. 441 U.S. 1 (1979).

[1233] For example, although fast-food franchisees formerly won suits against franchisors that required them to purchase foodstuffs from them or enter into restaurant leaseholds with them, more recently the franchisees have tended to lose these suits. See, *e.g.*, Principe v. McDonald's Corp., 631 F.2d 303 (4th Cir. 1980) (finding lawful a meter-pricing tie-in in which McDonald's required franchisees to rent their restaurants from it at rentals set to vary with the franchisees' respective sales-volumes).

(ii) Reciprocity

Direct challenges to reciprocity agreements are almost always made under Section 1 of the Sherman Act. I know of no case in which reciprocity has been condemned under Section 3 of the Clayton Act.[1234] The Federal Trade Commission has also not prohibited reciprocity under Section 5 of the Federal Trade Commission Act.

U.S. courts and the FTC recognize that reciprocity and tie-ins perform the same functions and have similar effects. They also use the same leverage, foreclosure, entry-barrier theories of illegality to analyze reciprocity that they use to analyze tie-ins.[1235] One would therefore predict that developments in the law of reciprocity would parallel those in the law of tie-ins.

I know of only one Supreme Court reciprocity case. *FTC v. Consolidated Foods Corp.* found a conglomerate acquisition of a producer of dehydrated onion and garlic by a processed-food reseller illegal on the ground that it would increase the extent to which the acquirer would engage in reciprocity (would condition its purchases of processed foods on the supplier's purchasing dehydrated onions and garlic from it):

> We hold at the outset that the "reciprocity" made possible by such an acquisition is one of the congeries of anticompetitive practices at which the antitrust laws are aimed. The practice results in "an irrelevant and alien factor"...intruding into the choice among competitive products, creating at the least "a priority on the business at equal prices." ...[R]eciprocal trading may ensue not from bludgeoning or coercion but from more subtle arrangements. A threatened withdrawal of orders if products of an affiliate cease being bought, or the conditioning of future purchases on the receipt of orders for products of that affiliate, is an anticompetitive practice.[1236]

The Supreme Court has never disavowed its *Consolidated Food* opinion. Nor has it subsequently affirmed the view of reciprocity that that opinion expressed. For a combination of three reasons, I would have predicted that the contemporaneous Supreme Court and the post-1965 lower federal courts would be far less likely to condemn reciprocity (or conglomerate mergers or acquisitions because they seemed likely to increase their participants' practice of reciprocity) than the *Consolidated Foods* opinion would commend. First, as already indicated, U.S. courts recognize that tie-ins and reciprocity perform the same functions and have similar effects. Second, as we also have seen, since 1965, U.S. courts have been increasingly willing to acknowledge that tie-ins can perform legitimate functions, such as reducing the cost their employer must incur to control the quality of the

---

[1234] In one case, the Fifth Circuit questioned whether Section 3 of the Clayton Act covered reciprocity though it concluded that in any event the test of illegality would be the same under the Clayton and Sherman Acts. See Spartan Grain & Mill Co. v. Ayres, 581 F.2d 419, 423 (5th Cir. 1978), cert. denied, 444 U.S. 831 (1979).

[1235] Thus, in Spartan Grain & Mill Co. v. Ayres, 581 F.2d 419, 425 (5th Cir. 1978), cert. denied, 444 U.S. 831 (1979), the court stated that, like tie-ins, reciprocity involves "the extension of economic power from one market to another market."

[1236] FTC v. Consolidated Foods Corp., 380 U.S. 592, 594 (1965).

complements its customers combine with its tying product (which is the analogue of the function that the reciprocity involved in *Consolidated Foods* would have performed—reducing the cost of controlling the quality of the inputs a supplier will incorporate into the product the reciprocal dealer buys as part of the arrangement): indeed, in 1960, in *Jerrold Electronics*, a District Court recognized the legitimacy of a complement-quality-controlling tie-in in an opinion that was affirmed *per curiam* in 1961 by the Supreme Court.[1237] Third, since 1961, when the Supreme Court replaced the *Standard Stations* quantitative-substantiality test for whether a (an alleged) foreclosure was legally problematic with the *Tampa Electric*[1238] qualitative-substantiality test, the Supreme Court has been increasingly insistent that, to pose a significant risk to competition, the "foreclosure" a tie-in entails must cover a substantial share of the sales made in the tied product.

In fact, the actual post-1965 decisions of the U.S. courts and the FTC have been far more hostile to reciprocity than my take on the developing law of tie-ins (which may be too optimistic) implies it would be. Two sets of cases are consistent with my prediction. The first contains cases in which lower courts concluded that "mutual dealing"—*i.e.*, cross-selling—between firms did not entail possibly-legally-problematic reciprocity.[1239] The second contains cases in which courts held that, to be illegal, reciprocity must be arranged by an actor with market power (presumably as either a buyer or a seller)[1240] and that even reciprocity that has been initiated by such an actor is *per se* illegal only if it was contractually required as opposed to being secured through a non-contractual purchasing or sales policy[1241] (a distinction that may affect whether a Sherman Act suit can be brought under Section 1 or Section 2 but otherwise has no legal significance). However, three sets of cases are inconsistent with my prediction. The first contains cases in which the court failed to recognize the legitimating-efficiency explanation of the

---

[1237] United States v. Jerrold Electronics Corp., 187 F. Supp. 545 (E.D. Pa. 1960), aff'd per curiam, 365 U.S. 567 (1961).

[1238] See Tampa Electric Co. v. Nashville Coal Co., 365 U.S. 320 (1961).

[1239] See, *e.g.*, Industria Siciliana Asfalti Bitumi v. Exxon Research & Eng. Co., 1977 Trade Cas. ¶61256 (S.D. N.Y) (fact that two firms buy from each other does not establish reciprocity since the transactions could be independently motivated); Ryals v. National Car Rental System, 404 F. Supp. 481 (D. Minn. 1975) (arrangement in which one firm agreed to purchase new cars from the other on condition that the other agree to buy back those cars as used cars found not to entail reciprocity because a single product was involved); United States v. Airco, 386 F. Supp. 915 (S.D. N.Y. 1974) (no illegality inferred from mutual dealings, internal use of reciprocity language, actual consideration of potential sales when making purchases); but see Carlos Cos. V. Sperry & Hutchinson Co., 1974 Trade Cas. ¶75153 at 97173 (D. Minn.): "Inferences of reciprocity can be drawn from the bare fact" of mutual dealing for summary-judgment purposes.

[1240] See, *e.g.*, Key Enterprises v. Venice Hospital, 919 F.2d 1550 (11th Cir. 1990), vacated, 979 F.2d 806 (11th Cir. 1992); Brokerage Concepts v. United States Healthcare, 140 F.3d 494 (3d Cir. 1988); and Great Escape v. Union City Body Co., Inc. 791 F.2d 532 (7th Cir. 1986).

[1241] Key Enterprises v. Venice Hospital, 919 F.2d 1550 (11th Cir. 1990), vacated 979 F.2d 806 (11th Cir. 1992).

reciprocity at issue.[1242] The second contains cases in which the court or FTC failed to focus on the qualitative substantiality of the "tied" sales—*i.e.*, on whether those sales constituted a sufficiently-high percentage of the sales of the product in question to make the alleged foreclosure problematic: the fact is that in virtually none of the post-1965 reciprocity cases did this issue get the attention that the tie-in cases recognize is warranted. And the third set of cases are those in which reciprocity was deemed illegal when I suspect it should not have been.[1243]

(D) Vertical Price Constraints on Resellers (Resale Price Maintenance) and Vertical Non-Price Constraints on Resellers (Vertical Territorial Restraints, Vertical Customer-Allocation Clauses, and Other Related Vertical Non-Price Constraints on Resellers)

(i) Resale Price Maintenance

(a) Minimum-Price-Setting Resale Price Maintenance In 2007, in *Leegin Creative Leather Products v. PSKS, Inc.*,[1244] the United States Supreme Court overruled a near-century-old precedent (*Dr. Miles*[1245]) and held that minimum-price-fixing resale price maintenance is not *per se* illegal (even when the price in question is fixed contractually in a sale to a buyer [as contrasted to being set in a consignment to an agent]). The Court held that the legality of individual minimum-price-fixing resale-price-maintenance agreements under the Sherman Act must be determined through a Rule-of-Reason analysis that takes into consideration both their "procompetitive effects" (by which the Court seems to have meant the benefits they could yield consumers by increasing inter-brand competition) and their anti-competitive effects (by which the Court seems to have meant the harm they could inflict on consumers by reducing intra-brand competition).[1246,1247] The Court went on to maintain that, in its view, the factors that determine whether RPM violates the

---

[1242] See, *e.g.*, Betaseed, Inc. v. U and I, Inc. 681 F.2d 1203 (9th Cir. 1982), which involved a reciprocity agreement in which a producer of sugar-beet seed conditioned its purchase of sugar beets on the supplier's using the sugar-beet-seed producer's seed or substantially-equivalent seed.

[1243] See, *e.g.*, Diamond Shamrock Corp. 5 Trade Reg. Rep. ¶22825 (May 11, 1990); Georgia-Pac. Corp., 103 F.T.C. 203 (1984); and Southland Corp., 101 F.T.C. 373 (1983).

[1244] 127 U.S. 2705 (2007).

[1245] Dr. Miles Medical Co. v. John D. Park & Sons Co., 220 U.S. 373 (1911).

[1246] For reasons that Section 1 of Chapter 4 articulated, I do not think that the Court's implicit buyer-equivalent-dollar-welfare test of illegality is a correct operationalization of the Sherman Act's test of illegality. (Indeed, it is also not a correct operationalization of the Clayton Act's test of illegality, to which it is admittedly more closely connected.)

[1247] As we shall see, the EC and the E.C./E.U. courts also believe that any tendency of RPM to inflict equivalent-monetary losses on consumers by reducing intra-brand competition counts against their legality under what is now Article 101 of the 2009 Treaty of Lisbon. In my judgment, this position is as wrong as a matter of E.C./E.U. law as its counterpart is as a matter of U.S. law.

Sherman act include (1) the number of manufacturers engaging in the practice, (2) whether the practice was initiated by the manufacturer or the reseller, and (3) the manufacturer's market power—none of which (with one possible exception) do I think is relevant to the impact of the practice on consumers or its legality under the Sherman Act. The possible exception is that RPM that originates with resellers may be slightly more likely to violate the Sherman Act by implementing a reseller horizontal price-fix: I say only slightly more likely for two related reasons—(1) in my judgment, few reseller-initiated RPM arrangements are devised to facilitate reseller cartels because such cartels are almost never profitable and (2) I suspect that, in a significant number of situations, full-service resellers induce their suppliers to cut off discount houses after convincing the supplier that discount distributors cost it more than they benefit it.

Although these criticisms of *Leegin* are important enough to be placed in the text, *Leegin* clearly represents a massive step in the legally-correct direction. Unfortunately, it is too early to tell how the lower courts and the Supreme Court will actually apply *Leegin*—whether in practice they will conclude that all exemplars of minimum-price-fixing RPM that do not effectuate either a reseller cartel or a producer cartel (*i.e.*, in my judgment, virtually all such RPM) are lawful under the Sherman Act.

In part because it is interesting for its own sake and in part because it may shed some light on E.C./E.U. law, which is hostile to RPM, I will now give a brief account of the U.S. antitrust precedents that *Leegin* overruled. Traditionally, the U.S. rule that minimum-price-fixing RPM is *per se* illegal is attributed to the 1911 *Dr. Miles* case. In fact, however, the *Dr. Miles* opinion focused primarily on the common law of resale price maintenance: its two brief references to the Sherman Act merely suggested that—in relation to RPM—the Sherman Act and the common law were probably the same. Obviously, the common law was concerned not with the legality of RPM under antitrust law but with the enforceability of RPM agreements. According to the common law, RPM agreements were enforceable unless (1) the supplier had a large market share or (2) the RPM was being used to effectuate horizontal price-fixing. However, *Dr. Miles* was never read as a common-law decision: from the start, it was interpreted to hold that RPM was a violation of the Sherman Act that could be challenged both by enforcement authorities and actors that were not parties to the RPM agreement (such as terminated dealers). Subsequent courts extended this interpretation of *Dr. Miles* by holding minimum-price-fixing RPM *per se* illegal even if the supplier did not have a large market share and the RPM was not being used to facilitate horizontal price-fixing.

Before proceeding to describe the two constraints on the coverage of this *per se* rule that U.S. courts developed, I want to comment on the four positive arguments that U.S. courts made or that seem likely to have influenced them to conclude that minimum-price-fixing RPM is *per se* illegal under the Sherman Act and some other beliefs of U.S. judges that may have inclined them to oppose RPM. The first of the four arguments assumes that one of the goals of the Sherman Act is to protect the liberty interests of economic actors and argues that RPM deprives distributors of the right to run their businesses as they see fit. Even if, contrary to fact, I could accept the claim that the Sherman Act was designed to protect liberty in the moral-right sense in which it is protected by the U.S. Constitution, I would find this argument misguided for at least four reasons: (1) it ignores the fact that the resellers in question agreed to the restriction in their ability to choose the prices for which they could resell the producer's product in circumstances in which one could not say that their will had been overborne; (2) it ignores the fact that RPM favors certain types of resellers and disfavors others; (3) it ignores the fact that, if producers are prohibited from using RPM and various vertical non-price constraints to control their independent distributors, they may well decide to integrate forward into distribution themselves; and (4) it incorrectly assumes that individuals have a liberty interest properly-so-called in being able to control the prices for which they resell a supplier's product (whereas in the liberal, rights-based societies of the U.S. and the member states of the E.C./E.U., liberty interests attach to choices that affect an individual's ability to develop his own conception of the good and to live a life in which he takes seriously both his moral obligations and his attempt to lead a life that is consistent with his conception of the good).[1248]

The second argument that some judges believe supports the conclusion that RPM is *per se* illegal is the claim that this conclusion is entailed by the *per se* illegality of other types of (*viz.*, horizontal) price-fixing. This wooden linguistic argument fails to address the functional and consequential differences between horizontal and vertical price-fixing.

The third argument that can be made for the *per se* illegality of minimum-price-fixing RPM purports to be an argument from Congressional intent. The supposed intent in question is not the intent of the 1890 Congress that passed the Sherman Act: RPM was almost totally ignored by the drafters of and legislators who passed the Sherman Act.[1249] The intent in question can also not be justifiably attributed to the 1937 Congress, which promulgated a so-called "fair-trade" amendment to Section 1 of the Sherman Act, which authorized individual states to permit producers to engage in RPM: that Congressional decision reflected the fact that the U.S. courts had held RPM *per se* illegal—a ruling that Congress may or may not have thought was correct as a matter of law. The relevant intent is the intent of the 1975 Congress, which repealed the "fair-trade" amendment to the Sherman Act in the belief that retail prices were higher in fair-trade states than in non-fair-trade states. This Congressional decision did reflect two Congressional conclusions: (1) that minimum-price-fixing RPM was undesirable and (2) that the courts would continue to hold such RPM *per se* illegal once the fair-trade exemption was removed. As the Supreme Court stated in 1977, by repealing the fair-trade statute, Congress "expressed its approval of a *per se* analysis of vertical price restrictions."[1250] However, in my judgment, this reality does not constitute the

---

[1248] See RICHARD S. MARKOVITS, MATTERS OF PRINCIPLE: LEGITIMATE LEGAL ARGUMENT AND CONSTITUTIONAL INTERPRETATION IN A LIBERAL, RIGHTS-BASED STATE (NYU Press, 1998).

[1249] Joseph E. Fortenberry, *A History of the Antitrust Law of Vertical Practices*, 11 RES. L. & ECON. 133, 209 and n. 161 (1988).

[1250] Between 1937 and 1975, when the "fair-trade" amendment was repealed, 46 states (at one time or another) passed "fair-trade" legislation, permitting producers to engage in RPM.

kind of legislative intent that is relevant in the United States to the determination of the interpretation of a statute that is correct as a matter of law. Even if the 1890 Congress that enacted the Sherman Act had clearly intended it to prohibit RPM, that fact would not affect my conclusion about the test of illegality the statute should be interpreted to have promulgated (a test under which RPM would be found illegal only if it had been used to effectuate either a reseller or a producer horizontal price-fix) *inter alia* because the specific policy conclusion in question would have been based on a misunderstanding of the function and effects of the practice—*i.e.*, would have reflected the 1890 Congress' erroneous belief that the test of illegality I believe it is legally correct to interpret the Sherman Act to have promulgated would condemn RPM. And as I have already indicated, in reality, Congress took no position on RPM during its Sherman Act deliberations. In my judgment, the fact that the 1975 Congress approved of the Supreme Court's conclusion that minimum-price-setting RPM is *per se* illegal under the Sherman Act has no bearing whatsoever on the legally-correct interpretation of a statute passed in 1890—is not in any way equivalent to changes in social realities that alter the legality of some conduct or decision under a statute whose test of illegality is goal-oriented by changing the consequences of the conduct or decision under scrutiny.

The fourth argument that has been made for the *per se* illegality of RPM is a narrow, precedent-based argument for continuing the rule that RPM is *per se* illegal.[1251] Although a moral and related legal case can be made for giving weight to even wrongly-decided precedents on which private parties could reasonably have relied, no such case can be made for continuing to apply the mistaken "*per se* illegal" rule for minimum-price-setting RPM because no private party has ever relied on that rule to its detriment.

Although I do not find any of the above four arguments persuasive, they clearly have influenced U.S. courts. I also think that the U.S. courts' position on RPM was affected as well by three other related "inclinations" or tendencies: (1) a tendency to give a lexical priority to the effect of any practice on price (to ignore or consider categorically less important all the other effects that RPM can have [an inclination that Congress seemed to share when it responded to claims that prices were higher in fair-trade states than in non-fair-trade states by eliminating the fair-trade amendment to the Sherman Act]); (2) an inclination to place a low positive or negative value on advertising and other types of sales or promotional activities; and (3) an inclination (present in most human beings) to respond to cognitive dissonance (*i.e.*, to information that is inconsistent with the conclusion one has reached [in this instance, to arguments that RPM can perform such useful functions as encouraging the supply of post-sales warranty service]) by denying the truth-value of that information (by claiming that suppliers could secure the same beneficial services for buyers equally proficiently without using RPM or any other practice that [in its judgment] was equally inimical to competition).

[1251] Continental T.V., Inc. v. GTE Sylvania, Inc. 433 U.S. 36, 51 n. 18 (1977).

I turn now to the two limitations in the coverage of the rule that RPM is *per se* illegal (usually mislabeled "exceptions" to that rule) that U.S. courts developed. The first—conventionally called the *Colgate* doctrine[1252] because it was enunciated in *United States v. Colgate & Co.*[1253]—declares that, although contracts in which suppliers require their distributors to charge specified prices for the supplier's product are *per se* illegal, suppliers can lawfully announce to prospective distributors their intention not to enter into contracts with resellers that charge lower prices than the supplier recommended/posted and can subsequently refuse to deal with resellers that charged lower prices. Although I recognize that the behavior the *Colgate* doctrine deems lawful is not covered by Section 1 of the Sherman Act (in that it involves no contract, agreement, or conspiracy), I would see no difficulty in condemning it under Section 2 if, contrary to fact, I agreed with the assumptions the U.S. courts then made about the functions of RPM that critically affected its profitability. In any event, lower courts interpreted the *Colgate* doctrine narrowly: if the producer went beyond announcing its intentions and refusing to deal by warning, threatening, or intimidating its retailers in any other way, its conduct would be deemed to be covered by the *per se* prohibition.[1254] Still, until *Leegin* did away with the *per se* rule, both the Supreme Court and lower federal courts upheld the *Colgate*[1255] limitation on its scope.[1256]

The second limitation on the coverage of the rule that RPM is *per se* illegal is the consignment limitation the Supreme Court promulgated in *United States v. General Electric Co.*[1257] According to this *General Electric* doctrine, the *per se* rule does not apply when the distributor is the producer's agent rather a reseller—*i.e.*, when the manufacturer consigned rather than sold the good to the distributor (when title to the merchandise remained with the manufacturer). Obviously, if producers could convert their arrangements from sales to consignments simply by redenominating

---

[1252] See, *e.g.*, the Supreme Court majority's reference to a "*Colgate* right" in Leegin Creative Leather Products v. PSKS, Inc. 555 U.S. 877, 902 (2007).

[1253] 250 U.S. 300 (1919).

[1254] See United States v. Parke, Davis & Co., 362 U.S. 29 (1960).

[1255] See Monsanto v. Spray-Rite Service Corp., 465 U.W. 752 (1984) and Russell Stover Candies, Inc. v. FTC, 718 F.2d 256 (8th Cir. 1983).

[1256] The text ignores a body of case-law that developed post-1979 that could be viewed as either expanding or narrowing the *Colgate* limitation of the coverage of the rule that minimum-price-fixing RPM is *per se* illegal. The relevant cases addressed the following question: Under *Colgate*, could a supplier lawfully terminate a distributor after receiving a complaint from a competing distributor that the former distributor was charging lower prices than the supplier had recommended or posted? The courts seem to have concluded that the answer to this question depends on whether an "agreement" can be inferred from the fact that the supplier terminated one or more resellers in response to one or more other resellers' complaints, though the outcome of some cases seems also to have been affected by the Supreme Court's statement in Business Electronics Corp. v. Sharp Electronics Corp., 485 U.S. 717, 728 (1988) that, for an agreement to be covered by the *per se* rule, it must be not just about price but about the particular price the dealer must charge. For an intelligent discussion of this body of case-law, see HOVENKAMP HORNBOOK 466–71.

[1257] 272 U.S. 476 (1926).

their arrangements, this "exception" would completely swallow the *per se* rule. The importance of this limitation therefore depends on the way in which courts determined whether a given arrangement involved a consignment or a sale. The intrinsically-correct way to do so is to follow the following three-step protocol. First, analyze the circumstances in which a consignment arrangement would be more profitable than an outright sale for the participating parties—*e.g.*, (1) when the cost to the reseller/consigner of the capital it would need to buy the merchandise was lower than the cost to the producer of supplying credit to the retailer, (2) when the cost to the reseller/consigner of the risk that a perishable good might deteriorate before it could be sold, that the good might be stolen or damaged by fire or some other calamity, or that the demand for the good might be higher than was anticipated was higher than the cost that these risks would impose on the producer (because the producer was less risk-averse than the reseller/consigner and/or because the possibilities in question confronted the producer with less risk in that the producer had a larger portfolio of risks whose possession reduced the additional risk that the contingencies in question would cause the producer to face), and (3) when the shift from the sale to the consignment does not reduce the producer's and distributor's joint gain by causing the distributor to take less-than-jointly-optimal care of the good in question (perhaps because it was inexpensive for the producer to obligate the distributor to take due care and to enforce that obligation). Second, determine whether in the situation in question, the conditions that would render consignment more jointly profitable than outright sales for the participants in the relevant transactions were fulfilled. And third, if the relevant conditions were fulfilled, determine whether in fact the arrangement between the parties did allocate the capital requirements and risk in the manner that a jointly-optimal consignment arrangement would have done. Early on, the courts that were applying the *General Electric* consignment/agency doctrine assessed the nature of the relationship between the producer and distributor by addressing such questions as "whether title to the relevant goods had passed from the producer to the distributor" in a metaphysical way that did not focus on the economic issues just articulated. In 1964, in *Simpson v. Union Oil Co.*,[1258] the Supreme Court used an approach to determining whether a given arrangement was a *General-Electric*-exempted consignment that attempted to focus on relevant economic realities. However, the reality that the Court stated justified its conclusion that Simpson Oil's arrangement with the retail gas stations that distributed the gasoline it refined was not a consignment within the meaning of the *General Electric* doctrine—*viz.*, that the arrangement was part of "a vast gasoline distribution system"—was not in fact relevant. My point is not that *Simpson Oil*'s arrangements were consignments (that the Court's resolution of this issue was wrong). The arrangements probably were not consignments: although the station operators leased their stations from the refiner—a fact that favors the consignment conclusion, that conclusion was strongly disfavored by the facts that the station operators bore all risk of loss and much of the

---

[1258] 377 U.S. 13 (1964).

risk of price fluctuation since their commissions varied with retail gasoline prices. Surprisingly, if from some perspectives encouragingly, only some lower courts followed the "giant distribution system" holding of *Simpson Oil*.[1259] Others worked around it by holding that, even when the producer can in one sense be found to use a large distribution network, a good-faith consignment can be given *General Electric* protection when the individual agent can be said not to be part of a *Simpson* giant distribution network.[1260] More intellectually coherently, starting in 1986, lower courts in effect renounced the "giant distribution system" holding of *Simpson Oil* in favor of an analysis that focused on whether the arrangement in question really was a consignment. In that year, in *Illinois Corporate Travel*,[1261] the Seventh Circuit based its finding that a travel agent is not a buyer-reseller of airlines tickets (was a consignee) despite being part of a giant distribution system because it carried no inventory, bore no risk of resale, and had nothing to do with the delivery of the purchased service itself—all facts that bear on whether the arrangement was in fact a jointly-profitable consignment. And in the next year, in *Ryko*,[1262] the Eighth Circuit gave *General Electric* protection to an arrangement in which a manufacturer of custom-made automatic car-washes that did in fact vary from buyer to buyer distributed its product through a network of independent distributors that found and made sales to buyers without incurring any risk of damage/loss or market-price decline in part because the manufacture did not produce the product or *a fortiori* deliver it to a distributor until the sale was closed.[1263]

I have focused so far on the positions that U.S. courts have taken on minimum-price-setting RPM. I have no doubt that the U.S. antitrust-enforcement agencies would attack RPM of this type that was used to effectuate a horizontal price-fix by either producers or resellers. However, with that exception, as the case-

[1259] For one case that did apply this holding faithfully, see United States v. General Electric, 358 U.S. 731 (S.D. N.Y. 1973).

[1260] See, *e.g.*, Mesirow v. Pepperidge Farm, Inc., 703 F.2d 339 (9th Cir. 1983), cert. denied, 464 U.S. 820 (1983), Hardwick v. Nu-Way Oil Co., Inc., 589 F.2d 806 (5th Cir. 1979), rehearing denied, 592 F.2d 1190 (5th Cir. 1979); and Pogue v. International Indus., Inc., 524 F.2d 342 (6th Cir. 1975).

[1261] Illinois Corporate Travel, Inc. v. American Airlines, 806 F.2d 722 (7th Cir. 1986), after remand, 889 F.2d 751 (7th Cir. 1989), cert. denied, 495 U.S. 919 (1990).

[1262] Ryko Manufacturing Co. v. Eden Services, 823 F.2d 1215 (8th Cir. 1987), cert. denied 484 U.S. 1026 (1988).

[1263] Other cases in which circuit courts have rejected *Simpson Oil* for an economically-sound approach to determining whether an arrangement is a consignment or sale include Ozark Heartland Electronics v. Radio Shack, 278 F.3d 759 (8th Cir. 2002); Belfiore v. New York Times Co., 826 F.2d 177 (2d Cir. 1987), cert. denied, 484 U.S. 1067 (1988); and Kowalski v. Chicago Tribune Co., 854 F.2d 168 (7th Cir. 1988). See also Miller v. W.H. Bristow, Inc., 739 F. Supp. 1044 (D. S.C. 1990) (stating that *inter alia* the determination of whether an arrangement constitutes a consignment or sale depends on whether the intermediary is responsible for payment immediately on delivery, makes substantial changes in the goods, bears risk of losses, and pays taxes on inventory [though this court's list of factors also includes whether the distribution system is vast and whether title has passed]).

citations to the preceding account of the courts' performance suggest, the U.S. antitrust-enforcement agencies no longer believe that minimum-price-selling RPM violates the Sherman Act.

(b) Maximum-Price-Setting Resale Price Maintenance In 1968, in *Albrecht v. The Herald Co.*,[1264] the U.S. Supreme Court held that maximum-price-setting RPM is illegal *per se*. In 1997, in *State Oil v. Khan*,[1265] the Supreme Court overturned *Albrecht* and held that the legality of maximum-price-setting RPM under the Sherman Act should be determined by the application of the Rule of Reason. The Supreme Court's opinion in *State Oil v. Khan* stated that maximum-price-setting RPM could perform some legitimate functions[1266] (though it did not articulate most of them). It also explained why the Court was not persuaded by the various alleged justifications for a *per se* rule against maximum-price-setting RPM:

(1) the Court countered the argument that such RPM undercut dealer freedom by pointing out that many producers responded to *Albrecht* by integrating forward into distribution[1267];
(2) it responded to the concern that maximum-price constraints would tend to deter distributors from offering buyers "essential or desired services" by arguing that, since the elimination of such services would be against the interest of the producer, one could assume that they would not set the maximum price at a level that would generate this effect[1268];
(3) it dismissed the claim that such RPM might favor larger, lower-cost distributors to the detriment of smaller, higher-cost distributors on the ground that injuries to inefficient dealers are not injuries to competition[1269]; and
(4) it acknowledged the possibility that RPM that purported to be maximum-price-setting RPM might in fact be minimum-price-fixing RPM, which under the doctrine that prevailed in 1997—*i.e.*, before *Leegin*—was *per se* illegal, but argued that this possibility could be addressed under the Rule of Reason (it should have said: could be handled by declaring the alleged maximum-price-setting RPM agreement a minimum-price-setting RPM agreement and applying the pre-*Leegin* rule of *per se* illegality for the latter type of RPM to the defendant's conduct).

* * *

The U.S. case-law on RPM resembles the U.S. case-law on tie-ins and reciprocity in the following ways: (1) the courts initially failed to understand the legitimate functions that the relevant practice can perform and, at least in part for this reason,

---

1264 390 U.S. 147 (1968).

1265 522 U.S. 3 (1997).

1266 *Id.* at 15–16.

1267 *Id.* at 17.

1268 *Id.*

1269 *Id.*

declared the practice *per se* illegal; (2) after coming to understand the legitimate functions that the relevant practice can perform, the courts concluded that its legality should be determined through a Rule-of-Reason analysis; (3) however, even contemporary courts seem to have mistaken notions of the Sherman Act test of illegality that applies to the relevant practice and appear to overestimate the likelihood that individual exemplars of the practice might be motivated in a way (or might produce effects) that would render it a violation of the antitrust laws; and (4) it is too early to tell the extent to which the mistakes delineated after "(3)" in this list will reduce the practical significance of the legally-correct doctrinal shift described after "(2)" in the list.

(ii) Vertical Territorial Restraints, Vertical Customer-Allocation Clauses, and Other Vertical Non-Price Constraints on Resellers

I will discuss in some detail the U.S. courts' handling of vertical non-price constraints, focusing on the relatively-modern case-law, starting with the 1963 case *White Motor v. United States.*[1270] Although it may be inaccurate as well as ungenerous for me to say so, I suspect that U.S. courts have always felt freer to deal with vertical *non-price* constraints than with vertical *price* restraints in a more individualized way because they felt less bound by precedents declaring (horizontal) *price*-fixing *per se* illegal. In any event, *White Motor* manifests this greater degree of freedom. The case addressed the legality under the Sherman Act of the vertical non-price restrictions that a small truck manufacturer (White Motor) engaged in competition with much larger producers (such as General Motors) "imposed" on its dealers. The Court held that the District Court had erred in holding prior to trial that, if established, White Motor's alleged inclusion of vertical territorial restraints in its contracts with its dealers and its reservation of certain named customers to itself would be *per se* illegal under the Sherman Act. The *White Motor* opinion did not hold that the legality under the Sherman Act of the type of conduct alleged in the case should be determined through a Rule-of-Reason analysis; much less did it specify the factors on which any such Rule-of-Reason analysis should focus. It just held (peculiarly in my judgment) that the trial court should have addressed these issues at the close of the trial or, at least, should not have fashioned an applicable *per se* rule until the close of the trial. The Court's opinion did contain one (to my mind, legally-incorrect) observation that might relate to the factors that should count in a Rule-of-Reason analysis or the determination of the substance of any "*per se* illegality" rule that might be warranted. In particular, the Court suggested that vertical restraints that enable small, marginal competitors to survive might be lawful under the Sherman Act on that account even though the same restraints arranged by a well-established concern would violate the Act. In his dissenting opinion in *White Motor*,[1271] Justice Clark claimed that the conduct

---

[1270] 372 U.S. 253 (1963).

[1271] *Id.* at 278 (Clark, J., joined by Warren, C.J. and Black, J., dissenting).

alleged in *White Motor* would be declared *per se* illegal under *Dr. Miles* because (1) *Dr. Miles'* condemnation of RPM was based on the fact that the practice reduced intra-brand competition (my words, not his) and (2) the vertical non-price restraints involved in *White Motor* were equally inimical to intra-brand competition. Four years later, in 1967, in *United States v. Arnold, Schwinn & Co.*,[1272] Clark's argument carried the day. The Court's *Schwinn* opinion justified its holding that all territorial restrictions imposed by a producer on either a wholesaler or retailer that has purchased the producer's product are *per se* illegal under the Sherman Act by asserting that all such restraints are "so obviously destructive of competition that their mere existence is enough"[1273] to warrant their condemnation.[1274] The clause "that has purchased the producer's product" appears in the preceding sentence because the *Schwinn* Court also concluded that producers could lawfully impose vertical non-price restraints on distributors who took the producer's product on consignment (*i.e.*, when the producer "completely retains ownership and risk of loss").[1275]

The *Schwinn* decision was short-lived. Lower courts refused to enforce it. In Herbert Hovenkamp's words: "Lower courts revolted against the *per se* rule in *Schwinn* because the value of territorial restrictions in certain distribution systems was obvious. Schwinn then became riddled with exceptions."[1276] In 1977, just 10 years after deciding *Schwinn*, the Supreme Court overruled it in *Continental T.V., Inc. v. GTE Sylvania, Inc.*[1277] Sylvania was a relatively-small television-manufacturer with 1–2 % of the national market. To improve its position, it instituted a marketing system in which its product was sold exclusively by a small group of carefully-selected dealers that were required to operate in specified locations. The strategy appears to have worked: Sylvania's share of the "national television-market" rose from 1 % to 2 % in 1962 when it was implemented to 5 % in 1965. Continental was an authorized Sylvania dealer in San Francisco that objected to Sylvania's licensing a second dealer in the city and responded to Sylvania's decision to do so both by selling more televisions produced by other manufacturers and by opening an unauthorized outlet in Sacramento. Sylvania reacted initially by reducing Continental's credit-line and finally by terminating Continental's franchise. The Supreme Court could have ruled in favor of Sylvania by carving out an exception

---

[1272] 388 U.S. 365 (1967).

[1273] *Id.* at 379.

[1274] As we shall see, even though the Supreme Court subsequently overturned the rule that vertical non-price constraints are *per se* illegal under the Sherman Act, it still thinks that the tendency of such restraints to reduce intra-brand competition should be counted against their legality in the Rule-of-Reason analysis it considers to be warranted.

[1275] United States v. Arnold, Schwinn & Co., 388 U.S. 365, 378–79 (1967). This distinction is no more persuasive in relation to vertical non-price restraints than it is in relation to vertical price restraints.

[1276] HOVENKAMP HORNBOOK 483. For a description of the exceptions, see Continental T.V., Inc. v. GTE Sylvania, Inc., 433 U.S. 36, 47–48 (1977).

[1277] *Id.*

to *Schwinn's per se* rule for small companies that need to use vertical restraints to survive. Although such a pari-mutuel approach would clearly be inconsistent with the U.S. antitrust law's "level playing-field" premise, the Court could have cited statements in *White Motor* to give such a carve-out a precedential grounding. However, the *Sylvania* Court rejected this (in some ways) more modest change in favor of overruling *Schwinn* altogether, holding that, regardless of the market share or financial condition of their perpetrator, non-price vertical territorial restrictions should be analyzed through the Rule of Reason. Because non-price vertical restraints can be used to execute either a producer or a reseller horizontal price-fix if they are employed in an appropriately-coordinated way by the vast majority of the members of any group of competitors, such vertical restraints *should be* subjected to a Rule-of-Reason analysis rather than being declared *per se* legal. Unfortunately, however, the *Sylvania* Court seriously mis-specified the structure of the Rule-of-Reason analysis that should be employed. Rather than focusing on the horizontal-price-fixing possibility on which a correct Rule-of-Reason analysis of vertical non-price restraints would exclusively focus, the *Sylvania* Court (implicitly) assumed that the Sherman Act promulgates a monetized buyer-welfare test of illegality and proposed a Rule-of-Reason analysis that focuses on whether the equivalent-dollar loss (I am elaborating) that the vertical restraint under scrutiny in a particular case imposed on Clayton-Act-relevant buyers (I am elaborating once more) by reducing intra-brand competition exceeded the equivalent-dollar gain it conferred on them by increasing inter-brand competition. This structure is incorrect for two related reasons: (1) the Sherman Act does not promulgate this type of buyer-welfare test of illegality and, relatedly, (2) the impact of a producer's conduct (including its decision to place vertical non-price restraints on the distributors to which it sells its products) on intra-brand competition is totally irrelevant to its Sherman-Act legality. (The execution of the trade-off the Supreme Court asserted was legally critical might also be flawed for a third reason: the applier might assume incorrectly that sellers that are prohibited from using vertical territorial restraints or vertical customer-allocation clauses would respond to this prohibition by dropping the restraints in question and changing nothing else when in fact the sellers would be likely to respond to such a prohibition either [1] by changing its pricing-technique [lowering its lump-sum fees and raising its per-unit prices] and making other adjustments to counteract the tendency of such a shift to deter its independent distributors from making jointly-profitable demand-increasing expenditures or resource allocations or [2] by vertically integrating forward into distribution—responses that would drastically and in almost all cases critically affect the net equivalent-dollar impact of the prohibition on relevant buyers.)

Lower U.S. courts have used a four-step protocol to resolve under *Sylvania* cases in which the plaintiff has attacked the defendant's non-price vertical restraint. First, they determine whether the conduct in question entailed an *agreement* between a producer and a distributor that had purchased the producer's product for resale (as opposed to either a sales policy that did not entail an agreement or a consignment). Second, if the court finds such an agreement, it determines the defendant's market power through an analysis that does not purport to be as rigorous as its counterpart in other monopolization or merger/acquisition cases and may not include a calculation of the defendant's market share.[1278] In some circuits, a finding that the defendant did not have market power in the market in which the allegedly-illegal conduct took place is decisive.[1279] The general practice among courts that have calculated the defendant's market share is to dismiss the complaint if the defendant's share is below 25 % and to require defendants whose market shares equal or exceed 25 % to establish justifications for their conduct whose exonerating strength increases with the defendant's market share. Third, if the defendant's market power is deemed to be sufficiently great to make its conduct legally problematic, the court proceeds to assess the magnitude of the legitimate benefits the conduct generates through analyses that take account of only some of the legitimate functions that vertical non-price restraints can perform and sometimes double-count the legitimate goal the conduct enables the perpetrator to achieve (*e.g.*, encouraging additional dealer services) and the means by which the conduct enables the perpetrator to achieve that goal (*e.g.*, preventing free-riding). Fourth, if the court concludes that the conduct in question does generate some legitimating benefits, it then determines whether those benefits are sufficiently large to render the conduct lawful. It is important to stress, however, that in no sense does this fourth step involve the kind of balancing of effects on intra-brand and inter-brand competition in which *Sylvania* seems to have instructed the lower courts to engage.

What has been the net result of all this effort—*i.e.*, since *Sylvania*, how frequently have plaintiffs prevailed in cases in which they alleged that a defendant's non-price vertical restraint should be declared illegal under the Rule-of-Reason analysis that *Sylvania* prescribed? According to Hovenkamp, "[i]f one counts

---

[1278] See Murrow Furniture Galleries v. Thomasville Furniture Industries (hereinafter *Murrow*), 889 F.2d 524, 528–29 (4th Cir. 1989); Ryko Manufacturing Co. v. Eden Services (hereinafter *Ryko*), 823 F.2d 1215, 1231 (8th Cir. 1987), cert. denied, 484 U.S. 1026 (1988); and Bi-Rite Oil Co. v. Indiana Farm Bureau Co-op Ass'n (hereinafter *Bi-Rite*), 908 F.2d 802, 810 (6th Cir. 1988).

[1279] See *Murrow* at 528–29, *Ryko* at 1231, *Bi-Rite* at 204, and Crane & Shovel Sales Corp. v. Bucyrus Erie Co., 854 F.2d 802, 810 (6th Cir. 1988). I should note that, even if (contrary to my conclusion) the impact of an actor's behavior on intra-brand competition were relevant to its legality under the Sherman Act, I would see no reason to believe that the negative impact of a defendant's conduct would increase with its market power or market share. To investigate the claim to the contrary, one would first have to define "intra-brand competition." Although no-one has ever to my knowledge even attempted to provide an operational definition of the concept of the intensity of such competition, I suspect that that operationalization would have to focus on the extent to which (1) price competition between or among a product's resellers drove the price that final consumers had to pay for the product in question (defined in physical terms?) below the price they would have been willing to pay for it if they could not buy it more cheaply from any source and (2) QV-investment competition between or among a product's resellers reduced its producer's profits (or perhaps increased its final consumers' buyer surplus directly) by increasing the QV investment in distribution above the level that was in the producer's interest. My point is that the extent of intra-brand competition defined in this or any other remotely-defensible way will depend not on the producer's market power but on its ability to prevent such competition by integrating forward into distribution itself or using RPM, non-price vertical restraints, *supra*-TSM-marginal-cost pricing, and/or other sorts of surrogates for vertical integration to prevent it, which ability does not depend at all on its competitive advantages as a producer of the good or its share of the "market" in which the good is sold.

litigated cases [as of the date on which he completed the third edition of his ANTITRUST HORNBOOK], there are no more than a half dozen plaintiff victories."[1280] Of course, as Hovenkamp also recognizes,[1281] plaintiffs may have prevailed in settlements reached before trial or even before a suit was filed. But the results of the litigated cases make it unlikely that this occurred very often. Hovenkamp's conclusion therefore seems almost certainly to be right: at least if one ignores some plaintiffs' attempts to circumvent *Sylvania* by classifying the defendant's conduct to be an illegal boycott as opposed to an illegal non-price vertical restraint (indeed, as we shall see next, even if one takes these attempts into account), the *Sylvania* Rule-of-Reason approach "has come close to creating complete nonliability for vertical nonprice restraints."[1282]

The second line of cases that *Sylvania* spawned manifests plaintiffs' attempts to circumvent *Sylvania* and the case-law applying its Rule-of-Reason approach by claiming that the defendant's conduct involved *inter alia* a boycott that was *per se* illegal. Only a small number of cases belong to this line, but it seems to me that at least some of those cases and some of the commentary[1283] on them manifest a misunderstanding not only of the legality of various types of boycotts under the Sherman Act, correctly interpreted and applied, but also of their legality under positive U.S. case-law. In particular, the relevant cases and commentary seem to reflect an incorrect assumption that under the Sherman Act both as correctly and as actually interpreted (1) individual refusals to deal (boycotts) cannot be illegal, (2) group boycotts of a rival by two or more competitors are always illegal, and (3) efforts by a reseller (or *a fortiori* group efforts by two or more resellers) to induce a supplier to stop supplying a rival reseller are always illegal. Section 9 of Chap. 11 explained that none of these claims is correct, either as a matter of law correctly found or as a matter of judicial practice. Admittedly, however, in at least one case, a reseller-plaintiff's claim that its supplier's decision to cut it off in response to a request by other franchisees that it do so constituted an illegal boycott did survive a motion for summary judgment.[1284] However, I would be very surprised if many suits based on this claim proved to be successful.

[1280] HOVENKAMP HORNBOOK 486. Hovenkamp cites the article David H. Ginsburg, *Vertical Restraints:* de Facto *Legality Under the Rule of Reason*, 60 ANTITRUST L.J. 67 (1991) to support his conclusion. Judge Ginsburg found three plaintiff victories in Circuit Courts and one remand for trial. The three victories are Graphic Product Distrib., Inc. v. Itek Corp., 717 F.2d 1560 (11th Cir. 1983); Multiflex, Inc. v. Samuel Moore & Co., 709 F.2d 980 (5th Cir. 1983); and Eiborger v. Sony Corp. of America, 622 F.2d 1068 (2d Cir. 1980). The case that was remanded for trial is Dimidowich v. Bell & Howell, 802 F.2d 1473 (9th Cir. 1986), modified, 810 F.2d 1517 (9th Cir. 1987). A preliminary injunction was issued in another case, Kohler Co. v. Briggs & Stratton Corp., 1986-1 Trade Cas. (CCH ¶ 67,047), 1986 WL 946 (E.D. Wis. 1986). The cites in this footnote, like the cites in many of the other footnotes in this section, are taken from HOVENKAMP HORNBOOK.

[1281] HOVENKAMP HORNBOOK 486.

[1282] *Id.*

[1283] See, *e.g.*, *id.* at 488–89.

[1284] Big Apple BMW v. BMW of North America, 974 F.2d 1358 (3rd Cir. 1992), cert. denied, 507 U.S. 912 (1993). See also Arnold Pontiac-GMC v. Budd Baer, 826 F.2d 1335 (3rd Cir. 1987).

Fortunately, the account of the U.S. antitrust-enforcement agencies' position on vertical non-price restraints can be much briefer. Although I have no doubt that the agencies would attack any such restraints that were being used to facilitate a horizontal price-fix, with that exception, the agencies do not oppose either non-price or price vertical restraints (have accepted the conclusion that all such restraints that are not effectuating horizontal price-fixes are performing legitimate functions).

* * *

A final comment on the U.S. case-law on vertical price and non-price restraints. The history of these cases parallels the history of the case-law on tie-ins and reciprocity. The early cases (or in the instance of vertical non-price restraints, the intermediate cases), which declare the practices *per se* illegal, manifest the judges' failure to appreciate the legitimate functions that the relevant practices can perform as well as their acceptance of clearly-fallacious arguments about the practices' tendencies to injure competition and/or the motives their perpetrators have to engage in them. The more recent cases manifest the judges' realization that the practices can perform some legitimate functions but also manifest the judges' continuing (1) failure to appreciate the range of such functions the practices can perform, (2) misapprehension of the Sherman Act's test of illegality, and (3) exaggeration of the likelihood that the practices' perpetrators might be motivated in a way that or that the conduct might produce effects that count against the practices' legality. The judges' increased understanding of the legitimate functions that these practices can perform has led them to conclude that the practices should not be declared *per se* illegal but that the legality of individual exemplars of these practices should be determined through a Rule-of-Reason analysis. The continuing gaps in the judges' understanding has led them to propose inappropriate structures for the Rule-of-Reason analysis they prescribe. However, although these Supreme Court mistakes have led lower courts to consider a wide variety of issues when applying the Rule of Reason to these practices that would be legally irrelevant if the law were correctly interpreted, the mistakes in question have only rarely led the lower courts to condemn as illegal exemplars that do not in fact violate the Sherman Act. I am optimistic that as time progresses the remaining errors will be rectified, fewer unjustified cases will be brought, and those unjustified cases that are brought will be handled more expeditiously and resolved (as a group) even more correctly than at present.

(E) Single-Brand Exclusive Dealerships

The U.S. case-law on single-brand long-term exclusive dealerships is analyzed in Sect. 9D(1)(B)(ii) of Chap. 11. My basic assessment of that case-law is similar to the assessment I made of the U.S. case-law on tie-ins and reciprocity and on vertical price and non-price restraints in this chapter. U.S. courts' understanding of both the legitimate functions of such exclusive dealerships and the conditions under which they will violate the Sherman Act and/or reduce competition has improved dramatically in recent years, though the courts still appear to be exaggerating the likelihood that producers establish dealerships to reduce inter-brand competition and misperceive the relevance of some factors (*e.g.*, the height of the barriers to entry) that they think affect the probability that such arrangements violate the Clayton Act or Sherman Act.

(F) Slotting Arrangements and Other Functionally-Related Types of Trade-Promotion Arrangements

Three lines of U.S. cases focus on (sometimes *inter alia*) slotting arrangements (fixed payments for a specified quantity and quality of shelf-space and floor-space) and other types of trade-promotion arrangements (distinguished by the fact that some or all of the payments the reseller receives are not up-front lump-sum fees but are "variable" [usually taking the form of per-unit product-price discounts]).

The first line of cases focuses on the possibility that the product-producer that has entered into the slotting arrangement or related trade-promotion arrangement in question did so predatorily in violation of the Sherman Act or overlapping state law. Some of these cases involve not just slotting or its equivalent but also arrangements in which resellers agree to charge lower prices for the payor's product than for its rivals' products. One of these cases (*Conwood*)[1285] involved a defendant that not only paid for a certain quantity and quality of shelf-space but also secured the arrangement by exaggerating its share of the market, discarded its rivals display-racks, and hiding its rivals' product in its own display-racks (to deprive rivals of valued "facings"). Although U.S. courts seem to believe that producers with large market shares (that produce products that ultimate consumers "require" retailers to offer for sale) can force resellers to provide them with promotional services[1286] (the same mistake that underlies the leverage theory of tie-ins and reciprocity and the EC's conclusion that producers of "must stock items" can force their potential distributors to accept contractual terms they would otherwise reject to obtain the items in question regardless of how those items were priced), they seem reluctant to find against defendants in these cases. *Conwood* is an exception. The Court of Appeals in that case rejected the defendant's argument that the trial court should not have submitted the case to the jury because the plaintiff had not put on acceptable evidence (1) to demonstrate that it or competition had been injured by the defendant's alleged illegal conduct[1287] or (2) to establish the damages that the

[1285] See Conwood Co. v. United States Tobacco Co. (hereinafter *Conwood*), 290 F.3d 768 (6th Cir. 2002).

[1286] Coca-Cola Company v. Harman Bottling Co. (hereinafter *Coca-Cola*), 218 S.W.3d 671–689 (Tex. 2006).

[1287] *Conwood* at 788–91.

plaintiff had sustained.[1288] In other cases in this category, Courts of Appeals (1) have made the standard mistake of requiring the plaintiff to demonstrate that the defendant had market power prior to engaging in the allegedly-predatory conduct,[1289] (2) have overturned jury verdicts on the ground that the plaintiff had failed to submit any evidence that competition had been harmed *in any relevant market*,[1290] and (3) have upheld a decision by a District Court to grant summary judgment for a defendant on the ground that the judge's decision to exclude an expert's testimony on causation and damages was not an abuse of discretion.[1291]

None of the decisions in this line of cases adequately operationalizes the Sherman Act's test of illegality—*i.e.*, none explains the conditions under which a slotting contract or functionally-analogous alternative arrangements that did or would be predicted to yield a producer some legitimate benefits would nevertheless be predatory. All correctly assess the relevance of any such arrangement's being short-term. But they all seem to put too much weight on whether or not the arrangement is exclusive and, more generally, on whether the percentage of shelf-space "locked up" exceeds the producer's *ex ante* market share. Some[1292] but not all of these cases pay attention to the developing law on single-brand exclusive dealerships and long-term requirements contracts, which does focus on the factors that determine whether the relevant practices will reduce competition by driving out established competitors or deterring QV investment.

The second line of cases are Robinson-Patman Act cases. These cases focus on the possibility that the product-producer may have paid the reseller more than that statute allows it to pay for the promotional services the reseller rendered and/or that the reseller consciously received "excess" payments that were not available to the reseller's rivals. Some of those cases assume that, for the slotting/trade-promotion arrangements in question to be illegal on this account, they must lessen competition in the (secondary) line or lines of commerce in which the favored and disfavored trade-promotion-service providers operate,[1293] while some at least leave the impression that slotting/trade-promotion arrangements can be illegal if they injure disfavored buyers (by worsening their ability to compete with favored buyers) even if they do not reduce secondary-line competition as a result.[1294] The courts in some of these cases also indicate that (1) to establish a functional (*i.e.*, cost-justification) defense in such a suit, the defendant need show that the relevant price-difference

[1288] *Id.* at 791–95.

[1289] See R. J. Reynolds Tobacco Co. v. Philip Morris Incorporated, 199 F. Supp. 2d 362, 381–86 (M.D. N.C. 2002).

[1290] See *Coca-Cola* at 689-90.

[1291] See El Aguila Ford Products, Inc. v. Gruma Corp., 131 Fed. Appx. 450, 2005 WL 1156090 (C.A. 5 Tex.).

[1292] For example, the District Court in R.J. Reynolds Tobacco Co. v. Philip Morris Incorporated, 199 F. Supp. 2d 362 (M.D. N.C. 2002) discussed this issue at 387–89.

[1293] See, *e.g.*, FTC v. McCormick (FTC Dkt. No. C-3939 [2000]).

[1294] See American Booksellers Assn., Inc. v. Barnes & Noble, Inc., 135 F. Supp. 2d 1031, 1057–58 (N.D. Cal. 2001).

equaled either the cost to the reseller of supplying the defendant with the promotional service in question (recognized to be an opportunity cost) or the value of the service in question to the defendant and that (2) the proof on these issues in this type of suit need not "satisfy the rigorous requirements of the cost-justification" defense in standard direct-price-discrimination cases.[1295] The sample of cases in this narrowly-defined line is admittedly very small. My impression is that (1) the courts are open to evidence that particular slotting arrangements do violate the relevant provisions of the Robinson-Patman Act[1296] but (2) they may be more demanding on matters of proof of business loss than at least I think is warranted.[1297]

The third "line of cases" contains just one case, *FTC v. H.J. Heinz, Co.*[1298] *Heinz* is actually a horizontal-merger case in which the defendants argued that the legality of their merger was favored by its tendency to lower the prices ultimate consumers would have to pay for the merger partners' products by eliminating competition between them for shelf-space—*i.e.*, by its tendency to lower the slotting fees the merged firm would have to pay below those its antecedents had to pay. The District Court based its decision to overturn the FTC's challenge to the merger in part on the FTC's rejection of this claim.[1299] The Court of Appeals reversed on the ground that the District Court had held the FTC to an inappropriately-high standard of proof.[1300] The associated legal and economic analyses were extremely dubious all along the line:

(1) although, as a matter of policy and possibly as a matter of law, it may be that reductions in buyer competition should be considered lawful, the U.S. antitrust laws have always been read (as their text in itself warrants) to condemn reductions in buyer competition as well as reductions in seller competition;
(2) because the fees that were being paid were fixed fees as opposed to product-unit-price discounts, their reduction would not affect the prices charged consumers by affecting the resellers' marginal costs (any reductions in such discounts would in any event tend to raise the prices charged final consumers by raising the marginal cost of goods sold to resellers);
(3) to the extent that any reduction in fixed fees would cause resellers to reduce the amount of shelf-space they had available, it might tend to cause prices to go down to the extent that additional eye-level displays encourage relatively-price-insensitive impulse buying; but
(4) it does not seem to me that even if the reduction in fixed (slotting) fees did reduce prices for the reasons alleged after "(3)," that fact would be legally relevant; I do not think that the antitrust laws should be interpreted to count as worthless or

---

[1295] See, *e.g.*, *id.* at 1058.
[1296] See, *e.g.*, *id.* at 1070–71.
[1297] The Intimate Bookshop, Inc. v. Barnes & Noble, Inc., 88 F. Supp. 2d 133 (S.D. N.Y. 2000).
[1298] 116 F. Supp. 2d 190 (D. D.C. 2000).
[1299] *Id.* at 197.
[1300] FTC v. H.J. Heinz Co., 246 F.3d 708, 719 (D.C. Cir. 2001).

undesirable the kind of "information-provision" that results in so-called "impulse buying": if such buying and its stimulation is deemed undesirable, the associated problem should be addressed in separate legislation, which might contain some provisions that bear on the antitrust laws' future application.

This discussion has focused on the case-law on slotting arrangements. The Antitrust Division has not brought any of the recent slotting cases. However, the FTC clearly is concerned about the practice and has sponsored both a conference and a separate report that focuses on its incidence in one industry and its possible consequences.[1301]

(G) Long-Term Full-Requirements Contracts

The U.S. case-law on long-term full-requirements contracts is analyzed in Sect. 9D(1)(B)(i) of Chap. 11. As that section discussed, early on, the U.S. courts used an economically-unsound and therefore legally-incorrect "quantitative-substantiality" test[1302] to assess the legality of such contracts, then shifted to a more-economically-and-legally-relevant qualitative-substantiality test,[1303] and more recently have been refining the application of the latter test to make it more responsive to the factors that actually do affect the likelihood that such a contract may reduce competition by driving an established firm out or deterring a QV investment or be critically motivated by the contracting supplier's interest in generating one or both of these effects.

* * *

The preceding discussion of the U.S. law on the various contractual surrogates for vertical integration has focused overwhelmingly on the case-law. Although occasional reference has been made to the positions that the U.S. antitrust-enforcement agencies have taken on the antitrust legality of the relevant practices, it might be well to close with a more general overview of this issue. As to general policy-statements or relevant non-case-initiation behaviors, I have already indicated that the DOJ's (Reagan era) 1985 Vertical Restraints Guidelines took positions that implied that virtually no vertical restraints (including RPM) violated the U.S. antitrust laws (the DOJ position on RPM was rejected by the State Attorneys General[1304]), that these Guidelines were withdrawn without explanation in 1993 during the Clinton

---

[1301] See Federal Trade Commission, Report on the Commission Workshop on Slotting Allowances and Other Marketing Practices in the Grocer Industry (2001) (summarizing the findings of a workshop held May 31-June 1, 2000) and Federal Trade Commission Staff Study, Slotting Allowances in the Retail Grocery Industries: Selected Case Studies in Five Product Categories (Government Printing Office, 2002).

[1302] Standard Oil Co. v. United States (Standard Stations), 337 U.S. 293 (1949).

[1303] See Tampa Electric Co. v. Nashville Coal Co., 365 U.S. 320 (1961).

[1304] National Association of Attorneys General (NAAG), Vertical Restraint Guidelines (1985), Antitrust and Trade Reg. Rep. 49 (BNA) No. 1243,996.

Administration, and that the FTC has commissioned various studies that manifest its concern that slotting arrangements may be harmful and illegal. In terms of case-initiation and handling, it appears that President Reagan's antitrust-enforcement agencies issued consent orders in only five vertical-restraint cases (all of which were based on investigations initiated during the Carter Administration), that no vertical-restraint complaint resulted from any investigation initiated during the Reagan Administration, and that the Administration of President H.W. Bush brought only four vertical cases, two of which dealt with resale price maintenance. During the Clinton Administration, only 16 vertical-restraint prosecutions were brought. These figures confirm that, even before the federal courts rejected their historic view that RPM and vertical territorial and customer-allocation restraints were *per se* violations of the Sherman Act, federal antitrust-enforcement-agencies had largely stopped prosecuting firms for engaging in these practices.[1305]

B. E.C./E.U. Competition Law

(1) E.C./E.U. Competition Law as Correctly Interpreted and Applied

Because Sect. 2 of Chap. 4's discussion of the E.C. (now E.U.) Treaty provisions that control the legality of the various surrogates for vertical integration appeared many pages ago and because the legality of many surrogates for vertical integration under the 1957 Treaty (whose relevant provisions have been incorporated into the 2009 Treaty of Lisbon), correctly interpreted and applied, depends on details of the Treaty provisions in question and on details of those provisions' correct interpretation, Sect. B(1) begins by reviewing eight sets of general points that pertain to the 1957 Treaty and its correct interpretation—points that are "general" in that they affect the legality under the 2009 Lisbon Treaty, correctly interpreted and applied, of two or more of the types of surrogates for vertical integration that Sect. 2 of this chapter distinguished—and then proceeds to use these general points to analyze the legality of each type of surrogate for vertical integration under E.C./E.U. competition law, correctly interpreted and applied.

(A) Eight General Points or Sets of General Points About E.C./E.U. Competition Law, Correctly Interpreted and Applied, That Are Relevant to the Legality of Surrogates for Vertical Integration

The first general point is that, correctly interpreted and applied, now-Article 101 covers not only clauses in contracts between a producer and reseller or between a

---

[1305] William E. Kovacic, *The Modern Evolution of U.S. Competition Policy Enforcement Norms*, 71 ANTITRUST L.J. 377, 382 (2003).

producer and consignee (because both types of contracts are agreements between undertakings) but also producer sales policies and consignment policies of dealing with or continuing to deal with only those resellers and consignees that conform to the producer's wishes on relevant issues when (1) the policies are at least partially successful at inducing the resellers/consignees to do what the producer wishes them to do, (2) at the time at which the reseller/consignee conformed to the producer's wishes, it understood that the reseller's objective was to prevent or restrict inter-brand competition, and (3) the reseller did not elicit the reseller's/consignee's collaboration by threatening to react to its non-collaboration by making it worse off than it would have been had it not dealt with the producer at all (because, when these three conditions are fulfilled—*i.e.*, when the reseller/consignee conforms to the producer's wishes to obtain a positive advantage—the policy in question can properly be said to have given rise to a concerted practice). As we shall see, the conclusions that now-Article 101(1) covers (1) consignment contracts and (2) some sales and consignment policies are salient because the EC and the E.C./E.U. courts have not always accepted them. I hasten to admit, however, that if I am correct in assuming that the EC (or, more recently, private plaintiffs) would bear the burden of persuasion on the "reseller/consignee understanding of producer object" issue and the non-coercion issue, only a small percentage of the sales and consignment policies that give rise to concerted practices that violate now-Article 101 will ever be proved to do so.

The second general point is that, although now-Article 102's coverage of the various surrogates for vertical integration is narrower than now-Article 101's insofar as now-Article 102 applies only to undertakings that are singly or collectively dominant, now-Article 102's coverage is broader than now-Article 101's in that it applies to (1) agreements between an undertaking and an individual and (2) undertaking sales policies and consignment policies toward both other undertakings and individuals that do not form the basis of a concerted practice because the reseller/consignee does not collaborate or because the reseller's/consignee's decision to collaborate was critically affected by the producer's threat to react to the other party's non-collaboration so as to leave the latter worse off than it would have been had it never dealt with the producer.

The third general point is that now-Article 101 does not render *prima facie* illegal covered conduct that has the object and/or effect of preventing or restricting *intra*-brand competition but does not have the object or effect of preventing or restricting *inter*-brand competition. This point is salient because, as we shall see, it has also been rejected by E.C./E.U. courts and the EC.

The fourth general point is actually a set of three general points or observations that relate to the object-branch of now-Article 101's test of *prima facie* legality. The least important of these observations is that this branch of now-Article 101's test of *prima facie* illegality condemns not only successful but also unsuccessful attempts to prevent, restrict, or distort competition in the common market through an agreement between undertakings, a trade-association decision, or a concerted practice. The most important of these observations relates to the following issue: for a covered agreement between undertakings, trade-association decision, or concerted practice to have as its object the prevention, restriction, or distortion of competition in the common market, must one or more of the perpetrators' *ex ante* beliefs that the conduct would be profitable have been critically affected by its or their perception that it would or might prevent, restrict, or distort such competition or is it sufficient that a perpetrator believed that the conduct would or might increase its profits in this way? For the reasons delineated in Sect. 2A(1)(B) of Chap. 4, I believe that the variant of the object-branch of now-Article 101(1)'s test of *prima facie* illegality that is correct as a matter of law is the variant that declares covered conduct *prima facie* illegal only if, *ex ante*, restricting or preventing competition was "a critical object" of the perpetrator-

The fifth set of general points consists of four observations that relate to the effect-branch of now-Article 101's test of illegality. First, when the kind of vertical conduct with which this chapter is concerned is at issue, the effect that the effect-branch of now-Article 101's test of illegality makes critical is not the effect of an individual firm's executing a covered agreement or engaging in a covered concerted practice but the effect of a rule permitting all members of a relevant set of rivals to engage in such conduct: the opposite conclusion seems incorrect to me as a matter of law because—given various features of now-Article 101(3)—it would often warrant pari-mutuel-handicapping decisions that prohibit well-established firms from using vertical contracts to organize their business cost-effectively while allowing marginal and potential competitors to employ such contracts to do so in order to keep the marginal firms in business and encourage entry. Even if (contrary to my view—see below) now-Article 102, correctly interpreted, would warrant such decisions (because it imposes a special obligation on dominant firms to preserve and foster competition), now-Article 101 does not do so. Second, for a rule allowing all members of a set of rivals to employ relevant types of vertical contracts or engage in concerted practices to prevent or restrict competition, three conditions must be fulfilled: (1) the contracts must be more advantageous for well-established firms than for marginal established competitors and/or otherwise-effective potential competitors; (2) the rule in question must, as a result, worsen the competitive-position array of marginal and otherwise-effective potential competitors; and (3) this deterioration in the competitive-position array of the marginal and otherwise-effective potential competitors in question must reduce competition by inducing the exit of a marginal competitor that would not be immediately replaced by an equally-effective competitor or critically raising the barriers to entry facing an otherwise-effective potential competitor. Third and relatedly, for two reasons, only rarely will a rule allowing all members of a set of rivals to execute vertical contracts or engage in vertical concerted practices have the effect of preventing or restricting inter-brand competition: (1) the relevant vertical agreements/concerted practices tend to be more advantageous for marginal and potential competitors (which, relative to well-established undertakings, are less able to integrate forward, less able to provide warranty services themselves, more needful of distributor/consignee promotional services, and more needful of distributors' and consignees' giving pre-sales advice) and (2) even when the relevant rule would disadvantage marginal and potential competitors, there is no reason to believe that it will often critically affect the exit decision of a marginal competitor that will not be immediately replaced by an equally-effective competitor or the barriers to entry confronting an otherwise-effective potential entrant. Fourth and finally, to determine the competitive effect of an agreement between undertakings, a trade-association decision, or a concerted practice under now-Article 101(1), one must consider "the counterfactual"—*i.e.*, the lawful conduct that the defendant(s) would have substituted for the covered conduct had it or they been prohibited from engaging in the relevant covered conduct. In many (indeed, quite possibly in the vast majority of) cases, the alternative conduct in which the defendants would have engaged (*e.g.*, vertical integration or increasing the per-unit price charged and decreasing the lump-sum fee charged) would have had at least as negative an effect on inter-brand competition (and, I should add, intra-brand competition) as the covered conduct will or did have.

The sixth set of general comments relates to the likelihood that the types of vertical conduct on which we are now focusing that would otherwise violate now-Article 101 because it violates the object-branch of its test of illegality on the "an object" reading of "their object" and not because it violates the effect-branch of its test of illegality on either the assumption that the relevant unit of analysis is an individual firm's or the assumption that the relevant unit of analysis is a rule allowing all competitors to engage in the conduct in question will merit a now-Article 101(3) exemption. First, as Sect. 2 of this chapter explained, many of the types of vertical conduct in question (1) induce independent resellers, consignees, and other sorts of buyers to alter their conduct in one or more ways that E.C./E.U. (and U.S.) antitrust-law analysis must assess to be economically efficient and/or (2) increase economic efficiency by reducing the private and presumptively the allocative transaction cost that producers incur/generate to secure the behavior-alterations they seek to engender. Second, the fact that the producer in question could induce the relevant buyer or consignee to alter its conduct in the way the producer desired without engaging in the vertical conduct under scrutiny was not necessary for the economic efficiency's generation. Unless, contrary to my belief, the relevant seller-conduct benefitted the seller by reducing inter-brand competition, the fact that the perpetrator chose to engage in the conduct under review to achieve the results the conduct achieved implies that it was a more-privately-cost-effective and presumptively-more-economically-efficient means of achieving those sorts of results than any alternative conduct would have been. Third, the now-Article 101(3) requirement that relevant consumers obtain a "fair share" of the "resulting benefit" is a requirement that the equivalent-monetary gains the relevant consumers obtained *from the conduct* in question as opposed to *from the efficiencies the conduct generated* constitute a fair share of the transaction-surplus increase generated *by the conduct* in question as opposed to *by the economic efficiencies the conduct in question generated.*

The seventh set of general points relates to the exclusionary-abuse branch of now-Article 102's test of illegality. First, any conduct by a singly-dominant or collectively-dominant undertaking that would violate the object-branch of now-Article 101(1)'s test of *prima facie* illegality if "their object" were read to refer to "a critical object"—*i.e.*, if the object-branch of now-Article 101(1)'s test of *prima facie* illegality were interpreted to be the same as the Sherman Act's test of illegality—violates the exclusionary-abuse branch of now-Article 102's test of illegality. Second, conduct for which restricting or preventing competition is "an object" but not "a critical object" does not violate the exclusionary-abuse branch of now-Article 102's test of illegality, even when its tendency to restrict or prevent competitors cannot be attributed to its increasing the perpetrator's organizational economic efficiency: I do not think that now-Article 102, correctly interpreted, places a special obligation on singly-dominant or collectively-dominant firms (1) to avoid conduct whose profitability does not depend on reducing or preventing an increase in competition but that does have such an effect even if the conduct does not increase the perpetrator's organizational economic efficiency or, *a fortiori*, (2) to commit unprofitable positive acts that have the effect of preserving or increasing the competition they face.

The eighth and final set of general comments relates to the exploitative-abuse branch of now-Article 102's test of illegality. First, I do not know whether the EC's and the E.C./E.U. courts' failure to condemn dominant-firm conduct as an exploitative abuse reflects the fact that, their statements to the contrary notwithstanding, they really do not believe that now-Article 102 prohibits exploitative abuses or their regretful realization that they cannot develop a judicially-cognizable operationalization of the concept of an exploitative abuse (presumably because they have concluded that courts cannot ascertain the facts that any conceptionally-defensible operationalization of the concept of an exploitative abuse or the related concept of the share of the gains from particular conduct that would be "fair" for consumers to obtain [if exploitation involves consumers being denied a fair share of some relevant gains]). Third, I assume that, in this context the concepts of "exploitation" and "fair share" relate to the percentage that relevant buyer surplus constitutes of the transaction surplus the relevant dominant firm's relevant sales generate as opposed to the absolute amount of surplus relevant buyers obtain or, more plausibly but still-unconvincingly, the percentage that the relevant buyer surplus constitutes of the transaction surplus that would have been generated by the production and "distribution" activities in question had the producer been vertically integrated forward into the buyer's activity and ideally controlled all its employees at no transaction cost. Fourth, regardless of how the relevant definitional/conceptual issue is resolved, I do not think that it would be more difficult or less practicable for the EC or for the E.C./E.U. courts to ascertain the facts that the "correct" definition of "exploitative abuse" or "fair share" deemed salient (to apply the definitions in individual cases) than to execute the empirical analyses that are required by their own approach or the legally-correct approach to applying the other tests of illegality that E.C./E.U. competition law promulgates (or has been incorrectly alleged to promulgate). Fifth, it is important to note that the "counterfactuals" that play an important role in determining whether a vertical contract will have or did have the effect of preventing or restricting competition under now-Article 101(1)—*i.e.*, the fact that the effect of the vertical conduct under scrutiny depends on the (lawful) conduct the producer in question would have substituted for it if prohibited from engaging in the conduct in question—has no counterpart in the analysis of any conduct or practice under the exploitative-abuse branch of now-Article 102's test of illegality. Assume that buyers that are exploitatively abused by a seller that is using one or more of the surrogates for vertical integration on which this chapter is focusing would not be better-off if the producer in question stopped using these surrogates because the producer would substitute for these behaviors other conduct (say, vertical integration or a shift to charging higher per-unit prices and lower lump-sum fees) that was not illegally exclusionary but that would not leave the buyers in question better-off. Although in these circumstances the dominant firm's exploitative abuse of its dominant position could not be attributed to its use of the particular surrogate for vertical integration it in fact employed, the legally-important conclusion would be that—regardless of the way in which the dominant firm chose to reduce its customers' share of the transaction surplus its sales to them generated to an unfairly-low percentage—its creation of this outcome would constitute an exploitative abuse of its dominant position in violation of now-Article 102.

(B) The Legality of the Various Types of Surrogates for Vertical Integration Under E.C./E.U. Competition Law as Correctly Interpreted and Applied

As Sect. 2A(1)(c) indicated, although the text of now-Article 101(1) contains no *de minimis* constraint on its coverage, the ECJ has decided that now-Article 101(1) does not prohibit at least some of the types of conduct it covers unless the conduct has more than a *de minimis* negative impact on competition, and the EC (1) has decided that, although now-Article 101 applies to all "hardcore restrictions"—agreements between competitors to fix prices, limit output, or allocate markets or customers—regardless of whether their impact on competition is *de minimis*, other categories of conduct will be deemed to violate now-Article 101 only if they have more than a *de minimis* negative impact and (2) has proceeded to promulgate operational rules for determining whether conduct in these categories should in effect be exempted from now-Article 101 coverage on "*de minimis* impact" grounds. In part because I consider these conclusions to be incorrect as a matter of law but primarily to save space, the analyses that follow will ignore the possibility that covered conduct may not be deemed illegal because its otherwise-critical negative impact is assessed to be *de minimis*.

(i) Non-Discriminatory Single Pricing, Non-Discriminatory Mixed Pricing That Combines a Lump-Sum Fee With a Supra-TSM-Marginal-Cost Per-Unit Price, Perfect Price Discrimination, and Conventional Price Discrimination

Non-discriminatory single pricing violates now-Article 101 if and only if (1) it is predatory or retaliatory in the service of contrivance and (2) either (A) it is practiced by one undertaking in relation to another undertaking or (B) it is practiced by one undertaking in relation to an individual who understood the character of the pricing in question at the time of sale and who participated in the relevant transaction to obtain an advantage (who was not coerced into buying the relevant good by a threat that the seller would react to non-participation by making the individual buyer worse off than he would have been had he not made the purchase in question). Non-discriminatory single pricing violates now-Article 102 if and only if (1) the seller is singly or collectively dominant and (2) the pricing is either (A) predatory or retaliatory in the service of contrivance or (B) exploitative in that it causes the relevant buyers' buyer surplus on the associated purchases to constitute an unfairly-low percentage of the transaction surplus the sales in question generated—*i.e.*, a percentage of that transaction surplus that is sufficiently low to justify the legal conclusion that the pricer has committed a now-Article 102 exploitative abuse of its customers.

The preceding general account of now-Articles 101 and 102 implies that the use of mixed pricing-techniques that combine some lump-sum fee with a supra-TSM-marginal-cost per-unit price violates now-Article 101 and now-Article 102 in the same circumstances in which non-discriminatory single pricing would do so. The use of a mixed pricing-technique (or the practice of perfect price discrimination, which will be discussed next) can be predatory or retaliatory in the service of contrivance if (in part for transaction-cost reasons) it is not inherently profitable but is employed nevertheless because the lower per-unit prices the mixed technique involves relative to its more-inherently-profitable alternative (or the lower per-unit prices on marginal and some intra-marginal units that perfect price discrimination involves) are designed to drive a target out or deter its QV investment by depriving it of profitable sales. It is worth pointing out that—at least when the relevant buyer is unable to protect itself by threatening to shift suppliers, not to buy at all, to integrate forward, or to secure the entry of an alternative supplier of the good in question—the use of the mixed technique is more likely to violate the exploitative-abuse branch of now-Article 102 than is any exemplar of non-discriminatory single pricing that the pricer in question would find profitable.

The same conclusions apply to perfect price discrimination in any of its forms. Indeed, since, as conventionally defined, perfect price discrimination deprives the relevant buyer of any surplus whatsoever, it would on that definition almost certainly constitute an exploitative abuse of a dominant position if practiced by a dominant undertaking. (This conclusion would not be warranted if the practice were defined to include any pricing strategy that [1] includes varying per-unit prices that prevent sales from dropping below the TSM level, [2] gives the seller more profits than it would earn if it charged no lump-sum fee and a per-unit price equal to TSM marginal cost, but [3] allows the buyer to obtain surplus by charging per-unit prices for intra-marginal units that are below the demand price and/or lump-sum fees that do not eliminate all the surplus the buyer would secure in their absence.)

I turn finally to conventional (inter-buyer) price discrimination. Conventional price discrimination violates now-Articles 101 and 102 when the conditions that result in the other single-product pricing-techniques' already discussed doing so are fulfilled. However, the likelihood that conventionally-discriminatory pricing will violate now-Article 101 or now-Article 102 is not the same as the likelihood that the other single-product pricing-techniques in question will do so, and two additional issues must be addressed in relation to the now-Article 101 legality of conventional price discrimination. In particular, conventional price discrimination is probably more likely to prevent or restrict competition in the now-Article 101 sense of that expression and to constitute an exclusionary abuse in the now-Article 102 sense of that expression than are any of the other single-product pricing-techniques in question because, as Chaps. 10 and 11 respectively argued, a firm is more likely to find it profitable to punish rivals that have refused to cooperate with its contrivance efforts by retaliating selectively than by cutting prices across-the-board. I should add that conventional price discrimination is more likely than non-discriminatory single pricing but less likely than the relevant mixed pricing-technique or perfect price discrimination to leave relevant consumers with a quantity of buyer surplus that constitutes a sufficiently-low percentage of the transaction surplus generated by the sales in question to justify the conclusion that the pricer (if it was singly or collectively dominant) had committed an exploitative abuse of its dominant position under now-Article 102. (Although conventional price discrimination can either increase or decrease buyer surplus, I suspect that, across all cases, it tends to reduce buyer surplus.)

The first of the two novel issues that conventional price discrimination raises relates to now-Article 101's *prima facie* prohibition of agreements between undertakings that *distort* competition in the common market—on my understanding, agreements that cause a buyer that would otherwise be privately (and presumptively allocatively) best-placed to supply one or more buyers further downstream to be privately-worse-than-best-placed to do so when the change in position cannot be attributed to the agreement's worsening the economic efficiency of the disadvantaged buyer's making the sale (in its role as a downstream supplier relative to the economic efficiency of its comparatively-advantaged rival's doing so). More concretely, the primary concern is that price discrimination between two undertaking-buyers that compete as sellers on the downstream (secondary-line) level may make a disfavored buyer that would otherwise have been privately-best-placed to supply some downstream buyer privately-worse-placed to do so than the favored buyer. (Although price discrimination could also "distort competition" in the sense in which economists understand this concept when the favored buyer does not compete against the favored buyer in a downstream "market" or when the favored buyer does not compete against the disfavored buyer in a downstream market, this possibility has never been considered.) Three legally-salient points need to be made in relation to this distortion-of-competition possibility:

(1) actual acts of discrimination will rarely distort secondary-line competition in the way described both (A) because upstream sellers will almost never find it profitable to engage in discrimination that renders privately-worse-than-best-placed a reseller/(buyer of an intermediate good) that would otherwise have been privately-best-placed since producers will almost always find it profitable to arrange their affairs so that the reseller/final-product producer that, absent discrimination, would be privately-best-placed (to resell its final good)/(to supply a downstream buyer of the final product that incorporates the producer's

intermediate good) remains so and (B) because of the point that is numbered "(3)" in this list;

(2) in the few cases in which the upstream seller would find it more profitable to practice discrimination that would render privately-worse-than-best-placed an "intermediary"—*i.e.*, a reseller of its final good or a producer of a final good for which the relevant producer's product is an input—that would otherwise be privately-best-placed than to supply that intermediary on a non-discriminatory basis—*viz.*, those in which the relevant intermediary was an effective potential entrant into or an effective potential expander in the discriminator's primary-line market and the discrimination in question would or might critically raise the barriers to entry or expansion facing the disfavored intermediary (by reducing its ability to finance the new QV investment internally, by depriving it of the opportunity to identify buyers in the primary-line market, to discover the special preferences of these buyers, and to make a good impression on them, and by depriving it of the opportunity to learn things about the discriminator's product by handling it), the conduct in question would prevent or restrict primary-line competition (by deterring the discriminated-against intermediary's entry or expansion or obviating the discriminator's and one or more other established firms' executing limit QV investments to deter the intermediary's new QV investment) even if it did not distort secondary-line competition, and the price discrimination in question would violate now-Article 101 on that account unless the perpetrator of the conduct in question could establish a now-Article 101(3) defense by demonstrating, *inter alia*, that its preventing the intermediary's QV investment increased economic efficiency by preventing the deflation of the perpetrator's incentives (A) to create the product in question (even though the intermediary's QV investment would not violate any IP right of the discriminator), (B) to identify buyers whose purchase of its product would be economically efficient, and (C) to provide those buyers with information that enables them to understand that they would gain by purchasing the product in question on the terms offered; and

(3) after (or if) the courts conclude that discrimination that has the object or effect of critically disadvantaging disfavored buyers violates now-Article 101, producers that might otherwise have practiced such discrimination to prevent potential entrants or expanders from making QV investments will find it more profitable to achieve this outcome by refusing to deal with the intermediaries in question since refusals to deal are not covered by now-Article 101 inasmuch as they do not involve an agreement between undertakings, a trade-association decision, or a concerted practice (though, admittedly, this argument will be less forceful if the perpetrator is singly or collectively dominant since such firms' refusals to deal are covered by now-Article 102).

The second special issue that price discrimination raises relates to the efforts that producers that want to practice price discrimination across national borders may find it profitable to make to prevent cross-national arbitrage (parallel trading) by dealers in those countries in which it wants to charge a lower price (say, because the country is poorer). A producer that is in this position may try to prevent cross-country arbitrage by including in its contracts of sale to the poor-country dealers to which it is charging lower prices clauses that forbid them from engaging in cross-country cross-selling, vertical-territorial-restraint-generating clauses that prohibit the favored dealers from selling to buyers in other countries, or vertical-customer-allocation clauses that limit such dealers to supplying buyers in their own country. Although some may think that such restrictions in intra-E.C./E.U. cross-country sales are precisely the kind of conduct that the 1957 Treaty was designed to prevent (conduct that militates against the development of an integrated Community market), I disagree. I consider such restrictions to be restrictions on intra-brand competition, which E.C./E.U. competition law, properly interpreted, does not prohibit. In part, my conclusion reflects the fact that efforts to prevent producers from deterring their independent distributors from engaging in cross-country arbitrage are likely to disserve the goal of encouraging cross-country trade and citizens' of one E.C./E.U. country learning about the tastes and consumption-patterns of citizens of other E.C./E.U. countries by inducing the producers in question to vertically integrate forward into distribution, to cease selling their products in poor countries at the discriminatorily-low prices that are profit-maximizing in those countries, or to cease selling their products in the poor countries altogether.

(ii) Contract Clauses/Consignment Policies That Obligate/Encourage Resellers/ Consignees to Make Out-of-Store-Advertising or In-Store-Promotional Decisions, Producer-Paid Subsidies of Such Reseller/Consignee Activities, and Sales/ Consignment Policies of Supplying/Hiring Only Resellers/Consignees That Make the Out-of-Store-Advertising and In-Store-Promotional Decisions the Producer Wishes Them to Make

Eight points or sets of related points are relevant. First, now-Article 101 covers both (1) contract clauses/consignment policies that (A) obligate/encourage resellers/ consignees to make certain advertising/promotional decisions and (B) obligate producers to subsidize the reseller/consignee decisions in question (since they constitute agreements between undertakings) and (2) sales and consignment policies that are designed to induce resellers and consignees to make the advertising and promotional decisions the producers wants them to make when those policies succeed and the reseller/consignee knowledge-and-profit conditions for their giving rise to a concerted practice are fulfilled.

Second, now-Article 102 covers not only (1) both of the types of contract clauses just delineated but also (2) the sales and consignment policies just described, regardless of whether they give rise to a concerted practice.

Third, if, correctly construed as a matter of law, the object-branch of now-Article 101(1)'s test of *prima facie* illegality declares *prima facie* illegal only those exemplars of covered conduct for which preventing, restricting, or distorting competition was "a critical object," the relevant contract clauses and covered sales/consignment policies will violate that branch of now-Article 101(1)'s test of *prima facie* illegality if and only if they are predatory or retaliatory in the service of contrivance.

Fourth, if the "their object" text of now-Article 101(1) is correctly interpreted to refer to "an object" but the object of restricting or preventing competition is correctly interpreted to refer to the object of restricting or preventing *inter*-brand but not *intra*-brand competition, the relevant contract clauses and covered sales/consignment policies violate the object-branch of now-Article 101(1)'s test of *prima facie* illegality both (1) when the conduct in question is predatory or retaliatory in the service of contrivance when the producer believed *ex ante* that the reseller/consignee advertising expenditures or in-store-promotion decisions that the clauses or policies in question would or might induce would or might increase its profits by reducing the absolute attractiveness of the offers against which it would have to compete by causing the exit of an established rival that would not be immediately replaced by an equally-effective competitor or by critically raising the barriers to QV investment confronting an otherwise-effective rival potential QV investor by improving the perpetrator's competitive-position array and concomitantly worsening the relevant established rival's competitive-position array and/or the relevant rival potential QV investor's prospective competitive-position array. I should add that, although I have no doubt that the second of these last two conditions is sometimes fulfilled, I do not know how often it is fulfilled and suspect that it is not fulfilled very often.

Fifth, if I am correct in concluding that—when the *prima facie* illegality of a vertical practice under the effect-branch of now-Article 101(1)'s test of *prima facie* illegality is at issue—the relevant analysand is the competitive impact of a rule permitting all members of a relevant set of rivals to engage in the practice in question rather than the competitive impact of an individual producer's engaging in the relevant vertical conduct, contract clauses and covered sales/consignment policies that are designed to increase a reseller's out-of-store advertising of or in-store promotion of a producer's product(s) violate the effect-branch of now-Article 101(1)'s test of *prima facie* illegality only if (1) the conduct in question (A) was predatory or retaliatory in the service of contrivance and (B) was at least partially successful or (2)(A) the conduct in question was less profitable for marginal competitors and otherwise-effective potential QV investors than for well-established firms and (B) a rule allowing all members of a relevant set of rivals to engage in the relevant conduct would reduce competition by causing the exit of a marginal firm (by worsening its array of competitive positions) that would not be immediately replaced by an equally-effective competitor and/or by critically raising the barriers to entry faced by an otherwise-effective potential QV investor (by worsening its prospective competitive-position array). I should add that, in my judgment, rules allowing all members of a set of rivals to use contract clauses and sales/consignment policies to induce resellers and consignees to increase their advertising and promotion of the producer's product will rarely reduce competition in either of the above ways and, when they do, the behavior in question will always satisfy the economic-efficiency-generating requirement (but perhaps not the "fair share" requirement) of now-Article 101(3)—at least if one assumes that, for the purpose of applying competition laws, all the advertising and in-store promotion of a product that is profitable for its producers and distributors combined (or at least all such profitable advertising/promotion that is not fraudulent) contributes to economic efficiency. Sixth, both types of contract clauses listed above and all the sales/consignment policies described above will violate the exclusionary-abuse branch of now-Article 102's test of illegality if and only if the perpetrator is singly or collectively dominant and the conduct is either predatory or retaliatory in the service of contrivance. Seventh, at least when the induced advertising is not fraudulent, none of the behaviors listed in the heading can constitute a now-Article 102 exploitative abuse of a dominant position: this conclusion reflects the combination of (1) "the fact" that competition-law appliers are not authorized to disvalue buyers' positive valuations of certain product-images or product-associations and (2) "the fact" that, although it is conceivable that advertising would change the demand curve a seller faced in a way that would make it profitable for the seller to reduce the amount of buyer surplus its possibly-changing customers obtained by patronizing it or the share of relevant transaction surplus that its possibly-changing customers' buyer surplus constituted, any such impact would rarely critically affect whether the producer had engaged in an exploitative abuse. Eighth, because I reject the claim that now-Article 102 imposes a special duty on dominant firms to foster competition or avoid reducing competition, I do not think that any of the types of conduct listed in the heading can violate now-Article 102 by worsening the competitive positions of extant or potential rivals.

(iii) Tie-Ins, Reciprocity, and Sales or Conceivably Consignment Policies That Are Designed to Achieve the Same Results That Tie-Ins and Reciprocity Can Achieve

Conventionally, a tie-in is defined to be (1) an *agreement* in which (usually) a seller that enjoys competitive advantages on one good (in standard terminology, that has "market power" when selling the good in question, which is denominated the "tying" product) conditions its obligation to supply that good to a buyer on specified terms on the buyer's agreeing to purchase a specified quantity or its full requirements of a second (so-called tied) good from the seller in question (or a third party the seller denominates) on specified terms or (2) an agreement in which (usually) a seller contracts to supply a buyer with a package of two or more goods (a "bundle" of goods) at a specified (total) price. Conventionally, a reciprocity agreement is defined to be a *contract* in which an undertaking that enjoys market power as a buyer of one good conditions its agreement to buy that product on specified terms from another undertaking on the latter undertaking's purchasing from the former undertaking or a third party that the former undertaking specifies a specified quantity or its full requirements of a second good on specified terms. However, sellers can sometimes use non-contractual sales or consignment policies as opposed to sales or consignment contracts to perform at least some of the functions that tie-ins (which by definition are contractual) can perform, and buyers can sometimes use non-contractual purchasing policies to perform some of the functions that reciprocity (which by definition is contractual) can perform.

I will make 14 points that relate to the legality of tie-ins and reciprocity and functionally-equivalent (non-contractual) sales and consignment policies under

E.C./E.U. competition law. First, now-Article 101(1) covers all tie-ins and reciprocity agreements that are executed by two undertakings.

Second, now-Article 101(1) covers the many tie-ins and reciprocity agreements that are executed between an undertaking and a non-undertaking (hereinafter between an undertaking and an individual) if but only if the agreement in question can correctly be said to have given rise to a concerted practice—more specifically, if and only if an object of the agreement was to prevent or restrict competition and the "individual" who entered into the agreement (1) was aware of this fact at the time of the agreement's formation and (2) entered into the agreement to obtain the short-run gains that the undertaking offered the individual to induce his or her collaboration: derivatively, if the undertaking secured the individual's collaboration by threatening to react to the individual's non-collaboration by making the individual worse off than he or she would have been had he or she had nothing to do with the undertaking, the tie-in or reciprocity agreement in question (which *ex hypothesis* was not an agreement between two undertakings) would not be covered by now-Article 101(1) because it would not have given rise to a concerted practice.

Third and relatedly, (1) tie-in-like non-contractual sales policies or consignment policies in which an undertaking-producer makes a practice of (supplying a buyer with one product)/(using a consignee to sell one product) on terms that are more attractive to the buyer/consignee in question than the terms the producer would otherwise have offered only if the buyer/consignee in question (purchases from it/ agrees to sell for it) without being contractually obligated to do so a specified quantity or its full requirements of a second product on terms that the buyer/ consignee in question would reject in a truly-independent transaction and (2) reciprocity-like non-contractual purchasing policies in which an undertaking-buyer/consignee lets it be known that it will (purchase or continue to purchase)/(sell as a consignee) one product from a supplier on terms the reciprocity-initiator would otherwise reject only if the trading-partner purchases from it (sells as a consignee) a specified quantity or its full requirements of a second product on terms the trading partner would reject in a truly-independent transaction are covered by now-Article 101(1) as concerted practices if but only if (1) the policy-creator's trading partner or consignee was aware at the time of its collaboration that the policy-creator's object was to prevent or restrict competition and (2) voluntarily agreed to collaborate to obtain short-run benefits.

Fourth, tie-ins, reciprocity, and related sales and consignment policies that function by concealing the existence, extent, or location of predation or retaliation in the service of contrivance can be covered by now-Article 101(1) either because they are agreements between undertakings or because they gave rise to a concerted practice (if the relevant conditions for coverage on these bases are fulfilled) even when—had it been prevented from using such conduct to execute and conceal the predation or contrivance in question—the predator or contriver in question would have practiced predation or contrivance in a way that would not have been covered by now-Article 101(1)—*e.g.*, by threatening and making predatory or retaliatory price-cuts or predatory or retaliatory QV-investments.

Fifth, although tie-ins, reciprocity agreements, and functionally-identical sales and consignment policies whose object is to effectuate and conceal predation or retaliation in the service of contrivance will violate the object-branch of now-Article 101(1)'s test of *prima facie* illegality and will violate the effect-branch of now-Article 101(1)'s test of *prima facie* illegality if they are at all successful, tie-ins, reciprocity agreements, and related sales and consignment policies that execute and conceal tax fraud, contract violations, maximum-price-regulation violations, or minimum-price-regulation violations do not violate the object-branch of now-Article 101(1)'s test of *prima facie* illegality, and will almost never violate the effect-branch of now-Article 101's test of *prima facie* illegality either.

Sixth, tie-ins that require buyers to purchase their full requirements of some product from the tying seller, reciprocity agreements that require a producer to supply a buyer with its total output, and sales policies and purchasing policies that are designed to induce respectively relevant buyers to purchase their full requirements of some product from the seller and relevant producers to supply their total output of some product to the buyer will violate the object-branch of now-Article 101's test of *prima facie* illegality if the perpetrator's or perpetrators' *ex ante* perception of these contractual provisions or sales/purchasing policies' profitability was (respectively) critically increased/increased at all by a belief that they would or might induct the exit of an existing rival that would not be immediately replaced by an equally-effective competitor or critically raise the barriers to entry confronting an otherwise-effective potential QV investor by locking in the buyers/suppliers in question and thereby reducing the demand curve the relevant existing competitors faced and the demand curve the relevant potential QV investor would anticipate facing.

Seventh, the possibilities on which the sixth point focuses seem extremely unlikely to be realized in practice. The conditions under which these kinds of conduct can reduce inter-brand competition by locking up buyers or suppliers (which were first discussed in Sect. 9 of Chap. 11) are set out in the discussion of single-brand exclusive dealerships that follows. The basic point is that the duration of the full-requirements obligation created by virtually all tie-ins that create such obligations and of the total-output-supply obligations created by virtually all reciprocity agreements that create such obligations is too short to have the "foreclosing" effect in question and that the relevant sales and purchasing policies will rarely foreclose because they do not impose any obligations at all.

Eighth, in the few cases in which foreclosure is a real possibility, the fact that the relevant full-requirements-purchasing or total-output-supplying obligations or incentives are created by tie-ins or reciprocity contracts or their sales/purchasing-policy analogues is legally relevant under now-Article 101(1) because the fact in question bears on the legitimate functions that the obligation-creating or incentive-creating conduct in question could be performing (functions that would be legally relevant under the Sherman Act's "critical-object" test of illegality since the prospect of their performance creates the possibility that their perpetrator might have believed *ex ante* that the conduct in question was *ex ante* profitable on their account alone).

Ninth, conduct that violates the object-branch of now-Article 101(1)'s test of illegality will violate the exclusionary-abuse branch of now-Article 102 only if the perpetrator was individually dominant or a member of a collectively-dominant set of rivals.

Tenth, full-requirements/total-output contracts and sales/purchasing policies that do not violate the "object" branch of now-Article 101(1)'s test of *prima facie* illegality could still violate the effect-branch of now-Article 101(1)'s test of *prima facie* illegality because it could still reduce competition.

Eleventh, the preceding analysis assumed that the appropriate unit for now-Article 101(1) "effect" analysis is the effect of an individual firm's using some surrogate for vertical integration. As previously stated, because the preceding analysand-conclusion would obligate the law's appliers to engage in pari-mutuel handicapping when analyzing the legality of surrogates for vertical interpretation, I believe that the proper unit of effect-branch analysis in all cases of non-predatory tie-ins or reciprocity is the effect of a rule allowing all members of a set of rivals to use a particular surrogate for vertical integration. If this is correct, the probability that these surrogates for vertical integration will violate now-Article 101(1)'s test of *prima facie* illegality will be substantially lower than it would be if the legally-correct analysand were the impact of an individual undertaking's using tie-ins, reciprocity, or related sales or consignment policies. In fact, for two reasons, I suspect that such conduct by a group of rivals will rarely violate now-Article 101(1)'s test of *prima facie* illegality: (1) tie-ins, reciprocity, and related sales and consignment policies will usually be more profitable for marginal and potential competitors than for well-established firms, and (2) even when they are less profitable for marginal and potential competitors, their use will often not critically affect the exit decision of a marginal competitor that will not be immediately replaced by an equally-effective competitor or critically raise the barriers to entry facing an otherwise-effective potential competitor. I should add that, even when a rule allowing all members of a set of rivals to use tie-ins, reciprocity, or related sales or consignment policies would reduce competition, the well-established perpetrators of such conduct may be eligible to receive a now-Article 101(3) exemption from Article 101(1) because many functional types of tie-ins and reciprocity generate economic efficiencies either or both by reducing allocative transaction costs or by achieving other results (*e.g.*, controlling the quality of complements) that are economically efficient and because some such efficiency-enhancing tie-ins and reciprocity do give the buyers they involve a fair share of the resulting benefits.

Twelfth, an individual undertaking's or a set-of-rivals' non-predatory or non-contrivance-related-retaliatory use of tie-ins, reciprocity, or sales/consignment policies can also have the effect of reducing competition if, relative to its alternatives, the conduct in question increases the unit sales of its employer(s) by lowering the per-unit price of the tying product in circumstances in which the associated reduction in the demand curve facing a marginal rival of the seller(s) in question or the prospective demand curve facing a potential competitor of the relevant seller(s) reduced competition by inducing the exit of the marginal rival in question when it would not be replaced by an equally-effective competitor or critically raising the barriers to entry facing the potential competitor in question when it otherwise would have been effective. I hasten to add that the preceding outcomes are unlikely to eventuate in more than a trivial number of cases, and (though this is irrelevant to our current concerns) I also doubt that courts will ever be able to determine that it would be likely to transpire or had transpired in any individual case.

Thirteenth, tie-ins and reciprocity and related sales and consignment policies that are used by singly-dominant or collectively-dominant sellers that reduce the private transaction cost of meter pricing or that increase the cost-effectiveness of supra-TSM-marginal-cost pricing by transferring its locus (in the case of tie-ins) to a segment of another demand curve (the full-requirements demand curve for the tied product) over which $\Delta SS+/\Delta BS-$ is higher can reduce buyer surplus (in the meter-pricing case by making it profitable for the seller to employ meter pricing that prevents it from allowing unnecessary buyer surplus to escape because it would otherwise charge too low a lump-sum fee for its durable machine or idea and in the "full-line forcing" case by making it profitable for the seller to substitute for single pricing a mixed lump-sum plus supra-TSM-marginal-cost per-unit price pricing-technique that eliminates surplus that the single pricing would have permitted to escape) and may therefore reduce the percentage of transaction surplus generated that buyer surplus constitutes to a level that justifies the conclusion that the seller in question was guilty of an exploitative abuse. I doubt that this last possibility has much practical legal significance both because I suspect that it eventuates only rarely and because I suspect that, even if the EC and the E.C./E.U. courts did conclude that the concept of an exploitative abuse was judicially cognizable, they would not be able to predict or postdict its eventuation when it was likely to or did in fact eventuate.

Fourteenth, in my judgment, now-Article 102 does not impose an obligation on a dominant seller to foster the competition it faces or to avoid reducing the competition it faces that makes it illegal for such a company to improve its competitive-position array and concomitantly worsen its rivals' competitive-position arrays by using tie-ins or related sales policies to control the quality of the complements its buyers combine with its product or by using reciprocity agreements or related purchasing policies to control the quality of the ingredients or other inputs that a potential supplier of a good it wishes to purchase use to produce that good.

(iv) Resale-Price-Maintenance Clauses, Vertical Contractual Territorial Restraints, Vertical Customer-Allocation Clauses, and Non-Single-Brand Exclusive Dealerships

For simplicity, I will ignore the possibility that a producer may attempt to achieve the goals that these types of arrangements can secure by substituting non-contractual sales or consignment policies for the arrangements in question. As Sect. 2 of this chapter explained, producers use contract clauses of these types (1) to deter independent resellers from driving down the prices that further-downstream buyers pay for the producer's product below the price those buyers would have been willing to pay if they could not purchase the producer's product more cheaply, (2) to deter independent resellers from placing more advertisements and engaging in more door-to-door salesmanship than is in the joint interest of the producer and all its distributors, (3) to induce its independent resellers to engage in more out-of-store advertising and in-store promotion of its products when the additional efforts in question are in its and all its distributors' joint interest, (4) to induce its independent resellers to provide pre-sales advice and post-sales warranty services whose provision is in its and its distributors' joint interest, and (5) to encourage its individual independent resellers to provide it and/or other resellers of its brand with valuable information about sales techniques that have proved effective or product-uses that some ultimate buyers value.

I want to make eight points that relate to the legality of these practices under now-Articles 101 and 102 of the 2009 Treaty of Lisbon. First, a reminder: non-single-brand exclusive dealerships (*i.e.*, agreements that give a dealer the exclusive right to sell the producer's product in a given territory or to a particular set of buyers) are simply in one sense the flip-side of vertical territorial restraints and vertical customer-allocation clauses—the latter arrangements are designed to enforce the non-single-brand exclusive-dealership rights of the dealer that has been given the exclusive right to sell the producer's product in a given territory or to a given set of buyers.

Second, the fact that all these arrangements have the object of preventing *intra*-brand competition does not make them even *prima facie* illegal under either the object-branch of now-Article 101(1)'s test of *prima facie* illegality or the exclusionary-abuse branch of now-Article 102's test of illegality.

Third, resale price maintenance that is practiced by resellers to facilitate their horizontal price-fix by inducing their suppliers to enforce it or that is being used by producers to facilitate their horizontal price-fix by reducing each's incentive to cut prices to resellers by precluding the resellers from passing on those price-cuts to ultimate consumers violate both the object-branch of the now-Article 101(1) test of *prima facie* illegality, the effect-branch of the now-Article 101(1)'s test of *prima facie* illegality when the relevant conduct is successful, and the exclusionary-abuse and possibly the exploitative-abuse branch of the now-Article 102 test of illegality.

Fourth, vertical territorial restraints and vertical customer-allocation clauses that are employed by either resellers or producers in a coordinated fashion to divide up territories or customers among themselves (ideally from the producers' perspective by assigning each territory or buyer to only one reseller of one brand) violate the object-branch of now-Article 101(1)'s test of *prima facie* illegality, the effect-branch of now-Article 101(1)'s test of *prima facie* illegality (if the effort at market division is at least partially successful), and the exclusionary-abuse and possibly the exploitative-abuse branch of now-Article 102's test of illegality.

Fifth, all these practices violate the effect-branch of now-Article 101(1)'s test of *prima facie* illegality if that branch is properly applied even if they do not have the object of restricting or preventing competition if a rule allowing all members of the relevant set of rivals to engage in such practices would reduce competition because the practices in question are more preferable for well-established producers than for marginal competitors and otherwise-effective potential QV investors and the other conditions that would result in such a rule's reducing competition on this account are satisfied.

Sixth, the possibility just delineated has relatively-little practical significance because (1) such practices tend to be more profitable for marginal and potential competitors than for well-established firms, (2) the other conditions for the relevant rule's reducing competition will often not be satisfied, and (3) the economic efficiency of the alterations in reseller non-pricing conduct that these practices elicit implies that they satisfy the economic-efficiency-generating condition for a now-Article 101(3) exemption.

Seventh, a point that would be legally salient if—contrary to my view—now-Article 101 does *prima facie* prohibit conduct that decreases *intra*-brand competition: in many if not most situations, RPM will not decrease intra-brand competition because its prohibition will tend to cause producers either to integrate forward into distribution or to reduce their lump-sum fees and increase their per-unit prices to prevent their independent distributors from competing down the prices the resellers' customers pay.

Eighth, given the fact that producers that are barred from using RPM, vertical territorial restraints, vertical customer-allocation clauses, and non-single-brand exclusive dealerships will tend to respond to such prohibitions by vertically integrating forward into distribution or raising their per-unit prices and lowering their lump-sum fees and given the fact that prohibitions of such vertical restraints will tend to reduce the amount of advertising-information, pre-sales advice, and post-sales warranty services buyers receive (all of which buyers positively value), there is little reason to believe that these practices tend to reduce the amount of buyer surplus relevant buyers secure and therefore even less reason to believe that the individual use of such practices by a dominant firm will make a firm of this sort that would not otherwise be guilty of committing an exploitative abuse of a dominant position guilty of doing so.

(v) Single-Brand Exclusive Dealerships

Seven points or sets of point are salient. First, as Sect. 9 of Chap. 11 explained, although single-brand exclusive dealerships can perform many legitimate functions and (I believe) are normally rendered profitable by the legitimate functions they perform, an individual firm's creation of an individual single-brand exclusive dealership, an individual firm's creation of multiple single-brand exclusive dealerships, and a group of established rivals' concerted creation of a series of single-brand exclusive dealerships can reduce inter-brand competition both (1) when the conduct worsens the distributive arrangements that one or more existing marginal rivals can make sufficiently to lead one or more of them to exit when it or they will not be immediately replaced by an equally-effective competitor or worsens the distributive arrangements that can be made by one or more otherwise-effective potential entrants or potential expanders sufficiently to critically raise the barriers to entry it or they face and (2) when the conduct plays a role in a successful horizontal market-division scheme.

Second, the likelihood that one or more single-brand exclusive dealerships will have the first of these effects will depend *inter alia* on (1) the duration of the single-brand exclusive dealerships in question, (2) (A) whether those dealerships leave uncommitted enough dealers to enable established rivals that do not have such arrangements or potential QV investors that do not have them either to distribute their products non-disadvantageously or (B) somewhat more sensitively, when particular distributors would be unusually-well-placed to distribute the product of a relevant marginal competitor or potential QV investor and could not prevent the producer from securing some profits from using them, whether the existing single-brand exclusive dealerships locked in enough of these particularly-well-placed distributors to disadvantage the relevant marginal competitors and potential QV investors, (3) the extent to which the (Π_D + R) barriers to vertical integration forward into distribution that the relevant marginal competitors and potential QV investors face exceed the average (Π_D + R) barriers faced by the locked-up distributors, (4) the extent to which the relevant marginal competitors and potential investors can reduce the (Π_D + R) barriers to their entering into the distribution business by participating in joint ventures, (5) the cost to the relevant marginal competitors and potential QV investors of inducing an independent entry into distribution (by providing relevant information to potential independent entrants, by subsidizing their entry with money, or by entering into full-requirements contracts with them) and the (Π_D + R) barriers to entry that the independent entrant in question would face relative to the (Π_D + R) barriers faced by the locked-up distributors, (6) the S barrier to forward integration into distribution that would confront the relevant marginal competitors and the S barriers to entry that would confront the independent entrants that might enter the relevant distributive space with or without the relevant producers' encouragement, (7) the probability that competitors that are prevented from using the locked-up distributors will be induced to exit by any given disadvantage and the probability that they would be immediately replaced by an equally-effective competitor, and (8) the probability that disadvantaged potential QV investors were effective and that any given related increase in the barriers to QV investment they faced would critically affect their willingness to invest if the (other) established firms did not make deterring limit QV investments.

Third, even if the perpetrator or perpetrators of single-brand exclusive dealerships knew that they will prevent or restrict competition by causing an established firm to exit when it will not be replaced by an equally-effective potential competitor and/or by critically raising the barriers to QV investment faced by an otherwise-effective potential QV investor, that fact does not guarantee that "the now-Article 101(1) object" of the creation of the single-brand exclusive dealerships in question was to prevent or restrict competition given that "their object" in now-Article 101(1) is correctly read to refer to "a critical object" because the creator or creators may have believed *ex ante* that the relevant single-based exclusive dealerships would be profitable even if they did not prevent or restrict competition.

Fourth, even if the single-brand exclusive dealerships in question do not violate the object-branch of now-Article 101(1)'s test of *prima facie* illegality, they might violate the effect-branch of now-Article 101(1)'s test of *prima facie* illegality if an individual undertaking's single-brand exclusive dealerships or (to my mind, more legally relevantly) a rule allowing all established undertakings to use single-brand exclusive dealerships did in fact prevent or restrict competition. This fact may be practically important because conduct that generates sufficient economic efficiencies not to violate the "critical-object" variant of the object-branch of now-Article 101(1)'s test of *prima facie* illegality might not qualify for or receive a now-Article 101(3) exemption: (1) the economic efficiencies the conduct in question generated might not fit into any of the categories of economic efficiency now-Article 101(3) recognizes, (2) the relevant consumers might not have obtained a fair share of the equivalent-monetary benefit the relevant distributorships yielded the producers and those distributors combined, and/or (3) the perpetrator(s) might not be able to prove that the conduct generated relevant efficiencies or gave relevant consumers a "fair share" of the resulting benefit.

Fifth, single-brand exclusive dealerships created by singly-dominant or collectively-dominant undertakings will violate the exclusionary-abuse branch of now-Article 102's test of illegality in the same circumstances in which they would violate the critical-object branch of now-Article 101(1)'s test of *prima facie* illegality.

Sixth, the reasons why vertical territorial restraints and vertical customer-allocation clauses are highly unlikely to violate the exploitative-abuse branch of now-Article 102 even when the perpetrator is a dominant firm imply that single-brand exclusive dealerships that are not exclusionary abuses of a firm's dominant position are also highly unlikely to constitute exploitative abuses of the firm's dominant position.

Seventh, the reasons for doubting that vertical territorial restraints and vertical customer-allocation clauses violate now-Article 102 because they are inconsistent with the special obligation of dominant firms to foster competition or at least not to disadvantage competitors (*inter alia*, that there is no such special obligation) also make it highly unlikely that single-brand exclusive dealerships created by dominant undertakings violate now-Article 102 on that account.

(vi) Slotting Contracts

Once more, for simplicity, I will assume that the slotting-oriented conduct in question involves the creation of contractual slotting obligations as opposed to slotting-oriented sales policies. Slotting-oriented conduct is directed at inducing resellers to supply in-store promotions (shelf-space and other sorts of in-store displays). Not surprisingly, then, the analysis of the legality of slotting contracts under E.C./E.U. competition law correctly interpreted and applied is identical to the analysis of the efforts of producers to employ contracts of various sorts to induce resellers to make expenditures on out-of-store advertising.

(vii) Long-Term Full-Requirements Contracts

The conditions under which full-requirements clauses in contracts that do not tie the sale of two or more products together or create reciprocal-trading obligations may prevent or restrict competition are identical to the conditions under which single-brand exclusive dealerships can do so. The analysis of the legality of long-term full-requirements contracts under E.C./E.U. competition law correctly interpreted and applied differs from the analysis of the legality of single-brand exclusive dealerships under E.C./E.U. competition law correctly interpreted and applied only to the extent that the legitimate functions of long-term full-requirements contracts differ from the legitimate functions of single-brand exclusive dealerships. The legitimate functions of both these practices are analyzed in Sect. 9 of Chap. 11.

(2) E.C./E.U. Competition Law as Actually Applied

Section 1B(2) of this chapter harshly criticized the way in which, historically, the U.S. courts and antitrust-enforcement agencies applied U.S. antitrust law to the various surrogates for vertical integration and argued that, although much progress has been made on this front over the past 30-plus years, the courts continue to make important errors. This section's criticism of the way in which E.C./E.U. competition law has actually been applied by the EC and various E.C./E.U. courts will be at least as harsh. In fact, in some respects, I will find even more fault with the way in which the EC and the E.C./E.U. courts have analyzed the legality of the various surrogates for vertical integration than I found with the way in which the U.S. courts and antitrust-enforcement agencies analyzed their legality under U.S. antitrust law. However, I want to state clearly at the outset that, to a very considerable extent, the fact that the relevant analyses of E.C./E.U. institutions contain more errors than their U.S. counterparts contain reflects the fact that the E.C./E.U. institutions have discussed the effect, "object," and other aspects of the character of the relevant conduct in far more detail than their U.S. counterparts ever did and therefore on this account had more occasions than did their U.S. counterparts to make economic mistakes when analyzing the conduct in question. I also want to point out at the outset that at least some of the more detailed analyses of surrogates for vertical integration that E.C./E.U. institutions have executed (for example, their analyses of the conditions under which single-brand exclusive dealerships or full-requirement contracts will decrease competition) are far better than their U.S. counterparts.

With that prologue as background, I will describe and criticize the ways in which the EC and various E.C./E.U. courts have analyzed particular surrogates for vertical integration. I will begin by pointing out some general errors that the EC and E.C./E.U. courts have made when analyzing these practices—errors that are general in the sense that they undermine those E.C./E.U. institutions' analyses of two or more of these practices.

The following account and critique of the EC's and the E.C./E.U. courts' handling of the various surrogates for vertical integration is divided into three parts. The first presents a general (but admittedly partial and selective) overview of the history of these institutions' application of what are now Articles 101 and 102 of the 2009 Lisbon Treaty to the vertical conduct in question[1306]; the second lists and briefly discusses initially the good and bad features of the EC's and E.C./E.U. courts' treatment of these types of conduct as a class; and the third focuses on the positions that the EC and the E.C./E.U. courts have taken on the various specific categories of surrogates for vertical integration that are useful to distinguish.

The history of the application of E.C./E.U. competition law to surrogates for vertical integration begins with a number of judicial opinions from the 1960s. The first set of these opinions held correctly as a matter of law (in my judgment) that vertical agreements (and, by extension, vertical concerted practices) are covered not only by then-Article 86 of the 1957 Treaty (now-Article 102 of the 2009 Lisbon Treaty) but also by then-Article 85 of the 1957 Treaty (now-Article 101 of the 2009 Lisbon Treaty).[1307] The second salient "set" of judicial opinions from the 1960s is a single opinion that held incorrectly as a matter of law (in my judgment) that then-Article 85(1) of the 1957 Treaty—now-Article 101(1) of the 2009 Lisbon Treaty (and presumably therefore then-Article 86 of the 1957 Treaty [now-Article 102 of the 2009 Lisbon Treaty])—declares *prima facie* illegal covered conduct whose object or effect is to reduce *intra*-brand competition as well as covered conduct whose object of effect is to reduce *inter*-brand competition.[1308] This decision—later confirmed by the ECJ[1309]—was motivated by the combination of (1) a correct premise that the 1957 Treaty was partially motivated by its ratifiers' desire to create an integrated community market and (2) an incorrect belief (see below) that the goals that led the Treaty's ratifiers to want to create an integrated community market would be furthered by prohibiting producers from preventing independent distributors in one country in the community from selling their respective products to buyers in other countries in the community. In the 1960s, before the introduction of "block-exemption regulations" (BERs), undertakings whose surrogates for vertical integration violated what was then Article 86(1)'s test of *prima facie* illegality because they had the object or effect of reducing *intra*-brand competition could secure exoneration only by following the procedure that the relevant EC regulation (Regulation 17/62[1310]) established for obtaining a then-Article-85(3)—now-Article 101(3)—exemption from what was then Article 85(1)—now-Article 101(1): that

[1306] The historical account this section of the text presents draws heavily on Luc Peeperkorn, Donncadh Woods, & Mario Filipponi (hereinafter Peeperkorn *et al.*), Chapter 9: *Vertical Agreements* in THE EC LAW OF COMPETITION 1131–1231 (Jonathan Faull and Ali Nikpay, eds.) (Oxford Univ. Press, 2d ed., 2007), KORAH 134–89, and MARCO COLINO, VERTICAL AGREEMENTS AND COMPETITION (hereinafter COLINO) (Hart Publishing, 2010).

[1307] See de Geus v. Bosch & van Rijh, Case 13/61, ECR 45, ¶¶ 53 and 69 (1962) and Italy v. Council and Commission, Case 32/65, ECR 389 (1966). See also Consten and Grundig v. Commission, Joined Cases 56/64 and 58/64, ECR 299 (1966). This conclusion was also endorsed by Advocate General Lagrange. See Peeperkorn *et al.* at 1131.

[1308] Consten and Grundig, OJ 161/245 (1964).

[1309] Consten and Grundig v. Commission, Joined Cases 56/64 and 58/64, ECR 299 (1966).

[1310] Council Reg. 17 of 13 March 962, JO 13-24 (1959–62) OJ Spec. Ed. 87 (1962).

procedure required the undertakings in question to notify the EC of their Article-85(1)-violating agreement (or, presumably, concerted practice) and to petition for an Article-85(3) exemption, which could be granted only through a formal decision by the EC. Not surprisingly, the volume of such petitions was overwhelming: "in 1963, 34,000 bilateral agreements had been notified, and by 1971 the figure for exclusive dealing agreements alone was 30,000."[1311] In most cases, the EC responded by sending the petitioning undertaking an informal "comfort letter," stating that the EC did not intend to move or rule against them, but for two reasons, this response was far from satisfactory: (1) the EC was not bound by the letter, and (2) since the letter was not published, it or it and the petition combined did not provide guidance to other undertakings.

The Council of Ministers responded to this systemic problem by authorizing the EC to issue block-exemption regulations (BERs) that declare certain categories of vertical agreements lawful under what was then Article 85 and thereby obviated such agreements' participants' notifying the EC of their agreement's existence.[1312] The EC responded by reviewing its conclusions in vertical-restraint "cases" to identify the categories of agreements that virtually always received exemptions and proceeded on this basis to issue "block exemptions" covering exclusive-distribution agreements, exclusive-purchasing agreements, franchising agreements, motor-vehicle-distribution agreements, and technology-transfer agreements.[1313]

Although these BERs clearly improved the EC's administrative efficiency, they were far from satisfactory. One problem was that the EC conditioned its block exemptions on the relevant undertakings' including certain positive terms in their agreements—positive terms that often were not well-articulated and frequently were not relevant in any case to the legality of the agreement under the Treaty, correctly interpreted and applied. Another problem was that the BERs that were issued did not cover some conduct (selective distribution and agency agreements)

[1311] See COLINO 63, citing for the first figure DANIEL GOYDER, COMPETITION LAW xli (Clarendon Press, 1998) and for the second, Commission of the EC, First Annual Report on Competition Policy (April 1972).

[1312] Council Regulation (EEC) No. 19/65 of 2 March 1965 on the Application of Article 85(3) of the Treaty to Certain Categories of Agreements and Concerted Practices, OJ L36 (1965).

[1313] Commission Regulation (EEC) 1983/83 of 22 June 1983 on the Application of Article 85(3) of the EEC Treaty to Categories of Exclusive Distribution Agreements, OJ L173/1 (1983), as amended at OJ L281/24 (1983); Commission Regulation (EEC) 1984/83 of 22 June 1983 on the Application of Article 85(3) of the EEC Treaty to Categories of Exclusive Purchasing Agreements, OJ L173/5 (1983), as amended at OJ L281/24 (1983); Commission Regulation 123/85 of 12 December 1984 on the Application of Article 85(3) of the EEC Treaty to Certain Categories of Motor Vehicle Distribution and Servicing Agreements, OJ L15/16 (1985) (subsequently replaced by Commission Regulation (EC) 1475/95 of 28 June 1995 on the Application of Article 85/(3) to Certain Categories of Motor Vehicle Distribution and Servicing Agreements), OJ L145/25 (1995), replaced by Commission Regulation (EC) 1400/202 of 31 July 2002 on the Application of Article 81/(3) of the Treaty to Categories of Vertical Agreements and Concerted Practices in the Motor Vehicle Sector, OJ L203/30 (2002); Commission Regulation (EEC) 4087/88 of 30 November 1988 on the Application of Article 83(3) of the EEC Treaty to Categories of Franchise Agreements, OJ L359/46 (1988).

they should have covered. A third problem was that the BERs on conduct that can reduce competition only when it locks in a critical percentage of the suppliers that an established firm or potential QV investor would have to trade with to prosper did not take appropriate account of whether the single-brand exclusive dealerships, long-term full-requirements contracts, or long-term full-requirements tying/ reciprocity contracts in question did leave free a problematically-small quantity of relevant trading partners for the firm the EC was concerned the agreement would lock out. A fourth problem—which (to be fair) had more to do with *Consten and Grundig*'s legal conclusion that the Treaty, correctly interpreted, prohibits any covered conduct that prevents cross-country sales within the Community (indeed, prohibits any covered conduct that would prevent such sales if the conduct's prohibition would not cause the perpetrator to change its behavior in any other way) is that the EC (and the E.C./E.U. courts) continued to apply the Treaty on the assumption that the above legal conclusion is correct as a matter of law. The final problem, which was fully appreciated by many European scholars, is that, more generally, both the EC's block-exemption decisions and its decisionmaking on other matters were insufficiently informed by economic analyses of the likely effects of the conduct in question. I hasten to add that economic analysis could have revealed to the EC not just that (1) those of its decisions that were made to achieve various non-economic goals prevented undertakings from committing acts that were not monopolizing in the U.S. sense and would not reduce competition but that (2) the decisions that it made to achieve at least some of the non-economic goals of the Treaty it was trying to secure would not in fact secure those "objects" (see below).

In any event, by the second half of the 1990s, criticism that the EC's handling of vertical restraints did not take appropriate account of the contribution that economics could make to the analysis of the relevant conduct's objects and effects—criticisms made by both European academics[1314] and E.C. courts (which, to be honest, talked a better game than they played)—began to bear fruit. (To an American, the fact that courts were more open to economic analysis than was an "administrative agency" is highly surprising.) The process began in 1997 and involved a Green Paper that elicited comments, a September 1998 Communication from the EC that summarized the comments on its Green Paper on the Application of EC Competition Law to Vertical Restraints and outlined the structure of its planned BER reform,[1315] the 1999 Commission Block Exemption Regulation,[1316] which was accompanied by a set

[1314] See, *e.g.*, Barry E. Hawk, *System Failure: Vertical Restraints and EC Competition Law*, 32 CML Rev. 973, 989 (1995), claiming that the EC and E.C. courts have created "doctrinal formalisms" instead of "relying on the valuable compass of economics."

[1315] Communication on the Application of the EC Competition Rules to Vertical Restraints, OJ C365/3 (1998), 4 CMLR 281 (1999).

[1316] Commission Regulation (EC) 2790/1999 of 22 December 1999 on the Application of Art. 81 (3) of the Treaty to Categories of Vertical Agreements and Concerted Practices (hereinafter 1999 BER), OJ L336 (1999).

of Guidelines on vertical agreements and concerted practices,[1317] the 2005 DG Competition Discussion Paper on the Application of Article 82 of the Treaty to Exclusionary Abuses, and the 2009 EC Guidance on the Commission's Enforcement Priorities in Applying Article 82 of the EC Treaty to Abusive Exclusionary Conduct by Dominant Undertakings.[1318]

Operationally, the most important of these documents were the 1999 Commission Regulation that promulgated the new BERs and the 2000 Commission Guidelines Notice that elaborated on them. These Regulations and Guidelines make the operational legality of vertical restraints depend on two considerations: (1) the market share of the producer/supplier involved (or, in appropriate cases, of the buyer involved) and (2) the substantive content of the vertical restraint.

Article 3 of the 1999 BER defines three market-share categories. Vertical agreements created by an undertaking whose relevant market share is below 15 % are deemed to fall outside now-Article 101; vertical agreements created by an undertaking whose relevant market share falls between 15 % and 30 % are exempted by the BER if they do not contain any black clause [see below] (if they contain a grey clause but no black clause, the agreement minus the grey clause will be exempted); and vertical agreements created by undertakings whose relevant market share is 30 % or higher are ineligible for block exemption.

The EC's conclusion about under-15 % cases could reflect either (1) its mistaken belief that agreements created by undertakings whose market shares are lower than 15 % will not produce more than *de minimis* effects (mistaken, *inter alia*, because it does not reflect the fact that the markets defined in the relevant cases vary tremendously in terms of the sales made within them) or (2) its mistaken beliefs that (A) vertical agreements can reduce competition only when created by firms with market power (its subscription to some variant of a leverage theory)[1319] and (B) market share is an accurate indicator of market power. The EC's differential treatment of vertical agreements created by undertakings with 15–30 % market shares on the one hand or market shares of 30 % or higher on the other probably

[1317] Commission Notice—Guidelines on Vertical Restraints, OJ C291 (2000).

[1318] C45/02 (2009). For additional citations to more specific twenty-first-century EC regulations, see notes 71 and 72 *supra*.

[1319] Admittedly, the probability that minimum-price-setting resale price maintenance and vertical territorial restraints or vertical customer-allocation clauses will have as their object effectuating horizontal price-fixing would increase with the total market share of their perpetrators if the relevant market could be defined non-arbitrarily, but the vast majority of the exemplars of these practices that are used by rivals with a collectively-high total market share will not have either the object or effect of decreasing inter-brand competition. Admittedly as well, the probability that single-brand exclusive dealerships or long-term full-requirements contracts or total-supply contracts will foreclose competition will increase with the percentage of buyers or suppliers that are locked up, but the correlation between their perpetrators' market shares and the probability that such arrangements will decrease competition by driving an established rival out or raising the barriers to QV investment confronting an otherwise-effective potential QV investor is undoubtedly very low.

does reflect its making the mistakes listed as (2)(A) and (2)(B) in the preceding sentence.

One other market-share-related feature of the BER should be noted: "Article 8 of the BER enables the Commission to exclude from the scope of the BER, by regulation, parallel networks of similar vertical restraints where these cover more than 50 % of a relevant market."[1320]

Before listing and discussing the vertical restrictions that the 1999 BER places into the "black clause" and "grey clause" categories, I want to make three preliminary points. The first is merely terminological. The "black clause" and "grey clause" terminology can be traced to the fact that the original BER contained a so-called "white list," which specified the restrictions that a distribution agreement could and in some instances had to have to be block-exempted. This point is substantive to the extent that it manifests the fact that the 1999 BER does not attempt to control nearly as much of the substance of distribution agreements as its predecessor did. The next two points are more substantive. The second is that the fact that a vertical agreement between undertakings or a concerted vertical practice does not qualify for a block exemption does not preclude their participants from seeking to obtain an exemption on an individual basis under what is now Article 101(3). The third point is that the 1999 BER does not override the more-specific vertical-restraint regulations the EC has promulgated. Thus, the 1999 BER does not apply to car-distribution agreements, which are covered by Commission Regulation (LEC) 1400/2002[1321] or to transfer-of-technology vertical agreements, which are covered by Commission Regulation (EC) 772/2004.[1322] The first two of these categories owe their presence on the "blacklist" at least to a substantial extent to the combination of (1) the EC's correct conclusion that the 1957 Treaty was designed, *inter alia*, to secure both the economic and the political and social benefits that an integrated community market would yield and (2) the EC's incorrect conclusion that prohibitions of producer-efforts to prevent independent distributors or agents in one community country from making sales in another community country (either indirectly by prohibiting potential resellers in one community country to which the producer was charging prices that were lower than the prices it was charging resellers in another community country from making sales in the second country by charging low prices in the second country or directly by restricting resellers to making sales only in the country in which they were respectively located) would further the more-ultimate goals that led the Treaty's ratifiers to pursue the proximate goal of increasing the integration of community markets.

The first category of black clauses, delineated in Article 4(a) of the 1999 BER, contains clauses that establish minimum resale prices. The 1999 BER condemns not only such clauses but also the combination of producer-issued

---

[1320] See Peeperkorn *et al.*

[1321] OJ L203 (2002).

[1322] OJ L123 (2004).

minimum-resale-price "recommendations" and other producer-policies that exert pressure on resellers to follow the "recommendations" in question (*e.g.*, sales policies of continuing to supply only those resellers that follow the minimum-resale-price recommendations of the supplier). (As the preceding sentence implies, the 1999 BER does not prohibit suppliers from recommending minimum resale prices so long as those recommendations are not combined with conduct that puts pressure on resellers to conform to the recommendations.) The Guidelines indicate that the "blacklisting" of minimum-price-setting clauses covers not only such clauses in agreements between suppliers and independent distributors but also clauses in agency agreements that prohibit the agent from lowering its price to a buyer by sharing its commission with the buyer (*i.e.*, without reducing the price obtained by the ultimate supplier). The 1999 BER does not put on its blacklist clauses that establish maximum resale prices. Of course, in a legal regime in which covered conduct that has as its object or effect decreasing *intra*-brand competition is *prima facie* illegal, the fact that maximum-price-setting RPM is not on the BER blacklist does not imply that it is lawful: in such a regime, to be lawful, individual exemplars of such RPM would have to be shown to qualify for a now-Article 101(3) exemption.

Article 4(b) delineates the second category of clauses in the 1999 BER's blacklist: clauses that restrict the territories within which a reseller can sell the producer's product or the buyers to which or whom a reseller can resell the producer's product. This prohibition covers not only direct prohibitions of such resales but also policies that are devised to deter such resales (refusals to pay bonuses, give discounts, or make profit-pass-over payments). The 1999 BER's prohibition of vertical territorial restraints and vertical customer-allocation clauses contains four exceptions: producers are allowed to restrict (1) resellers from making "active sales" (sales that result from the reseller's positive sales-efforts) as opposed to "passive sales" (sales that the reseller made without making any special effort to obtain them) into a territory or to a customer that the producer had allocated exclusively to itself or to another reseller when the restriction does not extend to the customers of the reseller, (2) wholesalers from making sales (in effect as retailers) to end-users either actively or passively, (3) resellers that are part of a selective-distribution system—*i.e.*, one in which the producer chooses to use only resellers whose personnel, organizational arrangements, and/or physical facility satisfy certain standards—from making sales either actively or passively to unauthorized distributors, and (4) resellers from reselling either actively or passively components supplied for the purposes of incorporation into the producer's product to rivals of the producer that would use them to produce goods that are competitive with the producer's goods.

The fact that the first exception to the BER's prohibition of inter-undertaking vertical territorial restrictions and vertical customer-allocation clauses draws a critical distinction between prohibitions of active sales (which under the indicated conditions are permitted) and prohibitions of passive sales (which are not permitted even when the indicated conditions are fulfilled) renders legally critical the classification as active or passive the making of sales through the use of the internet or a catalog. The EC's general conclusion is that the use of the internet or a catalog to obtain sales does not constitute active selling unless the website or catalog specifically targets buyers inside a territory exclusively allocated to another distributor or specified customers exclusively allocated to another distributor or the producer. The Guidelines also state that producers can set standards that its distributors' and consignees' internet websites (and presumably catalogs) must meet (just as it can establish standards for other sorts of advertising and promotional activities in which its distributors engage) but allow a producer to ban internet or catalog selling only when its doing so furthers health or safety goals. (In my judgment, this latter limitation is unwarranted—reflects the inclination of the EC [and E.C./E.U. courts] to second-guess the business decisions of producers or, more specifically and less ungenerously, to assume that a producer's decisions to control the image or presentation of its product by banning its distributors or consignees from using the internet or a catalog to sell it could not be the most-cost-effective way to secure this objective [could not be more profitable than setting and enforcing quality-standards] and therefore must either have been made to reduce competition in some unarticulated way or have constrained the liberty of the resellers or consignees in question for no legitimate reason.)

Article 4(c) delineates the third category of vertical restrictions blacklisted by the 1999 BER: restrictions in the active or passive sales of members of a selective retail-distribution system to end-users (be they professionals or final consumers). After prohibiting direct restrictions on such selected retailers' sales activities, Article 4(c) declares that it is permissible for a producer to influence the sales that the individual member of a selective retail-distribution system it has established can make by controlling the location(s) of their outlet(s). I have no idea why it might be desirable to prohibit a producer that uses a selective retail-distribution system from controlling the territories within which or customers to which its selective-retail-distribution system's individual members can make active or passive sales when it would not be desirable to prohibit a producer from placing similar limits on other sorts of resellers of its product. I also have no idea why, if the former difference were justified, it would make sense to permit a producer to control the buyers to whom its selected retailers make sales by controlling the location(s) of their retail establishment(s).

Article 4(d) prohibits "the restriction of cross-supplies between distributors within a selective-distribution system, including between distributors operating at different levels of trade." *Inter alia*, this provision (1) prohibits a producer from requiring its wholesale and retail distributors from purchasing their full requirements of the producer's product from it and (2) makes it far less likely that a producer that uses independent wholesalers and retailers will find it profitable to practice price discrimination in the economist's sense when selling to them.

Article 4(e) prohibits a buyer of a component from prohibiting its supplier from selling the component in question to end-users of the relevant buyer's product or to service providers "not entrusted by the buyer with the repair or servicing on its goods." The blacklisting of such clauses makes sense only if the component-buyer's conduct was predatory—*i.e.*, only if the component buyer in question's *ex ante* conclusion that the restrictions in question would be profitable was critically affected by its belief that the restrictions might critically raise the barriers that faced end-users of its product or independent service organizations when they were contemplating entry into the component-buyer's final-product-production business. For reasons that Sect. 10 of Chap. 11 explained, the vast majority of producer-attempts to control such after-market conduct are not predatory—indeed, do not have as even *an object* raising barriers to relevant rival QV investments but function instead by enabling the perpetrator to control the quality of the complements that are combined with its product and/or to use after-market services as metering devices.

Article 5 of the BER places three categories of vertical restrictions on a "grey list." Unlike restrictions that are blacklisted, the grey-listed restrictions (1) are not *per se* illegal—are just not block-exempted, indeed are to be individually assessed under Article 101(3) of the 2009 Treaty of Lisbon without any presumption of illegality—and (2) do not invalidate the rest of the agreement in which they are included. Article 5(a) places on the grey list clauses that impose so-called "non-compete obligations" whose duration exceeds 5 years: the to-my-mind peculiarly-named "non-compete obligations" are obligations to purchase from the supplier or a third party specified by the supplier at least 80 % of the buyer's previous-year purchases of the contract good and its substitutes. In situations in which the buyer resells the supplier's product "from premises and land owned by the supplier or leased by the supplier from third parties not connected with the buyer," the 5-year-duration limit is extended to cover the period during which the buyer occupies the land/premises in question. This extension of the time-limit may be justified by the land/premise owner's need to preserve its reputation in circumstances in which downstream buyers would attribute to the original supplier any deficiencies in the goods the buyer sold from the original supplier's land/premises. The Guidelines provide a number of detailed operationalizations of this grey-list provision, some of which may be ill-advised. For example, point 58 of the Guidelines specifies that a block exemption will be available for a supply-arrangement that includes a "non-compete obligation" whose duration is not disqualifying under which the supplier provides the buyer with equipment only if the buyer can purchase the equipment at its market value at the end of the non-compete obligation. Although I understand that this rule is included in the belief that the ability of the supplier to withdraw the relevant equipment extends the *de facto* duration of the buyer's "non-compete obligation," I find the rule unjustified both (1) because I reject its implicit assumption that the withdrawal of the equipment from a buyer that stops purchasing from the supplier the amount of the supplier's product the "non-compete obligation" required it to purchase from the supplier would be predatorily retaliatory and (2) because, in cases in which the supplier was in effect providing a buyer with a loan in the period covered by the "non-compete obligation" by underpricing the goods and services it provided the buyer during this period and had planned to have the loan repaid by extracting from the buyer *supra*-market-value compensation for the equipment it was providing the buyer during the post-"non-compete-obligation" period, the rule would preclude it from doing so.

Article 5(b) places on the grey list clauses that prohibit a buyer from competing against the supplier after the termination of their agreement by producing and/or selling the contract goods or services from other premises and land than the ones from which the buyer operated during the contract period or from the same premises and land that the buyer occupied during the contract period if the prohibition was "not indispensable to protect know-how transferred by the supplier to the buyer." Even considering the fact that a failure of such clauses to receive a block exemption does not preclude or even (in theory) make it more difficult for their perpetrator to obtain a now-Article 101(3) exemption, this provision seems far too restrictive to me from the perspective of administrative efficiency.

Article 5(c) places on the grey list clauses making the members of a selective-distribution system single-brand exclusive dealers—*i.e.*, clauses prohibiting such resellers from selling competing brands. Of course, any assessment of Article 5(c) must take account of the fact that perpetrators of such single-brand exclusive dealerships can justify their legality under now-Article 101(3) even in a legal regime in which covered conduct that reduces *intra*-brand competition is *prima facie* illegal. However, I suspect that the percentage of single-brand exclusive dealerships in selective-distribution systems that actually harm consumers is too low and the cost of individual-exemplar justification is too high for the grey-listing of such clauses to be cost-effective.

Basically, the EC has been applying its 1999 BER straightforwardly to prohibit undertakings from using agreements that include vertical restraints to deter cross-national sales within the Community/Union. The clauses that have been blacklisted for this reason (and perhaps for other reasons as well) include clauses setting minimum resale prices, clauses obligating authorized dealers to sell only to final consumers (to prevent dealers in one E.C./E.U. country that have been charged a lower price from cross-selling to dealers in another E.C./E.U. country that have been charged a higher price), clauses that in effect prohibit authorized dealers from purchasing from other authorized dealers (that require authorized dealers to purchase only from the supplier or one of its subsidiaries), clauses that obligate authorized dealers to inform the supplier before exporting through the internet, clauses that prohibit sales outside specified territories, clauses that create bonus schemes and other sorts of payments systems that render it less profitable for a distributor to make out-of-territory sales, clauses that restrict cross-selling between authorized distributors, clauses that prohibit "distant sales" through the internet, and sales policies of cutting off or eliminating supplies to distributors that fail to report to the supplier their purchasers' country of origin and their sales' final destination.[1323]

The preceding account of the EC's and the E.C./E.U. courts' treatment of surrogates for vertical integration has focused primarily on their handling of resale price maintenance, vertical territorial restraints, vertical customer-allocation clauses, and arrangements that obligate or are designed to induce buyers to purchase their full requirements or an amount that is close to their full requirements of some good from the seller involved. Section 9D of Chap. 11 also discussed the way

[1323] For a more detailed account of such cases, see Peeperkorn *et al.* at 1204–07.

in which the EC and the E.C./E.U. courts have analyzed the legality (in particular, the possible predatory character) of arrangements that substantially reduce the likelihood that a seller's customer (supplier) will deal with the seller's rivals. (In addition, Sect. 2E(2) of Chap. 11 discussed the EC's and the E.C./E.U. courts' treatment of price discrimination—*viz.*, of the possibilities that price discrimination [A] may be predatory and hence may violate now-Article 101 in that its object is preventing or restricting competition, [B] may be predatory and hence may constitute an exclusionary abuse of a dominant position in violation of now-Article 102 if practiced by a dominant firm or a member of a collectively-dominant set of rivals, and/or [C] regardless of whether it is predatory, may constitute an exploitative abuse of now-Article 102 if practiced by a dominant firm or a member of a collectively-dominant set of rivals.)

At this juncture, I must still describe and comment on the EC's and the E.C./E.U. courts' treatment of tie-ins and reciprocity agreements more generally. Six points or clusters of points are salient.

First, the EC and the E.C./E.U. courts clearly do think that tie-ins (and reciprocity agreements) would be covered by clause (e) of now-Article 101 if executed by two undertakings and would be covered by clause (d) of now-Article 102 if at least one of their participants was a dominant firm—*i.e.*, do believe that tying and reciprocity agreements "make the conclusion of contracts subject to the acceptance by the other parties of supplementary obligations which, by their nature or according to commercial usage, have no connection with the subject of such contracts." I have already explained why I believe that, both "by their nature and according to commercial usage," the tying and reciprocal-trading provisions of the overwhelming majority of the agreements that contain them are connected with the subject of the contracts that contain them.

Second, the EC and the E.C./E.U. courts have clearly accepted some inchoate version of the leverage theory of tie-ins and reciprocity—in particular, (1) believe that firms with market power over one of the products that tie-ins or reciprocity agreement involve can use and will find it profitable to use that power respectively to obtain a costless advantage when selling or buying the other product such contracts involve or to force their trading partner to make concessions on another product and (2) that, when firms with market power over the so-called tying good use that power to exert leverage, they will prevent, restrict, and/or distort competition and inflict losses on the trading partner that is participating in the contract in question. Thus, according to Mosso, Ryan, Albaek, and Centella,[1324] in now-Article 102 tie-in cases, "[c]oercion to purchase two products or services together" "has been considered a crucial element of the abuse" of a dominant position. As I have already explained, sellers with dominant positions or market power over one good cannot use that power to "coerce" buyers—can induce them to accept a deal on a

[1324] Carles Esteva Mosso, Stephen A. Ryan, Svend Albaek, and Maria Luisa Tierno Centella, *Article 82* in THE EC LAW OF COMPETITION 313, 370 (Jonathan Faull and Ali Nikpay, eds.) (Oxford Univ. Press, 2d ed., 2007).

second product that they would not have accepted in an independent transaction or can induce them to do something else that they would not have agreed to do in an independent transaction only by allowing them to retain surplus they could not otherwise have secured on the tying product—*i.e.*, only by "bribing" them, not by coercing them.

Third, like their U.S. counterparts, the EC and E.C./E.U. courts believe (1) that one can determine a tying seller's market power over the tying good from its share of the tying good's market and (2) that tie-ins are legally problematic when but only when that share exceeds some specified level. I have already explained why I reject both parts of this claim. I should add a related point: the contemporary EC and the E.C./E.U. courts not only believe in the appropriateness of using a market-oriented approach to foreclosure analysis but also are more concerned than their U.S. counterparts now are that tie-ins and other business practices that "lock up" (to my mind) modest percentages of the sales made in an allegedly-relevant market will prevent or restrict competition on that account by precluding the perpetrator's rivals from making the amount of sales they need to make to survive. In my judgment, this concern is unjustified and reflects the E.C./E.U. authorities' failure to realize (1) that the possible foreclosing effect of a seller's locking up sales depends not on the share of the relevant market's sales it has locked up but on the relationship between the quantity of sales that are not locked up and the quantity of sales (of the relevant kind) that an alleged target actual or potential competitor must make to break even and the quantity of such sales that are not locked up and (2) that targets can prevent themselves from being locked out by creating new sources of custom (or supply), by offering advantages to new-entrant buyers (suppliers), by entering into joint ventures, or by engaging in vertical integration.

Fourth, again like their U.S. counterparts, the EC and E.C./E.U. courts have struggled in tie-in cases to determine whether the items to be sold in a given "tie-in" case are two distinct products or services or components of a single product. The EC and E.C./E.U. courts have tried to resolve this issue by investigating "the nature of the products or services in question or by assessing whether they are normally sold together ('according to commercial usage')."[1325] I do not understand the referent of "the nature of the products or services in question" in this context, and, although the fact that two products are normally sold together may bear on the economic efficiency of their being sold together, it does not inform the analysis of whether one is dealing with two products or one product, at least in a now-Article 101 analysis in which the economic-efficiency issue is to be analyzed separately from the issue of whether the agreement in question prevents or restricts competition. (I admit that the fact that the two products are normally sold together may be more relevant in a now-Article 102 analysis, in which the economic-efficiency analysis is part of the analysis of whether the conduct in question constitutes an exclusionary abuse.) In any event, I regard the analysis that led (1) the E.C./E.U.

[1325] *Id.* at 369. See also Guideline 216, which deems critical the closely-related issue of whether buyers of either product want to purchase both products.

court to conclude in *Tetra Pak II*[1326] that the packaging machines and packaging materials involved in that case were separate products and (2) the EC to conclude in *IBM System 370*[1327] that computer main frames, memory devices, and basic software applications are separate products to be both beside the point and metaphysical.

Fifth, and one might say contrastingly, the EC and the E.C./E.U. courts have recognized the irrelevance of whether the conduct that they find legally problematic because it may foreclose a rival from making the sales it needs to survive is a decision to use a tie-in or to adopt some other policy such as a full-requirements obligation or a rebate scheme that may be predatory. If the feared wrong is predation, the E.C./E.U. authorities are correct in ignoring whether the predation is executed through a tie-in, a non-tie-in full-requirements contract, a rebate system, or a price-reduction. If the contract in question is predatory, it violates now-Article 101 on that account so long as the agreements each such type of conduct involves are agreements between undertakings, and if the conduct in question is predatory, it violates now-Article 102 so long as its perpetrator was individually dominant or a member of a collectively-dominant set of rivals.

Sixth, the EC and the E.C./E.U. courts do recognize that tie-ins are not used solely to generate leverage. In particular, the EC and the E.C./E.U. courts do recognize that tie-ins can enable producers of complex machinery to ensure that their customers use complements that will enable their machinery to perform as they should and that such tie-ins will increase economic efficiency both directly and by preserving the reputation of the machinery and its producer. On the other hand, the EC and the E.C./E.U. courts do not seem to realize that, even if—relative to doing nothing to control the complements its customers combine with its product—the machine-producer (or idea-discoverer) would find it profitable to specify the attributes of appropriate complements and (1) warn its customers of the cost of not using such complements, (2) obligate its customers to use complements with those attributes, investigate its customers' actual complement-choices, and sue customers that violate their complement obligations, or (3) persuade the government to require users of its machines to employ appropriate complements, in those instances in which the relevant seller would find it more profitable to use tie-ins to induce their customers to use appropriate complements, their use of the tie-in for this purpose will be presumptively more economically efficient than any of the alternative approaches just described (for a combination of transaction-cost and efficacy reasons).[1328] In addition, the EC and the E.C./E.U. courts do not seem to appreciate the fact that tie-ins can also perform a number of other Sherman-Act-licit functions

[1326] Tetra Pak International v. Commission, Case T-83/91, ECR II-755 (1994).

[1327] Bull CE 10/84, ¶ 3.4.1. See also Microsoft, 37.792, 4 CMLR 965 (2004).

[1328] In my view, this mistake partially accounts for the E.C. authorities' decisions to find illegal the tie-ins between packaging machines and packaging materials in *Tetra Pak II* and the tie-ins between nail guns on the one hand and nails and cartridges in *Hilti*. See respectively, Tetra Pak II, C-53/92P, ECR I-666 (1994) and Hilti, C-333/94P, ECR I-5951 (1996).

such as increasing the profitability of meter pricing,[1329] reducing the transaction cost of practicing lawful price discrimination, reducing the amount of transaction surplus destroyed by the use of supra-TSM-marginal-cost pricing to remove a relevant amount of buyer surplus that would otherwise be generated by the sale of final products, or reducing the amount of transaction surplus destroyed by the use of supra-TSM-marginal-cost pricing to remove a relevant amount of buyer surplus that would otherwise be generated by the sale of an input against which substitution is possible.

I will now give a brief assessment from the perspective of economics of the strengths and weaknesses of the EC's and the E.C./E.U. courts' analyses of the various surrogates for vertical integration I have distinguished. I start with six strengths. First, the EC and the E.C./E.U. courts have recognized (to a greater extent or at least earlier than their U.S. counterparts have done) that competition has not only a price dimension but a quality-and-variety dimension and that it is important to analyze separately the impact of a choice on what I call QV-investment competition (and to analyze separately as well the possibility that conduct may have as an object or a critical object reducing QV-investment competition).[1330] Second, these E.C./E.U. institutions seem also to be more aware than their U.S. counterparts are of the possibility that covered conduct may decrease what I call production-process-research competition.[1331] Third, the EC and the E.C./E.U. courts have recognized, again as their U.S. counterparts have not, that conduct can decrease what I call QV-investment competition by affecting the position not only of potential entrants but also of established undertakings that are possible QV-investment expanders.[1332] Fourth, although as the discussion of the economics deficiencies of the EC's and E.C./E.U. courts' treatment of surrogates for vertical integration will point out these institutions have never articulated an explicit definition of the concepts of barriers to entry or expansion, have defined these concepts implicitly in use both inconsistently and non-optimally (from the perspective of usefulness), and have totally ignored the impact that monopolistic QV-investment incentives and disincentives and natural oligopolistic QV-investment disincentives can have on potential expanders' QV-investment decisions, these institutions have done a better job than their U.S. counterparts have done of identifying at least some of the various sources of barriers to entry and expansion—"legal barriers" and "privileged access to essential inputs or natural resources, important technologies or an established distribution and sales network" (which can give rise to Π_D and/or R barriers in my terminology) and

[1329] I suspect that the tie-ins involved in *Tetra Pak II*, *Hilti*, and *Microsoft*, 4 CMLR 965 (2004), and Microsoft v. Commission, T-201/04, 4 CMLR 406 (2005) were performing this function as well as (at least in the former two cases) the function of increasing the profitability of controlling the quality of the complements a producer's customers combine with its product.

[1330] See, *e.g.*, Communication From the Commission—Guidance on the Commission's Enforcement Priorities in Applying Article 82 of the Treaty to Abusive Exclusionary Conduct by Dominant Undertakings (hereinafter 2009 EC Guidance Communication on Exclusionary Abuses) ¶¶ 5, 19, and 30, 2009/C 45/02 (2009).

[1331] See, *e.g.*, *id.* at ¶ 30.

[1332] See, *e.g.*, *id.* at ¶¶ 12, 16, and 20.

"economies of scale and scope" (which can give rise to either [Π_D + R] or S barriers in my terminology).[1333] Fifth, the EC and the E.C./E.U. courts have evinced a greater awareness than their U.S. counterparts have done of the fact that the foreclosing effect of any arrangement that locks in a potential customer or supplier of an established rival of the perpetrator(s) or of a rival potential QV investor in the area of product-space in which the perpetrator(s) is (are) operating depends not on the relationship between the quantity of purchases or sales that the possibly-foreclosed rival must make to be able to survive or break even and the quantity of sales or supplies in the relevant area of product-space that are not locked in but on the relationship between the former of the above two quantities and the quantity of non-locked-in sales *that a particular foreclosee was or would be well-placed to make* or the quantity of non-locked-in suppliers whose supply to the relevant foreclosee (given the products' attributes and the location of different suppliers) would have been most advantageous to it.[1334] Sixth, the EC and the E.C./E.U. courts have explicitly recognized in a way that their U.S. counterparts have not that the actual/prospective market share of an excluded established competitor may understate the negative competitive impact of its exclusion not only when it was unusually unwilling to collaborate in contrivance (was a "maverick" in U.S. terminology) but also (1) when (in my terminology) its market share is lower than the percentage of the dominant undertaking's customers it was uniquely-second-place to supply and/or, when it was the dominant undertaking's closest competitor, the amount by which it was better-placed than the third-placed supplier of the buyer in question was unusually high and (2) when it was unusually innovative (in my terminology, faced lower barriers to QV investment than the other potential QV investors faced).[1335] I should point out that both the fourth and the fifth strengths just listed reflect a greater awareness of the fact that—in our actual, monopolistically-competitive world—buyers, suppliers, and rivals are not identical or, from various analytic perspectives, fungible or interchangeable. Sixth and finally, in the last 15 or 20 years, first the E.C./E.U. courts and then the EC have become increasingly aware that, to be accurate, conclusions about the effects of successfully prohibiting an undertaking from using a particular surrogate for vertical integration must take account of the conduct the undertaking in question will substitute for the prohibited conduct in question—*i.e.*, must take account of what these institutions refer to as the "counterfactual."[1336] I list this strength last because in fact the EC and E.C./E.U. courts' recognition of this reality has been not only relatively recent but also only spotty—*i.e.*, because on this account this item provides a good segueway to the discussion of the 17 general weaknesses in these institutions' relevant analyses from the perspective of economics that I will discuss.

The first such weakness relates to the EC's and the E.C./E.U. courts' assumption that prohibiting producers from preventing their independent distributors from

[1333] See, *e.g.*, *id.* at ¶ 16.

[1334] See, *e.g.*, *id.* at ¶ 20 inset four.

[1335] See, *e.g.*, *id.* at ¶ 20 inset three.

[1336] See, *e.g.*, *id.* at ¶ 21.

making cross-E.C./E.U.-country sales of the producer's product would further the more-ultimate objectives behind the 1957 Treaty's ratifiers' goal of promoting the integration of community markets—enabling community undertakings to take better advantage of economies of scale, promoting greater social integration within the community by increasing the extent to which the citizens of and participants in each of its nations were familiar with the tastes of and products produced by the citizens of and participants in the other members of the community, increasing the economic interdependence and hence dependence of actors in different member-countries, and derivatively facilitating the political integration of the community. Had the EC and E.C./E.U. courts executed the appropriate economic analyses, they would have realized (1) that producers will respond to legal regimes that effectively prevent them from prohibiting their independent distributors from making cross-E.C./ E.U.-country sales by (A) integrating forward into distribution themselves, (B) ceasing to practice the between-country price discrimination that makes it profitable for favored dealers (in low-price countries) to cross-sell to disfavored dealers or end-users in high-price countries, (C) ceasing to sell their products at all in countries in which they otherwise would have sold them for discriminatorily-low prices, and/or (D) shifting from charging high lump-sum fees and low per-unit prices, which encourage between-country (as well as other types of) cross-selling, to charging low lump-sum fees and high per-unit prices and (2) to the extent that producers respond in one or more of these ways to legal prohibitions of their attempting to prevent their independent resellers from making inter-community-country cross-sales, such legal regimes (A) will not tend to enable community undertakings to take better advantage of economies of scale in production (because they will tend to reduce the unit sales of undertakings), (B) will not tend to increase the familiarity of the members of each community country with the tastes and products of other community countries (because they will not tend to increase the extent to which the products of one community country are sold in other community countries), (C) will not enhance inter-member-country actor financial interdependence and dependence, and therefore (D) will not tend to facilitate political integration by increasing cultural understanding (or at least cross-country consumption, understanding, and economic interdependence). I should add that, even if the prohibitions in question would not elicit the responses I have described, there would be no reason to believe that they would increase the extent to which E.C./E.U. distributors take advantage of economies of scale in distribution: indeed, since producers will profit from their distributors' taking advantage of economies of scale, prohibitions that prevent producers from organizing the distribution of their products in the non-inter-brand-competition-decreasing way that is most profitable will probably tend to reduce the extent to which distributors take advantage of economies of scale in distribution.

The second economics weakness in the EC's and E.C./E.U. courts' analyses of surrogates for vertical integration relates to these institutions' assumption that prohibitions of vertical restraints serve the Treaty-ratifier goal of eliminating constraints on the "liberty" of consumers and distributors. For current purposes, I will ignore the fact that "liberty" is being defined implicitly by the EC and the E.C./E.U. courts in this context in a way that renders the concept morally unimportant: the fact that a private or public choice reduces the opportunity-set from which an individual can choose does not imply that the choice harms the individual in a way that is morally problematic unless the reduction relates to a choice-option that would contribute significantly to the chooser's discovering the conception of the good to which he or she personally subscribes, actualizing his or her commitment to a particular conception of the good, or fulfilling his or her moral obligations. For current purposes, I will also ignore the fact that the EC's and E.C./E.U. courts' claim that vertical restraints restrict the liberty of distributors is undercut by the reality that the distributors in question were not coerced into accepting the restraints in question (a conclusion that the EC and the E.C./E.U. courts might have been led to reject by their subscription to the leverage theory, which assumes that a seller with competitive advantages can *impose* restraints, obligations, or unattractive terms on their trading partners without giving up anything in return—can have their cake and eat it too). For current purposes, the key point is not just that rules prohibiting vertical restraints deprive distributors of the opportunity to agree to such restraints in return for some direct or indirect type of compensation but that, given the ways in which producers that are forbidden to impose vertical restraints will respond to such prohibitions—*i.e.*, given the relevant counterfactuals, the prohibitions will not in any case actually increase the opportunity-set of the economic actors whose "liberty" or "freedom" they were designed to enhance. Thus, if producers that are forbidden to use contract clauses or sale/consignment policies to prevent independent distributors from making sales outside the territory allocated to them (say, in other countries) respond by integrating forward into distribution or abandoning the pricing-technique (price discrimination or the mixed technique that combines a high lump-sum fee with a low per-unit price) that made it profitable for one or more independent distributors to make out-of-territory (perhaps cross-E.C./E.U.-country) sales, the prohibition will not increase the opportunity-set of either independent distributors or their potential customers.

The third "economics" deficiency of the EC's and the E.C./E.U. courts' analyses of the legality under E.C./E.U. competition law of the various surrogates for vertical integration is their failure to define the now-Article 101 economic concepts of conduct whose "object" or conduct whose "effect" is to prevent, restrict, or distort competition. The EC and the E.C./E.U. courts have been as remiss in defining these concepts as their U.S. counterparts have been in defining such counterpart concepts as "agreements in restraint of trade," "monopolizing or attempting to monopolize," and "lessening competition." Chapter 4 analyzed the interpretation of each of the above E.C./E.U. competition-law concepts that is correct as a matter of E.C./E.U. law.

The fourth economics deficiency of the relevant analyses is related to the third. The EC and the E.C./E.U. courts often write as if, at least when the prohibition of the conduct in question does not serve the goal of increasing the integration of the Community/Union market or (perhaps) preserving end-user or distributor liberty, the legality of covered conduct under E.C./E.U. competition law depends on its impact on buyer (equivalent-dollar) welfare.[1337] Admittedly, this impact is relevant both (1) to

[1337] See, *e.g.*, *id.* at ¶¶ 5, 11, and 34.

whether covered conduct qualifies for a now-Article 101(3) "exemption" from now-Article 101(1) (in that one of the requirements for a now-Article 101(3) "exemption" is that buyers obtain a "fair share" of the benefit that results from the conduct in question) and (2) to whether the conduct of an undertaking that is singly or collectively dominant constitutes an exploitative abuse under now-Article 102. However, the fact that the conduct imposes a net equivalent-dollar loss on relevant buyers is neither a necessary condition for its ineligibility for a now-Article 101(3) exemption nor a sufficient condition for its violating the exploitative-abuse branch of the now-Article 102 test of illegality. Thus, in relation to both now-Article 101(1)'s test of *prima facie* illegality and the exclusionary-abuse branch of now-Article 102's test of illegality, this buyer (equivalent-dollar) welfare criterion ignores the legal salience of the distinction between (1) inflicting losses on buyers by taking better advantage of a given DD/MC combination for a given product or changing the product produced to one whose sales yields less buyer surplus and (2) inflicting losses on buyers by reducing the absolute attractiveness of the best offer they respectively receive from any inferior supplier.

The fifth economics deficiency of the EC's and the E.C./E.U. courts' treatment of surrogates for vertical integration also relates to the applicable Treaty-provisions' tests of illegality—in particular to the meaning of "object of preventing or restricting competition" in Article 101 and of "exclusionary abuse" as it is used in applying now-Article 102. The problem is that the EC and the E.C./E.U. courts (1) make some statements that implicitly define these concepts in the way in which I find legally correct—*viz.*, statements that competition on the merits cannot be deemed to be *prima facie* illegal either under now-Article 101(1) or (as exclusionary) under now-Article 102—and (2) make other statements that (A) conduct that a perpetrator realizes *ex ante* will reduce the competition it faces will be *prima facie* illegal under now-Article 101(1) even when the conduct in question constitutes competition on the merits and that (B) competition on the merits can be exclusionary in the now-Article 102 sense if its perpetrator is a dominant undertaking. Indeed, statements that respectively immunize and condemn competition on the merits often appear in close proximity to each other: in the now-Article 102 context, the apparent inconsistency is sometimes rationalized by an ambiguous reference to the "special responsibilities" of dominant undertakings.[1338]

[1338] See, *e.g.*, *id.* at ¶ 1: ". . .[A] dominant undertaking is entitled to compete on the merits. However, the undertaking concerned has a special responsibility not to allow its conduct to impair genuine undistorted competition on the common market." Although the reference to "undistorted" competition may make the second sentence compatible with the first, the word "However" is troubling, though the second sentence could be made consistent with the first by reading it to prohibit dominant undertakings from making any decision that would yield them private advantages not based on any economic-efficiency superiority even when their *ex ante* perception that the decision in question would be profitable was not critically affected by any belief that it would reduce the absolute attractiveness of the offers against which they would have to compete. Unfortunately, because I doubt that the EC had in mind the only type of decision that I can think of that would fall into this category—a decision to use an inherently-profitable pricing-technique that might in addition drive a rival out or deter a rival QV investment by increasing the unit sales of the perpetrator and thereby decreasing the profits that such actual and prospective rivals could earn, this charitable reading is something of a stretch.

The sixth economics deficiency in the EC's and E.C./E.U. courts' analyses of vertical restraints is the erroneous claim (made not only by them but also by U.S. courts and in the past by U.S. antitrust-enforcement agencies) that the probability that such restraints will be exclusionary in the Sherman Act sense or will reduce competition in the Clayton Act sense increases with the market power of the perpetrator.[1339]

The seventh economics mistake that E.C./E.U. institutions make when analyzing the surrogates for vertical integration is linked to the sixth economic mistake they make—their acceptance of the premise of the leverage theory of tie-ins that undertakings with competitive advantages can force potential buyers to accept obligations or other sorts of unfavorable terms without giving up anything in return (*e.g.*, can at no "cost" use their competitive advantages to induce their customers to make choices that exclude the perpetrator's established and/or potential rivals).[1340] As I have already explained, undertakings with competitive advantages cannot have their cake and eat it too.

The eighth and ninth economics mistakes that the EC and the E.C./E.U. courts make when analyzing surrogates for vertical integration are connected to the incorrect assumption that the exclusionary impact of vertical restraints is positively correlated with the perpetrator's market power. The eighth mistake is assuming that an undertaking's market power is more strongly and significantly correlated with its market share than it actually is. Although the EC and the E.C./E.U. courts acknowledge that market power cannot always be accurately inferred from market share, they exaggerate the strength and significance of the correlation between market share and marker power.[1341] The ninth mistake that the EC and the E.C./E.U. courts make in the current context is to assume that markets can be defined non-arbitrarily.

The tenth EC and E.C./E.U.-court economics mistake that affects these institutions' analyses of surrogates for vertical integration is their assumption that, for conduct to be illegally exclusionary in the sense of being predatory, the established rival it drives out or potential competitor it prevents from entering must be "equally efficient" as the perpetrator (in the Commission's words, must be an "equally efficient competitor").[1342] As I pointed out in Sect. 2D of Chap. 11 (when criticizing the irrebuttable presumption that prices that exceed average total cost are not predatory), an undertaking may find it profitable to engage in predation to drive

---

[1339] See, *e.g.*, *id.* at ¶ 85 and the market-share criteria of the EC's various BERs. European commentators generally agree with the EC's and E.C./E.U. courts' assumption that the risk of exclusion increases with the perpetrator's market share. See, *e.g.*, COLINO 118 and 145–46.

[1340] See, *e.g.*, 2009 EC Guidance Communication on Exclusionary Abuses ¶¶ 36, 39, and 54.

[1341] See *id.* at ¶¶ 14 and 15.

[1342] See *id.* at ¶¶ 23, 27, 60, and 67. Although at ¶ 24 the EC acknowledges that "in certain circumstances a less efficient competitor may also exert a constraint," the circumstances it had in mind appear to be ones that would result in the excluded undertaking's becoming equally efficient as the perpetrator in the future—in circumstances in which "in the absence of an abusive practice such a competitor may benefit from demand-related advantages, which will tend to enhance its efficiency."

out one or more rivals that are less efficient or deter the entry of one or more rivals that would be less efficient (in the sense of less profitable) than the undertaking is.

The eleventh through fourteenth economics deficiencies of the EC's and E.C./E.U. courts' analyses of surrogates for vertical integration all relate to which I call QV-investment competition. The eleventh is that the EC and the E.C./E.U. courts all assume that, as a general matter, established undertakings will respond to the presence of an effective potential competitor by engaging in limit pricing,[1343] an incorrect assumption that affects, *inter alia*, those institution's conclusion about the nature of the decrease in competition that will be generated by conduct that excludes an effective potential competitor.

The twelfth is that, as previously stated, the EC and the E.C./E.U. courts never offer an explicit definition of "barriers to entry" or "barriers to QV-investment expansion," never allude to the existence of a retaliation barrier to entry, totally ignore the existence of monopolistic and natural oligopolistic QV-investment disincentives and monopolistic QV-investment incentives, and seem to count as a barrier to entry or expansion the making of QV investments that render rival QV investments unprofitable without increasing the difference between the supernormal rate-of-return they will generate and the supernormal rate-of-return that will be generated post-entry or post-expansion by the most profitable QV investments in the relevant area of product-space.[1344]

Thirteenth and relatedly, although the EC's and E.C./E.U. courts' statements about this issue are not clear,[1345] they leave the impression that these institutions might consider what I call non-predatory limit QV investments to be illegal as exclusionary under now-Article 102 (when made by a dominant undertaking) (and, I suspect, *prima facie* illegal under now-Article 101(1) as well even if made by a non-dominant undertaking). As I indicated respectively in Sects. 4D and 4A of Chap. 11, the U.S. courts have not made this mistake, though it was made in a well-known article written by two deservedly-highly-respected U.S. economists.

Fourteenth, neither the EC nor the E.C./E.U. courts have executed an analysis of the conditions under which potential competition will be effective in a given area of product-space, the conditions under which a particular potential competitor will be effective, or the conditions under which a particular potential QV-investment expander will be effective in a given area of product-space—analyses that bear on whether conduct that disadvantages particular possible QV investors will tend to decrease competition on that account.

The fifteenth economics weakness of the EC's and the E.C./E.U. courts' analyses of the various surrogates for vertical integration is their failure to recognize that, except in unusual circumstances, an undertaking will find it most profitable to distribute its product through the independent distributor that is privately-best-placed to distribute its product rather than to distribute its product itself if it is less-well-placed to do so or through a privately-less-well-placed independent distributor. This

[1343] See, *e.g.*, *id.* at ¶¶ 16 and 68.

[1344] See, *e.g.*, *id.* at ¶ 17.

[1345] See *id.*

implies that, except in the unusual circumstances that will be described below, an undertaking will not find it profitable to (1) cut off an independent distributor and distribute its product itself when the independent distributor was privately-better-placed to distribute the producer's product than the producer was or (2) to discriminate against a distributor that would otherwise be privately-best-placed to distribute its product when doing so makes the favored distributor privately-best-placed to distribute the undertaking's product when the favored distributor would otherwise have been privately-worse-placed. I can think of two exceptions to the preceding conclusions: a producer may find it profitable to cut off or discriminate against a privately-better-placed distributor (1) when the latter has or would otherwise develop monopsony power over the producer and (2) when the latter's distribution of the producer's product would critically increase its ability to enter the relevant production business.

The sixteenth economics weakness of the EC's and the E.C./E.U. courts' analyses of the various surrogates for vertical integration has to do with these institutions' inability to determine the conduct that undertakings are likely to substitute for any contract-clause or sales-consignment-policy surrogate for vertical integration they are prohibited from using. Although the E.C./E.U. courts and, more recently, the EC have embraced the correct idea that the impact of any surrogate for vertical integration depends on the conduct its user will substitute for it if prevented from using it,[1346] in practice they are not adept at identifying the relevant "counterfactual."

The seventeenth and final general economic weakness in the EC's and E.C./E.U. courts' handling of surrogates for vertical integration is that these institutions have only a limited awareness of the legitimate functions that the various surrogates for vertical integration can perform. More specifically, those institutions say little more than that the various vertical restraints in question can promote economic efficiency (1) by giving future perpetrators appropriate incentives to make future QV investments that would create products whose marketings' profitability would be enhanced by the perpetrators' use of vertical restraints[1347] and (2) by preserving the incentive of future producers to provide independent distributors with training that would increase their proficiency but would not be supplied if it could subsequently be used by the independents to distribute the products of the perpetrator's rivals[1348]

[1346] See, *e.g.*, *id.* at ¶ 21.

[1347] For an interesting twist on this argument, see SA Binon & Cie v. SA Agence et Messageries de la Presse, Case 243/83, ECR 201 (1985), in which the ECJ stated: "...if the fixing of the retail price by publishers constitutes the sole means of supporting the financial burden resulting from the taking back of unsold copies and if the latter practice constitutes the sole method by which a wide selection of newspapers and periodicals can be made available to readers, the Commission must take account of these factors when examining an agreement for the purpose of Article 85(3) [now-Article 101(3)]."

[1348] See, *e.g.*, 2009 EC Guidance Communication on Exclusionary Abuses at ¶¶ 29, 30, 46, and 85; the exception to Article 5(b) of the BER's listing as a grey clause clauses that obligate buyers not to compete with their suppliers or clauses that prohibit buyers from doing so indefinitely or for over 5 years; see Pronuptia de Paris v. Pronuptia de Paris Irmgard Schillgalis, Case 161/84, ECR 374 (1996) and SPLR Louis Erauw-Jacquery v. La Hesbignonne SC, Case 27/87, ECR 1919 (1988), and Miller International Schallplatten GmbH v. Commission at ¶ 46, Case 19/77, ECR 131 (1978).

or to enter into the perpetrator's product-production business. Indeed, as previously stated, when the EC or an E.C./E.U. court acknowledge that in one sense some relevant type of conduct could be said to be performing another legitimate function, they tend to dismiss this possibility by arguing that the perpetrator could achieve this goal in another way that would be equally effective and proficient at achieving it but less injurious to competition. I should add that this last weakness of the EC's and E.C./E.U. courts' handling of vertical restraints undoubtedly lies behind its immediate predecessor—*i.e.*, the reason that these institutions have done a poor job of identifying the relevant counterfactuals is that they do not understand the functions that the conduct in question is performing and therefore cannot identify the alternative types of conduct that can perform the same functions.

I turn finally to a brief account of the EC's and E.C./E.U. courts' conclusions about the legality of the various surrogates for vertical integration. This account, which is partially anticipated by my earlier delineation of the black clauses and grey clauses in the EC's 1999 BER, will not attend to these institutions' pronouncements on the *de minimis* (appreciability) issue or, more generally, the details of the distinctions they draw between "object"-branch and "effect"-branch legal analysis under now-Article 101(1).[1349]

I start with qualitative and quantitative selective distribution—the practices in which a producer chooses respectively to have its product distributed only by wholesalers and/or retailers whose personnel, organization, and premises satisfy certain criteria (which presumably are relevant to the proficiency with which they will distribute its product) and to limit the number of distributors through which it sells its product. The E.C./E.U. courts have recognized the legitimacy of producers' using at least a qualitative selective-distribution system.[1350] However, rather than declaring decisions of producers to use such systems *per se* legal, they have concluded that the legality of such decisions should be assessed on a case-by-case, Rule-of-Reason-type basis.[1351] I think that the decision of E.C./E.U. courts to micro-manage producers' decisions about whether to use a qualitative selective-distribution system is both wrong as a matter of law and policy and a product of two other mistakes that the E.C./E.U. courts have made—(1) the legal mistake of concluding that E.C./E.U. competition law declares *prima facie* illegal covered acts that reduce *intra*-brand competition even if they do not reduce *inter*-brand competition and (2) the economics mistake of assuming that qualitative selective distribution tends to reduce intra-brand competition when, even if its prohibition would not lead producers to integrate forward into distribution, there would be no reason to believe that it would tend to reduce either the number of independent

---

[1349] Practitioners should look to Peeperkorn *et al.* for cogent discussions of the EC's and the E.C./E.U. courts' treatment of these practically-important issues.

[1350] Cabour SA et Nord Distribution Automobile SA v. Arnor SOCO SARL, Case C-230/96, ECR I-2055 (1998).

[1351] See, *e.g.*, Metro-SB-Grossmaerkte GmbH & Co. KG v. Commission and SABA, Case 26/76, ECR 1875 (ECJ) (1977).

distributors through which any particular brand is distributed or the extent to which a brand's distributors compete with each other. The EC originally declared quantitative selective distribution to be *per se* illegal[1352] (presumably on the assumption that it inevitably reduces intra-brand competition). However, like the E.C./E.U. courts, the EC has always been willing to acknowledge the legality of at least some exemplars of quantitative selective distribution both in particular industries[1353] and more generally. Thus, the 1999 BER grants a block exemption to selective-distribution choices of all kinds (including quantitative selective distribution) by any supplier whose market share is under 30 % and—at the third inset to Article 4(b)—declares block-exemptible clauses that prohibit authorized dealers from cross-selling to unauthorized distributors. Still, the 1999 BER does continue to manifest the beliefs (shared by the E.C./E.U. courts) that, at least when the market share of the supplier in question exceeds 30 %, selective distribution can decrease intra-brand competition (a result that the EC continues to assume disfavors the legality of covered conduct under now-Article 101) and can facilitate collusion among suppliers or buyers as well (though I see a connection only if the selective distribution is combined with single-brand exclusive dealership—see below). The 2000 EC Guidelines on Vertical Restraints state that, even if the supplier's market share is over 30 %, its use of a qualitative selective-distribution system is likely not to violate now-Article 101 if (1) the good's technological complexity, sophisticated image, high quality, or possible dangerousness make it necessary for the supplier to use selective distribution to preserve the product's quality-reputation and ensure its appropriate use, (2) the selection criteria are narrowly defined to achieve these objectives, and (3) the criteria are both objective and applied in a non-discriminatory manner. However, the 2000 Guidelines indicate that (1) the probability that an individual undertaking's selective-distribution arrangement will not be block-exempted and will violate now-Article 101 increases with the market share of the supplier,[1354] (2) the probability that selective-distribution arrangements entered into by two or more suppliers in the market will not be block-exempted and will violate now-Article 101 increases with the total market share of those suppliers that use selective-distribution systems (the Guidelines state that negative cumulative effects are unlikely to occur if the share of the market covered by selective distribution is lower than 50 % or if the cumulative market share of the five largest suppliers to use selective distribution is lower than

---

[1352] See Peeperkorn *et al.* at 1225 n. 342.

[1353] See Recital 4 of Commission Regulation (EC) 1475/95 (1995) (the automobile industry); Campari OJ L70/69 (1978); SABA, OJ L28/19 (1976); and BMW, OJ L29/1 (1975). I should add that the 1995 automobile-distribution regulation in question also contained a number of other provisions that, to my mind, manifest the EC's legally-unwarranted and independently-undesirable tendency to micro-manage the way in which producer-undertakings organize their affairs: for example, a white clause that establishes as conditions for the block exemption that the regulation grants automobile manufacturers a requirement that selected dealers be requested to provide repair and maintenance services on the manufacturer's vehicles (although a prospective distributor's possession of the ability to provide such services is one of the factors a car-producer would want to consider when deciding whether to select the distributor in question, there is no reason to believe that it would be a necessary condition for selection) and a number of other dubious black clauses.

[1354] See Commission Notice—Guidelines on Vertical Restraints at ¶ 187, OJ C291 (2000).

50 %),[1355] (3) the probability that selective distribution will reduce competition in the distribution business increases with the barriers to entry into the supply business[1356] (which is wrong, *inter alia*, because it assumes that the probability of entry into the supply business is primarily determined by the height of the barriers to entry into that business as opposed to by whether the barriers to entry facing the best-placed potential competitor are lower than the sum of the barriers to expansion and QV-investment incentives and disincentives facing the best-placed potential expander at the entry-barred, expansion-preventing QV-investment level), (4) the probability that selective distribution will reduce competition in the distribution business increases with the market power of the distributors[1357] (which will be true only in the unlikely case in which the distributors induce their suppliers to enforce a distributor cartel by cutting off distributors that undercut fixed prices on the ground that they no longer possess the qualifications the supplier requires its distributors to have), and (5) the probability that selective distribution decreases competition in the supplier market increases with the stagnancy of demand. The Guidelines do acknowledge that qualitative selectivity can yield efficiencies but claim that this result is likely to obtain only when the product is complex and product-quality cannot be accurately assessed prior to purchase.[1358]

I turn now to an account and critique of the EC's and E.C./E.U. courts' treatment of each of the surrogates for vertical integration I claim it is useful to distinguish. I begin with single-product pricing. Although both the EC and the E.C./E.U. courts have made statements that imply that the use of any pricing-technique by a dominant firm that reduces its customers' buyer surplus below some acceptable quantity or percentage of actual or maximum possible transaction surplus would constitute an exploitative abuse of its dominant position, they have never operationalized such statements or found a dominant firm to have violated what is now Article 102 for such a reason. Both the EC and the E.C./E.U. courts have recognized that conventional price discrimination (say, in the form of loyalty rebates) can violate what is now Article 101—*i.e.*, can be predatory.[1359] Indeed, the EC and ECJ have each concluded in some cases that price discrimination in the form of a rebate system that disadvantages smaller competitors is illegal because it is either unfair or anticompetitive (when adjudged to be systematic).[1360] Obviously, both the EC and the E.C./E.U. courts recognize that an undertaking's practice of cross-E.C./E.U.-country price discrimination may make it profitable for the

[1355] *Id.* at ¶ 189.

[1356] *Id.* at ¶ 190.

[1357] *Id.* at ¶ 191.

[1358] *Id.* at ¶ 195.

[1359] See, *e.g.*, Hoffman-La Roche v. Commission at ¶ 90, Case 85/76, ECR 461 (1979); Suiker Unie v. Commission, Case 40/73, ECR 1663 (1975); and Continental Can v. Commission, Case 6/72, ECR 215 (1973).

[1360] See Michelin v. Commission, Case T-203/01, ECRII-4071 (2003). See also Solvay SA v. Commission, OJ L152/21/(1991) and ICI v. Commission, OJ L152/40 (1991).

undertaking to include minimum-price-setting resale-price-maintenance clauses or vertical-territorial-restraint clauses in its distribution contracts or to adopt related sales/consignment policies to prevent the cross-E.C./E.U.-country sales that the price discrimination would otherwise render profitable for favored distributors—clauses and policies that these institutions (incorrectly, to my mind) believe violate what is now Article 101 of the 2009 Lisbon Treaty. However, the EC and the E.C./E.U. courts also appear to recognize that, even if the conduct that price discrimination makes profitable were illegal, that fact would not imply the illegality of the price discrimination itself. (The EC and the E.C./E.U. courts have never alluded to the related reality that an undertaking's decision to price its product by charging a high lump-sum fee and a low per-unit price will also tend to provide independent distributors with an incentive to make cross-E.C./E.U.-country sales and, concomitantly, the producer that uses this pricing-technique with an incentive to prevent its independent distributors from making cross-E.C./E.U.-country sales.) Not surprisingly, given the low probability of the relevant outcome and the difficulty of proving its likelihood *ex ante* or its occurrence *ex post*, the EC and the E.C./E.U. courts (like their U.S. counterparts) have never adverted (1) to the possibility that various single-product pricing-technique decisions that (relative to their alternatives) increase their perpetrator's unit sales may have the effect of reducing competition by inducing the exit of an established undertaking and/or critically raising the barriers to entry facing an otherwise-effective potential competitor by reducing the actual demand curve an established rival faced or the demand curve that a prospective QV investor would face or (2) to the related, though even-more-remote possibility that an undertaking's choice to charge prices or a particular combination of lump-sum fee and supra-TSM-marginal-cost per-unit price or to engage in perfect price discrimination was critically affected by its belief that the choice in question would or might have one or both of the above effects.

The EC's and E.C./E.U. courts' handling of tie-ins and reciprocity (*i.e.*, of multi-product pricing-techniques) has been thoroughly unsatisfactory—as bad as their U.S. counterparts' treatment of these practices at its worst. I will focus first on the EC's position and then on the E.C./E.U. courts' positions.

The EC continues to subscribe to a not-fully-articulated variant of the leverage theory of tie-ins.[1361] The 2009 BER does exempt tie-ins arranged by undertakings whose tying market shares are under 30 % (which would be consistent with the leverage theory if market shares were a reliable indication of market power and a 30 % market share created the requisite probability that the perpetrator's market power sufficed to allow its tie-ins to exert leverage). However, in part because the EC has (or, at least, its relevant pronouncements manifest) at best a very partial and imperfect understanding of the private functions that tie-ins (and reciprocity) can perform and in part because the EC has a strong, abiding belief that even when tie-ins can perform a legitimate function, the undertaking would be able to get that function performed equally proficiently in some other way that would be less likely

[1361] See 2009 EC Guidance Communication on Exclusionary Abuses at ¶¶ 49 and 54.

to reduce competition (even when that is almost certainly not the case),[1362] the EC has in essence decided that tie-ins arranged by sellers that have a market share of 30 % or more should not be given a block exemption. Indeed, although the fact that an agreement has not been given a block exemption is not supposed to create any presumption that it does not deserve a now-Article 101(3) exemption, the EC's subscription to the leverage theory implies that it does believe that tie-ins that do not merit a block exemption are highly likely to be illegal. I want to elaborate on my claim that the EC does not understand the functions that can be performed by or the economic efficiencies that can be generated by tie-ins. Specifically, this claim reflects the fact that the EC has never made any statement indicating that it understands that tie-ins can, *inter alia*, increase the proficiency with which their perpetrator (1) controls the quality of the complements its product's buyers combine with its product, (2) practices meter pricing, (3) practices lawful price discrimination, (4) prevents arbitrage, (5) reduces the amount of transaction surplus destroyed by a given amount of supra-marginal-cost pricing when the tying product is a final good and the tied product is not a complement of the tying product, or (6) keeps customers from making jointly-unprofitable substitutions of a complement of the perpetrator's product that is also a partial substitute for the perpetrator's product. Thus, even when the EC alludes to this last possibility, its discussion of the relevant possibility does not take account of the fact that the tie-in in question can perform this function.[1363] In one respect, the EC seems to have gotten things even more wrong than the U.S. courts and antitrust-enforcement agencies did at their worst: whereas the U.S. authorities asserted that tie-ins would reduce competition in the tied-product market, the EC declared without explanation that "[t]ying and bundling may lead to anticompetitive effects in the tied market, the tying market, or both at the same time."[1364] Hence, although the 1999 BER's blacklisting of tie-ins arranged by sellers whose market shares are 30 % or above is not supposed to create any kind of presumption against the legality of such agreements in now-Article 101(3) proceedings, I have little doubt that the EC believes that most such tie-in are illegal.

The E.C./E.U. courts' treatment of tie-ins has not been any better. As Professor Korah indicates,[1365] "[t]he E.C. case law does not contain much market analysis to see if a tie-in forecloses." Thus, in cases involving (1) the tie of the sale of machines to fill cartons with the aseptic cartons to be filled[1366] and (2) the tie of nails and nail cartridges to nailguns,[1367] the reviewing courts were no more willing than was the

---

[1362] See Commission Notice—Guidelines on Vertical Restraints at ¶ 222, OJ C291 (2000).

[1363] See *id.* at ¶ 56.

[1364] See *id.* at ¶52.

[1365] KORAH 163.

[1366] See Tetra Pak International SA v. EC Commission, C-333/948, ECR I-5951 (ECJ) (1996), reviewing Tetra Pak Rausing SA v. Commission, T-83/91, ECRII-755 (CFI) (1994), reviewing Commission Decision, Tetra Pak II, 92/163/EEC, OJ L72/1 (1992).

[1367] See Commission Decision Hilti, 88/138 EEC, OJ L65/19 (1988), confirmed in Hilti v. EC Commission, Case T-30/89, ECR-II 1439 (CFI) (1991).

EC (1) to acknowledge the possibility that the tie-ins in question might be more-cost-effective means of controlling complement-quality than writing contracts that specify the attributes of the complements that buyers must use, inspecting the complements that buyers actually do use to detect contract violations, and suing contract violators or (2) to grasp that the tie-ins in question may have been used in addition or instead to execute meter pricing. The preceding discussion did not focus on the special risks to competition that may be posed by tie-ins that obligate buyers to purchase their full requirements of the tied product from the seller: these risks will be discussed when considering long-term requirements contracts more generally. The preceding discussion also did not address reciprocity. This omission reflects the fact that, to my knowledge, neither the EC nor the E.C./E.U. courts have ever analyzed the legality of reciprocity under E.C./E.U. competition law (or noticed the fact that tie-ins and reciprocity perform the same or analogous functions, that an individual perpetrator's use of tie-ins and reciprocity will have the object and effect of reducing competition in the same rare circumstances, or that a general rule permitting all members of a set of rivals to use tie-ins or reciprocity will reduce competition only when the same, to my mind rarely-satisfied set of conditions is fulfilled). One final set of thoughts that also applies to the EC's and the E.C./E.U. courts' treatment of several of the other types of vertical-restraint clauses. Some commentators claim that these institutions' tendency to consider tie-ins and the relevant other sorts of vertical contract restraints illegal under now-Article 101 is justified by the fact that the original Article 85(1)(e)—now Article 101(1)(e)—lists as one of the categories of agreements that now-Article 101(1) might declare *prima facie* illegal agreements between undertakings that "make the conclusion of contracts subject to acceptance by the other parties of supplementary obligations, which by their nature or according to commercial usage, have no connection with the subject of such contracts." As I stated in Sect. 2A(1)(A) of Chap. 4, although I do not know whether the ratifiers of the 1957 Treaty believed that tie-ins (or reciprocity) belong in this category, for a combination of two reasons, I would not in any event find any such belief they had decisive on the legal-interpretation/application issue: (1) tie-ins and reciprocity clearly do not belong in category (e) both because such agreements are always intimately related to the "subject of the contracts" in which the clauses that create them are placed and because, almost always, all or at least the vast majority of the product-rivals of any seller that uses tie-ins or reciprocity use them as well and (2) legal interpreters are not bound by the mistaken views of ratifiers and drafters about the types of conduct that fit the abstract categories of conduct the legal text they ratified/drafted declares illegal or *prima facie* illegal. Although this last set of comments applies equally forcefully to the other categories of contract clauses that function as surrogates for vertical integration, to save space, I will not repeat them when addressing these other categories of conduct in the text that follows.

As we saw, minimum-price-setting RPM but not maximum-price-setting RPM is on the 1999 BER's blacklist. Of course, the fact that minimum-resale-price-setting contract clauses (and, I presume, related sales/consignment policies directed at independent distributors/consumers whose acquiescence has been secured by threats to make them worse off if they do not comply than they would have been had they not dealt with the perpetrator at all) are in the BER's black-clause list does not in itself imply their illegality under now-Article 101—indeed, in theory, does not create any type of presumption that they are even *prima facie* illegal. However, there is good reason to believe that both the EC and the E.C./E.U. courts do believe that the vast majority of such clauses are illegal.

My conclusion about the EC's assessment of the legality of such clauses reflects the following facts: (1) the EC believes that now-Article 101(1) makes efforts to reduce *intra*-brand competition *prima facie* illegal and one of the functions of minimum-price-setting RPM is to prevent intra-brand price competition for its own sake; (2) at least in some cases, minimum-price-setting RPM is used to prevent cross-E.C./E.U.-country sales by distributors that have been charged either discriminatorily-low prices (perhaps because their countries are poorer than the countries in which disfavored distributors are located and the end-user price that will maximize the producer's profits in these poorer countries is lower than its counterpart in richer countries) or low per-unit prices (and high lump-sum fees), and the EC believes that one of the proximate goals of the 1957 Treaty and its successors is to prevent producers from deterring cross-E.C./E.U.-country sales; (3) the EC does not appear to appreciate that the counterfactuals to a producer's minimum-price-setting RPM (*viz.*, the producer's vertically integrating forward into distribution or deciding to lower its lump-sum fees and increase its per-unit prices) may well decrease intra-brand competition and prevent cross-E.C./E.U.-country sales (relative to the intensity that such competition would have and the volume of such sales that would be made if the elimination of the minimum-price-setting RPM would not cause anything else to be changed) as much as the minimum-price-setting RPM did; and (4) the EC's pronouncements on minimum-price-setting RPM do not suggest that it understands in any detail (or that its decisions are influenced by a detailed understanding of) the legitimate functions such RPM can perform and the economic efficiencies it can generate.

The same facts support my conclusion that E.C./E.U. courts are disposed to find that minimum-price-setting RPM violates now-Article 101. E.C. case-law also supports this conclusion both through the courts' resolution of relevant cases[1368] and through the fact that the only justification under now-Article 101(3) for the practice that they recognize is the possibility that the relevant seller (and its future counterparts) would not supply the good in question at all if minimum-price-setting RPM did not enable it to earn extra profits by supplying it.[1369]

A final point. The BER does not place on its list of black "clauses" the practice in which a producer recommends a minimum resale price without threatening reprisals against non-conformists. If, contrary to my view, minimum-price-setting RPM that did not effectuate a reseller or producer cartel were illegal,

---

[1368] See, *e.g.*, SPRL Louis Erauw-Jacquery v. La Hesbignonne SC at ¶ 12, Case 27/87, ECR 1919 (1988) and Miller International Schallplatten GmBH v. Commission, Case 19/77, ECR 131 (1978).

[1369] See *id.* at ¶ 46.

minimum-price-setting recommendations that were not accompanied by threats that are accepted (*i.e.*, acted upon) by the reseller would be covered by now-Article 101(1) as a concerted practice if they benefitted the reseller as well as the producer and would usually violate now-Article 101 as a whole if, contrary to fact, the only economic efficiency such RPM generated was rendering profitable the economically-efficient QV investments that created the product in question.

As we saw, the combination of the 1999 BER and the Guidelines that elaborate on them creates an extremely-complicated set of rules for determining the blacklisting of a clause creating a vertical territorial restraint, a vertical customer-allocation clause, or a system of bonuses, discounts, or profit-pass-over obligations that is designed to deter distributors from making active sales in some territories or to some customers: (1) all restrictions on the territories in which or customers to which a supplier can make sales are block-exempted; (2) restrictions on passive sales by retailers (including internet sales and catalog-generated sales when the website or catalog message does not specifically target customers allocated to another retailer or to the supplier) are excluded from the block exemption; (3) restrictions on active sales by retailers into territories or to customers exclusively allocated to another retailer or reserved to the supplier are block-exempted; (4) restrictions on active or passive sales by wholesalers to end-users are block-exempted; (5) restrictions on active or passive sales by authorized members of a selective-distribution system to unauthorized distributors are block-exempted; (6) restrictions on the ability of a buyer to make active or passive sales of complements supplied for the purpose of incorporation into the supplier's product to a rival of the supplier that would use them to produce a good that is competitive with the supplier's product are block-exempted; (7) restrictions on active or passive sales by one member of a selective-distribution system to another member of a selective-distribution system are not block-exempted; (8) restrictions on active or passive sales to end-users by any individual member of a selective retail-distribution system are not block-exempted; and (9) although the rules applying to vertical customer-allocation clauses are the same, *mutatis mutandis*, as those that apply to vertical territorial restraints, the EC seems to think that exclusive customer allocations are unlikely to be lawful under now-Article 101. Thus, the 2000 Guidelines on Vertical Restraints' statement that an exclusive customer-allocation is unlikely to be individually exempted unless substantial economic efficiencies can be clearly established seems to imply the Commission's belief that this condition will be fulfilled less often than I suspect it will be, though the Commission does acknowledge that "[e]xclusive customer allocation may lead to efficiency, especially when the distributors are required to make investments in for instance specific equipment, skills or know-how to adapt to the requirements of their class of customers."[1370] My concern is that this admission does not cover the case in which a particular distributor is best-placed to supply a particular buyer because of their physical proximity to each other, because the distributor has knowledge of

[1370] See Commission Notice—Guidelines on Vertical Restraints at ¶ 180, OJ C291 (2000).

the buyer's special needs (whose possession may not count as skills or know-how), or because the buyer trusts the distributor in question (for reasons that would not be said to reflect the distributor's skills or know-how).

I suspect that the eighth BER rule in my list is included to keep restrictions on cross-E.C./E.U.-country (parallel) trade from being blocked-exempted. My problem is that I cannot see how point (8) in my list can be reconciled with point (3), which declares that restrictions on active sales by retailers into territories or to customers allocated to another retailer or reserved to the supplier are block-exempted. One could say that point (8) qualifies point (3) by declaring that point (3) is inapplicable to retailers that are part of a selective retail-distribution system, but I can imagine no reason why it would be desirable to make point (3) inapplicable to such retailers, and the text of the relevant BER provision—Article 4(c)—does not in any event, in any way, limit its applicability to situations in which the restraint in question would prevent cross-E.C/E.U.-country (parallel) trade.

As already indicated, I do not think that it is either correct as a matter of E.C./E.U. law or socially desirable (legal correctness aside) to declare illegal supplier-attempts to prohibit their retailers from making passive sales that violate territorial or customer allocations, to prohibit their wholesalers from making active or passive sales to end-users, to prohibit cross-sales among their authorized distributors, or to prohibit their distributors from making cross-E.C./E.U.-country sales. I also find it hard to understand how a decisionmaker who understands why it would be incorrect as a matter of law (and independently undesirable) to conclude that now-Article 101 made illegal a supplier's (1) restrictions on the sales it could make, (2) prohibition of its retailers' making active sales in violation of its territorial or customer allocations, (3) prohibition of authorized-distributor sales to unauthorized-distributor sales, and (4) prohibition of component-buyers' reselling the components to the component-supplier's potential final-product rivals could find it correct as a matter of law to exclude from block exemptions the vertical restraints that Article 4 of the 1999 BER places in its list of black clauses. Of course, this "inconsistency" is not greater than the inconsistency between the 1999 BER's treatment of minimum-price-setting RPM and the 1999 BER's treatment of those types of vertical territorial restraints and customer-allocation clauses to which Article 4 grants a block exemption.

I do not know whether the EC's refusal to grant block exemptions to many categories of vertical territorial restraints, vertical customer-allocation clauses, and related sales and consignment policies was a "product" of the case-law or *vice versa*. However, it is clear that the E.C./E.U. courts have been no more hospitable to such conduct than the EC has been. Admittedly, E.C./E.U. courts have recognized that exclusivity (and hence the vertical territorial restraints and vertical-customer-allocation clauses that yielded it) might be necessary to induce a distributor to incur the expense of setting up business.[1371] Still, there is a substantial difference

[1371] See Pronuptia de Paris v. Pronuptia de Paris Irmgard Schillgalis at ¶ 24, Case 161/84, ECR 374 (1996) and Bayerische Motorenwerke AG v. ALD Auto-Leasing D GmbH at ¶¶ 114–16, Case C-70/93, ECR I-3439 (1995).

between recognizing this fact and appreciating the various legitimate functions these surrogates for vertical integration can perform and the related economic efficiencies they can generate. The E.C./E.U. courts' hostility to these sorts of vertical restraints seems to have been generated not only by their failure to understand the legitimate functions of such restraints and their related possible economic efficiency but also by the combination of the fact that such restraints will often be used to prevent cross-E.C./E.U.-country trading and the courts' beliefs that (1) one of the most important proximate goals of the 1957 Treaty was to prevent undertakings from deterring such parallel trade and (2) the prohibition of vertical territorial and customer allocations would help to achieve this alleged Treaty goal.

The Guidelines that accompany the 1999 BER state that clauses that obligate resellers to display the supplier's brand name are not black clauses in the BER sense.[1372] However, I know of no EC or E.C./E.U.-court ruling on the legality of a producer's (1) obligating its distributors to make expenditures on out-of-store advertising or to supply in-store promotional displays or desirable shelf-space, (2) subsidizing such choices by its distributors, or (3) adopting sales policies that are designed to induce its distributors to engage in jointly-optimal advertising/ promotional activities.

As already indicated, non-single-brand exclusive dealerships are just the flip-side of vertical territorial restraints and vertical customer-allocation clauses. The preceding discussion of the EC's and E.C./E.U. courts' positions on such restraints and clauses should therefore apply to non-single-brand exclusive dealerships as well. However, the 2000 Vertical Restraint Guidelines also address separately what they call "exclusive distribution"—in U.S. terminology, non-single-brand exclusive dealerships (arrangements in which a supplier makes a distributor the sole authorized seller of the supplier's product in a specified territory or to a non-territorially-defined set of buyers). With two important qualifications, the 1999 BER block-exempts exclusive distribution. The two exceptions are created respectively by Article 4(b) and Article 4(c) of the 1999 BER: (1) the supplier cannot protect an "exclusive dealer" from passive sales made by other distributors of the supplier's product, regardless of whether the supplier has created a selective-distribution system, and (2) a supplier that uses a selective retail-distribution system cannot protect an exclusive dealer from either active or passive sales to end-users by members of the supplier's selective retail-distribution network. The Guidelines claim that five factors determine the risk that non-single-brand exclusive dealerships will reduce intra-brand or inter-brand competition: (1) the strength of the supplier's market position, which the EC considers relevant because it incorrectly believes that strong inter-brand competition will prevent end-users from being harmed by reductions in intra-brand competition; (2) the strength of the supplier's competitors' market positions, which cuts in two directions: in the one, the fact that the competitors of the supplier are strong favors the legality of the exclusive dealerships because, the EC believes, it causes reductions in intra-brand competition to be less damaging to

[1372] Commission Notice—Guidelines on Vertical Restraints at ¶ 49, OJ C291 (2000).

end-users (by reducing the strength of the supplier's market position?), and, in the other, the fact that the competitors of the supplier are strong disfavors the legality of the exclusive dealership by making it more likely that this arrangement will increase collusion[1373] (by precluding individual suppliers from increasing their sales in any territory by making price-cuts to other distributors in that territory that had not previously distributed its goods); (3) the participation of distributors that have substantial buying power disfavors the legality of exclusive dealerships because the EC believes that, for some reason it does not specify and I do not grasp, the amount by which such arrangements decrease intra-brand competition increases with the participating distributors' buying power and because the likelihood that the arrangement increases the risk of collusion among distributors is positively correlated with the distributors' buying power (which would be true if the distributors' individual buying power were positively correlated with the profitability of contrivance to them to the extent that non-single-brand exclusive dealerships reduce the number of dealers operating in the relevant product-area)[1374]; and (4) according to the Guidelines, the level of trade (wholesale or retail) at which the distributor that has been allotted an exclusive dealership operates also cuts in both directions in relation to the legality of the non-single-brand exclusive dealerships: in the one direction, for reasons I do not understand, the EC seems to think that the losses that exclusive distributorships inflict on consumers by reducing intra-brand competition are more likely to be fully offset or counterbalanced by the benefits the relevant consumers obtain from the economic efficiencies the exclusive dealerships generate when the exclusive dealers operate on the wholesale as opposed to the retail level while in the other direction the EC believes that exclusive dealerships created by more than one member of a set or rival suppliers are more likely to reduce inter-brand competition when they are created at the wholesale level than when they are created at the retail level (which would be true only if [1] the exclusive dealerships were single-brand exclusive dealerships and [2] the barriers that a potential entrant into the product-production business would face in relation to its entering into the wholesale-distribution business are likely to be greater than the barriers that such a firm would be likely to face in relation to its entering into the retail-distribution business and/or a potential entrant into the product-production business would find it more difficult to induce enough individual undertakings to enter into the wholesale business than to induce enough such undertakings to enter into the retail business to enable it to operate profitably).[1375] The Guidelines do acknowledge that non-single-brand exclusive dealerships can generate efficiencies not just by yielding "economies of scale in transport and distribution" but also by providing distributors with an appropriate incentive to "protect or build up brand image" and (though this is not fully spelled out) to provide buyers with information that encourages them to purchase new or complex products whose "qualities are

[1373] *Id.* at ¶ 164.
[1374] *Id.* at ¶ 167.
[1375] *Id.* at ¶ 170.

difficult to judge before consumption."[1376] Although the Guidelines' accounts of these possibilities could do with some elaboration, the Guidelines' relevant claims are essentially correct.

The Guidelines also address single-branding arrangements brought about through contractual clauses creating so-called non-compete obligations (prohibiting the buyer from selling competing products), so-called quantity-forcing clauses (which obligate the buyer to purchase a specified quantity of the supplier's product that effectively precludes the buyer from purchasing any or a significant amount of any rival product), so-called "English clauses" (which obligate the buyer to inform the supplier of any superior offer it received from a rival of the supplier and to patronize the supplier if it matches the rival offer), as well as quantity-rebate, fidelity-rebate, and mixed lump-sum plus per-unit-price pricing-schemes that have the same effect as the contractual clauses just listed.[1377] Single-branding is block-exempted by the 1999 BER when practiced by a producer whose market share is under 30 % or when the duration of the "not-compete obligation" in question is under five years or shorter than the period during which the buyer is occupying the supplier's premises.[1378] Single-branding that is grey-listed is not *per se* illegal: its legality must be assessed case by case through a Rule-of-Reason-type analysis.

According to the Guidelines, seven factors determine the now-Article 101 illegality of single-branding. The first is the market share of the supplier involved.[1379] As the Guidelines state, on the assumption that the supplier uses single-branding throughout its distribution network, the risk that the practice will reduce inter-brand competition by driving out an established rival and/or deterring a rival QV investment by depriving the rivals in question of the ability to make distribution arrangements that are as profitable as the ones they could otherwise have made will increase with the supplier's market share (though, as we have seen, many factors other than the supplier's market share affect the probability of this outcome). The Guidelines seem not to be sensitive to the fact stated in the preceding parenthetical: they declare that individual exemption will not be available for single-branding arrangements made by dominant sellers unless the practice is "objectively justified" in one of the ways now-Article 102 recognizes.

The "second" determinant of the legality of single-branding in an individual now-Article 101 proceeding that the Guidelines list is really just a modification of the first: it is the "incidence of the non-compete obligation," the percentage of distributors (it should be the percentage of resales) that are made by the supplier's single-branded distributors (the so-called "tied market share").[1380]

[1376] *Id.* at ¶ 174.

[1377] *Id.* at ¶ 152.

[1378] Thus, single-branding is not one of the black clauses delineated in Article 4. Clauses that create direct or indirect non-compete obligations are on Article 5's list of grey clauses, but Article 5(a), which places them on the grey list, creates the exceptions listed in the text.

[1379] *Id.* at ¶ 140.

[1380] *Id.* at ¶ 141.

The third such determinant in the Guidelines' list is the duration of the single-branding obligation: "obligations shorter than 1 year" are declared not legally problematic; the legality of those between "1 and 5 years" created by non-dominant undertakings is to be analyzed by balancing their (alleged) competition-lessening effects against any procompetitive effects the arrangement is deemed to have; and "obligations exceeding 5 year" will in most cases be deemed illegal either because their length is not necessary to achieve any associated efficiencies or because their supposed competition-lessening effects will outweigh the relevant impact of any efficiencies they generate.[1381]

The fourth determinant on this Guidelines list—the market position of the single-branding supplier's competitors—once more cuts in two directions. Thus, in the one direction, the EC claims that the likelihood that the single-branding will violate now-Article 101 by foreclosing the single-brander's established rivals will be inversely related to its individual rivals' market shares (a claim about which I am skeptical: I doubt that the single-brander's individual rivals' individual market shares will have much bearing on either the barriers they face to integrating forward into distribution or their ability to withstand the short-run losses that any single-branding-generated effective foreclosure inflicts on them, and I can see no other connection between the single-brander's individual rivals' individual market shares and the risk that such conduct will drive out an established rival or deter such a rival from making another QV investment in the single-brander's area of product-space). In the other direction, the Guidelines claim that the risk that single-branding will reduce inter-brand competition by facilitating collusion (by increasing "market rigidity" [whatever that is]) will increase with the individual market shares of the single-pricer's individual rivals. I admit that single-branding will tend to facilitate price-fixing by precluding the individual price-fixers from making additional sales to and through distributors of rival products by cutting their prices (violating the price-fix) and that this effect will be larger the greater the percentage of "market sales" made by single-branded distributors. However, I do not think that this latter percentage is strongly correlated with the market shares of the individual rivals of any single-branding suppler. Nor, for reasons that Chap. 10 explained, do I think that there is much of a connection between (1) the market share of the single-brander or the market shares of its larger individual rivals and (2) the probability that contrivance would be profitable or close to profitable without the single-branding (which is relevant because, even if single-branding increases the profitability of contrived oligopolistic pricing, it will not affect the amount of such pricing practiced if such pricing would still be unprofitable despite the practice of single-branding).

The fifth determinant of the legality of single-branding on the Guidelines list is the height of the barriers to entry into the relevant distribution market. It is true that, in situations in which single-branding would make entry into the product-production business less profitable for a potential competitor that could not

---

[1381] *Id.*

integrate forward into distribution or induce an independent entry into distribution and would make a QV-investment expansion less profitable for an established firm that could not integrate forward into distribution or induce an independent entry into distribution, the extent to which the single-branding would decrease the profitability of these potential QV investor's investment in product-production will increase with the extra "cost" they would have to incur to arrange for the distribution of their new product by entering the distribution business themselves or by inducing an independent to enter that business as opposed to distributing the product in question through one or more of the extant distributors that were locked in by single-branding arrangements. However, the connection between this "cost" and the "barriers to entry or expansion" into the relevant distribution business facing the potential entrants or expanders in the production business is at best obscure (given the failure of the EC to define "barriers to entry"), and this factor will not be relevant in the many situations in which (1) single-branding will not reduce such firms' prospective investment profits by reducing their distribution-options and/or (2) no firm that single-branding would disadvantage in this way would have been an effective potential QV investor in any event.

The sixth factor that the Guidelines claim will affect the legality of single-branding is the buying power of the distributors it involves. The scholarly analysis of the relevance of this factor assumes that single-branding can be imposed on buyers by sellers with market power and claims that "if single-branding were imposed on strong buyers the foreclosure effect would be magnified."[1382] I disagree with the assumption that buyers with market power can impose single-branding on potential distributors (which implicitly accepts some variant of the leverage theory and ignores the fact that single-branding is typically in the joint interest of the producer and distributor it involves) and see no reason why foreclosure is either more likely or likely to have more substantial consequences when the single-branded buyer is strong. To the contrary, the probability that a producer has engaged in single-branding (*i.e.*, has placed its customers under full-requirements obligations) predatorily—*i.e.*, has done so to drive an established rival out, prevent new entry, or prevent an established rival QV-investment—will be far lower when the individual customers in question distribute high percentages of the product the single-brander produces because, as Sect. 9A of Chap. 11 argued, predatory full-requirements contracts (including single-branding distribution agreements) (1) are against the interest of the buyers (distributors) they involve in that they reduce or prevent increases in competition in the associated product-production market and are usually against the joint interest of the seller and buyers they involve, (2) are sometimes rendered profitable for the seller that employs them despite that fact because the individual buyers (distributors) are tyrannized by their small decisions—*i.e.*, agree to lock themselves in for compensation that leaves them as a group worse off because each individual buyer believes that, regardless of what it does, enough of its colleagues will agree to lock themselves in to cause the target

[1382] See Peeperkorn *et al.* at 1221.

established firm to exit or deter the target firm from making a new QV investment and concludes for that reason that individually it can profit by accepting even a trivial amount of compensation for locking itself in (since little compensation is better than no compensation), and (3) the probability that the affected buyers will be tyrannized by their small decisions is inversely related to their market shares since the higher any individual buyer's (distributor's) market share the greater the probability that it could by itself enable the target established firm to survive or the prospective QV investor to at least break even on a new QV investment if it refused to lock itself in and the smaller the number of buyers (distributors) that would have to agree to keep themselves free to prevent the predator from succeeding the more likely it is that they will be able to reach an agreement to refuse to lock themselves in.

The Guidelines also claim that single-branding is less likely to violate now-Article 101 when the product involved is an intermediate as opposed to a final product and, when the product is a final product, when the distributor involved is a wholesaler as opposed to a retailer. The wholesaler/retailer point in part reflects the EC's concern that single-branding harms consumers by preventing *in-store* inter-brand competition—*i.e.*, by precluding end-users from assessing rival products by sight in one store and choosing between or among them in one store. The economics response to this last concern is: (1) to the extent that consumers value being able to choose between or among rival brands in one store, that reality will reduce the profitability (and economic efficiency) of single-branding; (2) if producers choose to single-brand despite that fact when their doing so will not reduce inter-brand competition, they must believe that the private losses in question are lower than the private benefits single-branding yields them by increasing the proficiency of the distribution of their product (the private counterparts to the associated economic efficiencies single-branding generates); and (3) there is no reason to think that it is either correct as a matter of law or desirable as a matter of policy for the government to review much less overturn such a business conclusion or prohibit the conduct in which it leads businesses to engage.

The Guidelines also note correctly that single-branding by multiple undertakings in a given area of product-space can cumulatively foreclose competition when no individual undertaking's single-branding would do so. The Guidelines state that no problem is likely to arise when total single-branded sales are below 40 %, though they acknowledge that the other factors they list should also be taken into account.[1383] I have two objections. First, I think that the 40 % figure is far too low: although my conclusion that markets cannot be defined non-arbitrarily causes me to hesitate to make any such statement, I suspect that the tied-up market share almost always has to be far higher than 40 % for the conduct to be problematic. Second, if the various single-branders have not agreed with each other to engage in single-branding and each finds its single-branding profitable in isolation, I doubt that their conduct is covered by now-Article 101.

[1383] Commission Notice—Guidelines on Vertical restraints at ¶ 149, OJ C291 (2000).

Finally, the Guidelines discuss the economic efficiencies that single-branding can generate that now-Article 101(3) makes relevant. The Guidelines refer to three categories of such efficiencies: (1) elimination of free-riding among suppliers; (2) surmounting hold-up problems (the Guidelines state that in situations in which the supplier has made substantial relationship-specific investments and transferred substantial know-how, single-branding in excess of 5 years may be legitimate); and (3) overcoming capital-market imperfections (by providing the producer with incentives to finance the creation of distributive outlets).[1384] The Guidelines state that this third "efficiency" can legitimate single-branding only "if the buyer is not prevented from terminating the non-compete obligation and repaying the outstanding part of the loan at any point in time and without payment of any penalty."[1385] This last position strikes me as another example of EC ill-advised micro-managing *inter alia* because, in situations in which the supplier charged the distributor lower interest rates and required lower repayments in early years to help the distributor get on its feet, it will be difficult to determine whether early-repayment charges really are penalties.

The final category of surrogates for vertical integration are long-term full-requirements purchasing contracts and long-term exclusive-supply contracts. Long-term full-requirements purchasing clauses can be included in contracts of sale in which only one good is being sold, in tying agreements that obligate the buyer to purchase its full requirements of the so-called tied product from the tying seller or a third party that the seller designates, and in reciprocity agreements in which a buyer of one product conditions its obligation to purchase that product from a second firm on the second firm's agreeing to purchase its full requirements of a second product (usually an input used to produce the first product) from the first firm or a third party the first firm designates. Long-term exclusive-supply clauses can be included both in contracts in which only one good is being sold and in reciprocity agreements. Single-brand exclusive dealing obligates the distributor it involves to purchase its full requirements of the category of product the producer is producing from the producer in question.

The most recent EC pronouncement on the legality under E.C. competition law of contract provisions that obligate buyers to purchase their full requirements of some product from a particular supplier or accept stocking obligations that in practice require exclusive purchasing is the 2009 Communication from the Commission—Guidance on the Commission's Enforcement Priorities in Applying Article 82 (now-Article 102) of the E.C. Treaty to Abusive Exclusionary Conduct by Dominant Undertakings.[1386] Although the Communication does not say so, I assume that this Communication also covers sales and consignment policies that in effect require buyers to purchase their full requirements of some good from the seller in question. Formally, these Comments cover only the behavior of dominant firms under a Treaty provision that declares "exclusionary abuses" illegal.

[1384] *Id.* at ¶ 116.

[1385] *Id.* at ¶ 156.

[1386] 2009/C 45/02 (2009).

However, since exclusionary abuses are conduct that have as their critical object preventing or restricting competition and since, if successful, exclusionary abuses will have the effect of preventing or restricting competition, the EC Communication on exclusionary abuses of dominant positions also bears on its position on the *prima facie* illegality of the relevant full-requirements contracts and related policies under now-Article 101 regardless of whether the perpetrator is a dominant or a non-dominant undertaking.

The EC Communication states that the likelihood that a seller's placing its customers under full-requirements purchasing obligations will constitute an exclusionary abuse depends on six factors. The first is "the position of the dominant undertaking" that is creating such obligations.[1387] Although the EC never explains why it believes that the likelihood of foreclosure increases with the "strength" (market power) of the perpetrator and although the leverage "argument" to which the EC subscribes elsewhere in the Communication cannot justify this conclusion because it is based on the silly premise that a seller can have its cake and eat it too (use its competitive advantages twice), the likelihood that the full-requirements-obligation-creating conduct of a seller that requires all its customers to purchase their full requirements from it will reduce competition by foreclosing rivals will, roughly speaking, increase with its market share in that, *ceteris paribus*, the higher the percentage of sales made to locked-in buyers the greater the likelihood that the sales that could be made to non-locked-in buyers will be insufficient to enable such buyers' alternative possible suppliers to break even.

The second factor that the EC Communication lists and discusses is the height of the entry and expansion barriers in the relevant area of product-space ("the conditions on the relevant market").[1388] As I have already explained, the Commission's discussion of this factor would have been more to the point if it had (1) provided explicit or even implicit definitions of "barriers to entry" and "barriers to expansion" and (2) recognized that the effectiveness that a particular potential entrant/expander would have if the perpetrator did not place its customers under full-requirements obligations depends not on the barriers to entry/expansion the potential entrant/expander in question faced but on whether the entry barriers in question are higher than (the expansion barriers [*plus* relevant QV-investment incentives/disincentives] that the best-placed potential expander at the entry-barred expansion-preventing QV-investment level would face) or on whether the relevant expansion barriers *plus* disincentives or incentives were higher than the barriers faced by the best-placed potential entrant.

A third factor that the EC correctly points out (under the heading "the position of the customers") is relevant to whether a given seller's full-requirements contracts will decrease competition by foreclosing competitors is the extent to which the reseller-buyers that are locked in are particularly well-placed to distribute a target

[1387] *Id.* at ¶ 20 inset one.

[1388] *Id.* at ¶ 20 inset two.

established rival's or potential QV investor's products.[1389] (This factor could be extended to include the extent to which the end-using buyers that are locked in are ones that the target established rival/potential QV investor are/would be particularly-well-placed to supply. I should add that U.S. authorities have not been alert to the relevance of the fact that neither distributors nor end-users are fungible to the possible foreclosing effect of particular exemplars of long-term full-requirements contracts).

A fourth factor ("the position of the dominant undertaking's competitors") that the EC claims affects the probability that a dominant seller's long-term full-requirements clauses will constitute an exclusionary abuse is whether the rival that could be damaged by its perpetrator's exclusionary conduct is one whose operations have been or would be particularly costly to the perpetrator because the damaged firm was more competitive with the perpetrator than with other sellers in the relevant area of product-space or was particularly inclined to undercut contrived oligopolistic prices.[1390] Once more, the EC is ahead of its U.S. counterparts in recognizing the importance of the fact that not all of a seller's rivals are fungible from the relevant perspective.

The fifth factor the EC recognizes is "the extent of the alleged abusive conduct"—the total sales or percentage of the total sales in the relevant market locked in and the duration of the obligations in question.[1391] Both these factors are obviously relevant, though the total sales or percentage of total sales locked in is an imperfect surrogate for the relationship between the amount of sales of the relevant kind not locked in and the amount of sales a potential target would have to make to break even.

The sixth and final factor that the EC believes determines the likelihood that a full-requirements-obligation-creating contract or a functionally-related sales policy will be foreclosing is relevant only when the contract in question is a tying agreement or the relevant sales policy involves two or more products. The EC believes that such arrangements are more likely to be foreclosing when one of the products (the "tying" product) is a "must stock" item.[1392] This claim manifests the EC's acceptance of the clearly-incorrect leverage "theory."

Although the EC's 2009 Communication on exclusionary abuses by dominant undertakings focuses almost entirely on long-term *full-requirements purchasing* contracts and related sales and consignment policies, the fact that the fourth inset to ¶ 20 actually is headed ("the position of the customers *or input suppliers*" [emphasis added]) implies that *mutatis mutandis* the EC intended its Communication's claims to apply as well to *full-output supply* contracts and related sales and consignment policies. The Commission's 2000 Notice on Vertical

[1389] *Id.* at ¶ 20 inset four.

[1390] *Id.* at ¶ 20 inset three.

[1391] *Id.* at ¶ 20 inset three.

[1392] *Id.* at ¶ 36.

Restrains[1393] (elaborating on its 1999 BER), which devotes considerable attention to "exclusive-supply" contracts (and by extension related purchasing policies), confirms this conclusion. The Notice states that the EC is concerned that such arrangements may violate now-Article 101 by reducing either or both inter-brand and intra-brand competition. It then lists and discusses five factors that will influence whether an exclusive-supply-securing contract or purchasing policy will be granted a block exemption from now-Article 101.

The first such factor is the buyer's market share, not just its share of the upstream purchase market (*i.e.*, the percentage of all "input" sales its exclusive-supply arrangement locks in), which is somewhat relevant, but its share of downstream sales, which I do not think is relevant at all. Thus, the Notice states that "[n]egative effects can. . .be expected when the market share of the buyer on the downstream supply market as well as the upstream purchase market exceeds 30 %" and that, more tellingly and worryingly, the Commission may also refuse to grant a block exemption when the upstream market share is below 30 % if the buyer's downstream market share exceeds 30 %.[1394] I should say that, in addition to doubting the relevance of the buyer's downstream market share, I find indefensible the EC's statement that, as a general matter, foreclosure is likely when the buyer has secured the exclusive supply of 30 % or more of the input in question. Although I recognize the importance of determining whether the locked-in suppliers were particularly well-placed to supply a target of the undertaking that is securing exclusive supplies, except in cases in which this factor is critical, the percentage of input-supply that would have to be locked in for foreclosure to be a possibility will be much higher than 30 % (as the U.S. case-law on full-requirements purchasing obligations recognizes).

The second factor in the Guidelines' list is the duration of the exclusive-supply arrangement. Arrangements that cover more than 5 years are deemed non-exemptible both because exclusivity for more than 5 years is not deemed necessary to achieve any economic efficiencies the arrangement might generate and because the benefits that the longer duration confers on consumers by enabling efficiencies to be generated are lower than the costs the longer duration imposes on consumers by foreclosing competition. I do not find either of these claims persuasive.

The EC believes that the third factor on which the Guidelines focus—the market position of the competitors of the producer securing exclusive supply—cuts in two directions, just as it does in relation to various other vertical practices already discussed.[1395] In the one direction, the EC believes that increases in the size of the down-market rivals of the undertaking obtaining exclusive supply relative to the size of the perpetrator favor the legality of the arrangement in question because foreclosure is likely only when such rivals have a lower downstream market share than does the undertaking that has secured exclusive supply. I see absolutely no

[1393] Commission Notice—Guidelines on Vertical Restraints, OJ C291 (2000).
[1394] *Id.* at ¶ 205.
[1395] *Id.* at ¶ 206.

reason to believe that this is the case. In the other direction, the EC believes that increases in the downstream market shares of the perpetrator's individual downstream rivals increases the likelihood that foreclosure will result from the cumulative effect of multiple firms' securing supplies. I have two reactions. First, I see no reason to believe that the market shares of the perpetrator's individual downstream rivals will bear at all on the likelihood that the perpetrator and those rivals will find it individually profitable for non-exclusionary reasons to secure exclusive supplies that reduce the amount of supplies not locked up to a foreclosing extent. Second, I do agree that increases in the market shares of the perpetrator's downstream rivals will tend to facilitate their engaging in concerted predation in violation of now-Article 101 by agreeing to make inherently-unprofitable exclusive-supply arrangements to reduce competition by driving out an established rival and/or critically raising the barriers to QV investment facing an otherwise-effective potential entrant or potential expander.

The fourth factor that the Guidelines claim is relevant to the likelihood that exclusive supply will reduce competition is the countervailing power of the suppliers involved.[1396] The Guidelines argue that strong suppliers are unlikely to agree to exclusive-supply arrangements unless those arrangements generate significant economic efficiencies whose private benefits they share. I suspect that the EC has reached this conclusion because it subscribes to the incorrect view that a buyer with market power can profit by forcing its individual suppliers to accept terms that are against not only their individual interests but against the joint interest of the buyer and supplier combined. However, a different, defensible argument can be made for the conclusion that exclusive-supply arrangements are less likely to reduce downstream competition when the upstream suppliers have substantial upstream market shares: exclusive-supply arrangements that are against the interest of the suppliers taken as a group because they reduce competition in the downstream market and thereby increase the buying power of downstream suppliers are less likely to be agreed to by strong suppliers because such suppliers are less likely to be tyrannized by their small decisions into entering into foreclosing exclusive-supply contracts that are individually profitable because no individual suppler can induce its rivals to follow its example of refusing to enter into an exclusive-supply arrangement. The smaller the number of upstream suppliers whose refusal to enter into such arrangements will preclude the downstream buyer(s) from foreclosing competition, the more likely it is that one or more upstream suppliers will find it individually profitable to reject a perpetrator's offered exclusive-supply contract or that an effective group of upstream suppliers will be able to get together and agree to reject the perpetrator's offered exclusive-supply contracts.

The fifth and final factor that the Guidelines claim affects the probability of foreclosure is the nature of the product in question—whether it is an intermediate or a final good and whether it is differentiated or homogeneous. There is some basis for the Commission's claim that the risk of foreclosure is lower when the product is

---

[1396] *Id.* at ¶ 208.

intermediate rather than final or homogeneous rather than differentiated. Product homogeneity matters and final products may be more likely to be differentiated than intermediate products: in particular, product homogeneity matters because there may be some tendency for (1) a particular differentiated product to be specially-well-placed to obtain the patronage of particular downstream distributors or producers and (2) particular downstream producers or distributors of differentiated products to be more competitive with a perpetrator than with other undertakings operating in the relevant downstream area of product-space.

In general, I think that the EC and E.C./E.U. courts vastly exaggerate the probability that exclusive-purchasing and exclusive-supply arrangements will reduce competition by foreclosing respectively particular sellers and particular buyers.

* * *

The EC's and E.C./E.U. courts' analyses of the various surrogates for vertical integration are in some respects superior to those of their U.S. counterparts. However, these European institutions still make at least the following ten significant errors when analyzing the legality of surrogates for vertical integration under E.C./E.U. competition law: (1) they assume that the Treaty is designed to protect intra-brand as well as inter-brand competition; (2) they accept the leverage-theory premise that a seller that has a competitive advantage when dealing for the patronage of a particular buyer can use that advantage to reduce or eliminate the cost it must incur to induce the buyer to accept burdensome terms of sale or other obligations; (3) they exaggerate the extent to which one can predict a firm's competitive advantages from its market share; (4) they assume that surrogates for vertical integration are more likely to reduce inter-brand competition when used by undertakings that have substantial competitive advantages and/or high market shares; (5) they overestimate the likelihood that various surrogates for vertical integration will reduce inter-brand competition; (6) they do not recognize many of the ways in which surrogates for vertical integration can increase economic efficiency and many of the non-efficiency-enhancing but also non-exclusionary functions that surrogates for vertical integration can perform; (7) because they do not understand the functions that non-exclusionary surrogates for vertical integration can perform, they often do not identify the kinds of conduct that an undertaking that uses a particular surrogate for vertical integration that is prohibited from doing so might substitute for the prohibited behavior in question or the likelihood that such an undertaking would substitute one or more of these functionally-equivalent kinds of conduct for the prohibited behavior; (8) because they do not predict accurately the relevant counterfactual(s), they exaggerate the likelihood that various surrogates for vertical integration will reduce intra-brand competition; and (9) because they do not appreciate the range and quantity of economic efficiencies that surrogates for vertical integration can generate, they underestimate the benefits that such efficiencies will confer on relevant consumers and therefore exaggerate the likelihood that such conduct would inflict a net equivalent-dollar loss on relevant consumers even if, contrary to fact, their estimates of the likelihood that or extent to which the conduct would reduce inter-brand and intra-brand competition were accurate.

4. The Functions and Possible Competitive Impact of Vertical Mergers and Acquisitions

Mergers and acquisitions are vertical when their participants are in a supplier-supplied relationship to each other. This section (A) delineates the various functions that vertical mergers and acquisitions can perform for their participants, (B) explains why such mergers and acquisitions can reduce competition in the Clayton Act sense (can have the effect of restricting, preventing, or distorting competition in the now-Article 101(1) terms) not only (1) when they violate the Sherman Act's test of illegality (have as a critical object restricting or preventing competition in now-Article 101 terms) and succeed but also (2) when they are not monopolizing in the Sherman Act sense (are not exclusionary in now-Article 102 terms), and (C) comments briefly on the "post-Chicago" economics literature that argues that in at least some circumstances vertical mergers and acquisitions will "reduce" or "fore-close" competition.

A. The Functions of Vertical Mergers and Acquisitions

It is useful to distinguish ten categories of functions that vertical mergers and acquisitions can perform. First, a vertical merger or acquisition can enable its upstream participant to increase its profits by controlling its downstream participant's conduct through hierarchical controls rather than through contractual clauses or sales policies.

Second, a vertical merger or acquisition can facilitate its participants' taking better advantage of continuous-flow economies.

Third, when one but not the other participant in a vertical merger or acquisition is subject to rate regulation, their vertical merger or acquisition can enable the regulated participant to conceal its rate-regulation violations more cost-effectively.

Fourth, a firm may execute a vertical merger with a second company to which it would find revealing information about its position or plans profitable if it were not for the risk that this second company would leak or sell the information to the firm's rivals to reduce the cost it would have to incur to prevent such leaks or sales.

Some elaboration of this last possibility is called for. In many situations, a firm will "need" to discuss its business plans with management consultants, lawyers, or financiers to secure business or legal advice or financing that would be profitable for it to obtain. In other situations, a firm might find it otherwise-profitable to reveal something or a lot about its business plans—*e.g.*, the particularities of the new products it expects to introduce in the future, the results of the market research it executed to determine the potential demand for the new products, how it intends to advertise the new products, and the quantities of the new products it intends to produce or the particularities of the market research it has done on the future demand for its old products and its planned advertising and outputs of its old products—(1) to input suppliers (to determine which input suppliers could best produce the needed quantity or at least a considerable quantity of the particular type of input the firm will use to produce its new and/or old products with acceptable degrees of quality control by revealing to them the products it intends to produce and its sales expectations) or (2) to distributors (to identify which distributors would be best-placed to distribute the firm's planned new and old products and persuade them to agree to distribute the firm's products). The information that the firm "needs" to supply to the business consultants, financers, lawyers, input suppliers, and distributors in question will be of value to the firm's actual and potential competitors, and its transmission to such competitors will reduce the firm's expected profits.

To some extent, a firm in this position will be able to rely on the following facts or legal options to keep the information they reveal to independent input suppliers or distributors from being conveyed to its rivals: (1) the relevant independents' ethical views, (2) Code of Ethics enforcement by relevant peak or professional associations (such as Bar Associations), (3) the combination of the value to the independents of preserving a reputation for not leaking or selling such information to rivals of the firms that supply them with it and their ability to control those of their own employees that receive this information, (4) contract law (when the firm has a contract with the independent in question—*e.g.*, with the lawyer or business consultant), (5) contract doctrines such as *culpa in contrahendo* (in civil-law countries) or (less likely) promissory estoppel (in common-law countries) that apply in cases in which the firm conveys the information to the independent in the course of dealings that are designed to yield contracts, (6) pre-contract contracts that focus specifically on the obligation to keep the relevant information secret, and (7) trade-secret law when the information in question qualifies as a trade secret and the firm has satisfied the other requirements for securing trade-secret-law protection. However, no individual protection of this kind and no combination of these protections is foolproof, and many that may be of some use are expensive to take advantage of.

Hence, in at least some situations, a firm will find that it can reduce the cost it must incur to prevent or allow such leaks by engaging in forward or backward vertical integration with one or more independents to which it would need to convey information it would not want to be revealed to its own rivals. Since such integration will perform this function only if hierarchical controls over employees (who may also be able to profit by selling such information to the firm's rivals for money or a better job) are a more-cost-effective way of dealing with this problem than any combination of the options that could be used to control independents, this fourth function is really just a subtype of the first function listed in this first category of functions. I have treated it separately and at length because it is sometimes ignored in the literature, the discussions of it that I have seen do not mention many of the factors or firm-actions that can deter independents from conveying the information in question to its provider's rivals, and (as we shall see) the EC Guidelines seem to take some note of this possible function of vertical integration.

The fifth category of functions of vertical mergers contains five direct functions that can also be performed by horizontal and conglomerate mergers and acquisitions and that do not in themselves relate to the merged (expanded) firm's engaging in oligopolistic or predatory conduct: creating a business organization with more buying power than either of its antecedents (when both antecedents purchase a given product or purchase different products supplied by one or more given suppliers); creating a business organization that can take better advantage of economies of scale in purchasing, financing, product and institutional advertising, and (when production and distribution have common operations) production and distribution; combining assets that are complementary for non-scale reasons (*e.g.*, when [1] one of the companies has "excess" research managers and the other has "excess" operational managers, [2] one of the companies has excess production managers and too few distribution managers and the other, excess distribution managers and not enough production managers, or [3] one company has substantial retained earnings but no attractive investment ideas and little ability to generate such ideas and the other company has lots of good investment ideas but no retained earnings and limited ability to obtain external financing for its ideas from other sources); for either scale or non-scale reasons, creating a company that can more-cost-effectively estimate its OCAs; for either scale or non-scale reasons, creating a company that can more-cost-effectively prevent arbitrage and, perhaps, for this reason, can profit more by engaging in conventional price discrimination, perfect price discrimination, or mixed lump-sum *plus* supra-TSM-marginal-cost per-unit pricing; creating a company that can take better tax advantage of the losses that one of the participants had realized; and enabling the owner of one of the participants to profit (perhaps profit more) by liquidating his or her assets and escaping managerial responsibilities.

The sixth category of functions that vertical mergers can perform contains those that relate to the practice of contrived oligopolistic pricing and are independent of any of the previously-listed types of economic efficiencies such conduct can generate, any increase in buying power it can yield, or any effect it has on the amount of predation the relevant actors practice. Specifically, in at least six ways, a vertical merger or acquisition will create a business organization that will find contrived oligopolistic pricing more profitable than one or both of its antecedents did: when one of the antecedents had a stronger reputation for contrivance or estimating its HNOPs accurately (which are relevant both because such reputations enable their possessor to communicate its contrived oligopolistic intentions simply by charging a contrived oligopolistic price and because, more generally, they make the firm's threats of retaliation and promises of reciprocation more credible by increasing its rivals' perception of the profitability of contrivance to the firm) than the other antecedent did, by creating a business organization that inherits the reputation of the antecedent with the stronger relevant reputation; by creating a business organization that can take better advantage of company-wide economies of scale in building and maintaining a reputation for contrivance or estimating HNOPs accurately; and when one of the antecedents has personnel that are more skilled in contrivance or estimating their employer's HNOP than any employee of the other antecedent is, by putting the post-merger/acquisition firm in a position to profit by using some of the personnel of the former antecedent to participate in the running of the other antecedent's business or using relevant personnel of the former antecedent to train up the personnel of the other antecedent. In addition, a vertical merger can also enable its participant to secure higher contrived oligopolistic margins by removing as an independent force a buyer that has the power and persistence to induce not only the upstream integrator but its upstream rivals to grant it discounts in violation of an upstream price-fixing scheme; when the economic efficiencies and increases in buying power that the merger or acquisition yields increase the frequency with which, relative to its antecedents, the business organization it creates is uniquely second-placed to obtain the patronage of buyers that a possible undercutter/underminer is best-placed to supply and the frequency with which it is only modestly worse-than-second-placed to supply such buyers, by decreasing on that account the cost it would have to incur to inflict any given amount of harm on such a rival through retaliatory pricing; and when the economic efficiencies and increases in buying power that the merger or acquisition yields increase the frequency with which, relative to its antecedents, the business organization it creates is uniquely second-placed to obtain the patronage of buyers a possible undercutter or underminer is best-placed to supply and/or the average amount by which, relative to its antecedents, it is better-placed than the third-placed supplier of those buyers when it is second-placed, by increasing the amount of benefits that it, relative to its antecedents, can confer on such rivals in exchange for their collaboration. (I should add before proceeding that, although a vertical merger can increase the profits the business organization it creates earns by practicing contrived oligopolistic pricing above the profits its antecedents realized by practicing oligopolistic pricing in all these ways, such mergers and acquisitions will also tend to reduce those profits by spreading the defenses of the perpetrators, generating economic efficiencies and buyer-power increases that raise the safe profits that, relative to its antecedents, the business organization it creates must put at risk to attempt to contrive any oligopolistic margin, and quite possibly reducing the frequency with which [relative to its antecedents] the business organization the merger or acquisition creates is second-placed or close-to-second-placed to supply relevant potential undercutters'/underminers' customers and the average amount by which, when it is second-placed, it is better-placed than the third-placed supplier of those buyers. I have no idea whether, across all cases, these last two outcomes are more or less likely than their opposites delineated at the end of the sentence immediately preceding this parenthetical.)

The seventh category of functions that vertical mergers can perform contains one that relates to the practice of natural oligopolistic pricing but is independent of any previously-listed economic efficiencies, increases in buying power, or predation that vertical mergers can generate: a vertical merger in an area of product-space in which across-the-board pricing is practiced can enable the business organization it creates to obtain more NOMs than its antecedents did on both levels by enabling the resulting organization to take better advantage than its antecedents could of economies of scale in changing advertised prices, prices on shelves, and (least importantly) prices in checkout-counter-computer price-lists (the last two listed effects will be possible only when the two firms involved are respectively a wholesaler and a retailer).

The eighth category of functions relates to the practice of predation. Vertical mergers can create a business organization that can profit more from and on that account may be inclined to practice more predation than its antecedents did by putting the resulting organization in a position to employ predatory price squeezes to drive out a downstream rival (to threaten predatory price squeezes to deter a rival QV investment in the downstream area of product space); by putting the resulting organization in a position to drive out either a downstream or an upstream rival (to deter a rival downstream or upstream QV investment) by refusing to deal predatorily (threatening to refuse to deal predatorily); by rendering predatory advertising, predatory QV investments (*e.g.*, fighting outlets), and predatory cost-reducing investments more profitable by creating a business organization that can take better advantage of real economies of scale in advertising, has more bargaining power as an advertiser, or faces a lower barrier to making the relevant predatory QV or cost-reducing investment than its antecedents did; by creating a business organization that can take better advantage than its antecedents would of company-wide economies of scale in building and maintaining a reputation for predation; and by creating a business organization whose threats of predation are more credible than those of one or both of its antecedents because the resulting company inherits the reputation for predation of the antecedent with the stronger reputation for predation and/or because, for the reasons stated earlier in this list, predation will be more profitable for the resulting company than for either of its predecessors.

I want to make four points that relate to the preceding list of reasons why vertical mergers can render predation more profitable for the resulting company than for its antecedents. First, I do not think that many of the items in this list are empirically significant. Thus, as Sects. 2 and 9 of Chap. 11 respectively indicated, I suspect that vertically-integrated firms rarely execute predatory price squeezes and rarely refuse to deal predatorily. Second, and somewhat relatedly, the fact that something makes predation profitable or more profitable for a business actor or for a newly-created organization than for its antecedents does not imply that more predation will be practiced: predation is illegal and immoral, and, on one or both of these accounts, many business organization will refuse to engage in it even if it would be profitable. Third, even if one knew that a vertical merger would create a business organization that engaged in more predation than did its antecedents, that fact might not affect the legality of the merger (as opposed to the predation) under either a specific-anticompetitive-intent (critical-object) or a Clayton-Act-type lessening-competition test of illegality: (1) it would not critically affect the legality of the merger under a specific-anticompetitive-intent test unless the participants' pre-merger conclusion that the merger would be profitable was critically affected by their belief that it would or might enable them to profit by engaging in additional predation (in which case it would not matter whether as a matter of law it would be incorrect to conclude that the relevant legislation/treaty was a "fence law," which could be properly applied to prevent subsequent, independent illegal acts) and (2) it would not critically affect the legality of the merger under a Clayton-Act-type lessening-competition test unless the prospect of the additional predation (or the reality of its practice) critically affected the merger's predicted or actual relevant effect on relevant buyers—*i.e.*, whether the merger should be expected to or did impose a net equivalent-monetary loss on relevant buyers by reducing the absolute attractiveness of the best offer they respectively received from any inferior supplier (assuming that as a matter of law it would be incorrect to conclude that the relevant legislation/treaty was a "fence law," which could be properly applied to prevent subsequent, independent illegal acts). Fourth, the preceding discussion of the impact of vertical mergers on predation (correctly) omitted a non-predatory possibility with consequences that may be similar to those of predation. In almost all cases, it will be most profitable for a vertically-integrated firm to instruct the managers of its downstream operation to determine the profitability of his or her decision-options on the assumption that the private marginal/incremental cost to his or her "division" of the company of any amount of any final good or input it obtains from the company's upstream division equals the private marginal or incremental cost to the upstream division of supplying the downstream division with the relevant amount of the final good or input in question. By way of contrast, for reasons I articulated when analyzing the most-inherently-profitable pricing-technique for a firm to use, in the vast majority of situations, the most-inherently-profitable way for a vertically-integrated firm to price its upstream product to an independent buyer will not be to charge that buyer a per-unit price equal to the supplier's marginal cost or a price for two or more units of its product equal to their incremental cost to it (even though the supplier can combine such per-unit or incremental-purchase "variable" prices with a lump-sum fee). In virtually all situations in which (1) an independent final-product producer coexists with one or more vertically-integrated firms that produce both the final product and an input used to produce the final product, (2) an independent distributor coexists with one or more vertically-integrated firms that both produce and distribute the final product in question, and (3) an independent retailer of a product coexists with one or more vertically-integrated wholesaler-retailers of that product, the combination of the shadow pricing of the vertically-integrated firm and its actual pricing to independents (A) will distort competition by placing the downstream independent at a competitive disadvantage vis-à-vis the downstream division of the integrated company that does not reflect the downstream independent's being less economically efficient than the downstream division of the integrated firm and (B) (here comes the predation-"analogy") could reduce competition in the downstream "market" by inducing the exit of the one or more disadvantaged downstream independents that would not be replaced by equally-effective competitors and/or by critically raising the barriers to downstream entry/expansion facing an otherwise-effective potential entrant into or potential (QV-investment) expander in the downstream "market." Producing this outcome would be a "function" of the vertical merger in question if the perpetrators understood *ex ante* that this outcome would or might result (since it would be positively valued by them) even when their recognition and positive valuation of it did not render the vertical merger in question predatory (Sherman-Act-violative or violative of the object-branch of now-Article 101 on its "critical-object" interpretation) because the perpetrators' *ex ante* perception of the profitability of their merger did not critically depend on their *ex ante* perception that it would or might reduce the competition they faced in this way.

The ninth category of functions of vertical mergers is related to the effect discussed at the end of the preceding paragraph in that the effect in question (a reduction in the competition faced by the merged firm relative to the competition faced by its antecedents) is the same as the effect of the function discussed at the end of the preceding paragraph and that, as in the case of that function, that effect is generated by other consequences of vertical mergers whose generation is not in itself legally problematic. More specifically, to the extent that the purchasing, production and distribution, QV-investment-related, PPR-related, plant-modernization-related economic efficiencies (as well as any increases in buying power) the vertical merger generates reduce the marginal cost of the merged firm below those of its antecedents or enable the merged firm to produce one or more different products whose competitive-position arrays are superior to those of the products of the antecedents for which it substitutes them, the vertical merger may reduce the competition its participants face by driving out one or more rivals that are not replaced by equally-effective competitors by worsening the exiting rivals' competitive-position arrays or by deterring an entry or rival QV-investment expansion by critically raising the barriers to entry or expansion an otherwise-effect potential QV investor faced by critically worsening its prospective competitive-position array. The fact that a vertical merger performs this last function will not render it illegal under the Sherman Act's specific-anticompetitive-intent test of illegality (or now-Article 101's critical-object test of *prima facie* illegality) unless the possibility that the merger might reduce competition in this way critically affected the merger partners' *ex ante* perception that it would be profitable. Moreover, with one exception, the fact that a vertical merger should be predicted to or actually has performed this last function (1) will not cause it to violate the Clayton Act if it is correct as a matter of law to read the organizational-economic-efficiency defense I have described into the Clayton Act and (2) will cause it to violate now-Article 101 even if it does cause it to generate the effect of injuring relevant buyers by restricting or preventing competition only if, all things considered, the relevant consumers do not obtain a fair share of the benefits the merger confers on them and the merger partners combined, given that any "competition-reducing" economic efficiencies the merger generates will satisfy now-Article 101(3)'s economic-efficiency requirements. The exception to which the expression that introduced the preceding sentence refers relates to vertical mergers that lessen competition in the way on which we are now focusing by increasing the buying power of the merged firm relative to that of its antecedents (for reasons unrelated to any purchasing economic efficiencies it generates): when such private advantages play a critical role, the merger partners will not be able to establish either a Clayton Act organizational-economic-efficiency defense or their entitlement to a now-Article 101(3) exemption from now-Article 101(1).

The tenth and final category of functions that vertical mergers can perform resembles the eighth in that it also results from effects of a vertical merger that are not themselves legally problematic. To the extent that a vertical merger increases the merged firm's BCAs by generating economic efficiencies or creating a merged firm that has more buying power than its antecedents had, it will tend to enable the merged firm to obtain OMs naturally from buyers from which its antecedents could not do so by increasing the merged firm's OCAs above its antecedents' OCAs both directly by raising its BCAs and indirectly by increasing the CMC the merged firm would have to incur to steal a remaining rival's customers above those a relevant antecedent would have had to incur to do so, thereby increasing those rivals' OCAs, thereby increasing the merged firm's OCAs by raising the CMC its relevant rivals would have to incur to charge the merged firm's customers a price that would result in its matching the merged firm's HNOP. (I should add that this effect will tend to make contrived oligopolistic pricing less profitable for the merged firm than for its antecedents by increasing the amount of safe profits the merged firm must put at risk to attempt to contrive an oligopolistic price above the amount its antecedents would have to put at risk to do so.)

B. The Possible Ways in Which an Individual Vertical Merger or a Rule Permitting the Individual Members of a Set of Product-Rivals to Execute Vertical Mergers Can Lessen Competition in the Clayton Act Sense

I will first list two sets of ways in which an individual vertical merger can reduce competition: (1) ways that reflect its performing one of the functions listed in the preceding section and (2) ways that do not relate to effects of such conduct that its perpetrators positively value. I will then analyze the conditions under which a rule permitting the members of some set of product rivals to execute vertical mergers will decrease competition. An individual vertical merger will lessen competition in the Clayton Act sense by performing one or more of the functions of vertical mergers just listed when it (1) increases the COMs the merged firm obtains relative to those its antecedents secured, (2) increases the NOMs the merged firm obtains relative to those its antecedents secured, (3) increases the amount of successful predation the merged firm practices relative to the amount that its antecedents practiced, (4) lessens competition by making it inherently profitable for the merged firm to charge downstream independents higher per-unit prices than the shadow prices on which the managers of its downstream operations base their decisions, and (5) lessens competition by causing a rival of the merged firm to exit or deterring a rival QV investment by generating economic efficiencies or increases in buying power that improve the merged firm's competitive-position array relative to the combined array of its antecedents and concomitantly critically worsen the competitive-position array of an established rival that will not be immediately replaced by an equally-effective competitor or the prospective competitive-position arrays of one or more otherwise-effective potential competitors. An individual vertical merger can also lessen competition in the Clayton Act sense in the following ways that are unrelated to any function that the merger performs because the merger-effect that lessens competition is not positively valued by the merger partners: (1) increasing the COMs that the merged firm's rivals can obtain by causing the merged firm to be more reluctant to undercut its rivals' contrived oligopolistic prices than its antecedents were by making the merged firm more vulnerable to retaliation than its antecedents were by increasing the merged firm's OCAs above its antecedents' and, when the rival in question is vertically integrated and operates at both the levels at which the merged firm operates, by spreading the merged firm's defenses (by enabling the merged-firm rival to retaliate against the merged firm at both levels) and enabling the rival to take advantage of any excess reciprocatory power it has at one level to reward the merged firm's cooperation at the other level and (2) creating a merged firm that is not an effective potential QV investor when one of the merger partners was or would have become an effective potential QV investor by making it profitable for the merged firm to devote to consolidation resources the antecedent would have used to create an additional QV investment and, when the merged firm faces a similarly-vertically-integrated rival, by increasing the retaliation barriers to QV investment the merged firm faces above those that confronted or would confront the relevant antecedent. (Of course, if the merger generates static efficiencies that will carry over to any QV-investment expansion it executes or specifically-dynamic efficiencies, it will increase Clayton Act competition on those accounts when the economic efficiencies in question reduce the barriers to expansion the merged firm faces critically below those that did or would face its relevant antecedent and the merged firm is an effective potential QV investor.)

I turn finally to the conditions under which a rule permitting the individual members of a set of product-rivals to execute vertical mergers (or acquisitions) will lessen competition in the Clayton Act sense. First and obviously, such a rule will lessen competition when the individual mergers it permits to be executed would lessen competition all things considered because they would reduce competition in one or more of the ways just listed. Second and somewhat overlappingly, such a rule will also lessen competition when the following conditions are fulfilled: (1) the rule permitting the individual members of a set of product-rivals to execute vertical mergers decreases the profits that one or more marginal established firms can realize by continuing to operate and/or the profits that one or more otherwise-effective potential QV investors will anticipate realizing on the most-profitable QV investment they can make and (2) the decrease in the profits that one or more marginal established firms can realize causes one or more of them to exit in circumstances in which they will not be immediately replaced by an equally-effective competitor and/ or the decrease in the profits that one or more otherwise-effective potential QV investors would realize on their perspective QV investments constitutes a critical increase in the barriers to QV investment they face.

I need to elaborate on the circumstances in which the rule now under consideration will decrease the actual profits of marginal competitors and the profits that otherwise-effective potential QV investors would realize on their planned investments. To facilitate the exposition, I will assume that the relevant vertical merger or acquisition is a vertical merger between a producer and a retailer and focus on the effect of the rule under consideration on marginal established firms in and potential QV investors in the production business. I will discuss two situations in which the rule under consideration will reduce the actual profits of marginal competitors and potential QV investors. In the first situation, all producers and retailers are originally not vertically integrated, all find it individually profitable to execute a vertical merger, and the vertical merger that each individual well-established firm can execute improves its competitive-position array by more than the amount by which the vertical merger that (each marginal established firm)/(each potential QV investor) can execute will improve its actual/prospective competitive-position array. In the second situation, all producers and retailers are originally not vertically integrated, the well-established producers find it profitable to execute vertical mergers with retailers that will improve the resulting company's competitive-portion arrays but marginal established producers and potential entrants that would be effective if vertical mergers were prohibited do not find vertical mergers profitable. In this section situation, the rule allowing all the firms in question to execute vertical mergers and the ensuing well-established firms' vertical mergers will worsen the competitive-position arrays of marginal established firms and potential QV investors both directly and possibly indirectly by preventing the non-integrators from selling through the retailers that have participated in the vertical mergers in question. The vertical mergers in question will produce this second indirect effect if two complex conditions are fulfilled: (1)(A) the quantity of retail capacity that the vertical mergers left non-integrated is lower than the quantity of such capacity required by non-integrating producers (because the integrating producers merged with [acquired] firms whose retail capacity exceeded the integrating producers' pre-merger sales) or (B) the vertical mergers eliminated as independents retailers that were best-placed to distribute at least some of the units of the non-integrating producers' products when pre-merger the integrating retailers shared at least some of the associated profits with the non-integrating producers and (2) the integrated firms in question either refused to resell the relevant non-integrated producers' products at all or agreed to resell them only on terms that were less profitable to the non-integrated producer than the terms the integrating retailers in question offered the non-integrating producers pre-merger either (A) because the integrated firms decided to refuse to deal or offer less-attractive terms predatorily or (B) because the merger rendered the refusals to deal or less-attractive offers in question inherently profitable by reducing the shadow price of the products that the integrated firm's production division supplied its retail division (the productions division's marginal cost) below the per-unit price the integrating producers offered the integrating retailers pre-merger and (3) applicable

S and (Π_D + R) barriers will prevent one or more truly-independent entries (see below) into retail, internal growth into retail by the relevant marginal established firms, independent entry into the retail business by the relevant potential entrants into the product-production business, joint-venture entry into the retail business by the relevant potential entrant into or marginal established firm in the production business, or efforts by the marginal established firms or potential entrants in question to induce not-quite-independent entries into the retail business by supplying potential entrants into that business with information, financial subsidies, long-term supply contracts, and/or exclusive dealerships from eliminating the losses that the rule under investigation and the well-established-firm vertical mergers it spawns from imposing actual/prospective equivalent-dollar losses on (marginal established producers)/(potential QV investors) in the production business in the second, indirect way that is now under consideration.

I should not close this discussion without making the following two points. First, because I believe that (1) vertical mergers are usually more profitable for the marginal established firms in and the potential entrants into any area of product space than for its well-established firms and (2) even when the rule in question does disadvantage marginal established firms and potential entrants, it will often not critically affect the exit decision of any marginal established firm that would not be replaced by an otherwise-effective competitor or the willingness of an effective potential entrant to make a QV investment if the established firms do not make limit QV investments, my judgment is that a rule allowing the independent members of any set of product rivals to execute vertical mergers will rarely reduce competition: this argument is perfectly analogous to the counterpart arguments I made when analyzing various surrogates for vertical integration. Second, as I indicated when analyzing the same possibility as it related to those surrogates for vertical integration, to the extent that the rule in question would disadvantage marginal and potential competitors because the vertical mergers it permitted well-established firms to execute would increase their organizational economic efficiency by more than the vertical merger it permitted marginal and potential competitors to execute would increase these latter two categories of firms' organizational economic efficiency, the perpetrators of the vertical mergers in question should be able to make out an organizational-economic-efficiency defense in any Clayton Act case and satisfy at least the increasing-economic-efficiency requirement for obtaining a now-Article 101(3) exemption in any now-Article 101 case.

C. A Brief Critique of the "Post-Chicago-School" Analysis of Vertical Mergers and Acquisitions

The Chicago school of economics has made substantial contributions to the economic analysis of vertical integration and what I call its various surrogates. Among other things, Chicago-school economists (1) pointed out that the traditional leverage theory of tie-ins was based on the indefensible assumption that firms with market power could have their cake and eat it too, (2) explained a large number of the legitimate functions that tie-ins, resale price maintenance, and vertical territorial restraints and vertical customer-allocation clauses can perform, and (3) revealed many of the problems with the traditional claims that single-brand exclusive dealerships, long-term full-requirements or total-output-supply contracts, and vertical mergers will reduce competition by "foreclosing competitors" in a wide variety of circumstances. Although my analysis of vertical integration and its surrogates recognizes some possibilities the Chicagoans overlook, adds some refinements to their analyses of possibilities they do consider, and concludes that such conduct is more likely to manifest specific anticompetitive intent than they acknowledge, I have learned and borrowed a great deal from their analyses of such conduct.

Over the last 30 years or so, several sophisticated economists have called into question a number of the basic conclusions that the Chicagoans reached about the functions, consequences, and legality under U.S. antitrust law of vertical integration and its various surrogates. This section will briefly summarize some of these post-Chicago revisionist economic and legal claims and explain why I find the arguments that underlie them largely unpersuasive.

I will begin with some general observations about three assumptions that those revisionists (all of whom are American and are focusing on U.S. law or policy) have taken over from the Chicagoans that they are criticizing. First, the revisionists do not distinguish policy analysis from legal analysis (perhaps more accurately and certainly more charitably, implicitly assume that U.S. antitrust law authorizes the courts to "regulate" the conduct they cover in the public interest). I do not think that U.S. (or E.C./E.U.) antitrust law authorizes antitrust-law-enforcement authorities to regulate the conduct the law covers in the public interest: in my view, U.S. antitrust law (and E.C./E.U. competition law) promulgate cognizable tests of illegality that do not make the legality of the conduct they cover depend on whether either that conduct or its prohibition serves the public interest (however that concept might be operationalized).

Second, the revisionists assume (1) that the U.S. antitrust laws promulgate either a decrease-in-relevant-buyer-equivalent-dollar-welfare or a decrease-in-economic-efficiency test of illegality or (2) that it would be most desirable as a matter of policy to regulate vertical integration through merger or acquisition (and the various surrogates for vertical integration) in the way that would generate the greatest possible increase in either the relevant buyers' equivalent-dollar welfare or economic efficiency. I do think that the Sherman Act, the Clayton Act, or the Federal Trade Commission Act promulgates either a decrease-in-relevant-buyer-equivalent-dollar-welfare or a decrease-in-economic-efficiency test of illegality. Moreover, unlike some of the revisionists (and some of the Chicagoans), I recognize that a decrease-in-relevant-buyer-equivalent-dollar-welfare test of illegality would yield very different conclusions from those that would be yielded by either a conduct-focused decrease-in-economic-efficiency test of illegality or a prohibition-focused increase-in-economic-efficiency test of illegality.

Third, the revisionists' analysis of the economic efficiency of vertical mergers—*e.g.*, of vertical mergers that have particular effects on the proportions in which particular inputs are used, on the output of some final product, and on the transaction costs the participating firms generate—assumes that it is appropriate to ignore The General Theory of Second Best. Thus, the revisionists assume theoretically unjustifiably and almost certainly empirically inaccurately that the mix of inputs that a vertically-integrated firm would find most profitable to employ is the most-economically-efficient input-mix for it to employ, that any decrease/increase in final-good output a vertical merger generates will be associated with a decrease/increase in economic efficiency, and that any private-transaction-cost reduction a vertical merger enables its participants to secure will equal its allocative counterpart.

As previously indicated, the Chicagoans attacked both the leverage theory of tie-ins and (more relevantly in this section) the foreclosure theory of vertical mergers and acquisition. The attempt to revivify the leverage theory of tie-ins focused on the mathematical fact that firms with competitive advantages could give their customers a non-infinitesimal benefit at no cost to themselves by reducing their price below its profit-maximizing level if they could make an infinitesimal reduction in their product's price. Unlike the revisionists, I do not think that this fact can provide a foundation for a leverage theory of tie-ins because, in the real world, firms cannot make an *infinitesimal* reduction in their product's price.

Recent attempts to revivify the foreclosure theory of vertical mergers (and by implication of long-term full-requirements or total-supply contracts) use various models to demonstrate that on certain assumptions vertical mergers in imperfectly-competitive "markets" (the scholars in question usually describe the "markets" in question as "concentrated") can reduce competition (they usually say, reduce output) by foreclosing established or potential competitors from dealing with the previously-independent downstream distributors or upstream suppliers with which they would otherwise have dealt. The literature in question does not pay appropriate attention to why the downstream or upstream "division" of the integrated company would not deal with the allegedly-foreclosed non-integrated concern: whether the predicted refusal to deal (or worsening of offers made) would be (1) predatory (in which case it would be illegal in itself—a fact that would warrant the conclusion that the vertical merger in question did not itself violate the Clayton Act[1397] if any subsequent predatory refusal to deal were detectable and provable) or (2) inherently profitable (rendered inherently profitable by the difference between the upstream-marginal-cost shadow price on which the downstream member of an integrated concern would base its decisions and the supra-upstream-marginal-cost per-unit price the downstream member of the integrated firm would have had to pay as a non-integrated downstream firm to the upstream non-integrated firm that participated in the merger). As Sects. 4A and B of this chapter indicated, I do not deny that participants

[1397] If the perpetrators' *ex ante* belief that the merger would or might permit them to refuse to deal predatorily critically affected their *ex ante* perception that the merger was profitable, that fact would render this merger illegal under the Sherman Act.

in vertical mergers can sometimes be critically motivated by a desire to foreclose competition or that individual vertical mergers or, *a fortiori*, all such mergers that would be executed in a relevant area of product-space if the law permitted its sellers to execute them might not reduce competition by foreclosing one or more established or potential competitors. However, I do not think that such motivations operate or effects occur nearly so often as the revisionists conclude or imply. I reject the revisionists' conclusions because (1) I reject their unexplained assumption that upstream firms that did not engage in contrivance prior to their vertical mergers would engage in contrivance after their mergers,[1398] (2) I reject their assumption that both the businesses that are executing vertical mergers and their rivals behave in the way that Cournot models assume they do,[1399] and (3) the models they use ignore the various ways in which vertical mergers can increase "competition" in the sense in which these scholars think the intensity of competition should be defined in the relevant legal and policy context.[1400]

Although, for reasons that will become obvious I hesitate to do so, I want to delineate and criticize one argument I have heard non-Chicago economists make on several occasions for the possible tendency of vertical mergers or acquisitions to lessen competition. The most simple variant of this argument begins by positing an initial situation in which there are two identical non-vertically-integrated producers and two identical non-vertically-integrated distributors (or input suppliers). The analyst then assumes that one of the producers in question acquires or merges with one of the independent distributors or input suppliers in question. The analyst next argues that the producer that integrates first will be able to obtain an advantage over its competitor by doing so because the producer that integrates first can secure a better deal from the firm it acquires or merges with because the first producer to integrate can play the independents with which it could combine off against each other whereas the other producer does not have this option. Even if one ignores (as perhaps one should) the possibilities that the second producer may be able to overcome any related disadvantage by integrating forward or backward through internal growth or inducing an independent entry, the fact is that in this scenario

---

[1398] This criticism was first made in David Reiffen and Michael Vita, *Comment: Is There New Thinking on Vertical Mergers* (hereinafter Reiffen and Vita), 63 ANTITRUST L.J. 917, 927 (1995). *Inter alia*, Reiffen and Vita discuss the following revisionist articles: Michael H. Riordan & Steven C. Salop, *Evaluating Vertical Mergers: A Post-Chicago Approach*, 63 ANTITRUST L.J. 513 (1995) and Janusz A. Ordover, Garth Saloner, & Steven C. Salop, *Equilibrium Vertical Foreclosure*, 80 AM. ECON. REV. 128 (1990). See also Thomas Krattenmaker & Steven Salop, *Anticompetitive Exclusion: Raising Rivals' Costs to Achieve Power Over Price*, 96 YALE L.J. (1986), Michael Winston, *Tying, Foreclosure and Exclusion*, 80 AMER. ECON. REV. 837 (1990), and Steve Salop, *Vertical Mergers and Monopoly Leverage* in 3 NEW PALGRAVE DICTIONARY OF ECONOMICS AND THE LAW 669 (P. Newman, ed., 1998). For two excellent articles critiquing *inter alia* the post-Chicago analysis of vertical integration, see Timothy J. Brennan, "*Vertical Market Power*" *as Oxymoron: Horizontal Approaches to Vertical Antitrust*, 12 GEO. MASON L. REV. 895 (2004) and *Understanding "raising rivals' costs,"* 33 ANTITRUST BULL. 95 (1988).

[1399] See note 31 *supra*.

[1400] See Reiffen and Vita at 929–30.

there is no reason to believe that the second integrator will be less-well-placed to strike a good deal than the first integrator was. Although the second integrator will not be able to play the two potential acquirees or merger partners off against each other, it will be able to take advantage of the fact that, unlike the first integrator, it is the only potential purchaser or merger partner available to the second distributor or input supplier. There is simply no reason why the second producer should be expected to secure worse terms than the first producer in this scenario. If the obviousness of this critique calls into question my claim to have heard several economists make the criticized argument, I sympathize with the skepticism of those who doubt the claim. But the fact is that I have heard this double-duopoly argument or a more complicated but essentially-identical variant of this argument made by several economists who ought to have known better.

I should add that the revisionists do accept two unit-output/economic-efficiency arguments that Chicagoans made in favor of the desirability and legality of vertical mergers (without distinguishing them). Unfortunately, each of these arguments has two important deficiencies that the revisionists have not recognized. The first Chicago argument in question focuses on situations in which a producer with competitive advantages originally distributed its product through a retailer with competitive advantages. On the assumption that both the producer and the retailer would engage in what I call single pricing, the Chicagoans explain that a vertical merger between these successive "monopolists" would lead to a reduction in the retail price of the good in question and an increase in the output of that good and then assert that the relevant increase in output is economically efficient. On the Chicagoans' single-pricing assumption, their price/output conclusions would be correct: since the shadow price on which the retail division of the vertically-integrated firm would base its pricing and output decisions (the marginal cost the firm's production division would have to incur to produce the good and deliver it to its retail division) would be lower than the most-profitable single price the non-integrated producer could charge the non-integrated retailer, the vertical merger would on the single-pricing assumption reduce the integrated retail division's marginal costs below the non-integrated retailer's marginal costs and therefore would reduce the integrated retailer's profit-maximizing resale price below its counterpart for the non-integrated retailer and increase the integrated retailer's profit-maximizing output above its counterpart for the non-integrated retailer, *ceteris paribus*. However, why should one assume that the non-integrated producer would find it most profitable to engage in single pricing? If the non-integrated producer found it most profitable to practice perfect price discrimination—say, by charging its independent retailers a lump-sum (franchise) fee for the right to purchase the product in question at the producer's TSM marginal cost, the vertical mergers between the producer and its distributors would not affect the retail price or quantity sold of the product in question. I admit that in almost all cases producers will find it most profitable to charge their independent retailers a per-unit price that exceeds their TSM marginal cost and to reduce their lump-sum fees accordingly. However, I suspect that most producers charge their independent distributors some lump-sum fee and a per-unit price that is lower than the most-profitable single price they could charge. If I am right, the Chicago argument exaggerates the extent to which vertical mergers will reduce price and increase quantity in "successive-monopoly" situations. In any event, the Chicago claim that any price-reduction and quantity-increases that vertical mergers generate on this account will be economically efficient is based on an implicit first-best argument—*i.e.*, ignores The General Theory of Second Best. Any such argument is indefensible. I acknowledge that, for the reasons that THE WELFARE ECONOMICS OF ANTITRUST POLICY AND U.S. AND E.U. ANTITRUST LAW will explore, any increase in unit output that vertical mergers generate in this way probably will be economically efficient, not as the Chicagoans think because the increase in output the vertical merger generates will prevent the final good in question from being underproduced relative to other goods in production to the extent that it otherwise would be but because the relevant increase in output will reduce the amount of economic inefficiency the economy generates by misallocating resources among unit-output-increasing, QV-investment-creating, and PPR-executing and plant-modernizing uses. However, the probable correctness of this Chicago economic-efficiency conclusion does not affect the woeful inadequacy of the Chicagoans' "argument" for this conclusion. In any event, the successive-monopoly Chicago argument in question has two deficiencies: (1) its micro-economic analysis is based on a false assumption about the way in which the producer in question would price its product to an independent retailer and (2) its economic-efficiency analysis ignores The General Theory of Second Best.

The second Chicago pro-vertical-merger argument I want to discuss has the same two weaknesses. The relevant argument focuses on situations in which the producer involved in the vertical merger produces an input against which substitution is possible. In such variable-proportion situations, it is argued,[1401] the vertical merger will prevent the downstream producer from making the substitutions against the upstream producer's input that it would otherwise be induced to make by the supra-marginal-cost price the input producer would charge the final-product producer for its input if the two companies were independent—substitutions that the Chicagoans claim would both reduce the joint profits of the input producer and final-product producer in question and decrease economic efficiency. The arguments that the Chicagoans explicitly made or implicitly relied on for those conclusions have the same two deficiencies that their successive-monopoly argument had. The micro-economic argument that the vertical mergers would prevent jointly-unprofitable substitutions against the input producer's input assumed unrealistically that the non-integrated input producer would sell their input separately and charge the non-integrated final-product producer single prices. In practice, I suspect, non-

[1401] See, *e.g.*, Masahiro Abiru, *Vertical Integration, Variable Proportions, and Successive Oligopolies*, 36 J. INDUS. ECON. 315 (1988); Parthasaradhi Mallela & Babu Nahata, *Theory of Vertical Control With Variable Proportions*, 36 J. POL. ECON. 1009 (1980); Michael Waterson, *Vertical Integration, Variable Proportions, and Oligopoly*, 92 ECON. J. 129 (1982); Frederick R. Warren-Boulton, *Vertical Control With Variable Proportions*, 82 J. POL. ECON. 783 (1974); and John Vernon & Daniel Graham, *Profitability of Monopolization by Vertical Integration*, 79 J. POL. ECON. 924 (1971).

integrated producers of inputs against which substitution is possible will (1) combine lump-sum fees with per-unit prices that equal their TSM marginal costs (in which case no jointly-unprofitable substitutions will be made), (2) combine smaller lump-sum fees with supra-marginal-cost per-unit prices that are below the most-profitable single price they could charge (in which case fewer jointly-unprofitable substitutions will be made than the Chicagoans suggest), (3) use agreements that tie the sale of their input to the buyer's agreeing to purchase from the producer their full requirements of the input that can be substituted for the tying seller's input or another input against which substitution is not possible for prices appropriately above their normal market price to prevent all jointly-unprofitable substitutions, (4) require the final-product producer to pay it an endproduct royalty for the right to purchase its full requirements of the input producer's input for a price equal to the input producer's TSM marginal cost (in which case no jointly-unprofitable substitutions will be made), or (5) require the final-product producer to agree to supply it with the final-product producer's total output of the final product for less than the price for which the final-product producer would otherwise sell that good in exchange for the right to purchase its full requirements of the input producer's input for a price equal to the input producer's TSM marginal cost (in which case no jointly-unprofitable substitutions will be made). Thus, if, instead of single pricing its input in a single-product transaction, the input producer uses technique (1), (3), (4), or (5) in the preceding list to price its input, the vertical merger will not prevent any jointly-unprofitable input substitutions because no such substitutions would be made in its absence. And if, instead of single pricing its input in a single-product transaction, the input producer uses technique (2) in the preceding list to price its product, the vertical merger will prevent far fewer jointly-unprofitable input substitutions than the Chicagoans claim because far fewer such substitutions would have been made in the absence of the vertical merger. In short, like the Chicagoans' analysis of the micro-economic effects of vertical mergers in successive-monopoly situations, their analysis of the micro-economic effects of vertical mergers in substitutable-input situations is severely compromised by their failure to identify accurately the relevant counterfactual—*i.e.*, the pricing-technique that the relevant producer would use to sell its product to the buyer in question if the two were independent.

The Chicagoan analysis of the substitutable-input situation goes on to assert that any jointly-unprofitable input-substitution that a vertical merger prevents would have been economically inefficient. Although they make no argument for their concomitant conclusion that vertical mergers that prevent jointly-unprofitable input-substitutions will increase economic efficiency on this account, I have no doubt that the argument they would make for this conclusion would be a first-best argument—*i.e.*, would ignore the possibility, on which Second-Best Theory focuses, that jointly-unprofitable input-substitutions might be economically efficient because externalities, imperfections in competition, taxes on the margin of income, *etc.* distort the private cost that the producer involved in the vertical merger must incur to produce its input, the private cost that the producer of the input that could be substituted for the integrating firm's input must incur to produce its input, or on the preceding or other accounts the private cost of the two inputs in question to the final-good producer involved in the merger in question. As we saw, this deficiency of the economic-efficiency branch of the Chicago substitutable-input argument is, in essence, the same as the deficiency in the economic-efficiency branch of the Chicago successive-monopoly argument.

5. The Legality of Vertical Mergers and Acquisitions Under U.S. and E.C./E.U. Antitrust Law, Both as Correctly Applied and as Actually Applied

A. The Legality of Vertical Mergers and Acquisitions Under U.S. Antitrust Law, Both as Correctly Interpreted and as Actually Applied

(1) The Legality of Vertical Mergers and Acquisitions Under U.S. Antitrust Law as Correctly Interpreted

The Sherman Act, properly interpreted, has always covered the execution of vertical mergers and acquisitions: exemplars of such conduct that manifest its participants' specific anticompetitive intent are both contracts in restraint of trade (prohibited by Section 1) and acts of monopolization or attempts to monopolize (prohibited by Section 2). Of course, this formal statement does not in itself reveal much amount the concrete circumstances in which vertical mergers or acquisitions will violate the Sherman Act or the percentage of such mergers or acquisitions that do violate the Sherman Act.

Vertical mergers and acquisitions can reduce the absolute attractiveness of the offers against which their perpetrators will have to compete in six ways:

(1) by "foreclosing" an upstream or downstream rival of the integrated firm (regardless of whether the decision of the integrated firm not to deal with the rival in question was predatory),
(2) by raising the rival's costs by raising the price it must pay for the product the upstream division of the integrated firm produces (regardless of whether the price-increase in question manifested predation by the integrated concern) and by reducing the rival's sales—see point (1)—and hence increasing its average total cost and/or marginal cost,
(3) by increasing the oligopolistic margins that the merged firm or the business organization that results from the acquisition in question contrives above those that its antecedents would have contrived,
(4) by increasing the amount of predatory conduct in which the merged firm or the business organization that results from the acquisition in questions engages above those that its antecedents would have engaged,

(5) by increasing the organizational economic efficiency of the merged firm or the business organization that results from the merger or acquisition in question in ways that make the competitive-position array of the merged firm or resulting business organization superior to the relevant portion of the combined arrays of its antecedents, thereby causing the exit of one or more established rivals that will not be immediately replaced by an equally-effective competitor by worsening their relevant competitive-position arrays (the frequency and average amount by which they were best-placed and the frequency with which they were worse-than-best-placed by a small enough amount to be able to profit by beating a rival's contrived oligopolistic offer) and/or critically raising the barriers to entry/expansion facing one or more otherwise-effective potential QV investors by worsening their relevant prospective competitive-position arrays, and
(6) by increasing the buying power of the merged company or the business organization created by the acquisition above that of its separate antecedents (*i.e.*, by enabling the merged firm or resulting business organization to secure price-concessions that its antecedents could not have obtained that were not based on the merged firm's/resulting business organization's greater economic efficiency as a buyer), thereby causing the merged firm/resulting business organization to have a superior competitive-position array to the (relevant portion of the) combined competitive-position array of its antecedents, thereby causing the exit of one or more established rivals that will not be immediately replaced by an equally-effective competitor by worsening these rivals' competitive-position arrays and/or critically raising the barriers to entry/expansion facing one or more otherwise-effective potential QV investors by worsening their relevant prospective competitive-position arrays.

On my view, the *ex ante* belief of the participants in a vertical merger or acquisition that their merger or acquisition would or might reduce the absolute attractiveness of the offers against which they would have to compete in one or more of the six ways just listed would not make their merger or acquisition illegal under the Sherman Act unless it critically affected their *ex ante* perception that the merger or acquisition was profitable. For three reasons, I think that vertical mergers and acquisitions rarely violate the Sherman Act. First, I believe that only a small percentage of vertical mergers and acquisitions reduce the absolute attractiveness of the offers against which their participants must compete by foreclosing competition, raising rival costs, and/or increasing the buying power of the merged firm/resulting business organization above its antecedents'. Second, I suspect that, in the vast majority of situations in which the participants in a vertical merger or acquisition believe *ex ante* that it would or might reduce the absolute attractiveness of the offers against which they will have to compete by increasing their organizational economic efficiency, the private benefits that the increases in organizational economic efficiency in question would confer on the participants even if the efficiencies would not reduce the competition they faced would suffice to render the merger or acquisition profitable *ex ante*. Third, although I am less confident about this claim, I suspect that few vertical mergers or acquisitions significantly increase the profits their participants realize through contrivance or predation. I should add (though this observation relates not to the actual illegality of vertical mergers and acquisitions but to their provable illegality) that I doubt that—even when the perpetrators' *ex ante* belief in the profitability of their vertical merger or acquisition was critically affected by their perceptions that it would or might enable them to make additional profits through contrivance or predation—a private plaintiff or the State would be able to establish the requisite probability of their intention or its criticality: internal written documents or convincing whistle-blower evidence will rarely be available, and it will rarely if ever be possible to prove that the merger/acquisition in question increased the amount of contrivance and/or predation in which its participants engaged.

I want to close this analysis of the legality of vertical mergers and acquisitions under the Sherman Act by pointing out that its list of six ways in which vertical mergers and acquisitions can reduce the absolute attractiveness of the offers against which their perpetrators will have to compete does not include (1) enabling a true monopolist to escape upstream price or rate-of-return regulation, (2) enabling a perpetrator to reveal to the resulting firm information about a third party's position that the third party communicated to the revealer when it was independent to increase the benefits the third party could obtain by dealing with the revealer—information that may be a trade secret of the third party or information to which the third party may have some other sort of intellectual-property right, or (3) enabling the merged firm or resulting business organization to profit or profit more than its antecedents could by breaching contracts. The first effect occurs but has no antitrust relevance (it is a matter that the relevant regulatory commission should address). I see no reason why the vertically-integrated firm would find it profitable to reveal such IP-protected information or trade secrets, but, if it does do this, that is a matter of IP trade-secret law, not antitrust law. And although contract breaches should be more profitable for vertically-integrated concerns than for their non-integrated antecedents if there are company-wide economies of scale in dealing with the associated disputes, this possibility is also irrelevant to antitrust law—is properly handled by contract law and the authorities that apply it. I mention these possibilities despite the above conclusions because, as the next section indicates, both U.S. antitrust courts and/or the Federal Energy Regulatory Commission (FERC), which has authority over vertical mergers and acquisitions in the power sector, have cited these alleged consequences of vertical mergers or acquisitions to justify prohibiting them.

Vertical mergers and acquisitions were not covered by the pre-1950 Clayton Act because the applicable Section—Section 7—prohibited mergers that were requisitely likely to lessen competition *between* the merger partners or *between* the acquired and acquiring firms. However, the 1950 Celler-Kefauver amendment to the Clayton Act revised Section 7 to eliminate the requirement that the critical lessening of competition be a lessening of competition between the participants in the merger or acquisition under review while its legislative history made it clear that the Congress that passed it wanted it to be interpreted to prohibit *ab initio* mergers and acquisitions that would reduce competition in the future (to prevent the lessening of competition at its "incipiency"). In any event, in my judgment, the post-1950 Section 7 of the Clayton Act prohibits vertical mergers and acquisitions if they are requisitely likely to inflict a net equivalent-dollar loss on the combination of the customers of the perpetrators and the customers of the perpetrators' rivals by reducing the absolute attractiveness of the best offer they respectively will receive from any inferior supplier unless this outcome has been critically affected by the merger or acquisition's driving out a rival that will not be immediately replaced by an equally-effective competitor or critically raising the barriers to QV investment facing an otherwise-effective potential QV investor by increasing the perpetrators' organizational economic efficiency, thereby making the merged firm's or the resulting business organization's competitive-position arrays better than the relevant portions of the combined competitive-position arrays of its antecedents, thereby worsening the competitive-position arrays of the relevant established rival and/or the relevant prospective competitive-position array(s) of the relevant potential QV investor(s) in question (in which case the perpetrators would be justified in asserting an organizational-economic-efficiency defense for their merger or acquisition if I am correct in reading such a defense into the Clayton Act).

Of course, this formal statement provides no more information about the concrete circumstances in which an individual vertical merger or acquisition will violate the Clayton Act and the percentage of such mergers or acquisitions that do violate the Clayton Act than the formal statement of the Sherman Act's test of illegality did about the counterpart Sherman-Act-related issues. The first step in any analysis of the conditions under which a vertical merger or acquisition can generate a Clayton Act lessening of competition is to list the ways in which it could do so. The relevant list includes the six ways in which participants in a vertical merger or acquisition can believe that the associated conduct can reduce the competition they face (or, at least, each of these "ways" that have some possibility of eventuating). However, the Clayton Act list also includes items that do not appear on the Sherman Act list because they refer to possible ways in which a vertical merger/acquisition can inflict relevant equivalent-dollar losses on Clayton-Act-relevant buyers without benefitting their perpetrators by reducing the competition they face:

(7) increasing the oligopolistic margins that the rivals of the perpetrators contrive by reducing the likelihood that the merged firm/resulting business organization will undercut their contrived oligopolistic prices below the likelihood that its antecedents would have done so *inter alia* by making it more vulnerable to retaliation than its antecedents were by increasing its OCAs and, when the rival in question is similarly vertically integrated, by making it more vulnerable to retaliation than its antecedents were by creating an organization whose defenses are more widespread than either of its antecedents' defenses were and by

enabling that rival to take advantage of any excess reciprocatory power it has vis-à-vis one perpetrator to compensate the merged firm for its cooperation (though these effects will be offset or possibly counterbalanced to the extent that the vertical merger increases the OCAs of the merged firm's rivals by increasing the merged firm's OCAs and HNOPs to its own customers by generating organizational economic efficiencies or increases its buying power and hence the CMCs the merged firm would have to incur to charge any given price to the relevant rival's customers),

(8) increasing the oligopolistic margins that the rivals of the perpetrators obtain naturally by increasing the OCAs of the rivals in question by increasing the prices the merged firm charges its customers above the prices its antecedents charged them and hence increasing the CMC the merged firm would have to incur to charge given prices to a relevant rival's customers above those its antecedents would have had to incur to charge the same price to them, and

(9) reducing the intensity of QV-investment competition in the relevant area of product-space when one or both of the perpetrators would on its/their own have found it profitable to bring total QV investment in the relevant area of product-space to a level to which it would not otherwise be brought by making it profitable for the merged firm/resulting business organization to devote to consolidation resources its relevant antecedent(s) would otherwise have devoted to creating a new QV investment in the relevant area of product-space or by critically increasing the retaliation barrier to QV investment the merged firm or new business organization faced above the retaliation barrier the relevant antecedent(s) would have faced by spreading the merged firm's/new business organization's defenses and increasing its OCAs and NOMs above those of its antecedents (though this effect will be offset or perhaps counterbalanced to the extent that the merger/acquisition generates dynamic efficiencies).

For six clusters of reasons, I think that few if any individual vertical mergers or acquisitions violate the Clayton Act. First, I think that few individual vertical mergers or acquisitions lessen competition by foreclosing rivals or raising rival costs. Second, I think that few individual vertical mergers and acquisitions increase the amount of contrived oligopolistic pricing or the amount of predation in which the perpetrators engage and believe that, even when a vertical merger or acquisition seems likely to increase the amount of contrivance and/or predation in which the perpetrators engage or can be shown to have done so, those facts should not affect the legality of a facilitating vertical merger or acquisition under the Clayton Act that would otherwise have been lawful unless the subsequent illegal acts in question are prohibitively expensive to prove: when this latter condition is not fulfilled, the merger or acquisition should be declared lawful and the illegal acts to which it leads should be addressed through a Sherman Act price-fixing or predation suit. I recognize that the fact that the 1950 revision of the Clayton Act was designed *inter alia* to prevent decreases in competition in their incipiency disfavors the preceding legal conclusion. Third, if I am correct in arguing that it is correct as a matter of law to read an organizational-economic-efficiency defense into the

Clayton Act, those individual vertical mergers and acquisitions that would not have inflicted a net equivalent-dollar loss on Clayton-Act-relevant buyers had they not increased the perpetrators' organizational economic efficiency do not violate the Clayton Act. Fourth, I suspect that only a tiny percentage of vertical mergers and acquisitions lessen competition in the Clayton Act sense by creating a merged firm/new business organization that has more buying power than its antecedents would have. Fifth, I suspect that only a few vertical mergers and acquisitions significantly harm Clayton-Act-relevant buyers by increasing the COMs of the product rivals of the perpetrators, by increasing the NOMs of those firms, or by reducing the intensity of QV-investment competition in the relevant area of product-space by increasing the (Π_D + R) and/or L barriers to QV investment that the merged firm/resulting business organization faces above the (Π_D + R + L) barriers its relevant antecedent (s) would have faced. Sixth and finally, I suspect that in many cases in which a vertical merger or acquisition does inflict an equivalent-dollar loss on Clayton-Act-relevant buyers for one or more of the six reasons that are relevant to its legality under the Sherman Act and the three additional reasons just listed that are not relevant to its legality under the Sherman Act, the merger or acquisition will confer enough benefits on those buyers by increasing the perpetrators' organizational economic efficiency for it not to inflict a net equivalent-dollar loss on them, all things considered.

I recognize that some might claim that the preceding analysis is misfocused in that the relevant issue is not the competitive impact of an individual vertical merger or acquisition but the competitive impact of an individual vertical merger or acquisition and any subsequent vertical mergers and acquisitions it would cause. Those that take this position might cite the 1950 legislative history, which indicates that the Congress that promulgated the Celler-Kefauver amendment to the Clayton Act was seeking to prevent in its incipiency any tendency a vertical merger or acquisition might have eventually to lessen competition as well as some prior U.S. federal cases in which courts appeared to subscribe to a kind of domino theory of vertical integration. I admit that, to the extent that vertical mergers and acquisitions can foreclose competition or raise barriers to QV investment by making it necessary for the investor to invest on two levels rather than one, one or a larger number of vertical mergers or acquisitions could induce non-integrated firms to integrate vertically to avoid being foreclosed. However, I doubt that individual vertical mergers often induce other firms to engage in vertical integration to avoid being foreclosed. In my judgment, when a substantial percentage, most, or all or virtually all members of a set of product rivals execute vertical mergers or acquisitions (or vertically integrate via internal growth), they do so because each has concluded that vertical integration will increase its organizational economic efficiency, not because they are seeking to avoid the foreclosing effects of their rivals having vertically integrated when the non-integrated firms have not, and, when this is the case, the whole series of vertical integrations is likely to confer an equivalent-dollar gain on Clayton-Act-relevant buyers. I want to add one further point that derives from the premise that the appropriate focus for the analysis of the legality of vertical mergers or acquisitions under the Clayton Act is not the competitive impact of an individual vertical merger but the collective impact of all the vertical mergers that all members of a relevant set of product rivals make. The argument in question admits that a significant number of vertical mergers or acquisitions could be executed in the area of product-space in question without competition's being reduced by foreclosure but claims (1) that the total number of such mergers and acquisitions that would be executed if the government did not prohibit their execution would generate competition-reducing foreclosures even if, as these experts assume, each of the vertical mergers or acquisitions was identical except for its placement in the series that was executed—*i.e.*, that after some number of identical vertical mergers and acquisitions have been executed, the next one will generate a competition-reducing foreclosure—and (2) that if the government has not prohibited the first vertical merger or acquisition in such a (predictable) series, it cannot prohibit the subsequent (say, *n*th) vertical merger or acquisition that would generate the competition-reducing foreclosure because (*ex hypothesis*) that *n*th vertical merger or acquisition is identical to its predecessors in the series and the government is morally and derivatively constitutionally obligated to treat like behavior alike. I reject this argument for three reasons. First, I believe that even if a series of individually-economically-efficient vertical mergers does for some reason induce the exit of one or more existing firms on one level or deter one or more QV investments on one level that would otherwise have been made, the vertical mergers in question will almost always confer an equivalent-dollar gain on Clayton-Act-relevant buyers. Second, I believe that, on the facts assumed, even if the mergers in question did inflict a net equivalent-dollar loss on Clayton-Act-relevant buyers, the perpetrators could make out organizational-economic-efficiency defenses. And third, I reject the premise that if the *n*th member of a series of vertical mergers or acquisitions is identical to its predecessors in all respects other than the fact that it is the *n*th such merger or acquisition to be executed and they were respectively the first, second,. . .(*n–1*)th such merger or acquisition to be executed that would imply that, from a legal perspective, the *n*th such merger was identical to its predecessors: in particular, I reject this premise because it ignores the relevance of the fact that the *n*th merger or acquisition takes place after (*n–1*) mergers or acquisitions have already been consummated—a fact that the experts in question admit is critical in that it causes the *n*th such merger or acquisition to reduce competition when its predecessors did not. If my first two objections were unsound, the government would not violate any right of the participants in the *n*th vertical merger or acquisition to be consummated in some area of product-space to be treated the same as their (*n–1*) predecessors were treated by prohibiting them from executing the *n*th vertical merger or acquisition in the relevant area of product-space after allowing their (*n–1*) predecessors to execute *otherwise*-identical vertical mergers or acquisitions because the *n*th such merger or acquisition is different from its (*n–1*) predecessors by virtue of being the *n*th member of the relevant series.

But what of the alternative unit for Clayton Act analysis to which I have referred—the competitive impact of a rule permitting all members of a set of rivals to execute vertical mergers and acquisitions? The advantage of using this unit of analysis is that its use precludes pari-mutuel handicapping—*i.e.*, precludes the decisionmaker from prohibiting well-established firms from engaging in conduct that would reduce competition by improving their competitive-position arrays and derivatively worsening the competitive-position arrays of marginal competitors sufficiently to induce them to exit and the prospective competitive-position arrays of otherwise-effective potential QV investors sufficiently to render them ineffective while allowing marginal competitors and potential QV investors to engage in the conduct in question respectively to enable them to survive and make them (more) effective as potential QV investors. The rejection of such pari-mutuel handicapping (in favor of a more-even-handed approach) is both advantageous from a policy perspective (since it allows well-established firms to increase their organizational economic efficiency, removes a disincentive to firms' making economically-efficient decisions that will render them well-established, and [if "well-established" is operationalized incorrectly in a way that makes a firm's market share or size as opposed to its rate-of-return a parameter of how well-established it is considered to be] removes an incentive for firms that might be considered to be well-established to break themselves up into smaller components when their doing so would be economically inefficient) and correct as a matter of law (to the extent that the relevant law is designed to establish a "level playing field," to allow firms to compete on the merits [as U.S. law clearly is and E.C./E.U. law seems to be (though I must acknowledge that the EC has sometimes stated that, contrary to my view, correctly interpreted as a matter of law, now-Article 102 requires dominant firms to forego moves that would increase their organizational economic efficiency to help their smaller rivals survive and grow)]). Admittedly, however, this possible advantage of focusing on the competitive impact of a rule allowing all members of a set of rivals to execute vertical mergers and acquisitions will be smaller if well-established firms whose vertical mergers and acquisitions would reduce competition by improving their competitive-position arrays could establish an organizational-economic-efficiency defense for their conduct—*i.e.*, if it were correct as a matter of law to read such a defense into the Clayton Act and practicable for the defendants to establish the relevant economic efficiencies and their critical impact on competition. Moreover, making the competitive impact of a universally-permissive rule the relevant unit for the analysis of the legality of vertical mergers and acquisitions under the Clayton Act will produce unsatisfactory results in what I take to be the rare case in which all the vertical mergers and acquisitions that would be executed under such a rule would, taken together, reduce competition in the Clayton Act sense by foreclosing some non-integrating firms and raising barriers to entry or QV-investment expansions but a smaller number of such vertical mergers and acquisitions would not decrease Clayton Act competition—indeed, would confer a net equivalent-dollar gain on Clayton-Act-relevant buyers—because the negative foreclosure/barrier effects of the last vertical mergers and acquisitions that would be executed would be greater than that of their predecessors while the positive organizational-economic-efficiency-generated effects of those last vertical mergers and acquisitions would not be greater than those of their predecessors—more specifically, because the last vertical mergers and acquisitions in question that would be executed under the rule in question would inflict an equivalent-dollar loss on Clayton-Act-relevant buyers that exceeds the equivalent-dollar gain its predecessors conferred on them. Although it may be improper to do so, I take refuge in my belief that this difficulty is unlikely to arise because even the totality of vertical mergers and acquisitions that would be executed under the universally-permissive rule in question will rarely if ever generate the foreclosure that could cause the rule to decrease competition in the Clayton Act sense.

Section 3 of this chapter argued that, for three reasons, a rule allowing all members of a set of product rivals to use such surrogates for vertical integration as tie-ins, reciprocity, resale price maintenance, and vertical territorial restraints and vertical customer-allocation clauses would rarely reduce competition in the Clayton Act sense or, *a fortiori*, violate the Clayton Act, properly interpreted and applied:

(1) such practices will tend to be more profitable for marginal established competitors and potential entrants than for well-established firms;
(2) even when they are less profitable for marginal established competitors and potential entrants than for well-established firms, the rule will generally not affect the survival of a marginal firm that would not be immediately replaced if it exited by an equally-effective competitor or critically raise the barriers to entry confronting an otherwise-effective potential competitor; and
(3) even when the rule would reduce competition in the Clayton Act sense by inducing the exit of one or more marginal established firms that were not immediately replaced by equally-effective competitors and/or by critically raising the barriers to entry confronting one or more otherwise-effective potential competitors, the well-established firms that the rule would or did permit to engage in the conduct the rule covered could make out an organizational-economic-efficiency defense of their behavior.

All three of these arguments apply equally forcefully when the focus of the relevant inquiry is the competitive impact of a rule that would prevent all members of a set of product rivals to execute vertical mergers or acquisitions. Admittedly, vertical mergers and acquisitions in which the merging or acquiring firms merge with or buy up more capacity on the other level than their pre-merger operation requires could create foreclosure or related barrier problems if the perpetrators subsequently refused to deal predatorily or if contextual marginal costs made it inherently profitable for the perpetrator to refuse deals that would create level playing fields or to offer terms of sale or purchase that would place non-integrated firms at a disadvantage that did not reflect the non-integrated firm's economic-inefficiency inferiority. However, I suspect that this outcome rarely if ever occurs. I therefore believe that in all or virtually all instances vertical mergers or acquisitions would not violate the Clayton Act's test of illegality if the legally-relevant question were the competitive impact of a rule allowing all members of a set of product rivals to execute vertical mergers or acquisitions.

(2) The Legality of Vertical Mergers and Acquisitions Under U.S. Antitrust Law as Actually Applied

This section describes and comments on both the U.S. case-law on vertical mergers and acquisitions (hereinafter vertical mergers) and the positions that the DOJ and FTC have taken on their execution. Because the original Clayton Act did not cover vertical mergers, the pre-1950 case-law on such conduct all dealt with their legality under the Sherman Act. That case-law combined (1) a legal conclusion that vertical mergers violated the Sherman Act if and only if they manifested one or both participants' "anticompetitive intent" (which I would deem correct if the enquoted expression referred to anticompetitive intentions that critically affected the perpetrators' *ex ante* perception that the vertical merger in question was profitable—*i.e.*, to "specific anticompetitive intent") and (2) an economic conclusion that vertical mergers often if not usually are undertaken to foreclose competition often if not usually have the effect of foreclosing competition.[1402] This economic conclusion was expressed already in 1911 in *United States v. American Tobacco Co.*—a case that focused on the Sherman-Act-legality of a tobacco trust created through a series of horizontal, conglomerate, and vertical acquisitions:

> [T]he conclusion of wrongful purpose and illegal combination is overwhelmingly established...[by the defendants'] gradual absorption of control over all the elements essential to the manufacture of tobacco products, and placing such control in the hands of seemingly independent corporations serving as perpetual barriers to the entry of others into the tobacco trade.[1403]

Although prior to 1950 the U.S. courts acknowledged that vertical mergers and acquisitions might be legitimately motivated, they continued to assume that many such mergers were designed to and succeeded in decreasing competition by foreclosing competitors. Thus, in 1948, in *United States v. Paramount Pictures*, the Supreme Court held that a vertical merger

> ...runs afoul the Sherman Act if it was a calculated scheme to gain control over an appreciable segment of the market and to restrain or suppress competition, rather than an expansion to meet legitimate business needs....[1404]

Note what I take to be the implication that vertical mergers that give (say) a producer control over "an appreciable segment of the (say, retail) market" will tend "to restrain or suppress competition"—an implication that I think will usually not be correct.

[1402] Hovenkamp attributes this economic conclusion to the courts' desire to protect "smaller, unintegrated" firms even from disadvantages they suffer because vertical integration increases the organizational economic efficiency of its participants. See HOVENKAMP, ANTITRUST HORNBOOK 387. I am more inclined to think that the courts honestly believed that vertical integration was associated with foreclosure that put non-integrated firms at a competitive disadvantage that did not reflect their lesser economic efficiency—*i.e.*, did not consist of competition on the merits, tilted the playing field in the vertically-integrated firms' favor.

[1403] United States v. American Tobacco Co., 221 U.S. 106, 182–83 (1911).

[1404] 334 U.S. 131, 174 (1948).

I hasten to add that, pre-1950, U.S. courts did not always find vertical mergers or even the combination of vertical acquisitions and decisions by the vertically-integrated firm to require its retailer subsidiaries (division) to use only the products its production division produced violative of the Sherman Act. Thus, in 1948, in *United States v. Columbia Steel Co.*, the Supreme Court rejected a foreclosure-argument case against a vertical merger involving a firm that it deemed to have only 3 % of the relevant (rolled-steel) market in circumstances in which it concluded the previous suppliers of the firm in question could easily market their output elsewhere.[1405] And in 1949 the Supreme Court affirmed a District Court conclusion finding that a taxi-manufacturing company's acquisition of taxi-operating companies and subsequent decision to require the acquired operators to purchase only the manufacturer's cabs did not violate the Sherman Act because neither was made to restrain or suppress competition. The relevant business and legal history of the latter case is complicated. In 1929, the Checker Cab Manufacturing Corporation started to acquire control of Yellow Cab and a number of other transportation companies. By 1937, Checker owned subsidiaries that had 53 % of the operating licenses in Chicago, 100 % of the operating licenses in Pittsburgh, 58 % of the operating licenses in Minneapolis, and 15 % of the operating licenses in New York City. Checker required all their subsidiaries to purchase all their taxis from it. The District Court dismissed the complaint against Checker on the ground that requirements that subsidiaries purchase exclusively from their parent "are common and are inherent in the acquisition by a manufacturer of outlets."[1406] The Supreme Court reversed and remanded the case for trial on the correct ground that the fact that "restraints" occurred inside a vertically-integrated enterprise does not guarantee their legality under the Sherman Act—correct because individual-firm refusals to deal can be predatory and therefore prohibited by the Sherman Act. At trial, the District Court judge, sitting without a jury, found for the defendants on the ground that they had no intention to suppress competition.[1407] The Supreme Court affirmed on the ground that the District Court's conclusion was not "clearly erroneous."[1408]

[1405] 334 U.S. 495, 507–10 (1948).

[1406] United States v. Yellow Cab Co., 69 F. Supp 170, 174 (N.D. Ill. 1946).

[1407] United States v. Yellow Cab Co., 69 F. Supp. 170 (N.D. Ill. 1946).

[1408] United States v. Yellow Cab Co., 338 U.S. 338 (1949). I should note one additional pre-1950 case that addressed the legality of a firm's extracting price-concessions from suppliers by executing vertical mergers or acquisitions, integrating vertically through internal growth, or threatening to vertically integrate in one way or another. Both the District Court and the Court of Appeals concluded that the extraction in these and other ways of price-concessions that put competitors at a disadvantage violate the Sherman Act. See United States v. New York Great Atlantic & Pacific Tea Co., 626 F. Supp. 626 (E.D. Ill. 1946), aff'd, 173 F.2d 70 (7th Cir. 1949). To my knowledge, the Justice Department did not even attempt to demonstrate in this case (1) that the defendant's *ex ante* perception that its efforts to obtain price-concessions by vertically integrating, threatening to vertically integrate, or in various other ways was profitable was critically affected by its belief that such price-concessions might or would reduce the absolute attractiveness of the offers against which it would have to compete by driving out a rival that would not be immediately replaced by an equally-effective competitor and/or by critically raising the barriers to QV investment faced by an otherwise-effective potential QV investor or (2) that the sought-after

For about 20 years after 1950, the U.S. courts—possibly under the influence of leading economists who believed that vertical integration often reduces competition by foreclosing competitors[1409]—were more hostile to vertical mergers and acquisitions than their predecessors had been. All the important post-1950 cases on vertical merger and acquisitions were brought under the Clayton Act.

The first of these cases, *United States v. E.I. du Pont de Nemours & Co.*,[1410] addressed the legality under the Clayton Act of the acquisition by du Pont (a manufacturer of finishes and fabrics for manufactured cars) of 23 % of the shares of General Motors. The Supreme Court's opinion, which reversed a lower-court dismissal of the suit, manifests the Court's hostility to vertical mergers and acquisitions in at least four ways. First, the Court decided that the suit should not be dismissed on the ground that, since the action was filed in 1949, the applicable version of the Clayton Act was the pre-Celler-Kefauver version, which does not apply to vertical acquisitions. The Court's implicit argument for ignoring this legal reality—*viz.*, that it is correct as a matter of law for it to apply the Congressional policy-preferences that motivated the Celler-Kefauver Act—is, to my mind, completely unpersuasive.

Second, the Court held that the likely effect of a vertical merger or acquisition should be determined "at the time of suit" rather than at the time of the merger's or acquisition's execution. Although the "time of suit" language is ambiguous on this issue, I take the Court to be saying not just that the legality of a vertical merger or acquisition under the Clayton Act depends on an assessment at the time of suit of the competitive impact it will have *from the date of execution* until the end of time but on an assessment at the time of suit of the competitive impact it will have *from the time of suit* until the end of time. In other words, I take the Court to be saying that a covered vertical merger or acquisition will violate the Clayton Act if at the time of suit it would be predicted to be requisitely likely to lessen competition *from the time of suit* onward even if at the time of suit it would not be post-dicted and predicted to be requisitely likely to lessen competition *from the time of execution* onward or even if at the time of execution it would not have been said to be requisitely likely to lessen competition from the time of execution onward. To see why the Court's choice is salient, note that at the time of suit GM's share of the national automobile market was about 50 % while at the time of acquisition its share of the national automobile-manufacturing market was about 11 % and there was no particular reason to believe that it would rise. Particularly when coupled with the Court's conclusion that, basically, the Government can wait as long as it likes to institute a suit against participants in a vertical merger or acquisition, these

---

price-concessions might, would, or did reduce competition in the relevant area of product-space in one or both of these ways.

1409 See, *e.g.*, Corwin D. Edwards, *Vertical Integration and the Monopoly Problem*, 17 J. MARKETING 404 (1953).

1410 353 U.S. 586 (1957).

time-perspective holdings are not only remarkable but also (I suspect) counterproductive from the perspective of the Congressional goal of increasing competition. Firms will be disinclined to execute vertical mergers and acquisitions that will increase competition from the date of their consummation forward if they know that they can be required to split up their enterprise, pay various other sorts of penalties, and incur the cost of litigation if there is a requisite probability that from some post-execution date forward their vertical merger or acquisition would lessen competition in the Clayton Act sense.

Third, the Supreme Court's *du Pont-GM* opinion manifests its hostility to vertical mergers and acquisitions by manifesting great concern that a potential supplier's ownership of 23 % of a potential buyer's stock will enable the supplier to induce the buyer to purchase its wares when it would be unprofitable for the buyer to do so. Perhaps I have overstated this objection: in fact, the opinion simply indicates that the legality of the acquisition would turn primarily on whether du Pont's 23 % holding of GM stock enables du Pont to make sales to GM not on the competitive merits.

Fourth, the Supreme Court's *du Pont-GM* opinion manifests its hostility to vertical acquisitions by appearing to assume that, if du Pont's ownership of GM stock enabled it to supply the 67 % of GM's paint and fabric requirements that it did supply when it would not have done so on the competitive merits, that fact would imply that du Pont's acquisition of GM stock would lessen competition by foreclosing competitors going forward. To see why that conclusion is problematic, note that it implies that the foreclosure of a maximum of 33 1/2 % of the contemporaneous automobile paint and fabric market would raise substantial competitive concerns: I indicate "a maximum of 33 ½ %" because, given GM's 50 % contemporaneous share of the national automobile-manufacturing market, the percentage of sales du Pont's acquisition of GM stock would have foreclosed would be 33 1/2 % = (67 %)(50 %) if du Pont would have made no sales to GM on the competitive merits.

The next important federal vertical-merger case was *Brown Shoe Co. v. United States*.[1411] *Brown Shoe* involved a mixed horizontal/vertical acquisition by Brown Shoe Co.—the third largest manufacturer of shoes by sales volume in the United States and a shoe retailer with over 1230 owned, operated, or controlled shoe-outlets—of Kinney, the eighth largest manufacturer of shoes in the United States and the owner of 350 retail shoe-outlets. If I accept for the sake of the argument the use of a national shoe market, the *Brown Shoe* opinion condemned under Section 7 of the Clayton Act, *inter alia*, a vertical acquisition by a shoe manufacturer with 5 % of a highly-unconcentrated national market of a retailer whose share of the "national shoe retail" market was 1 %. The Court expressed the concern that the acquisition in question would foreclose competition and would induce further foreclosures by "forcing" other shoe manufacturers to integrate forward into retail

[1411] 370 U.S. 294 (1962).

shoe distribution. The reality is that, at least at the time of trial, shoe manufacturers that were not vertically integrated forward into distribution were not being foreclosed: in 1963, a year after *Brown Shoe* was decided, fewer than 10 % of U.S.-made shoes were distributed through stores owned or operated by the manufacturer.[1412] The reality also is that the trend to vertical integration that the Supreme Court noted and was concerned by could best be explained by citing the ability of vertical integration to increase its participants' organizational economic efficiency rather than by declaring that the decision of some shoe manufacturers to integrate forward into distribution for some unexplained reason forced their non-integrated rivals to follow their example. Of course, since the Supreme Court that wrote the *Brown Shoe* opinion believed that Congress had consciously chosen to secure atomized production and distribution even when economic efficiency had to be sacrificed to do so, it would not find the economic-efficiency explanation of the "definite trend" toward vertical integration into distribution it noted legally salient.

By 1970, the U.S. courts' handling of Section 7 vertical-merger-and-acquisition cases led the highly-respected-economist author of a major study on industrial organization to conclude that "emerging from the leading court interpretations [of Section 7 of the Clayton Act] is a virtual *per se* prohibition of...vertical mergers likely to foreclose an appreciable share of some market."[1413]

The Supreme Court's last decision on vertical mergers or acquisitions—in a 1972 case, *Ford Motor Co. v. United States*[1414]—continues to manifest the Court's hostility to such transactions. In this opinion, the Court condemned Ford Motor Co.'s acquisition of Autolite, a manufacturer of spark plugs, not on the foreclosure theory on which its more recent preceding opinions had relied but on its "cousin"—the theory that the acquisition would reduce competition by raising the barriers to entry facing any firm that was considering entering either the spark-plug or the automobile-manufacturing business by making it necessary for them to enter both businesses. No careful consideration was given (1) to the conditions under which vertical integration would foreclose a non-integrated firm from making sales to the downstream or from purchasing from the upstream division of relevant vertically-integrated firms and/or from non-integrated firms operating downstream/upstream or (2) to the conditions under which such foreclosure would make entry less attractive to potential competitors at either level.

Although, as just indicated, the Supreme Court has not decided a vertical merger or acquisition case since *Ford Motor (Autolite)* in 1972, a number of such cases have been decided by the lower courts. The opinions in the 1970s were based on the foreclosure theory and seemed to find that foreclosures of 5–6 % were acceptable but foreclosures of 15 % or higher rendered the vertical mergers or acquisitions that yielded them Clayton-Act-violative. (I think that in most situations the percentage of sales foreclosed would have to be far higher than 15 % for the foreclosure to

---

[1412] See John L. Peterman, *The* Brown Shoe *Case*, 18 J. L. & ECON. 81, 117 (1975).

[1413] See F.M. SCHERER, INDUSTRIAL MARKET STRUCTURE AND ECONOMIC PERFORMANCE 480 (1970).

[1414] 405 U.S. 562 (1972).

be problematic and that, as the U.S. courts have realized in long-term full-requirements-contracts cases, the critical issue is not the percentage of sales foreclosed but [roughly speaking] the relationship between that percentage and the percentage of sales that established independents or possible potential entrants would have to be able to make to at least break even).

Hovenkamp discusses three cases from the 1970s to support the preceding lower-court-practice conclusion, which is his as well.[1415] In the first, the Fifth Circuit prohibited an automobile manufacturer's acquisition of a manufacturer of air conditioners for automobiles after defining the relevant market incorrectly in a way that yielded the conclusion that the acquisition would foreclose an extremely-high percentage of relevant sales—*viz.*, by defining the relevant market to be the market for "Volkswagen air conditioners" as opposed to the market for air conditioners for all brands of automobiles.[1416] In the second, the Second Circuit overturned an FTC ruling condemning a vertical merger under Section 7 and ordering divestiture in a case in which the merger partners were respectively a manufacturer of truck trailers that had the largest share (25 %) of the United States market (Truehauf) and a manufacturer of 15 % of the heavy-duty truck and trailer wheels sold in the United States (Kelsey-Hayes). The court stated that it was

> unwilling to assume that any vertical foreclosure lessens competition. Absent very high market concentration or some other factor threatening a tangible anticompetitive effect, a vertical merger may simply realign sales patterns, for insofar as the merger forecloses some of the market from the merging firms' competitors, it may simply free up that much of the market. . .for new transactions. . ..[1417]

In the third case in this category, the Ninth Circuit upheld the FTC's condemnation of two acquisitions by a cement manufacturer with 15 % of the relevant market of companies that respectively purchased 10 % and 3 % of the cement sold in the relevant market (and used it to produce ready-mix concrete for use in the construction industry).[1418]

By the late 1980s, the federal courts seem to have come to the conclusion that vertical mergers and acquisitions reduce competition only in rare, extreme situations. Thus, in 1987, the Third Circuit came close to rejecting the foreclosure theory as a basis for liability, arguing that the self-dealing that is associated with vertical acquisitions is almost always economically efficient.[1419] Also, in 1987, in a case that focused on a hospital chain's acquisition of an HMO, a District

---

[1415] See HOVENKAMP HORNBOOK 391.

[1416] Heat Transfer Corp. v. Volkswagenwerk, A.G., 553 F.2d 964 (5th Cir. 1977), cert. denied, 434 U.S. 1087 (1978).

[1417] Fruehauf Corp. v. FTC, 603 F.2d 345, 352 at n. 9 (2d Cir. 1979).

[1418] Ash Grove Cement v. FTC, 577 F.2d 1368 (9th Cir. 1978), cert. denied, 439 U.S. 982 (1978), affirming 85 F.T.C. 1123 (1975).

[1419] See Alberta Gas Chemicals Ltd. v. E.I. du Pont de Nemours & Co., 826 F.2d 1235 (3d Cir. 1987), cert. denied, 486 U.S. 1059 (1988).

Court declared that vertical acquisitions are not even a "suspect category" of business conduct.[1420]

More recently, the U.S. federal courts and the FTC (see below) seem to have been more concerned that vertical mergers and acquisitions may lessen competition in the Clayton Act sense by raising rivals' costs by precluding the rivals from taking advantage of relevant economies of scale without fully recognizing the connection between this argument and the foreclosure argument that they have rejected or came close to rejecting. On the whole, however, the decisions that both the FTC and the reviewing courts have made under the shadow of this concern have been far more permissive than the decisions the U.S. courts formerly make under the influence of the foreclosure and "raising barriers to entry" theories.[1421]

As previously stated, the Supreme Court has not decided a vertical merger or acquisition case since *Ford Motor (Autolite)* in 1972. However, the Court's post-1980 permissive decisions on tie-ins, maximum-and-minimum-price-setting RPM, vertical territorial restraints, vertical customer-allocation clauses, exclusive dealerships, and long-term full-requirements contracts and the lower federal courts' even-more-permissive operationalization of the Supreme Court's current announced or *de facto* Rule-of-Reason approach to these practices imply that both the Supreme Court and the lower federal courts are now far less likely to condemn vertical mergers and acquisitions than they were in the past: institutions that have come to recognize many of the legitimate functions that surrogates for vertical integration can perform and to realize that those surrogates will rarely violate the Sherman Act or Clayton Act seem likely to reach the same conclusions about mergers and acquisitions that yield the vertical integration for which the other practices are surrogates.

I turn now to the positions that the U.S. antitrust-enforcement agencies—the DOJ, FTC, and (as a kind of postscript) the Federal Energy Regulatory Commission (FERC)—have taken on vertical mergers and acquisitions (which the FERC denominates "convergence mergers"). Until around 1970, the Antitrust Division of the United States Department of Justice (DOJ) was as hostile to vertical mergers and acquisitions as were the U.S. courts. Since the DOJ brought many of the suits against participants in vertical mergers and acquisitions that I think were wrongly declared illegal as well as some of the vertical-merger/acquisition suits that were resolved in the defendants' favor during this period and argued in some cases that certain kinds of vertical integration should be deemed *per se* illegal in some industries (*e.g.*, argued in *United States v. Paramount Pictures* that "vertical integration of producing,

[1420] Reazin v. Blue Cross & Blue Shield, 663 F. Supp. 1360, 1489 (D. Kan. 1987), affirmed, 899 F.2d 951 (10th Cir. 1990), cert. denied, 497 U.S. 1005 (1990). See also United States v. Loew's, 882 F.2d 29, 33–34 (2d Cir. 1989) (approving a motion-picture producer's acquisition of an exhibitor) and O'Neill v. Coca-Cola Co., 669 F. Supp. 217, 224 (N.D. Ill. 1987) (asserting that consumers could not establish the injury necessary to give them standing to challenge a soft-drink producer's acquisition of a bottler). The cites in this footnote and its predecessor have been taken from HOVENKAMP HORNBOOK 392 and n. 25.

[1421] See, *e.g.*, United States v. Enora Corp., 107 F. Supp. 2d 10 (D.D.C. 2000).

distributing, and exhibiting motion pictures is illegal *per se*"), this account of the DOJ's pre-1970 position on vertical mergers and acquisitions should in one sense not be surprising. In 1968, the DOJ published Merger Guidelines that paid less attention to the possibility that vertical mergers and acquisitions involving producers and distributors might reduce competition in the upstream market by driving one or more established non-integrated producers out of that market by foreclosing them from the downstream (distributive) market and more attention (1) to the possibility that vertical mergers and acquisitions whose perpetrators are an input supplier and a producer might reduce competition in the final-product-production (downstream) market by driving one or more established non-integrated producers out of that market by subjecting them to "supply squeezes"—*i.e.*, by foreclosing them from making input purchases—and (2) to the possibility that vertical mergers and acquisitions might reduce competition in one or both of the levels they involve by raising barriers to entry. Equally important, although the position that the DOJ's 1968 Merger Guidelines took on the legality of vertical mergers and acquisitions may have been slightly less hostile to them than the U.S. courts were at that time, the 1968 Guidelines still stated that the Antitrust Division would challenge any vertical merger or acquisition that involved a supplier with at least a 10 % share of the relevant market's sales and a buyer that purchased at least 6 % of the goods sold in the market in question "unless it clearly appears that there are no significant barriers to entry into the business of the purchasing firm or firms"[1422]—*i.e.*, would challenge many vertical mergers and acquisitions that, in my judgment, would almost certainly not lessen competition in the Clayton Act sense.

Starting in about 1970, the combination of the Chicago-school critique of the traditional arguments against vertical mergers and acquisitions and the increased presence of economists and more-economically-sophisticated lawyers on the Antitrust Division's staff led to a dramatic change in the DOJ's enforcement-practice. According to one study, the number of purely-vertical mergers and acquisitions challenged by the DOJ and FTC fell from 27 between 1960 and 1970 to two between 1970 and 1980.[1423]

This change in enforcement-practice is implicitly explained by the DOJ's replacement of its 1968 Guidelines with the more-perpetrator-friendly 1982 and 1984 Guidelines. I will focus here on the 1984 Vertical Merger Guidelines.[1424] The 1984 Guidelines pay scant attention to the risk that vertical mergers and acquisitions might drive out (1) one or more downstream established firms by subjecting them to "supply squeezes" or (2) one or more upstream established firms by foreclosing them from distributing their final products or selling the inputs they made to downstream final-product producers. Instead, they focus on the risk

[1422] United States Department of Justice Merger Guidelines at ¶ 12 (1968), 4 Trade Reg. Rep. (CCH) ¶ 13,101.

[1423] See Alan A. Fisher and Richard S. Sciacca, *An Economic Analysis of Vertical Merger Enforcement Policy*, 6 RES. L. & ECON. 1, Table 8 (1984).

[1424] 49 Fed. Reg. 26,823 (1984).

that vertical mergers and acquisitions might lessen competition by increasing barriers to entry, by facilitating collusion, and by enabling the merged firm to avoid rate regulation.

Section 4.21 addresses the "barrier to entry" possibility. According to the 1984 Guidelines, there are three necessary but not sufficient conditions for a vertical merger's or acquisition's lessening competition by raising entry barriers.

First, vertical integration must be sufficiently extensive to necessitate a potential competitor's entering both markets simultaneously. The Guidelines indicate that this condition will not be fulfilled if there is sufficient non-integrated capacity at one level to supply the needs of two operations of minimum efficient scale at the other level involved in the merger. I am troubled by this operationalization because it assumes that non-integrated firms will be foreclosed from dealing with integrated firms at the level at which the non-integrated firm is not operating and (in the other direction) because it ignores the fact that not all distributors or input suppliers will be equally-well-placed to supply a particular potential foreclosee and because it does not cover the situation in which, absent foreclosure, three or more entries would be executed.

Second, the need to enter at two levels must significantly increase the barriers to entry that relevant potential competitors face (*e.g.*, by raising their weighted-average-expected costs and/or their risk costs). The 1984 Guidelines get some things that relate to this issue right. Thus, they state correctly that the fact that it takes more capital to enter at two levels rather than one does not in itself make the barriers to two-level entry higher than the barriers to one-level entry. And they recognize that, if the two-level entry is riskier than a single-level entry, that fact will make the barriers to executing a two-level entry higher than the barriers to executing a one-level entry (in my terminology, will raise the R barrier to a two-level entry above the R barrier to a one-level entry). However, surprisingly, the 1984 Guidelines do not appropriately address what I take to be the most important reason why the barriers to two-level entry are likely to be significantly higher than the barriers to one-level entry: the relevant potential competitors may be much less skilled at operating at one level than at the other or may not have enough personnel to enter at two levels and be in a situation in which their organizational proficiency would be significantly reduced if they had to hire enough new personnel to execute a dual entry (because of the expense of making the additional hires, the non-availability of personnel whose intrinsic attributes would make their employment as cost-effective as the company's use of its existing personnel, and/or the cost the company would have to incur to integrate the new personnel into its organization [or the extra costs it would have to incur because the new personnel did not know the identity of the colleagues they should ask for various types of information or advice, did not know who was authorized to make certain sorts of decisions, and did not know how to communicate or behave more generally within the organization]). Virtually the only statement that the 1984 Guidelines contain that relates to this Π_D issue is the assertion that the necessity of entering on two levels will be more likely to increase relevant barriers to entry when minimum efficient scale (MES) at the level at which the potential competitor really wants to enter is significantly smaller than MES at the other level at which its rivals' vertical integration is requiring it to enter. Such MES-differences will be relevant to only some of the Π_D issues I raised, and even when the MES-difference is relevant the factor that is really relevant is the absolute MES in the area of product-space into which *ex hypothesis* the potential competitor's rivals' vertical integration is requiring it to enter. I should add that the Guidelines also ignore the scale barrier to entry, which may be significant if the $H\Pi_E$ curve in the relevant ARDEPPS will not rise through time and MES in the primary entry market is large relative to the scale of that market. Finally, the Guidelines also do not consider the possibility that potential entrants that are foreclosed from dealing with vertically-integrated established firms may find two-level independent entry less profitable than entering as part of a joint venture or securing the entry of a non-integrated firm at the second level by incurring the expense of identifying a suitable potential entrant, informing it of the possibly-profitable entry possibility, and perhaps subsidizing its entry with cash, a favorable loan, or a favorable long-term (full-requirements) contract. Nor, concomitantly, do the Guidelines address the determinants of the attractiveness of these options relative to the option of two-level entry.

Third, the 1984 Guidelines assert that, for vertical mergers or acquisitions to create a risk that they will lessen competition by raising barriers to entry, the market in question must not be competitive. On this account, the 1984 Guidelines state that the Antitrust Division is unlikely to challenge a vertical merger or acquisition unless the HHI in one of the markets concerned is above 1800. Perhaps this abstract condition would be justified if by "competitive" the DOJ meant "perfectly competitive," though even in that case an increase in the barriers to entry (and expansion) would have an effect as the original perfect competitors exited as their plant and equipment wore out. But, more important, the 1984 Guidelines' operationalization of competitive—a market with an HHI below 1800—makes clear that, at least in practice, the DOJ does not intend to interpret "competitive" to mean "perfectly competitive." For reasons that I examined in detail in Chaps. 8, 10, and 12, I do not think that HHIs are good predictors of the intensity of price competition, QV-investment competition, or overall competition in any area of product-space and would not think otherwise even if I were convinced that markets could be defined non-arbitrarily. However, I have no doubt that competition in many "markets" whose HHIs will in practice be determined to be under 1800 will be far from perfect and that, if their established firms were not vertically integrated, some of the potential entrants into and potential QV-investment expanders in those markets would be effective. Because the authors of the 1984 Guidelines did not focus separately on QV-investment competition and have no conceptual scheme for analyzing the conditions under which a potential competitor or a potential QV-investment expander will be effective, they could not offer any useful comments on the factors that determine what they should have identified as the third condition that must be fulfilled for there to be a risk that vertical mergers or acquisitions will reduce competition by raising barriers to entry (and expansion)—*viz.*, that one or more potential competitors or potential QV investors would have been effective had vertical integration not taken place.

Section 4.22 of the 1984 Guidelines discuss the second way in which its authors believe that vertical mergers and acquisitions can lessen competition—

viz., by facilitating collusion. The 1984 Guidelines state that vertical mergers or acquisitions can increase collusion by eliminating a "disruptive buyer" in markets whose structural characteristics permit effective collusion. The Guidelines seem to imply that the DOJ will not conclude that an allegedly-disruptive buyer is in fact disruptive unless "it differs substantially in volume of purchases or other relevant characteristic from the other firms in its market" and that the DOJ will not consider the relevant market's structure to be requisitely conducive to collusion unless its HHI is above 1,800. I have four objections. First, unless "other relevant characteristics" is defined in a way that makes the operationalization redundant (*i.e.*, to include the characteristic of being disruptive), I reject the DOJ's test for disruptiveness—indeed, I do not even agree with its apparent implicit assumption that relatively-large buyers are likely to be more disruptive than relatively-small buyers. Second, I do not think that there is much of a connection between whether a market's HHI is over or under 1,800 and either the profitability of collusion-efforts to the sellers that operate in it or the likelihood that they will attempt to engage in collusion when it would be profitable for them to do so. Third, as Sect. 4 of this chapter explained, vertical mergers and acquisitions can affect the profitability of contrived oligopolistic pricing, of jointly (or individually) creating retaliation barriers to entry or expansion, and of concerted (or individual-firm) predation in a large number of ways that the 1984 Guidelines ignore. And fourth, it is not at all clear as a matter of law that any tendency of a merger to increase (illegal) collusion in the markets in which the MPs operated count against its Clayton Act legality (since one could permit the merger or acquisition that would otherwise be lawful and attack the collusion when it occurs), and any such tendency will critically affect the legality of a vertical merger or acquisition under the Sherman Act only if (1) the participants' *ex ante* belief that their merger or acquisition would or might enable them to engage in additional collusion critically affected their *ex ante* perception that the vertical merger or acquisition in question was profitable and/or (2) the merger or acquisition was a sufficiently-concrete step in the direction of committing a planned future illegal act to be actionable on that account.

Section 4.23 of the 1984 Guidelines discusses the third way in which the DOJ of that era believed vertical mergers and acquisitions can lessen competition in the Clayton Act sense—*viz.*, by enabling a participant whose prices or rate-of-return is regulated to evade rate-regulation. Although I agree that a vertical merger and acquisition can enable a regulated monopolist to evade rate-regulation and that the consequence of its doing so will be higher prices for consumers, on my interpretation, that consequence is irrelevant to the legality of the vertical merger or acquisition in question under either the Clayton Act or the Sherman Act. It is irrelevant to the legality of the relevant transaction under the Clayton Act because it does not involve relevant buyers' suffering an equivalent-dollar loss *because the best offer they have respectively received from any inferior supplier has worsened.* It is irrelevant to the legality of the relevant transaction under the Sherman Act because the associated gain to the perpetrators is not caused by a deterioration in the absolute attractiveness of the offers against which they have to compete.

I have criticized the 1984 Guidelines in such detail because the criticisms reveal the value of the conceptual systems and theories this study has developed. However, from the perspective of the concerns of this section, the important point is that the conditions that the DOJ's 1984 Guidelines state must be fulfilled for it to challenge a vertical merger or acquisition will be fulfilled at most infrequently. It therefore comes as no surprise that at least since 1984 the Antitrust Division has devoted few resources to investigating or challenging vertical mergers or acquisitions. (Admittedly, the FTC has paid somewhat more attention to such transactions.)

I want to close this section with what amounts to a brief postscript about the Federal Energy Regulatory Commission's treatment of vertical mergers and acquisitions. Until now, this study has ignored the fact that not only the DOJ and FTC but also the FERC enforce antitrust rules in the U.S.—in the FERC's case when the perpetrators are operating in relevant portions of the energy sector. I will limit myself to pointing out that some of the concerns that seem to have motivated the FERC's (generally-permissive) handling of vertical mergers and acquisitions—preventing businesses from being in a position in which they can learn and illicitly pass on another business' trade secrets or preventing firms from securing a position that will facilitate their evading price or rate-of-return regulation are not antitrust concerns, regardless of whether they are appropriate concerns for the FERC, other public-utility regulators, or private-law courts or legislators.[1425]

B. The Legality of Vertical Mergers and Acquisitions Under E.C./E.U. Competition Law, Both as Correctly Interpreted and as Actually Applied

(1) The Legality of Vertical Mergers and Acquisitions Under E.C./E.U. Competition Law as Correctly Interpreted

All vertical mergers and acquisitions are covered by the EMCR, which promulgates a Clayton-Act-type "lessening-competition" test of illegality. Any vertical merger or acquisition that has as a (critical) object or effect increasing the amount of contrived oligopolistic pricing the merged firm/resulting business organization practices relative to the amount that its antecedents would have practiced, increasing the retaliation barriers to entry or expansion the merged firm/resulting business organization erects relative to the retaliation barriers its antecedents would have erected, or increasing the amount of predation the merged firm/resulting business organization practices relative to the amount its antecedents would have practiced is covered by now-Article 101 and violates that Article if its participants cannot establish a now-Article 101(3) defense for the transaction. And any vertical merger or acquisition one or both of whose participants are dominant firms is covered by now-Article 102 and violates its terms if it reduces the buyer surplus that the customers of either participating firm

[1425] For an intelligent description and critique of the FERC's vertical-merger-and-acquisition decisions, see Timothy J. Brennan, *"Vertical Market Power" as Oxymoron: Horizontal Approaches to Vertical Antitrust*, 12 GEO. MASON L. REV. 895 (2004).

realize on their transactions with it to an absolute level or relevant percentage of some transaction-surplus figure that renders the seller in question guilty of an exploitative abuse or, possibly, if it leads the merged firm/resulting business organization to engage in more contrivance or predation than its antecedents would have done—in which case the merger or acquisition might be deemed to constitute an exclusionary abuse, though a strong argument can be made for not attributing to the merger or acquisition the subsequent, illegal exploitative abuses to which it led.

In part for reasons that Sect. 4A(1)'s analysis of the legality of vertical mergers and acquisitions under U.S. antitrust law properly interpreted reveals, vertical mergers and acquisitions rarely violate E.C./E.U. competition law. Thus, the earlier section's explanation of why few if any such transactions violate the Clayton Act imply that few if any of them are likely to violate the EMCR or the effect branch of Article 101's test of illegality. Similarly, the earlier section's analysis of why few such transactions are likely to increase the profits their participants can earn by contriving oligopolistic margins, erecting retaliation barriers, or practicing predation, the possibility that firms may not choose to make profits in these ways even when they could do so, and the earlier section's account of the various economic efficiencies such transactions can generate and the ways in which they can benefit relevant buyers all suggest that few vertical mergers and acquisitions violate the object branch of now-Article 101's test of illegality. Finally, the arguments that favor the conclusion that few vertical mergers and acquisitions violate now-Article 101 imply that few such transactions that involve a dominant firm violate either the exclusionary-abuse branch or the exploitative-abuse branch of now-Article 102. Indeed, the probability that a vertical merger or acquisition that involves a dominant firm will violate the exploitative-abuse branch of now-Article 102's test of illegality is even lower than the probability that such a transaction will violate now-Article 101 since conduct that reduces the buyer surplus of a dominant firm's customers may not reduce it critically from the perspective of the exploitative-abuse branch of the now-Article 102 test of illegality.

(2) The Legality of Vertical Mergers and Acquisitions Under E.C./E.U. Competition Law as Actually Applied

I will first describe and criticize in some detail the EC's handling of one non-internal-growth vertical-integration case (*MSG Media Service*[1426]) whose treatment by the EC was typical[1427] of the way in which the EC analyzed the legality of non-internal-growth vertical-integration cases prior to 2005 (2005 represents a turning point because in that year the CFI criticized the EC's handling of one

---

[1426] Case IV/M. 469, OJ L364/1 (1994).

[1427] See, *e.g.*, Nordic Satellite Distribution, Case IV/M. 490, OJ L53/20 (1996); RTL/Veronica/Endemol, Case IV/M. 1157, OJ L183/1 (1999); Vivendi Canal/Seagram, Case COMP/M. 2050, and AOL/Time Warner, Case COMP/M. 1845 (2000), OJ L268/28 (2001).

such case[1428] and the ECJ criticized the EC's handling of certain issues in conglomerate-merger cases that are equally relevant to the disposition of non-internal-growth vertical-integration cases[1429]). I will then consider the relevant sections of the EC's 2008 Non-Horizontal Merger Guidelines, which the EC published in part to indicate its intention to handle future non-internal-growth vertical-integration cases in the way that in 2005 the courts stated was legally required and in part to elaborate on the protocol for deciding such cases that the courts concluded was warranted.

The pre-2005 EC case I will consider will also be relevant in Chap. 15 since it addresses the legality of a vertical joint venture as opposed to a vertical merger or acquisition. (Joint ventures are classified as concentrations in E.C./E.U. competition law.) In *MSG Media Service*,[1430] the Commission prohibited a joint venture (MSG) that its parents—Bertelsmann AG, Deutsche Bundespost Telekom, and Kirch, two of which (Bertelsmann and Kirch) had substantial shares of the German pay-TV market—were proposing to create to supply pay-TV providers with technical and administrative services. The Commission condemned the proposed joint venture, grounding its conclusion that the joint venture violated the EMCR on a finding that the joint venture would entrench Bertelsmann's and Kirch's dominant positions in the pay-TV market (presumably by worsening the competitive-position arrays of their extant and possible future pay-TV rivals). More specifically, the EC stated that the joint venture would entrench its parents' dominant position because MSG would charge its parents' rivals prices for its services that exceeded the cost that MSG's parents would have to incur to obtain MSG's services (in reality, although the EC did not note this fact, any payments MSG's parents would make to MSG *plus* any losses or *minus* any profits the parents would make by creating and operating MSG) and because MSG would make smart-card and other technical/technological decisions that would place its parents' rivals at a disadvantage when marketing their programs. (The EC did not advert to the possibility that MSG might simply refuse to supply its services to its parents' rivals.)

The EC's analysis of the legal significance of these possibilities did not address whether the allegedly-competition-reducing conduct in which it believed MSG would engage would be predatory in the Sherman Act sense (exclusionary in the now-Article 102 sense)—*i.e.*, would have as a critical object preventing or restricting the competition that MSG's parents faced. If the decisions that the EC was concerned MSG might make would be predatory (exclusionary), the EC should have considered the likelihood that such conduct would itself violate the E.C./E.U. competition law because, if it would, that fact would both (1) reduce the likelihood

---

[1428] See General Electric v. Commission, Case T-201/01, ECRII-5575 (2005), an appeal from EC decision in General Electric/Honeywell, Case COMP/M. 2220 (2001), OJ L048/1, 2004/134 (2004).

[1429] Tetra Laval, Case C-13/03 (2005), ECR-I/1113 (2005), an appeal from Tetra Laval v. Commission, Case T-5/02 (2002), ECR-II 4381 (2002), 5 CMLR 1182 (2002).

[1430] Case IV/M. 469, OJ L364/1 (1994).

that MSG would engage in the conduct in question by making it even less attractive morally and by increasing the law-related cost of engaging in the conduct in question and (2) favor the conclusion that the response to the proposed joint venture that would be correct as a matter of law would be to permit the joint venture if it would not otherwise lessen competition and find illegal any illegal conduct in which the joint venture engaged.

I hasten to add that the legality of any predatory (exclusionary) conduct in which MSG might engage under E.C./E.U. competition law will depend on whether MSG or its parents would be deemed to be dominant firms. If (1) MSG would be deemed to be a dominant firm or if (2)(A) MSG's parents would be deemed to be individually or collectively dominant and (B) MSG's conduct was attributed to its parents (I think all three conclusions would be legally correct), any predatory conduct in which MSG engaged would violate the exclusionary-abuse branch of what is now-Article 102 of the Lisbon Treaty. The illegality of MSG's predicted conduct under Article 102 is critical because at least some and probably all of the conduct in question would not be covered by what is now Article 101 of the Lisbon Treaty even if it were exclusionary: thus, now-Article 101 (1) would not cover any of MSG's predatory refusals to deal or any of its unilateral predatory decisions to alter smart-cards or make other technological changes that would disadvantage its parents' rivals because such conduct would not constitute agreements between undertakings or concerted practices and would not be made by a trade association and (2) probably would not cover any MSG decisions to engage in predatory pricing to prevent or restrict the competition its parents face. (Although MSG's predatory pricing might appear to be covered by now-Article 101 when the buyers in question agree to pay the relevant prices since the prices would then be terms in agreements between undertakings, that conclusion does not imply that now-Article 101 would cover predatory pricing that deters all sales, and the conclusion that predatory pricing that does not prevent the formation of some sales-contracts is covered by now-Article 101 is disfavored by the fact that outright refusals to deal are not covered by now-Article 101 [on the logic that, if the greater evil is not covered, the lesser evil should also not be found to be covered].)

I should indicate as well that I am not at all convinced that—law-related costs aside—MSG would find it profitable to practice predation by refusing to deal with its parents' rivals or charging them predatorily-high prices: I see no reason to believe that such predation would be more profitable than predatory pricing by the parents. Moreover, although it is certainly possible that some smart-card or other technological maneuvers that would not otherwise be profitable might be rendered profitable by their tendency to disadvantage MSG's parents' actual and prospective rivals (might be a more-cost-effective method of predation than predatory pricing by the parents), the EC did not explain the relative-predation-proficiency of such technology-changes sufficiently to enable someone as ignorant as I am about the relevant facts to evaluate the likelihood that the parents would find some such business-moves by their joint venture to be the most-cost-effective method of predation available to them. I remain skeptical.

Of course, it is possible that MSG might find it inherently profitable to make pricing or technological decisions that would reduce the absolute attractiveness of the offers against which its parents would have to compete (1) by improving the parents' short-run competitive-position arrays and worsening the parents' rivals' (because the marginal or incremental cost of MSG's services to the parents were lower than the prices MSG would charge its parents' rivals even if MSG was not pricing predatorily) and/or (2) by improving the parents' long-run competitive-position arrays by inducing the exit of one or more of the parents' extant rivals in circumstances in which they would not be immediately replaced by equally-effective competitors or critically raising the barriers to entry facing one or more otherwise-effective potential competitors of MSG's parents by making it inherently profitable for its parents to lower their prices and/or improve their programming. However, the EC did not address either of these possibilities. Moreover, although it is true that, if the MSG conduct that would reduce competition is not independently illegal, one could not argue that the joint venture should be held legal under the EMCR (1) because the predicted behavior would not eventuate in that its law-related cost would be prohibitive and (2) because the predicted behavior could be attacked once it occurred, for two reasons, the fact that these arguments for finding a joint venture lawful under the EMCR will not be available when the allegedly-competition-reducing decisions that the joint venture might make are not independently illegal does not imply that vertical joint ventures or mergers or acquisitions that would create undertakings whose lawful behavior would tend to lessen competition if non-parents could not prevent themselves from being disadvantaged by it should be held to violate the EMCR (if the joint ventures, mergers, or acquisitions in question would not otherwise lessen competition—see below): (1) in at least some situations, non-parents will be able to protect themselves from disadvantagement by entering the joint venture's market individually, by creating their own joint ventures to enter the joint venture's market, by inducing independent entries into the joint venture's market, or by taking advantage of truly-independent entry into the joint venture's market, and (2) even if the parents' rivals cannot protect themselves in some such way, a decision to prohibit the joint venture because it lessens competition by improving the parents' competitive-position arrays would contravene the commitment of E.C./E.U. competition law to allowing undertakings to compete on the competitive merits (a commitment that the E.C./ E.U. courts and the EC are increasingly recognizing). The EC did not address any of these issues either.

In short, the EC's analysis of the legality of vertical joint ventures and by implication vertical mergers and acquisitions under the EMCR in *MSG Media Service* was seriously deficient. The EC did not adequately analyze (1) whether the joint venture would actually engage in the conduct through which the Commission predicted the joint venture would lessen the competition the parents faced or (2) whether the conduct in question would actually have such an impact, given the various moves the parents' rivals could make to protect themselves; it did not adequately consider whether the joint-venture conduct in question would be profitable for the parents even if it would not reduce the competition they faced; it did not consider whether the conduct in question would be independently illegal under E.C./E.U. law or the implications of its being independently illegal both for the probability that the joint venture would engage in it and for the relevance of any conclusion that the joint venture would engage in it for the legality of the joint venture itself; and it did not consider the implications for the legality of a joint venture of a finding that the joint venture would reduce the competition its parents faced even if it did not engage in predation simply by increasing the parents' organizational economic efficiency.[1431] All these deficiencies are also present in the EC's analyses of the legality of the vertical mergers and acquisitions they addressed between 1994 and 2005, the CFI's review of the EC's analysis of the GE/Honeywell vertical merger,[1432] and the ECJ's review of the EC's analysis of a conglomerate merger in a decision that addressed issues that are as salient in vertical-merger as in conglomerate-merger cases.[1433]

In *General Electric v. Commission*, the CFI reviewed *inter alia* the EC's decision that the vertical component of a merger between General Electric and Honeywell violated the EMCR. GE was the largest of three large manufacturers of engines for large commercial jet aircraft. GE also had a financial subsidiary (GE Capital) that financed the platform-program-development projects of aircraft manufacturers and had rescued at least one major airline. GE had an additional subsidiary—Capital Aviation Services (GECAS)—that purchased and leased aircraft—indeed, "was the world's largest buyer of airplanes,. . .[making] 10 % of all purchases of new commercial aircraft."[1434] Honeywell was the largest maker of engine starters for jet engines.

The EC found that GE was a dominant firm in the market for manufacturing jet engines for large commercial aircraft and large regional aircraft and that Honeywell was a dominant firm in the jet-engine-starter-manufacturing market. It then concluded that the vertical component of GE's merger with Honeywell would violate the EMCR both because the merger would strengthen GE's dominance of the large-commercial-jet-aircraft-engine market and because it would strengthen

---

[1431] Like the EC in *MSG Media Service*, the text ignores one ground for finding vertical joint ventures illegal under the EMCR that is arguable but I think wrong and three for doing so that will sometimes be justified. I have ignored these possibilities in the text of this chapter because they are peculiar to joint ventures and will be discussed in detail in Chapter 15. The EC cannot justify its failure to address these possibilities in this way. The contestable ground is that the EMCR should be interpreted to require the parents of a vertical joint venture to make participation in it available to all their rivals on "fair and equal" terms. The possible correct grounds are that the joint venture may facilitate the parents' engaging in contrived oligopolistic pricing or cooperative predatory pricing in the upstream market by affording them the opportunity to communicate with each other, may reduce competition in the downstream market by preventing entries into that market by two or more parents, and may reduce competition in upstream markets by enabling the parents to arrange not to enter into each other's markets when they would otherwise have done so and no-one else will do so either at all or as effectively as they would have done.

[1432] General Electric v. Commission, Case T-201/01, ECR-II 5575 (2005).

[1433] Tetra Laval, Case C-13/03 (2005), ECR-I/1113 (2005).

[1434] KORAH 420–21.

Honeywell's dominance of the jet-engine-starter-manufacturing market. In Korah's words, the EC believed that the GE/Honeywell combination would secure these results "through bundling, leveraging, and strategic behavior" that *inter alia* would induce buyers to shift enough of their patronage away from Honeywell's rivals to induce those rivals to exit.[1435] I have already explained why an individual firm's use of bundling and other forms of tie-ins and reciprocity agreements will almost never reduce competition in a way that is legally problematic. I suppose that the "firm" that the GE/Honeywell merger would have created might have engaged in predation by conditioning its provision of financing to aircraft manufacturers and airlines on their buying Honeywell starters or by conditioning its purchases of aircraft on the manufacturer's using Honeywell starters and GE engines when those conditions were not inherently profitable. Indeed, Korah's account of the case calls attention (for I suspect this reason) to the facts that pre-merger (1) GE had received an exclusive-purchase order for its jet engines from a major airline to which GE Capital had supplied a critical loan[1436] and (2) GECAS' "policy was to buy only planes fitted with GE engines."[1437] However, I doubt that GE would have found it more profitable to drive out its rivals in these ways (even if it had obligated the airline GE Capital rescued to purchase GE's engines) rather than more straightforwardly by charging predatorily-low prices for its engines: the tie-ins and reciprocity in question seem unlikely to have been rendered profitable by any ability to conceal GE's predation, and I can see no other way in which the arrangement in question would have increased the profitability of predation to GE. My own suspicion is that the facts in question have innocent explanations. The rescued airline gave GE an exclusive-purchase order because GE offered it a better deal than anyone else, and GECAS restricted its plane purchases to planes with GE jet engines because it thought those engines were superior and/or believed that it could maintain and repair them more cost-effectively than it could the engines of other manufacturers (if it had some obligation to maintain and repair the engines of aircraft it supplied others). Indeed, even if GE Capital's loan to the airline in question (indeed, to all airlines to which it made loans) was conditioned on its recipient's (respective recipients') purchasing jet engines exclusively from GE, that arrangement might be perfectly legitimate—might implement a meter-pricing scheme in which the rate of interest charged for the loan and other loan terms (the lump-sum-fee counterpart) was reduced and the recipient agreed to make additional payments by purchasing GE's engines for more than the recipient would otherwise have been willing to pay for them whose total would increase with the *ex post* value of the loan to them—*i.e.*, with the number of engines the loan made it profitable for them to buy by enabling them to survive.

In any event, the EC was particularly concerned that the GE/Honeywell merger would reduce competition in GE's jet-engine-manufacturing market (in which GE was already dominant) by creating a company that would have an incentive to and

---

[1435] *Id.* at 421.

[1436] *Id.* at 420.

[1437] *Id.* at 421.

would drive out GE's rivals by delaying or disrupting the supply of Honeywell starters to them or charging them predatorily-high prices for engine starters or their spares. The EC was concerned with this possibility because it found that (1) the major alternative existing source of jet-engine starters (Hamilton Sundstrand) had indicated that, even if the price of jet-engine starters increased, it would have no commercial interest in selling them to anyone other than the company to which it was currently supplying such starters exclusively (P&W) and (2) the barriers to entry into the jet-engine-starter business were prohibitively high.

The CFI did not question the EC's implicit assumption that the merged firm would find it more profitable to practice predation in one or both of the above ways than to do so straightforwardly by reducing the price of GE engines (an assumption I find dubious at best) and, more generally, did not reject the EC's bundling/leverage "theories." However, after repeating the ECJ's conclusions in the conglomerate-merger case *Tetra Laval* that (1) to justify a decision against a merger or acquisition on the ground that the resulting company would engage in future conduct that would lessen competition the EC would have to supply "convincing evidence" for its prediction and (2) the convincing evidence in question could consist of either "economic studies" or less-formal, "simple" accounts of the relevant "economic and commercial realities," the CFI pointed out that the EC had not relied on any formal economic study but had based its decision on a simple analysis of the economic and commercial realities that had ignored a possibly-critical legal reality—*viz.*, that both the predicted refusal to deal and the predicted price-increase might be deemed illegal under Article 82 (now-Article 102) as abuses of a dominant position. Indeed, according to the CFI, any price-increase on engine starters that would be big enough to drive out a rival of GE would be "so large that it would clearly amount to an abuse" and any "discriminatory" "disruption of supplies" to buyers of rival engines "would [also] clearly constitute abuse." The CFI concluded that, if the EC had taken this legal reality—*i.e.*, the associated "deterrent effect" of this legal reality—into account, "it could materially have influenced the Commission's appraisal of how likely it was that the conduct in question would be adopted." The CFI therefore held "that the [parts] of the contested decision relating to the strengthening of...[GE's] premerger dominant position on the market for large commercial jet aircraft engines, resulting from the vertical overlap between its engine-manufacturing business and Honeywell's manufacture of starters for those engines, is not sufficiently established...."[1438] I would have added that, even if the EC could establish that the merged company would engage in the relevant predation despite the legal disincentives in question, the fact that the conduct in question would be independently illegal would call into question the correctness as a matter of law of prohibiting the merger on this account: at least arguably, the legally-correct

[1438] I should make brief reference to one other feature of the CFI opinion. Like the EC's, the CFI's conclusion that GE was a dominant firm in the commercial-jet-engine-manufacturing market was partly based on its contestable attribution to GE of all the production of various joint ventures of which GE was just one parent.

response would be to allow the otherwise-not-illegal merger and move against the merged company's anticompetitive conduct when it occurred.

In 2008, after publishing Draft Guidelines and soliciting and obtaining comments on them, the EC promulgated Guidelines on the Assessment of Non-Horizontal [*i.e.*, Vertical and Conglomerate] Mergers Under the Council Regulation on the Control of Concentrations Between Undertakings.[1439] Since Chap. 13 already considered the sections of these Guidelines that relate to conglomerate concentrations and the Guidelines' treatment of vertical and conglomerate concentrations overlap in many ways, after summarizing the Guidelines' approach to vertical concentrations, I will comment primarily on the points the Guidelines make that are particularly relevant to vertical concentrations.

The 2008 Guidelines state[1440] that the net competitive impact of a vertical concentration depends on whether the amount by which it reduces competition (*i.e.*, the equivalent-euro losses it imposes on relevant buyers) (1) by "foreclosing" its participants' rivals from access to inputs (from upstream markets),[1441] (2) by foreclosing its participants' rivals from distributive services or downstream non-distributor buyers more generally (from downstream markets),[1442] (3) by giving the resulting entity access to "commercially sensitive information regarding the upstream or downstream activities of rivals" whose possession will "allow it to price less aggressively in the downstream market to the detriment of consumers" for reasons unrelated to coordination or "put competitors at a competitive disadvantage, thereby dissuading them to enter or expand in the market,"[1443] and (4) by increasing "coordination"[1444] *exceeds* the amount by which it increases competition (confers equivalent-euro gains on relevant buyers) by generating economic efficiencies.[1445] The 2008 EC Non-Horizontal Merger Guidelines articulate the correct and important general conclusion that "[n]on-horizontal mergers [including vertical mergers] are generally less likely to significantly impede effective competition than horizontal mergers"[1446] because they "do not entail the loss of direct competition between the merging firms"[1447] and conclude that "[t]he Commission is unlikely to find concern in non-horizontal mergers [including vertical mergers] be it of a coordinated or of a non-coordinated nature where the market share of the new entity in each of the markets concerned is below 30 % and the post-merger HHI is below 2,000,"[1448] except when the merged company is likely to "expand significantly in the near

---

[1439] 2008/C 265/07.

[1440] *Id.* at point 21.

[1441] *Id.* at points 40–46.

[1442] *Id.* at points 58–77.

[1443] *Id.* at point 78.

[1444] *Id.* at points 79–90.

[1445] *Id.* at points 13–14 and 54–57.

[1446] *Id.* at point 10.

[1447] *Id.* at point 12.

[1448] *Id.* at point 25.

future," market-share and market-concentration data is less informative because of "cross-shareholdings or cross-directorships among the market participants," one of the merging firms is a maverick, or there is evidence that market participants have engaged in or are still engaging in "coordination."[1449] This operational conclusion reflects the EC's beliefs that (1) vertical (and conglomerate) mergers are unlikely to yield competition-reducing foreclosures or increases in (illegal?) coordination unless at least one of the participants has market power in at least one of the markets concerned and the structure of at least one of the markets in question is conducive to foreclosure and/or coordination and that (2) except when one or more of the facts listed after the words "except when" in the preceding sentence obtain, market-share figures are accurate indicators of firm market power and HHI figures are good indicators of the profitability of foreclosure and "coordination." The 2008 EC Non-Horizontal Merger Guidelines also state that, although participant market power and favorable market structure (usually high market concentration) are necessary conditions for "competitive harm," they are not sufficient conditions.[1450] This conclusion might reflect the EC's realization that—at least if the feared "foreclosure" and "coordination" is independently illegal—vertical-concentration participants might not engage in foreclosing or illegal coordinated conduct out of respect for the law even if the possibility of legal sanctions does not render such conduct *ex ante* unprofitable. However, the Guidelines do not mention this possibility. Instead, the Guidelines' statement that participant market power and high market concentration are necessary but not sufficient conditions for competitive harm seems to have more to do with (1) the EC's belated recognition that, if the allegedly-competition-reducing conduct in question would violate E.C./E.U. competition law (or, presumably if it might be deemed to violate E.C./E.U. competition law), that fact might deter the resulting entity from engaging in it (a point made both by the ECJ in *Tetra Laval* and by the CFI in *GE/Honeywell*),[1451] (2) the EC's recognition that, in some cases in which foreclosure might otherwise be a risk, the potentially-foreclosed parties may be able to prevent the foreclosure by using "effective and timely counterstrategies,"[1452] the foreclosure may be prevented by new entry,[1453] or the ultimate buyers on which foreclosure would otherwise impose losses may be able to protect themselves from harm by exercising their buying power,[1454] and (3) the EC's realization that in some cases in which a vertical concentration will impose equivalent-euro losses on relevant buyers in one or more

---

[1449] *Id.* at point 26.

[1450] *Id.* at point 27.

[1451] *Id.* at point 46.

[1452] *Id.* at points 39 and 67.

[1453] This possibility is recognized implicitly in *id.* at points 49 and 64 and explicitly at *id.* at point 76.

[1454] *Id.* at point 76.

of the above-listed ways, the concentration will generate economic efficiencies that confer at least as large equivalent-euro gains on the buyers in question.[1455]

I will now criticize nine aspects of the 2008 EC Guidelines' discussion of vertical concentrations that I find incorrect or inadequate. First, although the Guidelines are correct in stating that input-foreclosure (*i.e.*, upstream foreclosure) can be achieved in many ways—*e.g.*, through absolute refusals to deal, partial restrictions of supply, price-increases, changes in product to variants that are incompatible with rival operations, and degradation of the inputs supplied[1456]—and that downstream foreclosure can also be secured in many ways—*e.g.*, through total refusals to purchase from upstream rivals, reductions in purchases from upstream rivals, and offering rivals less-favorable terms,[1457] the EC does not consider the possibility that in some circumstances the conduct in question might be inherently profitable (might not have as a critical object reducing the absolute attractiveness of the offers against which the vertically-integrated firm must compete)—*i.e.*, does not consider the reasons why or the conditions under which this would be the case or the legal implications of its being the case.

Second, the 2008 Guidelines do not explain when and why a vertically-integrated firm will find it more profitable to engage in predation in the ways just listed rather than by reducing the retail price it charges for the good it produces. Such an explanation is required because, as I explained earlier, unless some special conditions are fulfilled, a vertically-integrated (distributor)/(producer) (1) will find it profitable to purchase (the final goods it distributes)/(its inputs) from an independent concern that is better-placed to supply it than is its own (final-good)/(input)-production division and (2) will find it profitable to (distribute the final goods it produces)/(sell the inputs it produces) (through an independent distributor)/(to an independent final-good producer) that is better-placed (to distribute its output)/(to produce the relevant final good) than its (in-house distributors)/(in-house final-good-production division) are.

Third, the 2008 EC Guidelines' claim that foreclosure is more likely to be effective the higher the share that the resulting vertically-integrated entity has of the relevant market assumes incorrectly that relevant markets can be defined non-arbitrarily and ignores the fact that not all potential suppliers of potential distributors for a foreclosure target are equally-well-placed to deal with it—*i.e.*, the fact that the integrated undertaking may be a more-important (or less-important) potential customer or supplier of the foreclosed supplier than the integrated undertaking's market share might suggest. The latter objection will be important when (1) if no-one engaged in strategic behavior, the profits that the foreclosure target would earn by supplying the vertically-integrated concern would constitute a higher share of its total profits than the integrated firm's purchases and sales constituted of all purchases and sales made in the relevant market and (2) if

[1455] *Id.* at points 21 and 54–57.

[1456] *Id.* at point 33.

[1457] *Id.* at point 60.

no-one engaged in strategic behavior, the profits that the foreclosure target would earn by distributing the vertically-integrated concern's final product or using the input it produced to produce its own final product would constitute a higher share of its total profits than the integrated firm's purchases and sales constituted of all purchases and sales made in the relevant market.

Fourth, the 2008 EC Guidelines mis-state the factors that determine the extent to which the possible illegality of any foreclosing decisions a resulting vertically-integrated entity might make would reduce their profitability and hence the likelihood that the firm in question would make those choices. In particular, the Guidelines state that the EC will on this account take into consideration "(i) the likelihood that. . .[the] conduct [in question] would be clearly, or highly probably, illegal, (ii) the likelihood that this illegal conduct would be detected, and (iii) the penalties which could be imposed."[1458] The correct statement of the factors to be considered would substitute for the words that appear after "(i)" "the likelihood that the conduct in question would be challenged by the EC, the likelihood that it would be found illegal by the EC, the likelihood that it would be found illegal by the CFI, and the likelihood that it would be found illegal by the ECJ" and would substitute for the words after "(iii)" "the cost of defending the conduct in question before the EC, CFI, and ECJ, the likelihood that it would be found illegal by the last decisionmaker to consider that issue, and the penalties that could be imposed."

Fifth, although the list of "effective and timely counterstrategies" that the Guidelines mention includes one that might be significant—sponsoring new entry[1459]—and one that could work (though I doubt that it often will be available—"changing. . .production process so as to be less reliant on the input concerned,"[1460] it contains one other—"pricing more aggressively"[1461]—that seems unlikely to be of much use (will be useful only if the post-foreclosure profit-maximizing price of the foreclosed firms is lower) and does not explicitly consider the possibility that a foreclosed firm might be able to protect itself by engaging in independent vertical integration, participating in a vertical joint venture, or inducing an entry by an independent firm.

Sixth, the various critiques I made of the 2008 Guidelines' treatment of the ways in which conglomerate mergers can affect coordination (contrivance in my terms) apply fully to the Guidelines' treatment of the ways in which vertical concentrations can do so.

Seventh, the Guidelines' claim that a vertical concentration can harm relevant buyers in ways that are relevant to its legality by giving the "merged entity. . .access to commercially sensitive information" whose possession (1) enables it to "price less aggressively" and (2) deters rivals from entering or expanding is disturbing in that the first concern appears to assume that the fact that a concentration enables a

---

[1458] *Id.* at point 46.

[1459] *Id.* at point 39.

[1460] *Id.*

[1461] *Id.* at point 38.

seller to raise its prices without contriving by giving it more information about its rivals' competitive positions and pricing counts against its legality under the EMCR and the second concern appears to assume that the fact that a concentration deters entries and expansions by providing its participants with information that increases their organizational economic efficiency counts against its legality under the EMCR. But perhaps these criticisms do not really go to the relevant core concern of the EC. Although the EC never articulated this concern, perhaps the Commission is worried that (1) the legal permissibility of vertical mergers and acquisitions that would lead the integrated distribution or input-supply division to reveal to its in-house production-division business-reality or business-plan information that relates to the plans or positions of rivals of the production-division that the production-division's rivals previously supplied the formerly-independent but now-integrated distributor, input supplier, management consultant, financier, or lawyer to determine whether the independent actors in question would be good "trading partners" and to encourage them to "trade" with the relevant rival of the integrated production-division in question and that (2) the prospect of such leaks' occurring would reduce economic efficiency (A) by rendering unprofitable business-plan-information communications that are otherwise-profitable and antitrust-assumed economically efficient and (B) by deterring firms from making distribution arrangements and supply arrangements that would otherwise be profitable and the antitrust laws assume would be economically efficient, by deterring firms from securing financing in the way that would otherwise be most profitable (and presumptively economically efficient), and by deterring firms from securing management and legal advice that would otherwise be most profitable and (unless the advice's profitability reflected its enabling the firm to reduce the competition it faced) presumptively economically efficient. I do not think that this concern is idle. But my inclination is to handle this problem through an expanded trade-secret law or *culpa in contrahendo* or "promissory estoppel" doctrine rather than by prohibiting the vertical mergers and acquisitions that can cause it.

Eighth, the Guidelines' account of the economic efficiency that vertical concentrations can generate[1462]—though far from completely misguided—is not entirely satisfactory in that it (1) does not include any reference to continuous-flow economies, (2) classifies as an "efficiency" eliminating "pre-existing double-mark-ups"[1463] (when any such result would not constitute an economic efficiency and might not even tend to increase economic efficiency in our highly-Pareto-perfect economy, though it would benefit relevant buyers), (3) seems to assume that non-integrated firms would fail to respond to the losses that double markups would impose on them by using pure-lump-sum pricing-techniques that would eliminate the double markup or mixed lump-sum *plus* supra-marginal-cost per-unit-price techniques that would substantially reduce double markups, (4) does not distinguish between vertical-integration-permitted hierarchical controls that reduce purely-private losses that firms that are not vertically

[1462] *Id.* at points 54–57.

[1463] *Id.* at point 55.

integrated can suffer on that account from hierarchical controls that increase economic efficiency, (5) does not take account of the possibility that the economic-efficiency gains that vertical integration permits firms to secure by using hierarchical controls to influence their employees as opposed to using uncontrolled independent input suppliers and/or distributors would be smaller if the firms were allowed to use contract clauses or sales or consignment policies to control their independent distributors, and (6) does not take account of the economic efficiencies vertical integration can generate by enabling a firm to implement business plans without revealing to independents information whose communication to rivals would reduce the firm's profits.

Ninth and finally, the 2008 EC Guidelines give no indication that the Commission understands the determinants of the amount by which the various kinds of economic efficiencies vertical concentrations can generate will benefit relevant buyers.

The EC's 2008 Non-Horizontal Merger Guidelines make some improvements relative to the decisions that the EC had previously made in vertical-joint-venture and vertical-merger cases. However, they still contain important errors of omission and commission.

6. The Economic Functions and Competitive Consequences of Vertical Integration by Internal Growth

Chapter 12 does not address horizontal internal growth, and Chap. 13 does not explicitly address conglomerate internal growth. However, many of the points made in those and other chapters of this study do apply to horizontal internal growth and conglomerate internal growth. Thus, Sect. 4 of Chap. 10's analysis of the circumstances in which a QV investment will be predatory, the illegality of predatory QV investments, and the U.S. case-law on allegedly-predatory QV investments does apply to internal horizontal growth. Much of Sect. 1 of Chap. 12's analyses of the functions that horizontal mergers can perform and the ways in which horizontal mergers can increase or decrease competition apply *mutatis mutandis* to horizontal internal growth. And much of Sects. 1 and 3 of Chap. 13's analyses of the functions that conglomerate mergers can perform and the ways in which conglomerate mergers can increase or decrease competition apply *mutatis mutandis* to conglomerate internal growth.

I have decided to address vertical internal growth in Chap. 14 (if only briefly) in part to remedy (if only to a minor extent) this omission and in part because a few U.S. cases address the legality of vertical internal growth. The discussion of this section will partially make up for my failure to analyze horizontal and conglomerate internal growth in Chaps. 12 and 13 respectively because many of the points it will make about vertical internal growth apply to horizontal and conglomerate internal growth. The next section's discussion of the relevant U.S. cases is valuable not because they are curiosities but because they manifest the early hostility of the U.S. courts to vertical integration and the more contemporary courts' appreciation of the fact that vertical integration can perform many socially-valuable functions and usually does not violate U.S. antitrust law.

I will start by comparing the functions of vertical internal growth with those of vertical mergers and acquisitions. With the following exceptions, vertical internal growth can perform all the functions that vertical mergers and acquisitions can perform. Vertical internal growth cannot (1) generate economic efficiencies by combining companies that have assets that are complementary for non-scale reasons, (2) enable the resulting business organization to take advantage of what was another company's underutilized capacity to estimate its (HNOP + NOM)s accurately, to choose more profitable pricing-techniques, and/or to practice contrivance or predation profitably, (3) enable the resulting business organization to take better advantage of another firm's tax losses or the desire of the owner of another firm to liquidate his or her assets and escape managerial responsibilities, (4) enable two firms that wanted to engage in contrived oligopolistic pricing to substitute one communication for the two communications they originally had to make to an integrated rival, (5) enable the resulting business organization to inherit the stronger reputation for contrivance of one of its antecedents, (6) enable the resulting business organization to communicate its contrived oligopolistic intentions more cheaply simply by charging a contrived oligopolistic price by creating a new business organization that enjoys the stronger reputation for estimating its (HNOP + NOM)s accurately and for practicing contrivance than one of its antecedents had, (7) enable the resulting business organization to eliminate a buyer that disrupts price-fixing in one of the areas of product-space in question, and (8) enable the resulting business organization to practice predation by refusing to deal with non-integrated firms except (and this is a big exception) to the extent that the vertical internal growth causes the exit of a non-integrated firm or prevents the execution of a QV investment by a non-integrated firm.

Before proceeding to the various ways in which vertical internal growth can decrease competition in the Clayton Act sense, I want to make a few comments on the relative profitability of vertical integration through internal growth on the one hand and vertical integration through merger or acquisition on the other. Obviously, the fact that vertical internal growth cannot perform eight of the functions that vertical mergers and acquisitions can perform favors the conclusion that vertical mergers and acquisitions will be more profitable than vertical internal growth. Vertical mergers but not vertical acquisitions may also be more profitable than vertical internal growth because the capital costs of the merger is lower and because it may be possible for one MP to "pay less" for a merger partner than it is worth to the "paying" MP or for an acquiring firm to pay less for the acquired firm than it is worth to the acquirer. In the other direction, vertical internal growth will tend to be more profitable than vertical mergers or acquisitions to the extent that (1) it is more cost-effective for a firm to use its own otherwise-underutilized employees or hire additional employees from a variety of different sources to operate a new business than to integrate the employees of a merger partner or acquired firm into its organization, (2) the antitrust-law-related cost of a vertical merger or acquisition is higher than the antitrust-law-related cost of vertical internal growth, and (3) the internal growth raises QV investment in the market into which the firm in question is integrating whereas the merger or acquisition does not do so.

The fact that vertical internal growth cannot perform the functions of vertical mergers and acquisitions I indicated it could not perform implies (1) that vertical internal growth is less likely to impose equivalent-dollar losses on Clayton-Act-relevant buyers in Clayton-Act-relevant ways—*viz.*, (A) by driving out one or more established rivals that will not be replaced by equally-effective competitors by foreclosing them from supplies or distributive services, (B) by critically raising the barriers to entry facing an otherwise-effective potential QV investor by making it necessary for it to enter on two levels on its own, to participate in a joint-venture entry on the second level, or to solicit and perhaps subsidize a second-level entry by another non-integrated firm (perhaps by offering it a long-term requirements contract), and (C) by raising rival's costs, (2) that vertical internal growth is more likely than vertical mergers and acquisitions to confer equivalent-dollar gains on Clayton-Act-relevant buyers by increasing equilibrium QV investment or short-term actual QV investment in the relevant area of product-space, and (3) that vertical internal growth is less likely to confer equivalent-dollar gains by generating economic efficiencies because it will not generate such efficiencies by combining the assets of different firms that are complementary for non-scale reasons.

7. The Legality of Vertical Internal Growth Under U.S. Antitrust Law and E.C./E.U. Competition Law, Both as Correctly Interpreted and as Actually Applied

A. The Legality of Vertical Internal Growth Under U.S. Antitrust Law, Both as Correctly Interpreted and as Actually Applied

(1) U.S. Law as Correctly Interpreted

Vertical internal growth is covered by the Sherman Act but not by the Clayton Act. Section 5A of this chapter argued that vertical mergers and acquisitions rarely if ever violate the Sherman Act, correctly interpreted and applied. Section 6's account of the difference between the functions that vertical internal growth can perform on the one hand and vertical mergers and acquisitions can perform on the other does not suggest that a different conclusion about the legality of vertical internal growth under the Sherman Act is warranted: although vertical internal growth may be less able to generate legitimate profits in some ways, it is also sometimes more able to generate such profits and is also less able to generate profits illegitimately in various ways.

(2) U.S. Law as Actually Applied

In 1927, the Supreme Court concluded that a company's vertical internal growth violated the Sherman Act.[1464] The opinion manifested the fact that at that time U.S. courts believed that vertical integration was almost always motivated by anticompetitive intent. No more-recent Supreme Court decision addresses the legality of vertical internal growth under the Sherman Act. Fortunately, however, as Hovenkamp has stated, "the trend in recent lower court cases has been to permit vertical integration [by internal growth], even by the monopolist, unless there is clear evidence that the monopolist is attempting to use the integration to create a barrier to entry, or to increase the scope or duration of its monopoly in some other way."[1465] Hovenkamp cites two cases as evidence of this trend. In *Paschall v. Kansas City Star Co.*,[1466] the Eighth Circuit found lawful the decision of a daily newspaper to have its newspaper delivered by its own employees rather than by independent carriers, and in *Morris Communications Corp. v. PGA Tours, Inc.*,[1467] the Eleventh Circuit found lawful the choice of the Professional Golfers' Association to broadcast its own real-time golf-scores rather than using independent broadcasters to do so.

B. The Legality of Vertical Internal Growth Under E.C./E.U. Competition Law, Both as Correctly Interpreted and as Actually Applied

Vertical internal growth by a dominant firm is covered by now-Article 102 but not by the EMCR or now-Article 101, and vertical internal growth by non-dominant firms (even if it makes them dominant) is not covered by any provision of E.C./E.U. competition law. Vertical internal growth by a dominant firm that has the effect of leading the integrated firm to engage in additional predatory conduct or contrivance might violate the exclusionary branch of now-Article 102's test of illegality, though it is more than arguable that the legally-correct response would be to declare the predation or contrivance but not the vertical internal growth that led to it an exclusionary abuse of its perpetrator's dominant position. Vertical internal growth that leads the resulting business organization to engage in additional predation or contrivance or enables it to profit by using pricing-techniques that reduce the buyer surplus of the dominant firm's customers to an absolute level or a percentage of some amount of transaction surplus that is deemed unfair might also constitute an exploitative abuse of the firm's dominant position, though once more it is more than arguable that the legally-correct response is to declare the predation, contrivance, or

[1464] Eastman Kodak Co. of New York v. Southern Photo Materials Co., 273 U.S. 359 (1927).

[1465] HOVENKAMP ANTITRUST 159.

[1466] 727 F.2d 692 (8th Cir. 1984), en banc, cert. denied, 469 U.S. 872 (1984).

[1467] 364 F.3d 1288 (11th Cir. 2004).

use of the pricing-technique in question but not the vertical internal growth that led to it an exploitative abuse. I know of no E.C./E.U. competition-law case that addresses the legality of vertical internal growth.

* * *

Chapter 14 has argued that (1) vertical integration by merger or acquisition or by internal growth and its various surrogates can perform a large number of legitimate functions and can increase economic efficiency in a significant number of ways, (2) the vast majority of exemplars of vertical integration by merger or acquisition or by internal growth (hereinafter vertical integration) and its surrogates do not violate (the Sherman Act's specific-anticompetitive-intent)/(now-Article 101's critical-object or now-Article 102's exclusionary-abuse) test of illegality, (3) the vast majority of exemplars of vertical integration by merger or acquisition and its surrogates do not violate the Clayton Act/EMCR/Article 101 lessening-competition test of illegality, (4) a few exemplars of vertical integration and surrogates for vertical integration do violate the anticompetitive-intent/critical-object/exclusionary-abuse test of illegality, (5) a few exemplars of surrogates for vertical integration do violate the lessening-competition/effect-of-restricting-or-preventing competition test of illegality, (6) it might be incorrect as a matter of law to find exemplars of vertical integration that lessen competition because they lead their perpetrator(s) to engage in independently-illegal conduct illegal on that account, (7) exemplars of vertical integration and of various surrogates for vertical integration that impose equivalent-dollar losses on their perpetrator's or perpetrators' customers either in some way that implies that those losses are relevant to whether the conduct in question lessens competition in the Clayton Act sense or in some other way may violate the exploitative-abuse branch of now-Article 102, (8) the U.S. courts and antitrust-enforcement agencies originally believed that vertical integration and many of its surrogates always or usually violate U.S. antitrust law, (9) for the past 30 to 40 years, the U.S. antitrust-enforcement agencies have operated on the correct assumption that vertical integration and its various surrogates rarely violate U.S. antitrust law, (10) over the past 20 years, the U.S. Supreme Court and the lower federal courts have come to appreciate the fact that vertical integration and its surrogates can perform many legitimate and valuable functions and often do not violate U.S. antitrust law, though at least the Supreme Court remains attached to the incorrect notion that any tendency of such conduct to reduce intra-brand completion counts against its legality and that the correct approach to analyzing the legality of such behavior is to use a Rule-of-Reason analysis that balances any negative impact it has on intra-brand competition against any positive impact it has on inter-brand competition, (11) the EC and the E.C./E.U. courts were originally as hostile to vertical integration and many of its surrogates as the U.S. courts and antitrust-enforcement agencies were until the 1970s, (12) in the last 10 or so years, the EC and the E.C./E.U. courts have come to appreciate some of the economically-efficient functions that such conduct can perform and to assess somewhat more accurately the legality of such conduct under E.C./E.U. competition law, however (13) in my judgment, the EC and the E.C./E.U. courts still lag behind their U.S.

counterparts in assessing the legality under their respective laws of vertical integration and its various surrogates, (14) this difference reflects (A) the greater influence that economic analysis has on the application of antitrust law in the United States, (B) the fact that the E.C./E.U. antitrust-enforcement authorities still seem to think that the leverage theory is correct whereas their U.S. counterparts have come closer to rejecting this position, (C) the fact that the E.C./E.U. antitrust-enforcement authorities still seem to think that the probability that vertical integration or a surrogate for vertical integration will reduce competition has more to do with the market share of the vertically-integrated firm or the firm employing the surrogate for vertical integration than it actually does and that U.S. authorities now appear to believe that it does, (D) the fact that the EC and the E.C./E.U. courts take more seriously than the U.S. courts their (mistaken) conclusions respectively that E.C./E.U. competition law and U.S. antitrust law is designed to prevent reductions in intra-brand competition (although the Supreme Court continues to believe that U.S. law is designed *inter alia* to prevent reductions in intra-brand competition—has stated that the legality of some surrogates for vertical integration depends on whether they increase inter-brand competition by more than they decrease intra-brand competition, the lower courts seem not to be following that protocol [seem to always find that the increase in inter-brand competition exceeds the decrease in intra-brand competition]: in addition, the U.S. antitrust-enforcement agencies no longer believe that U.S. antitrust law is concerned with reductions in intra-brand competition), (E) although the EC and the E.C./E.U. courts recognize that relevant impacts of a surrogate for vertical integration depend on the conduct that the perpetrator would substitute for it if prohibited from using it, the fact that they are less cognizant of the actual functions that these practices can perform than their U.S. counterparts appear to be make them more likely than their U.S. counterparts are to conclude that such practices will have impacts that they find legally problematic, (F) the fact that the EC and the E.C./E.U. courts believe incorrectly that it is correct as a matter of law to interpret and apply E.C./E.U. competition law to promote cross-E.C./E.U.-country trade and that prohibiting firms from directly or indirectly restricting independent distributors from making cross-E.C./E.U.-country sales will promote cross-E.C./E.U.-country trade, and (G) the fact that the EC and E.C./E.U. courts believe incorrectly that it is correct as a matter of law to interpret E.C./E.U. competition law to promote the "freedom" of independent distributors to run their businesses as they see fit and the "freedom" of buyers to choose among as many products from as many sources as is possible and that legal decisions prohibiting producers from restricting the choices their independent distributors can make and, in particular, preventing them from making cross-E.C./E.U.-country sales will promote such distributor and consumer freedom (beliefs to which at least some of their U.S. counterparts used to subscribe but to which no contemporary U.S. court or antitrust-enforcement agency currently subscribes).

Chapter 15
Joint Ventures and Other Types of Functionally-Analogous Collaborative Arrangements

The concept of a "(business) joint venture" has been defined (usually implicitly) in a wide variety of ways. This study defines a "(business) joint venture" narrowly to refer to a business entity created by two or more other business entities (the parents) to engage in one or more business activities. Firms can collaborate in business activities without creating separate business entities that each collaborator partially owns—*e.g.*, by entering into long-term leases that may include restrictive covenants or by establishing joint committees to structure collaborative activities and, when cross-payments are or may be appropriate, to determine when cross-payments should be made and the magnitude of any cross-payments that should be made.

1. The Sherman-Act-Licit and Sherman-Act-Illicit Functions of Joint Ventures and Other Types of Functionally-Analogous Collaborative Arrangements

A. The Sherman-Act-Licit Functions of Joint Ventures and Other Types of Collaborative Arrangements

Joint ventures and other types of collaborative arrangements (hereinafter joint ventures) can perform 11 and perhaps 12 Sherman-Act-licit functions:

(1) reducing the transaction costs that the parents have to incur to supply each other with inputs of some type (*e.g.*, with news stories or the right to use product or production-process patents);
(2) reducing the production costs that the parents have to incur to supply themselves with an input they all use or some final product they all resell by enabling the parents to produce that input or product more cheaply by combining assets that are complementary for scale or non-scale reasons;

R.S. Markovits, *Economics and the Interpretation and Application of U.S. and E.U. Antitrust Law*, DOI 10.1007/978-3-642-24313-4_4,

(3) reducing the cost the parents have to incur to purchase inputs from others (when the parents are producers) or final products from others (when the parents are resellers) by enabling the parents to take advantage of economies of scale or scope in purchasing that relate to (A) the per-unit mechanical transaction cost of the transactions in question and (B) the benefits that assured sales give suppliers (i) by obviating their incurring costs to identify potential buyers, to advertise their products to them, and to direct more individualized sales-efforts at them and (ii) by reducing the risk costs that the suppliers incur because they do not know how many units of their product they will sell (when the related gains increase more than proportionately with the amount of sales that are assured);
(4) doing market research more proficiently than any individual parent could do such research by enabling the parents to combine relevant assets that are complementary for scale or non-scale reasons;
(5) increasing the proficiency with which the parents can establish credible quality-standards for the goods they produce and/or distribute as well as the proficiency with which they can grade the products that they and perhaps their rivals produce and/or distribute;
(6) increasing the proficiency with which the parents can control the quality of the goods the parents produce and/or distribute, can establish a brand name for those products, and can advertise that brand and/or the type of product the parents produce/distribute;
(7) increasing the proficiency with which the parents can assess the credit-worthiness of potential customers, bill actual buyers, and/or collect and process payments from actual buyers;
(8) increasing the proficiency with which the parents can execute a given innovative product-research or production-process-research project;
(9) increasing the proficiency with which the parents can make a non-innovative QV investment or plant-modernization investment;
(10) enabling the parents to execute a more profitable set of product-research or production-process-research projects without increasing the proficiency with which any individual project is executed by permitting the parents to substitute a more-privately-profitable because less-jointly-unprofitably-duplicative set of research projects for a less-privately-profitable because more-jointly-unprofitably-duplicative set of research projects (even if the two sets of projects are equally costly);
(11) enabling the parents to create one profitable innovative or non-innovative QV investment or to execute one profitable PPR project when they would not have done so when acting separately because—as independent agents—they would have confronted each other with natural oligopolistic QV-investment disincentives; and perhaps
(12) enabling the parents to purchase inputs or final products more cheaply from others by creating a joint-purchasing organization that has more buying power than the sum of any buying power the parents had when acting separately ("perhaps" because the courts, the DOJ and FTC, and some scholars believe that the Sherman Act prohibits buyer price-fixing just as it prohibits horizontal seller price-fixing).

B. The Sherman-Act-Illicit Functions of Joint Ventures and Other Types of Collaborative Arrangements

I should say at the outset that joint ventures will perform some of these functions only when the parents abuse the opportunity for communication that their participation in the joint venture affords them, will perform some of these functions because the joint-venture agreement contains one or more provisions that impose restraints on the parents and/or the joint venture, and can perform some of these functions even when (1) the parents do not abuse the opportunity for communication their participation in the joint venture affords them and (2) the joint-venture agreement does not impose any relevant restraints on the parents and/or the joint venture. I should also indicate at this juncture that the possibly-anticompetitive restraints that joint-venture agreements impose on the parents and/or the joint venture may not in fact reduce competition and, even if they do, may also perform Sherman-Act-licit functions—*i.e.*, may increase the joint venture's profits by increasing its organizational economic efficiency by increasing the amount of legitimately-valuable information or personnel the parents supply the joint venture (indeed, may critically affect the legitimate profitability of the joint venture in this way).

In any event, joint ventures can perform at least five and perhaps six Sherman-Act-illicit functions. The first Sherman-Act-illicit function that joint ventures can perform is increasing the profits the parents earn by practicing contrived oligopolistic pricing both by making it profitable for them to practice additional contrived oligopolistic pricing and by increasing the profits they realize by charging contrived oligopolistic prices they would have charged absent the joint venture. Joint-sales-agency joint ventures that prohibit the parents from making sales on their own perform this function most obviously: indeed, it would probably be more accurate to say that they obviate the parents' price-fixing in the same way that horizontal mergers obviate the merger partners' fixing each other's prices or horizontal acquisitions obviate the acquiring and acquired firms' fixing each other's prices. However, various sorts of joint ventures that do not in essence fix prices directly (that do not obviate the parents' engaging in price-fixing) can facilitate the parents' price-fixing. Thus, when the parents would find it inherently profitable to undercut or undermine each other's contrived oligopolistic prices, joint ventures can perform this illicit function by facilitating the parents' agreeing not to undercut each other's contrived oligopolistic prices and/or by enabling one or both parents to communicate their intention to retaliate against the other should the other not acquiesce in its contrivance and/or reciprocate to the other's cooperation. When the parents have one or more common rivals that could undercut or undermine the parents' contrived oligopolistic pricing, these other sorts of joint ventures can also facilitate the parents' contrived oligopolistic pricing by enabling them (1) to communicate to each other information about their own sales-records and about those rivals' sales-records that increase the ability of the parents in individualized-pricing contexts to determine whether undercutting from an inferior competitive position has taken place, to identify the undercutter, to identify opportunities to reciprocate to collaboration or to increase the benefits a parent can bestow on a cooperator through reciprocation when the parents are uniquely-equal-second-placed or respectively uniquely-second-placed and uniquely-third-placed to supply one or more buyers the cooperator was best-placed to supply, and to identify the customers of their undercutter to which it would be most-cost-effective to offer retaliatory price-cuts or at which it would be most-cost-effective to direct retaliatory advertising campaigns, (2) to put at each other's disposal any excess reciprocatory power each has in relation to a common rival that has cooperated with the other's contrivance, and (3) to retaliate cooperatively against each other's undercutters (in individualized-pricing contexts) or underminers (in across-the-board-pricing contexts), (4) when the joint venture is operating in a parent's market or in a market in which one or more of a parent's rivals are operating, to use the joint venture's sales-records to help the parent identify whether undercutting from a position of inferiority is taking place, to reciprocate to a cooperator, and/or to retaliate against an undercutter/underminer.

The second illicit function that joint ventures can perform is increasing the profits the parents can realize by confronting their rivals with retaliation barriers to entry or expansion, usually by increasing the effectiveness of their threats of retaliation but conceivably as well by enabling them to reward rival potential QV investors that choose not to invest. Joint ventures can yield the parents such benefits *inter alia* (1) by increasing the profits they can realize by confronting each other with retaliation barriers by facilitating their communication of relevant intentions to each other, (2) by enabling them to provide each other with information about another rival's competitive-position array that will enable each parent to retaliate more-cost-effectively or better to perceive its opportunities for reciprocation, (3) by increasing the amount of benefits the parents can provide cooperators by not beating their contrived oligopolistic offers (in situations in which the parents are uniquely-equal-second-placed or respectively uniquely-second-placed and uniquely-third-placed to supply one or more customers the cooperator is best-placed to supply), (4) by putting at each other's disposal any excess reciprocatory power either has in relation to a cooperator, (5) by facilitating their joint retaliation against an investor, and (6) by enabling them to use the joint venture to reciprocate to a non-investor and/or retaliate against an investor.

The third Sherman-Act-illicit function that joint ventures can perform is enabling the parents to profit more by engaging in other sorts of predation by enabling them better to coordinate their predatory pricing, predatory advertising, predatory investments, or predatory refusals to deal. For example, vertical joint ventures in which the parents agree to supply each other with inputs (say, news stories or other types of intellectual property [to allow each other to use patent-protected information]) or distributive services may contractually organize predatory refusals to deal by prohibiting the parents/participants from supplying the inputs or distributive services in question to any non-participant (for example, to each other's rivals) unless all participants, some burdensome percentage of participants, or the participant(s) that are rivals of the non-participant seeking membership consent to the latter's being supplied and/or unless the original non-participant accepts terms of participation that place it at a critical disadvantage. Of course, such contractual provisions will be predatory only if one or more of their perpetrators' *ex ante* perception that the provisions were profitable was critically affected by the perpetrators' belief that the provisions would or might reduce the absolute attractiveness of the offers against which they would have to compete.

The fourth Sherman-Act-illicit function that joint ventures can perform is enabling the parents to substitute one QV investment (a smaller number of QV investments) made by the joint venture for the two QV investments (a larger number of QV investments) the parents would have made absent the joint venture when no remaining rival would replace the deterred parent-QV-investment(s) immediately, at all, or with an equally-competitive QV investment. Sometimes, the joint venture will secure this result by including in its by-laws a provision precluding the parents from investing on their own in the joint venture's market. The parents might believe that they will be able to escape liability for including such a provision in the joint venture's by-laws by arguing that (1) no parent could have entered the joint venture's market on its own had it not learned things from the other parent(s) in the course of their participation in the joint venture and (2) the parents would not have found the joint venture profitable had they not been assured that the information they would supply it would not be used by any fellow parent to compete against the joint venture—*i.e.*, by arguing that the by-law provision in question was "ancillary" to the formation of a joint venture (ideally, that it increased competition [say] by causing a QV investment to be made that raised total QV investment in the relevant area of product-space to a level to which it would not otherwise have been raised). I should say that, in many situations, the parents may not need to include such a by-law provision in their joint-venture agreement to achieve this result: the mere fact that each parent (say, in a two-parent joint venture) owns 50 % of the joint venture and therefore would suffer 50 % of the loss that the parent's entry into the joint venture's market would impose on the joint venture may suffice to deter each parent from entering the joint venture's market.

The fifth Sherman-Act-illicit function that joint ventures can perform is enabling the parents to agree not to enter each other's markets when each was an effective potential competitor of the other. The joint venture could perform this function simply by facilitating the parents' communicating with each other. The joint venture could also perform this function more effectively by including in its by-laws a provision prohibiting the parents from entering each other's markets. Once more, even if such a by-law provision were purely anticompetitive, the parents might be able to persuade triers-of-fact that it was not anticompetitive (indeed, that it was procompetitive)—in particular, might be able to persuade triers-of-fact that the parents could not have entered each other's markets had they not participated in the joint venture, that the joint venture would enable them to profit by entering each other's markets because they would learn things necessary for doing so in the course of collaborating in the running of the joint venture, perhaps that none of them would have found the joint venture profitable had it not been able to prevent the other parent(s) from using against it information it conveyed to the other parent(s) in the course of participating in the joint venture, and perhaps that the joint venture increased competition in the market(s) in which it operated because it added one or more QV investments to the market(s) in which it operated that would not otherwise have been made or introduced QV investments into those markets that were more effective competitively than the QV investments of others the joint venture's QV investments deterred.

The sixth Sherman-Act-illicit function that joint ventures can perform is actually only possibly illicit. If the Sherman Act prohibits buyer price-fixing as well as seller horizontal price-fixing, joint ventures that create a purchasing agent that has more buying power than the sum of the buying power that each parent would have acting separately on its own will have performed a Sherman-Act-illicit function on that account.

Obviously, the price-fixing, erection of retaliation barriers to QV investment, predation, and anticompetitive agreements not to compete that I have just listed all (with the possible exception of the agreement not to compete as buyers) independently violate the Sherman Act. Still, it is worth noting that if the parents' *ex ante* belief that their joint venture would be profitable was critically affected by their perception that it would or might perform one or more of these functions for them (with the possible exception of increasing their buying power), that fact would render the joint venture itself illegal under the Sherman Act. And if one believes that as a matter of law it is correct to interpret the Sherman Act *inter alia* as a fence law, these possibilities are worth noting on this account as well.

2. The Ways in Which Joint Ventures and/or the Restraints That Joint-Venture Agreements Impose on the Joint Venture and/or Its Parents Can Confer Equivalent-Dollar Gains and Inflict Equivalent-Dollar Losses on Clayton-Act-Relevant Buyers

Although the legality of joint ventures under U.S. antitrust law does not depend on their competitive impact (since the Clayton Act does not cover joint ventures), the legality of so-called "concentrative" joint ventures under E.C./E.U. competition law does in part depend on their competitive impact (since the EMCR, which promulgates a Clayton-Act-type "lessening-competition" test of illegality, applies to "concentrative"—*i.e.*, full-function—joint ventures). With one minor qualification, a joint venture's performance of any of the Sherman-Act-licit functions that Section 1A of this chapter indicated such arrangements can perform will favor its legality under a Clayton-Act-type test of illegality by causing the joint venture to confer equivalent-dollar gains on Clayton-Act-relevant buyers on the account, and with one, different possible qualification, a joint venture's performance of any of the first five Sherman-Act-illicit functions that Section 1B of this chapter stated such arrangements can perform will favor its illegality under a Clayton-Act-type test of illegality. The qualification to the licit-function point is that, if (1) the joint venture increases the profits the parents realize by making an innovative or non-innovative QV investment, by executing a PPR project, or by engaging in plant modernization without inducing it to make additional investments of these kinds or (2) the joint venture causes the parents to execute a PPR project or plant-modernization investment that they would not otherwise have executed but the investment in question reduces their fixed costs or low-output variable costs but not their marginal costs at or beyond their pre-investment outputs, the joint venture's performance of the licit function in question will not benefit Clayton-Act-relevant buyers. The qualification to the illicit-function point is that, since the conduct that is associated with the joint venture's performance of the illicit functions in question is all or almost all independently illegal and the authorities could move against its perpetrators for engaging in it without attacking the joint venture, one might argue that the joint venture's legality should not be affected by the fact that it facilitates the parents' behaving in these illegal ways unless the prospect of obtaining profits in these illicit ways led the parents to execute a joint venture that would impose equivalent-dollar losses on Clayton-Act-relevant buyers even if the joint venture did not perform these illicit functions (*i.e.*, led the parents to participate in joint ventures that reduced the parents' organizational economic efficiency to put themselves in a position to make enough money by behaving independently illegally to offset the private losses the joint venture would otherwise have imposed on them) or the joint venture manifested specific anticompetitive intent (in which case its execution would be illegal because it would constitute a concrete step toward the completion of an illegal act). I hasten to add that this second qualification will not be applicable in cases in which the joint venture enables the parents to substitute the joint venture's one (smaller amount of) QV investment for the parents' two (larger amount of) QV investments even though the joint-venture agreement does not prohibit the parents from entering the joint venture's market because the individual parents' part-ownership of the joint venture makes it individually unprofitable for them to make an investment in the joint venture's market.

3. The Difficulty of Determining Whether a Joint Venture and/or the Restraints a Joint-Venture Agreement Imposes on the Joint Venture and/or Its Parents Violate the Specific-Anticompetitive-Intent Test and/or the Lessening-Competition Test of Illegality

I will make use of a hypothetical to illustrate my argument that one will not be able to assess whether a joint venture and/or any restrictive provision a joint-venture agreement contains manifest the parents' specific anticompetitive intent or lessen competition without knowing a great deal about the actual and prospective competitive positions of the parents, the actual and prospective competitive positions of their other rivals, and the Sherman-Act-licit functions that the joint venture and its restrictive provisions are performing or would perform. Assume that the joint venture (Trans-America Airline) is created in the U.S. in the 1920s, when the commercial passenger and freight aviation business was in its infancy, to transport passengers and goods through the air between various U.S. east-coast and U.S. west-coast locations by parents that are respectively a U.S. airline that transports passengers and goods over various routes between U.S. east-coast locations (East-Coast Airline) and a U.S. airline that transports passengers and goods over various routes between U.S. west-coast locations (West-Coast Airline). Assume as well that East-Coast Airline and West-Coast Airline respectively face competition from other east-coast and west-coast airlines but that Trans-America Airline will be the first commercial airline flying between the east coast and the west coast of the U.S. Assume finally that the agreement forming the joint venture prohibits the parents from entering the joint venture's trans-America market, the joint venture from entering the parents' coastal markets, and the parents from entering each other's coastal markets. My point is that on these facts

(1) the joint venture without the restrictions and the restrictive provisions in the joint-venture agreement could be lawful under the specific-anticompetitive-intent and lessening-competition tests of illegality,
(2) both the joint venture without the restrictions and the restrictions could both manifest the parents' specific-anticompetitive-intent and lessen competition,
(3) the joint venture without the restrictions could be lawful under the specific-anticompetitive-intent and lessening-competition tests of illegality but the restrictions could manifest the parents' specific anticompetitive intent and lessen competition, or
(4) the joint venture in itself could manifest the parents' specific anticompetitive intent, but the restrictions could not violate either the specific-anticompetitive intent or lessening-competition test of illegality.

I will now explain the conditions under which each of these sets of conclusions would be warranted, focusing separately on the parts of these conclusions that relate specifically to whether the joint venture or the restrictions in any joint-venture agreement violate first the specific-anticompetitive-intent test of illegality and second the lessening-competition or test of illegality. The analyses that follow will ignore the possibilities that the joint venture itself or any restrictive provisions the joint-venture agreement contains may increase the extent to which the parents profit from contrived oligopolistic pricing, raising the retaliation barriers to QV investment their rivals face, or practicing other types of predation or lessen competition by engaging in the strategic types of conduct just listed.

A. The Conditions Under Which the Parts of Each of the Four Preceding Conclusions That Relate to the Specific-Anticompetitive-Intent Test of Illegality Will Be Justified

The specific-anticompetitive-intent test of illegality is the test of illegality that applies in all Sherman Act cases in the United States, in all cases brought under the exclusionary-abuse branch of the test of illegality of now-Article 102 of the Lisbon Treaty, and (with a possible qualification that relates to contrivance and predation practiced exclusively through threats of harm-inflicting conduct and actual harm-inflicting conduct) in all cases brought under the object-branch of the test of illegality promulgated by what is now Article 101 of the 2009 Lisbon Treaty.

Since the U.S. Sherman Act covers all joint ventures that have a requisite impact on interstate commerce or commerce between the U.S. and foreign countries and all restrictive provisions in joint-venture agreements that have such an effect, Article 102 of the 2009 Lisbon Treaty covers all joint ventures created by one or more firms that are individually or collectively dominant and all restrictive provisions in joint-venture agreements that are created by one or more firms that are individually or collectively dominant, and Article 101 of the 2009 Lisbon Treaty covers all joint ventures that affect commerce between E.C./EU. member-nations and all restrictive provisions in joint-venture agreements that affect commerce between E.C./E.U. member-nations, the conclusions of this section are legally salient.

(1) The Conditions Under Which the Joint Venture Without Restrictions and Any Restrictive Provisions the Joint-Venture Agreement Contains Will Not Manifest Specific Anticompetitive Intent

The joint venture without the restrictions the joint-venture agreement contains will be lawful under the specific-anticompetitive-intent test if *ex ante* the parents believed that the joint venture would be *ex ante* profitable if did not cause them to suffer losses in the other markets in which they operated by creating a joint venture that would be their effective competitor in one or more of these markets or by making one parent or both parents an effective competitor of the other or a more-effective competitor of the other in one or more of the markets in which the parents operated by enabling one or both parents to learn things or gain access to personnel (or profits) by participating in the joint venture that they would not otherwise have learned/obtained that would reduce the (Π_D + R) barriers they faced in relation to the other parent's markets because (1) either (A) Trans-America would find it profitable to operate trans-America routes when neither East-Coast Airline nor West-Coast Airline would have found it profitable to do so or (B) one of the parents but not both of the parents as dual entrants would have found it profitable to enter the trans-America passenger and cargo air-transport business if Trans-America did not do so but the parent that would have entered if Trans-America did not would have made lower profits by doing so than Trans-America would make by doing so and (2) the supernormal profits that Trans-America would earn if neither parent would otherwise have entered its business or the positive difference between the supernormal profits that Trans-America would earn and any supernormal profits that would be earned by the parent that would have entered Trans-America's market had Trans-America not done so would constitute at least a normal rate-of-return on the transaction cost of trying to identify profitable joint-venture opportunities and creating the joint venture Trans-America Airline.

I should point out that there are at least five reasons why Trans-America Airline might be able to make more profits by entering the trans-America flight market than either parent (and perhaps anyone else) could realize by doing so: the joint venture's profits might be higher than the profits either parent could realize by entering the joint venture's market because

(1) the joint venture can take advantage of both East-Coast Airline's greater relevant knowledge and skills (related to locating appropriate sites for constructing additional airport facilities, actually constructing those facilities, hiring air-traffic-control personnel, airplane-maintenance personnel, ticket agents, airplane pilots, and other plane personnel, and obtaining necessary state and local government permissions) on the east coast of the U.S. and of West-Coast Airline's greater relevant knowledge and skills on the west coast;
(2) the joint venture can take advantage of the ability of both parents to supply their own personnel to the new venture (if, for example, East-Coast Airline has excess capacity in its airplane-maintenance department and West-Coast Airline has excess capacity in its route-coordination department);
(3) the joint venture can take advantage of both East-Coast Airline's greater skills at marketing air-transport services on the east coast of the U.S. and of West-Coast Airline's greater skills at marketing air-transport services on the west coast of the U.S.;
(4) the joint venture can reduce the finance cost of creating a trans-America air-service by pooling the financing that East-Coast Airline and West-Coast Airline could separately provide for the project themselves as well as by taking advantage of each parent's ability to obtain external financing for the project; and
(5) the joint venture inherits the superior reputation for safety and reliability of the parent that had that superior reputation (which would make it more profitable than an independent entry of the parent with the inferior reputation) or enjoys a superior reputation for safety and reliability than either parent would have enjoyed because potential customers assume that the cooperative effort of two established companies is likely to be superior to the effort of either.

I turn now to the conditions under which any provision of the joint-venture agreement that prohibits the joint venture from entering its parents' markets will not manifest the parents' specific anticompetitive intent. I should point out at the outset that this issue is salient because the parents' participation in the joint venture may give the joint venture access to information and/or personnel that would reduce the barriers to entering the parents' markets that the joint venture faced below those facing any other potential entrant to the parents' markets or at least below those facing the worst-placed potential entrant to any market of any parent that would otherwise have been an effective potential entrant.

I believe that two formally-different types of arguments can be made to justify the conclusion that a restrictive provision prohibiting a joint venture from entering its parents' markets does not violate the specific-anticompetitive-intent test of illegality. The first argument is the standard argument we have been using to analyze the legality of covered conduct under the Sherman Act. Two sub-cases need to be distinguished. In the first sub-case, the parents would respond to the prohibition of the restrictive provision at issue by deciding not to create the joint venture or not to increase its organizational economic efficiency by providing it with information, personnel, or other assets that would render it an effective or more-effective potential competitor of one or both parents. In this sub-case, under standard analysis, the restriction would be rendered lawful under the specific-anticompetitive-intent test of illegality both (1) by the fact that the parents would not have perceived *ex ante* that it would reduce the absolute attractiveness of the offers against which they would have to compete and (2) by the fact that, in an otherwise-Pareto-perfect world, the restrictions would increase economic efficiency by causing an economically-efficient joint venture to be created or by increasing the economic efficiency of a joint venture that would be created in any event. In the second sub-case, prohibition of the relevant restriction would not alter the parents' decisions to create the joint venture or to provide the joint venture with information, personnel, or other assets that would increase the joint venture's organizational economic efficiency. In such situations, the restrictions would not violate the specific-anticompetitive-intent test of illegality despite the fact that the parents' *ex ante* beliefs that the restriction was *ex ante* profitable were critically affected by their perceptions that the restriction would reduce the absolute attractiveness of the offers against which they would have to compete because the restriction would increase economic efficiency in an otherwise-Pareto-perfect economy by eliminating what would otherwise be a deflating distortion in the parents' incentives to create the competitive advantages they enjoy in their own markets and to search for profitable joint-venture opportunities (to eliminate the deflation in those incentives that would be generated by a rule that required them to give up some of the advantages they had in their original markets if they created a joint venture that could compete effectively against them in those markets).

The second argument combines (1) a premise that the relevant baseline not only for competitive-impact analysis but for specific-anticompetitive-intent analysis is the "do-nothing" baseline with (2) the claim that in this context the "do-nothing" option is not "not creating the joint venture" but "creating the joint venture without the restrictive provision at issue."

The two arguments in question are legally sound in themselves. And, not surprisingly, they have the advantage of producing legal conclusions that are consistent with the claim that firms have a legal right to prevent their knowledge, personnel, and assets from being used against them.

I turn next to the conditions under which any provision of the joint-venture agreement prohibiting the parents from entering the joint venture's market will not manifest the parents' specific anticompetitive intent. The concern is that the joint venture or the joint venture *plus* the restrictive provision in question is being used by parents that would each have entered the joint venture's market on its own to reduce the sum of the amounts of QV investments they make directly in their own names and indirectly via the joint venture below the sum of the amounts of QV investments they would have made in their own names had they not created the joint venture in circumstances in which no-one else will make QV investments in the joint venture's area of product-space that will "replace" the QV investments the parents do not make. A prohibition of the parents' not entering the joint venture's market (or the joint venture without such a prohibition) will not generate this effect if, absent the joint venture, (1) neither parent would have found it profitable to enter the joint venture's market even if no-one else did so or (2) one parent would have entered the joint venture's market with the same amount of QV investment as the joint venture made in that market.

I turn finally to the conditions under which any provision of the Trans-America joint-venture agreement that prohibits the parents from entering each other's markets will not manifest the parents' specific anticompetitive intent. Such prohibitions will not manifest the parents' specific anticompetitive intent if, absent the joint venture, (1) no parent would have found it profitable to enter the other's market if no-one else did or (2) one or more parents would have found it profitable to enter the other's market if no-one else did but one or more non-parents would have been at least as well-placed as the parents would have been to do so (and if those non-parents had entered or been deterred from entering by limit investments, the parent or parents in question would not have entered the other parent's market). When these conditions are fulfilled and (say) each parent's participation in (say) a two-parent joint venture would critically increase each's ability to enter the other parent's markets by giving each parent in question access to information or personnel that the other parent provided the joint venture, it would be legitimate for each parent to prevent the other parent from using the information and personnel that each parent provided the joint venture against it by including in the joint-venture agreement a provision prohibiting the parents from entering each other's markets. The argument for this conclusion is the same argument previously made for the legality of restrictive provisions in joint-venture agreements prohibiting the joint venture from entering the parents' markets.

(2) The Conditions Under Which Both the Joint Venture Without Restrictions and the Restrictions That the Joint Venture Imposes on the Joint Venture and Its Parents Will Manifest the Parents' Specific Anticompetitive Intent

Even if the joint-venture agreement does not contain any relevant restrictions, the joint venture will manifest the parents' specific anticompetitive intent if the parents' *ex ante* perceptions that the joint venture was *ex ante* profitable were critically affected by their beliefs that (1) absent the joint venture, two or more parents would have entered the joint venture's market, (2) the parents' respective part-ownerships of the joint venture would deter them from investing in the joint venture's market even if the joint-venture agreement did not prohibit them from doing so, and (3) no-one else would replace the QV investment(s) in the joint venture's market that the joint venture enables the parents not to make either with any QV investment or with a QV investment that would be as competitively effective as the "deterred" parent-QV-investment would have been.

Provisions of the joint-venture agreement prohibiting the parents from entering each other's markets will be purely anticompetitive if the parents' *ex ante* perceptions that the relevant restrictive provisions were *ex ante* profitable was critically affected by their beliefs that, absent those provisions, the parents would have been effective potential entrants into each other's markets—*i.e.*, if, absent those provisions, either (1) a parent and no-one else would have been willing to raise QV investment in another parent's market to some relevant level or (2) a parent would have been willing to make one or more QV investments in the other parent's market(s) that was (were) more rivalrous with the "invaded" parent's projects than the QV investments that any other rival would introduce into the invaded parent's market(s) if the invading parent did not enter the invaded parent's market(s). When these conditions are fulfilled, the provisions in the joint-venture agreement prohibiting the parents from entering each other's markets are simply agreements in which potential competitors that would have entered each other's markets if limit investments did not render their doing so unprofitable agree reciprocally not to compete against each other in this way.

If a joint venture that contained such a provision generated no economic efficiencies, it would be fair to characterize both the joint venture itself and the provision it contained as pure "shams." Both U.S. courts and E.C./E.U. competition-law-applying institutions have described some joint ventures as "pure shams."

(3) The Conditions Under Which the Joint Venture Will Not Manifest the Parents' Specific Anticompetitive Intent but the Restrictions the Joint-Venture Agreement Imposes on the Joint Venture and/or Its Parents Will Manifest the Parents' Specific Anticompetitive Intent

There is no reason why parents that have created a joint venture that will find it profitable to add a QV investment to an area of product-space when no parent and no-one else would find it profitable to add a QV investment (or a QV investment that would be as effective competitively as the joint venture's QV investment) to that area of product-space should not include a provision in their joint-venture agreement that prohibits them from entering each other's markets when they would otherwise have been each other's effective potential competitors and their participation in the joint venture would not have reduced in any way the barriers they faced to entering each other's markets. A full statement of the conditions under which (1) a joint venture would itself be lawful under the Sherman Act but (2) the restraints it imposed on the parents' entering each other's markets would manifest their specific anticompetitive intent are delineated respectively in Sects. 3A(1) and 3A(2) of this chapter.

(4) The Conditions Under Which the Joint Venture Will Manifest the Parents' Specific Anticompetitive Intent but the Restrictions It Imposed on the Joint Venture and Its Parents Will Not Manifest the Parents' Specific Anticompetitive Intent

A joint venture that imposes no restriction on the parents' investing in the joint venture's market will manifest the parents' specific anticompetitive intent when the parents' *ex ante* perceptions that the joint venture is *ex ante* profitable is critically affected by their beliefs that it will enable them to reduce the total amount of QV investment the parents make in the joint venture's market in their own names and via the joint venture when non-parents will not make up for the reduction in the parents' overall QV investment in the market in question (and/or by their beliefs that it will or may increase the profits they will earn by practicing contrived oligopolistic pricing, by raising the retaliation barriers to QV investment that rivals face, and/or by engaging in other types of predation). The conditions for the non-parenthetical results' obtaining are those listed at the beginning of Sect. 3A(2) of this chapter.

Parents whose creation of a joint venture manifests their specific anticompetitive intent may include in the joint-venture agreement a provision prohibiting them from entering each other's markets that do not manifest the parents' specific anticompetitive intent. This will occur when (1) the joint venture does generate some private (and presumably economic) efficiencies that make the joint venture's projects more profitable than any project either parent could create in the joint venture's market (just not enough such efficiencies to make the joint venture *ex ante* profitable on their account) and (2) the parents' participation in the joint venture would render them effective or more-effective potential competitors of each other because some of those efficiencies would carry over to the parents' QV investments in each other's markets.

* * *

The point of the preceding analysis is that (1) joint ventures may or may not manifest the parents' specific anticompetitive intent, (2) the restrictions that joint-venture agreements impose on the joint venture and its parents may or may not manifest the parents' specific anticompetitive intent, (3) joint ventures that do not manifest the parents' specific anticompetitive intent may contain restrictions that do manifest their specific anticompetitive intent, (4) joint ventures that do manifest the parents' specific anticompetitive intent may contain restrictions that do not manifest the parents' specific anticompetitive intent, (5) in order to determine whether a joint venture manifests the parents' specific anticompetitive intent, one must discover (roughly speaking) (A) whether the licit functions the joint venture performs are sufficient to render it *ex ante* profitable and, if there is some doubt, (B) whether the joint venture seems likely to be performing Sherman-Act-illicit functions—*viz*., whether the joint venture seems likely to enable the parents to reduce the amount of QV investment they collectively make in the joint venture's market in circumstances in which other firms will not make QV investments that replace the QV investments the joint venture enables the parents to avoid making and/or whether the joint venture will increase the profits the parents can make by engaging in contrived oligopolistic pricing, raising rivals' retaliation barriers to QV investment, and/or engaging in other types of predation, and (6) in order to determine whether a provision in a joint-venture agreement restricting the choices that the joint venture and/or the parents can make manifests the parents' specific anticompetitive intent, one must discover the same type of information needed to evaluate the legality under the Sherman Act of the joint venture without restrictions. Points (5) and (6) may be the most important because they imply that there is no simple way to determine whether joint ventures or the restrictive provisions joint-venture agreements contain violate the kind of specific-anticompetitive-intent test the Sherman Act promulgates.

B. The Conditions Under Which Joint Ventures, Other Types of Functionally-Analogous Collaborative Arrangements, and Any Restrictive Provisions in the Agreements or Understandings That Create Them Violate the (Organizational-Allocative-Efficiency-Defense-Qualified) Lessening-Competition Test of Illegality

Although the Clayton Act and its lessening-competition test of illegality do not apply to joint ventures or any restrictive provisions in joint-venture agreements (because Clayton Act Section 7 covers only the acquisition by a firm or person of the whole or any part of the assets, stock, or share capital of another firm or person—*i.e.*, covers only mergers and acquisitions), the Act—specifically, its Section 3—and its lessening-competition test of illegality does apply to some restrictive provisions in agreements that establish collaborative relationships that are functionally analogous to some joint ventures—specifically, agreements in which two or more firm or persons agree to leases of or sales-contracts relating to "goods, wares, merchandise, machinery, supplies, or other commodities" in which each participant is sometimes the lessee/buyer and sometimes the lessor/seller "on the condition, agreement, or understanding that the lessee or purchaser thereof shall not use or deal in the goods, wares, merchandise, machinery, supplies, or other commodities of a competitor or competitors of the lessor or seller...." I should admit that, for two reasons, Section 3 may cover only a small percentage of the joint-venture-like collaborative arrangements that involve such restrictive provisions: (1) many such arrangements (*e.g.*, patent pools and agreements by newspapers to allow the participants to publish each other's stories) may involve barter transactions rather than paradigmatic leases or "sales," and (2) many such arrangements may involve things of value (the right to use a patented product [as opposed to the product itself] or production process or the right to publish a newspaper story) that some would argue should not be classified as a Section 3 commodity. I hasten to add that I think that it would be correct as a matter of law to interpret Section 3 to cover pure barter arrangements involving the right to use patented products or production processes or the right to publish a newspaper story (to classify pure barter arrangements as Section 3 "sales" and the just-listed rights as Section 3 "commodities"). (I recognize that there is Clayton Act case-law to the contrary on the second of these two issues.)

The legality under E.U. competition law of many joint ventures and functionally-analogous collaborative arrangements that do not involve the creation of a separate business entity as well as of any restrictive provisions in the agreements or understandings that create them clearly does depend *inter alia* on whether they lessen competition in the Clayton Act sense of that expression. Thus, the EMCR, which in my judgement promulgates a lessening-competition test of illegality, covers "concentrative"—*i.e.,* full-function—joint ventures and any restrictive provisions that joint-venture agreements contain. And Article 101(1), whose "effect of restricting or preventing competition" language should in my judgement be interpreted in the same way that the Clayton Act's lessening-competition language should be interpreted, covers as agreements or concerted practices between undertakings all firm-created joint ventures, all restrictive provisions in joint-venture agreements, all joint-venture-like collaborations arranged through contract or understandings, and all restrictive provisions in the latter contracts or restrictive features of the latter understandings.

Now that I have established that the legality under U.S. antitrust law of some restrictive provisions in joint-venture-like collaborative arrangements created by lease or sales-contracts depends *inter alia* on whether they lessen competition in the Clayton Act sense of that expression and that the legality of all joint ventures, joint-ventures-like collaborative arrangements created by contract or understandings, and restrictive provisions in the contracts in question/restrictive features of the understandings in question under E.U. competition law depends *inter alia* on whether they lessen competition in the Clayton Act sense of that expression, I need to analyze the following two questions: (1) under what conditions will a joint venture or functionally-analogous collaborative arrangement that does not involve the creation of a separate business entity and that does not impose any restrictions on the joint venture or the parents of the joint venture or other participants in the other type of collaborative arrangement lessen competition in the Clayton Act sense of that expression and (2) under what conditions will the restrictive provisions in a joint-venture contract or the restrictions involved in a functionally-analogous collaborative arrangement that does not entail the creation of a separate business entity lessen competition in the Clayton Act sense of that expression?

My analysis of these questions will make use of the East-Coast/West-Coast Airline example even though, in the E.U. context, the relevant example should focus on North-Coast and South-Coast Airlines' creating a Trans-E.U. Airline joint venture. For simplicity, my discussion will ignore the possibility that the joint venture or other type of functionally-analogous collaborative arrangement in question may increase the extent to which the parents/participants engage in (illegal) contrivance or predation. As I have already indicated, although it is unclear whether any such tendency is relevant to the underlying conduct's legality under the Clayton Act (whether it is correct as a matter of law to interpret the Clayton Act to be a fence law), the text of Article 101—*viz.*, its clause (a) which indicates that covered conduct that "directly or *indirectly* [emphasis added] fix[es] purchase or selling prices or any other trading conditions"—warrants the conclusion that any tendency of a joint venture or other type of functionally-analogous collaborative arrangement to foster such subsequent conduct is relevant to its legality under the provision (at least when the conduct violates Article 101(1)—is neither contrivance initiated by a single firm that does not rely exclusively on threats and acts of retaliation or single-firm predation).

As to the first issue, a joint venture created by an agreement that does not include any restrictive provisions will not lessen competition in the Clayton Act's sense of that expression if (1)(A)(i) neither East-Coast Airline nor West-Coast Airline would have provided the trans-America air-service in question on its own and (ii) no-one else would have provided that service if neither East-Coast Airline nor West-Coast Airline nor Trans-America Airline did or (B)(i) East-Coast Airline or

West-Coast Airline or someone else but not more than one of them would have provided the service if Trans-America Airline did not but (ii) the buyers that would have patronized the firm that would have entered the joint venture's market had the joint venture not done so would not have obtained more buyer surplus from doing so than the joint venture's customers obtained or would obtain from patronizing it, presumably because the firm that would have provided the trans-America service if Trans-America Airline did not would not have been more proficient at doing so than the joint venture was, and (2)(A) East-Coast Airline's and West-Coast Airline's participation in the joint venture did not critically increase the barriers they faced to entering each other's markets (by allocating to the joint venture resources they could otherwise have used to enter each other's markets) in circumstances in which each would otherwise have been an effective potential competitor of the other or (B) if the parents' participation in the joint venture did critically increase the barriers one or both of them faced to entering the other's markets in circumstances in which each or both of the parents in question would otherwise have been an effective potential competitor of the other, the reduction in competition (equivalent-dollar loss to Clayton-Act-relevant buyers) that the formation of the joint venture would generate on that account would not be larger than the increase in competition (equivalent-dollar gain to Clayton-Act-relevant buyers) that the joint venture would generate for buyers of the joint venture's air services.

As to the second issue, the restrictions that are contained in any joint-venture agreement will clearly lessen competition if they manifest the parents' specific anticompetitive intent and were not incorporated into the agreement because the parents mistakenly believed that they would reduce the absolute attractiveness of the offers against which they would have to compete in some way that would render them illegal under the Sherman Act. If the restrictions do not violate the specific-anticompetitive-intent test of the Sherman Act, they may still violate the Clayton Act's lessening-competition test because they may lessen competition in ways that benefit the parents even when such effects are not critical to the parents' *ex ante* perception that the restrictions would be profitable and/or because they may lessen competition in ways that do not benefit the parents (say, by increasing the prices the parents' rivals charge the rivals' customers by causing the parents and joint venture to make these buyers less-attractive offers than the parents and joint venture would otherwise have made them) in both cases without generating enough equivalent-monetary gains for these buyers in other ways.

I want to close this discussion by pointing out that it implies that one will not be able to evaluate the legality of a joint venture or any restrictions a joint-venture agreement contains under a lessening-competition test of illegality without obtaining a considerable amount of information about some of the Sherman-Act-licit functions they perform, the competitive positions the parents and the joint venture occupy, and the competitive positions that some of their rivals occupy. There is no simple or easy-to-apply protocol for analyzing the legality of joint ventures or the restrictions that joint-venture agreements contain under either the lessening-competition or the specific-anticompetitive-intent test of illegality.

4. The Legality of Joint Ventures and Any Restrictive Provisions That Joint-Venture Agreements Contain Under U.S. Antitrust Law, Correctly Interpreted and Applied

Section 1 of the Sherman Act and its specific-anticompetitive-intent test of illegality clearly applies both to all joint ventures and to all restrictive provisions that joint-venture parents include in their joint-venture agreements. However, for reasons that Sect. 3 of this chapter explained, this conclusion does not imply that one can determine the Sherman Act legality of any joint venture or any restrictive provision in a joint-venture agreement without engaging in the kind of fact-intensive case-by-case analysis normally associated with the use of a Rule-of-Reason approach to antitrust-law analysis.[1468] Indeed, even joint ventures that create sales-cooperatives for rivals to use exclusively will not violate the Sherman Act if, had the parents addressed this possibility *ex ante*, they would have concluded that the *ex ante* profitability of the joint-sales-agency arrangement in question did not depend critically on their realization that it would eliminate the competition they waged against each other because it was secured by the ability of the arrangement to reduce the difference between the transaction costs the parents would have to incur to sell their products separately and the lower transaction costs they would have to incur to sell their products as a package.[1469]

Although in one case the U.S. Supreme Court assumed that joint ventures were covered by Section 7 of the Clayton Act,[1470] I think that this assumption is incorrect as a matter of law: Section 7 covers transactions in which a "person engaged in

[1468] I should add that, although the United States has passed two special joint-venture-focused pieces of antitrust legislation, neither alters the test of illegality U.S. law applies to joint ventures. Thus, although the National Cooperative Research Act of 1984 sought to encourage procompetitive R&D joint ventures by declaring that defendants that had notified the DOJ and FTC of their intended joint-venture—i.e., of the identities of the participating parents and the nature and goals of the undertaking—would not have a "per se illegal" rule applied to their conduct, would not have to pay treble as opposed to normal damages if found liable, and would be able to recover the attorney's fees and costs they had to incur to defend themselves against frivolous claims or litigant conduct, that legislation did not alter the test of illegality that applies to R&D joint ventures. See National Cooperative Research Act 1984, Publ. L. No. 98–462, 98 Stat. 1815 (1984). Similarly, although the National Cooperative Production Amendments Act 1993 sought to encourage procompetitive production joint ventures by declaring that joint ventures created by perpetrators that were either U.S. companies or companies from foreign countries whose joint-venture law does not discriminate against U.S. companies or persons and that provides appropriate notice to the FTC and DOJ would be analyzed through the Rule of Reason, would be exposed to actual rather than treble damages, and would be entitled to take advantage of special attorney-fee regulations related to cases in which the joint venture was challenged, that legislation also does not alter the test of illegality that applies to the joint ventures it covers (if I am correct that any truly *per se* rule would have been incorrect as a matter of law in any event). See National Cooperative Production Amendments 1993, Pub. L. No. 103–42, 107 Stat. 117, 107 Stat. 119 (1993).

[1469] See, *e.g.*, Broadcast Music, Inc. v. Columbia Broadcasting System, 441 U.S. 1 (1979).

[1470] See United States v. Penn-Olin Chemical Co., 378. U.S. 158 (1964).

commerce or in any activity affecting commerce...acquire[s], directly or indirectly, the whole or any part of the stock or other share capital...[or] the whole or any part of the assets of another person engaged also in commerce or in any activity affecting commerce" and joint ventures do not involve one such "person's" acquiring either the stock or the share capital or other assets of another such "person." However, I do think that Section 3 of the Clayton Act does cover collaborative arrangements that are functionally analogous to some joint ventures but do not entail the creation of a jointly-owned business that involve the parents' agreeing to supply each other with some good or service (including the right to use some asset such as a bridge or patent) at no charge or at a lower price than would otherwise have been charged either directly or through the auspices of the joint venture or some functionally-analogous arrangement on condition that one or more of the arrangement's participants, which may or may not be rivals, agree not to supply the relevant goods and services at all or on as advantageous terms to the other's or others' rivals (either separately or via the joint venture or its functional equivalent). Even if such an arrangement and any restraint it entails does not lessen competition in the Clayton Act's unqualified lessening-competition test of illegality sense of that expression, the restraint should be deemed to violate the Clayton Act unless (1)(A) it does not inflict a net equivalent-dollar loss on Clayton-Act-relevant buyers, all things considered, or (B) it does not do so by reducing the absolute attractiveness of the best offer they respectively receive from any inferior supplier or (2) the defendants can establish an organizational-economic-efficiency defense for the restraint by demonstrating that, although it did or will inflict a net equivalent-dollar loss on Clayton-Act-relevant buyers and did or will do so by reducing the absolute attractiveness of the best offer they respectively receive from any inferior supplier (by causing one or more non-collaborators to exit or deterring one or more non-collaborators from obtaining the good or service that the collaboration enables its participants to secure either at all or on terms that are as attractive as the terms on which collaborators can obtain them), the collaboration or restrictive provision generated this effect as a result of its increasing the collaborators' organizational economic efficiency. As a matter of law, defendants should sometimes be able to prevail under the Clayton Act because condition (1)(A) is not satisfied—*i.e.*, because the net equivalent-dollar benefits that the restraint confers on Clayton-Act-relevant buyers by improving the marginal-cost/value-of-product (competitive) position of the parents (say, by giving them access at no cost to each other's patents or news stories) by rendering the collaboration profitable or increasing the collaborators' organizational economic efficiency by preventing the sales to non-collaborators that would reduce the amount (measured by private value to the collaborators) of patentable discoveries the collaborators would make or the amount of news stories they would write *exceeds* the net equivalent-dollar loss the restraint imposes on Clayton-Act-relevant buyers by reducing the absolute attractiveness of the best offers they receive from any inferior supplier. As a matter of law, defendants should also sometimes be able to prevail under the Clayton Act on the ground that the restraint would not have inflicted a net equivalent-dollar loss on Clayton-Act-relevant buyers had it not eliminated or disadvantaged non-participants in the collaboration by increasing the collaborators' organizational economic efficiency.

5. The U.S. Case-Law and Antitrust-Enforcement-Agency Positions on Joint Ventures and Any Restrictive Provisions That Joint-Venture Agreements Contain

A. The U.S. Case-Law

I want to begin by making five points about the case-law. First, with one glaring Depression-era exception, U.S. courts have always recognized that joint-venture sales-cooperatives created by rivals whose *ex ante* perception that they would be profitable was critically affected by their belief that the joint ventures would reduce the competition that the parents waged against each other violate the Sherman Act. Second, U.S. courts have never explicitly addressed the possibility that a joint venture that would otherwise be lawful under the Sherman Act might be rendered illegal under that Act by its tendency to increase the extent to which the parents (and perhaps others) engaged in contrived oligopolistic pricing or raised the retaliation barriers to entry or expansion one or more rivals faced. Third, U.S. courts have addressed the possibility that a joint venture that does not contain any restraints might increase the extent to which the parents engage in predation only when considering the legality of joint-venture provisions that limit participation to the original parents or allow parents to make it more difficult or expensive for others to join the joint venture or secure the goods and services it supplies its members than it was for the parents to do so when there is no legitimating basis for the joint venture's refusing to deal with non-members at all or dealing with them on disadvantaging terms. In some such cases, U.S. courts have required joint ventures to make membership available on non-disadvantaging or non-discriminatory terms or to supply non-members the goods or services the joint venture supplies members on terms that do not place the non-members at a disadvantage without asking whether the parents' *ex ante* perception of the profitability of the joint venture itself or of the "discriminatory" membership or supplying-non-members provisions in question was critically affected by their belief that the joint venture or those provisions would reduce the absolute attractiveness of the offers against which they would have to compete. Fourth, to my knowledge, in only one case has a U.S. court recognized the possibility that a joint venture might be rendered illegal by either (1) the reality that or (2) the parents' *ex ante* perception that it would reduce the amount of QV investment in the joint venture's area of product-space by reducing the total amount of QV investment that the parents would make in that area of product-space (in their own names and in the joint venture's name) once they created the joint venture below the total amount of QV investment they would make in their own names if they did not create the joint venture. Fifth, U.S. courts have not addressed the legality under the Sherman Act of a joint venture whose parent-perceived *ex ante* profitability was critically affected by the parents' belief that it would enable them to make a set of QV investments (or investments in PPR) that would be more profitable than the investments of the same magnitude they would have made had they not created the joint venture because the investments the parents would make through the joint venture would be less duplicative than the investments the parents would have made on their own.

I now want to make three points or sets of points about the case-law on the legality under the Sherman Act of provisions in joint-venture agreements that restrain the conduct in which the joint venture and/or its parents can engage. The first set of points relates to the general doctrine that U.S. courts have used to resolve this issue. At the most abstract (formulaic) level, this doctrine is easy to describe. From early days, U.S. courts have held such restraints lawful under the Sherman Act if and only if they were deemed "ancillary" to a lawful joint venture. Unfortunately, the courts have never explicitly defined what they mean by "ancillary." Some statements by U.S. courts seem to imply that a "restraint" in a joint-venture agreement is lawful under the Sherman Act only if (1) the parents have a legitimate interest in preventing each other or the joint venture from engaging in the conduct that the restraining provision prohibits them from engaging in and (2) the restraint is necessary to preserve the profitability of a lawful joint venture. Other statements by U.S. courts seem to imply that only the first of the preceding two conditions must be satisfied for a restraint imposed by a provision in a joint-venture agreement to be "ancillary" and hence lawful under the Sherman Act. I think that the more-permissive position—the position delineated after (1) two sentences ago—is correct as a matter of law: the statement that a joint-venture parent has a legitimate interest in imposing a particular restraint on other parents of its joint venture or on the joint venture itself implies that the parents' *ex ante* perception that the imposition of the restraint was profitable did not depend on any belief they might have had that it would or might reduce the absolute attractiveness of the offers against which the restraint-imposing parents would have to compete, and that is all that is required for the restraint to be lawful under the Sherman Act.

The second point relates to the conclusions that U.S. courts have reached about the legality of certain kinds of restraints that some joint-venture agreements have imposed on the joint venture's parents. Some cases involving production/marketing joint ventures have declared illegal restraints that the joint-venture agreement imposed on the territories within which or customers to which the parents could resell the goods the joint venture supplied them because the courts deciding those cases misunderstood the functions that the vertical restraints in question were performing, misunderstood the test of illegality that it is correct as a matter of law to apply to such restraints, and hence misevaluated the legality of such restraints under the Sherman Act.

The third point is related to the third point in the preceding list. U.S. courts' evaluations of provisions in joint-venture agreements that prohibit members from supplying goods or services they supply members under the joint-venture agreement to non-members either at all or on non-disadvantaging terms often do not focus on whether the parents' *ex ante* perception of the profitability of such provisions was critically affected by their belief that the provisions would reduce the absolute attractiveness of the offers against which the parents would have to compete or whether the restraint in question would lessen competition.

I will now discuss briefly a number of canonical joint-venture cases that U.S. federal courts have decided, most of which have already been analyzed in Chaps. 10, 11, and 14. The first set of such cases focuses (1) on joint ventures that were created in some cases, *inter alia*, to market the product of parents that were horizontal competitors or (2) on trade-association or professional-association attempts to control the terms on which their members' services would be provided. With one exception and one qualification, U.S. courts have declared illegal such joint-sales-agency joint ventures and the attempts of trade or professional associations to control the terms on which the associations' members sold their services.

The set of non-exceptional cases in this category includes (1) *FTC v. Superior Court Trial Lawyers Association*,[1471] in which the Supreme Court declared illegal under the Sherman Act a decision by an organization of private trial lawyers whose members acted as court-appointed counsel in District of Columbia criminal-law cases to stop providing such representation until the District increased the compensation it provided for such services,[1472] (2) *FTC v. Indiana Federation of Dentists*,[1473] which struck down the efforts by an association of dentists to prevent insurance companies from controlling the dentists' use of X-rays, (3) *National Collegiate Athletic Association v. Board of Regents of the University of Oklahoma*,[1474] which struck down the NCAA's restrictions in the number of games for which its individual members could sell TV-transmission rights, (4) *National Society of Professional Engineers v. United States*,[1475] which deemed illegal under the Sherman Act efforts by the Society to prevent employers from selecting the consulting engineer they wished to hire on the basis of the prices candidates indicated in their initial interviews they would charge them for their services, and (5) *Goldfarb v. Virginia State Bar*,[1476] which deemed Sherman-Act-violative the efforts of the Virginia Bar Association to raise the minimum prices that its members charged for specified legal services. Moreover, if the Court's decision that the effort of the Maricopa County Medical Association to establish maximum prices for their members' medical services violated the Sherman Act was actually based on an assumption that the purported maximum-price fix in

[1471] 493 U.S. 413 (1989).

[1472] The Supreme Court opinion overruled the Court of Appeals' holding that, although the group boycott in question would (otherwise) be illegal *per se* under the Sherman Act, the Association could not constitutionally be found to have acted illegally because their action was intended (*inter alia*) to convey a political message that the members had a First Amendment (free-speech) right to communicate in the circumstances in question. For the Court of Appeals decision, see Superior Court Trial Lawyers Association v. FTC, 856 F.2d 226 (U.S. App. D.C. 1988).

[1473] 476 U.S. 447 (1986).

[1474] 468 U.S. 85 (1984). See also Chicago Professional Sport Ltd. Partnership v. National Basketball Association, 901 F.2d 667 (7th Cir. 1992).

[1475] 435 U.S. 679 (1978).

[1476] 421 U.S. 773 (1975).

question was really a minimum-price fix, (6) *Arizona v. Maricopa County Medical Society*[1477] would belong in this list as well. I would also place on this list (7) *Broadcast Music, Inc. v. Columbia Broadcasting System*[1478]: although the Supreme Court decided that the blanket-licensing of the music of the rival parents that created the BMI joint venture did not violate the Sherman Act in an opinion that failed to acknowledge either that the arrangement involved a horizontal price-fix or that it involved a tie-in whose positive-law legality was at best dubious at the time the decision was made, I think that *BMI* belongs in this list because its holding that the arrangement was rendered lawful under the Sherman Act by the sales-negotiation and use-monitoring transaction-cost economic efficiencies it generated implicitly assumes that, had the arrangement not generated such efficiencies, it would have violated the Sherman Act. The only true outlier in the set of U.S. cases that deals with this issue is *Appalachian Coals, Inc. v. United States*,[1479] a Depression-era case that found a joint-sales arrangement among rivals lawful on the false premise that the provision that gave Appalachian Coals the exclusive right to sell its members' coal was ancillary to the joint venture's performance of a number of other legitimate functions (as well as to its performance of some other, illegitimate functions whose performance the Court incorrectly assessed to be Sherman-Act-licit).

The second "set" of joint-venture opinions contains one opinion—a Supreme Court opinion in the 1964 case *United States v. Penn-Olin Chemical Co.*[1480]—that considered the possibility that the joint venture at issue might have reduced the sum of the amounts of QV investment the parents made in the joint venture's area of product-space in their own names and through the joint venture below the amounts they would have made in their own names absent the joint venture. The joint venture in question (Penn-Olin) was created by Pennsalt (a manufacturer of sodium chlorate in the American Northwest) and Olin (a purchaser and distributor of sodium chlorate that had patented certain uses of the product) to produce and distribute sodium chlorate in the American Southeast. The Supreme Court's opinion recognized that, since no-one else would otherwise have made a QV investment in the relevant market, a joint venture would violate U.S. antitrust law if it would reduce the amount of QV investment the parents would add, directly and indirectly, to the joint venture's area of product-space (if it would reduce the total amount of QV investment the parents would make in the relevant area of product-space in their own names and via the joint venture if they created the joint venture below the total amount of QV investment they would make in that area of product-space in their own names if they did not create the joint venture). Unfortunately, as the phrasing of the immediately-preceding sentence reflects, the *Penn-Salt* Court made the mistake of analyzing the legality of the joint venture at issue under the Clayton

[1477] 437 U.S. 332 (1982).
[1478] 441 U.S. 1 (1979).
[1479] 288 U.S. 344 (1933).
[1480] 378 U.S. 158 (1964).

Act rather than under the Sherman Act. After indicating that it was aware that a joint venture could violate U.S. antitrust law for the above reason, the Court concluded that it could not find the Penn-Olin joint venture illegal on this basis because it was bound by the lower court's finding that only one (not both separately) of the parents would have entered the joint venture's area of product-space had they not created the joint venture. However, rather than ruling in favor of Penn-Olin, the Court remanded the case back to a lower court to determine whether the joint venture might still have reduced competition because, in its absence, one parent would have entered and the other's presence as a "perceived potential entrant" would have led the established firms to engage in limit pricing to keep it out: this remand decision is "unfortunate" because (1) it implicitly accepts limit-pricing theory in circumstances in which the theory is almost certainly inapplicable, indeed (2) it accepts a falsely-perceived potential entrant variant of limit-pricing theory in a situation in which there was no factual basis for assuming that the incumbents would mistakenly conclude that, after the first potential parent entered, the potential parent that did not enter was an effective potential competitor, and (3) it ignores the fact that the limit pricing that it is concerned the joint venture would obviate would itself be illegal (would be predatory).

The third set of joint-venture cases I want to discuss contains three opinions that analyze the legality of restrictive provisions in either joint-venture agreements or functionally-equivalent contractual arrangements that control the prices that the parents/participants can charge for particular products, the territories within which or buyers to which the parents/participants can sell the products the joint venture involves, or the right of a participant to sell a particular category of product at all from a particular distributive outlet. Two of the opinions in question are Supreme Court opinions, and one was authored by a Court of Appeals.

The first opinion in this category is the 1967 Supreme Court opinion in *United States v. Sealy*.[1481] Sealy is a joint venture created by mattress manufacturers to design superior or at least more profitable mattresses, to promote the Sealy brand and Sealy products (mattresses and other bedding products), and to protect the Sealy trademark. The mattress-manufacturer members of the Sealy joint venture and no-one else were licensed to manufacture and sell Sealy-brand products in conformity with the product-attribute specifications established by the joint venture. Members of the joint venture were permitted to manufacture and sell other brands of mattresses and other bedding products from the outlets through which they distributed Sealy-brand products and/or from outlets in which they did not sell Sealy-brand products. However, the license that the joint venture's members received to manufacture and sell Sealy-brand products was restrictive in that it specified (1) the territory within which each licensee was authorized to manufacture and sell Sealy products as part of a system that gave each licensee an exclusive territory and (2) the prices that the licensees had to charge for Sealy-brand products. The District Court had held that, although the "price-fix" was illegal, the

[1481] 388 U.S. 350 (1967).

government had not established that the territorial restraint at issue was an unreasonable restraint of trade. The Supreme Court acknowledged that its prior decisions distinguished between horizontal market divisions (market allocations by rivals), which were deemed *per se* illegal, and vertical territorial restrictions (placed on independent distributors by manufacturers), which were to be analyzed under the Rule of Reason. However, the Court concluded that the territorial allocation at issue in *Sealy* was horizontal because, in the relevant joint-venture context, the actor that was in the position occupied by the manufacturer in the standard situation (Sealy) was the same party as the actors that were in the position occupied by the independent distributors in the standard situation (the individual manufacturers and sellers of mattresses that were the parents of Sealy). According to the Court, the legal conclusion that followed from its characterization of the territorial division in question as horizontal rather than vertical—*viz.*, the conclusion that the territorial division at issue was *per se* illegal—was confirmed by the fact that the territorial division was part of an "aggregation of trade restraints"—*i.e.*, was combined with a "price-fix" that was independently illegal.

Both the ruling that the "price-fix" involved in *Sealy* and the ruling that the territorial division involved in *Sealy* were illegal are wrong as a matter of law. There are two ways of explaining this conclusion. The first focuses on the fact that *Sealy* did not involve rivals' that already produced a particular product (1) agreeing to allocate among themselves the territories within which or buyers to which they could attempt to sell that product or (2) agreeing to sell that product at a particular price (*i.e.*, did not involve a standard horizontal territorial division or price-fix). *Sealy* involved firms' that may or may not have been rivals when selling other goods agreeing to produce and market a product or set of products they would not otherwise have produced and to impose restrictions on their individual marketing of that product that made it profitable or more profitable for them to engage in the activity in question. The net consequence of the Sealy joint venture was to increase competition in the manufacture and distribution of mattresses and other bedding products by introducing another brand into that market. The Sealy joint venture did not prohibit its members from producing and distributing non-Sealy mattresses and did not limit the extent to which they could compete against each other when doing so. One might be concerned that the Sealy parents' cooperation in Sealy would result or had resulted in their engaging in anticompetitive price-fixes and anticompetitive territorial divisions when producing and marketing non-Sealy brands, but neither the United States nor the Court mentioned this possibility or adduced any evidence to support this claim and, even if it were true, its relevance for the legality of the Sealy joint venture would be contestable: it would be relevant under the Sherman Act only if (1) the parents' *ex ante* perception of the profitability of the joint venture was critically affected by the possibility that it would enable them to profit more by engaging in such illegal conduct and/or (2) one concludes that it is correct as a matter of law to interpret the Sherman Act *inter alia* as a "fence law" that prohibits acts not otherwise illegal if they increase the probability that one or more perpetrators will engage subsequently in conduct that violates the antitrust laws.

The second (coincident) way to explain why the Sealy restrictions were not illegal is to focus on the functions they performed. The territorial restraints involved in *Sealy* performed the same functions that the vertical territorial restraints analyzed in Chap. 14 performed: *inter alia*, preserving the incentives of the individual manufacture/distributors that were Sealy-members to engage in the out-of-store advertising, in-store advice-giving and promotional activities, and post-sale warranty-service activities that are jointly optimal for all members of the joint venture by reducing the likelihood that the efforts of one parent will increase the sales made by another parent that offered lower prices. The "price-fix" involved in *Sealy* also performed the same legitimate functions that the vertical price-fixes analyzed in Chap. 14 performed: *inter alia*, preventing individual sellers of Sealy products from enabling buyers to purchase Sealy products for a lower price than they would have been willing to pay for them, preventing individual sellers of Sealy products from causing buyers to lower their assessment of the quality of Sealy products by lowering the price that is charged for them, preventing price-cutting from reducing the "organization's" total profits by deflating the incentives of individual members to spend money on out-of-store advertising, in-store promotional displays, in-store advice-giving, in-store salesmanship, and post-sale warranty-services when it would be jointly optimal for all members of the organization for them to spend money on these activities, and encouraging individual sellers of Sealy products to provide each other with information about sales-pitches and advertising that are cost-effective.

The second opinion in this category I want to discuss is the Supreme Court's 1972 opinion in *United States v. Topco Associates*.[1482] "Topco was founded in the 1940s by a group of small, local grocery chains, independently owned and operated, that desired to cooperate to obtain high-quality merchandise under private labels in order to compete more effectively with larger national and regional chains."[1483] In other words, Topco was a buying and private-label-promoting co-op. The Supreme Court's opinion does not make any reference to the ways in which Topco enables its members to obtain better deals when purchasing goods for resale: on the extents to which the profitability of the arrangement depend on its enabling Topco members to take better advantage of (1) economies of scale in developing or using skills to assess the quality of the products offered by and/or the reliability of different potential suppliers, (2) the mechanical-transaction-cost economies of scale related to the quantity of goods purchased from individual suppliers, (3) economies of scale related to the benefits an assured sale confers on a supplier by obviating its spending money to identify possible customers and convince them to give it their patronage and by reducing the risk costs the supplier in question incurs because it does not know how high its sales will be, (4) economies of scale in launching and promoting a private label, and (5) the fact that one buyer that is going to make a larger amount of purchases has more buying power than a series of

[1482] 405 U.S. 596 (1972).

[1483] *Id.* at 599.

individual buyers that collectively are going to make the same amount of purchases. I mention this fact because, although I disagree, the Supreme Court had held that the fact that covered conduct increases its perpetrators' buying power in the sense in which point (5) in the preceding list uses this expression disfavors its legality under the Sherman Act.

The Supreme Court's opinion focused and found illegal under Section 1 of the Sherman Act three features of the Topco joint-venture agreement: (1) a protocol under which "members have a veto of sorts over actual and potential competition in the territorial areas" in which they operate,[1484] (2) a provision restricting members to selling Topco-controlled brands only within territories allocated individually to them, and (3) a provision restricting the right of members to wholesale Topco-brand goods. In practice, the Court noted, the first two of these provisions gave each Topco member the exclusive right to distribute Topco-controlled brands within the territory allocated to it. In my judgment, all three of these restrictions are lawful for the same reason that the restrictions involved in *Sealy* and virtually all standard resale-price-maintenance agreements and standard vertical territorial restraints are legal. I assume but do not know that the prohibition on wholesaling was designed to prevent members from undermining the grant of exclusive territorial rights to fellow-members by wholesaling Topco-brand goods to non-members that could proceed to resell them in competition with members. If this is correct, this restriction is also lawful for the same reasons that the other restrictions are.

The Supreme Court reached the opposite conclusion. It based its decision on three legal claims, each of which I reject: (1) any impact of the restrictions on intra-brand competition is as legally relevant as their impact on inter-brand competition; (2) although the restrictions do increase inter-brand competition by enabling Topco members to compete more effectively with national chains and may increase competition overall, even if they do increase competition overall they are illegal because they decrease intra-brand competition and the fact that covered behavior reduces competition in "one sector of the economy" is determinative—Congress has precluded the courts from trading off against each other increases in competition in one or more sectors of the economy and decreases in competition in one or more sectors of the economy; and (3) even if that were not true so that the application of the Rule of Reason would lead to the conclusion that the restrictions were lawful, precedent in the form of decisions that conclude that this kind of constraint (which the Court deems horizontal) is *per se* illegal precludes the Court from entertaining this possibility—a conclusion that the Court attempts to justify by asserting that "courts are of limited utility in examining difficult economic

[1484] *Id.* at 602: "Membership must first be approved by the board of directors, and thereafter, by an affirmative vote of 75 % of the association's members. If, however, the member whose operations are closest to those of the applicant, or any member whose operations are located within 100 miles of the applicant, votes against approval, an affirmative vote of 85 % of the members is required for approval. . . .[A]s indicated by the record, members cooperate in accommodating each other's wishes. . . ."

problems."[1485] The first two of these claims are wrong for reasons I explained in Chap. 14: just as it is lawful for an integrated manufacturer/retailer to prevent intra-brand competition among its own distributive employees, it is lawful for a non-integrated manufacturer to prevent intra-brand competition among its independent distributors. The second claim is wrong because it extends a legal conclusion for which there is a textual basis (though I think it is wrong as a matter of law, all things considered)—*viz.*, that the Clayton Act prohibits covered conduct that lessens competition in one market even if it does not lessen competition on balance across all the Clayton-Act-relevant markets it affects—in two ways that clearly are wrong as a matter of law—*viz.*, (1) to cover conduct that lessens competition in a "sector of the economy" (whatever that means) when there is no reason to believe that that "sector" coincides with or contains a line of commerce (product market) or area of the country (geographic market) and (2) to apply in cases under the Sherman Act (which contains no text that favors it). The third of these claims is wrong because, as Justice Burger states in dissent in *Topco*, the Court's "role under the Sherman Act" "requires our 'examin[ation of]' difficult economic problems."[1486]

I hasten to add that I have included these cases not because I believe that the current Supreme Court would respond to similar restrictive provisions in similar joint-venture agreements in the same way that the *Sealy* and *Topco* majorities did. I do not think they would: the Court's understanding of the functions and legality of RPM and vertical territorial restraints and customer-allocation clauses has improved too much for it to make these mistakes now, and although the Supreme Court continues to believe that the U.S. antitrust law is designed to prohibit reductions in intra-brand competition as well as reductions in inter-brand competition, it now believes that the legality of relevant conduct depends on whether it increases inter-brand competition by at least as much as it decreases intra-brand competition. I have included these cases instead because they manifest the mistakes that U.S. courts formerly made when analyzing vertical integration and its surrogates, other mistakes that U.S. courts have made when interpreting U.S. antitrust law that we have encountered in other contexts, the tendency of U.S. judges to apply rigid rules to avoid having to consider the theories and facts that inform the resolution of the cases before them that are correct as a matter of law, and the negative consequences of the judges' or justices' refusing to grapple with "difficult economic problems."

The last opinion in this category that I want to discuss is the 1985 opinion by Court of Appeals Judge Frank Easterbrook in *Polk Bros. v. Forest City Enterprises*.[1487] I include this opinion in part because doing so enables me to close this discussion of this group of joint-venture cases on a positive note. Polk Bros. owns a chain of stores selling home appliances and furnishings. Forest City

---

[1485] *Id.* at 609.

[1486] *Id.* at 622.

[1487] 776 F.2d 185 (7th Cir. 1985).

owns a chain of stores that sell building materials, lumber, tools, and related products. The case involves not a joint venture but a restriction in a lease agreement. After obtaining Forest City's agreement to lease part of the building in question, Polk Bros. constructed a building large enough to accommodate one of its stores and one of Forest City's stores. It appears that the parties' *ex ante* belief that it would be profitable for them to occupy different parts of an internally-partitioned building was based on their perception that at least some buyers would find it convenient to purchase in one location home appliances, home furnishings, and the products necessary to repair and maintain a home. As part of the arrangement, the parties agreed on a list of products they both could sell and another list of products that one of them could sell but the other could not. The District Court found that Polk "would not have entered into this arrangement...unless it had received assurances that...[Forest City] would not compete with it in the sale of products that are the 'foundation of...[Polk's] business.'" According to Judge Easterbrook, those restrictions in the products that Forest City could sell from the building in question were necessary to prevent Forest City from taking a free ride on the substantial advertising, display, and in-store sales costs Polk incurred to attract appliance customers—one of the standard functions of and justifications for RPM and vertical territorial restraints and customer-allocation clauses. Easterbrook therefore concluded that these restraints were lawful under the Sherman Act—that they were ancillary to a building-construction/lease arrangement whose participants did not believe *ex ante* that its profitability was critically affected by the possibility that it would or might reduce the absolute attractiveness of the offers against which they would have to compete (and that was economically efficient and that presumably would benefit relevant buyers as well).

I am virtually certain that Easterbrook's account of the whole arrangement involved in *Polk Bros.* and the restrictive covenants in the lease in question is correct. It is conceivable that Polk Bros. would not have made this arrangement had the company not believed *ex ante* that Forest City's operation of the restricted outlet that it ran in the building in question would deter it from opening one or more other outlets that would have sold appliances in competition with Polk Bros. in circumstances in which no-one else would replace the QV investments the arrangement deterred Polk Bros. from making either at all or with equally-competitive projects, but to my knowledge there is no evidence in the record to support such a claim.

The fourth and final category of joint-venture opinions I want to consider are those that focus on the duty of the original members of a joint venture to make membership available to others available on non-discriminatory terms and/or to make the good that the joint venture produces or obligates its members to supply to each other available to non-members on non-discriminatory or at least less-discriminatory terms. Many of these cases have been resolved either explicitly or implicitly by the application of an "essential facilities" or "bottleneck" doctrine. Because those cases—the two most important Supreme Court opinions are *United*

States v. Terminal Railroad Association[1488] and *Associated Press v. United States*[1489]—have been discussed in great detail in Sect. 9 of Chap. 11 and because I will discuss most of the relevant issues once more at the end of this chapter's discussion of the E.C./E.U. case-law on joint ventures, I will confine myself here to repeating that I believe that no version of the "essential facilities" doctrine is correct as a matter of law and that I suspect that few if any of the membership-protocols or sales-to-non-member policies to which the "essential facilities" doctrine has been applied violate the Sherman Act's specific-anticompetitive-intent test of illegality.

B. The DOJ's and FTC's Positions on Joint Ventures and Any Restrictive Provisions That Joint-Venture Agreements Contain

(1) The DOJ's Position

Robert Kramer's statement in 1995[1490] holds true today:

> Since the repeal of the 1988 Antitrust Enforcement Guidelines For International Operations,[1491] the Antitrust Division has issued no comprehensive policy statement on joint ventures. To understand how the Division . . . view[s] joint ventures, . . . [one] needs to consult various sources. In the fields of intellectual property and health care, there are specific guidelines declaring Government enforcement policy. Business review letters issued by the Division and other Division actions may also give insight into how a contemplated business arrangement would be received by the Government.

The Antitrust Division appears to be assuming that the legality of joint ventures is to be assessed under the Clayton Act's "impact on competition" test rather than under the Sherman Act's specific-anticompetitive-intent test: perhaps it would be more accurate to state that the Division does not appear to distinguish between these two tests of illegality when considering joint ventures. Somewhat more concretely, the Antitrust Division follows a "Rule-of-Reason" approach to all joint ventures that are not pure shams.[1492] More concretely still, the Division assesses the legality of such joint ventures by balancing against each other the adverse competitive impacts and the economic efficiencies they (and their collateral restraints)

[1488] 224 U.S. 383 (1912).

[1489] 326 U.S. 1 (1945).

[1490] J. Robert Kramer II, Contractual Joint Ventures: The Enforcement View 7 (1995) (speech delivered at the Joint Venture Program of the 1995 American Bar Association Annual Meeting). Mr. Kramer was head of the Litigation II Section of the Antitrust Division. The text of the speech begins by indicating that the views expressed "do not necessarily reflect the views of the Department of Justice." However, I regard this statement to be *pro forma*.

[1491] Antitrust Division, United States Department of Justice, Antitrust Enforcement Guidelines For International Operations (1988), reprinted in 4 Trade Reg. Rep. (CCH) ¶ 13,109.

[1492] See Kramer, Contractual Joint Ventures: The Enforcement View 2.

generate.[1493] Since the Division has decided to treat joint ventures in much the same way that it approaches horizontal mergers,[1494] the fact that both the 1997-revised 1992 Horizontal Merger Guidelines and the 2010 Horizontal Merger Guidelines indicate that the metric for balancing the procompetitive economic efficiencies and independent anticompetitive impacts that horizontal mergers can generate is their net competitive impact in the Clayton Act's sense of that expression implies that the Antitrust Division will strike the relevant balance in this way in the context of joint ventures as well.[1495]

The Antitrust Division is fully aware of the fact that arrangements that appear at first sight to be economic-efficiency-enhancing joint ventures may actually be purely-anticompetitive shams.[1496] However, the Division seems to be optimistic about the likelihood that the procompetitive effects of the economic efficiencies generated by joint ventures that are not shams will outweigh their anticompetitive effects.[1497] For example, as Kramer indicates, the Division believes that R&D joint ventures "seldom raise antitrust issues."[1498]

Unfortunately, as we have seen, the basic horizontal-merger approach, which the Division carries over to joint ventures, is still more market-oriented than it should be. Although the "Division has not announced a formal screen for market power..., challenges have been brought only where firms possessed market power."[1499] More specifically, the DOJ believes that even joint ventures that create entities that operate in areas of product-space in which both parents are active rivals or could readily become active rivals will not raise antitrust concerns unless "the market is already concentrated."[1500] Obviously, both because I do not think that markets can be defined non-arbitrarily and because I do not think that the possible anticompetitive consequences of a joint venture have much to do with the pre-joint-venture concentration of the market in which it and its parents are (arbitrarily) said to operate (for example, because I recognize that parents that are uniquely-well-placed to invest in a particular "sub-market" may be able to profit by executing a joint venture to reduce their QV investments in this narrow area of product-space from

[1493] *Id.* at 12 and 18.

[1494] *Id.* at 2.

[1495] Kramer's account of the way that the Division is committed to balancing economic efficiencies against anticompetitive impacts is unclear, though it does refer to the procompetitiveness of economic efficiencies. See *id.* at 12.

[1496] See *id.* at 2—discussing the Division's position in United States v. Classic Care Network, 1995–1 Trade Cas. (CCH) ¶ 70,997 (E.D.N.Y., 1995)—and at 5–6—discussing the Division's position in United States v. Alliant Techsystems, Inc., Civ. No. 94–1026 (C.D. Ill. [complaint] 1994) and United States v. Alliant Techsystems, Inc., 1994–1 Trade Cas. ¶ 70,595 (C.D. Ill. [final judgment] 1994).

[1497] See Kramer, Contractual Joint Ventures: The Enforcement View 2 at the text preceding Kramer's footnote 5.

[1498] *Id.* at 5.

[1499] *Id.* at 16.

[1500] *Id.* at 3.

two to one even if the structure of the larger ARDEPPS defined to be the market is unconcentrated), I reject this market-oriented approach to joint-venture competitive-impact analysis just as I reject its counterpart to horizontal-merger competitive-impact analysis.

Admittedly, production joint ventures or product-R&D *plus* production joint ventures between parents that are active rivals in the joint venture's "product market" may be more likely to be designed to reduce QV-investment competition by substituting X QV investments executed by the joint venture for the (X + Y) QV investments that the parents would otherwise have made in the relevant ARDEPPS when the parents enjoy substantial BCAs on their own products in that ARDEPPS (since the parents will have more profits to protect against additional QV investment in this situation). However, for three reasons, this fact does not legitimate the creation of safe havens for joint ventures of this type whose parents have less than some specified percent of the relevant "market" or the use of a decision-standard that makes the likelihood of a finding of illegality increase (*a fortiori* increase strongly) with the parents' combined market share:

(1) as we have seen, a parent's market share is not strongly correlated with its total BCAs since the parent's market share indicates only the percentage of sales for which it is best-placed, not the average amount by which it is best-placed when it is best-placed,
(2) the parents' market shares do not indicate whether they would have chosen on their own to make QV investments in each other's more-narrowly-defined areas of product-space (whether they could have profited by making any additional QV investments in the relevant ARDEPPS and whether any such expansions they would have executed on their own would have been near the other's product-locations), and
(3) the parents' market shares also provide little if any information about whether they were uniquely-well-placed to invest near the locations of each other's extant products—whether other established or potential competitors would respond to the parents' decision not to invest by making QV investments that were equally competitive with the parents' pre-existing products as the parents' own expansions would have been.

For similar reasons, I reject the Agencies' "safety zone" approach to intellectual-property licensing-arrangements. The fact that "the parties to the agreement amount to no more than twenty percent of the relevant market"[1501] is perfectly compatible with the conclusion that the parents' *ex ante* beliefs in the *ex ante* profitability of their intellectual-property pool was critically affected by their perception that it would or might reduce the absolute attractiveness of the offers against which they

[1501] *Id.* at 8–9, citing United States Department of Justice and Federal Trade Commission, Antitrust Guidelines for the Licensing of Intellectual Property (1995), reprinted in Antitrust and Trade Reg. Rep. S-1 (1995).

would have to compete by inducing one or more non-members to exit by worsening these rivals' competitive-position arrays, and even if this is not the case, the members' *ex ante* beliefs in the *ex ante* profitability of their decision not to admit the non-members or to admit them only on disadvantageous terms (when the disadvantaging cannot be explained by the cost the original members had to incur to create and implement the patent pool or justified as an incentive to others to create economically-efficient patent pools) may have been critically affected by their perception that the decisions in question would reduce the absolute attractiveness of the offers against which they would have to compete by driving one or more non-members out and/or deterring the entry of one or more non-members. The same considerations lead me to reject the Division's decision to create a safe haven for joint ventures created to purchase, operate, and market high-technology equipment when the parents buy less than 35 % of the purchased product (and *a fortiori* to reject the Division's creation of a safe haven for such joint ventures when the parents' purchases amount to less than 20 % of the parents' revenues).[1502] Parents who have less than 35 % of the sales of an arbitrarily-defined market may still be best-placed and second-placed to supply particular buyers who operate in that market.

For the same reasons, I also consider inappropriate the 20 % "safety zone" for "physician network" joint ventures formed to help health-care providers "market their services jointly to health benefit plans and other purchasers."[1503] Equally unsound is the Division's practice of basing its decision on whether to challenge export agreements on the ground that the communications they involve may facilitate their participants' engaging in domestic contrived oligopolistic behavior—in the Division's words, may have undesirable domestic "spillover effects"—on the "concentration" of the relevant domestic market, the "ease of entry" into it, and the total domestic market share of its participants.[1504]

I also have objections to the Division's analysis of the legality of joint ventures created to produce and be the exclusive suppliers of inputs for their parents. The Division recognizes the risk that such joint ventures may enable the parents to restrict their production "as would a cartel"[1505]—*i.e.*, that the parents of such a joint venture may instruct the joint venture to predatorily refuse to supply inputs to the parents' rivals. I have two concerns. First, the Division's position that any tendency of such a joint venture to lead to such behavior disfavors its legality does not take

[1502] See Kramer, Contractual Joint Ventures: The Enforcement View 10.

[1503] See *id.* at 11, citing at notes 28–30 opinion letters written to health-care provider-networks, and United States Department of Justice and Federal Trade Commission, Antitrust Enforcement Policy Statements in the Health Care Area (1993), reprinted in 65 Antitrust & Trade Reg. Rpt. S-1 (Sept. 23, 1993).

[1504] See Kramer, Contractual Joint Ventures: The Enforcement View 13–14 and note 51—discussing the Export Trade Certificate application of the Construction Industry Manufacturers Association.

[1505] *Id.* at 4.

account of the possibility that the legally-appropriate response to any such tendency is to prosecute the predatory refusal to deal when it occurs. Second, the Division's apparent belief that competition from non-parents will prevent the joint venture from engaging in predatory refusals to deal if the relevant market is not concentrated ignores the possibility that the parents may have been best-placed and second-placed to supply the input to some final-product rivals when they produced the input themselves and that the joint venture would in such situations facilitate their engaging in a predatory refusal to deal through the joint venture as well as the possibility in situations in which the parents did not or would not otherwise have produced the input in question independently that the joint venture may be best-placed to supply the parents' rivals and operate in a situation in which, if it did supply the parents' rivals, it would not find it inherently profitable to price its product in a way that would remove all of the relevant buyers' buyer surplus.

Admittedly, many joint ventures of all these types are perfectly lawful. That is not the issue. My objection is to (1) using the Clayton Act's test of illegality rather than the Sherman Act's test of illegality to assess the legality of joint ventures, (2) using market-oriented approaches to assess their competitive impact and legality under the Clayton Act, and (3) establishing market-oriented "safe havens" or "safety zones" for them.

In addition to laying out and commenting on the Antitrust Division's basic approach to and assumptions about joint ventures, I want to pay some attention to a few "details" that reinforce my general conclusion that the Division has not only made real progress (in relation to joint ventures) in recent years but is on the threshold of analyzing the legality of such arrangements properly. First, the Division has clearly moved in the right direction by recognizing both that firms may use their participation in collective export agreements to collude domestically[1506] and that exclusive joint-licensing agreements may reduce competition (indeed, may be designed exclusively or *inter alia* to reduce competition) by disadvantaging or driving out the non-participating rivals of the participants. Second, the Division has made a real advance by recognizing that a joint venture that will operate in an area of product-space in which one parent is active and the other is a potential competitor may reduce competition if the potential-competitor parent is uniquely-well-placed to enter the relevant area of product-space.[1507] This

[1506] I do not know the significance of Kramer's somewhat cryptic statement that the Division is concerned that joint ventures that operate in a product or geographic market that is related to but separate from the market in which its parents operate may be directed by the parents in a way that reduces competition in the parents' market. Kramer, Contractual Joint Ventures: The Enforcement View 3–4. If the Division's fear is that the joint venture and its parents might cooperate in retaliating against and reciprocating to rivals that operate in both the joint venture's and the parents' markets or that the joint venture might be instructed not to enter the parents' market in circumstances in which the investor whose entry into the joint venture's market was deterred by the joint venture would have subsequently entered the parents' market had it entered the joint venture's market first, that fact would manifest real progress, but I suspect that this elaboration is too optimistic.

[1507] *Id.* at 4.

effort at what I call QV-investment-competition analysis represents substantial progress although it

(1) repeats the standard mistakes of ignoring the possibilities that a uniquely-well-placed potential entrant may still not be an effective potential entrant and that one or more potential expanders may be as well-placed to add a QV investment to the relevant area of product-space as is the best-placed potential-competitor parent,
(2) ignores the fact that a similar problem can arise when both parents are established in the joint venture's ARDEPPS—*i.e.*, when both parents are potential expanders, and
(3) ignores the fact that joint ventures can also decrease QV-investment competition when they operate in an area of product-space in which neither parent is currently active but both parents could enter.

Third, the Division is also correct in emphasizing the possibility that joint ventures can generate contrived oligopolistic pricing and predation in various ways. Fourth, the division deserves praise as well for its attempts to respond to these possibilities by requiring joint ventures whose contribution to the parents' organizational economic efficiency does not depend on the parents' exchanging information to hire independent agents, say, to negotiate the parents' joint purchases[1508] or to make export bids[1509] as well as by prohibiting the sharing of information whose dissemination is likely to reduce competition on balance in the Clayton Act sense.[1510]

A final report card on the DOJ's position on joint ventures. The Division deserves credit for recognizing that some joint ventures are purely-anticompetitive shams, that many joint ventures do generate economic efficiencies, that these economic efficiencies count in favor of the legality of the joint ventures that generate them, that joint ventures that are not shams can reduce competition both by promoting contrived oligopolistic pricing and predatory conduct in various ways and by restricting QV-investment competition in various ways, and that some of these negative tendencies can be reduced by restricting communications between the joint venture and the parents and between the parents themselves. Once again, however, the Division's approach is marred by its assumption that the legality of joint ventures depends on their competitive impact, by the market-oriented character of its competitive-impact analyses, by its creation of market-oriented safe havens, by its failure to develop a comprehensive analysis of the determinants of the profitability of contrived oligopolistic pricing and predation, and by its failure to develop an appropriate conceptual system for analyzing the impact of joint ventures on QV-investment competition.

[1508] *Id.* at 10.

[1509] *Id.* at 14.

[1510] *Id.*

(2) The FTC's Position

I am unaware of any general statements by the FTC about the legality of joint ventures or the restrictive provisions that joint-venture agreements may contain—much less any statements that compare or contrast the FTC's position on these matters with the DOJ's. However, I do want to describe the way in which the FTC handled one joint-venture proposal to which it responded in 1984. The case in question—*General Motors Corp.*[1511]—addressed the legality of a joint venture that General Motors and Toyota created to produce at a then-idle GM plant in California 200,000 to 250,000 units annually of a subcompact car based on Toyota's Sprinter, which at that time was sold only in Japan. The output was to be sold to GM at a price determined by an index in which the price of Toyota's Corolla figured prominently. After investigating the case, the FTC seems to have concluded that, at least for the next 12 years, the joint venture would increase competition on balance (1)(A) by introducing an additional QV investment into the relevant ARDEPPS (in the FTC's words, by "increas[ing] the number of small cars available in America," given the "restrictions on Japanese imports"[1512]) or (B) by substituting a better-placed QV investment for a worse-placed QV investment (which would have been introduced had GM had to rely on a different production-source) and/or (2) by increasing the organizational economic efficiency of GM's operations in general by enabling it "to complete its learning of more efficient Japanese manufacturing and management techniques."[1513]

Nevertheless, the FTC agreed to abandon formal proceedings only on condition that the parents enter into a consent agreement that

(1) prohibited any other joint venture between GM and Toyota,
(2) limited the duration of the joint venture under scrutiny to 12 years,
(3) limited the joint venture to producing 250,000 units annually, and
(4) prohibited the parents from discussing with each other non-public information about

    (A) current or future prices about new cars or components (except in the course of discussing possible sales between them),
    (B) costs of the parents' products,
    (C) sale or production forecasts or plans for any product other than the joint venture's product or marketing plans for any product, and/or (somewhat mysteriously), and
    (D) current or future model changes or designs for the joint venture's product, its sales or production forecasts, or the cost of components to be supplied to the joint venture by the parents except as necessary to the functioning of the joint venture.

[1511] 103 F.T.C. 374 (1984).

[1512] *Id.* at 388.

[1513] *Id.* at 387–88.

All of the restrictions that this consent agreement imposes on the joint venture and its parents strike me as either incorrect or dubious as a matter of law. Thus, there seems to be little or no justification for the requirement that GM and Toyota agree not to enter into other joint ventures (why not consider them when they are proposed) or for the limitation on the number of units the joint venture under scrutiny could produce. Furthermore, although the limitation of the joint venture to 12 years may in one sense be a sensible response to the fact that changes in conditions might make a joint venture that would increase competition for its first 12 years decrease competition thereafter, I doubt that the FTC has the legal authority to impose this kind of restriction on a joint venture that does not manifest its parents' specific anticompetitive intent and is not predicted to lessen competition over its lifetime (which would be relevant only if, contrary to my view, it were correct as a matter of law to interpret the FTC Act's unfair "method of competition" test of illegality to incorporate the Clayton Act's lessening-competition test of illegality as well as the Sherman Act's specific-anticompetitive-intent test of illegality). Even the prohibitions of the parents' exchanging various specified types of information seem legally questionable to me. Admittedly, parental exchanges of information about the prices they are currently charging for their own products or intend to charge for them in the future can facilitate their price-fixing by enabling them to detect when they are stealing each other's customers from a position of inferiority or to settle on a future fixed set of prices; parental exchanges of information about their own costs can facilitate their price-fixing by enabling them to identify each other as possible undercutters or underminers; parental exchanges of information about their production forecasts or plans can facilitate their price-fixing by enabling them to agree on output-restrictions; and parental exchanges of information about their own current or future model changes may be part of a process through which they agree to restrict their own QV investments when no rival will replace the investments they do not make. However, (1) the exchange of all of these types of information can also perform Sherman-Act-licit functions, particularly when the seller and/or buyer to which the information relates is identified—enabling sellers to identify their HNOPs, enabling sellers to detect the fact that their costs are unnecessarily high, enabling sellers to avoid producing more or fewer units of their products than is profitable, enabling sellers to avoid creating new models whose creation is less profitable, less beneficial to consumers, and less economically efficient than an alternative model the seller could have created with the same amount of resources would have been because the model it created was privately and economically excessively duplicative of the model its rival created—and (2) if *ex ante* the parents believed that the information-exchanges in question were rendered *ex ante* profitable by the prospect of their performing these Sherman-Act-licit functions, the exchanges would be lawful under the Sherman Act on that account even if the parents also believed *ex ante* that the exchanges would increase the profits they would make by engaging in contrivance (and/or predation) unless one concludes that it is correct as a matter of law to interpret the Sherman Act to be a fence law that prohibits conduct that is requisitely likely to lead to future illegal conduct even when the conduct's doing so is not essential to its perpetrators' *ex ante* perception that it was *ex ante* profitable.

In addition, the FTC's explanation of its apparent conclusion that the proposed joint venture would increase competition is not fully satisfactory. Even if Toyota were legally prohibited from entering on its own and GM could not enter as effectively on its own or through a joint venture involving someone else, might not the GM-Toyota joint venture have deterred someone else from entering or expanding its QV investments in the relevant ARDEPPS? Even if such an alternative QV investment would have been worse-placed, might it not have been more procompetitive, given that its product's price would not have been formally tied to the price of Toyota's Corolla? Admittedly, this analysis ignores the possible procompetitive impact of any organizational economic efficiencies the joint venture would enable GM to achieve in its other operations, but it also ignores the risk that the joint venture might lead its parents to engage in additional contrivance or other kinds of illegal conduct.

6. The Legality of Joint Ventures Under E.C./E.U. Competition Law, Correctly Interpreted and Applied

A. The Treaty Provision That Is Now Article 101 of the 2009 Treaty of Lisbon

I will address in this order (1) whether the formation of joint ventures and the decisions joint ventures make are covered by now-Article 101, (2) whether some joint ventures violate now-Article 101(1)'s test of *prima facie* illegality in that they have as "their object" or "effect" "the prevention, restriction, or distortion of competition within the common market," and (3) whether some joint ventures that violate now-Article 101(1)'s test of *prima facie* illegality are rendered lawful under now-Article 101 by their satisfaction of now-Article 101(3)'s requirements for receiving an "exemption" from now-Article 101(1)—in essence, by their satisfying the conditions for establishing a now-Article 101(3) economic-efficiency defense.

The first of these three issues is the simplest to resolve. Because virtually all joint ventures are created by agreements between undertakings, the formation of virtually all joint ventures are covered by what is now-Article 101 of the 2009 Treaty of Lisbon. Indeed, if joint ventures could also be said to be associations of undertakings in the now-Article 101(1) sense of that concept, their decisions would be covered by now-Article 101(1) on that basis as well.

The second of the above three issues can be resolved by combining (1) Sect. 2 of Chapter 4's explanations of why, correctly interpreted as a matter of E.C./E.U. law, the object-branch of Article 101(l)'s test of *prima facie* illegality is coincident with the Sherman Act's specific-anticompetitive-intent test of illegality and the meaning of "preventing or restricting competition" in the effect-branch of Article 101(1)'s test of *prima facie* illegality is coincident with the meaning of "lessening competition" in the Clayton Act's test of *prima facie* illegality, (2) Sect. 1 of this chapter's analysis of the possible Sherman-Act-illicit functions of joint ventures and/or the restrictive provisions that joint-venture agreements may contain and Sect. 3A of this chapter's analysis of the conditions under which joint ventures and/or any restrictive provisions that joint-venture agreements contain will manifest one or both parents' specific anticompetitive intent, and (3) Sect. 2 of this chapter's analysis of the conditions under which joint ventures and/or any restrictive provisions that joint-venture agreements may contain will violate the lessening-competition test of illegality by imposing a net equivalent-monetary loss on relevant buyers by reducing the absolute attractiveness of the best offer they respectively receive from any inferior supplier.

As to the third of the above three issues, some joint ventures that violate Article 101(1)'s test of *prima facie* illegality will not violate Article 101 because they qualify for a now-Article 101(3) exemption in that (1) they do not create a requisite "possibility" that "competition in respect to a substantial part of the product in question" will be "eliminate[ed]," (2) they do constitute the least restrictive means of "contribut[ing] to improving the production or distribution of goods or to promoting technical or economic progress, while allowing consumers a fair share of the resulting benefit," and (3) they do enable relevant "consumers [to obtain] a fair share of the resulting benefit." Nevertheless, for two reasons, the fact that now-Article 101 contains provision 101(3) does not make now-Article 101 as permissive of joint ventures as the Sherman Act is[1514]: (1) the requirement that "consumers [obtain]. . .a fair share of the resulting benefit" will render illegal under now-Article 101 many joint ventures that would be lawful under the Sherman Act and (2) now-Article 101(3)'s list of benefits whose generation could conceivably result in covered conduct's being "exempted" from now-Article 101(1) is not so extensive as the set of Sherman-Act-licit functions joint ventures can perform. Thus, "contribut[ing] to improving the production or distribution of goods or to promoting technical or economic progress" (1) would not appear to include (A) yielding real economies of scale in purchasing inputs or other sorts of real economies in purchasing inputs, (B) generating purely-private economies of scale or scope in purchasing by creating a joint venture that either on its own or in collaboration with its parents would have more bargaining power as buyers, and (C) rendering profitable non-innovative QV investments whose execution would be economically inefficient and (2) depending on how "promoting technical or economic progress" is interpreted, might not include yielding profits by enabling the parents to substitute a smaller number of research projects that will yield fewer discoveries for the larger number of research projects that would have yielded a larger number of

[1514] Article 101(3) resembles the Sherman Act's "efficiency defense" in that both place all variants of the relevant burden of proof (the burden of producing evidence, the burden of paying for relevant evidence, and the burden of persuasion on the issues in question) on the defendant(s).

discoveries that they would have executed had they not created the joint venture when the smaller set of research projects is more allocatively efficient than the larger set because the members of the smaller set are less-economically-inefficiently-duplicative than the members of the larger set would have been. (I assume that, like the Sherman Act, now-Article 101(3) should not be interpreted to permit joint ventures that increase economic efficiency by reducing the number of research projects that are executed when the reason that the reduction in research is economically efficient has nothing to do with differences in the extent to which the members of the two relevant sets of research projects are/would be economically-inefficiently-duplicative—*i.e.*, when it reflects the fact that, for other reasons [*e.g.*, the existence of non-perfectly-counteracting imperfections in price competition and/or IP law], the larger set of research projects includes one or more profitable projects that would be economically inefficient.)

B. The Treaty Provision That Is Now Article 102 of the 2009 Treaty of Lisbon

Only two of the three issues that were considered in relation to now-Article 101 must be considered in relation to now-Article 102: the coverage issue and the test-of-illegality issue. Now-Article 102 has no counterpart to now-Article 101(3): therefore, now-Article 102's test or tests of illegality are tests not of *prima facie* illegality but of final illegality.

Now-Article 102 covers all joint ventures created by one or more parents that are either individually dominant or (by interpretation) a member of a collectively-dominant set of rivals because now-Article 102 covers all conduct of such firms. Now-Article 102's test of illegality proscribes two categories of "abuses of a dominant position"—"exclusionary abuses," which in my judgment are acts or practices that violate the Sherman Act's specific-anticompetitive-intent test of illegality, and "exploitative abuses," which are acts or practices that reduce the buyer surplus of the dominant undertaking's actual and potential customers to an unacceptably-low magnitude, to an unacceptably-low percentage of the transaction surplus their transactions with the dominant firm generated, or to an unacceptably-low percentage of the transaction surplus their transactions with the dominant firm would have generated had it acted to maximize that transaction surplus or had its decisions given a "fair" weight to their equivalent-monetary effects on its potential customers. I have stated the exploitative-abuse branch of now-Article 102's "test" of illegality in the alternative because neither the text nor the history of now-Article 102 provides a basis for a definitive interpretation and no authoritative E.C./E.U. decisionmaker has ever offered an operational interpretation. As Sect. 2B of Chap. 4 indicated, although E.C./E.U. institutions have always insisted that now-Article 102's test of illegality does have an exploitative-abuse branch, they have virtually never condemned conduct as an exploitative abuse under now-Article 102.

In any event, it is clear that any joint venture and/or restrictive provision in a joint-venture agreement that violates the Sherman Act's specific-anticompetitive-intent test (because one or both of its perpetrators' *ex ante* perceptions that it was profitable were critically affected by their belief that it would or might reduce the absolute attractiveness of the offers against which they will have to compete by enabling them to engage in additional, profitable contrivance or predation, by prohibiting one or more of them from entering one or more of the others' markets when the prohibited parent would otherwise have been an effective potential competitor of the other parent, and/or by enabling the parents to reduce the amount of investment they make in the joint venture's area of product-space considering both the investments they make through the joint venture and the investments they make in their own names in circumstances in which the investments the parents do not make in the joint venture's area of product-space will not be replaced by investments by others) will also violate the exclusionary-abuse branch of now-Article 102's test of illegality. It is also clear that any joint venture or restrictive provision in a joint-venture agreement that reduces the buyer surplus of the parents' actual and potential customers because its performance of one or more of the just-listed functions imposes an equivalent-monetary loss on these parties that exceeds the equivalent-monetary gain the joint venture confers on them by generating economic and/or private efficiencies could violate the exploitative-abuse branch of now-Article 102's test of illegality under any of the possible operationalizations of the now-Article 102 concept of an "exploitative abuse."

C. The EMCR

Although, as I argued when explaining why Section 7 of the Clayton Act does not cover joint ventures, joint ventures are not mergers, a Council Regulation has declared that the EMCR (and its lessening-competition test of illegality) does cover a subset of joint ventures—namely, full-function (so-called "concentrative") joint ventures.[1515] I see no persuasive reason why—if it were desirable to use a lessening-competition test to determine the illegality of full-function joint ventures—it would not be desirable to use such a test to determine the illegality of limited-function (so-called "cooperative") joint ventures such as joint ventures

[1515] Council Regulation (EC) 139/2004 of 20 January 2004 on the Control of Concentrations Between Undertakings, OJ L24/1 (2004). The 1990 EMCR applied only to (1) full-function joint ventures that (2) created no risk of the parents' "coordinating" their behavior (in my terms, practicing contrivance) with each other or with the joint venture (in practice, applied only to joint ventures created by parents that were not active product rivals and would not *ab initio* be active product rivals of the joint venture). This second restriction of coverage was removed in 1997. See Council Regulation (EEC) 4064/89 of the Control of Concentrations Between Undertakings, OJ 1395/1 (19889); Council Regulation on Merger Control, Amending Regulation 4064/89, OJ L180/1 (1997); and KORAH at 428.

created exclusively (1) to perform joint-buying and private-brand-creating-and-promoting functions, (2) to perform joint-marketing functions, or (3) to execute joint R&D projects.[1516] However, the fact is that the EMCR and its lessening-competition test of illegality apply only to full-function joint ventures.

Full-function, concentrative joint ventures and/or any restrictive provisions contained in the joint-venture agreement creating them will violate the EMCR even if no parent is a dominant firm and/or the joint venture would not violate now-Article 102's specific-anticompetitive-intent (exclusionary-abuse) test of illegality if it is requisitely likely to or has imposed a net equivalent-monetary loss

[1516] As reported by Diaz, the "principle rationale for the distinction between [*i.e.*, for the divergent treatment of] co-operative and concentrative. . .[joint ventures is] that co-operative. . .[joint ventures] create greater risks of competitive harm and fewer opportunities for competitive benefits than [do] full mergers and acquisitions. . .." See Francisco Enrique Gonzalez Diaz, *Horizontal Co-operation Agreements* 659, 665 (hereinafter Diaz), Chapter 7 in The EC Law of Competition (Jonathan Faull and Ali Nikpay, eds.) (Oxford Univ. Press, 2d ed., 2007). For at least two reasons, this rationale cannot bear scrutiny. First, although partial-function joint ventures do "create fewer opportunities for competitive benefits than [do] full mergers and acquisitions," they also tend to create less competitive harm in that (1) unlike clearly-horizontal mergers and acquisitions, joint ventures created by parents that compete with each other do not automatically and often will not in practice end all competition between the participants and (2) unlike mergers and acquisitions between potential competitors, joint ventures created by parents that are potential competitors do not automatically and may not in practice deter one parent that would otherwise be an effective potential competitor of another parent from entering the other's market, enable two or more parents that would otherwise be effective potential competitors in one or more markets in which the joint venture is not operating to reduce the amount of QV investment they make in that market when it would be in their joint interest to do so, or enable two or more parents that would otherwise be effective potential competitors of the joint venture to reduce the amount of QV investment they make in the joint venture's market(s) in their own names and through the joint venture below the amount they would have made in that market or those markets in their own names absent the joint venture (even if the joint venture does prohibit the parents from entering the joint venture's market[s]). Second, the relevant comparison is not between cooperative joint ventures and mergers and acquisitions but between cooperative and concentrative joint ventures. I see no reason to believe either that (1) full-function (concentrative) joint ventures will be less likely than partial-function (cooperative) joint ventures to inflict an equivalent-monetary loss on relevant buyers or that (2) it would be more desirable to prohibit partial-function than full-function joint ventures that do not inflict an equivalent-monetary loss on relevant buyers but also do not confer on them a "fair share" of the equivalent-monetary gains the joint ventures yield in the ways listed in Article 101(3). I also see no reason to believe that it will be undesirable to investigate on a case-by-case basis whether particular partial-function joint ventures will inflict an equivalent-monetary loss on relevant buyers or whether particular partial-function joint ventures that do not inflict a net equivalent-monetary loss on relevant buyers but do not give such buyers a "fair share of the resulting benefits" should be prohibited as a matter of policy when it would be desirable to investigate these two issues on a case-by-case basis when full-function joint ventures are at issue.

I should point out that, in its White Paper on Modernization, the EC stated that it planned to bring within the coverage of the EMCR partial-function joint ventures whose assets at creation exceeded some minimum, to-be-specified amount. See Of the Rules Implementing Articles 85 and 86 of the E.C. Treaty [now-Articles 101 and 102 of the 2009 Treaty of Lisbon], Commission Program No. 99/027, ¶¶ 78-81a (1999). However, the EC has not yet issued a regulation declaring that such partial-function joint ventures are covered by the EMCR.

on "Clayton-Act-relevant" buyers as a result of its performing one or more of the four Sherman-Act-illicit functions delineated in Section B of this chapter. Still, since a finding that a joint venture is covered by the EMCR exempts it from now-Articles 101 and 102, the fact that some joint ventures (*viz.*, full-function, "concentrative" joint ventures) are covered by the EMCR will render at least some and I suspect many such collaborations lawful under E.C./E.U. competition law despite the fact that they would correctly be deemed to violate now-Article 101.[1517] This conclusion reflects two and perhaps three legal realities:

(1) the EMCR takes account of all the benefits that a joint venture can confer on "Clayton-Act-relevant" buyers, not just of the benefits that are generated in the limited set of ways that now-Article 101(3) specifies;
(2) the EMCR does not make relevant buyers' obtaining a "fair share" of the benefits a joint venture confers on the parents and buyers combined a necessary condition for the joint venture's legality—it requires only that the joint venture not impose more than a *de minimis* loss on Clayton-Act-relevant buyers; and perhaps
(3) in practice, defendants in EMCR joint-venture cases may not bear as heavy an evidentiary burden of establishing that their joint venture would have relevant-buyer-benefitting consequences as defendants in now-Article 101 joint-venture cases bear on this issue.

A comparison of the correctly-interpreted-and-applied E.C./E.U. and U.S. law on joint ventures may be illuminating. Three points or sets of points are salient. First, under E.C./E.U. law correctly interpreted and applied, limited-function joint ventures created by one or more parents that are individually dominant or belong to a collectively-dominant set of rivals are lawful unless they violate the Sherman Act's test of illegality (*i.e.*, unless they constitute an exclusionary abuse of a dominant prohibition prohibited by now-Article 102 or [at least in theory] unless they constitute an exploitative abuse of a dominant position [also prohibited by now-Article 102])—*i.e.*, will violate E.C./E.U. competition law in all cases in which they violate U.S. antitrust law (in particular, the Sherman Act) and in some cases in which they do not violate the U.S. antitrust law (the Sherman Act). Second, limited-function joint ventures none of whose parents is either individually dominant or a member of a collectively-dominant set of rivals (1) will virtually always violate E.C./E.U. competition law correctly interpreted and applied when they violate the U.S. Sherman Act's specific-anticompetitive-intent test of illegality because in such cases they will virtually always violate now-Article 101(1)'s test of *prima facie* illegality and will not qualify for a now-Article 101(3) exemption even if they do generate some economic efficiencies whose generation satisfies that requirement for a now-Article 101(3) exemption in that they will not satisfy now-Article 101(3)'s requirement that the conduct in question enables (relevant)

[1517] The text does not refer to now-Article 102 because any joint venture that would violate either of its branches would also violate the EMCR.

consumers to obtain a fair share of the resulting benefit (will violate now-Article 101 unless [A] the joint venture generates relevant economic efficiencies and [B] the joint venture and possibly its parents respond to the law by passing on sufficient gains to relevant consumers to qualify for a now-Article 101(3) exemption by making pricing and other decisions that would not otherwise be profitable [no such conduct has yet been reported]) and (2) will sometimes violate E.C./E.U. competition law correctly interpreted and applied when they do not violate the U.S. Sherman Act's specific-anticompetitive-intent test of illegality because (A) they do have the effect of reducing competition and (B) they (i) do not generate any now-Article 101(3)-qualifying efficiencies and/or (ii) do not confer on relevant buyers a fair share of the resulting benefit (perhaps, *inter alia*, because they increase the amount of contrivance and predation practiced). Third, full-function (so-called concentrative) joint ventures can violate E.C./E.U. competition law even when they do not violate U.S. antitrust law because (A) they are covered by and may violate the EMCR's lessening-competition test even when they would not violate the Sherman Act's specific-anticompetitive-intent test and (B) correctly interpreted, the U.S. Clayton Act with its lessening-competition test of illegality does not apply to full-function or any other type of joint venture.

For many years, the EC has stated that the legality of joint ventures can be determined only by executing economic analyses that reveal their likely effects.[1518] The CFI and ECJ clearly agree. Unfortunately, as the CFI's critique of a 1994 EC decision in a 1998 case pointed out,[1519] the EC has not always executed appropriate economic analyses. Unfortunately as well, the E.C./E.U. courts also are wedded to a market-oriented approach to many of the relevant issues that (in my judgment) is misguided.

Because the structure of this section is complicated, I will begin with an outline. The section starts by (1) delineating the issues made legally salient by now-Article 101, the Treaty provision that applies to all joint ventures other than the full-function joint ventures covered by the EMCR, (2) pointing out that (A) the relevant EC case-opinions, Regulations, Notices, and Guidelines, (B) the relevant CFI/ECJ opinions, and (C) the applicable portions of the leading E.C./E.U.-competition-law treatises do not explicitly or often even implicitly connect the points or facts whose

[1518] See, *e.g.*, Report on Competition Policy (Vol. XIII) 50–52 (1983) and Commission Notice on the Applicability of Article 81 to Horizontal Cooperation Agreements, OJ C3/2 (2001). See also the EC's 2001 Guidelines on the Applicability of Article 81 [now-Article 101] to Horizontal Cooperation: in particular, Guideline 14 second indent states that "cooperation between competing companies that cannot independently carry out the project or activity covered by the cooperation" is not covered by now-Article 101(1), and Guideline 20 indicates that under now-Article 101(1) agreements must be considered in their economic context. Guidelines 32–38 indicate that the economic efficiencies joint ventures can generate must be considered under now-Article 101(3). See also Commission on Regulation (EC) 2659/2000 on the Application of Article 81(3) [now-Article 101(3)] of the Treaty to Categories of Research and Development Agreements at ¶ 7, OJ L304/7 (2000) and EC Notice on Article 81(3) [now-Article 101(3)] at Guidelines 17 and 18, OJ C101/97 (2004).

[1519] European Night Services and Others v. Commission, T-374/94, ECR II-3141 (1998).

legal relevance they are asserting to the part of now-Article 101's text that makes or might make them legally relevant, and (3) explaining why there are fewer joint-venture-case-opinions (why the section discusses fewer joint-venture case-opinions) than one might expect. The section then proceeds to delineate and assess (1) the various reasons why the EC and the E.C./E.U. courts think that different types of joint ventures may violate now-Article 101(1)'s test of *prima facie* illegality and (2) the positions that the EC and E.C./E.U. courts have taken on various issues related to whether the parents of a joint venture can obtain a now-Article 101(3) economic-efficiency exemption from now-Article 101(1). *Inter alia*, the Article 101(3) analysis considers whether the EC's practice of declaring certain production or R&D joint ventures lawful but limiting the length of time during which the parents may (in essence) agree not to compete against each other as distributors of the jointly-produced product or the jointly-discovered product or production process—in R&D joint-venture cases, initially to 5 years[1520] and then to 7 years[1521] after any discovered product or production process was first distributed in the common market—can be legally justified in a way that, to my knowledge, the EC has never explicitly attempted to justify this practice—*viz.*, by arguing that the restriction in question is necessary to create the requisite probability that relevant buyers obtain a fair share of the benefit generated by the joint venture (a necessary condition for receiving a now-Article 101(3) exemption). Finally, the section discusses the case-law and any applicable EC Regulations, Notices, and Guidelines on (1) production joint ventures, (2) R&D joint ventures, (3) selling joint ventures, and (4) buying joint ventures.

Virtually all joint-venture cases that the EC and the E.C./E.U. courts have considered have been analyzed under now-Article 101 of the Treaty. This reality is primarily attributable to (1) the fact that the EMCR is of relatively-recent vintage, (2) the facts that (A) the EMCR covers only full-function joint ventures and (B) the vast majority of joint ventures are not full-function joint ventures, and (3) the fact that, even when a joint venture would be covered by now-Article 102, its legality would be more likely to be analyzed under now-Article 101 because it would be more likely to violate now-Article 101 than now-Article 102. This last claim reflects two legal facts: (1) now-Article 101(1)'s test of *prima facie* illegality contains an "effect" branch as well as a "critical object" branch and (2) now-Article 101(3) does not eliminate the difference between the exclusionary branch of now-Article 102's test of illegality and now-Article 101's overall test of illegality.

The analysis of the legality of joint ventures under now-Article 101 is not any different from the analysis of the legality under that provision of any other conduct it covers. Since all the joint ventures whose legality has been scrutinized have been agreements between undertakings, the only questions under now-Article 101(1) are (1) whether they prevent, restrict, or distort competition within the common market

[1520] See Commission Regulation (EEC) 418/85 of 19 December 1984 at Article 3(1.), OJ L53/5 (1985).
[1521] See Commission Regulation (EC) 2659/2000 at Article 5(g), OJ L304/7 (2000).

and (2) by interpretation, whether they do so to an appreciable extent, and the only questions under now-Article 101(3) are whether they (1) generate qualifying economic efficiencies, (2) do so at the smallest cost to competition that is possible, (3) confer a fair share of the resulting benefit on relevant (Clayton-Act-relevant) consumers, and (4) do not "afford...[the parents] the possibility of eliminating competition in respect of a substantial part of the products in question."

The preceding conclusions are obvious and widely shared. I am therefore surprised that neither the EC's various pronouncements on joint ventures, nor the E.C./E.U. courts' opinions in joint-venture cases, nor the major treatise-writers' treatment of these official pronouncements link the claims they make about the determinants of either the legality of various types of joint ventures under now-Article 101 or the legality of particular or most joint ventures under now-Article 101 to the just-delineated elements of the relevant legal analysis. For example, Professor Korah's belief that many joint ventures that have been given exemptions under now-Article 101(3) should have been cleared under now-Article 101(1)[1522] seems to me to ignore the fact that many joint ventures that satisfy now-Article 101(3)'s "economic-efficiency defense" requirements do have the effect of preventing or restricting competition—*i.e.*, do inflict some equivalent-money losses on relevant buyers by reducing the absolute attractiveness of the best offer they respectively receive from any inferior supplier. Similarly, as just stated, the EC has never attempted to justify its practice of approving relevant-economic-efficiency-generating production or R&D joint ventures that do reduce the competition for one or more relevant buyers' patronage only on the condition that the parents compete as distributors of the product jointly produced or the product or production process jointly discovered after it has been marketed in the common market for a specified period of years. This failure is made more surprising by the fact that at least in some and perhaps in many cases the imposition of such a condition might (in effect) create a joint venture that would be lawful despite the fact that the proposed joint venture violated the object-branch of Article 101 (1)'s test of *prima facie* illegality even though it generated Article 101(3) efficiencies by creating a joint venture that is eligible for an Article 101(3) exemption by critically increasing relevant consumers' share of the resulting benefits and might create a joint venture that would be lawful despite the fact that the proposed joint venture would violate the effect-branch of Article 101(l)'s test of *prima facie* illegality by creating a joint venture that, unlike the proposed joint venture, would not impose a net equivalent-monetary loss on relevant buyers. (I recognize that the EC might think [incorrectly for reasons I will discuss below] that this practice could be justified on the ground that the relevant agreements are agreements not to compete as distributors of the goods in question and that, if they extend beyond the stipulated number of years, they cannot be justified as being ancillary to a lawful joint venture.) Finally, the EC has never argued that its disposition to condemn joint ventures between parents with high market shares in a given market is justified by

[1522] See Korah at 435.

the now-Article 101(3) requirement that the conduct in question not give the parents "the possibility of eliminating competition in respect of a substantial part of the products in question."

The last introductory "point" consists of an admission and an explanation. The admission is that this section discusses fewer joint-venture cases than the combination of (1) the applicable law promulgated by the E.C./E.U. Treaty and EMCR, (2) the number of joint ventures executed in the E.C./E.U., and (3) the percentage of those joint ventures that had reducing or preventing competition as a critical object or as an effect should lead one to expect. The explanation is that (1) the EC has tended to respond to joint ventures that it deems lawful by issuing informal, unpublished comfort letters and (2) no joint-venture case was decided by the CFI or ECJ until 1998, partly because the EC condemned few proposed joint ventures before then and partly because parents of joint ventures that were approved (usually, exempted under now-Article 101(3)) subject to conditions and obligations chose not to challenge the restrictions in question. In this respect, the published case-opinions on the application of E.C./E.U. joint-venture law resemble the published materials on the post-1976 (post-Hart-Scott-Rodino) application of U.S. merger law: as we saw, post-1976, few mergers ever reached the U.S. courts; the *de facto* final official enforcers of U.S. merger law were the DOJ and FTC; and these "agencies" based their decisions on analyses that were never published (with the exception of a few lines in some general reports about a modest percentage of the merger proposals they reviewed).

7. The Legality of Joint Ventures Under E.C./E.U. Law as Actually Interpreted and Applied

I turn now to the general approach that the EC and the E.C./E.U. courts have taken when applying now-Article 101(1) and now-Article 101(3) to joint ventures. The EC and the E.C./E.U. courts have argued that joint ventures can violate now-Article 101(1)'s test of *prima facie* illegality in four different ways. At least on some formulations, three of these concerns are valid, both economically and legally. The fourth is legally unsound, even if on some definitions of a relevant concept it is economically sound. I will start with the three concerns of the EC that are justified.

The first justified concern is that, even if a joint venture does not lead the parents to execute contrived oligopolistic QV-investment restrictions, it may reduce QV-investment competition in the joint venture's area of product-space by reducing the amount of QV investment the parents make in the joint venture's area of product-space through the joint venture and in their own names combined below the total amount they would have made independently had they not executed the joint venture. As the EC and the E.C./E.U. courts have pointed out, the risk of such an outcome is increased by the fact that, even if the joint-venture agreement does not explicitly prohibit the parents from entering their joint venture's market, the parents' part-ownerships of the joint venture will often make it unprofitable for them to make otherwise-profitable QV investments in its market. Unfortunately, even in its most defensible (most abstract) form, the EC's and the E.C./E.U. courts' position on this possibility is seriously flawed in that it ignores the fact that non-parents might replace the QV investments the parents did not make in the joint venture's market (in their own names and through the joint venture combined). Obviously, when any reduction in relevant parental QV investment would induce equally-large and cost-effective non-parental QV investments, the joint venture will not prevent or restrict competition in this first way, regardless of whether the possibility of non-parental replacement QV investments deters the parents from reducing their relevant QV investments.

Clearly, this analytic error (omission) would tend to cause the EC and the E.C./E.U. courts to conclude that production and R&D joint ventures would violate now-Article 101(1)'s test of *prima facie* illegality by reducing QV-investment competition (by "preventing potential competition" in the EC's somewhat-misleading terminology) even if the EC correctly identified situations in which, absent the joint venture, two or more parents would have entered the joint venture's area of product-space. In fact, at least until 1983, the EC's proclivity to find that joint ventures reduced QV-investment competition in the joint venture's market was far stronger than the preceding omission can account for. The reason: until at least 1983, the EC implicitly and falsely assumed that, any time that the individual parents of a joint venture would find it individually inherently profitable to enter the joint venture's market independently after the joint venture was executed if they did not have to bear any of the loss their entry would impose on the joint venture, the joint venture would reduce the amount of QV investment they would make in the joint venture's area of product-space if they did not have to worry about non-parental QV investments.[1523] This assumption is wrong for two reasons. To start, it is based *inter alia* on the false premise that, any time that a joint venture's individual parents would be able to profit by entering the joint venture's market after the joint venture has been executed (or would have been able to do so had the joint venture not already increased the amount of QV investment in the relevant area of product-space—official statements on this issue are ambiguous), they would have been able to do so before the joint venture's execution. This premise is false because in many cases the parents' ability to enter the joint venture's market *ex post* will have been critically enhanced by the knowledge they obtained from each other or by knowledge they obtained in other ways by participating in the joint venture. Although the EC has taken account of joint-venture-generated parental learning when deciding whether a joint venture deserves a now-Article 101(3) exemption,[1524] for two reasons its failure to consider this reality when determining whether the joint venture violated now-Article 101(1)'s test of *prima facie* illegality

[1523] See Francisco Enrique Gonzales Diaz, Horizontal Cooperation Agreements, Chap. 7 in The E.C. Law of Competition 660, 670 (hereinafter Diaz) (Jonathan Faull and Ali Nikpay, eds.) (Oxford Univ. Press, 2d ed., 2007).

[1524] *Id.*

is not rendered inconsequential by its having done so: (1) not all joint-venture-generated economic efficiencies fall into one of the categories of economic efficiency whose generation is a necessary condition for a now-Article 101(3) exemption, and (2) defendants bear the burden of proof under now-Article 101(3) whereas the State bears the burden of proof under now-Article 101(1). In addition, the EC assumption in question is wrong because the fact that each of two or more parents would have found it profitable *ex ante* to enter the joint venture's market absent the joint venture if the parent in question were the only party to add a QV investment to the joint venture's area of product-space does not imply that both parents (or more than one parent when there are more than two parents) would have found it profitable to make QV investments in that area of product-space had they not created the joint venture—*i.e.*, that the parents would have made more relevant QV investments in their own names had they not created the joint venture than they made through the joint venture. I should add that, as previously indicated, the EC's estimate of the likelihood that joint ventures will reduce QV-investment competition in the joint venture's market is also inflated by its failure to take account of the facts that (1) in many situations, non-parents would replace any QV investments the parents chose not to make and (2) when that is the case, the joint venture will not reduce equilibrium QV investment in the joint venture's area of product-space even when it otherwise would have done so by reducing the amount of QV investment the parents make in it. I should also add that, as I will discuss below, post-1983, the number of mistaken legal conclusions the EC reached on the preceding account was substantially reduced by its increasing proclivity to undertake case-by-case investigations of the parents' pre-joint-venture abilities to enter the joint venture's market, which often led it to conclude that, absent the joint venture, neither parent would have entered the joint venture's market on its own.

The second way in which the EC and the E.C./E.U. courts believe joint ventures can violate now-Article 101(1)'s test of *prima facie* illegality is to increase the extent to which the parents engage in what they call coordination and I call contrivance. Some of the feared contrivance relates to the parents' QV-investment decisions. Thus, the EC recognizes that joint ventures may enable parents that are effective potential competitors of their joint venture to contrive QV-investment restrictions in their joint venture's product-production or R&D market when the parents' part-ownerships of the joint venture does not suffice to render individually unprofitable for each a QV investment in the joint venture's market. The EC also recognizes that joint ventures can enable parents that are each other's effective potential competitors in a non-joint-venture market to agree not to enter each other's other markets or can enable them to use threats of retaliation to deter themselves from entering each other's markets. (Obviously, such QV-investment contrivance could also be practiced by a subset of the set of two or more joint-venture parents.) The EC realizes as well that joint ventures can lead the parents to contrive price-increases or reductions in the attractiveness of other terms and conditions of sale in the joint venture's market if they operate independently in that market or in other markets in which they are both operating. The EC recognizes in addition that, even if sales joint ventures perform other functions than eliminating sales competition between the parents, they will always have the effect of eliminating the competition the parents wage against each other as sellers when the joint venture is given the exclusive right to sell its parents' relevant products (and, presumably, will always have the object of doing so as well in such cases, though that object may not have been critical to the parents' *ex ante* perception that their sales joint venture would be profitable). Finally, the EC realizes that buying joint ventures can enable the parents to contrive reductions in the prices they pay for the goods they purchase jointly and/or improvements in the other terms and conditions of their purchases.

Although I agree that joint ventures can generate all of these contrivance-related effects, I have three objections or clusters of objections to the EC's and the E.C./E.U. courts' treatment of those possibilities. The first is the same as one of the objections I had to the EC's position on the tendency of joint ventures to reduce QV-investment competition without increasing related contrivance: the EC's analysis ignores the fact that, if non-parents would find it profitable to "replace" any QV investments the parents might otherwise contrive not to make, the joint venture will not reduce QV-investment competition by enabling the parents to contrive QV-investment restrictions.

My second objection to the EC's and E.C./E.U. courts' contrivance analysis is that their analyses of the "price and other terms and conditions"-contrivance possibility is indefensibly market-oriented—assumes that the seriousness of the contrivance possibility increases with and is largely determined by the relevant market's concentration and the parents' market shares.[1525] I do not think that markets can be defined non-arbitrarily; I know that, even if they could, the relevance of market share and market concentration would be substantially reduced by the fact that, in almost all situations, the firms and products in a market would not be "equally competitive with each other" in any sense in which that phrase might be usefully defined; and I am certain that the profitability of such contrivance and the likely effect of a joint venture on the incidence of such contrivance will depend on many factors that the standard market-oriented analysis ignores. I have two more specific points to make in this connection. The first may reflect my misunderstanding of an EC pronouncement. The EC seems to believe that the risk that a joint venture will enable the parents to engage in contrivance increases with the extent to which the market of concern is "adjacent" to the joint venture's market. Thus, in 1993, the EC stated:

> When the JV [joint venture] operates on a market adjacent to that of its parents, competition can only be restricted when there is a high degree of interdependence between the two markets. This is generally the case when the JV manufactures products that are complementary to those of its parents.[1526]

[1525] See Korah at 431, quoting Francisco Enrique Gonzalez Diaz, Dan Kirk, Francisco Perez Flores, and Cécile Verkleij, Horizontal Agreements, Chapter 6 in THE E.C. LAW OF COMPETITION 333, 361 (Jonathan Faull and Ali Nikpay, eds.) (Oxford Univ. Press, 1st ed., 1999). At the time of the publication, the authors were all officials at the EC.

[1526] Commission Notice Concerning the Assessment of Co-operative Joint Ventures Pursuant to Article 85 of the EEC Treaty [now-Article 101 of the 2009 Treaty of Lisbon] at ¶ 41, OJ C43/2 (1993).

I see no reason to believe that there is any correlation between the weighted-average-expected extent to which a joint venture will make it profitable for the parents to engage in contrivance in some market in which both are actual or potential competitors and the proximity of that market to the joint venture's market.

The second is that the EC and the E.C./E.U. courts appear to believe that proof that a joint venture is requisitely likely to increase the amount of contrivance in which the parents would find it profitable to engage if such conduct were not illegal establishes its *prima facie* illegality under now-Article 101(1) and disfavors its legality under now-Article 102 and the EMCR when they are applicable—*i.e.*, the EC and the E.C./E.U. courts ignore the fact that the illegality of contrivance agreements under now-Article 101 and the illegality under now-Article 102 of all contrivance practiced by any firm that is individually dominant or a member of a set of collectively-dominant rivals disfavors the preceding two claims to the extent that the associated sanctions render the contrivance in question *ex ante* unprofitable for the undertakings in question and/or unattractive to those of their agents who value obeying the law (regardless of the relevant conduct's *ex ante* profitability to the undertakings).

Third, the EC's analysis of the *prima facie* illegality of joint buying under now-Article 101(1) ignores the Treaty-promulgator-goal argument for the conclusion that joint buying should not be deemed *prima facie* illegal if it benefits ultimate consumers. This legal conclusion is favored by the following facts: (1) most (certainly, at least some) buying joint ventures create bilateral-monopoly situations as opposed to monopsony situations in which the monopsonist faces sellers that have no bargaining power in relation to them, and (2) buying joint ventures that create buyers that can bargain more effectively with the non-perfectly-competitive sellers from which they purchase will reduce not just the average cost to the buyers of the good to be purchased but the marginal buying cost of those goods to them as well and hence the prices the joint buyers charge ultimate consumers (for the good the joint buyers are purchasing when the joint buyers are retailers [or wholesalers, indirectly] or for the good the joint buyers produce with the input they are joint buying when the joint buyers are final-good producers). (Admittedly, if the joint buyers are monopsonists that do not face non-perfectly-competitive suppliers and do not find it profitable to price discriminate as buyers, their joint buying could increase the marginal buying cost to them of the good involved [at the same time that it reduces the good's average buying cost to them] and hence could cause them to increase the prices they charge ultimate consumers.) I should explain this argument's legal premise that benefitting relevant consumers is the goal of E.C./E.U. competition law that is operative in this context. This premise is supported by (1) my surmise that the promulgators of now-Article 101 and the EMCR were influenced by the fact that, *ceteris paribus*, the reductions in competition that the Treaty article and regulation in question are designed to prevent will by definition always confer net equivalent-monetary losses on relevant consumers, (2) the fact that now-Article 101(3) makes consumers' obtaining a fair share of any resulting benefit a necessary condition for perpetrators' obtaining an economic-efficiency exemption to now-Article 101(1), (3) my surmise that the promulgators of now-Article 102 were influenced by the fact that the accurate enforcement of its prohibition of both exclusionary abuses and exploitative abuses will always confer equivalent-monetary gains on relevant consumers, and (4) the fact that joint-buying arrangements that would benefit ultimate consumers do not disserve the various social and political goals of the Treaty.

The third way in which the EC and the E.C./E.U. courts believe joint ventures can prevent, restrict, or distort competition is by "foreclosing" the parents' rivals from making sales to the joint venture and possibly its parents or from making purchases from the joint venture or possibly its parents. The referent of "foreclosure" as used by the EC and the E.C./E.U. courts in this joint-venture context is no clearer than it is in the other contexts in which they use this term. As we saw, "foreclosure" could refer to predatory refusals to deal (or, by extension, the predatory offer of unattractive terms of sale or purchase that are inherently unprofitable for the offeror), or it could be defined more broadly to include as well refusals to deal that are inherently profitable for the refuser but damaging to the refused. In any event, the EC and the E.C./E.U. courts are concerned that joint ventures may prevent, restrict, or distort competition by creating a company (the joint venture) that will refuse to deal as a buyer with upstream rivals of its parents or will refuse to deal as a seller with downstream rivals of its parents (distributors that distribute products that are rivalrous with the parents' products) without focusing either on whether the refusals in question will be predatory or on whether, even if they will not be, the prospect of their occurrence will still render a joint venture that is requisitely likely to lead to their occurrence *prima facie* illegal under now-Article 101(1) if the refusals to deal in question are requisitely likely to prevent, restrict, or distort competition.

I want to make five points about the EC's and the E.C./E.U. courts' treatment of this "foreclosure" possibility. First, since it is almost certainly correct as a matter of law to attribute a joint venture's refusal to deal to the joint-venture agreement even if that agreement does not require the joint venture to perpetrate the refusal to deal at issue, any finding that a joint venture was requisitely likely to create an entity that would engage in a predatory, competition-preventing, competition-restricting, or competition-distorting refusal to deal would justify the conclusion that it violated now-Article 101(1)'s test of *prima facie* illegality even if now-Article 101(1) were properly interpreted to render joint ventures *prima facie* illegal only if the competition-reducing/distorting conduct they induced were independently illegal (under now-Article 101 or possibly under either or both now-Article 101 or now-Article 102): the qualification in question would be legally critical on that assumption because now-Article 101(1) does not prohibit single-firm predation and single-firm predation is also not covered by now-Article 102 if the perpetrator is neither individually dominant nor a member of a collectively-dominant set of rivals.

Second, the EC and the E.C./E.U. courts have never adverted to the fact that joint ventures may facilitate their parents' engaging in other kinds of predation.

Third, the EC and the E.C./E.U. courts appear to believe that the likelihood that a joint venture will find it profitable to engage in predatory refusals to deal depends on its and the parents' market shares (and, to a lesser extent, the concentration of the relevant market)—a position that is wrong for the same reasons that the old U.S. "quantitative substantiality" test for the illegality of full-requirements contracts is wrong and that the U.S. "qualitative substantiality" test for the illegality of such contracts would be wrong if (contrary to fact) it were intended to be interpreted literally: in addition to ignoring the impossibility of defining markets non-arbitrarily, the position ignores the fact that not all suppliers in any area of product-space are equally-well-placed to supply given buyers in that area of product-space as well as the possibility that sellers that lose customers or buyers that lose suppliers may be able to reduce or eliminate the associate profit-losses by vertically integrating themselves, forming vertical joint ventures to enter the relevant input-production or distribution business, or inducing independents to enter the business in question by supplying them with information, monetary subsidies, and/ or long-term contracts.

Fourth, just as the EC and the E.C./E.U. courts appear to have ignored the fact that, for profit-related and/or other reasons, potential contrivers may choose not to engage in otherwise-profitable contrivance that is illegal, they ignore the fact that the illegality of predatory-refusal-to-deal agreements under now-Article 101 and of all predation under now-Article 102 (if the perpetrator is a dominant firm or a member of a set of collectively-dominant rivals) may deter joint ventures and their parents from engaging in otherwise-profitable refusals to deal.

Fifth, the EC and the E.C./E.U. courts erred in failing to distinguish between any tendency a joint venture has to result in predatory and non-predatory refusals to deal. Admittedly, for two reasons, in some cases, proof that a joint venture will result in non-predatory refusals to deal will justify the conclusion that it will prevent, restrict, or distort competition: (1) non-predatory refusals to deal can restrict and/or prevent competition by causing a refused rival to exit and/or by deterring a rival that would be refused from entering, and (2) when the inherent profitability of a joint venture's refusal to deal with one or more of the rivals of its parents reflects the fact that the joint venture has an interest in internalizing to itself what would otherwise be the surplus that non-parents would realize by dealing with it but no such interest in internalizing to itself its parents' surplus, the joint venture may distort competition by generating refusals to deal that result in downstream sales being made by allocatively-less-efficient suppliers. It may be that, correctly interpreted, now-Article 101(1) would be read to make *prima facie* illegal joint ventures that prevent, restrict, or distort competition by creating an entity that will engage in an inherently-profitable perfectly-legal refusal to deal. My complaint is that, because neither the EC nor the E.C./E.U. courts recognized that joint ventures could prevent, restrict, or distort competition by inducing either non-predatory or predatory refusals to deal, they never addressed this important legal issue.

As I have indicated, I agree with the EC's and E.C./E.U. courts' conclusion that joint ventures can violate now-Article 101(1)'s test of *prima facie* illegality in the three ways just discussed (the last two of which the Commission denominates the possible "spillover effects"[1527] of a joint venture). However, I do not agree with the EC's claim that joint ventures will also violate now-Article 101(1)'s test of *prima facie* illegality in the fourth set of circumstances in which it believes they

[1527] See Exxon/Shell, OJ L144/20 at ¶ 63 (1994).

will—*viz.*, when they are not as procompetitive as some alternative joint ventures (or alternative joint-venture agreements) that the parents might have found more profitable than doing nothing in the joint venture's market.

Some explanation is necessary. The EC has (admittedly implicitly) adopted this position in some cases that involve so-called "networks" of joint ventures created by a parent that produces an input or final product without which no QV investment would be made in any of the markets in which the joint ventures the parent has created operate when the associated joint-venture agreements include clauses that prohibit the individual joint ventures in question from competing against each other when selling the good they use the relevant parent's essential input to produce or distributing the final good with which the founding parent in question supplies them.[1528] Even if a law prohibiting founders of such joint-venture "networks" from prohibiting its members from competing against each other would increase competition in the relevant sense (which it might not do since such a law might lead the founder either not to enter the joint venture's markets at all or to enter them on its own with less-economically-efficient QV investments that leave relevant consumers worse off than they would have been had the essential parent created joint ventures that it prohibited from competing against each other), it would in my judgment, be incorrect as a matter of E.C./E.U. law to conclude that the joint ventures in question prevented or restricted competition. When measured against a do-nothing baseline, the joint-venture "network" clearly increased competition, and in this context the do-nothing baseline for competitive-impact measurement strikes me as correct as a matter of E.C./E.U. law. Thus, a series of joint ventures that increase competition above what it would have been had the participants done nothing cannot be said to have prevented or restricted competition because the participants could have altered their arrangements in a way that would have made the joint ventures they created even more procompetitive without rendering it unprofitable any more than a merger that increases competition above what it would have been had the merger partners executed no merger can be said to have lessened competition because one or both of the merger partners could have executed an even-more-procompetitive merger that would have been more profitable than no merger. I hasten to add that my conclusion that this fourth EC and E.C./E.U.-court concern is legally mistaken does not cover situations in which the creation of a "network" of joint ventures deters independent QV investments that may have been less economically efficient but would have been more beneficial to relevant consumers because the QV investors in question would have competed against each other. I should point out as well that the EC and E.C./E.U.-court mistake I am now discussing is akin to the error that the EC and the E.C./E.U. courts have made in prohibiting producers from preventing their independent distributors from waging *intra*-brand competition against each other.

The preceding discussion implies that the EC and E.C./E.U. courts are likely to find that far more joint ventures violate now-Article 101(1)'s test of *prima facie*

[1528] See, *e.g.*, Optical Fibres, OJ L235/30 (1986).

illegality than I believe is warranted. The record of the EC appears to me to be consistent with this "prediction." However, this "fact" does not imply that, historically, the EC (and, more recently, the E.C./E.U. courts) have declared too many joint ventures illegal under now-Article 101: the tendency of the EC and the E.C./E.U. courts to find joint ventures that would not prevent, restrict, or distort competition *prima facie* illegal under now-Article 101(1) would have little or no impact on the percentage of joint ventures found to violate now-Article 101 if all or the vast majority of joint ventures for which preventing, restricting, or distorting competition was found to be a critical object or an effect were granted now-Article 101(3) exemptions. In fact, that appears to be exactly what has happened, though (admittedly) a substantial number of the exemptions in question were granted subject to the parents' and the joint venture's accepting certain conditions and fulfilling certain obligations.

I want to make five points or clusters of points that relate to the EC's and the E.C./E.U. courts' now-Article 101(3) joint-venture practice or the assessment of that practice by European commentators. First, as I indicated earlier in this section, at least some prominent E.C./E.U.-competition-law scholars have argued that, as a matter of law, the EC and the E.C./E.U. courts should have cleared the vast majority of joint ventures those institutions considered under now-Article 101(1) rather than exempting them under now-Article 101(3).[1529] Even though I believe that many of the joint ventures that the EC concluded did violate now-Article 101(1)'s test of *prima facie* illegality did not do so, I think that these European scholars underestimate the percentage of proposed joint ventures that had as a critical object preventing or restricting competition or had the effect of preventing or restricting competition.

Second, my impression is that the EC has been far too willing to conclude that joint ventures generate economic efficiencies that satisfy the requirement of now-Article 101(3) that, to secure an exemption, a joint venture must improve the production or distribution of goods or promote technical or economic progress. I hasten to admit that, because so many of the relevant cases were resolved through unpublished consent letters, I am not in a position to assess the persuasiveness of most of the economic-efficiency claims that were made to the EC.

Third, the EC believes that proof that an R&D joint venture is requisitely likely to reduce the extent to which the R&D that a joint venture's parents execute (individually and/or through the joint venture) is economically-inefficiently-duplicative satisfies the economic-efficiency generation requirement of now-Article 101(3). I am skeptical. To my mind, if the expressions "improve the production or distribution of goods" and "promote technical or economic progress" are interpreted in a straightforward way, the fact that an R&D joint venture would prevent economically-inefficiently-duplicative R&D would not guarantee that the cooperation in question would either improve the production or distribution of goods or promote technical or economic progress. R&D joint ventures that reduce

[1529] See, *e.g.*, Korah at 435.

the economically-inefficiently-duplicative character of the R&D that is executed could simultaneously permit the parents to profit by restricting their R&D investments in the R&D market in question (because non-parents would not fully offset the reduction in the parents' investments). If an R&D joint venture that reduced the economically-inefficiently-duplicative character of the R&D that was executed simultaneously led to R&D restrictions, it might result in a smaller amount of R&D discoveries being made (measured by their allocative value)—*i.e.*, it might not lead to an improvement in the production or distribution of goods or to technical or economic progress. I do not know how often such an outcome would obtain. However, my impression is that the EC has not considered this possibility—has ignored the R&D-restriction possibility in cases in which an R&D collaboration would allegedly reduce the economically-inefficiently-duplicative character of the R&D that is executed.

Fourth, as I have already suggested, although to my knowledge the EC has never tried to justify its (to my mind, otherwise-unjustifiable) practice of conditioning its grant of a now-Article 101(3) exemption for production or R&D joint ventures on the parents' agreeing to compete against each other when distributing the good the production joint venture produced or the good or production process the R&D joint venture discovered starting some specified number of years after the product or production process in question was initially marketed in the common market on such a condition's lowering to the required level the probability that the relevant consumers would suffer a net equivalent-monetary loss or raising to the required level the probability that relevant consumers would obtain a fair share of the benefit the joint venture generated (alternatively, raising the relevant consumers' weighted-average-expected share of the resulting benefit to the required level), I suspect that the EC initiated and maintained this practice for the preceding reason. Unfortunately, even if one concedes that the EC is authorized to legislate (to promulgate operational decision-rules that diverge from Treaty meaning) to effectuate the Treaty's goals, this method of regulating proposed joint ventures to make them lawful under Article 101 is far too crude for the practice to be justifiable in these terms. Thus, whatever the referent of "a fair share of the resulting benefit," (1) the percentage of qualifying-economic-efficiency-generating joint ventures that would satisfy this "fair share" requirement if the parents never had to compete against each other as distributors of the good or production process concerned or had to compete against each other in this regard only after more than 5 or 7 years had passed since initial distribution in the common market is too high, (2) the percentage of economic-efficiency-generating joint ventures that will not satisfy this "fair share" requirement even when the parents are required to compete against each other as distributors after the specified time-period has passed is too low (a fact made more salient by E.C./E.U. competition law's recent recognition of "victim" interests and legal rights), (3) the cost of making more accurate individualized assessments of the "fair share" issue is too low, and (4) the cost-effectiveness of other methods of securing more benefits for relevant consumers is too high for this feature of the EC's joint-venture practice to be a defensible exercise of any legislative power it is correct to assume the EC has been granted. I should add that, if the joint venture in question is not a sham, it will usually not be possible to justify restricting the ability of the parents to prevent themselves from competing as distributors of the joint venture's output by arguing that the parents' efforts to avoid competing as distributors of the joint venture's output after a certain number of years have passed cannot be said to be ancillary: at least if, absent the joint venture, the parents would not have invested in the joint venture's market and there is not adequate proof that their joint venture would lead them to engage in contrivance or dubious foreclosing conduct, there is no legal basis for forcing them to compete as distributors. To do so is analogous to prohibiting (1) an undertaking that uses independent distributors from prohibiting those independent distributors from competing against each other or (2) an undertaking that has its own distribution network from prohibiting its own distributive outlets from competing against each other. The fact that the joint venture's output was produced by an entity created by two separate undertakings is economically and legally irrelevant.

The fifth and final point I want to make at this juncture is even more likely to derive from an hypothesis about the EC's decisionmaking that is factually inaccurate. As I indicated earlier, the EC has taken positions that seem to imply that it believes that the probability that a joint venture will lead the parents and/or the joint venture to engage in additional contrivance or foreclosing behavior (predation?) is directly related to their market shares. Sometimes, I have the impression that the relevant claims of the EC are connected less to any such beliefs and more to the Commission's concern that the joint venture might fail to qualify for a now-Article 101(3) exemption because "it afforded...[the parents] the possibility of eliminating competition in respect of a substantial part of the products in question"—a possibility that would be salient if the parents were product rivals of the joint venture or if the joint venture deterred both from investing in the joint venture's market even if it did not reduce the amount of QV investment in that market because (possibly to deter non-parents from investing) the joint venture made the same amount of QV investment in its market as the parents would have made in its absence.

I turn now to the EC's and E.C./E.U. courts' joint-venture case-opinions and the EC's relevant Regulations, Notices, and Guidelines. I will start by focusing on their production-joint-venture positions and then proceed to discuss their R&D-joint-venture, selling-joint-venture, and buying-joint-venture positions.

Because many of the most-revealing production-joint-venture cases antedate the currently-relevant Notices and Guidelines, I will begin by discussing the case-law, focusing primarily on the position that the case-opinion in question took on a relevant abstract issue. The initial case-opinion I want to discuss is a 1977 EC decision that sets the table for the discussion that follows. *GEC-Weir Sodium Circulators*[1530] focused on a joint venture to develop, produce, and sell sodium circulators. The EC's opinion stated that, for three reasons, the joint venture at issue

---

[1530] OJ L327/26 (1977).

violated now-Article 101(1)'s test of *prima facie* illegality—*i.e.*, had as its object or effect the prevention, restriction, or distortion of competition:

(1) because, even in the absence of an express agreement not to compete, a joint venture's parents' ownership of the joint venture will normally deter them from competing with it, the joint venture will restrict competition by substituting the joint venture for the two parents;
(2) the parents' joint management of the joint venture will cause the parents to collaborate (engage in what I call contrivance); and
(3) when the joint venture is vertically related to its parents, its creation will reduce competition because it will result in the foreclosure of the parents' rivals.

As we have seen, although each of these consequences might result, they will not inevitably obtain and the resulting "foreclosures" may not invalidate the joint venture even if they do cause it to prevent, restrict, or distort competition (because the foreclosures in question are not themselves illegal). Unfortunately, the EC's *GEC-Weir Sodium Circulators* opinion does not state the conditions under which the legally-problematic consequences in question would obtain, recount any evidence establishing that those conditions were fulfilled in the case at issue, or discuss the legal issue to which I have just referred.

I will now consider in turn the EC's and E.C./E.U. courts' pronouncements on each of the three possibilities just listed and previously discussed. Prior to 1983, when it published its XIIIIth Report on Competition Policy (1983), the EC came close to assuming that joint ventures would almost always reduce QV-investment competition—at least would do so whenever *ex post* each parent would have found it profitable to make a QV investment in the joint venture's market had the joint venture not been created. Post-1983, the EC was more likely to conclude that joint ventures would not prevent competition by causing the parents to reduce the amount of QV investment they made in the joint venture's market in their own and the joint venture's names combined below the amount of QV investment they would have made in that market in their own names had they not participated in the joint venture in circumstances in which the reduction in question would not be made up by non-parents. Thus, in 1985, in *BP/Kellogg*,[1531] the EC concluded that a joint venture between BP, which had discovered a catalyst for making ammonia, and Kellogg, which designed and built process plants, to create and use a plant to produce ammonia using BP's catalyst did not reduce QV-investment competition because neither BP nor Kellogg would have entered the joint venture's market on its own. And in 1986, in *Optical Fibres*,[1532] the EC concluded that a series of joint ventures between Corning Glass, which had developed optical fibres for use in telecommunications, and various E.C. undertaking telecommunication-facility suppliers, which sold such services to government post and telecommunication suppliers that tended to purchase only

[1531] OJ L369/6 (1985).
[1532] OJ L235/30 (1986).

from their own country's undertakings, did not directly reduce QV-investment competition in the joint ventures' markets since neither Corning nor its individual joint-venture partners could have profitably invested in the relevant joint ventures' separate national markets. The Commission's recognition that even well-established parents that possess considerable relevant technological and financial resources might not be able to enter their joint venture's market independently was also manifest in its 1987 *Mitchell Cotts/Solfiltra* decision,[1533] its 1988 *Oliveti/Canon* decision,[1534] and its 1990 *Odin* decision,[1535] all of which found that, absent the joint venture, the parents would not have been in a position to enter their joint venture's market on their own.

Moreover, even when the probability that a joint venture might reduce QV-investment competition by substituting the joint venture's QV investment for the larger amount of QV investment the parents would have made in the relevant area of product-space independently had they not created the joint venture is sufficiently high for the joint venture to violate now-Article 101(1)'s test of *prima facie* illegality (on the Commission's implicit and usually-uninvestigated assumption that the associated reduction in QV investment would not be fully offset by additional QV investments by others), the EC often granted the joint venture a now-Article 101(3) exemption. Thus, in 1993 in *Ford/Volkswagen*,[1536] the EC granted an exemption for a joint venture created by Ford and Volkswagen to develop and produce a range of multi-purpose vehicles (denominated "people carriers") despite the existence of a troubling probability that in its absence the parents would have both entered that market independently: the Commission did not consider whether any other firm would "replace" any resulting reduction in the parents' relevant QV investments. In part, the Commission's decision in this case reflected its conclusion that the parents would not develop and produce the vehicles in question as "rapidly and efficiently" on their own, and, in part, it reflected the fact that the parents agreed to differentiate the products they sold that incorporated the joint venture's output by installing different engines and varying their products' exterior and interior design. And in 2000 in *Engine Alliance*,[1537] the EC granted a now-Article 101(3) exemption to a joint venture created by GE and Pratt & Witney to produce and market a new jet engine for use in a new Airbus aircraft despite concerns that the joint venture might reduce QV investment in the jet-engine-design market because it found that the joint venture would accelerate development and reduce costs.[1538] In my judgment, in many cases of this kind, the EC was too willing

[1533] OJ L41/31 (1987).

[1534] OJ L52/51/(1988).

[1535] OJ L209/15 (1990).

[1536] OJ L20/14 (1993).

[1537] Case IV/36.213/F2 GEAE/P&W, OJ L58/16 (2000).

[1538] For another, more recent case in which the EC granted a joint venture a now-Article-101(3) exemption because of the economic efficiencies it found the joint venture would generate, see O2 UK Limited/T-Mobile UK Limited, OJ L200/59 (2003).

to accept the proffered economic-efficiency claims. It also failed to give legally-requisite attention to whether the relevant consumers would obtain a fair share of the resulting benefits,[1539] though the EC's concern about this issue may account for Ford's and Volkswagen's voluntarily agreeing to differentiate their "people carriers" and did account for the EC's conditioning its clearance in 2002 in *Austrian Airlines/Deutsche Lufthansa*[1540] of an airline joint venture on the parents' agreeing *inter alia* to admit competitors to their frequent-flier programs and to make up to 40 % of their seats on a route available to a new entrant that wants to operate on that route.

Although the preceding discussion may leave the impression that, at least since 1983, the EC has handled this QV-investment-competition issue consistently, as Korah points out, "the [EC] case law [on what she calls potential competition] has not been entirely consistent."[1541] Thus, in 1994, in its decision in *European Night Services*,[1542] the EC concluded that a joint venture between four established rail and train operators in different Member States created to provide passenger services through the Channel tunnel between distant cities at night was legally-disqualifyingly-likely to reduce competition *inter alia* by deterring the parents from providing such night services independently despite the absence of requisite proof that (1) the individual parents could do so independently or collaboratively with a different set of partners or (2) if the joint venture would reduce the total QV investment that the parents would make in the relevant area of product-space in their own names and through the joint venture, the shortfall in question would not be made up by investments by others. Fortunately, the CFI eventually overturned the EC's decision in this case in an opinion that (in essence) reprimanded the EC for failing to justify its findings on this and virtually all other issues the EC addressed.[1543]

The next series of cases I want to discuss relates to what I call the contrivance issue. The first case in this category is the 1978 case *Wano Schwarzpulver*.[1544] In its opinion in this case, the Commission asserted that the parents' collaboration in a joint venture to produce black powder would give them "opportunities and strong incentives" to divide up other markets in which they both participated, such as the safety-fuse market.[1545] Unfortunately, the EC gave no account of the conditions under which the parents would find it profitable to engage in contrivance in the safety-fuse market, provided no evidence about whether those conditions were fulfilled, and failed to acknowledge either that the illegality of such conduct may

---

[1539] See Diaz at 706.

[1540] OJ L242/25 (2002).

[1541] Korah at 431.

[1542] OJ L259/20 (1994).

[1543] European Night Services and Others v. Commission, T-374/94, ECR II-3143 (1998).

[1544] OJ L322/26 (1978).

[1545] *Id.* at ¶ 30. Thus, *inter alia*, this opinion expressed concern that the joint venture at issue would lead the parents to contrive QV-investment restrictions in markets other than the joint venture's market that would reduce QV-investment competition in those markets.

render it *ex ante* unprofitable or that undertakings may not engage in illegal conduct even when it would be *ex ante* profitable for them to do so.

The next opinions I will address that discuss the contrivance issue are the EC's 1992 opinion in *Ford/Volkswagen*[1546] and its 1996 opinion in *Atlas*.[1547] Although the EC did not declare the Ford/Volkswagen "people-carrier" design-and-production joint venture illegal for this reason, it did express the view that "the co-operation between Ford and VW will...lead to an extensive exchange and sharing of, *inter alia*, technical know-how which could affect the competitive behavior of the two partners in neighboring market segments like those of estate cars [stationwagons] or light vans." In *Atlas*, the EC exempted a joint venture created by France Telecom (FT) and Deutsche Telekom (DT) to provide international telecom services to corporate customers despite its concern that the parents' participation in this joint venture would deter them from entering each other's domestic markets after the regulatory changes scheduled for 1998 would make such entries possible.[1548] The opinion did not address whether FT and DT were effective potential entrants into each other's geographic markets—*inter alia*, whether they were better-placed than other potential entrants into those markets to execute entries that would have been inherently profitable for the parents.

The EC's 1994 opinion in *European Night Services*[1549] also asserted that the joint venture it involved would lead to its parents' engaging in various types of contrived behavior. The CFI rejected this finding as well,[1550] stating that it was not justified by any cogent explanation of how the parents' participation in ENS and a number of other related joint ventures would restrict competition. Although I agree with the CFI's assessment of the EC's treatment of this issue, the CFI's belief that the appropriate argument for the EC to have made is the standard market-oriented argument for conduct's increasing the profitability of contrivance to its perpetrators is regrettable.

The final joint-venture opinion on the contrivance possibility I will discuss is the EC's 1999 opinion in *Telia/Telenor/Schibsted*,[1551] a case that was analyzed under the EMCR since the joint venture at issue was deemed to be a concentrative, full-function joint venture. The joint venture at issue (Scandia OnLine) was to be created by the three defendants to provide particular internet services to consumers and businesses primarily in Sweden. At point 28 of its decision, the Commission stated:

> in order to establish a restriction in competition in the sense of Article 85(1) [now-Article 101(1)] EC-Treaty [a restriction that is also relevant to the joint venture's legality under the

---

[1546] OJ L20/14 (1993).

[1547] OJ L230/23 (1996).

[1548] Thus, the opinion also expressed concern that the joint venture at issue would lead the parents to execute contrived QV-investment restrictions in markets other than the joint-venture market that would reduce QV-investment competition in those other markets.

[1549] OJ L259/20 (1994).

[1550] See European Night Services and Others v. Commission, T-374/94, ECR II-3141 (1998).

[1551] OJ C220/28 (1999).

> EMCR], it is necessary that the coordination of the parent companies' competitive behavior is likely and appreciable and that it results from the creation of the joint venture, be it as its object or its effect.

The Commission proceeded to identify two markets in which the joint venture might cause coordination (contrivance in my usage): (1) website production and related services and (2) dial-up internet access. It then (1) rejected the claim that the joint venture would yield an appreciable increase in competition-restricting coordination in the website-production market on the ground that the combined market shares of the parents in the relevant market and the market share of the joint venture in the relevant market (both under 5 %) were too low for any resulting competition-restriction to be appreciable and (2) rejected the claim that the joint venture would restrict competition in the dial-up internet-access market on the ground that the market's high rate-of-growth and relatively-low barriers to entry as well as the high "price-sensitivity" of the consumer demand for individual products (a consequence of low switching-costs) would prevent the joint venture from critically increasing the profitability of contrivance. The EC's opinion in this case is important not because its arguments about appreciability and its assumptions about the determinants of the profitability of contrivance are sound: they are not.[1552] The opinion is important because it manifests (1) the EC's intention to execute case-specific analyses of the increase-in-coordination (contrivance) possibility and (2) its rejection of its historic, blithe assumption that joint ventures normally increase legally-problematic coordination. According to Diaz, all the joint-venture opinions that the EC has written since 1998 manifest these changes in the EC's position on coordination.[1553]

I will confine myself to discussing only one case that deals with the "foreclosure" possibility—*European Night Services*.[1554] One of the reasons why the EC concluded that the ENS joint venture would restrict or prevent competition was its belief that the joint venture would deny potential entrants access to resources they would need to enter the market in question. The CFI rejected this finding on the ground that the EC had failed to establish that such competitors did not have independent access to trains, crews, and track.

[1552] Since the volume of sales in markets varies enormously from market to market, market-share figures are not good indicators of absolute appreciability. I see no connection between a market's rate-of-growth and the profitability of its established firms' engaging in contrivance. The height of the barriers to entry into a market is a poor indicator of the effectiveness of its potential competitors. Although effective competition will reduce the profitability of contrived oligopolistic pricing, it will usually not critically reduce the profitability of such contrivance. And the sign of the correlation between the price-sensitivity of inter-product consumption choices (which tends to increase with product homogeneity) in different markets and the profitability of contrived oligopolistic pricing in those markets is uncertain.

[1553] See Diaz at 684, citing *inter alia* Sony/BMG, Case COMP/M.3333 (2004); M. Hutchinson/RCP/ECT, Case JV.55 (2001); Hutchinson/ECT, Case JV.56 (2001); BSkyB/KirchPay TV, Case JV.37 (2000); Mannesman/Bell Atlantic/Omnitel, Case JV.17 (2000); Alitalia/KLM, Case JV.19 (2000); Chronopost/Correos, Case JV.18 (1999); and Sony/Time Warner/CD Now, Case JV.25 (1999).

[1554] European Night Services and Others v. Commission, T-374/94, ECR II-3141 (1998), reviewing the Commission decision European Night Services, OJ L259/20 (1994).

I will conclude my discussion of the production-joint-venture cases with one case that is usually classified [1555] as a joint-buying case—*Rennett*.[1556] *Rennett* focused on the legality of a Dutch cooperative that produced 90 % of the rennet sold in the Netherlands. The EC concluded that the cost-saving and quality-control economic efficiencies the joint venture generated could have been secured even if the joint venture did not obligate the "parents" to purchase rennet exclusively through the cooperative. It therefore declared the exclusive-purchasing provisions of the cooperation agreement and the penalty provision enforcing them illegal under now-Article 101.[1557] I should add that the EC's general discussion of the "ancillarity" issue—usually under now-Article 101(3) as opposed to under now-Article 101(1)—has been no more precise than the U.S. courts' discussion of this issue.[1558]

In addition to its various case-opinions, the EC also published in 1993 a Notice Concerning the Assessment of Co-operative Joint Ventures Pursuant to Article 85 of the EEC Treaty [now-Article 101 of the 2009 Treaty of Lisbon][1559] and in 2001 a Commission Notice, Guidelines on the Applicability of Article 81 of the EEC Treaty [now-Article 101 of the 2009 Treaty of Lisbon] to Horizontal Co-operation Agreements[1560] that bear on its positions on the legality (*inter alia*) of production joint ventures. The 1993 Notice attempted to provide a general overview of the EC's position on joint ventures. The Notice indicates that, for a joint venture to violate now-Article 101(1)'s test of *prima facie* illegality, the parents must be actual or potential competitors (an anodyne claim) or the joint venture must have a deleterious impact on the ability of one or more third parties to compete (a claim that would be unobjectionable if the concern were that the joint venture might reduce a third party's ability to compete in that it would lead the joint venture and/or the parents to engage in a predatory refusal to deal, some other type of predation, or possibly a non-predatory refusal to deal that would reduce or distort competition, though it would be incorrect as a matter of law and undesirable as a matter of policy if the concern were that the joint venture might reduce a third party's ability to compete because the joint venture would be more economically efficient than any QV investment the parents could make independently and/or because the joint venture might increase the parents' economic efficiency in ways that would improve their competitive-position arrays in the joint venture's market [if they operated in them] and/or in other markets in which they operated). The 1993 Notice also indicates that, for now-Article 101(1)'s test of *prima facie* illegality to

[1555] See, *e.g.*, Diaz at 730.

[1556] OJ L51/19 (1979).

[1557] According to Korah, more recently, "the ECJ has held that cooperative buying and selling organisations with small market shares do not infringe Article 81(1) [now-Article 101(1)], even when members agree for long periods to buy largely from or sell to the organization and there is a penalty on leaving it, provided that the rules are proportional to the functions of the joint cooperation." See Korah at 440, citing Coberco, C-399/93, ECR I-4515, ¶¶ 9–20 (1995).

[1558] See Korah at 431.

[1559] OJ C43/2 (1993) (hereinafter 2001 Horizontal Cooperation Guidelines).

[1560] OJ C3/2 (2001).

be violated, the predicted reduction in competition must be appreciable. Chapter 3 of the 2001 Horizontal Cooperation Guidelines indicates *inter alia* that production joint ventures are unlikely to contravene Article 101(1)'s test of *prima facie* illegality if the parents are not competitors or if the parents are prospective customers of the joint venture that could not profitably enter the joint venture's market independently and the cost of the joint venture's product to the parents constitutes a small percentage of their respective total costs (in the EC's terminology, there is "low commonality of costs").[1561]

I turn next to the EC's and the E.C./E.U. courts' treatment of R&D joint ventures. The EC (and the E.C./E.U. courts) have been generally favorably disposed to R&D joint ventures and other sorts of R&D collaborations. According to Diaz[1562]:

> The Commission has often stated that it sees little problem with co-operative R&D[1563] and indeed, over the recent years it has actively encouraged, through the various Community research programs, co-operation in R&D and in the dissemination of its results. R&D agreements are also one of the few types of horizontal agreements to benefit from a block exemption.[1564] [internal footnote numbers not in the original text]

In part, this EC disposition reflects the fact, stated in paragraph (2) of the introduction to the 2000 Commission Regulation on the Application of Article 81(3) of the Treaty [now-Article 101(3) of the 2009 Treaty of Lisbon] to Categories of Research and Development Agreements,[1565] that "Article 163(2) of the [1957] Treaty calls upon the Commission to encourage undertakings, including small and medium-sized undertakings, in their research and technological development activities of high quality, and to support their efforts to cooperate with one another." And, in part, it reflects the EC's realization that (1) regardless of the size of the collaborators, R&D collaboration can avoid expensive duplications of effort (an economic-efficiency gain that, as I stated earlier, may be legally critical under now-Article 101(3) only if, all things considered, the joint venture that yields it will lead to additional technical or commercial progress) and can generate productive cross-fertilization of ideas and experience and (2) that R&D collaborations between SMEs (small and medium-sized enterprises) can enable them to compete more successfully against larger competitors[1566] (a fact whose recitation by the EC leaves the impression that the EC may be prone to engage in pari-mutuel handicapping that is unauthorized as a matter of law and unwise as a matter of policy). At various

[1561] For a case in which the low commonality of costs played a critical role, see Philips/Osram, OJ L378/37 (1994), in which the cost of the lead tubing for incandescent and fluorescent lamps that the joint venture at issue was created to manufacture typically constituted only 2 % of the cost of the final products in which it was used.

[1562] See Diaz at 685–86.

[1563] See Diaz at 685, citing Report on Commission Policy XIV (1984) and Report on Commission Policy XV (1985). See also 2001 Horizontal Cooperation Guidelines at ¶ 56.

[1564] See Diaz at 686, citing Commission Regulation (EC) 2659/2000 of 29 November 2000, OJ L304/7 (2000), replacing Regulation (EEC) 418/85 of 19 December 1984, OJ L53/5 (1985).

[1565] Commission Regulation 2659/2000 of 29 November 2000.

[1566] See Diaz at 685, citing 2001 Horizontal Guidelines at ¶ 40.

times such as prior to the EC's promulgation of the 1984 block-exemption regulation,[1567] this general disposition was reinforced by the EC's belief that the Europeans had to cooperate more in R&D to avoid falling behind Japan and the U.S. in technological development.

Nevertheless, the EC has been and still is concerned that R&D joint ventures may reduce competition in violation of now-Article 101(1)'s test of *prima facie* illegality in all the ways that I previously indicated the EC believes joint ventures in general can do so. Although the EC's treatment of these possibilities in relation to R&D joint ventures is not much different from its treatment of them in relation to production joint ventures, its handling of them in relation to R&D joint ventures does have some special features. Thus, the EC's treatment of the restriction-in-QV-investment-competition issue in relation to R&D joint ventures has had some special weaknesses and some special strengths. On the negative side of the ledger, the EC has adopted the incorrect presumption that, if the parents have some degree of market power on the product as opposed to the R&D market, they will be able "to reduce or delay innovations on that market,"[1568] and that, in its opinion, the likelihood that any reduction in the investment that the joint venture's parents make in the joint venture's R&D market will be offset by R&D expenditures of others is inversely related to the parents' market shares in and the concentratedness of the technology market in question (an incorrect claim that has the [rare] virtue of recognizing the relevance of the willingness of non-parents to invest).[1569] On the positive side of the ledger, the Commission has indicated that, in its judgment, the relevant likelihood increases with the number of existing "poles of [competitive] research,"[1570] has executed atypically-careful analyses of the ability of different potential researchers to engage in competitive R&D,[1571] and has explicitly recognized that the probability that an R&D joint venture will cause the parents to reduce the R&D they do in the joint venture's R&D market through the joint venture and in their own names combined relative to the amount they would have executed in their own names absent the joint venture will depend on whether any such reduction in their R&D would elicit R&D entry by one or more potential competitors.[1572]

In my judgment, the EC has also been particularly prone to make mistakes in relation to the contrivance issue in R&D joint-venture cases (though, as I indicated earlier, the decisions and Regulations in question might also have manifested an [unsuccessful] attempt by the EC to develop an operational decision-rule that would cost-effectively implement now-Article 101(3)'s requirement that, to obtain an

---

[1567] Commission Regulation (EEC) 418/85 of 19 December 1984, OJ L53/5 (1985).

[1568] See Diaz at 687.

[1569] 2001 Horizontal Cooperation Guidelines at ¶¶ 47–49.

[1570] See Diaz' discussion of the EC's position at 691.

[1571] See, *e.g.*, Pasteur Mérieux/Merck, OJ L309/1 (1994); Glaxo/Wellcome, Case IV/M555, OJ C65/3 (1995); Johnson & Johnson/Mercury Asset Managements, OJ C237/5 (2000), and Abbott/BASF, OJ C149/23 (2001).

[1572] 2001 Horizontal Cooperation Guidelines at ¶¶ 47–49.

economic-efficiency exemption, perpetrators must demonstrate that relevant consumers obtained or would obtain a fair share of the benefit generated by the conduct whose legality is at issue). More specifically, in R&D joint-venture cases, the EC has been particularly concerned that the joint venture would enable the parents to avoid competing against each other (in effect, to engage in contrivance) as distributors of the product or production process the joint venture discovered. This concern is justified in relation to R&D joint ventures that are shams: thus, if the parents could have made the joint venture's discovery just as proficiently themselves and marketed the goods or processes they discovered without violating each other's IP rights and the joint venture was really designed not just to reduce the amount of R&D the parents executed but to enable them to charge higher prices for the discovered good or production process (*i.e.*, to avoid competing against each other in the product market), it clearly would violate now-Article 101 on that account. The concern is also justified when the R&D joint venture is not a sham, but the parents would both have invested in the relevant R&D market absent the joint venture (even if their individual investments would be less economically efficient than their joint venture was). However, I do not think that this concern of the EC has been limited to these possibilities. In some contexts, the EC seems to think that now-Article 101(1) authorizes it to prevent the parents of an R&D joint venture that want to distribute the discovered product or process individually rather than jointly from allocating exclusive territories to each other even when the EC is assuming that no R&D projects would have been executed (the discovery would not have been made) absent the joint venture. Thus, in 1979, on that assumption, the EC held that, "to qualify for an exemption," the joint-research arrangement must permit the discoveries it yields to "be used by both parties [*i.e.*, the parents] freely and independently without any territorial or other restrictions on production or marketing within the common market."[1573] And in 1986, in a related non-R&D joint-venture case, the EC held that then-Article 81(1)—now-Article 101(1)—applied to various provisions of a production-joint-venture agreement that concerned the parents' functioning as distributors because, although the parents were not potential competitors in relation to the production of the good in question (high-quality air filters) prior to their joint venture, once their collaboration enabled them to produce suitable air filters they became potential competitors as distributors of the product in question.[1574] Admittedly, the Commission's 1984 and 2000 block-exemption Regulations permit the parents to assign to each other the exclusive right to make active sales within specified territories for some period (respectively 5 and 7 years) after the discovery is marketed in the common market,[1575] but these relaxations of

[1573] Beecham/Parke Davis, OJ L70/11 (1979).

[1574] Mitchell/Cotts/Sofiltra, OJ L41/31 (1987).

[1575] See Diaz at 698, citing Commission Regulation (EC) 2659/2000 at Article 5(g), OJ L304/7 (2000). I should also admit that the EC has permitted the parents of R&D joint ventures to market the discoveries they yield jointly when it finds that the parents could not market those discoveries individually. See, *e.g.*, Alcatel Espace/ANT Nachtrichtentechnik, OJ L32/19 (1990) and Konsortium ER 900, OJ L228/31 (1990).

its original stand do not extend to clauses prohibiting the parents from making passive sales outside territories assigned exclusively to them or clauses allocating exclusive territories to the parents more than 5 (originally) and 7 (subsequently) years after the discovered products were first marketed.[1576] Provisions in R&D-joint-venture agreements that create joint ventures that make discoveries that the parents would not otherwise have made that prohibit or prevent the parents from joint marketing the discoveries in question cannot be said to constitute contrivance.[1577] Nor, for reasons I discussed earlier, can these Regulations be justified as cost-effective rules for implementing now-Article 101(3)'s "fair share" requirement.

I do not want to leave the impression that the EC always prohibits the parents of R&D joint ventures from arranging the production and distribution of the discovered good or the distribution of the discovered production process so as to eliminate their competing against each other as producers and/or distributors of the discovered good or production process. In particular, in a number of decisions, the EC concluded that R&D joint ventures that involved joint production and marketing—which I would have concluded did not violate now-Article 101(1)'s test of *prima facie* illegality because the parents would not have "discovered" the good in question absent the joint venture—did not violate now-Article 101(1)'s test of *prima facie* illegality for a variety of different reasons. Thus, in *Elopak/Metal Box—Odin*,[1578] the EC ruled in favor of a joint venture created to develop, manufacture, and distribute a new type of packaging for certain types of processed foods on the ground that neither parent could have made the relevant discovery on its own; in *Alcatel Espace/ANT Nachtrichtentechnik*, the EC permitted joint marketing on the ground that "the benefits of joint R&D and joint manufacturer can only be achieved if they are combined with a degree of joint marketing;"[1579] and in *Korsortium ECR 900*, the EC concluded that a joint-marketing arrangement for mobile-phone technology did not raise now-Article 101(1) issues because the parents could not tender independently.[1580]

In all other respects, the EC's treatment of the contrivance issue in R&D joint-venture cases has been identical to its treatment of this possibility in production-joint-venture cases. Thus, although the EC believes that R&D joint ventures may "result in the coordination of the parties' behavior as suppliers of existing products"—in my terms, may increase the extent to which the parents agree to practice contrivance generally,[1581] it also believes that, in Diaz' words, for R&D joint ventures to induce

---

[1576] See Diaz at 699, citing Commission Regulation (EC) 2659/2000 at Article 5(f), OJ L304/7 (2000). See also Quantel International-Continuum/Quantel SA, OJ L235/9 (1992), confirming that the 1984 block-exemption regulation permitted the assignment of exclusive territories for only the first 5 years after the discovered product was marketed.

[1577] This criticism is perfectly analogous to my criticism of the EC decision prohibiting the parents of the production joint venture in *Optical Fibres* from assigning exclusive territories to the final-product-producing/distributive parents in question.

[1578] OJ L209/15 (1990).

[1579] OJ L32/19 (1990).

[1580] OJ L228/31 (1990).

[1581] See Diaz at 690, citing 2001 Horizontal Cooperation Guidelines at ¶¶ 44–46.

such additional contrivance, "it is essential that the parties have a strong market position with respect to both the existing product market and the R&D efforts."[1582] I do not know the referent of Diaz' "strong market position" concept. However, as we saw in Chaps. 6, 8 and 10, if by "strong market position" Diaz is referring to "high market share," high OCAs, high NOMs and/or COMs, or high (OCA + OM)s, there will not be much of a correlation between the strength of the parents' market positions and the extent to which their R&D joint venture will increase their COMs:

(1) market definitions and hence market-share calculations are inevitably arbitrary;
(2) high OCAs and NOMs tend to make contrived oligopolistic pricing less profitable; and
(3) high COMs make it more likely that an R&D joint venture will increase the parents' COMs only by eliminating the possibility that any related increase in the profitability of their engaging in contrivance will be inconsequential because, even after the R&D joint venture is executed and the profitability of contrived oligopolistic pricing is enhanced, such pricing will be unprofitable for the parents.

The EC's analysis of the "foreclosure" possibility in R&D joint-venture cases—*viz.*, that particular R&D joint ventures may "foreclose" potential purchasers of the joint venture's discovery (potential purchasers that compete against its parents in related non-technology product markets) from buying it—has been no different from its analysis of the analogous possibility in production-joint-venture cases. According to Diaz, the EC appears to be worried about this type of possible "foreclosure effect" "only" "when the degree of remaining actual and/or potential competition is considered to be insufficient."[1583]

I will conclude this discussion of the EC's and the E.C./E.U. courts' treatment of R&D joint ventures by summarizing and commenting on the EC's pronouncements on such joint ventures in its 2001 Horizontal Cooperation Guidelines and its Regulation (EC) No 2659/2000 of 29 November 2000 on the Application of Article 81(3) of the Treaty [now-Article 101(3) of the 2009 Treaty of Lisbon] to Categories of Research and Development Agreements (hereinafter 2000 Cooperative R&D Regulation).

I start with the EC's general position on the *prima facie* illegality of R&D joint ventures under now-Article 101(1) as expressed in its 2001 Horizontal Cooperation Guidelines:

(1) "most R&D agreements" do not violate now-Article 101(1)'s test of *prima facie* illegality[1584];
(2) "R&D cooperation between non-competitors" and "pure" R&D agreements—*viz.*, those that do not entail the joint exploitation of results—never or virtually never raise any concern[1585];

[1582] See Diaz at 690.
[1583] *Id.* at 694.
[1584] *Id.* at 686.
[1585] 2001 Horizontal Cooperation Guidelines at ¶ 58.

(3) R&D arrangements that are pure shams—*i.e.*, that disguise hardcore cartels—almost always violate not only now-Article 101(1)'s test of *prima facie* illegality but also Article 101, all things considered[1586]; and
(4) whether R&D joint ventures that do not fall into the second and third categories just delineated above violate now-Article 101(1)'s test of *prima facie* illegally must be determined on a case-by-case basis.

As my previous comments indicated, although I agree with points (3) and (4) in the preceding list, R&D cooperation between non-competitors and R&D agreements that do not entail the joint exploitation of results may have as a critical object or may have the effect of preventing or restricting competition, I am not convinced that "most R&D agreements" do not violate now-Article 101(1)'s test of *prima facie* illegality: indeed, even if I were so convinced, I would conclude that this issue should be investigated on a case-by-case basis.

I turn now to the EC's 2000 Regulation on the application of now-Article 101(3) to R&D agreements (which was originally scheduled to expire on 31 December 2010[1587]). The introduction to that Regulation declares that its goals are "ensuring effective protection of competition and providing adequate legal security for undertakings."[1588] (I assume that the latter goal is valued in this context only insofar as its furtherance "increases competition" by encouraging cooperative R&D that generates net equivalent-monetary gains for relevant consumers.) The Regulation's introduction proceeds to state that the EC's adoption of an "economics-based approach" is at least "consistent with" its pursuance of these goals.[1589] The introduction also explicitly states the EC's assumption that "[c]ooperation in research and development and in the exploitation of the results generally promotes economic progress. . .."[1590] It specifies that cooperation in R&D will generate such progress not only by "increasing the dissemination of know-how between the parties [parents]" but also by "avoiding [the economically-inefficient] duplication of research and development work" and "rationalising the manufacture or application of the processes" discovered by the R&D.[1591] Although it is hard to object to a claim that includes the word "generally," I suspect that I would be more disposed than the Commission has been to question the economic-efficiency claims that are made for particular R&D cooperations. Moreover, as I have already indicated, I believe that the fact that a cooperative-R&D arrangement will prevent economically-inefficiently-duplicative R&D does not guarantee that the arrangement will generate any of the kinds of economic efficiency that now-Article 101(3) requires conduct to generate to be eligible for an economic-efficiency-related exemption

[1586] *Id.* at ¶¶ 55–58 and 59.
[1587] 2000 R&D Regulation at Article 9.
[1588] *Id.* at ¶ (3) of introduction of the 2000 Cooperative R&D Regulation.
[1589] *Id.* at ¶ (7) of introduction of the 2000 Cooperative R&D Regulation.
[1590] *Id.* at ¶ (10) of introduction of the 2000 Cooperative R&D Regulation.
[1591] *Id.*

from now-Article 101—*viz.*, will increase production or distribution efficiency or will promote technical or economic progress. I also suspect that arrangements that purportedly "rationalize" production and distribution often will not be sufficiently likely to yield the types of economic-efficiency gains that have been claimed for them to merit an Article 101(3) exemption. In any event, although I agree that as paragraph (12) of the introduction to the 2000 Regulation asserts, now-Article 101(3)-relevant consumers will generally benefit from increases in the quantity of R&D and from increases in the effectiveness of a given quantity of R&D, they may not benefit from R&D cooperation that reduces the economically-inefficiently-duplicative character of the cooperators' research if it simultaneously reduces the quantity of research of the relevant type that is executed.[1592] The introduction to the 2000 Cooperative R&D Regulation also indicates that—unless the parents "agree not to carry out other research and development in the same field," "[a]greements on the joint execution of research work or the joint development of such research, up to but not including the stage of industrial application...do not fall within the scope of Article 81(1) of the Treaty [now-Article 101(1) of the 2009 Treaty of Lisbon]."[1593] Although the paragraph from which these quotations are taken speaks in broad terms, I take it actually to manifest an assumption that cooperative R&D agreements that do not explicitly prohibit the parents from executing independent research that would be competitive with the joint venture's R&D will not reduce QV investment in the relevant R&D market. I think that the EC's position on this issue puts too much weight on whether or not the parents have agreed not to compete with their joint venture in its R&D market. Even if the parents have not entered into such an agreement, their R&D joint venture may have as a critical object or may have the effect of reducing R&D competition—in particular, may be designed to achieve this result by giving each parent an R&D-deterring stake in the joint venture's earnings. The introduction to the 2000 Cooperative R&D Regulation also manifests the EC's acceptance of the reality that "[t]he joint exploitation of [the] results [of cooperative R&D] can be considered as a natural consequence of joint research and development."[1594] Given (1) the EC's optimism about both (A) the probability that R&D joint ventures will generate now-Article-101(3)-qualifying economic efficiencies and (B) the probability that they will reduce

---

[1592] I should point out in addition that, for reasons that the sequel to this study—THE WELFARE ECONOMICS OF ANTITRUST POLICY AND U.S. AND E.U. ANTITRUST LAW—will explain, even though now-Article-101(3)-relevant consumers will virtually always benefit from any business choice that increases the amount of product R&D or production-process R&D that relates to a product they purchase that is executed and even though increases in production-process R&D almost always increase economic efficiency, the increases in product R&D that antitrust policies generate probably tend to decrease economic efficiency (because, taken together, the various Pareto imperfections in contemporary developed economies tend to inflate the profitability of product R&D while deflating the profitability of production-process R&D). See also Richard S. Markovits *On the Economic Efficiency of Using Law to Increase Research and Development*, 39 HARV. J. ON LEG. 63 (2002).

[1593] See introduction of 2000 Cooperative R&D Regulation at ¶ (3).

[1594] See *id.* at ¶ (11).

QV-investment competition or decrease competition in other ways and (2) its recognition that the joint exploitation of the discoveries generated by collaborative R&D is "natural"—*i.e.*, legitimate if the joint R&D is lawful, it is not surprising that the Regulation proceeds to grant an exemption from now-Article 101(1) of seven years from the time the resulting discoveries (in its terms, the "contract products") "are first put on the market within the common market"[1595] to "joint research and development of products or processes and joint exploitation of the results of that research and development."[1596] However, in line with two statements in the introduction of the 2000 Cooperative R&D Regulation that indicate the EC's view that cooperative R&D is likely to do more harm than good when the perpetrators have significant market power,[1597] the 2000 Cooperative Research Regulation subsequently limits this exemption to cooperative arrangements between or among parties that the EC believes do not jointly have market power—in particular, between or among parties whose share of the relevant market (the market in which the contract products are sold) does not exceed 25 %. Specifically, because the EC believes that the "general" presumption that "the positive effects of research and development agreements [traceable, I presume, to the economic efficiencies they generate] will outweigh any negative effects [they will have] on competition" applies only when the relevant parties' total share falls "below a certain level"[1598]—in practice, below 25 % of the contract-product market, the full 7-year exemption applies only when the parties' total share of the contract-product market does not exceed 25 %. Thus, no exemption will be granted *ab initio* if the parents' combined share of the contract-product market exceeds 25 %[1599]; the exemption will continue beyond 7 years only so long as the participating undertakings' combined market share does not exceed 25 %[1600]; if the parents' and/or parents' and joint venture's market share is originally 25 % or lower but rises above 25 % to some level below 30 %, the exemption will continue for two years after the calendar year in which the relevant market share rose above 25 %[1601]; and if the relevant entities' combined market share is originally not above 25 % but rises above 30 %, the exemption will continue for one year after the calendar year in which the 30 % market-share level was exceeded.

I have two objections to this limitation in the EC's cooperative-R&D exemption. First I object to it both (1) because, for reasons that Chap. 8 explained, I do not think that one can measure an individual firm's market power by its market share or two or more firms' combined market power by their combined market shares and (2) because I do not think it appropriate to conclude that an agreement that enables

[1595] See 2000 Cooperative R&D Regulation at Article 4 ¶ 1.

[1596] See *id.* at Article 1 ¶ 1.

[1597] See introduction of the 2000 Cooperative R&D Regulation at ¶¶ (5) and (7).

[1598] See 2000 Cooperative R&D Regulation at Article 4 ¶¶ 1 and 2.

[1599] See *id.* at Article 4 ¶ 3.

[1600] See *id.* at Article 6 ¶ 2.

[1601] See *id.* at Article 5 ¶ 3.

the parents of an R&D joint venture to avoid competing against each other as distributors of a product or production process the joint venture discovers that would not otherwise have been discovered as early as the joint venture discovered it enables them "to eliminate competition in respect to a substantial part of the products" in the contract-product market regardless of the share of that market that the sales of the discovered product constitutes (and regardless of the parents' sales of any products they independently produce and sell in that market: if the cooperative R&D arrangement contributed to their engaging in contrivance on such sales, it would be illegal on that account regardless of whether the sales in question constituted a substantial part of the sales in the market in question). Second, even if I thought that two or more rivals' combined market power could be accurately inferred from their combined market shares, I would not think that the probability that their cooperative research would from the date of its inception onward yield relevant consumers a fair share of the benefits it generated was sufficiently connected to their market shares of the contract-product market at various points in time to justify the exemption-limitation on this basis.

I turn now to the EC's and the E.C./E.U.'s handling of sales joint ventures. In Korah's words, sales joint ventures "are usually treated by the Commission as classic cartels that enable parties to restrict production and raise price."[1602] In fact, the E.C./E.U. authorities' position is more complex (as is the position of the U.S. authorities).

In practice, the EC has distinguished between sales joint ventures (or other sorts of joint-sales arrangements) created by competitors with low market shares and sales joint ventures created by competitors with high market shares. In particular, for three reasons, the EC has often cleared or exempted sales joint ventures created by competitors with low market shares when it would not have done so had the parents' market shares been high:

(1) it assumed that the fact that the joint-sales arrangement was created by firms with low market shares implied that the joint venture's anticompetitive effect would not be appreciable[1603];
(2) it assumed that the fact that the sales-joint-venture's parents have low market shares rendered persuasive the claim that the arrangement would yield significant economic efficiencies by enabling the parents to take advantage of economies of scale in storage, salesmanship, and transportation[1604]; and

[1602] See Korah at 439–40.

[1603] For a case in which this consideration appears to have been critical, see SAFCO, OJ L13/44 (1972) where the fact that the parents (producers of preserves [fabricants des conserves alimentaires]) were small and medium-sized enterprises (SMEs) seems to have played a crucial role for this reason.

[1604] Thus, in both Floral, OJ L39/51 (1980) and ANSAC, OJ L152/54 (1990), the large size of the parents of the joint ventures at issue seems to have dissuaded the EC from accepting the claim that the joint ventures would generate economic efficiencies that would satisfy that requirement for a now-Article 101(3) exemption.

(3) it concluded that the fact that the parents had small market shares made it likely that the joint selling in question would critically affect the parents' ability to survive in competition with larger rivals[1605] (a position that would involve the EC in pari-mutuel handicapping [which I find as incorrect as a matter of E.C./ E.U. competition law as its *White Motor* counterpart is as a matter of U.S. antitrust law] if it led the EC to prohibit undertakings with large market shares from creating sales joint ventures that also would increase their organizational economic efficiency).[1606]

One final, important point: like the modern U.S. courts (*e.g.*, the Supreme Court in *Broadcast Music*), the EC has declared sales joint ventures lawful—in particular, has granted them now-Article 101(3) exemptions—when it concluded that the arrangement would yield substantial cost-savings. Thus, in 1989, in *UIP*,[1607] the EC exempted a joint-sales arrangement for films on this economic-efficiency ground.

I turn now to buying joint ventures. When discussing the legality of buying joint ventures under the U.S. Sherman Act, I argued that the fact that the Sherman Act was designed to benefit consumers by preventing businesses from engaging in presumptively-economically-inefficient conduct they would not have perceived to be *ex ante* profitable but for their belief that it would reduce the absolute attractiveness of the offers against which they would have to compete implies that it should not be interpreted to prohibit even those buying joint ventures for which no

---

[1605] Thus, the EC decision in SAFCO—OJ L13/44 (1972)—seems to have been influenced by its belief that the parents could not have penetrated the German market, which contained larger rivals, without engaging in joint selling. See Korah at 440.

[1606] In the other direction, the EC and the E.C./E.U. courts seem particularly likely to declare joint-selling joint ventures illegal when the joint venture has market power. Thus, in Stremsel v. Commission, 61/80, ECR 851 (1981), confirming the EC's decision in Rennett, ECR 851 (1981), the ECJ held that a joint-selling joint venture violates now-Article 101 when the joint seller has almost a monopoly. Admittedly, in one case—Finnpap, OJ C45/4 (1989)—the EC (through an informal clearance) allowed a joint-sales organization that had market power. However, this decision may have a political explanation—the EC may not have wanted to antagonize Finland just before it finally agreed to join the Community.

Two other EC decisions in cases the Commission considered to involve joint selling are also worth noting. In UEFA-Champions League, OJ L291/25 (2003), and in German Bundesliga, OJ L134/46 (2005) (summary of commitment decision), the EC conditioned UEFA's and the German football league's being allowed to restrict the ability of individual teams to market their games on the league's accepting a series of commitments. In my view, the imposition of these conditions are incorrect as a matter of E.C./E.U. competition law. UEFA (in its capacity as the organizers of the Champions League) and the Bundesliga (as the creator of the league in question), like the supplier of optical fibres in *Optical Fibres*, are the creators of a product (the *sporting* competitions they respectively organize) that would not exist but for their efforts and for that reason can prevent the individual teams that participate in the *sporting* competitions they organize from engaging in intrabrand *economic* competition without violating now-Article 101(1)'s test of *prima facie* illegality. In fact, because the leagues in question are really a single economic undertaking, I would not characterize the sales system they created as "joint selling"—a conclusion that underlies the wording of the first sentence of this paragraph.

[1607] OJ L226/25 at ¶ 44 (1989).

economic-efficiency defense can be established if the joint ventures in question benefit ultimate consumers by reducing their suppliers' marginal costs (although I admitted that valid textual and normative arguments to the contrary could be made). I believe that the same (in this case) treaty-promulgator-goal argument can be made for the legality under now-Articles 101 and 102 of E.C./E.U. competition law of buying joint ventures that confer net equivalent-monetary gains on relevant consumers (in my judgment, most buying joint ventures) despite the fact that textual and normative arguments can be made against this conclusion as well. Some might oppose this contention by pointing out that the E.C./E.U. Treaty was promulgated to promote a variety of social and political goals. However, for two reasons, I am not persuaded: (1) buying joint ventures do not disserve the social and political goals in question and (2) now-Article 101(3), both the exclusionary-abuse branch and the exploitative-abuse branch of now-Article 102's test illegality, and the EMCR all attest to the fact that E.C./E.U. competition law is designed to a considerable extent to promote relevant-consumer equivalent-monetary welfare.

Unfortunately, the EC and the E.C./E.U. courts have never explicitly adverted to this promulgator-goal argument for the legality of buying joint ventures under E.C./E.U. competition law and have not accepted the argument's conclusion that all such joint ventures and cognate arrangements that will confer an equivalent-monetary gain on relevant ultimate consumers—*viz.*, those that create (1) bilateral monopolists as opposed to (2) monopsonists that (A) face sellers that have no bargaining power and (B) do not practice something like perfect buyer price discrimination—are lawful under now-Articles 101 and 102.[1608]

I will begin by discussing briefly the EC's non-case pronouncements on buying joint ventures and then discuss equally briefly some of the EC major cases on such arrangements. The EC's 1968 Notice on Co-operation Between Enterprises[1609] did not explicitly address joint-buying arrangements. Although its Heading II(4) did refer to "agreements, which have as their sole object the joint use of...storing and transport equipment," the section in question does not apply to joint-buying arrangements whose functions extend beyond the mere joint storing and transport of goods. The EC's 1993 Notice Concerning the Assessment of Co-operative Joint Ventures Pursuant to Article 81[1610] (now-Article 101) takes a position on the legality of buying joint ventures that is far more favorable than the position the EC took in that Notice on the legality of selling joint ventures:

> Purchasing JVs [joint ventures] contribute to the rationalization of ordering and to the better use of transport and storage facilities but are at the same time an instrument for the setting of uniform purchase prices and conditions and often of purchase quotas. By combining their demand power in a JV, the parents can obtain a position of excessive influence vis-à-vis the other side of the market and distort competition between suppliers. Consequently, the disadvantages often outweigh the possible benefits, which can accompany purchasing

[1608] The EMCR is not applicable to joint-buying joint ventures because they are not full-function joint ventures.

[1609] OJ C84/14, CMR 2699 (1968).

[1610] OJ C43/2 (1993).

JVs, particularly those between competing producers. The Commission is correspondingly prepared to grant exemptions only in exceptional cases and then only if the parents can retain the possibility of purchasing individually.[1611]

I believe that the EC is justified in its concern that purchasing joint ventures created by parents that are actual competitors may lead the parents to engage in contrived oligopolistic pricing (in its words, to establish "purchasing quotas"). Indeed, I am concerned as well that (1) when such joint ventures are created by parents that are actual competitors, they may lead them to engage in additional predation and (2) when they are created by parents that are either actual or potential competitors, they may lead the parents to reduce their QV investments in markets in which one or both of them are operating in circumstances in which any such reduction in the parents' QV investments will not be fully offset by QV investments by others. However, I reject the claim that, any time that such a joint venture reduces the prices that the joint venture pays below the prices the parents would have paid independently for reasons unrelated to the joint venture's being more organizationally economically efficient than the parents were, the joint venture has exercised "excessive influence" on the relevant suppliers. Nor do I think that such joint ventures will tend to "distort competition between suppliers": indeed, to the extent that the joint venture can make better-informed purchasing decisions than its parents would have made because it can take advantage of economies of scale in purchasing or can for other reasons make better use of given purchasing agents, it will eliminate distortions in competition between suppliers by reducing the extent to which less-privately-well-placed suppliers make sales because the relevant buyer is unable to identify its privately-best-placed supplier (or possibly is unable to induce that supplier to beat the offers it receives from privately-worse-placed suppliers). Hence, although I agree that, if the relevant decision-criterion is the impact of the EC decision on relevant-buyer equivalent-monetary welfare, trade-offs will often have to be made (*i.e.*, that the legality of such joint ventures will depend on whether the equivalent-monetary gains that particular purchasing joint ventures confer on relevant consumers by generating passed-on economic efficiencies and passed-on input-price-concessions the joint venture's buying power enables it to secure exceed the equivalent-monetary losses it imposes on such buyers by enabling the parents to engage in contrivance and predation), the gains and losses that I think must be traded off are different from those the 1993 Notice references. Moreover, I suspect that, at least if appropriate attention is paid to deterring related contrivance and predation, the percentage of buying joint ventures that is lawful will be far higher than the 1993 Guidelines claim or imply. I should add that I also reject the 1993 Notice's contention that the parents' retaining the possibility of purchasing individually is often critical (indeed, is even relevant) to whether a buying joint venture violates now-Article 101. The only possible legal justification for this EC position is that, *inter alia*, the Treaty is designed to protect the liberty interests of individual businesses and contractual restrictions in the legal

[1611] *Id.* at Point 61.

right of parents to make independent purchases restricts their liberty. I admit that some promulgators or supporters of the 1957 Treaty may have intended the Treaty to preserve the ability of individual businesses to make any lawful choice they wish to make at any point in time in the view that doing so would protect their "liberty" in the sense that liberals believe liberty morally ought to be protected. However, I do not think there is any binding "legislative" history on this point and, in its absence, the facts that (1) these types of choices do not involve their prospective makers' liberty interests in the sense in which at least liberals are committed to valuing liberty and (2) the businesses in question have agreed to the restrictions in their options at issue when in their right minds under conditions in which they could not be said to have been coerced or to have operated under unacceptable duress disincline me to interpret the relevant Treaty provisions to preclude firms from accepting limitations in their legal right to make individual purchasing decisions.

The 2001 Horizontal Cooperation Guidelines'[1612] position on joint-buying arrangements is far more favorable to their legality, stating that joint-buying agreements between SMEs (small and medium-sized enterprises) are normally procompetitive because they enable the parents to achieve volumes and discounts similar to those their bigger competitors can secure: in particular, these Guidelines state that purchasing joint ventures are unlikely to raise concerns if the parents' combined market shares are below 15 %. I have three objections to the 2001 Horizontal Guidelines' position on buying joint ventures:

(1) they underestimate the probability that joint ventures between SMEs whose combined market share is below 15 % increase the amount of contrivance and predation in which the parents and/or the parents and their rivals engage (in part because they assume incorrectly that any resulting increase in contrivance and predation would not have appreciable effects and in part because they assume incorrectly that, to practice contrivance and predation successfully and profitably, a firm must have more than a small or a medium-sized market share and/or that the collaboration of a firm with a small or medium-sized market share cannot critically affect the profitability of contrivance or predation to an SME);
(2) they pay insufficient attention to whether the joint venture generates economic efficiencies of one or more kinds that are relevant to its eligibility for a now-Article 101(3) exemption—an issue that would clearly be relevant if Article 101(1) were deemed to cover reductions in buyer competition; and
(3) in making the argument that it is lawful for SMEs to create buying joint ventures because their doing so enables them to secure the buying advantages that larger rivals have, they imply that larger-firm buying joint ventures that improve the larger firms' competitive-position arrays either by increasing their buying power still further or, more disturbingly, by yielding additional

[1612] Commission Notice, Guidelines on the Applicability of Article 81 [now-Article 101] of the EC Treaty to Horizontal Cooperation Agreements, OJ C3/2 (2001).

economic efficiencies should be deemed to violate at least now-Article 101(1)'s test of *prima facie* illegality because they will put SMEs at a greater disadvantage.

Still, I do prefer the EC's 2001 position to its 1993 position: in this case, half a loaf is better than none.

I now turn to a few of the canonical buying-joint-venture cases decided by the EC. I begin with the 1968 case *Socemas*.[1613] Socemas was a joint venture created to import products into France from other Community countries. The parents (actually, parties to the relevant agreements) collectively had 9 % of the French food market, and their sales of the products imported through Socemas constituted 0.1 % of their turnover (a percentage that had remained constant over the years). The EC found the arrangement lawful on the ground that any relevant impact it might have had on competition would not have been appreciable.

In many ways, the EC's handling of the 1975 case *Intergroup* is similar.[1614] Intergroup was a buyer co-op created to import goods for food wholesalers and retailers that were members of SPAR chains established in a number of Community countries. In 1973, these chains contained 35,000 retailers and 180 wholesalers, and the goods imported for the 180 wholesalers by Intergroup constituted a percentage of their turnover that varied from 0.06 % to 0.89 %. In 1973, SPAR accounted for less than 4 % of total EC retail food turnover. SPAR members retained the right to set the resale prices they charged for the goods they obtained through Intergroup. The EC held that the arrangement fell outside then-Article 81(1) (now-Article 101 (1)), once more on the ground of appreciability—*i.e.*, because of the combination of (1) the fact that the goods that Intergroup supplied SPAR members constituted a small percentage of their total turnover and (2) the fact that the turnover of SPAR members itself constituted a small percentage of the total retail food sales in each Member State of the then EEC. Although I do not think that the Intergroup joint venture violated now-Article 101, my assessment of its legality reflects my belief that it benefitted ultimate consumers, not any belief that its effect was not appreciable: appreciability is a matter of equivalent-monetary effects, not market shares, and, in high-monetary-sales-volume "markets," practices that have a small percentage effect on the prices of firms with small market shares can still have an appreciable equivalent-monetary impact on relevant consumers.

I turn next to a 1990 case—*EEIG Orphe*.[1615] EEIG Orphe was created by seven small and medium-sized wholesalers of pharmaceuticals and pharmaceutical products to purchase such goods and create a common trademark. The EC concluded that this arrangement, under which the individual parents were permitted to determine their prices and other conditions of sale, did not violate now-Article 101(1)'s test of *prima facie* illegality primarily because it would enable the parents

---

[1613] OJ L201/4 (1968).

[1614] OJ L212/23 (1975).

[1615] EE1G Orphe, Report on Competition Policy (Vol. XX) 80, point 102 (1990).

to compete better against the very large wholesalers that dominated the procurement and, presumably, the wholesale resale markets. Insofar as this decision implies that the EC is willing to allow SMEs to engage in joint buying when it would not allow larger concerns to do so because both decisions enable the SMEs to compete more effectively against their larger competitors, it manifests the EC's adoption of something like the U.S. Supreme Court *White Motor* opinion's pari-mutuel-handicapping approach to antitrust, which I think is as wrong as a matter of E.C./E.U. competition law as it is as a matter of U.S. antitrust law.

I now want to discuss a case that manifests the fact that the EC is more disposed to allow at least SMEs to organize a joint-buying arrangement when the supply side of the market in which they are purchasing the good in question is highly concentrated. Before considering the case in question, I want to explain why I think that this disposition of the EC is almost always incorrect as a matter of E.C./E.U. law. Admittedly, an argument for the EC's position would be legally supportable if—as I suspect the EC clearly believes there is—there were a strong positive correlation between the concentration of the supply side of the market in which the buying joint venture would operate as a buyer and the probability that the joint-buying arrangement would yield a bilateral-monopoly situation as opposed to creating a monopsony situation in which the relevant sellers had no bargaining power and the resulting monopsonist would not find it profitable to engage in perfect or near-perfect price discrimination. In particular, on the assumption that there is a strong correlation between the concentration of the supply side of the relevant market and the probability that the suppliers of the joint buyer would have significant bargaining power, my "legislative"-goal argument that joint buying should be deemed lawful under E.C./E.U. competition law when it would yield equivalent-monetary gains to relevant ultimate consumers but should be deemed unlawful under E.C./E.U. competition law when it would impose equivalent-monetary losses on relevant ultimate consumers would imply that the EC is correct as a matter of law about the legal relevance of the concentratedness of the seller-side of the market in which the joint buyers are making purchases. Increases in the power of buyers that are operating in a bilateral-monopoly situation are likely to confer equivalent-monetary gains on relevant ultimate consumers by reducing not just the price that the joint buyers pay for the input/good in question but the marginal cost to them of purchasing it and thereby the price they charge for (the good they use the purchased input in question to produce)/(the purchased good in question when reselling it) whereas acts that give buyers monopsony power when they will not be operating in a bilateral-monopoly situation will tend to impose equivalent-monetary losses on relevant ultimate consumers because, if the relevant buyers do not practice close-to-perfect price discrimination when exercising their monopsony power in non-bilateral-monopoly situations, their monopsony will increase the marginal cost to them of the marginal units of the relevant input or final good and thereby increase the marginal cost they have to incur (to produce the final good they use the input in question to produce)/(to distribute the final good in question [including the marginal cost of goods resold]) and hence the price they charge ultimate consumers for the good they make/resell. My view that the EC's "concentratedness of the seller-side of the relevant market" "doctrine" is almost always incorrect as a matter of law reflects my judgment that—in the real world, in which market definitions are arbitrary because physical products, product images, and product-sale locations are differentiated in ways that matter differently to different consumers—there will be little if any correlation between the concentration of the seller-sides of defined markets and the likelihood that any buyers that obtain monopsony buyer by creating a buying joint venture or other type of joint-buying arrangement will be operating in a bilateral-monopoly situation—more particularly, that joint buyers will almost always be operating in bilateral-monopoly situations.

The "concentrated supplier side of the market" case I want to discuss is *National Sulfuric Acid Association.*[1616] The Association was formed by sulfuric-acid producers that collectively produced more than 80 % of the UK output of sulfuric acid and 100 % of the French output of sulfuric acid to purchase sulfur for sulfuric-acid production. The EC decided to grant the Association a now-Article 101(3) exemption that permitted its members to make up to 25 % of their purchases of sulfuric acid through the Association on condition that they eliminate a provision of the Association agreement that prohibited members from importing sulfur on their own. The EC indicated that the exemption was granted to give the Association members the ability to counteract the power of their major suppliers in a situation in which only eight major suppliers existed worldwide. I have three objections to this decision:

(1) I see no reason why the Association should have been limited to making 25 % of its members' purchases;
(2) I see no reason why the Association's members should have been prohibited from agreeing not to import sulfur independently (since I do not think that the Association's prohibition of such conduct disserves members' liberty interests, properly so-called); and
(3) if the EC were correct in deeming the joint-purchasing arrangement in question to constitute a violation of now-Article 101(1)'s test of *prima facie* illegality, the fact that the Association enabled its members to obtain price-concessions by increasing their bargaining power would not satisfy the now-Article 101(3) requirement that it generate economic efficiencies (though it may have generated economic efficiencies that the EC [and Diaz] did not discuss).[1617]

The final joint-buying case I want to discuss is a CFI 2002 decision *M6 and Others v. Commission,*[1618] annulling an EC decision to exempt under Article 101(3)

[1616] OJ L260/24 (1980) and OJ L190/22 (1989).

[1617] Diaz' account of the case does not warrant his discussing it under the heading "*Efficiencies*" in that he does not provide any evidence that the Association generated any economic efficiencies (did anything other than allow its members to exercise bargaining power that enabled them to obtain price-concessions). See Diaz at 729 and 730.

[1618] Joined Cases T-185/00, T-216/00, T-299/00, and T-300/00, ECR II-3805 (2002).

the creation of the European Broadcasting Union (EBU) system, a joint venture formed to jointly acquire and share TV rights for sporting events. EBU members were mostly broadcasters of free TV whose total market share (though declining) was deemed still to be sufficiently high to make it an attractive buyer for event organizers, who want a guaranteed large audience. The CFI overturned the EC's decision to exempt the arrangement because the CFI rejected the Commission's conclusion that the EBU's sub-licensing scheme gave EBU competitors sufficient transmission possibilities.

I want to make eight points about the decisions of the EC and the CFI in this case. First, neither the EC nor the CFI concluded that the joint venture was illegal in itself—*e.g.*, violated now-Article 101 by eliminating competition between EBU members as buyers of TV-transmission rights for sporting events. Second, neither the EC nor the CFI concluded that the EBU's failure to engage in additional sub-licensing was predatory/exclusionary—*i.e.*, entailed a refusal to deal that manifested its perpetrator's specific anticompetitive intent: this fact is not surprising, given the absence in the record of the evidence that would be necessary to support the opposite conclusion. Third, although both the EC and the CFI concluded that the EBU joint venture violated now-Article 101(1)'s test of *prima facie* illegality, I am not convinced that it did: for it to have done so, now-Article 101(1) must deem reductions in buyer-competition *prima facie* illegal even when they benefit ultimate consumers (in this case, by increasing the number of broadcasters offering free TV transmissions and, possibly, by reducing the prices ultimate consumers pay for a wide variety of products advertised by the broadcasters in question by reducing the price of that advertising), and I doubt that now-Article 101(1) should be so interpreted. Fourth, the CFI's decision to overturn the EC's grant of a now-Article 101(3) exemption to EBU must have reflected its belief that under the EBU's actual practice relevant TV-sport-programming consumers were not obtaining a fair share of the benefit the EBU joint venture generated for them and the members of the EBU "combined" but that the buyers in question would obtain a fair share of the resulting benefit if the EBU gave its members' competitors enough additional transmission possibilities: I do not believe that the record supports either of these two conclusions, regardless of how "a fair share of the resulting benefit" is interpreted. Fifth, I do not think one can justify the CFI's decision by arguing that the EBU has a special duty to help its competitors both (1) because the only official claims that undertakings have such a duty are now-Article-102-based claims that apply only to dominant firms and the EBU is not dominant and (2) because I think these now-Article-102-based claims are incorrect as a matter of E.C./E.U. competition law. Sixth, decisions to require joint ventures to treat undertakings that do not belong to the set of original parents more generously (1) by admitting them to membership on less-disadvantageous or non-discriminatory terms relative to the terms of membership that were available to original members and/or by offering to supply non-members with the good the joint venture purchases or produces—indeed, to supply them with those goods on less-advantageous or non-discriminatory terms relative to the terms available to members—may not increase competition or benefit buyers overall because (1) such decisions may deter potential-joint-venture founders from creating joint ventures that increase competition and benefit relevant buyers and (2) the associated long-run losses in question may exceed the short-run gains that would be generated by the decisions in question: the required analysis parallels the counterpart analysis for rules requiring patent-holders to license the use of their discoveries on reasonable terms. Seventh, since decisions that require otherwise-lawful joint ventures (roughly speaking) to treat non-members less-discriminatorily or non-discriminatorily seem to me to be inconsistent as a matter of law with the do-nothing baseline for competitive-impact analysis that, I believe, E.C./E.U. competition law (like U.S. antitrust law) adopts: they hold a joint venture that does not reduce competition in comparison with the *status quo ante* illegal on the ground that the substitution of a variant of that joint venture for the joint venture actually created would increase competition. Eighth, relatedly, and finally, even if one admits that it might be desirable from a defensible conception of the public interest to require joint ventures to treat non-members less-discriminatorily or non-discriminatorily, I think (1) that that choice (like the choice to require [say] dominant firms to divest part of their operation or the choice to impose compulsory licensing on patent-holders) is a legislative choice, not a choice commanded by current E.C./E.U. competition law, and (2) that antitrust-law-enforcement authorities are probably not the ideal institution for making decisions on such issues. THE WELFARE ECONOMICS OF ANTITRUST POLICY AND U.S. AND E.U. ANTITRUST LAW will make this last institutional point more persuasive by (A) explaining in great detail the difference between economic-efficiency analysis on the one hand and specific-anticompetitive-intent and competitive-impact analysis on the other and (B) by examining in great detail the relationship between the economic efficiency of a choice and its moral desirability from a variety of moral perspectives.

* * *

This account of the way in which the EC and the E.C./E.U. courts have actually applied E.C./E.U. competition law to joint ventures has been as complicated and, I fear, as contorted as the practice-reality it discusses. Although the EC and the E.C./E.U. courts have recognized that joint ventures can reduce competition by causing QV-investment restrictions that are not contrivance-based, by increasing contrivance of all kinds, and by generating both predatory and non-predatory foreclosures, they have not correctly analyzed the conditions under which such outcomes would be likely to obtain in part because they remain committed to a market-oriented approach to such issues and in part because they almost always have ignored such facts as the ability of non-parents to "replace" QV investments that joint-venture parents do not make and the reality that joint buying may reduce the prices that ultimate consumers must pay. In my judgment, the EC's and E.C./E.U. courts' handling of joint ventures has also been flawed by their undue optimism that such conduct will generate the kinds of economic efficiencies that put their perpetrators in a position to obtain a now-Article 101(3) exemption and will confer on relevant buyers the now-Article 101(3)-required fair share of the benefit yielded by the joint venture at issue for the parents and those consumers combined. Finally, it seems to me that the EC's and the E.C./E.U.'s treatment of joint ventures may have been undermined by a number of legal mistakes they may have made and by their failure to address what may be a contestable legal issue (a failure attributable to their not distinguishing between predatory and non-predatory refusals to deal):

(1) their possible belief that the law authorizes them to condition their approval of joint ventures that benefit relevant consumers relative to the state of the world that would have prevailed had the parents not created them (indeed, that give those consumers a fair share of the resulting benefit) on the parents' agreeing to compete against each other as distributors of the joint venture's output when such a decision would benefit the relevant consumers;
(2) their possible belief that the law authorizes them to permit SMEs to cooperate to help them compete with larger rivals when it would not permit larger undertakings to increase their organizational economic efficiency by cooperating;
(3) their failure to distinguish non-predatory and predatory foreclosures and to consider the possible legal significance of this distinction; and
(4) their unexamined assumption that any tendency of a cooperative R&D arrangement to reduce the extent of economically-inefficiently-duplicative R&D that is executed satisfies now-Article 101(3)'s requirement that covered conduct "impro[ve] the production or distribution of goods" or "promot[e] technical or economic progress."

Conclusion

Like and Unlike: U.S. Antitrust Law and E.C./E.U. Competition Law, Both as Written and as Applied

I have five children. The last two are non-identical twin girls. One (now an Associate Professor of Philosophy at MIT) took a painting class in her second term at university. The professor required the students to submit an end-of-term project—a painting 5 ft by 4 ft, to be executed with acrylic paint and entitled "Like and Unlike." My daughter painted a portrait of her twin sister and herself, sitting in the university art studio in which she worked. It now hangs in my law-school office.

"Like and Unlike." The title reminds me of U.S. antitrust law and E.C./E.U. competition law, though in this case the pair are more parent and child than twins. Nevertheless, I think it will be illuminating to conclude this study by comparing U.S. antitrust law and E.C./E.U. competition law both as written and as applied.

This Conclusion has three sections. Section 1 prepares the way for the comparisons the next two section make by reviewing (A) the definitions I have given to the various economic concepts that play an important role in the tests of illegality promulgated by U.S. antitrust legislation, the competition-law articles of the E.C./E.U. Treaty, and the European Merger Control Regulation (the EMCR), (B) the differences between subcategories of conduct that U.S. and E.C./E.U. antitrust officials should distinguish but often have not distinguished, (C) my reasons for rejecting market-oriented approaches to the analysis of any antitrust-law issue, and (D) the conceptual systems and theories I have created to analyze the competitive impact of various types of conduct, to generate tests for oligopolistic pricing (price-fixing) and predation of different sorts (*inter alia*, to establish the determinants of the profitability of such conduct for any alleged perpetrator[s]), and, relatedly, to analyze the impact of some types of conduct on the profitability of various types of monopolizing/exclusionary conduct to its possible perpetrator(s) and to the rivals of its possible perpetrator(s).

Section 2 compares post-1950 U.S. antitrust law as written with pre-EMCR and post-EMCR E.C./E.U. competition law as written. Rather than focusing separately on the U.S. and E.C./E.U. law as written on each category of business conduct covered by at least one of these jurisdictions' antitrust law, Sect. 2 will first make six points about the relationship between the tests of illegality that the relevant

R.S. Markovits, *Economics and the Interpretation and Application of U.S. and E.U. Antitrust Law*, DOI 10.1007/978-3-642-24313-4,

U.S. antitrust law and E.C./E.U. competition law promulgate and then discuss one shared conduct-coverage deficiency of U.S. antitrust law and E.C./E.U. competition law as written, three actual differences in the conduct-coverage of U.S. antitrust law and E.C./E.U. competition law, and one supposed difference between the pre-EMCR conduct-coverage of E.C./E.U. competition law as written and post-1950 U.S. antitrust law as written that I do not think exists.

Section 3 examines how the various errors that U.S. and E.C./E.U. antitrust-law implementers have made when interpreting and applying the laws they are charged with implementing have affected the relationship between U.S. antitrust law and E.C./E.U. competition law as applied. As it reveals, (1) one U.S. error has caused U.S. and E.C./E.U. antitrust law as applied to diverge less from each other than do U.S. and E.C./E.U. antitrust law as written, (2) some (which are made to an equal extent in both jurisdictions) leave U.S. and E.C./E.U. antitrust law as applied mistaken but equally different than U.S. and E.C./E.U. antitrust law as written, but (3) most of the errors in question cause U.S. and E.C./E.U. antitrust law as applied to diverge more from each other than do U.S. and E.C./E.U. antitrust law as written.

1. The Economic Definitions, Concepts, and Theories That the Study Develops and Uses

A. The Study's Operational Definitions of Economic Concepts That Play a Critical Role in the Interpretation or Application of the Tests of Illegality That U.S. Antitrust Law and E.C./E.U. Competition Law Do Promulgate and/or Have Been Interpreted to Promulgate

The study delineates and uses operational definitions for six such concepts or sets of such concepts that are either equivalent or related: two sets of such concepts that are equivalent for which, I think, the study's operational definitions are uniquely correct as a matter of law; one set of two related concepts one of whose members may not be definable in a uniquely-correct way in the E.C./E.U.-Treaty-article context in which it is relevantly used; another concept that plays different roles in the E.C./E.U. Treaty article in which it appears and in each of the two U.S. statutes to whose application it is important but whose correct operational definition is the same in all three of the Treaty articles or statutes in question; and one set of two related concepts and another individual concept for which it does not seem possible to generate non-arbitrary definitions in the relevant legal contexts.

Before discussing the concepts in question, I want to summarize without elaboration the tests of illegality that the three relevant U.S. antitrust statutes, the two relevant E.C./E.U.-Treaty articles, and the EMCR promulgate. I will begin with the U.S. statutes and then turn to the E.C./E.U. Treaty articles and the EMCR.

The U.S. Sherman Act (which covers virtually all types of business conduct) promulgates a specific-anticompetitive-intent test of illegality (which, with one qualification, prohibits business actors from engaging in conduct in which they would not have engaged had they not believed *ex ante* that it would or might reduce the absolute attractiveness of the offers against which they would have to compete when the conduct in question would not have been economically efficient in an otherwise-Pareto-perfect economy). The U.S. Clayton Act (which covers price discrimination, exclusive dealerships, full-requirements contracts, mergers, and acquisitions) prohibits the behavior it covers if that conduct lessens competition. I believe that, as a matter of law, the test of illegality promulgated by the Clayton Act should be interpreted to be qualified by an "organizational economic efficiency" defense—*i.e.*, should be read not to prohibit any covered conduct or transaction even if it did or was requisitely likely to lessen competition if it would not have had or would not have this effect but for the fact that it increased/would increase its perpetrators' "organizational economic efficiency." The Federal Trade Commission Act prohibits "unfair methods of competition." A subsequent statute makes it clear that this prohibition is properly interpreted to prohibit conduct covered by the Clayton Act if it violates the Clayton Act's lessening-competition test of illegality. The Federal Trade Commission Act's prohibition of "unfair methods of competition" has also been interpreted more straightforwardly to prohibit methods of competition that are unfair (see below) even when they do not violate the Sherman Act or the Clayton Act.

Now-Article 101 of the E.C./E.U. Treaty (which covers agreements by undertakings, decisions by associations of undertakings, and concerted practices) declares conduct it covers (which in my view is not more restrictively delimited by a list in now-Article 101(1) that is preceded in English by the words "in particular" and in other official languages by words that mean "especially" or "particularly") to be *prima facie* illegal if it has as its object preventing, restricting, or distorting competition in the common market (see Chap. 4 for an explanation of why the "*a critical* object" reading of "their object" is more persuasive than the "*an* object" reading). Now-Article 101(3) exempts conduct that would otherwise be prohibited by now-Article 101(1) if the conduct generates economic efficiencies that improve production or distribution and/or promote technical or economic progress, confers on relevant buyers a fair share of the benefit generated by the conduct for its perpetrators and the relevant buyers "combined," constitutes the least-restrictive-of-competition means of generating the economic efficiencies in question, and does not "eliminat[e] competition in respect of a substantial part of the products" directly involved. Now-Article 102 prohibits dominant firms or (by interpretation) the members of a set of collectively-dominant rivals from abusing their dominant positions—by interpretation, from committing exclusionary and/or exploitative abuses of such positions. The EMCR prohibits mergers and acquisitions and full-function joint ventures if they significantly impede effective competition.

With this as background, I can address six sets of economic concepts that play a role in the tests of illegality just delineated and/or in the way those tests have been interpreted or applied. I begin with two sets of equivalent economic concepts in this category for which I think operational definitions that are uniquely correct as a matter of law can be identified.

The first set of such economic concepts contains the concepts of "lessening competition" (U.S. Clayton Act), preventing or restricting competition (now-Article 101(1) of the E.U. Treaty), and "significantly impeding effective competition" (EMCR). I argue that, in U.S.-antitrust-law and E.C./E.U.-competition-law analyses, conduct should be said to lessen competition, to prevent or restrict competition, or to impede effective competition if and only if it imposes a net equivalent-monetary loss on the combination of the potential customers of its perpetrator or perpetrators and the potential customers of its perpetrator's or perpetrators' rivals by reducing the absolute attractiveness of the best offer they respectively receive from any inferior potential supplier. I also argue that, although the Clayton Act's "lessening competition" language has the same meaning as the EMCR's "significantly impeding effective competition" language, now-Article 101's reference to preventing or restricting competition should be correctly read as a matter of law to refer to any equivalent-monetary loss (that is collectively "appreciable") that the conduct in question would impose on relevant buyers by reducing the absolute attractiveness of the best offer they respectively receive from any inferior supplier if the conduct would generate no efficiencies and its perpetrators would take full advantage of its reducing the absolute attractiveness of the best offer relevant buyers receive from any of their respective inferior suppliers. This difference in interpretation is warranted because, if now-Article 101(1)'s language is interpreted in the way I claim the language of the Clayton Act and EMCR should as a matter of law be interpreted, now-Article 101(1) will render now-Article 101(3) irrelevant.

The second set of such concepts contains the Sherman Act's concepts of "agreements in restraint of trade," "monopolization," and "attempts to monopolize," now-Article 101(1)'s concept of conduct that has as "an object" the prevention or restriction of competition,[1619] and the concept of an "exclusionary abuse," which is one of the two types of abuses that now-Article 102 of the E.C./E.U. Treaty has been interpreted to prohibit dominant firms from committing. In my view, for conduct to involve a restraint of trade, monopolization, or an attempt to monopolize in the Sherman Act's sense of these expressions, to have as its object the prevention or restriction of competition in the Article 101(1) sense of those words, or to constitute an exclusionary abuse in the now-Article 102 sense, two conditions must be fulfilled:

[1619] This claim reflects my view that now-Article 101(1)'s reference to certain types of conduct that have as their object "preventing or restricting competition" is correctly interpreted as a matter of law to refer to covered conduct that has as *a critical* object (as opposed to as *an* object) preventing or restricting competition.

(1) its perpetrator's or perpetrators' *ex ante* perception that it was profitable must have been critically affected by their belief that it would or might reduce the absolute attractiveness of the offers against which it or they would have to compete, and
(2) the conduct must have been economically inefficient in an otherwise-Pareto-perfect economy.

In other words, for conduct to violate the Sherman Act's test of illegality, to violate the "object of preventing or restricting competition" branch of now-Article 101(1)'s test of *prima facie* illegality, or to constitute an exclusionary abuse under now-Article 102, its perpetrator-perceived tendency to reduce the absolute attractiveness of the offers against which the perpetrator(s) would have to compete must have rendered it *ex ante* profitable in the perpetrator's or perpetrators' eyes despite the fact that, in an otherwise-Pareto-perfect world, it would have been *ex ante* economically inefficient.

The third set of economic concepts the study defines that play a role in the tests of illegality that U.S. antitrust law and E.C./E.U. competition law either do promulgate or have been interpreted to promulgate has two related members—conduct that constitutes an "unfair method of competition" (prohibited by Section 5 of the U.S. Federal Trade Commission Act) and conduct that has the object or effect of "distorting competition" (which now-Article 101(1) declares to be *prima facie* illegal if the conduct itself is covered by the Article). At this juncture, I am not concerned with the part of the "interpreted" meaning of "unfair methods of competition" that covers all conduct that violates the Clayton Act's qualified lessening-competition test of illegality and/or the Sherman Act's specific-anticompetitive-intent test of illegality. For current purposes, the relevant point is that the expression "unfair methods of competition" has another, more straightforward meaning (which U.S. officials have also recognized)—*viz.*, methods of competition that attempt to give their practitioners a competitive advantage that is not based on the conduct's making the practitioner allocatively-better-placed than its disadvantaged rivals to supply the buyer in question or on their enabling relevant buyers to assess more accurately the relative value to them of the practitioner's product and its rivals' products and/or the relative cost to them of patronizing the practitioner and its rivals (methods of competition that attempt to persuade one or more buyers that the practitioner's product has a higher value to the buyer in question relative to the value to that buyer of the disadvantaged rival's product than it does and/or that the total cost to the buyer in question of buying and using the practitioner's product relative to the total cost to that buyer of buying and using the disadvantaged rival's product is lower than it actually is). The list of conduct that would constitute a method of competition that was "unfair" in this straightforward sense therefore includes (1) placing inaccurate or misleading advertising about one's product, (2) passing off one's product as the product of another firm that produces a product that is or is perceived to be a higher-quality product, (3) unjustifiably disparaging a rival's product, relatedly (4) promulgating industry quality-standards for products that one's own product passes and a target-rival's product does not (standards that create a false impression of the superiority of one's own product to the target-rival's product), (5) claiming that paid-for endorsements were disinterested endorsements, (6) making it unnecessarily difficult for buyers to assess the full cost of purchasing one's product by placing relevant terms and conditions of sale in unnecessarily-long written contracts, expressing relevant terms in language that is unnecessarily difficult to understand, and/or using fine print in the contract of sale, and/or, possibly, failing to point out that some of the lifetime costs of consuming the product in question (say, the cost of service and replacement parts) are higher than relevant buyers would expect, (7) exaggerating the full cost of purchasing a rival's product, *etc*. All such conduct is unfair because it does not involve competition on the economic-efficiency merits. I should add that conduct that is "unfair" in the straightforward sense just specified can reduce economic efficiency and unfairly harm its target even if it does not violate the Sherman Act's test of illegality—*i.e.*, even if it has no tendency to reduce the objective absolute attractiveness of the offers its perpetrator(s) will have to face in the future by causing the target to exit and/or deterring a new entry.

The concept in E.C./E.U. competition law that is consequentially related to the concept of an "unfair method of competition" is the Article 101(1) concept of "distorting competition." Conduct that "distorts competition" is consequentially related to conduct that is "an unfair method of competition" in the straightforward sense of that expression because the straightforward reading of "distorting competition" is enabling a seller that is not privately-best-placed (and would not be allocatively-best-placed in an otherwise-Pareto-perfect economy) to make a sale to a particular buyer in one or two ways: (1) by causing the seller in question's buyer-perceived buyer preference advantage (disadvantage) over the relevant buyer's actual privately-best-placed supplier to be higher than the seller's actual buyer preference advantage (smaller than its actual buyer preference disadvantage) is and/or (2) by causing the relevant buyer to overestimate the cost-savings it can secure by patronizing (underestimate the extra cost it would have to incur to patronize) the practitioner rather than the firm that was the buyer's actual privately-best-placed supplier. Although I can see no alternative to this straightforward reading of the "distorting competition" text of now-Article 101(1), I must admit that it is disfavored (if only slightly, given that [all things considered] the list to be referenced should be deemed illustrative rather than comprehensive) by the fact that the sentence that includes the words "distortion of competition" concludes with a list of the specific types of conduct that can have as their object or effect distorting (or preventing or restricting) competition that (1) is preceded in English by the words "in particular" and (2) includes none of the specific types of conduct that can "distort competition" in the "straightforward" sense in which I have just defined this concept.[1620] The fourth economic concept I want to consider at this juncture is the concept of "a business-conduct-generated increase in economic efficiency" as it relates to the legality of the economic-efficiency-generating conduct under the various tests of illegality promulgated by U.S. antitrust law and E.C./E.U. competition law. I want to make three comments or sets of comments about such increases in economic efficiency.

The first is simply the definition of "an increase in economic efficiency. In my usage, a natural event, non-government decision, or government decision increases economic efficiency if the equivalent-monetary gains it confers on its beneficiaries exceed the equivalent-dollar losses it inflicts on its victims.

The second is a set of comments that defines and exemplifies two broad categories of increases in economic efficiency that are important to distinguish because the legal significance of the fact that conduct generates increases in economic efficiency in one of these categories is quite different from the legal significance of the fact that conduct generates increases in economic efficiency in the other of these broad categories. The one category of increases in economic efficiency includes only those that result from the conduct's increasing the organizational economic efficiency of one or more of its perpetrators—*i.e.*, its increasing the allocative proficiency with which the perpetrator(s) run its/their business(es). Conduct can increase its perpetrator's or perpetrators' organizational economic efficiency (1) by enabling the perpetrator(s) to reduce the fixed, average variable, or marginal allocative costs it/they must generate to finance, produce, promote,

[1620] I should admit that, if the words "distort competition" stood alone, it might be appropriate to say that a horizontal merger in an individualized-pricing "market" that enables its perpetrators to raise the prices they charge some buyers (those for whose patronage they were either exclusively-equal-best-placed or respectively uniquely-best-placed and uniquely-second-placed pre-merger) *distorts competition*. In particular, such mergers might be said to distort competition for the patronage of buyers in relation to which the merged firm enjoys a lower BCA than it enjoys in relation to the buyers to which I have just referred by critically raising the contextual marginal costs the merged firm must incur to charge the latter buyers the prices it would have to charge them to secure their patronage above the contextual marginal cost that the merger partner that had a BCA in relation to those buyers pre-merger had to charge to secure their patronage and thereby creating a situation in which the merged firm does not supply the buyers in question despite the fact that it is allocatively-best-placed to supply them (*i.e.*, by making the merged firm a worse-than-privately-best-placed supplier of those buyers despite the fact that it is allocatively-best-placed to supply them by increasing critically the distorting contextual marginal costs the merged firm has to incur to supply them above the contextual marginal costs its relevant antecedent had to incur to supply them pre-merger). The same argument could also be used to demonstrate that competition was distorted by a predatory act/price-fix that makes a predator/price-fixer that was allocatively-best-placed to supply some buyer(s) and that would otherwise have been privately-best-placed to supply the buyer(s) in question worse-than-privately-best-placed to supply it/them by raising the prices that the predator/price-fixer charged other buyers and hence the contextual marginal costs it would have to incur to charge a given lower price to the buyer(s) in question. If conduct that "distorts competition" is interpreted to include conduct that cause sales to be made by firms that are allocatively-worse-placed for the above contextual-marginal-cost-related reason, the list that follows "in particular" in now-Article 101(1) would include types of conduct that could distort competition (*e.g.*, agreements to fix selling prices, limit production, share markets).

and/or marginal allocative costs it/they must generate to finance, produce, promote, and/or distribute the pre-conduct outputs of their pre-conduct set of products, (2) by enabling the perpetrator(s) to substitute a product variant whose supply is more allocatively efficient (and profitable) for one whose supply is less allocatively efficient (and profitable) because the new product's demand-curve/marginal-allocative-cost-curve combination is allocatively superior to the old product's combination without creating a QV investment, (3) by enabling the perpetrator(s) to make one or more-allocatively-efficient (and more-profitable) QV-investments or PPR-project investments than they otherwise could have made by increasing the allocative proficiency with which they can execute particular QV-investment or PPR projects or by increasing their ability to devise different, more-allocatively-efficient (and more-profitable) QV-investment or PPR projects, perhaps (4) by enabling two or more perpetrators to profit by making one QV investment or one PPR project that would be profitable in itself when they would have made none absent the conduct in question because any perpetrator's decision to make one such investment would have led one or more other perpetrators to make a QV investment when the multiple investments that would result would leave all of them worse-off, and/or perhaps (5) by enabling two or more perpetrators to increase the economic efficiency as well as the profitability of their QV investments or PPR projects by facilitating their making multiple investments that are less-economically-inefficiently (and less-jointly-unprofitably) duplicative.

The other category of increases in economic efficiency that conduct can generate covers increases in economic efficiency that conduct can yield without increasing the allocative proficiency with which the perpetrator(s) operate their businesses. This category includes increases in economic efficiency that conduct can generate by decreasing (1) the amount of unit-output to unit-output (UO-to-UO) misallocation the economy generates because, given the amount of resources it devotes to producing units of extant products, it allocates too many resources from the perspective of economic efficiency to the production of some products relative to the amount it allocates to the production of other products, (2) the amount of QV-investment to QV-investment (QV-to-QV) misallocation the economy generates because (A) given the amount of resources it devotes to creating QV investments, it allocates too many resources from the perspective of economic efficiency to creating QV investments in some areas of product-space relative to the amount it allocates to creating QV investments in other areas of product-space and/or (B) given the amount of resources it devotes to creating QV investments in some (arbitrarily-designated) area of product-space, the set of QV-investment projects in the area of product-space is less economically efficient because allocatively-inefficiently-duplicative than the set that could have been executed with the amount of resources in question, (3) the amount of PPR-to-PPR misallocation the economy generates because (A) given the amount of resources it devotes to executing PPR projects, it allocates too many resources from the perspective of economic efficiency to PPR in some areas of product-space relative to the amount it devotes to

PPR in other areas of product-space and/or (B) given the amount of resources it devotes to PPR in some (arbitrarily-designated) area of product-space, the set of PPR projects in that area of product-space is less economically efficient because allocatively-inefficiently-duplicative than the set that could have been executed with the amount of resources in question, and/or (4) the amount of total-UO/total-QV/total-PPR misallocation the economy generates because it allocates resources in economically-inefficient proportions to UO-production, QV-investment-creation, and PPR-execution. (I acknowledge that some of the increases in economic efficiency that are covered by item (4) in this paragraph's list are also covered by item (4) in the preceding paragraph's list are also covered by item (4) in the preceding paragraph's list and that some of the increases in economic efficiency that are covered by items (2)(B) and (3)(B) in this paragraph's list are also covered by item (5) in the preceding paragraph's list: that is why I inserted the word "perhaps" before item (4) and before item (5) in the preceding paragraph's list of organizational economic efficiencies.)

The third set of comments I want to make about "business-conduct-generated increases in economic efficiency" relate to the respective relevance of organizational-allocative-efficiency-connected and non-organizational-efficiency-connected increases in economic efficiency to the legality of the conduct that generated them under various U.S. antitrust laws and E.C./EU. competition-law provisions. I start with the relevance of these two broad categories of increases in economic efficiency to the legality of conduct under a specific-anticompetitive-intent test of illegality (the Sherman Act test of illegality, the object-branch of Article 101(1)'s test of illegality, and the exclusionary-abuse-branch of Article 102's test of illegality). Because the perpetrator(s) of conduct gain Sherman-Act-licit profits from the organizational economic efficiencies that conduct generates, any increase in economic efficiency that conduct generates because it increases the organizational economic efficiency of one or more of its perpetrators favors the conclusion that the conduct does not manifest specific anticompetitive intent. (Chapter 12 analyzes in detail the determinants of the ratio of the organizational economic efficiencies conduct generates to the amount of Sherman-Act-licit profits it yields on such efficiencies' account.) However, because the perpetrators of conduct gain no profits from any tendency it has to increase economic efficiency for reasons that are unrelated to the conduct's increasing one of more of their organizational economic efficiency, any increase in economic efficiency conduct generates without increasing the organizational economic efficiency of its perpetrators has no bearing on whether the conduct manifests the specific anticompetitive intent of its perpetrator(s).

I turn to whether the two broad categories of increases in economic efficiency I have distinguished respectively contain more-specific types of increases in economic efficiency whose generation Article 101(3) proclaims will form the basis for an exemption from Article 101(1) if various other conditions are satisfied. Some but not all of the various types of organizational economic efficiencies that conduct can generate belong to the set of efficiencies whose generation may enable the perpetrators of Article 101-covered conduct to obtain an Article 101(3) exemption. Thus, Article 101(3) counts as a relevant efficiency organizational economic efficiencies that result in better products being created or allocatively-cheaper production processes being discovered since such effects would constitute technical or economic progress. The organizational economic efficiencies that a joint venture (or merger or acquisition) generates by enabling the parents to reduce the extent to which their research is unprofitably and economic-inefficiently duplicative may not count as an Article 101(3) efficiency because the shift to the more profitable and more-allocatively-efficient set of research projects the conduct effectuates may reduce technical progress by reducing the quantity of resources the perpetrators allocate to research. (Admittedly, if "economic progress" is defined to include "increases in economic efficiency," all such increases in organizational economic efficiency will satisfy Article 101(3)'s efficiency requirement.) Similarly, unless economic progress is defined to include *all* increases in economic efficiency, the only non-organizational-economic-efficiency economic efficiencies that conduct can generate that would satisfy Article 101(3)'s efficiency requirement (because they would satisfy its "technological progress" criterion) would be reductions in QV-to-QV misallocation among QV-investment projects that are designed to yield technologically-innovative products, reductions in PPR-to-PPR misallocation reductions in PPR-to-(technologically-innovation QV) or (technologically-innovation QV)-to-PPR misallocation, reductions in PPR-to-UO misallocation, and reductions in (technologically-innovation QV)-to-UO misallocation—*i.e.*, the Article 101(3) efficiency condition would not be satisfied by conduct's tendency to reduce UO-to-UO misallocation, (non-innovative QV)-to-(non-innovative QV) misallocation, or UO-to-(non-innovative QV) or (non-innovative QV)-to-UO misallocation.

I address next the relevance of the two categories of increases in economic efficiency I have distinguished to whether the conduct that generates them violates the lessening-competition test of *prima facie* illegality (the basic Clayton Act test of *prima facie* illegality, an element of the effect-branch of Articles 101(1)'s test of illegality, and the EMCR's test of illegality). Because any increase in organizational economic efficiency that conduct generates will normally confer a net equivalent-monetary gain on the customers of the perpetrator(s) and the customers of the rivals of the perpetrator(s) combined, the fact that covered conduct generates organizational economic efficiencies will normally favor its legality under a lessening-competition test by reducing the probability that the conduct will impose a net (or more than a *de minimis* net) equivalent-monetary loss on the customers of the perpetrator(s) and the customers of the rivals of the perpetrator(s) "combined." (Chapter 12 analyzes in detail the determinants of the ratio of the organizational economic efficiencies conduct generates to the effect those efficiencies have on the net equivalent-monetary impact of the conduct in question on Clayton-Act-relevant buyers.) However, because any increases in economic efficiency that conduct generates without raising the organizational economic efficiency of its perpetrator(s) will have no "direct" bearing on the conduct's net equivalent-monetary impact on Clayton-Act-relevant buyers, any increase in economic efficiency that conduct generates without raising the organizational economic efficiency of its perpetrator(s) will have no "direct" bearing on its legality under a lessening-competition test of illegality. Thus, although the tendency of covered conduct to increase the amount of resources devoted to PPR in the relevant area of product-space confers a net equivalent-monetary gain on Clayton-Act-relevant buyers, the fact that the associated increase in PPR decreases PPR-to-QV/QV-to-PPR misallocation for reasons that THE WELFARE ECONOMICS OF ANTITRUST POLICY AND U.S. AND E.U. ANTITRUST LAW will explain is irrelevant to the equivalent-monetary impact on the tendency in question on Clayton-Act-relevant buyers and hence to the legality of the underlying conduct under a lessening-competition test of illegality.

I consider last the relevance of the two categories of increases in economic efficiency that conduct can generate that I have distinguished to whether conduct qualifies for the organization-economic-efficiency defense I claim it is correct as a matter of law to read into the Clayton Act. As the name of that defense should make obvious, only conduct-generated increases in organizational economic efficiency can form the basis of this defense, which should not be surprising given the connection between this defense and the specific-anticompetitive-intent test of illegality.

The fifth set of relevant economic concepts that I want to discuss contains the now-Article 102 concept of a "dominant position" and the concept of a firm's economic ("market" or "monopoly") power, which is used by both U.S. and E.C./E.U. officials when applying the bodies of antitrust and competition law they are respectively charged with implementing. Chapter 8 explains the complexities of those concepts and the reasons why they cannot be defined non-arbitrarily in the relevant legal context:

(1) a firm's dominance or market power is a function of both its ability to obtain prices above its marginal costs for the products it sells in a relevant area of product-space and its ability to secure supernormal profits on its QV investments in the relevant area of product-space;
(2) there is no non-arbitrary way to define the relevant area of product-space (see Chap. 6 and below);
(3) difficult interpretive problems are created by the fact that a part of a firm's ability to charge prices above its marginal costs and earn supernormal profits in any area of product-space is traceable not in one sense to its own power but to the exercised economic power of its rivals;
(4) even if one ignores the preceding two points, (A) there is no non-arbitrary way to determine whether a firm's dominance or market power over price should be measured by (P–MC), ([P–MC]/P), or ([P–MC]/MC) (where I am assuming that the P figures in question include the average per-unit magnitude of any lump-sum fee that is charged); (B) there is no non-arbitrary way to determine whether a firm's dominance or market power over QV investment should be determined by its total supernormal profits in the relevant area of

product-space, its average supernormal profit-rate on its QV investments in the relevant area of product-space, or its highest supernormal profit-rate on any QV investment it owns in the relevant area of product-space; and (C) there is no non-arbitrary way to define a firm's total dominance or market power as a function of its market power over price and its market power over QV investment; and

(5) even if one concludes that a firm's monopoly power over price and QV investment should not be defined to reflect its rivals' powers over price and QV investment—*e.g.*, even if one concludes that an individualized pricer's monopoly power over price relates solely to its BCAs and that a firm's monopoly power over QV investment relates solely to the difference between the Π_D, R, and S barriers and the monopolistic QV-investment incentives and disincentives it and its relevant rivals face, the three reasons delineated in item (4) of this list apply *mutatis mutandis* to the concept of a firm's monopoly power—*i.e.*, provide equally-forceful grounds for concluding that a firm's monopoly power in a market could not be defined non-arbitrarily even if markets could be defined non-arbitrarily.

The sixth and final concept whose definition I want to discuss at this juncture is the concept of a market. As Chap. 6 demonstrates, regardless of whether concrete market definitions or protocols for defining markets are to be evaluated by using ideal-type or functional criteria (regardless of whether one is seeking to identify so-called classical markets or so-called antitrust markets), there is no non-arbitrary way to define the concept of a market. Thus, attempts to define classical markets—*i.e.*, markets that satisfy certain ideal-type assumptions about the competitiveness of products placed inside a given market (ideally, that all such products are highly and equally competitive) and the difference between the competitiveness of products placed in the same market and products placed in different markets (ideally, that all pairs of products placed in the same market are far more competitive with each other than any product in that market is with any product placed in a different market)—confront at least the following issues that cannot be resolved non-arbitrarily that I will assert are critical in the sense that the way in which they are resolved will affect the set of market definitions that are deemed best by ideal standards:

(1) there is no non-arbitrary way to define the competitiveness of two products;
(2) even if there were a non-arbitrary way to define the competitiveness of two products, there would be no non-arbitrary way to define the inequality of the competitiveness of the different pairs of products placed in a given market;
(3) even if there were a non-arbitrary way to define the competitiveness of two products, there would be no non-arbitrary way to define the extent to which the condition that any pair of products placed in a given market must be more competitive than any product in that market is with any product placed in a different market would be satisfied if any particular set of market definitions were used; and

(4) when no set of market definitions is dominant—*i.e.*, when some sets do better at satisfying the "all market-insiders are highly competitive" condition, some do better at satisfying the "all market-insiders are equally competitive" condition, and some do better at satisfying the "all market-insiders are more competitive with any other market-insider than any market-insider is with any market-outsider" condition, there is no non-arbitrary way of ranking the different sets of market definitions (or the protocols that generate them).

One can also not define *antitrust* markets non-arbitrarily. In particular, attempts to identify the market definitions whose use in an antitrust-law decision-protocol would best promote the goals of the antitrust law of the jurisdiction in question are doomed to failure for at least three reasons:

(1) all market-oriented approaches to antitrust-law analysis are cost-ineffective—achieve the remarkable double of increasing cost while decreasing accuracy—because the non-market-aggregated data one uses to define a market have more predictive power than do the market-aggregated figures one can calculate after having gone through the extraordinarily-expensive process of defining relevant markets;
(2) even on the unrealistic assumption that the individuals who vote for antitrust legislation or ratify treaties that contain antitrust provisions had a well-thought-through maximand or objective function (knew their goals and the way in which they should be traded off against each other), it seems unlikely that one will be able (A) to develop correct protocols for ascertaining the objective function of the multi-member groups that pass antitrust laws or ratify treaties that contain antitrust provisions and (B) to determine the facts that any such protocol requires to be ascertained; and
(3) even if one assumes that the promulgators'/ratifiers' objective functions are ascertainable, the relevant "goal" for applying the law may be to maximize the extent to which the application has secured the rights of parties in associated litigations to have the relevant cases decided correctly as a matter of law and (perhaps) the interests of others in profiting from lawful behavior and not suffering the harm that illegal conduct would inflict on them, and there may be no non-arbitrary way to decide whether that "goal" is best served by a decision-protocol that minimizes the number of cases decided wrongly or one that minimizes the number of cases decided wrongly weighted by the seriousness of the errors made, and, if the seriousness of the relevant errors is to be taken into account, there may be no non-arbitrary way to define the seriousness of such errors (to decide the "weight" that should be given to [A] the losses suffered by the losing parties in incorrectly-decided cases, [B] the gains secured by the winning parties in incorrectly-decided cases, [C] the gains secured and losses suffered respectively by the beneficiaries and victims of the illegal behavior induced by false-negative findings on the illegality issue, [D] the gains secured and losses suffered respectively by the beneficiaries and victims of the deterrence -effects of false-positive findings of illegality, *etc.*).

B. The Study's Subdivision of Two Categories of Conduct—Coordinated Behavior and Refusals to Deal—That U.S. and E.C./E.U. Officials Do Not Always Subdivide, Though It Is Important to Do So for Both Legal and Policy Reasons

(1) The Study's Subdivision of Coordinated Conduct

Firms can correctly be said to "coordinate" their conduct when each makes its decision depend on the decision that the others will make in response to its decision and/or on the decisions the others have already made (if such past decisions will influence the future choices that the relevant others will make). For legal (and policy) reasons, it is important to distinguish between this kind of simple, two-step coordination and the more complex kind of three-step coordination that I denominate oligopolistic coordination. In my terminology, a behavior-sequence is said to manifest oligopolistic coordination (interaction) if the decision that the behavior-sequence initiator makes is influenced by its realization that its respondents know that it can react to their responses. The study further distinguishes two subcategories of oligopolistic interactions (whose legality is critically different under U.S. and E.C./E.U. law and which also are somewhat important to distinguish for policy reasons). The relevant distinction focuses on the reason why the initiator believed that the respondents would anticipate that the initiator would or might react to their responses by rewarding their cooperation and/or punishing their non-cooperation:

(1) if the initiator believed that the respondents would expect it to react to one or more of the responses they might make because the reactions in question would be inherently profitable for it to make, the oligopolistic interaction in question is said to be "natural," and
(2) if the initiator believed that the respondents would expect it to react to one or more of the responses they might make in ways that were inherently unprofitable for the initiator because the initiator had somehow communicated to the respondents its intention to punish their non-cooperation and/or reward their cooperation despite the fact that the punishing or rewarding moves in question were inherently unprofitable for the initiator (*i.e.*, had somehow communicated anticompetitive threats and/or promises to the respondents) in order to increase its profits by inducing the respondent(s) and others to cooperate with it in the future, the oligopolistic interaction is said to be "contrived."

The distinction between contrived and natural oligopolistic conduct is critical under U.S. law, which prohibits only contrived oligopolistic conduct. Article 101 of E.C./E.U. law covers natural oligopolistic conduct as a concentration. However, Articles 101 does not cover contrivance that is practiced by an individual initiator exclusively by making (and possibly carrying out) threats of retaliation. This feature of Article 101 is important because Article 102's prohibition of all variants of contrived oligopolistic conduct as exclusionary abuses applies to the behavior of only those firms that are individually dominant or members of a collectively-dominant set of rivals.

(2) The Study's Subdivision of Refusals to Deal

In many cases, U.S. and E.C./E.U. officials have also failed to distinguish two subcategories of refusals to deal: predatory refusals to deal (which, by definition, are inherently unprofitable) and inherently-profitable (non-predatory) refusals to deal. The distinction between predatory and non-predatory refusals to deal is critical for the legality of the refusal both under the Sherman Act (where it does tend to be recognized) and under now-Article 102 of the E.C./E.U. Treaty (where it is less likely to be recognized).

C. The Study's Critique of Market-Oriented Approaches to Antitrust-Law-Relevant Economic Issues

The study's critique of market-oriented approaches to antitrust-law analysis is based on two general claims that apply to such analyses of *any type* of business conduct and a series of more specific claims that relate to the accuracy and cost-effectiveness of specific market-oriented approaches to the analysis of *specific kinds* of business conduct. This section outlines both of these categories of critique.

(1) The Study's General Critique of Market-Oriented Approaches to Antitrust-Law-Relevant Economic Issues

The two general claims (which were made in essence most recently in Sect. 1A of this Conclusion) are:

(1) market-oriented analyses of antitrust-law-relevant issues are inherently arbitrary because the market definitions on which they are based are inherently arbitrary, and
(2) market-oriented analyses of antitrust-law-relevant issues would be less-cost-effective than one or more non-market-oriented approaches to such issues even if markets could be defined non-arbitrarily *inter alia* because (A) the process of moving from the non-market-aggregated data one uses to define the relevant market(s) to the market definition(s) in question is extremely expensive and (B) the non-market-aggregated data one uses to define markets (*e.g.*, data on how well-placed different pairs of products are to secure the patronage of particular buyers) have more relevant predictive power for any legally-relevant

factual issue than data on any market-aggregated parameter one could define (*e.g.*, on merger-partner market shares and seller-side concentration or on post-merger-HHI and merger-generated increase-in-HHI figures) could have.

(2) The Study's Critique of Market-Oriented Approaches to the Analysis of Specific-Conduct-Related Antitrust-Law-Relevant Economic Issues

(A) The Competitive Impact of Horizontal Mergers and Acquisitions

I will summarize three of the study's critiques of the market-oriented approach to this issue. The first is that, even if horizontal mergers and acquisitions (hereinafter horizontal mergers) never generated static economic efficiencies, one could not infer their impact on price competition acceptably accurately from market-aggregated data—more particularly, from the merger partners' market shares and the pre-merger concentration of the market in question (or from the post-merger HHI of the market and the merger-generated increase in the market's HHI)—*inter alia* because one cannot determine from two firms' shares of the sales made in a given market

(1) how frequently they are exclusively-equal-best-placed to secure the patronage of given buyers in that market,
(2) in those cases in which they are the only two best-placed firms, the average amount by which they are better-placed than the third-placed supplier of the buyer in question,
(3) how frequently they are respectively uniquely-best-placed and uniquely-second-placed to supply given buyers, and
(4) in those cases in which they are respectively uniquely-best-placed and uniquely-second-placed, the amount by which the second-placed merger partner is better-placed than the third-placed supplier of the buyer in question.

The second is that, even if horizontal mergers never generated dynamic efficiencies (which affect the barriers to expansion they face), one could not infer the impact of a horizontal merger on QV-investment competition acceptably accurately from market-aggregated data because one cannot tell from merger-partner market-share figures and traditional market-concentration figures (or from post-merger HHI figures and merger-generated increase-in-HHI figures) whether pre-merger one (both) of the merger partners was (were) the best-placed potential expander(s) in that market, whether potential competition was effective in that market, or the extent to which the resulting firm could reduce the amount by which any additional QV investment it made in the relevant market would reduce its pre-existing projects' profit yields by adjusting the product-space location of the new QV investment it executed.

The third is that, even if the first two problems could be ignored, one could not infer the competitive impact of a horizontal merger from the combination of (1) market-aggregated data on merger-partner market shares and market concentration (post-merger HHIs and merger-generated increases-in-HHIs) and (2) non-market-aggregated data on the magnitude and nature of the static and dynamic efficiencies the merger would generate because, for the following two reasons, the market-aggregated data in question would not enable an analyst to predict the competitive impact of merger-generated economic efficiencies of given kinds and magnitudes:

(1) the equivalent-monetary gains that the static marginal (say, marginal-cost) economic efficiencies a merger generates will confer on relevant buyers depends not just on the magnitude and kind of the economic efficiencies in question but also on the frequencies with which at least one of the merger partners was either second-placed or close-to-second-placed to secure the patronage of buyers that neither merger partner was best-placed to supply, and one cannot predict these frequencies from the frequencies with which the merger partners were best-placed (their market shares) and the concentration of the market in question, and
(2) the equivalent-dollar gains that the dynamic efficiencies that a horizontal merger generates will confer on relevant buyers depends not only on the magnitude of those economic efficiencies but also on whether potential competition was effective in the relevant area of product-space and on the extent to which the merger partner that was better-placed to expand pre-merger was worse-placed to expand than the best-placed potential expander in the relevant area of product-space pre-merger, and one cannot infer either of these facts from standard market-share and market-concentration data (or data on post-merger HHIs and the merger-generated increase in HHIs), though admittedly one could infer these facts from a combination of (A) "market"-aggregated data on barriers to entry, barriers to expansion, and monopolistic and natural oligopolistic QV-investment incentives/disincentives and (B) an appropriate account of the determinants of the intensity of QV-investment competition in any area of product-space and the way(s) in which they interact to determine the intensity of such competition.

(B) Market-Oriented Approaches to the Analysis of the Profitability of Contrived Oligopolistic Pricing

The conventional market-oriented approach to the profitability of what I call contrived oligopolistic pricing claims that the profitability of a firm's practicing contrived oligopolistic pricing increases primarily with the concentration of the seller-side of the market in question and the market share of the relevant firm. Obviously, one of my objections to this and any other market-oriented approach to predicting the profitability of contrived oligopolistic pricing for a particular firm is that all such approaches assume incorrectly that the relevant market can be defined non-arbitrarily. The preceding objection applies regardless of whether prices are set on an individualized or across-the-board basis by the seller in question.

The other objections I have to the market-oriented approach to analyzing the profitability of contrived oligopolistic pricing for a firm varies to some extent with whether it engages in individualized or across-the-board pricing. To save space, I will confine myself to listing the ten most important objections I have to this approach in cases in which the relevant seller is setting individualized prices:

(1) even if, contrary to fact, one could predict the number of sellers in a market from a particular inside-seller's market share or the market's seller-concentration however defined, one could not predict from the firm's market share and the relevant market's seller-concentration the number of rivals that would find it inherently profitable to beat a firm's contrived oligopolistic price to a buyer the firm was privately-best-placed to supply (*i.e.*, profitable assuming no reciprocation to the relevant rival's cooperation or retaliation against its non-cooperation) because (A) the average percentage of the sellers in any given market that are second-placed or close-to-second-placed to supply buyers in that market differs substantially from market to market and (B) in any given market, the average percentage of in-market sellers that are second-placed or close-to-second-placed to supply the buyers that particular in-market sellers are best-placed to supply often varies substantially from in-market seller to in-market seller: the number of rivals that would find undercutting a given firm's contrived oligopolistic price to a particular buyer inherently profitable affects both the cost the firm would have to incur to communicate the anticompetitive threats and/or promises it must communicate to contrive an oligopolistic price (by affecting the number of rivals to which it must make such communications) and the cost the firm would have to incur to identify its actual undercutter if its contrived oligopolistic price was beaten (by affecting the number of potential undercutters);

(2) data on a firm's market share and the relevant market's seller-side concentration also has no bearing on whether the firm can reduce the mechanical and legal cost of communicating the anticompetitive threats and offers whose communication contrived oligopolistic pricing entails by communicating them simply by charging contrived oligopolistic prices—*i.e.*, has no bearing on such determinants of the ability of firms to do so as (A) its reputation for estimating its highest non-oligopolistic price and natural oligopolistic margin accurately and (B) its reputation for engaging in contrivance;

(3) somewhat relatedly, a firm's market share and the concentration of the market in which it is operating are also poor indicators of its reputation among its rivals for carrying out its contrived oligopolistic threats and promises, which will affect the profitability of its engaging in contrivance by affecting the probability that its rivals will undercut its contrived oligopolistic prices;

(4) somewhat relatedly again, a firm's market share and the relevant market's seller-concentration are also poor predictors of the attention that the antitrust authorities are paying to its pricing behavior, the likelihood they will challenge it (given the quality and quantity of the other evidence at their disposal),

the penalties that will be imposed on the firm and its officials if the firm loses or decides to settle an associated government case, and the damages the firm will have to pay and expenses it will have to incur as a result of any claims made by its antitrust victims;

(5) for four reasons, a firm's market share is a poor predictor of its ability to infer the fact that a rival has undercut its contrived oligopolistic price from circumstantial evidence relating to the percentage of sales to its own former customers it retained relative to the percentage of such sales it usually retains, the percentage of the sales its rivals previously made to established buyers that it captures relative to the percentage of such sales it usually captures, and the percentage of the sales to new buyers in the relevant area of product-space it secures relative to the percentage of such sales it usually makes: (A) although, *ceteris paribus*, this ability increases with the number of buyers in each of the above three categories and a firm's market share is positively correlated with the number of buyers in the market in which the seller operates to which it has made sales in the past, the variation in the number of buyers in different markets implies that, cross-markets, one can tell little about the relative number of buyers that sellers in different markets will have historically supplied from those sellers' relative market shares in the different markets in which they are operating, (B) even if all markets had the same number of buyers, firms' market shares would be inversely related to the number of buyers their rivals formerly supplied, (C) a firm's market share is either uncorrelated or extremely weakly correlated with the number of new buyers in the market in which it is operating, (D) a firm's market share does not bear on the extent to which its market share varies through time or its ability to identify and measure the factors other than variations in its rivals' undercutting its prices that cause its market share to vary through time;

(6) the concentration of the seller-side of the market in which it is operating has no bearing on its ability to detect the fact that it has been undercut by an inferior from the kinds of circumstantial evidence listed after (5);

(7) a firm's market share and its market's concentration are poor predictors of the extent to which the firm can confer benefits on its potential undercutters by reciprocating to their cooperation by not undercutting the contrived oligopolistic prices they charge their own customers when it would have been inherently profitable for the firm in question to undercut those prices—is not a good predictor of either (A) the frequency with which the firm in question is uniquely-second-placed to obtain the patronage of buyers its potential undercutters are best-placed to supply (both because there is no obvious positive correlation between the frequency with which a firm is best-placed and the frequency with which it is uniquely-second-placed and because there is no obvious positive correlation between the frequency with which firm *X*2 is or is close to being the second-placed supplier of buyers that firm X1 is best-placed to supply and the frequency with which firm X1 is uniquely-second-placed to obtain the patronage of buyers that firm *X*2 is uniquely-best-placed

to supply) or (B) the average amount by which the firm in question is better-placed than the third-placed supplier of buyers the firm in question is second-placed to supply and its respective potential undercutters are uniquely-best-placed to supply;

(8) a firm's market share and its market's concentration are poor predictors of the cost the firm would have to incur to inflict enough monetary losses on an undercutting rival (which it identified as its undercutter) to render the undercutter's undercutting sufficiently unprofitable (given any reciprocation rewards the firm withholds from the undercutter) to deter the undercutter and its future potential counterparts from undercutting the firm in the future (where the magnitude of the losses that will be sufficient for this purpose depends on the profits the undercutting would have given the undercutter had it not elicited a strategic response, the number that future potential undercutters assign to the probability that the firm will detect their future undercutting and identify them as the undercutter, the extent to which the potential undercutters in question are risk averse, and the rate at which the potential future undercutters discount future losses) because a firm's market share and the relevant market's seller-concentration are poor predictors of the determinants of those costs (given the magnitude of the oligopolistic margins the seller in question was trying to contrive)—*viz.*, the frequency with which the potential contriver's individual potential undercutters were second-placed to secure the patronage of buyers to which the contriver was charging contrived oligopolistic prices or were worse-than-second-placed to supply such buyers by an amount that was smaller than the contrived oligopolistic margin the contriver was attempting to secure, the frequency with which the contriver was second-placed or close-to-second-placed to secure the patronage of buyers its individual potential undercutters were uniquely-best-placed to supply, the average magnitude of the (OCA + NOM)s the firm's potential undercutters enjoyed in their relations with buyers they were respectively uniquely-best-placed to supply and the potential contriver was uniquely-second-placed, equal-second-placed, or close-to-second-placed to supply;

(9) a firm's market share and the seller-concentration of the market in which it is operating is also a poor predictor of the safe profits the firm must put at risk to contrive any oligopolistic margin—its (OCA + NOM)s—which are inversely related to the profitability of its practicing contrived oligopolistic pricing; and

(10) a firm's market share and the seller-concentration of the market in which it might be practicing contrived oligopolistic pricing are either totally uncorrelated or extremely weakly positively correlated with the amount of sales the firm is best-placed to make outside the market in question—*i.e.*, with the extent to which there are organization-wide economies of scale in its practicing contrived oligopolistic pricing (in fact, all kinds of contrivance and predation) (with the magnitude of the profits that making and carrying out anticompetitive threats and promises in one market will enable it to realize in other markets by enabling it to build and maintain a reputation for engaging in strategic conduct).

(C) The Market-Oriented Approach to the Analysis of the Feasibility and Profitability of a Firm's Engaging in a Predatory Refusal to Deal or Entering Into One or More Predatory Long-Term Full-Requirements Contracts

The standard market-oriented analysis of the feasibility and profitability of a firm's engaging in a predatory refusal to deal or entering into a predatory long-term full-requirements contract assumes that the probability that a firm's refusal to deal or long-term full-requirements contract is predatory (that a firm will find it profitable to engage in predatory conduct of these kinds) increases with the firm's market share and the share of the market's sales that is foreclosed. In my judgment, this assumption ignores at least the following four considerations:

(1) even if all sellers and products in any relevant area of product-space were interchangeable, the risk that competition will be reduced depends not on the percentage of sales that are locked up but on the relationship between the amount of sales (or input purchases) the alleged target rival must make to break even and the amount of sales (purchases) that are not foreclosed;
(2) in reality, in most situations, all products and all sellers are not interchangeable—particular firms may have strong preferences for particular inputs or be especially-well-placed to supply particular buyers, and, as a result, their survival may depend not on the relationship between the amount of sales/supplies not locked up and the amount of sales/supplies they must make/purchase to survive but on the relationship between the amount of sales/supplies that (they are well-placed to make)/(fit their needs well) and the amount of *such* sales/supplies that are not locked up; relatedly,
(3) because some in-market rivals may be more competitive with an alleged predator than are other in-market rivals and any unusually-close actual or prospective competitor that is driven out or deterred from entering may not be replaced by a rival equally competitive with the predator, predation may be more profitable for a firm that faces (and therefore can target) an unusually-close competitor than for a firm all of whose in-market rivals are equally competitive with it; and
(4) the market-oriented approach to predatory refusals to deal and predatory long-term full-requirements contracts ignores the importance of the ability of a foreclosed target to limit the loss the foreclosure imposes on it by integrating forward or backward itself, executing such a vertical integration through a joint venture, or inducing someone else to enter the foreclosing firm's area of product-space by providing the potential investor in question with information, long-term contracts, or outright monetary subsidies.

I should say in addition that although the relevant E.C./E.U. officials have not made much progress in recognizing the inadequacy of the market-oriented approach to analyzing the profitability of predatory refusals to deal and predatory long-term full-requirements contracts, over the last 20 years, not only the U.S. DOJ and FTC but also the U.S. Supreme Court and, to an even greater extent, the U.S. lower courts have rejected that approach and worked out a non-market-oriented alternative that comes close to being right.

D. The Study's Non-Market-Oriented Approaches to Antitrust-Law-Relevant Economic Issues

I will delineate in the following order the approach the study argues should be taken to analyzing (1) the competitive impact of horizontal mergers, (2)(A) the kinds of evidence or tests that should be used to determine whether firms have engaged in contrived oligopolistic pricing and (B) the profitability of any given firm's practicing contrived oligopolistic pricing, (3) whether a firm's refusal(s) to deal or long-term full-requirements contract(s) are predatory, and (4) the functions, competitive impact, and monopolizing (exclusionary) character of vertical integration and its contractual surrogates.

(1) The Competitive Impact of Horizontal Mergers

I will first indicate an important feature of the structure of the non-market-oriented approach to this issue I am proposing, then delineate the six basic components of the recommended analysis, and finally provide some more detail about four of the basic components in question. The important feature of the approach I am recommending is that it initially analyzes the competitive impact of a horizontal merger on the often-counterfactual assumption that the merger will not generate any relevant economic efficiencies. The six basic components of the approach are:

(1) an analysis of the determinants of the effect that any horizontal merger would have in the relevant (arbitrarily-defined) area of product-space on price competition if it generated no relevant economic efficiencies and did not affect equilibrium QV investment in the relevant area of product-space;
(2) an analysis of the determinants of the effect that any horizontal merger would have on QV-investment competition in the relevant area of product-space if it generated no relevant economic efficiencies and did not affect the equilibrium QV-investment level in the relevant area of product-space by affecting prices at the pre-merger equilibrium QV-investment level;
(3) an analysis of the determinants of the effect that any static economic efficiencies a horizontal merger generates will have on price competition in the relevant area of product-space if those static efficiencies did not affect the intensity of price competition by affecting the equilibrium QV-investment level;
(4) an analysis of the determinants of the effect that any dynamic efficiencies a horizontal merger generates will have on QV-investment competition in the relevant area of product-space if the merger would not otherwise affect equilibrium QV investment in the relevant area of product-space;
(5) an analysis of the way in which a horizontal merger's impact on price competition at the relevant area of product-space's pre-merger equilibrium QV-investment level will affect the intensity of QV-investment competition in the relevant area of product-space in equilibrium; and

(6) an analysis of the way in which a horizontal merger's impact on the intensity of QV-investment competition and equilibrium QV investment will affect its impact on equilibrium price competition in the relevant area of product-space.

The analysis of the determinants of the effect that any no-efficiency-generating horizontal merger would have on price competition if it did not affect equilibrium QV investment in the relevant area of product-space (1) focuses separately on individualized-pricing situations and across the-board-pricing situations, (2) focuses separately on the prices charged by the perpetrators and the prices charged by the perpetrators' rivals, (3) considers the way in which the impact that a merger has on the perpetrators' prices affect its rivals' prices and the impact that a merger has on the perpetrators' rivals' prices affect the perpetrators' prices, (4) in the individualized-pricing situations on which I will now concentrate, focuses separately on the impact on the merged firm's and the merged firm's rivals' OCAs and highest non-oligopolistic prices (HNOPs), natural oligopolistic margins (NOMs), and contrived oligopolistic margins (COMs) (while taking account of the inter-connections between or among these impacts), and (5) again, in individualized-pricing contexts, considers separately the impact of horizontal mergers on the following subcomponents of respective relevant best-placed firms' (HNOP − MC) gaps in their relations with each buyer they are respectively best-placed to supply—their basic competitive advantage in their relations with each such buyer (their BCAs) and the contextual marginal costs their closest rival for each such buyer's patronage would have to incur to match their HNOP-containing offer to that buyer (the applicable $CMC_{\#2}$s). At a more refined level, the analysis establishes the following conclusions:

(1) the impact of a horizontal merger on the merged firm's BCAs relative to the merger partners' depends on the facts delineated as items (1)–(4) in the first list in Sect. 1C(2) of this Conclusion;
(2) the impact of a horizontal merger on the CMC that the merged firm's closest competitor for a particular buyer's patronage must incur to match the merged firm's HNOP-containing offer to that buyer—$CMC_{\#2}$—relative to the CMC that the closest competitor of the merger partner that would have been best-placed to supply that buyer would have had to incur to match that merger partner's HNOP-containing offer to that buyer (I am assuming *ad arguendo* that the merger would not generate static marginal efficiencies that would make the merged firm best-placed to supply the relevant buyer even though neither merger partner would have been best-placed to do so) depends on (A) the amount by which the merger has raised the merged firm's BCA in its relations with that buyer above the relevant merger partner's BCA in relations with the buyer (the greater the amount by which the merged firm's BCA exceeds the merger partner's, the more $CMC_{\#2}$ for the merged firm will be lower than $CMC_{\#2}$ for the merger partner because the less discriminatory the price #2 would have to charge to match the respective #1s' HNOP-containing offers) and (B) the amount by which the merger has raised the #2's (HNOP + NOM + COM)s to its own customers (*ceteris paribus*, the greater this amount, the larger the amount by which $CMC_{\#2}$ for the merged firm's closest rival for the relevant buyer exceed $CMC_{\#2}$ for the merger partner's closest rival for that buyer because the greater the extent to which the

merged-firm #2's matching-offer price will be more discriminatory than the merger-partner #2's matching-offer price would have been);

(3) the impact of a horizontal merger on the NOMs the merged firm can secure relative to those the merger partners would have secured depends in part on the amount by which it has increased the merged firm's average (HNOP – OMC) gap above the average (HNOP – OMC) gap that would have existed for the merger partners when they would have been best-placed, in part on the impact of the merger on the costs the merged firm must incur to change its initially-announced prices relative to those the relevant merger partners would have to incur to do so, and in part on the frequency with which pre-merger the costs the merger partners would have had to incur to change their initially-announced prices to buyers they were best-placed to supply exceeded by different amounts their OCAs in relation to those buyers; and

(4) the impact of a horizontal merger on the difference between the COMs the merged firm secures and the COMs the merger partners would have secured (an impact that is clearly relevant to the merger's legality under the EMCR, will be relevant to the merger's legality under the Sherman Act in cases in which the merger's *ex ante* profitability was not assured by the Sherman-Act-licit profits it should have been predicted to generate (so that the critical issue is whether the perpetrators had made a mistake or were expecting the merger to confer Sherman-Act-illicit profits on them), and would also be relevant to the merger's legality under the Clayton Act if that Act were interpreted in part to be a fence law and the obstacles to proving contrived oligopolistic pricing were as high as I believe them to be) depends *inter alia* on (A) the difference between the merged firm's average (HNOP + NOM – OMC) figure for the buyers it was best-placed to supply and the merger partners' average (HNOP + NOM – OMC) figures for the buyers they were best-placed to supply (where any positive difference of this kind will tend to cause the merged firm to practice less contrived oligopolistic pricing than the merger partners would have done by increasing the safe profits it must put at risk to do so above the safe profits the merger partners would have had to put at risk to do so), (B) the difference between the cost to the merged firm and the cost to the merger partners of communicating the anticompetitive threats and promises one has to communicate to practice contrived oligopolistic pricing (a difference that could result from [i] the fact that the average number of merged-firm rivals that would find undercutting its contrived oligopolistic prices inherently profitable could be either higher or lower than the average number of rivals of the merger partners that would have found undercutting any contrived oligopolistic prices they charged inherently profitable, [ii] the fact that the merged firm's reputation for estimating its (HNOP + NOM) figures accurately and engaging in contrivance was stronger than the counterpart reputations of the merger partners (which would affect the relative abilities of the merged firm and the merger partners to make the necessary anticompetitive communications more cheaply simply by charging contrived oligopolistic prices), and [iii] the tendency of the merger to cause the antitrust authorities to pay more attention to the merged firm's pricing decisions than they would have paid to the pricing decisions of the merger partners), (C) the difference between the reputations of

the merged firm and the merger partners for carrying out their anticompetitive threats and promises (where increases in the strength of these sorts of reputations make contrivance more profitable by reducing the probability that it will lead to undercutting), (D) the difference between the abilities of the merged firm/the merger partners to infer the fact that it has/they have been undercut by a competitive inferior from circumstantial evidence relating to the relationship between (the percentage of sales of former customers each retained in the period in question and the percentages of rivals' former customers and new buyers in the market whose patronage each secured in the period in question) and (the historical counterparts for those percentages)—a difference that a horizontal merger could create by enabling the merged firm (i) to pool the merger partners' sales records and information about rival sales and new-buyer purchases, (ii) to pool any information the merger partners have about both the identity and the historical and contemporary magnitudes of the causes of period-to-period variations in the percentages in question other than variations in inferior-rival price-cutting, and (iii) to take advantage of economies of scale in doing the associated research (including economies related to the ability of skilled personnel to train others), (E) the extent to which the merged firm is more able than its antecedents to identify their undercutters because (i) the merged firm can profit by pooling the merger partners' information about their rivals that bears on the identity of the rivals that would find beating the merged firm's contrived oligopolistic prices inherently profitable and/or on the proclivity of those individual rivals that would find such undercutting inherently profitable to engage in undercutting and (ii) the merged firm can take advantage of economies of scale in observing the delivery vans that are supplying relevant buyers or in examining these buyers' input inventories or final products to determine the identity of the contriver's rivals that are supplying them, (F) the difference between the amount of benefits the merged firm can confer on cooperative rivals and the total benefits the merger partners could confer on such rivals (a difference that will increase with [i] the frequency with which the merger partners were exclusively-equal-second-place or uniquely-second-placed and uniquely-third-placed to supply a potential undercutter's customers and the average amount by which the two exclusively-second-placed merger partners or the uniquely-second-placed merger partner [when the other merger partner was uniquely-third-placed] were better-placed than the fourth-placed supplier of the buyers in question and [ii] the frequency with which and the extent to which one merger partner had excess reciprocatory power and the other insufficient reciprocatory power in relation to a potential undercutter), (G) the difference between the merged firm's harm-inflicted to loss-incurred ratio for inflicting relevant equivalent-monetary losses on undercutters through retaliation and its counterpart for its merger partners—a positive difference that the merger will generate (i) by increasing the target's (HNOP + NOM – MC) gaps (by increasing the target's HNOPs by increasing the merged firm's prices to its own customers above those the merger partners would have charged those buyers and hence by increasing the contextual marginal costs the merged firm would have to incur to match its rivals' pre-merger HNOP-containing offers to buyers they are best-placed to supply above the contextual marginal costs the merger partners would have had to incur to match those rival offers in cases in which one of the merger partners would have been uniquely-second-placed to supply the rival-customer in question) and (ii) by enabling the merged firm to engage in more retaliation through one of the merger partners' products and less through the other merger partner's products than the merger partner would have practiced independently because the marginal harm-inflicted to loss-incurred ratio for the last act of retaliation one merger partner would have committed against particular undercutting rivals was higher than its counterpart for the last act of retaliation the other merger partner would have committed against the rival in question, and (H) the extent to which the merger makes it more profitable for the merged firm to contrive oligopolistic prices than it was for the merger partners to do so because the merged firm, being larger across all its operations, can take advantage of company-wide economies of scale in building and maintaining a reputation for contrivance (and strategic conduct more generally).

(2) The Determinants of the Profitability of a Firm's Practicing Contrived Oligopolistic Pricing and the Evidence That Supports a Contrived-Oligopolistic-Pricing Finding

(A) The Determinants of the Profitability of a Firm's Practicing Contrived Oligopolistic Pricing

The study recognizes that one cannot establish the claim that a firm has practiced contrived oligopolistic pricing by demonstrating that it would have been profitable for it to do so and that one cannot disprove the claim that a firm has practiced contrived oligopolistic pricing by establishing the unprofitability of its doing so: the fact that conduct is illegal usually deters a firm from engaging in it both by making it unprofitable and by making it unattractive to the firm's decisionmakers even if the law does not render the conduct unprofitable, and firms do sometimes engage in illegal conduct even when their doing so was *ex ante* unprofitable (do sometimes make such mistakes). Nevertheless, a demonstration that it would not have been *ex ante* profitable for a firm to have engaged in contrived oligopolistic pricing clearly does have some probative value in a contrived-oligopolistic-pricing suit against it.

The study's analysis of the *ex ante* profitability of contrivance for a particular firm can be inferred from Sect. 1C(3) of the Conclusion's critique of the market-oriented approach to this issue. In brief, in the one direction, the profitability of such contrivance for a firm will be directly related to (1) its reputation for estimating its (HNOP + NOM)s correctly and for practicing contrived oligopolistic pricing, (2) the number of buyers to which it has historically made sales, the number of other firm's customers whose patronage it has historically stolen, the number of new buyers in the relevant area of product-space whose patronage it has historically secured, the constancy of the above percentages through time, and the firm's theoretical and empirical knowledge of the determinants other than changes in the amount of undercutting by inferiors of variations in the above percentages,

(3) the amount of information it has about the identities of its closest rivals for the patronage of particular buyers and their willingness to steal customers of other firms when it is inherently profitable for them to do so and the cost it must incur to identify relevant buyers' suppliers by observing the delivery vans that supplied the buyers in question and/or the buyers' input inventories or final products, (4) the ratio of (A) (the product of [i] the number of times that the firm is uniquely-second-placed to obtain the patronage of customers of any particular potential undercutter and [ii] the average amount by which the firm is better-placed than the third-placed supplier of customers of the potential undercutter in question when it is uniquely-second-placed to secure their patronage) to (B) (the profits the potential undercutter in question could realize by stealing from a position of competitive inferiority those of the firm's customers to which the firm was charging contrived oligopolistic prices if the relevant rival's undercutting would not elicit a strategic reaction), (5) the ratio of (A) (the product of [i] the number of customers of the contriver's potential undercutters that the contriver was second-placed or close-to-second-placed to supply and [ii] the average size of the [HNOP + NOM – MC] gap of the potential contriver's potential undercutter in the latter's relations with buyers the potential undercutter was best-placed to supply and the potential contriver was second-placed or close-to-second-placed to supply) to (B) (the profits the potential undercutter in question could realize by stealing those of the potential contriver's customers to which the potential contriver charged contrived oligopolistic prices), and (6) the amount of sales the potential contriver made in other areas of product-space and the extent to which the contriver's communicating and making good on contrived oligopolistic promises and threats would help it establish and/or maintain a company-wide reputation for contrivance that would increase the profits it could make through contrivance (and possibly predation) in other areas of product-space. In the other direction, the profitability of contrived oligopolistic pricing for a firm will be inversely related to (1) its (HNOP + NOM – MC)s, (2) the number of its potential undercutters, (3) the attention that antitrust authorities are paying to its pricing conduct, and (4) its risk-averseness.

(B) The Evidence and Tests One Should Use to Determine Whether Contrived Oligopolistic Pricing Has Been Practiced

The study argues that five sorts of evidence or tests should be used to determine whether one or more defendants have engaged in contrived oligopolistic pricing:

(1) smoking-gun evidence such as confessions of defendant-actors, recordings of telephone calls or non-telephone recorded conversations, e-mails, other written communications, testimony of participants in or overhearers of relevant conversations or of individuals who saw relevant written communications;
(2) comparisons of the prices that a defendant actually charged with the firm's (HNOP + NOM)s (that also take into account relevant errors);
(3) analyses that determine whether observed inter-regional or inter-temporal price-differences can be explained by differences in the magnitudes of the

relevant firm's highest legitimate prices in the two time-periods or in the two locations in question (can be explained by differences in the two [HNOP + NOM]s and/or differences in error-related margins);

(4) behavioral evidence that supports the hypothesis that the defendant had engaged in contrived oligopolistic pricing (evidence that the defendant had communicated with its rivals prior to its alleged practice of contrivance, evidence that the defendant had tried to merge with or acquire its rivals, evidence that the defendant had tried to drive one or more of its rivals out of business, evidence that the defendant had foregone inherently-profitable opportunities to steal its rivals' customers, evidence that the defendant had stolen rival customers by charging them inherently-unprofitably-low prices); and

(5) evidence that establishes that the alleged contrived oligopolistic pricing would have been profitable for the defendant(s) (see Sect. 1D2(A) of the Conclusion)—traditionally misnamed "structural evidence" by analysts who believe in the efficacy of market-oriented approaches to this issue.

(3) The Analysis of Whether a Firm's Refusal(s) to Deal or (Long-Term) Full-Requirements Contract(s) Are Predatory

The study's non-market-oriented approach has six components. The first is an analysis of the legitimate profitability of the allegedly-predatory refusal(s) to deal or full-requirements contract(s): if the refusal(s) to deal or requirements contract(s) are inherently profitable, they cannot by definition be predatory. A producer may refuse to purchase an input from a particular source because it is inherently profitable for it to supply itself or patronize another supplier. A firm may refuse to distribute its output through a particular independent distributor because it is inherently profitable for it to integrate forward into distribution or to use other distributors. And a producer can refuse to supply an input it produces to a particular outsider because it is more profitable to supply those inputs to its own final-product-production division or to other outsiders. Using a particular distributor may be inherently unprofitable for many reasons—*e.g.*, because of the contextual marginal cost of doing so or because the distributor in question persists in making outlet-location, pricing, advertising, shelving, post-sales service, and other choices that reduce the producer's overall profits. Supplying an input to a particular independent final-product producer may also be inherently unprofitable for many reasons—*e.g.*, because of the contextual marginal cost of doing so or because the particular final-product producer's final product has deficiencies (absolute or relative) with which it would be reputationally-costly for the input-producer in question to be associated. Similarly, for many reasons, long-term or medium-term full-requirements provisions in contracts can be legitimately profitable for the sellers that include them in their contracts—(1) can reduce seller-sales-effort and buyer-search-for-best-deal costs and the sum of seller and buyer contract-negotiation-and-drafting transaction costs, (2) can generate profitable opportunities for the seller and buyer involved to increase the joint profits their relationship yields them by communicating to each other information about their capabilities and needs and by adjusting their operations in their joint interest, (3) can reduce the sum of the seller's and buyer's risk costs by giving the seller assured sales and the buyer assured supplies and providing each with more certainty about the terms and conditions that their sales and purchasing contracts will contain, relatedly (4) can enable the seller and buyer to make additional profitable investments by providing them with both greater financial security and relevant information, and (5) can enable sellers and buyers to profit by entering into tying and reciprocity agreements that perform a wide variety of jointly-profitable functions and that would not be profitable for one of their participants if they did not impose a full-requirements or total-output-supply obligation on the other party. In any event, the first component of the study's approach to analyzing the predatory character of a firm's refusal(s) to deal or use of full-requirements contract(s) is an analysis of the legitimate profitability of the conduct in question.

The second component of the approach to this issue that the study recommends is an analysis of supposed smoking-gun, direct evidence of the accused's predatory intent—recordings or oral statements or written statements by the alleged predator that might be construed to manifest its predatory intent or testimony by witnesses of the predator's predatory intent. The study emphasizes that this type of evidence is not always as dispositive as the State or private plaintiffs sometimes claim it is: (1) many of the statements in question—*e.g.*, "I am going to drive you out of business."—are compatible not only with the utterer's intention to engage in predation but also with its intention to engage in competition on the merits that will drive the alleged target of predation out of business, and (2) eyewitness testimony from certain sources—*e.g.*, disgruntled employees, former employees who have been fired, or the alleged target of the alleged predation—are suspect.

The third component of the approach the study recommends taking to the legal evaluation of these sorts of conduct is the consideration of other sorts of behavioral evidence that supports the conclusion that the accused really did have predatory intent—*e.g.*, evidence that the accused had offered to buy out the alleged predation-target for a price that was lower than the market value the target business would have were it not to be a predation-target or evidence that the accused had engaged in other kinds of conduct that harmed the alleged target and seems likely to have been predatory (predatory pricing directed at the alleged target, predatory advertising directed at the alleged target, attempts to disparage the alleged target's products that would not have been profitable had they not raised the probability of the target's exit, the opening up of inherently-unprofitable "fighting" stores near the alleged target's operations, attempts to blow up the alleged target's production plant or distributive outlet, attempts to hire the target's managers for salaries that exceed their legitimate value to the alleged predator, inherently-unprofitable efforts to prevent the alleged target's suppliers from dealing with it [promises of or actual payments of bribes to firms that refuse to supply the accused target or threats or acts of retaliation against suppliers of the alleged target]), *etc.*

The fourth component of the approach that the study recommends taking to accusations that a firm has predatorily refused to deal or entered into predatory full-requirements contracts is to investigate the loss the refusals and full-requirements contracts in question would impose on the alleged target. For this purpose, it is important to recognize two facts that cut in opposite directions:

(1) to the extent that the firm that refuses to sell to the refused party was its best-placed supplier or the refused party was the best-placed supplier of the refusing party, the joint-profit loss the refusal generated will be larger, and
(2) to the extent that it was possible and inherently profitable for the refusing firm to have bargained for terms and conditions of sale or purchase that would have left the refused party with no gains from the transaction had the refusing party decided to participate in it, the equivalent-dollar loss the refusal imposed on the refused party will be smaller.

The traditional market-oriented approach to the issue in question ignores the first of these facts because it does not acknowledge that one seller in a given area of product-space may be best-placed to supply a particular buyer in that area of product-space; it ignores the second of these facts for no reason that I can imagine.

U.S. courts and antitrust-enforcement agencies used to assume that refusals to deal or long-term requirements contracts would impose costs on targets if but only if they covered more than a specified quantity of transactions or, more recently, more than a specified percentage of sales in the relevant market. I do not think that either of these sorts of figures is relevant: even if one ignores the possibilities considered in the next paragraph, the important question is whether the supply opportunities or sales opportunities that are still available to the refused party are as profitable for it as the "foreclosed" opportunities would have been and the answer to that question depends not on the quantity or share of market supplies or sales "foreclosed" but on the quantity of sales or supplies not locked up relative to the quantity of sales or supplies the refused party would otherwise have found most profitable respectively to make or purchase and on the relationship between the profits that the refused party would have obtained by making the refused sales or purchasing the refused supplies had the refuser not behaved strategically and the profits the refused party can obtain by making other sales to or purchases from other existing sources. As I have already indicated, over the past 15–20 years, the U.S. antitrust-enforcement agencies, the Supreme Court, and the lower federal courts have progressively rejected the traditional market-oriented approach to refusals to deal and long-term requirement contracts in favor of something like the approach I find warranted. Unfortunately, the relevant E.C./E.U. authorities have not made similar progress.

Traditional analyses of the loss that accused refusals to deal and full-requirements contracts have imposed on the refused parties have also ignored the extent to which a refused party can reduce any loss the refusal would otherwise have imposed on it by integrating forward or backwards into the refuser's area of product-space on its own, by entering that area of product-space by participating in a joint venture, or by inducing another firm to enter the refuser's market by providing it with advice, by entering into supply or purchase contracts with it, or by financing the independent entry in an arrangement that may or may not involve subsidization. Admittedly, the loss-mitigating effect of these moves will be reduced by the fact that they all will tend to increase QV investment in the refuser's area of product-space, but the costs associated with any such effect will be lower to the extent that equilibrium QV investment in the relevant area of product-space would have risen in any case (say, because of population-growth-driven increases in "industry" demand). But even if the increase-in-QV-investment-generated cost of such moves is not lowered for the above reason, there will be many situations in which the refused-party responses on which I am now focusing will reduce the loss the refusal imposes on the refused party. The approach the study recommends takes these possible moves and considerations into account.

The fifth component of the analysis the study recommends taking to such predation claims is an analysis of the probability that the losses one has concluded the refusal(s) to deal or full-requirements contract(s) in question will impose on the alleged target(s) will critically affect its/their decision to continue to operate in the relevant area of product-space or to make a new QV investment in that area of product-space. That analysis focuses not only on (1) the magnitude of the predicted losses but also on (2) the amount of supernormal profits the established targets would otherwise have earned by continuing to operate in the relevant area of product-space, (3) the extent to which the assets of the established targets can be put to other uses, (4) the extent to which those assets are depreciated and the rate at which they will depreciate further in the future, (5) the amount of supernormal profits that the target potential investor(s) would otherwise have anticipated realizing on its/their planned QV investment(s) in the relevant area of product-space, (6) the cost to the potential investor(s) of reducing the alleged predator's incentive to make it/them a target of predation by choosing to make a QV investment in the relevant area of product-space that would be less competitive with the alleged predator's projects, and (7) the stake the target established firm(s) or potential investor(s) has/have in avoiding a reputation for succumbing to threats or predatory acts.

The sixth and last component of the analysis the study recommends taking to predatory-refusals-to-deal and predatory-full-requirements-contract claims is an analysis of the likelihood that and the speed with which the exited established rival or deterred prospective rival QV investor would be replaced by another firm, the extent to which the replacement rivals would be less competitive with the alleged predator than its alleged target(s) was/were or would have been, and the extent to which the alleged predator could reduce the loss that such prospective replacement-firms would impose on it by making additional (limit) QV investments in the relevant area of product-space itself.

(4) The Functions, Monopolizing Character, Competitive Impact, Exploitative Character, and Legality Under U.S. Antitrust Law and E.C./E.U. Competition Law of Vertical Integration and Its Surrogates

(A) Single-Product Pricing-Techniques

The function of non-strategic single pricing, conventional price discrimination, perfect price discrimination in any of its forms, and the mixed pricing-technique that combines a lump-sum fee with a per-unit price that exceeds the seller's transaction-surplus-maximizing (TSM) marginal cost is to enable the seller to maximize its profits without changing the absolute attractiveness of the offers against which it has to compete. The profits any such pricing-technique will yield the seller equals (1) the seller surplus it enables the seller to obtain from the demand-curve/marginal-cost-curve combination it ends up facing (which in part will reflect the additional surplus that the pricing-technique enables it to realize by making it profitable for independent distributors of its product to make jointly-profitable expenditures or resource allocations that increased the demand for its product) *minus* (2) the pricing costs the seller must incur to use the pricing-technique in question (which include the associated buyer-valuation research costs, checkout-counter-personnel training costs, checkout-counter-delay costs, arbitrage-related costs, the costs it must incur to overcome any tendency its pricing has to deter its distributors from making jointly-profitable demand-increasing expenditures or resource allocations, and the costs it must incur to overcome any tendency the pricing-technique has to induce its distributors to engage in organizationally-unprofitable intra-brand competition).

This study's analysis of the legality of price discrimination under E.C./E.U. competition law is based on the following premise: although clause (d) in what is now Article 101(1) of the 2009 Treaty of Lisbon and item (c) in the first paragraph of what is now Article 102 of that Treaty probably do manifest the fact that the drafters and ratifiers of the 1957 Treaty and its sequels believed that agreements between undertakings that "apply dissimilar conditions to equivalent transactions with other trading parties, thereby placing them at a competitive disadvantage" will respectively prevent, restrict, or distort competition or constitute an exclusionary abuse if perpetrated by a dominant firm, that belief would be irrelevant to the legality of price of other-terms-and-conditions-of-sale discrimination if (as I believe is the case) price discrimination that is not retaliatory in the service of contrivance or predatory will only rarely if ever prevent, restrict, or distort competition. By way of contrast, the study does accept that the U.S. Robinson-Patman Act's amendment of Section 2 of the Clayton Act does add a particular "injury to competitor" test of illegality to the Clayton Act's normal "lessening competition" test, though this addition is likely to have no practical significance since sellers are unlikely to find it profitable to discriminate against resellers that will be injured by the discrimination—will rather not deal with them at all if their distributive efforts are against the seller's interest and will want to keep them in business if their distributive efforts increase the seller's profits.

By definition, the non-strategic use of any of these single-product pricing-techniques does not manifest the pricer's specific anticompetitive intent (is not monopolizing or exclusionary). The non-strategic use of these techniques will lessen competition in the sense in which that concept is used in the Clayton Act and EMCR only in the extremely-rare case in which the substitution of one such technique for another (whose use has somehow been determined to constitute the relevant baseline for competitive-impact analysis) increases the pricer's unit sales and concomitantly decreases the demand curve an established rival faces or the demand curve an effective potential investor in the relevant area of product-space will anticipate facing and thereby induces the established rival to exit (when it will not be immediately replaced by an equally-effective competitor) or critically raises the barriers to entry facing an otherwise-effective potential investor. In all other cases, the non-strategic use of such pricing-techniques will not lessen competition or impede effective competition in the sense in which those expression are used in the Clayton Act and EMCR because, even when such a use of a particular technique inflicts an equivalent-monetary loss on relevant buyers (relative to some agreed-on baseline [profit-maximizing single pricing?]), it will not do so by reducing the absolute attractiveness of the best offer the relevant buyers respectively receive from any inferior supplier.

However, when a dominant firm's non-strategic use of single pricing, conventional price discrimination, perfect price discrimination, or the mixed pricing-technique in question reduces relevant buyers' buyer surplus to a level that is "unfair," the firm's use of the single-product pricing-technique in question will constitute an exploitative abuse of its dominant position in violation of what is now Article 102 of the 2009 Treaty of Lisbon.

(B) Multi-Product Pricing-Techniques: Tie-Ins and Reciprocity

Tie-ins and reciprocity can be used non-strategically (1) respectively to increase the cost-effectiveness of their employer's efforts (A) to control the quality of the complements its customer combines with its product or (B) to control the quality of the ingredients its employer's supplier uses to produce the product the employer purchases from the supplier, (2) to increase the cost-effectiveness of its employer's efforts to control its trading-partner's practice of arbitrage, (3) to eliminate or reduce the costs its employer would have to incur to determine the monetary value that particular potential customers or particular categories of potential customers place on individual products and to reduce the checkout-counter-delay costs of price discrimination, (4) to conceal the existence, extent of, or location of its employer's price discrimination, illegal retaliation, predatory pricing, maximum-or-minimum price-regulation violations, tax fraud, or contract fraud, and (5)(A) to reduce the amount of transaction surplus the employer must destroy to remove a relevant given amount of buyer/seller surplus from its trading partner by charging non-TSM-marginal-cost per-unit prices for final products or (B) to enable the producer of an input against which substitution is possible to prevent its supra-TSM-marginal-cost per-unit pricing of inputs from destroying transaction surplus by inducing its trading-partner to make jointly-unprofitable substitutions against the input.

This study's analysis of the legality of tie-ins and reciprocity under U.S. antitrust law and E.C./E.U. competition law is based on two critical, parallel conclusions:

(1) although the fact that Section 3 of the Clayton Act prohibits full-requirements tie-ins (and other contractual provisions or other sorts of efforts designed to

prohibit or prevent a buyer from patronizing a rival of the seller in question) when "the effect. . .may be substantially to lessen competition or tend to create a monopoly" may manifest the relevant legislators' beliefs that such conduct will often lessen competition, that belief is irrelevant to the application of the provision in question that is correct as a matter of U.S. law, and

(2) although clause (e) in what is now Article 101(1) of the 2009 Treaty of Lisbon and item (d) in the list in what is now Article 102 of that Treaty may indicate that the drafters and ratifiers of the 1957 Treaty and its various sequels believe that tie-ins and reciprocity agreements have "as their object or effect the prevention [or] restriction of competition" or will constitute abuses of a dominant position if perpetrated by a dominant firm in that they "make the conclusion of contracts subject to the acceptance by the other partner of supplementary obligations, which, by their nature or according to commercial usages, have no connection with the subject of such contracts," that belief (which is clearly wrong in that tie-in and reciprocity clauses are intimately related to the functioning of the contracts in which they appear and are acknowledged to be so by commercial usage) is irrelevant to the application of what are now Articles 101 and 102 of the 2009 Treaty of Lisbon that is correct as a matter of E.C./E.U. law.

With two qualifications, tie-ins and reciprocity agreements never manifest their initiator's specific anticompetitive intent—*i.e.*, never involve monopolization, never have as a critical object the prevention or restriction of competition, and never constitute a now-Article 102 exclusionary abuse of a dominant position. The first qualification relates to tie-ins and reciprocity that are designed to conceal the extent and/or location of their practitioners' contrivance-executing pricing or predatory pricing. Such tie-ins and reciprocity do violate U.S. antitrust law: indeed, if the non-initiator understood the conduct's function and profited from its collaboration with the initiator, it as well as the initiator would be guilty of a violation of the Sherman Act. If the initiator of such a tie-in or reciprocity agreement is individually dominant or a member of a collectively-dominant set of rivals, the perpetrator's use of such agreements will violate the exclusionary-abuse branch of now-Article 102's test of illegality. However, if the perpetrator is not dominant, its use of a tie-in or reciprocity agreement to conceal its contrivance-executing retaliation or predation may not violate what is now Article 101 of the 2009 Treaty of Lisbon except in cases in which the retaliation was against a rival that had entered into and then broken a price-fixing agreement. Now-Article 101 does not prohibit contrivance that does not involve the formation of an agreement and does not prohibit single-firm predation, and, given that fact, it seems to me that contracts covered by now-Article 101(1) that were designed to conceal lawful conduct (that admittedly did have both the critical object and the effect of preventing or restricting competition) do not violate now-Article 101. But perhaps there is no reason to worry about this issue; if the underlying conduct is not illegal, its perpetrator might not use a tie-in or reciprocity agreement to conceal it (though the actor might if it feared that it might be found to be dominant or that the EC and the E.C./E.U. courts might conclude that threat-contrivance and single-firm predation does violate now-Article 101).

The second exception to the claim that tie-ins and reciprocity are not monopolizing or exclusionary relates to full-requirements tie-ins and total-output reciprocity. Although (in part because such contracts rarely cover a sufficiently-substantial period of time to be exclusionary), I doubt that more than a trivial number of such tie-in and reciprocity agreements were entered into with specific anticompetitive intent, I cannot totally rule out this possibility.

An individual undertaking's use of tie-ins and reciprocity agreements to do things other than conceal contrivance or predation is also extremely unlikely to reduce competition by causing an established rival to exit or critically raising the barriers to investment facing an effective potential competition—an outcome that would be relevant to a full-requirements contract's legality under Section 3 of the Clayton Act or the legality of any tie-in agreed to by two undertakings under now-Article 101. Admittedly, I cannot rule this possibility out entirely: to the extent that tie-ins and reciprocity improve their practitioners' competitive positions by enabling them to control complement/input quality more cost-effectively or to the extent that they make it profitable for their practitioners to charge lower per-unit prices that increase their practitioners' unit sales and reduce the demand curves one or more of their rivals face, the relevant tie-ins and reciprocity agreements could conceivably inflict a net equivalent-monetary loss on relevant buyers by reducing the absolute attractiveness of the best offer they respectively receive from any inferior supplier by inducing the exit of an established firm that will not be immediately replaced by an equally-effective competitor or by critically raising the barriers to QV investment facing an otherwise-effective potential investor in the relevant area of product-space. However, I suspect that such a result will virtually never obtain and that it will rarely be possible for the State or a private plaintiff to establish the requisite probability that it will obtain or has obtained in those cases in which it would or has. In any event, if, contrary to my expectation, plaintiffs could sometimes establish the requisite probability that the tie-in or reciprocity agreement at issue violated the Clayton Act's "lessening competition" test of *prima facie* illegality, defendants in U.S. Clayton Act cases might still be able to exonerate themselves by establishing an organizational-economic-efficiency defense (*e.g.*, by demonstrating that the agreement would not have lessened competition had it not increased the cost-effectiveness of their efforts to control complement/input quality, reduced the cost they had to incur to prevent arbitrage to some given extent, or increased the extent to which they were able to induce their distributors to make jointly-profitable demand-increasing expenditures or resource allocations). Admittedly, "the fair share of the resulting benefit" condition for a now-Article 101(3) exemption makes it less likely that a defendant in any such now-Article 101(1) E.C./E.U. case will be able to make out the type of efficiency defense that Article 101(3) provides for.

The preceding analysis of the "lessening competition" possibility assumed that the relevant unit for the analysis in question is an individual undertaking's use of tie-ins or reciprocity. I believe that the level-playing-field norm of U.S. antitrust law, which the EC and the E.C./E.U. courts have also indicated plays an important role in E.C./E.U. competition law, implies that the relevant unit for the analysis of the competitive impact of the various surrogates for vertical integration is a rule allowing all members of a set of rivals to employ tie-ins and reciprocity: the individual-firm-usage focus is inconsistent with the level-playing-field norm because its adoption will result in well-established firms' being prohibited from engaging in organizational-proficiency-enhancing conduct in which marginal and potential competitors are allowed to engage because the well-established firm's conduct will tend to induce exits and deter entries by improving the competitive-position arrays of the well-established firms while the marginal established firm's and potential entrants' conduct will help them respectively survive and enter.

Tie-ins and reciprocity that make it profitable for their employer to remove buyer surplus the employer would not otherwise have found profitable to remove could violate the exploitative-abuse branch of the test of illegality promulgated by what is now Article 102 of the 2009 Treaty of Lisbon. This result will obtain only if (1) the perpetrator is individually dominant or a member of a collectively-dominant set of rivals and (2) the associate reduction in buyer surplus critically affects the fairness to the buyer of its transactions with the perpetrator.

(C) Resale Price Maintenance, Vertical Territorial Restraints, and Vertical Customer-Allocation Clauses

Almost all exemplars of the practices listed in this heading function by reducing intra-brand competition to increase the producer' profits by

(1) preventing intra-brand competition from enabling final customers to purchase the producer's product for less than they would be willing to pay for it (or enabling the producer to charge its independent distributors higher lump-sum fees and lower per-unit prices without creating this problem),
(2) preventing independent resellers from reducing the actual value of the producer's product to consumers or the consumers' perception of that value by reducing the price for which it is sold,
(3) preventing intra-brand competition from reducing the profits of the producer and its distributors by causing them to incur duplicative, jointly-unprofitable sales expenses and by allocating sales to worse-than-best-placed distributors, and
(4) inducing independent resellers to make demand-increasing expenditures on or resource allocations to out-of-store-advertising, in-store shelf-space or displays, in-store sales efforts, and warranty services that are in the joint interest of the producer and its distributors.

Rarely (in my opinion), a set of producer-rivals may agree to engage in these practices to facilitate their own horizontal price-fix (say, by preventing their distributors from passing on any price-cuts they give them or by limiting the territories within which and customers to which their respective individual sales-organizations can make sales so as to produce a horizontal market allocation among the producers). Even more rarely (in my opinion), a set of distributor-rivals may agree to require the producers from which they buy to practice RPM as part of a scheme in which these producers are used to enforce the resellers' price-fix.

Both the U.S. antitrust-law-enforcement authorities and the E.C./E.U. competition-law-enforcement authorities have always believed and continue to believe that the statutes/treaty-provisions they are charged with implementing place the same significance on reductions in intra-brand and reductions in inter-brand competition. Admittedly, the language of the relevant provisions ("restraint of trade," "lessen competition," "prevention [or] restriction" of competition, "imped[ing] effective competition") does not explicitly differentiate between inter-brand and intra-brand competition. However, the goals of the statutes and treaty provisions (and, in the U.S., the near-universally-held belief that antitrust law does not prohibit a firm from converting into profits as much of its legitimately-obtained competitive advantages as it can as well as the deontological and utilitarian beliefs that underlie that view [regardless of their persuasiveness]) all favor the conclusion that the relevant language should as a matter of law be interpreted to refer exclusively to inter-brand (*i.e.*, not to intra-brand) competition. That conclusion partially reflects and partially is independently supported by the fact that the responses that firms will make to prohibitions of their efforts to reduce intra-brand competition (*e.g.*, vertical integration, increasing their per-unit prices and reducing their lump-sum fees, substituting single pricing for price discrimination, ceasing to supply buyers [countries] in whose favor they would otherwise have discriminated) will prevent the prohibition from furthering the goals it might otherwise have helped to achieve. That conclusion is also favored by the peculiarity of prohibiting firms from using contractual clauses and sales policies to induce their independent distributors to make certain choices while allowing them to use hierarchical controls to induce the employees of their own distributive divisions to make the choices in question.

I will proceed on the assumption that U.S. and E.C./E.U. antitrust law are concerned with reductions in inter-brand competition but not directly with reductions in intra-brand competition. My first conclusions is: except for the exemplars of RPM, vertical territorial restraints, and vertical customer-allocation clauses that function by enabling producers or resellers to fix prices, these practices never involve restraints of trade or monopolization, never have as their critical object the prevention or restriction of competition, and never constitute an exclusionary abuse of a dominant position even when the practitioner has a dominant position. Second, an individual producer's use of those practices will prevent or restrict competition in the now-Article 101(1) sense or impede effective competition in the sense of the EMCR (which might be relevant if a covered merger, acquisition, or joint venture would increase the participants' engagement in these practices) (the practices are not covered by the Clayton Act) in only two circumstances:

(1) when it effectuates a price-fix or
(2) when it leads to the exit of a rival of a perpetrator that will not be immediately replaced by an equally-effective competitor or raises the barrier to QV investment faced by an otherwise-effective potential investor by improving the perpetrator's array of competitive positions and thereby critically worsening the competitive-

position array of an established rival or the prospective competitive-position array of a potential QV investor in the relevant area of product-space.

I suspect that an individual firm's use of these practices will never or virtually never effectuate a price-fix, that individual-firm uses of these practices will rarely if ever prevent, restrict, or impede competition in the second way listed above, that plaintiffs will be hard-put to demonstrate that such a practice has had or will have such an effect even when it did or would, and that in at least some of the rare cases in which an individual firm's use of the practice does lessen competition it will do so by increasing the firm's organizational allocative efficiency (which may put its perpetrator[s] in a position to establish a Clayton Act organizational-economic-efficiency defense, may render the conduct exemptible under now-Article 101(3), and may cause it not to impose a net equivalent-monetary loss on relevant buyers, which would critically affect its legality under all applicable U.S. and E.C./E.U. statutory/treaty/regulatory provisions). In fact, if the baseline for an analysis of the effect of these practices on relevant buyers is the behavior the perpetrator would substitute for the practice if it were prohibited from engaging in it, I suspect that the practice would rarely if ever be deemed to inflict a net equivalent-monetary loss on relevant buyers.

I should add that, with one qualification, the preceding conclusions would be strengthened if, as I believe, the relevant unit for competitive-impact analysis is the impact not of an individual firm's engagement in these practices but the impact of a rule permitting all members of a set of product-rivals to engage in these practices. The qualification is that the use of RPM, VTRs, and vertical customer-allocation clauses by all members of a set of rivals is more likely to manifest producer or reseller price-fixing.

The conclusion that the substitution of RPM, VTRs, and/or vertical customer-allocation clauses for the conduct they would replace will rarely if ever inflict a net equivalent-monetary loss on relevant buyers also implies that—even when the perpetrator of the RPM, VTR, or vertical customer-allocation clause in question is a dominant firm—its conduct will rarely (probably never) cause it to violate the exploitative-abuse branch of now-Article 102.

(D) Producer Subsidies of Reseller Out-of-Store or In-Store Promotional Expenses or Resource Allocations or Producer Uses of Contract Clauses or Sales Policies to Induce Resellers to Make Jointly-Profitable Promotional Expenditures or Resource Allocations

Although subsidies, contract clauses, or sales policies that are designed to increase reseller promotion-efforts may sometimes be retaliatory in the service of contrivance or predatory, I am confident that virtually all such subsidies, contract clauses, and sales policies are not. Few if any will therefore violate any specific-anticompetitive-intent test of illegality. Individual-firm choices to pay such subsidies, use such clauses, or adopt such sales policies could reduce competition even if they were not strategic if they improved the practitioner's competitive-position array and critically worsened the array of its established rivals and/or the prospective arrays of otherwise-effective potential investors in its area of product-space. I suspect that this outcome rarely if ever obtains, and, even when it does, it will be difficult to establish that fact, and the perpetrator may in any case be able to establish a Clayton Act organizational-economic-efficiency defense or a now-Article 101(3) exemption if the case is brought under now-Article 101 or prove that the conduct did not impose a net equivalent-monetary loss on relevant buyers if the practice is considered to be relevant in an EMCR case because the firm that will result from the merger, acquisition, or full-function joint venture at issue is predicted to engage in such behavior more than the participating firms would have done.

(E) Vertical Mergers and Acquisitions

Section 9 of Chap. 11 and Sect. 4 of Chap. 14 investigated the economic functions and possible competitive impacts of vertical mergers and acquisitions in great detail, and Sect. 5 of Chap. 14 examined the legality of vertical mergers and acquisitions under both U.S. and E.C./E.U. law in great detail. This section provides an extremely-condensed account of those sections' analyses.

The first economics comment or set of economics comments I want to make about vertical mergers and acquisitions is that, in addition to all the Sherman-Act-licit functions that horizontal and conglomerate mergers and acquisitions can perform, vertical mergers and acquisitions can perform four Sherman-Act-licit functions that horizontal and conglomerate acquisitions cannot perform:

(1) enabling the resulting business organization (which may bear the name of the acquiring firm or one of the merger partners) to increase its profits by using hierarchical controls to influence its own employees as opposed to using contractual controls and sales/consignment policies to influence independent distributors and consignees;
(2) creating a business organization that can take better advantage than its antecedents could of continuous-flow economies (*e.g.*, that can arrange to have smelting and refining operations proceed on a continuous basis);
(3) creating a business organization that can better circumvent upstream price or profit controls; and
(4) enabling a firm to avoid dealing with independents that are more inclined than the firm's own employees would be to reveal to the firm's product-rivals information about the firm's business plans whose communication to the independents would otherwise be in the firm's and the independents' joint interest.

The second set of economics comments I want to make about vertical mergers and acquisitions contains two comments about their impact on the amount of contrivance and predation that is practiced. On the one hand, vertical mergers and acquisitions will tend in a wide variety of ways to make contrivance and predation more profitable for the resulting firm than for its antecedents (and may tend to make contrivance more profitable for the antecedents' rivals as well). On the other hand, there are good reasons to believe that only a small percentage of vertical mergers and acquisitions actually increase the incidence of contrivance and predation. I think, for example, that the estimates of some experts of the probability that vertical mergers and acquisitions will lead to (predatory) price squeezes and predatory refusals to deal are highly exaggerated.

The third economics comment I want to make about vertical mergers and acquisitions is that transactions of this kind that eliminate an effective potential competitor can generate Sherman-Act-illicit profits on that account.

The fourth economics comment I want to make about vertical mergers and acquisitions is that they can reduce competition not only by increasing the incidence of contrivance and predation but also by enabling the resulting firm to obtain NOMs when its antecedents could not and by generating economic efficiencies that, by improving the resulting firm's competitive-position array and thereby critically worsening the competitive-position arrays of one or more of its established rivals and the prospective competitive-position arrays of one or more potential investors in its area of product-space, it may "lessen competition" in the Clayton Act's sense of that expression (though in such cases the perpetrators may be able to establish an organizational-economic-efficiency defense if the relevant case is brought in the U.S. under the Clayton Act).

The fifth economics point I want to make is that I doubt that an individual vertical merger or acquisition or that the decision of virtually all firms in a given area of product-space to vertically integrate will usually inflict an equivalent-monetary loss on relevant buyers. In part, my doubts on this issue reflect my doubts about the frequency with which such vertical integration will reduce QV-investment competition by making it necessary for potential competitors to enter at more than one level (remember: QV investments can also be added to the relevant area of product-space by expanding established firms). However, primarily, my doubts reflect the combination of (1) my assumption that vertical integration is usually executed because it generates economic efficiencies and (2) my belief that, when vertical integration does generate such efficiencies, relevant buyers will gain even if the vertical integration simultaneously reduces QV-investment competition.

The sixth economics comment I want to make about vertical mergers and acquisitions is that the argument of some economists that vertical combinations between "successive monopolists" will cause prices to drop exaggerates this effect because it assumes that the upstream independent would have engaged in single pricing when, in reality, I suspect that in these sorts of situations it would charge a lower per-unit price and a lump-sum fee.

The seventh and final economics comment I want to make at this juncture is that the argument of some economists that vertical integration between the producer of an input against which substitution is possible and a final-good producer that uses that input will increase economic efficiency by preventing economically-inefficient substitutions against the input in question is deficient not only in that it ignores The General Theory of Second Best but also in that it assumes that the non-integrated input producer would sell its input separately for a single per-unit price when in fact sellers in this situation prevent or reduce jointly-unprofitable substitutions against their input (1) by conditioning their input's sale at an appropriate price on the buyer's agreeing to purchase its full requirements of the input that would be substituted for the input-producer's input at an appropriate price, (2) by conditioning their input's sale at a TSM marginal-cost price on the buyer's agreeing to purchase its full requirements of another input against which substitution is not possible for a price appropriately above its normal market price, (3) by using an endproduct-royalty scheme, (4) by requiring the buyer to sell the buyer's output of the relevant final product to them for a price appropriately below the price that the buyer would otherwise charge for it, or (5) by charging the buyer a lump-sum fee for the right to purchase its full requirements of the input in question at the seller's TSM marginal cost.

As some of the preceding conclusions suggest, I believe (1) that very few individual vertical mergers or acquisitions violate the specific-anticompetitive-intent test of illegality of the Sherman Act, the "object of preventing or restricting competition" test of *prima facie* illegality of now-Article 101(1), or the exclusionary-abuse branch of now-Article 102's test of illegality and (2) that very few individual vertical mergers or acquisitions violate the "lessening competition" test of the Clayton Act or the "impeding effective competition" test of the EMCR. I also think that the appropriate unit for legal analysis under a lessening-competition-type test of illegality is the impact of a rule allowing all members of a set of rivals to participate in vertical mergers and acquisitions as opposed to the impact of an individual vertical merger or acquisition and that, because vertical mergers and acquisitions will tend to be more profitable for marginal and potential competitors than for well-established firms, such a rule will rarely reduce competition.

* * *

Both (1) this study's critiques of the market-oriented approaches that many economists, antitrust-enforcement agencies, and antitrust courts historically took and, to some extent, continue to take to the analysis of antitrust-law-relevant economic issues and (2) the study's recommended approaches to these issues use a number of novel conceptual systems and related novel economic theories. This reality might call into question the admissibility at trial of testimony based on its critiques and proposals. I am confident that no such problem would arise in the E.C./E.U.: because most of the member states of the E.C./E.U. are civil-law countries in which lay juries play relatively-minor roles in deciding adjudicatory cases, neither those countries nor the E.C./E.U. has ever found it necessary to adopt rules of evidence on expert testimony that are designed to prevent lay jurypersons from being bamboozled: civil-law countries and hence the E.C./E.U. trust judges to assess the quality of expert testimony.

The United States is different. Because of the important role that lay juries play in deciding adjudication cases, the United States Federal Rules of Evidence and the U.S. courts that interpret and apply those Rules screen out expert testimony whose validity is questionable because U.S. authorities do not trust lay juries to evaluate expert testimony properly. My impression is that, at least until fairly recently, the admissibility of expert testimony in the U.S. depended to a very considerable extent on the degree to which the theory being advanced or the empirical scientific technique being used had achieved "general acceptance" in the relevant scientific community. The theories this study has developed and applied may satisfy this criterion for admissibility: (1) I have given well-received talks about them at the DOJ; (2) the Horizontal Merger Guidelines have progressively incorporated many of the ideas I presented to the DOJ in a 1978 lecture (though I cannot prove causation); (3) I have given many talks on my antitrust work to many law-school and some economics-department faculties in the U.S., U.K., Germany, Switzerland, and Belgium; and I have published many articles on antitrust-law-relevant economic issues in law journals and law-and-economics journals.

However, even if the admissibility of my arguments in U.S. trials would have been contestable in the past, recent changes in relevant practice have vastly raised the probability that the arguments of this study would be admissible in U.S. courts: since 1993, the criterion that U.S. courts have used to determine whether expert testimony is admissible has shifted from one in which "general acceptance in the relevant scientific community" played the dominant role to one in which the demonstrated soundness of the testimony is critical. I am confident that my conceptual systems and theories would pass a soundness test of admissibility.

The change in U.S. practice was initiated by a Supreme Court decision in *Daubert v. Merrill Dow Pharmaceuticals.*[1621] Although *Daubert* does list "general acceptance" in the relevant scientific community as a criterion for the admissibility of scientific testimony[1622] and does state that "a known technique which has been able to attract only minimal support within the community. . .may properly be viewed with skepticism,"[1623] it undercuts the importance of the "general acceptance" criterion by stating that "a reliability assessment does not require, although it does permit, explicit identification of a relevant scientific community and an express determination of a particular degree of acceptance within that community."[1624] The *Daubert* opinion also seems to me to undercut the importance of acceptance and promote the importance of objective "reliability" by stating that, although the admissibility-decision should take account of "[w]hether the theory or technique has been subjected to peer review and publication," "[p]ublication (which is but one element of peer review) is not a *sine qua non* of admissibility; it does not necessarily correlate with reliability. . . ."[1625] The *Daubert* opinion also seems to me to undercut the importance of acceptance as opposed to objective reliability by listing as criteria for admitting testimony based on a particular empirical methodology (1) whether it "can be and has been tested"[1626] and (2) "the known or potential rate of error. . . ."[1627] Although, in

[1621] 509 U.S. 579 (1993).

[1622] *Id.* at 593.

[1623] *Id.*

[1624] *Id.*

[1625] *Id.*

[1626] *Id.*

[1627] *Id.*

Hovenkamp's words, antitrust "courts have shown varying degrees of sophistication in applying *Daubert*,"[1628] they have in my opinion based their admissibility decisions on their assessment of the reliability of the testimony as distinct from the general acceptance of the methodology on which it is based in the relevant scientific community.

It is important to note in addition that the DOJ and FTC economists and attorneys who make the government's enforcement-decisions are not bound by the Federal Rules of Evidence or the court decisions interpreting and applying them. If these enforcement personnel can be convinced of the soundness of a theoretical position or empirical technique, arguments that rely on them will often control antitrust-law outcomes even if they would not be admitted in court.

2. Post-1950 U.S. Antitrust Law and Current E.C./E.U. Competition Law as Written: A Comparison

I will start by making six points about the tests of illegality promulgated by post-1950 U.S. antitrust law and the tests of illegality promulgated by post-EMCR E.C./E.U. competition law. First, properly interpreted, the object branch of now-Article 101's test of illegality and the exclusionary-abuse branch of now-Article 102's test of illegality are identical to the Sherman Act's specific-anticompetitive-intent test of illegality. Second, the overall test of illegality created by the combination of the "effect branch" of now-Article 101(1)'s test of *prima facie* illegality and now-Article 101(3)'s *de facto* economic-efficiency defense is different from the Clayton Act's lessening-competition test of illegality even though both tests focus on the conduct's equivalent-monetary impact on relevant buyers and both define the set of relevant buyers to consist of the customers of the perpetrator(s) and the customers of the perpetrator's or perpetrators' rivals:

(1) properly interpreted, the effect branch of now-Article 101(1)'s test of *prima facie* illegality declares covered conduct *prima facie* illegal if it causes some relevant buyers to suffer an equivalent-monetary loss by reducing the absolute attractiveness of the best offer they respectively receive from any inferior supplier even if the conduct does not inflict a net equivalent-monetary loss on any relevant buyer or on all relevant buyers, all things considered, and provides an exemption to conduct deemed *prima facie* illegal under now-Article 101(1) only if (*inter alia*) it yields one or more types of economic efficiencies listed in now-Article 101(3) and gives all relevant buyers a "fair share of the benefit" the conduct generated for the perpetrator(s) and the relevant buyers "combined", whereas

[1628] Herbert Hovenkamp, Federal Antitrust Policy: The Law of Competition and Its Practice 645 (Thomson West, 3rd ed., 2005).

(2) properly interpreted, the Clayton Act's general test of illegality—see point (5)—declares covered conduct illegal only if it inflicts a net equivalent-monetary loss on all relevant buyers all things considered as a result of its reducing the absolute attractiveness of the best offer that one or more of them respectively received from any inferior supplier unless this outcome was critically affected by the conduct's increasing its perpetrator's or perpetrators' organizational economic efficiency—*i.e.*, by its causing one or more established rivals of the perpetrator(s) to exit or critically raising the barriers to QV investment confronting an otherwise-effective potential investor in the relevant area of product-space by worsening respectively their actual and prospective competitive-position arrays by improving the competitive-position array(s) of the perpetrator(s) by increasing its/their organizational economic efficiency.

Third, the EMCR's "impeding effective competition" test of illegality is identical to the Clayton Act's "lessening competition" test of *prima facie* illegality—*i.e.*, the Clayton Act's test without its organizational-economic-efficiency-defense component. Fourth, U.S. antitrust law has no counterpart to the exploitative-abuse branch of now-Article 102's test of illegality (which applies only to firms that are individually dominant or members of a set of collectively-dominant rivals). Fifth, E.C./E.U. competition law has no counterpart to the deviant, "injury to competitor" test of illegality that the 1936 Robinson-Patman Act amendment to the original Clayton Act promulgated when the relevant competitor is the disfavored buyer that is injured in its ability to compete with its favored rivals (a deviant test that I suspect will almost never be applicable since sellers whose discrimination would injure the disfavored buyer in this scenario will almost always refuse to deal with the buyer rather than discriminate against it). It is arguable that the sixth and final point I want to make at this juncture is a point about the application of the relevant tests of illegality rather than about those tests themselves. I believe that the answer to the question "Should the Clayton Act be interpreted to be a fence law?" is contestable—*i.e.*, I am not sure whether any predicted tendency of Clayton-Act-covered conduct to inflict an equivalent-dollar loss on Clayton-Act-relevant buyers by increasing the extent to which contrivance and predation is practiced should count against its legality under the Clayton Act. By way of contrast, at least in combination with my conclusion that now-Article 101(1) does cover mergers, acquisitions, and joint ventures, the fact that it lists as exemplars of the effects that covered conduct might have that would render the conduct *prima facie* illegal any tendency the conduct has to "(a) directly or indirectly fix purchase or selling prices or any other trading conditions. . .[and] (c) share markets or sources of supply. . ." seems to me to favor the conclusion that, as a matter of law, now-Article 101 should be interpreted to be a fence law since semantically these possibilities refer to post-conduct conduct in which the perpetrators might engage.

I now want to point out one unfortunate shared conduct-coverage deficiency of U.S. antitrust law and E.C./E.U. competition law, five actual differences between the conduct-coverage of post-1950 U.S. antitrust law and E.C./E.U. competition law, and one alleged difference between the conduct-coverage of post-1950 U.S. antitrust law as written and pre-EMCR E.C./E.U. competition law as written that I do not think actually exists. The common deficiency is that neither U.S. law nor E.C./E.U. law as written covers unsuccessful attempts to enter into contrived oligopolistic unilateral contracts by firms that do not have dominant positions. The U.S. Sherman Act does not cover such attempts because (1) Sect. 1 does not cover *attempts* to form contracts in restraint of trade and (2) given that fact, the U.S. government's failure to pass a general attempt statute, and the federal courts' refusal to read attempt provisions into federal legislation when their absence was clearly a legislative mistake, it would be incorrect as a matter of law to conclude that Sect. 2's "attempt to monopolize" prohibition covers attempts to enter into contracts in restraint of trade. Now-Article 101(1) does not cover such attempts because such attempts do not involve an "agreement between undertakings," a "decision[] by an association of undertakings," or a "concerted practice[]."

There are at least five differences in the conduct-coverage of post-1950 U.S. antitrust law and E.C./E.U. competition law. First, unlike U.S. law, E.C./E.U. competition law—specifically, now-Article 102—does cover unsuccessful attempts to form a contrived-oligopolistic agreement when at least one of the perpetrators is individually dominant or a member of a collectively-dominant set of rivals. Second and third, as written, unlike U.S. law (in particular, the Sherman Act), E.C./E.U. law does not cover contrivance by a non-dominant firm that involves only threats and acts of retaliation or single-firm predation by a non-dominant firm because neither of these categories of conduct involves the creation of an "agreement[] between undertakings," a "decision[] by an association of undertakings," or a "concerted practice[]." Fourth, because E.C./E.U. competition law promulgates an "exploitative abuse of a dominant position" test of illegality that has no U.S. counterpart, it covers on that account pricing-techniques and decisions not to invest or advertise (when used or made by dominant firms that U.S. antitrust law does not cover). Fifth, unlike U.S. law (which does not cover natural oligopolistic conduct), E.C./E.U. law (in particular, Article 101) does cover such conduct as a concerted practice.

I want to close this section by discussing an alleged difference between pre-EMCR E.C./E.U. competition law and U.S. antitrust law as written that I do not think existed. The allegation is that pre-EMCR E.C./E.U. competition law did not cover mergers or acquisitions. That claim has always been based on three claims or sets of claims:

(1) the claim that the list that appears in clauses (a)–(e) of now-Article 101(1) after the words "in particular" in the English version of that provision is comprehensive rather than illustrative;
(2) the claim that mergers and acquisitions do not generate any of the effects or entail any of the conduct listed in clauses (a)–(e);
(3) the claim that a merger or acquisition cannot constitute a now-Article 102 "abuse. . .of a dominant position" either because (A) for some unexplained semantic reasons mergers or acquisitions cannot constitute an "abuse" or (B) because the list in clauses (a)–(d) in now-Article 102 that is preceded by the

words in English "may, in particular, consist in" is comprehensive and does not refer to any effects mergers or acquisitions generate or conduct-categories into which mergers or acquisitions fit.

For five reasons, I disagree both with the conclusion that now-Articles 101 and 102 do not cover mergers or acquisitions and with each of the claims on which that conclusion has been based. First, although I acknowledge that the English words "in particular" normally imply that the list they precede is comprehensive, in this instance, the conclusion that the clause (a)–(e) list in Article 101(1) is comprehensive is disfavored (1) by the fact that the words that take the place of "in particular" in several of the other-official-language versions of the Treaty mean "particularly" or "especially" rather than "in particular" (*i.e.*, imply that the list is illustrative rather than comprehensive), (2) by the fact that the conclusion that the list is comprehensive is inconsistent with the now-Article 101(1) text that states that it covers "*all* agreements between undertakings [emphasis added]," (3) by the fact that the conclusion that the list is comprehensive implies that the Treaty as written will not achieve the goals it was designed to achieve (including benefitting relevant buyers), and (4) by the fact that the conclusion in question makes bad policy-sense.

Second, even if it were correct as a matter of E.C./E.U. law to conclude that the "clause (a)–(e) list" of now-Article 101(1) is comprehensive, some mergers and acquisitions—*viz.*, those that would be predicted to increase the incidence of price-fixing by sellers, other-term fixing by sellers, the fixing of technologically-innovative or not-technologically-innovative QV investments, the fixing of investments in PPR, market-sharing by sellers, and supplier-sharing by buyers—would be covered by items (a), (b), or (c) in the clause (a)–(e) list.

Third, there is absolutely no semantic reason to conclude that a merger that manifests the specific anticompetitive intent of a participant that is dominant does not constitute an abuse of its dominant position.

Fourth, the fact that the clause (a)–(d) list in now-Article 102 is introduced by the words "*may*, in particular consist of [emphasis added]" makes it clear that the item (a)–(d) list in question is illustrative rather than comprehensive.

Fifth, even if it were correct as a matter of E.C./E.U. law to conclude that the "clause (a)–(d)" list in now-Article 102 is comprehensive, some mergers or acquisitions will generate effects that are delineated by clauses (a) and (b) in that list—*viz.*, will result in the perpetrators' and/or one or more of their rivals' "directly or indirectly imposing unfair purchase or selling prices or other unfair trading conditions" and/or "limiting production, markets or technical development to the prejudice of consumers. . .."

Hence, although I recognize that the EC, the E.C./E.U. courts, and European E.C./E.U. competition-law scholars have virtually always maintained that neither now-Article 101 nor now-Article 102 covers mergers or acquisitions, I think that they are simply wrong as a matter of law. I therefore disagree with the claim that, prior to the promulgation of the EMCR, E.C./E.U. competition law differed from post-1950 U.S. antitrust law in that, unlike U.S. law, it did not cover mergers or acquisitions.

3. The Impact of Errors of Interpretation and Application on the Divergences Between U.S. and E.C./E.U. Competition Law as Applied

The final section focuses primarily on whether the mistakes that the U.S. courts, DOJ, and FTC have made when interpreting and applying U.S. antitrust law and the mistakes that the EC and the E.C./E.U. courts have made when interpreting and applying E.C./E.U. competition law have caused the two bodies of law as applied to converge or diverge. It makes seven points or clusters of points.

The first relates to the two most important mistakes that U.S. and E.C./E.U. institutions have made when interpreting and applying the bodies of antitrust law they have been charged with implementing:

(1) interpreting the laws in question to be as concerned with preventing reductions in intra-brand competition as with preventing reductions in inter-brand competition and
(2) adopting market-oriented approaches to analyzing the monopolizing/exclusionary character and predicting the competitive impact of covered conduct that proceed on the assumption (roughly but generously speaking) that the probability that conduct is monopolizing/exclusionary or will lessen competition increases with the market shares of the perpetrator(s) and, in relation to some conduct, the concentration of the seller-side of the relevant market.

Although these mistakes have had unfortunate consequences, during the long period in which they were being made to the same extent and in the same way by U.S. and E.C./E.U. institutions, they did not cause U.S. antitrust law as applied to diverge from E.C./E.U. competition law as applied either more or less than U.S. antitrust law as written diverges from E.C./E.U. competition law as written.

The second cluster of points I want to make in the current context relates to a mistake of interpretation that the U.S. Supreme Court made in one case and that the EC seems to be making in some of its pronouncements—the mistake I denominate pari-mutuel handicapping. Antitrust enforcers engage in pari-mutuel handicapping when they (1) allow marginal and potential competitors to engage in conduct that will increase their organization's proficiency and thereby improve their competitive-position arrays because such conduct will help them respectively survive and enter and (2) prohibit well-established firms from engaging in the same conduct because, by improving their competitive-position arrays, the conduct will tend to cause marginal competitors to exit and critically raise the barriers to entry confronting otherwise-effective potential competitors by worsening respectively their actual and prospective competitive-position arrays (by improving the established firm's competitive-position array). If U.S. and E.C./E.U. antitrust-law appliers made this mistake in the same way to the same extent, it would not cause U.S. antitrust law as applied to diverge from E.C./E.U. competition law as applied more or less than U.S. antitrust law as written diverges from E.C./E.U. competition law as written (though the error would have undesirable consequences in both jurisdictions). I have separated this second cluster of points out from the first because I do not know the extent to which either U.S. authorities or E.C./E.U. authorities ever did or would now make this mistake. Both sets of institutions make many statements about the law's valuing competition on the merits, and I do not know the extent to which U.S. and E.C./E.U. authorities violate that "principle" in practice.

The third cluster of points that is relevant at this juncture relates to the fact that U.S. courts and the DOJ and FTC (1) made and continue to make one mistake that their E.C./E.U. counterparts had and continue to have no opportunity to make that causes U.S. antitrust law as applied to be more similar to E.C./E.U. competition law as applied than U.S. antitrust law as written is to E.C./E.U. competition law as written and (2) have in the past made a mistake that E.C./E.U. authorities could have made but did not. The first (exclusively-U.S.) mistake in question is the error the U.S. Supreme Court made when it held that, to win a Section 2 Sherman Act monopolization case, the plaintiff or State must demonstrate that the defendant had market power prior to engaging in the conduct alleged to be exclusionary. This mistaken position makes U.S. antitrust law as applied much closer to E.C./E.U. competition law as applied than U.S. antitrust law as written is to E.C./E.U. competition law as written. To see why, recall that

(1) U.S. antitrust law as written (the Sherman Act) prohibits single-firm predation (one type of monopolization) by firms that do not have pre-existing market power as well as by firms that do have pre-existing market power,
(2) now-Article 101(1) does not cover single-firm predation, and
(3) now-Article 102 does cover single-firm predation as an exclusionary abuse (and perhaps as an exploitative abuse as well) but only when the perpetrator is either individually dominant or a member of a collectively-dominant set of rivals (a condition that resembles the Supreme Court's requirement that the defendant had market power prior to engaging in the conduct alleged to be exclusionary [if that is the relevant Supreme Court requirement as opposed to its being that the defendant had monopoly power after engaging in the conduct in question]).

The second exclusively-U.S. error is the mistake of interpreting the Clayton Act to prohibit behavior that lessens competition in one product or geographic market even if it does not lessen competition overall. So far as I know, U.S. courts have made this mistake (what I take to be a mistake despite the fact that a straightforward textual argument favors the conclusion I deem mistaken) only in dicta. However, this mistake seems to me to underlie the DOJ and FTC's allowing certain mergers to proceed only on condition that the merger partners divest specified business holdings when (from all appearances) the merger would not lessen competition overall in their originally-proposed form. If the U.S. antitrust-law-enforcement institutions but not E.C./E.U. competition-law-enforcement institutions make this mistake, the error in question would cause U.S. antitrust law as applied to diverge more from E.C./E.U. competition law as applied than U.S. antitrust law as written diverges from E.C./E.U. competition law as written.

The fourth cluster of points relates to a mistake that the EC and the E.C./E.U. courts have made when interpreting now-Articles 101 and 102 that has no U.S.

counterpart because the U.S. had no possible basis for making this mistake—*viz.*, the mistake of concluding that neither now-Article 101 nor now-Article 102 covers mergers or acquisitions. I have already explained why I think this conclusion is wrong as a matter of E.C./E.U. competition law. It should be clear that, prior to the passage of the EMCR, this mistake caused E.C./E.U. competition law as applied to diverge far more from U.S. antitrust law as applied than E.C./E.U. competition law as written diverged from U.S. antitrust law as written. The promulgation of the EMCR clearly eliminated most of the impact of this error. However, given the fact that the EMCR does not cover the many joint ventures that are partial-function joint ventures, it did not render this error irrelevant.

The fifth cluster of points relates to the fact that, over the past 20 years, U.S. antitrust-law-enforcement institutions have progressively abandoned the market-oriented approach to the analysis of the legality of many types of conduct and have done so to a much greater extent than their E.C./E.U. counterparts have done. Take, for example, the analysis of the competitive impact of horizontal mergers. The traditional U.S. approach at least purported to proceed by defining relevant markets and deriving conclusions primarily from the merger partners' market shares and the traditional four-firm or eight-firm seller concentration ratio of the defined markets. The approach that the 1992 U.S. Horizontal Merger Guidelines commit the DOJ and FTC to taking is less market-oriented in two respects. First, although the General Standards approach the Guidelines prescribe for what they assume are the vast majority of cases state that many mergers will be lawful solely on the basis of market-aggregated data on the post-merger HHI of the relevant markets and the merger-generated increase in that HHI and that other mergers will be deemed rebuttably illegal on the basis of such data, they also state that such data will sometimes lead the Agencies to assess the competitive impact of the horizontal merger to which it relates without any presumption in one direction or the other. Second, the Qualifying Factor section of the 1992 Horizontal Merger Guidelines explicitly acknowledges that, when the products in the relevant market are heterogeneous, the conclusions that would be generated by the General Standards' market-oriented approach will have to be adjusted (even when no adjustment is required by the conditions-of-entry, failing-firm, and efficiency considerations that the General Standards state are always relevant). Although I think that market-oriented approaches of any kind are unacceptable when the relevant products are homogeneous as well as when they are heterogeneous and have no doubt that, when the market-oriented approach is inapposite, one should derive conclusions directly from the kinds of non-market-aggregated realities whose obvious relevance led the DOJ and FTC to include the Qualifying Factor analysis in their Guidelines rather than begin with a market-aggregated-data-based conclusion and adjust that conclusion to reflect the non-market-aggregated realities in question, for current purposes the important point is that the Qualifying Factors section of the 1992 Horizontal Merger Guidelines manifest the DOJ's and FTC's realization that the market-oriented approach to analyzing the competitive impact of horizontal mergers is neither acceptably accurate nor cost-effective from any appropriate perspective for at least some classes of horizontal mergers. Post-1992 Agency conduct reflects the same reality. Since 1992 the Agencies have used a variety of non-market-oriented methods to analyze the competitive impact of particular horizontal mergers (including merger simulations and the consideration of natural experiments) and have reached conclusions about the legality of many horizontal mergers that are inconsistent with the various market-oriented presumptions of the 1992 Guidelines' General Standards. The 2010 DOJ/FTC Horizontal Merger Guidelines take a further step in this direction by abandoning (not just altering) the various market-oriented irrebuttable presumptions of the 1992 Guidelines. Moreover, although economists at the Agencies continue to insist that market definitions and market-aggregated data can sometimes contribute to the analysis of the competitive impact of horizontal mergers, when pressed to provide a theoretical reason why or an example in which this is the case, they are unable to do so.

I admit that I am les-well-informed about EC practice. But I see no similar trend in the EC's horizontal-merger Guidelines and decisionmaking. To the extent that U.S. antitrust-law enforcers have gone further than their E.C./E.U. counterparts in abandoning the market-oriented approach to the analysis of the competitive impact of horizontal mergers, the U.S. law on horizontal mergers as applied will differ more from its E.C./E.U. counterpart than the U.S. law on horizontal mergers as written differs from the E.C./E.U. law on horizontal mergers as written.

The second example of this move away from market-oriented approaches I want to cite relates to the analysis of the competitive impact and legality of tie-ins (and, by implication reciprocity). The traditional position in the U.S. (which was a corollary of the leverage theory of tie-ins to which U.S. authorities subscribed) was that tie-ins violated the Sherman Act's specific-anticompetitive-intent test of illegality if and only if the tying seller had market power in the so-called tying-product market. The U.S. courts and the DOJ and FTC have now in practice abandoned the leverage theory of tie-ins (though they have never explicitly acknowledged that it cannot bear scrutiny). Under the judicial face-saving Rule of Reason approach they now take to tying agreements, the market share of the tying seller appears to play no role. The EC and the E.C./E.U. courts appear still to subscribe to the leverage theory and to the market-oriented approach to critical-object/exclusionary-intent and competitive-impact analysis that is its corollary. Once more, to the extent that such a difference affects legal conclusions in the two jurisdictions, E.C./E.U. competition law as applied will diverge more from U.S. antitrust law as applied by more than E.C./E.U. competition law as written diverges from U.S. antitrust law as written.

The third example of the move away from market-oriented approaches relates to long-term full-requirements contracts and long-term total-output-supply contacts. The historical change in the U.S. is actually mixed: the move from the original "quantitative substantiality" test of illegality to the somewhat-mislabeled "qualitative-substantiality test" of illegality (which focused on the share of the relevant market's sales or supplies that was locked up) involved a shift from an (incorrect) non-market-oriented decision-protocol to an (incorrect) market-oriented decision-protocol. I want to focus on the more recent development in which both the Supreme Court and the lower courts have "adjusted" the so-called "qualitative-substantiality" test to take account of the market-disaggregated fact that not all sellers are equally-well-placed to supply all buyers in conventionally-defined markets—a fact that is relevant when assessing the possible exclusionary effect both of a long-term requirements contract that will prevent a particular seller from supplying a particular buyer and of a long-term total-output-supply contract that will prevent a particular buyer from being supplied by a particular buyer. I do not think that E.C./E.U. decisionmakers have moved away from the market-oriented "qualitative-substantiality" approach to analyzing the monopolizing/exclusionary character and competitive impact of long-term supply arrangements to the extent that the U.S. courts have done. Once again, to the extent that this is the case, U.S. antitrust law as applied will differ from E.C./E.U. competition law as applied by more than U.S. antitrust law as written differs from E.C./E.U. competition law as written.

The sixth cluster of points I want to make at this juncture relates to whether U.S. and/or E.C./E.U. antitrust law are concerned with preventing intra-brand competition. Historically, the U.S. courts insisted that covered conduct that reduces intra-brand competition was *per se* illegal. More recently, the Supreme Court has held that covered conduct that reduces intra-brand competition is illegal only if the reduction in intra-brand competition it generates is greater than any increase in inter-brand competition it generates. It is still early days, but my impression is that in practice the lower courts virtually always conclude that covered conduct that reduces intra-brand competition (in particular, resale price maintenance, vertical territorial restraints, and vertical customer-allocation clauses) increases inter-brand competition even more and is therefore lawful. Since I think that the relevant conduct violates U.S. antitrust law only in the rare instances in which it implements a producer or reseller price-fix, I believe that this combination of Supreme Court test-promulgation and lower-court implementation has produced correct legal results without requiring the Court to admit that its conclusion that U.S. antitrust law is concerned with preventing reductions in intra-brand competition was and is wrong as a matter of law. The EC and the E.C./E.U. courts have also consistently claimed that E.C./E.U. competition law is concerned with preventing reductions in intra-brand competition. The commentary justifies this conclusions not only linguistically by citing the fact that the reduction of intra-brand competition involves a "prevention or restriction" of competition (the U.S. authorities have made the same wooden textual claim) but also by arguing that conduct that reduces intra-brand competition frequently disserves the liberty interests of independent distributors and the proximate goal of promoting inter-E.C./E.U.-country trade (and hence the ultimate goals that the achievement of that proximate goal is alleged to serve). The E.C./E.U. competition-law-enforcement authorities have become less zealous in declaring illegal conduct that would reduce intra-brand competition if its perpetrators would respond to its prohibition by ceasing to engage in it and making no other alteration in their conduct because the authorities have come to realize that its perpetrators will actually be likely to respond to prohibitions of conduct that would reduce intra-brand competition on that assumption in various lawful ways that are equally inimical to the supposed liberty-interests of independent distributors and the promotion of inter-E.C./E.U.-member-country trade. However, at least in part (I suspect) because the relevant decisionmakers have a less-complete understanding than their U.S. counterparts do of the functions that the conduct in question performs and hence of the official-goal-defeating behaviors that its perpetrators will substitute for it if it is prohibited, it seems to me that they are still more prone than their contemporary U.S. counterparts are to find such conduct illegal. To the extent that my assessment of this comparative-enforcement-practice issue is correct, E.C./E.U. competition law as applied will diverge more from U.S. antitrust law as applied on this account than E.C./E.U. competition law as written diverges from U.S. competition law as written.

The seventh (oh, lucky seven) cluster of points I want to make relates to whether the combination of the promulgation of the EMCR and the recent increases in the divergence between the extent to which U.S. and E.C./E.U. authorities have abandoned market-oriented approaches and their historic commitments to protecting intra-brand competition have resulted in U.S. antitrust law as applied being closer or further from each other now than they were 20 years ago. In part because I am not sure of the metric on which such a comparison should be based and in part because I do not have enough information about the number and importance (on any plausible measure) of the cases that will be handled more similarly and less similarly today in the two jurisdictions than they would have been 20 years ago, I will not venture a guess on this issue. What I will say, however, is that if the E.C./E.U. authorities follow their historical practice of altering their positions and decisions after some passage of time in the same ways that their U.S. colleagues have done, E.C./E.U. competition law as applied will come increasingly to resemble U.S. antitrust law as applied. We all tend to resemble our parents more than we thought we would—often more than we wish we would.

* * *

For almost 50 years, I have been writing (*inter alia*) a series of articles each of which dealt with a subset of the economic theory that is relevant to the interpretation and application of antitrust law, the legality of a subset of the various types of conduct antitrust laws cover, or the economic efficiency of those various standards that could be utilized to regulate them. When I received an enquiry from Springer about my interest in writing a book for them on the economics of antitrust, I realized immediately (1) that the study would have to distinguish sharply between the analysis of antitrust-*law*-related economic issues and antitrust-*policy*-related economic issues, (2) that it would be useful to analyze not only the legally-relevant economic issues in the abstract but also the ways in which they were being addressed by U.S. and E.C./E.U. legislation/treaties, courts, and antitrust-enforcement authorities, and (3) that I would have to make a substantial effort to learn more about E.C./E.U. antitrust law both as written and as applied. However, I did not appreciate the extent to which writing a comprehensive book about *all* antitrust-law-related economics issues and about *all* legal issues that related to the antitrust law of two jurisdictions would improve my understanding of both the relevant economics and the relevant law. I believe that the effort to bring it all together has generated many synergistic benefits. I hope that reading this study confers as many of these benefits on its consumers as writing it conferred on its author.

Index

In this index, upright page-reference numbers refer to pages in Volume 1, and *italicized* page-reference numbers refer to pages in Volume 2.

R.S. Markovits, *Economics and the Interpretation and Application of U.S. and E.U. Antitrust Law*, DOI 10.1007/978-3-642-24313-4,

GPSR Compliance

The European Union's (EU) General Product Safety Regulation (GPSR) is a set of rules that requires consumer products to be safe and our obligations to ensure this.

If you have any concerns about our products, you can contact us on ProductSafety@springernature.com

In case Publisher is established outside the EU, the EU authorized representative is:

Springer Nature Customer Service Center GmbH
Europaplatz 3
69115 Heidelberg, Germany

Batch number: 10268263

Printed by Printforce, the Netherlands